HONEST WORK

HONEST WORK

A Business Ethics Reader

Joanne B. Ciulla
University of Richmond

Clancy Martin
University of Missouri, Kansas City

Robert C. Solomon
University of Texas at Austin

New York Oxford
OXFORD UNIVERSITY PRESS
2007

Oxford University Press, Inc., publishes works that further Oxford University's
objective of excellence in research, scholarship, and education.

Oxford New York
Auckland   Cape Town   Dar es Salaam   Hong Kong   Karachi
Kuala Lumpur   Madrid   Melbourne   Mexico City   Nairobi
New Delhi   Shanghai   Taipei   Toronto

With offices in
Argentina   Austria   Brazil   Chile   Czech Republic   France   Greece
Guatemala   Hungary   Italy   Japan   Poland   Portugal   Singapore
South Korea   Switzerland   Thailand   Turkey   Ukraine   Vietnam

Published by Oxford University Press, Inc.
198 Madison Avenue, New York, New York 10016
http://www.oup.com

Oxford is a registered trademark of Oxford University Press

Library of Congress Cataloging-in-Publication Data

Honest work : a business ethics reader / by Joanne B. Ciulla, Clancy Martin, Robert C. Solomon
    p. cm.
  ISBN-13: 978-0-19-516168-7 (pbk.)
    1. Business ethics. 2. Work—Psychological aspects. 3. Work ethic. 4. Quality of work
life. 5. Social justice. 1. Title: Business ethics reader. II. Ciulla, Joanne B. III. Martin,
Clancy W. IV. Solomon, Robert C.

HF5387.H663 2005
174′.4—dc22

                                                                        2005048827

Printing number: 9 8 7 6 5 4 3 2

Printed in the United States of America
on acid-free paper

We dedicate this book to our families, who have contributed to our lives and work.

This book is for Joanne's husband, René Kanters;
Clancy's wife, Rebecca; and in memory of Bob's
parents, Charles M. and Vita P. Solomon

CONTENTS

PREFACE

FOR THE STUDENT

This is a reader on business ethics, intended for undergraduate, graduate, and executive courses in that subject. It consists, for the most part, of classic and recent articles and cases across a broad spectrum of issues, topics, and concerns. The working premise of the book is that people in business want and need to be informed and educated about the values that they and their work embody because they know that they have to be ready to confront difficult situations that they will—inevitably—face on the job. They also want and need to know how to think and feel about the business world that they work in—its benefits and its liabilities, the ways in which it is just and fair and the ways in which it should not be expected to satisfy such high ideals, the ways in which it should be "socially responsible," and the realms of social life in which social responsibility is not appropriate for most businesses.

What people do at work affects and even structures their lives more generally, and there is, accordingly, no clean line between business ethics and that most ancient of ethical concerns, the search for the good life, a happy life, a life of productive virtue free of regrets. How people *think* about their work affects and structures their lives even more profoundly, for it determines their attitudes and their expectations. Thus if one believes that the business world is a "dog-eat-dog" jungle, one will act accordingly. On the other hand, insofar as one believes that free enterprise is the best economic system for everyone and accordingly has a built-in concern for justice and fair dealing, one will live a very different life in business. Ethics is not just a peripheral concern of business, a set of constraints on business enterprise. It stands at the very core of business activity and defines the overall concepts and context in which business plays its role.

Toward this end, we have selected pieces that, for the most part, have both practical import and wide application and have structured the narratives that open the book and each chapter as personal challenges, presenting the reader with real ethical issues and dilemmas. Unlike most textbooks, therefore, we have taken the liberty of addressing the reader in the second person—*you*—in our introductions and narratives. The various essays, articles, and cases have been picked and arranged according to questions and problems that you will face (or already have faced), rather than the large policy issues that are the primary responsibility of executive boards, governments, and their agencies. Again, the focus of the book is personal, on issues that will very likely affect you, the reader. This does not mean that the book lacks any reference to the great thoughts about ethics and business, however. Questions about how to think about business will be just as important to your life in business as the more immediate challenges of an unfair boss or a cheating coworker. It is how you think about business, in general, that will dictate your response to these issues. Interspersed in our introductions, moreover, we bring in advice from some of the great thinkers of history by way of the whimsical device of occasional email messages (as if there had been email back in ancient and medieval times!), in order to shake up, challenge, and encourage your thinking.

The readings here, as well as the philosophical email messages, are presented as resources to use as you work your way through the various issues and problems in business ethics. We thus hope to engage you directly and practically in business ethics, not just to offer up a potpourri of "interesting" debates and proclamations. The chapters, readings, and cases are presented in such a way that every instructor should feel free to organize the course as he or she sees fit. Although we have approximated a coherent narrative, the various chapters, readings, and cases can be pursued in almost any order, and you, the reader, are encouraged to browse and enjoy them in any order as well. Only so much of the book can be covered in class, but you may well find your own interests provoked by some of the other material in the book.

FOR THE INSTRUCTOR

Although this book is intended to serve the function of a general-purpose traditional business ethics reader, we have also made a special effort to incorporate readings that are not so traditional and reflect dominant current themes and concerns, for instance, the ever-new technology and the ongoing globalization of the business world. We have also set our focus on what we consider the central and often most neglected theme in business ethics—the nature, the rewards, the costs, the promises, and the betrayals of work as such. Work is not just the raw material, the given theme, around which business ethics finds its problems. Work is what business ethics is all about, and how students think about work—as an unpleasant but necessary way to make money, a curse, or a way of realizing who they are and making their mark in the world—makes all the difference. Work has a rich history, from Adam and Eve's curse in *Genesis* to the challenges of the Protestant ethic to the short-lived "New Economy" of the 1990s. Our students will work in a world in which the meaning of work is very much in question, and to ignore that question or to take it for granted is to do them an extreme disservice. While this is, to be sure, not the whole of business ethics, it is, we think, its necessary starting point. It catches the students where their central concerns are, *What do you want to do? Why? And what kind of life do you think you'll achieve by doing it?*

What we have not done is what many business ethics texts stubbornly insist on doing, namely, to begin our text with an overview of different (usually three) ethical theories and then to "apply" these various theories throughout the book. In our (cumulative) 40 years of teaching the subject, we have confirmed over and over again that (1) most business students are not interested in ethical theories and find the terms of the debate overly abstract and irrelevant to what they will be doing. Discussing ethical theories starts the class off with a dull *thud.* And (2) insofar as the students do "get" the debate between competing ethical theories, they tend to walk away with exactly the wrong conclusion, that ethics is all "relative" and what answers you get to the issues depend almost entirely on what theory you choose to apply. We do not see the central issue of the course as a competition between ethical theories. We see the central issue of the course as the students' plans to live their lives in business, and ethics grows naturally out of the conversations initiated by those plans. Questions about happiness, consequences, moral rules, and character, as well as about the nature of entitlement and contracts (social and otherwise) and the obligations they engender emerge quite effortlessly from the students' own stated interests. So, too, isolated introductions to "moral reasoning" do not fare much better. Although moral reasoning is essential to the skills and the ethical "toolbox" that the students will need, we have found it much more effective when these skills are learned while the students are wrestling with real problems that they care about. They need not be imposed or "applied" from the framework of the course.

Ethics, of course, is already on the minds of any student who has read a newspaper in the past two years or so. Business ethics, or the lack thereof, has been in the headlines. Accordingly, we have highlighted the questions and issues that have given rise to some of the most egregious and expensive recent scandals in the business world, although we have not tried to spend much time on those still-unfolding scandals themselves. Rather, we have tried to put the emphasis where it should be, on the many companies, large and small, that have acted well as well as profitably over the years and whose managers and employees, consequently, have lived and are living good and satisfying lives in business. We have also avoided focusing exclusively on the ethics and behavior of large corporations. Most of the businesses in America—and consequently most of the job opportunities—are not in giant corporations but in small businesses, often started and run by families or groups of friends. These businesses have ethical values and needs, too, perhaps not involving thousands of jobs or many millions of dollars like Enron or Johnston & Johnston, but more personal and therefore more poignant considerations of survival, fair competition, distributive justice, and good ethical practices. We assume—on the basis of both statistics and years of teaching—that many of our readers will become involved and engaged in such businesses. Indeed, many business students, in the current atmosphere of entrepreneurship, will try to start their own. (Michael Dell founded Dell Computer out of his dorm room at the University of Texas.) So our emphasis will be directed toward start-ups and small businesses, as well as the better-known national and international corporations. Many of the issues will also apply to nonprofit organizations. The premise of this book, and we think the premise of business ethics as a subject, is the idea that every job and every career has its responsibilities and its ethical issues, and it is necessary for all students who are even thinking of spending part of their lives in the business world to be prepared by being informed and thoughtful.

Some of the chapters in this text address the immediate work issues that students will face, but others are more thought provoking and abstract. We think, as we said earlier, that the two feed one another. Some issues require immediate action, but all require some thought and understanding about what goes and what does not go in the peculiar ethics of the business world. So, in addition to the "issues at work" sorts of chapters, there are also the "big issues in the business world" chapters, on justice, on social responsibility, on the nature of the market itself. There are also "how to live" chapters, in which the students are encouraged to think about how their planned careers in business fit into and help satisfy their larger life goals. It is often said that "no one dies wishing that he or she had spent more time at the office," but the profundity of that witticism often escapes business students. They underestimate the nature of the commitments that they are about to enter into, and their perspective on the good life—which many of them sample indulgently as students—is easily lost once they submerge themselves in various corporate and career cultures. So that, too, is the central theme of business ethics—not just work but work as it fits into and promotes the good life. In this book, we have tried to package some of the best and most prominent and most lively writings and issues, together with some of the most challenging cases and case studies, supplemented with philosophical insights, in a single volume that allows each instructor to design his or her own course, but in a package that already presents, we think, the materials for an exciting course.

ACKNOWLEDGMENTS

In putting this book together, we have benefited from discussions, advice, and help from many of our colleagues. We would especially like to thank University of Richmond students Matt Murphy, who helped us in our search and exploration of the enormous amount of literature that is available, and Joe Nagraj, who aided in the preparation of articles for the manuscript. We owe a deep debt of gratitude to Emily Voigt, of Oxford University Press, who guided us through the entire process, and to her assistants Fern Lin and Sarah Calabi. We are also grateful to our editor, Robert Miller, for encouraging us to work with Oxford and giving us good advice throughout the process, and to the reviewers for their thoughtful comments and insights.

INTRODUCTION

You are about to begin a most important part of your business education, the study, discussion, and practice of business ethics. Business ethics has a few simple and rarely contested premises. These premises have their exceptions, to be sure, but there is little doubt that they hold up in general. First, ethics is essential to the functioning of the business world and the market. The opposite of ethics is corruption, and we know how badly corrupt countries and systems perform, insofar as they perform at all. Ethics is a fundamental part of business education, not an embellishment. Every course you take is not simply about learning the techniques of marketing, finance, accounting, and so forth, but how to practice them in the right way. Second, sound ethical practices are what make a business viable and adaptable to change over time. We do not claim that ethics *always* pays, but we do know how much ethical failure costs, not just in financial terms but in terms of productivity, innovation, morale, and goodwill in organizations. The sheer weight of guilt and regret is hard to measure, but everyone who has ever done anything wrong (and that covers just about all of us) knows how much such feelings can take away from a happy life. Third, business ethics is *everybody's* business. Every business student, every businessperson, every employee, every manager, and every executive has as his or her primary responsibility, along with learning and doing his or her job, acting ethically and, on occasion, speaking up in the face of unethical behavior. On the down side, *not* being ethical—or even failing to speak up—can bring a career, no matter how successful, to a sudden, humiliating halt. Ethical failures invite bankruptcy, lawsuits, and even jail time.

We designed this text with the pervasiveness of ethics in business and the personal nature of everyone's responsibility regarding ethics in mind. It is made up of the some of the best writing on business ethics along a broad spectrum of issues. But the readings are all directed toward one end, a practical end, and that is to provide you with the material to think about and discuss and ultimately to practice ethics in business. There are readings that tackle some huge questions about the nature of free enterprise and the new world of business in a globalized economy. There are readings concerning the new technologies and the ethical questions they raise. There are readings that focus on the details of your job—your rights, duties, and responsibilities as an employee or manager. In every reading, we want you to "take it personally." Take each issue as *your* issue, grapple with it as if it is up to you to decide, sitting there at or on your desk. These are issues that demand a decision and a solution. Someday soon, one or more of them may well be yours.

So, this book is ultimately about you, about you in business, about you as a professional, and about you as a decent human being. Our introductions to the various chapters all begin by presenting you with a situation, sometimes an ethical problem or dilemma, of the sort you may face on the job and sometimes a broader ethical issue in the business or economic world. We make no assumptions about whether you are male or female, where or in what industry you work, your precise aspirations or talents, or your race or religion. You know who you are. But ethics isn't just a matter of intuition or "gut feelings." It involves thought; information; practice in moral reasoning; and, if possible, knowledge of other, similar case histories. So you need resources—thought-provoking essays, facts, case studies, and philosophical insights.

Philosophy? Isn't that for airheads? What does it have to do with the rough and tumble of business life? But virtually every business and every businessperson has a philosophy, whether he or she calls it that or not. A philosophy specifies what is most important and what is not. A philosophy in business is a view or a vision of the place of one's business activities in one's life, in the community, and in the larger social world. It is a personal policy concerning the right and wrong ways to go about making money and the right and wrong ways of treating people (and being treated yourself). It is keeping the big picture in mind, the idea that money isn't everything, the idea that not everything is for sale, the importance of family and friends and community. (If you disagree with any of these statements, you *really* need this course.) We should add the love of one's country and one's culture, a hope for the well-being of all humanity, and some sense of the transcendent or the spiritual. By this we mean not only your religious beliefs and feelings, but the more worldly aspiration to be more than just a practical person caught up in daily routines. There are larger questions of meaning that business and making money cannot answer, like "what is the point of all this?" (Again, if you really think that the point is *just* to make money, you really need this course.)

Many great philosophers and social thinkers have had many things to say about these questions. Some of them were suspicious or even hostile to business. They saw business and making money as a tempting distraction from the more important things in life. But many philosophers and social thinkers were positive and even enthusiastic about business. The most famous of them, at least as far as business students are concerned, was Adam Smith, a moral philosopher (as well as a classic economist) in eighteenth-century Scotland. Smith thought that business (or, more accurately, the free enterprise system) offered tremendous hope to the world. But he was also very clear about the ethical presuppositions of any business culture, some sense of community or "fellow-feeling," a concern for justice and fairness in business dealings, a "natural" sense of sympathy for our fellow human beings. He would not have hesitated for a moment to embed his philosophy of business in a much larger picture of human happiness and well-being. And that is the philosophy of this book and this course as well. It is not to deny or cast doubt on business, but to situate it in a larger setting.

But you are too busy, no doubt, to read the often-wordy treatises of the philosophers. (Adam Smith's book *The Wealth of Nations* is over 500 pages long; his earlier book, *The Theory of the Moral Sentiments,* is not much shorter.) So we have devised a painless and efficient way to offer you these philosophical probes and insights. Perhaps you barely remember that roommate you had in your freshman year who considered a career in business but ultimately decided to study philosophy. For a couple of years, you lost touch. But as you have gotten into business ethics, this roommate (whom you have come to call, "the philosopher") has made a point of getting back in touch with you by email. As you read through the chapters on business and ethics, the philosopher reminds you of some of the great thoughts about business, ethics, and the good life. The philosopher's responses to your questions and opinions on various ethical issues and problems in business appear in various boxes throughout the text, providing you with some wise reflections from great thinkers past and present. Think of these boxes and others in the text as those occasional email messages you receive from friends that provide you with thoughts and an occasional laugh while you study for your courses and for your future career.

HONEST WORK

Why We Work

The Meaning of Work

Introduction

In our society, work shapes your life and your identity. What you do, in other words, has a lot to do with who you are. Accordingly, we should begin this business ethics text by asking you to think about what you ultimately value and what your work means and will mean to you. What do you want out of your work? What do you want out of your life? In this chapter, we invite you to step back, take a long look, and reflect on the meaning of work, its place in your life and in the lives of others. Thinking about the meaning of work and life is not a touchy-feely luxury in a business course. It will provide a foundation for thinking about how you should behave at work and how you understand the work behavior of others. Typically, unethical behavior in business is the product of people who have lost their perspective on themselves, their work, and their lives. Success in business, by contrast, is usually the dessert of people who know who they are, what they are doing, and why.

Some of the most profound insights about work and life, curiously enough, are to be found in the famous fables of the ancient storyteller Aesop, who wrote about animals who act, think, and talk like human beings. Aesop wrote these fables sometime around 620 B.C., but some of the same stories show up in various forms on Egyptian papyri that date back to 1000–800 B.C. In the well-known fable, "The Grasshopper and the Ant," Aesop locked horns with the question, to work or not to work? He wrote:

> The ants were employing a fine winter's day in drying grain collected in the summer time. A grasshopper, perishing with famine, passed by and earnestly begged for a little food. The ants inquired of him, "Why did you not treasure up food during the summer?" He replied, "I had not leisure enough. I passed the days in singing," They then said in derision: "If you were foolish enough to sing all the summer, you must dance supperless to bed in winter.*

This is a cautionary tale. It does not say that a life of work is better than a life of singing, but rather that if you want to sing, you have to be willing to pay the price. The issue here is self-

Aesop's Fables trans. from the Greek by Rev. G. F. Townsend (New York: McLoughin Br., 1924), p.16.

sufficiency and fairness—if you don't work, you don't eat, and you shouldn't expect others to feed you. Aesop's story gives us a choice. You can lead the brief happy life of the grasshopper or the long prudent life of the ant. Yet it's not wholly clear what the wise person should choose.

Unlike the good Protestant who would come along later, Aesop was somewhat ambivalent about industriousness. Greed, miserliness, and covetousness sometimes accompany hard work. In another story, "The Ant," he tells us that the ant was once a farmer who kept a jealous eye on his neighbor and stole some of his produce. Zeus, angry, changed the man into an ant, and Aesop wrote, "Although his form has changed, his character has not, for he still goes around the fields gathering up the wheat and barley of others and storing it up for himself." Aesop worried that industriousness, when motivated by envy can lead to theft, avarice, and miserliness.

Aesop was kinder to the grasshopper's relative, the cicada. He said that once there were men who, when music was invented, were so happy that they just kept singing and forgot food and drink until they died. From these men came the cicadas, who don't require food and sing their lives away. The muses smile upon the cicadas because their singing brings joy. While Aesop did not exactly endorse the life of the cicada, he expressed a somewhat romantic admiration. The cicada's brief life is spent in pursuit of beauty.

The aesthetic virtues of the cicadas and the moral virtues of the ant come together in Aesop's story called the "Ant and the Bee." In it, the bee and the ant have a dispute over who is more prudent and industrious. They appeal to Apollo for a judgment. The god applauds the ant's care, foresight, and independence from the labors of others, but he says, "it is you alone that you benefit; no other creature shares any part of your hoarded riches. Whereas, the bee produces, by his meritorious and ingenious exertions, that which becomes a blessing to the world." Again we see chinks in the moral armor of hard work. It's good to provide for oneself, but it is even better to contribute a pleasing and useful product for society. We admire hard work much more if people do it for some purpose that lies beyond pure self-interest. The Buddhist scriptures use the bee as a model of the environmentally responsible businessperson. They tell us, "The wise and moral man, Shines like a fire on a hill top, Making money like a bee, Who does not hurt the flower."

Aesop's ant, grasshopper, and bee give us three ways of approaching life. Frugal, acquisitive, and hardworking, the antlike worker values security above all else. He spends all his time working at a moderately interesting job, makes cautious career choices, has little involvement in nonwork activities, and takes few vacations and fewer chances. Like the ant, this sort of person saves for retirement, mortgaging certain enjoyments for 65 years of his or her life, in the hopes of making up for it in the last 10 or 20. Ants work for the future, but don't always know what to do when (or if) they reach it. The merit of the ant's life plan is that his frugality saves him from want, prepares him for emergencies, and ensures self-sufficiency.

In contrast to the ant, the grasshopper lives for the present and sacrifices the future. His playing goes nowhere and leaves nothing behind. There is pleasure in a life of play, but is there meaning? The bee works like an ant, but takes pleasure and finds meaning in producing a good and useful product that is appreciated by others. The bee symbolizes a life of useful and rewarding work, the ant represents a life of work and security, while the grasshopper depicts a frivolous life of play and uncertainty.

But why is it that "all play and no work makes Jack a big jerk"? Today we sometimes legitimate play in a work-oriented society by playing squash to unwind, golf to woo clients, and basketball for cardiovascular health. Even animals aren't exempt from nonproductive play. You may notice how the narrator of a Discovery Channel show solemnly explains to the viewer that the frolicking lion cubs may *think* that they are playing, but they are *really* practicing the skills that will make them good hunters. Contrast this with the idea of play defended by the great Greek philosopher Plato. Plato suggested that play evolved from the desire of children and small animals to leap and run around. Think for a moment of the delight that children and puppies get simply from jumping up and down and running around for no particular reason.

Play is often illogical and/or inefficient. Games are intentionally inefficient. The things that people do when they play them have no meaning outside the game. For example, if your job required you to put little white balls into 18 holes, you certainly wouldn't do it by separating the holes by several hundred yards and hitting the ball with a long, thin stick over lakes, hills, and sand traps. The point of golf is to get the ball into 18 holes in the most inefficient way possible. Getting the ball into the hole is important to the player, but just placing the golf balls in the holes serves no purpose whatsoever.

Play, like the cicada's singing, is done for no reason, except, perhaps, for pleasure. While the Aesop's grasshopper starves because he is irresponsible, the cicada is the "starving artist"; it starves for love of music. But the two fables convey different messages. Dying because of one's love of art seems to have some nobility, whereas dying just because one prefers to play games does not. For most of us, the hard question is not whether or not to play (most of us would say, "of course"), but "given freedom to choose, what should we do with the time given to us in life?"

There are four values that essentially shape how we make choices about work. They are (1) meaningful work, or work that is interesting and/or important to you or to others in society; (2) leisure or free time to do the things you want; (3) money; and (4) security. These values carry different weights at different times in life. Ideally, it would be best to have a fascinating job, plenty of vacation time, a salary that allows you to buy anything you want, and guaranteed lifetime employment. Since few of us have jobs that provide all these things, we make trade-offs, and these trade-offs signify what we value most. Consider the following thought experiment, which we will repeat in different versions throughout this book. Suppose you are single and have just graduated from college. You have four job offers. The first is a well-paying position in an accounting firm, the second is with Amnesty International, the third is a civil service job, and the fourth is a place as a waiter at an Aspen ski resort that operates only in winter. Which one would you choose?

Your answer probably derives from another question: What are you willing to give up if you can't have it all? People who are driven by the values of meaningful work and leisure are often more willing to give up security and money. If meaningful work is most important, you may choose Amnesty International. This job entails long hours without much pay or financial security but a keen sense of making a positive difference to people's lives. The resort job may not give you much meaning, money, or security, but it will give you plenty of opportunities to do what you love best, namely, ski. Meaningful work and leisure may have a lot in common. People who insist on doing meaningful work often say that they do not really distinguish between their work and their leisure-time activities. What is important to them is doing what they want to do, whether for the value of the work itself or because of its significance.

Some people prefer leisure to meaningful work because they do not want to or cannot engage in the activity they love as paid work. They turn to other activities (hobbies, music, sports, and even crime) and other institutions (family, friends, church, and community orga-

To: You
From: The Philosopher
Subject: "Worthy Work"

Do you remember the summer jobs that we had when we were students? You and I earned money baby-sitting, waiting on tables, and digging ditches. Work had a different meaning to us than to our coworkers who didn't get to quit when school started in September. I think people are willing to endure the worst jobs if it is reasonable to hope that the jobs will get them where they want to go or, at least, feed them along the way. The English designer, craftsman, poet, socialist, and all-around workaholic, William Morris, wrote a great essay on the difference between useful work and useless toil that emphasizes the importance of hope in the meaning of work.

> [There] are two kinds of work—one good, the other bad; one not far removed from a blessing, a lightening of life; the other a mere curse, a burden to life. What is the difference between them, then? This: one has hope in it, the other has not. It is manly to do one kind of work, and manly to refuse to do the other. What is the nature of hope that makes it worth doing?*
>
> It is threefold, I think—hope of rest, hope of product, hope of pleasure in the work itself; hope of these also in some abundance of good quality; rest enough and good enough to be worth having: product worth having by one who is neither a fool nor and ascetic; pleasure enough for all for us to be conscious of it while we are at work; not a mere habit, the loss of which we shall feel as a fidgety man feels the loss of the bit of string he fidgets with.
>
> Thus worthy work carries with it hope of pleasure in rest, the hope of pleasure in using what it makes, and the hope of pleasure in using our daily creative skill. All other work is worthless; it is slaves' work—mere toiling to live that we may live to toil.

*William Morris, "Useless Work Versus Useless Toil," in *The Collected Works of William Morris,* vol. 23 (London: Russell & Russell, 1966), pp. 98–100.

nizations) for the psychological rewards that they can't get from work. Meaningful work and leisure consist of activities that aren't just instrumental, but are rewarding or pleasurable in their own their own right.

If you value money and security above other things, then work is primarily an *instrumental* activity, a means toward those ends. For example, the accounting job may not be exciting, and few people ever make it to partner, but as a new graduate, you will make good money to pay off your college loans and buy a condo, nice clothes, and maybe a sports car. Those who value material goods above and beyond what they need to live comfortably trade leisure for over-time or a second job to buy extra cars and the like. Their pleasure in buying and owning things overrides their desire for free time. (Money is also important to those who value security; however, they value saving it over spending it.) If you want security, the government job may fit the bill. Even though it may not be glamorous, and you'll make less money than you would if you were in industry, the benefits are excellent, you get all the standard holidays, and it's rel-atively stable employment. At different points in one's life, different values dominate. The new graduate may choose the resort job, the single parent may choose between a challenging and time-consuming career and one that allows more time to spend with his or her children. Here, free time is more important than money or an interesting job.

This chapter begins with a short history of the meaning of work. History offers insights into the moral and emotional baggage behind our ideas about work today. What does work mean? How does it shape who you are and your moral worth? The article "Hopping On and Off Career Path" challenges the notion that your career has to dominate your life. Does it make sense to have a career that makes you work the hardest during the time in your life when your children need you the most? "The Job Interview" is an excerpt from the 1950's classic, *The Man in the Gray Flannel Suit.* In a scenario that you will probably face many times in your life, Sloan Wilson depicts a job candidate's inner struggle with who he is and what he can truthfully say to the interviewer about himself and why he wants the job. The last article, "Less Heat More Light," offers a radical proposal—why not work less and enjoy it more? Can decreasing the quantity of time we spend at work improve the quality of work?

This chapter invites you to think about the meaning of work and its place in your life. It provides a basis for your thinking about business ethics not as an abstract subject, but as *your* life in business. As we said at the beginning, success in business is most often the reward for people who know who they are, what they are doing, and why.

Joanne B. Ciulla

From Curse to Calling: A Short History of the Meaning of Work

Joanne Ciulla is professor and Coston Family chair in leadership and ethics at the Jepson School of Leadership Studies at the University of Richmond.

How did we get from the idea that we work to live to the idea that we live to work? From ancient times to the early middle ages, hard work didn't get you into heaven, demonstrate your moral goodness, endear you to your neighbors, or promise insight into the meaning of your life. Over time, work emerged from a morally neutral and somewhat negative idea to one that is rich with moral and social value and fundamental to how we think of ourselves. It's not easy to pinpoint when work began its moral and personal ascent. By looking at some historical snapshots, we will see how religion and ideas about fate shaped the social, moral, and personal meanings of work that we carry with us today.

THE ANCIENTS

For the ancient Greeks work was a curse. Around the 8th or 9th century B.C. Homer wrote that the gods hated humans and made them toil out of spite.[1] In the same era, the poet and farmer Hesiod said that the gods were displeased with humans so they buried their food under the earth. His poem "Works and Days" deplores idleness and begging but sees no inherent dignity in work. Hesiod longs for the return of the Golden Age when people lived without working.[2] But he also tells us that "envy and strife" motivate people to work and that strife is good for mortals, "so potter is piqued with potter, joiner with joiner, beggar begrudges beggar, and singer, singer."[3] In the third century B.C., the historian Xenophon said that work was the price that people had to pay for the goods of life.[4] If work was a curse from the gods, it was best given to people who were cursed either because they were vanquished enemies or captured foreigners or children of slaves. Slaves freed the affluent ancient Greeks from work. The Greeks considered slavish all occupations that served the needs of the maintenance of life.[5]

Aristotle not only thought that work was something that should, if possible, be foisted off on slaves, he believed that work done for profit could be its own curse. Property (land and slaves), not work, was the basis of a person's livelihood. Aristotle distinguished between work done to produce things for use in the household and work done for commercial gain. He said that household work, done to produce the things we need to stay alive, is natural and finite because human needs are finite. He called household production "oeconomia." Retail trade or work done for financial gain is not natural to humans because, according to Aristotle, it is produced for human wants. Wants, unlike human needs, are unlimited.[6] Aristotle said that the most hated and unnatural way to make money is through usury and interest. Money should be used for exchange, not for the breeding of more money. Those who believe they should spend their lives working on getting or not losing money are, according to Aristotle, "intent on living only, and not upon living well."[7] People who are consumed with getting wealth use everything as a means to wealth. They are not able to enjoy anything for its own sake. Furthermore, people who work for wealth are never satisfied because the things that they want and the work that they do to get it are never ending.

EARLY CHRISTIANS

Like the ancient Greeks, the early Christians emphasized the importance of contemplation over work, but for ascetic, rather than aesthetic, reasons. Although a carpenter by trade, Christ preached that work is irrelevant. Counseling absolute trust in God, he said, don't worry about food, "Behold the fowls of the air;

for they sow not, neither do they reap or gather into barns; Yet your Heavenly Father feedeth them. Are ye not much better than they?"[8] Nor should we care about clothing, "Consider how the lilies of the field grow; they neither toil nor spin."[9] As noted earlier, the problem with work was that people sometimes used it to accumulate wealth and glory. In the Bible, Christ cautions us, "It is easier for a camel to go through the eye of a needle than for a rich man to enter into the Kingdom of God."[10] The pursuit of wealth offered all sorts of temptations and distractions that interfered with the journey to paradise. In the first few centuries after Christ, people believed that since they were just passing through life on earth on their way to heaven, it made sense to invest in eternity, through contemplation and prayer. While a few people, such as the early monks, took Christ's asceticism literally, for the most part, the Catholic attitude was that you should trust in divine providence and only do what is necessary to get by.

In the New Testament, St. Paul recognizes the importance of work for order, just rewards, and discipline. He counsels the Thessalonians to live regularly, "For we have heard that some among you are living irregularly, doing no work but busy at meddling." Do not burden others by eating their bread, he says, "If any would not work, neither should he eat."[11] There are three messages here. Work is a part of the rhythm of life, it keeps people from getting into trouble, and it's not fair to eat food that you didn't earn.

The Church distinguished between work done to supply the basics of life with "good works" or work done for others, and work done for personal or material gains. The seven deadly sins—pride, envy, greed, gluttony, lust, anger, and sloth—reflect the potential dangers of work done for material gain.

MEDIEVAL OCCUPATIONAL ETHICS

By the 13th century, the medieval Catholic Church had become more interested in a person's disposition to sin, which was rooted in concrete social and work-related situations. As historian Jacques Le Goff pointed out, "For them, the demon took the form not so much of the seven deadly sins as of the countless offenses against God that a trade or group might fos-

To: You
From: The Philosopher
Subject: "Sloth: The Noonday Demon"

Have you ever noticed how the seventh deadly sin, sloth, seems almost out of place with the first six? I always thought it was worse to be greedy or lustful than to be just plain lazy, but it turns out that sloth isn't simply about not wanting to work, it's about being bored, listless, and simply not caring about work. In the fourth century, the Egyptian monk Evagrius called sloth the "Noonday Demon" that attacked monks after lunch and made the day seem as if it lasted 50 hours. He said:

> [The Noonday Demon] causes the monk continually to look out the windows and forces him to step out of his cell and to gaze at the sun to see how far it is from the ninth hour and to look around, here and there, whether any of his brethren is near.*

It makes you wonder how many people are attacked by this demon every day at work either because of a mind-numbing job, a big lunch, or sheer exhaustion.

*Siegfried Wenzel, *The Sin of Sloth: Acedia* (Chapel Hill, NC: University of North Carolina Press, 1967), p. 5.

ter in a variety of ways.[12] In 1215, confession became mandatory for all Christians, and priests used confessional manuals to understand the moral dangers of various occupations. These manuals regarded sin as a type of occupational hazard. One such manual, the *Summa Confessorum* by John of Frieburg, began with a section on sins that are common to all people and was then arranged by sins that are common to 14 occupational categories, ranging from bishops and their vicars to manual laborers. The confessional manuals told priests what sins to look for and what questions to ask in confession. For example, one manual says, "A knight must not be questioned about the sins of a monk, or vice versa."[13] Work not only identified people, it identified their potential virtues and vices. Priests were told to keep an eye out for signs of lust in innkeepers, bathhouse keepers, and tavern keepers. Cooks were potential gluttons, while a dishwasher's and a laundry man's contact with the unclean made them generally suspicious and put them near the bottom of all work. The manuals also urged priests to watch merchants and lawyers closely for signs of greed. Some wealthy merchants bought confessional manuals, which were expensive, and used them as business ethics guides. The manuals contained advice on all sorts of things, such as fair prices, money lending, and doing business at fairs on the Sabbath.

This new emphasis on the relationship among spiritual life, intentions, and vocation theologically connected personal identity and morality with work. Meanwhile, the growing identity with one's work was already occurring as a result of the emerging craft guilds. In the early middle ages, people had only first names, such as Mary, William, and John. Their identity came from their patron saint, their father, or their town. A person could be named after St. Mary or be called "John's son" or "William of Stratford." By the 12th century, people started using surnames that identified a person with his or her work. Consider the number of common surnames that are derived from trades, like Baker, Carpenter, Thatcher, Smith, Weaver,

Goldsmith, and Cook. These names came from a time when you would call on Margaret Thatcher to fix your roof and James Baker for a loaf of bread.

THE RENAISSANCE: WORK AS CREATIVITY

Our most beloved picture of work came from the Renaissance—work as creation. Humanism rested on the idea that God created man who was a creator of art, music, and other things of beauty. Wealthy merchants and bankers had the ancient Greek classics dusted off, translated, and reinterpreted. For example, the myth of Prometheus took on new meaning and significance. Prometheus, whose name means "foreseeing," stole fire from Zeus so that man could use it to forge the articles of human life. For the ancients, Prometheus was a trickster who doomed humanity to hard labor. By the Renaissance, he was a hero who had allowed mankind to seize hold of fate. The value of work grew as more people began to feel that they could control their lives, rather than wait around for divine providence. Fourteenth-century Florence gave us the image of humans as creators who mold the world and reshape nature, the *homo faber.* The Renaissance "man" educated his mind, spirit, body, and hands and produced things of beauty and worth. If religion was the opiate of the Middle Ages, creativity was the amphetamine of the Renaissance.

The Renaissance had its own rendition of the work ethic. St. Antonious of Florence and Bernardi of Sienna condemned idleness and extravagance and lauded activity. Wealth was all right as long as the rich man did something with his money and did not cling to it like a miser. The 15th-century philosopher and architect Leon Battista Alberti praised laboriousness because it "fills so well the slow passage of the hours."[14] Time was something used and filled, not simply passed. Alberti was considered one of the first universal or Renaissance men. He believed that life was about doing things, not waiting for them to happen. To the ancient Greek belief in training the body and the mind, the Renaissance added the hand.

Tommaso Campanella's *City of the Sun,* written in 1602, emphasized a social order based on communal living and science. All classes of society are equal in Campanella's utopia, and everyone in it loves working because they have jobs that are suitable to their character. However, Campenella tells us that the most noble are people who work at more than one trade.[15] The person defines his or her work, not vice versa—the man makes the work, rather than the work makes the man. What we call the "Renaissance Man" is someone who is interested and accomplished in many areas and in control of who he is and what he does. The ideal of the Renaissance Man stands in sharp contrast to the modern view. While we admire well-rounded people, we tend to encourage and reward them for excelling in one profession or area of work.

THE REFORMATION: WORK AS A MORAL QUALITY

The moral and spiritual ascendancy of work was marked by the descent of the beggar from a figure of compassion to a lazy freeloader, from the one who was first into the pearly gates to the one who was locked out. There was massive unemployment across Europe in the 16th century. In England, the enclosure laws turned communal land that was farmed by peasants into private pasturage for nobles. These laws forced peasants off the land. Those who couldn't find work became vagrants and beggars. Also, some scholars estimate that the population of Europe doubled during the 16th century, outstripping the job market and the land available for people to farm.[16] Beggars and vagrants appeared in great numbers in cities from Rome to London.

As we look back at this history through the lens of modern economics, we can easily explain why the ranks of the unemployed swelled and understand why displaced people migrated into cities. But this was not the way that Luther and other leaders of the time saw the world. Vagrancy and unemployment were not the cause by economic conditions; they were the result of a personal moral deficiency. Luther railed against lazy beggars and vagrants whom he saw on the streets. He believed that people were poor and homeless because they didn't want to work (a view still held by some today).[17] Luther's attitude was a radical departure from the traditional views of other major religions. For example, in the Koran and the Bible, beggars are part of the natural order of the world, and almsgiving is a moral and spiritual duty.

Luther wasn't alone in his condemnation of beggars. Alarmed by vagrants in 16th-century Rome, Pope Sixtus V denounced people who *feigned* poverty in order to live off the community without labor. In 1536, Henry VIII of England outlawed begging except for old and deserving beggars who were issued begging licenses.[18] Charity to the poor was not abandoned in the 16th century, it was just more discriminating. The able-bodied beggar was out, but the blind cripple was still worthy of receiving alms. The world of work had become everyone's monastery. There was no sympathy for those who were capable of work but living on the outside.

WORK AS IDENTITY

We credit Calvin and Luther with the idea of work for work's sake and the abhorrence of rest and pleasure. This is but one of the many renditions of what is called the work ethic. For Calvin, work was a token of grace and the means of salvation. In contrast to the aesthetic views of the Renaissance, Calvin's call to work demanded a worldly asceticism that limited indulgence of pleasures and luxuries, but did not completely exclude them. The accumulation of wealth was a sign that you were among God's chosen. Laziness and poverty indicated that you probably were not. One of the Calvinists' favorite biblical passages was Proverbs xxii 29: "Seest thou a man diligent in his business? He shall stand before kings." According to Calvin, the wealthy burgers of his time weren't supposed to spend their money on excessive consumption; rather, they were supposed save and reinvest it. Nonetheless, the emphasis on work, saving, and investment resulted in a richer and more diverse material world, which was, as Calvin and the Catholic Church feared, *very* seductive. Little did Calvin know that despite his warnings against luxurious consumption, the work ethic would, for some, mutate from the belief that we are born to work into the belief that we are born to shop.

The Reformation had defined all work as *beruf,* or a calling.[19] A calling did not refer to a type of work, but an attitude toward work. The Protestant work ethic also implied that through work, you could find yourself and discover your salvation. Work provided a means of discovering and creating oneself. Unsure of salvation, work was a quest for identity and signs of God's favor. As Max Weber pointed out, the Reformation left modern man with "an unprecedented inner loneliness."[20] In the Middle Ages, the Catholic could attain grace with the help of priests and the sacraments. The Calvinist and Lutheran had to go it alone; no one could change what God had already decided.

Since the time of Calvin and Luther, the work ethic was more likely to make sense to middle-class craftsmen, farmers, owners of small businesses, and professionals. When these people worked diligently, they got something out of it—a better life, respect, and satisfaction, whereas for slaves, indentured servants, and early industrial workers, there was little to gain from working beyond what was necessary, except exhaustion. The Protestant work ethic took hold in the northern European countries and among early settlers of the northern United States, not in the predominately Catholic countries, such as Spain, Italy, and France and the American South during the time of slavery. Writing in the early 20th century, Max Weber observed that "the Protestant prefers to eat well, the Catholic, to sleep undisturbed."[21]

We have been looking at how religion shaped the moral value of work. The ancients saw work as a necessity and a curse. The medieval Catholic Church bestowed on work a simple dignity. Renaissance humanists gave it glamour, but the Protestants endowed work with the quest for meaning, identity, and signs of salvation. The notion of work as something beyond mere labor, as work-plus, indeed as a calling, highlighted the personal and existential qualities of work. Work became a kind of prayer. More than a means of living, it became a purpose for living.

NOTES

1. Adriano Tilghar, *Work: What It Has Meant to Men Through the Ages,* trans. Dorothy Canfield Fisher, (New York: Harcourt, Brace & World, 1958), p. 3.

2. Ibid., p. 40.

3. Hesiod, *Theogeny and Works and Days,* trans. M. L. West (Oxford: Oxford University Press, 1988), p. 37.

4. Ibid., p. 3.

5. See Hannah Arendt, *The Human Condition,* (Chicago: University of Chicago Press, 1958), p. 80.

6. Aristotle, *Politics,* Bk. I, 1257b18–1258b7, trans. Benjamin Jowett, *The Complete Works of Aristotle,* Vol. II, ed. Jonathan Barnes (Princeton, N.J.: Princeton University Press, 1984), pp. 1995–1997.

7. Ibid., p. 1996.

8. Matthew 6:27.

9. Matthew 6:29.

10. Mark 10:26.

11. 2 Thessalonians 3:6–12.

12. Jacques Le Goff, *Time, Work and Culture in the Middle Ages* trans. Arthur Goldhammer (Chicago: University of Chicago Press, 1980), p. 39.

13. Ibid., p. 119.

14. Tilgher, *Work,* p. 43.

15. Ibid., p. 43.

16. R. Davis *The Rise of Atlantic Economies* (Ithaca, N.Y.: Cornell University Press, 1973), p. 18.

17. Paul Bernstein, *American Work Values* (Albany: State University of New York Press, 1997), p. 43.

18. John A. Garraty, *Unemployment in History: Economic Thought and Public Policy* (New York: Harper & Row, 1978), pp. 27–28.

19. Ibid., p. 194.

20. Max Weber, *The Protestant Ethic and the Spirit of Capitalism,* trans. Talcott Parsons (New York: Scribners, 1958), p. 104.

21. Ibid., p. 41.

QUESTIONS

1. How did the values associated with work change the meaning of work?

2. What are the strengths and dangers of having work as a key part of your identity?

Michelle Quinn

Hopping On and Off Career Track

Michelle Quinn is a staff writer for the *San Jose Mercury.*

Jennifer Lee was torn between two loves: her career as a hardware designer and her 10-month-old baby girl. She couldn't see how devotion to both could coexist, so she chose to stay home.

Two years later, Lee still wrestles with her decision. But she has joined a group of San Jose women who are also "sequencing," temporarily dropping out of the work force to raise children.

Sequencing is not a new idea but is gaining popularity as one way to think about being a stay-at-home mom without losing professional identity. The original concept was simple: Work hard before the children arrive. Step off the career track to be at home when the kids are young. Step back on when the children are older with work that allows flexibility.

Clearly it is a choice of privilege, belonging primarily to women with financial resources. Many of these women were expected to take motherhood in their stride as they shattered the corporate glass ceiling. Some do just that. But others are choosing to be home with plans to return later.

"It's almost like our generation is trying to prove something," said Jennifer Juo, 33, of Oakland, Calif. She quit work as an international trade manager at a biotechnology incubator to stay home with her 2-year-old son. "It's not just climbing to the top of

From Michelle Quinn, "Hopping On and Off Career Track," *Madison State Journal,* May 10, 2004, p. C10.

the corporate ladder. Other things are important such as family and a good marriage."

AREA WOMEN, COMPANIES PART OF THE TREND

In Madison, the trend is alive and well—and being aided by helpful dads, said Roger Backes, a local career coach.

"It is very helpful to have a cooperative husband who participates to the extent of cutting down on their hours to take on some of the child-care burden so the woman can restart with a greater focus on her career effort," said Backes, whose business is Coaching by Roger Backes. "I have lots of male friends who have done that . . . wanting to be good fathers and wanting to support their wives."

Some critics and even women who sequence worry that the job market won't be welcoming to women who take time off. If they do return, will the time away hurt their advancement?

Backes suggests that women planning to return should try to stay professionally connected in some way—or, if they were unhappy in their previous career, to use the time off to explore new options.

"It doesn't take a whole lot of time . . . to stay connected with the professional associations," Backes said. And sometimes, "women who are motivated by their careers sometimes have that motivation enhanced by stepping out of it."

First appearing in the 1986 book "Sequencing," the concept has evolved to include mothers who work part time or change careers to accommodate their families. (Its cousin, the "mommy track," was hotly debated in the early 1990s over whether mothers working flexible schedules were marginalized in the workplace.)

Women used to feel they had to downplay their home lives and their ambivalence about leaving young children to work, said Joanne Brundage, who, in 1986, started Mothers & More, a national organization with a local chapter devoted to helping sequencing women.

Now, the group, with 7,000 members, has a mission to help mothers exiting and re-entering the work force. "There is no right way to do this," Brundage said.

The more education a new mother has, the more likely she is to be working full time, according to a 2003 Census report.

However, over the past decade, there's been a trend in the other direction, particularly among women with a child under 1 year old and who have a bachelor's degree or some graduate training. In 1990, 68 percent of these mothers were in the labor force. In 2002, that dropped to 63.5 percent.

Now pregnant with her second child, Juo began to ask herself, how much money did her family need? What was her definition of success?

The transition back into the work force can be more difficult than most people anticipate. Sequencing, as a concept, "blithely ignores the financial penalty" experienced by stay-at-home mothers, said Ann Crittenden, author of "The Price of Motherhood."

Ellen Galinsky, president of the Families and Work Institute, a New York research center that provides data on the work force, said younger workers often don't know that a female executive once took time off—and how she built her career back.

"One of our suggestions to companies is: Make the career paths of your successful leaders visible," Galinsky said.

Friends and colleagues point to Karen Brewer as an example that sequencing can work. In 1992, Brewer quit her job as director of sales at Macromedia. Her first son was 6 months old and she was told she couldn't work part time. "It killed me to hand off our son every day to our nanny," she said.

Over the next decade, Brewer had two more boys, did some consulting and became involved with the community.

But three years ago, when her husband lost his job, Brewer was catapulted into a job search. She called people she knew. Bought new clothes. Practiced explaining the seven-year gap in full-time work on her resume.

Two years ago, she found a managerial job at Autodesk. "You never lose what you learn," said Brewer, now a director of product marketing at Autodesk.

QUESTIONS

1. What values would have to change in the workplace and in society for sequencing to be a viable way of pursuing a career for both men and women?

2. Do businesses have an obligation to implement employment practices that help men and women care for their families' needs?

CASES

CASE 1.1
The Job Interview
Sloan Wilson

"Why do you want to work for the United Broadcasting Corporation?" Walker asked abruptly.

"It's a good company . . ." Tom began hesitantly, and was suddenly impatient at the need for hypocrisy. The sole reason he wanted to work for United Broadcasting was that he thought he might be able to make a lot of money there fast, but he felt he couldn't say that. It was sometimes considered fashionable for the employees of foundations to say that they were in it for the money, but people were supposed to work at advertising agencies and broadcasting companies for spiritual reasons.

"I believe," Tom said, "that television is developing into the greatest medium for mass education and entertainment. It has always fascinated me, and I would like to work with it. . . ."

"What kind of salary do you have in mind?" Walker asked. Tom hadn't expected the question that soon. Walker was still smiling.

"The salary isn't the primary consideration with me," Tom said, trying desperately to come up with stock answers to stock questions. "I'm mainly interested in finding something useful and worth while to do. I have personal responsibilities, however, and I would hope that something could be worked out to enable me to meet them . . ."

"Of course," Walker said, beaming more cheerily than ever. "I understand you applied for a position in the public-relations department. Why did you choose that?"

Because I heard there was an opening, Tom wanted to say, but quickly thought better of it and substituted a halting avowal of lifelong interest in public relations. "I think my experience in working with *people* at the Schanenhauser Foundation would be helpful," he concluded lamely.

"I see," Walker said kindly. There was a short silence before he added, "Can you write?"

"I do most of the writing at the Schanenhauser Foundation," Tom said. "The annual report to the

From Sloan Wilson, *The Man in the Gray Flannel Suit* (Simon & Schuster, 1955), pp. 13–14.

trustees is my job, and so are most of the reports on individual projects. I used to be editor of my college paper."

"That sounds fine," Walker said casually. "I have a little favor I want to ask of you. I want you to write me your autobiography."

"What?" Tom asked in astonishment.

"Nothing very long," Walker said. "Just as much as you can manage to type out in an hour. One of my girls will give you a room with a typewriter."

"Is there anything in particular you want me to tell you about?"

"Yourself," Walker said, looking hugely pleased. "Explain yourself to me. Tell me what kind of person you are. Explain why we should hire you."

"I'll try," Tom said weakly.

"You'll have precisely an hour," Walker said. "You see, this is a device I use in employing people—I find it most helpful. For this particular job, I have twenty or thirty applicants. It's hard to tell from a brief interview whom to choose, so I ask them all to write about themselves for an hour. You'd be surprised how revealing the results are. . . ."

He paused, still smiling. Tom said nothing.

"Just a few hints," Walker continued. "Write anything you want, but at the end of your last page, I'd like you to finish this sentence: 'The most significant fact about me is . . .'"

"The most significant fact about me is . . ." Tom repeated idiotically.

"The results, of course, will be entirely confidential." Walker lifted a bulky arm and inspected his wrist watch. "It's now five minutes to twelve," he concluded. "I'll expect your paper on my desk at precisely one o'clock."

Tom stood up, put on his coat, said, "Thank you," and went out of the room. . . .

Tom sat down in the chair, which had been designed for a stenographer and was far too small for him. Son of a bitch, he thought—I guess the laws about cruel and unusual punishment don't apply to personnel men. He tried to think of something to write, but all he could remember was Betsy and the drab little house and the need to buy a new washing machine, and the time he had thrown a vase that cost forty dollars against the wall. "The most significant

fact about me is that I once threw a vase costing forty dollars against a wall." That would be as sensible as anything else he could think of, but he doubted whether it would get him the job. He thought of Janey saying, "It isn't *fair!*" and the worn linoleum on the kitchen floor. "The most significant fact about me is . . ." It was a stupid sentence to ask a man to finish.

I have children, he thought—that's probably the most significant fact about me, the only one that will have much importance for long. Anything about a man can be summed up in numbers. Thomas R. Rath, thirty-three years old, making seven thousand dollars a year, owner of a 1939 Ford, a six-room house, and ten thousand dollars' worth of G.I. Life Insurance which, in case of his death, would pay his widow about forty dollars a month. Six feet one and a half inches tall; weight, 198 pounds. He served four and a half years in the Army, most of it in Europe and the rest in the South Pacific.

Another statistical fact came to him then, a fact which he knew would be ridiculously melodramatic to put into an application for a job at the United Broadcasting Corporation, or to think about at all. He hadn't thought about this for a long while. It wasn't a thing he had deliberately tried to forget—he simply hadn't thought about it for quite a few years. It was the unreal-sounding, probably irrelevant, but quite accurate fact that he had killed seventeen men. . . .

Such things were merely part of the war, the war before the Korean one. It was no longer fashionable to talk about the war, and certainly it had never been fashionable to talk about the number of men one had killed. Tom couldn't forget the number, "seventeen," but it didn't seem real any more; it was just a small, isolated statistic that nobody wanted. His mind went blank. . . .

"The most significant fact about me is that I detest the United Broadcasting Corporation, with all its soap operas, commercials, and yammering studio audiences, and the only reason I'm willing to spend my life in such a ridiculous enterprise is that I want to buy a more expensive house and a better brand of gin."

That certainly wouldn't get him the job.

"The most significant fact about me is that I've become a cheap cynic."

That would not be apt to get him the job.

"The most significant fact about me is that as a young man in college, I played the mandolin incessantly. I, champion mandolin player, am applying to you for a position in the public-relations department!"

That would not be likely to get him far. Impatiently he sat down at the typewriter and glanced at his wrist watch. It was a big loud-ticking wrist watch with a black face, luminous figures, and a red sweep hand that rapidly ticked off the seconds. He had bought it years ago at an Army post exchange and had worn it all through the war. The watch was the closest thing to a good-luck charm he had ever had, although he never thought of it as such. Now it was more reassuring to look at than the big impersonal clock on the wall, though both said it was almost twelve-thirty. So far he had written nothing. What the hell, he thought. I was a damn fool to think I wanted to work here anyway. Then he thought of Betsy asking, as she would be sure to, "Did you get the job? How did it go?" And he decided to try.

"Anybody's life can be summed up in a paragraph," he wrote. "I was born on November 20, 1920, in my grandmother's house in South Bay, Connecticut. I was graduated from Covington Academy in 1937, and from Harvard College in 1941. I spent four and a half years in the Army, reaching the rank of captain. Since 1946, I have been employed as an assistant to the director of the Schanenhauser Foundation. I live in Westport, Connecticut, with my wife and three children. From the point of view of the United Broadcasting Corporation, the most significant fact about me is that I am applying for a position in its public-relations department, and after an initial period of learning, I probably would do a good job. I will be glad to answer any questions which seem relevant, but after considerable thought, I have decided that I do not wish to attempt an autobiography as part of an application for a job."

He typed this paragraph neatly in the precise center of a clean piece of paper, added his name and address, and carried it into Walker's office. It was only quarter to one, and Walker was obviously surprised to see him. "You've still got fifteen minutes!" he said.

"I've written all I think is necessary," Tom replied, and handed him the almost empty page.

Walker read it slowly, his big pale face expressionless. When he had finished it, he dropped it into a drawer. "We'll let you know our decision in a week or so," he said.

QUESTIONS

1. What values does Tom struggle with in the job interview?

2. What does this story say to you about the relationship between the individual and the organization?

CASE 1.2
Less Heat, More Light
Nick Denton

STATE OF THE UNION: My next company will be different. No more late nights. No more monomaniac workaholics. Less heat, more light. Call it the 80% company.

My first job over here was with a company of 120%-ers. It said so on the web site, without further explanation, as if it were self-evident that employees of a successful startup would work more than humanly possible.

"Are you a 120%-er?" I was asked in my interview. Intoxicated with stories of kids with sleeping bags under their desks and a mission to change the world, I answered unhesitatingly: yes, totally. Just as I later put aside my awkward English reserve and joined in on the high-five celebratory greeting when the incompetent programmers produced another line of code.

That particular company went bankrupt; the frenetic activity of the dot.com years has produced about a dozen lasting companies and a generation of burned-out cynics. They will never again believe that a business can be built on enthusiasm—and venture capital—alone.

And this is why I intend my next company to be different. No more late nights. No more monomaniac workaholics. Less heat, more light. If I keep my nerve, I'm going to institute a four-day week as the norm. Call it the 80% company.

It is a controversial notion, particularly in the U.S., where people work longer hours than anywhere else in the developed world. In Silicon Valley, the connection between success and long hours is so much assumed that venture capitalists are said to make investment decisions, in part, on the number of cars at night in a company's parking lot.

I could say that I have come to that conclusion from a study of international productivity statistics.

The International Labour Organization points to labour productivity growth—that is, productivity growth allowing for the impact of capital spending.

In the 1980s and 1990s, as U.S. workers put in longer and longer hours—1,966 per annum compared with 1,560 in Germany—labour productivity rose much more rapidly in western Europe. This is despite the fact that annual working hours have been going up in the U.S., while they've been on the decline or remained steady in Germany, France and other western European countries.

One could draw conclusions from France's Loi Aubrey, which legislated for a 35-hour week. France outstrips the U.S. in output per man-hour. When workers in the UK had to work three days a week in the 1970s to save power, production dropped only marginally.

But I've dug out these statistics only to justify a gut feeling: that part-timers are simply more effective, and just plain nicer to have around.

At Moreover Technologies, we employed a marketing writer called Eric who did not really want the job. He was, and is, a novelist, but reluctantly supplements his income with part-time commercial work. Open about his lack of commitment, Eric would achieve more in three days than others in a week, and with much less fuss.

Generalizing a little, part-timers are better employees first of all because they are more disciplined. It is an item of faith among part-timers with young children that they are more efficient than their full-time (usually male) counterparts, because they can't procrastinate. They simply have to get everything done by 5.30 p.m. in order to relieve the child care.

Second, part-timers focus on the job rather than their own psychological needs. Someone who writes a novel out of hours—or looks after children, or scales cliffs on Fridays—is less likely to have a mental breakdown over the company's decision to target larger corporate customers.

Third, part-timers are more loyal. It is so hard in corporate America to find a part-time job with real status that no-one can easily afford to leave. Once an employee has tasted the delights of another 52 days off each year, they will not want to go back to the U.S. norm: most working Americans get less than three weeks of paid vacation each year.

It is true, that part-timers lack single-minded drive. To which I would counter: yes, thank God. The creative and driven individuals who populated the management of most dot.coms spent far too much of their time arguing strategy, concluding meaningless deals and politicking. Give me someone who is in it for the wage cheque, any day.

There is just one problem with hiring part-timers. The obsessive full-timers. They dislike the idea that someone else has a life outside work; they complain about absent part-time colleagues; and, above all, they resent reporting to someone who puts in fewer hours. That means, in practice, that it is difficult to put part-timers into management positions, even though they often have the right, calm and organized temperament.

So my solution: employ only 80%-ers. Close down on Fridays. That way an employer can hire people with a life outside work, and give them a career path. Yes, you too can become a CEO one day. An 80% CEO, that is.

QUESTIONS

1. What is the difference between a workaholic and someone who works hard?

2. Do you think that reducing the workweek or hiring more part-time workers will improve people's lives and make the workplace more productive?

CHAPTER QUESTIONS

1. What is the relationship between the meaning of work and moral behavior in the workplace?

2. How does the history of the meaning of work shed light on the meanings of work today?

Promises and Betrayals on the Job

Ethics in the Workplace

Introduction

Most workplaces are like zoos. They are filled with a variety of people, some like you and some quite exotic. When you go to work, you navigate your way through a complex web of relationships with people who often seem to be of different species. Some of them are dominant, some are docile, some are cooperative, others are contentious, some are kind, and some will bite you. When you think of it, work is basically about the interaction of people toward some common goals, and ethics is about how they treat each other. The work zoo is an emotional place where employees experience anger, pain, fear, joy, satisfaction, and even love, sometimes all at once and in the same building. Not only do these people have different titles and different job descriptions, they also carry with them different lives shaped by gender, race, ethnicity, religion, health, and personal values, experiences, and cultural and personal preferences. Almost everyone you work with lives in another world with other responsibilities at home and at play. Before they go to work, some drop their children off at day care or school, others leave behind an elderly parent or a seriously ill spouse or partner, and still others say good-bye to their faithful dog or an empty apartment. After work, there are those who go off to help their favorite charity, those who go to the health club, and still others who head for the nearest bar. But they are all fellow members of this human zoo that we call work and, as such, deserve to be treated fairly and with respect.

When you think about it, what most upsets you about your job are the times when you either don't feel like you are treated with respect or don't think you are treated fairly. Throughout the history of modern work, one hears the same refrain from workers, "We just want to be treated like adults!" In the workplace, respect means treating someone as an autonomous person on the job, while at the same time knowing where to draw the line between the employee's job and the employee's personal life. You may have noticed that this line between work and private life is not easy to draw, especially if you socialize with coworkers, check your office email from home or are on call after hours via a pager or cell phone. But as your work life and your "personal" life converge, the question becomes even more pressing: What is the relation between the two? Is it OK for you to do whatever you want to in your personal life as long as you do your job well? What is the proper realm of privacy? And what are the employer's and employee's rights and responsibilities to each other?

Many great thinkers have argued that a core principle of all ethics is respect for our common humanity. That is why this chapter begins with Norman Bowie's discussion of what this principle means (according to Immanuel Kant) and how it applies to the workplace. One aspect of respecting people is appreciating that they have feelings. In "Exploring the Managed Heart," Arlie Hochschild describes the emotional labor that flight attendants and others in the service industry do every day. Her article raises the question, When does the requirement to be nice to customers compromise the dignity and autonomy of a person? Where does one draw the line between politeness and humiliation? But what are your rights at work? Anita Superson's article is about the right of employees to know about hazards in the workplace and the responsibility of employers to tell them. Employers carry a heavy moral burden because when they hire and fire people, they have an enormous impact on people's lives. John Orlando's article on corporate downsizing explores this responsibility in detail, as does the case "A 'State of the Art' Termination."

People too easily forget the most basic moral principle when they become managers, the golden rule. "Do unto others as you would have them do unto you," or perhaps even the more important rule, "Do *not* do unto others what you would *not* want them do unto you." As you well know, fairness goes beyond rules. It requires good sense and, most important, good judgment. Businesses often try to devise objective standards for hiring, salaries, firing, and promotion, but these standards do not always take into account the fact that fallible human beings implement them and apply them to a varied pool of people, some of them very different from themselves. But fairness, which is at the very heart of business ethics, requires that all of us pay attention both to standards of fairness and to our own fallibilities in trying to apply them.

The last article on antigay jokes and the cases that follow are all about the different kinds of people we meet in the workplace and the things that they bring with them to their relationships at work. Some of these people are gay, some have AIDS, some are drug users and wife beaters, and some are women and/or minorities who can't seem to get a fair deal. All these cases challenge you to think about how to treat people fairly and with respect when they are different, difficult, or just having problems. Even sexual attraction can influence your judgment at work. After all, people have been known to fall "in lust" on the job.

Respect for persons and fairness are both moral obligations, but they are more than that. They are at the core of what makes us good people and a good part of what motivates us to cooperate with one another. Thus, a solid sense of what is personally fair (and unfair) lies at the heart of personal, social, and professional success as well. People have known this for a long time. Around the eighth century B.C., the poet Hesiod wrote, "Neither famine nor disaster ever haunt men who do true justice; but lightheartedly they tend the fields which are all their care."

Norman E. Bowie | # Respecting the Humanity in a Person

Norman E. Bowie is a professor of management at the University of Minnesota.

Part of the power of Kant's ethics lies in the extent of its ability to answer questions that Kant himself did not consider.

—Barbara Herman

INTRODUCTION

If the average American has a second moral principle to supplement the Golden Rule, it is probably a principle that says we should respect people. Respecting people is thoroughly interwoven into the fabric of American moral life. There is no one in the business community that has challenged the respect for persons principle as a principle in business ethics the way Albert Carr challenged the application of the Golden Rule in business. Yet, ironically, many of the moral criticisms of business practice are directed against policies that do not respect persons, e.g., that business human relations policies often invade privacy or relegate people to dead-end jobs where they cannot grow. In addition, there is considerable controversy, even among ethicists, as to what a respect for persons principle requires. . . .

I want to begin with an example which, although oversimplified, represents a standard discussion of the application of Kant's respect for persons principle to business. After presenting the example, I shall provide Kant's justification of the respect for persons principle and, using contemporary scholarship, explain what Kant means by the principle. With that in hand I will be able to apply the principle to more complex business examples.

I recall from my undergraduate ethics class more than 30 years ago that we struggled with the issue of whether buying a product, like vegetables in the supermarket, violated the respect for persons requirement of the second formulation of the categorical imperative. In buying our groceries did we merely use the clerk who rang up our purchases on the register? The first issue to be decided was whether we treated the sales person as a thing. Somewhat naively we decided that we did not merely use people in business transactions because we could accomplish our goal—buying carrots or potatoes—but that we could still show respect to those on the other end of the transaction. A casual observer in a supermarket can usually distinguish those patrons who treat the cashiers with respect from those who do not.

Our "solution" in this undergraduate class did not address business exchanges that involve tradeoffs between human and nonhuman sources. Any introductory economics text establishes that the efficient producer is instructed always to rearrange capital, land, machines, and workers so that their proportional marginal productivity is equal. The requirement of equal proportional marginal productivity works as follows: If the price of machines rises with respect to labor, substitute labor for machines. If the price of labor rises with respect to machines, substitute machines for labor. Both substitutions are equivalent.[1]

At first glance it looks as if a Kantian would say that the two substitutions are not morally equivalent. The first is morally permissible; the second is not morally permissible. It looks as if the employees are used as a means merely for the enhancement of the profits of the stockholders. It is morally permissible to use machines that way but it is not morally permissible to use people that way. Unlike the grocery-store example, the managers who act on behalf of the stockholders are not in a personal face-to-face relationship with the employees and thus they cannot avoid the charge of merely using the employees by saying that in the transaction they treated the other

From Norman E. Bowie, *Business Ethics: A Kantian Perspective* (Oxford: Blackwell Publishers, 1999), 63–78 (edited).

party to the transaction with respect. It doesn't matter if the manager was nice to the employees when she laid them off—a fact of some importance in contemporary discussions of downsizing because many managers think that when they fire people in a nice way, as opposed to firing them cruelly, they are off the moral hook. It is morally better to be nice than to be cruel, but the real issue is whether the firing can be morally justified. How would a Kantian using the respect for persons principle justify these contentions? To answer that question some explanation of Kant's respect for persons principle is in order.

THE RESPECT FOR PERSONS PRINCIPLE

Kant's second formulation of the categorical imperative says "Act so that you treat humanity whether, in your own person or in that of another, always as an end and never as a means only."[2] Kant did not simply assert that human beings are entitled to respect; he had an elaborate argument for it. Human beings ought to be respected because human beings have dignity. For Kant, an object that has dignity is beyond price. That's what is wrong with the principle that says a manager should adjust the inputs of production to the point where the marginal productivity of each is equal. And further, the denial of dignity is what makes much downsizing unjust. In these cases, that which is without price, human beings, are treated as exchangeable with that which has a price. Human employees have a dignity that machines and capital do not have. Thus, managers cannot manage their corporate resources in the most efficient manner without violating the respect for persons principle— or so it seems. But why do persons possess a dignity which is beyond all price?

They have dignity because human beings are capable of autonomy and thus are capable of self-governance. As autonomous beings capable of self-governance they are also responsible beings, since autonomy and self-governance are the conditions for responsibility. A person who is not autonomous and who is not capable of self-governance is not responsible. That's why little children or the mentally ill are

not considered responsible beings. Thus, there is a conceptual link between being a human being, being an autonomous being, being capable of self-governance, and being a responsible being.

Autonomous responsible beings are capable of making and following their own laws; they are not simply subject to the causal laws of nature. Anyone who recognizes that he or she is autonomous would recognize that he or she is responsible (that he or she is a moral being). As Kant argues, the fact that one is a moral being enables us to say that such a being possesses dignity.

> Morality is the condition under which alone a rational being can be an end in himself because only through it is it possible to be a lawgiving member in the realm of ends. Thus morality, and humanity insofar as it is capable of morality, alone have dignity.[3]

It is the fact that human beings are moral agents that makes them subjects worthy of respect.

As I read Kant this is his argument for the necessity of including other persons within the scope of the respect for persons principle (treating the humanity in a person as an end and never as a means merely). It is based on consistency. What we say about one case, namely ourselves, we must say about similar cases, namely about other human beings.

Kant begins the third section of the *Foundations* as follows:

> What else, then, can freedom of the will be but autonomy (the property of the will to be a law to itself?) The proposition that the will is a law to itself in all its actions, however, only expresses the principle that we should act according to no other maxim than that which can also have itself as a universal law for its object. And this is just the formula of the categorical imperative and the principle of morality. Therefore a free will and a will under moral laws are identical.[4]

Freedom and the ability to make laws are necessary and sufficient for moral agency. Moral agency is what gives people dignity. The importance of rationality comes when one explicates the meaning of freedom. Freedom is more than independence from causal laws. This is negative freedom. Freedom is also the ability to make laws that are universal and to act on those laws in the world. As Kant says:

> The sole principle of morality consists in independence from all material of the law (i.e., a desired object) and in the accompanying determination of choice by the mere form of giving universal law which a maxim must be capable of having. That independence, however, is freedom in the negative sense, while this intrinsic legislation of pure and thus practical reason is freedom in the positive sense.[5]

Thus, we have shown why Kant believes persons have dignity and in this world are the only beings who have dignity. Kant has thus grounded our obligation to treat humanity in a person as an end and never as a means merely. But what specific obligations follow from that general obligation? More specifically, what is the casuistry for applying the principle in a business context? I follow contemporary scholarship in arguing that respect for persons requires two steps and have divided this chapter accordingly. For example, O'Neill says:

> The maxim must not use them (negatively) as mere means, but also (positively) treat them as ends-in-themselves. Kant describes the first sort of failure as

action on maxims to which no other could possibly consent, and the second as pursuit of ends another cannot share.[6]

Now we finally have the framework that can address the basic question for this chapter. How does the respect for persons principle apply in a corporate business setting?

NOTES

1. Richard Parker has correctly pointed out that if the substitution of the machines made the jobs of the remaining workers more meaningful, then Kant would not oppose the substitution of machines for people just because the cost of machines went down relative to the costs of people.

2. Immanuel Kant, *Foundations of the Metaphysics of Morals,* (New York: Macmillian, 1990) p. 46.

3. Ibid. p. 52

4. ibid. p. 64

5. Immanuel Kant, *Critique of Practical Reason,* (Upper Saddle River, NJ: Prentice Hall, 1993), pp. 33–34.

6. Onora O'Neill, *Constructions of Reason,* (New York: Cambridge University Press, 1996), p. 113.

QUESTIONS

1. What does the "respect for persons" principle mean in terms of the policies and practices of an organization?

2. If you simply are a means to your employer's ends, and you understand that this is the case when you are hired, would you care if you were treated as a means?

Arlie Hochshild | # Exploring the Managed Heart

Arlie Hochshild is a professor of sociology at the University of California at Berkeley.

The one area of her occupational life in which she might be "free to act," the area of her own personality, must now also be managed, must become the alert yet obsequious instrument by which goods are distributed.

— *C. Wright Mills*

In a section in *Das Kapital* entitled "The Working Day," Karl Marx examines depositions submitted in 1863 to the Children's Employment Commission in England. One deposition was given by the mother of a child laborer in a wallpaper factory: "When he was seven years old I used to carry him [to work] on my back to and fro through the snow, and he used to work 16 hours a day. . . . I have often knelt down to feed him, as he stood by the machine, for he could not leave it or stop." Fed meals as he worked, as a steam engine is fed coal and water, this child was "an instrument of labor."[1] Marx questioned how many hours a day it was fair to use a human being as an instrument, and how much pay for being an instrument was fair, considering the profits that factory owners made. But he was also concerned with something he thought more fundamental: the human cost of becoming an "instrument of labor" at all.

On another continent 117 years later, a twenty-year-old flight attendant trainee sat with 122 others listening to a pilot speak in the auditorium of the Delta Airlines Stewardess Training Center. Even by modern American standards, and certainly by standards for women's work, she had landed an excellent job. The 1980 pay scale began at $850 a month for the first six months and would increase within seven years to about $20,000 a year. Health and accident insurance is provided, and the hours are good.[2]

The young trainee sitting next to me wrote on her notepad, "Important to smile. Don't forget smile." The admonition came from the speaker in the front of the room, a crewcut pilot in his early fifties, speaking in a Southern drawl: "Now girls, I want you to go out there and really *smile*. Your smile is your biggest *asset*. I want you to go out there and use it. Smile. *Really* smile. Really *lay it on*."

The pilot spoke of the smile as the *flight attendant's* asset. But as novices like the one next to me move through training, the value of a personal smile is groomed to reflect the company's disposition—its confidence that its planes will not crash, its reassurance that departures and arrivals will be on time, its welcome and its invitation to return. Trainers take it as their job to attach to the trainee's smile an attitude, a viewpoint, a rhythm of feeling that is, as they often say, "professional." This deeper extension of the professional smile is not always easy to retract at the end of the workday, as one worker in her first year at World Airways noted: "Sometimes I come off a long trip in a state of utter exhaustion, but I find I can't relax. I giggle a lot, I chatter, I call friends. It's as if I can't release myself from an artificially created elation that kept me 'up' on the trip. I hope to be able to come down from it better as I get better at the job."

As the PSA jingle says, "Our smiles are not just painted on." Our flight attendants' smiles, the company emphasizes, will be more human than the phony smiles you're resigned to seeing on people who are paid to smile. There is a smile-like strip of paint on the nose of each PSA plane. Indeed, the plane and the flight attendant advertise each other. The radio advertisement goes on to promise not just smiles and service but a travel experience of real happiness and calm. Seen in one way, this is no more than delivering a service. Seen in another, it

From Arlie Hochshild, *The Managed Heart* (Berkeley: University of California Press, 1983), pp. 3–9.

To: You
From: The Philosopher
Subject: "Robert C. Solomon, *The Passions*"

I have a British friend who is always amazed by how service employees act in America. The first time she went to a bank here she said, "the teller acted as if she just happened to be there and was delighted that I had dropped by to see her." Emotions are a part of your job and your life. You shouldn't abuse them or fail to cultivate the right ones. As philosopher Robert C. Solomon noted:

> Emotions are the meanings of life. It is because we are moved, because we feel, that life has a meaning. The passionate life is the meaningful life. Of course, it all depend on *which* passions. There are the grand passions, the driving forces of life, a life well-lived. And then there are the petty passions, defensive and self-undermining, "which drag us down with their stupidity," as Nietzsche says. Some meanings, in other words, are de-meaning.

estranges workers from their own smiles and convinces customers that on-the-job behavior is calculated. Now that advertisements, training, notions of professionalism, and dollar bills have intervened between the smiler and the smiled upon, it takes an extra effort to imagine that spontaneous warmth can exist in uniform—because companies now advertise spontaneous warmth, too.

At first glance, it might seem that the circumstances of the nineteenth-century factory child and the twentieth-century flight attendant could not be more different. To the boy's mother, to Marx, to the members of the Children's Employment Commission, perhaps to the manager of the wallpaper factory, and almost certainly to the contemporary reader, the boy was a victim, even a symbol, of the brutalizing conditions of his time. We might imagine that he had an emotional half-life, conscious of little more than fatigue, hunger, and boredom. On the other hand, the flight attendant enjoys the upper-class freedom to travel, and she participates in the glamour she creates for others. She is the envy of clerks in duller, less well-paid jobs.

But a close examination of the differences between the two can lead us to some unexpected common ground. On the surface there is a difference in how we know what labor actually produces. How could the worker in the wallpaper factory tell when his job was done? Count the rolls of wallpaper; a good has been produced. How can the flight attendant tell when her job is done? A service has been produced; the customer seems content. In the case of the flight attendant, the *emotional style of offering the service is part of the service itself,* in a way that loving or hating wallpaper is not a part of producing wallpaper. Seeming to "love the job" becomes part of the job; and actually trying to love it, and to enjoy the customers, helps the worker in this effort.

In processing people, the product is a state of mind. Like firms in other industries, airline companies are ranked according to the quality of service their personnel offer. Egon Ronay's yearly *Lucas Guide* offers such a ranking; besides being sold in airports and drugstores and reported in newspapers, it is cited in management memoranda and passed down to those who train and supervise flight attendants. Because it influences consumers, airline companies use it in setting their criteria for successful job performance by a flight attendant. In 1980 the *Lucas Guide* ranked Delta Airlines first in service out of fourteen airlines that fly regularly between the United States and both Canada and the British Isles. Its report on Delta included passages like this:

> [Drinks were served] not only with a smile but with concerned enquiry such as, "Anything else I can get you, madam?" The atmosphere was that of a civilized party—with the passengers, in response, behaving like civilized guests. . . . Once or twice our inspectors tested stewardesses by being deliberately exacting, but they were never roused, and at the end of the flight they lined up to say farewell with undiminished brightness. . . .

[Passengers are] quick to detect strained or forced smiles, and they come aboard wanting to *enjoy* the flight. One of us looked forward to his next trip on Delta "because it's fun." Surely that is how passengers ought to feel."[3]

The work done by the boy in the wallpaper factory called for a coordination of mind and arm, mind and finger, and mind and shoulder. We refer to it simply as physical labor. The flight attendant does physical labor when she pushes heavy meal carts through the aisles, and she does mental work when she prepares for and actually organizes emergency landings and

---

To: You
From: The Philosopher
Subject: "John Stuart Mill on the Greatest Good and Expediency"

A friend of mine just started working at a bank. On his first day of work, he had to take a drug test. He asked his manager why and she said, "The reason why new employees have to take drug tests is to help protect our clients and the bank from potential problems. After all, if we got in trouble, we'd have to let employees go. So, while it may be unpleasant for you, it's best everyone."

When I heard this argument, I thought, they certainly don't seem to believe in Kant's idea of treating people as ends in themselves. She sort of sounded like John Stuart Mill.

> The multiplication of happiness is, according to utilitarian ethics, the object of Virtue: the occasions on which any person (except one in a thousand) has it in his power to do this on an extended scale, in other words to be a public benefactor, are but exceptional; and on these occasions alone, is he called on to consider public utility; in every other case, private utility, the interest or happiness of some few persons, is all the he has to attend to.*

But Mill also made a distinction between utility and expedience:

> [T]he expedient, in the sense in which it is opposed to the Right, generally means that which is expedient for the particular interest of the agent himself. . . . When it means anything better than this, it means that which is expedient for some immediate object, some temporary purpose, but which violates a rule whose observance is expedient in a much higher degree, The Expedient, in this sense instead of being the same thing as what is useful, is a branch of the hurtful."**

*John Stuart Mill, "What Is Utilitarianism?" in *Utilitarianism and other Essays,* ed. Alan Ryan (New York: Penguin Books, 1987), p. 282.

**Ibid., p. 283.

evacuations. But in the course of doing this physical and mental labor, she is also doing something more, something I define as *emotional labor*.[4] This labor requires one to induce or suppress feeling in order to sustain the outward countenance that produces the proper state of mind in others—in this case, the sense of being cared for in a convivial and safe place. This kind of labor calls for a coordination of mind and feeling, and it sometimes draws on a source of self that we honor as deep and integral to our individuality.

Beneath the difference between physical and emotional labor there lies a similarity in the possible cost of doing the work: the worker can become estranged or alienated from an aspect of self—either the body or the margins of the soul—that is *used* to do the work. The factory boy's arm functioned like a piece of machinery used to produce wallpaper. His employer, regarding that arm as an instrument, claimed control over its speed and motions. In this situation, what was the relation between the boy's arm and his mind? Was his arm in any meaningful sense his *own?*[5]

This is an old issue, but as the comparison with airline attendants suggests, it is still very much alive. If we can become alienated from goods in a goods-producing society, we can become alienated from service in a service-producing society. This is what C. Wright Mills, one of our keenest social observers, meant when he wrote in 1956, "We need to characterize American society of the mid-twentieth century in more psychological terms, for now the problems that concern us most border on the psychiatric."[6]

When she came off the job, what relation had the flight attendant to the "artificial elation" she had induced on the job? In what sense was it her *own* elation on the job? The company lays claim not simply to her physical motions—how she handles food trays—but to her emotional actions and the way they show in the ease of a smile. The workers I talked to often spoke of their smiles as being *on* them but not *of* them. They were seen as an extension of the make-up, the uniform, the recorded music, the soothing pastel colors of the airplane decor, and the daytime drinks, which taken together orchestrate the mood of the passengers. The final commodity is not a certain number of smiles to be counted like rolls of wallpaper. For the flight attendant, the smiles are a *part of her work,* a part that requires her to coordinate self and feeling so that the work seems to be effortless. To show that the enjoyment takes effort is to do the job poorly. Similarly, part of the job is to disguise fatigue and irritation, for otherwise the labor would show in an unseemly way, and the product—passenger contentment—would be damaged.[7] Because it is easier to disguise fatigue and irritation if they can be banished altogether, at least for brief periods, this feat calls for emotional labor.

The reason for comparing these dissimilar jobs is that the modern assembly-line worker has for some time been an outmoded symbol of modern industrial labor; fewer than 6 percent of workers now work on assembly lines. Another kind of labor has now come into symbolic prominence—the voice-to-voice or face-to-face delivery of service—and the flight attendant is an appropriate model for it. There have always been public-service jobs, of course; what is new is that they are now socially engineered and thoroughly organized from the top. Though the flight attendant's job is no worse and in many ways better than other service jobs, it makes the worker more vulnerable to the social engineering of her emotional labor and reduces her control over that labor. Her problems, therefore, may be a sign of what is to come in other such jobs.

Emotional labor is potentially good. No customer wants to deal with a surly waitress, a crabby bank clerk, or a flight attendant who avoids eye contact in order to avoid getting a request. Lapses in courtesy by those paid to be courteous are very real and fairly common. What they show us is how fragile public civility really is. We are brought back to the question of what the social carpet actually consists of and what it requires of those who are supposed to keep it beautiful. The laggards and sluff-offs of emotional labor return us to the basic questions. What is emotional labor? What do we do when we manage emotion? What, in fact, is emotion? What are the costs and benefits of managing emotion, in private life and at work?

NOTES

1. Karl Marx, (1977) *Capital* Vol. 1. *Intro. By Ernest Mandel. Tr. Ben Fowkes. New York: Vintage. pp. 356–357, 358.*

2. For stylistic convenience, I shall use the pronoun "she" when referring to a flight attendant, except when a specific male flight attendant is being discussed. Otherwise I shall try to avoid verbally excluding either gender.

3. Lucas Guide 1980, pp. 66.

4. I use the term *emotional labor* to mean the management of feeling to create a publicly observable facial and bodily display; emotional labor is sold for a wage and therefore has *exchange value.* I use the synonymous terms *emotion work* or *emotion management* to refer to these same acts done in a private context where they have *use value.*

5. Lucas Guide 1980, pp. 66, 76. Fourteen aspects of air travel at the stages of departure, arrival, and the flight itself are ranked. Each aspect is given one of sixteen differently weighted marks. For example, "The friendliness or efficiency of the staff is more important than the quality of the pilot's flight announcement or the selection of newspapers and magazines offered."

6. C. Wright Mills, (1956) *White Collar.* New York: Oxford University Press. p. xx.

7. Like a commodity, service that calls for emotional labor is subject to the laws of supply and demand. Recently the demand for this labor has increased and the supply of it drastically decreased. The airline industry speed-up since the 1970s has been followed by a worker slowdown. The slowdown reveals how much emotional labor the job required all along. It suggests what costs even happy workers under normal conditions pay for this labor without a name. The speed-up has sharpened the ambivalence many workers feel about how much of oneself to give over to the role and how much of oneself to protect from it.

QUESTIONS

1. What are the various types of emotional labor found in the workplace today?

2. What kinds of emotional labor are acceptable and what kinds are unacceptable in the workplace? What ethical principles would you use to draw the line?

Anita M. Superson

The Employer-Employee Relationship and the Right to Know

Anita Superson is associate professor of philosophy at the University of Kentucky.

I

Dangers lurk in the workplace. It has been reported that more than 2,200,000 workers are disabled, and more than 14,000 are killed annually as a result of accidents on the job.[1] The causes include safety hazards such as fires, explosions, electrocution, dangerous machinery, as well as health hazards such as loud noise, harmful dusts, asbestos particles, toxic gases, carcinogens, and radiation.[2] The fact that these and other dangers exist is problem enough; but even more

problematic is that an employee's awareness of such dangers, prior to being exposed to them, is often minimal, at best. If an employee is to have any say in what happens to his person, what needs to be established—at least more firmly than it is currently—is an employee's[3] right to know about the presence of health and safety hazards in the workplace.

II

In the medical setting a person's right to know about risks involved in different kinds of treatment has been recognized under the guise of informed consent. Recently, there have been many attempts in the law

From *Business and Professional Ethics Journal*, 3, no. 1 (1983), 45–58. Reprinted by permission of the author. Notes were deleted from this text.

and in various health codes to ensure that patients have given informed consent to medical treatments or experimentation. In *Canterbury* v. *Spence,* 1972, Circuit Court Judge Spotswood W. Robinson III ruled that since "every human being of adult years and sound mind has a right to determine what shall be done with his own body," a physician has a "duty of reasonable disclosure of the choices with respect to proposed therapy and the dangers inherently and potentially involved."[4] Similarly, the American Hospital Association's *Patient's Bill of Rights* (1973) states that "The patient has the right to receive from his physician information necessary to give informed consent prior to the start of any procedure and/or treatment."[5] Again, the Nuremberg Code, which focuses on guidelines used in human experimentation carried out in Nazi Germany, specifies that the human subject "should have sufficient knowledge and comprehension of the elements of the subject matter involved as to enable him to make an understanding and enlightened decision."[6] These and other such examples show that through informed consent, a patient's or research subject's right to know about the risks and hazards involved in medical procedures is firmly entrenched. We shall see later that this right is protected by the law. Though the amount of information given to patients may vary among physicians, consent forms must be signed by the patient or by his next of kin. This is true for all patients undergoing most invasive forms of treatment (e.g., surgery).

But the headway that has been made in the medical setting is, unfortunately, unparalleled in the workplace. It was not until 1980 that the Occupational Safety and Health Administration (OSHA) of the United States Department of Labor established the legal right of an employee to "access to employer maintained exposure and medical records relevant to employees exposed to toxic substances and harmful physical agents."[7]

In *Borden Chemical,* an administrative law judge of the National Labor Relations Board determined that Borden had refused to bargain in good faith when it failed to release information to the labor union. It was then ordered to supply the information to the

union. The reason behind the ruling was that Borden failed to show that disclosure of the information would damage its competitive position.[8] Essentially, Borden failed to show how its trade secrets would reach its competitors. In *Colgate-Palmolive,* however, an administrative law judge ruled that the employer was obliged to reveal a list of chemicals in the workplace *except* those constituting trade secrets.[9] Colgate-Palmolive apparently showed how it would be disadvantaged were its trade secrets to be revealed. We can surmise from these two cases and from the OSHA and NIOSH rulings that an employee's right to know is not accorded full protection by the law, and, in fact, may be denied by the law.

III

Why is the right to know in the workplace not firmly grounded? It is the argument of this section that protection of such a right is limited because of the very nature of the employer-employee relationship.

Both the employer and employee normally do not enter into their relation thinking that they can trust each other to look out for the other's best interests. Probably the only form of trust existent between the two parties is that the employer will pay the employee a wage that at least matches the work he puts out, and that the employee will perform the job he is asked to do in a way that is normally expected. These are the roles both the employer and employee expect each other to take on. It would be difficult to establish a fiduciary relationship under such expectations. What adds to the difficulty is that often the employer and employee do not even know each other at any kind of personal level. I ask rhetorically: How can a fiduciary relationship be established if no relationship has been established?

Another feature of the employer–employee relationship which adds to its nonfiduciary nature is the reasons both the employee and the employer have for entering into their relationship. The employee enters a relationship with his employer primarily for monetary reasons; he seeks employment in order to earn wages with which he can secure the goods he needs to live. The employer, on the other hand, enters a relationship primarily for the sake of profit-making. His position in respect to that of the employee is one of power. It derives its power from the fact that the employer offers the employee a benefit—wages—if he accepts and performs a job. The employer stands to benefit directly from his employee. He needs a certain job to be done; the company's profits depend upon whether the task is accomplished. And the financial success of the company is directly related to the employer.

Both the expectations of the employee and employer, as well as the reasons for each entering into the relationship, make it likely that an employer would use his employee merely as a means to his own end, to borrow a notion from Kant. That is, the employer, seeking to augment his profits (the end), may use the employee merely as a means to achieve that end. One way in which he could do this is to fail to inform an employee about hazardous work conditions. Failure to inform an employee about these hazards is to deny him information that may affect his decision to stay on the job. And by remaining on the job, the employee works in part for the employer's benefit, that is, to increase the company's profits. In this way, the employee is used as a means to the employer's end.

More specifically, if the expectations of both the employer and employee of each other are as I have described, it is easy for the former to use the latter as a means to an end because being so far removed on a personal level from the employee, he does not feel a sense of obligation towards the employee's welfare. All he has invested in the relationship is that the job gets done. And since the employee does not view the relationship as a fiduciary one, he has no basis for trusting the employer to ensure that the workplace is free from hazards, or at least to inform him of the hazards that do exist. Indeed it would be nice for the employer to do either; yet the employee probably does not expect it, and certainly cannot trust his employer to do so.

And, if the reasons the employer and employee have for entering their relationship are as I have described, this is another reason why an employer may use his employee merely as a means to his own end. If the employer is aware of the power he holds over his employee, that is, that he to a large extent controls the employee's means of livelihood, he may feel no obligation to inform the employee about on-the-job hazards. In fact, somewhat ironically, the employer may even go so far as to view the employee as using *him,* the *employer,* as a means to an end. This belief is based upon the fact that the employee may take on a job solely for the purpose of obtaining money, perhaps with minimum effort put forth, and that the employee is free to leave when he so desires. If the employer has this attitude toward his employee, it becomes easier for him not to inform the employee of hazards in the workplace.

IV

The moral basis of the right to know lies in the principle of autonomy. Much talk has been generated about this principle since Mill and Kant recognized its importance. Although the literature offers a variety of definitions, this principle is usually defined in such a way as to include the notion of making one's own decisions affecting one's own life without coercion from others. In order for one to make a responsible decision, he must be informed about the choices with which he is faced. Just as a patient must be informed about the risks involved in a certain treatment in order for him to decide if he wants that treatment, an employee, too, must be informed about the hazards involved in working under certain conditions if he is to make a responsible, autonomous choice about whether or not to subject his person to such risks. In either case, if such information is not disclosed, the person's autonomy has been placed in jeopardy.

———————

One basis, then, for establishing a right to know in the workplace is that it ensures that an employee is given information necessary for him to be able to make a choice which may significantly affect his life. Informing an employee of workplace hazards puts him in the position of deciding whether or not he wants to be exposed to hazards, and thereby is one step in the direction of promoting his autonomy. Establishment of a right to know is especially important for the worker since he does not have much recourse against his employer if damages ensue.

Another basis for establishing this right lies in the notion of fairness of contract. When a person is hired for a job, there is an implicit contract made between the employer and employee, the terms of which spell out that person X will do job A and will be paid by person Y. This contract requires, like any fair contract, that both parties know what they are contracting to. It is insufficient that an employee know he is consenting to do a certain job in a certain way at a certain pace, and so on. If hazards which may produce harm to his person are involved, he should be made aware of them before he enters the contract. If he is not made aware of the hazards, and enters the contract with the employer, he is not giving fully informed consent to the relevant terms of the contract. The contract is thus unfair.

A third basis for establishing an employee's right to know is partly economic, partly moral. It lies in Milton Friedman's notion of business' social responsibility, namely, "to use its resources and engage in activities designed to increase its profits so long as it stays within the rules of the game, which is to say, engages in open and free competition, without deception or fraud."[10] The moral justification for the right to know, using Friedman's terms of business' social responsibility, lies in his normative judgment that business should not engage in deceptive practices. Though Friedman does not spell out what this entails, surely withholding information from the prospective employee—information which is likely to influence his decision—is a deceptive practice, prohibited even on Friedman's libertarian analysis of business in the free market system.

An economic justification for the right to know also can be found in Friedman and other free market advocates. It is this: in order to ensure that the free market really *is* free, persons should be able to enter the occupation of their choosing (at least insofar as they meet the qualifications). This choice must be informed. If information about job hazards is withheld, the choice will not be fully informed. And if the choice is not fully informed, it is not truly free. Thus, ignoring the right to know, besides violating moral principles such as autonomy and fairness of contract, violates one of the fundamental economic bases of the free market system.

V

If an employee's right to know becomes firmly established, certain implications are likely to follow. On the negative side, the employer will be faced with the difficult task of determining how much and what kind of information ought to be given to the employee. The employer will have to devote time and effort to find out just what hazards exist, and to convey the results of his findings to the employee. And if the risks involved in taking on a certain job are very high, or very serious, the employer may have difficulty in hiring someone for the job. Also, the company's trade secrets undoubtedly will sometimes be revealed.

While I do not wish to diminish the inconvenience these implications bring to the employer, none is too important to override the employee's right to know.

NOTES

1. Manuel G. Velasquez, *Business Ethics: Concepts and Cases* (Englewood Cliffs, NJ: Prentice-Hall, Inc., 1982), p. 311.

2. See Nicholas A. Ashford, *Crisis in the Workplace: Occupational Disease and Injury* (Cambridge, MA: The MIT Press, 1976), pp. 68–83, for a thorough and interesting description of these hazards.

3. Although I shall use the term 'employee' throughout this essay, my arguments shall apply also to the prospective employee since he is faced with a similar choice, that is, whether or not to accept a job in a hazardous work environment.

4. *Canterbury* v. *Spence,* US Court of Appeals, District of Columbia Circuit, May 19, 1972, 464 Federal Reporter, 2nd Series, 772.

5. "A Patient's Bill of Rights," American Hospital Association, reprinted in Mappes & Zembaty (eds.), *Biomedical Ethics* (New York: McGraw-Hill, Inc., 1981), pp. 87–89.

6. "Declaration of Helsinki," World Medical Association, reprinted in Mappes & Zembaty, *ibid.,* pp. 145–147.

7. *Federal Register,* Vol. 45, no. 102, Friday, May 23, 1980, Rules and Regulations, Dept. of Labor, Occupational Safety and Health Administration, 23CFR Part 1910, 35212.

8. Tim D. Wermager, "Union's Right to Information vs. Confidentiality of Employer Trade Secrets: Accommodating the Interests Through Procedural Burdens and Restricted Disclosure," 66 *Iowa Law Review,* 1333–1351, July, 1981.

9. Ibid., p. 1345.

10. Milton Friedman, *Capitalism & Freedom* (Chicago: U. Chicago Press 1962), p. 33.

QUESTIONS

1. Besides informing employees of hazards and implementing safety precautions, what other obligations do employers have to employees who work in hazardous environments?

2. In what cases do employers have a responsibility to keep an employee who wants to work in a hazardous environment from working in that environment?

John Orlando | # The Ethics of Corporate Downsizing

John Orlando is a California specialist in management.

I. THE ISSUE

A survey of contemporary business ethics literature leads one to believe that the primary ethical questions facing businesses today concern topics such as affirmative action, sexual harassment, and the environment. While these are without a doubt weighty concerns, many workers, especially manufacturing workers, would place corporate downsizing—the closing of whole plants or divisions in order to increase profits—at the head of their list of ethically contentious business practices. Though the issue has provoked considerable debate in the popular press, the philosophical community has largely ignored it.

This oversight is curious given that downsizing is arguably the major business trend of our era. . . . The statistics on downsizing's human costs are sobering. One study found that 15 percent of downsized workers lost their homes, and another that the suicide rate among laid-off workers is thirty times the national average.[1] Despite the rosy picture of the economy painted by the popular media, where attention is constantly drawn to the growth of the stock market, evidence suggests that trends such as downsizing have led to a general decline in employee earnings, as well as a widening of the gulf between rich and poor in America.[2] Added to this is the fact that since the loss of jobs is concentrated in a relatively small geographic area, these closings affect the entire community. Businesses that rely upon workers' spending will feel the pinch, often leading to secondary layoffs. Consequently, communities as a whole have been devastated by such closings.[3] Downsizing also carries with it serious nonquantifiable harms. News of mass layoffs sends psychological tremors across the nation, leading to general worker apprehension about job security and less job satisfaction.[4] Worse yet, the anxiety of unemployment often leads to psychological symptoms such as depression, or expresses itself through a variety of unpleasant behaviors: i.e., crime, domestic violence, child abuse, and alcohol and drug abuse.[5] . . .

From *Business Ethics Quarterly* 9 (April 1999). Copyright © 1999 The Society for Business Ethics. Reprinted by permission. Some notes omitted.

II. THE MORAL EQUALITY OF WORKERS AND SHAREHOLDERS

Property Rights

First, it must be understood that one cannot justify the position that shareholder concerns take precedence over all other groups simply by appeal to the fact that the shareholders are the legal owners of the corporation. In that case, all one has done is provide a definition of the term *shareholder;* one has yet to provide a morally relevant reason for privileging the interests of that group. This is analogous to arguing that abortion is impermissible after viability because that is the point where the fetus could survive outside of the womb.

The natural tack at this point is to assert that a legal owner has property rights that allow her to dispose of her property in any manner she sees fit. But this justification skews the issue in the shareholder's favor by appealing to a paradigm that does not apply in the case of corporate ownership. The term *property rights* conjures up images of property for personal *use,* not *profit.* For instance, property rights advocates normally worry about laws that place restrictions on the use of one's homestead, such as laws regulating the appearance of one's home. . . . We may harbor a deep-seated intuition that property is sacred, but that intuition is tied to property with which we are in some respect intimately connected, such as a home.

To avoid glossing over the distinction between property for private use and property for profit, we will need to narrow our inquiry to an example of property for profit. Imagine that I own an apartment which I have rented to a couple for ten or fifteen years (think Fred and Ethel from "I Love Lucy"). I discover that I can make more money by dividing up the apartment and renting it to college students. My intuition is that I have a responsibility to the people who rent from me. At the very least, I should assure the couple, who might be frightened about the prospect of being thrown into the street, that I will not have them leave until they have procured similar housing elsewhere at a similar cost. I would also feel obligated to ensure that their transition is as easy as possible by, for instance, helping them move. Moreover, the purpose of the money will have a bearing on the moral status of the act. The act is far easier to justify if it is needed to

pay for my wife's extended medical care, than if it merely allows me to buy a longer sailboat. Thus, the general appeal to property rights breaks down when the property in question is for profit, and when we turn to scenarios closer to the practice of downsizing itself.

Fiduciary Duties

Many theorists and business managers defend the moral superiority of shareholders on grounds that corporate managers are bound by a fiduciary duty to their shareholders that trumps any competing duties. The burden of proof is then taken to fall on the shoulders of those arguing against this position to demonstrate that the manager has equally strong duties to others as well. . . .

There is considerable evidence that the fiduciary duty of a corporate manager has been historically justified as a means of protecting the owner from that manager. The legal justification of this duty can be traced to the 1741 court ruling in *The Charitable Corporation v. Sir Robert Sutton,* where the court ruled that managers of corporations were "most properly agents of those who employ them." Interestingly, the suit was brought against the managers of The Charitable Corporation for "self-dealing by executives, theft, failure of inventory control, and a huge unmet financial commitment." Notice that the neglect of managerial duty cited involved not benevolent contributions to others, but rather acting in their *own* interest. . . .

Hence, there is good reason to believe that the legal basis of fiduciary duties of corporate managers to shareholders has been construed as the obligation to not advance their own interests against those of the shareholders. Adopting this view of the fiduciary relationship would mean that when a corporate manager takes into account the interests of stakeholders, even where that comes at the expense of profits, this does not conflict with a manager's fiduciary duty to shareholders.

Risk

Ian Maitland provides two justifications for the position that corporate managers have duties to shareholders over those to other parties. The first appeals to the fact that shareholders have invested capital in the corporation. Why is this fact morally relevant? According to Maitland, shareholders have taken a risk in placing their money in the hands of the corporation, and are thereby due compensation in the form of having their interests given privilege over those of other parties. Maitland states that:

> As a practical matter, no stakeholder is likely to agree to bear the risk associated with the corporation's activities unless it gets the commitment that the corporation will be managed for its benefit. That is logical because the stockholder alone stands to absorb any costs of mismanagement.[6]

It is strange, however, to think that the worker who loses his job has not absorbed any costs of mismanagement. Maitland's point must be that while workers stand to lose their jobs due to corporate mismanagement, they only lose future potential earnings, whereas shareholders lose something they have placed into the corporation. However, workers too have placed something at risk when accepting a job. At the very least, the worker has bypassed other possible job opportunities, opportunities that may have turned out to be financially more rewarding. Also, some have gone to school in the hopes of pursuing a career in the field, thereby investing substantial sums of money (or accruing substantial debt) in the process. Even more importantly, many workers have purchased homes in the expectation of a steady income, and in this manner have risked their homes on the corporation. We can also add to our list the various ways in which workers plant roots in the community which are disrupted when they are forced to relocate, such as placing their children in local schools or having their spouses accept jobs. While the worker's investment in a corporation is not of the same sort as the shareholder's, it constitutes a risk nevertheless, and so the worker's position is not dissimilar to that of the shareholder. The only difference between the risks taken by the two parties is one of degree, and the degree of that risk will depend upon the particular situation of each individual.

Contracts

Maitland's second argument is that corporations are fundamentally a "freely chosen . . . nexus . . . of con-

tracts" between its stakeholders, which establish both the "rights" and the "obligations" of each party.[7] These contracts stipulate that the worker will give the corporation her labor in return for a fixed wage, while the shareholder will receive all of the profits of the corporation in return for investing capital in it. When third parties tinker with that arrangement, they violate the right of self-determination of the members of the contract, who have determined the terms of the contracts under "free," "voluntary," and "uncoerced" bargaining circumstances.[8] . . .

However, Maitland's picture of the corporation simply does not square with reality. It turns out that most shareholders expect corporate managers to take into account the interests of other constituencies when making decisions about the welfare of the corporation. More importantly, shareholders tend to think of themselves not as owners of the corporation, but rather as investors in it. . . . For the vast majority of shareholders, dabbling in the stock market is thought of as one means among many of investing one's money, something chosen for its high rate of return, not in order to become a corporate owner. Thus, it is hard to understand how the investor can be acting under the assumption of an unstated contract between himself, management, and the company's employees. On the other side, employees have traditionally assumed that taking a job meant having it for life as long as they perform their duties well. Given these considerations, if we are basing such contracts on the implicit understandings and expectations of the parties involved, the evidence actually points in the very opposite direction to which Maitland argues.

Finally, one can raise serious doubts about the assertion that the worker/manager/shareholder relationship has been established under "free, voluntary, and uncoerced" circumstances. For one, the parties are by no means in an equal bargaining position. Despite Maitland's insistence that the disgruntled employee can always "fire his boss by resigning," employees often find that they have very few job options given their skills, the labor market, and the costs of moving to another area. Shareholders, however, have thousands of companies from which to choose, and a variety of mechanisms specifically designed to make movement in and out of the stock market as easy as possible. . . .

The Utilitarian Argument

. . . Utilitarianism is generally construed as the principle that the act that maximizes total utility is morally right. Thus, one could argue that downsizing benefits the majority of the population, and though it leaves some individuals by the wayside, the benefit to the whole outweighs the harm to the few. The entire economy, it might be argued, is becoming more efficient. Moreover, the stock market has skyrocketed, benefiting all those who have investments in mutual funds.

But there is reason to doubt whether downsizing has generated a net gain in utility. A group of researchers recently concluded a fifteen-year study which found that when acts of downsizing are not accompanied by careful restructuring of the corporation—in other words, when people are simply laid off in order to lower costs of production without thought of how the remaining employees will sustain levels of productivity—downsizing has always hurt the corporation in the long run.[9] Reich also notes that the downsizing trend has caused a general drop in employee loyalty in the United States.[10] Workers are far less likely to go the extra mile for firms who treat them as disposable cogs in the corporate machine. While loyalty is not easily quantifiable, and thus does not show up in a corporate ledger, it will affect the company's overall performance. . . .

But even if the case could be made that downsizing improves the overall health of the economy, there would still be a gap between this fact and the conclusion that overall utility has risen. If the argument were to terminate at this point, it would be assuming that one can equate well-being with financial gain; however, far more things go into determining one's well-being. For instance, it is indisputable that the anxiety from job loss has a profoundly negative influence upon one's psychic health. The harm of unemployment cannot simply be measured by the total loss of income; it produces fear for one's own well-being as well as the well-being of one's family, not to mention the anxiety experienced by those other groups themselves. When these factors are taken into account, it

becomes clear that utilitarian considerations do not clearly point in favor of downsizing. It might in fact be determined that downsizing improves net utility in the long run, but the empirical evidence is inconclusive. Our position on the issue, therefore, will need to be informed by other considerations.

III. ARGUMENTS AGAINST DOWNSIZING

Harming Some to Benefit Others

Up to this point I have argued only that defenders of downsizing have failed to establish that downsizing is morally permissible. Here I will present reasons for thinking that downsizing is often morally wrong. The first argument appeals to the widely held intuition . . . that causing a great harm for a lesser benefit, even to a great number of people, cannot be morally justified. Most people would even consider it wrong to incur a great harm to a few in order to produce a great benefit to the many, such as removing the eyes from a sighted man and implanting them in two blind persons so that they can now see (with only a drop off in peripheral vision and depth perception distinguishing them from those with two eyes). There are even some who believe that no amount of harm to an individual can be justified on grounds that it will benefit others, since harms and benefits are incommensurable commodities. Given that statistics demonstrate that downsizing often leads to the loss of home and even suicide, it seems hard to deny that at least some downsized workers incur a significant harm from the practice. On the other side, since investors in a large corporation tend to diversify their assets, they incur only a minor benefit when any one stock price rises. Thus, if the act of downsizing is not done as a means of saving the corporation—preventing more workers from losing their jobs—but rather to increase profits, it involves causing a great harm for a minor benefit.

We can also draw a distinction within the practice of downsizing which will serve to amplify its wrongfulness in certain circumstances. Ask yourself if there is a difference in the moral status of the following two acts: First, a country involved in a just war

Ethical Management of Uncertain Employment
Rosabeth Moss Kanter

Ideas for building an ethical workplace in a time when no one's job is secure:

- Recruit for the potential to increase in competence, not simply for narrow skills to fill today's slots.
- Offer ample learning opportunities, from formal training to lunchtime seminars—the equivalent of three weeks a year.
- Provide challenging jobs and rotating assignments that allow growth in skills even without promotion to higher jobs.
- Measure performance beyond accounting numbers and share the data to allow learning by doing and continuous improvement—turning everyone into self-guided professionals.
- Retrain employees as soon as jobs become obsolete.
- Emphasize team building, to help our diverse work force appreciate and utilize fully each other's skills.
- Recognize and reward individual and team achievements, thereby building external reputations and offering tangible indicators of value.
- Provide three-month educational sabbaticals, external internships, or personal time-out every five years.
- Find growth opportunities in our network of suppliers, customers, and venture partners.
- Ensure that pensions and benefits are portable, so that people have safety nets for the future even if they seek employment elsewhere.
- Help people be productive while carrying family responsibilities, through flex-time, provision for sick children, and renewal breaks between major assignments.
- Measure the building of human capital and the capabilities of our people as thoroughly and frequently as we measure the building and use of financial capital.
- Encourage entrepreneurship—new ventures within our company or outside that help our people start businesses and create alternative sources of employment.
- Tap our people's ideas to develop innovations that lower costs, serve customers, and create new markets—the best foundation for business growth and continuing employment, and the source of funds to reinvest in continuous learning.*

*Rosabeth Moss Kanter, *Men and Women of the Corporation,* 2nd ed., (New York: Basic Books, 1993, 330–331).

bombs the other side's munitions factory in order to end the war, knowing that the bombing will also destroy a grade school bordering the factory and thus killing ten children. Second, a country in a just war bombs the school where the leaders of the opposing country send their kids in order to get them to end the war (accidentally destroying the neighboring munitions factory in the process). Most people would agree that the latter act is far worse than the former. The best way to explain this intuition is that in the latter act, the death of the children is a means to ending the war, while in the former it is an unfortunate byproduct of that means. The children in the second act are being *used* in a way that they are not being used in the former act.

Now consider the case where a CEO downsizes under the knowledge that the mere news of these layoffs will be greeted favorably by the stock market, and thus cause stock prices to rise . . . as opposed to the case where downsizing will improve profits by increasing productivity. Here the very act that harms the workers—the loss of their jobs—itself produces the benefit to shareholders. Harm is not a simple byproduct of an act which independently brings benefit, but rather is the means to that benefit. This grates even more deeply against our intuitions that it is wrong to use individuals for others' benefit.

Legitimate Expectations

We might also approach the issue from the perspective of the legitimate expectations of the individuals involved. To illustrate this notion, consider the possibility that the federal government repeals the home interest tax break without any other modifications in the tax code. While I see no reason why homeowners, and not renters, deserve such a break, one could question the action on grounds that homeowners have made plans under the assumption that this break would continue. Those who lose their homes because of the change in the tax laws would have a legitimate complaint, even though there was never a written guarantee that current tax laws would remain forever unchanged. Similarly, workers have made plans under the assumption of a continued source of income. These are not simply plans for leisure activities such as vacations, but rather plans that impinge

upon their fundamental well-being as well as the well-being of their families. There are, however, no similar expectations on the part of the shareholder. For one, shareholders know that stock prices are volatile and that they take a risk when entering the market. Thus, no reasonable investor backs her home on the future performance of her securities. Investors may expect a certain average rate of return, but this is over the long term and they budget accordingly. They do not bank important items such as their homes on the assumption of the continued unprecedented rates of return seen in the past few years. Surely, these returns are treated as "icing on the cake," and thus if preserving jobs will diminish returns to the levels historically expected from the market, no critical expectations are thwarted. Also, as mentioned earlier, shareholders tend to consider the companies in which they invest to have obligations to parties other than themselves. Hence, one cannot plead that shareholders entered the market expecting that the company would be run solely for their own benefit.

Fairness

We may also appeal to the work of John Rawls to provide critical perspective on the issue. . . . I will draw upon what I consider his more central intuition: that the arbitrary conditions of one's situation ought not to count against one's life prospects. The idea here is that the individual does not deserve the rewards or punishments that come via things for which she is not responsible. At the very least, these factors include genetic endowments and the social institutions of the society in which she lives. . . .

To apply the principle here, we would first note that the worker who loses his job does so through no fault of his own. Someone fired due to incompetence is not downsized. Downsizing does not involve a surgical removal of all employees in a firm whose work is not up to snuff; instead, whole divisions are removed by virtue of their overall profitability, with no effort made to determine if individual members of those divisions are at fault. In fact, if a division or plant is unprofitable it is most likely due to mismanagement on the part of those running the corporation. This is perhaps one of the reasons why downsized workers feel betrayed, as no attempt is made by management to judge their actual job performance. Downsized workers find themselves harmed due to forces outside of their control. Moreover, these forces have conspired to selectively harm them since upper management tends to be insulated from these harms, by devices such as receiving a sizable "golden parachute" when dismissed. True, there are a variety of ways in which natural and social forces reward and punish arbitrarily but this does not make those harms permissible or release us from obligations to mitigate them.

On the other side, shareholders have done nothing to merit the sharp gains that downsizing produces. Perhaps they are owed good faith efforts at sound management by the corporation in virtue of their investment, but they cannot claim to deserve the special increases in the value of their investments due solely to laying off workers. The fact that we happen to live in a world where canning large numbers of workers is a quick means of increasing profits is not any of their doing. Note also that those shareholders who have invested through mutual funds have not themselves chosen to invest in this particular firm. These investors most likely have little idea as to which stocks their mutual funds actually hold, since one of the appeals of these funds is that they allow individuals to enter the market without the need to concern themselves with the intricacies of investing, or the day-to-day fluctuations of the market. . . .

IV. APPLYING THE RESULTS AND RELATED CONCERNS

How might the corporate manager apply the insights gathered here to a particular situation? First and foremost, an act of downsizing that prevents the collapse of the corporation can be justified on grounds that the organism is saved by amputating a limb. However, we must keep in mind that bankruptcy does not always mean the complete shutting down of shop. Bankruptcy courts make every effort to find a way of restructuring the debts of the corporation to keep it in business. In fact, corporations have been known to use bankruptcy as a means of avoiding a court settlement. But an act of downsizing that merely increases profits, which seems increasingly the case, requires a careful analysis of the harms and benefits it will incur to the parties involved. For a small firm, such as a fast-food franchise with a single proprietor, the owner may be at greater risk than her employees. The owner most likely has a large percentage of her personal fortune wrapped up in the company, whereas the workers are usually (but not always) high school students just earning extra spending money. However, with a large corporation, the results are likely to be quite different. It bears mention that the corporate entity is grounded in the principle that a separation exists between the corporation and the personal finances of its owners, a device created specifically to minimize the risk to shareholders. Thus, the owner of a corporation is not personally liable for its debts; if IBM dissolves, shareholders need not fear that IBM's creditors will come knocking at their doors. Legal protection to the shareholder is built into the corporation's charter. More importantly, since investors tend not to risk money that is required for their sustenance, their losses do not normally affect their immediate well-being. By contrast, the worker who banks his home on his job places his immediate well-being, as well as the well-being of his family, in far greater peril. Finally, investors today diversify their assets through mutual funds which own shares in thousands of corporations. Thus, losses from one stock create only a minor shift in the fund's overall value. This means that acts of downsizing can cause great harm to a few for a minor benefit to the many, something that I have argued is not morally permissible. Also, one can argue that the sole proprietor who has nursed the business from the ground up merits greater consideration than the mutual fund investor who may not even know that he or she owns shares in the corporation. Moreover, the worker who has purchased a home, and started a family, based on the assumption of the continued source of income, is deserving of greater consideration than the investor who finds that unprecedented gains in the stock market allow him to extend his vacation to Aruba by a week. . . .

NOTES

1. Richard L. Bunning, "The Dynamics of Downsizing," *Personnel Journal* 69, no. 9 (Sept. 1990): 69.

2. Interview with Secretary of Labor Robert Reich in *Challenge,* July/August 1996, 4. Reich notes that while the *average* wage is up, the *median* wage (the wage of the individual in the middle) is down. The discrepancy is due to the unprecedented rise in compensation for top executives during the 1980s and 1990s.

3. Downsizing by the auto industry in the 1970s and 1980s caused Flint, Michigan's unemployment rate to climb to the highest in the United States, and its crime rate to rise accordingly. *Facts About the Cities,* ed. Allan Carpenter (New York: H. W. Wilson Co., 1992).

4. Harvey M. Brenner, *Mental Illness and the Economy* (Cambridge: Harvard University Press, 1973); Ralph Catalano and David Dooley, "Economic Predictors of Depressed Mood and Stressful Life Events in a Metropolitan Community," *Journal of Health and Social Behavior* 18 (1977): 292–307; Jean Hartley, Dan Jacobson, Bert Klandermans, and Tinka van Vuuren, *Job Insecurity: Coping With Jobs at Risk* (Newbury Park: Sage, 1991); and John R. Reynolds, "The Effects of Industrial Employment Conditions on Job-Related Distress," *Journal of Health and Social Behavior* (June 1977): 105–18.

5. David Dooley, Ralph Catalano, and Karen S. Rook,

"Personal and Aggregate Unemployment and Psychological Symptoms," *Journal of Social Issues* 44 (1988): 107–23; David Dooley, Ralph Catalano, and Georjeanna Wilson, "Depression and Unemployment: Panel Findings from the Epidemiologic Catchment Area Study," *American Journal of Community Health* 22 (1994): 745–65.

6. Ian Maitland, "The Morality of the Corporation: An Empirical or Normative Disagreement?" *Business Ethics Quarterly* 4, no. 4 (1994): 445–57.

7. Ibid., 449.

8. Ibid., 450.

9. Wayne F. Cascio, Interview on National Public Radio, November 14, 1997.

10. Reich, op. cit.

QUESTIONS

1. What are the dangers of using downsizing as a means of saving a business or improving its profits?

2. The old social contract was, "You do your job well, and you get to keep it." Today some people do their job well and get laid off. How would you construct a responsible new social contract between employers and employees?

Annette Friskopp and Sharon Silverstein | # Antigay Jokes

Annette Friskopp and Sharon Silverstein are the authors of the groundbreaking book, *Straight Jobs, Gay Lives.*

ANTIGAY JOKES

Most gay professionals believe jokes about gay men or lesbians stem from a deep-seated dislike of gay people. Often they see these jokes as hostile, a form of bullying that sends the message that gay people will not be tolerated in the organization. Some acknowledge that these jokes may be told out of

ignorance or in the mistaken belief that they are really funny. Occasionally, they allege, the joke tellers are themselves gay, using jokes to mask their own sexual orientation.

Yet not all jokes people in the workforce tell about gay people are intended as attacks. Jokes about gay men and lesbians can be used to send a variety of signals. Sometimes we have seen open-minded coworkers trying to establish that they are in the know about a particular gay person in the news or an aspect of gay culture. Outside of diversity-training forums, many heterosexuals do not feel completely comfort-

---

From Annette Friskopp and Sharon Silverstein, *Straight Jobs, Gay Lives: Gay and Lesbian Professionals, Harvard Business School, and The American Workplace* (New York: Scribner, 1995), 120–26.

able having serious, in-depth discussions on anything having to do with gay people. Joking can be their way, however indelicate, of indicating a willingness to talk about the subject. Clumsy yet sympathetic colleagues expect gay colleagues to laugh or banter back. Prematurely deciding that a coworker is homophobic can prevent the very bonds a potential ally is hoping to create.

"A woman I work with occasionally told me Michael Jackson jokes. One day, I retorted with a joke about Catholic priests," Carla said. "If I had jumped to the conclusion she was antigay, I wouldn't have made a valuable friend in another division. After I came out to her, I told her another joke: 'What did Michael Jackson say to O. J. Simpson? "I'll watch the kids!"' I don't know if these jokes are in the best of taste, but we have a rapport going that I think we both enjoy. And I certainly haven't experienced any homophobia on her part."

Other gay professionals told us they did not always feel it was necessary to object to jokes with gay themes. One factor is who the players are and why the joke is being told. Sybil told us that jokes about sex between men were a form of male bonding for the guys in the construction industry. "They would pound each other on the back and thank each other 'for last night' with an obvious leer. I guess what made it funny was that these guys were obviously not gay. But they were imitating some of the more macho gay men I know, not the effeminate, limp-wristed queens. I have to admit I thought it was funny to see them carry male bonding to its logical extreme. I also thought it was interesting that they were sure enough of their masculinity to joke about it in that way."

Sometimes the signals sent by jokes are difficult to decode. Bart Rubenstein recalled that in a former company he heard lots of gay jokes by senior management. "It was nothing vicious or mean, but the jokes were homophobic, nonetheless. Usually it was something inane and juvenile. Like somebody would raise their hand at a meeting or do something, and somebody else would say, 'Oh well, you know what it means if you do that? It means you're homosexual.' And everybody would laugh. There was one person who was kind of a ringleader for these jokes.

"He was the president of one of our divisions, and he was having a very hard time. In fact, at one point I think he was pretty sure that he was about to be canned. What I observed is that he decided he had to ingratiate himself to the rest of management. Making these jokes was a way he got laughs and approval. I noticed that over time he was starting to be accepted as part of the inner circle.

"Now the division that he's president of is actually much more progressive and open and liberal, to my observation, than the rest of the company. So I viewed that he had read the politics of the situation correctly and was stooping to the level of others, and it was working. It was a little scary. I felt disappointed, because I had spent a lot of time working with this division and always loved when I was working with them, because I felt more comfortable when I was there. And then I came into these senior management meetings and saw him acting like that . . . it was really a shame.

"The people who he was trying to cozy up to laughed, but I never heard them say anything like that. That's the irony here. The ones I was really nervous about were the ones who weren't saying anything. They are the ones who I was afraid of coming out to. The guy who was making the jokes—everything I know about him said being gay would not have affected anything in my relationship with him. . . ."

STRATEGIES FOR OPPOSING ANTIGAY JOKES

Enlisting Management Support

Some felt it was important to express their own disapproval of antigay jokes. Others felt the message would carry more weight if it came from management. Being willing to complain to a boss or to the human resources department can result in companywide changes, we learned. Gordon told us that when he worked at a large advertising agency in New York, he overheard a coworker make a homophobic joke. He recalls that a manager pulled his colleague aside to reprimand him so quickly it made the guy's head spin. This incident made an impression on Gordon, who saw how much power management has to

More Men Are Saying "Stop"

Reed Abelson

More and more men are filing sexual harassment suits these days.

A gay hotel employee is constantly harassed by his coworkers. They make obscene gestures and sometimes come up behind him and simulate sex to make the others laugh.

The male supervisor of a straight Wall Street analyst demanded sexual favors in exchange for a larger bonus. It was unclear if he was serious or was trying to humiliate the analyst. In the lawsuit it stated that the supervisor told the analyst he "would be better off as a male prostitute."

At a used-car dealership the managers told lewd jokes all the time. They often referred to the salesmen by girls' names and jokingly groped them.

Source: Reed Abelson, "Men, Increasingly, Are the Ones Claiming Sex Harassment by Men," *New York Times,* June 10, 2001, p. 29.

enforce corporate culture, even at a time when nondiscrimination based on sexual orientation was not written in company policy.

Some companies cover antigay discrimination under general language. They say, "We do not discriminate based on race, gender, or any other non-work-related characteristic." However, the prevalence of antigay jokes suggests such an ambiguous policy is not enough. In the face of employee complaints, some companies have adopted more specific language against discrimination based on sexual orientation.

Such language sends an important message to gay professionals and heterosexuals alike. To the gay employee it says, "Your complaints will be taken seriously." To the heterosexual it warns, "Antigay jokes and comments are off-limits." Antigay jokes only continue because they are seldom opposed. Whether or not a comprehensive nondiscrimination policy is in place, gay employees who fail to counter these jokes allow this phenomenon to be perpetuated. The same applies to managers: A consistent and immediate response to antigay jokes is necessary to diminish hostility against gay people in the workplace. . . .

Fighting Humor with Humor

Some felt it was necessary for gay people to maintain a sense of humor and laugh along with the jokes if they're funny, as they would if they were told in a group of gay men or lesbians. A few felt humor can be an effective weapon if it is wielded in response to an antigay joke or innuendo. . . .

In dealing with customers and vendors from the South, Carrie found herself hearing antigay as well as racist and anti-Semitic jokes virtually every day. She recalls her most successful response was humorous and spontaneous. "We were looking at a map of the United States, and one of my distributors was making cracks about California being the home of fruits and nuts—all the usual stuff. Then he pointed to the map which showed each state in a distinct color and said, 'Look, California is pink, that must be because of all those fruits.' Recalling that he was originally from Texas, I decided to respond obliquely by joshing, 'Look, Texas is pink too. I wonder why that is?' He looked flustered for a minute, but he rose to the challenge. 'It's because we have a woman governor,' he retorted. I had to laugh myself." Carrie chuckled. "I think we came out about even in the verbal duel."

The "Ouch" Technique

Some of those we interviewed told us that diversity trainers for their companies recommended using the "ouch" technique. Brett explains, "That's what you say when someone says some general comment that hurts you." A workshop participant at a gay workplace conference held at Stanford University expanded: "It's a simple technique. When someone says something really offensive, you just say 'ouch.' Usually the other person will say 'What's wrong?' And then you just say, 'What you said offended me.' That leads into discussion and dialogue." But Brett and others commented it is easier to say "ouch" when someone is talking to you than when you just overhear the comments of others.

"I Don't Get It"

A diversity trainer we know has another approach. "I've got one sure-fire answer that always stops jokes. . . . People tell jokes because they want something back. People are looking for approval or they're looking for you to laugh. You know, it's a way of showing that they're hip, they're with it, or whatever. You pick and choose who you're going to tell jokes to. You don't tell a joke to somebody you don't think is going to think it's funny or isn't going to get it. What I have found is that the surest, most effective way to just shut the whole conversation up

is right after the joke is told, you just look at everybody and say quite seriously, 'I don't get it.'

"It embarrasses people so much when I say, 'I don't get it. Was that a joke? Was that supposed to be funny? I don't get it.' All of a sudden, people stop. Nobody wants to be the one to have to explain. It's amazing, because it shuts down not only that person who told the joke but all the laughter. All of it stops. There's that pause where everybody has to think about why was that joke supposed to be so funny. And nobody has to come out. I've done it with coworkers, customers, and clients. It just cuts to the chase and it's over. And they're too embarrassed to do it again. *They're* the ones who are embarrassed. . . ."

Coming Out

While all of the above techniques for ending antigay jokes can be somewhat effective, those who came out found the jokes stopped automatically. One reason seems to be the corporate norm of getting along with coworkers. Very few white-collar workers want to insult someone to their face. So if a gay professional comes out, he or she gives a message that insulting gay people generally will be seen as a personal insult. Those who were out at work say this is one of the important side benefits to coming out. Not only do the jokes stop, but the underlying attitudes that give rise to the jokes change as well, because most people who know someone gay develop a more positive attitude toward gay people. . . .

QUESTIONS

1. What are some of the moral and immoral uses of humor? To what extent is there truth in jest?

2. What do the jokes in an organization tell you about its ethical environment?

CASES

CASE 2.1

A "State of the Art" Termination
John R. Boatright

Monday had been the most humiliating day of Bill Collin's life. Rumors of downsizing had been swirling for months, and every computer analyst in Bill's department knew that the ax would fall on some of them. Bets had even been taken on who would stay and who would go. When the news was finally delivered, Bill was not surprised. He also understood the necessity of reducing the computer support staff in view of the merger that had made many jobs redundant, and he felt confident that he would find a new job fairly quickly. What upset him was the manner in which he had been terminated.

Bill arrived in the office at eight o'clock sharp to find a memo on his desk about a nine-thirty meeting at a hotel one block away. Since this site was often used for training sessions, he gave the notice little thought. Bill decided to arrive a few minutes early in order to chat with colleagues, but he found himself being ushered quickly into a small conference room where three other people from his department were already seated. His greeting to them was cut short by a fourth person whom Bill had never seen before. The stranger explained that he was a consultant from an outplacement firm that had been engaged to deliver the bad news and to outline the benefits the company was providing for them. Once he started talking, Bill felt relieved: The package of benefits was greater than he had dared hope. All employees would receive full salary for six months plus pay for accrued vacation time; medical insurance and pension contribution

would be continued during this period; and the out-placement firm would provide career counseling and a placement service that included secretarial assistance, photocopying and fax service, and office space. The consultant assured the four longtime employees that the company appreciated their years of service and wanted to proceed in a caring manner. It was for this reason that they hired the best consulting firm in the business, one that had a reputation for a "state-of-the-art" termination process.

Bill's relief was jolted by what came next. The consultant informed the four that they were not to return to their office or to set foot inside the corporate office building again; nor were they to attempt to contact anyone still working for the company. (At this point, Bill suddenly realized that he had no idea how many employees might be in other four-person groups being dismissed at the same time.) The contents of their desks would be boxed and delivered to their homes; directories of their computer files would be provided, and requests for any personal material would be honored after a careful review of their contents to make sure that no proprietary information was included. The consultant assured them that all passwords had already been changed, including the password for remote access. Finally, they were instructed not to remain at the hotel but to proceed to a service exit where prepaid taxis were stationed to take them home.

Bill regretted not being able to say goodbye to

From John R. Boatright, *Ethics and the Conduct of Business*, 2nd edition (Upper Saddle River, NJ: Prentice Hall, 1997), pp. 255–256. Notes were deleted from the text.

friends in the office. He would have liked some advance warning in order to finish up several projects that he had initiated and to clear out his own belongings. The manner in which he had been terminated was compassionate up to a point, Bill admitted, but it showed that the company did not trust him. A few days later, Bill understood the company's position better when he read an article in a business magazine that detailed the sabotage that had been committed by terminated employees who had continued access to their employer's computer system. Some disgruntled workers had destroyed files and done other mischief when they were allowed to return to their offices after being informed of their termination. One clever computer expert had previously planted a virtually undetectable virus that remained dormant until he gained access long enough through a co-worker's terminal to activate it. The advice that companies were receiving from consulting firms that specialize in termination was: Be compassionate, but also protect yourself. Good advice, Bill thought, but the humiliation was still fresh in his mind.

QUESTIONS

1. Is firing someone with dignity an oxymoron?
2. Is there a way to fire people that will encourage them to act with dignity?

CASE 2.2
AIDS in the Workplace
William H. Shaw and Vincent Barry

Carla Lombard always worked well with people. So when she opened her bagel shop Better Bagels seven years ago, she anticipated that managing her employees would be the easy part. She had worked for enough different bosses herself, she thought, to know what it took to be a good employer. Whether she was up to the financial side of running a business was her worry. As it turned out, however, Better Bagels flourished. Not only had Carla gone on to open three smaller branches of Better Bagels, but her bakery also made daily wholesale deliveries to dozens of coffee shops and restaurants around the city. No, the business was prospering. It was just that the personnel issues were more difficult than she had ever expected. Take this week, for example.

On Tuesday, Carla was in the main bagel shop when around noon Tom Walters's ex-wife, Frances, came in. Tom oversaw a lot of the early morning baking at that shop, and like most of Carla's employees put in his share of time working the sales counter. He was a good worker, and Carla had been considering promoting him next month to manager of one of the branch shops. After ordering a bagel, Frances took Carla aside. She beat around the bush for a few minutes before she got to her point, because she was there to tell Carla that Tom had AIDS. Frances said she was telling Carla because she "always liked her and thought she was entitled to know because she was Tom's employer." Carla barely knew Frances, and she was so taken aback that she was at a loss for words. She was shocked and embarrassed and didn't know whether she should even discuss Tom with Frances. While Carla was still trying to recover herself, Frances took her bagel and left.

Carla was still concerned and upset when she saw Tom the next day. Perhaps he had been thinner and

William H. Shaw and Vincent Barry, *Moral Issues in Business Ethics,* 9th edition, (Belmont, CA: Wadsworth, 2004), pp. 300–301.

looked tired more often the last few months, Carla thought to herself. But she couldn't be sure, and Tom seemed to be his usual upbeat self. Carla wanted to discuss Frances's visit with Tom, but she couldn't bring herself to mention it. She had always liked Tom, but—face it, she thought—he's my employee, not my friend. And it's his business. If I were an employee, I wouldn't want my boss asking me about my health.

Later, however, she began to wonder if it wasn't her business after all. She overheard some customers saying that people were staying away from the local Denny's franchise because one of its cooks was reported to have AIDS. The rumor was that some of his fellow employees had even circulated a petition saying that the cook should go, but a local AIDS support group had intervened, threatening legal action. So the cook was staying, but the customers weren't. Carla knew something about AIDS and thought some of what her customers were saying was bigoted and ill informed. She was pretty sure that you couldn't transmit HIV through food—including bagel—preparation, but she thought that maybe she should double-check her information. But what was really beginning to worry her were the business implications. She didn't want a Denny's-like situation at Better Bagels, but in her customers' comments she could see the possibility of something like that hap-

pening once the word got out about Tom, especially if she made him a manager. Carla was running a business, and even if her customers' fears might be irrational or exaggerated, she couldn't force them to visit her shops or eat her bagels.

Carla knew it was illegal to fire Tom for having AIDS, and in any case that's not the kind of person she was. But she couldn't afford to skirt the whole problem, she realized, as some large companies do, by simply sending the employee home at full pay. To be sure, doing that deprives the employee of meaningful work, but it removes any difficulties in the workplace, and the employee has no legal grounds for complaint if he or she is left on the payroll. And then, of course, there was always the question of Tom's future work performance. Putting the question of promotion aside, if he really was ill, as Frances had said, his work performance would probably decline, she thought. Shouldn't she begin developing some plan for dealing with that?

QUESTIONS

1. Who are the stakeholders in this case, and how would you describe Carla's moral obligations to each of them?

2. If you were in Carla's position, what would your moral priorities be, and how would you act to fill them?

CASE 2.3
Racial Discrimination at Texaco
Kurt Eichenwald

Michael Moccio knew exactly what to do when a complaint of racial discrimination landed on his desk at Texaco Inc.

A manager in the oil giant's Denver office, Mr. Moccio had read the company's equal-opportunity policies and guidelines on proper conduct toward

other employees. So when Mary Devorce, a black accountant in that office, filed a complaint with the Government in 1991, contending she had been subjected to racism at Texaco, Mr. Moccio was ready.

First he assured Ms. Devorce that, despite the complaint, her job was safe. He told her that Texaco

The Two Faces Of Texaco by Kurt Eichenwald. *New York Times (1857-Current file);* Nov 10, 1996; ProQuest Historical Newspapers The New York Times pg. F1. Reproduced with permission of the copyright owner. Further reproduction prohibited without permission.

would treat her fairly. To demonstrate the company's concern, Mr. Moccio even offered her new duties that would remove her from the situation she found discriminatory.

It was all going exactly as it should. Then Mr. Moccio, who is white, called his supervisor, Jim Woolly, a white assistant controller in Houston. He filled in his boss on the complaint and described how he had handled it.

Mr. Woolly was not impressed, according to a sworn affidavit by Mr. Moccio.

"I'd fire her black ass," Mr. Woolly responded. When Mr. Moccio protested that Texaco could not dismiss someone for contending she was a victim of discrimination—a move that saved Ms. Devorce's job—Mr. Woolly shrugged it off.

"I guess we treat niggers differently down here," he replied, according to the affidavit, filed in a 1994 discrimination suit brought by six other employees.

And there, for Texaco, lies the grim conundrum. The antidiscrimination policies are in place. The channels for complaint are in place. The surveys in which employees can gripe anonymously to management about what needs improvement are in place.

But the array of principles and policies can often be impotent, largely because midlevel or senior managers operate by their own rules—with almost no corporate oversight.

The equal-opportunity system at Texaco, the nation's 14th-largest corporation, has come under the microscope after the disclosure last week that senior company executives, in conversations secretly recorded in 1994, plotted to destroy documents demanded in the discrimination suit, and used racial epithets in discussing black employees.

But the explosive tapes are just part of the problem. Thousands of pages of sealed court records obtained by The New York Times from the discrimination suit, as well as Government documents and corporate records, portray a company that says all the right things but that has done far too little to insure they have meaning.

The documents filed in the discrimination suit, which was brought by Texaco employees, reflect an equal-opportunity program without teeth. For example, responsibility for meeting equal-opportunity obligations at the company is pushed down to more than three dozen company divisions, but senior Texaco executives impose no oversight on those divisions to insure that the lower-level executives abide by Federal regulations and company policy.

And unlike many other companies, Texaco does not audit the performance of its divisions to make sure company practices like employee-performance reviews are not unfairly derailing the careers of minority-group employees. Instead, the company relies on the divisions to police themselves, and on audits conducted by the Government every few years on each division.

The documents also indicate that Texaco has a long way to go in promoting members of minority groups and in assuring that its workplace is free of hurtful racism:

- African-Americans make up some 12 percent of the United States population, but of the 873 executives at Texaco who make more than $106,000 annually, only 6—or 0.7 percent—are black. And while the number of executives in the highest pay grade has grown 44 percent over the last four years, to 49, not a single black person has held such a job.
- A Labor Department audit this year of a Texaco controller division found that employees who were members of minority groups had to wait far longer than whites for promotions and were far less likely to receive evaluations that would help them in their careers. Last May the agency ordered Texaco to compensate the minority-group employees for lost wages and to revise the appraisal system, which is used throughout the company.
- A confidential statistical analysis prepared by the plaintiffs—and sharply disputed by Texaco—concluded that the total cost to nonwhite Texaco employees in lost wages as a result of these problems was $71.1 million.
- Scores of Texaco's nonwhite employees contend in the court papers that they were subjected to racially hostile behavior but did not report the infractions for fear of losing their jobs.

"Deficiencies in the affirmative-action programs suggest that Texaco is not committed to insuring comprehensive, facility by facility, compliance with the company's affirmative-action responsibilities," wrote Leonard J. Bierman, former acting director of the Federal agency that monitors affirmative-action programs of Federal contractors like Texaco. His comments were in a confidential report on behalf of the plaintiffs in the discrimination suit. Because of those deficiencies, he continued, "Texaco cannot determine whether its affirmative-action programs achieve their goals or whether the company's policies and practices are having an adverse impact on African-Americans."

The problems at Texaco reflect the slow and bumpy development of equal employment opportunity for minority groups at companies everywhere. To date, there has been widespread success in hiring minority employees, at Texaco and elsewhere. But now comes the next challenge: moving those employees into senior management and assuring that the growing number of minority-group employees are treated fairly and with respect.

The Texaco executives' slurs caught on tape—like "black jelly beans" and "niggers"—go to the heart of that challenge. Were these the words of renegade executives—including the former treasurer—who had abandoned the company's self-proclaimed values? Or was this the unvarnished voice of Texaco's true corporate culture finally being heard?

"The tapes really do raise some profound questions about the integrity of Texaco's commitment to equal opportunity," said Wade Henderson, the executive director of the Leadership Conference on Civil Rights, an umbrella group of 180 organizations. "With the litigation and the tapes, serious questions emerge about whether this is an isolated incident or something far deeper."

Over the last week, Peter I. Bijur, Texaco's chairman and chief executive only since July, has repeatedly stepped before the cameras and the press to express horror at the blatant racism captured on the tapes.

Those recorded words "are statements that represent attitudes we hoped and wished had long ago disappeared entirely from the landscape of our country—and certainly from our company," Mr. Bijur said at a news conference last week. "We believe unequivocally it is utterly reprehensible to deny another human of his or her self-respect and dignity because of race, color, religion or sex."

QUESTIONS

1. The author suggests that the problem at Texaco is that it has antidiscrimination guidelines and procedures in place, but they do not have any teeth. Do you see any other problems in this case?

2. If you were a senior manager at Texaco, what steps would you take to make the organization a good place to work for black and white employees?

CASE 2.4
The Energetic Boss
Joanne B. Ciulla

You just started working in a bank. The people in the office are great. Your boss George is a terrific guy. Everyone in the office loves George. His energy, enthusiasm, and wit keep the place going at a fast but merry pace. George is one of those people who does everything with gusto, whether it's eating, smoking cigars, or trading stock options.

It's been a particularly busy week, and you look forward to the weekend. Your older brother Jim is flying in from California to visit you and attend his college reunion. On Friday night, you and Jim will have dinner with Harry, Jim's old college roommate.

When Jim arrives, you both go to meet Harry at a steak house in town. After a big dinner and a number of drinks, Harry suggests that you come with him to his neighbor's birthday party. You all jump into a cab and drive off to the party. When you arrive, the party is in full swing.

After a few drinks, you head upstairs to find a bathroom. You open the door that you thought was to the bathroom and inside the room there is a group of people sitting around a low table. On the table white powder is laid out in rows on a mirror. One man is holding a short straw in his hand. Shocked and embarrassed, you mumble, "excuse me." Before you can close the door, the man holding the straw turns his head so that you can see his profile. In that instant, you recognize the familiar face of your boss, George. Fortunately, he didn't see you.

You immediately leave the party. All weekend you think about George, and you wonder whether you should say or do anything about what you witnessed at the party.

QUESTIONS

1. Does the company have a right to know what employees do in their free time?

2. What are your moral obligations to George and the company, and would your obligations be different if you were George's boss?

CASE 2.5
Does Home Life Matter at Work?
Joanne B. Ciulla

Over the past month, you and your colleagues have been reviewing applications for regional manager. The regional manager's job involves overseeing and coordinating the operations of a large portion of the Western United States. On Friday afternoon, your committee finally makes its selection and plans to announce its choice on Monday morning. Out of a number of talented managers, it selected John Deer. John's peers often used the words "brilliant" and "genius" to describe him. He held a consistent record of excellence in every task that he accomplished for the company.

A quiet, polite man, John rarely attended social functions, and when he did, he never brought his wife. When you arrive at your office on Monday morning, you are surprised to get a call from John's wife Edith, whom you've never met. Her voice sounds shaky, and you can hardly hear her. She says:

I'm sorry to be a bother, but I needed to talk to you. My husband John has been tense lately because he really wants the regional manager's job. Anyway, last night John gave me a very bad beating. Our two children saw the whole thing and were terrified. I took the children and ran out of the house. We are now staying at the Chicago shelter for battered women. Over the years, John has hit me on numerous occasions, but never like this. He's basically a good man, but he's very high strung. Anyway, the reason why I am calling is to beg you to give the job to John. Maybe then he'll feel happier and things will be better for our family.

The phone call is so bizarre that you decide to check out Mrs. Deer's story. You call the Chicago shelter to find out if she is indeed there. The shelter director says that it is against its policy to give out the identity of clients or any information on them. Then in the background you hear some confusion as Mrs. Deer grabs the phone from the director. Mrs. Deer tells the director to get on the other line and demands that she answer your questions. The director protests, but does as she is asked. She reports that Mrs. Deer and her two children, ages 2 and 6, were admitted to the shelter last night at midnight after being treated at City Hospital. Mrs. Deer had a broken rib and bruises on the face, arms, and neck that were apparently caused by a blunt object.

It is now 10:30 a.m. The formal announcement is scheduled for noon. At this point, John may already know that he got the job. You are angry and disgusted, but you know that you will have to put your personal feelings aside and consider a number of issues before you make any decisions about John. Since Mrs. Deer has no plans to press charges against her husband, you put aside legal considerations and think about your ethical obligations in this situation.

QUESTIONS

1. Given that there is no legal action taken against an individual, is the way that a person treats his or her spouse or other family member relevant in hiring and promotion decisions?

2. If you were the manager in this case, how would you fill your moral obligations to all the stakeholders who are involved in it?

CASE 2.6
Discrimination at Wal-Mart: Unequal Wages and Opportunities

DECLARATION SUMMARIES

Barbara Steele

Barbara Steele worked her way up to store manager after working in several stores around the country, including in Missouri, Texas, New Mexico, Idaho, and Washington. She currently lives in Arizona. Ms. Steele had been an assistant manager for six years with no disciplinary action and only positive evaluations. She is personally aware of several men who got promoted much more quickly than she did to store manager positions. In her four years as a store manager, Ms. Steele enhanced the performance of both stores in which she worked but, in 1999, she was quickly demoted to assistant manager for back-dating one employee's evaluation. Ms. Steele then spent the next three years trying to get re-promoted to store manager. She never got promoted past grocery co-manager and men received almost all of the more than 24 positions for which she applied. While Ms. Steele had over four years' store manager experience, many of these men had no experience as a store manager. The male district manager who demoted her was later fired for violation of the fraternization policy and then, within 90 days, was rehired into one of the store manager positions for which she applied.

Kim McLamb

Mrs. McLamb worked for Wal-Mart from 1991 to 2001 as an assistant manager throughout Virginia. She was an excellent employee who continuously received "exceeds expectations" ratings on her evaluations. From the beginning of her employment, Mrs. McLamb regularly expressed an interest in promotion to several store managers and district managers. At one point, she was required to commit, in writing, to working overnights for a full two years. Male assistant managers were only required to rotate through the overnight position on a six-month basis. Mrs. McLamb was also passed over for management positions in favor of less experienced and less qualified men. When Mrs. McLamb discovered that male employees made more than female employees working the same jobs, she complained to three different assistant managers. Each told her it was because the men "had families to support." At one point, in 2001, when Mrs. McLamb and a number of other female assistant managers were working around the clock to prepare for inventory, the male store manager and male assistant managers spent their time training for a triathlon. They would bring their bikes into the store and often left work early to train. Unlike the female assistant managers, the males would rarely work on weekends.

Ramona Scott

Ramona Scott worked for Wal-Mart in Florida from 1990 to 1998. While working in Pinellas Park, Florida, Ms. Scott was a personnel manager who had access to payroll records. She noticed that men generally made more than women who had as much or more seniority. When she asked the male store manager about the pay discrepancy, he told her, "Men are here to make a career and women aren't. Retail is for housewives who just need to earn extra money." When Ms. Scott later inquired about a raise that a male employee had received, she was told by a male assistant manager, "He has a family to support." When she pointed out that she was a single mother, the assistant manager ignored her and walked away. When Ms. Scott expressed an interest in promotion into the Management Training Program, her district manager merely told her there were no openings but did not give her guidance or information about how to get into the program. When a new male store manager took over her store, he laughed at Ms. Scott's pay rate and told her that the male personnel manager at his former store made "a lot more" than she did. This same store manager dismissed her renewed request to enter the Management Training Program. He then told her that if she wanted to get along with him, she would have to behave like his wife and frequently asked her to get coffee for him and other male managers.

Claudia Renati

Claudia Renati began working at a Sam's Club in Roseville, California in 1993 as a marketing membership team leader. Early on, Ms. Renati became responsible for running the marketing programs in the region after the regional sales manager left. After two years of performing the tasks of both positions without the additional pay or the correct job title, she asked the director of operations to promote her into the position. He refused because she had not gone through the Management Training Program. Over the next couple of years, the position of marketing manager was filled by several male next-door neighbors of the director of operations. None had gone through management training and none had experience in marketing. Ms. Renati was responsible for training these less qualified and less experienced men who were hired to be her supervisors. Over the next several years, Ms. Renati trained approximately 20 male managers, many of whom never went through the Management Training Program nor were required to relocate. Ms. Renati continued to be passed over for promotions for positions that were consistently filled by males with no prior management experience and less seniority. At one point, the director of operations told Ms. Renati that before she could become a manager, she would be required to stack 50-pound bags of dog food as a floor team leader. When Ms. Renati indicated that she could not repeatedly lift 50 pounds, he told her he could not help her advance. Ms. Renati is aware of several male employees who never had to become floor team leader, nor were required to stack 50-pound bags of dog food in order to enter the Management Training Program.

Christine Kwapnoski

Christine Kwapnoski has worked for Sam's Club since 1986 in a variety of positions with ever increasing responsibilities. Her evaluations have been outstanding, and she received a number of merit raises over the years. Nevertheless, despite frequent requests for promotion, she was not allowed to join the ranks of management. The director of operations claimed she had "people issues," in that she was too direct and outspoken. Finally, two weeks after this suit was filed, Chris was promoted to an area manager. Because this is a salaried position with no overtime pay, her hourly rate actually decreased. While in this position, she was told by the General Manager of the Club to "doll up" and "blow the cobwebs off her makeup." She stayed an area manager for 1½ years until, at his deposition, Executive Vice President of Sam's Club, Gregg Spragg learned she had not been promoted to assistant manager. Ms. Kwapnoski entered Management Training in March 2003.

Micki Earwood

Micki Earwood is a Springfield, Ohio resident [who] worked for Wal-Mart for 10 years. Ms. Earwood held jobs as an associate, department manager, support manager and personnel manager at three separate Ohio Wal-Mart stores. Despite consistently receiving highly rated performance evaluations, Wal-Mart denied Ms. Earwood's repeated requests to be placed into the Management Training Program, thus denying her the opportunity to obtain a salaried Wal-Mart manager position. During her tenure as a personnel manager, Ms. Earwood had access to employee payroll information and thus had the unique opportunity to witness first-hand Wal-Mart's discrimination against women with regard to compensation. Ms. Earwood reported these gender-based pay discrepancies to her superiors. Instead of addressing to Ms. Earwood's complaints of discrimination, Wal-Mart wrongfully terminated her in September, 2000, based upon her whistle-blowing activities.

Laverne Jones

Laverne Jones, currently resides in Pontotoc, Mississippi and began working for Wal-Mart in 1977 with high hopes of a long and successful career with the emerging company. Within six months, Wal-Mart promoted her to a Department Manager position, an hourly supervisory job that is just a step away from the higher-paying realm of salaried management. For the next 25 years Ms. Jones tried to make the jump into the Management Training Program, which would have opened the door for her to salaried positions. Despite making multiple requests to be promoted into management and a quarter-century of exemplary work history, Ms. Jones has remained an hourly associate making less than $29,000 per year. A fellow male employee, on the other hand, who also started at the Pontotoc, Mississippi store in 1977, was placed into the Management Training Program and is now a District Manager earning a base salary that significantly dwarfs Ms. Jones' meager wages.

Karla Rojas

Karla Rojas, who received a BSBA degree in Marketing from the University of Arkansas (Fayetteville) and lives in Dallas, Texas, began working for Wal-Mart in 1983. Ms. Rojas' Wal-Mart career spanned nearly 17 years. Recognizing her management potential, Wal-Mart hired Ms. Rojas directly into the Management Training Program after she graduated from college, which program grooms employees to become salaried Wal-Mart managers. Ms. Rojas worked as a Wal-Mart manager in positions of assistant manager, operations assistant manager, co-manager, acting store manager and store manager. Ms. Rojas also worked at the Wal-Mart Home Office in Bentonville, Arkansas as a fashion distributor and associate buyer. Ms. Rojas repeatedly made it known to her supervisors that she wanted to be a store manager of a large Wal-Mart store. For years, her supervisors instructed her to work in certain positions in order to ensure a promotion to store manager. Then, after Ms. Rojas would followed their advice and obtained the position in question, her supervisors would inform her that the promotion rules had changed and that she should pursue an alternative promotion path. Meanwhile, males with experience comparable to or less than that of Ms. Rojas were rapidly promoted into store manager positions. When Ms. Rojas finally achieved store manager status after 12 years of dedicated service to the company, Wal-Mart discriminatorily assigned her to a previously mismanaged and dysfunctional store, ensuring that she would not advance further.

Melissa Howard

Melissa Howard worked at Wal-Mart from 1992 to 2000. Despite excellent evaluations and her stores making a profit, Ms. Howard felt she had to leave Wal-Mart due to the abuse and mistreatment she received based on her gender. In 1998, when Ms. Howard was a store manager in Decatur, Indiana, she was required to attend district meetings at a Hooter's Restaurant. On one occasion, Ms. Howard and two male members of management were driving to a management meeting in Bentonville, Arkansas when the male managers insisted on stopping at a strip club. As she did not feel safe sitting by herself in the dark parking lot of the strip club, Ms. Howard felt she had no choice but to accompany the male managers into the club. While in the club, Ms. Howard was approached by a stripper and the male district manager proposed they all have a "threesome out back." On the return trip to Indiana, two more stops were made at strip clubs where Ms. Howard sat in the back of the club, but was able to observe several males up front paying for lap dances. On the return trip, the male managers insisted on stopping at two more strip clubs. Ms. Howard and another female manager sat in the back while observing several of the male managers pay for lap dances. Although Ms. Howard continued to receive "exceeds expectations" ratings on her performance evaluations, she was continuously criticized and berated for her job performance during her time at Wal-Mart. She was also paid at a lower rate than other male store management. By 2000, she was so fed up and felt so undermined in her management career, that and she felt she had no choice but to leave Wal-Mart.

Deborah "Dee" Gunter:

Dee Gunter worked at three different Wal-Mart stores in Southern California from April 1996 through August 1999. She had extensive retail and management experience prior to joining the company. Despite her qualifications, Wal-Mart repeatedly denied Ms. Gunter promotion opportunities. On three separate occasions, Ms. Gunter applied for, but was denied, the position of support manager in Wal-Mart's Tire Lube Express Specialty Division in favor of men who had less time with the company and who were often less qualified than she. Ms. Gunter was required to train each of these men immediately prior to their promotions. During the two years she worked as an overnight stocker, Ms. Gunter was paid approximately $2.00 an hour less than some of her male co-workers. She was only earning $7.50 an hour when she left the company.

Gina Espinoza-Price

Gina Espinoza-Price was employed by Wal-Mart from November 1990 through April 1997. She worked her way up from an hourly associate to International Liaison for the Photo Division. Ms. Espinoza-Price was an extremely valuable asset to Wal-Mart: she wrote many of Wal-Mart's Specialty Division Distribution Center procedures and she helped open Photo departments in new stores in Canada, Mexico, and the United States. Despite her qualifications, Ms. Espinoza-Price was repeatedly overlooked for promotion to regional photo manager in favor of male photo district managers who had less experience than she or whom she had trained. She also was subjected to sexist and racist comments by a male regional photo manager, including being called "the little Mexican princess."

Vicki Thornton

In 1998, Vicki Thornton quit her job as a store manager at another retail store and took a 30% pay cut to work for a Wal-Mart in Racine, Wisconsin. She believed it would be a good career move because she was promised that, within six months, she would be promoted into the management ranks and could easily work her way up in the company. After three years, despite her hard work and excellent evaluations, Ms. Thornton had still not been promoted to the Management Training Program. During this

Sexual Harassment Guidelines

Sexual harassment is covered under Title VII of the Civil Rights Act of 1964. The act states that it is unlawful for an employer to discriminate against an employee based on a person's sex. It prohibits discrimination in decisions involving compensation, terms, conditions, or privileges of employment. There are two types of sexual harassment:

1. *Quid pro quo:* Harassment that pressures an employee for sexual favors as a condition of employment or for benefits, such as promotions, job assignments, etc.
2. *Hostile Environment:* Behavior that does not affect an employee's economic benefits. It consists of unwelcome advances or sexual, verbal, and/or physical conduct of a sexual nature. This conduct has the purpose or effect of interfering with an individual's work performance or creating an intimidating, hostile, or offensive working environment.*

Key elements of sexual harassment:

1. Harassment was unwelcome
2. Harassment was based on gender
3. Harassment was sufficiently severe or pervasive
4. Hostile environment affects a person's ability to perform at work and/or causes psychological harm.

*Anja Angelica Chan, *Women and Sexual Harassment* (New York: Harrington Park Press, 1994), pp. 5–6.

time, she constantly asked to be considered for promotion to the Management Training Program but she was always told there were no openings. At the same time, she watched as male employees with less experience were admitted to the training program. In addition, Ms. Thornton was also sexually harassed by two male department managers during her Wal-Mart tenure. She complained many times to her store manager and assistant manager who told her to just "grin and bear it." Ms. Thornton left Wal-Mart in 2001.

QUESTIONS

1. In which of the cases is discrimination obvious and in which is it not clear?

2. Is there a relationship between a hostile work environment and disparities between wages and opportunities?

CASE 2.7
Prejudice or Preference?
Joanne B. Ciulla

Sam, one of your senior professionals, has resigned unexpectedly to join one of your competitors. He was responsible for transactions with Magnolia Corporation, where he had a close relationship with the CEO, J. W. Crawford. You know that there is a good chance that Magnolia may go with Sam if you don't put a knowledgeable and experienced person on the account. This is your largest account, and you don't want to lose it. In the past, both the company and Sam have made a lot of money from various deals with Magnolia.

You know from Sam's client notes and from your previous visits to Magnolia that J. W. belongs to the "old school" and is most comfortable dealing with "one of the boys." Last year, when Sam was visiting Magnolia, he went on a hunting trip with J. W. The final night of the trip, J. W. surprised them with a "special treat." He invited a stripper to entertain them after a long dinner and plenty of drinks. On another occasion, Sam invited Elaine Jones, one of the firm's top account executives, to attend a meeting with J. W. Sam wanted her advice on an investment. During the meeting, J. W. paid little attention to what Elaine had to say and kept referring to her as "honey." On the way out of the meeting, J. W. gave her a pat on her behind.

Elaine is really the only person who knows J. W.'s business and has the expertise and seniority to take Sam's place. Ordinarily, there would be no question of her taking over this client because of her experience and track record. Elaine is not known to turn down potentially lucrative deals; however, knowing what you do about J. W., you wonder if she's the person for the job.

QUESTIONS

1. Who should be responsible for making this decision?
2. What are the larger long-term ramifications of this decision for the firm and its stakeholders?

CASE 2.8
Attraction or Business As Usual?
Joanne B. Ciulla

Your company is in the process of opening a new office. You are in charge of purchasing software that will be used for billing and payroll. There are really only three software systems that will meet your businesses needs.

Last week, each of the three vendors came in to gave a demonstration of their product and get an assessment of your computing needs. You spoke with salespeople from two of the companies. However, the third company that you talked to, Agape, sent along a salesperson and a systems expert. The systems expert was named Hank Smith. The salesman explained that Agape likes its customers to meet the technician whom they would be working with if they purchased the system.

Hank Smith was very knowledgeable and

answered all your questions clearly. He was also honest about the strengths and weaknesses of the system. The three of you talked for about two hours, and then the salesperson said that he had another appointment, but that Hank would stay to answer any further questions. Hank suggested that you continue over lunch. You said that would be fine, but only if you could pay.

At lunch Hank talks more about the software system, but you realize that you aren't really listening. Hank isn't just handsome, he's gorgeous and *very* charming. You find yourself looking at his hands to see if he is married. There is no wedding ring, so you turn the conversation to other matters. He tells you that he has an apartment in the city and, through a series of questions, you finally discover that he is not married and that he lives alone. You sense that Hank feels a similar attraction to you. Nonetheless, you realize that you can't do or say anything because of your business relationship.

Over the next few days, you keep thinking about Hank and hoping that Agape will come in with the lowest bid. Finally the bids arrive. Agape and Hi-Tech come in at about the same price. The third company's bid is significantly higher. You discuss the three options with your manager. The software packages offered by Agape and Hi-Tech are similar; either system would be adequate. The more expensive system does not offer much more, so you eliminate it.

Your manager says that since it's a toss-up between Agape and Hi-Tech, the decision is up to you. For a moment you think, about your intense attraction to Hank. But then you think, "I am a professional woman, and this is a decision that could be made by the toss of a coin. So why not choose Agape?" You buy the Agape software, but to your great disappointment, they send another systems expert to work with your company. It makes you wonder if you really made the best decision and if the company sent Hank to work his charm on you.

QUESTIONS

1. Would it be wrong if Agape sent Hank because it knew a single woman was making the decision on the software?

2. Is this a conflict of interest on the purchaser's part, or is it just a case of her interests coinciding with the company's interests?

CASE 2.9
Innocent and Dangerous
Joanne B. Ciulla

You manage a data processing department. Three years ago, you hired Fred Jones, a 25-year-old computer programmer. He proved to be an excellent worker who consistently received high performance ratings. Jones was very quiet and rarely socialized with other employees; however, whenever anyone had a computer problem, you could count on him to solve it.

A few months ago, Jones didn't show up for work and didn't call in. The next day you received a call from his mother. She said that Jones had been arrested and charged with the murder of his girlfriend, who was beaten and stabbed. Later that week, you received a letter from Jones. He said that he was devastated by the loss of his girlfriend. He went on to explain that the reason why he was a suspect is because he had argued with his girlfriend in public prior to her death. When the police came to question him, he had no one to back up his alibi because he had taken a long run in the country at the time of the murder. Jones ended the letter by saying that he was now living a nightmare. He lost his loved one and is accused of a brutal crime that he did not commit. He asks for an unpaid leave of absence. The company grants his request.

Jones goes on trial, and the jury finds him guilty. His lawyer appeals the case on a technicality. Jones is given a new trial, and this time he is found innocent. One month later, Jones calls and says that he is ready to work again. You are ambivalent, but you see no reason why he shouldn't come back. After all, he has not been convicted of crime, and he is a valuable employee. You mention to a colleague that Jones will be returning to work.

The next morning a group of employees are waiting for you at your office. They tell you that they refuse to work with Jones because they are afraid that he is dangerous. They demand that he be fired.

QUESTIONS

1. What should you do?
2. Aside from your legal obligations, what are your ethical obligations to the various stakeholders in this situation?

CHAPTER QUESTIONS

1. What are the underlying conditions of the employer-employee relationship that make it a challenge for organizations to respect the humanity of persons in the workplace?

2. What claim does an employer have on a person's feelings, rights, and privacy? What moral guidelines would you use to decide what you are willing to give up to be an employee and what you would ask others to give up as an employer?

3

"The Check Is in the Mail"

Honesty and Trust in Business

Introduction

You have a job you like, and you work for a man named George. George is a bright ambitious, and energetic person, but his expectations often outreach his grasp, and he tends to take on more work than he can do. Working with him can be fun, but it's often frantic. Projects are frequently late, and you always seem to be on a tight if not impossible deadline.

The phones ring constantly in George's office. Typically, George tells his secretary to say that he is not in or that he will be out of town until the end of the week. Sometimes when people hear that George is not in, they call you. This puts you in the awkward position of not only having to back up the lie that the secretary was instructed to tell but sometimes having to make up new lies. Sometimes, you have to lie to confirm that George is where he says he is. Other times, you have to lie about what George is doing. There are times when George tells his manager that your group is working on or even almost finished with a project that the group hasn't even heard of, let alone started. In this way, George sometimes gets his team projects that they might not have gotten otherwise, but it also puts pressure on everyone in the group (including you) to lie about what the group is doing and how it is progressing.

Today George is away with his family on vacation. You get a call from his boss. He says, "I need to talk to you about that Franklin project—George told me that your team has been making great progress on it." You have no idea what the Franklin project is, so you lie, say "just fine," and tell George's manager that you are tied up in meetings all day. You agree to stop by first thing tomorrow.

Your first instinct is to contact George. But he is on a camping trip with his family, and he makes it a point not to check for messages when he is away from the office on personal time. You are positive that no one in your office is working on a Franklin project because you coordinate all the projects for George.

All along you knew that the lies would catch up to George. Every small lie seems to require 10 more lies. Yet the thing about George is that he has a way of turning his lies into truths. He reminds you of the French writer Andre Malraux. Malraux believed that the way to lead an exciting life was to tell big lies and then live your life so as to make them true. But this is not the time for philosophizing. You have been lying not because you are fabricating a better life for yourself, but because George has put you into this awkward situation. This not the first time you have had to lie for him or because of him, of course, but this time is much more serious. The little "white lies" that his secretary routinely tells—and you've been party to—seem innocent enough. After all, whom do you know who hasn't said or had someone say that they're "in a meeting" when, in fact, they are taking a nap or spending some time in the restroom? And how often have you said or heard someone say "the check is in the mail" when it is not, although just saying that usually motivates getting that check in the mail ASAP. Sure, it's a lie, but it's an innocent lie, even a productive lie. So what harm is done?

But now, what will you tell George's boss?

"Honesty is the best policy," we are told from childhood. But we see cheating and lying all around us. Why is honesty so important? Why is telling the truth important? Indeed, why is truth so important? If lies and deception help us get along in life, for example, when we don't tell our friends something true but offensive about themselves, isn't that more important than the truth? And whatever we think about the idea of lying to friends or deceiving one's family, business would seem to be another matter. No one expects a salesman to tell "the whole truth and nothing but the truth" about the advantages of his own versus his competitor's products. No one ever got ahead in an organization by being completely forthright about his or her abilities and deficiencies, although *pretending* to be completely forthright about one's deficiencies (for example, "I get so involved in a project that I cannot quit until it gets done") can get one ahead, to be sure. And what is a lie, after all? It is impossible to tell the whole truth; there are always details left out, perspectives left unexplored, presuppositions left unspoken. Given any situation or state of affairs, there are more or less positive, and more or less negative, ways of presenting it, which in today's politics is called "spin." Spin, strictly speaking, is not lying. It does not involve falsehood. It just imposes a positive (or a negative) way of interpreting the facts. Thus, two politicians may take exactly the same facts about the economy, for example, and one suggests that they show that the economy is getting better and the other insists that they show that the economy is in serious trouble. So, too, a salesman necessarily puts a positive spin on the facts about his product (as opposed to the facts about his competitor's product) but he need not tell any falsehood to do so. So what does it mean in business, that "honesty is the best policy"?

In the following selections, we will see a wide-range of discussions and opinions about the place of truth, lies, and secrets in business. In the first selection, Albert Z. Carr argues that something very much like lying, *bluffing,* is utterly fundamental to business. Business, he says, is a lot like poker. He expands this analogy into a general observation that the morality of ordinary life is not applicable to business. Needless to say, many people in the business community howled in indignation. They thought of themselves as moral, upstanding citizens, and they thought of their business activities as a legitimate and completely moral part of their citizenship, and their replies make that very clear. We have also included an argument by business ethicist Norman Bowie, who argues against Carr that bluffing just doesn't pay. We then include a surprising excerpt from the great philosopher Immanuel Kant, who makes the good point that telling the truth is not always the right thing to do. He also opens up the question of privacy, confidentiality, and secrets. Robert C. Solomon then further complicates the issues of lying in business.

But honesty is not the only good policy in business. One of the complications surrounding questions of truthfulness in business is a legitimate concern with confidentiality and keeping secrets. All businesses operate within a network of agreements and promises, some of them explicitly spelled out in contracts, others left unsaid and merely implicit. People in the financial industry, for example, are often bound by confidentiality agreements. That means that they are committed not to tell the truth (or, rather, to not tell the truth) even when someone directly asks them for information that breaches confidentiality. In a more informal way, businesses have an obligation to their customers to maintain a certain privacy. Again, sometimes this obligation is explicit and spelled out (as when a mail order house promises to send a product "in a discrete package") but more often it is left merely implicit. Thus, airline customers howled and some even sued when their airlines passed along personal travel information to the federal government under the Homeland Security Act. That information, they argued, was private and therefore protected, whether or not they had any explicit assurances from the airlines. Protecting someone's privacy (including one's own), it can be argued, is not fairly construed as an instance of lying.

Many businesses also require secrets, secret formulas for a soft drink, secret strategies for negotiations, secret or at any rate private arrangements with various customers, employees, and vendors. Businesses, like individuals, are entitled to have secrets, and having secrets. . . . Transparency International, takes the lack of transparency to be the central measure of international business corruption. But what is a legitimate secret, and what is not? We include pieces by Sissela Bok and Richard T. de George that discuss the role of secrets in business.

Telling the truth is hardest, to many people, when one's career is on the line. If you are a consultant, for example, the temptation is to tell your client what he or she wants to hear. Otherwise, human nature being what it is, there is a strong likelihood that you will not be invited back. This is also true within the workplace, especially with the new emphasis on 360-degree assessment and regular job evaluations. So we have included an excerpt from a consultant's consultant, Sue De Wine, on "Giving Feedback." But the question about consultants can be turned around. When can a manager trust his or her consultant? Consider the following polemic from another consultant's consultant, Evan M. Dudik, who understands the self-deception that goes along with the investment in "expert" advice. A similar point is made in the accompanying *Economist* excerpt.

What makes honesty the best policy? Part of the answer is, because of *trust.* It is trust that makes the business world possible, and without it, there would be no business, just varieties of strategy, fraud, robbery, and coercion. Business is all about trust. Dishonesty violates trust and raises suspicions. And for those who think only prudentially, a powerful answer to the "why not lie?" question is "because you probably won't get away with it." People usually don't get away with it, not only because they get tripped up by embarrassing facts, but because they trip themselves up. We have included a piece by psychologists Paul Ekman and Mark Frank who have worked extensively with police and security institutions, explaining why this so often happens. The risk of destroying trust is usually enough of a deterrent for most people. Finally, we have included a short piece on the complex nature of trust.

To: You
From: The Philosopher
Subject: "Aristotle, Kant, and Mill on Honesty"

The way you are discussing honesty suggests that you think that truth and deception are special concerns in business, but if there is one moral rule that seems to have always been around; it is the insistence that we should tell the truth. Philosophers of almost every persuasion have seen fit to condemn lying, albeit for different reasons. Twenty-five hundred years ago, Aristotle argued that

> The man who loves truth and is truthful where nothing is at stake will be still more truthful where something is at stake; he will avoid falsehood as something base, seeing that he avoided it even for its own sake. Such a man is worthy of praise. (*N. Ethics* Book IV, Ch. 7)

For Aristotle, truthfulness was a virtue. The lack of truthfulness was a vice. Lying was not so much a breach of rules as it was a betrayal of bad character.

Kant, on the other hand, was a rule man. Lying was wrong because it violated what he called "The Moral Law" (or what he characterized as "The Categorical Imperative"). Yet he, too, saw lying as a mark of a bad person, worthy of contempt, and quite independent of the consequences.

> The greatest violation of man's duty to himself considered only as a moral being is the opposite of veracity: lying. That no intentional untruth in the expression of one's thoughts can avoid this harsh name in ethics which derives no authorization from harmlessness, is clear of itself For dishonor, to be an object of moral contempt, which goes with lying accompanies the liar like his shadow (*Metaphysics of the Principles of Virtue* p. 429)

In other words, lying is wrong even if the consequences are good, and truth telling is right even if the results are disastrous.

John Stuart Mill, by contrast, insisted that consequences are all-important. Lying is wrong, accordingly, because it usually—perhaps almost always—has long-term bad consequences.

Albert Z. Carr | # Is Business Bluffing Ethical?

Albert Carr wrote this inflammatory piece in the *Harvard Business Review* in 1968. It continues to attract controversy.

A respected businessman with whom I discussed the theme of this article remarked with some heat, "You mean to say you're going to encourage men to bluff? Why, bluffing is nothing more than a form of lying! You're advising them to lie!"

I agreed that the basis of private morality is a respect for truth and that the closer a businessman comes to the truth, the more he deserves respect. At the same time, I suggested that most bluffing in business might be regarded simply as game strategy—much like bluffing in poker, which does not reflect on the morality of the bluffer.

I quoted Henry Taylor, the British statesman who pointed out that "falsehood ceases to be falsehood when it is understood on all sides that the truth is not expected to be spoken"—an exact description of bluffing in poker, diplomacy, and business. I cited the analogy of the criminal court, where the criminal is not expected to tell the truth when he pleads "not guilty." Everyone from the judge down takes it for granted that the job of the defendant's attorney is to get his client off, not to reveal the truth; and this is considered ethical practice. I mentioned Representative Omar Burleson, the Democrat from Texas, who was quoted as saying, in regard to the ethics of Congress, "Ethics is a barrel of worms"[1]—a pungent summing up of the problem of deciding who is ethical in politics.

I reminded my friend that millions of businessmen feel constrained every day to say *yes* to their bosses when they secretly believe *no* and that this is generally accepted as permissible strategy when the alternative might be the loss of a job. The essential point, I said, is that the ethics of business are game ethics, different from the ethics of religion.

He remained unconvinced. Referring to the company of which he is president, he declared: "Maybe that's good enough for some businessmen, but I can tell you that we pride ourselves on our ethics. In 30 years not one customer has ever questioned my word or asked to check our figures. We're loyal to our customers and fair to our suppliers. I regard my handshake on a deal as a contract. I've never entered into price-fixing schemes with my competitors. I've never allowed my salesmen to spread injurious rumors about other companies. Our union contract is the best in our industry. And, if I do say so myself, our ethical standards are of the highest!"

He really was saying, without realizing it, that he was living up to the ethical standards of the business game—which are a far cry from those of private life. Like a gentlemanly poker player, he did not play in cahoots with others at the table, try to smear their reputations, or hold back chips he owed them.

But this same fine man, at that very time, was allowing one of his products to be advertised in a way that made it sound a great deal better than it actually was. Another item in his product line was notorious among dealers for its "built-in obsolescence." He was holding back from the market a much-improved product because he did not want it to interfere with sales of the inferior item it would have replaced. He had joined with certain of his competitors in hiring a lobbyist to push a state legislature, by methods that he preferred not to know too much about, into amending a bill then being enacted.

In his view these things had nothing to do with ethics; they were merely normal business practice. He himself undoubtedly avoided outright falsehoods—never lied in so many words. But the entire organization that he ruled was deeply involved in numerous strategies of deception.

PRESSURE TO DECEIVE

Most executives from time to time are almost compelled, in the interests of their companies or themselves, to practice some form of deception when negotiating with customers, dealers, labor unions, government officials, or even other departments of their companies. By conscious misstatements, concealment of pertinent facts, or exaggeration—in short, by bluffing—they seek to persuade others to agree with them. I think it is fair to say that if the individual executive refuses to bluff from time to time—if he feels obligated to tell the truth, the whole truth, and nothing but the truth—he is ignoring opportunities permitted under the rules and is at a heavy disadvantage in his business dealings.

But here and there a businessman is unable to reconcile himself to the bluff in which he plays a part. His conscience, perhaps spurred by religious idealism, troubles him. He feels guilty; he may develop an ulcer or a nervous tic. Before any executive can make profitable use of the strategy of the bluff, he needs to make sure that in bluffing he will not lose self-respect or become emotionally disturbed. If he is to reconcile personal integrity and high standards of honesty with the practical requirements of business, he must feel that his bluffs are ethically justified. The justification rests on the fact that business, as practiced by individuals as well as by corporations, has the impersonal character of a game—a game that demands both special strategy and an understanding of its special ethics.

The game is played at all levels of corporate life, from the highest to the lowest. At the very instant that a man decides to enter business, he may be forced into a game situation, as is shown by the recent experience of a Cornell honor graduate who applied for a job with a large company:

- This applicant was given a psychological test which included the statement, "Of the following magazines, check any that you have read either regularly or from time to time, and double-check those which interest you most. *Reader's Digest, Time, Fortune, Saturday*

Evening Post, The New Republic, Life, Look, Ramparts, Newsweek, Business Week, U.S. News & World Report, The Nation, Playboy, Esquire, Harper's, Sports Illustrated."

His tastes in reading were broad, and at one time or another he had read almost all of these magazines. He was a subscriber to *The New Republic,* an enthusiast for *Ramparts,* and an avid student of the pictures in *Playboy.* He was not sure whether his interest in *Playboy* would be held against him, but he had a shrewd suspicion that if he confessed to an interest in *Ramparts* and *The New Republic,* he would be thought a liberal, a radical, or at least an intellectual, and his chances of getting the job, which he needed, would greatly diminish. He therefore checked five of the more conservative magazines. Apparently it was a sound decision, for he got the job.

He had made a game player's decision, consistent with business ethics.

A similar case is that of a magazine space salesman who, owing to a merger, suddenly found himself out of a job:

- This man was 58, and, in spite of a good record, his chance of getting a job elsewhere in a business where youth is favored in hiring practice was not good. He was a vigorous, healthy man, and only a considerable amount of gray in his hair suggested his age. Before beginning his job search he touched up his hair with a black dye to confine the gray to his temples. He knew that the truth about his age might well come out in time, but he calculated that he could deal with that situation when it arose. He and his wife decided that he could easily pass for 45, and he so stated his age on his résumé.

This was a lie; yet within the accepted rules of the business game, no moral culpability attaches to it.

THE POKER ANALOGY

We can learn a good deal about the nature of business by comparing it with poker. While both have a large element of chance, in the long run the winner is the man who plays with steady skill. In both games ultimate victory requires intimate knowledge of the rules, insight into the psychology of the other players, a bold front, a considerable amount of self-discipline, and the ability to respond swiftly and effectively to opportunities provided by chance.

No one expects poker to be played on the ethical principles preached in churches. In poker it is right and proper to bluff a friend out of the rewards of being dealt a good hand. A player feels no more than a slight twinge of sympathy, if that, when—with nothing better than a single ace in his hand—he strips a heavy loser, who holds a pair, of the rest of his chips. It was up to the other fellow to protect himself. In the words of an excellent poker player, former President Harry Truman, "If you can't stand the heat, stay out of the kitchen." If one shows mercy to a loser in poker, it is a personal gesture, divorced from the rules of the game.

Poker has its special ethics, and here I am not referring to rules against cheating. The man who keeps an ace up his sleeve or who marks the cards is more than unethical; he is a crook, and can be punished as such—kicked out of the game or, in the Old West, shot.

In contrast to the cheat, the unethical poker player is one who, while abiding by the letter of the rules, finds ways to put the other players at an unfair disadvantage. Perhaps he unnerves them with loud talk. Or he tries to get them drunk. Or he plays in cahoots with someone else at the table. Ethical poker players frown on such tactics.

Poker's own brand of ethics is different from the ethical ideals of civilized human relationships. The game calls for distrust of the other fellow. It ignores the claim of friendship. Cunning deception and concealment of one's strength and intentions, not kindness and open-heartedness, are vital in poker. No one thinks any the worse of poker on that account. And no one should think any the worse of the game of business because its standards of right and wrong differ from the prevailing traditions of morality in our society. . . .

'WE DON'T MAKE THE LAWS'

Wherever we turn in business, we can perceive the sharp distinction between its ethical standards and those of the churches. Newspapers abound with sensational stories growing out of this distinction:

- We read one day that Senator Philip A. Hart of Michigan has attacked food processors for deceptive packaging of numerous products.[2]
- The next day there is a Congressional to-do over Ralph Nader's book, *Unsafe At Any Speed,* which demonstrates that automobile companies for years have neglected the safety of car-owning families.[3]
- Then another Senator, Lee Metcalf of Montana, and journalist Vic Reinemer show in their book, *Overcharge,* the methods by which utility companies elude regulating government bodies to extract unduly large payments from users of electricity.[4]

These are merely dramatic instances of a prevailing condition; there is hardly a major industry at which a similar attack could not be aimed. Critics of business regard such behavior as unethical, but the companies concerned know that they are merely playing the business game.

Among the most respected of our business institutions are the insurance companies. A group of insurance executives meeting recently in New England was startled when their guest speaker, social critic Daniel Patrick Moynihan, roundly berated them for "unethical" practices. They had been guilty, Moynihan alleged, of using outdated actuarial tables to obtain unfairly high premiums. They habitually delayed the hearings of lawsuits against them in order to tire out the plaintiffs and win cheap settlements. In their employment policies they used ingenious devices to discriminate against certain minority groups.[5]

It was difficult for the audience to deny the validity of these charges. But these men were business game players. Their reaction to Moynihan's attack was much the same as that of the automobile manufacturers to Nader, of the utilities to Senator Metcalf, and of the food processors to Senator Hart. If the laws governing their businesses change, or if public opinion becomes clamorous, they will make the necessary adjustments. But morally they have in their view done nothing wrong. As long as they comply with the letter of the law, they are within their rights to operate their businesses as they see fit.

The small business is in the same position as the great corporation in this respect. For example:

- In 1967 a key manufacturer was accused of providing master keys for automobiles to mail-order customers, although it was obvious that some of the purchasers might be automobile thieves. His defense was plain and straightforward. If there was nothing in the law to prevent him from selling his keys to anyone who ordered them, it was not up to him to inquire as to his customers' motives. Why was it any worse, he insisted, for him to sell car keys by mail, than for mail-order houses to sell guns that might be used for murder? Until the law was changed, the key manufacturer could regard himself as being just as ethical as any other businessman by the rules of the business game.[6]

Violations of the ethical ideals of society are common in business, but they are not necessarily violations of business principles. Each year the Federal Trade Commission orders hundreds of companies, many of them of the first magnitude, to "cease and desist" from practices which, judged by ordinary standards, are of questionable morality but which are stoutly defended by the companies concerned.

In one case, a firm manufacturing a well-known mouthwash was accused of using a cheap form of alcohol possibly deleterious to health. The company's chief executive, after testifying in Washington, made this comment privately:

"We broke no law. We're in a highly competitive industry. If we're going to stay in business, we have to look for profit wherever the law permits. We don't make the laws. We obey them. Then why do we have to put up with this 'holier than thou' talk about ethics? It's sheer hypocrisy. We're not in business to promote ethics. Look at the cigarette companies, for God's sake! If the ethics aren't embodied in the laws by the men who made them, you can't expect businessmen to fill the lack. Why, a sudden submission to Christian ethics by businessmen would bring about the greatest economic upheaval in history!"

It may be noted that the government failed to prove its case against him.

CAST ILLUSIONS ASIDE

Talk about ethics by businessmen is often a thin decorative coating over the hard realities of the game:

- Once I listened to a speech by a young executive who pointed to a new industry code as proof that his company and its competitors were deeply aware of their responsibilities to society. It was a code of ethics, he said. The industry was going to police itself, to dissuade constituent companies from wrongdoing. His eyes shone with conviction and enthusiasm.

  The same day there was a meeting in a hotel room where the industry's top executives met with the "czar" who was to administer the new code, a man of high repute. No one who was present could doubt their common attitude. In their eyes the code was designed primarily to forestall a move by the federal government to impose stern restrictions on the industry. They felt that the code would hamper them a good deal less than new federal laws would. It was, in other words, conceived as a protection for the industry, not for the public.

  The young executive accepted the surface explanation of the code; these leaders, all experienced game players, did not deceive themselves for a moment about its purpose.

The illusion that business can afford to be guided by ethics as conceived in private life is often fostered by speeches and articles containing such phrases as, "It pays to be ethical," or, "Sound ethics is good business." Actually this is not an ethical position at all; it is a self-serving calculation in disguise. The speaker is really saying that in the long run a company can make more money if it does not antagonize competitors, suppliers, employees, and customers by squeezing them too hard. He is saying that oversharp policies reduce ultimate gains. That is true, but it has nothing to do with ethics. The underlying attitude is much like that in the familiar story of the shopkeeper who finds an extra $20 bill in the cash register, debates with himself the ethical problem—should he tell his partner?—and finally decides to share the money because the gesture will give him an edge over the s.o.b. the next time they quarrel.

I think it is fair to sum up the prevailing attitude of businessmen on ethics as follows:

We live in what is probably the most competitive of the world's civilized societies. Our customs encourage a high degree of aggression in the individual's striving for success. Business is our main area of competition, and it has been ritualized into a game of strategy. The basic rules of the game have been set by the government, which attempts to detect and punish business frauds. But as long as a company does not transgress the rules of the game set by law, it has the legal right to shape its strategy without reference to anything but its profits. If it takes a long-term view of its profits, it will preserve amicable relations, so far as possible, with those with whom it deals. A wise businessman will not seek advantage to the point where he generates dangerous hostility among employees, competitors, customers, government, or the public at large. But decisions in this area are, in the final test, decisions of strategy, not of ethics.

. . . If a man plans to make a seat in the business game, he owes it to himself to master the principles by which the game is played, including its special ethical outlook. He can then hardly fail to recognize that an occasional bluff may well be justified in terms of the game's ethics and warranted in terms of economic necessity. Once he clears his mind on this point, he is in a good position to match his strategy against that of the other players. He can then determine objectively whether a bluff in a given situation has a good chance of succeeding and can decide when and how to bluff, without a feeling of ethical transgression.

To be a winner, a man must play to win. This does not mean that he must be ruthless, cruel, harsh, or treacherous. On the contrary, the better his reputation for integrity, honesty, and decency, the better his chances of victory will be in the long run. But from time to time every businessman, like every poker player, is offered a choice between certain loss or bluffing within the legal rules of the game. If he is not resigned to losing, if he wants to rise in his company and industry, then in such a crisis he will bluff—and bluff hard.

Every now and then one meets a successful businessman who has conveniently forgotten the small or large deceptions that he practiced on his way to fortune. "God gave me my money," old John D. Rockefeller once piously told a Sunday school class. It would be a rare tycoon in our time who would risk the horse laugh with which such a remark would be greeted.

In the last third of the twentieth century even children are aware that if a man has become prosperous in business, he has sometimes departed from the strict truth in order to overcome obstacles or has practiced the more subtle deceptions of the half-truth or the misleading omission. Whatever the form of the bluff, it is an integral part of the game, and the executive who does not master its techniques is not likely to accumulate much money or power.

NOTES

1. *The New York Times,* March 9, 1967.
2. *The New York Times,* November 21, 1966.
3. New York, Grossman Publishers, Inc., 1965.
4. New York, David McKay Company, Inc., 1967.
5. *The New York Times,* January 17, 1967.
6. Cited by Ralph Nader in "Business Crime," *The New Republic,* July 1, 1967, p. 7.

QUESTIONS

1. Answer Carr's question: Is business bluffing ethical? Why or why not?

2. Are there "rules to the game" of business? Is a certain amount of deception necessary or even good in business? Explain your answer.

Timothy B. Blodgett | # Replies to Carr

Few articles that HBR [*Harvard Business Review*] has published have aroused a response as great and as vociferous as Albert Z. Carr's "Is Business Bluffing Ethical?" (January–February 1968). Mr. Carr contended that business's ethical standards differ from society's and that, in business, deception is accepted and indeed necessary if one is to succeed. He likened this "game strategy" of the businessman to the poker player's bluffing. Quoting liberally from letters, Mr. Blodgett, Associate Editor of HBR, reports readers' reactions. . . .

> This article presents a very realistic and accurate account of the standards used in business decisions, at least for those companies and individuals who are subject to competitive pressures and therefore feel that they must take every legally permissible advantage in order to survive and grow.
>
> Fortunately, Mr. Carr's view does not appear to be the prevailing view, except, perhaps, along the few remaining frontiers of civilization, such as the upper Amazon.

These two quotations—the first from a letter written by Rawson L. Wood, Chairman of the Board of Arwood Corporation, Rockleigh, New Jersey, and the second from a letter by Leon P. Chemlen, who is on the marketing staff of Dynamics Research Corporation, Stoneham, Massachusetts—distill the contrasting reactions of HBR readers to Mr. Carr's article.

Of the many readers who responded, more than twice as many are critical of the article as are favorable to it. Many others seem uncertain or are noncommittal about Mr. Carr's position, devoting themselves mainly to discussion of the state of business ethics today.

The tone of the letters ranges from enthusiastic to shocked. Interestingly, a couple of the most favorable letters have come from persons in the advertising business, an endeavor not noted for understatement about the virtues and powers of goods being marketed.

A few correspondents question HBR's motives in publishing the article. One indignant writer gives this title to a lengthy dissertation: "Is the Article on Business Bluffing Ethical?" Another even questions the existence of "A. Z. Carr" and suggests that the Editors may have been playing an early April Fool's joke.

But most readers have been as serious and thoughtful in answering Mr. Carr as he was in presenting his view of the way things are.

"NO MEDALS FOR HONESTY"

Was Mr. Carr "telling it like it is" (in the current expression)? One reader who thinks so is Richard O. Lundquist, an underwriter in Washington, D.C., with The Equitable Life Assurance Society of the United States. He cites this case:

"A young manager was upset because his boss had told a prospective salesman, 'The minimum income a new man earned with us last year was $8,900.' That was about $2,000 from the truth. When the senior manager was questioned about this, he answered, 'Well, that's not important. We are just trying to attract him into the business.'"

Mr. Lundquist mentions two similar examples and then concludes:

"What is universal about these examples is that these managers, each functioning on a different corporate level, are concerned with one thing—*getting the job done*. Most companies give numerous awards for achievement and accomplishment, for sales, for growth, for longevity and loyalty; but there are no medals in the business world for honesty, compassion, or truthfulness." . . .

A MATTER OF "MUTUAL TRUST"

Many readers have given careful thought to refutation of Mr. Carr's contention that deception is an integral part of the business "game." I shall try to present their views fairly by quoting representative selections from letters.

Some readers take particular exception to Mr. Carr's claim that deception succeeds:

"All of us in business know that 'playing the game' yields only short-term rewards. We'll admit our faults, but we'll not endorse them as part of our philosophy. To do so would bring the house of business down on itself." (John Valiant, New Product Manager, William H. Rorer, Inc., Fort Washington, Pennsylvania)

"My own experience in dealing with hundreds of companies has led me to believe that sharp dealing or the slightest prevarication on the part of a businessman usually results in informal excommunication to the back alleys of the business world or to obscurity." (Mark Rollinson, President, Greater Washington Industrial Investments, Inc., Washington, D.C.)

"I think a better strategy in business is to work hard, be honest, and be smarter than anyone else." (L.D. Barre, Vice President—Marketing, RTE Corporation, Waukesha, Wisconsin) . . .

Mr. Carr cited as an accurate description of "bluffing" in business and poker this utterance of a British statesman: "Falsehood ceases to be falsehood when it is understood on all sides that the truth is not expected to be spoken." This has moved Alan B. Potter, Vice President of the Dye Division (Dorval, Quebec) of Ciba Company Limited, to comment:

"But it is not at all the case that businessmen do not expect the truth to be spoken. On the contrary, almost all day-to-day business is conducted verbally or on the basis of nonlegal documents. The economic system would collapse without mutual trust on a practically universal scale among business executives.

"Mr. Carr apparently assumes that 'not telling the whole truth' is synonymous with 'telling a lie.' Businessmen know that it would be ridiculous to expect anything more than a straight answer to a straight question. Moreover, it is perfectly acceptable to withhold the truth by saying, 'I am sorry, I am not willing to discuss that subject.' There are many reasons of self-interest or discretion which would justify a refusal to answer any question, and businessmen do not expect that those reasons need be given."

Another recurrent theme in the letters is an insistence that business's ethics cannot be separated from those of society. Typical is the response of J. Douglas McConnell, Marketing Economist at Stanford Research Institute and Lecturer at San Francisco State College:

"Mr. Carr's argument would be sound if business functioned in a vacuum. Because business is an inte-

---

To: You
From: The Philosopher
Subject: "Nietzsche on Honesty"

The philosopher Friedrich Nietzsche had an interesting take on truth-telling and lying. He rather famously argued that a certain amount of deception (and self-deception) was necessary for life. (Art, after all, is essentially the telling of half-truths, embellished truths, and untruths.) But he nevertheless saw in lying a special problem, one that had less to do with breaking any rule than it did with the breach of personal trust. He said (in a book called *Beyond Good and Evil* § 183),

"Not that you lied to me, but that I no longer believe you, has shaken me."

gral part of society, however, it will always be judged by societal criteria.

"It is inevitable that the ethics of business and those of society will always have a considerable degree of commonality. For one thing, business as a group is large and powerful in our society, and many of its values are accepted by society at large. Business's goal is to function at a profit, and to a considerable extent making money is also a value of society.

"Another point of commonality is that most people are members of several groups. The business executive is likely to be a veteran, a member of a school or college board, a member of a local church, or a committee man for the Community Chest; and he and his family are also consumers. The norms of these other groups carry over to his business life to a greater or lesser extent.

"We live in a highly complex world, with diverse pressures and interests, where simple answers seldom fit simple questions such as 'Is business bluffing ethical?' Business's principal role is that of the wealth-generating group in society—and its ethics will always reflect this. However, the other groups in society—such as education, health services, religion, the military, government, and the consumer—will occasionally be in conflict with these ethics, and there will be (as there is now) pressure to bring business ethics more into conformity with those of society." . . .

Several readers object to Mr. Carr's poker analogy on the ground that it oversimplifies the process of decision making and the nature of personal relationships in business. One of these correspondents is Henry Johnson, President of The Johnson Wire Works Limited of Montreal. After acknowledging that "there is a substantial element of truth" in likening business to a game in which "duplicity" is an accepted practice, he goes on:

"But the fact is that the businessman is engaged in many games at the same time, with vastly differing rules. At one end of the spectrum, he may be engaged in a labor negotiation where the rules are well known and the protestations of either side are never seriously regarded. At the other pole, the businessman is dealing with an individual employee or customer. These people are not playing games. Anything but straightforward dealing should indeed cause the businessman some guilty insomnia.

"In between lie the ethical question marks, and I do not think we can avoid them as easily as Mr. Carr implies, simply by reason of the fact that we are 'in the office.' Each matter that arises poses its own question: 'How much gamesmanship, if any, can I use here?'"

"But it is surely the function of what we call conscience to extend the area where truth is used, and to 'play games' only on recognized playing fields."

Implicit or stated in many letters is the idea that Mr. Carr *approved* of what he called "game strategy" (a notion to which he vigorously objects). . . . The stricture of F. W. Henrici, Systems Analyst for Schering Corporation, Bloomfield, New Jersey, is typical:

"What really bothers me is Mr. Carr's attempt to give businessmen something with which to salve their consciences. Almost everyone knows that one doesn't reach a position of power in business, or even in the church, without a little hanky-panky. So be it. But if you lust for power, or money, or success, so that you are willing to put up with hanky-panky, then at least suffer those pangs of conscience. Know that other men scorn you in some small way for the things you condone.

QUESTIONS

1. Is business like poker, according to Blodgett? Why or why not?

2. Why is "mutual trust" important for business?

Norman E. Bowie | # Does It Pay to Bluff in Business?

Norman E. Bowie holds the Chair in Business Ethics at the University of Minnesota.

Albert Carr has argued in an influential article[1] that the ethics of business is best understood on the model of the ethics of poker.

Wouldn't it be in the best interest of business to adopt the poker model of business ethics? I think not. Let us consider labor relations, where Carr's poker model is implicitly if not explicitly adopted. In collective bargaining the relationship between the employer and the employee is adversarial. Collective bargaining is competitive through and through. The task of the union is to secure as much in pay and benefits as possible. The task of the employer's negotiators is to keep the pay and benefits as low as possible.

In the resulting give-and-take, bluffing and deception are the rule. Management expects the union to demand a percentage pay increase it knows it won't get. The union expects the company to say that such a pay increase will force it to shut down the plant and move to another state. Such demands are never taken at face value although they are taken more seriously on the ninetieth day of negotiations than they are on the first day.

Recently the conventional view of collective bargaining practice has been under attack. One of the most prominent criticisms of current practice is its economic inefficiency. The adversarial relationship at the bargaining table carries over to the workplace. As a result of the hostility between employee and employer, productivity suffers and many American products are at a competitive disadvantage with respect to foreign products. Japanese labor-management relations are not so adversarial and this fact accounts for part of their success. This particular criticism of collective bargaining has received much

attention in the press and in popular business magazines. The most recent manifestation of the recognition of the force of this criticism is the host of decisions General Motors has made to ensure that labor relations are different at its new assembly plant for the Saturn.

Second, the practice of bluffing and deception tends to undermine trust. As some American firms lost ground to foreign competition, the management of many of the firms asked for pay reductions, commonly called "give backs." Other managers in firms not threatened by foreign competition cited the "dangers" of foreign competition to request pay cuts for their employees—even though they were not needed. Use of this tactic will only cause future problems when and if the competitive threat really develops. This utilitarian point was not lost on participants in a labor-management relations seminar I attended.

Participant I: In the past, there was a relationship of mutual distrust.

Participant II: These are the dangers in crying "wolf." When the company is really in trouble, no one will believe them.

Participant III: To make labor/management participation teams work, you need to generate mutual trust. It only takes one bad deal to undermine trust.

These individuals are indicating that the practices of bluffing and deception have bad consequences in employer/employee relationships. These unfortunate consequences have been well documented by philosophers—most recently by Sissela Bok. Bok's critique of "white lies" and the use of placebos applies equally well to deception in the collective bargaining process.

Norman E. Bowie and Thomas Beauchamp, *Business Ethics* (Englewood Cliffs, NJ: Prentice Hall, 1988).

Triviality surely does set limits to when moral inquiry is reasonable. But when we look more closely at practices such as placebo-giving, it becomes clear that all lies defended as "white" cannot be so easily dismissed. In the first place, the harmlessness of lies is notoriously disputable. What the liar perceives as harmless or even beneficial may not be so in the eyes of the deceived. Second, the failure to look at an entire practice rather than at their own isolated case often blinds liars to cumulative harm and expanding deceptive activities. Those who begin with white lies can come to resort to more frequent and more serious ones. Where some tell a few white lies, others may tell more. Because lines are so hard to draw, the indiscriminate use of such lies can lead to other deceptive practices. The aggregate harm from a large number of marginally harmful instances may, therefore, be highly undesirable in the end—for liars, those deceived, and honesty and trust more generally.[2]

However, there is more at stake here than the bad consequences of lying. Bluffing, exaggeration, and the nondisclosure of information also undermine a spirit of cooperation that is essential to business success. The poker model, with its permitted bluffing and the like, is a competitive model. What the model overlooks is the fact that the production of a good or service in any given plant or office is a cooperative enterprise. Chrysler competes with General Motors and Toyota but the production of Chrysler K cars in that assembly plant in Newark, Delaware, is a cooperative enterprise. Lack of cooperation results in poor quality vehicles.

Hence the competitive model of collective bargaining sets wages and working conditions for what at the local level is a cooperative enterprise. Labor-management negotiators forget the obvious truth that the production of goods and services cannot succeed on a purely competitive basis. There have to be some elements of cooperation somewhere in the system. Why shouldn't the collective bargaining process use cooperative rather than competitive techniques? When bargaining is conducted industrywide, as it is with automobiles, the competitive mode seems natural. Auto production is a competitive industry. But

just because Chrysler is competitive with General Motors, why must Chrysler management be in a competitive relationship with its own employees? Indeed, couldn't it be argued that the fact that Chrysler's management does see itself in competition with its unionized employees undercuts its competitive position vis-à-vis other automobile producers. To use the language of competition, if Chrysler is at war with itself, how can it win the war against others?

As long as collective bargaining is essentially adversarial and characterized by bluffing and exaggeration on both sides, the cooperative aspect of business will be underemphasized. The costs of ignoring the cooperative aspect are great—both for society and for business itself.

Hence this distrust that so concerned the participants in the seminar is only in part a function of the deceit and bluffing that go on in collective bargaining. It is in large part a function of using the wrong model. We shouldn't look at collective bargaining as a game of poker.

With this discussion of collective bargaining as instance, let us evaluate Carr's proposal on utilitarian grounds. Should the stockholders applaud a chief executive officer whose operating procedure is analogous to the operating procedure of a poker player? In Carr's view, "A good part of the time the businessman is trying to do unto others as he hopes others will not do unto him." But surely such a practice is very risky. The danger of discovery is great, and our experience of the past several years indicates that many corporations that have played the game of business like the game of poker have suffered badly. Moreover, if business practice consisted essentially of these conscious misstatements, exaggerations, and the concealment of pertinent facts, it seems clear that business practice would be inherently unstable. Contemporary business practice presupposes such stability, and business can only be stable if the chief executive officer has a set of moral standards higher than those that govern the game of poker. The growth of the large firm, the complexity of business decisions, the need for planning and stability, and the undesirable effects of puffery, exaggeration, and deception all count against Carr's view that the ethics of business should be the ethics of a poker game.

NOTES

1. Albert Z. Carr, "Is Business Bluffing Ethical?" *Harvard Business Review,* 46 (January–February 1968): 143–153.

2. Sissela Bok, *Lying: Moral Choice in Public and Private Life* (New York: Pantheon Books, 1978), pp. 19, 31.

QUESTIONS

1. What is Bowie's main reply to Carr?
2. How does cooperation suffer because of bluffing?

Robert C. Solomon | # Is It Ever Right to Lie?

Robert Solomon teaches philosophy and business at the University of Texas at Austin.

Is it ever right to lie?

No.

Now, let's get down to business.

It may never be right to tell a lie, but nevertheless it is often prudent, preferable, and—if the way people behave is any indication at all of morals—popular as well.

Consider the familiar dilemma of HGT sales representative John G., who is asked whether his product is in fact as good as a Xerox. One curious fact is that John G. owns a Xerox himself, but another not insignificant fact is that he is employed by the HGT company to sell their line of products, not to express his personal preferences or conduct a neutral survey of product quality. What does he do? What can he do? Of course, he says, "Yes—and better besides." Is he lying? Or just doing his job? He is doing both, of course, but should we say that he is thereby doing wrong?

"Truth" and "falsehood" are evasive qualities even in an academic seminar or a scientist's laboratory; they are even more so in the real world. Is a lover lying to himself when he says that his love is the "most wonderful woman in the world"? Is a salesman lying to a customer when he praises an imperfect product? To be sure, there is such a thing as outright deception—the standard case in which a used-car salesman insists that an old convertible is in excellent mechanical condition, knowing full well that the unhappy new owner will be lucky to get the heap off the lot. But one can also argue that shopping at certain used-car lots (the kind advertised by a hand-painted sign that says "Honest Harry Has the Bargains") carries with it the knowledge of risk on the part of the buyer, risking a trade-off for the bargain. What counts as "honest" is already put into question. Of course, there are outright lies—falsification of the odometer reading or the false claim that the engine was overhauled 3,000 miles ago, but there is a certain latitude in lying that depends on the context, the customer, and the costs. Not only lying but giving misleading information is intolerable in the health-care industry—for example, not mentioning the side effects of a new drug. Showing hyperdramatic demonstrations of "action" toys to children or giving technical information to people who cannot possibly understand it may involve neither false nor misleading information but nevertheless may be morally dubious (given the huge proportion of the adult population that can be swayed by mere adjectives such as "scientific" or "natural"). Cost counts, too. Exaggerated claims for the cleaning powers of an inexpensive soap product or the convenience of a household gadget advertised on TV for (inevitably) $19.95 are more easily forgiven than even mildly bloated praise for the value of a new house or bulldozer. On the other hand, it is clear that it is not only self-defeating but cruel to tell a customer *everything* horrible that might befall him with his product. (Imagine the warnings that would have to accompany even such a simple household appliance as a food processor.)

Lying may always be wrong, but some lies are much more wrong than others. Truth may always be desirable, but the "whole truth and nothing but the truth" is just as likely to be a nightmare.

To say that it is never right to lie is not the same as to say that one should never lie. It is rather to say that a lie is always a later resort, a strategy that is not a first choice. If the salesman could sell his wares by saying nothing but the truth, he could, should, and would do so. But one must always excuse a lie, by showing that some greater evil would result from telling the truth or, most often, simply by showing that there is minimal harm done by lying and that, in this context, the lie was not wholly inappropriate. The one thing that a person cannot do is to think that telling a lie—*any* lie—is just as good or right as telling the truth, and so needs no special justification for doing so.

Lying has almost always been considered a sin or an immoral act. In a best-selling book, Sissela Bok has argued that lying is always wrong because, in a variety of ways, it always has bad consequences—worse, that is, than if the lie had not been told. Common experience indicates otherwise, perhaps, for the general attitude both in business and in society is that lies have a perfectly proper social place. Indeed there are clearly contexts in which it would be wrong *not* to lie. Lies can prevent family fights and quarrels among couples. They can prevent bad feelings and help avoid misunderstandings. And, often, they can help an employee keep his or her job. ("I was caught in traffic" is a transparent lie but sometimes an ac-

ceptable excuse for being late; "I hated the idea of coming to work so much that I forgot to set the alarm" is, though true, utterly unacceptable.)

We can all agree, looking only at short-term and immediate benefits, that the harm done by some lies is considerably less than the harm that would be done by telling the "unvarnished truth." An employer forced to fire a mediocre worker is certainly not to be blamed for saying that "financial exigencies" have forced him to lay off several low-seniority personnel, instead of telling the truth, which is that the fellow borders on incompetence and doesn't have either the charm or the imagination of a pocket calculator. An advertiser would be judged an idiot, not honest, if he baldly stated that this pain remedy is no more nor less effective than any other on the market, though its packaging is prettier. Nevertheless, there are reasons for saying that lying is always wrong.

The first reason has to do with the enormous amount of effort involved in telling a lie—any lie. The truth—even the incomplete truth—is an enormously complex network of interlocking facts. Anyone who has found himself caught in the nervous web of fabrications involved in even such a simple lie as "We don't know a thing about what our competitors are doing" ("Then how do you know that . . . ?") knows how many seemingly disparate facts can come crashing in when a lie has torn just a small piece out of the truth. As recent national politics has so prominently displayed, the cost of a cover-up is often many times more than the damage done by the lie itself, even if the cover-up is successful.

The second reason looks beyond the short-term benefits of lying to the longer-term damage, which may be harder to see. Every lie diminishes trust. A lie discovered is guaranteed to undermine faith in the liar, but, more subtly, *telling* a lie diminishes one's trust in others. ("If I'm lying to them, they are probably lying to me as well.") Most Americans now look at television advertising as if it were nothing but a tissue of lies—ironically making the more successful ads just those that ignore substantial content and concentrate on memorable associations and effects. A businessman may make many a profit through deception—for a while—but unless one wants to keep on the road for the rest of one's life (sounds good at twenty, not so good at forty), deception almost always catches up and destroys just the business it used to ensure. As long-term investments, lies are usually a bad risk.

The third and strongest reason for thinking that it is never right to lie was suggested by Kant. He asked himself the question, "What would happen if lying were generally accepted? For example, what would happen if it were an everyday and unexceptional feature of the business world that one person would borrow money from another with no intention whatever of repaying the loan?" His answer was that telling the truth and, in the example, borrowing money would both become impossible, so that if I were to approach you and ask for a $10,000 loan, which I would promise to repay on the first of the year, you would simply laugh in my face, since everyone by then would know that such promises were not to be taken seriously. Lying, in other words, must always be wrong, since to treat lying as acceptable undermines just that trust that makes telling the truth meaningful.

Does this mean that one should never lie? Well, no. But it does mean that it is never right to tell a lie; that telling a lie always requires extra thought and some very good reasons to show that this cardinal violation of the truth should be tolerated.

This said, perhaps we should clear up a few common misconceptions about the place of lying in business. It is sometimes suggested that advertising is always a lie, since it tells only one side of the story and that side, needless to say, in the best possible light. But now it is important to distinguish—in facing any such accusation—among the following:

1. telling less than the whole truth;
2. telling a biased truth, with one's own interests in mind;
3. idealizing one's products or services;
4. giving misleading information; that is, true statements that are intended to be misunderstood or misinterpreted;
5. stating obvious falsehoods;
6. stating vicious falsehoods.

An obvious falsehood, for example, is the displayed claim of some toothpaste manufacturers—that use of a certain gel will overnight convert Shy Sam or Plain Jane to Fabulous Fred or Super Sally, the heartthrob of the high-school prom. One might object to other aspects of such advertising, but "It isn't true" seems too silly to say.

Vicious falsehoods, on the other hand, are those that are not at all obvious and are a deliberate and possibly dangerous form of deception. Saying that a product will do such and such when it will not is vicious deception, as is intentionally withholding information—for example, the flammability of children's pajamas or the side effects of a popular over-the-counter drug. Misleading information can be as vicious as false information—indeed it is only a matter of logical nuance that allows us to distinguish between the two.

It is impossible to tell the "whole story," especially in the limited time of a fifteen-second radio or TV slot or in the small space available on a paper package. But advertising isn't supposed to be a scientific study, even if it utilizes some (more or less) scientific evidence on the product's behalf. Of course advertising expresses a bias on the behalf of the product. Of course it idealizes the product in its presentation. But neither bias nor idealization is lying, and it is surely foolish to insist that advertising, unlike almost every other aspect of social life, be restricted to the simple, boring truth—that is, that this product is not much different from its competitors and that people have lived for hundreds of thousands of years without any of them.

It is often challenged—these days with Orwellian overtones—that advertising in general and TV advertising in particular have turned the American consumer into something of a supermarket zombie, without a will of his or her own, without judgment, buying hundreds of innocuous but sometimes tasteless products that no one really needs. But the zombie image contradicts precisely what lies beneath the whole discussion of truth—namely, the confidence that we are, more or less, capable of making value judgments on our own, and that if we buy or even need to buy products that are of no particular cosmic importance, this does not signal either the end of civilization or the disintegration of the human mind. Encouraging someone to buy a product that is only a fad or a mark of status is not deception, and to call it that tends to undermine the ethical distinction that is of enormous importance—between vicious falsehoods and any number of other "varnishings" of the truth. These may be vulgar. They may encourage us to compete for some pretty silly achievements—the shiniest (and most slippery) floor, a car that can win the grand prix (to be driven in bumper-to-bumper traffic up and down the freeway), a soap that makes one speak in a phony Irish brogue. But to condemn all advertising is to make it impossible to attack vicious advertising and thus to bring about the logical conclusion imagined by Kant—an entire world in which no one believes anything, in which advertising serves at most as a source of amusement and seduction of the feebleminded.

Let's end our discussion of lying by commenting once again on Alfred Carr's suggestion that business is like poker, that it has its own rules, which are different from ordinary ethics. One of these rules, supposedly, is the permissibility of lying. But business (like poker) forbids lying. Contrary to Carr, a generally accepted practice of lying would undermine the business world faster than any external threat that has ever faced it. Promises and contracts, if not good faith, are the presuppositions of all business. The exact nature of truth in advertising may be controversial, but advertising in general must be not only based on fact but believable and trustworthy. If it were not, the commercial world in America would be about as effective as the provocations of Hari Krishnas in America's airports—an annoyance to be ignored as we all go on with the rest of our lives.

Honesty isn't just the best policy in business; it is, in general, the only possible policy.

QUESTIONS

1. What does Solomon mean when he says that "some lies are much more wrong than others"? How does he distinguish among kinds of lies?

2. What does Solomon think about telling "the unvarnished truth"? Give examples from your own life of times when "the unvarnished truth" would be counterproductive.

Sissela Bok

Defining Secrecy—Some Crucial Distinctions

Sissela Bok wrote one of the most popular books on the subject of lying. She followed it up with this book on secrets.

Lying and secrecy intertwine and overlap. Lies are part of the arsenal used to guard and to invade secrecy; and secrecy allows lies to go undiscovered and to build up. Lying and secrecy differ, however, in one important respect. Whereas I take lying to be prima facie wrong, with a negative presumption against it from the outset, secrecy need not be. Whereas every lie stands in need of justification, all secrets do not. Secrecy may accompany the most innocent as well as the most lethal acts; it is needed for human survival, yet it enhances every form of abuse. The same is true of efforts to uncover or invade secrets.

A path, a riddle, a jewel, an oath—anything can be secret so long as it is kept intentionally hidden, set apart in the mind of its keeper as requiring concealment. It may be shared with no one, or confided on condition that it go no farther; at times it may be

From Sissela Bok, *Secrets* (New York: Vintage Books, 1989). Notes were deleted from this text.

known to all but one or two from whom it is kept. To keep a secret from someone, then, is to block information about it or evidence of it from reaching that person, and to do so intentionally; to prevent him from learning it, and thus from possessing it, making use of it, or revealing it. The word "secrecy" refers to the resulting concealment. It also denotes the methods used to conceal, such as codes or disguises or camouflage, and the practices of concealment, as in trade secrecy or professional confidentiality. Accordingly I shall take concealment, or hiding, to be the defining trait of secrecy. It presupposes separation, a setting apart of the secret from the non-secret, and of keepers of a secret from those excluded. The Latin *secretum* carries this meaning of something hidden, set apart. It derives from *secernere,* which originally meant to sift apart, to separate, as with a sieve. It bespeaks discernment, the ability to make distinctions, to sort out and draw lines: a capacity that underlies not only secrecy but all thinking, all intention and choice. The separation between insider and outsider is inherent in secrecy; and to think something secret is already to envisage potential conflict between what insiders conceal and outsiders want to inspect and lay bare.

Several other strands have joined with this defining trait to form our concept of secrecy. Although they are not always present in every secret or every practice of secrecy, the concepts of sacredness, intimacy, privacy, silence, prohibition, furtiveness, and deception influence the way we think about secrecy. They intertwine and sometimes conflict, yet they come together in our experience of secrecy and give it depth.

Too exclusive an emphasis on the links between the secret and the sacred can lead one to see all secrecy as inherently valuable. And those who think primarily of the links between secrecy and privacy or intimacy, and of secrets as personal confidences, have regarded them as something one has a duty to conceal. Negative views of secrecy are even more common. Why should you conceal something, many ask, if you are not afraid to have it known? The aspects of secrecy that have to do with stealth and furtiveness, lying and denial, predominate in such a view. We must retain a neutral definition of secrecy,

rather than one that assumes from the outset that secrets are guilty or threatening, or on the contrary, awesome and worthy of respect. A degree of concealment or openness accompanies all that human beings do or say. We must determine what is and is not discreditable by examining particular practices of secrecy, rather than by assuming an initial evaluative stance.

It is equally important to keep the distinction between secrecy and privacy from being engulfed at the definitional stage. The two are closely linked, and their relationship is central. In order to maintain the distinction, however, it is important first to ask how they are related and wherein they differ. Having defined secrecy as intentional concealment, I obviously cannot take it as identical with privacy. I shall define privacy as the condition of being protected from unwanted access by others—either physical access, attention, or access to personal information. Claims to privacy are claims to control access to what one takes to be one's personal domain.

Privacy and secrecy overlap whenever the efforts at such control rely on hiding. But privacy need not hide; and secrecy hides far more than what is private. A private garden need not be a secret garden; a private life is rarely a secret life. Conversely, secret diplomacy rarely concerns what is private, any more than do arrangements for a surprise party or for choosing prize winners.

Why then are privacy and secrecy so often equated? In part, this is so because privacy is such a central part of what secrecy protects that it can easily be seen as the whole. People claim privacy for differing amounts of what they are and do and own; if need be, they seek the added protection of secrecy. In each case, their purpose is to become less vulnerable, more in control. When do secrecy and privacy most clearly overlap? They do so most immediately in the private lives of individuals, where secrecy guards against unwanted access by others—against their coming too near, learning too much, observing too closely. Secrecy guards, then, the central aspects of identity, and if necessary, also plans and property. It serves as an additional shield in case the protection of privacy should fail or be broken down. Thus you may assume that no one will read your diary; but you can also hide it, or write it in code, as did William Blake, or lock it up. Secret codes, bank accounts, and retreats, secret thoughts never voiced aloud, personal objects hidden against intruders: all testify to the felt need for additional protection.

Similarly, groups can create a joint space within which they keep secrets, surrounded by an aura of mystery. Perhaps the most complete overlap of privacy and secrecy in groups is that exemplified in certain secret societies. The members of some of these societies undergo such experiences that their own sense of privacy blends with an enlarged private space of the group. The societies then have identities and boundaries of their own. They come into being like living organisms, vulnerable; they undergo growth and transformation, and eventually pass away.

It is harder to say whether privacy and secrecy overlap in practices of large-scale collective secrecy, such as trade or military secrecy. Claims of privacy are often made for such practices, and the metaphors of personal space are stretched to apply to them. To be sure, such practices are automatically private in one sense so long as they are not public. But the use of the language of privacy, with its metaphors of personal space, spheres, sanctuaries, and boundaries, to personalize collective enterprises should not go unchallenged. Such usage can be sentimental, and distort our understanding of the role of these enterprises.

The obsessive, conflict-ridden invocation of privacy in Western society has increased the occasions for such expanded uses of the metaphors of privacy; so has the corresponding formalization of the professional practices of secrecy and openness. At times the shield of privacy is held up to protect abuses, such as corporate tax fraud or legislative corruption, that are in no manner personal.

While secrecy often guards what is private, therefore, it need not be so, and it has many uses outside the private sphere. To see all secrecy as privacy is as limiting as to assume that it is invariably deceptive or that it conceals primarily what is discreditable. We must retain the definition of secrecy as intentional concealment, and resist the pressure to force the concept into a narrower definitional mold by insisting that privacy, deceit, or shame always accompanies it. But at the same time we must strive to keep in mind

these aspects of our underlying experience of secrecy, along with the others—the sacred, the silent, the forbidden, and the stealthy.

Secrecy is as indispensable to human beings as fire, and as greatly feared. Both enhance and protect life, yet both can stifle, lay waste, spread out of all control. Both may be used to guard intimacy or to invade it, to nurture or to consume. And each can be turned against itself; barriers of secrecy are set up to guard against secret plots and surreptitious prying, just as fire is used to fight fire.

Conflicts over secrecy—between state and citizen, or parent and child, or in journalism or business or law—are conflicts over power: the power that comes through controlling the flow of information. To be able to hold back some information about oneself or to channel it and thus influence how one is seen by others gives power; so does the capacity to penetrate similar defenses and strategies when used by others. To have no capacity for secrecy is to be out of control over how others see one; it leaves one open to coercion. To have no insight into what others conceal is to lack power as well.

In seeking some control over secrecy and openness, and the power it makes possible, human beings attempt to guard and to promote not only their autonomy but ultimately their sanity and survival itself. The claims in defense of this control, however, are not always articulated. Some take them to be so self-evident as to need no articulation; others subsume them under more general arguments about liberty or privacy. But it is important for the purposes of considering the ethics of secrecy to set forth these claims. The claims in defense of some control over secrecy and openness invoke four different, though in practice inseparable, elements of human autonomy: identity, plans, action, and property. They concern protection of what we are, what we intend, what we do, and what we own. Some capacity for keeping secrets and for choosing when to reveal them, and some access to the underlying experience of secrecy and depth, are indispensable for an enduring sense of identity, for the ability to plan and to act, and for essential belongings. With no control over secrecy and openness, human beings could not remain either sane or free.

Against every claim to secrecy stands, however, the awareness of its dangers. Secrecy can harm those who make use of it in several ways. It can debilitate judgment, first of all, whenever it shuts out criticism and feedback. The danger of secrecy goes far beyond risks to those who keep secrets. Because it bypasses inspection and eludes interference, secrecy is central to the planning of every form of injury to human beings. It cloaks the execution of these plans and wipes out all traces afterward. It enters into all prying and intrusion that cannot be carried out openly. While not all that is secret is meant to deceive—as jury deliberations, for instance are not—all deceit does rely on keeping something secret. And while not all secrets are discreditable, all that is discreditable and all wrongdoing seek out secrecy (unless they can be carried out openly without interference).

Given both the legitimacy of some control over secrecy and openness, and the dangers this control carries for all involved, there can be no presumption either for or against secrecy in general. Secrecy differs in this respect from lying, promise breaking, violence, and other practices for which the burden of proof rests on those who would defend them. Conversely, secrecy differs from truthfulness, friendship, and other practices carrying a favorable presumption. The resulting challenge for ethical inquiry into the aims and methods of secrecy is great. Not only must we reject definitions of secrecy that invite approval or disapproval; we cannot even begin with a moral presumption in either direction. This is not to say, however, that there can be none for particular practices, nor that these practices are usually morally neutral.

I shall rely on two presumptions that flow from the needs and dangers of secrecy that I have set forth. The first is one of *equality*. Whatever control over secrecy and openness we conclude is legitimate for some individuals should, in the absence of special considerations, be legitimate for all. My second presumption is in favor of *partial individual control* over the degree of secrecy or openness about personal matters—those most indisputably in the private realm. Without a premise supporting a measure of individual control over personal matters, it would be impossible to preserve the indispensable respect for identity, plans, action, and belongings that all of us need and should legitimately be able to claim. Such individual control should extend, moreover, to what people choose to share with one another about themselves—in families, for example, or with friends and colleagues. Without the intimacy that such sharing makes possible, human relationships would be impossible. At the same time, however, it is important to avoid any presumption in favor of *full* control over such matters for individuals. Such full control is not necessary for the needs that I have discussed, and would aggravate the dangers. It would force us to disregard the legitimate claims of those persons who might be injured, betrayed, or ignored as a result of secrets inappropriately kept or revealed.

QUESTIONS

1. Why does Bok distinguish between lies and secrets? Is keeping a secret ever morally equivalent to telling a lie?

2. How does Bok distinguish between privacy and secrecy?

Richard T. De George | # Secrecy and Disclosure

Richard T. DeGeorge teaches philosophy and business ethics at the University of Kansas.

Banks have moral obligations of confidentiality on the one hand and disclosure on the other. The obligation to maintain confidentiality stems from the right of depositors to privacy. One aspect of that right is that their accounts and transactions should be kept confidential. How much money we have and what we do with our money is in most cases no one else's business. Yet the right to privacy does not preclude our having to report our holdings for tax or legitimate other purposes. Furthermore, our right to privacy does not enable us to conceal illegal payments we might receive or make. The government has the right to learn the details of our accounts if there is valid reason—for example, that the information is pertinent to the investigation of a felony.

What then of secret bank accounts?

Such accounts were long the rule, for instance, in Switzerland. What is wrong with secret accounts? The problem lies not in the fact that they are secret but in the illegitimate uses that unrestricted secrecy allows. The problem is clear if one thinks of illegally acquired money—for instance, from drug trafficking. Secret accounts allow drug dealers to deposit their ill-gotten funds and then to place that money in legal investments. Such "laundering" of money is impossible to trace if bank accounts are totally secret, even from governments with cause to suspect felonious actions. Other ethically dubious uses of such accounts are as storage places for individuals or corporations in underdeveloped countries who use such accounts as repositories for money that they remove from their country, often money that is earmarked for capital or other improvements in the country. The alleged secret bank accounts of former President

Marcos of the Philippines are a case in point. Secret accounts can thus become part of a plan for criminal and unethical activity. It is their part in such activity that renders secret accounts, at least in these circumstances, unethical. There may be legitimate reasons for secrecy, and governments have no right without sufficient cause to infringe on privacy by gaining access to information on private bank accounts. But when they have sufficient cause, the inability to trace money is a hindrance to justice. And it is a sufficient hindrance that it overcomes any right to privacy.

The rules of bank secrecy were an impediment in the investigation of U.S. insider trading cases. The U.S. government sought, initially unsuccessfully, to trace money through Swiss accounts. The Swiss ultimately changed their laws, allowing the United States to pursue its investigation.[1] But some strict limits on secrecy still stand. Balancing the right of individuals and firms to confidentiality with the right of governments to pursue evidence of felonious action through bank deposits and exchanges is a delicate task. Not all government investigations may be appropriate, and indiscriminate release of information on individual accounts to government would be a prima facie violation of an individual's right to privacy. Yet banks are no more allowed to take part in or abet criminal activity than anyone else or any other institution.

On the other end of the spectrum, banks are morally obliged to disclose to customers and potential customers complete and accurate information concerning, for instance, the loans they make to their customers. Banks are morally precluded from charging exorbitant interest rates—known as usury. The maximum permissible rate is often set by law. We have argued that for any transaction to be fair both parties must enter in it freely and both should have

From Richard T. De George, *Business Ethics* (Englewood Cliffs, NJ: Prentice Hall, 1995).

access to appropriate information. In cases in which the bank is the lender, it is clearly in the position of strength and power with respect to the borrower. There is therefore all the more need for banks to make completely clear to borrowers the conditions of any loan, the real interest (rather than simply monthly payments), and the conditions and penalties for defaulting. Clarity requires that customers be informed in language they can understand.

How banks are to treat their loans in statements of their financial positions is a topic on which we have already touched. Customers who place their savings with banks have the right to know the actual financial situation of the bank, and disclosure to them is as appropriate as to shareholders.

Banks have been among the institutions that have helped finance a great deal of the restructuring of American business. Banks and their employees thus come to have access to inside information about planned and impending corporate takeovers. As insiders they have the obligation to keep such informa-

tion confidential, as well as not to trade on it for their own accounts. On the other hand, they have the obligation to make pertinent information public and available to all at the same time. Disclosure in this case means that in principle no one is given the information and the opportunity to act on it before it is made known publicly.

NOTE

1. Stephen Labaton, "Group of 7 Asks Money-Laundering Curbs," *New York Times,* April 20, 1990, p. C1; Alan Riding, "New Rule Reduces Swiss Banking Secrecy," *New York Times,* May 6, 1991, p. C1; and "The End of Banking Secrecy in Liechtenstein," *International Living 9* (February 1990), p. 19.

QUESTIONS

1. What is wrong with secret bank accounts?
2. What are the disclosures required of banks when they are lending money?

Sue De Wine | # Giving Feedback: The Consultant's Craft

Sue De Wine's book on consulting contains lots of helpful hints and strategies.

We all like to receive feedback but are afraid to ask for it. If I asked you "How am I doing?" you may really tell me and I may not like the answer! Feedback requires active listening and careful description of observed behavior. These two skills are the cornerstones to effective feedback and impactful interventions into human behaviors.

Schein (1988) suggests that most of what the process consultant does when he or she intervenes

with individuals or groups is to manage the feedback process. The consultant makes observations that provide information, asks questions that direct the client's attention to the consequences of the individual's behavior, and provides suggestions that have implicit evaluations built into them (i.e., any given suggestion implies that other things that have not been suggested are less appropriate than what has been suggested) (p. 105).

Feedback comes in two forms: information on a person's behavior, and information on what impact that behavior can have on others. Remember that the

Sue de Wine; *The Consultant's Craft* (Boston: Bedford/St. Martin's, 2001), pp. 307–314.

overall purpose of feedback is to help, not attack. When giving feedback, make sure you can answer *yes* to these questions:

Timing: Have I checked with the receiver to determine the best time and place to give feedback?

Motivation: Am I being supportive while giving the feedback rather than ridiculing and hurting the receiver?

Language: Am I using positive or neutral rather than derogatory statements?

Tone: Am I using a friendly and caring tone of voice?

Value: Is the feedback useful to the receiver rather than an outlet for my feelings, frustrations, or anger?

Focus: Am I focusing on actions rather than attitudes or personalities?

Specificity: Am I using specific examples of observed behavior?

Information: Am I giving a manageable amount of helpful information rather than overloading the receiver with more information than is necessary?

Questions: Have I asked the receiver questions to ensure that my feedback was clear and helpful?

When receiving feedback, check for *yes* answers to these questions:

Timing: Have I agreed to the time and place for receiving feedback?

Trust: Do I trust the giver to accurately present information concerning my behavior?

Nondefensiveness: Am I prepared to listen to the feedback, rather than argue, refute, or justify my actions?

Specificity: If feedback is vague, am I requesting specific behavioral examples?

Tone: Am I using a neutral rather than a defensive tone of voice?

Questions: Have I asked questions that clarify the feedback?

Feedback is best when it is asked for and when there is a need for impartial knowledge. The client has to understand the difference between wisdom, which is a personal attribute of an individual, and knowledge, which is gained from books and facts. It is the consultant's job to be honest, direct, and non-threatening.

Sometimes I am surprised at how willingly organizational members receive feedback. Just when I would expect defensiveness and denial, they admit the picture I am painting is on target.

One illustration of this occurred with a colleague, Elizabeth Bernett, when we worked with a health-care organization. We conducted interviews and asked for written statements about what was preventing this group from moving forward and cooperating with each other.

Participants told Elizabeth and me some very negative examples of how this group was dysfunctional. Some of the traits attributed to the group included being distrustful, deceitful, uncompromising, and overly critical of each other. We decided we would take the plunge and list all of the statements made by the group. We expected resistance and defensiveness. When we finished describing the list of attributes there was a long pause, and then someone spoke up and said, "Yep, that's us." Another said, "Sure sounds like us, doesn't it?" Nods of heads and general agreement indicated they accepted this feedback. Now our task was to find out if they were ready to change some of these behaviors or would they resist change because somehow these behaviors suited their individual agendas.

TYPES OF FEEDBACK

There are a variety of methods to provide feedback, many of which cause defensiveness. The function of feedback is to describe another person's observable behavior, disclose your thoughts and feelings about that behavior, interpret motives, and prescribe specific remedies. These may be our objectives; however, my experience has been that when people are evaluated they often feel attacked and begin to defend themselves.

Feedback is a way of helping another person to consider changing his or her behavior. It is communication to a person (or group) that gives that person information about how she or he affects others. As in a guided missile system, feedback helps an individual keep his or her behavior "on target" and thus achieve individual goals.

People give three kinds of feedback to others:

Evaluative: observing the other's behavior and responding with one's critique of it. "You are always late for everything. You are undependable."

Interpretive: observing the behavior and trying to analyze why the person is behaving that way. "You are late to meetings. I think you are spreading yourself too thin—trying to do too many things at the same time, and consequently you don't do anything really well."

Descriptive: observing the behavior and simply feeding back to the person specific observations without evaluating them, but sharing with the person how her or his behavior affects the speaker. "At the meeting last week you were 30 minutes late, on Monday you came when the meeting was half over, and today you missed the first 45 minutes of the meeting. I am concerned about the information you are missing by not being here."

In the first example, *always* and *undependable* are evaluative terms and create a climate of defensiveness on the part of the receiver. Chances are the person isn't *always* late, and using an all-inclusive term like *always* serves only to make the person angry. The receiver then naturally looks for ways to refute the statement. "I wasn't late to the staff meeting on Friday! You're being unfair."

In the second example the observer is playing dime-store psychologist and trying to figure out why someone is behaving a certain way. Unless you are a trained psychologist, your business is not to analyze and interpret someone else's behavior. You don't know why someone acts a particular way. All you can observe is behavior. You can't observe attitudes, nor should you be critiquing them.

In descriptive feedback we are describing, as specifically as possible, what we have actually observed the individual doing. We present that factual information, without judging the rightness or wrongness of the behavior and without trying to figure out why the person may have behaved that way.

EFFECTIVE FEEDBACK

Feedback should describe problematic behavior that the receiver can correct. Ideally, it is offered in response to the receiver's request, but whether or not it is solicited, effective feedback should be timely, clear, and accurate.

Useful Content

We have already discussed why feedback is more useful if it is descriptive rather than judgmental. Describing one's reaction to problematic behavior leaves the individual free to use the feedback or not, as the individual sees fit. Avoiding judgmental language reduces the need for the receiver to react defensively. Specific observations are more convincing than general ones. To be told that one is inattentive will probably not be as useful as to be told that: "Just now when we were deciding how to assimilate new employees, you were reading your mail. It made me feel that you were not interested or involved in the discussion."

Effective feedback takes into account the needs of both the receiver and the giver of the feedback. Feedback can be destructive when it serves only the giver's needs and fails to consider the needs of the person on the receiving end. For example, I may need to complain about the lateness of a report. The report writer may not need to hear my complaints because she is already aware of the deadline and cannot change the fact that some missing data from another department prevented her from finishing it earlier. It may make me feel better to "blow off steam" but in this instance it may actually impede the other person's ability to complete the task.

Effective feedback is directed toward behavior that the receiver can change. Frustration is only increased when a person is reminded of some shortcoming over which she or he has no control. One receptionist was criticized for her high-pitched voice over the phone. She had actually worked with a speech therapist and had improved it as much as possible. To continue to criticize her for something she could not change was not helpful; in fact, it was harmful. If the problem was severe enough, then her supervisor should have discussed other career options, but simply to continue to provide feedback that the problem existed could do nothing to bring about change.

Feedback is most useful when it is solicited rather than imposed and when the receiver has formulated the kinds of questions that people observing can answer. Unfortunately, people don't ask for feedback often enough. Therefore, we should take advantage of those rare opportunities when someone does ask us to take the time to provide it. It is easy to miss opportunities because one may dismiss a request as superficial.

For example, someone recently asked me, "How are things going?" (referring to a project she was working on). I said, "Oh, just fine." Her response was, "No, I really mean, *how do you think things are going?*" Then I said, "Oh, you *really* want some feedback about your performance?" If the person had not persisted, I would have missed a very good opportunity to provide feedback about her work performance at a time when she was actually requesting it!

Timeliness

In general, feedback is most useful at the earliest opportunity after the given behavior has occurred (depending, of course, on the person's readiness to hear it and the support that is available from others). One of the most delayed examples of feedback I have witnessed occurred with two female trainers with whom I was working. We were designing a seminar and the two began discussing their earlier work together. Finally, one said, "Let's be sure we get straight what each person's role will be throughout the course of this seminar because we aren't always clear about how much we want someone to be involved." When she was asked to explain her point further, she described a workshop the two of them had designed in which she felt her talents were not fully used. In fact, she was unclear about the role she should take. I ended up being the mediator in this discussion, and I asked when this workshop had occurred only to discover it had been eight years earlier! Feedback that delayed is useless and unfair. It is unfair because the person who chose not to provide the feedback closer to the time the behavior occurred had been harboring resentment for a long time. Indirectly she may have been acting on that resentment in her behavior toward the other person, who could do nothing about it.

Another example of poor timing would be if I asked my husband, during a formal banquet, how he liked my new outfit. To actually give me straightforward feedback, which may have been negative, at that time would have been inappropriate. What I really wanted him to say was, "You look great" whether I did or not! Why? Because there was nothing I could do to correct my appearance at that moment. The next time I was selecting an outfit to wear or buying a new one, when I could make a reasonable decision about how to use this information, would be a more appropriate time to tell me the outfit makes me look unattractive (if he dares to tell me that at all!). To provide such criticism in the middle of a social event could make both of us miserable!

Clarity and Accuracy

One way of checking to ensure clear communication is to ask the receiver to rephrase the feedback to see if it corresponds to what the sender had in mind. In this way too, the sender is training the other person to provide descriptive feedback.

Both giver and receiver should have an opportunity to check with others about the accuracy of the feedback. Is this one person's impression or an impression shared by others? A teacher knows that an entire classroom of students will not always be happy with the way in which the class is structured. The teacher must therefore check for themes that exist among most of the students. When you get disturbing or confusing feedback, be sure to check it with co-workers and colleagues. "Have you ever noticed me behaving in this way . . . ?"

Feedback, then, is a way of giving help; it is a corrective mechanism for the individual who wants to learn how well his or her behavior and intentions match and a means for establishing one's identity—

for answering "Who am I?" Feedback can be informal or a formal evaluation process, like performance appraisal.

TIPS ON PROVIDING FEEDBACK

Negative feedback is misunderstood much more readily than positive feedback. Consequently, go slowly and be descriptive. I prefer never to put negative feedback in a memo. There are too many opportunities to misinterpret the language. I use memos for good news and face-to-face meetings for bad news. I want to be sure people have a chance to ask any questions they might have when I am telling them something they may not want to hear. However, once the negative information has been communicated face-to-face, follow-up written documents are absolutely necessary to maintain a "paper trail."

Positive feedback that is too general has little impact. We shouldn't assume when we tell employees that they're doing a "good job" that the information will positively affect their performance. If they don't know exactly what it is they did well, it is unlikely they will know what to continue doing! In fact, if the feedback is perceived as too general, it might also be interpreted as insincere.

Keep feedback impersonal. It is important that the person and the person's actions be separated in discussions. I can like the person, respect the person, but find a particular behavior unacceptable. I love my children deeply, but I dislike intensely their tendency to squabble with each other. It is their behavior I find distasteful, not their person. Thus, when you provide feedback, make it impersonal and attach it to a specific behavior, not to the personality of the individual with whom you are talking.

Tailor the feedback to fit the person. Some people appreciate receiving straightforward, direct feedback about their efforts. Others cannot tolerate such directness and need positive reinforcement before they are prepared to handle negative information. Others learn best by example. Still others must hear new information several times before they really listen.

Use humor when appropriate. Sometimes it is easier to tease someone and indirectly provide feedback. This works when the relationship is a good one. The humorous memo in the beginning of this chapter was sent anonymously to the president of a company. It would be great if the president had a sense of humor, recognized the criticism as valid, and responded with his own humorous memo (I can imagine a variety of scenarios!). However, many top-level executives might not be able to handle such forms of feedback. In another organization, a short story written about the head of the unit satirized a recent series of decisions (or lack of them!). The story was never mentioned by the unit head in public. In private he expressed his inability to accept the feedback in that form.

Sometimes subtlety works best. There are times when direct confrontation over an issue is not the best approach. You may be calling too much attention to a problem others can then trivialize. For example, one woman who was constantly asked to take the minutes at executive meetings simply placed the memo pad in front of the senior member's chair at the next meeting, and then offered to provide him with a pen so he could take the minutes at that meeting. He got the message without her having to make a big deal out of the issue and began rotating this secretarial function among all present.

We know who we are by "bumping up against" other people. Their feedback helps shape our identity, self-esteem, and self-concept. The more feedback we provide for others, the better they are able to perform. The more we *ask* for feedback from others about ourselves, the clearer image we have of how others see us.

QUESTIONS

1. What is "feedback"?

2. How do we make feedback effective? How do we make it ineffective?

Evan M. Dudick | # Do Management Gurus Lie?

Evan Dudik runs his own management consulting firm and holds a Ph.D. in philosophy as well. He is a leading management consultant.

The business of consulting to business is booming. Andersen Consulting is pulling in $9 billion a year; KPMG and PricewaterhouseCoopers are each a measly billion or two behind. McKinsey is closing in on $3 billion. While a good portion of those fees is for information technology consulting, a lot of it is for good old strategic planning advice. . . . AKA snake oil. All told, the top ten consulting firms extracted $40 billion dollars from clients in 1999.

That's a lot of Powerpoint presentations!

It's a good thing these firm's revenues are booming. They are going to need the money. Some of the big boys are being hauled into court by their clients. In 1999 Ernst and Young's consulting unit agreed to pay $185 million because of allegedly shoddy work at Merry-Go-Round, a clothing fashion retailer. According to Business Week, Merry-Go-Round says it took E&Y nearly a year to come up with a plan for a measly $11 million in cost savings when the company was losing 15 times that.

The folks at Merry-Go-Round should feel like they have company. According to Business Week again, PricewaterhouseCoopers' predecessor, Coopers and Lybrand, soaked up $8 million in fees from Sunbeam Corp. "Sunbeam claims that Coopers' only attempt to analyze a key manufacturing plant consisted of sending a junior staffer for a brief tour that lasted just a few hours. And Sunbeam alleges that the plan assembled by Coopers . . . left the company a mess—with factories lacking key parts, its financial reporting systems in disarray, and the company unable to process all the resulting returns from customers."

Of course, most consulting firms' clients believe that most of the work consulting firms do most of the time is solid, valuable and reliable. If the market is any judge, the very growth of these firms is testimony that consulting works.

But there may be something else at work—and I think the Coopers and E&Y fights are just the tip of the iceberg. Management is beginning to realize that just because they agree with their consultants every step of the way doesn't mean they are getting the value they deserve.

In fact, it wouldn't be surprising in the E&Y and Coopers cases, that if you really dug down into what really went on inside those projects, you would probably find that management was on board every step of the way. Every step down the garden path of wonderful intentions.

And that's because consultants have long ago learned that to make change happen in a company requires management's involvement, agreement and commitment. Thus they've become experts in making management accomplices to what can sometimes be described as nothing other than corporate murder. That's why I say that often consultants drive the gateway cars to corporate failure.

Why does this happen? Why does it happen even when the consultants provide advice that goes against the expectations of top management! Yes, while many consultants are brought in to sanitize, bless or confirm top management's gut instincts many consultants do earn their fees by finding out and expressing what appear to be unpalatable truths. Yet even here consultants are often driving those getaway cars.

The reason is that ninety-one percent of strategic management consulting advice simply replaces one set of prejudices for another. The second set of prejudices—the ones from the consultants—may be based on more research, more facts; it might be more orderly, better packaged, even better thought-through. But it remains one-eyed prejudice because typically it simply hasn't been tested.

After all, who is there to test it? Who watches the

watch-dogs? Long experience makes savvy management consultants bring their clients along with them through their thought-processes. As the project wears on, the consultants and the management team become more and more "bought-in" to the ideas they are uncovering. When there is conflict or something seems not quite right—either in the facts or in some lowly director's opinion, is it followed up on? Is the conflict heralded as the source of new insight? Far from it! Rather it is explained away, or the opinion absorbed gently into a corner of the final report. Very often this contradicting evidence is simply ignored as the overwhelming evidence in favor of the consultant's (and now management's) is sorted, documented and rendered into Powerpoint charts.

Although leading management consultants have long promised to help make the practice of management scientific, what I've just described is almost the exact opposite of the way science works. Science progresses by making hypotheses and then testing them—trying as best it can to break the hypothesis. Where science is vigorous there are always competing theories—behind which are competing institutions, reputations and careers. Suppose a scientific team at University X proposes to explain A and B by invoking theory Z. You can be sure that over at University Y there is a team burning the midnight oil to concoct an experiment—a test—to prove those X guys are all wet. How different this is from the subtle co-option which is the stock in trade of the best management consultants, where every ambiguity is smoothed over, every contrary piece of evidence hidden or explained away!

Scientists on the hunt for powerful new theories glory in finding the *exceptions* to the norm, *the anomalies*. For example, to find better how HIV infection becomes AIDS, scientists sought out that one percent or so of people in Africa who, though infected with HIV somehow never developed AIDS. As another example, to understand how people control their emotions, particularly anger, psychologists and neurologists look at how how behavior changes in those with head injuries suffered on the job or in wartime. To identify environments that are becoming too polluted, scientists don't target the mainstream species in the area. No, they seek out the anomalies—the frog embryos that are mutant, the bird's eggshells that are thin.

Penicillin wouldn't have been discovered if Alexander Fleming hadn't noticed how differently bacteria cultures grew (or failed to grow) after a garden-variety laboratory mistake—leaving the cover off a Petri dish where he'd been growing some bacteria for other purposes. Today's typical management consult would have pooh-poohed the evidence as the result of some incompetent housekeeping, ignored the whole thing—and counseled you to do the same.

Then too, there's the fact that you've paid these consultants beaucoup bucks to come up with the right answer. So they feel obligated to do just that, and look good in the process. Is it any wonder that they buy into the advice they're giving? It's just human nature. After two or three months and $50,000 or $500,000 or $5,000,000 it just doesn't seem seemly to tell a client that their most promising ideas about how to save the company are . . . just not standing up to the most rigorous tests.

They are not going to spend time trying to find out why your new retail store concept surprisingly scored low in a market research survey with one specific group when it scored high with all the others. No, they are going to spend time telling you how much evidence is that their bright idea of retail concept will attract scads of customers. And you *will* find overwhelming evidence to agree with them. And you'll implement their recommendations. And you'll be disappointed, very often, when the customers don't show up. Because probing that one low—scoring group would have told you something! It would have warned you away from a blunder you (and your consultants) just didn't see coming.

But in the meantime, you have a thick study; you're convinced; you've had some fine dinners with the director of the consulting team and you know he's convinced. Money is about to change hands. You don't see that he's just pulled the getaway car to the curb.

QUESTIONS

1. Do management gurus lie? How and why?
2. What good purpose may management gurus serve?

The Economist | # Self-Deception

For every corporate crook there are at least ten corporate deceivers: people who fool themselves that things are other than what they appear to be. At first they do not break the law, but eventually they find that corporate deceit is difficult to sustain. "Oh what a tangled web we weave when first we practise to deceive," wrote Sir Walter Scott in 1808. He might have been talking about Enron, Lucent, Xerox or any of the other big corporate deceivers that have come to light in recent years.

Deceit demands more deceit until eventually the pile collapses under the weight of its own incredibility. As Warren Buffett puts it, "Once a company moves earnings from one period to another, operating shortfalls that occur thereafter require it to engage in further accounting manoeuvres that must be even more 'heroic'. These can turn fudging into fraud."

The most outstanding recent example of this is Enron, an energy-trading company as widely praised as any online wonder at the height of the Internet euphoria. Analysts loved it. One predicted that it would come to dominate the wholesale market for electricity, natural gas, coal, energy derivatives and bandwidth, and on three continents. Investors loved it enough to value the company at $28 billion in October 2001, less than two months before it skidded into bankruptcy.

The media also loved it. Without irony, *Fortune* magazine voted it "The most innovative company of the year" for 2000. And *The Economist,* for its sins, wrote at the end of June last year that "Enron has created what may be the most successful Internet venture of any company in any industry anywhere"—noting that the banner which greeted visitors at Enron's Houston headquarters had recently been changed from "The world's leading energy company" to "The world's leading company". Rarely has pride come before a bigger fall.

Above all, though, consultants loved it. In "The War for Talent" (Harvard Business School Press, 2001), Ed Michaels, Helen Handfield-Jones and Beth Axelrod wrote that: "Few companies will be able to achieve the excitement extravaganza that Enron has in its remarkable business transformation, but many could apply some of the principles."

The authors, all consultants at McKinsey, heaped particular praise on Jeff Skilling, a former McKinsey consultant who became Enron's CEO. In August 2001 he suddenly resigned from Enron "for personal reasons". Mr Skilling tried to weld a new culture on to an established firm by recruiting fast-track mbas and traders. It turned out to be an explosive formula.

QUESTIONS

1. How did Enron depend upon deceit?

2. Explain why lies require more lies. Can you give an example (painful though it might be) from your own experience?

Self-Deception from *The Economist* (March 9, 2002).

Paul Ekman and Mark G. Frank

Lies That Fail

Paul Ekman is one of the preeminent researchers on emotions and their expression and an expert on lying who has worked widely with police, federal agencies, and the Department of Homeland security. Until recently he taught in the Psychiatry Department of the University of California, San Francisco.

Lies fail for many reasons. Some of these reasons have to do with the circumstances surrounding the lie, and not with the liar's behavior. For example, a confidant may betray a lie; or, private information made public can expose a liar's claims as false. These reasons do not concern us in this chapter. What concerns us are those mistakes made during the act of lying, mistakes liars make despite themselves; in other words, lies that fail because of the liars' behaviors. Deception clues or leakage may be shown in a change in the expression on the face, a movement of the body, an inflection to the voice, a swallowing in the throat, a very deep or shallow breath, long pauses between words, a slip of the tongue, a microfacial expression, or a gestural slip.

There are two basic reasons why lies fail—one that involves thinking, and one that involves emotions. Lies fail due to a failure of the liar to prepare his or her line, or due to the interference of emotions. These reasons have different implications for the potential behavioral clues that betray a lie.

LIES BETRAYED BY THINKING CLUES

Liars do not always anticipate when they will need to lie. There is not always time to prepare the line to be taken, to rehearse and memorize it. Even when there

has been ample advance notice, and a false line has been carefully devised, the liar may not be clever enough to anticipate all the questions that may be asked, and to have thought through what his answers must be. Even cleverness may not be enough, for unseen changes in circumstances can betray an otherwise effective line. And, even when a liar is not forced by circumstances to change lines, some liars have trouble recalling the line they have previously committed themselves to, so that new questions cannot be consistently answered quickly.

Any of these failures—in anticipating when it will be necessary to lie, in inventing a line which is adequate to changing circumstances, in remembering the line one has adopted—produce easily spotted clues to deceit. What the person says is either internally inconsistent, or at odds with other incontrovertible facts, known at the time or later revealed. Such obvious clues to deceit are not always as reliable and straightforward as they seem. Too smooth a line may be the sign of a well rehearsed con man. To make matters worse, some con men knowing this purposely make slight mistakes in order not to seem too smooth! This was the case with Clifford Irving, who claimed he was authorized by Howard Hughes to write Hughes' biography. While on trial, Irving deliberately contradicted himself (albeit minor contradictions) because he knew that only liars tell perfectly planned accounts. The psychological evidence supports Irving's notion that planned responses are judged as more deceptive than unplanned ones. However, we believe in general that people who fabricate without having prepared their line are more likely to make blatant contradictions, to give evasive and indirect accounts—all of which will ultimately betray their lies.

Lack of preparation or a failure to remember the

From Michael Lewis and Carolyn Saarni, eds., *Lying and Deception in Everyday Life* (New York: Guilford Press, 1993). References were deleted from this text.

line one has adopted may produce clues to deceit in *how* a line is spoken, even when there are no inconsistencies in *what* is said. The need to think about each word before it is spoken—weighing possibilities, searching for a word or idea—may be obvious in pauses during speech, speech disfluencies, flattened voice intonation, gaze aversion, or more subtly in a tightening of the lower eyelid or eye brow, certain changes in gesture, and a decrease in the use of the hands to illustrate speech. Not that carefully considering each word before it is spoken is always a sign of deceit, but in some circumstances it is—particularly in contexts in which responses should be known without thought.

LYING ABOUT FEELINGS

A failure to think ahead, plan fully, and rehearse the false line is only one of the reasons why mistakes are made when lying, which then furnish clues to the deceit. Mistakes are also made because of difficulty in concealing or falsely portraying emotion. Not every lie involves emotions, but those that do cause special problems for the liar. An attempt to conceal an emotion at the moment it is felt could be betrayed in words, but except for a slip of the tongue, it usually is not. Unless there is a wish to confess what is felt, the liar does not have to put into words the feelings being concealed. One has less choice in concealing a facial expression, or rapid breathing, or a tightening in the voice.

When emotions are aroused changes occur automatically without choice or deliberation. These changes begin in a split second; this is a fundamental characteristic of emotional experience. People do not actively decide to feel an emotion; instead, they usually experience emotions as happening to them. Negative emotions, such as fear, anger, or sadness, may occur despite either efforts to avoid them or efforts to hide them.

These are what we will call "reliable" behavioral signs of emotion, reliable in the sense that few people can mimic them at all or correctly. Narrowing the red margins of the lips in anger is an example of such a reliable sign of anger, typically missing when anger is feigned, because most people can not voluntarily make that movement. Likewise, when people experi-

ence enjoyment they not only move their lip corners upward and back (in a prototypical smile), but they also show a simultaneous contraction of the muscles that surround the eye socket (which raises the cheek, lowers the brow, and creates a "crows feet" appearance). This eye muscle contraction is typically missing from the smile when enjoyment is feigned or not felt. And, as in the case of the involuntary movement of the red margins of the lips in anger, most people cannot voluntarily make this eye muscle movement when they are not truly feeling enjoyment.

Falsifying an experienced emotion is more difficult when one is also attempting to conceal another emotion. Trying to look angry is not easy, but if fear is felt when the person tries to look angry, conflicting forces occur. One set of impulses, arising from fear, pulls in one direction, while the deliberate attempt to appear angry pulls in the other direction. For example, the brows are involuntarily pulled upward and together in fear, but to falsify anger the person must pull them down. Often the signs of this internal struggle between the felt and the false emotion betray the deceit.

Usually, lies about emotions involve more than just fabricating an emotion which is not felt. They also require concealing an emotion which is being experienced. Concealment often goes hand in hand with fabrication. The liar feigns emotion to mask signs of the emotion to be concealed. Such concealment attempts may be betrayed in either of two ways: (1) some signs of the concealed emotion may escape efforts to inhibit or mask it, providing what Ekman and Friesen termed *leakage;* or (2) what they called a *deception clue* does not leak the concealed emotion but betrays the likelihood that a lie is being perpetrated. Deception clues occur when only a fragment leaks which is not decipherable, but which does not jibe with the verbal line being maintained by the liar, or when the very effort of having to conceal produces alterations in behavior, and those behavioral alterations do not fit the liar's line.

FEELINGS ABOUT LYING

Not all deceits involve concealing or falsifying emotions. The embezzler conceals that she is stealing money. The plagiarizer conceals that he has taken the words of another and pretends they are his own. The vain middle-aged man conceals his real age, dying his gray hair and claiming he is seven years younger than he is. Yet even when the lie is about something other than emotion, emotions may become involved. The vain man might be embarrassed about his vanity. To succeed in his deceit he must conceal not only his age but his embarrassment as well. The plagiarizer might feel contempt toward those he misleads. He would thus have to conceal not only the source of his work and pretend an ability that is not his, but also conceal his contempt. The embezzler might feel surprise when someone else is accused of her crime. She would have to conceal her surprise or at least conceal the reason why she is surprised.

Thus, emotions often become involved in lies that were not undertaken for the purpose of concealing emotions. Once involved, the emotions must be concealed if the lie is not to be betrayed. Any emotion may be the culprit, but three emotions are so often intertwined with deceit to merit separate explanation: fear of being caught, guilt about lying, and delight in having duped someone.

Fear of Being Caught

In its milder forms, fear of being caught is not disruptive and may even help the deceiver to avoid mistakes by maintaining alertness. Moderate levels of fear can produce behavioral signs that are noticeable by the skilled lie catcher, and high levels of fear produce just what the liar dreads, namely, evidence of his or her fear or apprehension. The research literature on deception detection suggests that the behavior of highly motivated liars is different from that of less motivated ones. In other words, the behavior of liars who fear being caught is different from the behaviors of liars who do not fear being caught.

Many factors influence how the fear of being caught in a lie (or, *detection apprehension*) will be felt. The first determinant to consider is the liar's beliefs about his target's skill as a lie catcher. If the target (i.e., the person being lied to) is known to be gullible, there usually will not be much detection apprehension. On the other hand, a target known to be tough to fool, who has a reputation as an expert lie catcher, will increase the detection apprehension.

The second determinant of detection apprehension is the liar's amount of practice and previous success in lying. A job applicant who has lied about qualifications successfully in the past should not be overly concerned about an additional deception. Practice in deceit enables the liar to anticipate problems. Success in deceit gives confidence and thus reduces the fear of being caught.

The third determinant of detection apprehension is fear of punishment. The fear of being caught can be reduced if the target suggests that the punishment may be less if the liar confesses. Although they usually cannot offer total amnesty, targets may also offer a psychological amnesty, hoping to induce a confession by implying that the liar need not feel ashamed nor even responsible for committing the crime. A target may sympathetically suggest that the acts are understandable and might have been committed by anyone in the same situation. Another variation might be to offer the target a face-saving explanation of the motive for the behavior in which the lie was designed to conceal.

A fourth factor influencing fear of being caught is the personality of the liar. While some people find it easy to lie, others find it difficult to lie; certainly more is known about the former group than the latter. One group, called *natural liars,* lie easily and with great success—even though they do not differ from other people on their scores on objective personality tests. Natural liars are people who have been getting away with lies since childhood, fooling their parents, teachers, and friends when they wanted to. This instills a sense of confidence in their abilities to deceive such that they have no detection apprehension when they lie. Although this sounds as if natural liars are like psychopaths, they are not; unlike natural liars, psychopaths show poor judgment, no remorse or shame, superficial charm, antisocial behavior without apparent compunction, and pathological egocentricity and incapacity for love.

Such natural liars may need to have two very different skills—the skill needed to plan a deceptive strategy, and the skill needed to mislead a target in a face-to-face meeting. A liar might have both skills, but presumably one could excel at one skill and not the other. Regretably, there has been little study of the characteristics of successful deceivers; no research has asked whether the personality characteristics of successful deceivers differ depending on the arena in which the deceit is practiced.

So far we have described several determinants of detection apprehension: the personality of the liar and, before that, the reputation and character of the lie catcher. Equally important are the *stakes*—the perceived consequences for successful and unsuccessful attempts at deception. Although there is no direct empirical evidence for this assertion, research on the role of appraisal in the experience of emotion is consistent with our thinking. There is a simple rule: the greater the stakes, the more the detection apprehension. Applying this simple rule can be complicated because it is not always so easy to figure out what is at stake; for example, to some people winning is everything, so the stakes are always high. It is reasonable to presume that what is at stake in any deception situation may be so idiosyncratic that no outside observer would readily know.

Detection apprehension should be greater when the stakes involve avoiding punishment, not just earning a reward. When the decision to deceive is first made, the stakes usually involve obtaining rewards. The liar thinks primarily about what might be gained. An embezzler may think only about the monetary gain when he or she first chooses to lie. Once deceit has been underway for some time the rewards may no longer be available. The company may become aware of its losses and suspicious enough that the embezzler

is prevented from taking more. At this point, the deceit might be maintained in order to avoid being caught, and avoiding punishment becomes the only stake. On the other hand, avoiding punishment may be the motive from the outset, if the target is suspicious or the liar has little confidence.

There are two kinds of punishment which are at stake in deceit: the punishment that lies in store if the lie fails; and the punishment for the very act of engaging in deception. Detection apprehension should be greater if both kinds of punishment are at stake. Sometimes the punishment for being caught deceiving can even be far worse than the punishment the lie was designed to avoid.

Even if the transgressor knows that the damage done if caught lying will be greater than the loss from admitting the transgression, the lie may be very tempting. Telling the truth brings immediate and certain losses, while telling a lie promises the possibility of avoiding all losses. The prospect of being spared immediate punishment may be so attractive that the liar may underestimate the likelihood that he or she will be caught in the lie. Recognition that confession would have been a better policy comes too late, when the lie has been maintained so long and with such elaboration that confession may no longer win a lesser punishment.

Sometimes there is little ambiguity about the relative costs of confession versus continued concealment. There are actions which are themselves so bad

Transparency International—USA Program

Securing Transparency in Trade: TI-USA is working with the U.S. administration, the private sector, and TI chapters to promote transparency in procurement, investment, services, and customs. It has promoted a World Trade Organization Agreement on Transparency in Government Procurement and agreements with similar requirements in the FTAA and APEC. It advocates strong transparency requirements in U.S. bilateral trade agreements and requiring bidders on projects financed by the World Bank and multilateral development banks to have antibribery programs.

that confessing them wins little approval for having come forward, and concealing them adds little to the punishment which awaits the offender. Such is the case if the lie conceals child abuse, incest, murder, treason, or terrorism. Unlike the rewards possible for some repentant philanderers, forgiveness is not to be expected by those who confess these heinous crimes—although confession with contrition may lessen the punishment.

A final factor to consider about how the stakes influence detection apprehension is what is gained or lost by the target, not just by the liar. Usually the liar's gains are at the expense of the target. The embezzler gains what the employer loses. Stakes are not always equal; moreover, the stakes for the liar and the target can differ not just in amount but in kind. A philanderer may gain a little adventure, while the cuckolded spouse may lose tremendous self-respect. When the stakes differ for the liar and target, the stakes for either may determine the liar's detection apprehension. It depends upon whether the liar recognizes the difference and how it is evaluated.

Deception Guilt

Deception guilt refers to a feeling about lying, not the legal issue of whether someone is guilty or innocent. Deception guilt must also be distinguished from feelings of guilt about the content of a lie. Thus, a child may feel excitement about stealing the loose change off his parents' dresser, but feel guilt over lying to his or her parents to conceal the theft. This situation can be reversed as well—no guilt about lying to the parents, but guilt about stealing the money. Of course, some people feel guilt about both the act and the lie, and some people will not feel guilt about either. What is important is that it is not necessary to feel guilty about the content of a lie in order to feel guilty about lying.

Like the fear of being caught, deception guilt can vary in strength. It may be very mild, or so strong that the lie will fail because the deception guilt produces leakage or deception clues. When it becomes extreme, deception guilt is a torturing experience, undermining the sufferer's most fundamental feelings of self-worth. Relief from such severe deception guilt

may motivate a confession despite the likelihood of punishment for misdeeds admitted. In fact the punishment may be sought by the person who confesses in order to alleviate the tortured feelings of guilt.

When the decision to lie is first made, people do not always accurately anticipate how much they may later suffer from deception guilt. Liars may not realize the impact of being thanked by their victims for their seeming helpfulness, or how they will feel when they see someone else blamed for their misdeeds—as in the recent case of the "gentleman bandit" who felt so guilty about someone else being prosecuted for his robberies that he turned himself in to the police. Another reason why liars underestimate how much deception guilt they will feel is that it is only with the passage of time that a liar may learn that one lie will not suffice, that the lie has to be repeated again and again, often with expanding fabrications in order to protect the original deceit.

Shame is closely related to guilt, but there is a key qualitative difference. No audience is needed for feelings of guilt, no one else need know for the guilty person is his own judge. Not so for shame. The humiliation of shame requires disapproval or ridicule by others. If no one ever learns of a misdeed there will be no shame, but there still might be guilt. Of course there may be both. The distinction between shame and guilt is very important because these two emotions may tear a person in opposite directions. The wish to relieve guilt may motivate a confession, but the wish to avoid the humiliation of shame may prevent it.

There exists a group of individuals who fail to feel any guilt or shame about their misdeeds; these people have been referred to as sociopaths or psychopaths. For these individuals, the lack of guilt or shame pervades all or most aspects of their lives. Experts disagree about whether the lack of guilt and shame is due to upbringing or some biological determinants. There is agreement that the psychopath's lack of guilt about lying and lack of fear of being caught will make it more difficult for a target to detect a psychopath's lies.

Conversely, some people are especially vulnerable to shame about lying and deception guilt; for example, people who have been very strictly brought up to believe lying is one of the most terrible sins. Those with less strict upbringing, that did not particularly condemn lying, could more generally have been instilled with strong, pervasive guilt feelings. Such guilty people appear to seek experiences in which they can intensify their guilt, and stand shamefully exposed to others; this appears to be the case for psychiatric patients suffering from generalized anxiety disorders. Unfortunately, unlike the psychopathic personality, there has been very little research about guilt-prone individuals.

Whenever the deceiver does not share social values with the victim, odds are there will not be much deception guilt. People feel less guilty about lying to those they think are wrongdoers. A philanderer whose marital partner is cold and unwilling in bed might not feel guilty in lying about an affair. A similar principle is at work to explain why a diplomat or spy does not feel guilty about misleading the other side. In all these situations, the liar and the target do not share common goals or values.

Lying is authorized in most of these examples—each of these individuals appeals to a well-defined social norm which legitimizes deceiving an opponent. There is little guilt about such authorized deceits when the targets are from opposing sides, and hold different values. There also may be authorization to deceive targets who are not opponents, who share values with the deceiver. Physicians may not feel guilty about deceiving their patients if they think it is for the patient's own good. Giving a patient a placebo, a sugar pill identified as a useful drug, is an old, time-honored, medical deceit. If the patient feels better, or at least stops hassling the doctor for an unneeded drug which might actually be harmful, many physicians believe that the lie is justified. In this case, the patient benefits from the lie, and not the doctor. If a liar thinks he is not gaining from the lie he probably will not feel any deception guilt.

Even selfish deceits may not produce deception guilt when the lie is authorized. Poker players do not feel deception guilt about bluffing (but they do feel detection apprehension). The same is true about bargaining whether in a Middle East bazaar, Wall Street, or in the local real estate agent's office. The home owner who asks more for his house than he will actually sell it for will not feel guilty if he gets his asking price. This lie is authorized. Because the participants expect misinformation, and not the truth, bargaining and poker are not necessarily lies. These situations by their nature provide prior notification that no one will be entirely truthful.

Deception guilt is most likely when lying is not authorized. Deception guilt should be most severe when the target is trusting, not expecting to be misled because honesty is expected between liar and target. In such opportunistic deceits, guilt about lying will be greater if the target suffers at least as much as the liar gains. Even then there will not be much, if any, deception guilt unless there are at least some shared values between target and liar. A student turning in a late assignment may not feel guilty about lying to the professor if the student feels the professor sets unreachable standards and assigns undoable workloads. This student may feel fear of being caught in a lie, but he or she may not feel deception guilt. Even though the student disagrees with the professor about the workload and other matters, if the student still cares about the professor he or she may feel shame if the lie is discovered. Shame requires some respect for those who disapprove; otherwise disapproval brings forth anger or contempt, not shame.

Liars feel less guilty when their targets are impersonal or totally anonymous. A customer who conceals from the check-out clerk that he or she was undercharged for an expensive item will feel less guilty if he or she does not know the clerk. If the clerk is the owner, or if it is a small family owned store, the lying customer will feel more guilty than he or she will if it is one of a large chain of supermarkets. It is easier to indulge the guilt-reducing fantasy that the target is not really hurt, does not really care, will not even notice the lie, or even deserves or wants to be misled, if the target is anonymous.

Often there will be an inverse relationship between deception guilt and detection apprehension. What lessens guilt about the lie increases fear of being caught. When deceits are authorized there should be less deception guilt, yet the authorization usually increases the stakes, thus making detection apprehension high. In a high stakes poker game there is high detection apprehension and low deception guilt. The employer who lies to his employee whom he has come to suspect of embezzling, concealing his suspicions to catch him in the crime, also is likely to feel high detection apprehension but low deception guilt.

While there are exceptions, most people find the experience of guilt so toxic that they seek ways to diminish it. There are many ways to justify deceit. It can be considered retaliation for injustice. A nasty or mean target can be said not to deserve honesty. "The boss was so stingy, he didn't reward me for all the work I did, so I took some myself." Or the liar can blame the victim of his or her lies; for example, Machiavellian personality types tend to see their victims as so gullible that they bring lies upon themselves.

QUESTIONS

1. Why do lies fail? Why are failed lies interesting?
2. What is deception guilt? How does it differ from shame?

Robert C. Solomon and Fernando Flores | # Building Trust

Fernando Flores is a senator in Chile and formerly ran a successful consulting firm in Berkeley California. Robert C. Solomon teaches philosophy and business at the University of Texas at Austin. This selection is from their 1999 book, *Building Trust.*

In our experience, business people feel uncomfortable talking about trust, except, perhaps, in the most abstract terms of approbation. When the topic of trust comes up, they heartily nod their approval, but then they nervously turn to other topics. Executives are talking a great deal about trust these days, perhaps because they rightly suspect that trust in many corporations seems to be at an all-time low. One of our associates, who also consults for major corporations, recently gave a lecture on the importance of trusting your employees to several hundred executives of one of America's largest corporations. There was an appreciative but stunned silence, and then one of them—asking for all of them—queried, "but how do we control them?" It is a telling question that indicates that they did not understand the main point of the lecture, that trust is the very opposite of control. Or, perhaps, they understood well enough, but suffered a lack of nerve when it came time to think through its implications. Like the first-time skydiver who had eagerly read all of the promotional literature about the thrills of the sport and had listened carefully to instructions, he asked, incredulously, "but now you want us to *jump out of the plane!?*" We all know the importance of trust, the advantages of trust, and we all know how terrible life can be without it. But when it comes time to put that knowledge into practice, we are all like the novice skydiver. Creating trust is taking a risk. Trust entails lack of control, in that some power is transferred or given up to the person who is trusted. It is leaping from the dark, claustrophobic fuselage of our ordinary cynicism into what seems like the unsupported free-fall of dependency. And yet, unlike skydiving, nothing is more necessary.

Today, there is a danger that trust is being oversold. There is such a thing as too much trust, and then there is "blind trust," trust without warrant, foolish

This essay is one of two based on a talk given at the DePaul University Conference on Trust in Business, in Chicago, February 20–21, 1997. Special thanks to George Brenkert, Daryl Koehn, Ken Alpern and, especially, the terrific anonymous reviewers for *BEQ,* and to Business Design Associates in Alameda, CA. A companion piece appears in the *Journal for Professional and Business Ethics,* edited by Daryl Koehn, and both are part of a book now published by Oxford University Press, *Building Trust,* 2001.

trust. Trust alone will not, as some of our pundits promise, solve the problems that our society now faces. Thus we think there is good reason to listen to doubters like Daryl Koehn, who rightly asks, "should we trust trust?"[1] But the urgency remains, we believe, on the side of encouraging and understanding trust. There is a lot of encouraging going on today. What is lacking, we want to suggest, is understanding. The problem is not just lack of an adequate analysis. The problem is an aggressive *mis*understanding of trust that pervades most of our discussions. The problem, if we can summarize it in a metaphor or two, is that trust is treated as if it were a "medium" in which human transactions take place, alternatively, as "ground," as "atmosphere" or, even more vaguely, as "climate." Benjamin Barber, for instance, who is one of the early writers on trust and often appealed to by the current crop of commentators, says that trust is "the basic stuff or ingredient of social interaction." But as "stuff" or "ingredient," as a "resource" (Fukuyama[2]), as "medium," "ground," "atmosphere" or "climate," trust all too easily tends to seem inert, simply "there" or "not there," rather than a dynamic aspect of human interaction and human relationships.

This is our thesis: Trust is a *dynamic aspect of human relationships.* It is an ongoing process that must be initiated, maintained, sometimes restored and continuously authenticated. Trust isn't a social substance or a mysterious entity; trust is a social practice, defined by choices. It is always relational: A trusts B (to do C, D, E). We can say that A is "trusting," but by that we mean that he or she has a disposition to readily trust people. Indeed, the very word "trust" is misleading, insofar as it seems to point to an entity, a thing, some social "stuff." Although we will continue to use the word, it might better be thought of as "trusting," an activity, a decision, a transitive verb, not a noun. Accordingly, the discussion of trust, in other words, is shot through with what French existentialist Jean-Paul Sartre called "bad faith," the distancing of our own actions and choices and the refusal to take responsibility for them. The not very subtle message of too much of the talk about trust today is, *"The problem isn't me/us, it's them,"* as if WE are perfectly willing to trust oth-

ers—if they are trustworthy, that is, but, unfortunately, they are not or have not proven themselves so. Thus say the Bosnians and the Serbs, the Israelis and the Palestinians, many parents and their teenage kids, and all too many managers and their employees.

The misunderstanding of trust, accordingly, takes the form of a dangerous rationalization. Trust(ing) presupposes trustworthiness. Either one is trustworthy or one is not. So trusting takes the form of a kind of knowledge, the recognition (which may, of course, be fallible) that someone is trustworthy. So, if one trust, so the rationalization goes, then nothing need be said, and it is much better that nothing be said. That is the core of our problem. Trust is rendered inarticulate, unpresentable. According to this view, to even raise the question, "do you trust me?" or "Can I trust you?" is to already instigate, not only indicate, distrust. (Blaze Starr's mother warns her, "never trust a man who says, "Trust me.""[3]) If one does not trust, then nothing much is accomplished by saying so, except, perhaps, as an insult, a way of escalating an already existing conflict or, perhaps, as a confirming test ("If you tell me that I should trust you, then you are doubly a liar.") When a politician or a business leader says, "trust me," he takes a considerable risk. Those who support him may well wonder why he needs to say that, and become suspicious. For those who are already suspicious of him, such an intrusive imperative confirms their suspicions.[4] On the other hand, when someone says "I trust you," there is always the possibility of some sense of manipulation, even the unwanted imposition of a psychological burden, one of whose consequences may be guilt.

The reason for talking about trust is not just to "understand" the concept philosophically but to put the issue of trust "on the table" in order to be able to talk it through in concrete, practical situations. By talking through trust, trust can be created, distrust mitigated. Not talking about trust, on the other hand, can result in continuing distrust, and lack of trust is calamitous to one's flourishing as a business and as individuals.

Economic approaches to trust, while well-intended and pointing us in the right direction, are dangerously incomplete and misleading. Trust in business is not merely a tool for efficiency, although it does have important implications for dealing with complexity and therefore efficiency.[5] Moreover, it would hardly be honest to guarantee (as many authors do these days), that more trust will make business more efficient and improve the bottom line. Usually, of course, trust has this effect, but there is no necessary connection between trust and efficiency, and this is neither the aim nor the intention of trust. Indeed, trust as a mere efficiency-booster may be a paradigm of *inauthentic* or phony trust, trust that is merely a manipulative tool, a facade of trust that, over the long run, increases *dis*trust, and for good reason. Employees can usually tell when the "empowerment" they receive like a gift is actually a noose with which to hang themselves, a set-up for blame for situations which they cannot really control. Managers know what it is like when they are awarded more responsibility ("I trust you to take care of that") without the requisite authority. Like many virtues, trust is most virtuous when it is pursued for its own sake, even if there is benefit or advantage in view. (Generosity and courage both have their pay-offs, but to act generously or courageously *merely* in order obtain the pay-offs is of dubious virtue.) To think of trust as a business tool, as a mere means, as a lubricant to make an operation more efficient, is to not understand trust at all. Trust is, first of all, a central concept of ethics. And because of that, it turns out to be a valuable tool in business as well.

TRUST AS AN EMOTIONAL SKILL: SIMPLE TRUST, BLIND TRUST, AUTHENTIC TRUST

Trust is an emotional phenomenon. This is not to say that its significance is first of all "felt," or that it is merely transient. Trust, like love and indignation, finds its significance in the bonds it creates (or, better, in the bonds we create through such emotions), and it is the very essence of trust, like love (but unlike indignation), that it is enduring. Nevertheless (as with love) it may be cut short, betrayed, interrupted, and, on occasion, it may be all too fleeting, usually because it has been foolish. But trust, like all emotions, is dynamic. It defines our relationships and our relationship—our "being tuned"—to the world.

The importance of understanding emotion as a dynamic is essential to our view of emotion in general and trust in particular.[6] The contrast is the usual passivity picture of emotions as physiological interruptions of our lives that *happen to* us. Trust, in particular, is not something that simply happens, or is found or intuited. It is rather created through interaction and in the making of relationships. This is not to deny that there is an innate predisposition to trust, as evidenced so obviously in most babies, and it is compatible with the fact that trust may (tentatively) be established very quickly, within the first few minutes, of a relationship. But what this means is that we will have to be very careful how we talk about trust, careful that we do not collapse and confuse several very different phenomena.

Trust comes in various forms and degrees of sophistication and articulation. We can and ought to distinguish, just to begin with: *simple trust,* naive trust, trust as yet unchallenged, unquestioned (the faith of a well brought up child), *blind trust,* which is not actually naive but stubborn, obstinate, possibly even self-deluding, *basic trust,* which consists in the sense of physical and emotional security which most of us happily take for granted, which is most blatantly violated in war and in acts of random violence, and *authentic trust,* which is trust reflected upon, its risks and vulnerabilities understood, with *distrust* held in balance. (Distrust admits of similar distinctions and levels of sophistication.) Authentic trust, as opposed to simple trust, does not exclude or deny distrust but rather accepts it, even embraces it, but transcends it, absorbs it, overcomes it. With simple trust, one can always be surprised. The reasons for distrust are not even considered, much less taken seriously. Authentic trust can be betrayed, of course, but it is a betrayal that was foreseen as a possibility. There is no denial or self-deception, as in blind trust. There is no naivete, as in simple trust. Authentic trust need not be opposed to basic trust, but when basic trust is violated authentic trust sees clearly what trust remains. Once trust is spelled out, all sorts of new possibilities arise. It can be examined. It can be specified. It can be turned into explicit agreements and contracts. The mistake is to think that such agreements and contracts *precede* or *establish* trust. There can, of course, be agreements and contracts in the absence of trust, typically with elaborate enforcement mechanisms. But it is just as much of a mistake to conflate all trust with articulated trust as it is to conflate all trust with simple or basic (inarticulate) trust. The emotional life of trusting relationships is much more intricate and humanly complex than either contracts and cognitive interactive strategies or "non-cognitive security about motives" would alone allow.

Trust is created (and damaged) through dialogue, in conversation, by way of promises, commitments, offers, demands, expectations, explicit and tacit understandings. It is through such dialogue and conversation, including the rather one-way conversation of advertising, that producers make the nature and quality of their products known, that professionals and companies make their services and the abilities known, that expectations get initiated and intensified. This is not to say that trust is entirely linguistic, the product of promises and expectations verbally created. There is a good deal of trust embodied in our mere physical presence to one another, in our gestures, looks, smiles, handshakes and touches. Animals (especially "social" animals) have enormously complex trust relationships, often highly competitive at the same time, as any casual observation of two or more dogs (or wolves) together will confirm. Nor is the emphasis on dialogue and conversation suggested to imply—as so many social analyses too quickly conclude—that trust is an "agreement" or a "contract" (formal or informal). Contracts, too, are too static (although the negotiation of them, and negotiation out of them, may be dynamic indeed). Nor should trust be understood *primarily* in terms of limited or momentary interactions or transaction—or any number of them. Analyses of trust too often take as their paradigm either the most intimate of relationships—mother and child, husband and wife or lovers—or the most casual of them—notably, the one-shot business deal (for example, buying gas on the Interstate), or, the repeated one-shot business deal (buying gas at the same station on the way back down the Interstate). An interaction—even repeated interaction—is not yet a relationship, although, obviously, such repeated exchanges—and, occasionally,

even a single one, can easily turn into one. A relationship is by its very nature on-going and dynamic, in which one of the central concerns of the relationship is the relationship itself, its status and identity and, consequently, the status and identity of each and all of its members. Trust is an essential and "existential" dimension of that dynamic relationship.

With this in mind, we can understand why lying betrays trust and is so damaging. Even just one lie— or a serious exaggeration or attempt to "spin" the truth can undermine the accumulated trust and good will with which most of us approach new relationships and come to take for granted in established ones. Betrayal from a friend or neighbor may, with great difficulty, be overcome and eventually forgiven (though rarely forgotten), if only because these people are not easily eliminated from our lives. But betrayals in business, where associations are voluntary and there are always other possibilities, are typically fatal. Why work with or work a deal with someone you can no longer trust when there are so many others available?

REFERENCES

1. Daryl Koehn, "Should We Trust Trust?" *American Business Law Journal,* vol. 34(2), 1996: 184–203.

2. Francis Fukuyama, *Trust: The Social Virtues and the Creation of Prosperity* (New York: Free Press, 1996).

3. Blaze Starr was the long-time mistress of Louisana governor Earl Long. The line occurs in the movie, starring Paul Newman and Lolita Davidovich, *Blaze* (1989).

4. E.g., Dick Morris on Bill Clinton's campaign strategy, *Behind the Oval Office* (New York: Knopf, 1997)

5. Nicholas Luhmann, "Trust: A Mechanism for the Reduction of Social Complexity," in his *Trust and Power* (New York: Wiley, 1980) pp. 4–103.

6. Martin Heidegger, *Being and Time (Sein und Zeit),* trans. Joan Stambaugh (S.U.N.Y., 1996), esp. pp. 134–9.

QUESTIONS

1. Is there such a thing as too much trust? Explain.
2. What is "authentic trust"? What are the other forms of trust identified here?

CASES

CASE 3.1

Flying or Lying in Business Class

Robert C. Solomon

A few months ago, you graduated from business school and began working at National Inc. in New York City. It was exciting for you and your spouse to live in New York, but also very expensive, especially since you still have huge loans to pay off from college. Your boss at National is sending you to a conference in Amsterdam. This is a great opportunity for you to display your talents. New hires are watched closely to see if they have the maturity and sophistication to work with foreign clients.

At National employees have the option of getting an advance for their plane tickets, instead of paying for them and being reimbursed later. National also has a policy of sending employees business class on any flight of five hours or more. You were surprised at the amount of the advance for the business-class ticket and realize that you could use it to buy two coach tickets.

Your spouse has not yet found a job in New York and is getting a little depressed. When your spouse hears about the trip and expresses an interest in going with you, you agree that it is a good idea. You can't really afford a vacation, and it would be nice to stay in a good hotel and enjoy the sights in Amsterdam. Since the company is so large, and you submit your receipts to the accounting division, your boss would never know if you bought one or two tickets. Two coach tickets may even cost the company less money.

QUESTIONS

1. Should you ask your boss if you can use the money to buy two tickets?

2. Does the fact that the two coach tickets cost less justify not telling your boss?

CASE 3.2

Willful Ignorance? Or Deception?

Robert C. Solomon

Two contract hires have been working in the accounts department at a major bank for eight months. The manager of their section had worked with HR (human resources) in posting the job and had agreed to a starting salary of $29,500, which the two hires had accepted. In a review of the section, the manager received a list of employees and their salaries and noticed that the two were listed as being paid $35,900. The manager assumed that it was a typographical error, but notified HR for a correction. HR responded that the two were indeed receiving that amount. Neither employee had informed the manager at any time during his or her employment that the salary was higher than what they had been offered.

As their manager, what would you do?

QUESTIONS

1. What would you do if you were being (modestly) overpaid?
2. Should the employees have told? Why? Is it possible that they just didn't notice? If they didn't notice, does their responsibility change? Why?

CASE 3.3
Blindsided by Bankruptcy
Clancy Martin

You own a large chain of retail jewelry stores. Christmas was terrible and you are on the edge of bankruptcy. After a meeting with your attorneys and your banker, you realize it is, sadly, the time to file for a Chapter Eleven reorganization. Later that afternoon you are in your office and Rudolph Bultmann, your Rolex rep, calls you. "How was the season?" he asks. "Not what we hoped," you tell him. "Well don't worry. We are rolling out a whole new line and I want you to be the first to get it. It's a three million dollar commitment but I'll give you great terms on the credit." "What about the five million I already owe Rolex?" you ask him. "Don't worry so much. You'll catch up. You always do."

Rolex is an unsecured creditor, and you know they will be lucky to see pennies on the dollar for their debt. On the other hand, you desperately need the watches for your attempt to get through the Chapter Eleven. You remember what your attorney warned you: "Chapter Eleven is like an emergency room, and your inventory is the only medicine you've got. Stock up." You've been doing business with Bultmann for years. And you consider yourself to be a constitutionally honest person. On the other hand your company is at stake. What do you do?

QUESTIONS

1. You have two duties to yourself: a duty to be honest and a duty to your material prosperity. How do you decide between them?
2. What other duties do you have?

CASE 3.4
Testing for Honesty
William H. Shaw and Vincent Barry

"Charity begins at home." If you don't think so, ask the Salvation Army. Some years ago, one of the Army's local branches discovered that it had a problem with theft among its kettle workers, the people who collect money for the Army during the Christmas season. Some of the Army's kettlers were helping themselves to the Army's loot before the organization had a chance to dole it out. To put a stop to the problem, Army officials sought the assistance of Dr. John Jones, director of research for London House Management Consultants.

London House is one of several companies that market honesty tests for prospective employees. Some of these tests, such as London House's Personnel Selection Inventory (PSI), also measure the applicant's tendency toward drug use and violence. All three categories—honesty, drugs, and violence—play a major part in company losses, according to the makers of these tests.

The company losses in question are astronomical. The U.S. Chamber of Commerce estimates that employee theft costs U.S. companies $40 billion annually; some unofficial estimates run three times as high. Moreover, 20 percent of the businesses that fail do so because of employee crime. Compounding the problem is the cost of employee drug use in terms of absenteeism, lost initiative, inattentiveness, accidents, and diminished productivity. Employee violence also costs companies millions of dollars in damage, lost productivity, and lawsuits.

Honesty-test makers say that the only way to deal with these problems is before workers are hired, not after—by subjecting them to a preemployment psychological test that will identify those prospective employees who will be likely to steal, who have a history of violence or emotional instability, or who have used illegal drugs on a regular basis.

James Walls, one of the founders of Stanton Corporation, which has offered written honesty tests for twenty-five years, says that dishonest job applicants are clever at hoodwinking potential employers in a job interview. "They have a way of conducting themselves that is probably superior to the low-risk person. They have learned what it takes to be accepted and how to overcome the normal interview strategy," he says. "The high-risk person will get hired unless there is a way to screen him." For this reason, Walls maintains, written, objective tests are needed to weed out the crooks. [Walls]

Millions of written honesty tests are given annually. Since 1988 demand has been booming as a result of congressional restrictions on polygraph testing, which prohibit about 85 percent of applicant and employee polygraph testing in the United States. As a result, purveyors of written tests have also been in high demand: The British Maxwell Communication Corporation, for instance, spent $17.4 million to acquire London House; Business Risk International took over the Stanton Corporation; and Wackenhut Corporation of Coral Gables, Florida, acquired marketing rights to the Phase II Profile, a widely used honesty test.

In addition to being legal, honesty tests are also more economical than polygraph tests. They cost between $7 and $14 per test, compared with $90 or so for a polygraph. Furthermore, the tests are easily administered at the workplace by a staff member to any category of worker, are easily and quickly evaluated by the test maker, and assess the applicant's overall answers rather than a few isolated responses.

From William H. Shaw and Vincent Barry, *Moral Issues in Business* (Belmont, CA: Wadsworth, 2001). Notes were deleted from this text.

The tests are also nondiscriminatory. The Equal Employment Opportunity Commission's "Uniform Guidelines on Employee Selection Procedures" (1978) permits tests that measure psychological traits because the race, gender, or ethnicity of applicants has no significant impact on scores.

A typical test begins with some cautionary remarks. Test-takers are told to be truthful because dishonesty can be detected, and they are warned that incomplete answers will be considered incorrect, as will any unanswered questions. Then applicants ordinarily sign a waiver permitting the results to be known to their prospective employer and authorizing the testing agency to check out their answers. Sometimes, however, prospective employees are not told that they are being tested for honesty, only that they are being asked questions about their background. James Walls justifies this less-than-frank explanation by saying that within a few questions it is obvious that the test deals with attitudes toward honesty. "The test is very transparent, it's not subtle." [Walls]

Some questions do indeed seem transparent—for example, "If you found $100 that was lost by a bank truck on the street yesterday, would you turn the money over to the bank, even though you knew for sure there was no reward?" But other questions are more controversial: "Have you ever had an argument with someone and later wished you had said something else?" If you were to answer no, you would be on your way to failing. Other questions that may face the test-taker are: "How strong is your conscience?" "How often do you feel guilty?" "Do you always tell the truth?" "Do you occasionally have thoughts you wouldn't want made public?" "Does everyone steal a little?" "Do you enjoy stories of successful crimes?" "Have you ever been so intrigued by the cleverness of a thief that you hoped the person would escape detection?" Or consider questions like "Is an employee who takes it easy at work cheating his employer?" or "Do you think a person should be fired by a company if it is found that he helped employees cheat the company out of overtime once in a while?" These ask you for your reaction to hypothetical dishonest situations. "If you are a particularly kind-hearted person who isn't sufficiently punitive, you fail," says Lewis Maltby, director of the workplace rights office at the American Civil Liberties Union. "Mother Teresa would never pass some of these tests." [Maltby]

A big part of some tests is a behavioral history of the applicant. Applicants are asked to reveal the nature, frequency, and quantity of specific drug use, if any. They also must indicate if they have ever engaged in drunk driving, illegal gambling, traffic violations, forgery, vandalism, and a host of other unseemly behaviors. They must also state their opinions about the social acceptability of drinking alcohol and using other drugs.

Some testing companies go further in this direction. Instead of honesty exams, they offer tests designed to draw a general psychological profile of the applicant, claiming that this sort of analysis can predict more accurately than either the polygraph or the typical honesty test how the person will perform on the job. Keith M. Halperin, a psychologist with Personnel Decision, Inc. (PDI), a company that offers such tests, complains that most paper-and-pencil honesty tests are simply written equivalents of the polygraph. They ask applicants whether they have stolen from their employers, how much they have taken, and other questions directly related to honesty. But why, asks Halperin, "would an applicant who is dishonest enough to steal from an employer be honest enough to admit it on a written test?" It is more difficult for applicants to fake their responses to PDI's tests, Halperin contends.

Not everyone is persuaded. Phyllis Bassett, vice-president of James Bassett Company of Cincinnati, believes tests developed by psychologists that do not ask directly about the applicant's past honesty are poor predictors of future trustworthiness. This may be because, as some psychologists report, "it is very difficult for dishonest people to fake honesty." One reason is that thieves tend to believe that "everybody does it" and that therefore it would be implausible for them to deny stealing. In general, those who market honesty exams boast of their validity and reliability, as established by field studies. They insist that the tests do make a difference, that they enable employers to ferret out potential troublemakers—as in the Salvation Army case.

Dr. Jones administered London House's PSI to eighty kettler applicants, which happened to be the number that the particular theft-ridden center needed. The PSIs were not scored, and the eighty applicants were hired with no screening. Throughout the fund-raising month between Thanksgiving and Christmas, the center kept a record of each kettler's daily receipts. After the Christmas season, the tests were scored and divided into "recommended" and "not recommended" for employment. After accounting for the peculiarities of each collection neighborhood, Jones discovered that those kettlers the PSI had not recommended turned in on the average $17 per day less than those the PSI had recommended. Based on this analysis, he estimated the center's loss to employee theft during the fund drive at $20,000.

The list of psychological-test enthusiasts is growing by leaps and bounds, but the tests have plenty of detractors. Many psychologists have voiced concern over the lack of standards governing the tests; the American Psychological Association favors the establishment of federal standards for written honesty exams. But the chief critics of honesty and other psychological exams are the people who have to take them. They complain about having to reveal some of the most intimate details of their lives and opinions.

For example, until an employee filed suit, Rent-A-Center, a Texas corporation, asked both job applicants and employees being considered for promotion true-false questions like these: "I have never indulged in any unusual sex practices," "I am very strongly attracted by members of my own sex," "I go to church almost every week," and "I have difficulty in starting or holding my bowel movements." A manager who was fired for complaining about the test says, "It was ridiculous. The test asked if I loved tall women. How was I supposed to answer that? My wife is 5 feet 3 inches." A spokesman for Rent-A-Center argues that its questionnaire is not unusual and that many other firms use it.

Firms who use tests like Rent-A-Center's believe that no one's privacy is being invaded because employees and job applicants can always refuse to take the test. Critics disagree. "Given the unequal bargaining power," says former ACLU official Kathleen Bailey, "the ability to refuse to take a test is one of theory rather than choice—if one really wants the job." [Bailey]

QUESTION

1. Describe how you'd feel having to take a psychological test or an honesty test either as an employee or as a precondition for employment. Would you take the test? Why or why not?

CASE 3.5

The Columbia Shuttle Disaster: Should We Have Told the Astronauts the Truth?

Margaret P. Battin and Gordon B. Mower

The space shuttle Columbia exploded in 2003, killing all seven astronauts aboard. M. Battin and G. Mower teach at the University of Utah.

There is a deep ethical dilemma in the Columbia shuttle disaster that's been overlooked by both principals and commentators. Linda Ham didn't recognize it; neither did the Mission Management Team, or the Photo Working Group, or the Program Manger for Launch Integration, or the Debris Assessment Team, or commentators like Donovan and Green or Davis—or, perhaps, they somehow subliminally recognized it but all assumed it should be decided in the same way.

There was a genuine moral issue here. Assume that, as soon as the photos were taken, it became apparent that the tile damage was much greater than on any previous mission. Indeed, let us suppose that the gravity of the situation was fully recognized by ground control. There didn't seem to be any way out—once the shuttle was aloft, it wouldn't have been possible to dock with the space station, and it wouldn't have been possible to rescue the astronauts. This might lead us to think that, as Linda Ham apparently did, "there isn't anything I can do."

But there is something of significant ethical importance that you could do; the question is whether you *should* do it or not. After all, as we're assuming, you know there is a high probability that the astronauts will die on reentry—but *they* don't know it. Would you tell them? Ham, and apparently all others, have assumed no. Yet this is not at all obvious, and indeed different ethical approaches to the question may yield quite different answers.

We might wonder, to begin with, what it is about the ethical course of not disclosing to the astronauts their impending fate that seemingly makes it so appealing to our moral intuitions. Nobody told the astronauts what very well could happen on reentry, and without access to the discussions of those concerned with tile loss, they had no way to know it themselves. Can we find support in ethical reasoning for our reticence? To do so, perhaps our reasoning takes a certain direction that we might find in other kinds of moral decision-making: let's consider several different seemingly analogous cases.

First, let's say that there is a military operation in which the leaders of the operation know that there is a reasonable chance that certain units will be destroyed by the enemy. Nevertheless, other units in the operation are dependent on these doomed units performing their part of the operation. Should the leaders of the operation inform the members of the endangered units that they are most likely to die? Wouldn't this knowledge affect their performance, thereby jeopardizing the mission and the lives of others? Isn't it the case that in the military profession, sometimes leaders know that certain people are about to die, but not only do they not tell them, they also exaggerate their chances for survival? In this profession, the ethical perspective might be one that emphasizes a primarily Utilitarian view of things— that one ought to try to promote the greater good for the greater number, even at some cost to a few.

There are all kinds of ways we can imagine in which informing the astronauts of the real risks they faced might affect their performance in ways that could affect others. It is, after all, a very powerful

From *Teaching Ethics*, Fall 2003, pp 89–91. Reprinted with permission of the Board of Directors of *Teaching Ethics*.

impulse to pursue one's own survival. If they knew of the damage to the tiles, for example, would they perhaps engage in an unauthorized space walk in an attempt to jury-rig some kind of tile repair, perhaps forgetting their research projects or releasing uncharted debris into space, the tiniest fragment of which could have catastrophic effects on future shuttle and space missions? Would they collapse from emotional stress, or even harm each other there in their small, now-lethal cocoon? The astronauts are about to die in the performance of their own professional duties. Not performing them well could affect others. But if there is a chance of survival, even a slim one, wouldn't their performance level be diminished by the stress of knowing their fate? This is an argument for not telling them what we know.

But if this were a case in medical ethics, the assumption would be made just the other way around. Suppose, for example, that you're a physician, and have seven cancer patients, each of whom will die. Would you tell them the truth? Yes, of course; truthtelling even in fatal cancer diagnoses is now standard practice in medicine—though physicians try to do so with tact, empathy, and understanding. Among the standard arguments for truthtelling are that people who are facing death should be allowed to have time to say goodbyes, to set their affairs in order, to make amends, or, if they're religious, to make whatever final confessions and prayers they wish. This is what it is to respect persons, as Kant might put it, to recognize them as ends in themselves, able to determine in accord with their own values how they choose to spend the last moments of their lives. This is a deontological response to the deep moral problem here: whatever the consequences, it would be wrong to lie to the astronauts or to deprive them of the truth. It would be wrong to rob them of autonomous choice during their last moments, and of the knowledge that these are their last moments.

But isn't this just what happened, out there in space? If we know there's a reasonable chance the seven astronauts will die, and that there's nothing we can do to save them, shouldn't we tell them? Would they live that last week any differently? Surely, in undertaking a space mission in the first place, they would have made their wills, put their affairs in order, told their spouses and their children that they loved them. But now suppose that they knew the end was really coming. Would they communicate differently? Live differently among themselves, there in the spaceship? Try to extend the length of the voyage until their supplies ran out? Or vote to "reenter" earlier, so that the fearsome end would be over sooner? Plead for help? Or send consoling messages to Earth, recognizing that this is a risk they voluntarily assumed and that they are willing to bear? There are many possibilities for heroism and despair, insight and cowardice, and the whole range of human emotion and reflection—not easy to bear but part of full human life—even one about to be made abruptly short. How will they live this week, before what may be a catastrophic end? These are the things the astronauts themselves should have a hand in deciding, not that should be decided by others.

If we move in the direction favored by Linda Ham, Mission Management, Launch Integration, Debris Assessment, the various commentators, and perhaps our own initial inclinations, we opt for a high dose of paternalism at one of the most significant points in the lives of these people. Perhaps we believe that this knowledge really is more harmful to the astronauts and to others than keeping it from them. Under such a belief, perhaps consequentialism trumps deontology. If, however, we are simply keeping the astronauts in the dark to protect them against their own fears, or even to protect ourselves against our anxieties for them, then this seems an unreasonable cost to their autonomy. Of course it would be painful to know the end was coming; but it would take a resolute paternalism to shield them from this knowledge, something we would not tolerate in other professions who work with people who know they are about to die.

QUESTIONS

1. Should they have told the astronauts the truth? Why or why not?

2. Why might being lied to be a good thing? Are there times when you would rather be lied to?

CHAPTER QUESTIONS

1. In business (and in life), does honesty mean different things in different contexts? Is honesty on a used-car lot different from honesty in a classroom? Or honesty among friends? But once you contextualize honesty, do you open yourself up to deception? Is there such a thing as Enron-style honesty?

2. How does secrecy relate to honesty? What about bluffing? Should we feel guilty about keeping secrets? Why or why not? Should we feel guilty about bluffing? How, when, and why are we allowed to control the truth? When and why is complete disclosure or transparency obviously undesirable?

4

The Good Life

Introduction

Of course, you want to be a success in business or in whatever enterprise you engage in. But what is success? How do you measure it? How will you know when you have achieved it? It is naturally tempting to postpone these questions, perhaps with a glib answer like "when I've got more money than I can spend" or "when I have it, I'll know it." But the truth is less obvious. Many people achieve the success that they sought as students, whether measured in dollars or in status, and only then realize that they were working for the wrong goal, that what they have earned turns out not to be what they really want or wanted. In the worst cases, people come to realize that they have wasted the best years of their lives. Psychiatrists document so many cases of "workaholism" and self-destructive goal setting in which people work and strive because they feel compelled to, perhaps imitating their parents or following what they take to be their parents constant prodding and expectations. People ignore their families, working for success, only to realize too late that they have neglected their families even as they were supporting them, that they missed the opportunity to watch their children growing up or enjoy their hard-earned wealth when they were most able to do so. Success thus means not just wealth and "making a living." It involves the wise use of one's time, a sense of balance between one's career and one's "personal life," a continuing sense of what one wants and what is ultimately worthwhile, a "balance" between one's work and the rest of one's life, even where one loves one's work so much that it is difficult to separate the two.

Business ethics, like all ethics, is not just concerned with "doing the right thing." It is not all about ethical dilemmas and hard choices. Business ethics, like all ethics, is first of all concerned with living a good life, getting the most out of one's years, and forging the most satisfying relationships with one's family, friends, and community. What makes you happy is just as much a focus of business ethics as telling the truth and building trust with your colleagues and your customers. Indeed, it is hard to separate the two, insofar as it is difficult to imagine being happy while alienating your friends and being distrustful of everyone. So what this chapter is about is the larger frame within which business success is measured and meaningful. That frame is life itself, the good life, which in many ways remains much the same for you as it would have been back in ancient times. Aristotle built his entire ethics around the question "what is happiness (*eudaimonia*)?" And his answer was that happiness is a life of virtue as well as pleasure, friendship as well as excellence in whatever it is you do. But it is not as if one simply achieves this through luck or good fortune or good upbringing (although all these may be a big advantage). Happiness is the result of practical wisdom and understanding. It is the result of planning. So as you put so much effort into preparing for your career, you had better make some time to plan for your life as well, and not just fill in the decreasing number of spaces between job assignments and pressures with friends, romance, excitement, and happiness.

Even in Aristotle's time, the temptation to misjudge one's own needs and desires was pervasive. Aristotle's teacher, Plato, had a good word for it, *"pleonexia,"* "grasping," or what we would loosely translate as *greed.* We hear a great deal about greed these days—top executives who never seem to have enough, despite obvious excesses and extravagances; financial managers, stockbrokers, and other agents who bilk their clients and the customers just for the sake of a little bit *more;* shareholders and customers who insist on a bit more profit or a better bargain without regard for where that money or savings is coming from and whose lives may be damaged or destroyed. But the problem with greed is not just the often-innocent victims who are hurt by it. As Plato and Aristotle knew very well, and as the medieval saints who listed greed ("avarice") as one of the seven deadly sins knew, too, greed has its most horrendous effects on the greedy themselves. Greed ruins lives. Greed runs the hardest after goals that contribute nothing to happiness but distract and detract from it. And foremost among these goals today, as it has been for thousands of years, is the pursuit of wealth. The ancient story of King Midas is as much a lesion for today's aspiring business students as it was for the students of Plato's Academy. Midas was a man who treasured gold above all else, and when he got his wish, that whatever he touched would turn to gold (a wish often put in the same terms by many of today's business students), that magical success became a lethal curse. One cannot eat or drink gold. Money, we are told, cannot buy love. (Although it is sometimes quipped, it can rent it for a while.) Money is little comfort to the deeply unhappy, although the perverse nature of greed is such that even when it is wealth that it is the source of unhappiness (for instance, in terms of enemies made, "friends" who cannot be trusted, opportunities missed or wasted in the pursuit of narrow business "success"), the illusion is that more wealth will make things better. But quite to the contrary, the pursuit of wealth often blinds us to what we really want.

None of this is to attack wealth or aspiration or success. Plato and Aristotle hung out with the wealthiest and most powerful men in Greece. (Alexander the Great was one of Aristotle's students, for example.) But wealth has its place. It is a means and not an end in itself. Knowing what one wants is knowing, in part, what it will cost, not just in terms of money but in terms of time, friendship, opportunities for adventure, and any number of other considerations that cannot be easily valued or measured by the market. As one of our current California wise men, Sam Keen, has put it, "the most important thing is knowing just how little one needs to be happy." The good life is the measure of success, and how much money one makes is just one of its many ingredients.

The following readings have been chosen to help you think philosophically about what you ultimately want out of life, not in terms of material acquisitions (a house, a couple of cars, a second house), but in terms the essential ingredients in happiness, which includes thinking about what you want to do with wealth when you get it. So we start with some classic readings from Aristotle and Epicurus, two Greek philosophers who thought a great deal about the question of what it takes to be happy. Then Andrew Carnegie, one of America's richest men in the nineteenth century, offers a meditation on the question of what to do with wealth when you get it. On the other hand, too much emphasis on wealth acquisition can be injurious to your life and happiness. Solomon Schimmel offers us a historical picture of the "deadly sin" of greed. Then, shifting gears, Joanne Ciulla discusses the role of leisure and consumption in the good life, and the great English philosopher Bertrand Russell quips on "idleness" in response to the old warning that "the devil makes work for idle hands." Shifting gears again, philosophers Lynn McFall and Cheshire Calhoun discuss the all-important virtue of integrity. We then offer a longer piece from Bertrand Russell on the importance of "impersonal" interests (as opposed to those that look to self-interest). Finally, just to make sure that this doesn't seem too far removed from the business of ethics, a stark reminder from Robert Solomon about why ethics is essential to the life well lived, if only as matter of prudence. The cases, too, are designed to help you think philosophically about what you want out of life. Success? At what cost? Achievement of one's objectives? But can this become a distraction from more important values? Happiness? But what is this? How about a life of pure pleasure without responsibilities, cares, or disappointments? Finally, from one of America's great playwrights, an account of a life badly lived—from Arthur Miller's *Death of a Salesman*.

Robert C. Solomon

Strategic Planning— For the Good Life

Young business people are often encouraged these days to make out a "plan" for themselves—where they would like to be in a year, in five years, perhaps more. An entire course at Harvard Business School is devoted to career planning—what sort of position to seek first, when to move, etc. But what is tragically lacking is analogous *life* planning, with an eye not only to such obvious life stages as marriage, children, and retirement and one or two hobbies for one's "spare time" (a revealing phrase) but also to other interests and aspects of one's personality. Not surprisingly, an informal survey of 1983 MBAs six months out of Harvard showed that nearly half were already frustrated with their jobs and their lives, though they had been equipped to understand and analyze only the former.

There is a sense, of course, in which the good life cannot be planned. Emergencies and tragedies are usually not predictable, and in business the details of the job market, politics, and the business cycle—even if explicable to future historians—provide the wild cards in the game of life. Planning when to get married—when one does not already have a specific person in mind—strikes us as not only unromantic but also foolish. Risks are a part of life—and sometimes desirable. But risks can be foolish as well as invigorating, and they can be planned for. Chance may be as essential to life as the search for security, but chance—paradoxically—does not "just happen." Chance too can be planned and evaluated, and there is a world of difference between being ready to welcome unexpected opportunity and being shocked and unprepared for it. Much of our unhappiness, in fact, is not the result of misfortune or bad luck. It is bad planning, or no planning, no sorting out of priorities *before* we find ourselves neck-deep in responsibilities and obligations or over our heads in a life we never really wanted in the first place.

Life in today's fast-moving world is not so unpredictable as the future shockers would tell us. Modes of communication and transportation—not to mention warfare—may be evolving at a terrifying speed, but the essentials of the good life remain remarkably constant: friendship, family life and time to enjoy it, a sense of fulfillment, the respect of one's neighbors and self-respect besides, the basic comforts of life, good health and the "good things" that money will buy (whatever those happen to be this year or decade). Is there really so much difference between wanting to own an expensive car in this century and desiring a fine carriage in the last one? Were the food and wine better in the Middle Ages, or was friendship any more enjoyable in ancient Rome? As we become ever more efficient and productive, how is it that we seem to have less time rather than more, and have fewer ideas about what to do?

A plan for the good life means something more than listing one's career ambitions and possibilities and something more than listing the things that one enjoys. A plan for the good life means, first of all, knowing your needs, your ideals and aspirations as a human being. One joins a firm with business and management objectives in mind; it is not unreasonable to keep in mind also a set of life management goals. If one can set one's sights on a promotion by the end of the first year, why not set a goal of friendship for that period, too? One might argue that in life, "management by objective" is compulsive and neurotic—if indeed it is pursued in too businesslike a manner. But when business life is so carefully planned and orchestrated, the rest of life is too easily forced into the odd or spare moments, or neglected altogether. Strangely enough, the risks and shocks we think of as the challenge of business are reserved for our personal lives, where they are usually much

From Robert C. Solomon *It's Good Business: Ethics and Enterprise for the New Millennium,* (Lanham: Rowman/Littlefield, 1998). Reprinted with permission of the author.

less welcome. Ethics and the good life get sacrificed not because of immorality or stupidity but simply because they are not part of the only plan in town.

What kinds of questions go into a plan for the good life? First of all, questions about yourself, what you want, expect, enjoy and need: security, freedom, companionship, privacy, power, friendship, great wealth, or just to be recognized as a success.

1. What do you consider the most important things in life? Success, family, companionship, romantic love, money, status and position, respect, friendship. Which could you live without, or have only in small doses? Which could you not live without, or have only in substantial doses?   ·

2. What do you most enjoy doing? Imagine yourself left entirely to choose on your own, without financial pressures, without expecting rewards or compensations beyond the activity itself. What would (or do) you choose to do? Listen to music? Play tennis? Build things? Have a quiet dinner with an intimate friend? Be alone, doing nothing? Work?

3. What kind of people do you like to spend your time with? Work with? Are they the kind of people you are spending time with now? Are you the kind of person they would want to spend time with? Do you enjoy people who inspire you? What are your primary expectations in a friend? In a colleague? In a boss? (Most of us conscientiously choose our subordinates; it is much more important to be careful in choosing a boss.)

4. How do you see yourself, ideally? How would you describe yourself in a paragraph, say, for a future *Who's Who* emphasizing not positions and awards but character and accomplishments? How well are you working toward that now?

5. How important is so-called spare time to you? How much do you need? What do you (or would you) do with it? Is spare time to you just time to relax and get ready for more work? (Living to work used to be a virtue, until psychiatrists gave it a pathological name: "workaholism." But the fact remains that loving one's work is one of the few dependable roads to happiness.) Is your spare time more important than your work? (Then why are you working so hard?)

6. Where would you draw the line in your job? What would you not do, even at the risk of being fired? Work seventeen-hour days, and weekends? Have to fire a good friend? Make false reports? Lie to your boss? Get ahead at the expense of someone who deserves it more? Be responsible—even indirectly—for some innocent person's death? (Better to be clear about these things *before* the topic comes up unexpectedly, under pressure.)

7. What is your ethical style? What kinds of arguments do you use to support your ideas? What kind of person do you find immoral? Do you resent people who obey the letter of the law? Do you find people who don't give arguments to be frustrating?

8. Whom do you want to please? ("Yourself" is the fashionable but usually false answer. "My mother" and "my father" are a bit overworked, thanks to Freud. Try again.)

9. How much money do you need? How much do you want? Why? Suppose you suddenly inherit $400,000. What would you do with it? Is that so important?

10. What do you want to be doing next year, this time, in your job and out of it?

11. What do you want to be doing five years from now—what kind of job, what kind of life? Does the idea of doing just what you are doing now (plus a little status and some cost-of-living increases) horrify you? Or does it give you a sense of pleasant comfort?

12. Looking back over your life and career from your rocking chair, what would you like to remember—and how would you like to be remembered?

QUESTIONS

1. Can you plan your life—or is it all just luck or fate?

2. What are your top five values? If you had to eliminate one, which would it be? Could you live without love, for example, if you knew that by doing so you would earn a million dollars a year?

Aristotle | # On the Good Life

Aristotle was one of the two greatest Greek philosophers of ancient times. His ethics is wholly devoted to an examination of happiness (*eudaimonia*) and the good life.

Each man judges well the things he knows, and of these he is a good judge. And so the man who has been educated in a subject is a good judge of that subject, and the man who has received an all-round education is a good judge in general. Hence a young man is not a proper hearer of lectures on political science; for he is inexperienced in the actions that occur in life, but its discussions start from these and are about these; and, further, since he tends to follow his passions, his study will be vain and unprofitable, because the end aimed at is not knowledge but action. And it makes no difference whether he is young in years or youthful in character; the defect does not depend on time, but on his living, and pursuing each successive object, as passion directs. For to such persons, as to the incontinent, knowledge brings no profit; but to those who desire and act in accordance with a rational principle knowledge about such matters will be of great benefit.

These remarks about the student, the sort of treatment to be expected, and the purpose of the inquiry, may be taken as our preface.

What is the highest of all goods achievable by action [as opposed to mere good fortune and those achievable by pure thought and contemplation]? Verbally, there is very general agreement; for both the general run of men and people of superior refinement say that it is happiness, and identify living well and doing well with being happy; but with regard to what happiness is they differ, and the many do not give the same account as the wise. For the former think it is some plain and obvious thing, like pleasure wealth, or honour; they differ, however, from one another—and often even the same man identifies it with different things, with health when he is ill, with wealth when he is poor; but, conscious of their ignorance, they admire those who proclaim some great ideal that is above their comprehension.

To judge from the lives that men lead, most men, and men of the most vulgar type, seem (not without some ground) to identify the good, or happiness, with pleasure; which is the reason why they love the life of enjoyment. For there are, we may say, three prominent types of life—that just mentioned, the political, and thirdly the contemplative life. Now the mass of mankind are evidently quite slavish in their tastes, preferring a life suitable to beasts, but they get some ground for their view from the fact that many of those in high places share the tastes of Sardanapallus. A consideration of the prominent types of life shows that people of superior refinement and of active disposition identify happiness with honour; for this is, roughly speaking, the end of the political life. But it seems too superficial to be what we are looking for, since it is thought to depend on those who bestow honour rather than on him who receives it, but the good we divine to be something proper to a man and not easily taken from him. Further, men seem to pursue honour in order that they may be assured of their goodness; at least it is by men of practical wisdom that they seek to be honoured, and among those who know them, and on the ground of their virtue; clearly, then, according to them, at any rate, virtue is better. And perhaps one might even suppose this to be, rather than honour, the end of the political life. But even this appears somewhat incomplete; for possession of virtue seems actually compatible with being asleep, or with lifelong inactivity, and, further, with the greatest sufferings and misfortunes; but a man who was living so no one would call happy, unless he were

From the *Nicomachean Ethics* (translated by W. D. Ross, Oxford University Press, 1915).

maintaining a thesis at all costs. But enough of this; for the subject has been sufficiently treated even in the current discussions. Third comes the contemplative life, which we shall consider later.

The life of money-making is one undertaken under compulsion, and wealth is evidently not the good we are seeking; for it is merely useful and for the sake of something else. And so one might rather take the aforenamed objects to be ends; for they are loved for themselves. But it is evident that not even these are ends; yet many arguments have been thrown away in support of them.

The function of man is an activity of the soul which follows or implies a rational principle, and the function of a good man is the good and noble performance of these in accordance with the appropriate virtue or excellence, so the good for man turns out to be an activity of soul in accordance with virtue, and if there are more than one virtue, in accordance with the best and most complete. But we should add, "in a complete life." For one swallow does not make a summer, nor one day; and so too one day, or a short time, does not make a man blessed or happy.

So the argument has reached this point; Since there are evidently more than one end, and we choose some of these (e.g. wealth, flutes, and in general instruments) for the sake of something else, clearly not all ends are final ends; but the chief good is evidently something final. Therefore, if there is only one final end, this will be what we are seeking, and if there are more than one, the most final of these will be what we are seeking. Now we call that which is in itself worthy of pursuit more final than that which is worthy of pursuit for the sake of something else, and that which is never desirable for the sake of something else more final than the things that are desirable both in themselves and for the sake of that other thing, and therefore we call final without qualification that which is always desirable in itself and never for the sake of something else.

Now such a thing happiness, above all else, is held to be; for this we choose always for itself and never for the sake of something else, but honour, pleasure, reason, and every virtue we choose indeed for themselves (for if nothing resulted from them we should still choose each of them), but we choose them also for the sake of happiness, judging that by means of them we shall be happy. Happiness, on the other hand, no one chooses for the sake of these, nor, in general, for anything other than itself.

From the point of view of self-sufficiency the same result seems to follow; for the final good is thought to be self-sufficient. Now by self-sufficient we do not mean that which is sufficient for a man by himself, for one who lives a solitary life, but also for parents, children, wife, and in general for his friends and fellow citizens, since man is born for citizenship. But some limit must be set to this; for if we extend our requirement to ancestors and descendants and friends' friends we are in for an infinite series. Let us examine this question, however, on another occasion; the self-sufficient we now define as that which when isolated makes life desirable and lacking in nothing; and such we think happiness to be; and further we think it most desirable of all things, without being counted as one good thing among others—if it were so counted it would clearly be made more desirable by the addition of even the least of goods; for that which is added becomes an excess of goods, and of goods the greater is always more desirable. Happiness, then, is something final and self-sufficient and is the end of action.

———————

We must take as a sign of states of character the pleasure or pain that ensues on acts; for the man who abstains from bodily pleasures and delights in this very fact is temperate, while the man who is annoyed at it is self-indulgent, and he who stands his ground against things that are terrible and delights in this or at least is not pained is brave, while the man who is pained is a coward. For moral excellence is concerned with pleasures and pains; it is on account of the pleasure that we do bad things, and on account of the pain that we abstain from noble ones. Hence we ought to have been brought up in a particular way from our very youth, as Plato says, so as both to delight in and to be pained by the things that we ought; for this is the right education.

Again, if the virtues are concerned with actions and passions, and every passion and every action is accompanied by pleasure and pain, for this reason also virtue will be concerned with pleasures and pains. This is indicated also by the fact that punishment is inflicted by these means; for it is a kind of cure, and it is the nature of cures to be effected by contraries.

After these matters we ought perhaps next to discuss pleasure. For it is thought to be most intimately connected with our human nature, which is the reason why in educating the young we steer them by the rudders of pleasure and pain; it is thought, too, that to enjoy the things we ought and to hate the things we ought has the greatest bearing on virtue of character. For these things extend right through life, with a weight and power of their own in respect both to virtue and to the happy life, since men choose what is pleasant and avoid what is painful; and such things, it will be thought, we should least of all omit to discuss, especially since they admit of much dispute. For some say pleasure is the good, while others, on the contrary, say it is thoroughly bad—some no doubt being persuaded that the facts are so, and others thinking it has a better effect on our life to exhibit pleasure as a bad thing even if it is not; for most people (they think) incline towards it and are the slaves of their pleasures, for which reason they ought to lead them in the opposite direction, since thus they will reach the middle state. But surely this is not correct. For arguments about matters concerned with feelings and actions are less reliable than facts: and so when they clash with the facts of perception they are despised, and discredit the truth as well; if a man who runs down pleasure is once seen to be aiming at it, his inclining towards it is thought to imply that it is all worthy of being aimed at; for most people are not good at drawing distinctions. True arguments seem, then, most useful, not only with a view to knowledge, but with a view to life also; for since they harmonize with the facts they are believed, and so they stimulate those who understand them to live according to them.

Eudoxus thought pleasure was the good because he saw all things, both rational and irrational, aiming at it, and because in all things that which is the object of choice is what is excellent, and that which is most the object of choice the greatest good; thus the fact that all things moved towards the same object indicated that this was for all things the chief good (for each thing, he argued, finds its own good, as it finds its own nourishment); and that which is good for all things and at which all aim was *the* good. His arguments were credited more because of the excellence of his character than for their own sake; he was thought to be remarkably self-controlled, and therefore it was thought that he was not saying what he did say as a friend of pleasure, but that the facts really were so. He believed that the same conclusion followed no less plainly from a study of the contrary of pleasure; pain was in itself an object of aversion to all things, and therefore its contrary must be similarly an object of choice. And again that is most an object of choice which we choose not because or for the sake of something else, and pleasure is admittedly of this nature; for no one asks to what end he is pleased; thus implying that pleasure is in itself an object of choice. Further, he argued that pleasure when added to any good, e.g. to just or temperate action, makes it more worthy of choice, and that it is only by itself that the good can be increased.

This argument seems to show it to be one of the goods, and no more a good than any other; for every good is more worthy of choice along with another good than taken alone. And so it is by an argument of this kind that Plato proves the good *not* to be pleasure; he argues that the pleasant life is more desirable with wisdom than without, and that if the mixture is better, pleasure is not the good; for the good cannot become more desirable by the addition of anything to it. Now it is clear that nothing else, any more than pleasure, can be the good if it is made more desirable by the addition of any of the things that are good in themselves. What, then, is there that satisfies this criterion, which at the same time we can participate in? It is something of this sort that we are looking for.

In reply to those who bring forward the disgraceful pleasures one may say that these are not pleasant; if things are pleasant to people of vicious constitution, we must not suppose that they are also pleasant to others than these, just as we do not reason so about the things that are wholesome or sweet or bitter to sick

Adam Smith on Capitalism

If we examine, I say, all these things, and consider what a variety of labor is employed about each of them, we shall be sensible that without the assistance and co-operation of many thousands, the very meanest person in a civilized country could not be provided, even according to what we very falsely imagine the easy and simple manner in which he is commonly accommodated. Compared, indeed, with the more extravagant luxury of the great, his accommodation must no doubt appear extremely simple and easy; and yet it may be true, perhaps, that the accommodation of an European prince does not always so much exceed that of an industrious and frugal peasant, as the accommodation of the latter exceeds that of many an African king, the absolute master of the lives and liberties of ten thousand naked savages.

From *The Wealth of Nations*

---

people, or ascribe whiteness to the things that seem white to those suffering from a disease of the eye. Or one might answer thus—that the pleasures are desirable, but not from *these* sources, as wealth is desirable, but not as the reward of betrayal, and health, but not at the cost of eating anything and everything. Or perhaps pleasures differ in kind; for those derived from noble sources are different from those derived from base sources, and one cannot get the pleasure of the just man without being just, nor that of the musical man without being musical, and so on. . . .

No one would choose to live with the intellect of a child throughout his life, however much he were to be pleased at the things that children are pleased at, nor to get enjoyment by doing some most disgraceful deed, though he were never to feel any pain, in consequence. And there are many things we should be keen about even if they brought no pleasure, e.g. seeing, remembering, knowing, possessing the virtues. If pleasures necessarily do accompany these, that makes no odds; we should choose these even if no pleasure resulted. It seems to be clear, then, that neither is pleasure the good nor is all pleasure desirable, and that some pleasures *are* desirable in themselves, differing in kind or in their sources from the others. So much for the things that are said about pleasure and pain.

Since every sense is active in relation to its object,

and a sense which is in good condition acts perfectly in relation to the most beautiful of its objects (for perfect activity seems to be ideally of this nature; whether we say that *it* is active, or the organ in which it resides, may be assumed to be immaterial), it follows that in the case of each sense the best activity is that of the best-conditioned organ in relation to the finest of its objects. And this activity will be the most complete and pleasant. For, while there is pleasure in respect of any sense, and in respect of thought and contemplation no less, the most complete is pleasantest, and that of a well-conditioned organ in relation to the worthiest of its objects is the most complete; and the pleasure completes the activity. But the pleasure does not complete it in the same way as the combination of object and sense, both good, just as health and the doctor are not in the same way the cause of a man's being healthy. (That pleasure is produced in respect to each sense is plain; for we speak of sights and sounds as pleasant. It is also plain that it arises most of all when both the sense is at its best and it is active in reference to an object which corresponds; when both object and perceiver are of the best there will always be pleasure, since the requisite agent and patient are both present.) Pleasure completes the activity not as the corresponding permanent state does, by its immanence, but as an end which supervenes as the bloom of youth does on those in the flower of their age. So long, then, as both the intelligible or sensible object and the discriminating or contemplative faculty are as they should be, the pleasure will be involved in the activity; for when both the passive and the active factor are unchanged and are related to each other in the same way, the same result naturally follows.

1. Aristotle insists that a little money is essential to living a good life. Do you agree? Does that mean poor people cannot be good?

2. What is the function of human beings for Aristotle? How does Aristotle argue his way to that function? Rewrite his argument in clear steps.

| Epicurus | # On Pleasure |

Epicurus wrote persuasively about the virtues of an unperturbed life, but his constrained emphasis on pleasure gave him the eventual (unwarranted) reputation as a party animal. "Epicurean" now means someone who lives for pleasure.

Let no one when young delay to study philosophy, nor when he is old grow weary of his study. For no one can come too early or too late to secure the health of his soul. And the man who says that the age for philosophy has either not yet come or has gone by is like the man who says that the age for happiness is not yet come to him, or has passed away. Wherefore both when young and old a man must study philosophy, that as he grows old he may be young in blessings through the grateful recollection of what has been, and that in youth he may be old as well, since he will know no fear of what is to come. We must then meditate on the things that make our happiness, seeing that when that is with us we have all, but when it is absent we do all to win it. . . .

Become accustomed to the belief that death is nothing to us. For all good and evil consists in sensation, but death is deprivation of sensation. And therefore a right understanding that death is nothing to us makes the mortality of life enjoyable, not because it

adds to it an infinite span of time, but because it takes away the craving for immortality. For there is nothing terrible in life for the man who has truly comprehended that there is nothing terrible in not living. So that the man speaks but idly who says that he fears death not because it will be painful when it comes, but because it is painful in anticipation. For that which gives no trouble when it comes, is but an empty pain in anticipation. So death, the most terrifying of ills, is nothing to us, since so long as we exist death is not with us; but when death comes, then we do not exist. It does not then concern either the living or the dead, since for the former it is not, and the latter are no more.

But the many at one moment shun death as the greatest of evils, at another yearn for it as a respite from the evils in life. But the wise man neither seeks to escape life nor fears the cessation of life, for neither does life offend him nor does the absence of life seem to be any evil. And just as with food he does not seek simply the larger share and nothing else, but rather the most pleasant, so he seeks to enjoy not the longest period of time, but the most pleasant. . . .

We must then bear in mind that the future is neither ours, nor yet wholly not ours, so that we may not altogether expect it as sure to come, nor abandon hope of it, as if it will certainly not come.

From *Epicurus* (translated by C. Bailey, Oxford University Press, 1926).

We must consider that of desires some are natural, others vain, and of the natural some are necessary and others merely natural; and of the necessary some are necessary for happiness, others for the repose of the body, and others for very life. The right understanding of these facts enables us to refer all choice and avoidance to the health of the body and the soul's freedom from disturbance, since this is the aim of the life of blessedness. For it is to obtain this end that we always act, namely, to avoid pain and fear. And when this is once secured for us, all the tempest of the soul is dispersed, since the living creature has not to wander as though in search of something that is missing, and to look for some other thing by which he can fulfil the good of the soul and the good of the body. For it is then that we have need of pleasure, when we feel pain owing to the absence of pleasure; but when we do not feel pain, we no longer need pleasure. And for this cause we call pleasure the beginning and end of the blessed life. For we recognize pleasure as the first good innate in us, and from pleasure we begin every act of choice and avoidance, and to pleasure we return again, using the feeling as the standard by which we judge every good.

And since pleasure is the first good and natural to us, for this very reason we do not choose every pleasure, but sometimes we pass over many pleasures, when greater discomfort accrues to us as the result of them: and similarly we think many pains better than pleasures, since a greater pleasure comes to us when we have endured pains for a long time. Every pleasure then because of its natural kinship to us is good, yet not every pleasure is to be chosen: even as every pain also is an evil, yet not all are always of a nature to be avoided. Yet by a scale of comparison and by the consideration of advantages and disadvantages we must form our judgement on all these matters. For

the good on certain occasions we treat as bad, and conversely the bad as good.

And again independence of desire we think a great good—not that we may at all times enjoy but a few things, but that, if we do not possess many, we may enjoy the few in the genuine persuasion that those have the sweetest pleasure in luxury who least need it, and that all that is natural is easy to be obtained, but that which is superfluous is hard. And so plain savours bring us a pleasure equal to a luxurious diet, when all the pain due to want is removed; and bread and water produce the highest pleasure, when one who needs them puts them to his lips. To grow accustomed therefore to simple and not luxurious diet gives us health to the full, and makes a man alert for the needful employments of life, and when after long intervals we approach luxuries, disposes us better towards them, and fits us to be fearless of fortune.

When, therefore, we maintain that pleasure is the end, we do not mean the pleasures of profligates and those that consist in sensuality, as is supposed by some who are either ignorant or disagree with us or do not understand, but freedom from pain in the body and from trouble in the mind. For it is not continuous drinkings and revellings, nor the satisfaction of lusts, nor the enjoyment of fish and other luxuries of the wealthy table, which produce a pleasant life, but sober reasoning, searching out the motives for all choice and avoidance, and banishing mere opinions, to which are due the greatest disturbance of the spirit.

QUESTIONS

1. Is pleasure always a good? Should we define other goods in terms of the pleasure they give us?

2. Can suffering ever be good? What would Epicurus say?

Andrew Carnegie | # Wealth

Andrew Carnegie was one of the most power-ful American millionaires of the nineteenth century. He was also a great philanthropist.

The problem of our age is the proper administration of wealth, so that the ties of brotherhood may still bind together the rich and poor in harmonious rela-tionship. The conditions of human life have not only been changed, but revolutionized, within the past few hundred years. In former days there was little differ-ence between the dwelling, dress, food, and environ-ment of the chief and those of his retainers. The Indi-ans are today where civilized man then was. When visiting the Sioux, I was led to the wigwam of the chief. It was just like the others in external appear-ance, and even within the difference was trifling between it and those of the poorest of his braves. The contrast between the palace of the millionaire and the cottage of the laborer with us today measures the change which has come into civilization.

This change, however, is not to be deplored, but welcomed as highly beneficial. It is well, nay essen-tial, for the progress of the race, that the houses of some should be homes for all that is highest and best in literature and arts, and for all the refinements of civilization, rather than that none should be so. Much better this great irregularity than universal squalor. Without wealth there can be no Maecetions. When these apprentices rose to be masters, there was little or no change in their mode of life, and they, in turn, educated in the same routine succeeding apprentices. There was, substantially, social equality, and even political equality, for those engaged in industrial pur-suits had then little or no political voice in the State.

But the inevitable result of such a mode of manu-facture was crude articles at high prices. Today the world obtains commodities of excellent quality at prices which even the generation preceding this would have deemed incredible. In the commercial world similar causes have produced similar results, and the race is benefited thereby. The poor enjoy what the rich could not before afford. What were the luxuries have become the necessaries of life. The laborer has now more comforts than the farmer had a few generations ago. The farmer has more luxuries than the landlord had, and is more richly clad and better housed. The landlord has books and pictures rarer, and appointments more artistic, than the King could then obtain.

The price we pay for this salutary change is, no doubt, great. We assemble thousands of operatives in the factory, in the mine, and in the counting-house, of whom the employer can know little or nothing, and to whom the employer is little better than a myth. All intercourse between them is at an end. Rigid Castes are formed, and, as usual, mutual ignorance breeds mutual distrust. Each Caste is without sympathy for the other, and ready to credit anything disparaging in regard to it. Under the law of competition, the employer of thousands is forced into the strictest economies, among which the rates paid to labor fig-ure prominently, and often there is friction between the employer and the employed, between capital and labor, between rich and poor. Human society loses homogeneity.

The price which society pays for the law of com-petition, like the price it pays for cheap comforts and luxuries, is also great; but the advantages of this law are also greater still, for it is to this law that we owe our wonderful material development, which brings improved conditions in its train. But, whether the law be benign or not, we must say of it, as we say of the change in the conditions of men to which we have referred: It is here; we cannot evade it; no substitutes

First published in the *North American Review,* June 1889.

for it have been found; and while the law may be sometimes hard for the individual, it is best for the race, because it insures the survival of the fittest in every department. We accept and welcome, therefore, as conditions to which we must accommodate ourselves, great inequality of environment, the concentration of business, industrial and commercial, in the hands of a few, and the law of competition between these, as being not only beneficial, but essential for the future progress of the race. Having accepted these, it follows that there must be great scope for the exercise of special ability in the merchant and in the manufacturer who has to conduct affairs upon a great scale. That this talent for organization and management is rare among men is proved by the fact that it invariably secures for its possessor enormous rewards, no matter where or under what laws or conditions. The experienced in affairs always rate the MAN whose services can be obtained as a partner as not only the first consideration, but such as to render the question of his capital scarcely worth considering, for such men soon create capital; while, without the special talent required, capital soon takes wings. Such men become interested in firms or corporations using millions; and estimating only simple interest to be made upon the capital invested, it is inevitable that their income must exceed their expenditures, and that they must accumulate wealth. Nor is there any middle ground which such men can occupy, because the great manufacturing or commercial concern which does not earn at least interest upon its capital soon becomes bankrupt. It must either go forward or fall behind: to stand still is impossible. It is a condition essential for its successful operation that it should be thus far profitable, and even that, in addition to interest on capital, it should make profit. It is a law, as certain as any of the others named, that men possessed of this peculiar talent for affairs, under the free play of economic forces, must, of necessity, soon be in receipt of more revenue than can be judiciously expended upon themselves, and this law is as beneficial for the race as the others.

Objections to the foundations upon which society is based are not in order, because the condition of the race is better with these than it has been with any others which have been tried. Of the effect of any new substitutes proposed we cannot be sure. The Socialist or Anarchist who seeks to overturn present conditions is to be regarded as attacking the foundation upon which civilization itself rests, for civilization took its start from the day that the capable, industrious workman said to his incompetent and lazy fellow, "If thou dost not sow, thou shalt not reap," and thus ended primitive Communism by separating the drones from the bees. One who studies this subject will soon be brought face to face with the conclusion that upon the sacredness of property civilization itself depends—the right of the laborer to his hundred dollars in the savings bank, and equally the legal right of the millionaire to his millions. To those who propose to substitute Communism for this intense Individualism the answer, therefore, is: The race has tried that. All progress from that barbarous day to the present time has resulted from its displacement. Not evil, but good, has come to the race from the accumulation of wealth by those who have the ability and energy that produce it. But even if we admit for a moment that it might be better for the race to discard its present foundation, Individualism—that it is a nobler ideal that man should labor, not for himself alone, but in and for a brotherhood of his fellows, and share with them all in common, realizing Swedenborg's idea of Heaven, where, as he says, the angels derive their happiness, not from laboring for self, but for each other—even admit all this, and a sufficient answer is, This is not evolution, but revolution. It necessitates the changing of human nature itself—a work of aeons, even if it were good to change it, which we cannot know. It is not practicable in our day or in our age. Even if desirable theoretically, it belongs to another and long-succeeding sociological stratum. Our duty is with what is practicable now; with the next step possible in our day and generation. It is criminal to waste our energies in endeavoring to uproot, when all we can profitably or possibly accomplish is to bend the universal tree of humanity a little in the direction most favorable to the production of good fruit under existing circumstances. We might as well urge the destruction of the highest existing type of man because he failed to reach our ideal as to favor the destruction of Individualism, Private Property, the Law of Accumulation of Wealth, and the Law of Competition; for these are the highest results of human experience, the soil in which society so far has produced the best fruit. Unequally or unjustly, perhaps, as these laws sometimes operate, and imperfect as they appear to the Idealist, they are nevertheless, like the highest type of man, the best and most valuable of all that humanity has yet accomplished.

We start, then, with a condition of affairs under which the best interests of the race are promoted, but which inevitably gives wealth to the few. Thus far, accepting conditions as they exist, the situation can be surveyed and pronounced good. The question then arises—and, if the foregoing be correct, it is the only question with which we have to deal—What is the proper mode of administering wealth after the laws upon which civilization is founded have thrown it into the hands of the few? And it is of this great question that I believe I offer the true solution. It will be understood that *fortunes* are here spoken of, not moderate sums saved by many years of effort, the returns from which are required for the comfortable maintenance and education of families. This is not *wealth,* but only *competence,* which it should be the aim of all to acquire.

. . . Indeed, it is difficult to set bounds to the share of a rich man's estate which should go at his death to the public through the agency of the state, and by all means such taxes should be graduated, beginning at nothing upon moderate sums to dependents, and increasing rapidly as the amounts swell, until of the millionaire's hoard, as of Shylock's at least

. . . The other half

Comes to the privy coffer of the state.

This policy would work powerfully to induce the rich man to attend to the administration of wealth during his life, which is the end that society should always have in view, as being that by far most fruitful for the people. Nor need it be feared that this policy would sap the root of enterprise and render men less anxious to accumulate, for to the class whose ambition it is to leave great fortunes and be talked about after their death, it will attract more attention, and, indeed, be a somewhat nobler ambition to have enormous sums paid over to the state from their fortunes.

There remains, then, only one mode of using great fortunes; but in this we have the true antidote for the temporary unequal distribution of wealth, the reconciliation of the rich and the poor—a reign of harmony—another ideal, differing, indeed, from that of the Communist in requiring only the further evolution of existing conditions, not the total overthrow of our civilization. It is founded upon the present most intense individualism, and the race is prepared to put it in practice by degrees whenever it pleases. Under its sway we shall have an ideal state, in which the surplus wealth of the few will become, in the best sense, the property of the many, because administered for the common good, and this wealth, passing through the hands of the few, can be made a much more potent force for the elevation of our race than if it had been distributed in small sums to the people themselves. Even the poorest can be made to see this, and to agree that great sums gathered by some of their fellow-citizens and spent for public purposes, from which the masses reap the principal benefit, are more valuable to them than if scattered among them through the course of many years in trifling amounts.

The best uses to which surplus wealth can be put have already been indicated. Those who would administer wisely must, indeed, be wise, for one of the serious obstacles to the improvement of our race is indiscriminate charity. It were better for mankind that the millions of the rich were thrown into the sea than so spent as to encourage the slothful, the drunken, the unworthy. Of every thousand dollars spent in so-called charity today, it is probable that $950 is unwisely spent; so spent, indeed, as to produce the very evils which it proposes to mitigate or cure. A well-known writer of philosophic books admitted the other day that he had given a quarter of a dollar to a man who approached him as he was coming to visit the house of his friend. He knew nothing of the habits of this beggar; knew not the use that would be made of this money, although he had every reason to suspect that it would be spent improperly. This man professed to be a disciple of Herbert Spencer; yet the quarter-dollar given that night will probably work more injury than all the money which its thoughtless donor will ever be able to give in true charity will do good. He only gratified his own feelings, saved himself from annoyance—and this was probably one of the most selfish and very worst actions of his life, for in all respects he is most worthy.

In bestowing charity, the main consideration should be to help those who will help themselves; to provide part of the means by which those who desire to improve may do so; to give those who desire to rise the aids by which they may rise; to assist, but rarely or never to do all. Neither the individual nor the race is improved by alms-giving. Those worthy of assistance, except in rare cases, seldom require assistance. The really valuable men of the race never do, except in cases of accident or sudden change. Every one has, of course, cases of individuals brought to his own knowledge where temporary assistance can do genuine good, and these he will not overlook. But the amount which can be wisely given by the individual for individuals is necessarily limited by his lack of knowledge of the circumstances connected with each. He is the only true reformer who is as careful and an anxious not to aid the unworthy as he is to aid the worthy, and perhaps, even more so, for in alms-giving more injury is probably done by rewarding vice then by relieving virtue.

Thus is the problem of Rich and Poor to be solved. The laws of accumulation will be left free; the laws of distribution free. Individualism will continue, but the millionaire will be but a trustee for the poor; intrusted for a season with a great part of the increased wealth of the community, but administrating it for the community far better than it could or would have done for itself. The best minds will thus have reached a stage in the development of the race in which it is clearly seen that there is no mode of disposing of surplus wealth creditable to thoughtful and earnest men into whose hands it flows save by using it year by year for the general good. This day already dawns. But a little while, and although, without incurring the pity of their fellows, men may die sharers in great business enterprises from which their capital cannot be or has not been withdrawn, and is left chiefly at death for public uses, yet the man who dies leaving behind him millions of available wealth, which was his to administer during life, will pass away "unwept, unhonored, and unsung," no matter to what uses he leaves the dross which he cannot take with him. Of such as these the public verdict will then be: "The man who dies thus rich dies disgraced."

Such, in my opinion, is the true Gospel concerning Wealth, obedience to which is destined some day to solve the problems of the Rich and the Poor, and to bring "Peace on earth, among men Good-Will."

QUESTIONS

1. What is the "proper administration" of wealth? Is it being properly administered today?

2. What is the "one mode" of using great fortunes? How should the problem of "rich and poor" be solved?

Solomon Schimmel | # Greed

Solomon Schimmel wrote the book (or, at any rate, one of them) on the seven deadly sins. Here he presents a scholarly look at greed, the vice most tempting and prevalent in business life.

If money be not thy servant, it will be thy master.
The covetous man cannot so properly be said to
possess wealth, as that may be said to possess him.
                                                      —*Francis Bacon*

In 1990 Congress passed a law that provided for life imprisonment for certain financial crimes in recognition of the social damage and danger of greed gone amok. This law was a reaction to public anger at the Savings and Loan scandal of the 1980s in which avaricious bankers, lawyers, and accountants, seeking easy riches, fraudulently deprived thousands of Americans of their savings, causing immeasurable suffering. The greed of the 1980s brought with it a surge in criminal and unethical schemes, such as insider trading on the stock market, company takeovers that resulted in massive layoffs followed by bankruptcies, and scientific fraud. Greed inflicted catastrophe on many innocent victims, and its adverse social consequences will be felt for many years.

This should come as no surprise, since the pursuit of wealth is a dominant value in our society. The media feature adulatory stories about thirty-year-old multimillionaires who have achieved their college goal of amassing a fortune within a decade of graduation. Rarely do journalists who revel in the rich ask whether such a goal is commendable, at what psychological or spiritual cost it was achieved, if ruthless or immoral means were used, and what "good" will be done with all of this wealth. Our constitution guarantees the freedom to pursue happiness and our capitalist ethos simplistically equates freedom with

lack of restraint and happiness with wealth. The premise is that unrestrained pursuit of wealth will eventually makes us happier, because the more money we accrue the happier we will be. But in so worshipping money, placing our hope and trust in it—a form of idolatry—we blind ourselves to the social and personal costs of greed. The assumption that greed is good and that riches guarantee satisfying lives is false, and the teachings of the moralists about the sin of avarice illuminate why.

Greed (also known as avarice and covetousness) manifests itself in many ways. The cutthroat competitor, the workaholic, the swindler, the miser, and the gambler are all greedy. Sometimes even the spendthrift is guilty of greed. Basically, greed is the inordinate love of money and of material possessions, and the dedication of oneself to their pursuit. This love of money is fed by other vices and leads to many evils.[1] In trying to satisfy greed we can injure ourselves and others, psychologically and physically. This is the paradox of greed—though its aim is to increase our pleasure through the purchase of goods and services, it often does so at the expense of pleasure and happiness.

––––––––––

A patient of mine provides an example of this. He hadn't taken a much-needed vacation for years although he could easily have afforded to do so. He could never get himself to spend a substantial sum of money on either himself or his wife. He was always complaining that airlines and hotels overcharge, and maintained that he enjoyed staying at home. It was quite obvious, though, that for his emotional health and for his wife's sake they needed to get away from the monotonous routine and pressures of their regular environment. The truth was that he found it extremely

From *The Seven Deadly Sins* (New York: Oxford University Press, 1997).

difficult to part with money, particularly for a nontangible asset. Things that were touchable could be assigned some money-equivalent value, so he was able to exchange money for them and buy a VCR or a new car. But the scenic beauty of nature, the enhanced intimacy and love that a tranquil getaway with his wife would facilitate, were, to him, ephemeral intangibles that were no substitute for money. This man's stinginess nearly cost him his marriage.

Another of my clients had been successfully immersed in the frenzied greed of the financial markets' subculture of the 1980s. By day he was a workaholic, by night a hedonist. He came to see me because he was unhappy with what he was doing with his life and with what his life was doing to him. He was wise and sensitive enough to realize that his money wasn't making him happy, and that the moral and spiritual values he once cherished were being eroded by his pursuit of wealth and pleasure. Yet he found it difficult to rectify the situation as long as he remained in the environment which supported it.

After a period of sustained honest reflection about what he felt he would want to be remembered for if he were to die suddenly, he concluded that it wasn't his financial success or the gratifications of his body that his money bought. He decided to make a dramatic rupture with his present. He moved to a farm in rural Vermont where he now lives a life of material simplicity. He uses his business and organizational skills to consult with local government on projects to improve the lot of the rural poor. Although he earns only a small fraction of what he once did and lives more modestly, he is a much happier person than he ever was in the heyday of his high-flying life-style. Nor does he miss the wealth of earlier times, now that he has adapted to the less that is really more. As Epicurus put it, wealth consists not in having great possessions but in having few wants.

Although greed is a cause of much unhappiness, there are few contemporary therapies for it since it is rarely perceived as undesirable. Only when it results in criminal behavior or in extreme disruption of per-

Labor Day, 2004

"While the economy has been sliding downward, worker productivity has inched upward," said Professor Joanne B. Ciulla, author of *The Working Life: The Promise and Betrayal of Modern Work.* "The work ethic is alive and well, but after years of economic uncertainty, it is often a work ethic based on fear or necessity. Americans need a day to relax and enjoy the other things life has to offer."

In the past six months, 32 percent of U.S. adults who are employed full time have increased their workweek hours. Of those, 67 percent are working an additional five or more hours each week. And also of those who said their work week has increased, the survey identified the lack of efficient staffing, less people to do the same amount of work, and pressure to do more as the top three drivers for the increase. When asked if they expect any relief from the increased hours within the next six months, the majority answered no.

Another startling finding is that although more than half of employed adults have increased their job responsibilities in the past six months, 62 percent also have not received a pay raise. This statistic compliments information in a recent report (State of Working America, 2004–05) from the Economic Policy Institute. The report states that despite the onset of the economic recovery, fast productivity growth, and even the return of job growth, over the past year, weekly earnings for most workers have fallen by 1.5 percent after inflation.

sonal or family life is some intervention deemed necessary. The courts will punish crimes that result from greed and therapists will treat an inveterate gambler or a high-powered executive whose drive for financial success produces intolerable stress or physical illness. For the most part, though, society encourages greed, although euphemisms are usually used when doing so, such as "financial success," "economic security," "the good life," or "having it all." This avoidance of the word *greed* reflects our ambivalence about greed because we know that it is essentially selfish and that when practiced to an extreme it can be very dangerous, leading even to murder.

QUESTIONS

1. Can greed be "good" (as Gordon Gecko argued)? Why or why not?
2. How may greed be a source of unhappiness?

Joanne B. Ciulla | # Leisure and Consumption

Leisure is a special experience. It consists of activities that are freely chosen and good in themselves. Listening to music for pure enjoyment is one such pursuit. Aristotle believed that leisure was necessary for human happiness. Most people today think that we conduct business so that we can make money and buy things. And some trade time for leisure so that they can buy more things. Aristotle said we conduct business (or are "unleisurely") so that we can have leisure. Leisure brings out what is best and most distinctive about being human—our abilities to think, feel, reflect, create, and learn. We need leisure to develop wisdom.

The word for leisure in Greek is *skolé;* in Latin it is *otium.* In both languages the word for work is simply the negation of the word for leisure; *ascholia* and *negotium* both mean "not leisure." This is also true in Spanish. Today *negocio,* the word for business, means "no leisure." Greek, Latin, and Spanish words compare work to leisure as if to say that leisure is the center of life. The English word *leisure* comes from the Latin *licere,* which means "to be permitted." Our language compares leisure to work as if to say that work is the norm of life and leisure is when we are "permitted" to stop working. The British essayist and self-confessed workaholic G. K. Chesterton wrote there are three parts to leisure: "The first is being allowed to do something. The second is being allowed to do anything and the third (and perhaps most rare and precious) is being allowed to do nothing."[1] [Chesterton]

In his book *Of Time, Work, and Leisure,* sociologist Sebastian de Grazia observed that although work can ennoble us, wear us down, or make us rich, it is leisure that perfects us as human beings. Writing in 1962, de Grazia applied Aristotle's notion of leisure to the twentieth century. He wrote, "Leisure and free time live in two different worlds. . . ." Free time refers to a special way of calculating a special kind of time. Leisure refers to a state of being, a condition of man."[2] [de Grazia] It is a frame of mind or attitude of imaginative people who love ideas. Until World War I, educated Virginians defined a Yankee as a person who didn't understand how to use his leisure. For de Grazia, leisure is a special intellectual state that few people are capable of having. It is more than simply organized activities, amusements, relaxation, and free time.

The idea that leisure is something that only a few people attain leaves us to wonder: Is leisure elitist, or do people like Aristotle and de Grazia take an elitist

From *The Working Life* (New York: Random House, 2001). References were deleted from this text.

view of leisure? After all, who are they to make judgments on what is and is not leisure? Besides eating, sleeping, procreating, and getting ready for work, how we use our free time is a highly personal matter. Class, taste, income, education, and personal preference certainly influence what we choose to do. Just as there is a pecking order in work there is also one outside of it. Golfers look down on bowlers, tennis players look down on golfers, opera lovers sneer at soap opera fans, *New York Times* readers condescend to *National Enquirer* readers, Bloomingdale's shoppers scorn Wal-Mart shoppers. The prosperous and better-educated think (and have always thought) that their leisure pursuits are more enriching and self-fulfilling than those of the poor and the working class. But there

are larger questions behind de Grazia's and Aristotle's discussions of leisure that get to the heart of how people experience life. Before we move to these questions, however, we need to look at the relationship of work to the way we spend our free time.

WORK AND AMUSEMENTS

The Reformation, with its emphasis on work, did its best to make Sunday a boring day. Luther got rid of the saints and their holidays. The Protestants associated work with virtue and hence leisure with vice. In the Middle Ages holidays were times for music, dancing, and drinking, but later, in Protestant countries, they became days for silence and meditation. In

In Praise of Idleness

Bertrand Russell

Like most of my generation, I was brought up on the saying "Satan finds some mischief still for idle hands to do." Being a highly virtuous child, I believed all that I was told, and acquired a conscience which has kept me working hard down to the present moment. But although my conscience has controlled my actions, my opinions have undergone a revolution. I think that there is far too much work done in the world, that immense harm is caused by the belief that work is virtuous, and that what needs to be preached in modern industrial countries is quite different from what always has been preached. . . .

The wise use of leisure, it must be conceded, is a product of civilization and education. A man who has worked long hours all his life will be bored if he becomes suddenly idle. But without a considerable amount of leisure a man is cut off from many of the best things. There is no longer any reason why the bulk of the population should suffer this deprivation; only a foolish asceticism, usually vicarious, makes us continue to insist on work in excessive quantities now that the need no longer exists.

It will be said that, while a little leisure is pleasant, men would not know how to fill their days if they had only four hours of work out of the twenty-four. In so far as this is true in the modern world, it is a condemnation of our civilization; it would not have been true at any earlier period. There was formerly a capacity for light-heartedness and play which has been to some extent inhibited by the cult of efficiency. The modern man thinks that everything ought to be done for the sake of something else, and never for its own sake.

From *In Praise of Idleness.*

the 1640s the Puritans, who dominated the British Parliament, banned all Christmas festivities and enjoyments, including plum pudding and mince pie. In our own times, starting in the 1980s all workers began to lose holidays and paid vacation time, and some managers began acting like Scrooge on Christmas. In 1986, when Christmas fell on a Thursday, 46 percent of employers gave workers Friday off. In 1997, when Christmas fell on a Thursday, only 36 percent did. Holidays are more than days off; they are supposed to be public celebrations. But the public can't celebrate together if most people are working.

According to de Grazia, businesspeople liked the idea of making Sunday a dismal bore because that would make work more desirable.[3] If leisure were too rewarding and too much fun, people wouldn't want to go back to work. But the Protestants and employers were probably more concerned about amusements than leisure. *The Oxford English Dictionary* defines an amusement as a pleasurable occupation that distracts or diverts attention from something. Interestingly, it comes from the word *muse,* which in this context means to be "affected with astonishment" or to be put into a "stupid stare."[4]

In the industrial era the English took legal measures to repress popular amusements in order to develop conduct suitable for work discipline. The Poor Law Amendment Act of 1834 wiped out the infrastructure of working-class entertainment. By restricting people to their parishes, the law effectively got rid of traveling balladeers, entertainers, and itinerant salesmen. The 1835 Highways Act forbade all street "nuisances," including soccer players, street entertainers, and traders. In the same year the Cruelty to Animals Act outlawed activities such as cockfights, but allowed fox hunting and other aristocratic pursuits. Working-class amusements moved off the streets and into pubs, which began providing various forms of entertainment to their customers. America never took such harsh legal measures except during the Prohibition years. Supporters of Prohibition argued that a shorter workweek would surely lead to more drinking.

At the turn of the century, employers opposed giving Saturday off because they claimed that their employees would only get into trouble. For example, in the early 1900s a Massachusetts firm required

workers who were unwilling to attend church to stay indoors and "improve their time" by reading, writing, or performing other valuable duties. Mill owners of the time forbade drinking and gambling and justified the twelve-hour day and six-day week as means of keeping workers from vicious amusements. This was not a totally unfounded fear. As mentioned earlier, workers in the early industrial days of England often used their leisure time to drink, fight, and bet on animal contests, such as cockfights.

In early twentieth-century America, millions of workingmen spent their free time in bars and union clubs. There were more than ten thousand saloons in New York in 1900. In *Cheap Amusements,* Kathy Peiss estimates that workingmen in New York spent about 10 percent of their weekly income on personal expenses, the bulk of which were for beer and liquor, tobacco, and movie and theater tickets. An extensive study of workingmen's leisure found that married men spent half of their free time with their families. Workingmen felt that their work gave them a "right" to amusements after work—"I worked for someone else all day and now I deserve to have someone or something work to entertain me."[5]

Married women did not start going out for entertainment in great numbers until after the invention of the nickelodeon in 1905. When young women found job opportunities outside domestic labor, they flocked to work in industry, department stores, and restaurants. Having grown up seeing their mothers work from dawn to dusk and observing domestic servants work twelve-to-fourteen-hour days, they too felt they had a "right" to outside entertainment. Workingwomen who loved to party were called "rowdy girls" in the Victorian era. They relished the freedom of going out with their friends, dancing, and socializing in mixed company. A manager from Macy's complained that young girls went out dancing on weeknights and came in exhausted for work the next day. Women also integrated amusements into their work. Female factory workers practiced the latest dance steps outside the factory during their breaks. Female cigar rollers insisted on having someone read the newspaper to them while they worked. Women became very protective of their work hours and filed grievances when asked to work overtime or when detained after closing time. Women workers were largely responsible for getting the workweek shortened for all workers. The more women worked by the clock outside the home the more they too felt entitled to a good time—something to distract them or take them away from work. Life became more segmented into bouts of uninterrupted work and bouts of amusement.

Not only did employers worry about the effects of workers' leisure on job performance, they had misgivings about what might happen when employees socialized together outside work. Union halls were just one form of association. Groupings of nonunion workers were also a threat because they gave employees ample time to bond and discuss working conditions and complaints, providing a fertile field for union organization.

In 1914 Henry Ford established a sociological department in his company. The department's mission was to supervise workers' lives so that they would be thrifty, industrious producers. They urged employees not to smoke and drink. Today's reformers who want to control sex and violence on TV, cigarettes, drugs, and alcohol face an uphill battle. If people like to engage in these activities during their free time, they will until they find—or the market offers them—alternatives they like more.

TRADING LEISURE
FOR CONSUMPTION

In 1970 economist Steffan Linder published *The Harried Leisure Class.* In it he argued that in affluent societies, when people have to choose between more free time and more spending, most choose more spending. That is why he believed that an increase in income is not necessarily an increase in prosperity. In 1986, for example, Americans spent more than thirteen billion dollars on sports clothing, which meant that they traded 1.3 billion hours of potential leisure time for leisure clothing.[6] Spending money takes time—time to make the money, time to shop, and time to enjoy the things the money buys, such as cabin cruisers, package tours, and the like. Ameri-

cans not only have less vacation time than Europeans, but they spend three to four times as many hours shopping as Europeans do.

Consumption ties a tighter knot between work and free time than any of the schemes of reformers, employers, or governments. William H. Whyte was right to be concerned about the organization man's shallow roots in the community and deep roots in the organization. What he didn't calculate was the way that consumerism and credit reinforce the grip of work on people. Consumption creates a *need* to work even when the desire to work is weak. However, it can also make work feel more burdensome. The market tempts people with more leisure options than they can afford or have time to enjoy. We wish we didn't have to work so that we could enjoy what the market has to offer us in terms of toys, vacations, and other amusements—all of which cost money.

Even teenagers trade their leisure for consumption. In the past, teens often had to work to help their families or pay for college. Some still do, but now a growing number of middle-class teens work to buy luxury items for themselves. As we have seen, generations of Americans have encouraged young people to work, in the belief that it keeps them out of trouble and develops discipline. In a 1986 study, researchers Ellen Greenberger and Laurence Steinberg came to a radically different conclusion about work and teenagers. They found that teens often get into more trouble when they work too much than they do during free time. This is because they suffer the stress of work and school and they have the money to buy drugs and alcohol. But most interestingly, Greenberger and Steinberg also suggest that too much work not only interferes with teens' schoolwork but can cause an "adjusted blandness" at a time when they should be curious, imaginative, and combative.[7] This "adjusted blandness" is exemplified by the routine "have a nice day" patter of counter workers in fast-food restaurants. Greenberger and Steinberg think that this is unhealthy.

At first their argument seems to go against the Protestant work ethic. But Greenberger and Steinberg maintain that instead of fostering respect for work, teenage employment often leads to increased cynicism about the ability of work to provide any personal satisfaction beyond a paycheck, since teens often work in menial jobs. They ask us to consider the image of a sixteen-year-old boy, who comes home from a long afternoon of work in a fast-food restaurant, downs a few beers, and thinks to himself, "People who work harder at their jobs than they have to are a little bit crazy."[8] Work is "bogus"—you do the minimum necessary to get paid.

Other researchers believe that the social meaning of work determines whether work is good or bad for teens. In 1993 J. Schulenberg and J. G. Bachman found that teens suffered when they worked *only* for the money, for long periods of time, at boring jobs that were unconnected to future work. A study conducted by H. W. Marsh in 1991 indicated that when teens were working to save money for college, their grades improved, even when the teens had boring jobs. When teens worked to buy extras such as cars and CD players for themselves, their grades went down, regardless of the job.[9] During the Depression era, similar studies showed the beneficial value of any kind of work for young people who contributed to the support of their families at a time of crisis. The young people gained self-confidence and a sense of efficacy from helping to care for their families.

These studies on teens offer an insight into how the meaning of work changes when teens conform to the demands of the workplace in order to conform to the desires elicited in the marketplace. Sometimes the reasons *why* we work are more important than the work we actually do. The experience of working to support a family or go to college may well be more satisfying than working for clothing and CD players, because the goals themselves are more lasting and meaningful. Nonetheless, many would still argue that it is better for young people to earn money to buy what they want than to have it given to them.

When teens substitute consumer goods for leisure, they get caught up in the work-and-spend pattern of their parents and something is lost. If they give up their free time so that they can make money to buy things, they don't have the leisure to discover what they like to do. They don't have the time to discover what activities they find intrinsically good. Far from fearing it (as parents and others in authority do), there is something to be said for doing nothing and hanging out with one's friends. While there may be the

potential for trouble, there is also the potential to learn how to enjoy life on one's own terms and not those of the consumer market.

———————

Of course, critics of consumerism and materialist values are legion. Somewhere in every major world religion is a warning about the dangers of the unfettered desire for material objects. We noted earlier that most of the seven deadly sins concern desire for material things. Nonetheless, many economists and businesspeople are cheered by the fact that consumer demand is insatiable. In *Social Limits to Growth*, Fred Hirsch wrote that the satisfaction that people derive from goods and services doesn't depend on their own consumption, but on the consumption of others, or "keeping up with the Joneses," which makes desire limitless. Juliet Schor's recent book *The Overspent American* picks up where Hirsch left off in his 1976 work. She argues that in the past our neighbors ("the Joneses") set the standard for what we wanted and thought we should buy. Today, she says, people often don't know their neighbors, and they compare what they own and want to own against the standards set by a wider range of people, such as those at work, on TV, in advertisements, and elsewhere. When we kept up with the Joneses, we kept up with people who had similar incomes. When we try to keep up with people at work or in the news, we may be trying to keep up with people who make many times more than we do.[10] This draws one into a seamless cycle of spending, debt, and longer working hours. Schor tells us that people who had been sucked into this cycle, "increasingly looked to consumption to give satisfaction, even meaning to their lives."[11]

NOTES

1. C.K. Chesterton, "On Leisure," *Generally Speaking*, (London: 1928), p. 130.

2. Sebastian de Grazia, *Of Time Work and Leisure* (New York: Twentieth Century Fund, 1962), p. 7.

3. Ibid. pp. 202–203.

4. *The Compact Oxford English Dictionary*, new edition (Oxford: Clarendon Press, 1991), p. 421.

5. Kathy Peiss, *Cheap Amusements* (Philadelphia: Temple University Press, 1986), pp. 17–23.

6. Witold Rybczynski, *Waiting for the Weekend* (New York: Viking Penguin, 1991), p. 219.

7. Ellen Greenberger & Laurence Steinberg, *When Teenagers Work* (New York: Basic Books, 1960), pp. 6–8.

8. Ibid. p. 173

9. See, Jeylan T. Mortimer and Michael D. Finch, "Work, Family, and Adolesant Development," in eds. Jeylan T. Mortimer and Michael D. Finch, *Adolescents, Work, and Family* (Thousand Oaks, CA: Sage Publications, 1996), pp. 9–10.

10. Juliet Schor, *The Overspent American*, (New York: Basic Books, 1998), p. 4.

11. Ibid. p. 112.

QUESTIONS

1. Explain Ciulla's concept of "amusement." When did it arise, and why?

2. Why do we trade leisure for consumption? Is it a good idea to do so? Why or why not? What about "slackers"?

Lynne McFall | # Integrity

Lynne McFall has a Ph.D. in philosophy and is a novelist. She is author of *The One True Story of the World.*

Olaf (upon what were once knees)
does almost ceaselessly repeat
"there is some shit I will not eat"

—*e. e. cummings*

COHERENCE

Integrity is the state of being "undivided; an integral whole." What sort of coherence is at issue here? I think there are several.

One kind of coherence is simple consistency: consistency within one's set of principles or commitments. One cannot maintain one's integrity if one has unconditional commitments that conflict, for example, justice and personal happiness, or conditional commitments that cannot be ranked, for example, truth telling and kindness.

Another kind of coherence is coherence between principle and action. Integrity requires "sticking to one's principles," moral or otherwise, in the face of temptation, including the temptation to redescription.

Take the case of a woman with a commitment to marital fidelity. She is attracted to a man who is not her husband, and she is tempted. Suppose, for the purity of the example, that he wants her too but will do nothing to further the affair; the choice is hers. Now imagine your own favorite scene of seduction.

After the fact, she has two options. (There are always these two options, which makes the distinction between changing one's mind and weakness of the will problematic, but assume that this is a clear case.) She can (1) admit to having lost the courage of her convictions (retaining the courage of her mistakes) or (2) rewrite her principles in various ways (e.g., by making fidelity a general principle, with exceptions, or by retroactively canceling her "subscription"). Suppose she chooses the latter. Whatever she may have gained, she has lost some integrity. Weakness of the will is one contrary of integrity. Self-deception is another. A person who admits to having succumbed to temptation has more integrity than the person who sells out, then fixes the books, but both suffer its loss.

A different sort of incoherence is exhibited in the case where someone does the right thing for (what he takes to be) the wrong reason. For example, in Dos-

From *Ethics* 9: (Oct 1987), pp. 11–16. Reprinted with permission.

toevsky's *The Devils,* Stepan Verkhovensky says, "All my life I've been lying. Even when I spoke the truth. I never spoke for the sake of the truth, but for my own sake." Coherence between principle and action is necessary but not sufficient. One's action might *correspond* with one's principle, at some general level of description, but be inconsistent with that principle more fully specified. If one values not just honesty but honesty for its own sake, then honesty motivated by self-interest is not enough for integrity.

So the requirement of coherence is fairly complicated. In addition to simple consistency, it puts constraints on the way in which one's principles may be held (the "first-person" requirement), on how one may act given one's principles (coherence between principle and action), and on how one may be motivated in acting on them (coherence between principle and motivation). Call this *internal coherence.* . . .

To summarize the argument so far: personal integrity requires that an agent (1) subscribe to some consistent set of principles or commitments and (2), in the face of temptation or challenge, (3) uphold these principles or commitments, (4) for what the agent takes to be the right reasons.

These conditions are rather formal. Are there no constraints on the *content* of the principles or commitments a person of integrity may hold?

INTEGRITY AND IMPORTANCE

Consider the following statements.

> Sally is a person of principle: pleasure.
>
> Harold demonstrates great integrity in his single-minded pursuit of approval.
>
> John was a man of uncommon integrity. He let nothing—not friendship, not justice, not truth—stand in the way of his amassment of wealth.

That none of these claims can be made with a straight face suggests that integrity is inconsistent with such principles.

A person of integrity is willing to bear the consequences of her convictions, even when this is difficult, that is, when the consequences are unpleasant. A person whose only principle is "Seek my own pleasure" is not a candidate for integrity because there is no possibility of conflict—between pleasure and principle—in which integrity could be lost. Where there is no possibility of its loss, integrity cannot exist.

Similarly in the case of the approval seeker. The single-minded pursuit of approval is inconsistent with integrity. Someone who is describable as an egg sucker, brownnose, fawning flatterer cannot have integrity, whatever he may think of the merits of such behavior. A commitment to spinelessness does not vitiate its spinelessness—another of integrity's contraries.

The same may be said for the ruthless seeker of wealth. A person whose only aim is to increase his bank balance is a person for whom nothing is ruled out: duplicity, theft, murder. Expedience is *contrasted* to a life of principle, so an ascription of integrity is out of place. Like the pleasure seeker and the approval seeker, he lacks a "core," the kind of commitments that give a person character and that makes a loss of integrity possible. In order to sell one's soul, one must have something to sell. . . .

Most of us, when tempted to "sell out," are tempted by pleasure, approval, money, status, or personal gain of some other sort. The political prisoner under the thumbscrew wants relief, however committed he may be to the revolution. Less dramatically, most of us want the good opinion of others and a decent standard of living. Self-interest in these forms is a legitimate aim against which we weigh our other concerns. But most of us have other "higher," commitments, and so those who honor most what we would resist are especially liable to scorn.

This tendency to objectify our own values in the name of personal integrity can best be seen, I think, in a more neutral case. Consider the following claim:

> The connoisseur showed real integrity in preferring the Montrachet to the Mountain Dew.

Even if he was sorely tempted to guzzle the Mountain Dew and forbore only with the greatest difficulty, the connoisseur, we would say, did not show integrity in preferring the better wine. Why? Resisting temptation is not the only test of integrity; the challenge must be to something *important.* . . .

One may die for beauty, truth, justice, the objection might continue, but not for Montrachet. Wine is not that important. . . .

When we grant integrity to a person, we need not *approve* of his or her principles or commitments, but we must at least recognize them as ones a reasonable person might take to be of great importance and ones that a reasonable person might be tempted to sacrifice to some lesser yet still recognizable goods. It may not be possible to spell out these conditions without circularity, but that this is what underlies our judgments of integrity seems clear enough. Integrity is a personal virtue granted with social strings attached. By definition, it precludes "expediency, artificiality, or shallowness of any kind." The pleasure seeker is guilty of shallowness, the approval seeker of artificiality, and the profit seeker of expedience of the worst sort. . . .

INTEGRITY, FRIENDSHIP, AND THE OLAF PRINCIPLE

An attitude essential to the notion of integrity is that there are some things that one is not prepared to do, or some things one *must* do. I shall call this the "Olaf Principle," in honor of e. e. cummings's poem about Olaf, the "conscientious objector." This principle requires that some of one's commitments be unconditional.

In what sense?

There are, in ordinary moral thought, expressions of the necessity or impossibility of certain actions or types of actions that do not neatly correspond to the notions of necessity and impossibility most often catalogued by moral theorists. "I *must* stand by my friend (or "I *cannot* let him down") may have no claim to logical, psychological, rational, or moral necessity in any familiar sense. There is nothing logically inconsistent in the betrayal of friendship, or one could never be guilty of it. It is not psychologically impossible, since many have in fact done it and survived to do it again. Rationality does not require unconditional allegiance, without some additional assumptions, for one may have better reason to do a conflicting action, for example, where the choice is between betraying a friend and betraying one's coun-

try (although I am sympathetic to E. M. Forster's famous statement to the contrary). Nor is the necessity expressed one that has a claim to universality, for different persons may have different unconditional commitments. Impartiality and absoluteness are not what is at stake, for the choice may be between a friend and ten innocent strangers, and one person may have different unconditional commitments at different times. It is not clear, then, what sense of *unconditional commitment* is at issue.

Unless corrupted by philosophy, we all have things we think we would never do, under any imaginable circumstances, whatever we may give to survival or pleasure, power and the approval of strangers; some part of ourselves beyond which we will not retreat, some weakness however prevalent in others that we will not tolerate in ourselves. And if we do that thing, betray that weakness, we are not the persons we thought; there is nothing left that we may even in spite refer to as *I*.

I think it is in this sense that some commitments must be unconditional: they are conditions of continuing as ourselves.

Suppose, for example, that I take both friendship and professional advancement to be great goods, and my best friend and I are candidates for a promotion. Suppose, too, that I know the person who has the final decision has an unreasoned hatred of people who drink more than is socially required, as my friend does. I let this be known, not directly of course, with the predictable result that I am given the promotion.

Now in one sense I have not done anything dishonest. My friend may be the first to admit the pleasure he takes in alcohol. It may even be one of the reasons I value his friendship. (Loyal drinking companions are not easy to come by.) But this is clearly a betrayal of friendship. Is it so obviously a failure of integrity?

In *any* conflict between two great goods, I may argue, one must be "betrayed." And between you and me, I choose me.

What is wrong with this defense?

To beat someone out of a job by spreading vicious truths is proof that I am no friend. It is in the nature of friendship that one cannot intentionally hurt a friend in order to further one's own interests. So if I claim to be this person's friend, then I am guilty of incoherence, and therefore lack integrity.

Why does incoherence seem the wrong charge to make? The answer, I think, is that it is much too weak.

Some of our principles or commitments are more important to us than others. Those that can be sacrificed without remorse may be called *defeasible* commitments. For many of us, professional success is an important but defeasible commitment. I would like to be a successful philosopher, esteemed by my colleagues and widely published, but neither success nor failure will change my sense of personal worth.

Contrasted to defeasible commitments are *identity-conferring* commitments: they reflect what we take to be most important and so determine, to large extent, our (moral) identities. . . .

For many of us, friendship is an identity-conferring commitment. If we betrayed a friend in order to advance our careers, we could not "live with" ourselves; we would not be the persons we thought we were. This is what it means to have a "core": a set of principles or commitments that makes us who we are. Such principles cannot be justified by reference to other values, because they are the most fundamental commitments we have; they determine what, for us, is to *count* as a reason. . . .

QUESTIONS

1. What is the "Olaf principle"?
2. What does personal integrity require, according to McFall?

Cheshire Calhoun | # Standing for Something

Cheshire Calhoun teaches women's studies and philosophy at Colby College in Maine.

We admire and trust those who have integrity, take pride in our own, rue its absence in politics, and regret our own failures to act with integrity. Clearly, integrity is a virtue, but it is less clear what it is a virtue *of* or why we might prize it.

PERSONAL AND SOCIAL VIRTUES

. . . Some virtues are personal, others are social, yet others are both. A personal virtue, like temperance, consists in having the proper relation to oneself—in this case, to one's desires. Social virtues consist in having the proper relation to others. Civility, for instance, is a social virtue, a desirable mode of con-

ducting oneself among others. Some virtues are both personal and social. Self-respect, for instance, might be thought to involve having both a proper regard for one's own moral status (and thus the right relation to oneself) and a proper regard for one's place among other moral beings (and thus the right relation to others); it is a virtue exercised both by holding oneself to standards and by demanding rightful treatment from others. . . .

Characterizing integrity as a purely personal virtue does not imply that there is anything self-indulgent about striving to have integrity. But it does imply that integrity is not essentially connected to how we conduct ourselves among others and that its fitting us for proper social relations is not what makes it a virtue. Is there any reason to think that integrity is less like temperance, a purely personal virtue, and

From *Journal of Philosophy* XCII 5 (May) 1995, pp. 17–22.

more like self-respect, a personal and social virtue? Taking the notion of "standing for something" and the self-indulgence criticism of integrity in turn, I want to suggest two reasons for not confining the analysis of integrity to understanding its nature as a personal virtue. First, doing so fails to provide us with an adequate explication of what it means to stand for something. Second, although such analyses can counter the self-indulgence charge, they cannot make the person of integrity's relation to other persons central to that defense.

Standing For

I take it that the notion of standing for something is central to the meaning of integrity. Indeed, part of the intuitive appeal of the integrated-self, identity, and clean-hands pictures lay in their articulating part of what is meant by standing for something. When, however, the analysis of integrity is confined to understanding it as a personal virtue, "standing *for*" something ultimately reduces to "standing *by*" the line that demarcates self from not-self. On the integrated-self, identity, and clean-hands pictures, the adoption of principles and values as one's own establishes the line between self and not-self. Acting with integrity, that is, on one's own judgment, is thus intimately tied to protecting the boundaries of the self—to protecting it against disintegration, against loss of self-identity, and against pollution by evil. Acting without integrity undermines the boundaries of the self, whether that be accomplished through the abandonment of one's autonomy, the betrayal of one's deepest commitments, or the contamination of one's agency through association with evil. On all three views, loss of integrity signals loss of some important dimension of selfhood.

To the extent that integrity is, indeed, a personal virtue, this account of the significance of standing by one's principles and values rings true. What drops out of these accounts, however, is the centrality of standing *for* principles and values that, in one's own best judgment, are worthy of defense because they concern how *we,* as beings interested in living justly and well, can do so.

. . . I am strongly inclined to think that integrity is a *social* trait and that its fitting us for community membership is precisely what makes it a social *virtue.* Looking at integrity as a social virtue enables us to see persons of integrity as insisting that it is in some important sense for us, for the sake of what ought to be our project or character as a people, to preserve what ought to be the purity of our agency that they stick by their best judgment. It is to a picture of integrity as a social virtue that I now turn.

STANDING FOR SOMETHING

What then is the social virtue of integrity? I begin with this picture: I am one person among many persons, and we are all in the same boat. None of us can answer the question—'What is worth doing?'—except from within our own deliberative points of view. This 'What is worth doing?' question can take many specific forms. What evils, if any, ought one morally to refuse doing no matter the consequences? What, for philosophers, is worth writing about? What is worth keeping, what worth reforming in the social identity "Black" or "woman" or "gay"? What principles take precedence over what others? What is one, if not the only, worthwhile way of conducting a good life? That they are answerable only from within each person's deliberative viewpoint means that all of our answers will have a peculiar character. As one among many deliberators, each can offer only her own judgment. Although each aims to do more than this—to render a judgment endorsable by all—nothing guarantees success. The thought, "It is just my judgment and it may be wrong," cannot be banished no matter how carefully deliberation proceeds. But given that the only way of answering the 'What is worth doing?' question is to plunge ahead using one's own deliberate viewpoint, one's best judgment becomes important. As one among many deliberators who may themselves go astray, the individual's judgment acquires gravity. It is, after all, not *just* her judgment about what it would be wrong or not worthwhile to do. It is also her *best* judgment. Something now hangs for all of us, as co-deliberators trying to answer correctly the "What is worth doing?" question, on her sticking by her best judgment. Her standing for something is not just something she does for herself. She takes a stand for, and before, all deliberators who share the goal of determining what is worth doing.

To have integrity is to understand that one's own judgment matters because it is only within individual persons' deliberative viewpoints, including one's own, that what is worth our doing can be decided. Thus, one's own judgment serves a common interest of co-deliberators. Persons of integrity treat their own endorsements as ones that matter, or ought to matter, to fellow deliberators. Absent a special sort of story, lying about one's views, concealing them, recanting them under pressure, selling them out for rewards or to avoid penalties, and pandering to what one regards as the bad views of others, all indicate a failure to regard one's own judgment as one that should matter to others. The artist who alters his work of genius, making it saleable to a tasteless public, lacks integrity because he does not regard his best aesthetic judgment as important to anyone but himself. He abandons the co-deliberative perspective. And those who act for the sake of preserving their identity without asking whether it is worth preserving lack integrity, because they do not even raise the "What is worth doing?" question. "Whatever sells" and "whatever is me" cannot ground action with integrity because these reasons do not address the co-deliberative question of what is worth doing.

That hypocrites lack integrity is a common observation. Analyses of integrity as a personal virtue, however, do not plausibly explain why. On the integrated-self and identity pictures of integrity, one would have to say that hypocrites lack integrity because their actions are not integrated with their endorsements; or because in the course of pretending commitment, they are untrue to their real, identity-conferring commitments; or because sustained pretense undermines the agent's ability to be clear and un-self-deceived about what she really does endorse. Although hypocrisy may be bad in these ways for the hypocrite, this is not typically why we charge hypocrites with lacking integrity. Hypocrites mislead. And it is because they deliberately mislead us or others about what is worth doing that they lack integrity. Jim Bakker, for instance, persuaded a lot of people to invest money in his doing God's work. His embez-

zling revealed that he had misled them either about the value of doing God's work or the value of his doing it. Neither the integrated-self nor the identity picture of integrity can explain why misleading others, by itself and not because of its deleterious effects on the hypocrite, has anything to do with lacking integrity. If, however, integrity is not a merely personal virtue, but the social virtue of acting on one's own judgment because doing so matters to deliberators' common interest in determining what is worth doing, then hypocritical misrepresentation of one's own best judgment clearly conflicts with integrity.

This view of integrity also helps to explain the shame at failure to abide by one's own judgment as something more than mere shame at the unsturdiness of one's will or the guilty awareness of violating a standard. If an agent passes herself off as someone who insists on the importance of private spaces and then secretly indulges in reading another's private letters, the thoughts, "I have no self-control" and "This is wrong," are different from the thought, "I have no integrity." Neither the weakness nor the wrongness of the act immediately reveals lack of integrity. Rather, the thought, "I have no integrity," accompanies the revelation of one's inability to stand for something before others.

Finally, looking at integrity not as the personal virtue of keeping oneself intact but as the social virtue of standing for something before fellow deliberators helps explain why we care that persons have the courage of their convictions. The courageous provide spectacular displays of integrity by withstanding social incredulity, ostracism, contempt, and physical assault when most of us would be inclined to give in, compromise, or retreat into silence. Social circumstances that erect powerful deterrents to speaking and acting on one's own best judgment and undermine the possibilities for deliberating about what is worth doing. We thus have reason to be thankful when persons of integrity refuse to be cowed.

CONCLUDING REMARK

What I have had to say about integrity suggests that integrity may be a master virtue, that is, less a virtue in its own right than a pressing into service of a host of other virtues—self-knowledge, strength of will, courage, honesty, loyalty, humility, civility, respect, and self-respect. My aim was to understand that service. What is a person who tries to have integrity trying to do? I have not rejected (though I have revised) the ideas that she is trying to be autonomous, or loyal to deep commitments, or uncontaminated by evils. But I have tried to argue that this is not the whole story. She is also trying to stand for what, in her best judgment, is worth persons' doing.

QUESTIONS

1. What is the difference between personal and social virtues?

2. Why is integrity a "master virtue"?

Joe Dominguez and Vicki Robin

Your Money or Your Life

Joe Dominquez was an analyst on Wall Street before he and Vicky Robin founded the New Road Map Foundation in Seattle.

All our false notions about money thus far have one common flaw—they identify money as something external to ourselves. It is something we all too often don't have, which we struggle to get, and on which we pin our hopes of power, happiness, security, acceptance, success, fulfillment, achievement and personal worth. Money is the master and we the slaves. Money is the victor and we the vanquished.

What, then, is the way out? What is the one consistently true statement we can make about money that will allow us to be clear, masterful and powerful in our relationship with it?

Money is something we choose to trade our life energy for.

We will repeat this because you may have missed its full significance: *Money is something we choose to trade our life energy for.*

Our life energy is our allotment of time here on earth, the hours of precious life available to us. When we go to our jobs we are trading our life energy for money. This truth, while simple, is profound. Less obvious but equally true, when we go to the welfare office, we are trading our life energy for money. When we go to Reno, we are trading our life energy for money (we hope). Even windfalls like inheritances must in some way be "earned" to actually belong to the heir—life energy must be exchanged. Time is spent with lawyers, accountants, trustees, brokers and investment counselors to handle the money. Or time is spent in therapy working out the relationship with the deceased or the guilt at receiving all that money. Or time is spent investigating worthy causes to fund. All this is life energy traded for money.

This definition of money gives us significant information. Our life energy is more *real* in our actual experience than money. You could even say money *equals* our life energy. So, while money has no intrinsic reality, our life energy does—at least to us. It's tangible, and it's finite.

Life energy is all we have. It is precious because it is limited and irretrievable and because our choices about how we use it express the meaning and purpose of our time here on earth. . . .

From Joseph R. Dominguez and Vicki Robin, *Your Money or Your Life: Transforming Your Relationship with Money and Achieving Financial Independence* (New York: Viking 1992), pp. 27–30.

HAVING ENOUGH

Global citizens living sustainably in a global community—what kind of world would that be? Let's try to imagine for a moment such a world, a world in which everyone had enough—enough for his or her survival, enough for comforts and even enough extra for those special times that represent real pleasure. . . .

The dream of "everyone having enough" has been with us as a species for thousands of years, yet has never been fulfilled. . . . The dream of a sustainable world might begin to seem quite possible if what wasn't needed, the clutter of life, faded away. Does this sound like an impossible dream? Perhaps . . . but if you agree with Viktor Frankl that we each possess a will to have meaning, then possibilities abound.

The Japanese have a wonderful saying: "The gods only laugh when people ask them for money."

And the Tao Te Ching, the ancient Chinese book of wisdom, puts it this way: "He who knows he has enough is rich. . . ."

THE PLEASURES OF FRUGALITY

We looked up "frugal" in a 1986 Merriam-Webster dictionary and found "characterized by or reflecting economy in the expenditure of resources." That sounds about right—a serviceable, practical and fairly colorless word. None of the elegance or grace of the "enoughness" that . . . [some] experience. But when we dig deeper, the dictionary tells us that "frugal" shares a Latin root with *frug* (meaning virtue), *frux* (meaning fruit or value) and *frui* (meaning to enjoy or have the use of). Now we're talking. Frugality is *enjoying the virtue* of getting good value for every minute of your life energy and from everything you *have the use of.*

That's very interesting. In fact, it's more than interesting. It's transforming. Frugality means we are to *enjoy* what we have. If you have ten dresses but still feel you have nothing to wear, you are probably a spendthrift. But if you have ten dresses and have enjoyed wearing all of them for years, you are frugal. Waste lies not in the number of possessions but in the failure to enjoy them. Your success at being frugal is measured not by your penny-pinching but by your degree of enjoyment of the material world.

Enjoyment of the material world? Isn't that hedonism? While both have to do with enjoying what you have, frugality and hedonism are opposite responses to the material world. Hedonism revels in the pleasures of the senses and implies excessive consumption of the material world and a continual search for more. Frugal people, however, get value from everything—a dandelion or a bouquet of roses, a single strawberry or a gourmet meal. A hedonist might consume the juice of five oranges as a prelude to a pancake breakfast. A frugal person, on the other hand, might relish eating a single orange, enjoying the color and texture of the whole fruit, the smell and the light spray that comes as you begin to peel it, the translucence of each section, the flood of flavor that pours out as a section bursts over the tongue . . . and the thrift of saving the peels for baking.

To be frugal means to have a high joy-to-stuff ratio. If you get one unit of joy for each material possession, that's frugal. But if you need ten possessions to even begin registering on the joy meter, you're missing the point of being alive.

There's a word in Spanish that encompasses all this: *aprovechar*. It means to use something wisely—be it old zippers from worn-out clothing or a sunny day at the beach. It's getting full value from life, enjoying all the good that each moment and each thing has to offer. You can *"aprovechar"* a simple meal, a flat of overripe strawberries or a cruise in the Bahamas. There's nothing miserly about *aprovechar;* it's a succulent word, full of sunlight and flavor. If only "frugal" were so sweet.

The "more is better and it's never enough" mentality in North America fails the frugality test not solely because of the excess, but because of the lack of enjoyment of what we already have. Indeed, North Americans have been called materialists, but that's a misnomer. All too often it's not material things we enjoy as much as what these things symbolize: conquest, status, success, achievement, a sense of worth and even favor in the eyes of the Creator. Once we've acquired the dream house, the status car or the perfect mate, we rarely stop to enjoy them thoroughly. Instead, we're off and running after the next coveted acquisition.

Another lesson we can derive from the dictionary definition of "frugal" is the recognition that we don't need to possess a thing to enjoy it—we merely need to *use* it. If we are enjoying an item, *whether or not we own it,* we're being frugal. For many of life's pleasures it maybe far better to "use" something than to "possess" it (and pay in time and energy for the upkeep). So often we have been like feudal lords, gathering as many possessions as possible from far and wide and bringing them inside the walls of our castle. If we want something (or wanted it in the past, or imagine we might want it in the future), we think we must bring it inside the boundaries of the world called "mine." What we fail to recognize is that what is outside the walls of "mine" doesn't belong to the enemy; it belongs to "the rest of us." And if what lies outside our walls is not "them" but "us," we can afford to loosen our grip a bit on our possessions. We can gingerly open the doors of our fortress and allow goods (material and spiritual) to flow into and out of our boundaries.

Frugality, then, is also learning to share, to see the world as "ours" rather than as "theirs" and "mine." And, while not explicit in the word, being frugal and being happy with having enough mean that more will be available for others. Learning to equitably share the resources of the earth is at the top of the global agenda, and some creative frugality in North America could go a long way toward promoting that balance.

Frugality *is* balance. Frugality is the Greek notion of the golden mean. Frugality is being efficient in harvesting happiness from the world you live in. Frugality is right-use (which sounds, appropriately, like "righteous")—the wise stewarding of money, time, energy, space and possessions. Goldilocks expressed it well when she declared the porridge "not too hot, not too cold, but just right." Frugality is something like that—not too much, not too little, but just right. Nothing is wasted. Or left unused. It's a clean machine. Sleek. Perfect. Simple yet elegant. It's that magic word—enough. The peak of the Fulfillment Curve. The jumping-off point for a life of being fulfilled, learning and contributing to the welfare of the planet.

"Frugal, man." That's the cool, groovy way to say "far out" in the nineties. Surfers will talk about frugal waves. Teenage girls will talk about frugal dudes. Designers will talk about frugal fashions. Mark our words!

Keep this in mind as we explore ways to save money. We aren't talking about being cheap, making do or being a skinflint or a tightwad. We're talking about *creative* frugality, a way of life in which you get the maximum fulfillment for each unit of life energy spent.

In fact, now that you know that money is your life energy, it seems foolish to consider wasting it on stuff you don't enjoy and never use. . . . if you are 40 years old, . . . you have just 329,601 hours of life energy in your bank. That may seem like a lot now, but those hours will feel very precious at the *end* of your life. Spend them well now and you won't have regrets later.

In the end, this creative frugality is an expression of self-esteem. It honors the life energy you invest in your material possessions. Saving those minutes and hours of life energy through careful consuming is the ultimate in self-respect.

QUESTIONS

1. What are the pleasures of frugality?
2. How does frugality link with self-respect?

Bertrand Russell | # Impersonal Interests

Bertrand Russell was one of the great philosophers, logicians, and moralists of the twentieth
century. This is one of his many musings from
The Conquest of Happiness.

I wish to consider not those major interests about
which a man's life is built, but those minor interests
which fill his leisure and afford relaxation from the
tenseness of his more serious preoccupations. In the
life of the average man his wife and children, his
work and his financial position occupy the main part
of his anxious and serious thought. Even if he has
extra-matrimonial love affairs, they probably do not
concern him as profoundly in themselves as in their
possible effects upon his home life. The interests
which are bound up with his work I am not for the
present regarding as impersonal interests. A man of
science, for example, must keep abreast of research
in his own line. Towards such research his feelings
have the warmth and vividness belonging to something intimately concerned with his career, but if he
reads about research in some quite other science with
which he is not professionally concerned he reads in
quite a different spirit, not professionally, less critically, more disinterestedly. Even if he has to use his
mind in order to follow what is said, his reading is
nevertheless a relaxation, because it is not connected
with his responsibilities. If the book interests him, his
interest is impersonal in a sense which cannot be
applied to the books upon his own subject. It is such
interests lying outside the main activities of a man's
life that I wish to speak about in the present chapter.

One of the sources of unhappiness, fatigue and
nervous strain is inability to be interested in anything
that is not of practical importance in one's own life.
The result of this is that the conscious mind gets no
rest from a certain small number of matters, each of
which probably involves some anxiety and some element of worry. Except in sleep the conscious mind is
never allowed to lie fallow while subconscious
thought matures its gradual wisdom. The result is
excitability, lack of sagacity, irritability, and a loss of
sense of proportion. All these are both causes and
effects of fatigue. As a man gets more tired, his external interests fade, and as they fade he loses the relief
which they afford him and becomes still more tired.
This vicious circle is only too apt to end in a breakdown. What is restful about external interests is the
fact that they do not call for any action. Making decisions and exercising volition are very fatiguing, especially if they have to be done hurriedly and without
the help of the subconscious. Men who feel that they
must "sleep on it" before coming to an important
decision are profoundly right. But it is not only in
sleep that the subconscious mental processes can
work. They can work also while a man's conscious
mind is occupied elsewhere. The man who can forget
his work when it is over and not remember it until it
begins again next day is likely to do his work far better than the man who worries about it throughout the
intervening hours. And it is very much easier to forget work at the times when it ought to be forgotten if
a man has many interests other than his work than it
is if he has not. It is, however, essential that these
interests should not exercise those very faculties
which have been exhausted by his day's work. They
should not involve will and quick decision, they
should not, like gambling, involve any financial element, and they should as a rule not be so exciting as
to produce emotional fatigue and preoccupy the subconscious as well as the conscious mind.

A great many amusements fulfill all these conditions. Watching games, going to the theater, playing
golf, are all irreproachable from this point of view.

From Bertrand Russell, *The Conquest of Happiness* (New York: Viking 1936), pp. 36–40.

For a man of a bookish turn of mind reading unconnected with his professional activities is very satisfactory. However important a worry may be, it should not be thought about throughout the whole of the waking hours. . . .

All impersonal interests, apart from their importance as relaxation, have various other uses. To begin with, they help a man to retain his sense of proportion. It is very easy to become so absorbed in our own pursuits, our own circle, our own type of work, that we forget how small a part this is of the total of human activity and how many things in the world are entirely unaffected by what we do. Why should one remember this? you may ask. There are several answers. In the first place, it is good to have as true a picture of the world as is compatible with necessary activities. Each of us in the world for no very long time, and within the few years of his life has to acquire whatever he is to know of this strange planet and its place in the universe. To ignore our opportunities for knowledge, imperfect as they are, is like going to the theater and not listening to the play. The world is full of things that are tragic or comic, heroic or bizarre or surprising, and those who fail to be interested in the spectacle that it offers are forgoing one of the privileges that life has to offer.

Then again a sense of proportion is very valuable and at times very consoling. We are all inclined to get unduly excited, unduly strained, unduly impressed with the importance of the little corner of the world in which we live, and of the little moment of time comprised between our birth and death. In this excitement and overestimation of our own importance there is nothing desirable. True, it may make us work harder, but it will not make us work better. A little work directed to a good end is better than a great deal of work directed to a bad end, though the apos-tles of the strenuous life seem to think otherwise. Those who care much for their work are always in danger of falling into fanaticism, which consists essentially in remembering one or two desirable things while forgetting all the rest, and in supposing that in the pursuit of these one or two any incidental harm of other sorts is of little account. Against this fanatical temper there is no better prophylactic than a large conception of the life of man and his place in the universe. This may seem a very big thing to invoke in such a connection, but apart from this particular use, it is in itself a thing of great value. . . .

A man who has once perceived, however temporarily and however briefly, what makes greatness of soul, can no longer be happy if he allows himself to be petty, self-seeking, troubled by trivial misfortunes, dreading what fate may have in store for him. The man capable of greatness of soul will open wide the windows of his mind, letting the winds blow freely upon it from every portion of the universe. He will see himself and life and the world as truly as our human limitations will permit; realizing the brevity and minuteness of human life, he will realize also that in individual minds is concentrated whatever of value the known universe contains. And he will see that the man whose mind mirrors the world becomes in a sense as great as the world. In emancipation from the fears that beset the slave of circumstance he will experience a profound joy, and through all the vicissitudes of his outward life he will remain in the depths of his being a happy man. . . .

QUESTIONS

1. How do impersonal interests help us?
2. What is happiness, for Russell? How does it relate to "greatness of soul"?

Robert C. Solomon | # Why Ethics?

Our seminars in business ethics are typically sandwiched in between sessions on financial analysis and production planning. Not unreasonably, business people expect similarly hard-headed, decisive, pragmatic, issue-oriented, goal-directed, job-defined, bottom-line-minded, and imminently useful information. Not surprisingly, then, our seminars almost always begin with and are periodically brought back around to such practical questions as "What does this have to do with my job?" or "Will understanding ethics help me do my job better?"

Such questions deserve and demand three immediate, practical answers.

1. ETHICAL ERRORS END CAREERS MORE QUICKLY AND MORE DEFINITIVELY THAN ANY OTHER MISTAKE IN JUDGMENT OR ACCOUNTING.

To err is human, perhaps, but to be caught lying, cheating, stealing, or reneging on contracts is not easily forgotten or forgiven in the business world. And for good reason: Such actions undermine the ethical foundation on which the business world thrives. Almost everyone can have compassion for someone caught in an ethical dilemma. No one can excuse immorality.

For every glaring case of known unethical conduct that goes unpunished, a dozen once-promising careers silently hit a dead end or quietly go down the tubes. On relatively rare occasions, an unhappy executive or employee is singled out and forced to pay public penance for conduct that everyone knows—he or she and the attorney will loudly protest—"goes on all the time." But much more often, unethical behavior, though unearthed, will go unannounced; indeed, the executive or employee in question will keep his or her job and may not even find out that he or she has been found out—may never even realize the unethical nature of his or her behavior. A career will just go nowhere. Responsibilities will remain routine, promotions elusive.

What makes such career calamities so pathetic is that they are not the product of greed or immorality or wickedness. They are the result of ethical naiveté.

- They happen because an employee unthinkingly "did what he was told to do"—and became the scapegoat as well.
- They happen because a casual public comment was ill-considered and had clearly unethical implications—through nothing of the kind may have been intended.
- They happen because a middle manager, pressed from above for results, tragically believed the adolescent cliches that pervade the mid-regions of the business world, such as "In business, you do whatever you have to do to survive." (It is both revealing and instructive that although we often hear such sentiments expressed in seminars for middle managers, we virtually never hear them in similar seminars for upper-level executives.)
- They happen because upper management wasn't clear about standards, priorities, and limits, or wasn't reasonable in its expectations, or wasn't available for appeal at the critical moment.

From Robert C. Solomon, *It's Good Business: Ethics and Free Enterprise for the New Millennium* (Lanham: Rowman/Littlefield, 1998). Reprinted with the permission of the author.

- They happen because an anonymous employee or middle manager hidden in the complexity of a large organization foolishly believed that such safe anonymity would continue, whatever his or her behavior.
- They happen, most of all, because a person in business is typically trained and pressured to "think business," without regard for the larger context in which business decisions are made and legitimized.

Unethical thinking isn't just "bad business"; it is an invitation to disaster in business, however rarely (it might sometimes seem) unethical behavior is actually found out and punished.

2. ETHICS PROVIDES THE BROADER FRAMEWORK WITHIN WHICH BUSINESS LIFE MUST BE UNDERSTOOD.

There may be a few people for whom business is all of life, for whom family and friendship are irrelevant, for whom money means only more investment potential and has nothing to do with respect or status or enjoying the good life. But most successful executives understand that *business is part of life.* Corporations are part of a society that consists of something more than a market. Executives and employees do not disappear into their jobs as if into a well, only to reappear in "real life" at the end of the business day.

Successful managers, we now all know, stay close to their subordinates—and not just as subordinates. The best corporations in their "search for excellence" begin and remain close to their customers, and not just in their narrowest role as consumers. Money may be a scorecard, a measure of status and accomplishment, but it is not the ultimate end. Business success, like happiness, often comes most readily to those who do not aim at it directly.

Executives are most effective and successful when they retain their "real life" view of themselves, their position, and the human world outside as well as inside the corporation. Business ethics, ultimately, is just business in its larger human context.

A corporation's responsibilities include how the whole business is conducted every day. It must be a thoughtful institution which rises above the bottom line to consider the impact of its action on all, from shareholders to the society at large. Its business activities must make business sense.

Andrew Siglér, "The Business Roundtable," *New York Times,* February 1981

3. NOTHING IS MORE DANGEROUS TO A BUSINESS—OR TO BUSINESS IN GENERAL—THAN A TARNISHED PUBLIC IMAGE.

A few years ago, *Business and Society Review* reported the results of a Harris Poll—one among many—that showed that public confidence in the executives running major corporations had declined "drastically" from 55% in 1966 to 16% in 1976; 87% of the respondents in a parallel poll agreed that most businessmen were more interested in profits than in the public interest. Whether or not such suspicions seriously affect sales, they indisputably hurt the bottom line in a dozen other hurtful ways—not least among them the pressure for government regulation. The fact is that a tarnished image has direct consequences, for sales, for profits, for morale, for the day-to-day running of the business. Distrust of an industry ("big oil," "the insurance racket") can hurt every company, and distrust of an individual company can quickly drive it to bankruptcy.

The editors of the *Review* tried to find the reason for the "falling image of private enterprise" and the flawed image of the men and women who devote their lives to business. They surveyed the chief executives of some of the nation's large corporations, asking for their opinions about what had happened and what could be done. As one would expect, there was vast disagreement on causes—from blaming the press to blaming the universities to expressing the view that since Watergate, all people and institutions in power are inevitably suffering from a more general loss of confidence. But what all of the respondents agreed about was the need to correct the image of business and free enterprise as essentially antagonistic or indifferent to the public good and morality. That correction, in turn, depends on the ability of business people to speak out for themselves, to express in their own terms the ethics and economics of their work without depending on the press to do it for them. Indeed, business ethics is not so much a subject matter as an alternative language in which business people must articulate their own awareness and aims of the work that they do. (The alternative assumption: "If they won't even tell us what they're doing, they must be doing something wrong.")

QUESTIONS

1. What are the reasons Solomon offers in favor of running a business ethically?

2. How do "career calamities" happen, according to Solomon?

CASES

CASE 4.1
The Opportunist
James Fenimore Cooper

James Fenimore Cooper is the author of such American classics as *The Deerslayer* and *The Last of the Mohicans*. This short story is from his collection, *Home as Found*.

The service at Mr. Effingham's table was made in the quiet but thorough manner that distinguishes a French dinner. Every dish was removed, carved by the domestics, and handed in turn to each guest. But there were a delay and a finish in this arrangement that suited neither Aristabulus' go-ahead-ism, nor his organ of acquisitiveness. Instead of waiting, therefore, for the more graduated movements of the domestics, he began to take care of himself, an office that he performed with a certain dexterity that he had acquired by frequenting ordinaries—a school, by the way, in which he had obtained most of his notion of the proprieties of the table. One or two slices were obtained in the usual manner, or by means of the regular service; and then, like one who had laid the foundation of a fortune by some lucky windfall in the commencement of his career, he began to make accessions, right and left, as opportunity offered. Sundry *entremets,* or light dishes that had a peculiarly tempting appearance, came first under his grasp. Of these he soon accumulated all within his reach, by taxing his neighbors, when he ventured to send his plate here and there, or wherever he saw a dish that promised to reward his trouble. By such means, which were resorted to, however, with a quiet and unobtrusive

From James Fenimore Cooper, *Home as Found* (New York: G. P. Putnam's Sons, 1838) pp. 18–19.

assiduity that escaped much observation, Mr. Bragg contrived to make his own plate a sample epitome of the first course. It contained in the centre, fish, beef, and ham; and around these staple articles he had arranged croquettes, rognons, ragouts, vegetables, and other light things, until not only was the plate completely covered, but it was actually covered in double and triple layers; mustard, cold butter, salt, and even pepper garnishing its edges. These different accumulations were the work of time and address, and most of the company had repeatedly changed their plates before Aristabulus had eaten a mouthful, the soup excepted. The happy moment when his ingenuity was to be rewarded had now arrived, and the land agent was about to commence the process of mastication, or of deglutition rather, for he troubled himself very little with the first operation, when the report of a cork drew his attention towards the champagne. To Aristabulus this wine never came amiss, for, relishing its piquancy he had never gone far enough into the science of the table to learn which were the proper moments for using it. As respected all the others at table, this moment had in truth arrived, though, as respected himself, he was no nearer to it, according to regulated taste, than when he first took his seat. Perceiving that Pierre was serving it, however, he offered his own glass, and enjoyed a delicious instant as he swallowed a beverage that much surpassed anything he had ever known to issue out of the waxed and leaded nozzles that, pointed like so many enemies' batteries loaded with headaches and disordered stomachs, garnished sundry village bars of his acquaintance.

Aristabulus finished his glass at a draught, and when he took breath he fairly smacked his lips. That was an unlucky instant; his plate, burdened with all its treasures, being removed at this unguarded moment; the man who performed this unkind office fancying that a dislike to the dishes could alone have given rise to such an *omniumgatherum.*

It was necessary to commence de novo, but this could no longer be done with the first course, which was removed, and Aristabulus set to with zeal forthwith on the game. Necessity compelled him to eat, as the different dishes were offered; and such was his ordinary assiduity with the knife and fork, that, at the end of the second remove, he had actually disposed of more food than any other person at table.

QUESTIONS

1. Is Aristabulus happy or unhappy? Why?
2. Why is the story entitled "the opportunist"? What does it tell us about our own society?

CASE 4.2
The Parable of the Sadhu
Bowen H. McCoy

Bowen H. McCoy is a managing director of Morgan Stanley & Co., Inc., and president of Morgan Stanley Realty, Inc. He is also an ordained ruling elder of the United Presbyterian Church.

Last year, as the first participant in the new six-month sabbatical program that Morgan Stanley has adopted, I enjoyed a rare opportunity to collect my thoughts as well as do some traveling. I spent the first three months in Nepal, walking 600 miles through 200 villages in the Himalayas and climbing some 120,000 vertical feet. On the trip my sole Western companion was an anthropologist who shed light on the cultural patterns of the villages we passed through.

From *Harvard Business Review,* Sept–Oct 1983, pp 103–104. Reprinted with permission.

During the Nepal hike, something occurred that has had a powerful impact on my thinking about corporate ethics. Although some might argue that the experience has no relevance to business, it was a situation in which a basic ethical dilemma suddenly intruded into the lives of a group of individuals. How the group responded I think holds a lesson for all organizations no matter how defined.

THE SADHU

The Nepal experience was more rugged and adventuresome than I had anticipated. Most commercial treks last two or three weeks and cover a quarter of the distance we traveled.

My friend Stephen, the anthropologist, and I were halfway through the 60-day Himalayan part of the trip when we reached the high point, an 18,000-foot pass over a crest that we'd have to traverse to reach to the village of Muklinath, an ancient holy place for pilgrims.

Six years earlier I had suffered pulmonary edema, an acute form of altitude sickness, at 16,500 feet in the vicinity of Everest base camp, so we were understandably concerned about what would happen at 18,000 feet. Moreover, the Himalayas were having their wettest spring in 20 years; hip-deep powder and ice had already driven us off one ridge. If we failed to cross the pass, I feared that the last half of our "once in a lifetime" trip would be ruined.

The night before we would try the pass, we camped at a hut at 14,500 feet. In the photos taken at that camp, my face appears wan. The last village we'd passed through was a sturdy two-day walk below us, and I was tired.

During the late afternoon, four back-packers from New Zealand joined us, and we spent most of the night awake, anticipating the climb. Below we could see the fires of two other parties, which turned out to be two Swiss couples and a Japanese hiking club.

To get over the steep part of the climb before the sun melted the steps cut in the ice, we departed at 3:30 A.M. The New Zealanders left first, followed by Stephen and myself, our porters and Sherpas, and then the Swiss. The Japanese lingered in their camp. The sky was clear, and we were confident that no spring storm would erupt that day to close the pass.

At 15,500 feet, it looked to me as if Stephen were shuffling and staggering a bit, which are symptoms of altitude sickness. (The initial stage of altitude sickness brings a headache and nausea. As the condition worsens, a climber may encounter difficult breathing, disorientation, aphasia, and paralysis.) I felt strong, my adrenaline was flowing, but I was very concerned about my ultimate ability to get across. A couple of our porters were also suffering from the height, and Pasang, our Sherpa sirdar (leader), was worried.

Just after daybreak, while we rested at 15,500 feet, one of the New Zealanders, who had gone ahead, came staggering down toward us with a body slung across his shoulders. He dumped the almost naked, barefoot body of an Indian holy man—a sadhu—at my feet. He had found the pilgrim lying on the ice, shivering and suffering from hypothermia. I cradled the sadhu's head and laid him out on the rocks. The New Zealander was angry. He wanted to get across the pass before the bright sun melted the snow. He said, "Look, I've done what I can. You have porters and Sherpa guides. You care for him. We're going on!" He turned and went back up the mountain to join his friends.

I took a carotid pulse and found that the sadhu was still alive. We figured he had probably visited the holy shrines at Muklinath and was on his way home. It was fruitless to question why he had chosen this desperately high route instead of the safe, heavily traveled caravan route through the Kali Gandaki gorge. Or why he was almost naked and with no shoes, or how long he had been lying in the pass. The answers weren't going to solve our problem.

Stephen and the four Swiss began stripping off outer clothing and opening their packs. The sadhu was soon clothed from head to foot. He was not able to walk, but he was very much alive. I looked down the mountain and spotted below the Japanese climbers marching up with a horse.

Without a great deal of thought, I told Stephen and Pasang that I was concerned about withstanding the heights to come and wanted to get over the pass. I took off after several of our porters who had gone ahead.

On the steep part of the ascent where, if the ice steps had given way, I would have slid down about 3,000 feet, I felt vertigo. I stopped for a breather,

To: You
From: The Philosopher
Subject: "A Happiness Box"

You wrote in your last email message, "All I want is to be happy and enjoy my life!" I detect some frustration in that outburst. But is that all that you really want out of life? I was thinking the other day: imagine an invention—which today is not at all implausible—that is the following. It is a box, cushioned and comfortable (not unlike a coffin, but don't let that association turn you off). You lie in the box, and we hook you up with electrodes, but nothing painful or discomforting and after a few minutes you forget that they are even there. The electrodes are connected to a computer that sends out signals that stimulate your brain, sending waves of pleasure and satisfaction. Within minutes, you completely stop caring about anything else. No worries, no problems. Of course, you can get out of the box anytime that you want to, but it isn't necessary because technicians take care of all your bodily needs, making sure you have water and nutrition, that your body stays at a healthy temperature, and so on. And as a matter of fact (we can imagine), no one has ever decided to get out of the box. With time, your body starts looking like a bean bag from lack of exercise, and your friends and family all forget about you, but you don't care. You're happy. You're completely satisfied with your life and enjoying every minute of it.

OK. There's your life of enjoyment, satisfaction, and happiness. Would you like to try out the box?

---

allowing the Swiss to catch up with me. I inquired about the sadhu and Stephen. They said that the sadhu was fine and that Stephen was just behind. I set off again for the summit.

Stephen arrived at the summit an hour after I did. Still exhilarated by victory, I ran down the snow slope to congratulate him. He was suffering from altitude sickness, walking 15 steps, then stopping, walking 15 steps, then stopping. Pasang accompanied him all the way up. When I reached them, Stephen glared at me and said: "How do you feel about contributing to the death of a fellow man?"

I did not fully comprehend what he meant.
"Is the sadhu dead?" I inquired.
"No," replied Stephen, "but he surely will be!"

After I had gone, and the Swiss had departed not long after, Stephen had remained with the sadhu. When the Japanese had arrived, Stephen had asked to use their horse to transport the sadhu down to the hut. They had refused. He had then asked Pasang to have a group of our porters carry the sadhu. Pasang had

resisted the idea, saying that the porters would have to exert all their energy to get themselves over the pass. He had thought they could not carry a man down 1,000 feet to the hut, reclimb the slope, and get across safely before the snow melted. Pasang had pressed Stephen not to delay any longer.

The Sherpas had carried the sadhu down to a rock in the sun at about 15,000 feet and had pointed out the hut another 500 feet below. The Japanese had given him food and drink. When they had last seen him he was listlessly throwing rocks at the Japanese party's dog, which had frightened him.

We do not know if the sadhu lived or died.

QUESTIONS

1. Who is responsible for the well-being of the sadhu? What are the duties of the people involved? What action would best serve the good of everyone?

2. How are the problems here similar to problems that arise in organizations every day? What kinds of sadhus do people confront in everyday life?

CASE 4.3
A Life Badly Lived
Arthur Miller

Arthur Miller was one of America's great playwrights, and *Death of a Salesman* is his masterpiece. This is the Requiem that ends the play

CHARLEY: It's getting dark, Linda.
Linda doesn't react. She stares at the grave.

BIFF: How about it, Mom? Better get some rest, heh? They'll be closing the gate soon.
Linda makes no move. Pause.

HAPPY (*deeply angered*): He had no right to do that. There was no necessity for it. We would've helped him.

CHARLEY (*grunting*): Hmmm.

BIFF: Come along, Mom.

LINDA: Why didn't anybody come?

CHARLEY: It was a very nice funeral.

LINDA: But where are all the people he knew? Maybe they blame him.

CHARLEY: Naa. It's a rough world, Linda. They wouldn't blame him.

LINDA: I can't understand it. At this time especially. First time in thirty-five years we were just about free and clear. He only needed a little salary. He was even finished with the dentist.

CHARLEY: No man only needs a little salary.

LINDA: I can't understand it.

BIFF: There were a lot of nice days. When he'd come home from a trip; or on Sundays, making the stoop; finishing the cellar; putting on the new porch; when he built the extra bathroom; and put up the garage. You know something, Charley, there's more of him in that front stoop than in all the sales he ever made.

CHARLEY: Yeah. He was a happy man with a batch of cement.

LINDA: He was so wonderful with his hands.

BIFF: He had the wrong dreams. All, all, wrong.

HAPPY (*almost ready to fight Biff*): Don't say that!

BIFF: He never knew who he was.

CHARLEY (*stopping Happy's movement and reply. To Biff*): Nobody dast blame this man. You don't understand: Willy was a salesman.
And for a salesman, there is no rock bottom to the life. He don't put a bolt to a nut, he don't tell you the law or give you medicine. He's a man way out there in the blue, riding on a smile and a shoeshine. And when they start not smiling back—that's an earthquake. And then you get yourself a couple of spots on your hat, and you're finished. Nobody dast blame this man. A salesman is got to dream, boy. It comes with the territory.

BIFF: Charley, the man didn't know who he was.

HAPPY (*infuriated*): Don't say that!

BIFF: Why don't you come with me, Happy?

HAPPY: I'm not licked that easily. I'm staying right in this city, and I'm gonna beat this racket (*He looks at Biff, his chin set.*) The Loman Brothers!

BIFF: I know who I am, kid.

HAPPY: All right, boy. I'm gonna show you and everybody else that Willy Loman did not die in vain. He had a good dream. It's the only dream you can have—to come out number-one man. He fought it out here, and this is where I'm gonna win it for him.

BIFF (*with a hopeless glance at Happy, bends toward his mother*): Let's go, Mom.

LINDA: I'll be with you in a minute. Go on, Charley. (*He hesitates.*) I want to, just for a minute. I never had a chance to say good-by.

Charley moves away, followed by Happy. Biff remains a slight distance up and left of Linda. She sits there, summoning herself. The flute begins, not far away, playing behind her speech.

LINDA: Forgive me, dear. I can't cry. I don't know what it is, but I can't cry. I don't understand it. Why did you ever do that? Help me, Willy, I can't cry. It seems to me that you're just on another trip. I keep expecting you. Willy, dear, I can't cry. Why did you do it? I search and search and I search, and I can't understand it, Willy. I made the last payment on the house today. Today, dear. And there'll be nobody home. (*A sob rises in her throat.*) We're free and clear. (*Sobbing more fully, released.*) We're free. (*Biff comes slowly toward her.*) We're free . . . We're free . . .

Biff lifts her to her feet and moves out up right with her in his arms. Linda sobs quietly. Bernard and Charley come together and follow them, followed by Happy. Only the music of the flute is left on the darkening stage as over the house the hard towers of the apartment buildings rise into sharp focus, and
The Curtain Falls

QUESTIONS

1. Is Willy Loman a hero or a just a failure? Why might his son insist on the heroism of Willy Loman?
2. What went wrong for Willy Loman?

CASE 4.4
Rags to Riches to Rags
Ruth Capriles

The Pemón are an indigenous people who inhabit the region of the tepuyes (Auyan, Chimanta, Akopan, Roraima). Although some anthropologists say the Pemón do not exist as a separate ethnic group from the Caribes, and whoever their ancestors may be, today they identify themselves as a tribal unit, scattered over the plains, living in more or less extended family groups, or in Catholic missions. Some of these Amerindians have been Westernized: they have been clothed, converted, taught to read and write, aided by social and missionary programs and have been taught to play the violin, work in the mines and cut diamonds. They appear to learn fast and yet have maintained a considerable ethnic rigidity (the community disapproves of inter racial mixing); their family-type social structure and their way of life are adapted to the plains, forests and rivers that constitute their natural environment, and to which they seem to make a straightforward return following their contact with modern civilization. The history that I am about to relate is more about my own astonishment than an exact description of the experience of this community. . . . I will tell the story in three moments or observation times.

THE UTOPIA

The story has a central figure, the current leader of a group of Pemón who lived on the other side of the tepuys, independent from the rest of the ethnic groups, escaping from the influence of Catholic missions and from the state control and urban influence.

From Ruth Capriles, "Rags to Riches to Rags," *Leadership and Organizational Development* vol 21, no 4, 2000, pp 195–199.

Having left the riverbank of the Alto Caroní at the age of seven, our leader reached Urimán where a pilot offered to take him to Ciudad Bolívar. Here the pilot handed him over to a good doctor who took him into his family and brought him up with his own son who was slightly younger. He was catechized by this Catholic family and he attended school; he lived in Caracas and began his high school diploma. But at the age of 16 he decided to return to his native land. For the next 15 years, we know little about him except that he returned to his native environment and made a living from the usual local economic activities: fishing, hunting, raising crops and pigs, finding the occasional alluvial diamond whose value to civilization he fully recognized.

Fifteen years later, his step brother went looking for him, found him now the captain of the Pemón at the other side of the Tepuy, and they joined forces in a mining venture. They obtained the concession to exploit the mines from the Ministry of Energy and Mines (MEM) and through heroic, pioneering work, they cleared a landing strip and set up a mining camp in the middle of the unending jungle; then they started production. They also began to learn the art of cutting diamonds for which they showed an immediate knack.

Five years later they lost the mining concession for various reasons that need not concern us here. The non-Indian workers left the site and went back to their city lives. But the Pemón did not. They live there, and so they stayed and continued to work the mine. For the next 15 years, the captain dedicated himself to building an organized community. With the surplus income from the mine, and with the collaboration of the community, he rebuilt an old and lost small village, turning it into a political, economic and social center. He joined forces with some North American Baptist missionaries and built a church; they installed an electrical plant and built four school rooms and a dispensary.

The village functions as the political and social center for the Pemón and although they do not live there all the time, it serves as a religious, social and political center to reunite them as a tribe or extended family. Anyone who comes in is a relative; although the extended family extends beyond the village itself and is spread throughout the upper Caroní. The church, the school and the dispensary, now run by a doctor who visits the region every two weeks (paid for by the community from income from mining activity) serve important functions, attracting inhabitants and promoting social cohesion. Children learn Spanish in the school and read the Bible in Pemón. There is no malaria, there are no serious infantile diseases, and appropriate vaccines are administered. In case of sickness or for specific needs, including cases of mercury poisoning, they can seek medical attention in Ciudad Bolívar.

The political representation of the organization is non-democratic. The captain has been elected and reelected by the heads of every family (women included if they are the head of the family, which is normal) and not by all adult members of the community. However, this seems to be a legitimate form of representation and meets little opposition or challenge from other parties. The captain exercises uncontested authority over the 38,000 hectares and the most astonishing thing is that he rules over the heterogeneous extractive population that has invaded the territory. Anyone who enters the area submits to the captain's authority, must ask permission to mine, contributes a percentage of the income from exploitation to the community, and restricts their activity to the area specified by the captain. Brazilian diamond-hunters, adventurers from the city, be they Arabs, natives of Caracas, US citizens, Canadians, contractors or independent workers, accept and cooperate with the order established by the captain and contribute to the indigenous community. The mining camps under the captain's authority adhere to the rules of behavior and are starting to have an obligation to save the damaged environment (an ecological conscience). There are no venereal diseases and no prostitution. In all conflicts the captain mediates, moving constantly throughout the region to settle disputes. Only the large foreign mining concerns, authorized by the CVG (Guayana Corporation) or the MEM in Pemón territory, restrict access to their camps, expropriate the natives and force them off the land (some concessions have been granted on lands covering existing indigenous villages (i.e. Morrocoy); these do not contribute to the community and cause greater, more widespread damage to the ecosystem.

The struggle to survive as an organized community in the face of the national interests of the state, that grants concessions and the interests of the transnational mining companies, is just starting. The Pemón have already lost several battles but they have achieved some miraculous results: being able to run mining operations without official concessions and having established order in all the regional camps with the exception of the foreign permit holders. This means that the Pemón's spontaneous form of organization seems to be capable of resolving the region's major problems, including mercury contamination of waterways.

———————

I hope that the mere existence of this indigenous group gives us food for thought for reflecting upon forms of organization, representation and local governability.

AFTERMATH—THIS IS NOT A HAPPY ENDING

Four years later, bliss is gone and the Pemón community is unstable. Our utopia went well until its leader lost the lead. Too many lives to live by the same person; too much money. In practice, our Cacique was leading three lives. He had to direct and oversee the mine territory and rule over Pemóns and interlopers. He had to be present at the religious and political center, and fly to the city to deal and sell. And the city had the worst of him. He forgot his extended family and the political project. He was surrounded, advised, and helped by outsiders pursuing their own interest: military with interest in mining; women in diamond trade; private entrepreneurs or companies ready to offer their services to extract and market diamonds, or even as partners in the mining business.

He certainly needed alliances to deal with the state policies on mining and he would hear anyone promising to help the community get the concession to oper-

ate the mines. Somehow, to get the concession and renew the permits of agrarian land rights became the main purpose of the leader. A number of factors combined to create instability in the Pemón' community.

The Catholic Church was one of his main opponents, competing for religious influence and contesting the Protestant influence over the community. The mission down river used its influence in government and demanded the control of education in the Pemón community, based on ancient privileges of the church to catechize and educate in the region. Teachers of the community had to be taught at the mission. This assured Catholic education in a village which had adopted the Baptist worship, which must have introduced certain ethical splits in the community. The intervention of the national education system through the mission control (and thereby the intervention of the national health system) also forced the leader to have the classrooms rebuilt in concrete blocks and zinc, rejecting the traditional hut, which is considered health hazardous. That meant a high cost of river transport in small boats (or curiaras) of heavy materials and a cost in time to build the needed classrooms.

The military (the National Guard[2]) are fundamental actors in this story. They are the authority in the region and exercise it at discretion. Corruption in the military at the region is a public secret. They decide who passes by road and river posts, who can extract gold or diamonds and who can export them without paying taxes; they get a share on each pile or wash; they even distribute the mercury which miners shouldn't use; they deal in the business. Sometimes they play on the same side of the Pemóns (it is to their interest that the Indians keep the concession, so it will not be given to a foreign company, which extracts and does not share with anyone). By the same token, they are a plague to the Indians who must negotiate with the military every inch of the way.

State decisions have dissolving influence on the community. Decisions supporting the mission's demands (strengthened by a social Christian national government) puts an area of the Cacique's authority under control of the Catholic Church, introducing the problems mentioned above. Even more vital to the community's unfolding are the mining policies. The

Ministry of Mining holds the mining concession pending. The Pemóns keep on extracting diamonds and gold in a lawless situation, under the permissive but discrete eyes of the National Guard. This is an unstable situation, obviously, that can be changed suddenly by state policies and decisions or by a switch in the military moods. Getting the concession becomes a survival goal of the community.

CORRUPTION OF THE LEADER

Staying too long in the city, women, processed alcohol, the company of adventurers detracts the leader from his purpose. He loses touch with the community and his legitimacy to rule diminishes rapidly. This has happened to leaders throughout history, regardless of their cultural background.

Mercury, used in mining not only by them, but by *garimpeiros* and other illegal miners up river, have contaminated the waters and the fish; and so also land animals and people. The shortage of fish had been a previous consequence of the Guri Dam built in the 1970s down river, which altered the ecosystem and interrupted the fish cycles. Having focused on the mining project as economic survival activity, the Indians did not attend to any other means of production of food. Their crops, mainly roots, do not provide the basic nutritional needs. By the end of the 1990s, the community was having real problems of nourishment, specially in proteins.

Intensive invasion of foreign miners or adventurers adds instability to the maintenance of authority. If becomes difficult to control mining activities, behavior in camps, sexual diseases, respect of the Indian women. . . .

THE UNSTABLE SOLUTION—
A NEW HAPPIER ENDING

One year later, descendants of the Pemón leader, his pupils and aids in the management of things (sons, nephews) called a Council of Family Chiefs to decide on the leadership of the community. The Council decided to ask the resignation of the Cacique, to establish a new form of government and

to choose new government. Addressed by his colleagues, the Cacique accepted, not without pain, the community decision and offered his assistance as adviser to the young leaders.

The new form of government is a triumvirate of Caciques: one is chief over the mining production and occupation of mining territory; another is the religious-political chief in the town; and the third is in charge of foreign relations, including trade and procuring state permissions and concessions. They are still pending on the concession and are having the same basic problems of uncertainty, invasion, lack of nutritional food. But the impetus of the young seems to have regrouped them. Some I know went back from the city to the jungle to help in the recuperation and control of the territory. The young men of each family were given sectors of responsibility, forming a controlling team. The success of which I can not yet say. In a future paper I will report, for this is history and leadership in the making under local, national, global forces. I can imagine they keep on extracting mines without the concession and, although under a lot of obstacles, they might be managing some recuperation, even if uncertain. According to reports, their situation is in an unstable equilibrium.

A new Constitution of Venezuela seems to open new possibilities for the Indians. It formally recognizes the collective property to ethnic groups and indigenous communities: article 119 says, "The State will recognize the existence of ethnic groups and indigenous communities, their social, political and economic organization; their culture, uses and costumes, languages and religions; and also their habitat and original rights over the land they have occupied from ancestry and tradition and which are needed to develop and guarantee their forms of life." It gives the Indian people the right to demarcate and claim ownership of their lands as collective property. This new constitutional provision would give the Indians autonomy and stability in their lands. But the probabilities of obtaining it are not high, considering that if all Venezuelan Indians (a population of approximately 300,000) claim rights over their ancestral lands, they would own in collective regimes more than half of Venezuelan territory. We can expect the rest of the country will object to such arrangement on the making. Neither would collective property over land solve the mining rights, for the new constitution reinstated the ownership of the State over underground products, which keeps miners submitted to State policies.

QUESTIONS

1. What leadership challenges did the Cacique face?
2. What factors led to the downfall of the Cacique?

CHAPTER QUESTIONS

1. What is the most important thing in life to you? How does your career fit into your life? Or is your career the most important thing in your life?

2. How does pleasure differ from happiness? And what about the difference between short-term pleasure and long-term pleasure? Many hedonists have insisted carpe diem—seize the day—and you might wonder how far you should defer your pleasures. On the other hand, will you get the "big pleasures" if you don't sacrifice a lot of pleasure in the short term?

5

Money, How We Get It, and Where It Goes

Accounting, Finance, and Investment Ethics

Introduction

"It's all about the money." Well, maybe. But we have already seen that it's about a lot more as well. It's about success. It's about satisfaction and self-satisfaction. It's about doing well and living well. Nevertheless, it's about the money. That's what business is, among other things. And that's what is involved in understanding business ethics as well. "Follow the money." That's good advice in both investigative journalism and in business ethics. Even if money is not all of what business is about, it certainly dictates an awful lot of what it is about. So what money is, where it comes from, how and where it gets invested and by whom, and where it goes are all crucial questions in business ethics.

What is money? That sounds like a naive question, until one actually starts to pay attention to it. What makes gold and silver, for example, so valuable? These "precious metals" have limited uses (filling teeth and making photo film, for instance, neither of which are all that impressive). Yet, since ancient times, they have been desired enough to kill for. To be sure, both are relatively rare. But so are hen's teeth and baby unicorns, although there would be little interest in the market for them if they existed. But even given the extraordinary value of precious metals and precious gems, the desirability of money is something else again. Most money is paper, of no value in itself, and even metal coins are rarely worth their face value. Paper money is a promissory note, and behind the promise is an enormous network of trust. (Think about what happens when even a hint of scandal or devaluation hits the banking community.) But what allows people to invest their trust this way? Why not just collect gold and hide it under one's mattress? In the final analysis, money is worth something only because people believe and trust that it is worth something. It is worth nothing at all in itself.

This mystery of money, as opposed to the illusion that money itself is what is ultimately desired and desirable, pervades the financial world and its ethics. Money depends entirely on trust, and trust is the stuff of ethics. Thus, the story of money and business, like the story of business ethics, is the story of trust and how it is gained and lost, how it is betrayed and, if lost, again regained. And the more abstract money becomes, the more it depends upon trust.

Today most financial transactions do not even involve pieces of paper, except perhaps as back-up records. Hence, we can readily understand the trauma and the seriousness of the recent failure of one of the biggest auditing companies—Arthur Andersen, as well as the seriousness of conflicts of interest in the financial markets, not only as violations of authority and professional responsibility but as potentially undermining the whole financial system.

Money doesn't just sit there. Money gets invested. Indeed, as any financial adviser will tell you, money that is just sitting there (e.g., in a low-interest savings or money market account) is nevertheless invested; it is just invested unwisely. Money is always at work. Money that is "just sitting there" still plays its passive role in the flow of markets and financial exchange. Indeed, money owed is also part of the flow of markets and financial exchange, and people who owe thousands of dollars in debt on their credit cards and corporations that owe billions to local and foreign banks are very much players in the system. But if everyone, whether a solvent, active investor or an insolvent, even bankrupt, debtor is part of the market, then those who actively control the market—bankers, brokers, bureaucrats, and others—have special obligations—fiduciary obligations—to those who are not so active or not so smart. The hard-edged position here is that everyone—except, perhaps, children and the feeble-minded—is or ought to be fully informed about and responsible for his or her own financial state. But this is naive, not only in the sense that it is harsh treatment of responsibility, but that, given the abstraction and ultimate mystery of the financial world, it is expecting much too much of the average and perhaps even the aggressive investor. A few years ago, for example, when derivatives came into existence as a hedge on the market, even the "experts" were forced to admit that they did not understand these instruments and thus, at least to some extent, could not be held responsible for what happened with them. But for

---

To: You
From: The Philosopher
Subject: "Accounting and Mergers"

Congratulations on the good news that your accounting firm is performing the due diligence and audit on the new merger. The stock offering will be the interesting part. We sometimes think that mergers and IPOs (and the accountants who manage them) are a new phenomenon, something the twentieth century invented. But when you are doing the numbers, remember these cautionary words from Daniel Defoe (he was writing in the early 1700s):

> Some in clandestine companies combine,
> Erect new stocks to trade beyond the line,
> With air and empty names beguile the town
> And raise new credits first, then cry 'em down,
> Divide the empty nothing into shares,
> And set the crowd together by the ears.

most investors (keeping in mind the passivity of most people's investment histories), even such seemingly simple concepts as stocks and bonds, insurance, and annuities are mysterious, even if these instruments have now become (in the absence of government "welfare" systems) part and parcel of almost everyone's life. It is not enough to say "investor beware!" The financial markets are now complex and mysterious enough, and most people are vulnerable enough, to require special efforts and responsibilities on the part of those who manage and advise them.

In this chapter, we want to give at least some suggestions about a field that has been too long neglected in discussions of business ethics. In part, it has been neglected because it has seemed to many people too technical to be included in business ethics discussions. On the other hand, it has often seemed to be just another part of professional ethics. Accountants and money managers have been considered just professionals like doctors, lawyers, and architects and thus subject to the rules of their own peculiar institutions. But the collapse of Arthur Andersen convinced just about everyone in the financial world that the role of the accountant and the financial manager is something more than that of an economic technician or just another professional. And for the past 15 years, after the financial scandals of the late 1980s, it has been evident that the financial markets can be as corrupted by unfair dealings (like insider trading and ignoring conflicts of interest) as it can be by outright theft and fraud. Behind all this concern is a new awareness that it is not enough to say investor beware!" It is the responsibility of the financial community—in other words, all of us—to have some concern for what we might call *the innocent investor,* not just the proverbial feeble old lady on a pension, but most likely all of us. The forces of the market are brutal enough and sufficiently beyond our control that we all need and have a right to expect some protection, which means, minimally, ethical behavior on the part of those who are centrally responsible for making markets run in the first place.

Richard T. De George begins the chapter by providing an overview of the ethical issues that accountants face in "Ethical Issues for Accountants." Carol J. Loomis canvasses several major accounting scandals and explains how accountants fall under enormous pressure to "manage earnings" in "Lies, Damned Lies, and Managed Earnings." Ed Cohen briefly reflects on "What Went Wrong" for Arthur Andersen in the recent Enron-related accounting scandal that closed the gigantic and prestigious accounting firm. Robert E. Frederick and W. Michael Hoffman look at the ethical duties that companies have to the individual investor and the limitations on these duties. John R. Boatright gives a large perspective on finance ethics generally. Jennifer Moore shows how ethically complicated the stock market is in her "What Is Really Unethical About Insider Trading?" Finally, Frank Partnoy, a former Wall Street trader himself, explains the many dangers that are associated with derivative stock instruments.

Richard T. De George | # Ethical Issues for Accountants

Richard T. De George is professor of philosophy at the University of Kansas.

ETHICAL ISSUES FOR ACCOUNTANTS

Accountants face a great many pressures from clients who want them to do what is illegal: underreporting income, falsifying accounts, taking questionable deductions, illegally evading income tax, and engaging in outright fraud. None of these pose difficult conceptual issues from a moral point of view. They are illegal and unethical. This fact does not lessen the pressure to act unethically that many CPAs feel and to which they are subject. But the ethically correct thing to do in these issues is not in question.

Other difficulties involve requests to alter financial statements in order to achieve certain purposes (e.g., so the company will be able to get loans the client could not otherwise get) and requests that accounts deviate from standard accounting practices for any number of reasons. Corporations prefer to have their earnings rise in a gently sloping line. They prefer to avoid spikes in earning charts and to balance out windfall earnings over several quarters or years. Some would prefer to keep some assets in reserve in case of a poor quarter or year. They would prefer, therefore, that sometimes their reports not accurately reflect their actual situation. Sometimes this is legal, as when a company defers receipts or defers shipments so that they fall in another quarter or year. Sometimes it is not, and companies seek creative bookkeeping techniques to achieve their goals. The pressure to supply such techniques or to approve them often falls on the CPAs.

Fee setting, billing clients whom one knows are on the verge of bankruptcy, working for clients who can no longer afford their services, and resisting offers to work on a contingency fee basis form another set of issues with an ethical dimension. Still another set of issues involves deciding how to handle mistakes, especially when some accountants feel they are unable to keep up with the constant changes in regulations, law, and accounting practices and rules. A CPA should undertake only those tasks that he or she is competent to perform; but the knowledge that one is over one's head sometimes emerges only as one is sinking. Similarly, the temptation to overcommit oneself and to allow too little time for carrying out one's tasks with the proper care all possibly lead to unethical behavior and practices.

The American Institute of Certified Public Accountants (AICPA) publishes professional rules to guide and govern certified public accountants. Accountants are governed by three codes: Generally Accepted Accounting Principles (GAAP), Generally Accepted Auditing Standards (GAAS), and a Code of Professional Ethics (COPE). The AICPA Rules require independence of the firm or accountant from the client. This means they cannot hold any financial interest in the company. The intent is clearly to avoid conflict of interest. If the accounting firm is to certify a company's financial statements, it should have no incentive, owing to financial holdings in the company, to make the firm's financial situation look better than it is. The Code demands integrity, objectivity, competence, and compliance with standards set forth in GAAS and GAAP. The Rules guard client confidentiality, prohibit contingency fees (e.g., according to which no fee is charged unless a certain specified finding is attained), and preclude encroachment on the client of another accountant or accounting firm and the payment of commissions to obtain a client.

The client is responsible for the financial statements. The CPA does not guarantee the accuracy of

From Richard T. De George, *Business Ethics,* 4th Edition (Englewood Cliffs, NJ: Prentice-Hall, 1995).

Six Principles of Ethical Accounting

PRINCIPLE	AICPA DIRECTIVE
1. Responsibilities	In carrying out their responsibilities as professionals, members should exercise sensitive professional and moral judgments in all their activities.
2. The public interest	Members should accept the obligation to act in a way that will serve the public interest, honor the public trust, and demonstrate commitment to professionalism.
3. Integrity	To maintain and broaden public confidence, members should perform all professional responsibilities with the highest sense of integrity.
4. Objectivity and independence	A member should maintain objectivity and be free of conflicts of interest in discharging professional responsibilities. A member in public practice should be independent in fact and appearance when providing auditing and other attestation services.
5. Due care	A member should observe the profession's technical and ethical standards, strive continually to improve competence and the quality of services, and discharge professional responsibility to the best of the member's ability.
6. Scope and nature of services	A member in public should observe the Principles of the Code of Professional Conduct in determining the scope and nature of services to be provided.

From the American Institute of Certified Public Accountants. Reprinted with permission.

the statements. The accountant is neither required nor expected to investigate in depth the accuracy of the data presented in the reports. A CPA might become suspicious of some entries and question them, and must refuse to certify a statement that is misleading. But the client, not the CPA, is responsible for maintaining accurate records, and it is not the CPA's job routinely to check those records against all other documents or inventories. The CPA certifies that the financial statements conform with generally accepted accounting principles.

For many practicing accountants, obeying the Rules is the guide to ethical behavior. However, for some critics, it is not the honesty of individual accountants as they try to live up to the Rules that is the problem. They attack the rules and the system itself as ethically deficient.

THE ACCOUNTING RULES

The major issue is the (at least) apparent conflict of interest, to which we already referred, that is built into the American accounting system. Critics claim that, although the purpose of certifying the accounts of a corporation is to assure the general public that the corporation's accounts are correct as reported, the system is not set up to guarantee this result. The major stumbling block is that the accounting firm certifying a company's accounts works for the company whose accounts it is auditing. Although the accounting firm is independent, in the sense that it has no financial holdings in the company it is examining, its client—the one who pays its bills—is the company it is examining. It may be fired by that company and replaced by another accounting firm as the client wishes. There is at least on the surface an unavoidable conflict of interest in the operation of any accounting firm. It has the temptation to do nothing to cause disfavor with the company that hires it. Hence, although it is supposed to strive for objectivity, objectivity is not easy to achieve under the circumstances.

A second complaint stems from the fact that the accounting firm simply certifies that the company's accounts are correctly presented and are in accord with the generally accepted accounting and auditing standards. The accounting firm has no responsibility to verify the information it is given by the company whose accounts it is certifying. Furthermore, it has no responsibility to make public any internal discrepancies, fraud, or other irregularities it may discover, even though it may not, of course, itself engage in any cover-up or falsification of the records it does certify. The CPAs are caught between the requirement of confidentiality with respect to the client and the public's interest. Because this is the case, the system does not really assure those interested in the financial health of the company—shareholders, potential shareholders, and to some extent the general public who do business with the company—that the company's records are accurate and reflect its actual financial situation. Furthermore, there are various acceptable methods of handling debits and credits, and those reading financial reports are not always appraised of which alternative methods might have been used and why the one that is used was chosen over the others. Loans and debt are cases in point. If a loan is not likely to be recoverable in full, it is misleading to carry it at its full value. How and when to reduce it for accounting purposes, however, is open

to a good deal of discretion, nor can a CPA always know which loans or investments may turn sour and lead to a company's failing.

The public often wonders when businesses go bankrupt how it is that the financial reports did not indicate the seriousness of their plight. The reply that this is not the obligation of the auditor is formally correct, but it is an indication of the problem, rather than an answer to the problem. If it is not the auditor's job to do this, then whose job is it? Can the public interest be protected if it is no one's job to reveal when a corporation is in financial difficulty? If accountants performing audits were paid by the government and required to report an instance of fraud or financial irregularity to the government rather than to the client, would the public be better served than it currently is? The answer is at least arguably yes.

In 1988, the Financial Accounting Standards Board (FASB), which sets standards that the Securities and Exchange Commission requires corporations to follow, proposed requiring that corporations carry as a liability their exposure in terms of retirees' health care benefits. The proposal was adopted as FAS Standard 106 and took effect for large companies in 1993 and for smaller companies in 1995. This method more accurately reflects the company's financial exposure than does the former practice of simply listing the amount paid for this purpose in the past year. Yet, because the new reporting method would at least initially diminish annual corporate earnings considerably, the proposal generated great opposition. Opponents also claimed that future projections were no better than a guess. What do fairness and accuracy in reporting require in this case? What do they amount to when actual liabilities such as this need not be reported? Should corporate opposition be sufficient to preclude and determine reporting regulations? Are the regulations for the benefit of the firms or of the public? These are legitimate questions, raising ethical concerns that deserve at least discussion. Critics claim that accounting firms would take the lead in changing reporting requirements to better serve the public if the firms were not paid by their clients, whose interests are not always served by such reporting regulations.

If there is a conflict between public interest and the interest of their clients, which interest is an accounting firm to put first? If the point of audits and certification were truly to protect the public interest, then accountants and accounting firms would be ethically obliged to place that interest above the interests of their clients. But they are not clearly required to do that, and hence they are in an ethically ambiguous position.

To the extent that accounting firms have taken on the additional task of consulting firms, they have increased the potential for conflict of interest. If the same company both suggests a policy and then audits the results, it is likely to be tempted to make the results look as favorable as possible. Faced with this temptation, some firms have attempted to construct "chinese walls" between their auditing departments and their consulting departments, such that neither knows what the other is doing.

Critics would prefer changing the system so as preclude the present built-in conflicts of interest. As yet, no widely acceptable alternative has emerged.

The accounting profession itself has responded to public concern by scrutinizing and revising its own rules, yet the AICPA has not been conspicuous in its ability or desire to police itself, enforce its codes, and take punitive actions against those who violate them. In this respect, it fares no better than other professional associations.

QUESTIONS

1. Does regulation make accountants more or less efficient? Why do accountants need ethically informed rules?

2. Give three examples of ethical conflict that accountants are likely to encounter.

Carol J. Loomis

Lies, Damned Lies, and Managed Earnings

Carol J. Loomis is a reporter for *Fortune* magazine.

Someplace right now, in the layers of a *Fortune* 500 Company, an employee—probably high up and probably helped by people who work for him—is perpetrating an accounting fraud. Down the road that crime will come to light and cost the company's shareholders hundreds of millions of dollars.

Typically, the employee will not have set out to be dishonest, only to dodge a few rules. His fraud, small at first, will build, because the exit he thought just around the corner never appears. In time, some subordinate may say. "Whoa!" But he won't muster the courage to blow the whistle, and the fraud will go on.

Until it's uncovered. The company's stock will drop then, by a big percent. Class-action lawyers will

leap. The Securities and Exchange Commission will file unpleasant enforcement actions, levy fines, and leave the bad guys looking for another line of work.

Eventually someone may go to jail.

And the fundamental reason, very often, will be that the company or one of its divisions was "managing earnings"—trying to meet Wall Street expectations or those of the boss, trying also to pretend that the course of business is smooth and predictable when in reality it is not.

Jail? This is not a spot that CEOs and other high-placed executives see themselves checking into, for any reason. *Jail for managing earnings?* Many corporate chiefs would find that preposterous, having come to believe that "making their numbers" is just what executives do. Okay, so the pressure might lead some of them to do dumb (but legal) things—like

Learning to Cheat?

Former Stanford University President Donald Kennedy blamed "infirmities" in the institution's accounting practices for overcharging the federal government more than $160 million over the past decade, including $180,000 for depreciation of the Stanford Sailing Association yacht and $185,000 for administrative costs for a profitable Stanford-owned shopping center. Kennedy said his institution billed the government for many of the expenses "merely because it was lawful to do so."

—*Quarterly Review of Doublespeak*, January 1992

making off-price deals at the end of a quarter that simply steal from full-priced business down the road. Who cares? Others might even be driven to make hash of the rules that publicly owned companies are required to abide by, Generally Accepted Accounting Principles, known as GAAP. Sure, that might mean crossing a legal line, but so what. . . .

What's at stake, he [Arthur Levitt chairman of the SEC] says, is nothing less than the credibility of the U.S. financial-reporting system, traditionally thought to be the best in the world. It will not now, he vowed, be undermined by managements obsessed with making their numbers. "It's a basic cultural change we're asking for," he said, "nothing short of that."

For those who can't get with the program, the punishment increasingly could be criminal prosecution. The SEC does not itself have the ability to bring criminal actions, so the chairman has been out jawboning people who do, like Attorney General Janet Reno and various U.S. Attorneys. Levitt would particularly like to see these folk nail brokers who cheat investors, but there are accounting-fraud cases in which he wants indictments as well.

One U.S. Attorney in tune with the SEC's tough new line is Mary Jo White, of New York's Southern District. White has brought a string of accounting-fraud actions and says she still has "a lot" in the pipeline. Her district has two bigtime criminal cases even now—Livent and Bankers Trust, both stem-

ming from managed earnings. However, as White points out. "On the criminal side, we don't use that polite a term: we call it accounting fraud or 'cooking the books.' " White has also prosecuted smaller cases that she prizes for their deterrence value. Object lessons don't work in most areas of the law, she says, but "significant jail time" for a white-collar executive is apt to give others of his ilk severe shakes.

What qualifies as significant? In March, Donald Ferrarini, the 71-year-old former CEO of a New York insurance brokerage. Underwriters Financial Group (UFG), got 12 years. (He is appealing.) Ferrarini had cooked the most basic recipes in the book: He overstated revenues and understated expenses, a combo that magically converted UFG from a loser into a moneymaker. The scam, uncovered in 1995, cost shareholders, policyholders, and premium finance companies close to $30 million . . .

Whether all this is enough to change the culture at the top of U.S. business remains to be seen. In taking on earnings management, Levitt is threatening a practice many CEOs regard as part of their bill of rights. The former communications director of a prominent *Fortune* 500 company remembers the blast his CEO once let loose at the financial managers and lawyers trying to tell him that the quarterly earnings he proposed to announce weren't accurate. Roared the CEO: "Stop fooling around with my numbers! The No. 1 job of management is to smooth out earnings . . ."

The fundamental problem with the earnings-management culture—especially when it leads companies to cross the line in accounting—is that it obscures facts investors ought to know, leaving them in the dark about the true value of a business. That's bad enough when times are good, like now. Let business go south, and abusive financial reporting can veil huge amounts of deterioration.

The cult of consistent earnings imposes opportunity costs as well. To start with, even the least offensive kinds of earnings management take time, mainly because executives have to decide which of several maneuvers to go for. Then there are the related tasks, especially the need to talk extensively to analysts and massage their earnings-per-share expectations. Custom says those expectations must not be disappointed by even a penny, since a management's inability to come up with a measly cent, when so many opportunities to manipulate earnings exist, will often be interpreted as a stark sign of failure and a reason to bomb the stock.

One well-regarded *Fortune* 500 CEO said recently that he probably spends 35% of his time talking to analysts and big shareholders, and otherwise worrying about the concerns of the Street. Would his company's bottom line be better off if he devoted that time to the business? "Of course," he answered. But there is always the stock price to think about—and naturally the CEO's compensation is structured to make sure he thinks about it a lot. . . .

What has sparked Chairman Levitt's war on falsified earnings reports, however, isn't the occasional distracted CEO. It's the continual eruption of accounting frauds. The accumulation of cases, in fact, keeps suggesting that beneath corporate America's uncannily disciplined march of profits during this decade lie great expanses of accounting rot, just waiting to be revealed.

Right now, among big cookers of books, the grand prize for rot is shared by the two caught up in criminal proceedings, Livent and Bankers Trust. Livent, for its part, vaporized close to $150 million in market value last August when new controlling shareholders (among them Hollywood bigwig Michael Ovitz) asserted that Livent's books had been cooked for years. Prosecutors went on to charge the company's

former CEO, *Ragtime* and *Fosse* producer Garth Drabinsky, with creating another showpiece, in which Livent starred as a thriving operation when in reality it was crumbling. Indeed, Livent kept looking presentable only because financial facts were being whisked around like props in a stage set. Drabinsky was indicted in January and even earlier had exited from the U.S., stage north: He is holed up in his homeland, Canada, where he has denied wrongdoing and has said he will fight extradition proceedings. He has also sued both Livent and its auditors, KPMG.

At Bankers Trust, prosecutors say that employees working in the securities-processing business in the mid-1990s met top management's call for good results by misappropriating money that belonged to security holders but hadn't been claimed (and that was required to be escheated to the state). The funds were used to cover the department's general expenses, a procedure that increased profits. The evidence has already caused Bankers Trust to plead guilty and agree to a $63 million fine. In addition, at least three former BT managers, including B.J. Kingdon, the boss of the division that included securities processing, are reported to have been issued "target letters" that signal they may be indicted.

Kingdon, through his lawyer, neither confirms nor denies the existence of a target letter. The lawyer says Kingdon has reacted to reports about this matter with "astonishment" and "outrage." Kingdon, says the lawyer, was not aware that anything unlawful was being done. The lawyer also says that "whatever took place, took place in daylight, with the appropriate levels of the bank monitoring the activity."

That comment raises a question already begging for an answer: whether executives up the line at Bankers Trust, like former CEO Charles Sanford, will be pulled into this affair. The SEC's attempts to curb accounting fraud have always emphasized "tone at the top," and Bankers Trust's management has given a great impression of being tone-deaf. A few years ago the company got into deep trouble for unprincipled selling of derivatives, and even now, in the midst of its securities-processing mess, it has the SEC on its neck because of possible problems with its loan-loss reserves. . . .

Never fear that the SEC will run out of accounting

cases to examine and perhaps move in on, because seldom does a month pass that those ugly words "restatement of earnings" do not fasten themselves to a new company. Joining the crowd recently from the FORTUNE 1,000 were drugstore chain Rite Aid, holding company MCN Energy Group, and drug wholesaler McKesson HBOC. Ironically, this is McKesson's second brush with accounting infamy this century . . .

Like any good general Arthur Levitt has a strategy for going after this enemy called managed earnings. In his September speech, in fact, he unveiled a list of five accounting problems that would get the unremitting attention of the SEC. They were "big bath" restructuring charges, acquisition accounting, "cookie-jar reserves," the abuse of "materiality," and revenue recognition.

Of these, that last item—the wrongful booking of sales—seems the closest to outright fraud. GAAP includes some firm rules for recognizing revenue, and most don't leave a lot of room for playing around. That hasn't stopped the bad guys. A recent study done for the Committee of Sponsoring Organizations of the Treadway Commission (called COSO), which is supported by various accounting and financial bodies, studied 200 alleged frauds carried out by publicly owned companies in the 11 years ended in 1997. Roughly 50% had a revenue-recognition component. Many of the cases involved small companies, which for that matter pack the list when it comes to fraud of any kind.

Even so, some of the biggest accounting scandals of the past few years (and now McKesson's to boot) have also featured revenue-recognition schemes. Executives at Sensormatic held the books open at the end of quarters so that they could get enough sales in the door to meet their earnings targets. Richard Rubin, former CEO of apparel company Donnkenny, is awaiting sentence for creating false invoices that he used to book sales. And Al Dunlap, who was fired as CEO of Sunbeam by its board, is alleged to have carried out (among other things) a "bill and hold" scam. In other words, Sunbeam recorded the sale of goods but simply held them in its own warehouse, a forbidden combo unless a customer has taken bona fide ownership of the goods and requested they be stored. . . . Walter Schuetze, chief accountant of the SEC's Division of Enforcement, sees in these scandals a simple theme: "When it comes to cooking the books, revenue recognition is the recipe of choice."

Lately, though, the other earnings-management techniques on Levitt's list have been . . . suddenly and sweepingly popular. Take, first, the charges that hit earnings when a company restructures on its own or as the result of an acquisition. Say that a company commits itself at these junctures to exit a business or close a factory in the near future. Under GAAP, it must today, in what we'll call year one, estimate the costs it will eventually incur in the restructuring—for severance payments, plant closings, and the like—and charge them off, even though many of the expenses won't actually be paid until, say, year two or three. These charges, which end up in a liability called a reserve, tend to put craters in year one's profits. But analysts generally ignore the bottom-line damage these write-offs do, focusing instead on operating earnings. In fact, all too often analysts cheer these charges, figuring that they clear the decks for good results in the future.

Earnings often *do* shine in the wake of a restructuring—but not necessarily because business has improved. Maybe all that happened was that the restructuring change was a "big bath," deliberately made larger than the monies to be paid out, which allows the excess to be channeled back into earnings in year two or year three. Abracadabra!—higher profits than would otherwise have materialized.

Or maybe the company made the restructuring charge a kitchen disposal, using it to gobble up all kinds of costs that by rights should be hitting this year's operating earnings or next. Schuetze recently ticked off some of the impermissible costs the SEC has found in restructuring charges: services to be provided in some future period by lawyers, accountants, and investment bankers; special bonuses for officers, expenses for retraining people.

Since Levitt's speech, the SEC has sent a letter to about 150 companies that took large restructuring charges last year. The letter warned that their annual reports might be selected for review. It also reminded the companies that they are required to make disclosures about the status of their restructuring reserves—

Ethical Decision Making

As a guide in deciding on a course of action, follow these steps:

1. *Recognize the Event, Decision or Issue*
   - You are asked to do something that you think might be wrong
   - You are aware of potentially illegal or unethical conduct on the part of others at PwC or a client
   - You are trying to make a decision and are not sure about the ethical course of action

2. *Think Before You Act*
   - Summarize and clarify your issue
   - Ask yourself, why the dilemma?
   - Consider the options and consequences
   - Consider who may be affected
   - Consult with others

3. *Decide On a Course of Action*
   - Determine your responsibility
   - Review all the relevant facts and information
   - Refer to applicable firm policies or professional standards
   - Assess the risks and how you could reduce them
   - Comtemplate the best course of action
   - Consult with others . . .

4. *Test Your Decision*
   - Review the "Ethics Questions to Consider" again
   - Apply the Firm's values to your decision
   - Make sure you have considered Firm policies, laws and professional standards
   - Consult with others—enlist their opinion of your planned action

5. *Proceed With Confidence*

ETHICS QUESTIONS TO CONSIDER

- *Is it legal?*
- *Does it feel right?*
- *How would it look in the newspapers?*
- *Will it reflect negatively on you or the firm?*
- *Who else could be impacted by this (others in the firm, clients, you, etc.)?*
- *Would you be embarrassed if others knew you took this course of action?*
- *Is there an alternative action that does not pose an ethical conflict?*
- *Is it against firm or professional standards?*
- *What would a reasonable person think?*
- *Can you sleep at night?*

how many dollars paid out so far, how many employees terminated vs. the original plan, and so forth. The implication was that the SEC would be looking to see that the companies were adhering to their restructuring plans and not emerging with reserves that could be popped into earnings at a propitious moment. The disclosure requirements had been there for years but were often ignored. Not anymore.

That's especially true because the SEC has followed through with tough reviews, both of annual reports and registration statements. One SEC target was Rite Aid, which took a large restructuring charge in fiscal 1999 (a year that ended in February) in anticipation of closing 379 stores. The SEC later compelled the company to reduce the size of its restructuring charge (from $290 million to $233 million), add major expenses to its operating costs, and restate its profits from the unaudited figure of $158 million it had reported in March—a figure even then far below "analysts' expectations"—to $144 million. This year, to date, Rite Aid has lost close to $7 billion in market cap, and class-action lawyers are all over its case. . . .

Let us dip now, if you will pardon the expression, into another item on Levitt's list, cookie-jar reserves. GAAP, of course, is too stiffly worded to include a term like that. But not even the accounting-challenged have trouble visualizing that these are earnings held back from the period in which they should have been recognized and kept instead for a rainy day. Maybe the husbander is truly worried about bad weather hitting its business (as many banks, for example, claim to be), or maybe it just wants to manage earnings. It doesn't matter: GAAP says companies cannot establish reserves for "contingencies," because such costs can't be estimated. They should hit income statements when they actually arrive.

Beyond that, cookie jars are innately a problem because investors usually can't detect that they exist. Even outside directors, said one recently, typically wouldn't be told that managers had hidden cookies away. That makes it difficult for anyone to fairly value a company, says Harvey Goldschmid, general counsel of the SEC. A second problem, he says, is that managements will often use reserves to "dim the signals" going to both the public and their boards when business turns down.

The SEC says it is looking at a number of companies suspected of harboring improper reserves . . . The SEC's most elaborate reserve case, is the one it launched last December against W.R. Grace, not just attacking cookie jars but also roping in another item on Levitt's list, "materiality." This term acknowledges that the preparation of financial statements is a complex job and that neither managements nor their outside auditors, however well intentioned, can testify that the figures are accurate down to the penny. Auditors deal with this uncertainty by attesting that a company's statements are accurate "in all material respects." Unfortunately, auditors also lean on materiality when they are trying to convince themselves it's okay for managers to slip intentional misstatements into their financial reports.

The SEC is right now busy drawing a line in the sand about materiality. In the past it has sometimes permitted managements to get by with irregularities in their financial reports just as long as the deliberate misstatements could be classed, often by some ad hoc mathematical logic, as immaterial. But it is now preparing to say—in a staff bulletin soon to appear— that intentional errors made for the purpose of managing earnings just won't be tolerated.

In the W.R. Grace case, moreover, it went after intentional errors made several years back. It seems that in the early 1990s a division of that company, National Medical Care (NMC), made more in profits than it had expected. So NMC, according to the SEC, deliberately underreported its earnings (thereby creating an "irregularity"), stuffing the excess into a cookie-jar reserve that in time got to be $60 million in size. Then in 1993, when profits needed a sugar fix, NMC started feeding the reserve into earnings (thereby compounding the irregularities). Meanwhile, Grace's auditors, Price Waterhouse, went along with these contortions on the grounds that they weren't material.

The SEC, launching its case, objected to the entire goings-on. By June it had exacted cease-and-desist consents from two PricewaterhouseCoopers partners and from Grace itself, which agreed as well to set up a $1 million educational fund to further awareness of GAAP. The commission has also filed cease-and-desist proceedings against seven former Grace officers (among them CEO J.P. Bolduc), of whom three get special attention. These three, who include Grace's former chief financial officer, Brian Smith, are licensed CPAs whom the SEC views as having engaged in "inappropriate professional conduct." So the commission wants an administrative judge to bar them from practicing before the SEC. That means they could not play *any* part in preparing the financial statements of publicly owned companies or any other SEC registrant. . . .

The Grace case is important to Levitt's initiative because it sends such a strong message to other companies, some of which should be thinking, "There but for the god of Grace go I." In an entirely different way, the Cendant case demands attention because it displays such gross behavior. The misdeeds are fully documented as well, in a remarkable and unsparing 146-page report done for the audit committee of Cendant's board by the law firm of Willkie Farr & Gallagher and auditors imported for the project, Arthur Andersen. Here are some of the report's findings:

- In the three years 1995–97, CUC's operating income before taxes was improperly inflated by $500 million, which was more than one-third of its reported pretax income for those years.
- Though many of the improprieties occurred in CUC's biggest subsidiary, Comp-U-Card, they reached to 16 others as well. No fewer than 20 employees participated in the wrongdoing.
- Several CUC employees who were interviewed said they understood that the purpose of inflating earnings was to meet "analysts' expectations."
- In the first three quarters of each of the infected years, CUC put out unaudited financial statements that headquarters deliberately falsified, mostly by "adjusting" Comp-U-Card's revenues upward and its expenses downward. These favorable "adjustments" grew: They were $31 million in 1995, $87 million in 1976, and $176 million in 1997.
- At the end of each year, before its outside auditors, Ernst & Young, came in to make their annual review. CUC undid those improprieties (which would almost certainly have been dis-

covered in the audit process) and instead created the earnings it needed mainly by plucking them from cookie-jar reserves.
- In most cases, the explanations that CUC gave Ernst & Young for these reserve infusions satisfied the accounting firm, which in general did not display impressive detective skills. On one occasion, however, E&Y could not find justification for $25 million transferred helpfully from a reserve—and this it let pass as "immaterial." (Cendant has sued E&Y, which has responded that it was the victim of deception and is "outraged" to be blamed for Cendant's own fraud.)
- In one particularly colorful incident, CUC used a merger reserve it had established in 1997 to swallow up $597,000 of private airplane expenses that its CEO Walter Forbes, had paid in 1995 and 1996, and for which he had requested reimbursement. Had these expenses not been allocated to the reserve, they would have turned up where they should have: in operating costs.

Naturally, Willkie Farr questioned Forbes about his knowledge of CUC's wrongdoing. He denied knowing anything about it. . . .

Michael Young, a Willkie Farr litigator and a student of accounting frauds, says they tend to follow a predictable trajectory. The Cendant case was no exception. It started small and grew out of control. It also dragged in employees who were troubled by what they were asked to do but did it anyway. Young remembers one case in which he was about to interview a woman implicated in a fraud. She suddenly burst into tears and said the totally unexpected: "I'm so glad to have someone to talk to about this."

Levitt understands well that the SEC is facing an enormous challenge in trying to get the cultural change it wants. Wall Street itself is an obstacle: It wants consistent earnings, however attained. Speaking at a recent investor-relations conference, one stock analyst, Gary Balter of DLJ, baldly urged that companies consider "hiding earnings" for future use. "If you don't play the game," he said, "you're going to get hurt."

On a second front, the SEC has already run into roadblocks on certain new rules it would like to impose on audit committees . . . Levitt himself has grown used to visits from business leaders not happy at all with accounting changes disturbing their lives. Even some feds are up in arms. The SEC, brandishing GAAP, is arguing that certain banks have overstated their reserves; banking regulators, perfectly happy with a little conservatism, have risen in protest.

Another issue is whether really egregious cases can be made criminal actions. For a U.S. Attorney, whose alternatives include going after drug dealing, espionage, and bank robbery, it is no easy decision to take on a white-collar case stuffed with the arcana of accounting. According to Levitt's chief policeman, director of enforcement Richard Walker, the cases that ought to wind up in criminal court are those in which a company or executive has exhibited a, high level of what lawyers call *scienter*—that is, knowing and willful conduct—and acted "to violate the law, misapply accounting standards, and affect financial reporting." Prosecutors may also weigh aggravating factors such as lies told to auditors or profitable trades made by an executive as he paints a false picture of his company's financial health. Walker, who has been at the SEC for eight years, thinks Levitt's message is in any event getting through. "I'm seeing more acceptance of these cases by U.S. Attorneys today than in all the time I've been here . . ."

Meanwhile, some corporations continue to behave in ways that make you question whether they've even heard of Levitt. Companies are not in the least required to make forecasts about earnings. Yet this spring, as McKesson was conceding that it had no real handle on the profits of its accounting-troubled unit, HBOC, it was still saying it was comfortable with projections that it could make $2.50 a share for its fiscal year ending next February. McKesson's nervy statement supports the opinion of class-action lawyer William Lerach that it is always good to allow time for the actors in frauds, especially CEOs, to make the self-destructive public statements they almost always do.

If tales like McKesson's confirm the challenge that Levitt faces, there is another that puts a slightly different complexion on things. The SEC's Turner says he knows a largish FORTUNE 500 company that in a recent reporting period ended up with earnings well beyond Street expectations. The boss said to the CFO: "Let's hold some of those back." "Wait a minute," objected the CFO, "don't even go there. Don't you know what the SEC is doing to people?" And the boss looked at the CFO, told him he was in "career limiting" territory, and once again ordered the earnings hid.

And what happened then? Turner's answer: "The CFO, the auditors, and the audit committee got together and managed to convince the boss he was wrong."

That's just one time, at one company. But at least it's a start.

QUESTIONS

1. What is the "fundamental problem" with the earnings-management culture?

2. What are several obstacles that the SEC faces in pursuing corporate criminals?

Ed Cohen

Arthur Andersen Refugees Reflect on What Went Wrong

Ed Cohen is an associate editor of *Notre Dame Magazine.*

Two Notre Dame alumni who held leadership positions with Arthur Andersen say mind-boggling corporate structures, pressure to keep earnings looking good to Wall Street, and negligent board directors all contributed to the wave of scandals that rocked the business world and toppled their long-venerated accounting firm at the turn of the 21st century.

They also say Arthur Andersen was unfairly scapegoated for having been Enron's and World-Com's auditor but that the accounting profession as a whole strayed from its traditional concern for keeping business on the straight and narrow.

Before being implicated in scandal, Arthur Andersen enjoyed a reputation for high ethical standards and quality work. . . .

Thomas Fischer . . . was managing partner of the Andersen's Milwaukee office until January 2002, when he took an already-planned retirement. Later that month it became known that the Justice Department intended to seek criminal obstruction-of-justice charges against the firm for its employees having shredded documents in the Enron case.

Fischer says he never witnessed any wrongdoing or felt pressure to cook books while at Andersen. So he believes it was unfair that the company was put out of business by the notoriety. Its demise cost more than 80,000 employees their jobs. . . .

Before the Whistle Blew . . .

Sherron Watkins

An excerpt from an August 2001 memo to Enron CEO Ken Lay:

> Has Enron become a risky place to work? For those of us who didn't get rich over the last few years, can we afford to stay?
>
> Skilling's abrupt departure will raise suspicions of accounting improprieties and valuation issues. Enron has been very aggressive in its accounting—most notably the Raptor transactions and the Condor vehicle. . . .
>
> It sure looks to the layman on the street that we are hiding losses in a related company and will compensate that company with Enron stock in the future.
>
> I am incredibly nervous that we will implode in a wave of accounting scandals. . . .

Ed Cohen, "Arthur Andersen Refugees Reflect on What Went Wrong," *Notre Dame Magazine* Jan, 2004. Reprinted with permission of the editor.

"A lot of people would like to believe that Arthur Andersen was doing some kind of drive-by auditing and all the bad things that happened in the accounting profession were all centered in Arthur Andersen," he says. "Nothing is farther from the truth. All firms were run basically the same way."

Fischer blames the wave of corporate scandals on what he calls a "social and economic blow-off" that occurred in the United States in the late 1990s. People thought the good times would never end, and many were willing to bend rules to keep them rolling, he says. One of the symptoms of the culture, he says, was excessive compensation paid to CEOs.

"Accountants used to be the part of business that stood up and said, 'This is not right, this doesn't make sense,'" Fischer says. He says he hopes the profession will one day "stand up and be the backbone and the moral compass of the business world that it used to be and is not today."

Joe J. Tapajna, former worldwide managing tax practice director for Arthur Andersen, is now national professional practice director for tax at Deloitte and Touche in Chicago. He also teaches a graduate-level course in tax accounting at Notre Dame.

Tapajna says that when he entered the profession in the 1970s, accounting emphasized professionalism and caution. Accountants were outspoken about following procedures and adhering to the spirit rather than merely the letter of the law. . . .

Tapajna says that in the 1980s and '90s accurate accounting became much more difficult as businesses became more complex and the investment community demanded information faster. He notes that Enron, the giant energy-trader, consisted of thousands of subsidiaries with management acquiring and disposing of companies on almost a daily basis.

"[A]t best, you were always trying to come up with approximately the right answer instead of the right answer."

Both professionals also say that board members failed in their responsibility to provide appropriate oversight of management's activities.

"It isn't really ethics," says Fischer, "it's 'do your job.'"

QUESTIONS

1. What do you think went wrong at Arthur Andersen? Did the firm deserve the consequences?

2. If (as a management guru) you had to give advice to Arthur Andersen executives *before* the Enron debacle, what would you say?

Robert E. Frederick
and W. Michael Hoffman

The Individual Investor in Securities Markets: An Ethical Analysis

Robert E. Frederick is professor of philosophy at Bentley College. W. Michael Hoffman taught at Bentley College.

Securities markets are full of pitfalls for individual investors. Examples of fraud and regulatory violations in the markets are common. For instance, a recent *Business Week* cover story reports that investors are being duped out of hundreds of millions a year in penny stock scams in spite of SEC regulations.[1] A report in the *Wall Street Journal* on the Chicago futures trading fraud highlights the "danger of being ripped off in futures markets" by unscrupulous floor brokers filling customers' "market orders"—a type of order that "individual investors should avoid using."[2]

But securities markets present risks to individual investors that go beyond clear violations of regulations and fraud. The above *Wall Street Journal* story, for example, also issued a more general warning to investors:

> Futures are fast moving, risky investment vehicles that are unsuitable for anyone who can't afford to lose and who doesn't have time to pay close attention to trading positions?[3]

Furthermore, it is not only the high risk futures and commodities markets that are perilous for investors. . . . Even the bond markets, which in the past at least gave the outside appearance of stability, are in increasing turmoil. . . .

In light of these and many other examples that could be given, suppose the SEC announced that individual investors, for their own protection, no longer have access to securities markets. They are no longer permitted to buy stocks, bonds, or commodities or futures options. If this were to happen there surely would be a public outcry of protest, even moral outrage. The reasons for such outrage probably would revolve around the belief that some fundamental right had been violated, perhaps the presumed right that markets should be free and open so that everyone has an opportunity to better his or her position and enjoy the goods and services of society.

A quick look, however, reveals that not all markets have unrestricted access. Nor is there a generally accepted belief that any rights are being unjustifiably violated in such cases. In consumer markets, for example, individuals under a certain age are prohibited from voting, buying alcoholic beverages, and seeing certain movies. Regardless of age, not just anyone can buy a fully automatic rifle or order a few dozen hand grenades. In fact, not just anyone can drive a car; one must pass a test and be licensed to do that. Furthermore, even after being allowed to drive, this privilege can be revoked if it is abused. And, of course, none of our citizens is legally permitted to participate in certain drug markets, such as cocaine.

But it will be argued that there is good reason for these and other such restrictions. We are attempting to prevent people, the argument goes, from harming themselves or causing harm to others. This is what makes it morally permissible, or even obligatory, to restrict access to certain kinds of consumer products. The ethical principle here is that, when possible, persons ought to be protected from undue harm. Hence, the restrictions in question are justified.

Journal of Business Ethics 9 (1990): 579–89. © 1990 Kluwer Academic Publishers. Reprinted by permission of Kluwer Academic Publishers.

Yet might not this be exactly the rationale behind a possible SEC ban against individual investors entering securities markets? Just as unrestricted access to some drugs is thought to present unacceptable risks to consumers, trading in today's securities markets may present unacceptable risks to many investors, resulting in great financial rather than physical harm. And since we feel justified in prohibiting consumers from buying what we take to be highly dangerous drugs or other consumer products, shouldn't we, by analogy, be justified in prohibiting certain investors from buying highly risky financial instruments? . . .

EXACTLY WHAT KIND
OF INVESTOR ARE
WE TALKING ABOUT?

The type of investor we will be concerned with, and the type we take to be the most likely candidate for the SEC prohibition mentioned earlier, is one that (a) is at relatively *high risk,* where risk is a function of the probability of a certain market event occurring and the degree of harm the investor would suffer were the event to occur, and (b) an investor who is relatively *unsophisticated* about the functioning of the market and hence unappreciative of the degree of risk he or she faces. For example, suppose Jones invests his life savings in high yield bonds . . . and suppose a few months later the company that issued the bonds suddenly announces that it is going into Chapter 11 bankruptcy. The value of the bonds drops precipitously and, for all practical purposes, in a matter of hours Jones' savings are wiped out. If Jones did not realize that the high return he was initially receiving was a reflection of the risky nature of the bonds, then he would fall within the category of investors with which we are concerned even assuming he had several million dollars invested. . . .

WHAT SORT OF JUSTIFICATION
MIGHT BE OFFERED FOR
RESTRICTING THE INVESTMENTS
OF AT-RISK INVESTORS?

One kind of justification that might be proposed is paternalistic. By paternalism we roughly mean interfering with a person's actions or preferences by restricting their freedom of action or the range of choices normally available to them for the reason that such a restriction promotes or preserves their good, welfare, happiness, or interests. A paternalistic justification for restricting at risk investors would be that exposure to risk for many investors is too great to permit them to continue without some sort of protection that reduces the risk to an acceptable degree. For certain investors an acceptable degree may be no risk at all. For others some risk may be permissible. In either case, the argument goes, as long as the intent of intervention is to protect or promote the good of at risk investors, and as long as it does not wrong other persons, then intervention is at least permissible and may be obligatory. It is only in this way that harm to many investors can be prevented.

The standard objection to paternalistic justifications is something like this: If people choose to run the risk to gain what they believe will be the rewards, who are we to interfere? From where do we derive a special dispensation to overrule their choices and interfere with their lives?

Although there is a kernel of truth in this objection, it is much too facile. Some paternalistic acts are clearly justified. Paternalistic reasoning is commonly used to justify restricting the choices of children and people judged incompetent or otherwise unable rationally to consider the consequences of their acts. Moreover, paternalistic justifications are not obviously unreasonable even in cases where the competence of the person is not in question. It is at least initially credible that some consumer products, such as prescription drugs, are not in unrestricted circulation precisely because of paternalistic reasons.

Let us confine our discussion to those persons ordinarily taken to be competent and rational. We still do not believe that paternalism per se justifies restricting at-risk investors that fall within this category. One reason is that it may be impossible to find out just what the good or welfare of an individual investor is. Not only is there the thorny problem of trying to reach a common and precise understanding of the vague idea of the "good" of a person, there are immense practical difficulties in discovering whether a certain individual's good is served by restricting his or her access to the market. There may be situations where an individual's good is not served, and inter-

Dire Consequences . . .

The number of bankruptcy petitions filed in federal courts rose 15.1 percent in the 12-month period ending March 31, 2002, according to statistics released by the Administrative Office of the U.S. Courts. The total filings broke the bankruptcy filing record for any 12-month period. Bankruptcy filings rose from 1,307,857 in the 12-month period ended March 2001 to 1,504,806 in the same time period in 2002. The previous highest total of filings for any 12-month period was in the 12-month period ending December 31, 2001, with a total of 1,492,129.

Business filings totaled 39,845, up 10.7 percent from 35,992 in 2001. Non-business filings totaled 1,464,961, up 15.2 percent from the total non-business filings of 1,271,865, in the 12-month period ending March 31, 2001.

Business and Non-business Filings (Years Ended March 31, 1997–2002)

YEAR	TOTAL	NON-BUSINESS	BUSINESS
2002	1,504,806	1,464,961	38,845
2001	1,307,857	1,271,865	35,992
2000	1,301,205	1,263,096	38,109
1999	1,419,199	1,378,071	41,128
1998	1,423,128	1,370,490	52,638
1997	1,247,065	1,193,057	54,008

*Source: Bureau of U.S. Statistics.

vention in those cases would be a wrongful violation of his or her rights.

But suppose regulators do know the good of some individuals. Would paternalism then justify intervening to preserve or promote their good? We believe not in cases where regulators and the person in question have differing conceptions of that person's good. Even if regulators happen to know a person's "true" good better than he or she does themselves, imposing on that person a conception of his or her good they do not accept is not justified. Regulators may attempt to persuade at-risk investors to take a different course or provide them with information that they need to make an informed decision, but it is not permissible to deny them the right to direct their lives. . . .

Although paternalism as characterized thus far does not justify interference with the choices of at-risk investors, there are circumstances in which intervention is justified. This can best be explained by using an example not related to investing. Suppose Jones mistakenly believes the food he is about to eat is wholesome but we have good reason to think it is contaminated with botulism. As he raises the fork to his mouth, we only have time to strike it away. At first he is angry, but after we explain the reason for our action he is grateful. The act of striking the fork away is an example of paternalistic intervention since it is done for Jones' good but against his wishes. It seems obvious, however, that we acted properly. Intervention in this case is justified since if

Jones were fully aware of the circumstances he would act differently or would agree to have us intervene on his behalf. He would consent to our action. Hence, intervention here respects his right to freedom since it is compatible with his goals and does not force upon him some version of his good he would not accept.

Note that it is not merely our superior knowledge of the situation that justifies interference, but also our judgment that Jones would agree that our actions preserve or promote his good. The case would be different were Jones attempting suicide instead of trying to have a decent meal. Paternalistic intervention may not be justified when a person voluntarily undertakes an action harmful to him- or herself, provided that person has a reasonably complete understanding of his or her circumstances and the consequences of the action. But it is at least prima facie justified, we suggest, when an action is based on incomplete information and thus is, in one sense, less than fully voluntary.

Now suppose there are compelling grounds to believe that some otherwise competent investors are unappreciative of the high degree of risk they face, and that if they were presented with information about those risks they would act either to reduce or eliminate them, or would consent to having restrictions placed on the kinds of investments they could make. Since they would consent to intervention or act differently were they fully aware of the circumstances, intervention on their behalf is justified just as it was justified for Jones. Their rights are not violated since nothing is imposed on them that they would not consent to were they fully aware of the dangers they faced.

A major difference between the Jones case and at-risk investors is that we dealt with Jones as an individual, but a regulatory or legislative body would have to deal with at-risk investors as a group. There simply is no way to reach them all individually. Furthermore, although such bodies may be able to make reasonable assumptions about the kinds of risks acceptable to most at-risk investors, and about the kinds of restrictions to which most of them would agree, it seems inevitable that there will be some investors who would not consent to restrictions because, for example, they have an unusual concep-

tion of their good or welfare, or because they find the restrictions highly offensive. For these people restrictions on investing will impose a foreign conception of their good on them and thus is not compatible with their right to direct their lives. . . .

If the *reason* given for intervening is promoting the good of at-risk investors as a group, then, as we have tried to argue, it is not justified. Suppose, however, the reason is not only that the good of some investors is promoted, but that there is a duty to intervene to protect certain *rights,* in particular, the right of investors not to be harmed. The argument would go something like this: There is good reason to believe that some at-risk investors would consent to having restrictions placed on them to protect their financial position and prevent them from suffering financial harm. Since it is a basic function of government to protect its citizens from harm, there is a duty to protect these investors. Hence, placing restrictions on their investment activities is justified even though such restrictions may violate the right of other investors to direct their lives as they see fit.

If this argument is plausible, then there is a conflict of rights between two groups of at-risk investors. This is a genuine moral dilemma that can only be resolved by deciding whose rights are to prevail. We believe it should be the right not to be harmed. An analogy with prescription drugs may be helpful here. One reason there are restrictions on access to drugs is to prevent harm to persons who do not know how to use them correctly. These restrictions are justified, in our view, even supposing there are some individuals willing to take the risk. The right to freedom of this latter group should be and should remain a serious consideration in devising restrictions on drugs, but it does not override the right of others not to be exposed to excessive risk and possible serious harm.

The same holds true of at-risk investors. The right of some of them not to be exposed to excessive risk and possible serious financial harm overrides the right of others to invest without restrictions. We emphasize, however, that the right to freedom cannot be lightly dismissed, and must be given due consideration when formulating policies and regulations governing the markets. . . .

IF SOME INVESTORS ARE RESTRICTED, HOW SHOULD IT BE DONE?

Since we are not experts in the regulation of securities markets, the best we can do here is make a few suggestions that seem to us worthy of additional investigation. It is a basic premise, essential for any just system of regulation and law, that relevantly different classes of persons be treated in relevantly different ways. Hence, it clearly would be unjust to restrict the activities of all investors to protect some of them. It also follows from this basic premise that distinctions must be drawn within the class of at-risk investors. It may turn out in the end that there is no workable method of protecting some at-risk investors while preserving the rights of all of them, but it would be a mistake to begin with this assumption.

In light of this it might be suggested that the only plausible course of action is to make sure that at-risk investors have all the information they need to make investment decisions. This has at least three advantages. The first is that providing information does not seriously infringe any rights. And establishing stringent policies to ensure that the information is received also may be reasonable. For example, suppose that to demonstrate a minimum level of competence persons must pass an examination before investing, just as they have to pass a driving exam before driving. Different kinds of exams could be given for different kinds of investments. Would such a procedure violate any rights? It certainly would be costly and inconvenient, but we doubt that it is an inordinate restriction on the right to freedom.

A second advantage is that providing information is already one function of the Securities and Exchange Commission. According to the Commission's pamphlet "Consumers' Financial Guide" the three main responsibilities of the Commission are:

1. To require that companies that offer their securities for sale in "interstate commerce" register with the Commission and make available to investors complete and accurate information.
2. To protect investors against misrepresentation and fraud in the issuance and sale of securities.

3. To oversee the securities markets to ensure they operate in a fair and orderly manner.

Although the pamphlet goes on to advise investors that "whatever the choice of investment, make sure that you have complete and accurate information before investing to ensure that you use your funds wisely," it also emphasizes that the SEC does not see itself as the guarantor of investments:

> Registration . . . does not insure investors against loss of their investments, but serves rather to provide information upon which investors may base an informed and realistic evaluation of the worth of a security.

Thus, providing information to at-risk investors is consistent with the mission of the SEC and would not require massive restructuring of the Commission.

The third advantage is that providing information would be the most direct way to discover whether investors would consent to restrictions. Earlier we argued that restrictions on some at-risk investors are justified because they would consent to intervention if they were fully aware of the risk they faced. But instead of imposing regulations based on what investors *would* do were they to have all the relevant information, it is preferable to give them the information whenever possible and see what they *actually* do. This would avoid the danger of imposing on them a conception of their good that they do not accept.

We agree that providing information to at-risk investors is a good idea, and propose that methods be initiated that ensure that investors receive the information, rather than just having it available for those that seek it out. However, this may not be enough to eliminate unacceptable risks for at-risk investors. Consider the prescription drug market again, and assume that the FDA made strenuous efforts to provide consumers with complete information about drugs. Supposing for a moment that it is legally permissible for consumers to buy drugs, as it is in some countries, this might be enough to eliminate unacceptable risk of harm from drugs for the few that had the time, energy, and expertise to use the information. But for most people it would be an overwhelming blizzard of paper that would be of no real use.

The same reasoning applies in the securities markets. So much information is available and it is so complex that for many investors beyond a certain point it would be too costly to make the investment in time required to assimilate it all. Having "complete and accurate information," as the SEC suggests, is not enough. Leaving aside the issue of how one determines whether it is complete and accurate (note that not even the SEC does that), there remains the problem of understanding it well enough to make a wise investment decision. Perhaps it could be done, but would it be done by most at-risk investors? We are inclined to think not. So we suggest that, just as with prescription drugs, at-risk investors be required by law to engage the services of an expert. This would go a long way toward eliminating unacceptable risks for them, and given the significant possibility of harm many investors face, we do not feel it would be an excessive restriction on their freedom. Exceptions would have to be made for those investors willing to become expert in the markets (since they would no longer meet the definition of an at-risk investor), and some system of qualifications would need to be established to identify investment counselors capable of advising the other investors. . . .

NOTES

1. "The Penny Stock Scandal," *Business Week,* 23 (January 1989), pp. 74–82.
2. "Investors Can Take a Bite Out of Fraud," *Wall Street Journal,* (January 24, 1989), p. C1.
3. *Wall Street Journal,* (January 24, 1989), p. C1.

QUESTIONS

1. What is an individual investor, and why are individual investors a special category of investor?
2. How should some investors be restricted from risk in securities markets? Why should they be?

John R. Boatright | # Finance Ethics

John R. Boatright teaches at Loyola University in Chicago.

- *Financial markets* are vulnerable to unfair trading practices (fraud and manipulation), unfair conditions (an unlevel playing field), and contractual difficulties (forming, interpreting, and enforcing contracts). The main aim of federal securities laws and the self-regulation of exchanges is expressed in the phrase "fair and orderly" markets, which reflects the need in financial markets to balance the twin goals of fairness and efficiency.

- Many individuals and institutions serve as financial intermediaries, providing *financial services* on behalf of others. Financial intermediaries commonly make decisions as agents for principals in an agency relation, and they often become fiduciaries with fiduciary duties. Agents and fiduciaries have an obligation to act solely in the interests of other parties and, especially, to avoid conflicts of interest. Although financial services providers are often merely sellers in a buyer-seller relation, they still have the obligations of any seller to avoid deceptive and abusive sales practices.

From Robert E. Frederick, ed., *A Companion to Business Ethics,* (Malden, MA: Blackwell, 1999), pp 153–163. Reprinted by permission.

• *Financial Management:* Business firms are legally structured as the financial instruments of shareholders, and officers and directors are agents of firms, and have a fiduciary duty to manage the firms with the objective of maximizing shareholder wealth. Ethical issues in financial management concern the actions that violate the duties of financial managers and the discretion of financial managers to serve the interests of nonshareholder groups, commonly called "stakeholders."

All financial activity takes place in a larger economic, political, and social setting and so ethical issues arise about the overall impact of financial activity. Although financial decision making is generally limited to the financial factors of risk and return over time, ethics includes a consideration of the ethical treatment of everyone affected by a decision, and the consequences for the whole of society.

FINANCIAL MARKETS

The fundamental ethical requirement of financial markets is that they be *fair.* Fairness may be defined either *substantively* (when the price of a security reflects the actual value) or *procedurally* (when buyers are enabled to determine the actual value of a security). In the USA, some state securities laws aim at substantive fairness by requiring expert evaluation of new securities (so-called "blue-sky" laws), but the federal Securities Act of 1933 and the Securities Exchange Act of 1934 attempt to secure fairness procedurally by requiring adequate disclosure. The rationale for mandatory disclosure is that securities transactions are more likely to be fair when material information must be disclosed, and investors have easy access to information.

Unfair Trading Practices

Fraud, manipulation, and other unfair trading practices lead not only to unfair treatment in securities transactions but to a loss of investor confidence in the integrity of financial markets. Speculative activity also produces excess volatility, which was blamed

for the stock market crashes of 1929 and October 1987.

Both fraud and manipulation are defined broadly. Section 17(a) of the 1933 Securities Act and Section 10(b) of the 1934 Securities Exchange Act prohibit anyone involved in the issue or exchange of securities to make a false statement of a material fact, to omit a fact that makes a statement of material facts misleading, or to engage in any practice or scheme that would serve to defraud. Whereas fraud generally involves the disclosure or concealment of information that bears on the value of a security, manipulation consists of trading for the purpose of creating a misleading impression about a security's value.

Fraud is obviously committed by an initial stock offering that inflates the assets of a firm or fails to disclose some of its liabilities. Insider trading has been prosecuted as a fraud on the grounds that nonpublic material information ought to be disclosed before trading. In the 1920s, the stock market was manipulated by traders who bid up the price of stock in order to sell at the peak to unwary investors. In recent years, concern has been expressed about a form of program trading known as index arbitrage, in which traders are able to create volatility in different markets, solely for the purpose of trading on the resulting price differences.

Fair Conditions

Fairness in financial markets is often expressed by the concept of a level playing field. A playing field may be unlevel because of inequalities in information, bargaining power, resources, processing ability, and special vulnerabilities.

Unequal information, or *information asymmetry,* may refer either to the fact that all parties to a transaction do not possess the same information or that they do not have the same *access* to information. The possession of different information is a pervasive nature of markets that is not always ethically objectionable. Indeed, investors who invest resources in acquiring superior information are entitled to exploit this advantage. And they perform a service by making markets more efficient. The unequal possession of information is unfair only when the information has not been legitimately acquired or when its use violates some right or obligation. Other arguments against insider trading, for example, are that the information has not been acquired legitimately but has been misappropriated from the rightful owner (the "misappropriation theory") and that an insider who trades on information that has been acquired in a fiduciary relation violates a fiduciary duty. Equal access to information is problematical because accessibility is not a feature of information itself but a function of the investment that is required to obtain information. To the objection that an inside trader is using information that is inherently inaccessible, some reply that anyone can become an insider by devoting enough resources.

Similarly, inequalities in bargaining power, resources, and processing ability—which are pervasive in financial markets—are ethically objectionable only when they are used in violation of some right or obligation and especially when they are used coercively. The main ethical requirement is that people not use any advantage unfairly. For example, American stock markets permit relatively unsophisticated investors with modest resources and processing ability to buy stocks on fair terms, and some changes, such as increased use of program trading or private placements, are criticized for increasing the advantages of institutional investors. (The growth of mutual funds has served to reduce the adverse consequences of inequalities among investors.) Vulnerabilities, such as impulsiveness or overconfidence, create opportunities for exploitation that can be countered by such measures as a "cooling off" period on purchases and loans, and the warning to request and read a prospectus before investing.

Financial Contracting

Some financial instruments, such as home mortgages and futures options, are contracts which commit the parties to a certain course of action, and many financial relations, such as being a trustee or corporate officer, are contractual in nature. Contracts are often vague, ambiguous, or incomplete, with the result that disagreements arise about what is ethically and legally required.

First, beyond the written words of *express contracts* lie innumerable tacit understandings that constitute *implied contracts*. Financial affairs would be impossible if every detail had to be made explicit. However, whatever is left implicit is subject to differing interpretations, and insofar as implied contracts are not legally enforceable, they may be breached with impunity. Not only financial instruments but the relations of corporations with employees, customers, suppliers, and other stakeholders consist of implied contracts, from which each party receives some value. . . .

Second, contracts are sometimes imperfect because of limitations in our cognitive ability, especially incomplete knowledge, bounded rationality, and future contingencies. In addition, some situations may be too complex and uncertain to permit careful planning. As a result, the parties may fail to negotiate contracts that produce the maximum benefit for themselves. Disputes in contractual relations also arise over what constitutes a breach of contract and what is an appropriate remedy.

Agency and fiduciary relations are one solution for the problems of imperfect contracting because they replace specific obligations with a general duty to act in another's interests. In particular, the fiduciary relations of managers to shareholders has arisen because of the difficulties of writing contracts for this particular relation. Similarly, supplier relations are not easily reduced to contractual terms. The term *relational contracting* has been coined to describe the building of working relations as an alternative to rigid contracts.

FINANCIAL SERVICES

The financial services industry—which includes commercial banks, securities and investment firms, mutual and pension funds, insurance companies, and financial planners—provides a vast array of financial services to individuals, businesses, and governments. Financial services firms act primarily as financial *intermediaries,* which is to say that they use their capital to provide services rather than to trade on their own behalf. In providing financial services, these firms sometimes act as agents or fiduciaries with respect to clients; at other times, they act as sellers in a typical buyer—seller relation. Thus, a broker who is authorized to trade for a client's account is an agent, but a broker who makes a cold call to a prospect is merely a salesperson. Many ethical disputes result from misunderstandings about the nature of a financial service provider's role.

Fiduciaries and Agents

A fiduciary is a person who is entrusted to act in the interests of another. Fiduciary duties are the duties of a fiduciary to act in that other person's interest without gaining any material benefit except with the knowledge and consent of that person. Similar to the fiduciary relation is the relation of *agent* and *principal,* in which one person (the agent) is engaged to act

on behalf of another (the principal). Whereas fiduciary relations arise when something of value is entrusted to another person, agency relations are due to the need to rely on others for their specialized knowledge and skill. In both relations, the specific acts to be performed are not fully specified in advance and fiduciaries and agents have wide latitude.

A major source of unethical conduct by fiduciaries and agents is conflict of interest, in which a personal interest of the fiduciary or agent interferes with the ability of the person to act in the interest of the other person. Fiduciaries and agents are called upon to exercise judgment on behalf of others, and their judgment can be compromised if they stand to gain personally by a decision. For example, a conflict of interest is created when a brokerage firm offers a higher commission for selling in-house mutual funds. The conflict

The Wake-Up Call

"We must usher in a new era of integrity in corporate America," Mr. Bush said in a speech before Wall Street leaders today.

"The business pages of American newspapers should not read like a scandal sheet. . . . I am calling for a new ethic of personal responsibility in the business community—an ethic that will increase investor confidence, make employees proud of their companies and regain the trust of the American people."

The president vowed his administration would "end the days of cooking the books, shading the truth and breaking our laws."

"Self-regulation is important, but it is not enough." . . .

The president announced he would create a Corporate Fraud Task Force which would operate like a "financial crimes SWAT team, overseeing the investigation of corporate abusers and bringing them to account." . . .

The president urged Congress to pass a $20 million emergency funding request for the SEC to allow the agency to hire 100 enforcement agents. Mr. Bush asked legislators to approve an additional $100 million for the SEC in his 2003 budget. . . . Other proposals in the president's ten-point plan included doubling prison terms for mail and wire fraud to ten years, and toughening laws for document shredding and other ways of obstructing federal investigations. . . .

—*Online NewsHour,* http://www.pbs.org/newshour/updates/corporateμ_07-09-02.html, July 9, 2002 arises because the broker has an incentive to sell funds that may not be in a client's best interests. Whether mutual fund managers should be permitted to trade for their own account is a controversial question because of the perceived conflict of interest. Fiduciaries and agents also have duties to preserve the confidentiality of information and not to use the information for their own benefit. Thus, "piggyback" trading in which a broker copies the trades of a savvy client, is a breach of confidentiality. Agency relations are subject to some well-known difficulties that arise from the inability of principals to monitor agents closely. These difficulties are opportunism, moral hazard, and adverse selection. Opportunism, or shirking, occurs because of the tendency of agents to advance their own interests despite the commitment to act on behalf of another. In agency theory, which is the study of agency relations, whatever in principal loses from opportunism is known as agency loss. The total of the agency loss and expenditures to reduce it are called agency costs. Moral hazard arises when the cost (or risk) of an activity is borne by others, as when a person seeks more medical care because of insurance. Moral hazard can be reduced in insurance by requiring deductibles and copayments, which provide an insured person with an incentive to lower costs. Insurance companies can also seek out better insurance prospects, but this leads to the problem of adverse selection. Adverse selection is the tendency, in insurance, of less suitable prospects to seek more insurance, which increases the risk for insurers who cannot easily identify good and bad insurance prospects. More generally, principals are not always able to judge the suitability of agents, and agents have an incentive to misrepresent themselves.

Many ethical problems, ranging from churning of client accounts by stockbrokers to the empire-building tendencies of CEOs, result from the difficulties inherent in agency relations. These problems can be addressed by closer monitoring and by changes in the structure of the relation. For example, the incentive for brokers to churn could be reduced by basing compensation more on the performance of clients' portfolios and less on the volume of trades. In addition, compensating executives with stock options aligns their interests more closely with those of the shareholders and thus prevents empire building. The most effective solutions for ethical problems in agency relations are twofold: first, there must be a strong sense of professionalism accompanied by professional organizations with codes of ethics; second, a high degree of trust must be present. Trust is essential in the financial services industry, and companies generally pay a heavy price for violating the public's confidence.

Sales Practices

Financial products are susceptible to abusive sales practices, such as "twisting," in which an insurance agent persuades a client to replace an existing policy merely for the commission, and "flipping," which is the practice of replacing one loan with another in order to generate additional fees. The poor are frequent targets of abuses by loan providers who offer high-interest loans and add on various "options" of little value. Finally, financial products should meet certain standards of integrity. Just as automobiles and houses can be shoddily made, so too are there shoddy financial products. The sale of limited partnerships, for example, has been criticized in recent years for dubious valuation of assets and questionable practices by developers.

Victims of fraud or abuse by financial services firms generally have recourse to the courts, but the securities industry in the USA requires most customers (and employees) to sign a predispute arbitration agreement (PDAA) that commits them to binding arbitration of disputes. Mandatory arbitration is spreading to the holders of credit cards, insurance policies, and other financial products. Although arbitration has many advantages over litigation, critics charge that the process is often unfair and denies investors adequate protection. The controversy over compulsory arbitration in the securities industry focuses on three issues: the requirement that investors sign a PDAA as a condition of opening an account, the alleged industry bias of arbitration panels, and the permissibility of punitive damages. In addition, the requirement that employees submit complaints about such matters as discrimination and harassment to arbitration denies them of the right to sue in court, a right that employees outside the securities industry take for granted.

Financial Services Firms

Financial services firms are themselves businesses, and the management of such a business raises some ethical issues, especially in the treatment of institutional clients. For example, underwriters of municipal bonds have been criticized for making political contributions in city elections in order to gain access. Firms as well as individuals encounter conflicts of interest, such as the reluctance of brokerage firms to issue a negative analysis of a client company's stock. In recent years, rogue traders have caused great losses at some firms, including the collapse of a major bank.

The managers of large investment portfolios for mutual funds, insurance companies, pension funds, and private endowments face two important ethical questions.

1. Should they consider social factors in making decisions, such as how a corporation treats its employees or its record on the environment?
2. Should they vote the stock that they hold, and if so, what criteria should they use to evaluate the issues that are submitted to a vote?

Some large institutional investors take a hands-off approach, while others are becoming actively involved as shareholders in a movement known as relationship investing.

FINANCIAL MANAGEMENT

Financial managers have the task of actively deploying assets rather than investing them. Unlike a portfolio manager who merely buys stocks of corporations for a client, a corporate financial manager is involved in the running of a corporation. Investment decisions in a corporation are concerned not with which securities to hold but with what business opportunities to pursue. These decisions are still made using standard financial criteria, however. Finance theory can be applied to the operation of a corporation by viewing the various components of a business as a portfolio with assets that can be bought and sold. Option pricing theory, in particular, suggests that all of the possibilities for a firm can be regarded options to buy and sell assets. Bankruptcy, for example, is exercising an option to "sell" the corporation to the debtholders. (However, one critic has called this a "thoroughly immoral view of finance.")

The ethical issues in financial management are twofold.

- Financial managers, as agents and fiduciaries, have an obligation to manage assets prudently and especially to avoid the use of assets for personal benefit. Thus, managers, who have preferential access to information, should not engage in insider trading or self-dealing. For example, management buyouts, in which a group of managers take a public corporation private, raise the question whether people who are paid to mind the store should seek to buy it.
- Financial managers are called upon to make decisions that impact many different groups, and they have an obligation in their decision making to balance some competing interests. For example, should the decision to close a plant be made solely with the shareholders' interests in mind or should the interests of the employees and the local community be taken into account?

Balancing Competing Interests

In finance theory, the objective of the firm is shareholder wealth maximization (SWM). This objective is reflected in corporate law, according to which officers and directors of corporations are agents of the corporation and have a fiduciary duty to operate the corporation in the interests of the shareholders. Despite the seemingly unequivocal guide of SWM, financial managers still face the need, in some situations, to balance competing interests. In particular, decisions about levels of risk and hostile takeovers reveal some difficulties in the pursuit of SWM.

The Level of Risk

Maximizing shareholder wealth cannot be done without assuming some risk. A critical, often overlooked, task of financial management is determining the appropriate level of risk. Leveraging, for example, increases the riskiness of a firm. The capital asset pricing model suggests that, for properly diversified shareholders, the level of risk for any given firm, called *unique* risk, is irrelevant and that only market or *systemic* risk is important. Finance theory treats bankruptcy as merely an event risk that is worth courting if the returns are high enough. If a firm is in distress, then a high risk, "bet-the-farm" strategy is especially beneficial to shareholders, because they will reap all the gains of success, while everyone will share the losses of failure (the moral hazard problem). Consequently, a financial manager should seek the highest return adjusted for risk, no matter the actual consequences.

However, a high-risk strategy poses dangers for bondholders, employees, suppliers, and managers themselves, all of whom place a high value on the continued operation of the firm. Employees, in particular, are more vulnerable than shareholders to unique, as opposed to systemic, risk because of their inability to diversify. Is it ethical for financial managers to increase risk in a firm so as to benefit shareholders, at the expense of other corporate constituencies? Does the firm, as an ongoing entity, have value that should be considered in financial decision making? Some have argued that managing purely by financial criteria, without regard for the level of risk, is immoral.

Hostile Takeovers

Hostile takeovers are often epic battles with winners and losers. For this reason, the rules for acquiring controlling interest should be fair to all parties involved. Managers of target companies feel entitled to a fair chance to defend their jobs; shareholders who sell their shares, and those who do not, have a right to make a decision in a fair and orderly manner; bondholders often lose in takeovers because of the increased debt; and employees and residents of local communities, who usually have no say in the decision, are generally the groups most harmed. . . .

The directors of a target company, whose approval is often necessary for a successful takeover, have a fiduciary duty to act in the best interests of the firm itself, which may not be identical with the interests of either the preexisting shareholders or those who seek control. A majority of states have adopted so-called "other constituency statutes" that permit boards of directors to consider other constituencies, such as employees, suppliers, customers, and local communities, in evaluating a takeover bid. Many other laws govern the conduct of raiders and defenders alike, so that the market for corporate control is scarcely a pure market. In general, courts and legislatures have created rules for takeovers that seek both fairness and efficiency.

QUESTIONS

1. What are unfair trading practices? Give several examples.

2. What are the important ethical distinctions between stockholders and stakeholders?

Jennifer Moore

What Is Really Unethical About Insider Trading?

Jennifer Moore is an author and an attorney.

The term *insider trading* needs some preliminary clarification. Both the SEC and the courts have strongly resisted pressure to define the notion clearly. In 1961, the SEC stated that corporate insiders—such as officers or directors—in possession of material, nonpublic information were required to disclose that information or to refrain from trading. But this "disclose or refrain" rule has since been extended to persons other than corporate insiders. People who get information from insiders ("tippees") and those who become "temporary insiders" in the course of some work they perform for the company, can acquire the duty of insiders in some cases. Financial printers and newspaper columnists, not "insiders" in the technical sense, have also been found guilty of insider trading. Increasingly, the term *insider* has come to refer to the kind of information a person possesses rather than to the status of the person who trades on that information. My use of the term will reflect this ambiguity. In this paper, an "insider trader" is someone who trades in material, nonpublic information—not necessarily a corporate insider.

1. ETHICAL ARGUMENTS AGAINST INSIDER TRADING

Fairness

Probably the most common reason given for thinking that insider trading is unethical is that it is "unfair." For proponents of the fairness argument, the key feature of insider trading is the disparity of information between the two parties to the transaction. Trading should take place on a "level playing field," they argue, and disparities in information tilt the field toward one player and away from the other. There are two versions of the fairness argument: the first argues that insider trading is unfair because the two parties do not have *equal* information; the second argues that insider trading is unfair because the two parties do not have equal *access* to information. Let us look at the two versions one at a time.

According to the equal information argument, insider trading is unfair because one party to the transaction lacks information the other party has, and is thus at a disadvantage. Although this is a very strict notion of fairness, it has its proponents, and hints of this view appear in some of the judicial opinions. One proponent of the equal information argument is Saul Levmore, who claims that "fairness is achieved when insiders and outsiders are in equal positions. That is, a system is fair if we would not expect one group to envy the position of the other." As thus defined, Levmore claims, fairness "reflects the 'golden rule' of impersonal behavior—treating others as we would ourselves."[1] If Levmore is correct, then not just insider trading, but *all* transactions in which there is a disparity of information are unfair, and thus unethical. But this claim seems overly broad. An example will help to illustrate some of the problems with it.

Suppose I am touring Vermont and come across an antique blanket chest in the barn of a farmer, a chest I know will bring $2,500 back in the city. I offer to buy it for $75, and the farmer agrees. If he had known how much I could get for it back home, he probably would have asked a higher price—but I failed to disclose this information. I have profited from an informational advantage. Have I been unethical? My suspicion is that most people would say I have not. While knowing how much I could sell the chest for in the city is in the interest of the farmer, I am not morally obligated to reveal it. I am not morally obligated to tell those who deal with me *everything* that it would be in their interest to know. . . .

In general, it is only when I owe a *duty* to the other party that I am legally required to reveal all information that is in his interest. In such a situation, the other party believes that I am looking out for his interests, and I deceive him if I do not do so. Failure to disclose is deceptive in this instance because of the relationship of trust and dependence between the parties. But this suggests that trading on inside information is wrong, *not* because it violates a general notion of fairness, but because a breach of fiduciary duty is involved. Cases of insider trading in which no fiduciary duty of this kind is breached would not be unethical. . . .

The "equal information" version of the fairness argument seems to me to fail. However, it could be argued that insider trading is unfair because the insider has information that is not *accessible* to the ordinary investor. For proponents of this second type of fairness argument, it is not the insider's information advantage that counts, but the fact that this advantage is "unerodable," one that cannot be overcome by the hard work and ingenuity of the ordinary investor. No matter how hard the latter works, he is unable to acquire nonpublic information, because this information is protected by law.[2]

This type of fairness argument seems more promising, since it allows people to profit from informational advantages of their own making, but not from advantages that are built into the system. Proponents of this "equal access" argument would probably find my deal with the Vermont farmer unobjectionable, because information about antiques is not in principle unavailable to the farmer. The problem with the argument is that the notion of "equal access" is not very clear. What does it mean for two people to have equal access to information?

Suppose my pipes are leaking and I call a plumber to fix them. He charges me for the job, and benefits by the informational advantage he has over me. Most

of us would not find this transaction unethical. True, I don't have "equal access" to the information needed to fix my pipes in any real sense, but I could have had this information had I chosen to become a plumber. The disparity of information in this case is simply something that is built into the fact that people choose to specialize in different areas. But just as I could have chosen to become a plumber, I could have chosen to become a corporate insider with access to legally protected information. . . .

One might argue that I have easier access to a plumber's information than I do to an insider trader's, since there are lots of plumbers from whom I can buy the information I seek. The fact that insiders have a strong incentive to keep their information to themselves is a serious objection to insider trading. But if insider trading were made legal, insiders could profit not only from trading on their information, but also on selling it to willing buyers. Proponents of the practice argue that a brisk market in information would soon develop—indeed, it might be argued that such a market already exists, though in illegal and clandestine form.[3] . . .

The most interesting thing about the fairness argument is not that it provides a compelling reason to outlaw insider trading, but that it leads to issues we cannot settle on the basis of an abstract concept of fairness alone. The claim that parties to a transaction should have equal information, or equal access to information, inevitably raises questions about how informational advantages are (or should be) acquired, and when people are entitled to use them for profit. . . .

Property Rights in Information

As economists and legal scholars have recognized, information is a valuable thing, and it is possible to view it as a type of property. We already treat certain types of information as property: trade secrets, inventions, and so on—and protect them by law. Proponents of the property rights argument claim that material, nonpublic information is also a kind of property, and that insider trading is wrong because it involves a violation of property rights.

If inside information is a kind of property, whose

property is it? How does information come to belong to one person rather than another? This is a very complex question, because information differs in many ways from other, more tangible sorts of property. But one influential argument is that information belongs to the people who discover, originate, or "create" it. As Bill Shaw put it in a recent article, "the originator of the information (the individual or corporation that spent hard-earned bucks producing it) owns and controls this asset just as it does other proprietary goods."[4] Thus, if a firm agrees to a deal, invents a new product, or discovers new natural resources, it has a property right in that information and is entitled to exclusive use of it for its own profit.

It is important to note that it is the firm itself (and/or its shareholders), and not the individual employees of the firm, who have property rights in the information. To be sure, it is always certain individuals in the firm who put together the deal, invent the product, or discover the resources. But they are able to do this only because they are backed by the power and authority of the firm. The employees of the firm—managers, officers, directors—are not entitled to the information any more than they are entitled to corporate trade secrets or patents on products that they develop for the firm. It is the firm that makes it possible to create the information and that makes the information valuable once it has been created. . . .

If this analysis is correct, then it suggests that insider trading is wrong because it is a form of theft. It is not exactly like theft, because the person who uses inside information does not deprive the company of the use of the information. But he does deprive the company of the *sole* use of the information, which is itself an asset. The insider trader "misappropriates," as the laws puts it, information that belongs to the company and uses it in a way in which it was not intended—for personal profit. It is not surprising that this "misappropriation theory" has begun to take hold in the courts, and has become one of the predominant rationales in prosecuting insider trading cases. . . .

This theory is quite persuasive, as far as it goes. But it is not enough to show that insider trading is always unethical or that it should be illegal. If insider information is really the property of the firm that produces it, then using that property is wrong *only when the firm prohibits it.* If the firm does not prohibit insider trading, it seems perfectly acceptable. (Unless there is some other reason for forbidding it, such as that it harms others.) Most companies do in fact forbid insider trading. But it is not clear whether they do so because they don't want their employees using corporate property for profit or simply because it is illegal. Proponents of insider trading point out that most corporations did not prohibit insider trading until recently, when it became a prime concern of enforcement agencies. . . .

A crucial factor here would be the shareholders' agreement to allow insider information. Shareholders may not wish to allow trading on inside information because they may wish the employees of the company to be devoted simply to advancing shareholder interests. We will return to this point below. But if shareholders did allow it, it would seem to be permissible. Still others argue that shareholders would not need to "agree" in any way other than to be told this information when they were buying the stock. If they did not want to hold stock in a company whose employees were permitted to trade in inside information, they would not buy that stock. Hence they could be said to have "agreed."

Manne and other proponents of insider trading have suggested a number of reasons why "shareholders would voluntarily enter into contractual arrangements with insiders giving them property rights in valuable information."[5] Their principal argument is that permitting insider trading would serve as an incentive to create more information—put together more deals, invent more new products, or make more discoveries. Such an incentive, they argue, would create more profit for shareholders in the long run. Assigning employees the right to trade on inside information could take the place of more traditional (and expensive) elements in the employee's compensation package. Rather than giving out end of the year bonuses, for example, firms could allow employees to put together their own bonuses by cashing in on inside information, thus saving the company money. In addition, proponents argue, insider trading would improve the efficiency of the market. We will return to these claims below.

If inside information really is a form of corporate

property, firms may assign employees the right to trade on it if they choose to do so. The only reason for not permitting firms to allow employees to trade on their information would be that doing so causes harm to other investors or to society at large. Although our society values property rights very highly, they are not absolute. We do not hesitate to restrict property rights if their exercise causes significant harm to others. The permissibility of insider trading, then, ultimately seems to depend on whether the practice is harmful.

Harm

There are two principal harm-based arguments against insider trading. The first claims that the practice is harmful to ordinary investors who engage in trades with insiders; the second claims that insider trading erodes investors' confidence in the market, causing them to pull out of the market and harming the market as a whole. I will address the two arguments in turn.

Although proponents of insider trading often refer to it as a "victimless crime," implying that no one is harmed by it, it is not difficult to think of examples of transactions with insiders in which ordinary investors are made worse off. Suppose I have placed an order with my broker to sell my shares in Megalith Co., currently trading at $50 a share, at $60 or above. An insider knows that Behemoth Inc. is going to announce a tender offer for Megalith shares in two days, and has begun to buy large amounts of stock in anticipation of the gains. Because of his market activity, Megalith stock rises to $65 a share and my order is triggered. If he had refrained from trading, the price would have risen steeply two days later, and I would have been able to sell my shares for $80. Because the insider traded, I failed to realize the gains that I otherwise would have made.

But there are other examples of transactions in which ordinary investors *benefit* from insider trading. Suppose I tell my broker to sell my shares in Acme Corp., currently trading at $45, if the price drops to $40 or lower. An insider knows of an enormous class action suit to be brought against Acme in two days. He sells his shares, lowering the price to $38 and trig-

gering my sale. When the suit is made public two days later, the share price plunges to $25. If the insider had abstained from trading, I would have lost far more than I did. Here, the insider has protected me from loss. . . .

The truth about an ordinary investor's gains and losses from trading with insiders seems to be not that insider trading is never harmful, but that it is not systematically or consistently harmful. Insider trading is not a "victimless crime," as its proponents claim, but it is often difficult to tell exactly who the victims are and to what extent they have been victimized. The stipulation of the law to "disclose *or* abstain" from trading makes determining victims even more complex. While some investors are harmed by the insider's trade, to others the insider's actions make no difference at all; what harms them is simply *not having complete information* about the stock in question. Forbidding insider trading will not prevent these harms. Investors who neither buy nor sell, or who buy or sell for reasons independent of share price, fall into this category.

Permitting insider trading would undoubtedly make the securities market *riskier* for ordinary investors. Even proponents of the practice seem to agree with this claim. But if insider trading were permitted openly, they argue, investors would compensate for the extra riskiness by demanding a discount in share price. . . . If insider trading were permitted, in short, we could expect a general drop in share prices, but no net harm to investors would result. Moreover, improved efficiency would result in a bigger pie for everyone.

The second harm-based argument claims that permitting insider trading would cause ordinary investors to lose confidence in the market and cease to invest there, thus harming the market as a whole. As former SEC Chairman John Shad puts it, "if people get the impression that they're playing against a marked deck, they're simply not going to be willing to invest."[6] Since capital markets play a crucial role in allocating resources in our economy, this objection is a very serious one.

The weakness of the argument is that it turns almost exclusively on the *feelings* or *perceptions* of ordinary investors, and does not address the question of whether these perceptions are justified. If permitting insider trading really does harm ordinary investors, then this "loss of confidence" argument becomes a compelling reason for outlawing insider trading. But if, as many claim, the practice does not harm ordinary investors, then the sensible course of action is to educate the investors, not to outlaw insider trading. It is irrational to cater to the feelings of ordinary investors if those feelings are not justified. We ought not to outlaw perfectly permissible actions just because some people feel (unjustifiably) disadvantaged by them.

II. IS THERE ANYTHING WRONG WITH INSIDER TRADING?

My contention has been that the principal ethical arguments against insider trading do not, by themselves, suffice to show that the practice is unethical and should be illegal. The strongest arguments are those that turn on the notion of a fiduciary duty to act in the interest of shareholders, or on the idea of inside information as company "property." But in both arguments, the impermissibility of insider trading depends on a contractual understanding among the company, its shareholders and its employees. In both cases, a modification of this understanding could change the moral status of insider trading.

Does this mean that there is nothing wrong with insider trading? No. If insider trading is unethical, it is so *in the context* of the relationship among the firm, its shareholders, and its employees. It is possible to change this context in a way that makes the practice permissible. But *should* the context be changed? I will argue that it should not. Because it threatens the fiduciary relationship that is central to business management, I believe, permitting insider trading is in the interest neither of the firm, its shareholders, nor society at large.

Fiduciary relationships are relationships of trust and dependence in which one party acts in the interest of another. They appear in many contexts, but are absolutely essential to conducting business in a complex society. Fiduciary relationships allow parties with different resources, skills, and information to cooperate in productive activity. Shareholders who wish to invest in a business, for example, but who cannot or do not wish to run it themselves, hire others to manage it for them. Managers, directors, and to some extent, other employees, become fiduciaries for the firms they manage and for the shareholders of those firms.

The fiduciary relationship is one of moral and legal obligation. Fiduciaries, that is, are bound to act in the interests of those who depend on them even if these interests do not coincide with their own. Typically, however, fiduciary relationships are constructed as far as possible so that the interests of the fiduciaries and the parties for whom they act *do* coincide. Where the interests of the two parties compete or conflict, the fiduciary relationship is threatened. . . .

Significantly, proponents of insider trading do not dispute the importance of the fiduciary relationship. Rather, they argue that permitting insider trading would *increase* the likelihood that employees will act in the interest of shareholders and their firms. We have already touched on the main argument for this claim. Manne and others contend that assigning employees the right to trade on inside information would provide a powerful incentive for creative and entrepreneurial activity. It would encourage new inventions, creative deals, and efficient new management practices, thus increasing the profits, strength, and overall competitiveness of the firm. Manne goes so far as to argue that permission to trade on insider information is the only appropriate way to compensate entrepreneurial activity, and warns: "[I]f no way to reward the entrepreneur within a corporation exists, he will tend to disappear from the corporate scene."[7] The entrepreneur makes an invaluable contribution to the firm and its shareholders, and his disappearance would no doubt cause serious harm.

If permitting insider trading is to work in the way proponents suggest, however, there must be a direct and consistent link between the profits reaped by insider traders and the performance that benefits the firm. It is not at all clear that this is the case—indeed, there is evidence that the opposite is true. There appear to be many ways to profit from inside information that do not benefit the firm at all. I mention four possibilities below. Two of these (2 and 3) are

Ethics Matter

Roel C. Campos

One of my duties as a Commissioner is not only to support and implement the securities laws, but also at times to urge practices that go beyond the letter of the law. I believe that this is such a time.

I am sure that I speak for the Chairman and my fellow Commissioners in observing that it is not enough for reporting companies simply to have a code of ethics. No matter how well or beautifully the language of the code of ethics reads, if the code is relegated to the back of a policy manual or a cluttered website, it is of no use. I submit that having a code of ethics that is not vigorously implemented is worse than not having a code of ethics. It smacks of hypocrisy.

We all know that having rules in life is not enough. Indeed, if it were enough, the existence of the Ten Commandments would ensure proper conduct among human beings. For this reason, I urge all CEOs and senior management of reporting companies to live and practice on a daily basis the principles contained in their codes of ethics.

Senior management should make it clear to employees through their words and conduct that ethics matter. Senior management and boards of directors should establish practices that acknowledge and commend acts of honesty and ethical behavior.

Just as good deeds in life create unforeseen blessings, I believe it is fundamental that honesty and integrity will ultimately create business success. Creating an ethical business culture should not be viewed as a sacrifice. Indeed, it is good business to be open and honest with your shareholders. It is good business to have fair dealings with your business partners. It is good business to reward employees for being honest and ethical. It is good business to be known as a company that deals fairly in its business transactions. It is good business for shareholders to know that a company not only has a code of ethics but that the code is followed every day. It is also good business to select CEOs and Presidents largely based on their integrity and commitment to ethical behavior. . . .

SEC Commissioner Roel C. Campos, Washington, D.C., October 16, 2002; http://www.sec.gov/news/speech/spch593.htm

---

simply ways in which insider traders can profit without benefiting the firm, suggesting that permitting insider trading is a poor incentive for performance and fails firmly to link the interests of managers, directors, and employees to those of the corporation as a whole. The others (1 and 4) are actually harmful to the corporation, setting up conflicts of interest and actively undermining the fiduciary relationship.

1. Proponents of insider trading tend to speak as if all information were positive. "Information," in the proponents' lexicon, always concerns a creative new deal, a new, efficient way of conducting business, or a new product. If this were true, allowing trades on inside information might provide an incentive to work even harder for the good of the company. But information

can also concern *bad* news—a large lawsuit, an unsafe or poor quality product, or lower-than-expected performance. Such negative information can be just as valuable to the insider trader as positive information. If the freedom to trade on positive information encourages acts that are beneficial to the firm, then by the same reasoning the freedom to trade on negative information would encourage harmful acts. At the very least, permitting employees to profit from harms to the company decreases the incentive to avoid such harms. Permission to trade on negative inside information gives rise to inevitable conflicts of interest. Proponents of insider trading have not satisfactorily answered this objection.

2. Proponents of insider trading also assume that the easiest way to profit on inside information is to "create" it. But it is not at all clear that this is true. Putting together a deal, inventing a new product, and other productive activities that add value to the firm usually require a significant investment of time and energy. For the well-placed employee, it would be far easier to start a rumor that the company has a new product or is about to announce a deal than to sit down and produce either one—and it would be just as profitable for the employee. If permitting insider trading provides an incentive for the productive "creation" of information, it seems to provide an even greater incentive for the nonproductive "invention" of information, or stock manipulation. The invention of information is in the interest neither of the firm nor of society at large.

3. Even if negative or false information did not pose problems, the incentive argument for insider trading overlooks the difficulties posed by "free riders"—those who do not actually contribute to the creation of the information, but who are nevertheless aware of it and can profit by trading on it. . . . Unless those who do not contribute can be excluded from trading on it, there will be no incentive to produce the desired information; it will not get created at all.

4. Finally, allowing trading on inside information would tend to deflect employees' attention from the day-to-day business of running the company and focus it on major changes, positive or negative, that lead to large insider trading profits. This might not be true if one could profit by inside information about the day-to-day efficiency of the operation, a continuous tradition of product quality, or a consistently lean operating budget. But these things do not generate the kind of information on which insider traders can reap large profits. Insider profits come from dramatic changes, from "news"—not from steady, long-term performance. If the firm and its shareholders have a genuine interest in such performance, then permitting insider trading creates a conflict of interest for insiders. The ability to trade on inside information is also likely to influence the types of information officers announce to the public, and the timing of such announcements, making it less likely that the information and its timing is optimal for the firm. And the problems of false or negative information remain.

If the arguments given above are correct, permitting insider trading does not increase the likelihood that insiders will act in the interest of the firm and its shareholders. In some cases, it actually causes conflicts of interest, undermining the fiduciary relationship essential to managing the corporation. This claim, in turn, gives corporations good reason to prohibit the practice. But insider trading remains primarily a private matter among corporations, shareholders, and employees. It is appropriate to ask why, given this fact about insider trading, the practice should be *illegal.* If it is primarily corporate and shareholder interests that are threatened by insider trading, why not let corporations themselves bear the burden of enforcement? Why involve the SEC? There are two possible reasons for continuing to support laws against insider trading. The first is that even if they wish to prohibit insider trading, individual corporations do not have the resources to do so effectively. The second is that society itself has a stake in the fiduciary relationship. . . .

The notion of the fiduciary duty owed by managers and other employees to the firm and its shareholders has a long and venerable history in our society. Nearly all of our important activities require some sort of cooperation, trust, or reliance on others, and the ability of one person to act in the interest of another—as a fiduciary—is central to this cooperation. The role of managers as fiduciaries for firms and shareholders is grounded in the property rights of shareholders. They are the owners of the firm, and bear the residual risks, and hence have a right to have it managed in their interest. The fiduciary relationship also contributes to efficiency, since it encourages those who are willing to take risks to place their resources in the hands of those who have the expertise to maximize their usefulness. While this "shareholder theory" of the firm has often been challenged in recent years, this has been primarily by people who argue that the fiduciary concept should be widened to include other "stakeholders" in the firm. I have heard no one argue that the notion of managers' fiduciary duties should be eliminated entirely, and that managers should begin working primarily for themselves.

III. CONCLUSION

I do believe that lifting the ban against insider trading would cause harms to shareholders, corporations, and society at large. But again, these harms stem primarily from the cracks in the fiduciary relationship caused by permitting insider trading, rather than from actual trades with insiders. Violation of fiduci-

ary duty, in short, is at the center of insider trading offenses.

NOTES

1. Saul Levmore, "Securities and Secrets: Insider Trading and the Law of Contracts," 68 *Virginia Law Review* 117.

2. The equal access argument is perhaps best stated by Victor Brudney in his influential article, "Insiders, Outsiders and Informational Advantages Under the Federal Securities Laws," 93 *Harvard Law Review* 322.

3. Manne, *Insider Trading and the Stock Market* (Free Press, New York, 1966), 75.

4. Bill Shaw, "Should Insider Trading Be Outside the Law?" *Business and Society Review* 66: 34. See also Macey, "From Fairness to Contract: The New Direction of the Rules Against Insider Trading," 13 *Hofstra Law Review* 9 (1984).

5. Carlton and Fischel, "The Regulation of Insider Trading," 35 *Stanford Law Review* 857. See also Manne, *Insider Trading and the Stock Market.*

6. "Disputes Arise Over Value of Laws on Insider Trading," *The Wall Street Journal,* November 17, 1986, 28.

7. Manne, *Insider Trading and the Stock Market,* 129.

QUESTIONS

1. What *is* really unethical about insider trading? What does Moore conclude?

2. How might you argue that insider trading is really a good thing that should be allowed?

Frank Partnoy | # F.I.A.S.C.O.

Frank Partnoy is an author and former Wall Street trader.

Keeping tabs on the derivatives obituaries column is nearly a full-time job these days, especially with the recent surge in activity. By the time you read this, the market is likely to be more than $100 trillion (it was estimated at $65–80 trillion as of mid-1998), headed for the astronomical $1 quadrillion mark. I can't resist the urge to abuse the late Senator Everett Dirksen's famous quote: a quadrillion here and a quadrillion there and pretty soon you're talking about some serious money.

———

. . . Derivatives, once again, are a horror show. The structured notes and leveraged swaps that rocked the financial markets with billion-dollar losses in 1994–95 are back. The same specters that haunted, and then broke Barings, and Orange County, and took a slice out of Procter & Gamble have returned from the dead. And in my opinion, the sequel is even more scary.

Derivatives remain unseen, yet ubiquitous. Time bombs are ticking away, concealed in the underbelly of our investment portfolios. Whether you realize it or not, most of you investors continue to have exposure to derivatives, typically through investments in mutual funds . . . and pension funds. . . . I was not happy to discover that my new hometown, sleepy San Diego, has a $3.3 billion public-employee pension fund chock full of derivatives. I own derivatives, indirectly, through a mutual fund I bought, and I'll bet you own them, too. If you still don't believe me, just call your mutual fund manager or read your prospectus. And get ready to weep.

Of course, Wall Street isn't weeping one tear. Derivatives continue to be hugely profitable for bankers, in part because fund managers who buy derivatives will pay a premium to take on risks they can hide from shareholders, and in part because other buyers don't fully understand what they are buying. Derivatives have helped Wall Street to its best year ever—bonuses were up more than 30 percent last year. Sellers of derivatives are ecstatic. Many buyers are happy, for now; ignorance is bliss. Yet 70 percent of derivatives professionals say they expect big losses in the coming year.

Opinion about derivatives remains sharply divided, George Soros, billionaire trader, warns that derivatives traders cause instability that will "destroy society." . . . [I believe that] derivatives carry hidden seeds of destruction, and that no one truly understands their risks. . . .

ASIAN FALLOUT

Much of the [recent] derivatives action . . . has been in Asia, where the derivatives market is estimated to be in the tens of trillions of dollars, though no one really knows how big it is. Market participants are worried, and Hong Kong pension fund regulators even proposed forbidding derivatives use. Japan and the Asian "tigers"—Korea, Indonesia, Malaysia, the Philippines, Singapore, Taiwan, Thailand—were doing just fine until the summer of 1997. On July 2, 1997, Thailand, which had pegged its currency, the baht, to a basket of foreign currencies, based on Thailand's trade with other countries, finally had to eliminate the peg. The baht plunged more than 17 percent against the U.S. dollar that day, just as the Mexican

Peso had collapsed on December 20, 1994. The effects were cataclysmic.

[For instance, there was a] mouth-watering Thai baht structured note. . . . That note, and similar foreign exchange-linked notes, were issued by highly-rated corporations and government sponsored enterprises, such as General Electric Credit Corporation and the Federal Home Loan Banks. The notes looked safe, and paid a deliciously high coupon. But if you were an unlucky holder of a Thai baht structured note on July 2, 1997, you were suffering from more than mild digestive problems. A mountain of pink bismuth powder couldn't block the financial dysentery as the note ripped through the innards of your balance sheet, faster than a plate of bad paed ped.

The other Asian tigers followed Thailand into the dumpster. Asian banks had been feasting, like the fat Mexican banks of the early 1990s, making leveraged bets on their own markets and currencies using equity swaps, total return swaps, options, futures, forwards, and more complex derivatives. Now, they faced annihilation. Within months, the foreign currency value of investments in East Asia dropped by 50 percent or more.

Structured notes and swaps did far more than cause localized commercial collywobbles in Asia. They ensured that the ripple effects of the baht devaluation would reach well beyond the domestic markets. If a butterfly flapping its wings in Thailand can affect weather in the U.S., imagine what a currency devaluation can do. Individual investors, money managers, even hedge fund operators throughout the world were hurting.

Most of the derivatives causing the pain were "over-the-counter" rather than traded on any exchange. That means, for example, that Asian banks engaging in swaps had a counterparty, typically a U.S. or European bank, who expected repayment on the swap, just as I would expect repayment if you and I had bet $10 on whether the Asian markets would falter. In other words, the Asian banks and companies hadn't lost money to any centralized exchange; they had lost money to other companies, primarily Western banks. The bottom line was that if the Asian banks went bust, their counterparties might lose the entire amounts the Asian banks owed.

The over-the-counter nature of these derivatives trades created enormous potential for loss. For example, banking regulators warned that U.S. banks had more than $20 billion of exposure to Korea. One Korean investment firm, SK Securities Company, had bet with J. P. Morgan that the Thai baht would rise relative to the Japanese yen, and when the baht collapsed, SK owed J. P. Morgan about $300 million. Other banks—including Citicorp, Chase Manhattan, and Bankers Trust—each disclosed more than a billion dollars of exposure to Asia. This exposure to a counterparty's inability or unwillingness to repay is called "credit risk." Credit risk is a banal non-issue irrelevant to a counterparty until a so-called credit event actually occurs; then, credit risk is a central issue mattering all too much. Credit risk from derivatives was a major reason the U.S. was so concerned about rescuing Asia (and its banking counterparties) from financial meltdown.

One man who was suffering more than most during this period of financial indigestion in Asia was Victor Niederhoffer, the celebrated, and often barefooted, squash/derivatives maestro and hedge fund manager extraordinaire. Niederhoffer's imbroglio illustrates the interconnectedness of modern capital markets, and the amazing velocity of investments in derivatives.

In June 1997, Niederhoffer was on top of the world. His excellent autobiography, *The Education of a Speculator,* was selling well, and he was managing more than $100 million of investments, including much of his own considerable wealth. He was both popular and respected, and had an incredible track record: returns of 30 percent per year for fifteen years, with a 1996 return of 35 percent.

Unfortunately, Niederhoffer also had made a big bet on the baht. And when the Thai butterfly flapped its wings, he lost about $50 million, almost half of his fund.

Derivatives traders who lose $50 million, or more, seem to follow a pattern. I used to fall into that pattern playing blackjack in Las Vegas. Perhaps you've had a similar experience. You play a hand of blackjack for $100, thinking it wouldn't kill you to lose that much money. You lose the hand. Then, you play another hand, thinking it wouldn't be a big deal to

To: You
From: The Philosopher
Subject: "Aristotle on Money"

You probably remember Aristotle's idea of the "Golden Mean." Aristotle argued that if we consider almost any activity, the virtue of that activity lies in the mean between a "defect" or a "deficiency" and an "excess." Moderation is the key to virtue and happiness. True, he was not an accountant or an investment adviser, but Aristotle certainly has some helpful advice on how we relate to money:

> With regard to giving and taking of money the mean is liberality, the excess and the defect prodigality and meanness. They exceed and fall short in contrary ways to one another; the prodigal exceeds in spending and falls short in taking, while the mean man exceeds in taking and falls short in spending. With regard to money there are also other dispositions—a mean, magnificence (for the magnificent man differs from the liberal man; the former deals with large sums, the latter with small ones), an excess, tastelessness and vulgarity, and a deficiency, miserliness.

From Aristotle, *Nicomachean Ethics,* 1107b8–22.

lose $200. Besides, maybe you'll win the hand and get back to even. You lose that hand, too. Then, you lose another hand, and another hand, and another. Pretty soon, you're down $500, an amount of money you really would prefer *not* to lose. What do you do? Do you quit? Or course not. You do the opposite. You increase your wagers, and start betting to get even. That's the pattern. You look up to the eye-in-the-sky, and a little voice in your head trembles. "If only I could win that money back; *then* I would stop gambling. Forever."

Imagine adding five zeros to that $500. What does that voice sound like, now? It might sound awfully depressing if the $50 million was your money. But what if the money was, in the words of Justice Louis Brandeis, "other people's money"? Suddenly betting to get even doesn't seem foolish at all. Wouldn't you double-down, at least once, for $50 million of *someone else's* money? Why not? If you win, you're even and no one will ever care about your temporary loss. And if you lose, do you really think it matters much if you lose another $50 million of someone else's

money. After the first $50 million, you've pretty much guaranteed that special someone won't be inviting you to thanksgiving dinner.

So Niederhoffer, like others before him—Nick Leeson of Barings, Joseph Jett of Kidder, Peabody, Yasuo Hamanaka of Sumitomo, Toshihide Iguchi of Daiwa—began betting to get even, taking on additional risk in the hope that he could make back enough money to overcome his losses on the baht. Academics would refer to Niederhoffer, at this point in his life, as a rogue trader.

He had recovered a bit of the Thai loss by September, but was still down about 35 percent for the year. Going into October, Niederhoffer began doubling down by selling put options on the Standard & Poor's 500 index futures contract. This was a truly gutsy move. The S & P 500 index futures contract allows speculators to make leveraged bets on the performance of the S & P 500 index, an index that tracks 500 large stocks. You can sell put options on this contract in the same way you can sell put options on any other instrument.

. . . A put option is the right to sell some underlying financial instrument or index at a specified time and price. In the trader's parlance, or Corvette lingo, if you bought a put option, you might pay $1,000 today for the right to sell a Corvette for $40,000 some time during the next month. You would make money if the price of Corvettes dropped. If the price of a Corvette dropped to $30,000, you would make $10,000—the $40,000 you could sell a Corvette for, using the put option, minus the $30,000 you could buy a Corvette for in the market (less the $1,000 premium you had paid).

Whereas the buyer of a put option wants the price to go down, the seller of a put option wants the price to stay the same or go up—but definitely, *please,* not to go down. The more the price goes down, the more the seller of the put option must pay the buyer. In our example, if the price of Corvettes dropped to $30,000, and we had sold put options on 100 Corvettes, we would lose $900,000 ($1 million less the $100,000 premium we had received). The strategy of selling put options does not carry the one benefit Morgan Stanley touted for some of the riskier products it sold: "downside limited to size of initial investment." In this case, you could lose *more* than everything. A put seller's downside is limited only by the size of his or her imagination (and the fact that prices don't usually drop below zero).

Niederhoffer was looking OK through the weekend of October 25–26. October had not been an especially eventful month, the publication of my book notwithstanding. Niederhoffer was waiting, hoping the options would expire worthless so he could keep the premium and get back closer to even. Remember, he wanted the market to stay the same or go up—but definitely, *please,* not to go down.

On Monday, October 27, 1997, the U.S. stock market plummeted 554 points, or about 7 percent. The S & P index fell 64.67 points to 876.97. It had been almost exactly 10 years since the stock market crash of 1987, dubbed "Black Monday," October 19, 1987. A 7 percent drop didn't meet the definition of market crash, and it certainly couldn't match Black Monday. But for Niederhoffer, that Monday delivered a death blow. By noon, he was broke. By Wednesday, his funds had been liquidated. The $100 million plus of his investor's money was gone.

Take a guess at who Niederhoffer's investors were? That's right, believe it or not, my hometown favorite, the $3.3 billion San Diego public-employee pension fund was right there in the thick of it with Niederhoffer's other put option sellers. Well done, San Diego!

QUESTIONS

1. What was the fiasco?
2. What are derivatives? Why do they tend to create unique ethical dilemmas?

CASES

CASE 5.1

A Modern History of "Creative" Accounting
The Democratic Policy Committee

A timeline of corporate misconduct and accounting irregularities, offered in "A Special Report by the Democratic Policy Committee 7/11/02" follows.

April 1998: Waste Management/Arthur Andersen. Andersen approved a series of audits that overstated Waste Management's profits by $1.4 billion, the largest ever at the time. Andersen paid a $7 million fine, also the largest ever at the time. The SEC determined that Andersen had noticed the accounting irregularities but knowingly allowed the audits to go through with false numbers. . . .

December 1999: Tyco International/PricewaterhouseCoopers. The SEC reopened its investigation into conglomerate Tyco International, alleging accounting irregularities, including that Tyco had used reserves and other creative accounting strategies to increase its stock prices—problems that auditor PricewaterhouseCoopers had not disclosed. PricewaterhouseCoopers also provided consulting services to Tyco—amounting to $37.9 million in 2001 alone. In addition, Tyco CEO Dennis Kozlowski resigned after having been indicted for tax evasion, and information has come out that his successor, John F. Fort III, has been involved in questionable accounting transactions that may indicate a significant conflict of interest. In 1999, the SEC investigated Tyco for not having reported the details of 700 acquisitions costing over $8 billion.

July 2000: Rite Aid/KPMG. Several former executives at Rite Aid have been indicted for securities and accounting fraud that led to a $1.6 billion restatement of earnings—a problem that Rite Aid's then-auditor, KPMG, never discovered. . . .

November 2001: Enron/Arthur Andersen. Enron restated its 1997–2001 financial statements to reflect a $1.2 billion reduction in shareholder equity; it had improperly inflated earnings and hidden debt through business partnerships. An Arthur Andersen partner who objected to the accounting standards used in the Enron audit was removed from his oversight role after Enron pressured Andersen to do so. Earlier this year, Andersen was convicted of obstruction of justice.

January 2002: ImClone Systems. ImClone Systems CEO Samuel Waksal resigned over a major conflict of interest, which culminated in his recent arrest. In its criminal probe, the FBI accused Waksal of selling his stock in the company and alerting family members and friends to do so after he found out that ImClone's cancer drug would not be approved by FDA.

From *A Special Report by the Democratic Policy Committee,* 7/11/02.

February 2002: Global Crossing/Arthur Andersen. Global Crossing, a fiber optic network provider, is an example of myriad conflicts of interests and accounting problems that have led to over 60 investor fraud lawsuits. First, it has admitted to having shred documents after the SEC and the Justice Department began investigating potential fake network-access transactions it conducted in order to boost its revenue. These transactions involved counting revenue from long-term contracts immediately, rather than properly recording them over the period of the entire contract. Second, the SEC is also investigating stock sales and purchases by Global Crossing executives, several of whom made large sums of money before the company declared bankruptcy and cut 12,000 jobs. Third, Global Crossing appears to have had questionable ties to stock analyst Jack Grubman of Salomon Smith Barney. Grubman had a close relationship with Global Crossing's chairman for many years and purportedly influenced several of the company's key decisions. Grubman maintained a "buy" rating on Global Crossing's stock until just two months before the company filed for bankruptcy, despite signs that the company was in serious trouble.

March 2002: Qwest/Arthur Andersen. The SEC is investigating Qwest for overstating its revenue through capacity swaps and equipment sales— questionable transactions that were never questioned by auditor Arthur Andersen.

April 2002: Xerox/KPMG. KPMG found no irregularity in its audit of Xerox, even though Xerox had overstated its profits by $1.5 billion over 4 years. As a result, Xerox paid a $10 million civil penalty, the largest ever for fraud charges. More recently, PricewaterhouseCoopers re-audited Xerox's books and found that Xerox had improperly recorded over $6 billion in revenue over five years.

May 2002: PeopleSoft/Ernst & Young. The SEC has charged auditor Ernst & Young with vio-

lating federal securities law when it entered into business deals with its audit client PeopleSoft, a software maker. Ernst & Young had agreed to sell and install PeopleSoft's software—including to its audit clients.

May 2002: Halliburton/Arthur Andersen. The SEC is investigating Halliburton for accounting irregularities in which the company apparently changed its accounting practices in order to report a disputed $100 million in construction overruns as profit. Its accounting method, approved by auditor Arthur Andersen, allowed it to postpone losses and was never disclosed to the SEC.

May 2002: Peregrine Systems/KPMG/Arthur Andersen. Peregrine Systems, Inc. fired KPMG after it was revealed that Peregrine's previous auditor, Arthur Andersen, had not caught a $100 million overstatement in earnings, which led to a 3-year restatement of earnings. The problem? $35 million of this had come from transactions between KPMG Consulting and Peregrine—a clear conflict of interest that neither the auditing nor consulting arms of KPMG had revealed to Peregrine.

May 2002: Adelphia Communications/Deloitte & Touche. Adelphia Communications, one of the largest cable companies in the United States, never reported $2.3 billion in debt—and its auditor, Deloitte & Touche, never caught it. The money had been loaned to the Rigas family, Adelphia's owner, who used it to buy Adelphia stock. Deloitte served as both Adelphia's accountant and auditor for the Rigas-controlled entities, creating a conflict of interest, and Deloitte never revealed to Adelphia's audit committee that the Rigases were using the company's credit lines to buy Adelphia stock. This information caused Adelphia's stock to plummet to its lowest level since 1997. The SEC is investigating both Adelphia and Deloitte.

June 2002: WorldCom/Arthur Anderson. World-Com recently reported that it had overstated its earnings by $3.8 billion—even though its figures were approved by auditor Arthur Andersen. According to the SEC, WorldCom illegally manipulated its earnings in order to bolster its stock price. Bankruptcy is now imminent for WorldCom. The current scandal comes in the wake of a class action lawsuit filed by shareholders, charging that WorldCom had misrepresented its earnings in official SEC filings. The SEC is also investigating World-Com for loaning former CEO Bernie Ebbers

$366 million so that he would not have to sell any of his WorldCom stock.*

QUESTIONS

1. What do all these scandals have in common? How might they have been avoided?

2. What constraints should be placed on accounting firms in order to avoid scandals like these? What about criminal penalties?

CASE 5.2

Merger Mania

Lisa H. Newton and David P. Schmidt

Lisa Newton and David Schmidt are leading contemporary business ethicists.

People seem to love hating Martha Stewart, the homemaking queen known for her ingenious decorating ideas, linens, and housewares. Perhaps they resent her seemingly inexhaustible ability to transform mundane junk into all manner of beautiful and ingenious things. Or perhaps they believe the rumors that she is a harshly demanding chief executive of Martha Stewart Living Omnimedia. Whatever the reason, an entire nation sat up and eagerly took notice when Stewart joined the ranks of CEOs charged with corporate misdeeds. More than a few observers outwardly delighted in her troubles.

On December 27, 2001, Stewart sold 4,000 shares of ImClone Systems, a biotech company that was started and run by Stewart's friend, Samuel D. Waksal. According to Stewart's lawyers, she and her stockbroker, Peter E. Baconovic, had long before agreed that he should sell ImClone if the price dropped below $60 a share. Stewart denies that her

decision to sell the shares was based on any inside information from Waksal or anyone else. It was simply a coincidence, she maintained, that her sale of ImClone took place just before the company released the bad news that the Food and Drug Administration (FDA) was not going to approve a new ImClone anti-cancer drug.

By the late 1990s, "merger mania" was once again becoming a force to reckon with. Just halfway into 1998, for example, takeovers and acquisitions engineered by Wall Street had soared past $1.2 trillion dollars, compared to just $920 billion in the entire preceding year. When many companies are taken over and sold, the conditions are ripe for abusing nonpublic information that can affect the stock prices of companies. Apparently, that is precisely what has been happening in recent years.

The Securities and Exchange Commission has lately redoubled its efforts to catch insider traders. It is especially interested in the trading patterns of senior executives who have been linked to the various accounting and disclosure scandals that rocked the

Lisa H. Newton, David P. Schmidt "*Merger Mania*" in *Wake-Up Calls: Classic cases in Business Ethics,* 2nd ed. © 2004 by South Western (Thomson).

business world in 2001–2002. The SEC also wants to pursue anyone who profited illegally from the sudden declines in the stock market following the dot-com bust. It is hard to say whether there is more insider trading going on now than in the 1990s. Clearly, however, we now live in a troubled business climate in which the public is much less tolerant of any illegal trading that is taking place. In an effort to restore public confidence in Wall Street, the SEC is now imposing tougher penalties on those who get caught. In the fiscal year ended September 30, 1997, the Commission brought forward 57 insider trading cases.

Some things about insider trading have not changed significantly since the 1980s. For example, as was the case back then, there still is no statutory definition of insider trading. The reason for this continues to be that a clear definition of insider trading would only help crafty lawyers find legal loopholes. We continue to use certain theories to interpret whether insider trading has occurred. One of these is the so-called "misappropriation theory," which says that people who acquired material nonpublic information through a special relationship with a company could not "misappropriate" this information for their own financial gain. Since the 1980s, prosecutors have had mixed success using this theory to convict inside traders. But in 1997, the Supreme Court strengthened the misappropriation theory when it upheld the insider-trading conviction of James H. O'Hagan. O'Hagan was a Minneapolis lawyer who sought to profit from information gleaned from his law firm's representation of Grand Metropolitan, a company who had tried to take over the Pillsbury Company. While O'Hagan's law firm worked for Grand Met, he bought call options and shares of Pillsbury stock. He sold these options and stock when Grand Met announced its tender offer, for a profit of more than $4.3 million. A case was made against O'Hagan. However, a federal appeals court overturned the conviction, saying that O'Hagan was neither an employee nor a fiduciary of Pillsbury. But the Supreme Court reversed the federal appeals court, saying that a person who obtains inside information, under conditions in which that person knows the information is supposed to remain nonpublic, may not use that information for trading. As a consequence, people who buy and sell securities today still

need to be mindful of legal interpretive principles that were first hammered out in the 1980s.

At the same time, some things about insider trading today are very different than in the 1980s. Charges of insider trading today arise in a context of widespread public disgust with corporate scandals and ethical misconduct of senior executives. It galls many people that CEOs continue to enjoy huge salaries, bonuses, and perks while their companies' profits evaporate, employees are laid off, and long-term investors get hammered. There may be literally dozens of cases in which corporate insiders have legally sold millions of dollars of shares shortly before revised earnings projections drove down the prices of their companies' shares. It looks like insider trading. Why is it allowed to happen?

The problem was created, in part, by the growing practice of companies compensating their chief executives with generous stock options. One purpose of these options was to align the executives' self-interest with the interests of their corporations. But the executives needed a way to exercise their stock options without being accused of insider trading. By the end of 2000, then SEC Chairman Arthur D. Levitt led the Commission to adopt a rule allowing executives to set prearranged schedules for selling their stock. This so-called "safe harbor" approach insulated the executives from charges of insider trading, since they were selling according to fixed, pre-arranged schedules.

Levitt's rule may have helped to curb insider trading, but it did little to soften the growing public outcry over whether executives and the markets can be trusted. Kenneth Borovina is a thirty-four-year-old carpenter whose grandmother's life savings has shrunk from $600,000 to $200,000 in 2001–2002 in the dismal stock market. Of the senior executives who recently have been investigated and arrested for shady financial dealings, Borovina says, "They're getting what they deserve. That makes me feel great." He no doubt speaks for many Americans who have turned their backs on corporate America in disgust.

QUESTIONS

1. Do you trust corporate America? Why or why not? Is "trust" appropriate in this context?

2. What is merger mania? What fuels it? Is it new, or has it been around for a while?

CASE 5.3
Annuities to Seniors
Ron Duska

The growth of the annuities market has been a boon for insurance companies accounting for a large portion of their sales. According to the ACLI fact book:

> The mix of premiums from life insurance and annuity considerations has changed markedly over the last 25 years. In 1978 the share of premium receipts from life policies (46%) was more than double the 21 percent from annuities. By 2002, this trend had reversed: Life policies accounted for only one-quarter of premium receipts (26%) while annuity considerations contributed more than half (53%). [American Council of Life Insurers: *Life Insurers Fact Book,* 2003. p. 53]

But the growth in the annuities market brings a set of problems for the industry that some say have the potential to lead to ethical scandals that could be devastating for the industry

There is much concern about potentially unsuitable sales of variable annuities to seniors. The NASD in one of its alerts states the following:

> The marketing efforts used by some variable annuity sellers deserve scrutiny—especially when seniors are the targeted investors. Sales pitches for these products might attempt to scare or confuse investors. One scare tactic used with seniors is to claim that a variable annuity will protect them from lawsuits or seizures of their assets. Many such claims are not based on facts, but nevertheless help land a sale. [*NASD Investor Alert,* "Variable Annuities: Beyond the Hard Sell", May 27, 2003. This Alert focuses solely on *deferred variable* annuities and the unique issues they raise for investors.]

The *Wall Street Journal* reports that one company offers training sessions on how to sell annuities to senior citizens. "Treat them like they're children." "Don't be sophisticated. "They buy based upon emotions! Emotions of fear, anger and greed." "Show them their finances are all screwed up so that they think, "Oh, no, I've done it all wrong." This will make you money, and it's probably a product they need." Tell them you can protect their life savings from nursing home and Medicaid seizure of assets. They don't know what that is, but it sounds scary. It's about putting a pitchfork in their chest."

What's an annuity? "There's the technical answer, and there's the senior answer. Tell them it's like a CD—it's safe, it's guaranteed."

On June 27, 2002 The SEC filed civil fraud charges against a California Broker, Gregory W. The SEC alleged that W. defrauded scores of retired customers by recommending they replace existing investments in variable annuities with new investments in similar variable annuities. The switches would enable him to receive significant commissions. W. recommended approximately 57 such switches in less than four years. W. told the customers they needed to switch in order to stem investment losses caused by declines in the stock market. The switching did not halt their losses and they could have achieved that objective by simply electing another investment option within the original variable annuity. The customers either received no economic benefit or lost money in the switch transactions and together incurred more than $200, in needless transactions costs, while W. received approximately $275,000 in commissions for the unsuitable switches.

Simultaneously the Commission proceeded against W.'s supervisor for failing to reasonably supervise W. and not investigating red flags raised by certain switches when she reviewed the transactions.

1. How can companies ensure that their annuity sales to seniors are suitable—that the product is both needed and understood by the client?

2. What are the ramifications of having multiple pricing and commission structures available on identical products? How can the company be confident that the agent is selling the right product for each client? What disclosures about product choices and compensation are appropriate?

CASE 5.4
An Auditor's Dilemma
John R. Boatright

Sorting through a stack of invoices, Alison Lloyd's attention was drawn to one from Ace Glass Company. Her responsibility as the new internal auditor for Gem Packing is to verify all expenditures, and she knew that Ace had already been paid for the June delivery of the jars that are used for Gem's jams and jellies. On closer inspection, she noticed that the invoice was for deliveries in July and August that had not yet been made. Today was only June 10. Alison recalled approving several other invoices lately that seemed to be misdated, but the amounts were small compared with the $130,000 that Gem spends each month for glass jars. I had better check this out with purchasing, she thought.

Over lunch, Greg Berg, the head of purchasing, explains the system to her. The jam and jelly division operates under an incentive plan whereby the division manager and the heads of the four main units—sales, production, distribution, and purchasing—receive substantial bonuses for meeting their quota in pre-tax profits for the fiscal year, which ends on June 30. The bonuses are about one-half of annual salary and constitute one-third of the managers' total compensation. In addition, meeting quota is weighted heavily in evaluations, and missing even once is considered to be a death blow to the career of an aspiring

executive at Gem. So the pressure on these managers is intense. On the other hand, there is nothing to be gained from exceeding a quota. An exceptionally good year is likely to be rewarded with an even higher quota the next year, since quotas are generally set at corporate headquarters by adding 5 percent to the previous year's results.

Greg continues to explain that several years ago, after the quota had been safely met, the jam and jelly division began prepaying as many expenses as possible—not only for glass jars but for advertising costs, trucking charges, and some commodities, such as sugar. The practice has continued to grow, and sales also helps out by delaying orders until the next fiscal year or by falsifying delivery dates when a shipment has already gone out. "Regular suppliers like Ace Glass know how we work," Greg says, "and they sent the invoices for July and August at my request." He predicts that Alison will begin seeing more irregular invoices as the fiscal year winds down. "Making quota gets easier each year," Greg observes, "because the division gets an ever increasing head start, but the problem of finding ways to avoid going too far over quota has become a real nightmare." Greg is not sure, but he thinks that other divisions are doing the same thing. "I don't think corporate has

From *Ethics and the Conduct of Business,* 2nd edition by John R. Boatright, © 1993. Reprinted by permission of Prentice Hall, Inc., Upper Saddle River, NJ.

caught on yet," he says. "But they created the system, and they've been happy with the results so far. If they're too dumb to figure out how we're achieving them, that's their problem."

Alison recalls that upon becoming a member of the Institute of Internal Auditors, she agreed to abide by the IIA code of ethics. This code requires members to exercise "honesty, objectivity, and diligence" in the performance of their duties, but also to be loyal to the employer. However, loyalty does not include being a party to any "illegal or improper activity." As an internal auditor, she is also responsible for evaluating the adequacy and effectiveness of the company's system of financial control. But what is the harm of shuffling a little paper around? she thinks. Nobody is getting hurt, and it all works out in the end.

QUESTIONS

1. Is the IAA code of ethics really helpful in resolving Alison's dilemma? Why or why not?

2. Greg blames the incentive system for the dilemma. Is he right?

CASE 5.5

Enron and Employee Investment Risk

David Lawrence and Tom L. Beauchamp

In order to determine appropriate and acceptable levels of risk in their retirement funds, employee-investors must be knowledgeable about how those funds are invested. Often employees are unaware of the level of risk taken by their employers in maintaining a fund. A famous recent case of the problem emerged from the ashes of the collapse of Enron.

After greatly expanding its operations during the 1990s, Enron, an energy broker, experienced unprecedented financial growth and soaring stock prices. Much of this growth, however, was not legitimate, and the details, as a result, were not disclosed to investors or to employees.

Using the lawful practice of "mark-to-market" accounting, Enron's financial analysts and advisors were able to record potential, future profits as immediate gains. To boost these apparent profits even more, Enron also created businesses and partnerships to hide its debt. These practices inflated stock prices while falsely establishing the company's financial position and stability. The success and prominence of the company seemed to minimize concerns about investment risk in Enron stock. Seeing immediate and extensive gains, however, such employee-investors saw little incentive in questioning the risk of their investments. They were not concerned when Enron used company stock as the sole unit of deposit in employee 401(k) earnings. While this involved tremendous risk, given Enron's true instability, the details of the company's financial state remained undisclosed. Only after uncovering the fraudulent accounting practices was the true level of the risk assessed. By this time, however, employee-investors and employees with retirement savings invested in stock had lost all of their investments and all of their retirement funds.

Enron-style investing is commonplace in employee retirement accounts, where diversification in types of investment is not generally recognized as a

In Tom L. Beauchamp and Norman E. Bowie, *Ethical Theory and Business,* 7th ed. (Englewood Cliffs, NJ: Prentice Hall, 2004), p. 251. Reprinted with the permission of the authors.

legal or a moral requirement. While the collapse of Enron is everywhere recognized to be a scandal, the underlying questions of investor risk in company retirement plans is one feature of this scandal that remains largely unaddressed.

QUESTIONS

1. Should businesses, like Enron, encourage employees to buy stock in their own companies? Why or why not?

What are some of the risks involved in permitting such practices?

2. While, legally, not all information must be disclosed, should companies be obligated to reveal the true nature of investor risk? Or, are investors individually responsible for determining such risk?

3. Does Enron's overstating of profit amount to a manipulation of investors? Was the manipulation intentional? Should investors assume a high level of risk unless expressly told otherwise?

CHAPTER QUESTIONS

1. What are the basic conflicts that arise in helping other people with their money? Should we rely on experts when it comes to money? How do we know when an expert's own pocketbook is guiding a decision, rather than an interest in our financial success? Are there ways of guaranteeing that our financial success, the expert's financial success, and good ethical principles are all in agreement?

2. One commentator described the Enron–Arthur Andersen debacle as "the half-full problem"—the tendency for analysts to insist that the glass is half-full rather than half-empty. How can financial managers both stimulate financial success and yet be wary of the dangers of excessive optimism? Is there a place for optimism in accounting? In the sale of derivatives?

6

Who Gets What and Why?

Fairness and Justice

Introduction

Businesses and corporations are not just legal entities. They are communities. Small businesses are more like extended families, perhaps, but even giant corporations try to maintain something of a family identity in order to encourage family-like loyalty and foster a sense of belonging that "work-for-hire" and other contract workers do not feel. (Of course, there are unhappy as well as dysfunctional families and communities, but it is already a significant step to understand that joining a company is not just a matter of "taking a job.") As a member of a family or a community, however, you will, of course, be sensitive to considerations that pertain not just to yourself, for example, your salary, your job skills, and your responsibilities, but to you as a member of a group, the sort of motivation that is summarized in most corporations as "team spirit." But being a member of a group is not just becoming submerged in the group. One retains one's identity and interests as an individual. And that means that among the most important factors in a good job and the satisfaction that goes along with it is fairness, a *comparative* measure of how people are treated. It is a conclusion of a great deal of research, often confirmed, that people care about their comparative (ordinal) worth more than they care about their absolute (cardinal) worth. Most people, given the choice between a salary of, say, $60,000—while other people at the same level are making $64,000—and a salary of, say, $56,000—while other people at the same level are making $50,000—will choose the latter observer the former. In the abstract, you may think, "How stupid! Choosing the lower salary." But in the context of a work situation, comparative rewards mean a great deal, in terms of one's sense of worth, one's sense of being appreciated, and one's sense of being fairly treated. Even trivial differences in salary or bonuses can cause seething and poisonous resentment.

Of course, considerations of fairness cut across careers and professions and involve both rewards and burdens, including punishments, of various kinds. In other words, considerations of fairness are not confined to peers and pay. A company that gives out awards or promotions, whether or not they involve any monetary reward, will find quickly the huge cost of favoritism and other forms of unfair competition. When the boss's nephew wins the award for "Best New Employee," he had better have the on-the-job record to back it up. Indeed, it may have been an injustice for him to get the job in the first place. But this is not to say that everyone should be treated or paid equally. Few people deny that top executives deserve more in salary than does the ordinary manager, but the question *how much more* is a controversial question these days. (It used to be a multiple of 35 or so. It is now over 500. In 2003, the average CEO of a major company received $9.2 million in total compensation, according to a study by compensation consultant Pearl Meyer & Partners for the *New York Times*.) The nurse who takes care of your sick aunt or the teacher who spends six hours a day with your eight-year-old niece in public school makes far less money for (arguably) just as much work. A stockbroker or investment banker readily makes a six-figure income; the nurse and the teacher make a fraction of that, with little possibility of a dramatic increase or substantial bonus.

Justice has two basic forms: *retributive* justice and *distributive* justice. Distributive justice is concerned with the distribution of goods, in the context of a job, salaries, bonuses, promotions, but also opportunities and responsibilities. Retributive justice is essentially concerned with penalties and punishments, with assigning blame and, when necessary, reprimanding or punishing people in proportion to their mistakes or misdeeds. Business, for the most part, is concerned with distributive justice. (In the wake of some of the serious scandals of recent years, retributive justice also becomes a major issue, but it becomes a matter

---

To: You
From: The Philosopher
Subject: "Plato and Aristotle on Justice"

The subject of justice is as old as human civilization. In really ancient times, perhaps, the rule was "might makes right." Some people still think that it does. But for most of history thoughtful people have seen beyond mere force and power to the idea that there is a *fairer* way of thinking about what people should get and give from and to society. Plato, through his spokesman Socrates in *The Republic,* argued that everyone should get his or her due— what he or she deserves—based on his or her place in a just society. Aristotle, Plato's student, had a more economically sophisticated version of this idea. He insisted that justice requires a principle of *equality,* by which he meant not (as in more recent philosophies) that everyone should get the same but, rather, that justice requires that everyone should get the proportion he or she deserves, depending on his or her position in the society. It is "equal" in the sense that it is neither too much nor too little. (Aristotle suggests, insightfully, that the best way to test a person's sense of fairness is to watch the person when he or she is in charge.)

of law and the business of the courts, rather than an issue in business ethics as such.) The one thing that we should say about retributive justice is that it is based on the idea that everyone should be treated fairly and equally, so that one person should not be punished for another person's mistakes and one person should not be punished more harshly than another who has made the same mistake. No matter how effective it may be to make an example of an innocent employee in order to deter other employees who may be thinking about cheating on their expense accounts, we feel strongly that it is unfair and an *injustice* to punish someone who has not, in fact, done something wrong. But in distributive justice, too, what is essential is that a person be rewarded in accordance with what he or she *deserves.* Two people who do the same job equally well deserve the same rewards. Different rewards (e.g., larger and smaller bonuses) had better be based on differences in the quality or quantity of work. Extraneous considerations—whether a person is male or female, his or her race or religion, his or her personal preferences or idiosyncrasies—should make no difference at all.

We start the chapter with a few bits from the great philosophers Plato and Aristotle on justice and, in particular, the famous "Ring of Gyges" example from Plato's *Republic,* in which the question is posed, Why would you care about doing the right thing and being fair if you could get away with anything? Then Adam Smith considers the value of fair exchange in the marketplace. The antithesis of justice in the marketplace is *exploitation,* and we offer a couple of different perspectives on its, from the very abstract (Karl Marx) to the very concrete (Wal-Mart's behavior in Latin America) and something in between, Joanne B. Ciulla on exploitation in the job market. Then we open up our horizons to the world more generally. The late philosopher John Rawls summarizes his classic theory of justice, and Princeton ethicist Peter Singer sums up the argument against the extreme gap between rich and poor in the world. Then Irving Kristol and Friedrich von Hayek offer two more conservative views of justice, Kristol on how justice fits into the free market and von Hayek on how it does not. Eduard Garcia weighs the risks of a society in which the "winner takes all." Finally, Gerald W. McEntee considers the question of gender equality and "comparable worth," the shameful fact that in a society in which people are supposed to be paid for the work they do, women are paid considerably less than are men for doing exactly the same job. Finally, the cases are intended to provoke your thinking about concrete concerns about justice, for instance, the fact that you may be contributing to the exploitation and injustice in the world by buying some of the products that you are wearing right now.

Plato | # Ring of Gyges

Plato was one of the two greatest Greek philosophers of ancient times. This is the infamous "Ring of Gyges" story from his dialogue, *The Republic,* told by one of Socrates philosophical sparring partners, Glaucon.

GLAUCON (TO SOCRATES): I have never yet heard the superiority of justice to injustice maintained by anyone in a satisfactory way. I want to hear justice praised in respect of itself; then I shall be satisfied, and you are the person from whom I think that I am most likely to hear this; and therefore I will praise the unjust life to the utmost of my power and my manner of speaking will indicate the manner in which I desire to hear you too praising justice and censuring injustice. Will you say whether you approve of my proposal?

SOCRATES: Indeed I do; nor can I imagine any theme about which a man of sense would oftener wish to converse.

GLAUCON: I am delighted to hear you say so, and shall begin by speaking, as I proposed, of the nature and origin of justice.

They say that to do injustice is, by nature, good; to suffer injustice, evil; but that there is more evil in the latter than good in the former. And so when men have both done and suffered injustice and have had experience of both, any who are not able to avoid the one and obtain the other, think that they had better agree among themselves to have neither; hence they began to establish laws and mutual covenants; and that which was ordained by law was termed by them lawful and just. This, it is claimed, is the origin and nature of justice;—it is a mean or compromise, between the best of all, which is to do injustice and not be punished, and the worst of all, which is to suffer injustice without the power of retaliation; and justice, being at a middle point between the two, is tolerated not as a good but as the lesser evil, and honoured where men are too feeble to do injustice. For no man who is worthy to be called a man would ever submit to such an agreement with another if he had the power to be unjust; he would be mad if he did. Such is the received account Socrates, of the nature of justice, and the circumstances which bring it into being.

Now that those who practise justice do so involuntarily and because they have not the power to be unjust will best appear if we imagine something of this kind: having given to both the just and the unjust power to do what they will, let us watch and see whither desire will lead them; then we shall discover in the very act the just and unjust man to be proceeding along the same road, following their interest, which all creatures instinctively pursue as their good; the force of law is required to compel them to pay respect to equality. The liberty which we are supposing may be most completely given to them in the form of such a power as is said to have been possessed by Gyges, the ancestor of Croesus the Lydian. According to the tradition, Gyges was a shepherd in the service of the reigning king of Lydia; there was a great storm, and an earthquake made an opening in the earth at the place where he was feeding his flock. Amazed at the sight, he descended into the opening, where, among other marvels which form part of the story, he beheld a hollow brazen horse, having doors, at which he stooping and looking in saw a dead body of stature, as appeared to him, more than human; he took from the corpse a gold ring that was on the hand, but nothing else, and so reascended. Now the shepherds met together, according to custom, that they might send their monthly report about the flocks to

From *Republic,* Book 2, trans. Benjamin Jowett (Oxford University Press, 1924).

the king; into their assembly he came having the ring on his finger, and as he was sitting among them he chanced to turn the collet of the ring to the inside of his hand, when instantly he became invisible to the rest of the company and they began to speak of him as if he were no longer present. He was astonished at this, and again touching the ring he turned the collet outwards and reappeared; when he perceived this, he made several trials of the ring, and always with the same result—when he turned the collet inwards he became invisible, when outwards he was visible. Whereupon he contrived to be chosen one of the messengers who were sent to the court; where as soon as he arrived he seduced the queen, and with her help conspired against the king and slew him, and took the kingdom. Suppose now that there were two such magic rings, and the just put on one of them and the unjust the other; no man can be imagined to be of such an iron nature that he would stand fast in justice. No man would keep his hands off what was not his own when he could safely take what he liked out of the market, or go into houses and lie with any one at his pleasure, or kill or release from prison whom he would, and in all respects be like a god among men. Then the actions of the just would be as the actions of the unjust; they would both tend to the same goal. And this we may truly affirm to be a great proof that a man is just, not willingly or because he thinks that justice is any good to him individually, but of necessity; for wherever anyone thinks that he can safely be

unjust, there he is unjust. For all men believe in their hearts that injustice is far more profitable to the individual than justice and he who argues as I have been supposing will say that they are right. If you could imagine anyone obtaining this power of becoming invisible, and never doing any wrong or touching what was another's, he would be thought by the lookers-on to be an unhappy man and a fool, although they would praise him to one another's faces, and keep up appearances with one another from a fear that they too might suffer injustice. Enough of this.

Now, if we are to form a real judgement of the two lives in these respects, we must set apart the extremes of justice and injustice; there is no other way; and how is the contrast to be effected? I answer: Let the unjust man be entirely unjust, and the just man entirely just; nothing is to be taken away from either of them, and both are to be perfectly furnished for the work of their respective lives. First, let the unjust be like other distinguished masters of craft; like the skillful pilot or physician, who knows intuitively what is possible or impossible in his art and keeps within those limits, and who, if he fails at any point, is able to recover himself. So let the unjust man attempt to do the right sort of wrongs, and let him escape detection if he is to be pronounced a master of injustice. To be found out is a sign of incompetence; for the height of injustice is to be deemed just when you are not. Therefore I say that in the perfectly unjust man we must assume the most perfect injus-

---

To: You
From: The Philosopher
Subject: "Would You Rather Earn More or Just More Than the Other Fellow?"

Suppose that you are given a choice between two jobs, one with a salary of $60,000, but you know that other new hires at the same level have been offered $64,000, and the other with a salary of $56,000, and you know that other new hires have only been offered $50,000. Other things being equal (the job description, the working conditions, the people you will be working with), which would you chose?

tice; there is to be no deduction, but we must allow him, while doing the most unjust acts, to have acquired the greatest reputation for justice. If he has taken a false step he must be able to recover himself; he must be one who can speak with effect, if any of his deeds come to light, and who can force his way where force is required, by his courage and strength and command of wealth and friends. And at his side let us place the just man in his nobleness and simplicity, wishing, as Aeschylus says, to be and not to seem good. There must be no seeming, for if he seems to be just he will be honoured and rewarded, and then we shall not know whether he is just for the sake of justice or for the sake of honours and rewards; therefore, let him be clothed in justice only, and have no other covering; and he must be imagined in a state of life the opposite of the former. Let him be the best of men, and let him be reputed the worst; then he will have been put to the test and we shall see whether his justice is proof against evil reputation and its consequences. And let him continue thus to the hour of death; being just and seeming to be unjust. When both have reached the uttermost extreme, the one of justice and the other of injustice, let judgement be given which of them is the happier of the two.

SOCRATES: Heavens! my dear Glaucon . . . how energetically you polish them up for the decision, first one and then the other, as if they were two statues.

QUESTIONS

1. What would you do if you had the ring of Gyges? What do you think your best friend would do?

2. The consequences of unjust actions are one kind of constraint upon justice. What are some other constraints? Why might we want to appeal to more than consequences?

Adam Smith | # On Human Exchange and Human Differences

This division of labor, from which so many advantages are derived, is not originally the effect of any human wisdom which foresees and intends that general opulence to which it gives occasion. It is the necessary, though very slow and gradual, consequence of a certain propensity in human nature which has in view no such extensive utility: the propensity to truck, barter, and exchange one thing for another.

Whether this propensity be one of those original principles in human nature, of which no further account can be given; or whether, as seems more probable, it be the necessary consequence of the faculties of reason and speech, it belongs not to our present subject to enquire. It is common to all men, and to be found in no other race of animals, which seem to know neither this nor any other species of contracts. Two greyhounds, in running down the same hare, have sometimes the appearance of acting in some sort of concert. Each turns her toward his companion, or endeavors to intercept her when his companion turns her toward himself. This, however, is not the effect of any contract, but of the accidental concurrence of

From Adam Smith, *The Wealth of Nations* (New York: Hafner, 1948).

their passions in the same object at that particular time. Nobody ever saw a dog make a fair and deliberate exchange of one bone for another with another dog. Nobody ever saw one animal by its gestures and natural cries signify to another, this is mine, that yours; I am willing to give this for that. When an animal wants to obtain something either of a man or of another animal, it has no other means of persuasion but to gain the favor of those whose service it requires. A puppy fawns upon its dam, and a spaniel endeavors by a thousand attractions to engage the attention of its master who is at dinner, when it wants to be fed by him. Man sometimes uses the same arts with his brethren, and when he has no other means of engaging them to act according to his inclinations, endeavors by every servile and fawning attention to obtain their good will. He has not time, however, to do this upon every occasion. In civilized society he stands at all times in need of the co-operation and assistance of great multitudes, while his whole life is scarce sufficient to gain the friendship of a few persons. In almost every other race of animals each individual, when it is grown up to maturity, is entirely independent, and in its natural state has occasion for the assistance of no other living creature. But man has almost constant occasion for the help of his brethren, and it is in vain for him to expect it from their benevolence only. He will be more likely to prevail if he can interest their self-love in his favor, and show them that it is for their own advantage to do for him what he requires of them. Whoever offers to another a bargain of any kind, proposes to do this. Give me that which I want, and you shall have this which you want, is the meaning of every such offer; and it is in this manner that we obtain from one another the far greater part of those good offices which we stand in need of. It is not from the benevolence of the butcher, the brewer, or the baker, that we expect our dinner, but from their regard to their own interest. We address ourselves, not to their humanity but to their self-love, and never talk to them of our own necessities but of their advantages. Nobody but a beggar chooses to depend chiefly upon the benevolence of his fellow-citizens. Even a beggar does not depend upon it entirely. The charity of well-disposed people, indeed, supplies him with the whole fund of his subsistence. But though this principle ulti-

mately provides him with all the necessaries of life which he has occasion for, it neither does nor can provide him with them as he has occasion for them. The greater part of his occasional wants are supplied in the same manner as those of other people, by treaty, by barter, and by purchase. With the money which one man gives him he purchases food. The old clothes which another bestows upon him he exchanges for other old clothes which suit him better, or for lodging, or for food, or for money, with which he can buy either food, clothes, or lodging, as he has occasion.

As it is by treaty, by barter, and by purchase that we obtain from one another the greater part of those mutual good offices which we stand in need of, so it is this same trucking disposition which originally gives occasion to the division of labor. In a tribe of hunters or shepherds a particular person makes bows and arrows, for example, with more readiness and dexterity than any other. He frequently exchanges them for cattle or for venison with his companions; and he finds at last that he can in this manner get more cattle and venison than if he himself went to the field to catch them. From a regard to his own interest, therefore, the making of bows and arrows grows to be his chief business, and he becomes a sort of armorer. Another excels in making the frames and covers of their little huts or movable houses. He is accustomed to be of use in this way to his neighbors, who reward him in the same manner with cattle and with venison till at last he finds it his interest to dedicate himself entirely to this employment, and to become a sort of house carpenter. In the same manner a third becomes a smith or a brazier; a fourth a tanner or dresser of hides or skins, the principal part of the clothing of savages. And thus the certainty of being able to exchange all that surplus part of the produce of his own labor, which is over and above his own consumption, for such parts of the produce of other men's labor as he may have occasion for, encourages every man to apply himself to a particular occupation, and to cultivate and bring to perfection whatever talent or genius he may possess for that particular species of business.

The difference of natural talents in different men is, in reality, much less than we are aware of; and the very different genius which appears to distinguish men of different professions, when grown up to maturity, is not upon many occasions so much the cause as the effect of the division of labor. The difference between the most dissimilar characters, between a philosopher and a common street porter, for example, seems to arise not so much from nature as from habit, custom, and education. When they came into the world, and for the first six or eight years of their existence, they were, perhaps, very much alike, and neither their parents nor play-fellows could perceive any remarkable difference. About that age, or soon after, they come to be employed in very different occupations. The difference of talents comes then to be taken notice of, and widens by degrees, till at last the vanity of the philosopher is willing to acknowledge scarce any resemblance. But without the disposition to truck, barter, and exchange, every man must have procured to himself every necessary and conveniency of life which he wanted. All must have had the same duties to perform, and the same work to do, and there could have been no such difference of employment as could alone give occasion to any great difference of talents.

As it is this disposition which forms that difference of talents so remarkable among men of different professions, so it is this same disposition which renders that difference useful. Many tribes of animals acknowledged to be all of the same species derive from nature a much more remarkable distinction of genius than what, antecedent to custom and education, appears to take place among men. By nature a philosopher is not in genius and disposition half so different from a street porter as a mastiff is from a greyhound, or a greyhound from a spaniel, or this last from a shepherd's dog. Those different tribes of animals, however, though all of the same species, are of scarce any use to one another. The strength of the mastiff is not in the least supported either by the swiftness of the greyhound, or by the sagacity of the spaniel, or by the docility of the shepherd's dog. The effects of those different geniuses and talents, for want of the power or disposition to barter and exchange, cannot be brought into a common stock, and do not in the least contribute to the better accommodation and conveniency of the species. Each animal is still obliged to support and defend itself separately and independently, and derives no sort of advantage from that variety of talents with which nature has distinguished its fellows. Among men, on the contrary, the most dissimilar geniuses are of use to one another; the different produces of their respective talents, by the general disposition to truck, barter, and exchange, being brought, as it were, into a common stock, where every man may purchase whatever part of the produce of other men's talents he has occasion for.

QUESTIONS

1. Why does Smith believe that "self-love" is a good thing?

2. Why does Smith discuss the differences in people's talents? Why is it important that the difference in talents is not so large as we often suppose?

Latin Trade | # A Latin Viewpoint: The Bentonville Menace

Latin Trade is a South American business magazine.

If you wonder why more Latin American countries aren't jumping on the free-trade bandwagon, look no further than the cutthroat business practices of the world's largest private company, US$245 billion-in-revenues Wal-Mart Stores.

Taking screw-the-workers capitalism to new depths, this modern-day robber baron has pushed its Latin American suppliers to cut costs to the bone or lose their contracts to China. They are even trying to force down labor costs in emerging Asia. It seems even $0.40 cents an hour—the estimated wage in China—is too high for the heartless executives at the front offices in Bentonville, Arkansas.

In some 40 lawsuits reportedly filed in the United States, the corporate behemoth—its annual sales is greater than the gross domestic product (GDP) of all but two Latin American economies—has been accused of using third-party contractors who hire illegal immigrants to work below minimum wage; of forcing employees to work overtime without pay; of busting up attempts to unionize; and of skimping on worker and retirement compensation. The company's official line is anti-union.

An internal audit at Wal-Mart three years ago—as reported in the *The New York Times*—showed extensive violations of child labor laws. Meanwhile, a federal judge in San Francisco is considering a sexual discrimination suit that could encompass as many as 1.6 million women, making it the largest civil rights class-action case in U.S. history.

If Wal-Mart stands accused of engaging in such shenanigans in the United States, imagine its corporate behavior in far-less-litigious Latin America.

"Many Latin Americans concerned about economic development see little benefit from the Wal-Mart model of maximizing profits by paying poverty wages," says Kent Wong, director of the Center for Labor Research and Education at the University of California at Los Angeles.

It was a *Los Angeles Times* exposé published in November that noted how Wal-Mart's global network of 10,000 suppliers is under constant pressure to reduce costs. The article described the unhappy life of a Honduran woman named Isabel Reyes, who works for a textile company in San Pedro Sula that makes shirts and shorts for Wal-Mart. With quotas constantly rising, she now works 10 hours a day, sewing sleeves onto 1,200 shirts a day for about $35 a week. The 37-year-old seamstress can't hold her infant daughter without gulping anti-inflammatory pills.

To be sure, nobody is forcing Reyes to work there. "It's easy to compare a $35 a week salary with a U.S. salary," Wal-Mart spokesman Bill Wertz told me. "But I don't know what the alternatives are in that country."

He's right—to an extent. What choice does Reyes have in a nation where 53% of the population lives below the poverty line, and 28% of the work force is unemployed?

Latin American governments are grappling with weak economies and need all the jobs they can get. Wal-Mart offers lots of them. The retail chain is now Mexico's largest private employer, with 663 stores and 100,000 employees. The chain generates $11 billion a year there—more than the country's entire tourism sector, or about 2% of Mexico's GDP. Puerto Rico has 53 Wal-Mart stores with 11,600 workers. Brazil has 25 stores and 6,600 employees; Argentina 11 stores and 4,200 employees.

And customers all over the world love bargain prices. In 1995, I covered the opening of Wal-Mart's first store in São Paulo. I remember Brazilians rhap-

From *Latin Trade,* May 2004.

sodizing over the store's mantra of "everyday low prices." So many people lined up to get inside during the first week of business that the manager had to lock out some customers.

Still, it's time to hold this mega-corporation accountable. Latin American leaders must not be forced to cower to foreign investors who threaten to move elsewhere if they don't play by the rules of take-no-prisoners U.S. capitalism.

Free trade was supposed to create decent paying jobs that ultimately offer Latin American families a middle-class life style and turn them into consumers. Unfortunately, fairness has never been part of the free trade blueprint. Nor, in my view, is fairness uppermost in the mind of Wal-Mart's corporate masters.

Consumers should think twice about patronizing any business that perpetuates economic injustice. Everyday social justice is more important than low prices at any cost.

QUESTIONS

1. What is the problem with Wal-Mart in Latin America?

2. Is economic justice more important than low prices? Should we be shopping at Wal-Mart?

Joanne B. Ciulla | # Exploitation of Need

The fact that a person can choose his or her work does not necessarily justify ill-treatment by an employer. Part of the question is how many options a person really does have. A common myth is that all people really have a wide range of choices when it comes to making a living. The most important part of the American dream was that anyone could become anything. This was a land not only of opportunity but of options. But what about the destitute person whose only options are degrading ones?

The practice of self-enslavement had been around for a long time. It was common among the Germanic and Anglo-Saxon peoples in the Middle Ages. A person in need of support and/or protection would sell himself to another. This choice, though more or less freely made, was grounded in the same fears of starvation and violence found in other forms of slavery. Self-enslavement raises some interesting questions. Does a frightened and starving person *freely* choose to enter into a contract with someone who can provide him or her with food and safety? This is a question that lies beneath the way Americans think about employment. Is any kind of work or any set of working conditions okay as long as a person freely chooses it? We may be quicker to defend people's right to do any job they want to do, but what about the right of employers to hire people for physically dangerous or personally demeaning work?

The philosopher John Locke offers some insight into these questions. The desire to be free from the yoke of one's master or employer is at the heart of some of our most treasured political ideals. In the first of his two treatises on government, Locke asks, "And how is it that property in land gives a man power over another?" Here Locke is disputing the natural right of kings over property and their subjects. Locke argues that people own the work of their hands and the labor of their bodies. He also notes that we have a moral obligation to help those in need and not take advantage of them: "Charity gives every man a title to so much out of another's plenty, as will keep him from extreme want, where he has no means to subsist otherwise; and a man can no more justly make use of another's necessity, to force him to become his vassal, by withholding that relief."

Locke then goes on to raise one of the biggest tensions of the employer-employee relationship. He writes that "the subjugation of the needy does not begin with the consent of the Lord, but with the consent of the poor man, who preferred being his [another person's] subject to starving." So, it's wrong to force a needy person to be your slave, but it's not wrong for the needy person to choose to be your slave or indentured servant. Are the two really that different? This is like the employer who says to a single mother of four, "If you don't like working here you are free to leave" or "If you didn't like the working conditions here, then you shouldn't have taken the job in the first place." A single mother who lives in a small town and has four children to support has the freedom to choose where to work, but little to chose from. When it comes to work, everyone has freedom of choice, but not everyone has viable options.

The actual difference between the indentured servant and the slave rests on his or her consent, even if a person really has only one viable choice. The indentured servant's bondage may be short-term and tempered by the voluntary contractual arrangements between the two people. The slave's bondage is involuntary and long-term, and there is no restriction on the master's power over the slave. In theory at least, it is not wrong to take away a person's freedom as long as he or she consents to the arrangement. This begs the larger question of exploitation. How much freedom and human dignity can an employer morally justify buying because someone is willing to sell it? The fourteen-year-old runaway on Sunset Boulevard in Los Angeles is willing to sell his body to buy the drugs he desperately needs. To what extent does he "freely" enter into the transaction? The answer to a question like this has always been hotly contested. Some would argue that the boy could choose other-

---

To: You
From: The Philosopher
Subject: "Marx on Alienated Labor"

There are a lot of people who feel alienated from their jobs and don't want to be identified with their work. The guy who serves you fries at McDonald's probably does not want his work to identify who he is. His job is to make food exactly the way he is told and wait on you fast. This isn't rocket science. Some people are much bigger than their jobs. Karl Marx understood this. He might have been misguided in his economics, but he was a keen observer of what happens to people when they are alienated from their work:

> . . . he does not confirm himself in his work, he denies himself, feels miserable instead of happy, deploys no free physical and intellectual energy, but mortifies his body and ruins his mind. Thus the worker only feels a stranger. He is at home when he is not working and when he works he is not at home.
>
> The result we arrive at then is that man (the worker) only feels himself freely active in his animal functions of eating, drinking, and procreating, at most also in his dwelling and dress, and feels himself in his animal functions. Eating, drinking, procreating, etc. are indeed truly human functions. But in the abstraction that separates them from the other round of human activity and makes them into final and exclusive ends they become animal.

From Karl Marx, *Capital*, Penguin Classics, 1992

wise, others that given his physical and psychological condition, he is not free.

MONKEY LABOR

It is easy to slip into a logic of exploitation that says that those in need who are exploited are better off than they would be if they weren't exploited. *The Economist* ran a tongue-in-cheek report on working monkeys that illustrates this logic. In southern Thailand several thousand monkeys are "employed" every year to pick the 1.5 million-ton crop of coconuts. Village families train the monkeys and rent them out to plantation owners. The monkeys "earn" about twelve dollars per month in "monkey wages" of eggs, rice, and fruit from the plantation owner. Working monkeys are given names; they are groomed, bathed, and fed three times a day. Sometimes their owners even give them a ride to work, on the back of their motor scooters. When a monkey is ill, it gets the day off. When it is too old to work, it "retires," either back into the wild or as a family pet. The downside of the monkeys' work is that they are kept on chains and not allowed to breed at will. However, the article points out, this practice of "employment" keeps some species such as the crab-eating macaque from becoming extinct because their habitat is being destroyed by humans.

There is a striking parallel between this case and the way that colonists—and some people today—have justified their treatment of indigenous or tribal people in Africa, the Americas, and Australia. They would argue that although the farmers take away the monkeys' freedom, the monkeys are "better off" than they would be on their own in the wild, especially since their habitat has been largely taken over by the farmers. We don't know what the monkeys think. Would they prefer to give up their monkey wages, their names, their daily baths and motor scooter rides to take their chances in the wild? The justification for this arrangement is simple. It's okay for farmers to take away the monkey's freedom because they supply the monkey with what *they* think the monkey needs, even if it is not what the monkey wants.

This extreme (and, to some, frivolous) case illustrates how the logic of exploitation justifies taking advantage of those in need by arguing that one is taking care of people's needs. Exploitation is also about using one's power over others to determine what people need and what they *should* be willing to trade to have their needs filled. Similarly, the farmer decides that the monkey *needs* three meals a day and assumes that the monkey is willing to give up its freedom for them. As we'll see later, sometimes employers fill "needs" that employees do not have or want.

WAGES FOR TIME AND FREEDOM

We own our labor and we own our freedom. Freedom, like labor, is something that we can barter. Most paid employment involves some loss of freedom for the employee. All of us must sell, in varying degrees, our work and our time to earn a living. Both John Locke and Adam Smith realized that employees are not really paid for what they produce. Smith said workers receive compensation for their loss of freedom at work, not for the product they make. Here loss of freedom means a restriction of their liberty to do and say or not to do and say certain things during the time that they are working. Usually when we take a job we implicitly or explicitly agree to do it when, where, and how our employer wants it done. For instance, think about a receptionist's job. She has to sit at the front desk all day, greet people, and answer the phone. She is not totally free to come and go when she pleases. Someone has to cover for her when she goes to the rest room, or takes a break for coffee or lunch. *Being there* is a fundamental part of her job. She is paid for her time as well as for what she does. She can't say what she wants when she answers the phone, she has to be polite and say the name of the company. Today managers would argue that she is paid for the value she adds to the organization—her "value added."

The idea that wages are compensation for loss of freedom also leads to some absurd possibilities. Would this mean that the less freedom a person has on the job the more he or she should get paid? Quite the contrary: jobs with more surface freedom tend to signal higher status and pay more money. In his book *Class,* Paul Fussell argues that the amount of freedom one has on the job is a better indicator of class than salary. The idea of selling freedom often goes hand and hand with selling labor, especially when a person is in desperate need of a job and has little choice.

QUESTIONS

1. Tom desperately needs a job. Tom will work for $1 an hour because he cannot find a job that pays more.

Although some of my workers (who perform comparable work) are paid $7 an hour or more, I offer Tom the job at $1 an hour. I do not force Tom to take the job. He happily accepts the job. Have I done something wrong in offering Tom a job he was grateful to accept? Why or why not, according to Ciulla?

2. What does Ciulla mean by "self-enslavement"? Can you give examples from your own experience of self-enslavement?

John Rawls | **Justice as Fairness**

John Rawls was the premier American political philosopher of the twentieth century. This is from his groundbreaking book, *A Theory of Justice.*

My aim is to present a conception of justice which generalizes and carries to a higher level of abstraction the familiar theory of the social contract as found, say, in Locke, Rousseau, and Kant. In order to do this we are not to think of the original contract as one to enter a particular society or to set up a particular form of government. Rather, the guiding idea is that the principles of justice for the basic structure of society are the object of the original agreement. They are the principles that free and rational persons concerned to further their own interests would accept in an initial position of equality as defining the fundamental terms of their association. These principles are to regulate all further agreements: they specify the kinds of social cooperation that can be entered into and the forms of government that can be established. This way of regarding the principles of justice I shall call justice as fairness.

Thus we are to imagine that those who engage in social cooperation choose together, in one joint act, the principles which are to assign basic rights and duties and to determine the division of social benefits. Men are to decide in advance how they are to regulate their claims against one another and what is to be the foundation charter of their society. Just as each person must decide by rational reflection what constitutes his good, that is, the system of ends which it is rational for him to pursue, so a group of persons must decide once and for all what is to count among them as just and unjust. The choice which rational men would make in this hypothetical situation of equal liberty, assuming for the present that this choice problem has a solution, determines the principles of justice.

In justice as fairness the original position of equality corresponds to the state of nature in the traditional theory of the social contract. This original position is not, of course, thought of as an actual historical state of affairs, much less as a primitive condition of culture. It is understood as a purely hypothetical situation characterized so as to lead to a certain conception of justice. Among the essential features of this situation is that no one knows his place in society, his class position or social status, nor does any one know his fortune in the distribution of natural assets and abilities, his intelligence, strength, and the like. I shall even assume that the parties do not know their con-

From *A Theory of Justice* (Cambridge, Mass.: Harvard University Press, 1971).

ceptions of the good or their special psychological propensities. The principles of justice are chosen behind a veil of ignorance. This ensures that no one is advantaged or disadvantaged in the choice of principles by the outcome of natural chance or the contingency of social circumstances. Since all are similarly situated and no one is able to design principles to favor his particular condition, the principles of justice are the result of a fair agreement or bargain. For given the circumstances of the original position, the symmetry of everyone's relations to each other, this initial situation is fair between individuals as moral persons, that is, as rational beings with their own ends and capable, I shall assume, of a sense of justice. . . .

I shall maintain instead that the persons in the initial situation would choose two . . . principles: the first requires equality in the assignment of basic rights and duties, while the second holds that social and economic inequalities, for example inequalities of wealth and authority, are just only if they result in compensating benefits for everyone, and in particular for the least advantaged members of society. These principles rule out justifying institutions on the grounds that the hardships of some are offset by a greater good in the aggregate. It may be expedient but it is not just that some should have less in order that others may prosper. But there is no injustice in the greater benefits earned by a few provided that the situation of persons not so fortunate is thereby improved. The intuitive idea is that since everyone's well-being depends upon a scheme of cooperation without which no one could have a satisfactory life, the division of advantages should be such as to draw forth the willing cooperation of everyone taking part in it, including those less well situated. Yet this can be expected only if reasonable terms are proposed. The two principles mentioned seem to be a fair agreement on the basis of which those better endowed, or more fortunate in their social position, neither of which we can be said to deserve, could expect the willing cooperation of others when some workable scheme is a necessary condition of the welfare of all. Once we decide to look for a conception of justice that nullifies the accidents of natural endowment and the contingencies of social circumstance as counters in quest for political and economic

advantage, we are led to these principles. They express the result of leaving aside those aspects of the social world that seem arbitrary from a moral point of view.

———————

I shall now state in a provisional form the two principles of justice that I believe would be chosen in the original position. The first statement of the two principles reads as follows.

- First: each person is to have an equal right to the most extensive basic liberty compatible with a similar liberty for others.
- Second: social and economic inequalities are to be arranged so that they are both (a) reasonably expected to be to everyone's advantage, and (b) attached to positions and offices open to all.

By way of general comment, these principles primarily apply, as I have said, to the basic structure of society. They are to govern the assignment of rights and duties and to regulate the distribution of social and economic advantages. As their formulation suggests, these principles presuppose that the social structure can be divided into two more or less distinct parts, the first principle applying to the one, the second to the other. They distinguish between those aspects of the social system that define and secure the equal liberties of citizenship and those that specify and establish social and economic inequalities. The basic liberties of citizens are, roughly speaking, political liberty (the right to vote and to be eligible for public office) together with freedom of speech and assembly; liberty of conscience and freedom of thought; freedom of the person along with the right to hold (personal) property; and freedom from arbitrary arrest and seizure as defined by the concept of the rule of law. These liberties are all required to be equal by the first principle, since citizens of a just society are to have the same basic rights.

The second principle applies, in the first approximation, to the distribution of income and wealth and to the design of organizations that makes use of differences in authority and responsibility, or chains of command. While the distribution of wealth and income need not be equal, it must be to everyone's advantage, and at the same time, positions of authority and offices of command must be accessible to all. One applies the second principle by holding positions open, and then, subject to this constraint, arranges social and economic inequalities so that everyone benefits.

These principles are to be arranged in a serial order with the first principle prior to the second. This ordering means that a departure from the institutions of equal liberty required by the first principle cannot be justified by, or compensated for, by greater social and economic advantages. The distribution of wealth and income, and the hierarchies of authority, must be consistent with both the liberties of equal citizenship and equality of opportunity.

QUESTIONS

1. What does Rawls mean by the "initial situation"? Why does he posit an initial situation?

2. What are Rawls's two principles of justice? How do they guarantee justice? How does Rawls's more general conception of justice emerge from them?

Peter Singer | # Rich and Poor

Peter Singer is an Australian philosopher who teaches at Princeton University's Institute for Values and is most famous for his defense of "animal liberation."

SOME FACTS ABOUT POVERTY

. . . Consider these facts: by the most cautious estimates, 400 million people lack the calories, protein, vitamins and minerals needed to sustain their bodies and minds in a healthy state. Millions are constantly hungry; others suffer from deficiency diseases and from infections they would be able to resist on a better diet. Children are the worst affected. According to one study, 14 million children under five die every year from the combined effects of malnutrition and infection. In some districts half the children born can be expected to die before their fifth birthday.

Nor is lack of food the only hardship of the poor. To give a broader picture, Robert McNamara, when president of the World Bank, suggested the term "absolute poverty." The poverty we are familiar with in industrialised nations is relative poverty—meaning that some citizens are poor, relative to the wealth enjoyed by their neighbours. People living in relative poverty in Australia might be quite comfortably off by comparison with pensioners in Britain, and British pensioners are not poor in comparison with the poverty that exists in Mali or Ethiopia. Absolute poverty, on the other hand, is poverty by any standard. In McNamara's words:

Poverty at the absolute level . . . is life at the very margin of existence. The absolute poor are severely deprived human beings struggling to survive in a set of squalid and degraded circumstances almost beyond the power of our sophisticated imaginations and privileged circumstances to conceive.

Compared to those fortunate enough to live in developed countries, individuals in the poorest nations have:

- An infant mortality rate eight times higher
- A life expectancy one-third lower
- An adult literacy rate 60 per cent less
- A nutritional level, for one out of every two in the population, below acceptable standards;

• And for millions of infants, less protein than is sufficient to permit optimum development of the brain.

McNamara has summed up absolute poverty as "a condition of life so characterised by malnutrition, illiteracy, disease, squalid surroundings, high infant mortality and low life expectancy as to bo beneath any reasonable definition of human decency." . . .

Death and disease apart, absolute poverty remains a miserable condition of life, with inadequate food, shelter, clothing, sanitation, health services and education. The Worldwatch Institute estimates that as many as 1.2 billion people—or 23 per cent of the world's population—live in absolute poverty. For the purposes of this estimate, absolute poverty is defined as "the lack of sufficient income in cash or kind to meet the most basic biological needs for food, clothing, and shelter." Absolute poverty is probably the principal cause of human misery today. . . .

The problem is not that the world cannot produce enough to feed and shelter its people. People in the poor countries consume, on average, 180 kilos of grain a year, while North Americans average around 900 kilos. The difference is caused by the fact that in the rich countries we feed most of our grain to animals, converting it into meat, milk, and eggs. Because this is a highly inefficient process, people in rich countries are responsible for the consumption of far more food than those in poor countries who eat few animal products. If we stopped feeding animals on grains and soybeans, the amount of food saved would—if distributed to those who need it—be more than enough to end hunger throughout the world.

These facts about animal food do not mean that we can easily solve the world food problem by cutting down on animal products, but they show that the problem is essentially one of distribution rather than production. The world does produce enough food. Moreover, the poorer nations themselves could produce far more if they made more use of improved agricultural techniques.

So why are people hungry? Poor people cannot afford to buy grain grown by farmers in the richer nations. Poor farmers cannot afford to buy improved seeds, or fertilisers, or the machinery needed for drilling wells and pumping water. Only by transferring some of the wealth of the rich nations to the poor can the situation be changed.

That this wealth exists is clear. Against the picture of absolute poverty that McNamara has painted, one might pose a picture of "absolute affluence." Those who are absolutely affluent are not necessarily affluent by comparison with their neighbours, but they are affluent by any reasonable definition of human needs. This means that they have more income than they need to provide themselves adequately with all the basic necessities of life. After buying (either directly or through their taxes) food, shelter, clothing, basic health services, and education, the absolutely affluent are still able to spend money on luxuries. The absolutely affluent choose their food for the pleasures of the palate, not to stop hunger; they buy new clothes to look good, not to keep warm; they move house to be in a better neighborhood or have a playroom for the children, not to keep out the rain; and after all this there is still money to spend on stereo systems, video-cameras, and overseas holidays.

At this stage I am making no ethical judgments about absolute affluence, merely pointing out that it exists. Its defining characteristic is a significant amount of income above the level necessary to provide for the basic human needs of oneself and one's dependents. By this standard, the majority of citizens of Western Europe, North America, Japan, Australia, New Zealand, and the oil-rich Middle Eastern states are all absolutely affluent. To quote McNamara once more:

> The average citizen of a developed country enjoys wealth beyond the wildest dreams of the one billion people in countries with per capita incomes under $200.

These, therefore, are the countries—and individuals—who have wealth that they could, without threatening their own basic welfare, transfer to the absolutely poor.

At present, very little is being transferred. Only Sweden, the Netherlands, Norway, and some of the oil-exporting Arab states have reached the modest target, set by the United Nations, of 0.7 per cent of gross national product (GNP). Britain gives 0.31 per cent of its GNP in official development assistance and a small additional amount in unofficial aid from voluntary organisations. The total comes to about £2 per month per person, and compares with 5.5 per cent of GNP spent on alcohol, and 3 per cent on tobacco. Other, even wealthier nations, give little more: Germany gives 0.41 per cent and Japan 0.32 per cent. The United States gives a mere 0.15 per cent of its GNP. . . .

THE OBLIGATION TO ASSIST

The Argument for an Obligation to Assist

The path from the library at my university to the humanities lecture theatre passes a shallow ornamental pond. Suppose that on my way to give a lecture I notice that a small child has fallen in and is in danger of drowning. Would anyone deny that I ought to wade in and pull the child out? This will mean getting my clothes muddy and either cancelling my lecture or delaying it until I can find something dry to change into; but compared with the avoidable death of a child this is insignificant.

A plausible principle that would support the judgment that I ought to pull the child out is this: if it is in our power to prevent something very bad from happening, without thereby sacrificing anything of comparable moral significance, we ought to do it. This principle seems uncontroversial. It will obviously win the assent of consequentialists; but non-consequentialists should accept it too, because the injunction to prevent what is bad applies only when nothing comparably significant is at stake. Thus the principle cannot lead to the kinds of actions of which non-consequentialists strongly disapprove—serious violations of individual rights, injustice, broken promises, and so on. If non-consequentialists regard any of these as comparable in moral significance to the bad thing that is to be prevented, they will automatically regard the principle as not applying in those cases in which the bad thing can only be prevented by violating rights, doing injustice, breaking promises, or whatever else is at stake. Most non-consequentialists hold that we ought to prevent what is bad and promote what is good. Their dispute with consequentialists lies in their insistence that this is not the sole ultimate ethical principle: that it is an ethical principle is not denied by any plausible ethical theory.

Nevertheless the uncontroversial appearance of the principle that we ought to prevent what is bad when we can do so without sacrificing anything of comparable moral significance is deceptive. If it were taken seriously and acted upon, our lives and our world would be fundamentally changed. For the principle applies, not just to rare situations in which one can save a child from a pond, but to the everyday situation in which we can assist those living in absolute poverty. In saying this I assume that absolute poverty, with its hunger and malnutrition, lack of shelter, illiteracy, disease, high infant mortality, and low life expectancy, is a bad thing. And I assume that it is within the power of the affluent to reduce absolute poverty, without sacrificing anything of comparable moral significance. If these two assumptions and the principle we have been discussing are correct, we have an obligation to help those in absolute poverty that is no less strong than our obligation to rescue a drowning child from a pond. Not to help would be wrong, whether or not it is intrinsically equivalent to killing. Helping is not, as conventionally thought, a charitable act that it is praise-worthy to do, but not wrong to omit; it is something that everyone ought to do.

QUESTIONS

1. What does Singer mean by "absolute poverty"? Why does he distinguish it from relative poverty?
2. What is Singer's argument for "an obligation to assist"?

Irving Kristol | # A Capitalist Conception of Justice

Irving Kristol was, for many years, the editor of the conservative journal *The Public Interest.*

It is fashionable these days for social commentators to ask, "Is capitalism compatible with social justice?" I submit that the only appropriate answer is "No." Indeed, this is the only possible answer. The term "social justice" was invented in order *not* to be compatible with capitalism.

What is the difference between "social justice" and plain, unqualified "justice?" Why can't we ask, "Is capitalism compatible with justice?" We can, and were we to do so, we would then have to explore the idea of justice that is peculiar to the capitalist system, because capitalism certainly does have an idea of justice.

"Social justice," however, was invented and propagated by people who were not much interested in understanding capitalism. These were nineteenth-century critics of capitalism—liberals, radicals, socialists—who invented the term in order to insinuate into the argument a quite different conception of the good society from the one proposed by liberal capitalism. As it is used today, the term has an irredeemably egalitarian and authoritarian thrust. Since capitalism as a socioeconomic or political system is neither egalitarian nor authoritarian, it is in truth incompatible with "social justice."

Let us first address the issue of egalitarianism. In a liberal or democratic capitalist society there is, indeed, a connection between justice and equality. Equality before the law and equality of political rights are fundamental to a liberal capitalist system and, in historical fact, the ideological Founding Fathers of liberal capitalism all did believe in equality before the law and in some form of equality of political rights. The introduction of the term "social justice" represents an effort to stretch the idea of justice that is compatible with capitalism to cover *economic* equality as well. Proponents of something called "social justice" would persuade us that economic equality is as much a right as are equality before the law and equality of political rights. As a matter of fact, these proponents move in an egalitarian direction so formidably that inevitably *all* differences are seen sooner or later to be unjust. Differences between men and women, differences between parents and children, differences between human beings and animals—all of these, as we have seen in the last ten or fifteen years, become questionable and controversial.

A person who believes in "social justice" is an egalitarian. I do not say that he or she necessarily believes in perfect equality; I do not think anyone believes in perfect equality. But "social justice" advocates are terribly interested in far more equality than a capitalist system is likely to deliver. Capitalism delivers many good things but, on the whole, economic equality is not one of them. It has never pretended to deliver economic equality. Rather, capitalism has always stood for equality of economic opportunity, reasonably understood to mean the absence of official barriers to economic opportunity.

We are now in an egalitarian age when Harvard professors write books wondering whether there is a problem of "social justice" if some people are born of handsome parents and are therefore more attractive than others. This is seriously discussed in Cambridge and in other learned circles. Capitalism is not interested in that. Capitalism says there ought to be no *official* barriers to economic opportunity. If one is born of handsome or talented parents, if one inherits a musical skill, or mathematical skill, or whatever, that is simply good luck. No one can question the person's right to the fruits of such skills. Capitalism believes that, through equal opportunity, each individual will pursue his happiness as he defines it, and as far as his natural assets (plus luck, good or bad) will permit. In pursuit of that happiness everyone will, to use that familiar phrase of Adam Smith, "better his condition."

Thus, capitalism says that equal opportunity will result in everyone's bettering his or her condition. And it does. The history of the world over the past 200 years shows that capitalism did indeed permit and encourage ordinary men and women in the pursuit of their happiness to improve their condition. Even Marx did not deny this. We are not as poor as our grandparents. We are all better off because individuals in pursuit of happiness, and without barriers being put in their way, are very creative, innovative, and adept at finding ways for societies to be more productive, thereby creating more wealth in which everyone shares.

Now, although individuals do better their condition under capitalism, they do not better their conditions equally. In the pursuit of happiness, some will be more successful than others. Some will end up with more than others. Everyone will end up with *somewhat* more than he had—everyone. But some people will end up with a lot more than they had and some with a little more than they had. Capitalism does not perceive this as a problem. It is assumed that since everyone gets more, everyone ought to be content. If some people get more than others, the reason is to be found in their differential contributions to the economy. In a capitalist system, where the market predominates in economic decision making, people who—in whatever way—make different productive inputs into the economy receive different rewards. If one's input into the economy is great, one receives a large reward; if one's input is small, one receives a modest reward. The determination of these rewards is by public preferences and public tastes as expressed in the market. If the public wants basketball players to make $400,000 a year, then those who

are good at basketball can become very, very rich. If the public wants to purchase certain paintings for $1 million or $2 million, then certain artists can become very, very rich. On the other hand, croquet players, even brilliant croquet players, won't better their condition to the same degree. And those who have no particular skill had better be lucky.

This is the way the system works. It rewards people in terms of their contribution to the economy as measured and defined by the marketplace—namely, in terms of the free preferences of individual men and women who have money in their pockets and are free to spend it or not on this, that, or the other as they please. Economic justice under capitalism means the differential reward to individuals is based on their productive input *to the economy*. I emphasize "to the economy" because input is measured by the marketplace.

Is it "just" that Mr. Ray Kroc, chairman of the board of McDonald's, should have made so much money by merely figuring out a new way of selling hamburgers? They are the same old hamburgers, just better made, better marketed. Is it fair? Capitalism says it is fair. He is selling a good product; people want it; it is fair. It is "just" that he has made so much money.

However, capitalism doesn't say only that. It also understands that it is an exaggeration to say that literally *everyone* betters his condition when rewards are based on productive input. There are some people who are really not capable of taking part in the race at all because of mental illness, physical illness, bad luck, and so on. Such persons are simply not able to take advantage of the opportunity that does exist.

Capitalism as originally conceived by Adam Smith was not nearly so heartless a system as it presented itself during the nineteenth century. Adam Smith didn't say that people who could make no productive input into the economy through no fault of their own should be permitted to starve to death. Though not a believer, he was enough of a Christian to know that such a conclusion was not consistent with the virtue of charity. He understood that such people had to be provided for. There has never been any question of that. Adam Smith wrote two books. The book that first made him famous was not

to each according to his/her ——————.

contribution to economy

The Wealth of Nations but *The Theory of Moral Sentiments,* in which he said that the highest human sentiment is sympathy—the sympathy that men and women have for one another as human beings. Although *The Wealth of Nations* is an analysis of an economic system based on self-interest, Adam Smith never believed for a moment that human beings were strictly economic men or women. It took some later generations of economists to come up with that idea. Adam Smith understood that people live in a society, not just in an economy, and that they feel a sense of social obligation to one another, as well as a sense of engaging in mutually satisfactory economic transactions.

In both these books, but especially in *The Theory of Moral Sentiments,* Adam Smith addressed himself to the question, "What do the rich do with their money once they get it?" His answer was that they reinvest some of it so that society as a whole will become wealthier and everyone will continue to be able to improve his or her condition to some degree. Also, however, the rich will engage in one of the great pleasures that wealth affords: the expression of sympathy for one's fellow human beings. Smith said that the people who have money can only consume so much. What are they going to do with the money aside from what they consume and reinvest? They will use it in such a way as to gain a good reputation among their fellow citizens. He said this will be the natural way for wealthy people to behave under capitalism. Perhaps he was thinking primarily of Scotsmen. Still, his perceptiveness is interesting. Although capitalism has long been accused of being an inhumane system, we forget that capitalism and humanitarianism entered the modern world together. Name a modern, humane movement—criminal reform, decent treatment of women, kindness to animals, etc. Where does it originate? They all came from the rising bourgeoisie at the end of the eighteenth century. They were all middle-class movements. The movements didn't begin with peasants or aristocrats. Peasants were always cruel to animals and aristocrats could not care less about animals, or about wives, for that matter. It was the bourgeoisie, the capitalist middle class, that said animals should be treated with consideration, that criminals should not be tortured,

that prisons should be places of punishment, yes, but humane places of punishment. It was the generation that helped establish the capitalist idea and the capitalist way of thinking in the world that brought these movements to life. Incidentally, the anti-slavery movement was also founded by middle-class men and women who had a sense of social responsibility toward their fellow citizens.

So it is simply and wholly untrue that capitalism is a harsh, vindictive, soulless system. A man like Adam Smith would never have dreamed of recommending such a system. No, he recommended the economic relations which constitute the market system, the capitalist system, on the assumption that human beings would continue to recognize their social obligations to one another and act upon this recognition with some degree of consistency. Incidentally, he even seems to have believed in a progressive income tax.

However, something very peculiar happened after Adam Smith. Something very odd and very bad happened to the idea of capitalism and its reputation after the first generation of capitalism's intellectual Founding Fathers. The economics of capitalism became a "dismal science." One cannot read *The Wealth of Nations* and have any sense that economics is a dismal science. It is an inquiry into the causes of the wealth of nations that tells people how to get rich. It says, "If you organize your economic activities this way, everyone will get richer." There is nothing pessimistic about that, nothing dismal about that. It was an exhilarating message to the world.

Unfortunately, what gave capitalism a bad name in the early part of the nineteenth century was not the socialist's criticism of capitalism but, I fear, the work of the later capitalist economists. We do not even have a really good intellectual history of this episode because people who write histories of economic thought tend not to be interested in intellectual history, but in economics. For some reason, Malthus and then Ricardo decided that capitalist economics should not deal with the production of wealth but rather with its distribution. Adam Smith had said everyone could improve his condition. Malthus said the situation was hopeless, at least for the lower classes. If the lower classes improved their condition,

Adam Smith: trickle down through generosity spending

Cristol: Capitalist doesn't mean benevolence

he argued, they would start breeding like rabbits and shortly they would be right back where they started. Ricardo came along and said that the expanding population could not all be fed because there is a shortage of fertile land in the world. In his view, the condition of the working class over the long term was unimprovable.

This was the condition of capitalist economics for most of the nineteenth century. It is a most extraordinary and paradoxical episode in modern intellectual history. Throughout the nineteenth century, ordinary men and women, the masses, the working class, were clearly improving their condition. There is just no question that the working classes in England were better off in 1860 than they had been in 1810. In the United States there was never any such question and in France, too, it was quite clear that the system was working as Adam Smith had said it would. Yet all the economists of the School of Malthus and Ricardo kept saying. "It cannot happen. Sorry, people, but you're doomed to live in misery. There is nothing we can do about it. Just have fewer children and exercise continence." To which the people said, "Thank you very much. We do not much like this system you are recommending to us," as well they might not.

When the possibility of helping the average man and woman through economic growth is rejected loudly and dogmatically by the leading economists of the day, many will believe it. When they conclude that their condition cannot be improved by economic growth, they will seek to improve it by redistribution, by taking it away from others who have more. It is nineteenth-century capitalist economic thought, with its incredible emphasis on the impossibility of improving the condition of the working class—even as the improvement was obviously taking place—that gave great popularity and plausibility to the socialist critique of capitalism and to the redistributionist impulse that began to emerge. This impulse, which is still so appealing, makes no sense. A nation can redistribute to its heart's content and it will not affect the average person one bit. There just isn't ever enough to redistribute. Nevertheless, once it became "clear" in the nineteenth century that there was no other way, redistribution became a very popular subject.

Because capitalism after Adam Smith seemed to be associated with a hopeless view of the world, it provoked egalitarian impulses. Is it not a natural human sentiment to argue that, if we're all in a hopeless condition, we should be hopeless equally? Let us go down together. If that indeed is our condition, equality becomes a genuine virtue. Egalitarianism became such a plausible view of the world because capitalist apologists, for reasons which I do not understand, kept insisting that this is the nature of capitalism. Those who talk about "social justice" these days do not say that the income tax should be revised so that the rich people will get more, although there may be an economic case for it. (I am not saying there is, even though there might be.) "Social justice," the term, the idea, is intimately wedded to the notion of egalitarianism as a proper aim of social and economic policy, and capitalism is criticized as lacking in "social justice" because it does not achieve this equality. In fact, it does not, cannot, and never promised to achieve this result.

However, I think the more important thrust of the term "social justice" has to do with its authoritarian meaning rather than its egalitarian meaning. The term "social" prefixed before the word "justice" has a purpose and an effect which is to abolish the distinction between the public and the private sectors, a distinction which is absolutely crucial for a liberal society. It is the very definition of a liberal society that there be a public sector and a large, private sector where people can do what they want without government bothering them. What is a "social problem?" Is a social problem something that government can ignore? Would anyone say we have a social problem but it is not the business of government? Of course not.

The term "social justice" exists in order to identify those issues about which government should get active. A social problem is a problem that gives rise to a governmental policy, which is why people who believe in the expansion of the public sector are always inventing, discovering, or defining more and more social problems in our world. The world has not become any more problematic than it ever was. The proliferation of things called "social problems" arises out of an effort to get government more and

Executive Compensation

- "Over the past decade, rank-and-file wages have increased by 36%, pay for chief executive officers climbed 340%." (*Business Week*)
- In 1980, the average executive in the United States made 42 times more than did the average worker (in the same company).
- In 2003, the average executive in the United States made 500 times more than did the average worker (in the same company). (In Japan and Germany, the figure was 15–20 times.)
- "No one should make more than five times the income of an ordinary worker." Plato, 428–348 B.C.E.
- "No leader should make more than 20 times the lowest paid employee" (Peter Drucker, management guru, 1980).

more deeply involved in the lives of private citizens in an attempt to "cope with" or "solve" these "problems." Sometimes real problems are posed. Rarely are they followed by real solutions.

The idea of "social justice," however, assumes not only that government will intervene but that government will have, should have, and can have an authoritative knowledge as to what everyone merits or deserves in terms of the distribution of income and wealth. After all, if we do not like the inequality that results from the operation of the market, then who is going to make the decision as to the distribution of services and wealth? Some authority must be found to say so-and-so deserves more than so-and-so. Of course, the only possible such authority in the modern world is not the Church but the State. To the degree that one defines "social justice" as a kind of protest against the capitalist distribution of income, one proposes some other mechanism for the distribution of income. Government is the only other mechanism that can make the decisions as to who gets what, as to what he or she "deserves," for whatever reason.

The assumption that the government is able to make such decisions wisely, and therefore that government should make such decisions, violates the very premises of a liberal community. A liberal community exists on the premise that there is no such authority. If there were an authority which knew what everyone merited and could allocate it fairly, why would we need freedom? There would be no point in freedom. Let the authority do its work. Now, we have seen the experience of non-liberal societies, and not all of it is bad. I would not pretend that a liberal society is the only possible good society. If one likes the values of a particular non-liberal society, it may not be bad at all. There are many non-liberal societies I admire: monasteries are non-liberal societies, and I do not say they are bad societies. They are pretty good societies—but they are not liberal societies. The monk has no need for liberty if he believes there is someone else, his superior, who knows what is good for him and what reward he merits.

Once we assume that there is a superior authority who has authoritative knowledge of the common good and of the merits and demerits of every individual, the ground of a liberal society is swept away, because the very freedoms that subsist and thrive in a liberal society all assume that there is no such authoritative knowledge. Now, this assumption is not *necessarily* true. Maybe there is someone who really does have an authoritative knowledge of what is good for all of us and how much we all merit. We who choose a liberal society are skeptical as to the possibility. In any case, we think it is more likely that there will be ten people all claiming to have different versions of what is good for all of us and what we should all get, and therefore we choose to let the market settle it. It is an amicable way of not getting involved in endless philosophical or religious arguments about the nature of the true, the good, and the beautiful.

The notion of a "just society" existing on earth is a fantasy, a utopian fantasy. That is not what life on earth is like. The reason is that the world is full of other people who are different from you and me, alas, and we have to live with them. If they were all like us, we would live fine; but they are not all like us, and the point of a liberal society and of a market economy is to accept this difference and say, "Okay, you be you and I'll be I. We'll disagree, but we'll do business together. We'll mutually profit from doing business together, and we'll live not necessarily in friendship but at least in civility with one another."

I am not saying that capitalism is a just society. I am saying that there is a capitalist conception of justice which is a workable conception of justice. Anyone who promises you a just society on this earth is a fraud and a charlatan. I believe that this is not the nature of human destiny. It would mean that we all would be happy. Life is not like that. Life is doomed not to be like that. But if you do not accept this view, and if you really think that life can indeed be radically different from what it is, if you really believe that justice can prevail on earth, then you are likely to start taking phrases like "social justice" very seriously and to think that the function of politics is to rid the world of its evils: to abolish war, to abolish poverty, to abolish discrimination, to abolish envy, to abolish, abolish, abolish. We are not going to abolish any of those things. If we push them out one window, they will come in through another window in some unforeseen form. The reforms of today give rise to the evils of tomorrow. That is the history of the human race.

If one can be somewhat stoical about this circumstance, the basic precondition of social life, capitalism becomes much more tolerable. However, if one is not stoical about it, if one demands more of life than life can give, then capitalism is certainly the wrong system because capitalism does not promise that much and does not give you that much. All it gives is a greater abundance of material goods and a great deal of freedom to cope with the problems of the human condition on your own.

QUESTIONS

1. What is the difference between social justice and plain, unqualified justice?

2. Is Adam Smith's understanding of capitalism harsh and "soulless"? What makes Smith's understanding of capitalism more humane than some other versions of capitalism?

Friedrich von Hayek | # Justice Ruins the Market

Friedrich Hayek was a classic neoconservative and a staunch defender of the unfettered, unregulated market. This is from his book, *The Road to Serfdom.*

THE IMMORAL CONSEQUENCES OF MORALLY INSPIRED EFFORTS

Though in the long perspective of Western civilization the history of law is a history of a gradual emergence of rules of just conduct capable of universal application, its development during the last hundred years has become increasingly one of the destruction of justice by "social justice," until even some students of jurisprudence have lost sight of the original meaning of "justice." We have seen how the process has mainly taken the form of a replacement of the rules of just conduct by those rules of organization which we call public law (a "subordinating law"), a distinction which some socialist lawyers are trying hard to obliterate. In substance this has meant that the individual is no longer bound only by rules which confine the scope of his private actions, but has become increasingly subject to the commands of authority. The growing technological possibilities of control, together with the presumed moral superiority of a society whose members serve the same hierarchy of ends, have made this totalitarian trend appear under a moral guise. It is indeed the concept of "social justice" which has been the Trojan Horse through which totalitarianism has entered.

The values which still survive from the small end-connected groups whose coherence depended upon them, are, however, not only different from, but often incompatible with, the values which make possible the peaceful coexistence of large numbers in the Open Society. The belief that while we pursue the new ideal of this Great Society in which all human beings are regarded as equal, we can also preserve the different ideals of the small closed society, is an illusion. To attempt it leads to the destruction of the Great Society.

The possibility of men living together in peace and to their mutual advantage without having to agree on common concrete aims, and bound only by abstract rules of conduct, was perhaps the greatest discovery mankind ever made. The "capitalist" system which grew out of this discovery no doubt did not fully satisfy the ideals of liberalism, because it grew up while legislators and governments did not really understand the modus operandi of the market, and largely in spite of the policies actually pursued. Capitalism as it exists today in consequence undeniably has many remediable defects that an intelligent policy of freedom ought to correct. A system which relies on the spontaneous ordering forces of the market, once it has reached a certain level of wealth, is also by no means incompatible with government providing, outside the market, some security against severe deprivation. But the attempt to secure to each what he is thought to deserve, by imposing upon all a system of common concrete ends towards which their efforts are directed by authority, as socialism aims to do, would be a retrograde step that would deprive us of the utilization of the knowledge and aspirations of millions, and thereby of the advantages of a free civilization. Socialism is not based merely on a different system of ultimate values from that of liberalism, which one would have to respect even if one disagreed; it is based on an intellectual error which makes its adherents blind to its consequences. This must be plainly said because the emphasis on the alleged difference of the ultimate values has become the common excuse of the socialists for

From Friedrich von Hayek, *The Road to Serfdom* (Highpoint Press, 1940). Reprinted with permission.

shirking the real intellectual issue. The pretended difference of the underlying value judgments has become a protective cloak used to conceal the faulty reasoning underlying the socialist schemes.

IN THE GREAT SOCIETY "SOCIAL JUSTICE" BECOMES A DISRUPTIVE FORCE

Not only is it impossible for the Great Society to maintain itself while enforcing rules of "social" or distributive justice; for its preservation it is also necessary that no particular groups holding common views about what they are entitled to should be allowed to enforce these views by preventing others to offer their services at more favourable terms. Though common interests of those whose position is affected by the same circumstances are likely to produce strong common opinions about what they deserve, and will provide a motive for common action to achieve their ends, any such group action to secure a particular income or position for its members creates an obstacle to the integration of the Great Society and is therefore anti-social in the true sense of this word. It must become a divisive force because it produces not a reconciliation of, but a conflict between, the interests of the different groups. As the active participants in the struggle for "social justice" well know, it becomes in practice a struggle for power of organized interests in which arguments of justice serve merely as pretexts.

The chief insight we must hold on to is that not always when a group of people have strong views about what they regard as their claims in justice does this mean that there exists (or can be found) a corresponding rule which, if universally applied, would produce a viable order. It is a delusion to believe that whenever a question is represented as one of justice it must be possible to discover a rule capable of universal application which will decide that question. Nor does the fact that a law endeavours to meet somebody's claim for justice prove that it is a rule of just conduct.

All groups whose members pursue the same or parallel aims will develop common views about what is right for members of those groups. Such views, however, will be right only for all those who pursue the same aims, but may be wholly incompatible with any principles by which such a group can be integrated into the overall order of society. The producers of any particular commodity or service who all aim at a good remuneration for their efforts will regard as unjust the action of any fellow producer who tends to reduce the incomes of the others. Yet it will be precisely the kind of actions by some members of the group that the rest regard as harmful which will fit the activities of the members of the group into the overall pattern of the Great Society and thereby benefit all.

It is certainly in itself not unjust if a barber in one city receives $3 for a haircut while in another city only $2 is paid for the same work. But it would clearly be unjust if the barbers in the first prevented any from the second city from improving their position by offering their services in the first for, say, $2.50 and thus, while improving their position, lowering the income of the first group. Yet it is precisely against such efforts that established groups are today permitted to combine in defence of their established position. The rule "do nothing which will decrease the income of the members of your own group" will often be regarded as an obligation of justice toward one's fellow members. But it cannot be accepted as a rule of just conduct in a Great Society where it will conflict with the general principles on which the activities of that society are co-ordinated. The other members of that society will have every interest and moral right to prevent the enforcement of such a rule that the members of a special group regard as just, because the principles of integration of the Great Society demand that the action of some of those occupied in a particular manner should often lead to a reduction of the incomes of their fellows. This is precisely the virtue of competition. The conceptions of group justice would often proscribe all effective competition as unjust—and many of the "fair competition" demands aim in effect at little less.

It is probably true that in any group whose members know that their prospects depend on the same circumstances, views will develop that represent as unjust all conduct of any member which harms the others; and there will in consequence arise a desire to prevent such conduct. But by any outsider it will rightly be regarded as unjust if any member of such a group is prevented by his fellows from offering him more advantageous terms than the rest of the group are willing to offer. And the same is true when some "interloper" who before was not recognized as a member of the group is made to conform to the standards of the group as soon as his efforts compete with theirs.

The important fact which most people are reluctant to admit, yet which is probably true in most instances, is that, though the pursuit of the selfish aims of the individual will usually lead him to serve the general interest, the collective actions of organized groups are almost invariably contrary to the general interest. What in fact leads to the condemnation as anti-social of that pursuit of individual interests which contributes to the general interest, and to the commendation as "social" of the subservience to those sectional interests which destroy the overall order, are sentiments which we have inherited from earlier forms of society. The use of coercion in this kind of "social justice," meaning the interests of the

particular group to which the individual belongs, will thus always mean the creation of particular preserves of special groups united against the outsiders—interest groups which exist because they are allowed to use force or pressure on government for the benefit of their members. But, however much the members of such groups may agree among themselves that what they want is just, there exists no principle which could make it appear as just to the outsider. Yet today, if such a group is only large enough, its representation of the demands of its members as just is commonly accepted as one view of justice which must be taken into account in ordering the whole, even though it does not rest on any principle which could be generally applied.

QUESTIONS

1. How does justice ruin the market, according to Hayek?

2. How would Hayek deal with the problem of monopolies?

<hr>

Eduard Garcia | # The Winner-Take-All Game

Eduard Garcia is a senior manager with Deloitte MCS, Strategy & Operations in London.

In 1981, when the world was at the deep end of the so-called Second Oil Crisis, Marvin Harris, an American anthropologist, published a short essay entitled "America Now: the Anthropology of a Changing Culture." In it he analyzed the underlying economic phenomena that had ultimately generated a wide cultural change, and he found out that the problem could to a large extent be traced back to the general lack of reliability of goods and services produced in Amer-

ica at that time, and that this, in turn, was attributable to the short-term-oriented management style that had increasingly dominated corporate America since the end of World War II:

> "The observers [agree] that there is something in the way today's executives relate to their companies that makes them different from the previous generation of corporate leaders. De Lorean, for example, depicts them as 'short-term professional executives' that remain in a company less than ten years and that are driven by the need to produce immediate profits during their short tenure. Due to the frequent change

from one company to another, their economic position does no longer depend mainly on owning assets in the company they work for, and therefore do not need to worry about what will happen if, say, the reputation of their firm regarding quality falls to pieces soon after they left. . . .

In the wake of the most recent corporate scandals it has once again become fashionable to criticize this myopia of bad behavior often in fairly apocalyptic terms and in a tone that seems to imply that "something" should be done about it. However, without an understanding of the underlying causes of this phenomenon, the recent outcry is not likely to be any more effective than its predecessors apart from, perhaps, encouraging the deployment of government regulatory measures that, as public intervention usually does, are more likely to impair the efficiency of the system as a whole rather than solving any real problem.

Therefore, the objective of this paper is to put forward a potential explanation of this phenomenon that is consistent with its remarkable resilience over time as well as its presence in economic systems that otherwise are quite healthy. Specifically, the phenomenon can be interpreted as a side effect of free market competition and, therefore, not only are there no "magic bullets" available, but solutions based on radical forms of intervention are likely to do more harm than good. Instead, just as in the case of a chronic illness, it will be suggested that it is better not to try to fix it once and for all, but rather to consistently monitor its evolution and fine-tune the balance of long vs. short-term incentives within the organization whenever they deviate too much from the desired "balance," which, incidentally, may also change over time.

――――――――

Imagine a country with ten cities, in each one of which lives a single doctor, and let's assume there are strong limitations for people to go visit physicians in cities other than their own, be it due to a deficient transport system, to a legal system that requires them to depend upon a local doctor, or to any other reason. The income of each one of the physicians, assuming the size and morbidity of the different cities to be roughly the same, will thus also tend to be more or less the same. The physicians, under these conditions, will not have many incentives to invest in advertising themselves, as there is no pressure for competition, and the control by each one of them of his/her own city market will have monopolistic characteristics, with the corresponding impact on price and quality. On the other hand, the planning investment horizon of each one of the physicians will tend to be relatively long, as the expectation is that each city market will belong to its local doctor for a long time, and perhaps even pass to his or her descendants.

Now suppose that the barriers to free competition disappear: communications improve across the cities, and there are no legal restrictions to prevent people from freely choosing any doctor. What happens now? To begin with, of course, people will tend to go to the doctor with the best reputation. Thus, other things being equal, the income of the best physicians will rise, and that of the worst will decline. At the extreme (e.g., if the best physician can really deal with all the patients and, thus, all the other doctors have no business), this is just a winner-take-all game. There will be competitive pressure both on prices and quality and on the proportion of their income the physicians spend on advertising themselves. There will also be a strong tendency for success (or failure) to retro-feed itself: the most successful doctors will make more money and, therefore, be able to afford both better equipment and more expensive advertising. This means that winning in the next few rounds of the game has a potentially very high relevance, as it determines to a large extent the conditions under which the player is going to have to compete afterwards. Yet success will always have the potential of being short-lived because tomorrow an unfortunate mistake in a difficult surgery procedure or the appearance of a new, better advertised or genuinely more gifted competitor can trigger the vicious cycle of failure for the physician that today is at the top of the world. This provides an incentive for market leaders to stay "on their toes" for sure, but it also discounts any long-term investment at a heavy risk premium, especially if it reduces the chances of immediate success. At this point, the reader may have spotted a seeming contradiction: if the physician "on top" keeps focusing on his short-term marketability and downplaying longer-term investments (such as his own retraining), isn't he implicitly digging his own grave in the long run? The answer is yes, of course, as this is precisely the nature of the dilemma.

This is what we could call "Hollywood-style economics," as it is indeed how the Hollywood star system has worked almost from the beginning. The Hollywood cinema industry is a very competitive industry with global reach. Every weekend, people in the whole world are free to chose what movie they want to watch, and they do so based on a few parameters such as the name of the featured actors or a trailer they saw last week. The value of the theatre ticket of each one is minimal, but there is almost no limit to the number of people who can go to a given movie, and, therefore, the potential revenue from a film can swing from zero (no one was interested) to many millions (Everyone went to watch it, and some even went twice.). In other words: as in the case of the doctors after the barriers between the cities was removed, the difference between the physician (or, in this case, the actor) on top and the one at the bottom of the ranking is potentially huge. Under these conditions, of course, the stakes are very high, and the competition must be cut-throat. Therefore, reputation is everything, and the salaries of the actors at the top of the system are an almost obscene multiple of those of many others who are only slightly less gifted, or simply have been a bit less lucky or a bit less ruthless.

Our modern economy, increasingly global, competitive and meritocratic as it is, just cannot be excluded from this same rule: as competition grows on a global scale, the pressure for performance will increase, which is a stimulating factor but, at the same time, the planning horizon of corporations and even individuals will tend to become somewhat shorter simply because none of them can count on retaining his/her position in the marketplace in the long run. This, of course, generates interesting and seemingly paradoxical effects. For example, as long as the top leadership of Marks & Spencer in the UK

was securely in the hands of a member of the founding family (as it was always the case from the company's foundation in 1894 until 1984), the CEO never needed to justify a long-term-oriented policy of sustained product quality and client service, even when facing temporary losses, simply because he/she did not face the risk of dismissal. In fact, the problems that ended up in the spectacular nosedive of this firm in 1999 can to a large extent be attributed to a series of policies increasingly aimed at improving measurable results in the short term that M&S applied throughout the 90s. This is by no means an exceptional situation. Anderson and Reeb (2003), working on U.S. data from S&P 500 companies over the period 1992 to 1999, found statistically robust evidence that "family firms perform better than non-family firms" and that, even within the set of family-controlled firms, "when family members serve as CEO, performance is better than with outside CEOs." They link these findings directly to those of James (1999) in the sense that family firms can attain greater investment efficiency due to their longer investment horizons.

Conversely, for a hired CEO who is exposed to being fired if short-term results are below the board's expectations, reputation represents a large portion of his/her market value, and reputation is built upon sustained, demonstrated success. The stakes are high and, thus, it is not at all surprising that, as research found, they discount their companies' investments at a rate higher than that applied by the shareholders they serve. Interestingly, the same paper also found that "at the time of the survey, the fall of 1990, U.S. CEOs believed that their firms had systematically shorter time horizons than their major competitors in Europe and (especially) Asia," which is consistent with the general observation that the U.S. market is still freer and more internally competitive than most of the European and Asian ones. This is also consistent with findings which suggest that CEO performance-related turnover rates are generally higher in the U.S. than in either Europe and Asia, although the long-term tendency is for the latter to gradually approach the US rates over time.

The pressure, of course, rarely stays at the CEO

level, as it tends to spread top down throughout the whole organization culture. For example, while one should always take comments on a failed business with more than a grain of salt (it is just too easy to pontificate on what went wrong in a business after it has failed), the analysis of Enron's case suggest that it was to a large extent their aggressive culture of internal competition as represented by the annual performance review. Informally known as "rank and yank," whose focus on measurable results within the period being appraised meant that, in the words of a former employee, "people went from being geniuses to idiots overnight" and which typically resulted in the bottom 10–20% performers being regularly fired. It meant, too, unyielding focus on results. According to a former employee, "they were so goal-oriented toward immediate gratification that they lost sight of the future," and this is what ultimately led them to catastrophe.

QUESTIONS

1. What is "the winner-take-all-game"? Is it a good thing or a bad thing? Why?

2. What does Garcia mean by "Hollywood-style" economics? Do you think Hollywood-style economics should be encouraged or discouraged? How would you do so?

Gerald W. McEntee

Comparable Worth: A Matter of Simple Justice

Gerald W. McEntee was president, American Federation of State, County and Municipal Employees.

On December 31, 1985, the American Federation of State, County, and Municipal Employees (AFSCME) and the state of Washington reached a historic comparable worth agreement. They negotiated a settlement of the *AFSCME* v. *Washington State* pay equity lawsuit. The $106.5 million payout is historic because it is the largest comparable worth settlement in history, and it ended over a decade of resistance by the state to rectify sex-based wage discrimination in its wage scales, as documented by Washington's own studies.

In spite of this historic ruling, however, there is evidence that public sector employers still practice intentional wage discrimination and job segregation policies that funnel women into lower-paying, female-dominated jobs. Is this segregation intentional? And are the pay scales for these particular jobs based on sex-based wage discrimination?

AFSCME believes that the answer to both is "yes."

Take the Washington State example. According to the state's own studies, a laundry operator working in a large state institution should have been paid more than a farm equipment operator. But the salaries for farm equipment operators were seventeen pay grades higher than those of the laundry workers. The difference? One job was male-dominated; the other, female-dominated.

Also in Washington, clerk-typists working in state government and beginning warehouse workers were rated at the same level. But typists earned salaries ten pay grades below those of warehouse workers.

In both the public and the private sector workforce, these examples of pay discrimination are

This article first appeared in *The Humanist* issue of May/June 1986 and is reprinted with permission.

repeated hundreds of times in various job classifications. This translates into a national problem for working women, who still earn only sixty-four cents for every dollar working men earn, in spite of increased education and growing workforce participation by women.

The Washington State settlement capped off a year of comparable worth successes for AFSCME. Comparable worth moved from the courts to the bargaining table and state legislatures in 1985. Public employers are beginning to negotiate with their employees and their unions to work out practical and affordable solutions to the historic problem of sex-based wage discrimination.

However, in spite of the gains made on the comparable worth front this past year, the debate over this method of eradicating sex-based wage discrimination continues. Unfortunately, the discussion too often remains mired in the same kind of mean-spirited arguments used against every major piece of civil rights legislation. Opponents include U.S. Civil Rights Commission Chairman Clarence Pendleton, Phyllis Schlafly, and President Reagan. They have constructed their own definition of what comparable worth is, how it can be accomplished, how much it will cost, and what its effects will be. Their dire predictions fly in the face of the experience of AFSCME and public sector employers across the country. Many employers have voluntarily begun to correct disparities in their wage scales due to sex discrimination. The main arguments of comparable worth opponents are the following:

The gap between men's earnings and women's earnings is due to women's more recent entry into the workforce and their lesser education, training, and experience. Once you have allowed for legitimate differences in pay between men and women, such as seniority, experience, and collective bargaining agreements, there is still a gap that has remained constant for most of the years women have been in the workforce. At least half of this gap is due to sex discrimination by employers. AFSCME defines pay equity, or comparable worth, as a means of closing the gap between men's salaries and women's salaries that can be attributed only to sex discrimination.

Instituting comparable worth will upset the free market economy and require new laws and government wage-setting boards. The U.S. economy is partly controlled by minimum wage laws, civil rights laws, child labor laws, and the Equal Pay Act of 1963. AFSCME contends that the so-called free market has historically discriminated against women. Otherwise, nurses would be handsomely paid, because over the years they have been in critically short supply. But in 1981, for example, full-time registered nurses earned an average of only $331 a week—less than ticket agents and drafters.

Similarly, laws requiring women to be paid the same as men if they are doing comparable work are already on the books—all that remains is the will to enforce the law. In 1981, the Supreme Court ruled that the prohibition of *Title* VII of the 1964 Civil Rights Act against discrimination in wage compensation was not limited to the claims of working women for equal pay for equal work. The Court made it clear that *Title* VII prohibits all forms of discrimination in wage setting, including instances in which the male and female jobs being compared are dissimilar.

No advocate of comparable worth has urged that a government board set wages. Comparable worth requires only that *each individual employer* remove sex bias from his or her wage scale. If, say, a truck driver and a secretary within the same organization are evaluated as doing comparable work, they should be paid comparably.

Dissimilar jobs—like apples and oranges—cannot be compared. Think again. You *can* compare apples and oranges on a basis of their weight, their color, and their percentages of vitamins and fluid. Likewise, jobs have certain common characteristics: training, experience, responsibility, working conditions, and other criteria. Employers have been comparing jobs for as long as they have been hiring workers. Two-thirds of all workers are covered by some form of job evaluation system. The federal government has had an evaluation system to compare dissimilar jobs for one hundred years.

Comparable worth costs too much. AFSCME's on-the-job experience has shown that comparable worth has never cost more than 4 percent of a jurisdiction's payroll. In its first four years of implementation on the state level in Minnesota (which is now implementing pay equity on the county and local level), comparable worth was expected to cost 4 percent of the state's total payroll. Actually, it will cost about 3.5 percent.

Interestingly, the same cost argument was made during the debate over civil rights legislation in the 1960s. Critics charged that paying blacks more would reduce the salaries of white workers. Critics of comparable worth argue that paying women more will reduce men's salaries.

Charging that pay equity will cost too much is an empty argument; it is inflammatory rhetoric designed to alienate women from men. Just because it carries a price, we should not be diverted from our goal of ending discrimination.

Unions promote pay equity because they want to keep women segregated in traditionally female-dominated jobs. Sex segregation in the workforce is a fact of life. A recent National Academy of Sciences report found that, despite recent progress, most American women who are employed will continue to work in largely low-paying occupations dominated by women for the foreseeable future.

Fifty-one percent of AFSCME's members are working women. The concerns of the union's women members are part of the union's overall agenda for the 1980s. Career ladders and career development programs are two of the contract provisions AFSCME negotiates to help move women into better-paying, more skilled jobs.

At the same time, a worker should be paid fairly for his or her work. Today, nearly 60 percent of mothers in families with children under-eighteen are working; 80 percent of all working women are segregated into only twenty of the jobs listed by the *Dictionary of Occupational Titles*. Comparable worth is a means to bring the wages of working women into the mainstream. There are side benefits, also. For example, in Minnesota, during the first four years of pay equity, there has been an increase of 19 percent in the number of women entering nontraditional jobs.

AFSCME believes that comparable worth is the civil rights issue of the eighties. By using collective bargaining and legislative lobbying, AFSCME is pursuing the vestiges of sex-based wage discrimination. Its pay equity lawsuits on behalf of workers in Hawaii, Connecticut, New York City, Philadelphia, and Nassau County, New York, are making their way through the federal courts. Tens of thousands of workers—both women and men—in female-dominated jobs across the country are beginning to be paid based upon fairness and worth. It's a matter of simple justice.

QUESTIONS

1. What is comparable worth?

2. What are several strong arguments in favor of comparable worth? What are some arguments opposed to it? Can comparable worth ever result in injustice?

CASES

CASE 6.1
Revolution Without Ideology
Naomi Klein

Naomi Klein is the author of No Logo *and* Fences and Windows.

An extraordinary chapter in capitalist history is being written today in Argentina. Call it revolution without ideology, or serendipitous employee ownership. Call it a reminder that property rights originate at the point of a gun. Whatever words we use cannot do justice to the remarkable events themselves. In Buenos Aires, every week brings news of a new worker occupation—a four-star hotel now run by its cleaning staff, a supermarket taken over by its clerks, a regional airline about to be turned into a cooperative by the pilots and attendants. In Trotskyist journals around the world, Argentina's occupied factories are giddily hailed as the dawn of a socialist utopia, because workers have "seized the means of production." In *The Economist,* the worker-run factories are described as a threat to the sacred principle of private property. The truth lies in between.

Take the Brukman textile factory in Buenos Aires. Brukman has been producing men's suits for 50 years, and since December it's been doing it without managers. The means of production weren't seized—they were simply picked up after being abandoned by their owners. The factory had been in decline for years, with debts to utility companies piling up. Seamstresses had seen salaries slashed from 100 pesos a week to two pesos—not enough for bus fare.

In December 2002, the workers demanded a travel allowance. The owners, pleading poverty, told them

to wait at the factory while they looked for the money. "We waited until night," said Brukman worker Celia Martinez. "No one came."

Getting the keys from the doorman, workers slept at the factory that night. They've been running it ever since. They've paid the outstanding bills, attracted new clients and—without profits and management salaries to worry about—paid themselves steady salaries. All these decisions have been made by vote in open assemblies of the 58 workers. "I don't know why the owners had such a hard time," Martinez says. "I don't know much about accounting, but for me it's easy: addition and subtraction."

Like other garment factories, Brukman is filled with women hunched over sewing machines, eyes straining and fingers flying. What makes Brukman different are the sounds. Along with the roar of machines is the Bolivian folk music, coming from a tape deck at the back of the room. And there are soft voices, as older workers show younger ones new stitches. "Before," says Martinez says, "they wouldn't let us get up from our workspaces or listen to music. But why not listen to music, to lift the spirits a bit?"

In dozens of cases like Brukman's, workers have been awarded legal expropriation by the courts—much like squatters allowed to claim ownership of occupied buildings. Lawyers of the Brukman workers argue that factory owners have violated principles of business by failing to pay employees and creditors, while collecting huge subsidies from the state. Why can't the state now insist that the indebted com-

From *Business Ethics,* Summer 2003, p. 6. Reprinted by permission of Bell Globemedia Interactive Inc.

panies' assets continue to serve the public with steady jobs?

In Brukman's case, the argument hasn't worked. A federal judge has ordered the workers evicted, writing—in a remarkable statement—that "Life and physical integrity have no supremacy over economic interests." Property rights trump all other rights.

Those preeminent rights were enforced in April, when police carried out the judge's eviction order in the middle of the night. They turned the entire block into a military zone guarded by machine guns and attack dogs. Unable to get into the factory and complete an order for 3,000 pairs of dress trousers, the workers gathered a huge crowd of supporters and announced it was time to go back to work. At 5 p.m., 50 middle-aged seamstresses in no-nonsense haircuts, sensible shoes, and blue smocks walked up to the police fence. Someone pushed, the fence fell. The Brukman women—unarmed and arm in arm—slowly walked through.

They had taken only a few steps when the police began shooting: tear gas, water cannons, rubber bullets, then lead. Dozens were injured—for the crime of trying to sew trousers.

"They are afraid of us because we have shown that, if we can manage a factory, we can also manage a country," Martinez said. "That's why this government decided to repress us." There may also be fear of the sheer magnitude of what is underway. In the past 18 months, almost 200 factories employing more than 10,000 nationwide have been taken over and run by workers.

It's a new kind of labor movement, based not on the power to stop working (the traditional union tactic) but on the dogged determination to keep working no matter what. It's a demand driven not by dogma but by realism: In a country where 58 per cent of the population is in poverty, workers are a paycheck away from having to scavenge to survive. A revolution may be underway, but it's not driven by ideology. The specter haunting Argentina's occupied factories is not communism, but indigence.

QUESTIONS

1. Did these women have a moral justification for taking over their factory?

2. Aside from the legal arguments, did the factory owners have a good moral argument for stopping the women from running the factory?

CASE 6.2
Going Down the Road
Jim Hightower

[handwritten margin notes: Mexico - 3rd trader to us; Maquiladora factories - produce goods shipped to us + others; 1,000 of workers]

Jim Hightower was Texas Railroad commissioner and is a popular talk show host.

A couple of years ago, Susan DeMarco and I were doing our radio talk show, *Chat & Chew*, on the topic of sweatshop goods. A lady from Jackson, Mississippi, called to say that whenever she goes into a store to shop for clothing, she always tries to find a manager and asks, "Can you tell me where your made-in-the-USA section is?" Good questions. Go into any clothing department and everything in there—from overcoats to undies, hats to shoes—bears labels that shout: made in China, Bangladesh, El Salvador, the Philippines . . . everywhere but the US of A. This is not only in the Wal-Marts and Targets but also in the upscale Talbotses and Abercrombie & Fitches.

"Going Down the Road" *The Nation*, June 24, 2002.

It is not that Americans are unable to make quality stuff, but the ugly fact is that corporations have abandoned US workers and communities in hot pursuit of ever-fatter profits, rushing off to the lowest-wage hellholes they can find to cut and sew their garments. Instead of paying even a minimum wage of $5.15 an hour here, they can get wage slaves at 13 cents an hour in China—then ship the goods back here without lowering the price they charge us. The corporations gleefully pocket the difference in labor costs—and claim that this is the "magic" of the new global market at work. It certainly is magic for them.

For us it is globaloney—just the same old greed. But what's a consumer to do? Even if a garment is made in the United States, some companies also run sweatshops here, with workers, usually recent immigrants, crammed into basement "contract shops," making less than minimum wage. How can we combat the scourge of sweatshops everywhere? Government could take action, but even under Bill Clinton, it was Nike, Gap, Ralph Lauren and other bigwigs that dominated the discussion, so Washington did nothing but dabble and dawdle. Of course, under King George the W, even discussion has stopped.

SWEATX IS CHIC

The goods news is that people themselves—especially children and young people—see sweatshops as a moral abomination, putting them (yet again) well ahead of officialdom. Major groups like United States Against Sweatshops, the National Labor Committee, Global Exchange and the garment union UNITE have been aggressively exposing, agitating and organizing against sweatshop labor. As this political organizing expands, an important assault on sweatshops has come from the one place the multibillion-dollar industry least expects: The marketplace itself.

SweatX is a new brand of garment in every sense of the word. The Hot Fudge Social Venture Fund, set up by Ben Cohen, the puckish entrepreneur and social activist of Ben & Jerry's ice cream fame, has invested $1 million to date in a brand-new garment business in Los Angeles. The business, called *teamX,* is based on a thoroughly radical principle: "Garment workers

don't have to be exploited in order to operate a financially successful apparel factory." Imagine.

Inspired and informed by Spain's Mondragon Industrial Cooperatives (a fifty-year-old network of successful employee-owned businesses: *www.mcc .es*), *teamX* is organized as a worker-owned co-op that (1) is a union shop organized by UNITE; (2) pays a living wage starting at $8.50 an hour; (3) provides good health care, a pension and a share of profits through co-op ownership; (4) practices the "solidarity ratio," in which no executive is paid more than eight times what the lowest-paid worker gets; and (5) intends to make a profit, grow and spread its progressive seed.

This is no touchie-feelie, froufrou social exercise but a bottom-line business initiative to show that doing well can also mean doing good. Pierre Ferrari's twenty-five years in the corporate world ranges from being VP of Coca-Cola to being director of Ben & Jerry's . . . to now being CEO of *teamX.* These entrepreneurial folks believed that there had to be a better way than sweatshops. Ferrari immersed himself in the economics of garment production. His most shocking (and enlightening) discovery was that a sweatshop worker in the United States gets about 25 cents to make a T-shirt that retails for as much as 18 bucks. Let's say that a worker grosses about $9,000 a year. Poverty. What if you doubled the wage—to 50 cents per shirt? The increase would not affect the buyer, but that worker would suddenly be getting $18,000 a year. Not exactly a fortune, but a livable wage. "Come on," says Ferrari, "they're exploiting people for a lousy 25 cents?"

BUILDING THE BRAND

This March, twenty *teamX* employee-owners, many of whom previously had been sweatshop workers, began production in Los Angeles on their company's first line of stylish shirts, shorts, caps and other casual wear, working with state-of-the-art equipment in a brand-new factory. "I've been working in clothing for twenty years, and I never had a paid holiday before this," one of the employees told the *Los Angeles Times.* A small, experienced team of managers has been assembled, drawing especially on some older managers who are not merely chasing bucks but looking to add a moral dimension to their work lives.

To build the brand identity, *teamX* is initially targeting the activist community—campuses, unions, churches, local governments, nonprofits, etc. (The T-shirts for my Rolling Thunder Downhome Democracy. Tour proudly bear the SweatX label.) This "market of conscience" alone has a huge and virtually untapped potential—as Ferrari discovered, for example, unions buy a lot of T-shirts for rallies, organizing drives and such. After Oprah recently featured *teamX* on her show, the phones began ringing off the hook with orders, and Ferrari now expects this upstart startup to break even by July—an investment miracle by anyone's standards.

By tapping this growing market of conscience, SweatX not only can be successful but will put the lie to the garment industry's cynical assertion that low wages are an inevitable component of globalization. We can help by talking to our local organizations, clothing store managers, school board members and others, introducing them to the SweatX possibility . . . showing with our dollars that commerce and conscience can cohabitate.

QUESTIONS

1. Are sweatshops "moral abominations"? Why?
2. What should we do about sweatshops?

CASE 6.3

The Problem with Dudley Less

Joanne B. Ciulla

Dudley Less is an account manager. Dudley started working for A. H. Miller soon after he got out of high school. He is now 55 years old. Today, Dudley's coworkers took him to dinner to celebrate 30 years of service to the company. You are Dudley's manager. At the end of the party, he asks to see you. Dudley takes you aside and says, "I've been thinking. I've been doing the same job for this company for 30 years. But, today I realized that I want a change. I'd like to take the leadership program to qualify for a more senior position in our new division. I've received above-average evaluations for many years and believe that my experience will be a real asset to this division."

You are flabbergasted. Dudley came into this business in another era. In his day, account managers took three-hour lunches and had personal ties with clients. Dudley has made some attempt to keep up with the hectic pace of the office. He is a steady worker and a pleasant guy. His work has always been quite average, but because of his personality and long tenure with the company, he has always received very good performance ratings. He never displayed any ambition to move up in the organization before, nor had you ever seen him demonstrate management potential. Now he is asking you to send him to a company leadership program that is designed for fast-track managers. The program is three months long, and the cost per employee is very high. Managers are encouraged to be selective about who they send. Your office is allowed to send only one employee a year. You were thinking of sending Carol Thompson through the program this year. You think Carol has a bright future with the company. You tell Dudley that you will consider his request.

QUESTIONS

1. What does the company owe an employee like Dudley?
2. What would you tell Dudley?

CASE 6.4
Overworked and Ready to Blow
Joanne B. Ciulla

You have been working at the Regent Corporation for 15 years. Because of a recent downsizing, your job has become extremely hectic. You now do a job that had been done by three employees. You've been working late and on weekends. Recently you had to cancel a much-needed vacation because you had to work. You are afraid to raise any questions about overtime because your manager keeps telling you that the company values committed and loyal employees.

All your family members have suffered from your heavy work schedule. You missed your daughter's Christmas play and have been unable to take a few hours off to watch your son's soccer games. When you get home at night, you are exhausted, but there is still dinner to make, clothes to wash, and the children's homework to check. Your husband is also tired when he comes home, and because he often arrives home late, he is not able to help much around the house. The two of you have had numerous fights over who should do what. These fights have strained your marriage and upset your children. Lately, your son has been misbehaving in school. You feel like your life is spinning out of control and you are ready to explode.

Today you went to your manager and explained to him that you needed two days off. You told him about the stress that you were under at home and pointed out how helpful it would be to take Thursday and a Friday off as vacation leave. This would allow you time to catch up on work at home and time to go and talk to your son's teacher.

Your manager said he understood your problem, but that your request was not very professional. He said, "Professionals don't ask for time off to catch up on their housework. We'd all like to have time off to do things at home. You don't see any of the guys in this office coming in to ask for time off to cut the grass or wash the car. This is a business. If you want to keep up with your housework, don't work—stay at home. When things slow down around here next month, you can take some vacation days." You left his office feeling angry and humiliated.

QUESTIONS

1. What do loyalty and commitment mean to the manager in this case? What should the terms mean to a business from an ethical point of view?

2. Would it have been wiser for you simply to call in sick on Thursday and Friday?

CASE 6.5
Poverty Area Plants
Rogene A. Buchholz

Paperboard Company did not have a contributions program and was being pressured by other companies in the city to help make a better community by contributing to some aspect of community welfare. The company was being accused of being a free rider and benefiting from other companies' concern about city problems. Company management wanted to be a responsible company, but it doubted the wisdom of establishing a contributions program. The company wanted to do something different.

Paperboard had heard of Control Data's program to build plants in disadvantaged areas to employ local people and thus help the area to establish a sound economic base. The management of the company wondered if this strategy would work well for Paperboard and if it could make a better contribution to the community in this manner. Its manufacturing process lent itself to small plants that could make specialized products. The company also did not need many highly skilled employees to operate a typical plant.

The company was also aware that the federal gov-ernment was considering a bill to create enterprise zones in disadvantaged areas to encourage companies to locate there. Due to budgetary considerations, however, political experts were saying that the bill had little chance of passage during the current congressional session. Paperboard was thus wondering whether to wait and see if this bill could be salvaged, or whether to go ahead on its own and plan to build plants in disadvantaged areas of the community.

QUESTIONS

1. What factors should the company consider in building plants in disadvantaged areas? What problems are likely to be encountered? Will small plants of this nature really make much of an impact on disadvantaged areas of communities?

2. Should the company lobby for passage of federal legislation to establish enterprise zones? Or should it begin to work at the state level for passage of similar legislation? Which would be the most socially responsible course of action?

Rogene A. Buchholz, *Business Environment and Public Policy: Implications for Management,* 5th ed. (Englewood Cliffs, NJ: Prentice Hall, 1995), p. 301.

CASE 6.6
Poverty in America
William H. Shaw and Vincent Barry

In recent years the U.S. Census Bureau has brought some glad tidings: The median income of American households has been increasing. Meanwhile, the number of families with incomes below the poverty line—defined as $17,960 for a family of four—has declined, and overall the poverty rate has fallen to 11.3 percent, about what it had been back in the 1970s. Still, despite the long economic boom of the 1990s, 32.3 million Americans continue to live in poverty, a third of them children. That's more than one out of every nine people. Moreover, the average adult American has a 60 percent chance of living at least one year below the poverty line and a 33 percent chance of experiencing dire poverty.

Most people think that those described as "poor" in the United States are pretty well off by world standards. The truth is, in life expectancy twenty-year-old U.S. males rank thirty-sixth among the world's nations, and twenty-year-old U.S. females rank twenty-first. Our infant mortality rate is worse than that in twenty-one other Western nations. Moreover, millions of Americans endure hunger. According to the U.S. Department of Agriculture, 31 million Americans lack "food security," and in 3 million American households one or more persons go hungry during the year. Figures from the Food Research and Action Center are even more alarming; it reports that 5 million children under age twelve go hungry each month. In addition, one out of every four Americans lives in substandard housing, and in most cities one sees people roaming the streets in tattered clothing, picking their food out of garbage cans. Homeless people—many of them former mental patients released from state hospitals, others jobless individuals and families unable to afford housing—live in aban-doned cars and shacks or simply sleep in doorways and on subway grates. Precise figures are impossible to obtain. One recent survey found 280,000 people homeless, but other experts estimate that 600,000–700,000 Americans are homeless on any given night and that 3 to 12 million Americans are homeless sometime during the year.

People in different walks of life and in different circumstances experience poverty. Many others live on the edge of poverty and are in continual danger of falling into it through illness, job loss, or other misfortune. In the United States today, the "working poor"—that is, those who work full time, year around, while earning an income below the poverty line—number 2.8 million. They represent a higher percentage of the workforce than in the 1970s as well-paid unionized manufacturing jobs have been replaced by nonunion service jobs. In 1997, the minimum wage was increased to $5.15 per hour, but it is still less in real terms than it was in 1969. Someone working forty hours a week, every week, for that wage cannot raise his or her family out of poverty. In fact, according to a housing advocacy group, a minimum-wage earner can't afford to rent a two-bedroom home anywhere in the United States.

Many poor people are unable to work and depend on outside assistance. Recent legislative efforts to reform the welfare system rely on certain myths about welfare recipients. Investigation shows, for instance, that most people do not stay on the welfare rolls for years. They move on and off, and less than 1 percent remain on welfare for ten years. Contrary to popular mythology, the majority of those who receive welfare are young children whose mothers must remain at home. They are not able-bodied

From William H. Shaw and Vincent Barry, *Moral Issues in Business,* 9th ed. (Belmont, CA: Wadsworth, 2004), pp. 127–129. Reprinted by permission of the editors.

adults who are unwilling to work. Nor do welfare mothers differ from non-welfare mothers in the number of children they have. About 70 percent of welfare families have only one or two children, and there is little financial incentive to have more. Half of the families who receive welfare include an adult who works full or part time, and research consistently demonstrates that poor people have the same strong desire to work that the rest of the population does. Two-thirds of the mothers on welfare did not grow up in families that received welfare—contrary to the stereotype of intergenerational welfare dependency—and only 7.6 percent of them are under eighteen and unmarried.

There has never been a way to live well on welfare. Under the old system of AFDC (Aid to Families with Dependent Children), by 1996 welfare benefits had fallen, in real terms, to 51 percent of what they had been in 1971. With annual cash allowances for a family on AFDC ranging from $1,416 in Mississippi to $6,780 in New York, even in the most generous states stipends were never enough to allow a family to escape from poverty. In 1996 Congress replaced AFDC with TANF (Temporary Assistance to Needy Families). Under the new system, the entitlement of poor people to support has been replaced by block grants to the states to run their own welfare programs. The grants are limited to a certain amount of money; if they run out, the states are not required to make additional expenditures. Welfare recipients are required to work for pay or to enroll in training programs, and financial support is limited to a lifetime maximum of five years. This shift in policy has been controversial. Since the TANF system began, the number of people receiving welfare benefits has declined, but experts disagree about the reasons: Is it a growing economy offering more opportunities, the success of the new approach in encouraging welfare recipients to make themselves employable, or simply people who are not able to take care of themselves being denied support?

One thing that is clear is the large number of women living in poverty. This includes women with inadequate income following divorce, widowhood, or retirement, as well as women raising children alone. Wage discrimination against women is one factor. Women who work full time, year round earn only about two-thirds of what men earn. And millions of women hold full-time jobs that pay wages near or below the poverty line.

Women's responsibilities for child rearing are another important factor. Despite many changes in recent years, women continue to have primary responsibility in this area. When marriages break up, mothers typically take custody and bear the major financial burden. Fewer than half the women raising children alone are awarded child support, and fewer than half of those entitled to it receive the full amount. Of family households headed by women, 52 percent have incomes below $25,000 and 19.7 percent have incomes below $10,000.

Most poor people in our nation—about two-thirds of them—are white, but blacks are about three times more likely to be poor. Whereas fewer than one out of every ten white Americans is poor, more than one of every five African Americans and Hispanics are below the poverty line. Many members of the minority communities have succeeded in moving up the economic ladder, but the overall picture is bleak. African-American family income, for instance, is only 62 percent that of white family income.

QUESTIONS

1. Does the existence of poverty imply that our socioeconomic system is unjust? Does the concentration of poverty in certain groups make it more unjust than it would be otherwise?

2. Surveys show that Americans, even poor Americans, favor individualistic explanations of poverty (such as lack of effort or ability, poor morals, poor work skills) over structural explanations (such as inadequate schooling, low wages, lack of jobs), whereas Europeans favor structural explanations of poverty over individualistic explanations. What are the causes of poverty? How is one's answer to this question likely to affect one's view of the justice or injustice of poverty?

CASE 6.7

Burger Beefs

William H. Shaw and Vincent Barry

When seventeen-year-old Wendy Hamburger (her real name) applied for a summer job at a Wendy's Old Fashioned Hamburgers outlet near her Barrington, Illinois, home, she hoped to earn some money for college. But after working there for only three months, she quit when a manager threatened to fire her if she refused to work an extra shift on a holiday.

Wendy wasn't too upset about losing her job. "It seemed like the job cost me more than I made," she says. She does concede, however, that Wendy's International did pay her a little attention during her brief connection with the company. It used her to get a lot of free publicity in Chicago-area newspapers, and its president and founder, R. David Thomas, mailed her an autographed photograph of himself, which presumably she didn't have to return when she quit.

Actually, there's nothing atypical about Wendy's experience. Rock-bottom pay, unpleasant working conditions, and bossy bosses—all are familiar to the millions of teenage employees in the fast-food industry. Little wonder the average teenage worker quits in disgust within four months of being hired.

Such rapid turnover would disembowel most businesses. Not so for those that peddle billions of burgers, fries, and shakes a year. For them, frequent turnover is the rank fodder for their multimillion-dollar operations, at least according to critics. Instead of relying upon a small, stable workforce of well-paid and well-trained employees, the fast-food industry seeks out part-time, unskilled workers who are willing to accept low pay. Teenagers, of course, fit this bill perfectly. These days the nation's approximately 3.5 million fast-food workers are the largest group of minimum-wage earners in the country— only migrant farm workers consistently earn a lower

hourly wage—and two-thirds of them are less than twenty years old.

"The whole system is designed to have turnover," says Robert Harbrant, secretary-treasurer for the AFL-CIO Food and Beverage Trades Department in Washington, D.C. That way the industry averts pay increases and thwarts union efforts to organize workers. Moreover, the fast-food chains work hard at making their machines and operating systems as foolproof as possible. That way their jobs require no skills, and any individual worker can be quickly replaced.

Industry executives deny such nefarious motives. They point out, correctly, that for most youngsters a fast-food job is their first work experience. Such unseasoned workers usually are undisciplined and unreliable. No sooner are they trained, say fast-food executives, than they up and leave.

Harlow E. White, president of Systems for Human Resources, Inc., thinks otherwise. He publicly wonders whether the 300 percent annual turnover of fast-food workers is the cause or effect of industry operations. He suspects that "the industry has managed to manufacture a self-fulfilling prophecy: 'We're going to have turnover. And by God, we do.'" While admitting that the teenage part-timer is crucial to fast-food success, industry officials insist that they do not purposely encourage turnover. "Turnover costs us money," asserts a spokesperson for Burger King, even while conceding that it takes little time to train a new worker.

Despite the industry's declared good intentions, discontent among fast-food workers is widespread. That's not surprising given that the vast majority of them are paid an hourly wage, provided no benefits, and scheduled to work only as needed. If the restau-

From William H. Shaw and Vincent Barry, *Moral Issues in Business,* 9th ed. (Belmont, CA: Wadsworth, 2004), pp. 298–299. Reprinted by permission of the editors.

rant's busy, they're kept longer than usual. If business is slow, they're sent home early. For example, one teenage part-timer at a New York McDonald's shop says management there routinely has workers appear up to an hour ahead of work time and then "wait in the back room and punch in later when they need you." (A McDonald's official insists that this is an isolated case, that McDonald's does not condone such a policy.) And a teenage waitress in an Atlanta Steak n' Shake complains that she is scheduled for a two-hour workday, although it takes her that much time to make a round-trip from home to work. (A company official says this is a management problem, that the policy of Steak n' Shake is to pay workers for a minimum of three hours.)

Some believe that the companies' insistence that such problems lie with local management, not the home office, is buck passing. Richard Gilber, a compliance officer in the U.S. Labor Department's wage and hour division, places the blame squarely on the store-manager training programs conducted by the home offices. He says, "We find in many cases that the 20-year-old managers are sales oriented and cleanliness oriented. But they aren't taught much about employee relations. And the Wage Hour Law is just another three pages in the operating manual."

Wendy Hamburger agrees. "I went through three managers in the short time I was at Wendy's," she recalls. "They needed managers so badly they hired anyone. They got a lot of young guys in there who think they're Mr. Macho and want to exercise their power. They don't know anything."

A Burger King official conceded that much of the criticism is warranted. The industry, he says, has put people in their early twenties in charge of a million-dollar restaurant and sometimes forty employees under age eighteen and expects them to function like professionals. The results are often less than ideal. "You can train someone to fix a piece of equipment a lot easier than you can to deal with people," he says.

To be sure, a manager's job is no bowl of cherries. Ask the young woman who is paid not much more than minimum wage to run a McDonald's outlet that grosses $750,000 annually. "They don't pay managers enough," she complains. "I'm on my feet from 6 A.M. to 6 P.M. Often I don't have time to eat all day. On days off I come in a couple of hours or call in to check on my assistant managers. And I have to take work home, like weekly scheduling."

Low pay is the chronic complaint of fast-food employees. Most chains come under minimum-wage and overtime-pay laws, but they don't always abide by them. Although enforcement of the laws is often lax, fast-food franchises across the country have been found guilty of underpaying their workers and not keeping proper wage reports. In 1997, for example, a Washington State jury found that Taco Bell had systematically coerced employees into working off the clock in order to avoid paying them overtime. In addition, the industry routinely ignores child-labor laws that restrict the hours that young teenagers can work. A few years ago the Labor Department fined Burger King $500,000—the largest child-labor penalty in history—for letting fourteen- and fifteen-year olds work late into the night on school nights.

Over at Starbucks Coffee, things are a little different. In contrast to the giant fast-food chains, Starbucks recently became the first U.S. company to give its part-time, hourly employees full health care benefits and stock options—even though, like the burger chains, part-time workers make up most of the company's workforce. "It's not viewed as a professional job in America to work behind a counter," says the owner of Starbucks, Howard Schultz. "We don't believe that. We want to provide our people with dignity and self-esteem, and we can't do that with lip service. So we offer tangible benefits."

QUESTIONS

1. Do you think the fast-food industry dislikes turnover? Do you think it encourages turnover?

2. Are wages in the fast-food industry fair? Does the industry exploit teenage workers? Compare the attitude of Starbucks to its workers with that of the fast-food industry.

3. How would you evaluate personnel procedures and working conditions in the fast-food industry? Are they reasonable? Could they be improved?

CASE 6.8
Nike's Suppliers in Vietnam
Sasha Lyutse

Following allegations of worker abuse, an investigation was launched in 1998 of Nike practices in subcontracted factories in Vietnam. This investigation created a public relations problem for the American manufacturer of athletic apparel. The report found that by not directly running the factories where its products were being made, Nike had little direct control over how employees were treated.

The report focused on Nike subcontracted factories in and around Ho Chi Minh City. It found local supervisors using abusive and humiliating practices to punish Vietnamese workers. Nike insisted that it did not tolerate abuse and required its manufacturers to take "immediate and effective measures to deal with it." A Nike training manager, the company said, works with subcontractors on sexual harassment, physical and verbal abuse, as well as on listening skills. The report found that Nike had "a fine code of conduct," but that its local contractors often violated it.

In 1998 Nike employees at the Sam Yang factory, just outside Ho Chi Minh City, were paid $1.84 a day. Their average monthly salary was $48—slightly better than Vietnam's $45 minimum wage for this region. With this salary, Nike workers could meet needs for food and shelter, but little else. In a 1998 survey, however, Nike suppliers were found to be paying competitive wages—no worse and no better than those paid by other foreign shoemakers.

Phillip Knight, founder of Nike's $9 billion sports-apparel empire, signs sports superstars to multimillion dollar contracts to advertise Nike sneakers that sometimes sell for $100 or more on the American market. A pair of Nike sneakers is unattainable for a worker at the Sam Yang factory, who works six days a week and makes roughly $600 a year, half the average income in Ho Chi Minh City, but about four times the annual earnings in more remote rural regions of Vietnam.

In 1999 Nike responded to mounting pressures by creating a labor monitoring department and translated its code of conduct into 11 languages so that more workers could read it. At the Sam Yang factory the local owners issued a 10-point "action plan" based on many of the 1998 report's recommendations. They held a union election, signed a labor contract with workers, and improved working conditions. The factory also got a new manager, increased trainees' wages and cut overtime. Most workers got a 5 percent raise, which came to about 8 cents more a day.

However, a 2001 report by the Global Alliance, an initiative sponsored by Nike in response to persistent criticism, documented proof of continued abusive labor practices in Southeast Asia, including physical, verbal and sexual abuse. According to the report, 96 percent of workers stated that they did not make enough money to meet their basic needs.

In its early days, before costs escalated and orders shifted to lowercost suppliers in Taiwan and South Korea, Nike imported all of its shoes from Japan. Soon, even Taiwan and South Korea became expensive, and suppliers moved their factories to China and Indonesia. In its global search for low-cost labor, Nike found Vietnam. By 1998, one out of every 10

This case was written by Sasha Lyutse. Basic sources were: *"The Living Wage Project to Brief Members of Congress on Nike Labor Abuses,"* PR Newswire Association, Inc., Copyright 2001, April 3, 2001; *"Labor-rights Group: Nike, Knight not Living up to 1998 Promises,"* The Associated Press State & Local Wire, May 16, 2001; and *"Nike battles Labour Charges U.S. Firm makes Changes after Alleged Worker Abuses in Vietnam,"* Toronto Star Newspapers, Ltd., Copyright 1998, April 2, 1998.

pairs of Nike shoes came from subcontractors in Vietnam.

Vietnam is one of Southeast Asia's poorest countries. It has an official rural unemployment of about 27 percent in some regions. It aggressively seeks foreign investment to create jobs and bring manufacturing expertise. However, unlike those countries that turn a blind eye to worker abuses by overseas employers, Vietnam pays close attention to foreign investors' behavior and has some of the region's toughest laws aimed at protecting workers; it ensures a minimum wage, sets overtime limits, permits strikes, etc.

At the same time, Vietnamese government officials sometimes appear to have divided priorities. They feel that they are duty-bound to defend workers (which union leaders say is their primary responsibility), but they also feel that they must accommodate investment planners who want trade unions to back off and not scare away desperately needed foreign investments.

In 1998 Nike employed more workers than any other foreign business in Vietnam (through its five Nike-aligned shoe factories). At the time, shipments of Nike shoes accounted for 5 percent of Vietnam's total exports. If Nike were to pull out of Vietnam, 35,000 Vietnamese would be out of work.

QUESTIONS

1. Is an average monthly salary of $48 morally indefensible, or is such a judgment relative to the expectations of a given society?

2. Are there issues of economic justice in this case, or are prices always fair when set in competitive markets?

3. If Nike were to close its factories and leave Vietnam for a country with a lower minimum wage, would this decision be morally indefensible?

CHAPTER QUESTIONS

1. Is capitalism just? Why should we even ask the question? Is the fairest society produced by capitalism? Is there even a tension between capitalism and fairness?

2. We are the wealthiest society the world has even seen. Does wealth create responsibilities? If so, how should these responsibilities be distributed or shared?

7

Is "the Social Responsibility of Business . . . to Increase Its Profits"?

Social Responsibility and Stakeholder Theory

Introduction

Business ethics has been around a long time, in fact, as long as there has been business in the world. The ancient Greeks were concerned about it, although it must be admitted that they were not particularly sympathetic to business, which was considered a grubby and parasitic way to make a living. (The much better way to make one's fortune was to inherit it or, even better, to loot it from a conquered adversary.) The early Romans, who were much more sympathetic to business, worried at some length about fair trade practices. Cicero, for example, expressed a contemporary concern about whether someone who was selling a house or a horse was obliged to tell the potential buyer of its existing flaws and defects. (The familiar warning, Caveat emptor—"buyer beware"—is in Latin, after all.) And throughout the ages, the main concern of business ethics has remained the lure of profit as opposed to larger social responsibilities, one's loyalty to one's country, for instance, or the local consequences of a business deal.

That question, what is now called (since the nineteenth century) "the profit motive" as opposed to broader social responsibilities, including questions of fairness as well as patriotism and consequences, still occupies a large part of business ethics. Civic-minded corporate executives worry about how they can maximize the bottom line without breaking the rules of their society and without betraying their own integrity. Small businesses fight to keep up with the competition while keeping in mind their obligations to their customers and the local community. You, no doubt, want the best job you can get, but there are all sorts of lines you do not want to cross—breaking the law, acting contrary to your religious beliefs, violating your own personal morality, turning your friends and neighbors against you. So the question is, what are your social responsibilities, and how do they tie into your own sense of personal worth and morality? How much can you serve and fulfill what you take to be your social responsibilities (responsibilities to your family, your friends, your neighbors, your religious group, your country, the world at large) and at the same time make the kind of living that you would like to make?

In the past 30 years, business ethics has gotten a great deal of mileage out of a polemic that Nobel prize-winning economist Milton Friedman published in the *New York Times Magazine* (September 1971). Friedman took on the raising chorus of demands that businesses, now the wealthiest and most powerful segment of society, have a greater sense of social responsibility. (That demand can be traced back to a Medieval notion, noblesse oblige, the obligation of the most powerful and most privileged members of society—whether the Church and the clergy or the army and its officers or the aristocracy and its nobles—to use some of their wealth and power to benefit the whole society.) But Friedman said *no,* the demand is misplaced, and business is not in a position to do more than it is created to do. Business is not social work, although a business is, of course, a valuable source of jobs and livelihoods. Business is not an educator, except, of course, in business. Business is not an arbiter of artistic taste, although what it sells may well be in better or worse taste. The business of business is, in short, business. That is what it can do well, and the benefits of a prosperous business community, Friedman says, will spill over into benefits for the whole society. (This part, the reader will note, comes directly from Adam Smith and his classic treatise on the benefits of the free market system.) But business does not—and *should not*—aim at this result. It will follow naturally, not by design.

What Friedman actually wrote—the now-famous title of his piece—was that "The Social Responsibility of Business Is to Increase its Profits." He was immediately pounced upon by business ethicists—and by a great many businessmen—who insisted that his pronouncements were themselves irresponsible and misleading, as well as insulting to the many business leaders, managers, and employees who took their sense of social responsibility very seriously, and as business leaders, managers, and employees, not just as citizens. The question was raised whether business would have the benign effects that Friedman predicted if everyone in business did, in fact, follow his prescription and think of nothing but profits. It was pointed out that businesses do, in fact, have and recognize any number of other responsibilities and obligations, for example, to their employees and to their customers. Friedman responded, predictably enough, that, of course, they had to treat their employees decently, or the employees would quit their jobs and work for somebody else and, of course, that they had to treat their customers well, or the customers would buy from someone else. In other words, the free market would take care of such things. The owners of a business or the leaders of a corporation know full well that to be profitable, they need to treat their employees and their customers well, and therefore they can and should just focus on profitability. The market will take care of the rest.

Needless to say, the debate did not stop there. The question became whether the obligation of a corporation to its stockholders was indeed its primary obligation or rather just one of many obligations to its *stakeholders,* that is, all those who are effected by the actions of a company, whether they had any market power or not. The question turned to the nature of profits and how they could be distinguished, nonarbitrarily, from income and assets in general. And the question remained just what was meant by that red-button phrase, "social responsibility." Just what is the social responsibility of a business? Is it just to pay its debts and make a good-quality (or, at least, a not unexpectedly dangerous) product? Is it to clean up any mess it makes, whether pollution or increased traffic around a site? Is it to help educate the people it will or, at least, may employ? Is it to solve such social problems as poverty and racial tension? Is it to enrich the society through its support of the arts and various cultural events and institutions? Of course, we recognize that many corporations do all these things, but then the question turns to the *motive* for doing so. Friedmanites will insist that companies have found that it is good publicity and good public relations to be associated with such projects. Anti-Friedmanites will say that this shows that corporations (or their leaders) do have a conscience and a sense of social responsibility that goes beyond their insistence on profitability. And that is where the question still stands today.

Following Friedman's piece is a rebuttal by University of Southern California professor Christopher D. Stone from his book *Where the Law Ends.* Of course, it doesn't make any sense to say that corporations have social responsibilities if it doesn't make sense to say that they have any responsibilities at all, that is, if they are not agents who can be praised or blamed for their actions, a widespread view in the business community. But Peter A. French, in "Corporate Moral Agency," takes issue with this notion and claims that corporations are agents in the appropriate sense and can indeed be praised or blamed for their actions. Then R. Edward Freeman advances the now-standard conception of a stakeholder (instead of just talking about stockholders) in his now-classic "A Stakeholder Theory of the Modern Corporation." Kenneth J. Arrow then approaches the social responsibility question from a different angle, that of economic efficiency," in his "Social Responsibility and Economic Efficiency." Finally, J. Maurice Clark considers the changing basis of economic responsibility.

Milton Friedman | # The Social Responsibility of Business Is to Increase Its Profits

Milton Friedman wrote this seminal piece in the *The New York Times Magazine.* It continues to attract considerable controversy.

When I hear businessmen speak eloquently about the "social responsibilities of business in a free-enterprise system," I am reminded of the wonderful line about the Frenchman who discovered at the age of 70 that he had been speaking prose all his life. The businessmen believe that they are defending free enterprise when they declaim that business is not concerned "merely" with profit but also with promoting desirable "social" ends; that business has a "social conscience" and takes seriously its responsibilities for providing employment, eliminating discrimination, avoiding pollution and whatever else may be the catchwords of the contemporary crop of reformers. In fact they are—or would be if they or anyone else took them seriously—preaching pure and unadulterated socialism. Businessmen who talk this way are unwitting puppets of the intellectual forces that have been undermining the basis of a free society these past decades.

The discussion of the "social responsibilities of business" are notable for their analytical looseness and lack of rigor. What does it mean to say that "business" has responsibilities? Only people can have responsibilities. A corporation is an artificial person and in this sense may have artificial responsibilities, but "business" as a whole cannot be said to have responsibilities, even in this vague sense. The first step toward clarity to examining the doctrine of the social responsibility of business is to ask precisely what it implies for whom.

Presumably, the individuals who are to be responsible are businessmen, which means individual proprietors or corporate executives. Most of the discussion of social responsibility is directed at corporations, so in what follows I shall mostly neglect the individual proprietors and speak of corporate executives.

In a free-enterprise, private-property system, a corporate executive is an employee of the owners of the business. He has direct responsibility to his employers. That responsibility is to conduct the business in accordance with their desires, which generally will be to make as much money as possible while conforming to the basic rules of the society, both those embodied in law and those embodied in ethical custom. Of course, in some cases his employers may have a different objective. A group of persons might establish a corporation for an eleemosynary purpose—for example, a hospital or a school. The manager of such a corporation will not have money profit as his objectives but the rendering of certain services.

In either case, the key point is that, in his capacity as a corporate executive, the manager is the agent of the individuals who own the corporation or establish the eleemosynary institution, and his primary responsibility is to them.

Needless to say, this does not mean that it is easy to judge how well he is performing his task. But at least the criterion of performance is straight-forward, and the persons among whom a voluntary contractual arrangement exists are clearly defined.

Of course, the corporate executive is also a person in his own right. As a person, he may have many other responsibilities that he recognizes or assumes voluntarily—to his family, his conscience, his feelings of charity, his church, his clubs, his city, his country. He may feel impelled by these responsibilities to devote part of his income to causes he regards as worthy, to refuse to work for particular corporations, even to

leave his job, for example, to join his country's armed forces. If we wish, we may refer to some of these responsibilities as "social responsibilities." But in these respects he is acting as a principal, not an agent; he is spending his own money or time or energy, not the money of his employers or the time or energy he has contracted to devote to their purposes. If these are "social responsibilities," they are the social responsibilities of individuals, not of business.

What does it mean to say that the corporate executive has a "social responsibility" in his capacity as businessman? If this statement is not pure rhetoric, it must mean that he is to act in some way that is not in the interest of his employers. For example, that he is to refrain from increasing the price of the product in order to contribute to the social objective of preventing inflation, even though a price increase would be in the best interests of the corporation. Or that he is to make expenditures on reducing pollution beyond the amount that is in the best interests of the corporation or that is required by law in order to contribute to the social objective of improving the environment. Or that, at the expense of corporate profits, he is to hire "hardcore" unemployed instead of better qualified available workmen to contribute to the social objective of reducing poverty.

In each of these cases, the corporate executive would be spending someone else's money for a general social interest. Insofar as his actions in accord with his "social responsibility" reduce returns to stockholders, he is spending their money. Insofar as his actions raise the price to customers, he is spending the customers' money. Insofar as his actions lower the wages of some employees, he is spending their money.

The stockholders or the customers or the employees could separately spend their own money on the particular action if they wished to do so. The executive is exercising a distinct "social responsibility," rather than serving as an agent of the stockholders or the customers or the employees, only if he spends the money in a different way than they would have spent it.

But if he does this, he is in effect imposing taxes, on the one hand, and deciding how the tax proceeds shall be spent, on the other.

This process raises political questions on two levels: principle and consequences. On the level of political principle, the imposition of taxes and the expenditure of tax proceeds are governmental functions. We have established elaborate constitutional, parliamentary and judicial provisions to control these functions, to assure that taxes are imposed so far as possible in accordance with the preferences and desires of the public—after all, "taxation without representation" was one of the battle cries of the American Revolution. We have a system of checks and balances to separate the legislative function of imposing taxes and enacting expenditures from the executive function of collecting taxes and administering expenditure programs and from the judicial function of mediating disputes and interpreting the law.

Here the businessman—self-selected or appointed directly or indirectly by stockholders—is to be simultaneously legislator, executive and jurist. He is to decide whom to tax by how much and for what purpose, and he is to spend the proceeds—all this guided only by general exhortations from on high to restrain inflation, improve the environment, fight poverty and so on and on.

The whole justification for permitting the corporate executive to be selected by the stockholders is that the executive is an agent serving the interests of his principal. This justification disappears when the corporate executive imposes taxes and spends the proceeds for "social" purposes. He becomes in effect a public employee, a civil servant, even though he remains in name an employee of a private enterprise. On grounds of political principle, it is intolerable that such civil servants—insofar as their actions in the name of social responsibility are real and not just window-dressing—should be selected as they are now. If they are to be civil servants, then they must be elected through a political process. If they are to impose taxes and make expenditures to foster "social" objectives, then political machinery must be set up to make the assessment of taxes and to determine through a political process the objectives to be served.

This is the basic reason why the doctrine of "social responsibility" involves the acceptance of the socialist view that political mechanisms, not market mechanisms, are the appropriate way to determine the allocation of scarce resources to alternative uses.

On the grounds of consequences, can the corporate executive in fact discharge his alleged "social responsibilities"? On the one hand, suppose he could get away with spending the stockholders' or customers' or employees' money. How is he to know how to spend it? He is told that he must contribute to fighting inflation. How is he to know what action of his will contribute to that end? He is presumably an expert in running his company—in producing a product or selling it or financing it. But nothing about his selection makes him an expert on inflation. Will his holding down the price of his product reduce inflationary pressure? Or, by leaving more spending power in the hands of his customers, simply divert it elsewhere? Or, by forcing him to produce less because of the lower price, will it simply contribute to shortages? Even if he could answer these questions, how much cost is he justified in imposing on his stockholders, customers and employees for this social purpose? What is his appropriate share and what is the appropriate share of others?

And, whether he wants to or not, can he get away with spending his stockholders', customers' or employees' money? Will not the stockholders fire him? (Either the present ones or those who take over when his actions in the name of social responsibility have reduced the corporation's profits and the price of its stock.) His customers and his employees can desert him for other producers and employers less scrupulous in exercising their social responsibilities.

This facet of "social responsibility" doctrine is brought into sharp relief when the doctrine is used to justify wage restraint by trade unions. The conflict of interest is naked and clear when union officials are asked to subordinate the interest of their members to some more general purpose. If the union officials try to enforce wage restraint, the consequence is likely to be wildcat strikes, rank-and-file revolts and the emergence of strong competitors for their jobs. We thus have the ironic phenomenon that union leaders—at least in the U.S.—have objected to Government interference with the market far more consistently and courageously than have business leaders.

The difficulty of exercising "social responsibility" illustrates, of course, the great virtue of private competitive enterprise—it forces people to be responsible for their own actions and makes it difficult for them to "exploit" other people for either selfish or unselfish purposes. They can do good—but only at their own expense.

Many a reader who has followed the argument this far may be tempted to remonstrate that it is all well and good to speak of Government's having the responsibility to impose taxes and determine expenditures for such "social" purposes as controlling pollution or training the hard-core unemployed, but that the problems are too urgent to wait on the slow course of political processes, that the exercise of social responsibility by businessmen is a quicker and surer way to solve pressing current problems.

Aside from the question of fact—I share Adam Smith's skepticism about the benefits that can be expected from "those who affected to trade for the public good"—this argument must be rejected on grounds of principle. What it amounts to is an assertion that those who favor the taxes and expenditures in question have failed to persuade a majority of their fellow citizens to be of like mind and that they are seeking to attain by undemocratic procedures what they cannot attain by democratic procedures. In a free society, it is hard for "evil" people to do "evil," especially since one man's good is another's evil.

I have, for simplicity, concentrated on the special case of the corporate executive, except only for the brief digression on trade unions. But precisely the same argument applies to the newer phenomenon of calling upon stockholders to require corporations to exercise social responsibility (the recent G.M. crusade for example). In most of these cases, what is in effect involved is some stockholders trying to get other stockholders (or customers or employees) to contribute against their will to "social" causes favored by the activists. Insofar as they succeed, they are again imposing taxes and spending the proceeds.

The situation of the individual proprietor is somewhat different. If he acts to reduce the returns of his enterprise in order to exercise his "social responsibility," he is spending his own money, not someone else's. If he wishes to spend his money on such purposes, that is his right, and I cannot see that there is any objection to his doing so. In the process, he, too, may impose costs on employees and customers.

However, because he is far less likely than a large corporation or union to have monopolistic power, any such side effects will tend to be minor.

Of course, in practice the doctrine of social responsibility is frequently a cloak for actions that are justified on other grounds rather than a reason for those actions.

To illustrate, it may well be in the long-run interest of a corporation that is a major employer in a small community to devote resources to providing amenities to that community or to improving its government. That may make it easier to attract desirable employees, it may reduce the wage bill or lessen losses from pilferage and sabotage or have other worthwhile effects. Or it may be that, given the laws about the deductibility of corporate charitable contributions, the stockholders can contribute more to charities they favor by having the corporation make the gift than by doing it themselves, since they can in that way contribute an amount that would otherwise have been paid as corporate taxes.

In each of these—and many similar—cases, there is a strong temptation to rationalize these actions as an exercise of "social responsibility." In the present climate of opinion, with its widespread aversion to "capitalism," "profits," the "soulless corporation" and so on, this is one way for a corporation to generate goodwill as a by-product of expenditures that are entirely justified in its own self-interest.

It would be inconsistent of me to call on corporate executives to refrain from this hypocritical window-dressing because it harms the foundations of a free society. That would be to call on them to exercise a "social responsibility"! If our institutions, and the attitudes of the public make it in their self-interest to cloak their actions in this way, I cannot summon much indignation to denounce them. At the same time, I can express admiration for those individual proprietors or owners of closely held corporations or stockholders of more broadly held corporations who disdain such tactics as approaching fraud.

Whether blameworthy or not, the use of the cloak of social responsibility, and the nonsense spoken in its name by influential and prestigious businessmen, does clearly harm the foundations of a free society. I have been impressed time and again by the schizophrenic character of many businessmen. They are capable of being extremely far-sighted and clearheaded in matters that are internal to their businesses. They are incredibly short-sighted and muddleheaded in matters that are outside their businesses but affect the possible survival of business in general. This short-sightedness is strikingly exemplified in the calls from many businessmen for wage and price guidelines or controls or income policies. There is nothing that could do more in a brief period to destroy a market system and replace it by a centrally controlled system than effective governmental control of prices and wages.

The short-sightedness is also exemplified in speeches by businessmen on social responsibility. This may gain them kudos in the short run. But it helps to strengthen the already too prevalent view that the pursuit of profits is wicked and immoral and must be curbed and controlled by external forces. Once this view is adopted, the external forces that curb the market will not be the social consciences, however highly developed, of the pontificating executives; it will be the iron fist of Government bureaucrats. Here, as with price and wage controls, businessmen seem to me to reveal a suicidal impulse.

The political principle that underlies the market mechanism is unanimity. In an ideal free market resting on private property, no individual can coerce any other, all cooperation is voluntary, all parties to such cooperation benefit or they need not participate. There are no values, no "social" responsibilities in any sense other than the shared values and responsibilities of individuals. Society is a collection of individuals and of the various groups they voluntarily form.

The political principle that underlies the political mechanism is conformity. The individual must serve a more general social interest—whether that be determined by a church or a dictator or a majority. The individual may have a vote and say in what is to be done, but if he is overruled, he must conform. It is appropriate for some to require others to contribute to a general social purpose whether they wish to or not.

Unfortunately, unanimity is not always feasible. There are some respects in which conformity appears unavoidable, so I do not see how one can avoid the use of the political mechanism altogether.

But the doctrine of "social responsibility" taken seriously would extend the scope of the political mechanism to every human activity. It does not differ in philosophy from the most explicitly collectivist doctrine. It differs only by professing to believe that collectivist ends can be attained without collectivist means. That is why, in my book "Capitalism and Freedom," I have called it a "fundamentally subversive doctrine" in a free society, and have said that in such a society, "there is one and only one social responsibility of business—to use its resources and engage in activities designed to increase its profits so long as it stays within the rules of the game, which is to say, engages in open and free competition without deception or fraud."

QUESTIONS

1. How does business benefit society by increasing its profits?

2. Can profit ever harm society, according to Friedman? What do you think?

Christopher D. Stone

Why Shouldn't Corporations Be Socially Responsible?

Business responsibility to make money)

Christopher Stone teaches law at the University of Southern California.

The opposition to corporate social responsibility comprises at least four related though separable positions. I would like to challenge the fundamental assumption that underlies all four of them. Each assumes in its own degree that the managers of the corporation are to be steered almost wholly by profit, rather than by what they think proper for society on the whole. Why should this be so? So far as ordinary morals are concerned, we often expect human beings to act in a fashion that is calculated to benefit others, rather than themselves, and commend them for it. Why should the matter be different with corporations?

THE PROMISSORY ARGUMENT

The most widespread but least persuasive arguments advanced by the "antiresponsibility" forces take the form of a moral claim based upon the corporation's supposed obligations to its shareholders. In its baldest and least tenable form, it is presented as though management's obligation rested upon the keeping of a promise—that the management of the corporation "promised" the shareholders that it would maximize the shareholders' profits. But this simply isn't so.

Consider for contrast the case where a widow left a large fortune goes to a broker, asking him to invest and manage her money so as to maximize her return. The broker, let us suppose, accepts the money and the conditions. In such a case, there would be no disagreement that the broker had made a promise to the widow, and if he invested her money in some venture that struck his fancy for any reason other than that it would increase her fortune, we would be inclined to advance a moral (as well, perhaps, as a legal) claim against him. Generally, at least, we believe in the keeping of promises; the broker, we should say, had violated a promissory obligation to the widow.

But that simple model is hardly the one that obtains between the management of major corporations and their shareholders. Few if any American shareholders ever put their money into a corporation upon the express promise of management that the company would be operated so as to maximize their returns. Indeed, few American shareholders ever put their money directly *into* a corporation at all. Most of the shares outstanding today were issued years ago and found their way to their current shareholders only circuitously. In almost all cases, the current shareholder gave his money to some prior shareholder, who, in turn, had gotten if from B, who, in turn, had gotten it from A, and so on back to the purchaser of the original issue, who, many years before, had bought the shares through an underwriting syndicate. In the course of these transactions, one of the basic elements that exists in the broker case is missing: The manager of the corporation, unlike the broker, was never even offered a chance to refuse the shareholder's "terms" (if they were that) to maximize the shareholder's profits.

There are two other observations to be made about the moral argument based on a supposed promise running from the management to the shareholders. First, even if we do infer from all the circumstances a "promise" running from the management to the shareholders, but not one, or not one of comparable weight running elsewhere (to the company's employees, customers, neighbors, etc.), we ought to keep in mind that as a moral matter (which is what we are discussing here) sometimes it is deemed morally justified to break promises (even to break the law) in the furtherance of other social interests of higher concern. Promises can advance moral arguments, by way of creating presumptions, but few of us believe that promises, per se, can end them. My promise to appear in class on time would not ordinarily justify me from refusing to give aid to a drowning man. In other words, even if management *had* made an express promise to its shareholders to "maximize your profits," (a) I am not persuaded that the ordinary person would interpret it to mean "maximize *in every way you can possibly get away with,* even if that means polluting the environment, ignoring or breaking the law"; and (b) I am not persuaded that, even if it were interpreted as so blanket a promise, most people would not suppose it ought—morally—to be broken in some cases.

Finally, even if, in the face of all these considerations, one still believes that there is an overriding, unbreakable, promise of some sort running from management to the shareholders, I do not think that it can be construed to be any stronger than one running to *existent* shareholders, arising from *their* expectations as measured by the price *they* paid. That is to say, there is nothing in the argument from promises that would wed us to a regime in which management was bound to maximize the income of shareholders. The argument might go so far as to support compensation for existent shareholders if the society chose to announce that henceforth management would have other specified obligations, thereby driving the price of shares to a lower adjustment level. All future shareholders would take with "warning" of, and a price that discounted for, the new "risks" of shareholding (i.e., the "risks" that management might put corporate resources to *pro bonum* ends).

THE AGENCY ARGUMENT

Related to the promissory argument but requiring less stretching of the facts is an argument from agency principles. Rather than trying to infer a promise by management to the shareholders, this argu-

ment is based on the idea that the shareholders designated the management their agents. This is the position advanced by Milton Friedman in his *New York Times* article. "The key point," he says, "is that . . . the manager is the agent of the individuals who own the corporation. . . ."[1]

Friedman, unfortunately, is wrong both as to the state of the law (the directors are *not* mere agents of the shareholders) and on his assumption as to the facts of corporate life (surely it is closer to the truth that in major corporations the shareholders are *not,* in any meaningful sense, selecting the directors; management is more often using its control over the proxy machinery to designate who the directors shall be, rather than the other way around).

What Friedman's argument comes down to is that for some reason the directors ought morally to consider themselves more the agents for the shareholders than for the customers, creditors, the state, or the corporation's immediate neighbors. But why? And to what extent? Throwing in terms like "principal" and "agent" begs the fundamental questions.

What is more, the "agency" argument is not only morally inconclusive, it is embarrassingly at odds with the way in which supposed "agents" actually behave. If the managers truly considered themselves the agents of the shareholders, as agents they would be expected to show an interest in determining how their principals wanted them to act—and to act accordingly. In the controversy over Dow's production of napalm, for example, one would expect, on this model, that Dow's management would have been glad to have the napalm question put to the shareholders at a shareholders' meeting. In fact, like most major companies faced with shareholder requests to include "social action" measures on proxy statements, it fought the proposal tooth and claw. It is a peculiar agency where the "agents" will go to such lengths (even spending tens of thousands of dollars of their "principals'" money in legal fees) to resist the determination of what their "principals" want.

THE ROLE ARGUMENT

An argument so closely related to the argument from promises and agency that it does not demand extensive additional remarks is a contention based upon *ease of entry* *roles to workers*

supposed considerations of *role*. Sometimes in moral discourse, as well as in law, we assign obligations to people on the basis of their having assumed some role or status, independent of any specific verbal promise they made. Such obligations are assumed to run from a captain to a seaman (and vice versa), from a doctor to a patient, or from a parent to a child. The antiresponsibility forces are on somewhat stronger grounds resting their position on this basis, because the model more nearly accords with the facts—that is, management never actually promised the shareholders that they would maximize the shareholders' investment, nor did the shareholders designate the directors their agents for this express purpose. The directors and top management are, as lawyers would say, fiduciaries. But what does this leave us? So far as the directors are fiduciaries of the shareholders in a legal sense, of course they are subject to the legal limits on fiduciaries—that is to say, they cannot engage in self-dealing, "waste" of corporate assets, and the like. But I do not understand any proresponsibility advocate to be demanding such corporate largesse as would expose the officers to legal liability; what we are talking about are expenditures on, for example, pollution control, above the amount the company is required to pay by law, but less than an amount so extravagant as to constitute a violation of these legal fiduciary duties. (Surely no court in America today would enjoin a corporation from spending more to reduce pollution than the law requires.) What is there about assuming the role of corporate officer that makes it immoral for a manager to involve a corporation in these expenditures? A father, one would think, would have stronger obligations to his children by virtue of his status than a corporate manager to the corporation's shareholders. Yet few would regard it as a compelling moral argument if a father were to distort facts about his child on a scholarship application form on the grounds that he had obligations to advance his child's career; nor would we consider it a strong moral argument if a father were to leave unsightly refuse piled on his lawn, spilling over into the street, on the plea that he had obligations to give every moment of his attention to his children, and was thus too busy to cart his refuse away.

Like the other supposed moral arguments, the one from role suffers from the problem that the strongest moral obligations one can discover have at most only prima facie force, and it is not apparent why those obligations should predominate over some contrary social obligations that could be advanced.

Then too, when one begins comparing and weighing the various moral obligations, those running back to the shareholder seem fairly weak by comparison to the claims of others. For one thing, there is the consideration of alternatives. If the shareholder is dissatisfied with the direction the corporation is taking, he can sell out, and if he does so quickly enough, his losses may be slight. On the other hand, as Ted Jacobs observes, "those most vitally affected by corporate decisions—people who work in the plants, buy the products, and consume the effluents—cannot remove themselves from the structure with a phone call."[2]

THE "POLESTAR" ARGUMENT

It seems to me that the strongest moral argument corporate executives can advance for looking solely to profits is not one that is based on a supposed express, or even implied promise to the shareholder. Rather, it is one that says, if the managers act in such fashion as to maximize profits—if they act *as though* they had promised the shareholders they would do so—then it will be best for all of us. This argument might be called the polestar argument, for its appeal to the interests of the shareholders is not justified on supposed obligations to the shareholders per se, but as a means of charting a straight course toward what is best for the society as a whole.

Underlying the polestar argument are a number of assumptions—some express and some implied. There is, I suspect, an implicit positivism among its supporters—a feeling (whether its proponents own up to it or not) that moral judgments are peculiar, arbitrary, or vague—perhaps even "meaningless" in the philosophic sense of not being amenable to rational discussion. To those who take this position, profits (or sales, or price-earnings ratios) at least provide some solid, tangible standard by which participants in the organization can measure their successes and failures, with some efficiency, in the narrow sense, resulting for the entire group. Sometimes the polestar position is based upon a related view—not that the moral issues that underlie social choices are meaningless, but that resolving them calls for special expertise. "I don't know any investment adviser whom I would care to act in my behalf in any matter except turning a profit. . . . The value of these specialists . . . lies in their limitations; they ought not allow themselves to see so much of the world that they become distracted."[3] A slightly modified point emphasizes not that the executives lack moral or social expertise per se, but that they lack the social authority to make policy choices. Thus, Friedman objects that if a corporate director took "social purposes" into account, he would become "in effect a public employee, a civil servant. . . . On grounds of political principle, it is intolerable that such civil servants . . . should be selected as they are now."[4]

I do not want to get too deeply involved in each of these arguments. That the moral judgments underlying policy choices are vague, I do not doubt—although I am tempted to observe that when you get right down to it, a wide range of actions taken by businessmen every day, supposedly based on solid calculations of "profit," are probably as rooted in hunches and intuition as judgments of ethics. I do not disagree either that, ideally, we prefer those who have control over our lives to be politically accountable; although here, too, if we were to pursue the matter in detail we would want to inspect both the premise of this argument, that corporate managers are not *presently* custodians of discretionary power over us anyway, and also its logical implications: Friedman's point that "if they are to be civil servants, then they must be selected through a political process"[5] is not, as Friedman regards it, a reductio ad absurdum—not, at any rate, to Ralph Nader and others who want publicly elected directors.

The reason for not pursuing these counterarguments at length is that, whatever reservations one might have, we can agree that there is a germ of validity to what the "antis" are saying. But their essential failure is in not pursuing the alternatives. Certainly, *to the extent* that the forces of the market and the law can keep the corporation within desirable bounds, it may be better to trust them than to have corporate managers implementing their own vague and various notions of what is best for the rest of us. But are the "antis" blind to the fact that there are circumstances in which the law—and the forces of the market—are simply not competent to keep the corporation under control? The shortcomings of these traditional restraints on corporate conduct are critical to understand, not merely for the defects they point up in the "antis'" position. More important, identifying where the traditional forces are inadequate is the first step in the design of new and alternative measures of corporate control.

NOTES

1. *New York Times,* September 12, 1962, sect. 6, p. 33, col. 2.
2. Theodore J. Jacobs, "Pollution, Consumerism, Accountability," *Center Magazine* 5, 1 (January–February 1971): 47.
3. Walter Goodman, "Stocks Without Sin," *Harper's,* August 1971, p. 66.
4. *New York Times,* September 12, 1962, sec. 6, p. 122, col. 3.
5. Ibid., p. 122, cols. 3–4.

QUESTIONS

1. What is the promissory argument?
2. Explain the agency and the role arguments. How do they differ?

Peter A. French | # Corporate Moral Agency

Peter A. French runs the Lincoln Center for Applied Ethics and teaches philosophy at Arizona State University.

1

In one of his *New York Times* columns of not too long ago Tom Wicker's ire was aroused by a Gulf Oil Corporation advertisement that "pointed the finger of blame" for the energy crisis at all elements of our society (and supposedly away from the oil company). Wicker attacked Gulf Oil as the major, if not the sole, perpetrator of that crisis and virtually every other social ill, with the possible exception of venereal disease. I do not know if Wicker was serious or sarcastic in making all of his charges; I have a sinking suspicion that he was in deadly earnest, but I have doubts as to whether Wicker understands or if many people understand what sense such ascriptions of moral responsibility make when their subjects are corporations. My interest is to argue for a theory that accepts corporations as members of the moral community, of equal standing with the traditionally acknowledged residents—biological human beings—and hence treats Wicker-type responsibility ascriptions as unexceptionable instances of a perfectly proper sort without having to paraphrase them. In short, I shall argue that corporations should be treated as full-fledged moral persons and hence that they can have whatever privileges, rights, and duties as are, in the normal course of affairs, accorded to moral persons.

2

There are at least two significantly different types of responsibility ascriptions that I want to distinguish in

ordinary usage (not counting the laudatory recommendation, "He is a responsible lad.") The first type pins responsibility on someone or something, the who-dun-it or what-dun-it sense. Austin has pointed out that it is usually used when an event or action is thought by the speaker to be untoward. (Perhaps we are more interested in the failures rather than the successes that punctuate our lives.)

The second type of responsibility ascription, parasitic upon the first, involves the notion of accountability. "Having a responsibility" is interwoven with the notion "Having a liability to answer," and having such a liability or obligation seems to imply (as Anscombe has noted) the existence of some sort of authority relationship either between people, or between people and a deity, or in some weaker versions between people and social norms. The kernel of insight that I find intuitively compelling is that for someone to legitimately hold someone else responsible for some event, there must exist or have existed a responsibility relationship between them such that in regard to the event in question the latter was answerable to the former. In other words, a responsibility ascription of the second type is properly uttered by someone Z if he or she can hold X accountable for what he or she has done. Responsibility relationships are created in a multitude of ways, e.g., through promises, contracts, compacts, hirings, assignments, appointments, by agreeing to enter a Rawlsian original position, etc. The "right" to hold responsible is often delegated to third parties; but importantly, in the case of moral responsibility, no delegation occurs because no person is excluded from the relationship: moral responsibility relationships hold reciprocally and without prior agreements among all moral persons. No special arrangement needs to be established between parties for anyone to hold someone morally responsible for his or her acts or, what amounts to the same thing, every person is a party to a responsibility relationship with all other persons as regards the doing or refraining from doing of certain acts: those that take descriptions that use moral notions.

Because our interest is in the criteria of moral personhood and not the content or morality, we need not pursue this idea further. What I have maintained is that moral responsibility, although it is neither contractual nor optional, is not a class apart but an extension of ordinary, garden-variety responsibility. What is needed in regard to the present subject, then, is an account of the requirements in *any* responsibility relationship.

3

A responsibility ascription of the second type amounts to the assertion that the person held responsible is the cause of an event (usually an untoward one) and that the action in question was intended by the subject or that the event was the direct result of an intentional act of the subject. In addition to what it asserts, it implies that the subject is liable to account to the speaker (who the speaker is or what the speaker is, a member of the "moral community," a surrogate for that aggregate). The primary focus of responsibility ascriptions of the second type is on the subject's intentions rather than, though not to the exclusion of, occasions.

4

For a corporation to be treated as a responsible agent it must be the case that some things that happen, some events, are describable in a way that makes certain sentences true, sentences that say that some of the things a corporation does were intended by the corporation itself. That is not accomplished if attributing intentions to a corporation is only a shorthand way of attributing intentions to the biological persons who comprise, for example, its board of directors. If that were to turn out to be the case, then

on metaphysical if not logical grounds there would be no way to distinguish between corporations and mobs. I shall argue, however, that a corporation's CID Structure (the *C*orporate *I*nternal *D*ecision Structure) is the requisite redescription device that licenses the predication of corporate intentionality.

It is obvious that a corporation's doing something involves or includes human beings' doing things and that the human beings who occupy various positions in a corporation usually can be described as having reasons for *their* behavior. In virtue of those descriptions they may be properly held responsible for their behavior, *ceteris paribus*. What needs to be shown is that there is sense in saying that corporations, and not just the people who work in them, have reasons for doing what they do. Typically, we will be told that it is the directors, or the managers, etc. that really have the corporate reasons and desires, etc. and that although corporate actions may not be reducible without remainder, corporate intentions are always reducible to human intentions.

5

Every corporation must have an internal decision structure. The CID Structure has two elements of interest to us here: (1) an organizational or responsibility flow chart that delineates stations and levels within the corporate power structure and (2) corporate decision recognition rule(s) (usually embedded in something called "corporate policy"). The CID Structure is the personnel organization for the exercise of the corporation's power with respect to its ventures, and as such its primary function is to draw experience from various levels of the corporation into a decision-making and ratification process. When operative and properly activated, the CID Structure accomplishes a subordination and synthesis of the intentions and acts of various biological persons into a corporate decision. When viewed in another way the CID Structure licenses the descriptive transformation of events seen under another aspect as the acts of biological persons (those who occupy various stations on the organizational chart) as corporate acts by exposing the corporate character of those events. A functioning CID Structure *incorporates* acts of biological persons. For illustrative purposes, suppose we imagine that an event E has at least two aspects, that is, can be described in two nonidentical ways. One of those aspects is "Executive X's doing *y*" and one is "Corporation C's doing *z*." The corporate act and the individual act may have different properties: indeed they have different causal ancestors though they are causally inseparable.

Although I doubt he is aware of the metaphysical reading that can be given to this process, J. K. Galbraith rather neatly captures what I have in mind when he writes in his recent popular book on the history of economics:

> From [the] interpersonal exercise of power, the interaction . . . of the participants, comes the *personality* of the corporation.[1]

I take Galbraith here to be quite literally correct, but it is important to spell out how a CID Structure works this "miracle."

In philosophy in recent years we have grown accustomed to the use of games as models for understanding institutional behavior. We all have some understanding of how rules of games make certain descriptions of events possible that would not be so if those rules were nonexistent. The CID Structure of a corporation is a kind of constitutive rule (or rules) analogous to the game rules with which we are familiar. The organization chart of, for example, the Burlington Northern Corporation distinguishes "players" and clarifies their rank and the interwoven lines of responsibility within the corporation. The Burlington chart lists only titles, not unlike King, Queen, Rook, etc. in chess. What it tells us is that anyone holding the title "Executive Vice President for Finance and Administration" stands in a certain relationship to anyone holding the title "Director of Internal Audit" and to anyone holding the title "Treasurer," etc. Also it expresses, or maps, the interdependent and dependent relationships that are involved in determinations of corporate decisions and actions. In effect, it tells us what anyone who occupies any of the positions is vis-à-vis the decision structure of the whole. The organizational chart provides what might be called the grammar of corporate decision-making. What I shall call internal recognition rules provide its logic.[2]

Recognition rules are of two sorts. Partially embedded in the organizational chart are the procedural recognitors: we see that decisions are to be reached collectively at certain levels and that they are to be ratified at higher levels (or at inner circles, if one prefers the Galbraithean model). A corporate decision is recognized internally not only by the procedure of its making, but by the policy it instantiates. Hence every corporation creates an image (not to be confused with its public image) or a general policy, what G. C. Buzby of the Chilton Company has called the "basic belief of the corporation,"[3] that must inform its decisions for them to be properly described as being those of that corporation. "The moment policy is side-stepped or violated it is no longer the policy of that company."[4]

Peter Drucker has seen the importance of the basic policy recognitors in the CID Structure (though he treats matters rather differently from the way I am recommending). Drucker writes:

> Because the corporation is an institution it must have a basic policy. For it must subordinate individual ambitions and decisions to the *needs* of the corporation's welfare and survival. That means that it must have a set of principles and a rule of conduct which limit and direct individual actions and behavior.[5]

6

Suppose, for illustrative purposes, we activate a CID Structure in a corporation, Wicker's favorite, the Gulf Oil Corporation. Imagine then that three executives X, Y, and Z have the task of deciding whether or not Gulf Oil will join a world uranium cartel (I trust this may catch Mr. Wicker's attention and hopefully also that of Jerry McAfee, current Gulf Oil Corporation president). X, Y, and Z have before them an Everest of papers that have been prepared by lower echelon executives. Some of the reports will be purely factual in nature, some will be contingency plans, some will be in the form of position papers developed by various departments, some will outline financial considerations, some will be legal opinions, and so on. Insofar as these will all have been processed through Gulf's CID Structure system, the personal reasons, if any, individual executives may have had when writing their reports and recommendations in a specific way will have been diluted by the subordination of individual inputs to peer group input even before X, Y, and Z review the matter. X, Y, and Z take a vote. Their taking of a vote is authorized procedure in the Gulf CID Structure, which is to say that under these circumstances the vote of X, Y, and Z can be redescribed as the corporation's making a decision: that is, the event "X Y Z voting" may be redescribed to expose an aspect otherwise unrevealed, that is quite different from its other aspects, e.g., from X's voting in the affirmative.

But the CID Structure, as already suggested, also provides the grounds in its nonprocedural recognitor for such an attribution of corporate intentionality. Simply, when the corporate act is consistent with the implementation of established corporate policy, then it is proper to describe it as having been done for corporate reasons, as having been caused by a corporate desire coupled with a corporate belief and so, in other words, as corporate intentional.

An event may, under one of its aspects, be described as the conjunctive act "X did a (or as X intentionally did a) and Y did a (or as Y intentionally did a) and Z did a (or as Z intentionally did a)" (where a = voted in the affirmative on the question of Gulf Oil joining the cartel). Given the Gulf CID Structure—formulated in this instance as the conjunction of rules: when the occupants of positions A, B, and C on the organizational chart unanimously vote to do something and if doing that something is consistent with an implementation of general corporate policy, other things being equal, then the corporation has decided to do it for corporate reasons—the event is redescribable as "the Gulf Oil Corporation did j for corporate reasons f" (where j is "decided to join the cartel" and f is any reason [desire + belief] consistent with basic policy of Gulf Oil, e.g., increasing profits) or simply as "Gulf Oil Corporation intentionally did j." This is a rather technical way of saying that in these circumstances the executives voting are, given its CID Structure, also the corporation

deciding to do something, and that regardless of the personal reasons the executives have for voting as they do, and even if their reasons are inconsistent with established corporate policy or even if one of them has no reason at all for voting as he does, the corporation still has reasons for joining the cartel; that is, joining is consistent with the inviolate corporate general policies as encrusted in the precedent of previous corporate actions and its statements of purpose as recorded in its certificate of incorporation, annual reports, etc. The corporation's only method of achieving its desires or goals is the activation of the personnel who occupy its various positions. However, if X voted affirmatively purely for reasons of personal monetary gain (suppose he had been bribed to do so), that does not alter the fact that the corporate reason for joining the cartel was to minimize competition and hence pay higher dividends to its shareholders. Corporations have reasons because they have interests in doing those things that are likely to result in realization of their established corporate goals regardless of the transient self-interest of directors, managers, etc. If there is a difference between corporate goals and desires and those of human beings, it is probably that the corporate ones are relatively stable and not very wide ranging, but that is only because corporations can do relatively fewer things than human beings, being confined in action predominately to a limited socioeconomic sphere. It is, of course, in a corporation's interest that its component membership view the corporate purposes as instrumental in the achievement of their own goals. (Financial reward is the most common way this is achieved.)

It will be objected that a corporation's policies reflect only the current goals of its directors. But that is certainly not logically necessary nor is it in practice totally true for most large corporations. Usually, of course, the original incorporators will have organized to further their individual interests and/or to meet goals which they shared. But even in infancy the melding of disparate interests and purposes gives rise to a corporate long-range point of view that is distinct from the intents and purposes of the collection of incorporators viewed individually. Also corporate basic purposes and policies, as already mentioned, tend to be relatively stable when compared to those of individuals and not couched in the kind of language that would be appropriate to individual purposes. Furthermore, as histories of corporations will show, when policies are amended or altered it is usually only peripheral issues and matters of style that are involved. Radical policy alteration constitutes a new corporation. This point is captured in the incorporation laws of such states as Delaware. ("Any power which is not enumerated in the charter or which cannot be inferred from it is *ultra vires* (beyond the legal competence) of the corporation.") Obviously underlying the objection is an uneasiness about the fact that corporate intent is dependent upon policy and purpose that is but an artifact of the sociopsychology of a group of biological persons. Corporate intent seems somehow to be a tarnished, illegitimate, offspring of human intent. But this objection is a form of the anthropocentric bias that pervades traditional moral theory. By concentrating on possible descriptions of events and by acknowledging only that the possibility of describing something as an agent depends upon whether or not it can be properly described as having done something for a reason, we avoid the temptation of trying to reduce all agents to human referents.

The CID Structure licenses redescriptions of events as corporate and attributions of corporate intentionality while it does not obscure the private acts of executives, directors, etc. Although X voted to support the joining of the cartel because he was bribed to do so, X did not join the cartel: Gulf Oil Corporation joined the cartel. Consequently, we may say that X did something for which he should be held morally responsible, yet whether or not Gulf Oil Corporation should be held morally responsible for joining the cartel is a question that turns on issues that may be unrelated to X's having accepted a bribe.

Of course Gulf Oil Corporation cannot join the cartel unless X or somebody who occupies position A on the organization chart votes in the affirmative. What that shows, however, is that corporations are collectivities. That should not, however, rule out the possibility of their having metaphysical status and being thereby full-fledged moral persons.

This much seems to me clear: We can describe many events in terms of certain physical movements of human beings and we also can sometimes describe those events as done for reasons by those human beings, but further we also can sometimes describe those events as corporate and still further as done for corporate reasons that are qualitatively different from whatever personal reasons, if any, component members may have for doing what they do.

Corporate agency resides in the possibility of CID Structure licensed redescription of events as corporate intentional. That may still appear to be downright mysterious, although I do not think it is, for human agency, as I have suggested, resides in the possibility of description as well. On the basis of the foregoing analysis, however, I think that grounds have been provided for holding corporations *per se* to account for what they do, for treating them as metaphysical persons *qua* moral persons.

A. A. Berle has written:

> The medieval feudal power system set the "lords spiritual" over and against the "lords temporal." These were the men of learning and of the church who in theory were able to say to the greatest power in the world: "You have committed a sin; therefore either you are excommunicated or you must mend your ways." The lords temporal could reply: "I can kill you." But the lords spiritual could retort: "Yes that you can, but you cannot change the philosophical fact." In a sense this is the great lacuna in the economic power system today.[6]

I have tried to fill that gap by providing reasons for thinking that the moral world is not necessarily composed of homogeneous entities. It is sobering to keep in mind that the Gulf Oil Corporation certainly knows what "You are held responsible for payment in full of the amount recorded on your statement" means. I hope I have provided the beginnings of a basis for an understanding of what "The Gulf Oil Corporation should be held responsible for destroying the ecological balance of the bay" means.

NOTES

1. John Kenneth Galbraith, *The Age of Uncertainty* (Boston: Houghton Mifflin, 1977), p. 261.

2. By "recognition rule(s)" I mean what Hart, in another context, calls "conclusive affirmative indication" that a decision on act has been made or performed for corporate reasons. H. L. A. Hart, *The Concept of Law* (Oxford: Clarendon Press, 1961), Chap. VI.

3. G. C. Buzby, "Policies—A Guide to What a Company Stands For," *Management Record* (March 1962), p. 5.

4. Ibid.

5. Peter Drucker, *Concept of the Corporation* (New York: John Day Co., 1946/1972), pp. 36–37.

6. A. A. Berle, "Economic Power and the Free Society," *The Corporate Take-Over,* ed. Andrew Hacker (Garden City, N.Y.: Doubleday, 1964), p. 99.

QUESTIONS

1. Explain French's idea that corporations should be treated as full-fledged moral persons. What motivates this argument? What are his goals? What problems may this account provoke?

2. How do internal decisions structures influence his account? Explain the significance of the CID.

R. Edward Freeman | # A Stakeholder Theory of the Modern Corporation

R. Edward Freeman teaches business ethics at the University of Virginia.

INTRODUCTION

Corporations have ceased to be merely legal devices through which the private business transactions of individuals may be carried on. Though still much used for this purpose, the corporate form has acquired a larger significance. The corporation has, in fact, become both a method of property tenure and a means of organizing economic life. Grown to tremendous proportions, there may be said to have evolved a "corporate system"—which has attracted to itself a combination of attributes and powers, and has attained a degree of prominence entitling it to be dealt with as a major social institution.

—A. Berle and G. Means, The Modern Corporation
                                        and Private Property

Despite these prophetic words of Berle and Means (1932), scholars and managers alike continue to hold sacred the view that managers bear a special relationship to the stockholders in the firm.[1] Since stockholders own shares in the firm, they have certain rights and privileges, which must be granted to them by management, as well as by others. Sanctions, in the form of "the law of corporations," and other protective mechanisms in the form of social custom, accepted management practice, myth, and ritual, are thought to reinforce the assumption of the primacy of the stockholder.

The purpose of this paper is to pose several challenges to this assumption, from within the framework of managerial capitalism, and to suggest the bare bones of an alternative theory, *a stakeholder theory of the modern corporation.* I do not seek the demise of the modern corporation, either intellectually or in fact. Rather, I seek its transformation. In the words of Neurath, we shall attempt to "rebuild the ship, plank by plank, while it remains afloat."[2]

My thesis is that I can revitalize the concept of managerial capitalism by replacing the notion that managers have a duty to stockholders with the concept that managers bear a fiduciary relationship to

From Norman E. Bowie and Thomas L. Beauchamp, eds., *Ethical Theory and Business,* (Englewood Cliffs, NJ: Prentice Hall, 1994), 66–74.

stakeholders. Stakeholders are those groups who have a stake in or claim on the firm. Specifically I include suppliers, customers, employees, stockholders, and the local community, as well as management in its role as agent for these groups. I argue that the legal, economic, political, and moral challenges to the currently received theory of the firm, as a nexus of contracts among the owners of the factors of production and customers, require us to revise this concept. That is, each of these stakeholder groups has a right not to be treated as a means to some end, and therefore must participate in determining the future direction of the firm in which they have a stake.

The crux of my argument is that we must reconceptualize the firm around the following question: For whose benefit and at whose expense should the firm be managed? I shall set forth such a reconceptualization in the form of a *stakeholder theory of the firm*. I shall then critically examine the stakeholder view and its implications for the future of the capitalist system.

THE ATTACK ON MANAGERIAL CAPITALISM

The Legal Argument

The basic idea of managerial capitalism is that in return for controlling the firm, management vigorously pursues the interests of stockholders. Central to the managerial view of the firm is the idea that management can pursue market transactions with suppliers and customers in an unconstrained manner.

The law of corporations gives a less clearcut answer to the question: In whose interest and for whose benefit should the modern corporation be governed? While it says that the corporations should be run primarily in the interests of the stockholders in the firm, it says further that the corporation exists "in contemplation of the law" and has personality as a "legal person," limited liability for its actions, and immortality, since its existence transcends that of its members. Therefore, directors and other officers of the firm have a fiduciary obligation to stockholders in the sense that the "affairs of the corporation" must be conducted in the interest of the stockholders. And stockholders can theoretically bring suit against

those directors and managers for doing otherwise. But since the corporation is a legal person, existing in contemplation of the law, managers of the corporation are constrained by law.

Until recently, this was no constraint at all. In this century, however, the law has evolved to effectively constrain the pursuit of stockholder interests at the expense of other claimants on the firm. It has, in effect, required that the claims of customers, suppliers, local communities, and employees be taken into consideration, though in general they are subordinated to the claims of stockholders.

For instance, the doctrine of "privity of contract," as articulated in *Winterbottom v. Wright* in 1842, has been eroded by recent developments in products liability law. Indeed, *Greenman v. Yuba Power* gives the manufacturer strict liability for damage caused by its products, even though the seller has exercised all possible care in the preparation and sale of the product and the consumer has not bought the product from nor entered into any contractual arrangement with the manufacturer. Caveat emptor has been replaced, in large part, with caveat venditor. The Consumer Product Safety Commission has the power to enact product recalls, and in 1980 one U.S. automobile company recalled more cars than it built. Some industries are required to provide information to customers about a product's ingredients, whether or not the customers want and are willing to pay for this information.

The same argument is applicable to management's dealings with employees. The National Labor Relations Act gave employees the right to unionize and to bargain in good faith. It set up the National Labor Relations Board to enforce these rights with management. The Equal Pay Act of 1963 and Title VII of the Civil Rights Act of 1964 constrain management from discrimination in hiring practices; these have been followed with the Age Discrimination in Employment Act of 1967. The emergence of a body of administrative case law arising from labor-management disputes and the historic settling of discrimination claims with large employers such as AT&T have caused the emergence of a body of practice in the corporation that is consistent with the legal guarantee of the rights of the employees. The law has protected the due process rights of those employees who enter into collective bargaining agreements with management. As of the present, however, only 30 percent of the labor force are participating in such agreements; this has prompted one labor law scholar to propose a statutory law prohibiting dismissals of the 70 percent of the work force not protected.

The law has also protected the interests of local communities. The Clean Air Act and Clean Water Act have constrained management from "spoiling the commons." In an historic case, *Marsh v. Alabama,* the Supreme Court ruled that a company-owned town was subject to the provisions of the U.S. Constitution, thereby guaranteeing the rights of local citizens and negating the "property rights" of the firm. Some states and municipalities have gone further and passed laws preventing firms from moving plants or limiting when and how plants can be closed. In sum, there is much current legal activity in this area to constrain management's pursuit of stockholders' interests at the expense of the local communities in which the firm operates.

I have argued that the result of such changes in the legal system can be viewed as giving some rights to those groups that have a claim on the firm, for example, customers, suppliers, employees, local communities, stockholders, and management. It raises the question, at the core of a theory of the firm: In whose interest and for whose benefit should the firm be managed? The answer proposed by managerial capitalism is clearly "the stockholders," but I have argued that the law has been progressively circumscribing this answer.

The Economic Argument

In its pure ideological form managerial capitalism seeks to maximize the interests of stockholders. In its perennial criticism of government regulation, management espouses the "invisible hand" doctrine. It contends that it creates the greatest good for the greatest number, and therefore government need not intervene. However, we know that externalities, moral hazards, and monopoly power exist in fact, whether or not they exist in theory. Further, some of the legal apparatus mentioned above has evolved to deal with just these issues.

The problem of the "tragedy of the commons" or the free-rider problem pervades the concept of public

goods such as water and air. No one has an incentive to incur the cost of clean-up or the cost of nonpollution, since the marginal gain of one firm's action is small. Every firm reasons this way, and the result is pollution of water and air. Since the industrial revolution, firms have sought to internalize the benefits and externalize the costs of their actions. The cost must be borne by all, through taxation and regulation; hence we have the emergence of the environmental regulations of the 1970s.

Similarly, moral hazards arise when the purchaser of a good or service can pass along the cost of that good. There is no incentive to economize, on the part of either the producer or the consumer, and there is excessive use of the resources involved. The institutionalized practice of third-party payment in health care is a prime example.

Finally, we see the avoidance of competitive behavior on the part of firms, each seeking to monopolize a small portion of the market and not compete with one another. In a number of industries, oligopolies have emerged, and while there is questionable evidence that oligopolies are not the most efficient corporate form in some industries, suffice it to say that the potential for abuse of market power has again led to regulation of managerial activity. In the classic case, AT&T, arguably one of the great technological and managerial achievements of the century, was broken up into eight separate companies to prevent its abuse of monopoly power.

Externalities, moral hazards, and monopoly power have led to more external control on managerial capitalism. There are de facto constraints, due to these economic facts of life, on the ability of management to act in the interests of stockholders.

A STAKEHOLDER THEORY OF THE FIRM

The Stakeholder Concept

Corporations have stakeholders, that is, groups and individuals who benefit from or are harmed by, and whose rights are violated or respected by, corporate actions. The concept of stakeholders is a generalization of the notion of stockholders, who themselves have some special claim on the firm. Just as stockholders have a right to demand certain actions by management, so do other stakeholders have a right to make claims. The exact nature of these claims is a difficult question that I shall address, but the logic is identical to that of the stockholder theory. Stakes require action of a certain sort, and conflicting stakes require methods of resolution.

Freeman and Reed distinguish two senses of *stakeholder*. The "narrow definition" includes those groups who are vital to the survival and success of the corporation. The "wide-definition" includes any group or individual who can affect or is affected by the corporation. I shall begin with a modest aim: to articulate a stakeholder theory using the narrow definition.

Stakeholders in the Modern Corporation

Figure 1 depicts the stakeholders in a typical large corporation. The stakes of each are reciprocal, since each can affect the other in terms of harms and benefits as well as rights and duties. The stakes of each are not univocal and would vary by particular corporation. I merely set forth some general notions that seem to be common to many large firms.

Owners have financial stake in the corporation in the form of stocks, bonds, and so on, and they expect some kind of financial return from them. Either they have given money directly to the firm, or they have some historical claim made through a series of morally justified exchanges. The firm affects their livelihood or, if a substantial portion of their retirement income is in stocks or bonds, their ability to care for themselves when they can no longer work. Of course, the stakes of owners will differ by type of owner, preferences for money, moral preferences, and so on, as well as by type of firm. The owners of AT&T are quite different from the owners of Ford Motor Company, with stock of the former company being widely dispersed among 3 million stockholders and that of the latter being held by a small family group as well as by a large group of public stockholders.

Employees have their jobs and usually their livelihood at stake; they often have specialized skills for which there is usually no perfectly elastic market. In return for their labor, they expect security, wages, benefits, and meaningful work. In return for their loyalty, the corporation is expected to provide for them and carry them through difficult times. Employees are expected to follow the instructions of management most of the time, to speak favorably about the company, and to be responsible citizens in the local communities in which the company operates. Where they are used as means to an end, they must participate in decisions affecting such use. The evidence that such policies and values as described here lead to productive company-employee relationships is compelling. It is equally compelling to realize that the opportunities for "bad faith" on the part of both management and employees are enormous. "Mock participation" in quality circles, singing the company song, and wearing the company uniform solely to please management all lead to distrust and unproductive work.

Suppliers, interpreted in a stakeholder sense, are vital to the success of the firm, for raw materials will determine the final product's quality and price. In turn the firm is a customer of the supplier and is therefore vital to the success and survival of the supplier. When the firm treats the supplier as a valued member of the stakeholder network, rather than simply as a source of materials, the supplier will respond when the firm is in need. Chrysler traditionally had very close ties to its suppliers, even to the extent that led some to suspect the transfer of illegal payments. And when Chrysler was on the brink of disaster, the suppliers responded with price cuts, accepting late payments, financing, and so on. Supplier and company can rise and fall together. Of course, again, the particular supplier relationships will depend on a number of variables such as the number of suppliers and whether the supplies are finished goods or raw materials.

Customers exchange resources for the products of the firm and in return receive the benefits of the products. Customers provide the lifeblood of the firm in the form of revenue. Given the level of reinvestment of earnings in large corporations, customers indirectly pay for the development of new products and services. Peters and Waterman have argued that being close to the customer leads to success with other stakeholders and that a distinguishing charac-

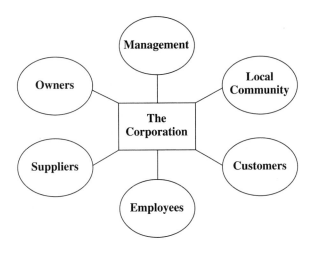

Figure 1   A stakeholder model of the corporation.

teristic of some companies that have performed well is their emphasis on the customer. By paying attention to customers' needs, management automatically addresses the needs of suppliers and owners. Moreover, it seems that the ethic of customer service carries over to the community. Almost without fail the "excellent companies" in Peters and Waterman's study have good reputations in the community. I would argue that Peters and Waterman have found multiple applications of Kant's dictum, "Treat persons as ends unto themselves," and it should come as no surprise that persons respond to such respectful treatment, be they customers, suppliers, owners, employees, or members of the local community. The real surprise is the novelty of the application of Kant's rule in a theory of good management practice.

The local community grants the firm the right to build facilities and, in turn, it benefits from the tax base and economic and social contributions of the firm. In return for the provision of local services, the firm is expected to be a good citizen, as is any person, either "natural or artificial." The firm cannot expose the community to unreasonable hazards in the form of pollution, toxic waste, and so on. If for some reason the firm must leave a community, it is expected to work with local leaders to make the transition as smoothly as possible. Of course, the firm does not have perfect knowledge, but when it discovers some danger or runs afoul of new competition, it is expected to inform the local community and to work with the community to overcome any problem. When the firm mismanages its relationship with the local community, it is in the same position as a citizen who commits a crime. It has violated the implicit social contract with the community and should expect to be distrusted and ostracized. It should not be surprised when punitive measures are invoked.

I have not included "competitors" as stakeholders in the narrow sense, since strictly speaking they are not necessary for the survival and success of the firm; the stakeholder theory works equally well in monopoly contexts. However, competitors and government would be the first to be included in an extension of this basic theory. It is simply not true that the interests of competitors in an industry are always in conflict. There is no reason why trade associations and other multi-organizational groups cannot band together to solve common problems that have little to do with how to restrain trade. Implementation of stakeholder management principles, in the long run, mitigates the need for industrial policy and an increasing role for government intervention and regulation.

The Role of Management

Management plays a special role, for it too has a stake in the modern corporation. On the one hand, management's stake is like that of employees, with some kind of explicit or implicit employment contract. But, on the other hand, management has a duty of safeguarding the welfare of the abstract entity that is the corporation. In short, management, especially top management, must look after the health of the corporation, and this involves balancing the multiple claims of conflicting stakeholders. Owners want higher financial returns, while customers want more money spent on research and development. Employees want higher wages and better benefits, while the local community wants better parks and day-care facilities.

The task of management in today's corporation is akin to that of King Solomon. The stakeholder theory does not give primacy to one stakeholder group over another, though there will surely be times when one group will benefit at the expense of others. In general, however, management must keep the relationships among stakeholders in balance. When these relationships become imbalanced, the survival of the firm is in jeopardy.

When wages are too high and product quality is too low, customers leave, suppliers suffer, and owners sell their stocks and bonds, depressing the stock price and making it difficult to raise new capital at favorable rates. Note, however, that the reason for paying returns to owners is not that they "own" the firm, but that their support is necessary for the survival of the firm, and that they have a legitimate claim on the firm. Similar reasoning applies in turn to each stakeholder group.

A stakeholder theory of the firm must redefine the purpose of the firm. The stockholder theory claims that the purpose of the firm is to maximize the welfare of the stockholders, perhaps subject to some moral or social constraints, either because such maximization leads to the greatest good or because of property rights. The purpose of the firm is quite different in my view.

"The stakeholder theory" can be unpacked into a number of stakeholder theories, each of which has a "normative core," inextricably linked to the way that corporations should be governed and the way that managers should act. So, attempts to more fully define, or more carefully define, a stakeholder theory are misguided. Following Donaldson and Preston, I want to insist that the normative, descriptive, instrumental, and metaphorical (my addition to their framework) uses of 'stakeholder' are tied together in particular political constructions to yield a number of possible "stakeholder theories." "Stakeholder theory" is thus a genre of stories about how we could live. Let me be more specific.

A "normative core" of a theory is a set of sentences that includes among others, sentences like:

(1) Corporations ought to be governed . . .
(2) Managers ought to act to . . .

where we need arguments or further narratives which include business and moral terms to fill in the blanks. This normative core is not always reducible to a fundamental ground like the theory of property, but certain normative cores are consistent with modern understandings of property. Certain elaborations of the theory of private property plus the other institutions of political liberalism give rise to particular normative cores. But there are other institutions, other political conceptions of how society ought to be structured, so that there are different possible normative cores.

So, one normative core of a stakeholder theory might be a feminist standpoint one, rethinking how we would restructure "value-creating activity" along principles of caring and connection. Another would be an ecological (or several ecological) normative cores. . . .

If we begin with the view that we can understand value-creation activity as a contractual process among those parties affected, and if for simplicity's sake we initially designate those parties as financiers, customers, suppliers, employees, and communities, then we can construct a normative core that reflects the liberal notions of autonomy, solidarity, and fairness as articulated by John Rawls, Richard Rorty, and others. Notice that building these moral notions into the foundations of how we understand value creation and contracting requires that we eschew separating the "business" part of the process from the "ethical" part, and that we start with the presumption of equality among the contractors, rather than the presumption in favor of financier rights.

The normative core for this redesigned contractual theory will capture the liberal idea of fairness if it ensures a basic equality among stakeholders in terms of their moral rights as these are realized in the firm, and if it recognizes that inequalities among stakeholders are justified if they raise the level of the least well-off stakeholder. The liberal ideal of auton-omy is captured by the realization that each stakeholder must be free to enter agreements that create value for themselves, and solidarity is realized by the recognition of the mutuality of stakeholder interests.

QUESTIONS

1. What is a stakeholder? What is the stakeholder's role in guiding the corporation?

2. How and why do "corporate systems" complicate the moral responsibility of the corporation?

Kenneth J. Arrow

Social Responsibility and Economic Efficiency

Kenneth J. Arrow is Professor Emeritus at Stanford University and one of the most prominent economic theorists of the twentieth century.

Let us first consider the case against social responsibility: the assumption that the firms should aim simply to maximize their profits. One strand of that argument is empirical rather than ethical or normative. It simply states that firms *will* maximize their profits. The impulse to gain, it is argued, is very strong and the incentives for selfish behavior are so great that any kind of control is likely to be utterly ineffectual. This argument has some force but is by no means conclusive. Any mechanism for enforcing or urging social responsibility upon firms must of course reckon with a profit motive, with a desire to evade whatever response of controls is imposed. But it does not mean that we cannot expect any degree of responsibility at all.

One finds a rather different argument, frequently stated by some economists. It will probably strike the noneconomist as rather strange, at least at first hearing. The assertion is that firms *ought* to maximize profits; not merely do they like to do so but there is practically a social obligation to do so. Let me briefly sketch the argument:

Firms buy the goods and services they need for production. What they buy they pay for and therefore they are paying for whatever costs they impose upon others. What they receive in payment by selling their goods, they receive because the purchaser considers it worthwhile. This is a world of voluntary contracts; nobody *has* to buy the goods. If he chooses to buy it, it must be that he is getting a benefit measured by the price he pays. Hence, it is argued, profit really represents the net contribution that the firm makes to the social good, and the profits should therefore be made as large as possible. When firms compete with each other, in selling their goods or in buying labor or other services, they may have to lower their selling prices in order to get more of the market for themselves or raise their wages; in either case the benefits which the firm is deriving are in some respects shared with the popu-

Kenneth J. Arrow, "Social Responsibility and Economic Efficiency," *Public Policy* 21 (Summer 1973). Reprinted by permission.

lation at large. The forces of competition prevent the firms from engrossing too large a share of the social benefit. Now, as far as it goes this argument is sound. The problem is that it may not go far enough.

Under the proper assumptions profit maximization is indeed efficient in the sense that it can achieve as high a level of satisfaction as possible for any one consumer without reducing the levels of satisfaction of other consumers or using more resources than society is endowed with. But the limits of the argument must be stressed. I want to mention two well-known points in passing without making them the principal focus of discussion. First of all, the argument assumes that the forces of competition are sufficiently vigorous. But there is no social justification for profit maximization by monopolies. This is an important and well-known qualification. Second, the distribution of income that results from unrestrained profit maximization is very unequal. The competitive maximizing economy is indeed efficient—this shows up in high average incomes—but the high average is accompanied by widespread poverty on the one hand and vast riches, at least for a few, on the other. To many of us this is a very undesirable consequence.

Profit maximization has yet another effect on society. It tends to point away from the expression of altruistic motives. Altruistic motives are motives whose gratification is just as legitimate as selfish motives, and the expression of those motives is something we probably wish to encourage. A profit-maximizing, self-centered form of economic behavior does not provide any room for the expression of such motives.

———

[Even] if the three problems above were set aside . . . there are [still] two categories of effects where the arguments for profit maximization break down: The first is illustrated by pollution or congestion. Here it is no longer true (and this is the key to these issues) that the firm in fact does pay for the harm it imposes on others. When it takes a person's time and uses it at work, the firm is paying for this, and therefore the transaction can be regarded as a beneficial exchange from the point of view of both parties. We have no similar mechanism by which the pollu-

tion which a firm imposes upon its neighborhood is paid for. Therefore the firm will have a tendency to pollute more than is desirable. That is, the benefit to it or to its customers from the expanded activity is really not as great, or may not be as great, as the cost it is imposing upon the neighborhood. But since it does not pay that cost, there is no profit incentive to refrain.

The same argument applies to traffic congestion when no charge is made for the addition of cars or trucks on the highway. It makes everybody less comfortable. It delays others and increases the probability of accidents; in short, it imposes a cost upon a large number of members of the society, a cost which is not paid for by the imposer of the cost, at least not in full. The person congesting is also congested, but the costs he is imposing on others are much greater than those he suffers himself. Therefore there will be a tendency to overutilize those goods for which no price is charged, particularly scarce highway space.

There are many other examples of this kind, but these two will serve to illustrate the point in question: some effort must be made to alter the profit-maximizing behavior of firms in those cases where it is imposing costs on others which are not easily compensated through an appropriate set of prices.

The second category of effects where profit maximization is not socially desirable is that in which there are quality effects about which the firm knows more than the buyer. Let me illustrate by considering the sale of a used car. (Similar considerations apply to the sale of new cars.) A used car has potential defects and typically the seller knows more about the defects than the buyer. The buyer is not in a position to distinguish among used cars, and therefore he will be willing to pay the same amount for two used cars of differing quality because he cannot tell the difference between them. As a result, there is an inefficiency in the sale of used cars. If somehow or other the cars were distinguished as to their quality, there would be some buyers who would prefer a cheaper car with more defects because they intend to use it very little or they only want it for a short period, while others will want a better car at a higher price. In fact, however, the two kinds of car are sold indiscriminately to the two groups of buyers at the same price, so that we can argue that there is a distinct loss of consumer satisfaction imposed by the failure to convey information that is available to the seller. The buyers are not necessarily being cheated. They may be, but the problem of inefficiency would remain if they weren't. One can imagine a situation where, from past experience, buyers of used cars are aware that cars that look alike may turn out to be quite different. Without knowing whether a particular car is good or bad, they do know that there are good and bad cars, and of course their willingness to pay for the cars is influenced accordingly. The main loser from a monetary viewpoint may not be the customer, but rather the seller of the good car. The buyer will pay a price which is only appropriate to a lottery that gives him a good car or a bad car with varying probabilities, and therefore the seller of the good car gets less than the value of the car. The seller of the bad car is, of course, the beneficiary. Clearly then, if one could arrange to transmit the truth from the sellers to the buyers, the efficiency of the market would be greatly improved. The used-car illustration is an example of a very general phenomenon. . . .

Defenders of unrestricted profit maximization usually assume that the consumer is well informed or at least that he becomes so by his own experience, in repeated purchases, or by information about what has happened to other people like him. This argument is empirically shaky; even the ability of individuals to analyze the effects of their own past purchases may be limited, particularly with respect to complicated mechanisms. But there are two further defects. The risks, including death, may be so great that even one misleading experience is bad enough, and the opportunity to learn from repeated trials is not of much use. Also, in a world where the products are continually changing, the possibility of learning from experience is greatly reduced. Automobile companies are continually introducing new models which at least purport to differ from what they were in the past, though doubtless the change is more external than internal. New drugs are being introduced all the time; the fact that one has had bad experiences with one drug may provide very little information about the next one.

Thus there are two types of situation in which the simple rule of maximizing profits is socially inefficient: the case in which costs are not paid for, as in

pollution, and the case in which the seller has considerably more knowledge about his product than the buyer, particularly with regard to safety. In these situations it is clearly desirable to have some idea of social responsibility, that is, to experience an obligation, whether ethical, moral, or legal. Now we cannot expect such an obligation to be created out of thin air. To be meaningful, any obligation of this kind, any feeling or rule of behavior has to be embodied in some definite social institution. I use that term broadly: a legal code is a social institution in a sense. Exhortation to do good must be made specific in some external form, a steady reminder and perhaps enforcer of desirable values. Part of the need is simply for factual information as a guide to individual behavior. A firm may need to be told what is right and what is wrong when in fact it is polluting, or which safety requirements are reasonable and which are too extreme or too costly to be worth consideration. Institutionalization of the social responsibility of firms also serves another very important function. It provides some assurance to any one firm that the firms with which it is in competition will also accept the same responsibility. If a firm has some code imposed from the outside, there is some expectation that other firms will obey it too and therefore there is some assurance that it need not fear any excessive cost to its good behavior.

———————

Let me turn to some alternative kinds of institutions that can be considered as embodying the possible social responsibilities of firms. First, we have legal regulation, as in the case of pollution where laws are passed about the kind of burning that may take place, and about setting maximum standards for emissions. A second category is that of taxes. Economists, with good reason, like to preach taxation as opposed to regulation. The movement to tax polluting emissions is getting under way and there is a fairly widely backed proposal in Congress to tax sulfur dioxide emissions from industrial smokestacks. That is an example of the second kind of institutionalization of social responsibility. The responsibility is made very clear: the violator pays for violations.

A third very old remedy or institution is that of

legal liability—the liability of the civil law. One can be sued for damages. Such cases apparently go back to the Middle Ages. Regulation also extends back very far. There was an ordinance in London about the year 1300 prohibiting the burning of coal, because of the smoke nuisance.

The fourth class of institutions is represented by ethical codes. Restraint is achieved not by appealing to each individual's conscience but rather by having some generally understood definition of appropriate behavior. . . . [w]hen there is a wide difference in knowledge between the two sides of the market, recognized ethical codes can be a great contribution to economic efficiency. Actually we do have examples of this in our everyday lives, but in very limited areas. The case of medical ethics is the most striking. By its very nature there is a very large difference in knowledge between the buyer and the seller. One is, in fact, buying precisely the service of someone with much more knowledge than you have. To make this relationship a viable one, ethical codes have grown up over the centuries, both to avoid the possibility of exploitation by the physician and to assure the buyer of medical services that he is not being exploited. I am not suggesting that these are universally obeyed, but there is a strong presumption that the doctor is going to perform to a large extent with your welfare in mind. Unnecessary medical expenses or other abuses are perceived as violations of ethics. There is a powerful ethical background against which we make this judgment. Behavior that we would regard as highly reprehensible in a physician is judged less harshly when found among businessmen. The medical profession is typical of professions in general. All professions involve a situation in which knowledge is unequal on two sides of the market by the very definition of the profession, and therefore there have grown up ethical principles that afford some protection to the client. Notice there is a mutual benefit in this. The fact is that if you had sufficient distrust of a doctor's services, you wouldn't buy them. Therefore the physician wants an ethical code to act as assurance to the buyer, and he certainly wants his competitors to obey this same code, partly because any violation may put him at a disadvantage but more especially because the vio-

lation will reflect on him, since the buyer of the medical services may not be able to distinguish one doctor from another. A close look reveals that a great deal of economic life depends for its viability on a certain limited degree of ethical commitment. Purely selfish behavior of individuals is really incompatible with any kind of settled economic life. There is almost invariably some element of trust and confidence. Much business is done on the basis of verbal assurance. It would be too elaborate to try to get written commitments on every possible point. Every contract depends for its observance on a mass of unspecified conditions which suggest that the performance will be carried out in good faith without insistence on sticking literally to its wording. To put the matter in its simplest form, in almost every economic transaction, in any exchange of goods for money, somebody gives up his valuable asset before he gets the other's; either the goods are given before the money or the money is given before the goods. Moreover there is a general confidence that there won't be any violation of the implicit agreement. Another example in daily life of this kind of ethics is the observance of queue discipline. People line up; there are people who try to break in ahead of you, but there is an ethic which holds that this is bad. It is clearly an ethic which is in everybody's interest to preserve; one waits at the end of the line this time, and one is protected against somebody's coming in ahead of him.

In the context of product safety, efficiency would be greatly enhanced by accepted ethical rules. Sometimes it may be enough to have an ethical compulsion to reveal all the information available and let the buyer choose. This is not necessarily always the best. It can be argued that under some circumstances setting minimum safety standards and simply not putting out products that do not meet them would be desirable and should be felt by the businessman to be an obligation.

QUESTIONS

1. How does Arrow propose to improve the efficiency of business?

2. Explain Arrow's "used-car" argument. What does it show?

J. Maurice Clark | # The Changing Basis of Economic Responsibility

J. Maurice Clark taught economics at the University of Chicago.

FORECAST OF THE ARGUMENT

Twenty years ago an economist writing under this title would have been expected to deal chiefly or solely with the responsibility of the individual for his own economic destiny: his responsibility for paying his debts and keeping out of the poor-house. Economic responsibility meant self-reliance and self-dependence. Today any treatment of the subject from such a limited standpoint would be an anachronism. The ideas of obligation which embody the actual relations of man to man in the twentieth century, and answer the needs of the twentieth century, are radically different from the ideas which dominated the nineteenth.

Some have failed to realize what the change means and have resisted it uncomprehendingly. Interdependence means no more to them than it did in the days when free exchange seemed adequate to organize the world, and enlist the far islands of the seas to furnish London breakfast tables. That was one kind of interdependence, marvelously far-reaching and marvelously effective—but not the interdependence that is putting its peculiar stamp on the life of the present generation.

Some have gone to the other extreme and have lost their old sense of personal accountability in an easy philosophy that lays the burdens on the impersonal state, and the blame on heredity and environment. But most of us have not gone so far as that. We do not want a state that shall prohibit all our vices, syndicate all our virtues, and render old-fashioned self-reliance

obsolete, if indeed that were remotely possible! Instead, many men are honestly seeking to know what their obligations are in this new era, that they may meet them on their own initiative. More knowledge is wanted, that men may guide themselves. The modern prayer is not so much for strength as for wisdom.

In the economic world this issue is presented more clearly perhaps than anywhere else. We have inherited an economics of irresponsibility. We are in an economy of control with which our intellectual inheritance fits but awkwardly. To make control really tolerable we need something more; something which is still in its infancy. We need an economics of responsibility, developed and embodied in our working business ethics.

THE SWING OF THE PENDULUM

We have gone through a revolution of late in many realms of thought and policy. We have swung far away from narrow individualism toward a sense of solidarity and social-mindedness. In religion the dominant ideal is no longer a narrowly personal salvation granted from above as a reward of personal faith, but rather an attitude of love and service to one's fellows which are in themselves salvation. The old idea of free will is giving way to determinism, individualism to public control, personal responsibility to social responsibility.

This changed attitude shows itself in economic matters in a hundred ways. The common law treated industrial accidents as matters of personal responsibility and attempted to fix a personal blame. The results were intolerable. Something was wrong. Contrast the attitude of a system of compulsory compen-

From *The Journal of Political Economy* (Vol. 24, No. 3, 1916) 209–229.

sation which blames nobody, and seems almost to take away all responsibility, distributing it between the state and the employer and treating the employer impersonally, as the representative of the industry. This policy expresses a new idea of responsibility.

Not long ago we were almost morbidly afraid to do anything to relieve distress, for fear of undermining people's independence and perpetuating the disease we aimed to cure. If these unfortunates could not quickly be put in a condition of doing for themselves there was danger in doing too much for them. Anything looking toward permanent assistance was a confession of failure in the present and an omen of evil to come. Meanwhile poverty continued to breed poverty. Now free meals for school children are becoming more and more common, the minimum wage in a mild form is being seriously tried out, and we seem to be on the threshold of similar experiments with old-age pensions, mothers' pensions, and insurance against unemployment.

The old-time lumber-gang boss or division superintendent promoted men or discharged them at will. He was responsible to his superior officer for getting results, and to his conscience, if he had one, for the rights and wrongs of his actions. Often he adopted a policy of rewards or punishments that were sudden, unexpected, and intentionally arbitrary, his object being to keep the men in proper awe of what might happen, and to keep them on their good behavior in little things: things so small in themselves that only the momentary impulse of an arbitrary autocrat would take any notice of them. It was every man's own lookout that the blow did not fall on his head. This system could work tolerably well in a young country, so rich in opportunity that most men could "fall on their feet" whatever happened and whenever and wherever they might be cast adrift.

But today the consequences are too serious to be treated thus cavalierly. Compare the situation of the modern official dealing with a strong union. He cannot discharge men without the possibility of having to face a committee of their fellow-laborers who will make him give an account of his actions. A group has assumed responsibility for its members and a new responsibility of an individual toward the group is being enforced. How shall the group, the union, have brought home to it its own responsibility to the larger group of which it is a part? That is the next chapter of the story, and the end is not yet written.

Unemployment used to be considered largely a matter of personal fitness and willingness to work; now it is spoken of as a disease of our economic system. Criminals and prostitutes used to be regarded quite simply as wicked people. Now they are quite as often looked upon as victims of the social order. In fact this explanation is so much in the air that it has become a habit, an unthinking reaction to anything and everything that goes wrong, and anyone and everyone who goes to pieces. There is little room to question that our habit of overworking this conveniently impersonal scapegoat is closely connected with what Miss Repplier has called our national "loss of nerve." It is all a most disquieting phase of the spread of deterministic ideas among people ready to absorb them one-sidedly.

But it is all part of a movement we cannot escape, with its successes and its failures, its inspiration for the man big enough to catch it, and its enervating effect on those without the vision. It is the product of new situations and new knowledge, and we must use the knowledge to make the best of the situations. We must take what it gives and fight to keep whatever of good it threatens to take away.

It is the product of many things, from psychology to life insurance and from bacteriology to large-scale manufacturing. The bottom facts are, first, that we are becoming interdependent in new and unforeseen ways, and, second, that we are finding out more about the remote causes of things, which we used to take for granted.

Psychology shows us our minds as products of inherited tendencies and the environment to which they react. This makes the living conditions of the slum responsible for the gangster's criminal tendencies and many lesser personal faults and failures. Mortality tables show us occupational environments as killing so many men out of a thousand every year, and statisticians correlate hot weather and suicide, and attempt to correlate crime and heredity.

Indeed, statistics, together with the mass-phenomena they measure, have been the instrument of a surprising deal of altered thinking. When we are looking at John Smith alone, we cannot tell just what he will do in a given situation or what a change in environment will do to him. He is still an independent personality and a law unto himself. But we can tell in advance what such a change will do to a thousand John Smiths. It may kill so and so many, or save so and so many alive, and we become accustomed to the idea that enfeebling environments have made so and so many criminals, and so and so many good-for-nothing idlers, who would otherwise have remained on the safe side of respectability and self-support. The environment has become responsible for John Smith.

But at the same time John Smith has become responsible for the environment. A knowledge of bacteria makes criminal neglect out of what were once matters of purely private concern, and the outcome is to make medicine more and more a matter of maintaining a healthful environment and hence a matter of public prevention rather than of private cure.

Man is ever in the presence of powers too strong for him to cope with, and never knows when they may reach out and take his life. Where the environment that threatens and the powers that kill are the environment and the powers of nature, he worships and watches his priming, learns to sleep lightly, to read footprints, and to know the signs of water. Where the environment is man-made and the powers are those of machinery, he ceases to worship, and he may begin instead to resent, to protest, and ultimately to revolt. Large-scale industry puts the laborer in surroundings, no more dangerous perhaps than the forest or desert which faced the old-time frontiersman, but surroundings which, dangers and all, are the work of human hands and human brains. All these things have given us new ideas of causes and effects, and these have given us new ideas of responsibility. We are finding out that many things' are not to be taken for granted as of old, because they are things over which someone can exercise control, and that means they are things for which someone is responsible.

RESPONSIBILITY
AND THE LIBERAL ECONOMICS

By comparison with the scope of responsibility as it has been conceived and presented here the laissez-faire economics may well be characterized as the economics of irresponsibility, and the business sys-

tem of free contract is also a system of irresponsibility when judged by the same standard. Of static theory we must simply say that while it does not deny social responsibilities it does to a large extent ignore them. Since its abstract premises leave out most of the facts on which they are based, they are left to be taken account of in other departments of the science. Liberal economics or business economics in general accomplishes much the same result by separating business sharply off from the rest of life.

"Business is business," and while men are unselfish and recognize many kinds of obligations to their fellows beyond the letter of the law, their unselfishness is not carried into business relations, and the extralegal responsibilities are not business responsibilities, except such as have become so firmly established in business morals as to have the binding force of laws. In business, men do not render services without being paid such price as they are willing to accept nor undergo sacrifices except for a consideration which they deem sufficient. From this it may be concluded that both parties are better off for every business transaction, at least in their own minds at the moment, than if the transaction had not been made.

With this dangerously inadequate idea of bargaining and contract, and with the equally inadequate idea of business competition as a sort of Darwinian struggle for survival, constantly tending toward the natural selection, of the fit, it is small wonder if the business man is willingly convinced that in the struggle for financial success he is fulfilling the whole duty that society can reasonably impose upon his business hours. In other words, theory and practice combine to further an irresponsible attitude among leaders of industry and laborers alike.

Meanwhile the demand for control has grown with amazing speed, and in every direction experiments are being tried. This should properly be regarded as a recognition of special kinds of responsibility which the business economics leaves out of account and which the machinery of free contract furnishes no way of bringing home to the proper persons. But instead, this regulation is looked on by too many as a phase of the old irresponsible struggle, merely translated from the field of business into the field of politics. It is under suspicion as being mere irresponsible class legislation, and unfortunately the suspicion has some justification.

Hence employers often feel either contemptuous or deeply injured when laws begin to interfere with customary business practices, and when investigating committees ask prying questions which imply a demand for a righteousness that shall exceed the righteousness of the scribes and Pharisees. Business men with this point of view oppose the growth of public control with a resistance that is now adroit and now stubborn but nearly always powerful. The economics of control is at war with the economics of irresponsibility.

Beyond all the special issues of this struggle there stand out certain general questions of attitude and interpretation that are most real and most vital. Are these new policies of regulation to be regarded as exceptions to our general economic philosophy or are they an integral part of it? Are they special and disconnected cases or are they phases of one consistent program whose central features can be formulated? And above all, are they mere matters of political struggle and political compromise; matters to be temporarily settled by a show of hands, or of teeth, and perpetually unsettled again with every real or fancied change in the strength of the contending parties? Or are they matters of economic law, with a solid foundation in real relationships of cause and effect which no party in the many-sided struggle can permanently ignore? Do our economic regulations mean merely the creation and attempted enforcement of arbitrary requirements or do they mean the recognition and bringing home of existing and very real responsibilities? And, if the answer to this last be in the affirmative, is there a twilight zone of obligations not yet enforced by law or custom but no less real for that? If there is such a twilight zone, how shall we act toward it?

It is good and necessary that new proposals should be first treated as exceptions to economic theory, for they need to be settled on their merits, but it is not good that they should remain permanently unassimilated. It is good and necessary that they be urged by men intensely devoted, each to his special cause, but it is also good ultimately to absorb them all into a broadly constructive plan. It is good when political force breaks down stereotyped codes and precepts masquerading as "natural rights" and natural law, but it is not good to imagine that there are no laws to which men and groups of men are responsible other than the law of getting all they can.

The task of economic theory in these matters is clear, and the importance of this task is often too little realized. There are principles underlying our multifarious social policies—principles as general and far-reaching as those underlying the "theory of value and distribution." In fact, they are all phases of one process, social housekeeping. And until "free exchange" and "social reform" are both interpreted as governed by one consistent set of laws, they are not interpreted correctly. The crucial task of such a theory is to unify, to reveal those causes and consequences of things men do which transcend the scope of free exchange. These create responsibilities which, in turn, the policy of regulation is attempting to enforce. In a broad sense the great task of the theorist of our tremendously dynamic age is to substitute an economics of responsibility for the economics of irresponsible conflict. That is his part in furthering the growth of willing co-operation in the endless process of adapting our organization and industrial ways to the unforeseen needs and relationships which machinery and science are continually thrusting, upon us.

QUESTIONS

1. How has economic responsibility evolved over time?

2. Do you consider yourself to be primarily responsible for your own economic well-being? How may your case differ from that of the so-called trustafarians (trust-fund babies). The welfare mother?

CASES

CASE 7.1

Mondragon Cooperatives

Ana G. Johnson and William F. Whyte

The Basque region of Spain contains the world's most successful industrial cooperative, the Mondragon system. The Mondragon system is a group of more than 80 cooperatively owned firms with a combined total of over 18,000 employee owners. These profitable co-ops are the product of a single cooperative firm begun in 1956 under the guidance of a Spanish priest, José Maria Arizmendi.

The system of employee-owned businesses is supported by a cooperative educational system that provides well-educated workers and, most importantly, by a credit union that provides the capital required to sustain cooperative firms in their early years. The credit union's capital is raised from deposits by local residents. Its funds are used to supply loans to cover 60 percent of the startup costs of new cooperative enterprises and also to cover any deficits that accrue during the first two years of the firm's existence. The credit union also supplies invaluable organizational assistance by assigning credit union specialists to assist the cooperative's management in running the new firm. None of the 56 new cooperatives begun through the credit union between 1961 and 1976 has failed.

The cooperative firms maintain a maximum disparity between workers' wages of three to one. Since entry level employees are paid wages comparable to those in non-cooperative firms, higher level employ-

ees have wages below the norm in other firms. This may be compensated for by the fact that most profits of the firm eventually return to the worker owners. But the distribution of annual profits is controlled by a policy which mandates that 10 to 15 percent of the profits be returned to support community activities such as the school system, 15 percent be reinvested in the firm, and the remaining 70 percent be invested in accounts within the firm in the names of individual employees. These accounts pay employees interest, but the principal cannot be withdrawn until the worker retires. This policy for controlled profit distribution solves one of the most common problems of cooperative enterprises—the lack of operating capital due to too little reinvestment.

Mondragon policies also protect against another tendency of cooperatives—to revert to traditional private ownership by non-employee stockholders. At Mondragon, the worker owners cannot sell their shares or continue to own stock after leaving the company. In addition, every new employee is required to buy shares in the firm (purchase of those shares can be facilitated by personal loans from the credit union).

Internal governance of the Mondragon cooperatives had until recently been primarily hierarchical and autocratic. Work at Mondragon differed little from the most routinized American factory. How-

This case was prepared from information found in the following sources: "The Mondragon System of Worker Production Cooperatives," Ana G. Johnson and William F. Whyte, *Industrial and Labor Relations Review,* vol. 31, no. 1, 18–30; *Working Together,* John Simmons and William Mares (New York University Press, 1985) 136–142.

ever, in the 1970s the Mondragon system began to evolve a more participatory system of governance in response to labor unrest at one of the larger cooperatives. Now most cooperatives have employee-elected boards to oversee management, direct involvement at the shop floor, and employee social councils which consider issues related to working conditions.

QUESTIONS

1. How could a reliable source of initial capital for cooperative firms be created in the United States?

2. What do you imagine prevents most U.S. cooperatives from adopting a Mondragon-like policy for controlling shares?

3. Is a narrow range of wage levels necessary for maintaining a successful cooperative enterprise?

CASE 7.2
The Social Audit
Rogene A. Buchholz

Monolith, a large conglomerate, has recently come under fire from a variety of federal agencies and/or offices because of alleged problems in some of its operations. The Occupational Safety and Health Administration has charged it with certain violations in its steel plants, the Office of Federal Contract Compliance Programs is threatening to cancel some of the government contracts the company enjoys because of its failure to meet affirmative action guidelines, and the Federal Trade Commission is taking a close look at certain aspects of the corporation's advertising strategies. A management consultant called in to study the situation has advised that the company would not be in this predicament if it had periodically conducted a social audit. The consultant recommends that such an audit be taken systematically in the future.

The company is thus considering doing something along these lines, but it is finding that there is no agreement on what a social audit should look like. It has run across various proposals as to what kinds of things should appear on a social audit and what measures are appropriate. There is also the question as to whether such an audit should be used for internal management purposes only or disclosed to the outside public. Nonetheless, the company is committed to developing some kind of means to determine how well it is doing in areas that cannot be measured by the traditional financial statements. It has formed a team to deal with this problem and make proposals to top management as to what exactly ought to be done in this regard.

QUESTIONS

1. What types of regulations may the conglomerate have violated based on the agencies mentioned in the case? Be as specific as possible. Would an audit of the areas covered by these regulations help the company with its compliance efforts?

2. What do you think of the suggestion to conduct a social audit? As far as the issues raised in this case are concerned, what type of social audit might be most useful to alleviate some of the problems the company is currently facing?

From Rogene A. Buchholz, *Business, Environment and Public Policy,* (Englewood Cliffs, NJ: Prentice Hall, 1995).

CASE 7.3

The NYSEG Corporate Responsibility Case

Kelley MacDougall, Tom L. Beauchamp, and John Cuddihy

We are responsible to the communities in which we live and work and to the world community as well. We must be good citizens and support good works and charities. . . . We must encourage civic improvements and better health and education.[1]

Many large corporations currently operate consumer responsibility or social responsibility programs, which aim to return something to the consumer or to the community in which the company does business. New York State Electric and Gas (NYSEG) is one company that has created a program to discharge what its officers consider to be the company's responsibility to its public.

NYSEG is a New York Stock Exchange-traded public utility with approximately 60,500 shareholders. It supplies gas and electricity to New York State. NYSEG currently earns 89 percent of its revenues from electricity and 11 percent from gas sales. The company is generally ranked as having solid but not excellent financial strength. Earnings per share have declined in recent years because of the regulatory climate and the company's write-offs for its Nine Mile Point #2 nuclear unit. In order to finance the unit, the company at one point had to absorb delay costs of several million dollars per month. The setback reduced shareholders' dividends for the first time in many years. NYSEG's financial base is now less secure than in the past because of the lowered earnings per share and the increased plant costs.

The company's corporate responsibility program has been in effect throughout this period of financial reversal. NYSEG designed the program to aid customers who are unable to pay their utility bills for various reasons. The program does not simply help customers pay their bills to the company. Rather,

NYSEG hopes the program will find people in the community in unfortunate or desperate circumstances and alleviate their predicament. The two objectives often coincide.

NYSEG has created a system of consumer representatives, social workers trained to deal with customers and their problems. Since the program's 1978 inception, NYSEG has maintained a staff of 13 consumer representatives. Each handles approximately 40 cases a month, over half of which result in successful financial assistance. The remaining cases are referred to other organizations for further assistance.

The process works as follows: When the company's credit department believes a special investigation should be made into a customer's situation, the employee refers the case to the consumer representative. Referrals also come from human service agencies and from customers directly. Examples of appropriate referrals include unemployed household heads; paying customers who suffer serious injury, lengthy illness, or death; and low-income senior citizens or those on fixed incomes who cannot deal with rising costs of living. To qualify for assistance, NYSEG requires only that the customers must be suffering from hardships they are willing to work to resolve.

Consumer representatives are primarily concerned with preventing the shutoff of service to these customers. They employ an assortment of resources to put them back on their feet, including programs offered by the New York State Department of Social Services and the federal Home Energy Assistance Program (HEAP), which awards annual grants of varying amounts to qualified families. In addition the consumer representatives provide financial counseling and help customers with their medical bills and education planning. They arrange assistance from churches and social services, provide food stamps, and help arrange VA benefits.

NYSEG also created a direct financial assistance program called Project Share, which enables paying customers who are not in financial difficulty to make charitable donations through their bills. They are asked voluntarily to add to their bill each month one, two, or five extra dollars, which are placed in a special fund overseen by the American Red Cross. This special Fuel Fund is intended to help those 60 years and older on fixed incomes who have no other means of paying their bills. Help is also provided for the handicapped and blind who likewise have few sources of funds. Many Project Share recipients do not qualify for government-funded assistance programs but nonetheless face energy problems. Through December 1990 Project Share had raised over $1.5 million and had successfully assisted more than 8,000 people.

The rationale or justification of this corporate responsibility program is rooted in the history of public utilities and rising energy costs in North America. Originally public utilities provided a relatively inexpensive product. NYSEG and the entire industry considered its public responsibility limited to the business function of providing energy at the lowest possible costs and returning dividends to investors. NYSEG did not concern itself with its customers' financial troubles. The customer or the social welfare system handled all problems of unpaid bills.

However, the skyrocketing energy costs in the 1970s changed customer resources and NYSEG's perspective. The energy crisis caused many long-term customers to encounter difficulty in paying their bills, and the likelihood of power shutoffs increased as a result. NYSEG then accepted a responsibility to assist these valued customers by creating the Consumer Representative system.

NYSEG believes its contribution is especially important now because recent reductions in federal assistance programs have shifted the burden of addressing these problems to the private sector. Project Share is viewed as "a logical extension of the President's call for increased volunteerism at the local level."[3] NYSEG chose the American Red Cross to cosponsor Project Share because of its experience in providing emergency assistance.

The costs of NYSEG's involvement in the program are regarded by company officers as low. NYSEG has few additional costs beyond the consumer representatives' salaries and benefits, which total $462,625 annually and are treated as operating expenses. To augment Project Share's financial support, NYSEG shareholders give the program an annual, need-based grant. In the past, shareholder grants have ranged from $40,000 to $100,000. NYSEG also pays for some personnel and printing costs through consumer rate increases, despite a recent ruling by the New York State Supreme Court that forbids utilities from raising consumer rates to obtain funds for charitable contributions (*Cahill v. Public Service Commission*). The company has also strongly supported Project Share by giving $490,000 over a seven-year period. The company's annual revenues are in the range of $1.5 billion, and the company's total debt also runs to approximately $1.5 billion.

The company views some of the money expended for the corporate responsibility program as recovered because of customers retained and bills paid through the program. NYSEG assumes that these charges would, under normal circumstances, have remained unpaid and would eventually have been written off as a loss. NYSEG's bad-debt level is 20 percent lower than that of the average U.S. utility company. The company believes that its corporate responsibility policy is *both* altruistic *and* good business, despite the program's maintenance costs, which seem to slightly exceed recovered revenue.

NOTES

1. "The Johnson and Johnson Way" (from the Johnson and Johnson Company credo), 1986, p. 26.

2. NYSEG, Project Share Procedures Manual, 1988, p. 2.

QUESTIONS

1. Do you agree that NYSEG's Project Share is both altruistic and good business? Why or why not?

2. To what extent, if any, is Project Share an example of stakeholder management principles?

3. Could adherents to a stockholder theory of corporate responsibility and adherents to a stakeholder theory both endorse Project Share as socially responsible? Why or why not?

CASE 7.4
Beech-Nut's Imitation Apple Juice
Thomas I. White

In 1988, the Beech-Nut Nutrition Corporation and two of its top executives admitted that they had knowingly sold adulterated apple juice. In fact, the baby food, although described on the label as "100% fruit juice," contained little if any apple juice. The company agreed to pay a $2 million fine, but the ultimate cost to Beech-Nut was closer to $25 million when the settlement of a class action suit, legal fees, and lost sales are included. The two executives, Neils L. Hoyvald, the firm's former president and CEO, and John F. Lavery, former vice-president of manufacturing, were fined $100,000 each and sentenced to jail terms of a year and a day. (A major part of the conviction and Hoyvald's imprisonment were dismissed when an appeals court ruled that the trial had taken place in the wrong court.)

This example of corporate wrongdoing combines fraud with a coverup and was apparently driven by ongoing and intense financial pressure at Beech-Nut. In 1977, Beech-Nut changed suppliers of the concentrate used to produce its apple juice when it was offered the product at 20 percent below market rates by Interjuice Trading Corporation. This resulted in an annual savings of $250,000—no small amount for a company that was financially strapped. Despite misgivings about the juice by Jerome LiCari, Beech-Nut's director of research and development, laboratory tests could not prove that the juice was counterfeit. By 1981, however, LiCari believed that there was enough circumstantial evidence to suggest that the concentrate was a blend of synthetic ingredients, and he claims that he notified senior management of his belief. By that time, however, Hoyvald had apparently promised Nestlé, the Swiss food concern that had bought Beech-Nut, that the company would

turn around financially in 1982. Beech-Nut had been sold to Nestlé in 1979 and had lost $2.5 million in fiscal 1981. But Hoyvald pledged a profit of $700,000 for the following year, and the parent company apparently communicated to him that he must deliver. As Hoyvald put it, "The pressure was on." Changing suppliers and buying a more expensive concentrate would have made a profit impossible to achieve. Also, some Beech-Nut officials still pointed to the fact that there was no absolute proof that the apple juice was adulterated. (It is worth noting, however, that although Beech-Nut's policy was to stay with the concentrate as long as it could not be proven that it was counterfeit, other companies reversed the burden of proof and terminated a supplier if it could not prove that its product was genuine.) Some Beech-Nut officials also claimed that even if the juice were fake, it was not doing anyone any harm. The juice in the bottles might not be apple juice, but it was not a health hazard.

By mid-1982, however, a private detective hired by an industry association found proof that the concentrate was synthetic and presented it to Beech-Nut. The company did stop buying the concentrate at that time. But instead of publicly admitting the error, destroying or relabeling the inventory, and paying a fine, Hoyvald chose a strategy that would buy enough time to see the $3.5 million worth of juice sitting in warehouses. The company refused to cooperate with an investigation against the suppliers and waited a few months before r\the United States. The product then was offered at large discounts to offshore distributors. To keep one step ahead of state law enforcement officials, inventory was even moved from one state to another. Hoyvald apparently

From Thomas I. White, *Business Ethics: A Philosophical Reader* (New York: Macmillan, 1993).

believed that Beech-Nut's very existence was at stake. When asked by one of the prosecutors why the juice had simply not been destroyed, he replied, "And I could have called up Switzerland and told them I had just closed the company down. Because that is what would have been the result of it."

REFERENCES

Buder, Leonard, "2 Former Executives of Beech-Nut Guilty in Phony Juice Case," *New York Times*, February 18, 1988, A1, D3.

Traum, James, "Into the Mouths of Babes," *This World*, August 7, 1988, 14–15.

"What Led Beech-Nut Down the Road to Disgrace," *Business Week*, February 22, 1988, 124–128.

QUESTIONS

1. How seriously unethical is what Beech-Nut did? How seriously wrong is what Hoyvald and Lavery did?

2. How do you distinguish corporate from personal responsibility? Should the parent company, Nestlé, be held responsible for anything that happened?

3. Is the company's difficult financial condition an extenuating circumstance?

4. How relevant is the claim that the counterfeit juice did not hurt any babies who drank it?

5. If you were the judge in this case, what punishments would you assign the corporation and the individual executives?

6. What would the punishments look like if you used French's Hester Prynne Sanction, Shipp's modified vendetta, or Rafalko's beheading proposal?

CASE 7.5

Sentencing a Corporation to Prison

Thomas I. White

In 1988, Federal Judge Robert G. Doumar handed down an extremely unusual punishment for a corporation convicted of wrongdoing—he sentenced it to three years in prison. The Maryland-based Allegheny Bottling Company was found guilty of three years of price-fixing, and Judge Doumar wanted a penalty that would be sterner than the typical fine. "The corporation," explained the jurist, "cannot come in here, profit to the tune of $10 million and walk away with a $1 million fine." The punishment he chose, on top of such a fine, was clearly unexpected.

Judge Doumar later suspended the sentence and $50,000 of the fine, but he placed the company on probation. The judge explained that in the case of a corporation, imprisonment amounted to placing restrictions on the company's ability to operate. He ordered that four of the company's senior executives perform up to two years of full-time community service. And he threatened that if the company failed to do so, he would close down its operations.

Allegheny Bottling, a Pepsi bottling franchise, was accused of collaborating with the Mid-Atlantic Coca-Cola Bottling Company to set wholesale prices. Before Allegheny's sentencing, the price-fixing scheme had already led to convictions of Morton Lapides, former chairman of Allegheny, and James Harford, former president of Mid-Atlantic Coca-Cola. Both men were sentenced to three years in prison, with all but six months suspended. Harford

From Thomas I. White, *Business Ethics: A Philosophical Reader* (New York: Macmillan, 1993).

was also sentenced to three years of community service. In his order that four of Allegheny's executives perform community service, Judge Doumar specified that their positions and salaries must be similar to those of the executives already sentenced.

Attorneys for the company objected, pointing out that there was no precedent for imprisoning a corporation.

REFERENCE

Hicks, Jonathan P., "Corporate Prison Term for Allegheny Bottling," *New York Times,* September 1, 1988, D2.

QUESTIONS

1. It is obviously difficult to punish a corporation, and one of the most frustrating aspects of trying to do is that a fine can ultimately be passed along to stockholders, employees, or consumers—that is, people who had no hand in the wrongdoing pay the penalty. Is the Allegheny case a model of how to address this particular problem?

2. Two specific top executives were sentenced to prison and community service, Allegheny was ordered to have four other senior managers perform community service, and the company was ordered to pay a fine. How does this serve justice, broadly understood? Is such a model appropriately retributive for the crime? Would it deter other corporations? Most important, does it make any sense to sentence a corporation to imprisonment?

CHAPTER QUESTIONS

1. Is the social responsibility of business to increase its profits? Why or why not?

2. How are corporations like persons? How are they different? Why do stakeholders matter?

8

When Innovation Bytes Back

Ethics and Technology

Introduction

It is hard to talk about contemporary business without talking at the same time about technology. Some of the problems of business ethics, to be sure, are pretty much the same as they were in ancient times. The Roman philosopher Cicero expounded at length about the risks and responsibilities involved in buying or selling a house or a chariot, and the ethics surrounding such exchanges were not much different from our current concerns when we are buying or selling a modern condo or a new or used car. But even these transactions are permeated by ever-more-difficult questions that have to do with the new technologies. People buy cars and even houses on-line, without ever actually seeing them. They exchange funds and make contracts over the Internet without anything so tangible as paper currency, much less gold coins ever changing hands. They make promises and offers by email that may go out to hundreds of thousands of consumers (most of whom are more irritated than enticed). One might argue that all that has changed is the speed of business and personal transactions—from days, weeks, or (until the nineteenth century) months to fractions of a second or even nanoseconds, but this would be a very unimaginative view. What has changed is not just the speed, but the very nature of business and business transactions.

Whether this is an unmixed blessing, needless to say, is the subject of considerable debate. What were introduced as dramatic aids to efficiency and productivity have, ironically, seemingly increased the time that most of us spend in our jobs, whether in or out of the office (if one even *has* an office). Mobile phones make us accessible to our bosses and supervisors 24 hours a day, 7 days a week, at home, in our cars, and at the beach, and many employers insist that we "stay in touch" or have our phones turned on and available even while we're supposedly not at work or "on vacation." Laptop computers and wireless connections mean that we can work on projects anywhere. Email, even forgetting about the time it takes most of us to delete the "spam" we receive, seems to increase the demands on our time, rather than decrease it, making us less rather than more efficient. What used to be short, concise to-the-point memos have given way to long rambling verbose documents that take time and patience to read, with little reward. It is an observation that has become commonplace: With the dramatic improvements in communication technology, we spend more time on the job; have less time to ourselves; have less privacy; and, in many cases, get no more done than when we walked from office to office, working, talking, and negotiating with people face to face. In fact, many of us miss that interpersonal experience. Not going to the office may save many of us an hour or more of commuting time, but it also deprives many people of the camaraderie that is often (though surely not always) one of the satisfactions of working life.

Technology also raises new and novel legal and ethical problems. The law, as plodding as it is, can't keep up with the new technologies. (A famous statue in the Palace of Justice in Paris depicts a famous judge, his foot on a turtle, thus complaining about the slowness of the legal process even in the eighteenth century.) And just as compliance is difficult when the rules no longer apply, ethics is equally difficult when there are few precedents and no clear traditions or customs to guide us. For example, there are the intricacies of copyright and intellectual property law and the ethics that gives rise to them. Music and movies used to be played on the radio or shown in theaters, where there were no ready ways of copying or reproducing them. Now, "downloading" from the web, near-perfect digital copies, and handheld recorders and videocameras make stealing such things easy. But what counts as stealing? It used to be that if you owned something and I took it, I now had it and you didn't. That makes it theft. But if I download a song from the Internet, you (who ever you are—the musician, the producer, the recording company) still own it. I just happen to have a copy, too. So is this stealing? The general consensus is, yes (though many students still seem to have the idea that music, by its very

---

To: You
From: The Philosopher
Subject: "Locke on Property"

Who hasn't downloaded a song from the Internet? Or shared files? Or perhaps used bootlegged or pirated software? (It was paid for once, what is the harm if *I* use it?). There is a lot of material on the web that doesn't seem to belong to *anyone*. But could that be right? How did it get on the web? And who created the content? For Locke, our notion of property is inseparable from our notion of labor. If you have invested work into the creation of something, if it is what it is because of your labor, then it ought to belong to you (imagine how controversial this idea was in the 17th century, when Locke wrote it—especially among the wealthy English landowners). Now, if we think about it that way, do we still feel OK about downloading the latest *Outkast* release (and avoiding paying 99 cents for it)? Here's Locke:

> Though the earth and all inferior creatures be common to all men, yet every man has a *property* in his own *person*. This nobody has any right to but himself. The *labour* of his body and the *work* of his hands, we may say, are properly his. Whatsoever, then, he removed out of the state that nature hath provided and left it in, he hath mixed his labour with it, and joined to it something that is his own, and thereby makes it his property. . . . Thus, the grass my horse has bit . . . and the ore I have digged in any place, where I have a right to them in common with others, become my property without the assignation or consent of any body. The labour that was mine, removing them out of that common state they were in, hath fixed my property in them.

From John Locke, *The Second Treatise on Government*, Oxford, England: Clarendon Press, 1690, pp. 26–27.

nature, is or ought to be free and belong to none). But what does that mean? If I buy a piece of software and install it on my computer at work, but then I want to install it on my computer at home (which I also use for work), is that stealing, too? What if I give the same software to my officemate? If I want to back up my purchase of a DVD movie in case of loss or damage, is that stealing? And if some companies (Linux, for instance) choose to make their intellectual property free and "open" to everyone, does that in any way change the status of those who vigorously insist on their ownership (Microsoft, for example)? We all appreciate the complexity of these questions, even if we disagree on the exact answers to them.

Or consider the new privacy issues that have come with the new technology. It used to be, if you didn't want anyone to know what you have written, you could burn the paper (or, if you're a spy in a desperate situation, you could eat it). Now, everyone knows that erasing an email message doesn't make it disappear, should your computer be seized and searched by experts. Private correspondence is vulnerable to hackers of all stripes. (And, by the way, is hacking ethical? It is a matter of violating another's privacy—even if nothing is "taken" [e.g., credit card numbers], but when is violating another person's privacy unethical, and when is it a case not so different from listening to—and not merely overhearing—a neighbor's audible argument with his or her spouse?) Office email is no longer considered private. And then there are questions about personal correspondence on the office computer. If, after hours, you want to use your office computer to chat with a friend overseas, is that stealing? It does not cost the company anything (as opposed, say, to a long distance overseas call, which used to cost quite a lot). If you do some on-line shopping during your lunch hour, does that violate some new ethical principle? When you are on the Internet, whether it's business or personal, do you have an obligation to reveal your true identity, when now it is so easy to hide or disguise it? The truth is that all such questions are very much in play, as companies and managers try to decide what is legitimate and what is not. And while they are doing so, the technology keeps changing. When you can merely think thoughts that are automatically transmitted to colleagues across town or across an ocean, does the company have some sort of claim to your mental processes? And when the software becomes so sophisticated that it can reproduce YOUR job, is your company justified in letting you go to be replaced by a piece of machinery that never stops working, expects no benefits, and wastes no time at the water cooler? Such questions are no longer the stuff of science fiction but the source of tomorrow's ethical dilemmas.

First, Deborah C. Johnson discusses the problem of intellectual property rights in computer software. Who should own what, why, and for how long? She discusses the tension between creativity and freedom and considers a labor theory of property. Turning to a different kind of right, the right to privacy, Richard A. Spinello argues that employers' rights to their employees' email messages must be strictly controlled. Elizabeth A. Buchanan argues that the Internet has opened up opportunities, but with those opportunities comes a duty to disseminate beneficial information worldwide, especially to those persons whom it will most benefit. Deborah C. Johnson argues in "Hacker Ethics" that hackers must be governed by the same moral principles that govern the rest of us with respect to other people's property." But the internet has created new opportunities and, with them, new responsibilities. Bill Joy, in "Why The Future Doesn't Need Us," argues that technology must be carefully curtailed by prudent people (especially scientists) today. Technology must serve us, not the other way around. We are in danger of destroying the world through a slavish dedication to "technology for its own sake." Finally, a cautionary note that we should curb our enthusiasm. Theodore Roszak, who describes himself as a Luddite, argues, "In Defense of the Naked Mind," that technology cannot provide the meaning of life.

Deborah C. Johnson

Intellectual Property Rights and Computer Software

Deborah Johnson is Olsson Professor of Applied Ethics Technology, Culture, and Communication at the University of Virginia.

THE PHILOSOPHICAL BASIS OF PROPERTY

Property is by no means a simple notion. Property is created by law. Laws specify what can and cannot be owned, how things may be acquired and transferred. Laws define what counts as property and create different kinds of property.

... [S]oftware has challenged our traditional notions of ownership in that the system of laws created specifically to deal with invention in the useful arts and sciences in the U.S. does not seem to grant property rights in software that are comparable to the property rights of inventors in other fields. In discussing this situation we often implicitly or explicitly make assumptions about or argue for moral (and not just legal) rights in property. These assumptions and arguments need to be fully articulated and critically examined. . . .

The reasoning behind both the patent and copyright systems is consequentialist in that the system's primary aim is to create property rights which will have good effects. Invention is encouraged and facilitated so that new products and processes will be made available. Nevertheless, many discussions of property rights assume that property is not a matter of social utility, but rather a matter of justice or natural right. We will consider this approach first, as it applies to the ownership of software.

NATURAL RIGHTS ARGUMENTS

The strongest natural rights argument that can be made for private ownership of software is based on the idea that a person has a natural (and, therefore, moral) right to what he or she produces and this natural right ought to be protected by law. John Locke's labor theory of property bases the natural right of ownership on the labor one puts into a thing in creating it.

According to this theory, a person acquires a right of ownership in something by mixing his labor with it. Thus, in a state of nature (that is, before laws and civilized society), *if* an individual were to come upon a piece of land that looked suitable for cultivation, and *if* this person were to cultivate the land by planting seed, tending to the crops daily, nourishing them and so on, *then* the crops would belong to the person. The person has a strong claim to the crops because his labor produced them and they would not exist without this labor. It would be wrong for someone else to come along and take the crops. The intruder would, in effect, be confiscating the creator's labor.

On the face of it, this Lockean account seems plausible. Locke's theory is tied to the notion of individual sovereignty. A person cannot be owned by another and since a person's labor is an extension of her body, it cannot be owned by another. If an individual puts her labor in something and then someone else takes it, the laborer has been rendered a slave.

Using a Lockean theory of property, a software developer could argue that the program she developed is rightfully "hers" because she created it with her labor. . . .

From *Computer Ethics*, pp. 70–79 © 1994 by permission of Prentice-Hall, Inc.

Critique of Moral Rights In Software

Now, while this argument seems plausible, it can be countered in several ways. First, we can imagine a just world in which we did not acquire rights to what we created. To be sure, it would be unjust if others acquired rights to what we created, but if there were no property rights whatsoever, then there would be no injustice. Those who created things would simply create things. If one mixed one's labor with something, one would simply lose one's labor. Robert Nozick alludes to the possibility of such an arrangement when he questions Locke's theory in *Anarchy, State and Utopia:*

> Why does mixing one's labor with something make one the owner of it? Perhaps because one own one's labor, and so one comes to own a previously unowned thing that becomes permeated with what one owns. Ownership seeps over into the rest. But why isn't mixing what I own with what I don't own a way of losing what I own rather than a way of gaining what I don't? If I own a can of tomato juice and spill it in the sea so that its molecules (made radioactive, so I can check this) mingle evenly throughout the sea, do I thereby come to own the sea, or have I foolishly dissipated my tomato juice?

A second counter to the Lockean theory applies only to intellectual or nontangible things, such as computer software. Though software's primary function is for use in computers, software is intelligible as a nontangible entity. The software designer can describe how the software works and what it does. Another person can comprehend, and even use this information as instructions—without the software ever being put into a machine.

The point is that with intellectual things, many people can "have" or use them at the same time. If a second person eats or sells food that I have grown, I have lost the products of my labor altogether. But one can continue to have and use software when others have and use it. So, when a person copies a program that I have created, she has not taken it from me. I am not deprived of it by her act. Rather, what is usually the case is that by copying my program, the person has taken my *capacity to profit from my creation,* either by making it difficult for me to sell it (since it becomes available at no cost), or by taking my com-

petitive advantage in using the program (since my competitors can now also use it).

Once this difference between intellectual and tangible things is recognized, the natural rights argument appears much weaker than at first sight. The claim of software developers turns out *not* to be a claim to their creations (this they still have when others have their software), but a claim to a right to profit from their creations. However, to show that a person has a right to profit from his creation requires more than showing that he has created it. If he ever has a right to profit, it would seem that such a right would be socially created. It would be defined by an economic system with laws about what can be owned, what can be put into the marketplace, under what conditions, and so on. In other words, the right would derive from a complex set of rules structuring commercial activity.

The natural rights argument is, therefore, not convincing on its own. To be sure, there is a moral issue when it comes to confiscation for profit. It is unfair for one person (or company) to take a program written by someone else, and sell it. However, from a moral point of view software need never enter the commercial realm. It might be declared unownable or public property.

So, the claims of software developers must be understood not to be claims to a natural or moral right, but rather to a social right. Deciding whether or not such a social right should be created is a consequentialist issue. In a moment we will explore the consequentialist reasons for creating property rights in software, as already suggested by the rationale of the patent and copyright. For now it may be useful to point out that a natural rights argument could be made against private ownership of software.

Against Ownership

Some of the early legal literature on ownership of programs and some of the court cases focused on the idea that a patent on a program might violate "the doctrine of mental steps." This doctrine states that a series of mental operations like addition or subtraction cannot be owned. Discussion of the doctrine was based on the possibility that computers, in effect, perform, or at least duplicate, mental steps. It is acknowledged that the operations are performed quickly on the machine so that in a short time a large number of steps can take place. Still, it might be argued, the operations performed by the computer are in principle capable of being performed by a person. If this is so, then ownership of programs could be extremely dangerous for it might interfere with freedom of thought. Those who had patents on programs would have a monopoly on mental operations and might be able to stop others from performing those operations in their heads.

If this is right, then we have the basis of a natural rights argument against ownership of computer software. The argument would be that individuals have a natural right to freedom of thought, and ownership of software will interfere with that right. The argument is worthy of further reflection, especially in light of research in artificial intelligence. . . .

CONSEQUENTIALIST ARGUMENTS

As suggested earlier the claims of software developers make most sense as arguments for a social right to ownership. They can and do claim that good consequences result from ownership and bad consequences result when there is no or inadequate protection. Unless individuals and companies have some proprietary rights in what they create, they will not invest the time, energy, and resources needed to develop and market software. Without protection, they can never make money at producing software. Why develop a new program if the moment you introduce it, others will copy it, produce it more cheaply, and yours will not sell? If we, as a society, want software developed, we will have to give those who develop it the protection they need; otherwise society will lose because the great promise of computers will not be realized. There must be an incentive to create programs and that incentive is profit—so the argument goes.

Objections can be made to this very important argument. In particular, we can argue that there are incentives other than profit to create software. For one thing, people will create software because they need it for their own purposes: they can use it and make it available to others or keep it to themselves, as they choose.

Another possibility is that we could create a credit system similar to what we have now with scientific publications, in which individuals are given credit and recognition for new knowledge they create when they publish it and make it available to others. (Admittedly, credit may not be enough of an incentive to encourage the development of expensive and elaborate programs, and it may lead to more secrecy.)

Another possible incentive on which we might rely, if software were not ownable, would be the incentive of hardware companies to create software to make their computers marketable. A company's computers are useless without good software to go with them. Indeed, the better the software available for a type of computer, the better the computer is likely to do in the marketplace.

The point is that if ownership of software were disallowed, software development would not come to a complete standstill. There would be other incentives for creating software. So, while the consequentialist argument for ownership is a good argument—ownership does encourage development—it is not such an overwhelming argument that we should reject all other considerations.

Indeed, as already explained, both the copyright and the patent system recognize reasons for limiting ownership. Both recognize that the very thing we want to encourage—development of the technological arts and sciences—will be impeded if we fail to limit ownership. Both the copyright and patent systems recognize that invention will be retarded if ideas and other building blocks of science and technology are owned.

This gets us to the dilemmas that we presently face in both copyright and patent law: How can we draw a line between what can and cannot be owned so that software developers can own something of value but not something which will interfere, in the long run, with development in the field?

CONCLUSIONS FROM THE PHILOSOPHICAL ANALYSIS OF PROPERTY

The preceding philosophical analysis of property rights in software supports a consequentialist framework for analyzing the property rights issues surrounding software (and not a natural rights framework). The consequentialist framework puts the focus on deciding ownership issues in terms of effects on continued creativity and development in the field of software. This framework suggests that we will have to delicately draw a line between what is ownable and what is not ownable when it comes to software, along the lines already delineated in patent and copyright law. . . .

IS IT WRONG TO COPY PROPRIETARY SOFTWARE?

We must now turn our attention to the individual moral issue. Is it wrong for an individual to make a copy of a proprietary piece of software? You will see that the answer to this question is somewhat connected to the preceding discussion of policy issues.

To begin, it will be helpful to clarify the domain of discussion. First, making a backup copy of a piece of software, which you have purchased, for your own protection is generally not illegal, and is, in any case, not at issue here. Second, while I have labeled this the "individual" moral issue, it is not just an issue for individuals but applies as well to collective units such as companies, agencies, and institutions. The typical case is the case in which you borrow a piece of software from someone who has purchased it and make a copy for your own use. . . . This case does not differ significantly from the case in which a company buys a single copy of a piece of software and makes multiple copies for use within the company in order to avoid purchasing more.

We can begin with the intuition (which many individuals seem to have) that copying a piece of software is *not wrong* (that it is morally permissible). This intuition seems understandable enough at first glance. After all, making a copy of a piece of software is easy, and seems harmless, and the laws aimed at preventing it seem ill-suited for doing the job. Nevertheless, when we examine the arguments that can be made to support this intuition, they are not very compelling. Indeed, after analysis, it seems difficult to deny that it is morally wrong to make an illegal copy of a piece of software. The key issue here

has little to do with software per se and everything to do with the relationship between law and morality.

Perhaps the best way to begin is by laying out what seem to be the strongest arguments for the moral permissibility of individual copying. The strongest arguments claim (1) the laws protecting computer software are bad, and either (2a) making a copy of a piece of software is not intrinsically wrong, or (2b) making a copy of a piece of software does no harm, or (2c) *not* making a copy of a piece of software actually does some harm.

. . . [I]t is important to be clear on what could be claimed in Premise (1). Here are some of the possibilities: (1a) All property law in America is unjust and the software laws are part of this; (1b) all intellectual property laws are unjust and software laws are part of this; (1c) most property law in America is just, but the laws surrounding computer software are not; and (1d) while the laws surrounding the ownership of software are not unjust, they could be a lot better. The list could go on and just which position one holds makes much of the difference in the copying argument.

We will not be able to analyze each of the possibilities here, but it should be clear . . . that I believe that the system of intellectual property rights in America (in particular patent, trade secrecy, and copyright laws) may not be the best of all possible laws in every detail but they are roughly just. That is, copyright and patent laws aim at a utilitarian system of property rights and aim essentially to draw the right kind of line between what can and cannot be owned. I recognize that there are problems in extending these laws to software, and I recognize the system could be improved. Nevertheless, I do not believe that the system is blatantly unjust or wholly inappropriate for software.

Now, the next step in my argument is to claim that an individual has a *prima facie* obligation to obey the law of a roughly just system of laws. . . . The prima facie obligation to obey the law can be overridden by higher-order obligations or by special circumstances that justify disobedience. Higher-order obligations will override when, for example, obeying the law will lead to greater harm than disobeying. . . . For example, the law prohibiting us from driving on the left side of the road is a good law but we would be justified in breaking it in order to avoid hitting someone.

Seven Theses for Business Ethics and the Information Age

Richard de George

THESIS 1

The IT Head-in-the-Sand Syndrome

Many businesses either fail to realize that we have entered the information age or fail to appreciate its importance.

THESIS II

The Abdication of IT Ethical Responsibility

The lack of awareness of the ethical implications of the information age is what I call the "myth of amoral computing and information technology." The myth says that computers are not good or bad, information systems are not good or bad—they simply have a logic and rationale of their own.

THESIS III

Where are the Business Ethicists when you need them?

The task of the business ethicist in the present period of transition—and a task in which few are engaged—is to help anticipate the developments and ease the transition by not losing sight of the effects on people.

THESIS IV

Surmounting the Information Nexus

If by "information" we mean not simply data but *useful* data, we see immediately that what we are interested in is useful information. Information, as generally used, stands for true knowledge in some area. Its opposites are disinformation, misinformation, and falsehood. Information is not simply data, but data that represents reality. It's true and not false.

Two virtues appear immediately. One is truth (and so truthfulness), the other is accuracy.

THESIS V

Confronting the Communication Complex

Information is not useful, even if truthful and accurate, unless it is used. Hence, it needs to be communicated. The communication process, which is developing at an exponential rate, is central to the information age. The virtues of truthfulness and accuracy carry over into communication. But there are elements of communication that pose their own ethical issues: communication of what, to whom, in what form?

THESIS VI

The American Information Privacy Schizophrenia

The U.S. is schizophrenic about information privacy, wanting it in theory and giving it away in practice.

Information must be communicated, but it must also be about something. Information about people has become much more important than it was previously because of the great opportunity for a revolution in marketing in which manufacturers can target potential customers in ways not previously possible.

THESIS VII

Mickey Mouse isn't a Program

Information is very different from machines and tangible products, and so requires a new conception of property and property protection applicable to it.

Until fairly recently, a copyright granted protection to the expression of ideas in books and similar forms for 28 years (renewable for another 28 years). The protected period was then changed to the life of the author plus 50 years and to 75 years for a corporate author. In 1998, Congress extended the already-extended period, to the life of the author plus 70 years and to 95 years for a corporate author. The change came just in time to save Mickey Mouse from falling into the public domain, much to the pleasure of the Walt Disney Company.

So I am not claiming that people always have an obligation to obey the law; I claim only that the burden of proof is on those who would disobey roughly good laws. Given that extant laws regarding computer software are roughly good and given that a person has a prima facie obligation to obey roughly good laws, the second premise carries the weight of the argument for the moral permissibility of copying. In other words, the second premise must provide a reason for disobeying roughly just laws.

Premises (2a)–(2c) must, then, be examined carefully. Premise (2a) to the effect that there is nothing intrinsically wrong with making a copy of a piece of software is true, but it doesn't make the argument. The claim is true in the sense that if there were no laws against copying, the act of copying would not be wrong. Indeed, I argued earlier that property rights are not natural or moral in themselves but a matter of social utility. They acquire moral significance only when they are created by law and only in relatively just systems of law. Still, premise (2a) does not support copying because copying has been made illegal and as such is prima facie wrong: There have to be overriding reasons or special conditions to justify breaking the law.

According to premise (2b), making a copy of a piece of software for personal use harms no one. If we think of copying taking place in a state of nature, this premise is probably true; no one is harmed. However, once we are in a society of laws, the laws create legal rights, and it seems that a person harms another by depriving him of his legal right. When a person makes a copy of a piece of *proprietary* software, she deprives the owner of his legal right to control use of that software and to require payment in exchange for the use of the software. This is a harm, (Those who think this is not a harm should think of small software companies or individual entrepreneurs who have gone into the business of developing software, invested time and money, only to be squeezed out of business by customers who would buy one copy and make others instead of buying more.) So premise (2b) is false. Making a copy of a piece of proprietary software in our society harms someone.

Premise (2c) has the most promise as an argument for copying in that if it were true that one was doing harm by obeying the law, then we would have a moral reason for overriding the law, even if it were relatively good. Richard Stallman and Helen Nissenbaum have both made arguments of this kind. Both argue that there are circumstances in which not making a copy or not making a copy *and* providing it to a friend does some harm. However, in their arguments, the harm referred to does not seem of the kind to counterbalance the effects of a relatively just system of property rights. Both give examples of how an individual

---

To: You
From: The Philosopher
Subject: "Foucault and the Panopticon"

The English philosopher Jeremy Bentham designed the first Panopticon, in the hope of improving the dismal conditions in the prisons of his day. At the center of a huge octagon stood a tower, from which the guards could monitor any cell. Ringed around the tower were the prisoners in their cells, entirely visible to the guards (and largely visible to one another. In fact, many prisons that were built in the United States in the 1960s and 1970s followed closely the architectural model that was first designed and drawn by Bentham.

But Bentham did not anticipate the effects on the human psyche that constant surveillance would have. Unfortunately, today the possibilities of such constant surveillance (by the government? By marketers? By big business?) grow and grow. In his great study of the emergence of the modern prison, the 20th-century French philosopher Foucault has a chilling meditation on the Panopticon:

> Hence the major effect of the Panopticon: to induce in the inmate a state of conscious and permanent visibility that assures the automatic functioning of power. So to arrange things that the surveillance is permanent in its effects, even if it is discontinuous in its action; that the perfection of power should tend to render its actual exercise unnecessary; that this architectural apparatus should be a machine for creating and sustaining a power relation independent of the person who exercises it; in short, that the inmates should be caught up in a power situation of which they are themselves the bearers. To achieve this, it is at once too much and too little that the prisoner should be constantly observed by an inspector; too little, for what matters is that he knows himself to be observed; too much, because he has no need in fact of being so. In view of this, Bentham laid down the principle that power should be visible and unverifiable. Visible: the inmate will constantly have before his eyes the tall outline of the central tower from which he is spied upon. Unverifiable: the inmate must never know whether he is being looked at at any one moment; but he must be sure that he may always be so.

From Michel Foucault, *Discipline and Punish: The Birth of the Prison,* trans. Alan Sheridan (New York: Random House, 1979), p. 201.

might be able to help a friend out by providing her with an illegal copy of a piece of proprietary software. Both argue that laws against copying have the effect of discouraging altruism.

Still, this argument ignores the harm to the copyright or patent holder. Even if we were to grant that not providing a copy to a friend does harm, we have to compare that harm to the harm to the owner and choose the lesser.

Given what I said above about the prima facie obligation to obey the law, it follows that there may be some situations in which copying will be justified, namely when some fairly serious harm can only be prevented by making an illegal copy of a piece of proprietary software and using it. In most cases, however, the claims of the software owner to her legal rights would seem to be much stronger than the claims of someone who needs a copy to make her life easier.

If the position I have just sketched seems odd, consider an analogy with a different sort of property. Suppose I own a private swimming pool and I make a living by renting the use of it to others. I do not rent the pool every day and you figure out how to break in undetected and use the pool when it is not opened and I am not around. The act of swimming is not intrinsically wrong, and swimming in the pool does no obvious harm to me (the owner) or anyone else. Nevertheless, you are using my property without my permission. It would hardly seem a justification for ignoring my property rights if you claimed that you were hot and the swim in my pool made your life easier. The same would be true, if you argued that you had a friend who was very uncomfortable in the heat and you, having the knowledge of how to break into the pool, thought it would be selfish not to use that knowledge to help your friend out.

Of course, there are circumstances under which your illegal entry into my pool might be justified. For example, if someone else had broken in, was swimming, and began to drown, and you were innocently walking by, saw the person drowning, broke in, and jumped in the pool in order to save the other. Here the circumstances justify overriding my legal rights.

There seems no moral difference between breaking into the pool and making a copy of a proprietary piece of software. Both acts violate the legal rights of the owner—legal rights created by reasonably good laws. I will grant that these laws do prevent others from acting altruistically, but this, I believe, is inherent to private property. Private property is individualistic, exclusionary, and, perhaps, selfish. So, if Stallman and Nissenbaum want to launch an attack on all private property laws, I am in sympathy with their claims. However, I would press them to explain why they had picked out computer software law when private ownership of other things, such as natural resources or corporate conglomerates, seems much more menacing.

I conclude that it is prima facie wrong to make an illegal copy of a piece of proprietary software because to do so is to deprive someone (the owner) of their legal rights, and this is to harm them.

QUESTIONS

1. Why does computer software complicate the question of property?

2. How does Johnson use Locke's notion of property to solve the problem?

Elizabeth A. Buchanan

Information Ethics in a Worldwide Context

Elizabeth A. Buchanan is an assistant professor at the School of Information Studies, University of Wisconsin–Milwaukee.

Alkalimat begins his eloquent essay, "The New Technological Imperative in Africa: Class Struggles on the Edge of Third-Wave Revolution" by stating the "twentieth century is ending as a global drama full of conflict and change, with humanity torn between hope and despair. For a few the new century offers the wonders of a high-tech future, with wealth amid the birth of a new civilization; but for the majority there is fear of war, starvation, homelessness, poverty, and plagues. . . . " As information professionals, what are our ethical obligations in this worldwide context? . . . The information age is a time of mythology, a time for fantasies of wealth, power, ownership. The ethics of information services in this time, however, are very real, and don't necessarily correspond to these fantasies.

How do we as information professionals respond? Do we contribute to the fantasies? the non-truths? Or do we recognize the conditions Alkalimat describes and respond to them? . . .

The information society (now understood as a global society) or information age possesses a number of characteristics or qualities, among them a growing reliance on computer technologies, a large knowledge sector work force, a growing division of labor—a division which has major international implications, a movement from an analog to a digital model of informational and commercial transfer, and the consideration of information as a major commodity, analogous to the physical goods of the indus-trial age. And, nearly two decades ago, Smith recognized the global significance of information as a major commodity and defining feature of this age. Smith then declared that information lay at the heart of the world economy and cannot be separated from the other conflicts of which international and national policies are composed. Thus, the information society is considered an international phenomenon, with potential benefits and detriments to the world as a whole.

. . . [New] ethical dilemmas range from the fair and equitable distribution of resources to the availability and provision of education and training, to a mutual respect and consideration of cultural specificity and values. For instance, while the information age has encouraged a major increase in the amount of information produced, in the number of available channels through which information is accessible, and the apparent ease with which information is readily available, a growing disparity continues to set apart the now all-too-familiar "haves" and the "have-nots." While the information society offers an abundance of goods to some peoples, it is contributing to an expansive "digital divide," keeping peoples and nations on unequal planes. This inequality is promulgated on a number of levels.

AN OVERVIEW OF INFORMATION INEQUITY

In 1979, Mustapha Masmoudi's seminal paper "The New World Information Order" drew attention to the growing inequities and imbalances across the world in terms of information access, control, dissemina-

From *Ethics And Information Technology 7 (1999),* © 193 *Kluwer Academic Publishers (author).* Notes were deleted from the text.

tion, and content construction. In it, he cites seven prominent forms of inequities existing in the world in terms of information.

1. A flagrant quantitative imbalance between North and South;
2. An inequality in information resources;
3–4. A de facto hegemony and a will to dominate;
5. A lack of information on developing countries;
6. Survival of the colonial era. An alienating influence in the economic, social, and cultural spheres.
7. Messages ill-suited to the areas in which they are disseminated.

. . . Smith highlighted cultural domination of the South by the North through the control of major media outlets, through the unstinted flow of its cultural products throughout the world, and the cultural, political, and economic powers wielded by the North over the South. Ultimately, Smith's *Geopolitics of Information* thoroughly documented the ways in which information dissemination and commoditization fuel international domination, inequality, and suppression of cultural uniqueness and traditional values. Following Masmoudi and Smith, Morehouse called attention to another level of inequality, in the quantitatively biased distribution of resources, including information-based resources, across the world; he states

> . . . the late twentieth century world is a highly unequal place in energy consumption, income distribution, materials deprivation, economic and political power, and science-based problem solving capacity. Ninety-seven percent of the world's expenditure on research and development is made by a handful of industrialized countries. . . . Technology is rapidly emerging as a major instrument for global domination as other economic and military forms of power decline for stronger nations in the international system.

Nearly twenty years after Masmoudi, Smith, and Morehouse questioned the ethics of the information age and its supposed free flow of information and related commodities, the inequities in information transfer across the globe have changed very little. For example, flagrant inequities exist on a number of levels where the transfer of information or commodities is involved. Of particular significance, the unjust state of intellectual resource allocation severely affects contemporary scientists. If knowledge is power, the creation and dissemination of knowledge contribute to power. Thus, in relation to the science-based problem solving capacity to which Morehouse referred, Gibbs reviews the poor showing of third world researchers in the *Science Citation Index,* the leading index to cited scientific journal literature. This poor showing has third world researchers caught in a "vicious circle."

Third world scientists denied the possibility to contribute suggests that their information is less valuable, or less esteemed to the western eye. Less developed countries are held at a distance in terms of research and development, forcing continuous cycles of dependence. On another level, Gibbs considers telephone access, and notably, Haywood suggests that "one approach to measuring the impact of the 'information economy' as it evolves is the rate at which a country gains access to telephone lines." A dramatic example comes from Africa, a continent representing more than one tenth of the world's population, yet the least technologically and informationally developed. "The entire continent of Africa . . . contains fewer telephone lines than does Manhattan. African customers who sign up for service today are put on a waiting list 3.6 million people deep; in sub-Saharan regions, the wait is currently about nine years." Equally dismal, Haywood relates that "portable radios are probably the most widespread technology to be found in rural Africa, but even these lie silent for want of batteries."

It is significant to note that within Africa, great inequities exist. "South Africa has 9.5 main telephone lines per hundred people, giving a teledensity twenty times higher than the rest of sub-Saharan Africa. But only 11.6% of Africans have telephones in their homes, compared with 87.4% of whites, and 47.6% of Africans have no access to any phone, compared to only 6.6% of whites." This suggests that while North to South information flow is dramatically inequitable, internal inequities exist as well. In many ways, these inequities parallel the disparity between suburban, urban, and rural regions within the United States.

QUALITATIVELY-GROUNDED INEQUITIES

While a quantitative evaluation of information equity is dim for many nations, a more qualitatively-based assessment of the information society and its international flow of information reveals an equally disturbing picture. . . .

First, information transfer from the North to the South may contribute to serious disruption in the social fabric of a nation. Given that the majority of information entering a country is from the United States or constructed with a western viewpoint, cultural values and perspectives are transferred as well. The potential for serious social fragmentation is at hand and Woodrow draws attention to four major areas of potential conflict or tension that result from this international telecommunications or transfer of information. These include conflict over basic values embedded within the information infrastructure; tensions at the industry levels, at which western corporate interest may take precedence over the indigenous interests; conflict among nations over views on liberal or conservative approaches to information dissemination; and finally, tension, which arises when information holds great economic and political power; the power remains in the hands of the developers or transmitters of information, not in the hands of the receivers. Furthermore, social disruption may ensue, leading to potential dangerous situations; for instance, the Tiananmen Square incident in China was further aggravated by incoming fax memos and email messages from dissidents in the United States.

INFORMATION COMMODITIZATION, OR, "FREE IS OUT, FEE IS IN"

Next, the commoditization of information brings potentially unnecessary or undesirable forms of information to a region or country. . . . The increasing commoditization of information is removing information from public sectors or public agencies to the private realm. . . . If we are of the belief that information wants to be free and should be free, an age old adage of librarianship, this intense commoditization of information comprises a most significant issue facing information professionals today. As wealth is concentrated in fewer and fewer hands through monopolization and centralization, information professionals must more actively seek alternative outlets of information. Uniformity and monotony dominate, as we see American and western privatization strangle choice and options. While we have hundreds of channels, millions of Internet sites, and a plethora of media outlets, we still suffer from a paucity of choice. On the global level, fewer countries, fewer cultures have a chance to promote their own forms of indigenous knowledge, and they are increasingly forced to accept irrelevant, futile, and ineffective information.

Furthermore, the continual neglect of developing nations as *potential* information suppliers smacks of imperialism and colonialism, while it continues to deny any economic power or autonomy to the developing nations. . . . The myth of the information age strikes again—providing computers to the average citizens of the third world is insufficient, at best. . . . [T]he information society is grounded in commoditization and profit for some, while simultaneously, for many, social necessities and resources are in danger. . . .

THE INTERNET: PERPETUATING INEQUITY WORLD WIDE

Increasingly, the information age is defined by the "world-wide" presence of the Internet. The NTIA offers a familiar sentiment "Now that a considerable portion of today's business, communication, and research takes place on the Internet, access to the computers and networks may be as important as access to traditional telephone service." The Internet has been heralded as a means to ensure equitable access to information and democratic ideals, as well as a destroyer of cultural sovereignty and polluter of values. Due to the inherent nature of the Internet, including its many-to-many mode of communication, its immediacy, and its anonymity, the world's population can potentially have access to any and all forms of information, regardless of where or when it was released, or irregardless of its subject. Yes, information might be free in the philosophical sense, but at what expense, in the monetary sense and in terms of cultural values?

Shapiro optimistically acknowledges the liberating characteristics of the Internet; these sentiments comprise the many myths surrounding the information age and its technologies.

Using the Net and other new media, individuals can take back power from large Institutions, including government, corporations, and the media. Trends like personalization, decentralization, and dis-intermediation . . . will allow us each to have more control over life's details: what news and entertainment we're exposed to, how we learn and work, whom we socialize with, even how goods are distributed and political outcomes are reached. . . . The Net will allow us to transcend the limitations of geography and circumstance to create new social bonds.

Conversely—some would say more realistically—the Net can contribute to "social fragmentation;" it can cause cultural splintering and loss of tradition, . . . "What happens to the special history of people situated in microsocial niches when information is directed to people en masse? Does this universality of information destroy particularity of social life?" Many issues demand the attention of information professionals in considering these questions. Firstly, the mass release of information fails to consider cultural sensitivity; peoples and nations may take objection to such forms of information as governmental, for instance.

Secondly, the immediacy of the international information flow denies opportunities for peoples and nations to prepare for the onslaught of foreign cultural viewpoints, and the rapidity with which information is released denies the chance for contemplation and consideration.

Thirdly, cultural particularity is under siege by the prevalence of the English language on the Internet; some 90% of the material on the Internet is in the English language, thus raising concerns over language imperialism and literacy issues.

Fourthly, cultural specificity should be cherished and protected. With mass releases of information,

information that continues to be homogenous and often monotonous, individual thought is diminishing and communal integrity is lessening, Cultural niches fight for survival in a world of sameness, and despite the many predictions and hopes of virtual communities and virtual neighborhoods, individuality in the truest sense and the communal sense is taking a severe beating. . . .

Receptivity to information between cultures is increasingly at an exciting or alarming rate, depending on your point of view. The upside of this is that different races can now understand more about each other as language barriers break down in favor of English; the downside is that, as language is the main conduit of cultural heritage and the key to distinctiveness, there will be less to fascinate and excite us because the richness of difference will be replaced by the poverty of sameness. . . .

CONCLUSION

Masmoudi demands a reevaluation and readjustment to the inequitable conditions surrounding information access, control, dissemination, and content construction. Yet, it is critical however, that developing countries make their own decisions concerning the flow of information; while no country should be denied access or control of information, cultural sensitivity demands that self-reliance and self-control dictate that flow of information. Cultural specificity demands respect. An imperialistic or colonialist approach to information will only set the worlds further apart, at a time when information and its conveyers promise to bring the world closer together.

In summary, it is useful to consider an episode which begins Richard Sclove's *Democracy and Technology:*

> During the 1970s, running water was installed in the houses of Ibieca, a small village in northeast Spain. With pipes running directly to their houses, Ibiecans no longer had to fetch water from the village fountain. Families gradually purchased washing machines, and women stopped gathering to scrub laundry by hand at the village washbasin.
>
> Arduous tasks were rendered technologically superfluous, but village social life unexpectedly

changed. The public fountain and washbasin, once scenes of vigorous social interaction, became nearly deserted. Men began losing their sense of familiarity with the children and the donkeys that had once helped them to haul water. Women stopped congregating at the washbasin to intermix their scrubbing with politically empowering gossip about men and social life. In hindsight, the installation of running water helped break down the Ibiecans' strong bonds—with one another, with their animals, and with the land—that had knit them together as a community.

Sclove's premise in *Democracy and Technology* involves participatory design and a democratic adoption of information and technology. Participatory design and development holds the key to ensuring that all peoples will be able to choose among alternatives, these choices will reflect their personal aspirations and their view of the common good, and will contribute to the best social conditions possible according to the perspective of those affected by the information flow or technological development.

Sclove asserts that participatory design and development will "ensure a more diverse range of social needs, concerns, and experiences." Such an approach is requisite if the information age is to be equitable and ethical. Consequently, information transfer in terms of access, dissemination, control, and content construction must be designed according to a principle or set of principles that respect cultural specificity, subjectivity, and values. The information age holds great potential to unite disparate peoples and ideas; nevertheless, it is imperative to safeguard the cultural uniqueness and social microcosms which furnish the regions of the world with independence, freedom of choice, and freedom of access.

QUESTIONS

1. Why does the "worldwide context" of information change its ethical situation?
2. Why might a free on-line library (containing much or most of the world's recorded knowledge) be a good thing? Why might it be a bad thing?

Deborah C. Johnson | # Hacker Ethics

Deborah C. Johnson is Olsson Professor of Applied Ethics Technology, Culture, and Communication at the University of Virginia.

I am going to use the term *hacker* to refer to a person who engages in behavior that attacks the Internet and *hacking* to refer to the activity. . . . When hacker and hacking were first coined, hacker referred to a computer enthusiast and hacking referred to the feats such enthusiasts were able to accomplish. Hackers were individuals who loved computers and would spend hours and hours figuring out how to do clever things with them. Usually hackers were young men who had

acquired a good deal of knowledge about computers, and they shared this knowledge with one another through the first electronic bulletin boards. Often hackers organized computer clubs and user groups, circulated newsletters, and even had conventions.

Only later did the term *hacker* acquire negative connotations. Hacker began to be used to refer to those who used computers for illegal actions, especially gaining unauthorized access to computer systems, and stealing (and then sharing) proprietary software. Resisting this change in usage, many old-line computer enthusiasts pushed for a distinction between *crackers* and *hackerrs*. Hacker, they hoped

From Deborah C. Johnson *Computer Ethics*, Prentice Hall © 2001, pp. 97–102.

would continue to have its original, heroic meaning, while cracker would refer to those who engage in illegal activities—cracking into systems.

This distinction has not, however, taken hold. Hacker and hacking are now routinely used to refer to those who gain unauthorized access and accomplish other disruptive feats. Still, such a wide variety of illegal activities now occur on the Internet that it seems most useful to reserve the term hacking for only a subset of these. I propose to use the term hacking to refer to the subset of illegal behaviors that involve unauthorized access and aim at disruption and damage. Such acts undermine the security and the integrity of the Internet. On this definition, such acts as intentionally sending viruses or worms that damage computer systems, denial of service attacks, and unauthorized taking control of a Web site all count as hacking.

. . . . In most cases, hacking is illegal and the harmfulness of the activity is apparent. Most Internet users want a system that is reliable; works without interruption; has privacy and integrity; and doesn't require a lot of effort or resources to make secure. Thus, from the perspective of most Internet users, hackers are a nuisance or worse. They snoop around trying to get access to systems they are not authorized to access; they plant viruses and worms bringing systems down and making them unreliable; they copy and distribute proprietary software; they cause expensive denial of service delays. They force everyone to invest more and more effort and resources in security.

There are interesting sociological and psychological questions to be asked about hackers and why they hack. For example, why is it mostly male teenagers who hack? Why do they believe they can get away without being detected even though the technology is now highly traceable? Why is it that individuals who probably wouldn't break into a store on the street are willing to try to break into a computer system? While these are fascinating questions, from an ethical perspective the behavior is transparently undesirable and, therefore, not at all controversial or difficult. Hacking behavior generally doesn't pose difficult or complicated ethical challenges or dilemmas.

The situation was not always like this. In the early days of computing, the situation was different. Computers were just beginning to be used more and more, and the technology to connect computers to one another via telecommunications lines had just become available. At this time, there were no laws specifying what could or couldn't be done via remote access. There weren't laws specifically prohibiting unauthorized access; the idea of designing a worm or virus to infect a computer system had not yet occurred, let alone been prohibited. . . . [T]here were a multitude of policy vacuums.

In those days, the ethical questions were pressing because the policy vacuums had to be filled and there were substantial ethical questions about what rules would be fair and would lead to the best consequences. Perhaps the most pressing issue had to do

An Internet Culture?

C. Kluckhorn

Culture: "the total way of life for a people," "the social legacy an individual acquires from his group," "a way of thinking, feeling and believing," "a mechanism for the regulation of behavior."

C. Kluckhorn, *Mirror for Man*

with the ownership of software.... [M]any of the first computer enthusiasts had an alternative vision of the potential of computers. They saw in the reproducibility of computer information and software, the enormous potential to spread information and knowledge across the globe. They saw the parallel between computing and the printing press and envisioned how computing could exponentially extend the spread of knowledge. The fact that electronic information could be reproduced without loss to the original and without loss to the original holder of the information meant the availability of information at essentially no cost. This was a vision of *sharing* of knowledge, not one of property and commercialization. Many enthusiasts resisted the idea of making software into intellectual property. They argued that information should be free (i.e., un-ownable).

Unfortunately, this vision of the potential of computer and information technology has largely been lost. Instead, it is now taken for granted that most information is (or could be or should be) proprietary. Acts of accessing, replicating, and distributing information without permission are immediately seen as privacy- or property-rights violations. Compared to the early days of computing, a good deal of legislation—specifying what is and is not allowed on the Internet—now exists. Most of the policy vacuums have been filled. Thus, the arguments that hackers used to give in their defense now seem somewhat anachronistic. Still, the arguments in defense of hacking are enlightening and for this reason, I will discuss several of them briefly.

The arguments that hackers gave in their defense in the early days of computing can be sorted into four arguments. I have already suggested the first argument; it is the argument to the effect that all information should be free. . . .

The second argument is that break-ins illustrate security problems to those who can do something about them. Remember the Robert Morris case at the beginning of this chapter. Morris claimed that he was trying to expose a flaw in the system. He had tried other means to get the problem fixed but system administrators had not listened to him. Hence, he defended his action on grounds that he was doing a service to computer system administrators and users

by demonstrating the seriousness of the problem. In fact, he confessed that he didn't mean to do as much damage as he had done; the worm got out of control.

The argument, in effect, claims that hacking does some good. Hacking illustrates the weaknesses—the vulnerabilities—of computer systems to those who can repair them, before more serious damage is done.

Under careful scrutiny, this argument falters. It suggests that hacking into a system should be understood as an act of whistle-blowing. Individuals "blow the whistle" on illegal or dangerous activities so as to draw attention to a situation, to prevent harm and get the situation fixed. The literature on whistle-blowing suggests that whistle-blowers should always try first to fix the problem through internal channels because it is better to get a bad situation fixed with the least risk or danger (to those who are in danger as well as to the whistle-blower). Yes, we can imagine cases in which an individual is frustrated in her attempts to get a flaw fixed and we can imagine cases in which the flaw is serious enough for severe action. . . . Still, such cases are going to be rare, not the typical motive for hacking in or using a virus.

Arguing by analogy, Spafford gives a convincing counter to the whistle-blowing argument. Spafford suggests that the hacker defense amounts to saying that "vigilantes have the right to attempt to break into the homes in my neighborhood on a continuing basis to demonstrate that they are susceptible to burglars" (Spafford, 1992). Since we would never accept this argument made in defense of burglars, we should not accept it for hacking. Spafford also points out that online break-ins, even when done to call attention to flaws in security, wastes time and money, and pressures individuals and companies to invest in security. Many do not have the resources to fix systems or implement tighter security, yet the "vigilante behavior" forces upgrades.

An analogy with automobile security seems relevant here. Thirty years ago, depending on where you lived, many individuals were able to leave their automobiles on city streets without locking them and without fear of the car being stolen. Now, in many parts of the world, owners not only must lock their automobiles, they must invest in elaborate security devices to protect against stealing. Indeed, automobile manufacturers now routinely include such devices on cars. All the resources put into automobile security (the owner's money, the police force's time, automobile manufacturers' expertise) could have been invested elsewhere, if so many individuals were not trying to steal automobiles.

Analogously, those who attempt to gain unauthorized access, plant viruses, make denial of service attacks, and so on, compel the investment of time, energy, and other resources into making the Internet secure, when these resources could be used to improve the Internet in other ways. It is important to see that this applies as much to the energies and resources of the designers and manufacturers of computer and information technology as to service providers and individual users.

This defense of hacking does not, then, seem to have force. It is unquestionably a good thing for those who become aware of flaws in the security of computer systems to inform computer administrators and urge them to fix these flaws. We can even imagine cases in which the flaws in security are extremely serious and an individual's reports of the threat to security fall on deaf ears. It is difficult, nevertheless, to imagine a case that justifies using viruses, denial of service attacks, or accessing private files as a means to get the problem fixed.

Another argument, used in defense of gaining unauthorized access to computer systems, is that breaking into a computer system does no harm as long as the hacker changes nothing. And, if the hacker learns something about how computer systems operate, then, something is gained at no loss to anyone.

A little thought reveals the weakness of the first part of this argument, for individuals can be harmed simply by the unauthorized entry. After all, nonphysical harm is harm nonetheless. If individuals have proprietary rights and rights to privacy, then they are harmed when these rights are violated, just as individuals are harmed when they are deprived of their right to vote or their right to due process. Moreover, hackers can do physical harm. For example, hackers could gain access to computer systems used in hospitals where patients are at risk or systems running industrial processes where workers are at physical risk from dangerous chemicals or explosions. Sup-

pose a hacker were to access and tamper with the computer system used to match donated organs with those in need of organs. Here time is absolutely critical. A slow down in the system caused by tampering could make the difference between life and death.

So, the hacker defense that they are doing no harm and actually learning about computer systems is not convincing. Hacking can be dangerous and can put people at unnecessary risk.

To be sure, hackers may learn about computing and computer systems from their hacking activities. It may be argued in particular that hacking is a good way to learn about how to design computer systems to make them more secure. This argument is complex and tricky. The fact that one learns from an activity does not justify it. Giving electric shocks to learners when they make mistakes may promote learning, but this does not make it a good teaching method. Allowing children to stick things in electric outlets might result in their learning the dangers of the outlets, but there are less dangerous ways to teach this lesson. So, just because hackers learn from hacking does not make it a good thing.

Hacking is not the only way to learn about computing or computer security. Aside from the standard ways one learns in the classroom (by reading, listening to a teacher, doing problems), one can imagine a variety of creative ways to teach people about computers and computer security. These might include challenging games or tournaments that encourage learners to be creative and clever.

To justify hacking as a means to learning about computing and computer security, an argument would have to show not just that hackers learn but that hacking is the only way or the best way to learn. Showing that hacking is the "best way" would have to show that the improvement in knowledge and skill was so great as to counterbalance the risks and dangers to those who might be harmed by the hacking. In other words, if hacking promotes learning, the good of the learning would have to be weighed against the negative consequences of this method of learning. So, this defense of hacking is also not convincing.

Finally, hackers used to argue that they would help keep Big Brother at bay. This argument may be more understandable after . . . comprehending the threats to privacy that have arisen because of the use of computer and information technology. The thrust of the argument is that computers and information technology are being used to collect information about individuals and to do things to individuals that they don't want done. Hackers have the computer savvy to find out what is going on and tell us about it. They can assure us that covert illegalities and abuse will not go undetected. In short, the argument suggests that hackers are good vigilantes. Imagine government agencies gathering information they are not authorized or justified in gathering. Imagine companies maintaining secret databases of information that is prohibited by law from being collected or used. Hackers provide protection against this. By gaining unauthorized access to government and commercial systems, they can see when abuse is occurring and alert the public.

The argument is correct in suggesting that the public needs protection against abuses of information and Big Brother. Still, are hackers the best agents for this kind of protection? Would the cost of tolerating hackers be worth what we gain in protection? Do hackers solve the problem or make it worse?

We have many options to monitor for such things as information abuse and government surveillance. We could create a national data protection commission that would have the authority to monitor information practices, propose legislation, and prosecute violators. Commission or no commission, we could develop better laws and clearer guidelines for information practices. We could assign special obligations to computer professionals calling upon them to report any information they acquire about data abuse and/or illegal surveillance. We could encourage users to report suspicious behavior. In short, there are a variety of strategies that could be adopted to protect the public from Big Brother.

While toleration of hackers is one such strategy, it is not the most attractive. The problem is that the public would get rid of one problem by creating another. We might reduce the threat of data abuse and covert surveillance by government and by commercial interests, but in exchange we would be at the mercy of vigilantes. The vigilantes might decide to take a look at our files or explore our computer sys-

tems, in the name of protection. Suffice it to say that we would have exchanged the rule of law and protection by formal authorities, for rule by vigilantes.

So, hacking is not justified. It causes harm; it violates legitimate privacy and property rights; it often deprives users of access to their own computer systems and to the Internet; and, it compels investment in security when the invested resources might have been used for other activities. The arguments in defense of hacking are not convincing. Hacking is unethical and has rightly been made illegal.

Nevertheless, a note of caution is in order lest some of the arguments made by hackers be too quickly dismissed. Several of the arguments point to potentials of the Internet that are being neglected—to the detriment of the Internet. Implicit in the hacker arguments is a concern to take advantage of the enormous potential of the Internet for spreading and sharing information. The reproducibility of the Internet makes it possible for information to be reproduced at negligible cost; in theory this means information and knowledge could be spread across the globe at little cost. On the other hand, this potential is undermined by extensive property rights that restrict distribution of information. Hackers seem aware of this, as well as of the vulnerability of computer systems to attack and failure. This vulnerability is often underappreciated when important information and activities are put online without adequate security. Finally, hackers' concerns about Big Brother are worthy of consideration. . . . [P]rivacy on the Internet is rapidly shrinking.

So, while hacking is disruptive, dangerous, and unjustified, discussion provoked by hackers and hacking—of what should be allowed and not allowed on the Internet—should not be squelched too quickly. Hacking represents a countercurrent in the development of the Internet, and to take advantage of the enormous potential of the Internet, it behooves us to listen to countercurrents.

QUESTIONS

1. Why should hackers be ethical?
2. Does hacking ever serve a social good? How and why (or why not)?

| Bill Joy | Why The Future Doesn't Need Us |

Bill Joy, cofounder and chief scientist of Sun Microsystems, was cochair of the presidential commission on the future of IT research.

From the moment I became involved in the creation of new technologies, their ethical dimensions have concerned me, but it was only in the autumn of 1998 that I became anxiously aware of how great are the dangers facing us in the 21st century. I can date the onset of my unease to the day I met Ray Kurzweil, the deservedly famous inventor of the first reading machine for the blind and many other amazing things. . . .

In the hotel bar, Ray gave me a partial preprint of his then-forthcoming book *The Age of Spiritual Machines,* which outlined a utopia he foresaw—one in which humans gained near immortality by becoming one with robotic technology. On reading it, my sense of unease only intensified; I felt sure he had to be understating the dangers, understating the probability of a bad outcome along this path.

I found myself most troubled by a passage detailing a *dys*topian scenario:

THE NEW LUDDITE CHALLENGE

First let us postulate that the computer scientists succeed in developing intelligent machines that can do all things better than human beings can do them. In that case presumably all work will be done by vast, highly organized systems of machines and no human effort will be necessary. . . .

If the machines are permitted to make all their owndecisions, we can't make any conjectures as to the results, because it is impossible to guess how such machines might behave. We only point out that the fate of the human race would be at the mercy of the machines. . . . The human race might easily permit itself to drift into a position of such dependence on the machines that it would have no practical choice but to accept all of the machines' decisions. As society and the problems that face it become more and more complex and machines become more and more intelligent, people will let machines make more of their decisions for them, simply because machine-made decisions will bring better results than man-made ones. Eventually a stage may be reached at which the decisions necessary to keep the system running will be so complex that human beings will be incapable of making them intelligently. At that stage the machines will be in effective control. People won't be able to just turn the machines off, because they will be so dependent on them that turning them off would amount to suicide.

On the other hand it is possible that human control over the machines may be retained. . . . Due to improved techniques the elite will have greater control over the masses; and because human work will no longer be necessary the masses will be superfluous, a useless burden on the system.

In the book, you don't discover until you turn the page that the author of this passage is Theodore Kaczynski—the Unabomber. . . .

Kaczynski's dystopian vision describes unintended consequences, a well-known problem with the design and use of technology, and one that is clearly related to Murphy's law—"Anything that can go wrong, will." . . . Our overuse of antibiotics has led to what may be the biggest such problem so far: the emergence of antibiotic-resistant and much more dangerous bacteria. Similar things happened when attempts to eliminate malarial mosquitoes using DDT caused them to acquire DDT resistance; malarial parasites likewise acquired multi-drug-resistant genes.

The cause of many such surprises seems clear: The systems involved are complex, involving interaction among and feedback between many parts. Any changes to such a system will cascade in ways that are difficult to predict; this is especially true when human actions are involved. . . .

THE SHORT RUN (EARLY 2000S)

Biological species almost never survive encounters with superior competitors. Ten million years ago, South and North America were separated by a sunken Panama isthmus. South America, like Australia today, was populated by marsupial mammals, including pouched equivalents of rats, deers, and tigers. When the isthmus connecting North and South America rose, it took only a few thousand years for the northern placental species, with slightly more effective metabolisms and reproductive and nervous systems, to displace and eliminate almost all the southern marsupials.

In a completely free marketplace, superior robots would surely affect humans as North American placentals affected South American marsupials (and as humans have affected countless species). Robotic industries would compete vigorously among themselves for matter, energy, and space, incidentally driving their price beyond human reach. Unable to afford the necessities of life, biological humans would be squeezed out of existence.

There is probably some breathing room, because we do not live in a completely free marketplace. Government coerces nonmarket behavior, especially by collecting taxes. Judiciously applied, governmental coercion could support human populations in high style on the fruits of robot labor, perhaps for a long while.

A textbook dystopia—and Moravec is just getting wound up. He goes on to discuss how our main job in the 21st century will be "ensuring continued cooperation from the robot industries" by passing laws decreeing that they be "nice," and to describe how seriously dangerous a human can be "once transformed into an unbounded superintelligent robot." Moravec's view is that the robots will eventually succeed us—that humans clearly face extinction.

I decided it was time to talk to my friend Danny Hillis. Danny became famous as the cofounder of Thinking Machines Corporation, which built a very powerful parallel supercomputer. Despite my current job title of Chief Scientist at Sun Microsystems, I am more a computer architect than a scientist, and I respect Danny's knowledge of the information and physical sciences more than that of any other single person I know. Danny is also a highly regarded futurist who thinks long-term—four years ago he started the Long Now Foundation, which is building a clock designed to last 10,000 years, in an attempt to draw attention to the pitifully short attention span of our society. . . . Danny's answer—directed specifically at Kurzweil's scenario of humans merging with robots—came swiftly, and quite surprised me. He said, simply, that the changes would come gradually, and that we would get used to them.

———————

The 21st-century technologies—genetics, nanotechnology, and robotics (GNR)—are so powerful that they can spawn whole new classes of accidents and abuses. Most dangerously, for the first time, these accidents and abuses are widely within the reach of individuals or small groups. They will not require large facilities or rare raw materials. Knowledge alone will enable the use of them.

Thus we have the possibility not just of weapons of mass destruction but of knowledge-enabled mass destruction (KMD), this destructiveness hugely amplified by the power of self-replication.

I think it is no exaggeration to say we are on the cusp of the further perfection of extreme evil, an evil whose possibility spreads well beyond that which weapons of mass destruction bequeathed to the nation-states, on to a surprising and terrible empowerment of extreme individuals.

Nothing about the way I got involved with computers suggested to me that I was going to be facing these kinds of issues.

———————

In designing software and microprocessors, I have never had the feeling that I was designing an intelligent machine. The software and hardware is so fragile and the capabilities of the machine to "think" so clearly absent that, even as a possibility, this has always seemed very far in the future.

But now, with the prospect of human-level computing power in about 30 years, a new idea suggests itself: that I may be working to create tools which will enable the construction of the technology that may replace our species. How do I feel about this? Very uncomfortable. Having struggled my entire career to build reliable software systems, it seems to me more than likely that this future will not work out as well as some people may imagine. My personal experience suggests we tend to overestimate our design abilities.

Given the incredible power of these new technologies, shouldn't we be asking how we can best coexist with them? And if our own extinction is a likely, or even possible, outcome of our technological development, shouldn't we proceed with great caution? . . .

How soon could such an intelligent robot be built? The coming advances in computing power seem to make it possible by 2030. And once an intelligent robot exists, it is only a small step to a robot species—to an intelligent robot that can make evolved copies of itself.

A second dream of robotics is that we will gradually replace ourselves with our robotic technology, achieving near immortality by downloading our consciousnesses. . . . But if we are downloaded into our technology, what are the chances that we will thereafter be ourselves or even human? It seems to me far more likely that a robotic existence would not be like a human one in any sense that we understand, that the robots would in no sense be our children, that on this path our humanity may well be lost.

———————

Molecular electronics—the new subfield of nanotechnology where individual molecules are circuit elements—should mature quickly and become enormously lucrative within this decade, causing a large incremental investment in all nanotechnologies.

Unfortunately, as with nuclear technology, it is far easier to create destructive uses for nanotechnology than constructive ones. Nanotechnology has clear military and terrorist uses, and you need not be suicidal to release a massively destructive nanotechnological device—such devices can be built to be selec-

tively destructive, affecting, for example, only a certain geographical area or a group of people who are genetically distinct.

An immediate consequence of the Faustian bargain in obtaining the great power of nanotechnology is that we run a grave risk—the risk that we might destroy the biosphere on which all life depends.

. . . "Plants" with "leaves" no more efficient than today's solar cells could out-compete real plants, crowding the biosphere with an inedible foliage. Tough omnivorous "bacteria" could out-compete real bacteria: They could spread like blowing pollen, replicate swiftly, and reduce the biosphere to dust in a matter of days. Dangerous replicators could easily be too tough, small, and rapidly spreading to stop—at least if we make no preparation. We have trouble enough controlling viruses and fruit flies.

Among the cognoscenti of nanotechnology, this threat has become known as the "gray goo problem." Though masses of uncontrolled replicators need not be gray or gooey, the term "gray goo" emphasizes that replicators able to obliterate life might be less inspiring than a single species of crabgrass. They might be superior in an evolutionary sense, but this need not make them valuable.

The gray goo threat makes one thing perfectly clear: We cannot afford certain kinds of accidents with replicating assemblers.

Gray goo would surely be a depressing ending to our human adventure on Earth, far worse than mere fire or ice, and one that could stem from a simple laboratory accident. Oops.

———————

These possibilities are all thus either undesirable or unachievable or both. The only realistic alternative I see is relinquishment: to limit development of the technologies that are too dangerous, by limiting our pursuit of certain kinds of knowledge.

Yes, I know, knowledge is good, as is the search for new truths. We have been seeking knowledge since ancient times. Aristotle opened his *Metaphysics* with the simple statement: "All men by nature desire to know." We have, as a bedrock value in our society, long agreed on the value of open access to information, and recognize the problems that arise with attempts to restrict access to and development of knowledge. In recent times, we have come to revere scientific knowledge.

But despite the strong historical precedents, if open access to and unlimited development of knowledge hence-forth puts us all in clear danger of extinction, then common sense demands that we reexamine even these basic, long-held beliefs.

It was Nietzsche who warned us, at the end of the 19th century, not only that God is dead but that "faith in science, which after all exists undeniably, cannot owe its origin to a calculus of utility; it must have originated *in spite of* the fact that the disutility and dangerousness of the 'will to truth,' of 'truth at any price' is proved to it constantly." It is this further danger that we now fully face—the consequences of our truth-seeking. The truth that science seeks can certainly be considered a dangerous substitute for God if it is likely to lead to our extinction.

If we could agree, as a species, what we wanted, where we were headed, and why, then we would make our future much less dangerous—then we might understand what we can and should relinquish. Otherwise, we can easily imagine an arms race developing over GNR technologies, as it did with the NBC technologies in the 20th century. This is perhaps the greatest risk, for once such a race begins, it's very hard to end it. This time—unlike during the Manhattan Project—we aren't in a war, facing an implacable enemy that is threatening our civilization; we are driven, instead, by our habits, our desires, our economic system, and our competitive need to know. . . .

As Thoreau said, "We do not ride on the railroad; it rides upon us"; and this is what we must fight, in our time. The question is, indeed, Which is to be master? Will we survive our technologies?

We are being propelled into this new century with no plan, no control, no brakes. . . .

And yet I believe we do have a strong and solid basis for hope. Our attempts to deal with weapons of mass destruction in the last century provide a shining example of relinquishment for us to consider: the unilateral U.S. abandonment, without preconditions, of the development of biological weapons. This relinquishment stemmed from the realization that while it would take an enormous effort to create these terrible weapons, they could from then on easily be duplicated and fall into the hands of rogue nations or terrorist groups.

––––––––––

Where can we look for a new ethical basis to set our course? I have found the ideas in the book *Ethics for the New Millennium,* by the Dalai Lama, to be very helpful. As is perhaps well known but little heeded, the Dalai Lama argues that the most important thing is for us to conduct our lives with love and compassion for others, and that our societies need to develop a stronger notion of universal responsibility and of our interdependency.

The Dalai Lama further argues that we must understand what it is that makes people happy, and acknowledge the strong evidence that neither material progress nor the pursuit of the power of knowledge is the key—that there are limits to what science and the scientific pursuit alone can do.

Clearly, we need to find meaningful challenges and sufficient scope in our lives if we are to be happy in whatever is to come. But I believe we must find alternative outlets for our creative forces, beyond the culture of perpetual economic growth; this growth has largely been a blessing for several hundred years, but it has not brought us unalloyed happiness, and we must now choose between the pursuit of unrestricted and undirected growth through science and technology and the clear accompanying dangers.

––––––––––

Do you remember the beautiful penultimate scene in *Manhattan* where Woody Allen is lying on his couch and talking into a tape recorder? He is writing a short story about people who are creating unnecessary, neurotic problems for themselves, because it keeps them from dealing with more unsolvable, terrifying problems about the universe.

He leads himself to the question, "Why is life worth living?" and to consider what makes it worthwhile for him: Groucho Marx, Willie Mays, the second movement of the *Jupiter Symphony,* Louis Armstrong's recording of "Potato Head Blues," Swedish movies, Flaubert's *Sentimental Education,* Marlon Brando, Frank Sinatra, the apples and pears by

Cézanne, the crabs at Sam Wo's, and, finally, the showstopper: his love of Tracy's face.

Each of us has our precious things, and as we care for them we locate the essence of our humanity. In the end, it is because of our great capacity for caring that I remain optimistic we will confront the dangerous issues now before us.

QUESTIONS

1. Why doesn't the future need us? Or does it need us, but only in certain ways?

2. Does regulation ever encourage creativity? How can we both encourage innovation and avoid the dangers that technological innovation often creates?

Theodore Roszak | # In Defense of the Naked Mind

Theodore Roszak is the author of *Making of a Counter Culture* and *The Cult of Information*.

THE COMPUTER AND GENERAL LUDD

There are computer enthusiasts I have met who will hear no evil spoken of the machine they hold dear. They tend to regard every critic they encounter as the latest species of "Luddite" those notorious machine-wreckers of the early industrial revolution who are remembered in the textbooks as mindless enemies of progress. . . .

The Luddites have come to play a peculiar role in technological history. They are usually invoked as convenient whipping boys whose function is to squelch critical discussion of machines and their uses. Once the label "Luddite" has been attached to you, the inevitable next question is, "How would you like to go back and live in a cave?"

Historians now tell us that the original Luddites may have taken a bad rap. The hard-pressed weavers of northern England who rallied around the mythical General Ludd appear to have had no grudge against technology in and of itself; their grievance was with those who used machines to lower wages or eliminate jobs. General Ludd's "army of re-dressers" as they named themselves, never attacked one of the new power looms unless its owner had violated the workers' interests. Though they were desperate men fighting to feed their families, their hostility was carefully targeted. They asked how the machines were being used, by whom, for whose benefit—and then normally tried negotiating a better deal with their employers. Only when that effort failed did they feel forced to resort to violence. But to begin with, theirs was essentially an appeal for justice and humane treatment. . . .

Like all the works of *homo faber,* high tech, this latest chapter in humanity's ongoing industrial saga, deserves to be honored as a manifestation of the astonishingly inventive genius of our species. I use a computer to earn my way as a writer; I might even qualify as a highly proficient user. I marvel each time I boot the machine at the cunning that has found a way to translate so much of human culture—numbers, words, graphics, music, three-dimensional design, animation, fractals—into simple digital symbols that can be read as electrical signals. I am astonished at the speed and compaction that has been achieved by computational devices in little more than

From *The Cult of Information* (Berkeley: University of California Press, 1986), pp. xvii–xlvi, 16–19. Notes were deleted from the text.

a generation. I can even understand how some might (though mistakenly, I think) identify an accomplishment of this magnitude as an incipient form of superior intelligence. . . .

I value having plenty of data readily available as much as the next person. *Unless,* that is, the next person happens to be a computer manufacturer, a software mogul, an advertising executive in charge of the IBM account, or an Artificial Intelligence expert under contract to AT&T. Whenever I hear vested interests like these speaking of information as if it were *all* the human mind needs to think with, I begin to feel as if I might have strayed into some strange sect where all about me I find people worshipping light bulbs. No question but that light bulbs are useful devices; I would not want to live without them. But I never would have thought of them as objects of veneration.

So too with information. The cultlike status it has attained both bewilders and troubles me. The eagerness some enthusiasts (as well as many academics, intellectuals, and journalists who should know better) display to globalize the word until it covers all the cultural ground in sight seems to me blatantly wrong—especially when it comes to teaching the young. If they had their way, they would flatten the natural hierarchy of the mind until people cannot tell the difference between the telephone directory and Homer's *Iliad.* So in these pages I raise a small protest on behalf of the naked human mind, its creative powers, its animal resiliency, its undiscovered evolutionary potentiality, its deep enigmas of aspiration and self-transcendence. I seek to remind readers of the obvious that so often goes unobserved. There have been works of genius, indeed whole golden ages of culture—many of them the creation of peasant peoples and tribal folk—based upon nothing more than human speech, imagination, and memory. The heights of intellect and vision have been scaled by people gathered around campfires to tell stories, by poets scratching away with a quill by candlelight, by scribes bending over a sheet of parchment, by inspired painters working on the wall of a cave. There is, of course, no reason why we should not, in our time, look for other, more expressive media of

communication, but I find it important to recall that mind has never been dependent on machinery to reach the peaks of achievement.

Though that reminder is not meant as a rejection of machinery, which is itself a glory of our species, I am sure some will see it as a typical humanist response to the overweening claims of the technician. Well, perhaps it is. But where high tech is concerned the disposition of forces ought to be obvious to anyone who has as much as a passing acquaintance with the shape of the global economy. High tech is the biggest thing going in the world of financial and political decision; it enjoys the unstinting support of governments and great corporations. . . .

MEANWHILE, BACK
AT THE CARNIVAL

. . . [t]he merchandising of hardware and software remains as much of a carnival act as ever, with endless new attractions along the midway, all of them being brazenly oversold. While the price of such basic items as memory chips and hard disks continues to fall, new fascinations like desktop publishing multimedia, and interactivity serve to keep the consumers consuming. New hardware and software constantly push toward the purchase of bigger, faster equipment and more complex programs, none of which is nearly as necessary to have, as cheap to buy, or as friendly to use as the advertising pretends. . . .

And what, overwhelmingly, do the hardware and the software get used for outside their day-to-day business applications? The computer industry remains embarrassingly dependent upon much that is simply tawdry. Games and amusements continue to be the mainstay of the technology in the mass market. As of the early 1990s American parents were paying more for video games (over *$5 billion*) than for tickets to the movies. Manufacturers are hoping to increase that figure tenfold by the end of the decade by including 3-D, virtual reality, adult versions of "Star Trek" and "Yoshi's Cookies"—probably spiked with a heavy dose of pornware, or "erototronics," as it is called in *Future Sex,* a magazine that specializes in computer-mediated titillation. "Adult" bulletin boards have proven to be one of the growth areas of the technology. Advertising "A Hundred Lines of Hot Modem Fun At Your Fingertips! With Both Straight and Gay Sections," the language and imagery have grown potent enough to raise issues of censorship. Responding to police raids in some cities, system operators have addressed the question of X-rated material at conferences with some urgency. In Austria kids can now purchase neo-Naziware videogames called *Aryan Test* and *KZ Manager* which allow players to run death camps and gas inferior races.

Even the business community gets suckered into wasting precious resources on expensive computer digressions like chasing fonts through desktop publishing programs and cranking out 256-color graphics-laden fast-step CD-ROM "presentations" that are more sizzle than substance. One study I have come across estimates the amount of time spent fussing with in-house newsletters, especially trying out this and that font, may cost American industry tens of millions of dollars in lost time. . . .

THE END OF THE WAR MACHINE?

Another issue [is] . . . the power of the computer to concentrate ever-greater decision-making power in the wrong few hands. . . . What I refer to as "the War Machine," the computerized control of thermonuclear weaponry, has receded as a threat to our freedom and survival in recent years. Though the Russian government that has taken over from the former Soviet leadership still possesses more than thirty thousand nuclear weapons (ten thousand of them capable of reaching targets in the United States), the complex of international political changes we refer to as "the end of the cold war" has made the forty-year balance of terror seem far less terrifying. The worst danger to which I addressed myself in dealing with the military uses of high tech—that of all-out Soviet-American nuclear war initiated by computer error or by the hair-trigger response of forces kept on instant alert—has all but disappeared. . . . The underlying concern I voice in dealing with nuclear weapons is not really tied to the particular facts and figures of the arms race at a given point in history. Rather, it has to do with the overweening confidence of computer scientists in their systems—and with our willingness as a society to believe what those scientists tell us about the absolute reliability of their programs.

At the same time, we should bear in mind that much of that military technology still exists and is as error-prone as ever. In one respect, we may even be worse off than before. As nuclear weapons proliferate around the world, the chance of regional conflicts achieving nuclear proportions increases. We now have more nuclear powers than ever before, many of them living side by side in deep distrust, their armed forces on round-the-clock alert, their under-trained technicians nervously fingering the red button. As Daniel Ellsberg warns us, "Worldwide, although the risk of nuclear war between NATO and the former Warsaw Pact powers has virtually vanished, the chance that some nuclear weapons will kill humans somewhere may be higher than before." Another study by Scott Sagan reminds us that computerized weapons systems must still remain a cause for serious concern precisely because the cold war has ended. . . .

As things now stand, our military leaders can have no clear idea who controls the world's remaining thermonuclear weapons systems; all accountability is being lost in the progressively fragmenting international community. Nor can anybody say with certainty what programs those weapons now obey, or how competent their new and anonymous keepers may be in dealing with this delicate and deadly technology. The "War Machine" is far from being a historical curiosity.

THE ADVENT
OF THE MONEY MACHINE

. . . To the other categories of computer abuse . . . I would now add "the Money Machine." As in the worlds of law enforcement, political campaigning, and the military, so now in the world of high finance the computer has fallen into the wrong hands and is being used in ways that have radically altered international economic affairs. Programmed trading, a form of Expert System that has been steadily under development since the 1970s by some of the best mathematical brains in the nation, has at last become a disruptive and all but dictatorial force in world finance—to such a degree that patterns of investment and speculation generated by computers have become an independent factor determining the shape of the market.

Electronic cash management and funds transfers using the speed of computers and global telecommunications networks date well back into the 1960s; but the first indication the public received that the technological magic that made same-day funds possible might be a mixed blessing came in May 1984 when, following little more than rumors in the press, Continental Illinois Bank of Chicago, the seventh-largest bank in the United States, was reported to be insolvent. Foreign banks, mainly Japanese, responding to rumors about Continental's dubious financial health, had suddenly withdrawn billions of dollars in one-day overnight deposits. A massive run on the bank had begun in the international banking community. Continental, it was feared, was carrying far too many bad loans and was not financially stable. The reports turned out to be true; the bank had made many big, bad investments, mainly in oil companies. Poor judgment in the banking world is nothing new; what was new about the story were the scale of the misjudgment and the way in which such immense mismanagement could be kept out of sight. As the story unfolded, it became clear that Continental had been covering up its true condition by using its state-of-the-art instant-communications capacity to execute the sort of rapid electronic transfers of short term funds that computers and global telecommunications make possible. The transfers amounted to as much as $8 billion in overnight funds and $35 billion in one-week deposits. Now Continental had fallen victim to its own sleight-of-hand methods; the same electronic network it had been using to stay afloat had turned against it to produce a bank failure so huge that the federal government had no choice but to bail Continental out at the public expense.

A year after the collapse of Continental Illinois, a major brokerage house, E.F. Hutton, was indicted by the Justice Department in a multimillion-dollar computer scam. Hutton was caught fast-shuffling funds between scores of banks throughout the United States in such a way that the company could write checks against deposits that did not exist except as computer records flashing across the electronic network—a form of high-tech check kiting.

Front page sensations like these were the public's first significant experience of the destabilizing potential that computers had assumed in the financial markets. Over the next year, commentators raised questions about another new computer-driven business practice: programmed trading. Might it be introducing too much speed and speculation into the markets? Not everybody saw much to worry about; there was certainly nothing illegal about the practice. *Time* magazine quoted optimistic insiders who even believed the new high-speed technology represented the "threshold of a golden age of capitalism." Other observers were more skeptical; they saw in the growing use of neural networked systems ominous possibilities for new forms of financial manipulation that would be dominated by a handful of institutional investors and programmed traders equipped with the best expert investment systems money can buy.

The skeptics turned out to be right. In October 1987, programmed decisions to buy and sell by large institutional investors triggered the worst collapse in the history of the New York Stock Exchange. In effect, too many of the programs that had been cleverly devised *by* the "rocket scientists" (as the hackers of the financial world are called) at major brokerage firms were doing the same thing at the same time. What each of the institutional investors was seeking to do was to protect itself by choosing the safest selection of risk-reducing options and futures: "portfolio insurance," as it is termed. But the net result was a cascading series of self-fulfilling prophecies operating as a feedback loop. The market went haywire.

After the crash, the Securities and Exchange Commission imposed "circuit-breakers" to head off any future disaster of this kind. But these are of limited value in a financial marketplace that has become round-the-clock and international; damping the panic in one stock exchange will only divert it elsewhere.

The simple fact is that, thanks to the computer, information about money has now become as valuable as money itself. And those who can process the most information the fastest are in the best position to profit—often in ways that escape any effective legal control. The computerized hand can move faster than the regulatory eye. As a result, the instability produced by high-speed computerized operations has become endemic.

———————

Inevitably, restless and globally foot-loose capital drifts toward the international electronic casino where the returns come at the speed of light. Writes Kurtzman:

> Over the years, especially during the 1980s, real-economy companies have been hit by wave after wave of corporate takeovers, with the stock market conspiring in those takeovers by camouflaging rather than revealing true value. These companies have also been handed a big bill from the firms that sell their stocks for the thrill of participating in financial markets that are rigged against real-economy companies.

So Kurtzman asks of the high-flying "megabyte marketplace" that now devours the true wealth of nations: "When the economic unit is the globe, where do people fit in?"

Like the other examples I offer of computer power "in the wrong hands," the money machine raises issues about the social value of the computer that make for neo-Luddite pessimism. The question of balance once again is central. List the pros and the cons of the technology and give them their proper weight. Granted, it is now possible for concerned citizens with PCs and Macs to log into electronic conferences on their local bulletin board, to debate, to gripe, to complain and petition. On the other hand we have the money machine, which makes possible the electronic hijacking of the world's financial markets by a small number of privileged traders who play the game for paper billions. As a result, the capital

resources that we need to generate paychecks, useful products, research and development, and helpful services are diverted from long-term investment to short-term speculation. What citizenly use of this technology can counterbalance a shift of power on this scale?

One comes back to the basic economic fact of the matter: computer technology, both the hardware and the software, is a commodity on sale to those who can afford it—and the most powerful machines continue to be in the wrong hands.

EDUTAINMENT

. . . Even though there are more computers than ever in our schools (since the early 1980s, the number of personal computers in U.S. schools has risen from fifty thousand to 2.4 million), their place in the curriculum remains highly uncertain. Certainly the predictions that were being made a few decades ago that public education would be revolutionized by the advent of the electronic classroom have fallen flat. In 1969, for example, the National Education Association confidently predicted (in a report titled "The Teacher and His Staff") that by 1994 every student in the United States would be equipped with "computer information bank consoles" and international video phones.

Computers are only the most recent wave of educational technology; since the 1950s educators have been through two generations of hype about all the good things they can expect from various kinds of "teaching machines." They have learned to be skeptical.

An increasing number of educators have begun to recognize that classroom technology is emphatically *not* neutral but carries with it significant (if subliminal) cultural, ethical, and epistemological presuppositions. The computer is inherently a Cartesian device embedded in the assumptions of a single intellectual style within a single culture of the modern world. The very metaphors that surround it bespeak a conception of the mind as logical machinery; the constant references to the "productivity" that the computer promises endorse the values of the marketplace and the western ethos of progress.

––––––––––––––

If the data merchants have their way, the main thrust of edutaining technology will be toward ever-more-expensive gimmickry with ever-less quality control. But they are pushing a costly substitute for books and blackboards, one that many school districts, plagued by a backlog of social issues, simply cannot afford.

That factor has shown up dramatically in an unusually comprehensive and conscientious survey of computers in our schools that was sponsored in the early 1990s by *Macworld* magazine. The findings were sobering. Charles Piller, who headed the study, concluded that we are rapidly creating a "technological underclass in America's public schools." While the survey did find schools where computers were being used imaginatively as an integrated part of a high-level curriculum, it found many more schools where the machines were limited to drill-and-practice sessions, and far too many where computers were simply going unused. This led to an important insight: *Mere statistics, like computer-to-student ratios, tell us nothing about the real on-site value of the technology.* Many computers that get tallied in superficial studies turn out to be broken relics stacked away in closets and storerooms. This is poignantly true of schools in minority neighborhoods. "Poor schools," the *Macworld* study observes, "tend to use computers so rigidly and ineptly as to repel students. Poor schools create refugees from technology." In a follow-up article for *The New York Times,* Piller concluded, "Instead of becoming instruments of reform, computers are reinforcing a two-tier system of education for the rich and poor."

Moreover, even if the will and the skill were there to use the machines well, in many school districts the funds educators divert to computers will have to come out of urgently necessary programs like vaccinations or school lunches or campus security. There are schools where controlling the handguns on campus counts for more than teaching computer literacy.

We are reminded that our nation's schools are woven into a dense political and sociological fabric that has everything to do with morale, teachability, opportunity, safety, and survival. . . .

Computers raise another issue in the classroom. By far the strongest argument for going high tech in the schools has been the promise of employment; computer literacy supposedly represents the royal road to a good job. But, by a cruel irony, in the greater global economy that surrounds our schools, the main effect of automation and cybernation is to deskill, disempower, and disemploy people from the assembly line up through middle management. Computers have come to play a central role in downsizing companies and in the creation of a part-time, temporary, low-paid, nonbenefited workforce. The brutal economic fact of life in today's marketplace is that we could generate more good jobs by outlawing computers than by multiplying them. Once again the basic truth about public education is clear: our schools do not exist in a vacuum. They are surrounded by and permeated by social and economic forces that pose more problems in the lives of our children than any machine will ever solve—unless videogames are intended to be the circus that will keep otherwise restless citizens preoccupied in the New World Order.

THE IDEAL OF THE ONLINE COMMONWEALTH

Does it *have* to be like this? Does this remarkable technology *have* to be swamped by silly commercial novelties and abusive social power? Of course not. There is no law that says information technology *must* fall victim to mindless consumption and technocratic manipulation. . . .

If information is what our embattled democracy needs, people—at least those who can afford the bill—should soon have no great difficulty filling the need in the "wired world" that some predict. In fact, navigating the surplus may be the great problem. There are difficulties and expenses involved in making use of the opportunity, but these need not be insurmountable. With enough skill, anyone owning a cheap second-hand computer and a modern can access many networking services. It is now possible to exchange mail, news, and expertise across the globe at a cost that may be as low as a local phone call or a subscription to a daily newspaper.

And there are other good possibilities. . . . [T]he nation's libraries might become the vital center that would provide maximum democratic access to the burgeoning electronic plenty within an ethic of public service. The libraries are, I suggest, our best hope of turning the sprawling potentiality of information technology into a true public utility.

For all the reservations I may express about computes and their uses, my heart goes out to the heroic spirits who recognize what power we have here to do the right thing—and who struggle to keep that power under democratic control. They are the conscience of the technology. . . .

Whenever I find myself having doubts whether increasingly powerful media . . . will ever be brought under the creative control of mature aesthetic minds, I try to remind myself that once upon a time the printing press, the camera, the piano, the orchestra, and motion pictures were innovations with no cultural track record. But one thing I know for certain: the minds that use these powers well will still have to master the art of thinking. Though the medium may be zero-cost infinite bandwidth networks, the media users will have to exercise the same mental muscles as the artists of Lascaux and draw upon the same creative sources. If there is anything particularly pernicious in the lore of high tech it is the facile assumption that just maybe the machines will do the thinking (and the feeling, and the judging, and the creating) for us, and do it better. The irony behind this technology is the tendency it encourages in some of its most talented and enthusiastic developers to cheapen—or even try to replace—the mind that created the technology in the first place.

A FEW WORDS FOR THE REST OF US

Despite the problems I mention here, I fully accept that information technology is here to stay—at least for as long as the world industrial economy survives.

(No guarantees about that, to be sure.) It has the permanence of a mature technology.

What is a mature technology?

One that finally generates as many problems as it solves.

As we have learned from every earlier wave of invention, machines are jinnis that get out of control. They reshape the world in unforeseen ways. The railroad and the automobile "solved" the problem of rapid transportation—only to finish by depleting our store of nonrenewable fossil fuels, fouling the air, and destroying the integrity of cities. Modern medicine "solved" the problem posed by numerous infectious diseases, only to finish by giving us the population explosion, ever-more-resistant strains of bacteria, and the ethical dilemma of protracted senility.

The computer "solved" the problem of fast, cheap data processing in a business culture drowning in red tape and paperwork, only to finish by destroying the rights of privacy, concentrating the political and commercial control of information in ever fewer hands, mesmerizing our children with bad art and pernicious nonsense, and menacing us with "computer errors" vast enough to paralyze whole societies. A clever few find ways to work around these vices and maximize the advantages of each new technology; the computer-proficient can sound quite smug about their command of databases and online resources. Many earn well from new, more sophisticated media. But the sum total of good and bad gets visited on the rest of us—and especially on the generations to come, who are simply born into the technology's inevitable downside. . . .

There is the problem, right before our eyes. The machines may not be smarter than we are, but we may not be proficient enough or moneyed enough to hold our own with those who own and exploit the machines. The cult of information is theirs, not ours. They use it, and they use it against us. What "the rest of us" are offered as "access" to the information society is hardly enough to make us real citizens of the information age: it may be little more than a diversion. True, we can now use our modems to send email to the new online White House, but there is no law that says anybody has to read what we send. And if there were, would it matter? We may soon have programs that make it possible to defeat the purpose of rapid, personal communications. A teaching colleague of mine, swamped by the email he receives from the students in one college course—much of which he finds repetitious, garbled, or witless—has developed a program that scans what he receives for keywords and generates boilerplate responses.

"The rest of us" get games to play and programs that will balance our checkbooks and catalogue our recipes. Maybe eventually we will get 3-D subscription virtual sex. We can rent CompuServe or log onto the local electronic bulletin board to check the running file of light-bulb jokes or to flame away on an issue or two. But even if we can buy the technology, we don't own it—not in any substantial way that gives us power. I, for example, am grateful that high tech has provided me with a great substitute for my old Smith-Corona on which to write my neo-Luddite lament. Perhaps one day I will become proficient enough to find my way through a MUD (a Multi-User Dungeon) on the Internet. But all the while I keystroke away, I suspect that the data-surfers at the IRS and the FBI and TRW are gliding through every secret I ever thought I had, and that the hot young quants at Morgan Stanley are using their rather more powerful machines to vandalize the banking systems of six nations. While the rest of us cling to the margins, the power and the profit of the technology gravitate elsewhere. The solution is once again becoming the problem.

But then the history of technology has always been a faltering search for Promethean power and utopian perfection. Every mature technology brings a minimal immediate gain followed by enormous long-term liabilities. The computer is the latest entry in that history, still bright with promise for its enthusiasts but surely destined to join the lengthening file of modern technological treachery that Aldous Huxley began compiling in his prophetic *Brave New World*. By now we should know what the Luddites of old learned before us: every tool ever invented is a mixed blessing. How things will balance out is a matter of vigilance, moral courage, and the distribution of power.

Whenever I begin to despair over such matters, I conjure up a few consoling images: Charlie Chaplin sliding woefully down the gullet of the assembly line, Laurel and Hardy fleeing for their lives before a runaway trolley car. There is a certain healthy amusement to be enjoyed in the irony of seeing our species victimized by the machines we invent to liberate ourselves—*provided,* that is, we heed the great lesson that underlies the human comedy. Namely, that there will never be a machine that leaves us wiser or better or freer than our own naked mind can make us—nor any that helps us work out our salvation with diligence.

QUESTIONS

1. Why might we be better off without technology? What are examples of technologies that have harmed rather than helped us?

2. Do you think your quality of life is better because of television? email? What would Roszak argue?

CASES

CASE 8.1
The Digital Divide
Joel Rudinow and Anthony Graybosch

The National Telecommunications and Information Administration (NTIA) issued a report on access to computer information services in July 1998. (See the suggested readings at the end of this chapter to find the full report.) The report found as follows:

> Despite this significant growth in computer ownership and usage overall, the growth has occurred to a greater extent within some income levels, demographic groups, and geographic areas, than in others. In fact, the "digital divide" between certain groups of Americans has *increased* between 1994 and 1997 so that there is now an even greater disparity in penetration levels among some groups. There is a widening gap, for example, between those at upper and lower income levels.

Additionally, even though all racial groups now own more computers than they did in 1994, Blacks and Hispanics now lag *even further behind* [emphasis in original] Whites in their levels of PC-ownership and online access.

QUESTIONS

1. Do you think that lack of access to computers and computer-based information services places the children of the poor and minority groups in an unfair educational and financial situation that amounts to a competitive disadvantage in the emerging information based economy?

2. What role, if any, should government take to encourage computer literacy and information access in public schools?

CASE 8.2

Hacking into the Space Program
Joel Rudinow and Anthony Graybosch

Hackers regularly gain access to highly sensitive Internet sites. For instance, a hacker overloaded the National Aeronautics and Space Administration (NASA) communications system in 1997 as the United States space shuttle was docking with the Russian space station, Mir. The hacker, intentionally or unintentionally, interfered with medical monitor-

ing and communication with the astronaut on the shuttle. NASA was forced to rely upon an alternative communications route.

QUESTIONS

1. Because hackers have proved able at gaining access to sensitive sites guarded by the latest security systems, do

Joel Rudinow and Anthony Graybosch, *Ethics and Values in the Information Age,* Wadsworth, 2001. (cases 8.1–8.3)

you think it reasonable to protect military information systems by threat of criminal prosecution?

2. Or should sensitive information remain off the Internet and decisions about the use of weapons systems always require a human decision maker?

CASE 8.3

The I Love You Virus

Joel Rudinow and Anthony Graybosch

The I Love You virus was ". . . estimated to have hit tens of millions of users and cost billions of dollars in damage." Cyber attacks against commercial sites such as Yahoo and e-Bay not only cause direct financial losses but shake the confidence of both corporations and consumers in electronic commerce. Assume that these attacks were motivated by curiosity or spite and not by a political concern.

QUESTIONS

1. Would Arquilla consider such attacks instances of information warfare?

2. Would just war theory consider the attacks terrorism? Are these terrorist attacks?

CASE 8.4

Privacy Pressures: The Use of Web Bugs at HomeConnection

Tom L. Beauchamp and Norman E. Bowie

As Matthew Scott, president of HomeConnection, sat in his office waiting for several members of his executive team to arrive, he grew more worrisome about a story featuring his company in the morning paper. His impulse was to fight back and go on the defensive, but Scott knew that he had to be careful. However, he did not accept the article's implicit conclusion that HomeConnection had no regard for the privacy rights of its customers, and he was anxious to hear what his colleagues had to say about the matter.

HomeConnection was an Internet Service Provider (ISP) with several million customers, primarily clustered in the mid-West. An ISP links people and businesses to the Internet, usually for a monthly fee. HomeConnection was much smaller than the industry leader, America OnLine (AOL), but it was still seen as a formidable player in this industry. Thanks to Scott's management, the company had recorded increasing profits for the past three years, 1999 through 2002. One feature that attracted customers was the opportunity to create their own personal Web page. HomeConnection made this process easy and convenient.

From Tom L. Beauchamp and Norman E. Bowie, *Ethical Theory and Business* (Englewood Cliffs, NJ: Prentice Hall, 2004). Reprinted with permission. *Case Studies in Information Technology Ethics*, 2/E by Spinello, Richard A., copyright Reprinted by permission of Pearson Education, Inc., Upper Saddle River, NJ.

In the past year HomeConnection had devised an innovative promotion to help increase its subscriber base. The company encouraged its users with their own personal Web pages to carry an ad for Home-Connection. The ad would offer new subscribers a heavily discounted rate for the first year of membership. In addition, as an incentive to display the ad on their personal Web pages, the company agreed to pay its users $25 for any new members who signed up for a subscription by clicking on the ad. The response to the promotion was stronger than expected, and HomeConnection's membership had risen by over 6.5 percent since the program's inception eight months ago. Scott was quite enthused about the results, and he did not anticipate that one aspect of the program would attract some negative attention.

In consultation with his marketing manager, Scott had authorized the use of Web bugs so that when users placed the ad on their Web pages they would also get a Web bug. A Web bug is embedded as a miniscule and invisible picture on the screen and it can track everything one does on a particular Web site. Web bugs, also called "Web beacons," are usually deployed to count visitors to a Web site or to gather cumulative data about visitors to those sites without tracking any personal details. In this case the Web bug transmitted information to a major on-line ad agency, DoubleDealer. DoubleDealer would collect data about those who visited these Web pages, which ads they clicked on, and so forth.

The newspaper report cited HomeConnection as well as other ISPs and e-commerce sites for using this protocol without the permission of their customers. They quoted a well-known privacy expert: "It's extremely disturbing that these companies are using technology to gather information in such a clandestine manner; I don't see how it can be morally justified." The article had clearly resonated with some of HomeConnection's users, and the switchboard had been busy most of the afternoon with calls from irate customers. Some wanted to cancel their subscription.

Scott felt that the company had done nothing wrong but was a victim of a pervasive paranoia about privacy. HomeConnection was not using these bugs for any untoward purposes—its purpose was to track the results of the advertising promotion, that is, how many people were clicking on these ads. Also, Scott himself had modified the company's privacy policy to indicate that Web bugs might be used sometimes. (However, there was no indication that Web bugs would be placed on the personal Web pages of its user base.)

As several of his managers made their way into the conference room adjoining his office, Scott made one last check with customer service. By now it was late in the day and the volume of calls and emails was dying down. It was now up to Scott to determine a response—did the company face a serious problem or was this just a tempest in a teapot?

QUESTIONS

1. Had HomeConnection done something wrong? Why or why not?

2. What might be ethical or legal limitations you would place on HomeConnection?

CHAPTER QUESTIONS

1. Is technology a good or a bad thing in your life, on balance? List 10 ways in which technology has improved your life and 10 ways in which it has been detrimental. How can we find the right role for technology in society, in business, and in our individual lives? Has technology assumed a godlike role in our culture?

2. Why do new technologies create problems for old laws and regulations? How does new technology create new definitions of property? How might ethical principles solve these problems?

9

The Art of Seduction

The Ethics of Advertising, Marketing, and Sales

Introduction

It's Saturday morning. You're taking it easy, sitting with your kids who are watching cartoons. During one of the intervals, the sound volume doubles, and a new cartoon character appears, but this one in the service of an ad for a new double-sugared and chocolate-covered cereal. The character is cute if obnoxious, and the ad features a photo of delighted children ecstatic as they munch. The cereal itself is presented with special-effects sparkles, making it look magical. This is followed by an ad for one of the big fast-food outfits, Mr. B's, which is offering a cheap but colorful toy with every kiddy meal. The company has become renowned for its nonnutritional high-calorie foods, and one of your kids is already showing a weight problem. Immediately he turns to you excitedly and asks, "Can we go to Mr. B's, for lunch, huh, please, please, please?" A family negotiation follows, in which it becomes evident that it is the toy, rather than the meal, that has moved your youngsters and the ad, not the cereal, that attracted their attention. But it gets you thinking. What is the justification for making such unhealthy appeals to young children? And at a time when most parents are not there, as you are now, to monitor and discuss the true desirability of these artificially created desires. Indeed, what is the difference between appealing to kids' actual needs and wants as opposed to creating artificial desires that are the opposite of their actual needs and wants? And shouldn't there be some restrictions on advertising to the young and vulnerable?

That last question you answer right away. Restrictions on advertising violate the right to free speech. You, like most Americans, are against censorship, particularly by the government and its agencies. But then you start thinking again. What if what is advertised is unhealthy? What if, as in the case of cigarettes and other tobacco products, it is downright deadly? The problem is not just kids and sugary, fattening foods. There is a similar problem with teenagers, who are subject to peer pressure that is artfully manipulated by advertisers, not only in the case of smoking, but across the whole range of teenage fads, clothes, and habits. But then, there are adults, too. It's not as if they are privy to the skills and secrets of contemporary marketing and advertising techniques. Ads for cars, ads for real estate, ads for detergents and cosmetics and beers and now even pharmaceuticals and plastic surgery. It is all seduction. But is seduction always wrong? How about the truth of the claims? "The best beer in the world." Who knows? The fastest-acting cleanser? Has anyone measured this? (Probably Consumer Reports, but who has read it? And doesn't the company keep repeating the ad—now disproved—anyway?) There are lies, but then there are white lies and partial truths and "spin," which has some basis in truth but is powerfully prejudiced toward a certain bias. Where does advertising fit in? What makes it legitimate? What would make it illegitimate? Is it allowable to tell a lie in order to sell something?

At this point, we may want to go back to our honesty chapter, but most of us would argue that honesty, full disclosure, may be too high a standard for most advertising and marketing. No one expects a salesperson to tell you the flaws in the product or the advantages of a competitor's version. And advertising and marketing, which are by their very nature biased, play a critical role in a free market system. People have to know about a product to have any interest in buying it. People have to be appealed to and made to pay attention to learn about a product. And the products themselves must be made appealing and distinguished from the many other products on the market. Merely providing the information to the consumer is rarely enough. In a world filled with ads and products, much more dramatic methods are called for. But once we get beyond the honest presentation of information, the ethical questions get rather difficult. What do we do about advertising to kids and teenagers and people who are vulnerable (which means, ultimately, all of us)? What are the limits of exaggeration and self-promotion? What are the effects of not just supplying what people want and need, but creating their desires, which then become created needs? And what about those needs that are satisfied by the ads themselves?

The great economist John Kenneth Galbraith begins, in "The Dependence Effect," by showing how advertising may actually create consumer demands, rather than merely serve consumer needs. Friedrich von Hayek offers a vigorous counterargument to Galbraith's position in "The Non Sequitur of the 'Dependence Effect.'" Robert L. Arrington offers an analysis of ways in which advertising actually does determine consumer behavior in his "Advertising and Behavior Control." Alan Goldman offers a powerful argument in defense of the usefulness and, ultimately, the ethical importance of advertising in his "The Justification of Advertising in a Market Economy." Leslie Savan details more ways in which advertising and the market more generally may undermine the freedom of consumers in "The Bribed Soul." Finally, Thomas L. Carson explains the ethical duties of salespeople in his "The Ethics of Sales."

John Kenneth Galbraith | # The Dependence Effect

John Kenneth Galbraith was one of the most influential economists of the twentieth century.

The theory of consumer demand, as it is now widely accepted, is based on two broad propositions, neither of them quite explicit but both extremely important for the present value system of economists. The first is that the urgency of wants does not diminish appreciably as more of them are satisfied or, to put the matter more precisely, to the extent that this happens it is not demonstrable and not a matter of any interest to economists or for economic policy. When man has satisfied his physical needs, then psychologically grounded desires take over. These can never be satisfied or, in any case, no progress can be proved. The concept of satiation has very little standing in economics. It is neither useful nor scientific to speculate on the comparative cravings of the stomach and the mind.

The second proposition is that wants originate in the personality of the consumer or, in any case, that they are given data for the economist. The latter's task is merely to seek their satisfaction. He has no need to inquire how these wants are formed. His function is sufficiently fulfilled by maximizing the goods that supply the wants.

The notion that wants do not become less urgent the more amply the individual is supplied is broadly repugnant to common sense. It is something to be believed only by those who wish to believe. Yet the conventional wisdom must be tackled on its own terrain. Intertemporal comparisons of an individual's state of mind do rest on doubtful grounds. Who can say for sure that the deprivation which afflicts him with hunger is more painful than the deprivation which afflicts him with envy of his neighbour's new car? In the time that has passed since he was poor his soul may have become subject to a new and deeper searing. And where a society is concerned, comparisons between marginal satisfactions when it is poor and those when it is affluent will involve not only the same individual at different times but different individuals at different times. The scholar who wishes to believe that with increasing affluence there is no reduction in the urgency of desires and goods is not without points for debate. However plausible the case against him, it cannot be proved. In the defence of the conventional wisdom this amounts almost to invulnerability.

However, there is a flaw in the case. If the individual's wants are to be urgent they must be original with himself. They cannot be urgent if they must be contrived for him. And above all they must not be contrived by the process of production by which they are satisfied. For this means that the whole case for the urgency of production, based on the urgency of wants, falls to the ground. One cannot defend production as satisfying wants if that production creates the wants.

Were it so that man on arising each morning was assailed by demons which instilled in him a passion sometimes for silk shirts, sometimes for kitchenware, sometimes for chamber-pots, and sometimes for orange squash, there would be every reason to applaud the effort to find the goods, however odd, that quenched this flame. But should it be that his passion was the result of his first having cultivated the demons, and should it also be that his effort to allay it stirred the demons to ever greater and greater effort, there would be question as to how rational was his solution. Unless restrained by conventional attitudes, he might wonder if the solution lay with more goods or fewer demons.

So it is that if production creates the wants it seeks to satisfy, or if the wants emerge *pari passu* with the production, then the urgency of the wants can no longer be used to defend the urgency of the production. Production only fills a void that it has itself created.

The even more direct link between production and wants is provided by the institutions of modern advertising and salesmanship. These cannot be reconciled with the notion of independently determined desires, for their central function is to create desires—to bring into being wants that previously did not exist.[1] This is accomplished by the producer of the goods or at his behest. A broad empirical relationship exists between what is spent on production of consumers' goods and what is spent in synthesizing the desires for that production. A new consumer product must be introduced with a suitable advertising campaign to arouse an interest in it. The path for an expansion of output must be paved by a suitable expansion in the advertising budget. Outlays for the manufacturing of a product are not more important in the strategy of modern business enterprise than outlays for the manufacturing of demand for the product. None of this is novel. All would be regarded as elementary by the most retarded student in the nation's most primitive school of business administration. The cost of this want formation is formidable. In 1956 total advertising expenditure—though, as noted, not all of it may be assigned to the synthesis of wants—amounted to about ten thousand million dollars. For some years it had been increasing at a rate in excess of a thousand million dollars a year. Obviously, such outlays must be integrated with the theory of consumer demand. They are too big to be ignored.

But such integration means recognizing that wants are dependent on production. It accords to the producer the function both of making the goods and of making the desires for them. It recognizes that production, not only passively through emulation, but actively through advertising and related activities, creates the wants it seeks to satisfy.

The businessman and the lay reader will be puzzled over the emphasis which I give to a seemingly obvious point. The point is indeed obvious. But it is one which, to a singular degree, economists have resisted. They have sensed, as the layman does not, the damage to established ideas which lurks in these relationships. As a result, incredibly, they have closed their eyes (and ears) to the most obtrusive of all economic phenomena, namely modern want creation.

This is not to say that the evidence affirming the dependence of wants on advertising has been entirely ignored. It is one reason why advertising has so long been regarded with such uneasiness by economists. Here is something which cannot be accommodated easily to existing theory. More pervious scholars have speculated on the urgency of desires which are so obviously the fruit of such expensively contrived campaigns for popular attention. Is a new breakfast cereal or detergent so much wanted if so much must be spent to compel in the consumer the sense of want? But there has been little tendency to go on to examine the implications of this for the theory of consumer demand and even less for the importance of production and productive efficiency. These have remained sacrosanct. More often the uneasiness has been manifested in a general disapproval of advertising and advertising men, leading to the occasional suggestion that they shouldn't exist. Such suggestions have usually been ill received.

And so the notion of independently determined wants still survives. In the face of all the forces of modern salesmanship it still rules, almost undefiled, in the textbooks. And it still remains the economist's mission—and on few matters is the pedagogy so firm—to seek unquestioningly the means for filling these wants. This being so, production remains of prime urgency. We have here, perhaps, the ultimate triumph of the conventional wisdom in its resistance to the evidence of the eyes. To equal it one must imagine a humanitarian who was long ago persuaded of the grievous shortage of hospital facilities in the town. He continues to importune the passers-by for money for more beds and refuses to notice that the town doctor is deftly knocking over pedestrians with his car to keep up the occupancy.

And in unravelling the complex we should always be careful not to overlook the obvious. The fact that wants can be synthesized by advertising, catalysed by salesmanship, and shaped by the discreet manipulations of the persuaders shows that they are not very urgent. A man who is hungry need never be told of his need for food. If he is inspired by his appetite, he is immune to the influence of Messrs. Batten, Barton, Durstine and Osborn. The latter are effective only with those who are so far removed from physical want that they do not already know what they want. In this state alone men are open to persuasion.

The general conclusion of these pages is of such importance for this essay that it had perhaps best be put with some formality. As a society becomes increasingly affluent, wants are increasingly created by the process by which they are satisfied. This may operate passively. Increases in consumption, the counterpart of increases in production, act by suggestion or emulation to create wants. Or producers may proceed actively to create wants through advertising and salesmanship. Wants thus come to depend on output. In technical terms it can no longer be assumed that welfare is greater at an all-round higher level of production than at a lower one. It may be the same. The higher level of production has, merely, a higher level of want creation necessitating a higher level of want satisfaction. There will be frequent occasion to refer to the way wants depend on the process by which they are satisfied. It will be convenient to call it the Dependence Effect.

The final problem of the productive society is what it produces. This manifests itself in an implacable tendency to provide an opulent supply of some things and a niggardly yield of others. This disparity carries to the point where it is a cause of social discomfort and social unhealth. The line which divides our area of

Plato on the Danger of Believing Bad Arguments

There is one danger that we must guard against, Socrates said.

What sort of danger? I asked.

Of becoming misologic [hating logic], he said, in the sense that people become misanthropic. No greater misfortune could happen to anyone than that of developing a dislike for argument. Misology and misanthropy arise in just the same way. Misanthropy is induced by believing in somebody quite uncritically. You assume that a person is absolutely truthful and sincere and reliable, and a little later you find that he is shoddy and unreliable. Then the same thing happens again. After repeated disappointments at the hands of the very people who might be supposed to be your nearest and most intimate friends, constant irritation ends by making you dislike everybody and suppose that there is no sincerity to be found anywhere. . . .

The resemblance between arguments and human beings lies in this: that when one believes that an argument is true without reference to the art of logic, and then a little later decides rightly or wrongly that it is false, and the same thing happens again and again . . . they end by believing that they are wiser than anyone else, because they alone have discovered that there is nothing stable or dependable either in facts or in arguments, and that everything fluctuates just like the water in a tidal channel, and never stays at any point for any time. . . .

But suppose that there is an argument which is true and valid but someone spent his life loathing arguments and so missed the chance of knowing the truth about reality—would that not be a deplorable thing?

—Plato, *Phaedo* 89d–90e, fourth century B.C. *Hugh Tredennick,* The Last Days of Socrates (Harmondsworth, MD: Penguin, 1954).

wealth from our area of poverty is roughly that which divides privately produced and marketed goods and services from publicly rendered services. Our wealth in the first is not only in startling contrast with the meagreness of the latter, but our wealth in privately produced goods is, to a marked degree, the cause of crisis in the supply of public services. For we have failed to see the importance, indeed the urgent need, of maintaining a balance between the two.

This disparity between our flow of private and public goods and services is no matter of subjective judgment. On the contrary, it is the source of the most extensive comment which only stops short of the direct contrast being made here. In the years following World War II, the papers of any major city— those of New York were an excellent example—told daily of the shortages and shortcomings in the elementary municipal and metropolitan services. The schools were old and overcrowded. The police force was under strength and underpaid. The parks and playgrounds were insufficient. Streets and empty lots were filthy, and the sanitation staff was underequipped and in need of men. Access to the city by those who work there was uncertain and painful and becoming more so. Internal transportation was overcrowded, unhealthful, and dirty. So was the air. Parking on the streets had to be prohibited, and there was no space elsewhere. These deficiencies were not in new and novel services but in old and established ones. Cities have long swept their streets, helped their people move around, educated them, kept order, and provided horse rails for vehicles which sought to pause. That their residents should have a non-toxic supply of air suggests no revolutionary dalliance with socialism.

The contrast was and remains evident not alone to those who read. The family which takes its mauve and cerise, air-conditioned, power-steered, and power-braked car out for a tour passes through cities that are badly paved, made hideous by litter, blighted buildings, billboards, and posts for wires that should long since have been put underground. They pass on into a countryside that has been rendered largely invisible by commercial art. (The goods which the latter advertise have an absolute priority in our value system. Such aesthetic considerations as a view of the countryside accordingly come second. On such matters we are consistent.) They picnic on exquisitely packaged food from a portable icebox by a polluted stream and go on to spend the night at a park which is a menace to public health and morals. Just before dozing off on an air-mattress, beneath a nylon tent, amid the stench of decaying refuse, they may reflect vaguely on the curious unevenness of their blessings. Is this, indeed, the American genius?

The case for social balance has, so far, been put negatively. Failure to keep public services in minimal relation to private production and use of goods is a cause of social disorder or impairs economic performance. The matter may now be put affirmatively. By failing to exploit the opportunity to expand public production we are missing opportunities for enjoyment which otherwise we might have had. Presumably a community can be as well rewarded by buying better schools or better parks as by buying bigger cars. By concentrating on the latter rather than the former it is failing to maximize its satisfactions. As with schools in the community, so with public services over the country at large. It is scarcely sensible that we should satisfy our wants in private goods with reckless abundance, while in the case of public goods, on the evidence of the eye, we practice extreme self-denial. So, far from systematically exploiting the opportunities to derive use and pleasure from these services, we do not supply what would keep us out of trouble.

The conventional wisdom holds that the community, large or small, makes a decision as to how much it will devote to its public services. This decision is arrived at by democratic process. Subject to the imperfections and uncertainties of democracy, people decide how much of their private income and goods they will surrender in order to have public services of which they are in greater need. Thus there is a balance, however rough, in the enjoyments to be had from private goods and services and those rendered by public authority.

It will be obvious, however, that this view depends on the notion of independently determined consumer wants. In such a world one could with some reason defend the doctrine that the consumer, as a voter, makes an independent choice between public and private goods. But given the dependence effect—given that consumer wants are created by the process by which they are satisfied—the consumer makes no such choice. He is subject to the forces of advertising and emulation by which production creates its own demand. Advertising operates exclusively, and emulation mainly, on behalf of privately produced goods and services.[2] Since management and emulative effects operate on behalf of private production, public services will have an inherent tendency to lag behind. Car demand which is expensively synthesized will inevitably have a much larger claim on income than parks or public health or even roads where no such influence operates. The engines of mass communication, in their highest state of development, assail the eyes and ears of the community on behalf of more beer but not of more schools. Even in the conventional wisdom it will scarcely be contended that this leads to an equal choice between the two.

The competition is especially unequal for new products and services. Every corner of the public psyche is canvassed by some of the nation's most talented citizens to see if the desire for some merchantable product can be cultivated. No similar process operates on behalf of the nonmerchantable services of the state. Indeed, while we take the cultivation of new private wants for granted we would be measurably shocked to see it applied to public services. The scientist or engineer or advertising man who devotes himself to developing a new carburetor, cleanser, or depilatory for which the public recognizes no need and will feel none until an advertising campaign arouses it, is one of the valued members of our society. A politician or a public servant who dreams up a new public service is a wastrel. Few public offences are more reprehensible.

So much for the influences which operate on the decision between public and private production. The calm decision between public and private consumption pictured by the conventional wisdom is, in fact, a remarkable example of the error which arises from viewing social behaviour out of context. The inherent tendency will always be for public services to fall behind private production. We have here the first of the causes of social imbalance.

NOTES

1. Advertising is not a simple phenomenon. It is also important in competitive strategy and want creation is, ordinarily, a complementary result of efforts to shift the demand curve of the individual firm at the expense of others or (less importantly, I think) to change its shape by increasing the degree of product differentiation. Some of the failure of economists to identify advertising with want creation may be attributed to the undue attention that its use in purely competitive strategy has attracted. It should be noted, however, that the competitive manipulation of consumer desire is only possible, at least on any appreciable scale, when such need is not strongly felt.

2. Emulation does operate between communities. A new school or a new highway in one community does exert pressure on others to remain abreast. However, as compared with the pervasive effects of emulation in extending the demand for privately produced consumers' goods there will be agreement, I think, that this intercommunity effect is probably small.

QUESTIONS

1. Does advertising serve our needs or create them? Or both? Explain and provide examples.

2. Think of three or four television commercials that you like. Briefly describe them on paper. Now ask yourself: how many lies or half-truths are expressed by those ads?

Friedrich von Hayek

The Non Sequitur of the "Dependence Effect"

Friedrich von Hayek was the most eminent of the Austrian economists and the author of *Road to Serfdom.*

For well over a hundred years the critics of the free enterprise system have resorted to the argument that if production were only organized rationally, there would be no economic problem. Rather than face the problem which scarcity creates, socialist reformers have tended to deny that scarcity existed. Ever since the Saint-Simonians their contention has been that the problem of production has been solved and only the problem of distribution remains. However absurd this contention must appear to us with respect to the time when it was first advanced, it still has some persuasive power when repeated with reference to the present.

The latest form of this old contention is expounded in *The Affluent Society* by Professor J. K. Galbraith. He attempts to demonstrate that in our affluent society the important private needs are already satisfied and the urgent need is therefore no longer a further expansion of the output of commodities but an increase of those services which are supplied (and presumably can be supplied only) by government. Though this book has been extensively discussed since its publication in 1958, its central thesis still requires some further examination.

I believe the author would agree that his argument turns upon the "Dependence Effect" [p. 389 of this book]. The argument of this chapter starts from the assertion that a great part of the wants which are still unsatisfied in modern society are not wants which would be experienced spontaneously by the individual if left to himself, but are wants which are created

by the process by which they are satisfied. It is then represented as self-evident that for this reason such wants cannot be urgent or important. This crucial conclusion appears to be a complete *non sequitur* and it would seem that with it the whole argument of the book collapses.

The first part of the argument is of course perfectly true: we would not desire any of the amenities of civilization—or even of the most primitive culture—if we did not live in a society in which others provide them. The innate wants are probably confined to food, shelter, and sex. All the rest we learn to desire because we see others enjoying various things. To say that a desire is not important because it is not innate is to say that the whole cultural achievement of man is not important.

This cultural origin of practically all the needs of civilized life must of course not be confused with the fact that there are some desires which aim, not as a satisfaction derived directly from the use of an object, but only from the status which its consumption is expected to confer. In a passage which Professor Galbraith quotes, Lord Keynes seems to treat the latter sort of Veblenesque conspicuous consumption as the only alternative "to those needs which are absolute in the sense that we feel them whatever the situation of our fellow human beings may be." If the latter phrase is interpreted to exclude all the needs for goods which are felt only because these goods are known to be produced, these two Keynesian classes describe of course only extreme types of wants, but disregard the overwhelming majority of goods on which civilized life rests. Very few needs indeed are "absolute" in the sense that they are independent of social environment or of the example of others, and that their satisfaction is an indispensable condition for the preservation of the individual or of the species. Most needs which make us act are needs for things which only civilization teaches us to exist at all, and these things are wanted by us because they produce feelings or emotions which we would not know if it were not for our cultural inheritance. Are not in this sense probably all our esthetic feelings "acquired tastes"?

How complete a non sequitur Professor Galbraith's conclusion represents is seen most clearly if we apply the argument to any product of the arts, be it music, painting, or literature. If the fact that people would not feel the need for something if it were not produced did prove that such products are of small value, all those highest products of human endeavor would be of small value. Professor Galbraith's argument could be easily employed without any change of the essential terms, to demonstrate the worthlessness of literature or any other form of art. Surely an individual's want for literature is not original with himself in the sense that he would experience it if literature were not produced. Does this then mean that the production of literature cannot be defended as satisfying a want because it is only the production which provokes the demand? In this, as in the case of all cultural needs, it is unquestionably, in Professor Galbraith's words, "the process of satisfying the wants that creates the wants." There have never been "independently determined desires for" literature before literature has been produced and books certainly do not serve the "simple mode of enjoyment which requires no previous conditioning of the consumer." Clearly my taste for the novels of Jane Austen or Anthony Trollope or C. P. Snow is not "original with myself." But is it not rather absurd to conclude from this that it is less important than, say, the need for education? Public education indeed seems to regard it as one of its tasks to instill a taste for literature in the young and even employs producers of literature for that purpose. Is this want creation by the producer reprehensible? Or does the fact that some of the pupils may possess a taste for poetry only because of the efforts of their teachers prove that since "it does not arise in spontaneous consumer need and the demand would not exist were it not contrived, its utility or urgency, ex contrivance, is zero?"

The appearance that the conclusions follow from the admitted facts is made possible by an obscurity of the wording of the argument with respect to which it is difficult to know whether the author is himself the victim of a confusion or whether he skillfully uses ambiguous terms to make the conclusion appear plausible. The obscurity concerns the implied assertion that the wants of the consumers are determined by the producers. Professor Galbraith avoids in this connection any terms as crude and definite as "determine." The expressions he employs, such as that wants are "dependent on" or the "fruits of" production, or that "production creates the wants" do, of course, suggest determination but avoid saying so in plain terms. After what has already been said it is of course obvious that the knowledge of what is being produced is one of the many factors on which it depends what people will want. It would scarcely be an exaggeration to say that contemporary man, in all fields where he has not yet formed firm habits, tends to find out what he wants by looking at what his neighbours do and at various displays of goods (physical or in catalogues or advertisements) and then choosing what he likes best.

In this sense the tastes of man, as is also true of his opinions and beliefs and indeed much of his personality, are shaped in a great measure by his cultural environment. But though in some contexts it would perhaps be legitimate to express this by a phrase like "production creates the wants," the circumstances mentioned would clearly not justify the contention that particular producers can deliberately determine the wants of particular consumers. The efforts of all producers will certainly be directed towards that end: but how far any individual producer will succeed will depend not only on what he does but also on what the others do and on a great many other influences operating upon the consumer. The joint but uncoordinated efforts of the producers merely create one element of the environment by which the wants of the consumers are shaped. It is because each individual producer thinks that the consumers can be persuaded to like his products that he endeavours to influence them. But though this effort is part of the influences which shape consumers' tastes, no producer can in any real sense "determine" them. This, however, is clearly implied in such statements as that wants are "both passively and deliberately the fruits of the process by which they are satisfied." If the producer could in fact deliberately determine what the consumers will want, Professor Galbraith's conclusions would have some validity. But though this is skillfully suggested, it is nowhere made credible, and could hardly be made credible because it is not true. Though the range of choice open to the consumers is the joint result of, among other things, the efforts of all producers who vie with each other in making their respective products appear more attractive than those of their competitors, every particular consumer still has the choice between all those different offers.

A fuller examination of this process would, of course, have to consider how, after the efforts of some producers have actually swayed some consumers, it becomes the example of the various consumers thus persuaded which will influence the remaining consumers. This can be mentioned here only to emphasize that even if each consumer were exposed to pressure of only one producer, the harmful effects which are apprehended from this would soon be offset by the much more powerful example of his fellows. It is of course fashionable to treat this influence of the example of others (or, what comes to the same thing, the learning from the experience made by others) as if it amounted all to an attempt of keeping up with the Joneses and for that reason was to be regarded as detrimental. It seems to me that not only the importance of this factor is usually greatly exaggerated but also that it is not really relevant to Professor Galbraith's main thesis. But it might be worthwhile briefly to ask what, assuming that some expenditure were actually determined solely by a desire of keeping up with the Joneses, that would really prove? At least in Europe we used to be familiar with a type of persons who often denied themselves even enough food in order to maintain an appearance of respectability or gentility in dress and style of life. We may regard this as a misguided

effort, but surely it would not prove that the income of such persons was larger than they knew how to use wisely. That the appearance of success, or wealth, may to some people seem more important than many other needs, does in no way prove that the needs they sacrifice to the former are unimportant. In the same way, even though people are often persuaded to spend unwisely, this surely is no evidence that they do not still have important unsatisfied needs.

Professor Galbraith's attempt to give an apparent scientific proof for the contention that the need for the production of more commodities has greatly decreased seems to me to have broken down completely. With it goes the claim to have produced a valid argument which justifies the use of coercion to make people employ their income for those purposes of which he approves. It is not to be denied that there is some originality in this latest version of the old socialist argument. For over a hundred years we have been exhorted to embrace socialism because it would give us more goods. Since it has so lamentably failed to achieve this where it has been tried, we are now urged to adopt it because more goods after all are not important. The aim is still progressively to increase the share of the resources whose use is determined by political authority and the coercion of any dissenting minority. It is not surprising, therefore, that Professor Galbraith's thesis has been most enthusiastically received by the intellectuals of the British Labour Party where his influence bids fair to displace that of the late Lord Keynes. It is more curious that in this country it is not recognized as an outright socialist argument and often seems to appeal to people on the opposite end of the political spectrum. But this is probably only another instance of the familiar fact that on these matters the extremes frequently meet.

QUESTIONS

1. Would Hayek regulate advertising? Why or why not?
2. What is the "non sequitur" of the dependence effect?

Robert L. Arrington | # Advertising and Behavior Control

Robert L. Arrington is professor of philosophy at Georgia State University.

Consider the following advertisements:

1. "A woman in *Distinction Foundations* is so beautiful that all other women want to kill her."
2. Pongo Peach color from Revlon comes "from east of the sun . . . west of the moon where each tomorrow dawns." It is "succulent on your lips" and "sizzling on your finger tips (And on your toes, goodness knows)." Let it be your "adventure in paradise."
3. "Increase the value of your holdings. Old Charter Bourbon Whiskey—The Final Step Up."
4. Last Call Smirnoff Style: "They'd never really miss us, and it's kind of late already, and it's quite a long way, and I could build a fire, and you're looking very beautiful, and we could have another martini, and its awfully nice just being home . . . you think?"
5. A Christmas Prayer. "Let us pray that the blessings of peace be ours—the peace to build and grow, to live in harmony and sympathy with others, and to plan for the future with confidence." New York Life Insurance Company.

These are instances of what is called puffery—the practice by a seller of making exaggerated, highly fanciful or suggestive claims about a product or service. Puffery, within ill-defined limits, is legal. It is considered a legitimate, necessary, and very successful tool of the advertising industry. Puffery is not just bragging; it is bragging carefully designed to achieve a very definite effect. Using the techniques of so-called motivational research, advertising firms first identify our often hidden needs (for security, conformity, oral stimulation) and our desires (for power, sexual dominance and dalliance, adventure) and then they design ads which respond to these needs and desires. By associating a product, for which we may have little or no direct need or desire, with symbols reflecting the fulfillment of these other, often subterranean interests, the advertisement can quickly generate large numbers of consumers eager to purchase the product advertised. What woman in the sexual race of life could resist a foundation which would turn other women envious to the point of homicide? Who can turn down an adventure in paradise, east of the sun where tomorrow dawns? Be at the pinnacle of success—drink Old Charter. Or stay at home and dally a bit—with Smirnoff. And let us pray for a secure and predictable future, provided for by New York Life, God willing. It doesn't take very much motivational research to see the point of these sales pitches. Others are perhaps a little less obvious. The need to feel secure in one's home at night can be used to sell window air conditioners, which drown out small noises and provide a friendly, dependable companion. The fact that baking a cake is symbolic of giving birth to a baby used to prompt advertisements for cake mixes which glamorized the 'creative' housewife. And other strategies, for example involving cigar symbolism, are a bit too crude to mention, but are nevertheless very effective.

Don't such uses of puffery amount to manipulation, exploitation, or downright control? In his very popular book *The Hidden Persuaders,* Vance Packard points out that a number of people in the advertising world have frankly admitted as much:

> As early as 1941 Dr. Dichter (an influential advertising consultant) was exhorting ad agencies to recognize themselves for what they actually were—"one of the most advanced laboratories in psychology".

Excerpted from "Advertising and Behavior Control," published in *Journal of Business Ethics,* vol. 1, no. 1 (February 1982), pp. 3–12. Copyright © 1982 by D. Reidel Publishing Company, Dordrecht, Holland. Notes were deleted from the text.

He said the successful ad agency "manipulates human motivations and desires and develops a need for goods with which the public has at one time been unfamiliar—perhaps even undesirous of purchasing". The following year *Advertising Agency* carried an ad man's statement that psychology not only holds promise for understanding people but "ultimately for controlling their behavior."[1]

Such statements lead Packard to remark: "With all this interest in manipulating the customer's subconscious, the old slogan 'let the buyer beware' began taking on a new and more profound meaning."[2]

B. F. Skinner, the high priest of behaviorism, has expressed a similar assessment of advertising and related marketing techniques. Why, he asks, do we buy a certain kind of car?

> Perhaps our favorite TV program is sponsored by the manufacturer of that car. Perhaps we have seen pictures of many beautiful or prestigeful persons driving it—in pleasant or glamorous places. Perhaps the car has been designed with respect to our motivational patterns: the device on the hood is a phallic symbol; or the horsepower has been stepped up to please our competitive spirit in enabling us to pass other cars swiftly (or, as the advertisements say, 'safely'). The concept of freedom that has emerged as part of the cultural practice of our group makes little or no provision for recognizing or dealing with these kinds of control.[3]

In purchasing a car we may think we are free, Skinner is claiming, when in fact our act is completely controlled by factors in our environment and in our history of reinforcement. Advertising is one such factor. . . .

Puffery, indirect information transfer, subliminal advertising—are these techniques of manipulation and control whose success shows that many of us have forfeited our autonomy and become a community, or herd, of packaged souls?[4] The business world and the advertising industry certainly reject this interpretation of their efforts. *Business Week,* for example, dismissed the charge that the science of behavior, as utilized by advertising, is engaged in human engineering and manipulation. It editorialized to the effect that "it is hard to find anything very sinister about a science whose principle conclusion is that you get along with people by giving them what

they want."[5] The theme is familiar: businesses just give the consumer what he/she wants; if they didn't they wouldn't stay in business very long. Proof that the consumer wants the products advertised is given by the fact that he buys them, and indeed often returns to buy them again and again.

The techniques of advertising we are discussing have had their more intellectual defenders as well. For example, Theodore Levitt, Professor of Business Administration at the Harvard Business School, has defended the practice of puffery and the use of techniques dependent on motivational research.[6] What would be the consequences, he asks us, of deleting all exaggerated claims and fanciful associations from advertisements? We would be left with literal descriptions of the empirical characteristics of products and their functions. Cosmetics would be presented as facial and bodily lotions and powders which produce certain odor and color changes; they would no longer offer hope or adventure. In addition to the fact that these products would not then sell as well, they would not, according to Levitt, please us as much either. For it is hope and adventure we want when we buy them. We want automobiles not just for transportation, but for the feelings of power and status they give us. Quoting T. S. Eliot to the effect that "Human kind cannot bear very much reality," Levitt argues that advertising is an effort to "transcend nature in the raw," to "augment what nature has so crudely fashioned." He maintains that "everybody everywhere wants to modify, transform, embellish, enrich and reconstruct the world around him." Commerce takes the same liberty with reality as the artist and the priest—in all three instances the purpose is "to influence the audience by creating illusions, symbols, and implications that promise more than pure functionality."

The defense of advertising which suggests that advertising simply is information which allows us to purchase what we want, has in turn been challenged. Does business, largely through its advertising efforts, really make available to the consumer what he/she desires and demands? John Kenneth Galbraith has denied that the matter is as straightforward as this.[7] In his opinion the desires to which business is supposed to respond, far from being original to the consumer, are often themselves created by business. The producers make both the product and the desire for it, and the "central function" of advertising is "to create desires." Galbraith coins the term 'The Dependence Effect' to designate the way wants depend on the same process by which they are satisfied.

David Braybrooke has argued in similar and related ways.[8] Even though the consumer is, in a sense, the final authority concerning what he wants, he may come to see, according to Braybrooke, that he was mistaken in wanting what he did. The statement 'I want x,' he tells us, is not incorrigible but is "ripe for revision." If the consumer had more objective information than he is provided by product puffing, if his values had not been mixed up by motivational research strategies (e.g., the confusion of sexual and automotive values), and if he had an expanded set of choices instead of the limited set offered by profit-hungry corporations, then he might want something quite different from what he presently wants. This shows, Braybrooke thinks, the extent to which the consumer's wants are a function of advertising and not necessarily representative of his real or true wants.

The central issue which emerges between the above critics and defenders of advertising is this: do the advertising techniques we have discussed involve a violation of human autonomy and a manipulation and control of consumer behavior, *or* do they simply provide an efficient and cost-effective means of giving the consumer information on the basis of which he or she makes a free choice. Is advertising information, or creation of desire?

To answer this question we need a better conceptual grasp of what is involved in the notion of autonomy. This is a complex, multifaceted concept, and we need to approach it through the more determinate notions of (a) autonomous desire, (b) rational desire and choice, (c) free choice, and (d) control or manipulation. In what follows I shall offer some tentative and very incomplete analyses of these concepts and apply the results to the case of advertising.

AUTONOMOUS DESIRE

Imagine that I am watching T.V. and see an ad for Grecian Formula 16. The thought occurs to me that if

I purchase some and apply it to my beard, I will soon look younger—in fact I might even be myself again. Suddenly I want to be myself! I want to be young again! So I rush out and buy a bottle. This is our question: was the desire to be younger manufactured by the commercial, or was it 'original to me' and truly mine? Was it autonomous or not?

F. A. von Hayek has argued plausibly that we should not equate nonautonomous desires, desires which are not original to me or truly mine, with those which are culturally induced.[9] If we did equate the two, he points out, then the desires for music, art, and knowledge could not properly be attributed to a person as original to him, for these are surely induced culturally. The only desires a person would really have as his own in this case would be the purely physical ones for food, shelter, sex, etc. But if we reject the equation of the nonautonomous and the culturally induced, as von Hayek would have us do, then the mere fact that my desire to be young again is caused by the T.V. commercial—surely an instrument of popular culture transmission—does not in and of itself show that this is not my own, autonomous desire. Moreover, even if I never before felt the need to look young, it doesn't follow that this new desire is any less mine. . . .

This shows that there is something wrong in setting up the issue over advertising and behavior control as a question whether our desires are truly ours *or* are created in us by advertisements. Induced and autonomous desires do not separate into two mutually exclusive classes. To obtain a better understanding of autonomous and nonautonomous desires, let us consider some cases of a desire which a person does not *acknowledge* to be his own even though he *feels* it. The kleptomaniac has a desire to steal which in many instances he repudiates, seeking by treatment to rid himself of it. . . .

There may be some desires I feel which I have picked up from advertising and which I disown—for instance, my desire for A-1 Steak Sauce. If I act on these desires it can be said that I have been led by advertising to act in a way foreign to my nature. In these cases my autonomy has been violated. But most of the desires induced by advertising I fully accept, and hence most of these desires are autonomous. The most vivid demonstration of this is that I often return to purchase the same product over and over again, without regret or remorse. And when I don't, it is more likely that the desire has just faded than that I have repudiated it. Hence, while advertising may violate my autonomy by leading me to act on desires which are not truly mine, this seems to be the exceptional case. . . .

What are we to say in response to Braybrooke's argument that insofar as we might choose differently if advertisers gave us better information and more options, it follows that the desires we have are to be attributed more to advertising than to our own real inclinations? This claim seems empty. It amounts to saying that if the world we lived in, and we ourselves, were different, then we would want different things. . . .

RATIONAL DESIRE AND CHOICE

Braybrooke might be interpreted as claiming that the desires induced by advertising are often irrational ones in the sense that they are not expressed by an agent who is in full possession of the facts about the products advertised or about the alternative products which might be offered him. Following this line of thought, a possible criticism of advertising is that it leads us to act on irrational desires or to make irrational choices. It might be said that our autonomy has been violated by the fact that we are prevented from following our rational wills or that we have been denied the "positive freedom" to develop our true, rational selves. It might be claimed that the desires induced in us by advertising are false desires in that they do not reflect our essential, i.e., rational, essence.

The problem faced by this line of criticism is that of determining what is to count as rational desire or rational choice. If we require that the desire or choice be the product of an awareness of *all* the facts about the product, then surely every one of us is always moved by irrational desires and makes nothing but irrational choices. How could we know all the facts about a product? If it be required only that we possess all of the *available* knowledge about the product advertised, then we still have to face the problem that not all available knowledge is *relevant* to a rational choice. If I am purchasing a car, certain engineering features will be, and others won't be, relevant, *given*

what I want in a car. My prior desires determine the relevance of information. Normally a rational desire or choice is thought to be one based upon relevant information, and information is relevant if it shows how other, prior desires may be satisfied. It can plausibly be claimed that it is such prior desires that advertising agencies acknowledge, and that the agencies often provide the type of information that is relevant in light of these desires. To the extent that this is true, advertising does not inhibit our rational wills or our autonomy as rational creatures.

FREE CHOICE

It might be said that some desires are so strong or so covert that a person cannot resist them, and that when he acts on such desires he is not acting freely or voluntarily but is rather the victim of an irresistible impulse or an unconscious drive. Perhaps those who condemn advertising feel that it produces this kind of desire in us and consequently reduces our autonomy.

This raises a very difficult issue. How do we distinguish between an impulse we *do* not resist and one we *could* not resist, between freely giving in to a desire and succumbing to one? A person acts or chooses freely if he does so for a reason, that is, if he can adduce considerations which justify in his mind the act in question. Many of our actions are in fact free because this condition frequently holds. Often, however, a person will act from habit, or whim, or impulse, and on these occasions he does not have a reason in mind. Nevertheless he often acts voluntarily in these instances, i.e., he could have acted otherwise. And this is because if there *had been* a reason for acting otherwise of which he was aware, he would in fact have done so. Thus acting from habit or impulse is not necessarily to act in an involuntary manner. If, however, a person is aware of a good reason to do *x* and still follows his impulse to do *y,* then he can be said to be impelled by irresistible impulse and hence to act involuntarily. Many kleptomaniacs can be said to act involuntarily, for in spite of their knowledge that they likely will be caught and their awareness that the goods they steal have little utilitarian value to them, they nevertheless steal. Here their "out of character" desires have the upper hand, and we have a case of compulsive behavior.

Applying these notions of voluntary and compulsive behavior to the case of behavior prompted by advertising, can we say that consumers influenced by advertising act compulsively? The unexciting answer is: sometimes they do, sometimes not. I may have an overwhelming. T.V. induced urge to own a Mazda Rx-7 and all the while realize that I can't afford one without severely reducing my family's caloric intake to a dangerous level. If, aware of this good reason not to purchase the car, I nevertheless do so, this shows that I have been the victim of T.V. compulsion. But if I have the urge, as I assure you I do, and don't act on it, or if in some other possible world I could afford an Rx-7, then I have not been the subject of undue influence by Mazda advertising. Some Mazda Rx-7 purchasers act compulsively; others do not. The Mazda advertising effort *in general* cannot be condemned, then, for impairing its customers' autonomy in the sense of limiting free or voluntary choice. Of course the question remains what should be done about the fact that advertising may and does *occasionally* limit free choice.

———————

Let me summarize my argument. The critics of advertising see it as having a pernicious effect on the autonomy of consumers, as controlling their lives and manufacturing their very souls. The defense claims that advertising only offers information and in effect allows industry to provide consumers with what they want. After developing some of the philosophical dimensions of this dispute, I have come down tentatively in favor of the advertisers. Advertising may, but certainly does not always or even frequently, control behavior, produce compulsive behavior, or create wants which are not rational or are not truly those of the consumer. Admittedly it may in individual cases do all of these things, but it is innocent of the charge of intrinsically or necessarily doing them or even, I think, of often doing so. This limited potentiality, to be sure, leads to the question whether advertising should be abolished or severely curtailed or regulated because of its potential to harm a few poor souls in the above ways. This is a very difficult question, and I do not pretend to have the answer. I only hope that the above discussion, in showing some of the kinds of harm that can be done by advertising and by indicating the likely limits of this harm, will put us in a better position to grapple with the question.

NOTES

1. Vance Packard, *The Hidden Persuaders* (Pocket Books, New York, 1958), pp. 20–21.

2. Ibid., p. 21.

3. B. F. Skinner, 'Some Issues Concerning the Control of Human Behavior: A Symposium', in Karlins and Andrews (eds.), *Man Controlled* (The Free Press, New York, 1972).

4. I would like to emphasize that in what follows I am discussing these techniques of advertising from the standpoint of the issue of control and not from that of deception. For a good and recent discussion of the many dimensions of possible deception in advertising, see Alex C. Michalos, "Advertising: Its Logic, Ethics, and Economics" in J. A. Blair and R. H. Johnson (eds.), *Informal Logic: The First International Symposium* (Edgepress, Pt. Reyes, Calif., 1980).

5. Quoted by Packard, op. cit., p. 220.

6. Theodore Levitt. 'The Morality (?) of Advertising', *Harvard Business Review* 48 (1970). 84–92.

7. John Kenneth Galbraith, *The Affluent Society;* reprinted in Tom L. Beauchamp and Norman E. Bowie (eds.), *Ethical Theory and Business* (Prentice-Hall, Englewood Cliffs, 1979), pp. 496–501.

8. David Braybrooke, "Skepticism of Wants, and Certain Subversive Effects of Corporations on American Values," in Sidney Hook (ed.), *Human Values and Economic Policy* (New York University Press, New York, 1967); reprinted in Beauchamp and Bowie (eds.), op. cit., pp. 502–508.

9. F. A. von Hayek, "The *Non Sequitur* of the 'Dependence Effect,'" *Southern Economic Journal* (1961); reprinted in Beauchamp and Bowie (eds.), op. cit., pp. 508–512.

QUESTIONS

1. Does advertising control our behavior? How? Why might you argue that advertising is just another kind of information

2. Give a definition of freedom. Then list the various constraints upon your own, personal freedom. Are there non-material as well as material restraints?

Alan Goldman

The Justification of Advertising in a Market Economy

Alan Goldman is professor of philosophy at the University of Miami.

The first virtue of a market economy is its efficiency in allocating economic resources, capital, and labor to satisfy collective needs and wants for products and services. In theory, maximum efficiency obtains given certain ideal conditions of pure competition. These conditions include: (1) competition within industries among firms, each of which is too small to dictate prices to the market; (2) fluidity of labor and capital; (3) perfect knowledge on the part of consumers of prices and features of various products and services; and (4) knowledge on the part of producers of consumer demand for various goods. Given such conditions, the market, through its price mechanisms, guides profit seeking producers to allocate economic resources in ways that optimize the aggregate satisfaction of demand—that is, the sum total of wants in society. Goods are distributed in turn to those with greatest demand, the degree of demand being measured by willingness to pay. The result approximates to maximization of utility, understood as the greatest sum of the satisfaction of wants over the whole society. Those goods are produced and distributed that yield the greatest surplus of value over economic costs.

The market mechanism theoretically underlying efficiency of resource allocation was first described by Adam Smith. When a certain good is under-supplied in relation to the demand for it, its price is bid upward. Consumers are willing to pay more for a product they want when it is in short supply, and producers can improve their profits by selling the limited supply at a higher price. The possibility of higher profits will attract new resources (that is, capital and labor) to the industry, until supply is increased and the margin of profit falls again to approximate that of other industries. Thus supply adjusts to demand. Conversely, oversupply of a good means that some of it will have to be sold at a loss, driving resources from the industry and adjusting the production downward. The tendency is toward an equilibrium at which the marginal value of all goods is equal and, taken collectively, maximal in relation to the relative social demand for the various goods.

This process is dynamic and progressive. At the same time as optimal efficiency is achieved in allocating resources so as to satisfy particular wants at particular times, competition generates progress through improvement of productive techniques and processes. Each competitor is motivated to modernize production so as to increase volume and cut unit costs of products. The price a producer pays for obsolescence is being undersold by the more efficient competition and thereby driven out of business. Thus the free market is theoretically efficient over time. It guarantees not only the most efficient use of resources in the present, but the production of more and more goods and services in the future.

A further virtue of the competitive market economy, given ideal conditions, is its maximization of individual freedoms. All transactions within this economy are to be voluntary. Individuals are free to choose their occupations, investors to invest where they like, and consumers to buy or refuse what is offered for sale. For a transaction to take place, given the ideal condition of full knowledge of its features

Just Business: New Introductory Essays in Business Ethics, ed. Tom Regan (New York: Random House, 1983, 235–270). Reprinted with permission of McGraw Hill Co.

and alternatives, it must be perceived as mutually beneficial to the parties involved.

If we accept this model as a morally defensible economic system, where in it can we find a place for the institution of advertising? The ideal requires relevant knowledge on the part of consumers of the existence, quality, and prices of products, and it is unclear that advertising, at least as we know it, accomplishes this goal. Second, the model also assumes that consumer demands are given and judges the efficiency of the market by the extent to which they are satisfied. Advertising, however, sometimes aims to *create* desires in the consuming public, and it is unclear whether the satisfaction of these desires should likewise be counted as a gain in utility or social value. An even more fundamental difficulty may be explained as follows. Our model assumes that consumer demand for a product dictates prices to individual firms, which then manufacture goods until the marginal costs equal the price (that is, until no more profit can be made from additional units). But some economists have argued that advertising contributes to conditions in which producers can control prices, by creating demand to match planned levels of supply at fixed prices. Similarly, advertising often seeks to create *consumer loyalty,* which arguably makes it more difficult for new competitors to enter the market—specifically, more expensive, since it requires extensive advertising campaigns to overcome consumer loyalty. Brand loyalty may also be inefficient in itself, since it leads consumers to perceive differences among products when there may be no real differences in quality, which might cause them to forgo savings in price among identical products, (for example chemically identical aspirin tablets), thereby diminishing maximum utility.

More recently, however, economists have taken the opposite stand on this issue. Some have argued that advertising actually facilitates entry of new competitors by allowing them to publicize their products and lure customers away from established firms. The purpose of ad campaigns, it is now said, is to create brand *dis*loyalty. Campaigns are typically directed not at those who already are customers, but at potential new customers. In response to the claim that ads lead consumers to make ungrounded and costly prod-

uct differentiations, it is pointed out that brand recognition and even brand loyalty create benefits for consumers as well. When shoppers can identify products and their manufacturers, the latter are pressured to maintain quality. At the same time comparison shopping is facilitated among retailers, so that they must sell within price limits.

In assessing this debate, it appears that the claims of the opposing sides may all be true, showing only that advertising produces *both* positive *and* negative effects upon competition and prices for consumers. It seems clear, first, that there have been successful advertising campaigns of both sorts, those that reinforce brand loyalty and help to retain a clientele (perhaps by reinforcing a favorable image of the brand in consumers' minds), and those that lure new customers away from established brands. Furthermore, while brand loyalty may raise successful entry costs, advertising may simultaneously ease entry for those with the capital to mount extensive campaigns. Finally, while ads may create the illusion of product differences where none exist and hence prevent choice of cheaper alternatives, brand recognition, achieved through exposure to ads, does facilitate comparison shopping among retailers. In the absence of data weighing these opposing tendencies across many industries, it seems impossible to justify or condemn advertising by its effects on the degree of competition in various product markets. There is no good reason at present, in short, for believing that advertising is inconsistent with the free market's aims of eliminating monopolies and encouraging competition.

Principal among the direct benefits claimed to result from advertising is the benefit of consumers' having relevant knowledge of the existence, quality, and price of products. How well advertising provides this benefit will concern us shortly. First, though, let us consider an indirect social benefit attributed to the institution of advertising: namely, that it subsidizes the media. Commercial radio and television, as well as most newspapers and magazines, could not survive without this subsidy, certainly not in the forms we know them and at the prices we are used to paying. It can be argued, then, that since these media themselves add much to the social environment in the way of information and entertainment, the institution of advertising is indirectly but importantly valuable in making this possible.

Once again, however, one must recognize as well the negative influence of advertising, especially upon the broadcast media. The main problem, of course, is the desire of the stations, pressured by the sponsors, to appeal to the largest possible audience with every show. The result is the reduction of content and style to the lowest common denominator of taste. Commercial television can be held responsible for debasing American taste, certainly for failing to elevate it and contribute culturally and aesthetically as it could. Advertising sponsors are the main culprits. Not only the "highbrow," but also the innovative, daring, or controversial is shunned as possibly offensive, when sponsors exercise effective censorship over programming. This is true not only of cultural and entertainment shows, but perhaps more seriously, sometimes of news and information programs as well. . . .

Thus once more we find a mixed blessing at best in the social effect of advertising. Here we can begin to draw some morals for advertisers. The service provided by advertising in subsidizing the media seems clearly preferable when sponsors do not act as censors. When commercial considerations come first, this priority is clearly detrimental to the aesthetic value of programs. This may be even more clearly true of the informative value of news and information programming. Very large audiences can be expected to be attracted only to the familiar and aesthetically un-innovative. But the judgment of artistic merit, as well as that of newsworthiness, ought to be made on intrinsic grounds by those with some expertise, rather than on strictly commercial grounds, if the media are to realize their potential for educating and not simply tranquilizing the public. In order to accomplish this, self-restraint, sometimes at the expense of the short-term self-interest of particular advertisers and their business clients, is required.

If advertising is to be ethically justified, given the free-market approach, it is not enough to argue for its consistency in a free-market economy, or that it is not wasteful of economic resources, or even that it provides certain indirect social benefits. The positive jus-tification must include the direct benefit that allegedly accrues from this institution: namely, the provision of relevant information. Maximal value can be obtained by consumers only if they know all the alternative ways of satisfying their desires and the costs of doing so. For any beneficial transaction to occur, people must be acquainted with products available. Advertising so informs them, also often providing data on product features, changes, and prices. Such information must be continuously provided because of the arrival of new consumers, new products, and new product features. So advertising seems justified in a free market as a valuable source of information. Even when it attempts mainly to persuade rather than to inform directly, it will tell of a product's availability and perhaps of its prominent features.

Certain moral demands appear to follow quite obviously from this justification. If advertisements are to be justified as sources of information for consumers then they ought to be truthful and avoid deception. If, in the area of consumer decisions, free choice is most likely to satisfy genuine desires and maximize welfare, then lies in the marketplace tend to subvert the entire rationale of the free-market economy. If consumers are misled, they will no longer be free in their choices and will no longer be maximizing utility; the virtues of the free market will be lost.

A central function of much advertising is to persuade people to buy products. One method of persuading someone to buy something is simply to inform him of its features and availability. This suffices when the object is known to satisfy some pre-existing desire. A slightly more complex method that better fits our usual concept of persuasion consists in showing someone that he *should* desire something because it is a means to achieve something else that he desires. This is still a typical form of rational persuasion—one provides reasons for desiring that are to be consciously weighed by the person addressed.

A more controversial method of persuasion by-passes reason and even conscious thought processes, attempting rather to create an association in the consumer's mind between the product and some image that expresses a subconscious wish or desire. A possibly more sinister variation on this persuasive strategy seeks to establish an association between the lack or absence of the product and some unconscious fear or anxiety. The consumer is then to choose the product as a way of fulfilling his unconscious wish or avoiding the object of his unconscious anxiety.

The psychological theory behind typical variations on this method is eclectic, a mixture of Freudian ideas and behavioral conditioning methods. Notions of subconscious wishes, fears, and sublimations combine with techniques to induce association by conditioning. Methods of advertising (like simple repetition of a brand name or slogan) that make little sense if we think of them as means of providing information become intelligible under this alternative analysis. But though economically successful at least some of the time, such advertising might be condemned on moral grounds. Why?

Persuasion by rational means respects the right of the intended object of persuasion to free and informed choice. But when the influence is intended to be subconscious, the persuasion appears similar to deception. The method appears then to violate a central requirement of at least one major moral tradition, the imperative to treat other persons as equals and to respect their rationality and freedom of choice. It also seems to contradict a major justification of the free economic market: that the system permits all economic transactions to be voluntary. A consumer's decision to buy is not voluntary, it can be argued, when he has been unduly influenced in this way.

Suppose we grant that there is a right to advertise. Businesses have the right to promote their products and services, and advertisers have the right to provide this service to them. Advertising is a form of speech, and as such it seems to require no further justification than appeal to the right of free expression. There remains a constitutionally supported distinction between commercial and other relevant forms of speech, that is, political and literary. Congress is granted the right to control commerce, but not to abridge other forms of speech. Granted that certain economic freedoms are central—for example, the freedom of individuals to work, invest, and consume as they choose—even in these areas there are limitations to protect others as well as the agents themselves. One cannot buy dangerous explosives or work on certain jobs without wearing safety equipment; one cannot invest in the heroin trade. In the realm of speech, the right to advertise does not include a right to defraud, or moral license to mislead people into buying harmful products. Legally, the Federal Trade Commission requires that advertisements be truthful and that their factual claims be substantiated. Such requirements, of course, would not be tolerated in other realms of discourse. We would not trust the government to prohibit political speech it judges to be untrue or literary works it holds misleading or even subversive ...

In endorsing regulation of advertising we must recognize certain negative consequences. First, strict scrutiny of factual claims may lead advertisers to reduce their content, relying instead upon nonrational methods of persuasion. One could argue that the net result is less information to consumers. We can reply that less information is better than false or misleading information. In addition, information that gives good reasons to prefer the product remains valuable for use in ads. The public can still recognize substantiated claims of superiority in product features, and such claims are likely to be more persuasive than meaningless jingles, with less repetition required. Second, it has been argued that regulation makes ads more believable in the eyes of the public, which only makes it easier for the less scrupulous to deceive. But to argue in that way against holding advertisers to the truth suggests more generally that we ought not to encourage honesty, since honesty as a rule makes deception in particular cases easier. This argument is absurd.

We must recognize, secondly, that not all morally objectionable practices on the part of advertisers can be made illegal or regulated. Fair regulation requires objectively verifiable criteria on which to base enforcement. It must therefore center on fraud and deception in factual claims and upon limiting promotion of obviously harmful products such as cigarettes. Non-rational persuasion that creates false associations or insecurities, or that encourages pretentious and unfulfilling patterns of consumption and lifestyles, cannot be prohibited, since enforcement of the prohibitions could not be fair and non-controversial. Such practices nevertheless remain morally objectionable. . . .

Despite the limitations on regulation, then, it is clear that the right to advertise does not include a moral right to deceive, mislead, or harass, or to create or foster insecurities or self-defeating values. The legal right to advertise is narrower than the corresponding right to free non-commercial speech. The moral right to engage in specific advertising practices is narrower still, not including certain activities that cannot be legally sanctioned (because of the costs involved). . . .

The social effect of advertising subsidies to print and broadcast media is optimized when sponsors restrain their inclinations to censor program material in order to appeal to uniformly large audiences and avoid offending them. Only uncensored media can educate public taste rather than accommodating to its lowest common denominator. Here is the first case of a moral demand that may run counter to the profit-maximizing motive of the advertiser and his client. The injunction against censorship is a genuinely moral requirement, since the social effect of commercial censors seems no less pernicious than that of government censors.

A function more intrinsic to advertisements themselves is the provision of information to consumers enabling them to make more rational choices among products so as to better satisfy their desires. The performance of this function requires that advertisements be truthful and verifiable in their explicit and implied factual claims. "Puffery" or hyperbole must be clearly distinguishable from factual claims by the audience, this requirement becoming broader and stricter when the product is potentially harmful and the intended audience less worldly wise (for example, children). While the advertiser is not morally required to aim at providing complete information, material omitted must not negate claims made or implied, or relate to probable harm from the product.

. . . The basic principle regarding effects of persuasion is that advertisers ought not to create desires whose fulfillment would be more harmful than beneficial to consumers. More broadly, the principle we propose would prohibit encouraging irrational desires. Desires are irrational if their targets are falsely believed to be means to ends sought, if their satisfaction blocks that of other more important desires, or if the costs of their satisfaction are too high. Proscribed are desires for specific products known by the advertiser to be harmful, as well as yearnings for a lifestyle out of reach or ultimately low in overall satisfaction. The advertiser's ignorance of the harmfulness of the product he advocates is normally no excuse. Since he shares responsibility for the consumer's buying the product, he must share the blame for the harm that results. To avoid such blame he is obligated to find out, within reasonable limits, the nature of the products he sells. . . .

Turning to the methods of non-rational persuasion, important moral considerations include the resistibility of the appeal to the audience, that is, whether the choices under its influence remain free, and the importance of the choices at stake. The former is especially relevant in the case of children, where the advertiser must exercise extreme caution and restraint. . . .

Weaker moral demands relate also to the aesthetics of advertising. The advertiser ought not to harass or irritate us intentionally or pollute our natural or aesthetic environments in order to get our attention.

QUESTIONS

1. How does Goldman justify advertising in a market economy?

2. Suppose I am a Nazi propagandist "advertising" the good of concentration camps for the German people (pay your taxes! It supports the camps!). What would Goldman say to me?

Leslie Savan	# The Bribed Soul

Leslie Savan is the advertising columnist for the *Village Voice* and was twice a finalist for the Pulitzer Prize in criticism.

Television-watching Americans—that is, just about *all* Americans—see approximately 100 TV commercials a day. In that same 24 hours they also see a host of print ads, billboard signs, and other corporate messages slapped onto every available surface, from the fuselages of NASA rockets right down to the bottom of golf holes and the inside doors of restroom stalls. Studies estimate that, counting all the logos, labels, and announcements, some 16,000 ads flicker across an individual's consciousness daily. . . .

Most admakers understand that in order to sell to you they have to know your desires and dreams better than you may know them yourself, and they've tried to reduce that understanding to a science. Market research, in which psychologists, polling organizations, trends analysts, focus group leaders, "mall-intercept" interviewers, and the whole panoply of mass communications try to figure out what will make you buy, has become a $2.5 billion annual business growing at a healthy clip of about 4.2 percent a year (after adjustment for inflation). Yet this sophisticated program for the study of the individual consumer is only a starter kit for the technological advances that will sweep through the advertising-industrial complex in the 1990s. Today, the most we can do when another TV commercial comes on—and we are repeatedly told that this is our great freedom—is to switch channels. But soon technology will take even that tiny tantrum of resistance and make it "interactive," providing advertisers with information on the exact moment we became bored—vital data that can be crunched, analyzed, and processed into the next set of ads, the better to zap-proof *them.*

Impressive as such research may be, the real masterwork of advertising is the way it uses the techniques of art to seduce the human soul. Virtually all of modern experience now has a sponsor, or at least a sponsored accessory, and there is no human emotion or concern—love, lust, war, childhood innocence, social rebellion, spiritual enlightenment, even disgust with advertising—that cannot be reworked into a sales pitch. The transcendent look in a bride's eyes the moment before she kisses her groom turns into a promo for Du Pont. The teeth-gnashing humiliation of an office rival becomes an inducement to switch to AT&T.

In short, we're living the sponsored life. From Huggies to Maalox, the necessities and little luxuries of an American's passage through this world are provided and promoted by one advertiser or another. The sponsored life is born when commercial culture sells our own experiences back to us. It grows as those experiences are then reconstituted inside us, mixing the most intimate processes of individual thought with commercial values, rhythms, and expectations. It has often been said by television's critics that TV doesn't deliver products to viewers but that viewers themselves are the *real* product, one that TV delivers to its advertisers. True, but the symbiotic relationship between advertising and audience goes deeper than that. The viewer who lives the sponsored life—and that is most of us to one degree or the other—is slowly re-created in the ad's image.

Inside each "consumer," advertising's all-you-can-eat, all-the-time, all-dessert buffet produces a build-up of mass-produced stimuli, all hissing and sputtering to get out. Sometimes they burst out as sponsored speech, as when we talk in the cadences of sitcom one-liners, imitate Letterman, laugh uproariously at lines like "I've fallen and I can't get up," or mouth the words of familiar commercials, like the entranced high school student I met in a communication class who moved his lips with the voiceover of a Toyota spot. . . .

To lead the sponsored life you don't really have to do anything. You don't need to have a corporate sponsor as the museums or the movies do. You don't even have to buy anything—though it helps, and you will. You just have to live in America and share with the nation, or at least with your mall-intercept cohorts, certain paid-for expectations and values, rhythms and reflexes. . . .

The chief expectation of the sponsored life is that there will and always should be regular blips of excitement and resolution, the frequency of which is determined by money. We begin to pulse to the beat, the one-two beat, that moves most ads: problem/solution, old/new, Brand X/hero brand, desire/gratification. In order to dance to the rhythm, we adjust other expectations a little here, a little there: Our notions of what's desirable behavior, our lust for novelty, even our visions of the perfect love affair or thrilling adventure adapt to the mass consensus coaxed out by marketing. Cultural forms that don't fit these patterns tend to fade away, and eventually *everything* is commercial culture—not just the 30-second spot but the drama, news segment, stage performance, novel, magazine layout—comes to share the same insipid insistence on canned excitement and neat resolution.

What's all the excitement about? Anything and nothing. You know you've entered the commercial zone when the excitement building in you is oddly incommensurate with the content dangled before you: does a sip of Diet Coke really warrant an expensive production number celebrating the rebel prowess of "ministers who surf," "insurance agents who speed," and "people who live their life as an exclamation not an explanation"?!? Of course not. Yet through the sympathetic magic of materialism we learn how to respond to excitement: It's less important that we purchase any particular product than that we come to expect resolution *in the form of* something buyable. . . .

Irony has become the hallmark of the sponsored life because it provides a certain distance from the frustration inherent in commercial correctness. For some time now the people raised on television, the baby boomers and the "Generation Xers" that followed, have mentally adjusted the set, as it were, in order to convince themselves that watching is cool. They may be doing exactly what their parents do—but they do it *differently.* They take in TV with a Lettermanesque wink, and they like it when it winks back. In many cases (as Mark Crispin Miller has described it so well in *Boxed In*), the winkers have enthusiastically embraced the artifice, even the manipulativeness, of advertising as an essential paradox of modern life, a paradox that is at the crux of their own identity.

The winkers believe that by rolling their collective eyes when they watch TV they can control *it,* rather than letting it control them. But unfortunately, as a defense against the power of advertising, irony is a leaky condom—in fact, it's the same old condom that advertising brings over every night. A lot of ads have learned that to break through to the all-important boomer and Xer markets they have to be as cool, hip, and ironic as the target audience likes to think of itself as being. That requires at least the pose of opposition to commercial values. The cool commercials—I'm thinking of Nike spots, some Reeboks, most 501s, certainly all MTV promos—flatter us by saying we're too cool to fall for commercial values, and therefore cool enough to want their product.

If irony is weak armor, how do we ward off the effect of billions of words and images from our sponsors? No perfect wolfsbane exists, but I can suggest some tactics to keep in mind:

When watching, watch out. Literally. Watch as an outsider, from as far a distance as you can muster (farther even than irony)—*especially* when watching ads that flatter you for being an outsider, as more and more are doing.

Big lie, little lie. All advertising tells lies, but there are little lies and there are big lies. Little lie: This beer tastes great. Not all ads tell little lies—they're more likely to be legally actionable (while big lies by definition aren't). And many products do live up to their modest material claims: This car runs. But all ads *must* tell big lies: This car will attract

To: You
From: The Philosopher
Subject: "Conspicuous Consumption"

Thorstein Veblen was an American economist and social theorist. He argued that the reason our society loves consumer goods is that they give us prestige. Why do we buy a Porsche instead of a Previa? Because people admire Porsche owners. Why do people buy Rolexes instead of Timexes, despite the notorious unreliability of the former? Simply because they cost more. The logical conclusion of consumption, Veblen argues, is systematic waste.

> Conspicuous consumption of valuable goods is a means of reputability to the gentleman of leisure. As wealth accumulates on his hands, his own unaided effort will not avail to sufficiently put his opulence in evidence by this method. The aid of friends and competitors is therefore brought in by resorting to the giving of valuable presents and expensive feasts and entertainments. . . .
>
> The basis on which good repute in any highly organised industrial community ultimately rests is pecuniary strength; and the means of showing pecuniary strength, and so of gaining or retaining a good name, are leisure and a conspicuous consumption of goods. . . . No class of society not even the most abjectly poor, foregoes all customary conspicuous consumption. The last items of this category of consumption are not given up except under stress of the direst necessity. Very much of squalor and discomfort will be endured before the last trinket or the last pretence of pecuniary decency is put away.
>
> . . . It appears that the utility of both alike for the purposes of reputability lies in the element of waste that is common to both. In the one case it is a waste of time and effort, in the other it is a waste of goods. Both are methods of demonstrating the possession of wealth, and the two are conventionally accepted as equivalents. The choice between them is a question of advertising expediency simply, except so far as it may be affected by other standards of propriety springing from a different source. On grounds of expediency the preference may be given to the one or the other at different stages of the economic development. The question is, which of the two methods will most effectively reach the persons whose convictions it is desired to affect. . . .
>
> Throughout the entire evolution of conspicuous expenditure, whether of goods or of services or human life, runs the obvious implication that in order to effectually mend the consumer's good fame it must be an expenditure of superfluities. In order to be reputable it must be wasteful. . . . *

*From Thorstein Veblen, *The Theory of the Leisure Class: An Economic Study of Institutions* (New York: Macmillan, 1902), pp. 68–101.

babes and make others slobber in envy. Don't be shocked that ads lie—that's their job. But do try to distinguish between the two kinds of lies.

Read the box. Look not just at whether an ad's claims are false or exaggerated, but try to figure out what portion of an ad is about the culture as opposed to the product. Read the contents as you would a cereal box's: Instead of how much sugar to wheat, consider how much style to information. Not that a high ratio of sugar to wheat is necessarily more malevolent than the other way around. But it's a sure sign that they're fattening you up for the shill.

Assume no relationship between a brand and its image. Marlboro was originally sold as a woman's cigarette, and its image was elegant, if not downright prissy. It wasn't until 1955 that the Marlboro Man was invented to ride herd on all that. The arbitrary relationship between a product and its ads becomes even clearer when you realize how much advertising is created to overcome "brand parity"—a plague more troubling to marketers than bodily odors. Brand parity means that there is little or no difference between competing brands and that the best a brand can do is hire a more appealing image. When advertising works at all, it's because the public more or less believes that something serious is going on between a product and its image, as if the latter reveals intrinsic qualities of the former. Peel image off item, and you too can have more of the freedom that ads are always promising. Likewise . . .

We don't buy products, we buy the world that presents them. Over the long run, whether you actually buy a particular product is less important than that you buy the world that makes the products seem desirable. Not so long ago a BMW or a Mercedes was required if you seriously bought the worldview that their ads conveyed. Still, buying an attitude doesn't automatically translate into product purchase. If your income precluded a BMW, you might have bought instead a Ralph Lauren polo shirt or even a Dove bar (which is how yuppie snack foods positioned themselves—as achievable class). Sure, GE wants you to buy its bulbs, but even more it wants you to buy the paternalistic, everything's-under-control world that GE seems to rule. Buying *that* will result, GE is betting, not only in more appliance sales but also in more credibility when spokesmen insist that defrauding the Pentagon is not *really* what GE is all about. That is to say . . .

The promotional is the political. Each world that commercials use to sell things comes packed with biases: Entire classes, races, and genders may be excluded for the coddling of the sponsored one. Lee Jeans' world (circa 1989) is a place where young people are hip, sexual, and wear jeans, while old peo-

ple are square, non-sexual, and wear uniforms. The class and age politics here is more powerful than the Young Republicans'. There is politics in all advertising (and, more obviously, advertising in all politics). It makes sense that these two professions call what they do "campaigns."

Advertising shepherds herds of individuals. When Monty Python's mistaken messiah in *The Life of Brian* exhorts the crowd of devotees to "Don't follow me! Don't follow anyone! Think for yourselves! . . . You are all individuals!" they reply in unison, "We are all individuals!" That is advertising in a nutshell.

Advertising's most basic paradox is to say: Join us and become unique. Advertisers learned long ago that individuality sells, like sex or patriotism. The urge toward individualism is a constant in America, with icons ranging from Thomas Jefferson's yeoman farmer to the kooky girl bouncing to the jingle "I like the Sprite in you!" Commercial nonconformity always operates in the service of . . . conformity. Our system of laws and our one-man-one-vote politics may be based on individualism, but successful marketing depends on the exact opposite: By identifying (through research) the ways we are alike, it hopes to convince the largest number of people that they need the exact same product. Furthermore, in modern pop culture, we construct our individuality by the unique combination of mass-produced goods and services we buy. I sip Evian, you slug Bud Light; I drive a Geo, you gun a Ford pickup; I kick sidewalk in cowboy boots, you bop in Reeboks. Individuality is a good angle for all advertising, but it's crucial for TV commercials. There you are sitting at home, not doing anything for hours on end, but then the very box you're staring at tells you that you are different, that you are vibrantly alive, that your quest for freedom—freedom of speech, freedom of movement, freedom to do whatever you damn well choose—will not be impeded! And you can do all that, says the box, without leaving your couch.

It's the real ad. The one question I'm most often asked is, Does advertising shape who we are and what we want, or does it merely reflect back to us our own emotions and desires? As with most nature-or-nurture questions, the answer is both. The real ad in any campaign is controlled neither by admakers nor adwatchers; it exists somewhere between the TV set and the viewer, like a huge hairball, collecting bits of material and meaning from both. The real ad isn't even activated until viewers hand it their frustrations from work, the mood of their love life, their idiosyncratic misinterpretations, and most of all, I think, their everyday politics. On which class rung do they see themselves teetering? Do they ever so subtly flinch when a different race comes on TV? In this way, we all co-produce the ads we see. Agency people are often aghast that anyone would find offensive meanings in their ads because "that's not what we intended." Intention has little to do with it. Whatever they meant, once an ad hits the air it becomes public property. That, I think, is where criticism should aim—at the fluctuating, multi-meaning thing that floats over the country, reflecting us as we reflect it.

Follow the flattery. I use the word "flattery" a lot. When trying to understand what an ad's really up to, following the flattery is as useful as following the money. You'll find the ad's target market by asking who in any 30-second drama is being praised for qualities they probably don't possess. When a black teenager plays basketball with a white baby boomer for Canada Dry, it's not the black youth that's being pandered to. It's white boomers—the flattery being that they're cool enough to be accepted by blacks. Ads don't even have to put people on stage to today up to them. Ads can flatter by style alone, as do all the spots that turn on hyper-quick cuts or obscure meanings, telling us—uh, *some* of us—that we're special enough to get it.

We participate in our own seduction. Once properly flattered, all that's left is to close the sale—and only we can do that. Not only do we co-produce the ads, but we're our own best voiceover—that little inner voice that ultimately decides to buy or not. The best ads tell us we're cool *coolly*—in the other meaning of the word. McLuhan used to say that a cool medium, like television, involves us more by not giving us everything; the very spaces between TV's flickering dots are filled in by our central nervous system. He refers to "the involvement of the viewer with the completion of 'closing' of the TV image." This is seduction: We're stirred to a state so that not only do we close the image but, given the right image at the right time, we open our wallet. All television is erotically engaged in this way, but commercials are TV's G-spot. The smart ads always hold back a little to get us to lean forward a little. Some ads have become caricatures of this tease, withholding the product's name until the last second to keep you wondering who could possibly be sponsoring such intrigue. The seduction may continue right to the cash register, where one last image is completed: you and product together at last. It'd be nice to say that now that you've consumed, you've climaxed, and everyone can relax. But sponsorship is a lifetime proposition that must be renewed every day.

QUESTIONS

1. Is your soul bribed? Why or why not? Give examples?

2. How is it that our souls come to be "bribed"? How can we free our souls?

Thomas L. Carson

The Ethics of Sales

Thomas L. Carson is professor of philosophy at Loyola University, Chicago.

PRELIMINARIES: A CONCEPTUAL ROADMAP

We need to distinguish between lying, deception, withholding information, and concealing information. Roughly, deception is intentionally causing someone to have false beliefs. Standard dictionary definitions of lying say that a lie is a false statement intended to deceive others. The *Oxford English Dictionary* (1989) defines a lie as: "a false statement made with the intent to deceive." *Webster's* (1963) gives the following definition of the verb *lie:* "to make an untrue statement with intent to deceive." The word *deception* implies success in causing others to have false beliefs, but lying is often unsuccessful in causing deception. A further difference between lying and deception is that, while a lie must be a false statement, deception needn't involve false statements; true statements can be deceptive and many forms of deception do not involve making statements of any sort. Thus, many instances of deception do not constitute lying. Withholding information does not constitute deception. It is not a case of *causing* someone to have false beliefs; it is merely a case of failing to correct false beliefs or incomplete information. On the other hand, actively concealing information usually constitutes deception.

THE COMMON LAW PRINCIPLE OF CAVEAT EMPTOR

According to the common law principle of *caveat emptor,* sellers are not required to inform prospective buyers about the properties of the goods they sell. Under *caveat emptor,* sales and contracts to sell are legally enforceable even if the seller fails to inform the buyer of serious defects in the goods that are sold. Buyers themselves are responsible for determining the quality of the goods they purchase. In addition, English common law sometimes called for the enforcement of sales in cases in which sellers made false or misleading statements about the goods they sold (Atiyah 464–65).

Currently, all U.S. states operate under the Uniform Commercial Code of 1968. Section 2-313 of the code defines the notion of sellers' warranties (Preston 52). The code provides that all factual affirmations or statements about the goods being sold are warranties. This means that sales are not valid or legally enforceable if the seller makes false statements about the goods s/he is selling. The American legal system has developed the concept of an "implied" (as opposed to an express or explicit) warranty. Implied warranties are a significant limitation on the principle of *caveat emptor.* According to the Uniform Commercial Code, any transaction carries with it the following implied warranties: 1) that the seller owns the goods he is selling and 2) that the goods are "merchantable," i.e., suitable for the purposes for which they are sold (Preston 56–57). Many local ordinances require that people who sell real estate inform buyers about all known serious defects of the property they sell. These ordinances are also a significant limitation on the traditional principle of *caveat emptor.*

Deceptive sales practices also fall under the purview of the Federal Trade Commission (FTC). The FTC prohibits deceptive sales practices—practices likely to materially mislead reasonable consumers (FTC Statement 1983). . . .

HOLLEY'S THEORY

Holley's theory is based on his concept of a "voluntary" or "mutually beneficial" market exchange (Holley uses the terms *voluntary exchange* and *mutually beneficial exchange* interchangeably). He says that a voluntary exchange occurs "only if" the following conditions are met (Holley takes his conditions to be *necessary* conditions for an acceptable exchange):

1. Both buyer and seller understand what they are giving up and what they are receiving in return.
2. Neither buyer nor seller is compelled to enter into the exchange as a result of coercion, severely restricted alternatives, or other constraints on the ability to choose.
3. Both buyer and seller are able at the time of the exchange to make rational judgments about its costs and benefits. (Holley 463)

These three conditions admit of degrees of satisfaction. An ideal exchange is an exchange involving people who are fully informed, fully rational, and "enter into the exchange entirely of their own volition" (Holley 464). The conditions for an ideal exchange are seldom, if ever, met in practice. However, Holley claims that it is still possible to have an "acceptable exchange" if the parties are "adequately informed, rational, and free from compulsion."

According to Holley, "the primary duty of salespeople to customers is to avoid undermining the conditions of an acceptable exchange." He makes it clear that, on his view, acts of omission (as well as acts of commission) can undermine the conditions of an acceptable exchange (Holley 464).

Because of the complexity of many goods and services, customers often lack information necessary for an acceptable exchange. Careful examination of products will not necessarily reveal problems or defects. According to Holley, caveat emptor is not acceptable as a moral principle, because customers often lack information necessary for an acceptable exchange. In such cases, sales-people are morally obligated to give information to the buyer. The question then is: *What kind of information* do salespeople need to provide buyers in order to ensure that the buyer is adequately informed? Holley attempts to answer this question in the following passage in which he appeals to the golden rule:

> Determining exactly how much information needs to be provided is not always clear-cut. We must in general rely on our assessments of what a reasonable person would want to know. As a practical guide, a salesperson might consider, "What would I want to know, if I were considering buying this product?" (Holley 467)

This principle is very demanding, perhaps more demanding than Holley realizes. Presumably, most reasonable people would *want* to know *a great deal* about the things they are thinking of buying. They might want to know *everything* relevant to the decision whether or not to buy something (more on this point shortly).

CRITICISMS OF HOLLEY

First, when time does not permit it, a salesperson cannot be morally obligated to provide all information necessary to ensure that the customer is adequately informed (all the information that a reasonable person would *want* to know if she were in the buyer's position). In many cases, reasonable customers would *want* to know a great deal of information. Often salespeople simply don't have the time to give all customers all the information Holley deems necessary for an acceptable exchange. Salespeople don't always know all the information that the buyer needs for an acceptable exchange. It cannot be a person's duty to do what is impossible—that statement that someone *ought* to do a certain act implies that she *can* do that act. Further, in many cases, salespeople don't know enough about the buyer's state of knowledge to know what information the buyer needs in order to be adequately informed. A salesperson might know that the buyer needs certain information in order to be adequately informed but not know whether or not the buyer possesses that information. One might reply that salespeople *should* know all the information necessary for an adequate exchange. However, on examination, this is not a plausible view. A salesperson in a large retail store cannot be expected to be knowledgeable about every product he sells. Often, it is impossible for realtors and used car salesmen to know much about the condition of the houses and cars they sell or the likelihood that they will need expensive repairs.

Second, Holley's theory implies that a salesperson in a store would be obligated to inform customers that a particular piece of merchandise in her store sells for less at a competing store if she knows this to be the case. (Presumably, she would *want* to know where she can get it for the lowest price, were she herself considering buying the product.) Not only do salespeople have no duty to provide this kind of information, (ordinarily) it would be wrong for them to do so.

Third, Holley's theory seems to yield unacceptable consequences in cases in which the buyer's alternatives are severely constrained. Suppose that a person with a very modest income attempts to buy a house in a small town. Her options are severely constrained, since there is only one house for sale in her price range. According to Holley, there can't be an acceptable exchange in such cases, because condition number 2 is not satisfied. However, it's not clear what he thinks sellers ought to do in such cases. The seller can't be expected to remove these constraints by giving the buyer money or building more homes in town. Holley's view seems to imply that it would be wrong for anyone to sell or rent housing to such a person. This result is unacceptable.

TOWARD A MORE PLAUSIBLE THEORY ABOUT THE ETHICS OF SALES

I believe that salespeople have the following moral duties regarding the disclosure of information when dealing with *rational adult consumers* (cases involving children or adults who are not fully rational raise special problems that I will not try to deal with here):

1. Salespeople should provide buyers with safety warnings and precautions about the goods they sell. (Sometimes it is enough for salespeople to call attention to written warnings and precautions that come with the goods and services in question. These warnings are unnecessary if the buyers already understand the dangers or precautions in question.)
2. Salespeople should refrain from lying and deception in their dealings with customers.
3. As much as their knowledge and time constraints permit, salespeople should fully answer questions about the products and services they sell. They should answer questions forthrightly and not evade questions or withhold information that has been asked for (even if this makes it less likely that they will make a successful sale). Salespeople are obligated to answer questions about the goods and services they sell. However, they are justified in refusing to answer questions that would require them to reveal information about what their competitors are selling. They are not obligated to answer questions about competing goods and services or give information about other sellers.
4. Salespeople should not try to "steer" customers toward purchases that they have reason to think will prove to be harmful to customers (financial harm counts) or that customers will come to regret.

These are prima facie duties that can conflict with other duties and are sometimes overridden by other duties. A prima facie duty is one's actual duty, other things being equal; it is an actual duty in the absence of conflicting duties of greater or equal importance. For example, my prima facie duty to keep promises is my actual duty in the absence of conflicting duties of equal or greater importance. The above is a *minimal list* of the duties of salespeople concerning the disclosure of information. I believe that the following are also prima facie duties of salespeople, but I am much less certain that these principles can be justified:

5. Salespeople should not sell customers goods or services they have reason to think will prove to be harmful to customers or that the customers will come to regret later, without giving the customers their reasons for thinking that this is the case. (This duty does not hold if the seller has good reasons to think that the customer already possesses the information in question.)

6. Salespeople should not sell items they know to be defective or of poor quality without alerting customers to this. (This duty does not hold if the buyer can be reasonably expected to know about the poor quality of what he is buying.)

I have what I take to be strong arguments for 1–4, but I'm not so sure that I can justify 5 and 6. I believe that reasonable people can disagree about 5 and 6. (I have very little to say about 5 and 6 in the present essay. See Carson [2001] for a discussion of arguments for 5 and 6.)

There are some important connections between duties 2, 4, and 6. Lying and deception in sales are not confined to lying to or deceiving customers about the goods one sells. Many salespeople misrepresent their own motives to customers/clients. Almost all salespeople invite the trust of customers/clients and claim, implicitly or explicitly, to be acting in the interests of customers/clients. Salespeople often ask customers to defer to their judgment about what is best for them. For most salespeople, gaining the trust of customers or clients is essential for success. Many salespeople are *not* interested in helping customers in the way they represent themselves as being. A salesperson who misrepresents her motives, and intentions to customers violates rule 2. This simultaneous inviting and betrayal of trust is a kind of treachery. In ordinary cases, rules against lying and deception alone prohibit salespeople from steering customers toward goods or services they have reason to think will be bad for them. It is difficult to steer someone in this way without lying or deception, e.g., saying that you believe that a certain product is best for someone when you don't believe this to be the case. Similar remarks apply to selling defective goods. Often, it is impossible to do this without lying to or deceiving customers. In practice, most or many violations of rules 4 and 6 are also violations of rule 2. . . .

The Golden Rule

I think that the golden rule is most plausibly construed as a consistency principle (those who violate the golden rule are guilty of inconsistency). The following version of the golden rule can be justified.

GR. Consistency requires that if you think that it would be morally permissible for someone to do a certain act to another person, then you must consent to someone else doing the same act to you in relevantly similar circumstances.

How the Golden Rule Supports My Theory

Given this version of the golden rule, any rational and consistent moral judge who makes judgments about the moral obligations of salespeople will have to accept rules 1–4 as prima facie duties. Consider each duty in turn:

1. All of us have reason to fear the hazards about us in the world; we depend on others to warn us of those hazards. Few people would survive to adulthood were it not for the warnings of others about such things as oncoming cars, live electric wires, and approaching tornadoes. No one who values her own life can honestly say that she is willing to have others fail to warn her of dangers.

2. Like everyone else, a salesperson needs correct information in order to act effectively to achieve her goals and advance her interests. She is not willing to act on the basis of false beliefs. Consequently, she is not willing to have others deceive her or lie to her about matters relevant to her decisions in the marketplace. She is not willing to have members of other professions (such as law and medicine) make it a policy to deceive her or lie to her whenever they can gain financially from doing so.

3. Salespeople have questions about the goods and services they themselves buy. They can't say that they are willing to have others evade or refuse to answer those questions. We want our questions to be answered by salespeople or else we wouldn't ask them. We are not willing to have salespeople evade or refrain from answering our questions. (Digression. Rule 3 permits salespeople to refuse to answer questions that would force them to provide information about their competitors. Why should we say *this*? Why not say instead that salespeople are obligated to answer *all questions* that customers

Ask Me No Questions . . .

Every fat commission check has a price tag. For Matt Cooper the cost of earning up to $150,000 per sale was spending every day lying to his customers. It was the promise of huge bonus checks—not his $40,000 base salary—that lured him to join the sales force of a large, well-known Internet company two years ago. In his early twenties, hungry, and aggressive, Cooper fit the dot-com's sales culture mold, but what he didn't realize was that dishonesty was the price of admission.

The New York-based start-up formed a big-deals team, a group that sold multimillion-dollar advertising campaigns to some of the world's largest companies. The sales force's key strategy? Do whatever it took to close those deals. Almost 100 percent of the time that meant lying to the client. "If you didn't lie you were fired," Cooper says. "It always came down to careful wording and fudging numbers." Among various other deceptive tactics, the Internet company's salespeople would book $2 million deals, promising a certain amount of impressions on the client's banner ads for the first million and guaranteeing a certain amount of sales for the second million dollars. . . .

Finally Cooper couldn't take it anymore. "I started selling only what I knew worked, because I couldn't lie anymore—so my managers told me to either close more deals or find another job," he says. "It was the kind of culture where they broke you down and rebuilt you to be an animal." . . .

Such deception may be more common than we think. In the SMM survey, 36 percent of respondents said salespeople now conduct business in a less ethical manner than they did five years ago, and 36 percent believe there's been no change at all. What kind of fabrications do salespeople resort to? The survey shows that 45 percent of managers have heard their reps lying about promised delivery times, 20 percent have overheard their team members give false information about the company's service, and nearly 78 percent of managers have caught a competitor lying about their company's products or services. "It appears that misrepresentation of products or services is prevalent among salespeople," [Andy] Zoltners [a marketing professor at Northwestern University's Kellogg School of Management] says. "This is a losing strategy, and this kind of behavior is not what the best salespeople do."

Erin Stroud, "Kellogg in the Media." *Sales & Marketing Management,* July 2002, Kellogg School of Management

ask? The answer is as follows: A salesperson's actions affect *both* her customers and her employer. In applying the golden rule to this issue she can't simply ask what kind of information she would want were she in the customer's position [Holley poses the question in just this way]. Rule 3 can probably be improved upon, but it is a decent first approximation. A disinterested person who was not trying to give preference to the interests of salespeople, employers, or customers could endorse 3 as a policy for salespeople to follow. We can and must recognize the legitimacy of employers' demands for loyalty. The role of being an advocate or agent for someone who is selling things is legitimate within certain bounds—almost all of us are willing to have real estate agents work for us. A rational person could consent to the idea that everyone follow principles such as rule 3.)

4. All of us are capable of being manipulated by others into doing things that harm us, especially in cases in which others are more knowledgeable than we are. No one can consent to the idea that other people (or salespeople) should manipulate us into doing things that harm us whenever doing so is to their own advantage. Salespeople who claim that it would be permissible for them to make it a policy to deceive customers, fail to warn them about dangers, evade their questions, or manipulate them into doing things that are harmful to them whenever doing so is advantageous to them are inconsistent because they are not willing to have others do the same to them. They must allow that 1–4 are prima facie moral duties.

Rules 1–4 are only prima facie duties. The golden rule can account for the cases in which 1–4 are overridden by other more important duties. For example, we would be willing to have other people violate rules 1–4 if doing so were necessary in order to save the life of an innocent person. In practice, violating 1, 2, 3, or 4 is permissible only in very rare cases. The financial interests of salespeople seldom justify violations of 1, 2, 3, or 4. The fact that a salesperson can make more money by violating 1, 2, 3, or 4 would not justify her in violating any of these unless she has very pressing financial obligations that she cannot meet otherwise. Often, salespeople need to meet certain minimum sales quotas to avoid being fired. Suppose that a salesperson needs to make it a policy to violate 1–4 in order to met her sales quotas and keep her job. Would this justify her in violating 1–4? *Possibly.* But, in order for this to be the case, the following conditions would have to be met: a) she has important moral obligations such as feeding and housing her family that require her to be employed

(needing money to keep one's family in an expensive house or take them to Disney World wouldn't justify violating 1–4); and b) she can't find another job that would enable her to meet her obligations without violating 1–4 (or other equally important duties). Those salespeople who can't keep their jobs or make an adequate income without violating 1–4 should seek other lines of employment. . . .

EXAMPLES

I will discuss several cases to illustrate and clarify my theory.

Example A

I am selling a used car that I know has bad brakes; this is one of the reasons I am selling the car. You don't ask me any questions about the car, and I sell it to you without informing you of the problem with the brakes.

Example B

I am selling a used car that starts poorly in cold weather. You arrange to look at the car early in the morning on a very cold day. I don't own a garage so the car is out in the cold. With difficulty, I start it up and drive it for thirty minutes shortly before you look at it and then cover the car with snow to make it seem as if it hasn't been driven. The engine is still hot when you come and the car starts up immediately. You then purchase the car, remarking that you need a car that starts well in the cold to get to work, since you don't have a garage.

Example C

While working as a salesperson, I feign a friendly concern for a customer's interests. I say, "I will try to help you find the product that is best suited for your needs. I don't want you to spend any more money than you need to. Take as much time as you need." The customer believes me, but she is deceived. In fact, I couldn't care less about her welfare. I only want to sell her the highest priced item I can as quickly as I can. I don't like the customer; indeed, I am contemptuous of her.

In example A, I violate rule 1 and put the buyer and other motorists, passengers, and pedestrians at risk. In example B, I violate rules 2 and 5. In example C, I violate rule 2. In the absence of conflicting obligations that are at least as important as the rules I violate, my actions in cases A–C are morally wrong.

Example D: A Longer Case (an Actual Case)

In 1980, I received a one-year fellowship from The National Endowment for the Humanities. The fellowship paid for my salary, but not my fringe benefits. Someone in the benefits office of my university told me that I had the option of continuing my health insurance through the university if I paid for the premiums out of my own pocket. I told the benefits person that this was a lousy deal and that I could do better by going to a private insurance company. I went to the office of Prudential Insurance agent Mr. A. O. "Ed" Mokarem. I told him that I was looking for a one-year medical insurance policy to cover me during the period of the fellowship and that I planned to resume my university policy when I returned to teaching. (The university provided this policy free of charge to all faculty who were teaching.) He showed me a comparable Prudential policy that cost about half as much as the university's policy. He explained the policy to me. I asked him to fill out the forms so that I could purchase the policy. He then told me that there was a potential problem I should consider. He said roughly the following:

> You will want to return to your free university policy next year when you return to teaching. The Prudential policy is a one-year terminal policy. If you develop any serious medical problems during the next year, Prudential will probably consider you "uninsurable" and will not be willing to sell you health insurance in the future. If you buy the Prudential policy, you may encounter the same problems with your university policy. Since you will be dropping this policy *voluntarily,* they will have the right to underwrite your application for re-enrollment. If you develop a serious health problem during the next year, their underwriting decision could

be "Total Rejection," imposing some waivers and/or exclusions, or (at best) subjecting your coverage to the "pre-existing conditions clause," which would not cover any pre-existing conditions until you have been covered under the new policy for at least a year.

If I left my current health insurance for a year, I risked developing a costly medical condition for which no one would be willing to insure me. That would have been a very foolish risk to take. So, I thanked him very much and, swallowing my pride, went back to renew my health insurance coverage through the university. I never bought any insurance from Mr. Mokarem and never had occasion to send him any business.

I have discussed this case with numerous classes through the years. It usually generates a lively discussion. Most of my students do not think that Mr. Mokarem was morally obligated to do what he did, but they don't think that what he did was wrong either—they regard his actions as supererogatory or above and beyond the call of duty.

My View About Example D

On my theory, this is a difficult case to assess. If rules 1–4 are a salespersons's only duties concerning the disclosure of information, then Mr. Mokarem was not obligated to inform me as he did. (In this case, the information in question was information about a competing product—the university's health insurance policy.) If rule 5 is a prima facie duty of salespeople, then (assuming that he had no conflicting moral duties of greater or equal importance) it was his duty, all things considered, to inform me as he did. Since I am uncertain that 5 can be justified, I'm not sure whether or not Mr. Mokarem was obligated to do what he did or whether his actions were supererogatory. This case illustrates part of what is at stake in the question of whether rule 5 is a prima facie duty of salespeople.

NOTES

This essay is a revised and abridged version of material from two earlier essays, "Deception and Withholding Information in Sales," *Business Ethics Quarterly* 11 (2001): 275–306, and "Ethical Issues in Selling and Advertising,"

The Blackwell Guide to Business Ethics, ed. Norman Bowie (Oxford: Blackwell, 2002), 186–205. Many thanks to Ivan Preston for his very generous and helpful advice and criticisms. Everyone interested in these topics should read his work.

REFERENCES

Atiyah, P. S. (1979) *The Rise and Fall of Freedom of Contract.* Oxford: The Clarendon Press.

Carson, Thomas. (1988) "On the definition of lying: a reply to Jones and revisions." *Journal of Business Ethics,* 7:509–14.

Carson, Thomas. (2001) "Deception and withholding information in sales." *Business Ethics Quarterly* 11:275–306.

FTC policy statement on deception. (1983—still current) Available on the Web at: http://www.ftc.gov/bcp/guides/guides.htm then click on FTC Policy Statement on Deception.

Gensler, Harry. (1986) "A Kantian argument against abortion." *Philosophical Studies* 49:83–98.

Holley, David. (1993) "A moral evaluation of sales practices." In Tom Beauchamp and Norman Bowie, eds., *Ethical Theory and Business,* fourth edition, 462–72. Englewood Cliffs, NJ: Prentice Hall.

QUESTIONS

1. What ethical constraints should be placed on salespeople, according to Carson?

2. Can a lie to a customer ever be justified? What about withholding information? Do salespeople have a duty to explain every detail of a product to a customer?

CASES

CASE 9.1
Toy Wars
Manuel G. Velasquez

Tom Daner, president of the advertising company of Daner Associates, was contacted by the sales manager of Crako Industries, Mike Teal.[1] Crako Industries is a family-owned company that manufactures children's toys and had long been a favorite and important client of Daner Associates. The sales manager of Crako Industries explained that the company had just developed a new toy helicopter. The toy was modeled on the military helicopters that had been used in Vietnam and that had appeared in the "Rambo" movies. Mike Teal explained that the toy was developed in response to the craze for military toys that had been sweeping the nation in the wake of the Rambo movies. The family-owned toy company had initially resisted moving into military toys, since members of the family objected to the violence associated with such toys. But as segments of the toy market were increasingly taken over by military toys, the family came to feel that entry into the military toy market was crucial for their business. Consequently, they approved development of a line of military toys, hoping that they were not entering the market too late. Mike Teal now wanted Daner Associates to develop a television advertising campaign for the toy.

The toy helicopter Crako designers had developed was about one and one-half feet long, battery-operated, and made of plastic and steel. Mounted to the sides were detachable replicas of machine guns and a detachable stretcher modeled on the stretchers used to lift wounded soldiers from a battlefield. Mike Teal of Crako explained that they were trying to develop a toy that had to be perceived as "more macho" than the top-selling "G. I. Joe" line of toys. If the company was to compete successfully in today's toy market, according to the sales manager, it would have to adopt an advertising approach that was even "meaner and tougher" than what other companies were doing. Consequently, he continued, the advertising clips developed by Daner Associates would have to be "mean and macho." Television advertisements for the toy, he suggested, might show the helicopter swooping over buildings and blowing them up. The more violence and mayhem the ads suggested, the better Crako Industries was relying heavily on sales from the new toy, and some Crako managers felt that the company's future might depend on the success of this toy.

Tom Daner was unwilling to have his company develop television advertisements that would increase what he already felt was too much violence in television aimed at children. In particular, he recalled a television ad for a tricycle with a replica machine gun mounted on the handlebars. The commercial showed the tricycle being pedaled through the woods by a small boy as he chased several other boys fleeing before him over a dirt path. At one point the camera closed in over the shoulder of the boy, focused through the gun sight, and showed the gun sight apparently trying to aim at the backs of the boys as they fled before the tricycle's machine gun. Ads of that sort had disturbed Tom Daner and had led him to think that advertisers should find other ways of promoting these toys. He suggested, therefore, that instead of promoting the Crako helicopter through

violence, it should be presented in some other manner. When Teal asked what he had in mind, Tom was forced to reply that he didn't know. But at any rate, Tom pointed out, the three television networks would not accept a violent commercial aimed at children. All three networks adhered to an advertising code that prohibited violent, intense, or unrealistic advertisements aimed at children.

This seemed no real obstacle to Teal, however. Although the networks might turn down children's ads when they were too violent, local television stations were not as squeamish. Local television stations around the country regularly accepted ads aimed at children that the networks had rejected as too violent. The local stations inserted the ads as spots on their non-network programming, thereby circumventing the Advertising Codes of the three national networks. Daner Associates would simply have to place the ads they developed for the Crako helicopter through local television stations around the country. Mike Teal was firm: if Daner Associates would not or could not develop a "mean and tough" ad campaign, the toy company would move their account to an advertiser who would. Reluctantly, Tom Daner agreed to develop the advertising campaign. Crako Industries accounted for $1 million of Daner's total revenues.

Like Crako Industries, Daner Associates is also a family-owned business. Started by his father almost fifty years ago, the advertising firm that Tom Daner now ran had grown dramatically under his leadership. In 1975 the business had grossed $3 million; ten years later it had revenues of $25 million and provided a full line of advertising services. The company was divided into three departments (Creative, Media, and Account Executive), each of which had about 12 employees. Tom Daner credited much of the company's success to the many new people he had hired, especially a group with M.B.A.s who had developed new marketing strategies based on more thorough market and consumer analyses. Most decisions, however, were made by a five-person executive committee consisting of Tom Daner, the Senior Account Manager, and the three department heads. As owner-president, Tom's view tended to color most decisions, producing what one of the members called a "benevolent dictatorship." Tom himself was an enthusiastic, congenial, intelligent, and widely read person. During college he had considered becoming a missionary priest but had changed his mind and was now married and the father of three daughters. His personal heros included Thomas Merton, Albert Schweitzer, and Tom Dooley.

When Tom Daner presented the Crako deal to his Executive Committee, he found they did not share his misgivings. The other Committee members felt that Daner Associates should give Crako exactly the kind of ad Crako wanted: one with a heavy content of violence. Moreover, the writers and artists in the Creative Department were enthused with the prospect of letting their imaginations loose on the project, several feeling that they could easily produce an attention-grabbing ad by "out-violencing" current television programming. The Creative Department, in fact, quickly produced a copy-script that called for videos showing the helicopter "flying out of the sky with machine guns blazing" at a jungle village below. This kind of ad, they felt, was exactly what they were being asked to produce by their client, Crako Industries.

But after viewing the copy, Tom Daner refused to use it. They should produce an ad, he insisted, that would meet their client's needs but that would also meet the guidelines of the national networks. The ad should not glorify violence and war but should somehow support cooperation and family values. Disappointed and somewhat frustrated, the Creative Department went back to work. A few days later they presented a second proposal: an ad that would show the toy helicopter flying through the family room of a home as a little boy plays with it; then the scene shifts to show the boy on a rock rising from the floor of the family room; the helicopter swoops down and picks up the boy as though rescuing him from the rock where he had been stranded. Although the Creative Department was mildly pleased with their attempt, they felt it was too "tame." Tom liked it, however, and a version of the ad was filmed.

A few weeks later Tom Daner met with Mike Teal and his team and showed them the film. The viewing was not a success. Teal turned down the ad. Referring to the network regulations, which other toy advertisements were breaking as frequently as motorists broke the 55 mile per hour speed law, he said, "That commercial is going only 55 miles an hour when I want one that goes 75." If the next version was not "tougher and meaner," Crako Industries would be forced to look elsewhere.

Disappointed, Tom Daner returned to the people in his Creative Department and told them to go ahead with designing the kind of ad they had originally wanted: "I don't have any idea what else to do." In a short time the Creative Department had an ad proposal on his desk that called for scenes showing the helicopter blowing up villages. Shortly afterwards a small set was constructed depicting a jungle village sitting next to a bridge stretching over a river. The ad was filmed using the jungle set as a background.

When Tom saw the result he was not happy. He decided to meet with his Creative Department and air his feelings. "The issue here," he said, "is basically the issue of violence. Do we really want to present toys as instruments for beating up people? This ad is going to promote aggression and violence. It will glorify dominance and do it with kids who are terrifically impressionable. Do we really want to do this?" The members of the Creative Department, however, responded that they were merely giving their client what the client wanted. That client, moreover, was an important account. The client wanted an aggressive "macho" ad, and that was what they were providing. The ad might violate the regulations of the television networks, but there were ways to get around the networks. Moreover, they said, every other advertising firm in the business was breaking the limits against violence set by the networks. Tom made one last try: why not market the toy as an adventure and fantasy toy? Film the ad again, he suggested, using the same jungle backdrop. But instead of showing the helicopter shooting at a burning village, show it flying in to rescue people from the burning village. Create an ad that shows excitement, adventure, and fantasy, but no aggression. "I was trying," he said later, "to figure out a new way of approaching this kind of advertising. We have to follow the market or we can go out of business trying to moralize to the market. But why not try a new approach? Why not promote toys as instruments that expand the child's imagination in a way that is positive and that promotes cooperative values instead of violence and aggression?"

A new film version of the ad was made, now showing the helicopter flying over the jungle set. Quick shots and heightened background music give the impression of excitement and danger. The helicopter flies dramatically through the jungle and over a river and bridge to rescue a boy from a flaming village. As lights flash and shoot haphazardly through the scene the helicopter rises and escapes into the sky. The final ad was clearly exciting and intense. And it promoted saving of life instead of violence against life.

It was clear when the final version was shot, however, that it would not clear the network censors. Network guidelines require that sets in children's ads must depict things that are within the reach of most children so that they do not create unrealistic expectations. Clearly the elaborate jungle set (which cost $25,000 to construct) was not within the reach of most children, and consequently most children would not be able to recreate the scene of the ad by buying the toy. Moreover, network regulations stipulate that in children's ads scenes must be filmed with normal lighting that does not create undue intensity. Again clearly the helicopter ad, which created excitement by using quick changes of light and fast cuts, did not fall within these guidelines.

After reviewing the film Tom Daner reflected on some last-minute instructions Crako's sales manager had given him when he had been shown the first version of the ad: The television ad should show things being blown up by the guns of the little helicopter and perhaps even some blood on the fuselage of the toy; the ad had to be violent. Now Tom had to make a decision.

QUESTIONS

1. Should he risk the account by submitting only the rescue mission ad? Or should he let Teal also see the ad that showed the helicopter shooting up the village, knowing that he would probably prefer that version if he saw it?

2. And was the rescue mission ad really that much different from the ad that showed the shooting of the village?

3. Did it matter that the rescue mission ad still violated some of the network regulations?

4. What if he offered Teal only the rescue mission ad and Teal accepted the "rescue approach" but demanded he make it more violent; should he give in?

5. And should Tom risk launching an ad campaign that was based on this new untested approach?

6. What if the ad failed to sell the Crako toy?

7. Was it right to experiment with a client's product, especially a product that was so important to the future of the client's business?

NOTE

1. Although the events described in this case are real, all names of the individuals and the companies involved are fictitious; in addition, several details have been altered to disguise the identity of participants.

CASE 9.2
Advertising at Better Foods
Rogene A. Buchholz

The Better Foods Corporation had been producing a cereal that tasted good and was nutritious for children as well as adults. When first introduced, the product captured a significant share of the market and had held this market share for several years. The company did not tout the health benefits of its cereal because of regulations that prevented companies from making such claims. Thus, its advertisements stressed the taste features of the product as well as other characteristics such as crispiness that might appeal to consumers.

When the government relaxed restrictions on making health claims, the company's competitors began to tout the benefits their cereals had on cholesterol levels as well as other areas of health that were of concern to consumers. The companies knew many of these claims were misleading to consumers because they implied that eating regular amounts of the cereal would have such health benefits. Actually, consumers would have to consume prodigious amounts of cereals to receive any such benefits. But consumers were not made aware of this fact and were beginning to be influenced by all the hype about health benefits of these cereals.

Better Foods Corporation experienced its first drop in market share in several years because of this new type of advertising. As an employee in charge of the advertising program, you have been asked to come up with a new advertising campaign that will stress the nutritious aspects of the company's product. This assignment puts you in something of a bind, as you find some of the outrageous claims being made by your competitors offensive from a moral standpoint. Yet, if you don't do the same, the sales of your company's product may continue to decline and your job itself may be in jeopardy.

QUESTIONS

1. What is the purpose of advertising in a free market society? Are there minimum standards of honesty that should be adhered to, or are advertisers free to do whatever the market will bear? How can consumers tell the outrageous health claims from honest ones so they can make a reasonable decision?

2. What advertising strategy should Better Foods adopt? Should it follow the lead of its competitors? Could it point out the misleading advertising its competitors are doing? Should it advertise more honestly and take the moral high ground even if it leads to a further decrease in sales?

From Rogene A. Buchholz, *Business, Environment, and Public Policy* (Englewood Cliffs, NJ: Prentice Hall, 1995).

CASE 9.3
Advertising's Image of Women
Joseph R. Desjardins and John J. McCall

It has been estimated that U.S. children between the ages of two and five watch an average of 30 hours of television each week. At this rate, the average young person will watch some 350,000 television commercials by the end of high school. Given all forms of advertising (magazines, newspapers, packaging, radio, television) the average American will have seen some 50 million commercials by age 60. Thus advertising is inescapable in our culture, and its socializing impact cannot be ignored. Ads not only describe products but also present images, values, and goals; they portray certain concepts of normalcy and sexuality, and they promote certain types of self-images. Advertising not only aims to provide information to consumers but also aims to motivate them. What images of women does it present, and what motivations does it appeal to?

Many ads seek to motivate women by suggesting that they are inadequate without a particular product. Cosmetic ads purvey an ideal form of female beauty—a form that is unattainable. Women are portrayed as having no facial wrinkles, no lines, no blemishes—indeed no pores. If you do not look like this, the ads suggest, you are not beautiful, and since no one (including the model) really looks like this, women need cosmetics to look beautiful. Beauty thus results from products and not from the woman herself. Advertising tells women that they should change their age (the "little-girl look"), weight, bust size, hair color, eye color, complexion—and even their smell. In many ads a woman's worth is measured not by her intelligence or her character or even her natural appearance. A woman's worth is measured by how closely she approaches an ideal created by an advertising agency.

Many ads also portray women as inferior to other women and to men. Women are seen as engaged in a constant competition with other women for the attention of men. When they are pictured with men, women are often shown as clinging to the male, as passive, as submissive. Men are seen in control, active, and dominant.

Besides feelings of inadequacy, many ads also use guilt to motivate women. The "housewife" is constantly being chided because the laundry is not as white nor does it smell as clean as the neighbor's. Her dishes have spots, her meals are unappealing, her floors and furniture have "wax buildup," and her clothes are out of style. Even when women are shown in the more realistic setting of worker rather than homemaker, feelings of guilt and inadequacy are still reinforced. The working woman is portrayed as a superwoman who harmonizes perfectly the roles of career woman, mother, wife, and homemaker. Despite all of these demands, the woman still looks like a model. In those few cases where the harmony breaks down, the woman is shown as being responsible for the breakdown or in need of drugs to cope with the stress. On the other hand, men are seldom seen as responsible for cooking, cleaning, and child care, or in need of drugs in order to cope.

QUESTIONS

1. What kind of influence has advertising had on your own views of beauty, attractiveness, sexuality?

2. How does advertising influence our understanding of social role based on gender?

3. To what degree have your family, friends, and classmates been socialized by advertising?

From Joseph R. Desjardins and John J. McCall, *Contemporary Issues in Business Ethics,* 2nd ed. (Belmont, CA: Wadsworth, 1990).

CASE 9.4

Hucksters in the Classroom

William H. Shaw and Vincent Barry

Increased student loads, myriad professional obligations, and shrinking school budgets have sent many public school teachers scurrying for teaching materials to facilitate their teaching.

They don't have to look far. Into the breach has stepped business, which is ready, willing, and able to provide current print and audiovisual materials for classroom use. These activities and industry-supplied teaching aids are advertised in educational journals, distributed to school boards, and showcased at educational conventions. The Dr Pepper Company, for example, displays at such conventions a recipe booklet titled *Cooking with Dr Pepper.* Each recipe includes sugar-filled Dr Pepper soda.

One collective tack taken by the business community has been the ABC Education Program of American Industry, whose annual publication, *Resource-book,* consists of product-specific "sponsored pages" or ads with accompanying teacher guide sheets. Food and toiletry products are featured, as in the following:

A is for AGREE: the Creme Rinse and Conditioner that helps the greasies.

C is for COCONUT: a tantalizing tropical treat from Peter Paul candies.

E is for EFFECTIVE double deodorant system in Irish Spring (soap).

Advertising space in *Resourcebook* doesn't come cheap: A single ad can run as much as $30,000. But ABC official Art Sylvie thinks it's worth it. After all, he asks, where else are manufacturers going to get such widespread and in-depth product exposure? He has a point: About 2.7 million or 35 percent of all junior high school students in the United States participate in the ABC program, not to mention their 95,000 teachers.

An integral part of the ABC program is an annual essay-writing contest. Essays must deal with some aspect of a product in *Resource-book*—its production and marketing, the history or importance of an industry to a community or nation, and so on. To be eligible, entries must be signed by a teacher and include a product label or reasonable facsimile. Student writers can earn up to $50 for entering.

The people at ABC say they want to reflect the positive aspects of the world outside the classroom. And they're convinced that the way to do it is through depicting the wonders and genius of industry. "Thus," says researcher Sheila Harty, "history is taught in terms of 'innovative industrial genius,' as students write their essays on the value of soft drinks (C is for Canada Dry) or the production of tires (G is for Goodyear)."

Evidently teachers go for corporate freebies with all the gusto of a softball player at a company picnic. In a survey of its members, the National Educational Association found that about half its members were using industry audiovisual materials and the ten resource guides published annually by Educators Progress Services (EPS). A cursory look at the guides suggests that the offerings are comprehensive and impartial. A closer look reveals that most are privately, not publicly, sponsored.

Some people think corporate-sponsored teaching materials do more than fill curriculum needs. They are also public relations gambits. Thus, in his book *Corporate Response to Urban Crisis,* professor of sociology Ken Neubeck writes:

Corporations must continually respond to problems which they had a hand in creating in the first place. From this perspective, corporate social responsibility becomes a defensive strategy to be employed

William H. Shaw and Vincent Barry, *Moral Issues in Business,* 5th ed. (Belmont, CA: Wadsworth, 1992).

whenever the social and political climate become hostile to the active pursuit of corporate economic goals. It is a strategy of "enlightened self-interest."

Corporate America's latest and most dramatic venture into the classroom, however, goes beyond a defensive public relations strategy. In 1989, Whittle Communications began beaming into high schools in six cities its controversial Channel One, a television newscast for high school students, and by June 1991 the number of schools receiving Channel One had grown to 8,600. Although Whittle has grander plans for the future, the broadcasts at present are twelve minutes long—ten minutes of news digest with slick graphics and two minutes of commercials for Levi's jeans, Gillette razor blades, Head & Shoulders shampoo, Snickers candy bars, and other familiar products.

The schools in the program receive thousands of dollars worth of free electronic gadgetry, including television monitors, satellite dishes, and video recorders. And students seem to like the program. "It was very interesting and it appeals to our age group," says student Angelique Williams. "One thing I really liked was the reporters were our own age. They kept our attention."

But Whittle Communications, and interested competitors like Turner Broadcasting and the Discovery Channel, formed in Maryland by four large cable operators, have more in mind than simply making the news interesting to students like Angelique.

The prospect of being able to deliver a captive and narrowly targeted audience to its customers promises to be breathtakingly profitable—so profitable, in fact, that advertisers on Channel One pay $150,000 for each thirty seconds of commercial time.

That captive audience is just what worries the critics. Peggy Charren of Action for Children's Television calls the project a "great big, gorgeous Trojan horse. . . . You're selling the children to the advertisers. You might as well auction off the rest of the school day to the highest bidders." This development worries many educators, and New York and New Jersey have banned Channel One and its potential clones from public classrooms.

On the other hand, Principal Rex Stooks-bury of Central High School in Knoxville, which receives Channel One, takes a different view. "This is something we see as very, very positive for the school," he says. And as student Danny Diaz adds, "we're always watching commercials" anyway.

QUESTIONS

1. What explains industry's thrust into education? Is it consistent with the basic features of capitalism?

2. What moral issues, if any, are involved in the affiliation between education and commercial interests?

3. Do you think students have a "moral right" to an education free of commercial indoctrination?

CASE 9.5
Marketing Malt Liquor
Tom L. Beauchamp and Norman E. Bowie

During the summer of 1991, the surgeon general of the United States and advocacy groups led by the Center for Science in the Public Interest (CSPI) launched a campaign to remove G. Heileman Brewing Company's malt liquor PowerMaster from store shelves. The LaCrosse, Wisconsin-based brewer had experienced a series of financial setbacks. In January 1991 the company filed for protection from creditors in a New York bankruptcy court, claiming to be "struggling under a huge debt load." (Alix Freedman, "Heileman Will Be Asked to Change Potent Brew's Name," *The Wall Street Journal,* June 20, 1991, p. B1.) In an attempt to reverse its financial decline, Heileman introduced PowerMaster with a 5.9 percent alcohol content. Most malt liquors (defined by law as beers with alcohol levels above 4 percent) have a 5.5 percent average content, as compared with the typical 3.5 percent alcohol level of standard beers.

PowerMaster came under fire from both anti-alcohol and African-American activists. These groups charged that Heileman had created the name and the accompanying advertising campaign, which featured a black male model, with the intent of targeting young black men, who consume roughly one-third of all malt liquors. U.S. Surgeon General Anto-nia Novello joined the Heileman critics, calling the PowerMaster marketing campaign insensitive. Citing the economic burden that a legal contest to retain the brand name would entail, the company discontinued the product. However, beer industry executives and members criticized the government's role in the controversy. One newspaper columnist cited race as the critical factor in the campaign to remove PowerMaster, noting that the "It's the power" advertising slogan used in the marketing of Pabst Brewing Co.'s Olde English 800 malt liquor had gone unchallenged. James Sanders, president of the Washington, DC-based Beer Institute, contended that the government focused on the PowerMaster label to avoid having to focus on other factors such as unemployment and poverty, the real problems that the black community confronts.

QUESTIONS

1. Would it be deceptive or manipulative advertising to call your beer "PowerMaster" and to use black male models?

2. Is it ethically insensitive for a company to target a specific market identified by race and gender?

Tom L. Beauchamp and Norman E. Bowie *Ethical Theory and Business*, 7th ed. (Englewood Cliffs, NJ: Prentice Hall, 2004), p. 465.

CHAPTER QUESTIONS

1. Explain how advertising may influence autonomy. Are there ways that advertising creates freedom? How would you regulate advertising, if you would regulate it at all?

2. Is some level of deception necessary or inevitable in all sales? What would a perfectly transparent sales pitch look like? Would it persuade anyone? What are the duties of truthfulness of advertisers and salespeople? And how much product information do we really want or need)?

10

Things Fall Apart

Product Liability and Consumers

Introduction

During a brief strike at your company, all the managers—regardless of their status or position—are farmed out to the various company functions that are normally handled by the striking employees. You are put in charge of the walk-in Complaint Department. The second day, a fellow walks in with one of your company's products, mangled almost beyond recognition. It is immediately obvious to you that the consumer has misunderstood the assembly instructions, and his rambling explanation confirms it. You tell him, politely, that you think that this is what happened, but he, in turn, gets irritated and a bit abusive. He threatens to sue. You are not used to this sort of behavior, and you are getting pretty irritated yourself. You think of a number of terse and sarcastic responses, but you keep your cool and some semblance of a smile. Your manager has told you to handle all cases as best you can and has given you a free hand to give refunds or replace products at your discretion. But there is no advice or policy about what to do when a customer abuses the product through stupidity or incompetence. In your view, should the company honor the complaints of this customer? Or should you (politely) tell him what he should do?

"Sooner or later, life makes philosophers of us all" wrote minor French philosopher Maurice Riseling. In the same vein, "Shit Happens" is the crude philosophical message of one of the ruder bumper stickers you see around town these days "Accidents happen," the more polite way of putting the same point, is an inescapable part of business life. Even high-quality products break. Good intentions get frustrated. It would be good and useful experience for every manager and employee, in whatever industry, to spend a few days working in the Complaint Department. (In the most trusted corporations, every person in the company is, in effect, a mini-Complaint Department, responsible for making good on the company's claims and liabilities.) The aim of a business, we are told, is to make a profit by selling high-quality products at a reasonable price. But this makes it sound as if most business transactions are one-shot deals, without an aftermath, sort of like buying something on E-Bay or at a garage sale. But most business is not like this. It involves multiple transactions, often over a prolonged period. (It is often pointed out that getting a new customer costs a business 10 times what it costs to retain an old one.) It thus involves the building of relationships, and this means not just continuing to provide high-quality products and services, but "making good" when they go wrong. How a business responds to flaws and failure, whether or not the company is strictly responsible, can fix the fate of a business relationship. A dissatisfied consumer will end his or her relationship and, even after many years, cease to do business with the company. The defensive response that we hear too often, "so what d'ya want me to do about it?" signals the end of many business relationships.

Businesses are responsible for what happens because of their operations and products. The extent and nature of that responsibility depends on the product, the situation, the extent of the damage caused, the character of the company, the consumer, and the community. If something bad happens because an already-hated company or industry does something wrong, the reaction will be much more ferocious than when a well-loved local business makes a mistake. Sometimes, the mistake in question is a broken or flawed product. Sometimes, as was described earlier, the mistake is the consumer's, not the company's at all, but, nevertheless, the company has to deal with it. Sometimes the harm done is inherent to the product itself. No one any longer pretends that smoking doesn't cause cancer and all sorts of other horrid diseases, but there is still considerable controversy surrounding the selling and marketing of tobacco products. An important question is to what extent the consumer is a fully responsible agent, which is why marketing to teenagers is so much in focus. Sometimes the harm is not from the product, but from the production process, for example, when a manufacturing process causes severe pollution or building a new factory strains the infrastructure of a small community. Sometimes the potential harm of a product or a line of products is just not known, for instance, the new bioengineered foods or the radiation from cell phones. But after the fact, companies may still be liable, as evidenced by the still-lingering asbestos-poisoning cases from decades ago.

Complicating the basic observation that most people consider companies to be responsible for their products and services are a number of issues that are both basic to human psychology and emergent in the new world of tort law and strict liability. On the human psychology side, there is the fact that when something goes wrong, people want to *blame* someone. Thus, the relationship between company and consumer when something goes wrong often starts on a confrontational, if not hostile, note, and the first concern of any wise company or agent of the company is to defuse the accusations of blame and re-present the situation as a shared problem. On the side of tort law, there has been a ballooning—especially in America—of product liability and malpractice cases and verdicts. Some of these verdicts have been well publicized and quite understandably strike fear in the hearts of anyone who tries to supply products or services to the public. Some strike most people as ridiculous—the original multi-million-dollar award to the woman who spilled MacDonald's hot coffee on herself (the award was considerably reduced on appeal), but others, for instance, when medical products have caused serious illnesses and deaths, do not strike most people as ridiculous. Deterring such irresponsibility, of course, is why the plaintiffs' attorneys defend the current system of sometimes-huge verdicts. It is not enough to punish an allegedly wrong-doing company (when it is usually possible to absorb the verdict as just another cost of doing business). The aim is to put the company out of business.

Further complicating the emerging portrait of the tort system is the concept of "strict liability." Most people accept the idea that when someone does something wrong or causes harm that could or should have been avoided, he or she should be held responsible. But strict liability bypasses that commonsense practice and holds companies responsible—at least financially responsible—even in the absence of any argument that they could have or should have avoided the harm in question. Thus, it has become common practice for plaintiffs to sue not only those who are immediately responsible for a harm, but those who are simply in the chain of causation. For instance, after an automobile accident, one might expect the wrongful or careless driver to be sued. But current law allows for the pursuit of the company that manufactured the car as well, even if there was no design flaw that contributed to the accident. Feeding this practice is the notion of "deep pockets," the idea that those who are immediately responsible may not have funds to pay any substantial award, but someone down the line may well have the resources to do so. It is, in part, because of this practice, but also the enormous size of some of the recent awards, that tort law has been declared a kind of "crisis" by many in the business community.

In this chapter, we explore a family of issues surrounding the concepts of risk and responsibility, both on an individual and on a corporate level, and their effects on society as a whole. The issues are economic, to be sure, but they also have a great deal to do with fairness and our attitudes toward life. Accordingly, they are of interest to both the law and philosophy and the basic question of how much risk are we willing to take in our lives. Economically, on the one hand, there is the need to provide recourse for consumers and communities who are hurt by business practices and products and to deter and punish companies that act irresponsibly. On the other hand, the cost of litigation and the irresponsible use of litigation do indeed hurt innocent businesses and compromises the free enterprise system. In the readings that follow, we take a look at some of the situations that are most in the news and both some of the charges against the tort system and the arguments for it. We start with Peter Huber's polemical book on the liability crisis and the need for tort reform, which has now become a major campaign by many prominent politicians. The numbers are still in dispute, but the seriousness of the problem is very much on the national agenda.

In response to Huber, we offer different perspectives on the problem, including various considerations about both the difficulties of risk assessment and fairness. From inside the insurance industry, Stanley J. Modic explains "How We Got into This Mess," but then a philosopher, George G. Brenkert, who directs **the** Georgetown Business Ethics Institute, defends the current strict products liability in terms of compensatory justice. Henry Fairlie chastizes us all for failing to acknowledge the role of risks in our lives in his "Fear of Living," and former Chief Justice Warren E. Burger reflects on the situation of "Too Many Lawyers, Too Many Suits" in *The New York Times* (1991). Finally, we focus on one of the most publicized liability cases in the past several decades, the case of the once-popular Ford Pinto, which exploded on impact because of a fixable design flaw. Mark Dowie presents the original case in his "Pinto Madness," from *Mother Jones* in 1977, but philosopher and business ethicist Patricia Werhane urges us to be cautious in considering such cases. She compares the Pinto case with the classic Japanese movie, *Rashamon,* in which we get four different accounts of a murder and no clear resolution in favor of any one of them. In the cases, you will be asked to examine more examples of liability and the law.

Peter Huber | # Liability

Peter W. Huber is a lawyer, a Senior Fellow of the Manhattan Institute for Policy Research, and the author of *Liability*.

It is one of the most ubiquitous taxes we pay, now levied on virtually everything we buy, sell, and use. The tax accounts for 30 percent of the price of a stepladder and over 95 percent of the price of childhood vaccines. It is responsible for one-quarter of the price of a ride on a Long Island tour bus and one-third of the price of a small airplane. It will soon cost large municipalities as much as they spend on fire or sanitation services.

Some call it a safety tax, but its exact relationship to safety is mysterious. It is paid on many items that are risky to use, like ski lifts and hedge trimmers, but it weighs even more heavily on other items whose whole purpose is to make life safer. It adds only a few cents to a pack of cigarettes, but it adds more to the price of a football helmet than the cost of making it. The tax falls especially hard on prescription drugs, doctors, surgeons, and all things medical. Because of the tax, you cannot deliver a baby with medical assistance in Monroe County, Alabama. You cannot buy several contraceptives certified to be safe and effective by the Food and Drug Administration (FDA), even though available substitutes are more dangerous or less effective. If you have the stomach upset known as hyperemesis, you cannot buy the pill that is certified as safe and effective against it. The tax has orphaned various drugs that are invaluable for treating rare but serious diseases. It is assessed against every family that has a baby, in the amount of about $300 per birth, with an obstetrician in New York City paying $85,000 a year.

Because of the tax, you cannot use a sled in Denver city parks or a diving board in New York City schools. You cannot buy an American Motors "CJ" Jeep or a set of construction plans for novel airplanes from Burt Rutan, the pioneering designer of the *Voyager*. You can no longer buy many American-made brands of sporting goods, especially equipment for amateur contact sports such as hockey and lacrosse. For a while, you could not use public transportation in the city of St. Joseph, Missouri, nor could you go to jail in Lafayette County in the same state. Miami canceled plans for an experimental railbus because of the tax. The tax has curtailed Little League and fireworks displays, evening concerts, sailboard races, and the use of public beaches and ice-skating rinks. It temporarily shut down the famed Cyclone at the Astroland amusement park on Coney Island.

The tax directly costs American individuals, businesses, municipalities, and other government bodies at least $80 billion a year, a figure that equals the total profits of the country's top 200 corporations. But many of the tax's costs are indirect and unmeasurable, reflected only in the tremendous effort, inconvenience, and sacrifice Americans now go through to avoid its collection. The extent of these indirect costs can only be guessed at. One study concluded that doctors spend $3.50 in efforts to avoid additional charges for each $1 of direct tax they pay. If similar multipliers operate in other areas, the tax's hidden impact on the way we live and do business may amount to a $300 billion dollar annual levy on the American economy.

The tax goes by the name of *tort liability*. It is collected and disbursed through litigation. The courts alone decide just who will pay, how much, and on

From Peter Huber, *Liability* (New York: Basic Books, 1990), pp. 3–39. Reprinted with permission.

what timetable. Unlike better-known taxes, this one was never put to a legislature or a public referendum, debated at any length in the usual public arenas, or approved by the president or by any state governor. And although the tax ostensibly is collected for the public benefit, lawyers and other middlemen pocket more than half the take.

The tort tax is a recent invention. Tort law has existed here and abroad for centuries, of course. But until quite recently it was a backwater of the legal system, of little importance in the wider scheme of things. For all practical purposes, the omnipresent tort tax we pay today was conceived in the 1950s and set in place in the 1960s and 1970s by a new generation of lawyers and judges. In the space of twenty years they transformed the legal landscape, proclaiming sweeping new rights to sue. Some grew famous and more grew rich selling their services to enforce the rights that they themselves invented. But the revolution they made could never have taken place had it not had a component of idealism as well. Tort law, it is widely and passionately believed, is a public-spirited undertaking designed for the protection of the ordinary consumer and worker, the hapless accident victim, the "little guy." Tort law as we know it is a peculiarly American institution. No other country in the world administers anything remotely like it.

FROM CONSENT TO COERCION

Tort law is the law of accidents and personal injury. The example that usually comes to mind is a two-car collision at an intersection. The drivers are utter strangers. They have no advance understanding between them as to how they should drive, except perhaps an implicit agreement to follow the rules of the road. Nor do they have any advance arrangement specifying who will pay for the damage. Human nature being what it is, the two sides often have different views on both these interesting questions. Somebody else has to step in to work out rights and responsibilities. This has traditionally been a job for the courts. They resolve these cases under the law of *torts* or civil wrongs.

But the car accident between strangers is comparatively rare in the larger universe of accidents and injuries. Just as most intentional assaults involve assailants and victims who already know each other well, most unintended injuries occur in the context of commercial acquaintance—at work, on the hospital operating table, following the purchase of an airplane ticket or a home appliance. And while homicide is seldom a subject of advance understanding between victim and assailant, unintentional accidents often are. More often than not, both parties to a transaction recognize there is some chance of misadventure, and prudently take steps to address it beforehand.

Until quite recently, the law permitted and indeed promoted advance agreement of that character. It searched for understandings between the parties and respected them where found. Most accidents were handled under the broad heading of *contract*—the realm of human cooperation—and comparatively few relegated to the dismal annex of tort, the realm of unchosen relationship and collision. The old law treated contract and tort cases under entirely different rules, which reflected this fairly intuitive line between choice and coercion.

Then, in the 1950s and after, a visionary group of legal theorists came along. Their leaders were thoughtful, well-intentioned legal academics at some of the most prestigious law schools, and judges on the most respected state benches. They were the likes of the late William Prosser, who taught law at Hastings College, John Wade, Professor of Law at Vanderbilt University, and California Supreme Court Justice Roger Traynor. They are hardly household names, but considering the impact they had on American life they should be. Their ideas, eloquence, and persistence changed the common law as profoundly as it had ever been changed before. For short, and in the absence of a better term, we will refer to them as the founders of modern tort law, or just the *Founders*. If the name is light-hearted, their accomplishments were anything but.

The Founders were to be followed a decade or two later by a much more sophisticated group of legal economists, most notably Guido Calabresi, now Dean of the Yale Law School, and Richard Posner of the University of Chicago Law School and now a federal judge on the Seventh Circuit Court of Appeals. There were many others, for economists seem to be almost as numerous as lawyers, and the application of economic theory to tort law has enjoyed mounting popularity in recent years as tort law has itself become an industry. An economist, it has been said, is someone who observes what is happening in practice and goes off to study whether it is possible in theory. The new tort economists were entirely true to that great tradition. Indeed, they carried it a step forward, concluding that the legal revolution that had already occurred was not only possible but justified and necessary. Mustering all the dense prose, arcane jargon, and elaborate methodology that only the very best academic economists muster, they set about proving on paper that the whole new tort structure was an efficient and inevitable reaction to failures in the marketplace. Arriving on the scene of the great tort battle late in the day, they courageously congratulated the victors, shot the wounded, and pronounced the day's outcome satisfactory and good.

Like all revolutionaries, the Founders and their followers, in the economics profession and elsewhere, had their own reasons for believing and behaving as they did. Most consumers, they assumed, pay little attention to accident risks before the fact. Ignoring or underestimating risk as they do, consumers fail to demand, and producers fail to supply, as much safety as would be best. As a result, manufacturers, doctors, employers, municipalities, and other producers get away with undue carelessness, and costly accidents are all too frequent. To make matters worse, consumers buy less accident insurance than they really need, so injuries lead to unneeded misery and privation and some victims become public charges.

With these assumptions as their starting point, the new tort theorists concluded that the overriding question that the old law asked—how did the parties agree to allocate the costs of the accident?—was irrelevant or worse. The real question to ask was: How can society best allocate the cost of accidents to minimize those costs (and the cost of guarding against them), and to provide potential victims with the accident insurance that not all of them currently buy or can

afford? The answer, by and large, was to make producers of goods and services pay the costs of accidents. A broad rule to this effect, it was argued, can accomplish both objectives. It forces providers to be careful. It also forces consumers to take accident costs into account, not consciously but by paying a safety-adjusted price for everything they buy or do. And it compels the improvident to buy accident insurance, again not directly but through the safety tax. It has a moral dimension too: People should be required to take care before the accident and to help each other afterward, for no other reason than that it is just, right, and proper to insist that they do so.

The expansive new accident tax is firmly in place today. In a remarkably short time, the Founders completely recast a centuries-old body of law in an entirely new mold of their own design. They started sketching out their intentions only in the late 1950s; within two short decades they had achieved virtually every legal change that they originally planned. There were setbacks along the way, of course; the common law always develops in fits and starts, with some states bolder and others more timid, and the transformation of tort law was no exception. But compared with the cautious incrementalism with which the common law had changed in centuries past, an utter transformation over a twenty-year span can fairly be described as a revolution, and a violent one at that.

The revolution began and ended with a wholesale repudiation of the law of contract. Until well into the 1960s, it was up to each buyer to decide how safe a car he or she wanted to buy. Then as now, the major choices were fairly obvious: large, heavy cars are both safer and more expensive; economy cars save money but at some cost in safety. In case after case today, however, the courts struggle to enforce a general mandate that all cars be *crashworthy*. That term is perfectly fluid; it is defined after the accident by jury pronouncements; it is defined without reference to preferences and choices deliberately expressed by buyer and seller before the transaction. A woman's choice of contraceptives was once a matter largely under the control of the woman herself and her doctor, with the FDA in the background to certify the general safety and efficacy of particular drugs or devices. Today tort law has shifted that authority too from the doctor's office to the courtroom. Balancing the risks and benefits of childhood vaccination was once a concern of parents, pediatricians, the FDA, and state health authorities. But here again, the views of the courts have become the driving force in determining what may be bought and sold. Not long ago, workplace safety was something to be decided between employer and employees, often through collective bargaining, perhaps with oversight from federal and state regulators, while compensation for accidents was determined by state workers' compensation laws. Today the courts supervise a free-for-all of litigation that pits employees against both employers and the outside suppliers of materials and equipment, the latter two against each other, and both against their insurers.

What brought us this liability tax, in short, was a wholesale shift from consent to coercion in the law of accidents. Yesterday we relied primarily on agreement before the fact to settle responsibility for most accidents. Today we emphasize litigation after the fact. Yesterday we deferred to private choice. Today it is only public choice that counts, more specifically the public choices of judges and juries. For all practical purposes, contracts are dead, at least insofar as they attempt to allocate responsibility for accidents ahead of time. Safety obligations are now decided through liability prescription, worked out case by case after the accident. The center of the accident insurance world has likewise shifted, from *first-party* insurance chosen by the expected beneficiary, to *third-party* coverage driven by legal compulsion.

STRICT LIABILITY

The old negligence rules had always been open to the reproach of stinginess. With the death of contract, they now promised to be hopelessly cumbersome as well. The prospect of running an ever-growing number of cases through a full postaccident inquest on how all the players had performed was discouraging; the sheer task threatened to overwhelm the courts, and the outcome would too often be compensation deferred or denied altogether. This was most vexing.

The Founders had labored hard to cross the high mountains of contractual language, only to find that the valley of tort below was not exactly flowing with milk and honey.

As we saw earlier, their initial response was to rely on the contractual material already at hand, using it to spin out liability through the implied warranty. If the Mammoth Corporation had somehow *promised* to pay for any and all accidents involving its product, everything else was simple. No one had to worry about whether there had been negligence; somewhere or other down there between the lines the contract itself promised payment. The content was novel, but the forms were reassuringly familiar.

For a while, then, the reinterpretation of contract terms sufficed as a basis for inventing liability standards much stricter than negligence. And a while was all the Founders really needed. Most people are eager to believe good news, even when it is too good to be true. The public and press didn't at all mind the idea that manufacturers had suddenly begun promising (tacitly, mind you) to pay for accidents resulting from all defects in their products, regardless of negligence. Within a few years, this legal notion of "strict" producer liability had become familiar and obvious. At that point, several state courts were ready to discard the roundabout legal fictions and take a more direct route to the same result. In 1962, the California Supreme Court led the way.

For Christmas in 1955, William Greenman's wife had bought her husband a Shopsmith, a new power tool that served as a combination saw, drill, and wood lathe. Greenman was making a wooden chalice on his Shopsmith one day when a piece of wood flew out of the machine and struck him on the forehead. He sued the manufacturer, maintaining that "inadequate[ly] set screws were used to hold parts of the machine together so that normal vibrations caused the tailstock of the lathe to move away from the piece of wood being turned, permitting it to fly out of the lathe." No contract claim was possible: Greenman was not the actual buyer of the lathe, and he had failed, in any event, to comply with California contract rules that require timely notice of a pending claim. By 1962, however, when the case reached it, the California Supreme Court was already growing tired of contracts and all their troublesome formalities and rules. It contemptuously brushed aside the notice requirement as a "booby trap for the unwary." Strict liability, the court bluntly declared, would no longer be rationalized in terms of implied warranties, fictional contracts, or anything of that sort. Product manufacturers would instead be held "strictly liable" to consumers for accidents caused by a "defect in manufacture" of their product.

This was a great leap. The need to find implied warranties and such had been a bothersome and often embarrassing barrier to contractual theories of liability. The need to find negligence had been an equally troublesome barrier to tort theories of liability. Now, at one bound, the courts could leap directly to the desired goal, at least so long as a product defect was at issue.

But there was important work still to be done. Though somewhat obscure on the point, *Greenman* seemed to cover *manufacturing defects,* which are in fact quite rare. *Design defects,* however, were quite another matter, and had not yet been officially incorporated into the new doctrine. So Barbara Evans learned in 1966. Driving her station wagon across an intersection one day, Barbara's husband was broadsided by another car and killed. The 1961 Chevrolet had an X-shaped frame; at the time, other manufacturers still used a box frame. Barbara sued General Motors, claiming misdesign. Her suit was quickly dismissed. "Perhaps it would be desirable to require manufacturers to construct automobiles in which it would be safe to collide," the court of appeals declared, "but that would be a legislative function, not an aspect of the judicial interpretation of existing law." Errors in manufacture were one thing. But in 1966 the courts were not yet ready to examine product design and declare it defective.

Greenman, however, had its own inexorable logic. If General Motors can be held liable for leaving a frame strut loose accidentally, why shouldn't it be liable for leaving it out deliberately? By mid-decade the design defect barrier was beginning to crumble.

David Larsen broke through this last major conceptual wall in 1968, just two years after Barbara Evans lost her case. His 1963 Chevrolet Corvair collided head on with another car, thrusting the steering column into his head. He sued General Motors, complaining that "the design and placement of the solid steering shaft, which extends without interruption from a point 2.7 inches in front of the leading surface of the front tires to a position directly in front of the driver, exposes the driver to an unreasonable risk of injury from the rearward displacement of that shaft in the event of a left-of-center head-on collision." This time, a federal appeals court was ready to move ahead. Thereafter, the court announced, juries would be free to pin liability on defects in design as well as manufacture.

Like so many other changes in the tort rules, the step from manufacturing defects to design defects was presented as the soul of modesty. But with that simple change the courts plunged into a new and daunting enterprise. To begin with, the takes in design defect cases are much higher. A manufacturing-defect verdict condemns only a single item coming off the assembly line. But a defect of design condemns the entire production, and a loss in one case almost inevitably implies losses in many others. Moreover, design is a much more subtle business than manufacture, and identifying deficiencies is vastly more difficult.

Before long, juries across the country were busy redesigning lawn mowers, electrical switches, glass and plastic bottles, pesticides, and consumer and industrial products of every other description. A product can be defectively designed because a safety device has been omitted (e.g., a paydozer without rearview mirrors) or because certain parts are not as strong as they might have been (e.g., a car roof is not strong enough to withstand a rollover, or the impact of a runaway horse that lands on the roof after a front-end collision). A jury can find that a single-control shower faucet is defective because if one turns it on all the way to one side, it will allow only hot water to spray, or that children's cotton sleepwear is defective because it has no flame-retardant chemicals added. Sears lost a $1.2 million judgment to a man who suffered a heart attack caused (he alleged) by a lawn mower rope that was too hard to pull. The Bolko Athletic Company paid $92,500 for defectively designing the second base on a baseball diamond; a concrete anchor, the jury concluded, was unsafe for amateur-league players. Recent cases have attempted to extend strict liability (at least for the condition rather than the design of a product) to persons who sell used goods, even ordinary citizens selling cars through the classified ads, though so far most courts have declined to take this seemingly logical step.

Drugs and pharmaceutical devices were among the last products to be swept up in design defect litigation. Until well into the 1970s, most courts accepted that potent drugs often have unavoidable side effects, and they declined to repeat the difficult balancing of risks and benefits already conducted by the FDA. But this line was crossed in the end as well. Courts began to find design defects in contraceptive pills (one brand contained more hormone than another, making it both more effective and riskier), vaccines (the live but weakened polio virus is both more effective and more dangerous than the killed virus), morning sickness drugs, and intrauterine devices.

QUESTIONS

1. What is "liability"? How does a business acquire it?
2. What are the limits on liability? How are they justified?

| John Nesmith | Calculating Risks: It's Easier Said Than Done |

WASHINGTON—What's more dangerous? A terrorism attack involving anthrax or being struck by lightening? A plane trip or a long country drive? In these terror-haunted times, we must constantly balance risks.

We often fear the wrong things and spend money to protect ourselves from lesser evils, says David Ropeik, director of risk communications at Harvard Center for Risk Analysis.

Government and industry together spend more than $30 million a year to deal with hazardous products even though the number of people whose health is at risk from this special kind of garbage is quite low. The annual expenditure on anti-smoking campaigns, on the other hand, is only about $500 million a year, even though smoking is one of the leading preventable causes of death in America.

"This irrational response kills people," Ropeik says. "In a world of finite resources, we can only protect ourselves from so many things."

But fear often is stronger than reason.

Ropeik likes to cite the example of a hiker walking through the woods who sees a dark, crooked shape on the ground. Before he has time to ask himself whether it is a stick or a snake, and then reason that if it is a snake it could be dangerous, he jumps away, impelled by a fear programmed deep in his brain, perhaps even in his genes.

Nerve circuits convey information to the brain's fear center, or amygdala, much faster than other circuits serve the cortex, where thought and rational learning occur, Ropeik says. These messages not only trigger the physical response, but also reinforce the fear itself.

That means to Ropeik that fear and the emotional processes linked to it are more powerful than the rational processes with which we might make more valid assessments of our risks.

In addition to such biological factors, Ropeik says, social psychologists have identified "universal

Reprinted by permission of John Nesmith of the Cox News Washington Bureau.

What's Risky? Chances of Death?

The annual risks of dying of various causes in the United States:

Heart disease, 1 in 397

Cancer, 1 in 511

Stroke, 1 in 1,699

Accidents (all kinds), 1 in 3,014

Accidents (motor vehicle), 1 in 6,745

Alzheimer's disease, 1 in 5,752

Alcohol (including liver disease), 1 in 6,210

Suicide, 1 in 12,091

Homicide, 1 in 15,440

Food poisoning, 1 in 56,031

Fire, 1 in 82,977

Bicycle accidents, 1 in 376,165

Lightning, 1 in 4,478,159

Bioterrorism attack involving anthrax, 1 in 56,424,800

Harvard Center for Risk Analysis, from U.S. Centers for Disease Control and Prevention data.

perception factors" that underlie group fears and help shape behavior. Among them are:

- Control vs. no control: We normally fear something more if we are not personally in control of it. Thus, you feel safer driving your own car through several hundred miles of bad traffic than traveling the same distance in an airliner, even though you are safer in the plane.
- Immediate vs. chronic: We are more afraid of something that can kill us suddenly and violently than we are of chronic, long-term dangers.
- Natural vs. manmade: We're less afraid of radiation from the sun than of the radiation from power lines and cell phone towers, even though the risk from the sun is far greater.
- Risk vs. benefit: We find reasons to overlook the risks brought to us by something we like. The acetone in fingernail polish is less fearsome to those who use it than the same chemical encountered in another form.
- Imposed vs. voluntary: Nonsmokers are often fearful of tobacco smoke. Smokers usually aren't.

There's even some risk in assessing risk, at least politically. The Harvard center has been criticized for accepting contributions from government-regulated industries eager to promote any suggestion that their products pose relatively little danger. Thus, the center is controversial with environmental and consumer groups.

Ropeik, who authored "Risk: A Practical Guide for Deciding What's Really Safe and What's Really Dangerous in the World Around Us," insists that some of our most expensive risks are actually "bogeymen" on which society spends inordinate sums.

"I think some people have used this to advance

political or corporate agendas," he said. "Obviously, there are environmental risks that are bigger and demand more attention than we're giving them."

He cited indoor air pollution. Most Americans draw nine out of 10 breaths in indoor environments that are polluted with molds, germs and chemicals, he said.

So, with crooked sticks, solar radiation, acetone, mosquitoes and dirty indoor air surrounding us, what is our biggest risk?

Ropeik hesitated.

"Obesity," he replied. "There is better than a 50-50 chance that any given American is obese, and this causes 300,000 deaths a year. Tobacco causes about 400,000 deaths a year, but only 47 million Americans smoke. They are really neck-and-neck."

QUESTIONS

1. What are the "universal perception factors" that are used in explaining group fear?

2. What are your biggest fears as a consumer? As a citizen? How do they control your behavior?

Stanley J. Modic | # How We Got into This Mess

Stanley J. Modic is a journalist and a member of the Press Club of Cleveland's Hall of Fame. John Anderson is a retired vice president of All-state Insurance Co.

Product-liability problems continue to vex U. S. industry. Just about everyone concedes that something must be done, but consensus as to a solution remains elusive.

Some accuse the insurance industry of contriving a crisis to justify raising premiums. Others blame the legal profession's obsession with using tort law to extract high settlements.

Just where *does* the fault lie? And where do we go from here? Are legislative curbs needed?

The search for a remedy is mired in confusion. And the confusion stems primarily from the way in which liability insurance and tort law have combined into an organic system which has evolved over the years.

The principal catalysts feed on each other. As the system of tort law has grown and its scope has expanded, the insurance industry has responded by increasing the amounts of coverage it offers and, naturally, its premiums. Each system has prospered, in a

sense, from the activities of the other. And, over the years, that has caused the product-liability problem to spiral out of control.

Roy R. Anderson, who retired as a vice president of Allstate Insurance Cos., has pondered this dilemma. As an actuary, a strategic planner, and a futurist, he has extensively analyzed the problems of our society and of the insurance industry. In retirement, he continues his interest in futurism. And, though he readily admits that accurately predicting the future is impossible, he believes that the way to get a fix on the future is to study how our systems are working today and how they got that way.

WHO PAYS?

"It is critical," Mr. Anderson stresses, "to understand that both liability insurance and tort law are organic, man-made systems that operate in accordance with the perceptions, beliefs, and values of human beings—all of which continually are shifting."

As he explains it, the tort system was originally intended to achieve two goals in situations where one person, through negligence, injured another person.

Stanley J. Modic, "How We Got into This Mess," *Industry Week,* Jan 12, 1987.

"The first was to heal the victim; the second was to punish the person at fault by making him compensate the victim."

The advent of liability insurance drastically changed things. "No longer was the person at fault punished by having to bear the full cost of compensating the victim," Mr. Anderson explains. "Instead, this 'punishment' was spread across society by means of insurance premiums."

To illustrate how social systems evolve, Mr. Anderson points out that in some respects we are returning to the days when the guilty party had to bear the full burden of compensating the victim. This happens when a person (or corporation) forgoes liability insurance—because it's not available or because the premiums are too high. It also happens when the amount of the plaintiff's award greatly exceeds the amount of liability insurance carried—an increasingly common situation which alarms many manufacturers.

IT'S NOT WORKING

For those individuals and corporations priced out of the insurance market, the system is no longer working. The expansion of the tort system has warped beyond all reason both the financial settlements and the legal definition of what constitutes being "at fault."

"The most invidious and illogical of these distortions has been the increase in awards for punitive damages," Mr. Anderson contends. He feels that if a guilty person is to be punished for behavior that caused injury to another person, that punishment should come in the form of a fine payable to the state, rather than punitive damages awarded in a civil suit to the individual.

"This is especially true," Mr. Anderson asserts, "in the case of a guilty corporation where the fine must be very large before it gets the attention of the wrongdoer. Clearly, such cases should come under the criminal section of the law—with both the corporation and the guilty corporate executives subject to the penalty process."

Other shifts, too, have distorted the legal system. The initial concept that the guilty person had to be 100% at fault and that the victim had to be totally blameless in the cause of the injury has been eroded,

Mr. Anderson points out. In addition, the definition of what constitutes an "injury" and the conditions under which a party can be deemed liable have changed; and class-action and cumulative-injury precedents have been established.

WHY IT'S HAPPENING

The reasons for these shifts, Mr. Anderson says, include: The liberality of juries in awarding damages; the attitude of the public toward insurance companies' ability to pay; and public outrage against the questionable behavior of some corporations and professionals.

"In a nutshell, the system of liability insurance has been transformed from a system that originally compensated only blameless victims to a system that is steadily expanding to take care of all injured persons [regardless of fault]," Mr. Anderson claims.

It comes into play in our lives in many ways. The skyrocketing cost of liability insurance impacts the repair of our automobiles and the quality of our health care. It increases the cost of new products being developed—and keeps some of them off the market. More recently, it has even affected civic affairs, Little League baseball, and our leisure hours.

"If you stop to consider how much it is messing up so much of what we do, you have to wonder how we let it get so bad," says Mr. Anderson.

The former insurance executive believes that the tort law-liability insurance system started going sour with the explosion in automobile ownership following World War II. Prior to that time, liability insurance was almost a luxury for the lower and middle classes. Ordinarily, they carried only collision and comprehensive insurance, usually provided by the dealer as part of the financing package, Mr. Anderson explains. But the enactment of financial-responsibility laws shifted liability insurance from a luxury to a necessity.

"Steadily, it became apparent to the plaintiffs' [attorneys] that each time there was an automobile accident, there was a good chance that there was also an injured person—and another person involved who was at fault," Mr. Anderson says. "The existence of the 'contingent fee' provision in the tort system made it possible for the plaintiff's lawyer to finance the lawsuit for his client—and to be rewarded handsomely for his initiative if he won the case."

In terms of coverage—typically $10,000 for bodily injury and $5,000 for property damage—the amount of insurance in force in the 1950s was "peanuts," reflects Mr. Anderson. "But it was enough to support a training ground for the plaintiffs' bar as it learned to expand the scope of the fledgling system."

IMPETUS FROM DETROIT

At the same time, a symbiotic relationship was evolving between the auto-insurance industry and the car manufacturers, Mr. Anderson points out. "With the growth of property-damage liability insurance, together with collision insurance, the automakers knew that adequate money would be available for the repair of the great majority of damaged cars. . . . Typically, the owner of the damaged car has not been concerned about what he was charged for repairs, as long as it was covered by insurance."

This knowledge influenced how auto manufacturers built and priced their cars. The philosophy was: "Keep the price of new cars low to encourage sales and make up the difference on repair and replacement parts," Mr. Anderson notes. "It also occurred to them that it might be in their financial interest to design cars that were easily damaged. For example, look at what Detroit has done to bumpers over the years, designing them to be more like ornaments that provide little or no protection, thus adding substantially to repair costs."

Mr. Anderson claims that the insurance industry played a useful role in improving the construction of automobile bumpers. "It was the advertising and lobbying efforts of the insurance companies that led to state and federal laws requiring sensible bumpers rather than fragile ornaments."

TWO CRISES

The first major crisis in the tort law/auto insurance system arose in the mid-1970s with the proposal for "no-fault" auto insurance. "In essence, it would have meant the elimination of tort law in the case of auto accidents. It would have been replaced by a 'first-party' system which would compensate the injured parties for medical expenses and economic loss, regardless of fault," the former insurance executive explains.

He recalls that the auto-insurance business was deeply divided on the no-fault issue. Proponents were mainly those carriers writing auto insurance for large corporate clients. Opponents of no-fault were the companies doing business primarily with individuals.

"Unfortunately, what finally emerged from the battle over no-fault was 'modified no-fault,' which included the poorer parts of both systems and ended up costing the public more than the old 'fault' system."

The next crisis in the system occurred with the huge growth in medical-malpractice suits. As Mr. Anderson sees it, the medical profession did "a miserable job" of policing itself. "Incompetent doctors remained at large because medical societies took little action. In those days, doctors operated under their version of the Mafia's *omerta* or 'vow of silence'—which precluded doctors from testifying against each other."

Mr. Anderson credits the plaintiffs' bar and the judicial system for cracking this "vow of silence" and turning the spotlight on the shabby performance of the medical profession—"even though its motives were hardly altruistic."

Cultivating the Market

Initially, the average damage settlements were relatively small, Mr. Anderson points out. Even so, studies indicated that the insurance industry could economically provide higher amounts of coverage. And carriers jumped at the chance to tap a new market; they urged policyholders to buy higher limits on liability coverage.

Although it seemed to be in the best interests of the public, "from a systems standpoint it proved to be ill-advised," Mr. Anderson reflects. "The plaintiffs' bar reacted to the higher limits like a cat to catnip.

"Here again," he says, "it is obvious that the system that has evolved is not the best way to 'monitor' the quality of medical care. The sooner the plaintiffs' bar is removed from the picture, the better."

As Mr. Anderson sees it, the experience in the auto and medical arenas set the stage for the legal profession's pursuit of greener pastures—product liability. "It is in the area of product liability that some of the most significant precedents of tort law have been established and enhanced," he points out. The legal system has accepted new thinking on joint and several liability, punitive damages, class-action suits, and cumulative injury (due, for example, to repeated exposure to a toxic substance).

In product liability the stakes are high. Injury, and the number of people affected, can accumulate over long periods.

Mr. Anderson says the classic case may be asbestosis. "The amount of damages that corporations now have to pay are astronomically so much higher than the direct economic loss that they can bankrupt a company."

A GLOOMY PROSPECT

As bad as the asbestos case has been, it pales in comparison with potential damage claims against companies, or even entire industries, stemming from toxic chemicals or long-term environmental degradation.

"The explosive nature of the present product-liability system is [such] that it will ultimately be beyond the capacity of the insurance business to carry it," Mr. Anderson contends. "The systems are so out of control that our economy and society can no longer bear the cost."

Mr. Anderson believes that the public, as well as federal and state legislators, recognize that something must be done. The problem, however, transcends the issues of law, insurance, and compensation.

"In fact," he claims, "what we are dealing with is the very value structure of our society." Mr. Anderson warns that change will come slowly, because "the legal fraternity has a great vested interest in the system."

Solutions Coming

But, as bleak as the situation seems today, this futurist sees a light at the end of the tunnel. A start is likely this year; Congress is expected to pass legislation to cap the amount of damages that can be awarded.

That legislation, however, will not solve the basic problem of a tort law-liability insurance system run-

ning amok. Nevertheless, Mr. Anderson believes there is reason to hope for a long-range solution. Congressional action, he predicts, will break a log-jam and set into motion waves of change that will ripple through other aspects of tort law.

Organic, man-made systems have life cycles and ultimately run their course, Mr. Anderson observes. "The system of liability insurance is well into the stage of decline," he believes.

He thinks that the system of tort law is also in a state of decline. "However, the course of its future and the timing of its demise will differ greatly from that of the insurance system. Because tort law is an important part of the much broader system of civil and criminal law, its future—and its demise—will be tied to its broader parent system," he concludes.

Tort-Law Change

As for tort law, the futurist makes this prediction: The two purposes served under the present system—compensating the injured persons and punishing those at fault—eventually will be served by two different systems.

"The compensation of injured people will be included under a much broader system that will compensate or cure injured persons, regardless of the cause of the injury," he anticipates.

The "punishment" purpose, Mr. Anderson predicts, will be handled under the criminal justice system. "There would be standards of performance required for the various professions; those who failed to adhere to those standards would be punished by their profession—or under criminal law."

The same would apply to manufactured products. "Standards would be established and tests would be required. Manufacturers failing to follow the standards, thereby causing injury, would be punished under criminal law."

QUESTIONS

1. How did we "get into this mess," according to Modic? What is the mess we are in? How does Modic think we can get out of the mess?

2. How did the major crises in the tort law/auto insurance system complicate the issues of liability?

George G. Brenkert

Strict Products Liability
and Compensatory Justice

George Brenkert teaches business ethics at Georgetown University and is editor of *Business Ethics Quarterly.*

Strict products liability is the doctrine that the seller of a product has legal responsibilities to compensate the user of that product for injuries suffered because of a defective aspect of the product, even when the seller has not been negligent in permitting that defect to occur. Thus, even though a manufacturer, for example, has reasonably applied the existing techniques of manufacture and has anticipated and cared for nonintended uses of the product, he may still be held liable for injuries a product user suffers if it can be shown that the product was defective when it left the manufacturer's hands.

To say that there is a crisis today concerning this doctrine would be to utter a commonplace which few in the business community would deny. The development of the doctrine of strict products liability, according to most business people, threatens many businesses financially. Furthermore, strict products liability is said to be a morally questionable doctrine, since the manufacturer or seller has not been negligent in permitting the injury-causing defect to occur. On the other hand, victims of defective products complain that they deserve full compensation for injuries sustained in using a defective product whether or not the seller is at fault. Medical expenses and time lost from one's job are costs no individual should have to bear by himself. It is only fair that the seller share such burdens.

In general, discussions of this crisis focus on the limits to which a business ought to be held responsible. Much less frequently, discussions of strict products liability consider the underlying question of whether the doctrine of strict products liability is rationally justifiable. But unless this question is answered it would seem premature to seek to determine the limits to which business ought to be held liable in such cases. In the following, I discuss this underlying philosophical question and argue that there is a rational justification for strict products liability which links it to the very nature of the free enterprise system.

II

It should be noted at the outset that strict products liability is not absolute liability. To hold a manufacturer legally (and morally) responsible for any and all injuries which product users might sustain would be morally perverse. First, it would deny the product user's own responsibility to take care in his actions and to suffer the consequences when he does not. It would therefore constitute an extreme form of moral and legal paternalism.

Second, if the product is not defective, there is no significant moral connection between anything the manufacturer has done or not done and the user's injuries other than the production and sale of the product. This provides no basis for holding the manufacturer responsible for the user's injuries. If, because of my own carelessness, I cut myself with my new pocket knife, the fact that I just bought my knife from Blade Manufacturing Company provides no moral reason to hold Blade Manufacturing responsible for my injury.

Finally, though the manufacturer's product might be said to have harmed the person, it is wholly implausible, when the product is not defective and the manufacturer not negligent, to say that the manufacturer has harmed the user. Thus, there would seem to be no moral basis upon which to maintain that the manufacturer has any liability to the product user. Strict products liability, on the other hand, holds that the manufacturer can be held liable when the product can be shown to be defective, even though the manufacturer himself has not been negligent.

Two justifications of strict products liability are predominant in the literature. Both, I believe, are untenable. They are:

1. To hold producers strictly liable for defective products will cut down on the number of accidents and injuries which occur by forcing manufacturers to make their products safer.
2. The manufacturer is best able to distribute to others the costs of injuries which users of his defective products suffer.

There are several reasons why the first justification is unacceptable. First, it has been argued plausibly that almost everything that can be attained through the use of strict liability to force manufacturers to make their products safer can also be attained in other ways through the law. Hence, to hold manufacturers strictly liable will not necessarily help reduce the number of accidents. The incentive to produce safer products already exists, without invoking the doctrine of strict products liability.

Second, at least some of the accidents which have been brought under strict liability have been caused by features of the products which the manufacturers could not have foreseen or controlled. At the time the product was designed and manufactured, the technological knowledge required to discover the hazard and take steps to minimize its effects was not available. It is doubtful that in such cases the imposition of strict liability upon the manufacturer could reduce accidents. Thus, again, this justification for strict products liability fails.

Third, the fact that the imposition of legal restraints and/or penalties would have a certain positive effect—for example, reduce accidents—does not show that the imposition of those penalties would be just. It has been pointed out before that the rate of crime might be cut significantly if the law would

imprison the wives and children of men who break the law. Regardless of how correct that claim may be, to use these means in order to achieve a significant reduction in the crime rate would be unjust. Thus, the fact—if fact it be—that strict liability would cut down on the amount of dangerous and/or defective products placed on the market, and thus reduce the number of accidents and injuries, does not justify the imposition of strict liability on manufacturers.

Finally, the above justification is essentially a utilitarian appeal which emphasizes the welfare of the product users. It is not obvious, however, that those who use this justification have ever undertaken the utilitarian analysis which would show that greater protection of the product user's safety would further the welfare of product users. If emphasis on product user safety would cut down on the number and variety of products produced, the imposition of strict liability might not enhance product user welfare; rather, it might lower it. Furthermore, if the safety of product users is the predominant concern, massive public and private education safety campaigns might do as much or more to lower the level of accidents and injuries as strict products liability.

The second justification given for strict products liability is also utilitarian in nature. Among the factors cited in favor of this justification are the following:

1. "An individual harmed by his or her use of a defective product is often unable to bear the loss individually."
2. "Distribution of losses among all users of a product would minimize both individual and aggregate loss."
3. "The situation of producers and marketers in the marketplace enables them conveniently to distribute losses among all users of a product by raising prices sufficiently to compensate those harmed (which is what in fact occurs where strict liability is in force)."

This justification is also defective.

First, the word "best" in the phrase "best able to distribute to others the cost" is usually understood in a nonmoral sense; it is used to signify that the manufacturer can most efficiently pass on the costs of injuries to others. Once this use of "best" is recognized, surely we may ask why these costs ought to be passed on to other consumers and/or users of the same product or line of products. Even if the imposition of strict liability did maximize utility, it might still be unjust to use the producer as the distributor of losses. Indeed, some have objected that to pass along the costs of such accidents to other consumers of a manufacturer's products is unjust to them. The above justification is silent with regard to these legitimate objections.

Second, manufacturers may not always be in the best (that is, most efficient and economical) position to pass costs on to customers. Even in monopoly areas, there are limitations. Furthermore, some products are subject to an elastic demand, preventing the manufacturer from passing along the costs. Finally, the present justification could justify far more than is plausible. If the reason for holding the manufacturer liable is that the manufacturer is the "best" administrator of costs, one might plausibly argue that the manufacturer should pay for injuries suffered not only when he is not negligent but also when the product is not defective. Theoretically, at least, this argument could be extended from cases of strict liability to that of absolute liability.

Whether this argument holds up depends upon contingent facts concerning the nature and frequency of injuries people suffer using products, the financial strength of businesses, and the kinds and levels of products liability insurance available to them. It does not depend on any morally significant elements in the relationship between the producer and the product user. Such an implication, I believe, undercuts the purported moral nature of this justification and reveals it for what it is: an economic, not a moral, justification.

Accordingly, neither of the major current justifications for the imposition of strict liability appears to be acceptable. If this is the case, is strict products liability a groundless doctrine, willfully and unjustly imposed on manufacturers?

III

This question can be asked in two different ways. On the one hand, it can be asked within the assumptions of the free enterprise system. On the other hand, it could be raised with the premise that the fundamental assumptions of that socioeconomic system are also open to revision and change. In the following, I will discuss the question *within* the general assumptions of the free enterprise system. Since these assumptions are broadly made in legal and business circles it is interesting to determine what answer might be given within these constraints. Indeed, I suggest that only within these general assumptions can strict products liability be justified.

To begin with, it is crucial to remember that what we have to consider is the relationship between an entity doing business and an individual. The strict liability attributed to business would not be attributed to an individual who happened to sell some product he had made to his neighbor or a stranger. If Peter sold an article he had made to Paul and Paul hurt himself because the article had a defect which occurred through no negligence of Peter's, we would not normally hold Peter morally responsible to pay for Paul's injuries.

Peter did not claim, we may assume, that the product was absolutely risk-free. Had he kept it, he himself might have been injured by it. Paul, on the other hand, bought it. He was not pressured, forced, or coerced to do so. Peter mounted no advertising campaign. Though Paul might not have been injured if the product had been made differently, he supposedly bought it with open eyes. Peter did not seek to deceive Paul about its qualities. The product, both its good and bad qualities, became his when he bought it.

In short, we assume that both Peter and Paul are morally autonomous individuals capable of knowing their own interests, that such individuals can legitimately exchange their ownership of various products, that the world is not free of risks, and that not all injuries one suffers in such a world can be blamed on others. To demand that Peter protect Paul from such dangers and/or compensate him for injuries resulting from such dangers is to demand that Peter significantly reduce the risks of the product he offers to Paul and to protect Paul from encountering those risks. However, this demand smacks of paternalism and undercuts our basic moral assumptions about such relations. Hence, in such a case, Peter is not morally responsible for Paul's injuries or, because of this transaction, obligated to aid him. Perhaps Peter owes Paul aid because Paul is an injured neighbor or person. Perhaps for charitable reasons Peter ought to help Paul. But Peter has no moral obligation stemming from the sale itself to provide aid.

It is different for businesses. They have been held to be legally and morally obliged to pay the victim for his injuries. Why? What is the difference? The difference is that when Paul is hurt by a defective product from corporation X, he is hurt by something produced in a socioeconomic system purportedly embodying free enterprise. In other words, among other things:

1. Each business and/or corporation produces articles or services it sells for profit.
2. Each member of this system competes with other members of the system in trying to do as well as it can for itself not simply in each exchange, but through each exchange for its other values and desires.
3. Competition is to be "open and free, without deception or fraud."
4. Exchanges are voluntary and undertaken when each party believes it can benefit thereby. One party provides the means for another party's ends if the other party will provide the first party the means to its ends.
5. The acquisition and disposition of ownership rights—that is, of private property—is permitted in such exchanges.
6. No market or series of markets constitutes the whole of a society.
7. Law, morality, and government play a role in setting acceptable limits to the nature and kinds of exchange in which people may engage.

What is it about such a system which would justify claims of strict products liability against businesses? Calabresi has suggested that the free enterprise system is essentially a system of strict liability. Thus the very nature of the free enterprise system justifies such liability claims. His argument has two parts. First, he claims that "bearing risks is both the function of, and justification for, private enterprise in a free enterprise society." "Free enterprise is prized, in classical economics, precisely because it fosters the creation of entrepreneurs who will take such uninsurable risks, who will, in other words, gamble

on uncertainty and demonstrate their utility by surviving—by winning more than others."

Accordingly, the nature of private enterprise requires individual businesses to assume the burden of risk in the production and distribution of its products. However, even if we grant that this characterization of who must bear the risks "in deciding what goods are worthy of producing and what new entrants into an industry are worth having" is correct, it would not follow that individual businesses ought to bear the burden of risk in cases of accidents.

Calabresi himself recognizes this. Thus in the second part of his argument he maintains that there is a close analogy which lets us move from the regular risk-bearing businesses must accept in the marketplace to the bearing of risks in accidents: "although . . . [the above characterization] has concerned *regular* entrepreneurial-product risks, not accident risks, the analogy is extremely close." He proceeds to draw the analogy, however, in the following brief sentence: "As with product-accident risks, our society starts out by allocating ordinary product-production risks in ways which try to maximize the chances that incentives will be placed on those most suited to 'manage' these risks." In short, he asserts that the imposition of strict products liability on business will be the most effective means of reducing such risks.

But such a view does not really require, as we have seen in the previous section, any assumptions about the nature of the free enterprise system. It could be held independently of such assumptions. Further, this view is simply a form of the first justificatory argument we discussed and rejected in the previous section. We can hardly accept it here just by attaching it to the nature of free enterprise.

Nevertheless, Calabresi's initial intuitions about a connection between the assumptions of the free enterprise system and the justification of strict products liability are correct. However, they must be developed in the following, rather different, manner. In the free enterprise system, each person and/or business is obligated to follow the rules and understandings which define this socioeconomic system. Following the rules is expected to channel competition among individuals and businesses to socially positive results. In providing the means to fulfill the ends of others, one's own ends also get fulfilled.

Though this does not happen in every case, it is supposed to happen most of the time. Those who fail in their competition with others may be the object of charity, but not of other duties. Those who succeed, qua members of this socioeconomic system, do not have moral duties to aid those who fail. Analogously, the team which loses the game may receive our sympathy but the winning team is not obligated to help it to win the next game or even to play it better. Those who violate the rules, however, may be punished or penalized, whether or not the violation was intentional and whether or not it redounded to the benefit of the violator. Thus, a team may be assessed a penalty for something that a team member did unintentionally to a member of the other team but which injured the other team's chances of competition in the game by violating the rules.

This point may be emphasized by another instance involving a game that brings us closer to strict products liability. Imagine that you are playing table tennis with another person in his newly constructed table tennis room. You are both avid table tennis players and the game means a lot to both of you. Suppose that after play has begun, you are suddenly and quite obviously blinded by the light over the table—the light shade has a hole in it which, when it turned in your direction, sent a shaft of light unexpectedly into your eyes. You lose a crucial point as a result. Surely it would be unfair of your opponent to seek to maintain his point because he was faultless—after all, he had not intended to blind you when he installed that light shade. You would correctly object that he had gained the point unfairly, that you should not have to give up the point lost, and that the light shade should be modified so that the game can continue on a fair basis. It is only fair that the point be played over.

Businesses and their customers in a free enterprise system are also engaged in competition with each other. The competition here, however, is multifaceted as each tries to gain the best agreement he can from the other with regard to the buying and selling of raw materials, products, services, and labor. Such agreements must be voluntary. The competition which

leads to them cannot involve coercion. In addition, such competition must be fair and ultimately result in the benefit of the entire society through the operation of the proverbial invisible hand.

Crucial to the notion of fairness of competition are not simply the demands that the competition be open, free, and honest, but also that each person in a society be given an equal opportunity to participate in the system in order to fulfill his or her own particular ends. Friedman formulates this notion in the following manner:

> . . . the priority given to equality of opportunity in the hierarchy of values . . . is manifested particularly in economic policy. The catchwords were free enterprise, competition, laissez-faire. Everyone was to be free to go into any business, follow any occupation, buy any property, subject only to the agreement of the other parties to the transaction. Each was to have the opportunity to reap the benefits if he succeeded, to suffer the costs if he failed. There were to be no arbitrary obstacles. Performance, not birth, religion, or nationality, was the touchstone.

What is obvious in Friedman's comments is that he is thinking primarily of a person as a producer. Equality of opportunity requires that one not be prevented by arbitrary obstacles from participating (by engaging in a productive role of some kind or other) in the system of free enterprise, competition, and so on in order to fulfill one's own ends ("reap the benefits"). Accordingly, monopolies are restricted, discriminatory hiring policies have been condemned, and price collusion is forbidden.

However, each person participates in the system of free enterprise *both* as a worker/producer *and* as a consumer. The two roles interact; if the person could not consume he would not be able to work, and if there were no consumers there would be no work to be done. Even if a particular individual is only (what is ordinarily considered) a consumer, he or she plays a theoretically significant role in the competitive free enterprise system. The fairness of the system depends upon what access he or she has to information about goods and services on the market, the lack of coercion imposed on that person to buy goods, and the lack of arbitrary restrictions imposed by the market and/or government on his or her behavior.

In short, equality of opportunity is a doctrine with two sides which applies both to producers and to consumers. If, then, a person as a consumer or a producer is injured by a defective product—which is one way his activities might arbitrarily be restricted by the action of (one of the members of) the market system—surely his free and voluntary participation in the system of free enterprise will be seriously affected. Specifically, his equal opportunity to participate in the system in order to fulfill his own ends will be diminished.

Here is where strict products liability enters the picture. In cases of strict liability the manufacturer does not intend for a certain aspect of his product to injure someone. Nevertheless, the person is injured. As a result, he is at a disadvantage both as a consumer and as a producer. He cannot continue to play either role as he might wish. Therefore, he is denied that equality of opportunity which is basic to the economic system in question just as surely as he would be if he were excluded from employment by various unintended consequences of the economic system which nevertheless had racially or sexually prejudicial implications. Accordingly, it is fair for the manufacturer to compensate the person for his losses before proceeding with business as usual. That is, the user of a manufacturer's product may justifiably demand compensation from the manufacturer when its product can be shown to be defective and has injured him and harmed his chances of participation in the system of free enterprise.

Hence, strict liability finds a basis in the notion of equality of opportunity which plays a central role in the notion of a free enterprise system. That is why a business which does *not* have to pay for the injuries an individual suffers in the use of a defective article made by that business is felt to be unfair to its customers. Its situation is analogous to that of a player's unintentional violation of a game rule which is intended to foster equality of competitive opportunity.

A soccer player, for example, may unintentionally trip an opposing player. He did not mean to do it; perhaps he himself had stumbled. Still, he has to be penalized. If the referee looked the other way, the tripped player would rightfully object that he had been treated unfairly. Similarly, the manufacturer of a product may be held strictly liable for a product of his which injures a person who uses that product. Even if he is faultless, a consequence of his activities is to render the user of his product less capable of equal participation in the socioeconomic system. The manufacturer should be penalized by way of compensating the victim. Thus, the basis upon which manufacturers are held strictly liable is compensatory justice.

In a society which refuses to resort to paternalism or to central direction of the economy and which turns, instead, to competition in order to allocate scarce positions and resources, compensatory justice requires that the competition be fair and losers be protected. Specifically, no one who loses should be left so destitute that he cannot reenter the competition. Furthermore, those who suffer injuries traceable to defective merchandise or services which restrict their participation in the competitive system should also be compensated.

Compensatory justice does not presuppose negligence or evil intentions on the part of those to whom the injuries might ultimately be traced. It is not perplexed or incapacitated by the relative innocence of all parties involved. Rather, it is concerned with correcting the disadvantaged situation an individual experiences due to accidents or failures which occur in the normal working of that competitive system. It is on this basis that other compensatory programs which alleviate the disabilities of various minority groups are founded. Strict products liability is also founded on compensatory justice.

An implication of the preceding argument is that business is not morally obliged to pay, as such, for the physical injury a person suffers. Rather, it must pay for the loss of equal competitive opportunity—even though it usually is the case that it is because of a (physical) injury that there is a loss of equal opportunity. Actual legal cases in which the injury which prevents a person from going about his or her daily activities is emotional or mental, as well as physical, support this thesis. If a person were neither mentally nor physically harmed, but still rendered less capable of participating competitively because of a defective aspect of a product, there would still be grounds for holding the company liable.

For example, suppose I purchased and used a cosmetic product guaranteed to last a month. When used by most people it is odorless. On me, however, it has a terrible smell. I can stand the smell, but my co-workers and most other people find it intolerable. My employer sends me home from work until it wears off. The product has not harmed me physically or mentally. Still, on the above argument, I would have reason to hold the manufacturer liable. Any cosmetic product with this result is defective. As a consequence my opportunity to participate in the socioeconomic system is curbed. I should be compensated.

IV

There is another way of arriving at the same conclusion about the basis of strict products liability. To speak of business or the free enterprise system, it was noted above, is to speak of the voluntary exchanges between producer and customer which take place when each party believes he has an opportunity to benefit. Surely customers and producers may miscalculate their benefits; something they voluntarily agreed to buy or sell may turn out not to be to their benefit. The successful person does not have any moral responsibilities to the unsuccessful person—at least as a member of this economic system. If, however, fraud is the reason one person does not benefit, the system is, in principle, undermined. If such fraud were universalized, the system would collapse. Accordingly, the person committing the fraud does have a responsibility to make reparations to the one mistreated.

Consider once again the instance of a person who is harmed by a product he bought or used, a product that can reasonably be said to be defective. Has the nature of the free enterprise system also been undermined or corrupted in this instance? Producer and consumer have exchanged the product but it has not been to their mutual benefit; the manufacturer may have benefited, but the customer has suffered because of the defect. Furthermore, if such exchanges were universalized, the system would also be undone.

Suppose that whenever people bought products from manufacturers the products turned out to be defective and the customers were always injured, even though the manufacturers could not be held negligent. Though one party to such exchanges might benefit, the other party always suffered. If the rationale for this economic system—the reason it was adopted and is defended—were that in the end both parties share the equal opportunity to gain, surely it would collapse with the above consequences. Consequently, as with fraud, an economic system of free enterprise requires that injuries which result from defective products be compensated. The question is: Who is to pay for the compensation?

There are three possibilities. The injured party could pay for his own injuries. However, this is implausible since what is called for is compensation and not merely payment for injuries. If the injured party had simply injured himself, if he had been negligent or careless, then it is plausible that he should pay for his own injuries. No compensation is at stake here. But in the present case the injury stems from the actions of a particular manufacturer who, albeit unwittingly, placed the defective product on the market and stands to gain through its sale.

The rationale of the free enterprise system would be undermined, we have seen, if such actions were universalized, for then the product user's equal opportunity to benefit from the system would be denied. Accordingly, since the rationale and motivation for an individual to be part of this socioeconomic system is his opportunity to gain from participation in it, justice requires that the injured product user receive compensation for his injuries. Since the individual can hardly compensate himself, he must receive compensation from some other source.

Second, some third party—such as government—could compensate the injured person. This is not wholly implausible if one is prepared to modify the structure of the free enterprise system. And, indeed, in the long run this may be the most plausible course of action. However, if one accepts the structure of the free enterprise system, this alternative must be rejected because it permits the interference of government into individual affairs.

Third, we are left with the manufacturer. Suppose a manufacturer's product, even though the manufacturer wasn't negligent, always turned out to be defective and injured those using his products. We might sympathize with his plight, but he would either have to stop manufacturing altogether (no one would buy such products) or else compensate the victims for their losses. (Some people might buy and use his products under these conditions.) If he forced people to buy and use his products he would corrupt the free enterprise system. If he did not compensate the injured users, they would not buy and he would not be able to sell his products. Hence, he could partake of the free enterprise system—that is, sell his products—only if he compensated his user/victims. Accordingly, the sale of this hypothetical line of defective products would be voluntarily accepted as just or fair only if compensation were paid the user/victims of such products by the manufacturer.

The same conclusion follows even if we consider a single defective product. The manufacturer put the defective product on the market. Because of his actions others who seek the opportunity to participate on an equal basis in this system in order to benefit therefrom are unable to do so. Thus, a result of his actions, even though unintended, is to undermine the system's character and integrity. Accordingly, when a person is injured in his attempt to participate in this system, he is owed compensation by the manufac-

turer. The seller of the defective article must not jeopardize the equal opportunity of the product user to benefit from the system. The seller need not guarantee that the buyer/user will benefit from the purchase of the product; after all, the buyer may miscalculate or be careless in the use of a nondefective product. But if he is not careless or has not miscalculated, his opportunity to benefit from the system is illegitimately harmed if he is injured in its use because of the product's defectiveness. He deserves compensation.

It follows from the arguments in this and the preceding section that strict products liability is not only compatible with the system of free enterprise but that if it were not attributed to the manufacturer the system itself would be morally defective. And the justification for requiring manufacturers to pay compensation when people are injured by defective products is that the demands of compensatory justice are met.

QUESTIONS

1. What is strict product liability? How does it differ from absolute liability?

2. Why might we argue that strict product liability imposes an unjust burden on manufacturers?

Henry Fairlie | # Fear of Living

Henry Fairlie writes for *The New Republic* magazine.

In January 1967 the first Apollo spacecraft caught fire during a test on the launchpad. Three astronauts were killed. The nation was shocked and horrified, all the more so because the screams and scrambles of the astronauts could be clearly heard. But although there was a congressional hearing, and some delay of the manned flights, the Apollo program went smartly

ahead, with the full understanding and support of the nation, and within 18 months Apollo 11 landed on the moon, ahead of the deadline set by John Kennedy. The Apollo disaster was not graven on the public mind as a rebuke to America's confidence in its technology, or taken as the occasion to preach that Americans must learn the limits to their energy and power.

Nineteen years later, the space shuttle Challenger was destroyed before our eyes on television. It was a spectacular tragedy, the result of human miscalcula-

From *The New Republic,* Jan 23, 1989.

tion and technical failure, neither of which should have been present, perhaps, but both of which are understood risks in the still dangerous enterprise of space flight. Yet the prevailing mood in America so panicked NASA that it took almost three years to send up another shuttle. NASA even reached the stage, as members of its staff said, of taking so many precautions that it was in danger of enlarging, instead of diminishing, the possibility of malfunction.

In the 19 years between these tragedies, the idea that our individual lives and the nation's life can and should be risk-free has grown to be an obsession, driven far and deep into American attitudes. Indeed, the desire for a risk-free society is one of the most debilitating influences in America today, progressively enfeebling the economy with a mass of safety regulations and a widespread-fear of liability rulings, and threatening to create an unbuoyant and uninventive society. As many studies show, this is strikingly an American phenomenon, one that seems to have taken root in yet another distortion of the philosophy of rights underlying the Constitution, as if the Declaration of Independence had been rewritten to include freedom from risk among the self-evident rights to life, liberty, and the pursuit of happiness. This morbid aversion to risk calls into question how Americans now envision the destiny of their country.

If America's new timorousness had prevailed among the Vikings, their ships with the bold prows but frail hulls would have been declared unseaworthy. The Norsemen would have stayed home and jogged. Columbus's three tubs would not have been allowed to sail; as it was, one was left wrecked on American shores. The Vikings and Columbus were exploring what was as unknown to them then as our solar system is to us today, and it is not only the practical achievements of such venturing that are frustrated by the desire for a risk-free society. Something of the questing endeavor of the human spirit is also lost. The Vikings made sagas of their explorations, as European and English literature flowered during the great Age of Exploration. There once was, but there is not now, a promise of saga in America. Its literature has retreated into a preoccupation with private anxieties and fretting.

At Three Mile Island, the fail-safe system worked.

The power station switched itself off. There was a scare, but no disaster. Yet Three Mile Island in the American mind is an emblem of catastrophe. Nuclear power in America, as in no equivalent industrial or industrializing nation, has been almost paralyzed, although it is the only sufficient, efficient, and *relatively* safe source of energy that can avoid the greater risks of pollution and the "greenhouse effect." Of course there is a risk in nuclear power, and there should be thorough inspections and safeguards. Of course, also, there is such a thing as a level of risk that is unacceptable. But in America the threshold of tolerable risk has now been set so low that the nation is refusing to pay the inevitable costs of human endeavor. Stand beneath the majesty of the Grand Coulee Dam, or gaze up at the marvel of the Brooklyn Bridge—"O Harp and Altar," as Hart Crane sang of it—and count the number of lives lost in their construction. But then feel the power, even the beauty, of both dam and bridge, and weigh the cost of lives against the benefits they have brought.

The origins of the widespread refusal to accept a sometimes high level of risk as a normal and necessary hazard of life lie in the early 1970s. As America lost heart in the prosecution of the war in Vietnam, the energy of the dissenters—the vanguard of the "Me Decade"—turned to lavish care for the environment, the snail darter, and their own exquisite, often imagined, physical and emotional well-being. The simultaneous loss of faith in American technology was part of the same phenomenon; technology, it was observed, not only fouled the environment, but had proved incapable of winning a war against guerrillas in the jungle. And beyond this, of course, has been the growth of the larger belief that science itself has somehow betrayed us, that it promises evil and not beneficence.

This loss of courage and faith has manifested itself in many ways, but it has found its most immediately dangerous expression in tort (liability) law. Tort law is not only threatening to make the economy uncompetitive, it is warping the American legal system and its judicial philosophy. As Peter W. Huber observes in *The Legal Revolution and Its Consequences*, "No other country in the world administers anything like it." Tort law was "set in place in the

1960s and 1970s by a new generation of lawyers and judges. . . . Some grew famous and more grew rich in selling their services to enforce the rights they themselves invented."

In November a court in Albany had seriously to consider a claim for $1 million in damages against New York state, brought by a woman who, while she was sunbathing on the beach in a public park on Long Island, was hit in the neck by a Frisbee being tossed between a nine-year-old boy and a 20-year-old woman. Her lawyer contended that the Frisbee was a "dangerous instrument" that should not have been allowed on the beach. (Since the idea of the Frisbee was taken from the bakery of that name where the workers whizzed pie plates to each other, rather than laboriously carry them, are we to assume that today the Occupational Safety and Health Administration would have stepped in to stop this skilled, efficient, rapid, but clearly "dangerous" method of conveyance?) At least this woman's claim was thrown out: the judge observed that she could have moved to another part of the beach if she feared injury from these alarming flying objects. Consider also the mother who sued a baseball club because her son was injured by a ball fouled back to their seats. It may well be that they had chosen seats there because her son had hopes of capturing a foul ball as a trophy, in which case the risk was known and invited by the mother; in any event, blame cannot be said to lie with the club, the hitter, or the ball. Here we see one pernicious moral effect of America's growing fear of risk: a commensurate diminution of the notion of individual responsibility for one's actions.

Claims of others' liability for our plights are, with the support of judges, lawyers, and juries, producing a "tort tax" on goods and services. They amount to a $300 billion levy on the American economy, observes Huber, that "accounts for 30 percent of the price of a stepladder and 95 percent of the price of childhood vaccines." The development of tort law has been particularly vicious in its effect because of another phenomenon peculiar to the United States—the award of huge punitive damages (as opposed to nominal damages, intended only to compensate the victim for the actual injury inflicted). The flagrant injustice of many of these awards was illustrated in a case brought against the Monsanto Company that sought damages for 65 plaintiffs for alleged personal injuries from one of the company's products used to make wood preservatives. After the longest-running trial in American history, the jury awarded each plaintiff one dollar in nominal damages, but then, "in a burst of tortured reasoning," as Monsanto Chairman Richard J. Mahoney says, awarded $16 million to the plaintiffs in punitive damages.

There is no justification for this. The Supreme Court has recently agreed to hear a case in which the constitutionality of huge punitive damages will be tested. In an earlier case, Justices Antonin Scalia and Sandra Day O'Connor observed that "this grant of wholly standardless discretion to determine the severity of punishment appears inconsistent with due process." Meanwhile, the awards further frustrate, if they are not crushing, the spirit of innovation in American business. The Conference Board in 1988 conducted a survey of chief executive officers. It showed that uncertainty over potential liability had led almost 50 percent to discontinue product lines, and nearly 40 percent to withhold new products, including beneficial drugs. The fault lies not only with the "wholly standardless discretion" allowed to juries to determine the severity of the punishment, but with the present power of a single jury to decide what conduct is liable for punitive damages.

The result of all this, says Justice Richard Neely of the West Virginia Supreme Court, author of *The Product Liability Mess,* is that "as a state court judge much of my time is devoted to ways to make business pay for everyone else's bad luck." When the step of a stepladder breaks because it was made of defective material, the payment of reasonable damages to the injured party is just. But as anyone with any household experience knows, sometimes a broken stepladder is just a broken stepladder, the result of bad luck; and surely each of us has the individual responsibility to approach any stepladder with some circumspection. The prevailing attitude in America is that people should be safeguarded against not only negligence but bad luck; it has become all too easy for lawyers to manipulate jurors who generally are scientifically ignorant and believe that they can be guaranteed a risk-free society.

One confirmation that the obsessive American aversion to risk is a growth of the last two decades is the proliferation in that time of academic and quasi-academic literature on risk, with such titles as "Public Perceptions of Acceptable Risks as Evidence of Their Cognitive, Technical, and Social Structure." The conclusions of much of this literature were drawn together in 1982 by Mary Douglas and Aaron Wildavsky in *Risk and Culture,* their own still impressive critique of this phenomenon. Among the interesting questions asked by the authors is "Why is asbestos poisoning now seen to be more fearsome than fire," especially when asbestos was introduced and welcomed as a prevention of injury or death by fire? The question is made even more interesting by Mahoney's revelation that Monsanto "abandoned a possible substitute product for asbestos just before commercialization, not because it was unsafe or ineffective, but because a whole generation of liability lawyers had been schooled in asbestos liability theories that could possibly be turned against the substitute." In principle, Douglas and Wildavsky note, a society selects which risks it will worry, and perhaps even legislate, about in the hope of diminishing or eliminating them. But why do Americans seem to be more concerned about the risks of pollution than about the budget deficit, economic stagnation, and even war?

Who are the people who promote the intolerance of risk in contemporary America, and select which risks the society should worry about? It is reasonable and almost certainly correct to assume a link between the attitudes that have led to the slowing of such new and promising industries as space technology and nuclear power, the gross development of liability law and litigation, the concern about environmental pollution, and the finicky attention to one's bodily health, comfort, and even purity. Together they form a syndrome. The people who are environmental extremists are likely also to be exorbitantly fussy about the risks to their bodily purity from a multitude of pollutants, natural and artifical, not much concerned about the progress of the space and nuclear power industries, automatically against manufacturing companies in liability cases, and generally uninterested in creating and maintaining a productive industrial economy.

From such people are drawn the staffs and membership of the special interest groups that have sedulously promoted America's risk aversion. Douglas and Wildavsky counted some 75 national environmental groups alone, and thousands more at state and local levels. By something like sleight of hand they represent themselves as public interest groups, but in fact these risk-averse groups speak for a very clear special interest: those who work not in manufacturing industries, but in the now vast services sector, including government and corporate bureaucracies, and who manufacture nothing. In short, they do not get their hands dirty. So it is easy for them—it does not violate their "class interest"—to be indifferent to creating a productive industrial economy. It is no sweat off their backs if a manufacturer is closed down, and its workers laid off for environmental reasons. The risk-averse groups are drawn from a privileged class.

Since it is in the interest of these groups to multiply regulations and strengthen their control of the economy, they have encouraged the growth of government bureaucracy (federal, state, and local). The federal environmental agencies have grown like a coral reef into this bureaucracy and are as indestructible. Since their bureaucrats also wish to keep their paper-shuffling jobs, they work hand in glove to promote yet more regulation of the manufacturing sector of the economy.

One of the reasons why an aversion to risk has taken hold in America is the manner in which the American political system has developed during precisely the same two decades as the growth of the movement for a risk-free society. All the influences that have been observed and analyzed—the decline of parties, the proliferation of committees and subcommittees and the undermining of seniority in Congress, and the development of the primary electoral system—have given advantage to single-issue special interest groups. Direct-mailings have provided special interest groups, as well as candidates, with direct access to the voters without having to work through the established political institutions that would have forced them to adjust their own aims to accommodate the broader national interest. Never has it been so evident that, as Macaulay wrote to his

American correspondent H. S. Randall, the biographer of Jefferson, "your Constitution is all sail and no anchor." Those now filling the sails are the special interest groups, of whom the risk-averse are the most successful. European countries, in contrast, simply have not permitted the sacrifice of their political systems to the single-issue special interests. Strong parties compel these special interests to adjust to the national interests.

But these groups could not have been so destructively successful if Americans had not already suffered a loss of faith in their nation—a loss of faith in the science and technology on which American progress has been built (while paradoxically they look to science to create their version of a risk-free country); a loss of faith in America's inexhaustible possibilities, its sense of limitlessness; a loss of faith in the ever-advancing frontier, even, as Kennedy proclaimed, the exploration of the new frontier in space. And with it all, a loss of the American adventuring spirit, of the American gusto whose absence the world now laments, the gusto that, until the 1960s,

blew like a fresh wind around the globe, showing what could be accomplished in so short a time by a nation that did not shrink from risk but found it a challenge.

There is something grossly at fault in the conception of the Vietnam War Memorial and the false veneration it excites. It is not, like the Iwo Jima Memorial, a monument to heroism, or even to sacrifice. It is a monument to a loss of life that is seen as wasteful and dishonorable. The feelings it excites reflect a nation that is coming to believe that even war should be fought without risk to its fighting men or risk of defeat.

A nation should lament the deaths, and succor the survivors. But it cannot forever be counting its dead.

QUESTIONS

1. What is the "fear of living"? Should we have it? How can we escape it?

2. What groups encourage the fear of living? Why do they do so?

Warren E. Burger | # Too Many Lawyers, Too Many Suits

Warren E. Burger was the Chief Justice of the U.S. Supreme Court from 1969 to 1986 and presided over several of the most important cases in recent American history.

In a speech to the American Bar Association convention in 1906, the famous legal philosopher and Harvard Law School Dean, Roscoe Pound, criticized lawyers for making litigation a "sporting contest." The A.B.A. did not like the criticism and at first refused to publish the speech. In "The Litigation

Explosion," Walter K. Olson echoes and amplifies Pound's indictment of the legal profession.

Writing especially for nonlawyers, Mr. Olson, a journalist and a senior fellow at the Manhattan Institute, argues that the decline in ethics and the profession's abandonment of age-old constraints on lawyers has created the "litigation business." Lawyers, he tells us, are moving from a profession to a trade, with a corresponding decline in ethics, and they are developing many of the attitudes exhibited by used car dealers. Lawyers' behavior, Mr. Olson says, is largely respon-

From the *New York Times,* May 12, 1991. Reprinted with permission.

sible for the alarming increase in the number of lawsuits in the United States in comparison to other countries that share the basic structure of our legal system. Mr. Olson adds that this rise parallels the rise in the number of law schools and lawyers—producing a kind of "chicken and egg" situation. . . .

To demonstrate that our society is drowning in litigation, one only has to look at the overworked system of justice, the delays in trials, the clogs businessmen face in commerce and a medical profession rendered overcautious for fear of malpractice suits. The litigation explosion, which developed in barely more than a decade beginning in the 1970's, has affected us at all levels, including, as Mr. Olson notes, "the most sensitive and profound relationships of human life." The consequences of the explosion have become painfully obvious. Suits against hospitals and doctors, which went up 300-fold since the 1970's, increased doctors' medical insurance premiums more than 30-fold for some. We have more lawyers per 100,000 people than any other society in the world. We have almost three times as many lawyers per capita as Britain, with whom we share the common law system.

Mr. Olson notes that lawyers who got their start advertising on late-night television are moving from automobile cases into commercial litigation—or any litigation that earns fees. Another recent book, "Shark Tank," by Kim Isaac Eisler, tells the dismal tale of a mega-law firm, Finley Kumble, and reveals, among other things, the growing use of public relations consultants to tout a law firm's skills and accomplishments. The United States stands alone as the glorifier of lawyers and litigation. And who pays? All of us! Malpractice insurance (which can cost a doctor upward of $50,000 a year), higher automobile insurance rates and other such expenses are a "sales tax" paid by all of us, but one that goes into lawyers' pockets.

There was a time, Mr. Olson indicates, when litigation was viewed as undesirable and, at best, like war, a necessary evil. Strict professional standards, tough laws and social stigma discouraged shyster lawyers from the temptation to stir up litigation. Professional ethics were alive and on the minds of most attorneys. Today, however, success at the bar is measured by salaries and bonuses, while many lawyers, Mr. Olson notes, justify their new role in our litigious society by asserting that they are preserving and protecting people's rights—giving more "access to justice." In short, as he aptly puts it, lawyers want Americans to believe that "the more lawsuits there are . . . the closer to perfect the world will become."

The author says this idea—that lawsuits can be used to deter wrongdoing—is one reason for the litigation explosion. Lawsuits, he argues; have become known as assertions of "rights." Lawyers have justified a wide range of grossly unprofessional actions, like flying off to Bhopal, India, to solicit cases, or to Alaska in a chase for cases on oil spills. To those who have praised litigation as having social value per se, one is tempted to cite Judge Learned Hand: "I must say that as a litigant, I should dread a lawsuit beyond almost anything else short of sickness and death."

One way Mr. Olson documents the disintegration of professional ethics is by examining lawyer advertising on television and in print. In 1977, in Bates v. Arizona, the Supreme Court held 5 to 4 that such advertising was protected by the First Amendment; prior to that time, lawyers were forbidden to advertise or to solicit clients. Apart from a handful of "ambulance chasers," only the shysters went further than sending a business card to a potential client or joining the right clubs. Clearly, the disintegration accelerated after the Bates case. But Mr. Olson's argument that the decision itself changed legal ethics attributes too much to it. The author ignores the difference between a profession, like the law, and a trade or business where advertising is more acceptable.

For centuries, the standards of the legal profession were higher than simply compliance with the law. Yet after the Bates ruling, the American Bar Association quickly relaxed its traditional Canons of Professional Ethics, leading some commentators to wonder whether the A.B.A. had become more interested in a large membership than in traditional ethical standards. Today, the ancient and hallowed concept that lawyers are officers of the court is too often treated with an indulgent smile, not only by shyster advertisers, of course, but unfortunately even by some members of the legal profession who have been entrusted with teaching law students.

Legal academia is one of Mr. Olson's frequent targets. For example, he takes on a law professor who argues that in the "contemporary social context" it may be appropriate for lawyers to sponsor and finance litigation. Mr. Olson also perceptively criticizes the tricky business of champerty, allowing a third party, a bank for instance, to finance litigation, with the attorney often agreeing to pay back that third party, or even putting up collateral. Transactions of this kind reflect what has gone on in the savings and loan and the bank scandals—and in the Ivan Boesky and Michael Milken cases. Champerty, as Mr. Olson explains, developed from another form of legal gambling, the contingency fee.

Mr. Olson would be on even sounder ground if he were to expand his discussion and say that a contingency fee is unethical and dishonest, and ought to be unlawful whenever liability is certain, as it often is, for example, in multiple-victim disasters like plane crashes or railroad collisions. Admittedly, unless the measure of damages is fixed by statute, the *amount* of a recovery can vary, even when liability is certain. A highly experienced litigator is likely to get a larger settlement or verdict than an amateur. But if a lawyer soliciting a case is required to tell a client whenever liability is certain, that should at least rule out unconscionable contingency fees of 33 percent and 50 percent in those certain-recovery cases.

Mr. Olson contrasts lawyers' contingency fees with the ethical prohibition against doctors charging a fee contingent on the success of the treatment of a patient. The American Medical Association, unlike the American Bar Association, has not thought that the constitutional protection of advertising called for a change in medical ethics. The Hippocratic oath still prevails among doctors. Because a doctor may *constitutionally* advertise has not meant that doctors may do so *ethically*. Compare this with the A.B.A.'s tentative standard forbidding only "false and misleading" advertising. Shyster advertisers stimulate litigation with their advertisements, offering a "free" conference. This kind of advertising is reminiscent of that old poem we recited in our school days: "'Come into my parlor,' said the spider to the fly."

There is some hope, Mr. Olson points out, of curbing the litigation explosion through third-party arbitration and other forms of "alternative dispute resolution." In 1976, the Judicial Conference of the United States and the A.B.A. sponsored a conference to celebrate the 70th anniversary of Pound's famous speech. That meeting introduced "alternative dispute resolution" into our vocabulary. With hordes of unneeded lawyers flooding the country, perhaps the surplus could be used as arbitrators and mediators.

Who, finally, is to blame for the current problem? Journalists? Lawyers? Law professors? The A.B.A.? The Supreme Court? Mr. Olson indicts all of us; and while there is much to this, those charged with legal stewardship, pre-eminently the A.B.A., can especially be called to account.

The legal and the medical professions are monopolies. Historically, each has largely regulated itself with codes and creeds. Medicine has the Hippocratic oath. Lawyers have no counterpart, but over centuries they have developed common law ethical standards. Up till now, legislative bodies and courts have left regulation to the organized bar. Will that continue? One can only hope that Mr. Olson's book will stimulate moves to control unethical lawyers.

In an era noted for corruption in business, the clergy, academia, science, the political arena—and even among Federal judges—it should not be surprising that there has been a deterioration in the standards and practices of the legal profession. More Federal judges have been found guilty of bribe-taking and tax fraud in the past decade than in the first 190 years of our history. Mr. Olson need not be totally correct in all his criticisms to make "The Litigation Explosion" a valuable contribution to the public interest. Will the legal profession, especially the A.B.A., do anything to clean its own house? It remains uncertain.

QUESTIONS

1. Why does Justice Berger think there are too many lawyers?

2. Can you argue, against Burger, that we need more lawyers?

Mark Dowie | # Pinto Madness

Mark Dowie is a multiple award-winning journalist. He wrote this explosive piece for *Mother
Jones.*

One evening in the mid-1960s, Arjay Miller was
driving home from his office in Dearborn, Michigan,
in the four-door Lincoln Continental that went with
his job as president of the Ford Motor Company. On
a crowded highway, another car struck his from the
rear. The Continental spun around and burst into
flames. Because he was wearing a shoulder-strap seat
belt, Miller was unharmed by the crash, and because
his doors didn't jam he escaped the gasoline-
drenched, flaming wreck. But the accident made a
vivid impression on him. Several months later, on
July 15, 1965, he recounted it to a U.S. Senate sub-
committee that was hearing testimony on auto safety
legislation. "I still have burning in my mind the
image of that gas tank on fire," Miller said. He went
on to express an almost passionate interest in controlling fuel-fed fires in cars that crash or roll over.
He spoke with excitement about the fabric gas tank
Ford was testing at that very moment. "If it proves
out," he promised the senators, "it will be a feature
you will see in our standard cars."

Almost seven years after Miller's testimony, a
woman, whom for legal reasons we will call Sandra
Gillespie, pulled onto a Minneapolis highway in her
new Ford Pinto. Riding with her was a young boy,
whom we'll call Robbie Carlton. As she entered a
merge lane, Sandra Gillespie's car stalled. Another
car rear-ended hers at an impact speed of 28 miles per
hour. The Pinto's gas tank ruptured. Vapors from it
mixed quickly with the air in the passenger compart-
ment. A spark ignited the mixture and the car
exploded in a ball of fire. Sandra died in agony a few
hours later in an emergency hospital. Her passenger,

13-year-old Robbie Carlton, is still alive; he has just
come home from another futile operation aimed at
grafting a new ear and nose from skin on the few
unscarred portions of his badly burned body. (This
accident is real; the details are from police reports.)

Why did Sandra Gillespie's Ford Pinto catch fire
so easily, seven years after Ford's Arjay Miller made
his apparently sincere pronouncements—the same
seven years that brought more safety improvements
to cars than any other period in automotive history?
An extensive investigation by *Mother Jones* over the
past six months has found these answers:

- Fighting strong competition from Volkswagen
  for the lucrative small-car market, the Ford
  Motor Company rushed the Pinto into production in much less than the usual time.
- Ford engineers discovered in pre-production
  crash tests that rear-end collisions would rupture the Pinto's fuel system extremely easily.
- Because assembly-line machinery was already
  tooled when engineers found this defect, top
  Ford officials decided to manufacture the car
  anyway—exploding gas tank and all—*even
  though Ford owned the patent on a much safer
  gas tank.*
- For more than eight years afterwards, Ford successfully lobbied, with extraordinary vigor and
  some blatant lies, against a key government
  safety standard that would have forced the company to change the Pinto's fire-prone gas tank.

By conservative estimates Pinto crashes have
caused 500 burn deaths to people who would not
have been seriously injured if the car had not burst
into flames. The figure could be as high as 900. Burning Pintos have become such an embarrassment to
Ford that its advertising agency, J. Walter Thomp-

son, dropped a line from the end of a radio spot that read "Pinto leaves you with that warm feeling."

Ford knows the Pinto is a firetrap, yet it has paid out millions to settle damage suits out of court, and it is prepared to spend millions more lobbying against safety standards. With a half million cars rolling off the assembly lines each year, Pinto is the biggest-selling subcompact in America, and the company's operating profit on the car is fantastic. Finally, in 1977, new Pinto models have incorporated a few minor alterations necessary to meet that federal standard Ford managed to hold off for eight years. Why did the company delay so long in making these minimal, inexpensive improvements?

- Ford waited eight years because its internal "cost-benefit analysis," *which places a dollar value on human life,* said it wasn't profitable to make the changes sooner. . . .

———————

Cost-benefit analysis was used only occasionally in government until President Kennedy appointed Ford Motor Company President Robert McNamara to be Secretary of Defense. McNamara, originally an accountant, preached cost benefit with all the force of a Biblical zealot. Stated in its simplest terms, cost-benefit analysis says that if the cost is greater than the benefit, the project is not worth it—no matter what the benefit. Examine the cost of every action, decision, contract, part, or change, the doctrine says, then carefully evaluate the benefits (in dollars) to be certain that they exceed the cost before you begin a program or—and this is the crucial part for our story—pass a regulation.

As a management tool in a business in which profits matter over everything else, cost-benefit analysis makes a certain amount of sense. Serious problems come, however, when public officials who ought to have more than corporate profits at heart apply cost-benefit analysis to every conceivable decision. The inevitable result is that they must place a dollar value on human life.

Ever wonder what your life is worth in dollars? Perhaps $10 million? Ford has a better idea: $200,000.

Remember, Ford had gotten the federal regulators to agree to talk auto safety in terms of cost-benefit analysis. But in order to be able to argue that various safety costs were greater than their benefits, Ford needed to have a dollar value figure for the "benefit." Rather than be so uncouth as to come up with such a price tag itself, the auto industry pressured the National Highway Traffic Safety Administration to do so. And in a 1972 report the agency decided a human life was worth $200,725. (For its reasoning, see [Table 1].) Inflationary forces have recently pushed the figure up to $278,000.

Furnished with this useful tool, Ford immediately went to work using it to prove why various safety improvements were too expensive to make.

Nowhere did the company argue harder that it should make no changes than in the area of rupture-

TABLE 1 What's Your Life Worth? Societal Cost Components for Fatalities, 1972 NHTSA Study

Component	1971 Costs
Future productivity losses	
Direct	$132,000
Indirect	41,300
Medical costs	
Hospital	700
Other	425
Property damage	1,500
Insurance administration	4,700
Legal and court	3,000
Employer losses	1,000
Victim's pain and suffering	10,000
Funeral	900
Assets (lost consumption)	5,000
Miscellaneous accident costs	200
Total per fatality: $200,725	

Here is a chart from a federal study showing how the National Highway Traffic Safety Administration has calculated the value of a human life. The estimate was arrived at under pressure from the auto industry. The Ford Motor Company has used it in cost-benefit analyses arguing why certain safety measures are not "worth" the savings in human lives. The calculation above is a breakdown of the estimated cost to society every time someone is killed in a car accident. We were not able to find anyone, either in the government or at Ford, who could explain how the $10,000 figure for "pain and suffering" had been arrived at.

prone fuel tanks. Not long after the government arrived at the $200,725-per-life figure, it surfaced, rounded off to a cleaner $200,000, in an internal Ford memorandum. This cost-benefit analysis argued that Ford should not make an $11-per-car improvement that would prevent 180 fiery deaths a year. (This minor change would have prevented gas tanks from breaking so easily both in rear-end collisions, like Sandra Gillespie's, and in rollover accidents, where the same thing tends to happen.)

Ford's cost-benefit table [Table 2] is buried in a seven-page company memorandum entitled "Fatalities Associated with Crash-Induced Fuel Leakage and Fires." The memo argues that there is no financial benefit in complying with proposed safety standards that would admittedly result in fewer auto fires, fewer burn deaths and fewer burn injuries. Naturally, memoranda that speak so casually of "burn deaths" and "burn injuries" are not released to the public. They are very effective, however, with Department of Transportation officials indoctrinated in McNamarian cost-benefit analysis.

TABLE 2 $11 vs. a Burn Death: Benefits and Costs Relating to Fuel Leakage Associated With the Static Rollover Test Portion of FMVSS 208

Benefits

Savings: 180 burn deaths, 180 serious burn injuries, 2,100 burned vehicles.
Unit cost: $200,000 per death, $67,000 per injury, $700 per vehicle.
Total benefit: 180 × ($200,000) + 180 × ($67,000) + 2,100 × ($700) = $49.5 million.

Costs

Sales: 11 million cars, 1.5 million light trucks.
Unit cost: $11 per car, $11 per truck.
Total cost: 11,000,000 × ($11) + 1,500,000 × ($11) = $137 million.

From Ford Motor Company internal memorandum: "Fatalities Associated with Crash-Induced Fuel Leakage and Fires."

The Nixon Transportation Secretaries were the kind of regulatory officials big business dreams of. They understood and loved capitalism and thought like businessmen. Yet, best of all, they came into office uninformed on technical automotive matters. And you could talk "burn injuries" and "burn deaths" with these guys, and they didn't seem to envision children crying at funerals and people hiding in their homes with melted faces. Their minds appeared to have leapt right to the bottom line—more safety meant higher prices, higher prices meant lower sales and lower sales meant lower profits.

So when J. C. Echold, Director of Automotive Safety (which means chief anti-safety lobbyist) for Ford wrote to the Department of Transportation—which he still does frequently, at great length—he felt secure attaching a memorandum that in effect says it is acceptable to kill 180 people and burn another 180 every year, *even though we have the technology that could save their lives for $11 a car.*

Furthermore, Echold attached this memo, confident, evidently, that the Secretary would question neither his low death/injury statistics nor his high cost estimates. But it turns out, on closer examination, that both these findings were misleading.

First, note that Ford's table shows an equal number of burn deaths and burn injuries. This is false. All independent experts estimate that for each person who dies by an auto fire, many more are left with charred hands, faces and limbs. Andrew McGuire of the Northern California Burn Center estimates the ratio of burn injuries to deaths at ten to one instead of the one to one Ford shows here. Even though Ford values a burn at only a piddling $67,000 instead of the $200,000 price of life, the true ratio obviously throws the company's calculations way off.

The other side of the equation, the alleged $11 cost of a fire-prevention device, is also a misleading estimation. One document that was *not* sent to Washington by Ford was a "Confidential" cost analysis *Mother Jones* has managed to obtain, showing that crash fires could be largely prevented for considerably *less* than $11 a car. The cheapest method involves placing a heavy rubber bladder inside the gas tank to keep the fuel from spilling if the tank ruptures. Goodyear had developed the bladder and had demonstrated it to the automotive industry. We have in our possession crash-test reports showing that the Goodyear bladder worked well. On December 2, 1970 (*two years before* Echold sent his cost-benefit memo to Washington), Ford Motor Company ran a rear-end crash test on a car with the rubber bladder in the gas tank. The tank ruptured, but no fuel leaked. On January 15, 1971, Ford again tested the bladder and again it worked. The total purchase and installation cost of the bladder would have been $5.08 per car. That $5.08 could have saved the lives of Sandra Gillespie and several hundred others.

QUESTIONS

1. What was the fundamental moral mistake made by Ford?

2. Insurers place dollar values on human lives all the time—otherwise they would go out of business. When is it permissible to assign a cash value to a human life, and when not? What differentiates between the cases?

Patricia Werhane

The Pinto Case and the Rashomon Effect

Patricia Werhane teaches business ethics at the University of Virginia and currently holds the Wicklander Chair in Business Ethics and is Director of the Institute for Business and Professional Ethics at De Paul University in Chicago. This is from her book, *Moral Imagination and Management Decision-Making.*

The Academy Award-winning 1950 Japanese movie *Rashomon* depicts an incident involving an outlaw, a rape or seduction of a woman, and a murder or suicide of her husband. A passerby, who is also the narrator, explains how the story is told to officials from four different perspectives: that of the outlaw, the woman, the husband, and himself. The four narratives agree that the outlaw, wandering through the forest, came upon the woman on a horse led by her husband; the outlaw tied up the husband; the woman and the outlaw had intercourse in front of the bound husband; and the husband was found dead. The narratives do not agree on how these events occurred or who killed the husband. The outlaw contends that consensual intercourse occurred between him and the wife, and he claims to have killed the husband. The wife depicts the sexual act as rape and claims that because of her disgrace, she killed her husband. The husband, through a medium, says that the sexual act began as rape and ended as consent, and that, in shame after being untied by the outlaw, he killed himself. The passerby's story confirms the husband's account of the sexual contact but claims that the bandit was initially afraid to kill the husband. The passerby depicted both men as cowards, preferring to save their own lives rather than protect the wife. Eventually, however, the husband was killed by the bandit. Interestingly, because the passerby is also the narrator of the film, recounting to friends the strange contradictory reportings of this event, we tend to believe his version. But what actually took place is never resolved.

In the preceding chapters I used a series of cases or narratives that depicted incidents in corporate decision-making. In this chapter I examine the role of narratives and make the following claim: the ways

From Patricia Werhane, *Moral Imagination and Management Decision-Making* (New York: Oxford University Press, 1999), pp. 69–75 we present or re-present a story, the narrative we employ, and the conceptual framing of that story affect its content, its moral analysis, and the subsequent evaluation (Chambers, 1996, 25). Sometimes, narratives of a particular set of events contradict each other. Other times, when one narrative becomes dominant, we appeal to that story for reinforcement of facts, assuming it represents what actually happened, even though it may have distorting effects. The result in either case is a *Rashomon* effect. Yet we seldom carefully examine the narrative we use, often unaware of the "frame" or mental model at work. If my thesis is correct, it is important, morally important, to understand the constructive nature and limits of narratives. . . .

We are at once byproducts of, characters in, and authors of, our own stories (e.g., Johnson, 1993, 153; Sartre, 1956). Still, sometimes we become so embroiled in a particular set of narratives, of our own making or not, that we fail to compare it with other accounts or evaluate its implications. . . .

Let us begin with some accounts of the Ford Pinto. The accounts of these cases are Mark Dowie's "Pinto Madness" from *Mother Jones,* later revised and reprinted in *Business and Society;* "Beyond Products Liability" by Michael Schmitt and William W. May from the *University of Detroit Journal of Urban Law;* Manuel Velasquez's treatment of the Pinto in his book *Business Ethics* (second edition); Dekkers L. Davidson and Kenneth Goodpaster's Harvard Business School case, "Managing Product Safety: The Ford Pinto"; Ford Motor Company's statements from its lawsuit, *State of Indiana vs. Ford Motor Company;* and Michael Hoffman's case/essay, "The Ford Pinto." Reporting on these incidents, different commentators present "independently supportable facts" (Schmitt and May, 1979, 1022). In each instance, the commentator claims to be presenting facts, not assumptions, commentary, or conjecture. Yet these "facts" seem to differ. One report, Mark Dowie's, one of the earliest accounts of the case, becomes the dominant narrative despite some of its suspect claims.

The Grimshaw/Pinto case began the documentation of a series of Pinto automobile fires involving rear-end collisions, usually at low speeds, that caused the gas tanks in the Pintos to explode. There is *one* indisputable set of data upon which all commentators agree:

> On May 28, 1972 Mrs. Lily Gray was driving a six-month old Pinto on Interstate 15 near San Bernardino, California. In the car with her was Richard Grimshaw, a thirteen-year old boy. . . . Mrs. Gray stopped in San Bernardino for gasoline, got back onto the freeway (Interstate 15) and proceeded toward her destination at sixty to sixty-five miles per hour. As she approached Route 30 off-ramp, . . . the Pinto suddenly stalled and coasted to a halt in the middle lane. . . . [T]he driver of a 1962 Ford Galaxie was unable to avoid colliding with the Pinto. Before impact the Galaxie had been braked to a speed of from twenty-eight to thirty-seven miles per hour.
>
> At the moment of impact, the Pinto caught fire and its interior burst into flames. The crash had driven the Pinto's gas tank forward and punctured it against the flange on the differential housing. . . . Mrs. Gray died a few days later. . . . Grimshaw managed to survive with severe burns over 90 per cent of his body. (*Grimshaw v. Ford Motor Co.,* 1978, 359; Velasquez, 1988, 122)

What is the background behind the development of the Pinto? Lee Iacocca, then CEO of Ford, stated publicly that in order to meet Japanese competition, Ford decided to design a subcompact car that would weigh less than 2,000 pounds and cost less than $2,000 (Davidson and Goodpaster, 1983). According to Davidson and Goodpaster, Ford began planning the Pinto in June 1967 and began producing it in September 1970. This represented a 38-month turnaround time as opposed to the industry average of 43 months for engineering and developing a new automobile (Davidson and Goodpaster, 1983, 4). Mark Dowie claims that the development was "rushed" into 25 months (1977, 20); Velasquez says it occurred in "under two years" (1988, 120); Hoffman, claims that Ford "rushed the Pinto into production in much less than the usual time" (1984, 133). Although the actual time of development may seem unimportant, critics of the Pinto design argue that *because* it was "rushed into production," the Pinto was not as carefully designed or as carefully checked for safety as a model created over a 43-month time span (Dowie, 1977; Velasquez, 1988). But if it took 38 months rather than 25, perhaps the Pinto was not rushed into production after all.

The Pinto was designed so that the gas tank was placed behind the rear axle. According to Davidson and Goodpaster, "[a]t that time almost every American-made car had the fuel tank located in the same place" (1983, 4). Dowie wonders why Ford did not place the gas tank over the rear axle, Ford's patented design for its Capri models. This placement is confirmed by Dowie, Velasquez, and some Ford engineers as the "safest place." Yet, according to Davidson and Goodpaster, other studies at Ford showed that the Capri placement actually increased the likelihood of ignition inside the automobile (1983, 4). Moreover, such placement reduces storage space and precludes a hatchback design. Velasquez says that "[b]ecause the Pinto was a rush project, styling preceded engineering" (Velasquez, 1988, 120), thus accounting for the gas tank placement. This notion may have been derived from Dowie's quotation, allegedly from a "Ford engineer, who doesn't want his name used," that "[t]his company is run by salesmen, not engineers; so the priority is styling, not safety" (1977, 23).

Dowie claims that in addition to rushing the Pinto into production, "Ford engineers discovered in preproduction crash tests that rear-end collisions would rupture the Pinto's fuel system extremely easily" (1977, 18). According to Dowie, Ford crash-tested the Pinto in a secret location, and in every test made at over 25 mph the fuel tank ruptured. But according to Ford, Pinto's gas tank exploded during many of its tests, because, following government guidelines, Ford had tested the car using a fixed barrier standard, wherein the vehicle is towed backwards into a fixed barrier at the speed specified in the test. Ford argued that Pinto behaved well under a less stringent moving-barrier standard, which, Ford contended, is a more realistic test (Davidson and Goodpaster, 1983; *State of Indiana v. Ford Motor Company,* 1979).

Ford Motor Company and the commentators on this case agree that in 1971, before Ford launched the automobile, an internal study showed that a rubber bladder inner tank would improve the reliability of Pinto's gas tank placement. The bladder would cost perhaps $5.08 (Dowie, 1977, 29; Schmitt and May,

1979, 1023), $5.80 (Davidson and Goodpaster, 1983), or $11 (Velasquez, 1988, 120). The $11 figure probably refers to a design adjustment required to meet a later government rollover standard. However, the idea of this installation was discarded, according to Ford, because of the unreliability of the rubber at cold temperatures, a conjecture not mentioned by commentators. Dowie also contends that Ford could have reduced the dangers from rear-end collisions by installing a $1 plastic baffle between the gas tank and the differential housing to reduce the likelihood of gas tank perforation. I can find no other verification of this contention.

All commentators claim that Ford did a cost/benefit analysis to determine whether it would be more costly to change the Pinto design or to assume the liability costs for burn victims, and memos to that effect were cited as evidence at the Grimshaw trial (*Grimshaw v. Ford Motor Co.,* 1978, 570). However, according to trial evidence submitted by Ford in *Grimshaw,* this estimate was made in 1973, the year *after* the Grimshaw accident, after Ford had evaluated a proposed new government rollover standard. According to evidence presented by Ford in *Grimshaw,* Ford calculated that it would cost $11 per auto to meet the rollover requirement. Ford used government data for the cost of a life ($200,000 per person), and projected an estimate of 180 burn deaths from rollovers. The study was not applicable to rear-end collisions, as some commentators, following Dowie's story, claimed.

Many reports of this case noted the $200,000 figure as Ford's price of a human life. Dowie says, for example, "Ever wonder what your life is worth in dollars? Perhaps $10 million? Ford has a better idea: $200,000" (1977, 24). In fact, it was the National Highway Traffic Safety Administration's 1973 figure.

How many people have died as a result of being inside a Pinto during a rear-end collision? "By conservative estimates Pinto crashes have caused 500 burn deaths to people who would not have been seriously injured had the car not burst into flames. The figure could be as high as 900," Dowie claimed (1977, 18). Hoffman repeats Dowie's figures, word for word (1984, 133). A more cautious Velasquez claims that by 1978 at least 53 people had died and "many more had been severely burnt" (Velasquez, 1988, 122). Schmitt and May, quoting a 1978 article in an issue of *Business and Society Review* that I could not find, estimate the number as "at least 32" (1979, 1024, and 1024 at note 16). Davidson and Goodpaster claim that by 1978, NHTSA estimated that 38 cases involved 27 fatalities (1983, 5).

In the 1978 trial that followed the Grimshaw accident, a jury awarded Grimshaw at least $125 million in punitive damages. *Auto News* printed a headline, "Ford Fights Pinto Case: Jury Gives 128 Million" on February 13, 1978. The commonly cited figure of $125 million is in the court records as the total initial punitive award. The $128 million might be the total award including punitive damages. This award was later reduced on appeal to $3.5 million, a fact that is seldom cited.

A second famous Pinto accident led Indiana to charge Ford with criminal liability. Hoffman reports the incident that led to the charges, on which all agree:

> On August 10, 1978, a tragic automobile accident occurred on US Highway 33 near Goshen, Indiana. Sisters Judy and Lynn Ulrich (ages 18 and 16, respectively) and their cousin Donna Ulrich (age 18) were struck from the rear in their 1973 Ford Pinto by a van. The gas tank of the Pinto ruptured, the car burst into flames, and the three teenagers were burned to death. (1984, 132)

There are two points of interest in this case that apparently led the jury to find Ford not guilty. First, in June 1978 Ford recalled 1.5 million Pintos in order to modify the fuel tank. There was some evidence that the Ulrich auto had not participated in the recall (*State of Indiana v. Ford Motor Company,* 1979). Second, Ulrich's Pinto was hit from behind at 50 mph by a van driven by a man named Duggar. Dug-

gar later testified that he looked down for a "smoke" and then hit the car, although, according to police reports, the Ulrich car had safety blinkers on. Found in Duggar's van were at least two empty beer bottles and an undisclosed amount of marijuana. Yet this evidence, cited in the *State of Indiana v. Ford Motor Co.* case, is seldom mentioned in the context of the Ulrich tragedy, and Duggar was never indicted.

The purpose of this exercise is not to exonerate Ford or to argue for bringing back the Pinto. Rather, it is to point out a simple phenomenon—a story can become a narrative and can be taken as fact even when other alleged equally verifiable facts contradict that story. Moreover, one narrative can dominate as *the facts.* Dowie's interesting tale of the Pinto became the prototype for Pinto cases; many authors accepted his version without going back to check whether his data were correct or to question why some of his data contradicted Ford and government claims. Dowie's reporting of Grimshaw became a prototype for the narrative of the Ulrich case as well, so that questions concerning the recall of the Ulrich auto and Duggar's performance were virtually ignored. Such omissions not only make Ford look better, they also question the integrity of these reports and cases. Thus, this set of cases illustrates pitfalls that develop when a particular narrative becomes the paradigm for data and fact.

QUESTIONS

1. What is the "Rashomon effect?" How does it affect the Pinto case?

2. How do the stories we tell about ourselves (and to ourselves) influence our moral decisions? Do you ever see yourself as a character in a drama that you are creating? But what about when the drama becomes all too real? What about the other characters in this drama?

CASES

CASE 10.1
The Skateboard Scare
William H. Shaw and Vincent Barry

Colin Brewster, owner of Brewster's Bicycle Shop, had to admit that skateboard sales had salvaged his business now that interest in the bicycle seemed to have peaked. In fact, skateboard business was so brisk that Brewster could hardly keep them in stock. But the picture was far from rosy.

Just last week a concerned consumer group visited his shop. They informed Brewster that they had ample evidence to prove that skateboards present a real and immediate hazard to consumer safety. Brewster conceded that the group surely provided enough statistical support; the number of broken bones and concussions that had resulted directly and indirectly from accidents involving skateboards was shocking. But he thought the group's position was fundamentally unsound because, as he told them, "It's not the skateboards that are unsafe but how people use them."

Committee members weren't impressed with Brewster's distinction. They likened it to saying automobile manufacturers shouldn't be conscious of consumer safety because it's not the automobiles that are unsafe but how we drive them. Brewster objected that automobiles present an entirely different problem, because a number of things could be done to ensure their safe use. "But what can you do about a skateboard?" he asked them. "Besides, I don't manufacture them, I just sell them."

The committee pointed out that other groups were attacking the problem on the manufacturing level. What they expected of Brewster was some responsible management of the problem at the local retail level. They pointed out that recently Brewster had run a series of local television ads portraying young but accomplished skateboarders performing fancy flips and turns. The ad implied that anyone could easily accomplish such feats. Only yesterday one parent had told the committee of her child's breaking an arm attempting such gymnastics after having purchased a Brewster skateboard. "Obviously," Brewster countered, "the woman has an irresponsible kid whose activities she should monitor, not me." He pointed out that his ad was not intended to imply anyone could or should do those tricks, no more than an ad showing a car traveling at high speeds while doing stunt tricks implies that you should drive that way.

The committee disagreed. They said Brewster not only should discontinue such misleading advertising but also should actively publicize the potential dangers of skateboarding. Specifically, the committee wanted him to display prominently beside his skateboard stock the statistical data testifying to its hazards. Furthermore, he should make sure anyone buying a skateboard reads this material before purchase.

Brewster argued that the committee's demands were unreasonable. "Do you have any idea what effect that would have on sales?" he asked them.

Committee members readily admitted that they were less interested in his sales than in their children's safety. Brewster told them that in this matter their children's safety was their responsibility, not his. But the committee was adamant. Members told Brewster that they'd be back in a week to find out what positive steps, if any, he'd taken to correct the

William H. Shaw and Vincent Barry, *Moral Issues in Business,* 5th ed. (Belmont, CA: Wadsworth, 1996).

problem. In the event he'd done nothing, they indicated they were prepared to picket his shop.

NOTE

1. *BUSINESS AND SOCIETY REVIEW* 69 (Spring 1989): 67; "Tobacco's Toll," *Newsweek* (international edition), November 9, 1979; and James Shriver, "Sharp Drop in Cigaret Smokers," *San Francisco Chronicle,* May 31, 1989, A4.

QUESTIONS

1. With whom do you agree—Brewster or the committee? Why?

2. Would you criticize Brewster's advertisements? Do you think the demand that he publicize the dangers of skateboarding is reasonable?

3. What responsibilities, if any, do retailers have to ensure consumer safety? Compare the responsibilities of manufacturers, skateboarders, and parents.

CASE 10.2

Aspartame: Miracle Sweetener or Dangerous Substance?

William H. Shaw and Vincent Barry

Diet Coke stands alone as the greatest overnight success in the marketplace. But when you quaff a Diet Coke on a hot summer's day, you may be doing more than quenching your thirst. You could be inviting a headache, depression, seizure, aggressive behavior, visual impairment, or menstrual disturbances. You might even be loading your tissues with a carcinogen. The reason, say most nutritionists and medical scientists, is that soft drinks like Diet Coke—and a host of other products—contain the low-calorie sweetener aspartame, which goes by the name NutraSweet.

In 1983 the Reagan administration's commissioner of the Food and Drug Administration, Dr. Arthur Hull Hayes, Jr., approved the use of aspartame in carbonated beverages. In one stroke, he seemed to end the prolonged controversy over the safety of the artificial sweetener. That controversy erupted in 1974, when the FDA first approved aspartame as a food additive.

No sooner had aspartame's manufacturer, G. D. Searle & Co., begun to celebrate the FDA's initial approval of its profits-promising sweetener than things turned sour. Largely as a result of the rancorous protests of lawyer James Turner, author of a book about food additives, the FDA suspended its approval. Armed with the results of animal experiments conducted at Washington University, Turner insisted that aspartame could damage the brain, especially in infants and children. Searle pooh-poohed the charges, citing experiments of its own that, it said, established the safety of its chemical sweetener. Unconvinced, Dr. Alexander M. Schmidt, then FDA commissioner, appointed a task force of six scientists to examine Searle's experiments.

The task force's findings did not corroborate Searle's rosy assurances of safety. In fact, it concluded that Searle had distorted the safety data to win FDA approval of aspartame. According to the task force's 1976 report, "Searle made a number of deliberate decisions which seemingly were calculated to minimize the chances of discovering toxicity and/or to allay FDA concern." Schmidt not only endorsed the task force's findings but told Congress in April 1976 that he saw in Searle's experiments "a pattern of conduct which compromises the scientific integrity of the studies." He added: "At the heart of the FDA's regulatory process is the ability to rely upon the integrity of the basic safety data submitted by the sponsors of regulated products. Our investigation clearly demonstrates that, in the G. D. Searle Co., we have no basis

William H. Shaw and Vincent Barry, *Moral Issues in Business* 5th ed. (Belmont, CA: Wadsworth, 1996).

for such reliance now." Specifically addressing the tests of aspartame, the commissioner and other FDA officials reported such irregularities as test animals recorded as dead on one date and alive on another and autopsies on rats conducted a year after the rodents had died during a feeding experiment. Schmidt further branded Searle's animal studies as "poorly conceived, carelessly executed, or inaccurately analyzed or reported."

Understandably, Searle wasn't about to allow these broadsides to pass unanswered. In a May 1976 letter to Schmidt, the firm's executive vice president, James Buzard, asserted that the FDA task force investigators "totally failed to find fraud, totally failed to find concrete evidence of an intent to deceive or mislead the agency or any advisory committee, or a failure to make any required report."

Sticking to his opinions, Schmidt asked the Justice Department to investigate the possibility that Searle had deliberately misled the FDA. After looking into the matter, a grand jury brought no indictment against the company. Nevertheless, under FDA pressure Searle enlisted the services of Universities Associated for Research and Education in Pathology (UAREP), a private group of fifteen universities that work under contracts and grants for paying clients. UAREP was to scrutinize eight of the fifteen as yet unreviewed aspartame studies to check Searle's conclusions. Under the terms of its agreement with Searle, UAREP would submit its findings to the company before submitting them to the FDA. Searle said that procedure was necessary to ensure accuracy. But Adrian Gross, a task force member and senior FDA scientist, expressed misgivings about the arrangement to his superiors. The report that UAREP submitted, Gross argued, "may well be interpreted as nothing short of an improper whitewash."

Despite Gross's concern, the UAREP body proceeded, focusing solely on the microscopic slides produced by Searle in its animal experiments. In the end, the consortium could find nothing improper in Searle's interpretation of the slides. But James Turner complained that the review was unacceptably narrow and incomplete because it had failed to consider either the design or execution of Searle's experiments. He was assured in writing that these and other relevant matters would be taken up by a public board of inquiry.

That board, made up of three independent scientists, had plenty to do. By January 1980, when the panel convened, the FDA had amassed 140 volumes of data on aspartame. Unable to deal with the mountain of information, the board concentrated on the same studies UAREP had examined. On September 30, 1980, the panel recommended that the FDA withdraw approval of aspartame. In making its recommendation, the board said it couldn't exclude the possibility that aspartame causes cancer in rats.

It thus appeared that the FDA would keep aspartame off the market for good. But in November 1980 the country elected a new president, and within a few short months, the chemical would be sweetening a multitude of products and making millions of dollars for its manufacturer.

The day after Ronald Reagan was inaugurated president of the United States, Searle repetitioned the FDA to approve the sale of aspartame. It based its appeal on the same data it had previously submitted. Six months later, on July 24, 1981, the new FDA commissioner, Dr. Hayes, approved the sale of aspartame as a "tabletop sweetener and ingredient of dry foods."

In approving the product for sale, Hayes discounted the possible cancer connection. He cited a study done in 1981 by Ajinomoto, a Japanese chemical firm. Its study found that, while rats fed with aspartame did develop more brain tumors than untreated rats, the increase was not statistically significant. The commissioner took the results as breaking the tie between two similar experiments conducted earlier by Searle, which had produced differing results.

Some scientists immediately discredited the Ajinomoto experiments, claiming that they used a strain of rat different from the one used in earlier Searle studies. In reply, Searle insisted that all three rat studies demonstrated that aspartame was noncarcinogenic.

In 1983 Searle successfully petitioned the FDA to permit aspartame to be used in carbonated beverages. Hayes gave FDA approval on July 8, 1983. Worldwide sales of aspartame the next year were estimated at $600 million.

One month after granting Searle permission to use aspartame in soft drinks, Dr. Hayes resigned from the FDA to become dean of New York Medical College. Three months later, in November 1983, he also took a job as senior scientific consultant to Burson-

Marsteller, the public relations firm that has Searle's account for aspartame.

QUESTIONS

1. Does the aspartame controversy tend to support or belie the assumption that regulatory agencies are sufficient to ensure consumer safety?

2. Who do you think should have primary responsibility for ensuring product safety—manufacturer or government agency?

3. Does requiring a label warning consumers that a food or beverage contains carcinogenic chemicals sufficiently discharge a government agency's obligation to protect the public? Or should such products be banned? What if the product contains a substance that is only possibly carcinogenic?

CASE 10.3
Children and Reasonably Safe Products
Joseph R. Desjardins and John J. McCall

When children are involved, how safe need a "reasonably safe" product be? How vigilant should manufacturers be in forseeing misuse? Consider two cases.

In *Ritter v. Narragansett Electric Co.,* a four-year-old girl was injured when she used an oven door as a stepstool to stand on so that she could peak into a pot on the top of the stove. Her weight caused the stove to tip over, causing serious injury to the child. The first question concerns a possible defective design. Was the stove defective because it could not support thirty pounds on the oven door without tipping? A for-seeable use of the stove could involve placing a heavy roasting pan on the oven door while checking food during preparation. If the stove tipped over and injured the cook during this use, it is very likely that a court would rule against the manufacturer on the grounds of a design defect. The manufacturer should have forseen the use of the door as a shelf. Could the manufacturer forsee the use of the door as a stepstool? Should it matter, since the product was defective in this regard anyway?

Vincer v. Esther Williams Swimming Pool Co.
concerned a two-year-old boy who climbed the ladder of an above-ground swimming pool at his grandparents' house and fell into the pool. He remained under water for some time before being rescued. As a result, he suffered severe and permanent brain damage. His family sued the manufacturer, claiming that the pool should have had a self-closing gate and/or an automatically retractable ladder. Knowing that children are attracted to swimming pools and knowing that many children drown each year because of such accidents, should the manufacturer have forseen this possibility? Was it "unreasonable" not to include protections against such an accident in the design of the swimming pool?

QUESTIONS

1. Courts ruled against the manufacturer in *Ritter,* and in favor of the manufacturer in *Vincer.* Do you agree? Why or why not?

2. Does your determination of "reasonably safe product" depend on the person who is using it? If so, are any products "reasonably safe" where children are concerned? If so, who decides what is "reasonable"?

Joseph R. Desjardins and John J. McCall, *Contemporary Issues in Business Ethics,* 2nd ed. (Belmont, CA: Wadsworth, 1990).

CASE 10.4
Living and Dying with Asbestos
William H. Shaw and Vincent Barry

Asbestos is a fibrous mineral used for fireproofing, electrical insulation, building materials, brake linings, and chemical filters. If exposed long enough to asbestos particles—usually ten or more years—people can develop a chronic lung inflammation called asbestosis, which makes breathing difficult and infection easy. Also linked to asbestos exposure is mesothelioma, a cancer of the chest lining that sometimes doesn't develop until forty years after the first exposure. Although the first major scientific conference on the dangers of asbestos was not held until 1964, the asbestos industry knew of its hazards more than sixty years ago.

As early as 1932, the British documented the occupational hazards of asbestos dust inhalation. Indeed, on September 25, 1935, the editors of the trade journal *Asbestos* wrote to Summer Simpson, president of Raybestos-Manhattan, a leading asbestos company, asking permission to publish an article on the dangers of asbestos. Simpson refused and later praised the magazine for not printing the article. In a letter to Vandivar Brown, secretary of Johns-Manville, another asbestos manufacturer, Simpson observed: "The less said about asbestosis the better off we are." Brown agreed, adding that any article on asbestosis should reflect American, not English, data.

In fact, American data were available, and Brown, as one of the editors of the journal, knew it. Working on behalf of Raybestos-Manhattan and Johns-Manville and their insurance carrier, Metropolitan Life Insurance Company, Anthony Lanza had conducted research between 1929 and 1931 on 126 workers with three or more years of asbestos exposure. But Brown and others were not pleased with the paper Lanza submitted to them for editorial review. Lanza, said Brown, had failed to portray asbestosis as

milder than silicosis, a lung disease caused by long-term inhalation of silica dust and resulting in chronic shortness of breath. Under the then-pending Workmen's Compensation law, silicosis was categorized as a compensable disease. If asbestosis was worse than silicosis or indistinguishable from it, then it, too, would have to be covered. Apparently Brown didn't want this and thus requested that Lanza depict asbestosis as less serious than silicosis. Lanza complied and also omitted from his published report the fact that more than half the workers examined—67 of 126—were suffering from asbestosis.

Meanwhile, Summer Simpson was writing F. H. Schulter, president of Thermoid Rubber Company, to suggest that several manufacturers sponsor additional asbestos experiments. The sponsors, said Simpson, could exercise oversight prerogatives; they "could determine from time to time after the findings are made whether we wish any publication or not." Added Simpson: "It would be a good idea to distribute the information to the medical fraternity, providing it is of the right type and would not injure our companies." Lest there be any question about the arbiter of publication, Brown wrote to officials at the laboratory conducting the tests:

> It is our further understanding that the results obtained will be considered the property of those who are advancing the required funds, who will determine whether, to what extent and in what manner they shall be made public. In the event it is deemed desirable that the results be made public, the manuscript of your study will be submitted to us for approval prior to publication [Brown].

Industry officials were concerned with more than controlling public information flow. They also

William H. Shaw and Vincent Barry, *Moral Issues in Business,* 9th ed, (Belmont, CA: Wadsworth, 2004). Notes were deleted from this text.

sought to deny workers early evidence of their asbestosis. Dr. Kenneth Smith, medical director of a Johns-Manville plant in Canada, explained why seven workers he found to have asbestosis should not be informed of their disease:

> It must be remembered that although these men have the X-ray evidence of asbestosis, they are working today and definitely are not disabled from asbestosis. They have not been told of this diagnosis, for it is felt that as long as the man feels well, is happy at home and at work, and his physical condition remains good, nothing should be said. When he becomes disabled and sick, then the diagnosis should be made and the claim submitted *by the Company*. The fibrosis of this disease is irreversible and permanent so that eventually compensation will be paid to each of these men. But as long as the man is not disabled, it is felt that he should not be told of his condition so that he can live and work in peace and the Company can benefit by his many years of experience. Should the man be told of his condition today there is a very definite possibility that he would become mentally and physically ill, simply through the knowledge that he has asbestosis.

When lawsuits filed by asbestos workers who had developed cancer reached the industry in the 1950s, Dr. Smith suggested that the industry retain the Industrial Health Foundation to conduct a cancer study that would, in effect, squelch the asbestos-cancer connection. The asbestos companies refused, claiming that such a study would only bring further unfavorable publicity to the industry and that there wasn't enough evidence linking asbestos and cancer industrywide to warrant it.

Shortly before his death in 1977, Dr. Smith was asked whether he had ever recommended to Johns-Manville officials that warning labels be placed on insulation products containing asbestos. He testified as follows:

> The reasons why the caution labels were not implemented immediately, it was a business decision as far as I could understand. Here was a recommendation, the corporation is in business to make, to provide jobs for people and make money for stockholders and they had to take into consideration the effects of everything they did, and if the application of a caution label identifying a product as hazardous would cut out sales, there would be serious financial implications. And the powers that be had to make some effort to judge the necessity of the label vs. the consequences of placing the label on the product.

Dr. Smith's testimony and related documents have figured prominently in hundreds of asbestos-related lawsuits. In the 1980s these lawsuits swamped Manville (as Johns-Manville is now called) and forced the company into bankruptcy. A trust fund valued at $2.5 billion was set up to pay Manville's asbestos claimants. To fund the trust, shareholders were required to surrender half the value of their stock, and the company had to give up much of its projected earnings over the next twenty-five years. Claims, however, soon over-whelmed the trust, which ran out of money in 1990. After various legal delays, the trust fund's stake in Manville was increased to 80 percent, and Manville was required to pay it an additional $300 million in dividends. The trust fund itself was restructured to pay the most seriously ill victims first, but average payments to victims were lowered significantly—from $145,000 to $43,000.

Meanwhile, in 1997 the U.S. Supreme Court struck down a landmark $1.3-billion class-action settlement between some twenty former asbestos producers and their injured workers. A few years earlier, the companies involved had approached the workers' lawyers and agreed to settle thousands of existing health complaints, in a deal that netted the lawyers millions of dollars in fees. Then the lawyers and companies devised a settlement agreement involving people who had not filed claims against the company by a specified date. It was this aspect of the settlement that was the main sticking point. Although a lower court had praised the settlement for "forging a solution to a major social problem," the Supreme Court balked at the fact that future claimants were not allowed to opt out of the agreement. A class-action agreement, the Court said, was not the best way to resolve thousands of different claims involving different factual and legal issues. In 1999, the Court rejected a second proposed settlement. As a result, thousands of lawsuits that would have been settled by the agreements continue to clog federal dockets.

The situation is made worse by the fact that in the last few years asbestos-related litigation has expanded exponentially—spun out of control, some would say—as workers who did not make asbestos, but only handled it every now and then or worked in the vicinity of those who did, are suing companies that never made the stuff but only used it. Altogether more than 200,000 cases are pending nationwide against more than 1,000 companies. In fact, of the 91,000 cases filed in 2001, only 6 percent of the plaintiffs have actually suffered from asbestos-related diseases. Almost all of the other claimants are seeking compensation for anxiety they have experienced over the risk that they might have asbestosis.[5]

QUESTIONS

1. Hand-of-government proponents would say that it's the responsibility of government, not the asbestos industry, to ensure health and safety with respect to asbestos—that in the absence of appropriate government regulations, asbestos manufacturers have no responsibility other than to operate efficiently and profitably. Do you agree?

2. What responsibilities do asbestos manufacturers now have to their injured workers? How should society respond to these workers' claims for restitution? Is our legal system adequate for handling this problem? Should the asbestos companies be punished in some way, or is their liability to civil lawsuits sufficient?

3. Do you see any parallels between this case and the tobacco industry's response to the health risks of smoking?

CASE 10.5
Merck and Vioxx
Kenneth B. Moll and Associates

On October 5, 2004, Kenneth B. Moll & Associates, Ltd. filed the first worldwide class action lawsuit against Merck, on behalf of all persons who were prescribed the potentially deadly arthritis drug rofecoxib, also known as Vioxx (Ceoxx outside the United States).

The law firm has already received inquiries from persons who believe they were injured by Vioxx in over 14 countries (China, South Africa, Italy, Canada, Iceland, Israel, Chile, United Kingdom, New Zealand, Brazil, The Netherlands, Singapore, the United States, and other countries). Merck estimates that over 24 million patients have been prescribed the drug worldwide.

The lawsuit, known as the "VIOXX Class Action," was filed in the Federal District Court for the Northern District of Illinois.

On September 30, 2004, Merck officially announced a voluntary withdraw of Vioxx from all markets worldwide in light of unequivocal results from a clinical trial demonstrating that Vioxx almost triples the risk of heart attack and stroke for those who take the product long term. The company's decision is based on three-year data from a prospective, randomized, placebo-controlled clinical trial, the APPROVe (Adenomatous Polyp Prevention on VIOXX) trial.

The APPROVe study followed the 1999 VIGOR (Vioxx Gastrointestinal Outcomes Research Study) study. In the VIGOR study, analysis of the cardiovascular data by the Safety Monitoring Board focused on "the excess deaths and cardiovascular adverse experiences in [the Vioxx group] compared to [the Naproxen group].

Attorney Kenneth Moll said, "a primary goal of the Vioxx Class Action is to inform consumers and physicians worldwide of the potentially deadly side

Source: Kenneth B. Moll and Associates. Reprinted by permission of Kenneth B. Moll and Associates.

effects of Vioxx." Mr. Moll said he is concerned that thousands of people have been injured by the drug and are not aware of their injuries. According to our experts, a person is susceptible to a Vioxx injury beginning from the initial dosage, up to and including a week after discontinuing use of the drug.

The lawsuit will request that a medical monitoring fund be established to enable people who have taken Vioxx to monitor the existence of dangerous side effects.

IMPORTANT: Injuries from Vioxx may occur days after usage.

Our offices are working in conjunction with attorneys around the world to address the enormous public health issue created by Merck in its manufacture, marketing and distribution of the prescription drug Vioxx (marketed as Ceoxx outside of the United States). The drug has been marketed around the world since 1999 and has been prescribed tens of millions of times. In light of the millions of patients around the world who were taking Vioxx, even if a fraction of a percent of patients experience cardiovascular events, that would translate into thousands of affected people. The Italian consumer protection group, ADUC, has addressed the health concerns surrounding Vioxx and has issued a press release.

QUESTIONS

1. What duties does Merck have in the Vioxx case?
2. Should attorneys always be the ones to "solve" liability problems? Why or why not?

CHAPTER QUESTIONS

1. When should producers be responsible for harms that are caused by their products? What moral responsibilities do producers have? What are the responsibilities of consumers? Where (and how) do we draw the line?

2. Is life becoming more dangerous? Is greater fear one of the costs of greater convenience and greater luxury? How can we regulate business—if we should—to manage the escalating risks created by mushrooming production?

11

"You Know How to Whistle, Don't You?"

Whistle-Blowing, Company Loyalty, and Employee Responsibility

Introduction

One of the wise-guy employees of a local, particularly vicious, crime family, let's call them the Baritones, finds himself increasingly repulsed by some of his assignments, which involve, among other things, the breaking of various bones and the noncosmetic rearrangement of unresponsive clients' faces. He starts to feel sorry for his victims, most of whom are perfectly law-abiding citizens who just happen to have small businesses in Baritone territory and find themselves unable to make the extortion payments that have been demanded of them. Eventually, his conscience gets the better of him, and he has a change of heart. He gets in touch with the FBI (though he by no means feels all that good about doing so) and offers to testify ("rat," in his lexicon) on his bosses. There is no doubt that they have been doing wrong (to put it mildly). There is no doubt that their activities have been both destructive of the community and corrupting to the real free enterprise system (which, as Adam Smith warned years ago, can be ruined by "Force and Fraud"). But this guy took an oath, a blood oath, in fact, to keep his secrets and not betray his employers, who have come to seem to him, over the years, like a literal family. And the question that bugs him, over and over, is how he can justify violating that oath, however evil his "family" may be.

Whatever our affection for fictional crime families may be—indeed, whatever misplaced affection we may have for real-life criminals in the news—we recognize or should recognize evil for what it is, evil. We're not talking here about bending the law or cutting corners. We're not talking about wrongdoers who deserve one another. We're talking about terrorizing and ruining the lives of hardworking, innocent people. But even so, we can understand the turmoil of the wise guy, torn between his belated recognition of evil and his sense of loyalty. And if that is so, we should be all the more sympathetic toward those who see less than evil—shoddy business practices, dangerous situations for employees, pollution or destruction of the environment, the violation of tax laws, and the systematic misleading of investors—and are moved to say something about it. Whistle-blowing, as it has come to be called, is always a painful and desperate course of action. But sometimes, it is heroic and nec-

Martin Luther King on Silence

Our lives begin to end the day we become silent about things that matter.

—*From an Enron Company notepad*

essary. And that becomes a question for all of us. Most of us will, at some time in our lives, work for a corporation or an institution with flaws. At what point might we feel justified, indeed even compelled, to speak out, first, of course, with a more or less polite internal memo. But if that memo gets no results, are we ever justified in violating our own sense of loyalty—and others' expectations of loyalty—to go outside the company? This, of course, has been the dilemma of several high-placed whistle-blowers in recent years. Erin Brockovich became a national heroine (and had superstar Julia Roberts depict her in a movie) for blowing the whistle on corporate polluters. Jeffrey Wigand went through utter Hell exposing the lethal lies told by his employers in the tobacco industry, but he also emerged a hero (played by Russell Crowe in the movie, *The Insider*) for daring to risk his life and career for the sake of the truth and public safety. More recently, Sherron Watkins (along with Cynthia Cooper of WorldCom and Coleen Rowley of the FBI) made the cover of *Time* magazine for writing a now-famous memo to Enron CEO Kenneth Lay, warning of an "implosion" if Enron's accounting practices ever came to light, and then testified against her superiors in the much-awaited criminal cases that followed.

Most of us will never find ourselves in such a difficult position, but we all need to keep that possibility in mind. First of all, we all need to have some sense of what lines we will not cross, what sorts of things we would refuse to do, what sorts of activities we will not tolerate, even if we ourselves are not direct participants but only observers (and therefore nonetheless complicit). And second, we need to keep in mind how painful such a dilemma must be for those who are so involved, rather than simply retreat to the knee-jerk (or perhaps just jerk) reaction that "they should not have gotten themselves into that situation in the first place" or "I would never rat on my employer." (No? Never? No matter what?) What's more, the opposition is not always (or usually) the company versus the public, but the very existence of the company. An early whistle-blower (especially if he or she is heeded *within* the company) can prevent the massive Enron-type collapse and bankruptcy. Not only the ethics but the health of the free enterprise system depends on the freedom of everyone in it to speak up and to criticize or expose wrongdoing. This is not to say that speaking up is easy or that all criticism is warranted criticism. But unless we acknowledge and even celebrate those who are willing to act as correctives when our market system goes wrong, we are in danger of finding ourselves in a world that is no longer free or a true market but, as wrongdoing tends to find its imitators, what Smith warned us about, a system of Force and Fraud.

Sissela Bok offers a general characterization of the ethical foundations of whistle-blowing in her "Whistleblowing and Professional Responsibility." Michael Davis explains the many tensions and difficulties in an adequate characterization of the moral obligation to blow the whistle in his "Some Paradoxes of Whistleblowing." Ronald Duska emphasizes the particular difficulties posed by the conflict between loyalty and a moral obligation to blow the whistle in his "Whistleblowing and Employee Loyalty." David E. Soles offers a comprehensive analysis of the ethical foundations of employee loyalty in his "Four Concepts of Loyalty." Finally, George D. Randels expands the idea of loyalty to include loyalties between employees and corporations, corporations and communities, and corporations to employees in his "Loyalty, Corporations, and Community."

Sissela Bok | # Whistleblowing and Professional Responsibility

Sissela Bok is a member of the American Academy of Political and Social Science and is an Eleanor Roosevelt Fellow. She was formerly professor of philosophy at Brandeis University.

"Whistleblowing" is a new label generated by our increased awareness of the ethical conflicts encountered at work. Whistleblowers sound an alarm from within the very organization in which they work, aiming to spotlight neglect or abuses that threaten the public interest.

The stakes in whistleblowing are high. Take the nurse who alleges that physicians enrich themselves in her hospital through unnecessary surgery; the engineer who discloses safety defects in the braking systems of a fleet of new rapid-transit vehicles; the Defense Department official who alerts Congress to military graft and overspending: all know that they pose a threat to those whom they denounce and that their own careers may be at risk. . . .

NATURE OF WHISTLEBLOWING

Three elements, each jarring, and triply jarring when conjoined, lend acts of whistleblowing special urgency and bitterness: dissent, breach of loyalty, and accusation.

Like all dissent, whistleblowing makes public a disagreement with an authority or a majority view. But whereas dissent can concern all forms of disagreement with, for instance, religious dogma or government policy or court decisions, whistleblowing has the narrower aim of shedding light on negligence or abuse, or alerting to a risk, and of assigning responsibility for this risk.

Would-be whistleblowers confront the conflict inherent in all dissent: between conforming and sticking their necks out. The more repressive the authority they challenge, the greater the personal risk they take in speaking out. At exceptional times, as in times of war, even ordinarily tolerant authorities may come to regard dissent as unacceptable and even disloyal.

Furthermore, the whistleblower hopes to stop the game; but since he is neither referee nor coach, and since he blows the whistle on his own team, his act is seen as a violation of loyalty. In holding his position, he has assumed certain obligations to his colleagues and clients. He may even have subscribed to a loyalty oath or a promise of confidentiality. Loyalty to colleagues and to clients comes to be pitted against loyalty to the public interest, to those who may be injured unless the revelation is made.

Not only is loyalty violated in whistleblowing, hierarchy as well is often opposed, since the whistle-

From Sissela Bok, "Whistleblowing and Professional Responsibility," *New York University Education Quarterly,* 11 (Summer 1980): 2–7. Reprinted with permission. Notes were deleted from the text.

blower is not only a colleague but a subordinate. Though aware of the risks inherent in such disobedience, he often hopes to keep his job. At times, however, he plans his alarm to coincide with leaving the institution. If he is highly placed, or joined by others, resigning in protest may effectively direct public attention to the wrongdoing at issue. Still another alternative, often chosen by those who wish to be safe from retaliation, is to leave the institution quietly, to secure another post, then to blow the whistle. In this way, it is possible to speak with the authority and knowledge of an insider without having the vulnerability of that position.

It is the element of accusation, of calling a "foul," that arouses the strongest reactions on the part of the hierarchy. The accusation may be of neglect, of willfully concealed dangers, or of outright abuse on the part of colleagues or superiors. It singles out specific persons or groups as responsible for threats to the public interest. If no one could be held responsible—as in the case of an impending avalanche—the warning would not constitute whistleblowing.

The accusation of the whistleblower, moreover, concerns a present or an imminent threat. Past errors or misdeeds occasion such an alarm only if they still affect current practices. And risks far in the future lack the immediacy needed to make the alarm a compelling one, as well as the close connection to particular individuals that would justify actual accusations. Thus an alarm can be sounded about safety defects in a rapid-transit system that threaten or will shortly threaten passengers, but the revelation of safety defects in a system no longer in use, while of historical interest, would not constitute whistleblowing. Nor would the revelation of potential problems in a system not yet fully designed and far from implemented.

Not only immediacy, but also specificity, is needed for there to be an alarm capable of pinpointing responsibility. A concrete risk must be at issue rather than a vague foreboding or a somber prediction. The act of whistle-blowing differs in this respect from the lamentation or the dire prophecy. An immediate and specific threat would normally be acted upon by those at risk. The whistleblower assumes that his message will alert listeners to something they do not know, or whose significance they have not grasped because it has been kept secret.

The desire for openness inheres in the temptation to reveal any secret, sometimes joined to an urge for self-aggrandizement and publicity and the hope for revenge for past slights or injustices. There can be pleasure, too—righteous or malicious—in laying bare the secrets of co-workers and in setting the record straight at last. Colleagues of the whistleblower often suspect his motives: they may regard him as a crank, as publicity-hungry, wrong about the facts, eager for scandal and discord, and driven to indiscretion by his personal biases and shortcomings.

For whistleblowing to be effective, it must arouse its audience. Inarticulate whistleblowers are likely to fail from the outset. When they are greeted by apathy, their message dissipates. When they are greeted by disbelief, they elicit no response at all. And when the audience is not free to receive or to act on the information—when censorship or fear of retribution stifles response—then the message rebounds to injure the whistleblower. Whistleblowing also requires the possibility of concerted public response: the idea of whistleblowing in an anarchy is therefore merely quixotic.

Such characteristics of whistleblowing and strategic considerations for achieving an impact are common to the noblest warnings, the most vicious personal attacks, and the delusions of the paranoid. How can one distinguish the many acts of sounding an alarm that are genuinely in the public interest from all the petty, biased, or lurid revelations that pervade our querulous and gossip-ridden society? Can we draw distinctions between different whistleblowers, different messages, different methods?

We clearly can, in a number of cases. Whistleblowing may be starkly inappropriate when in malice or error, or when it lays bare legitimately private matters having to do, for instance, with political belief or sexual life. It can, just as clearly, be the only way to shed light on an ongoing unjust practice such as drugging political prisoners or subjecting them to electroshock treatment. It can be the last resort for alerting the public to an impending disaster. Taking such clear-cut cases as benchmarks, and reflecting on what it is about them that weighs so heavily for or against speaking out, we can work our way toward the admittedly more complex cases in which whistleblowing is not so clearly the right or wrong choice, or where different points of view exist regarding its legitimacy—cases where there are moral reasons both for concealment and for disclosure and where judgments conflict. Consider the following cases:[1]

A. As a construction inspector for a federal agency, John Samuels (not his real name) had personal knowledge of shoddy and deficient construction practices by private contractors. He knew his superiors received free vacations and entertainment, had their homes remodeled and found jobs for their relatives—all courtesy of a private contractor. These superiors later approved a multimillion no-bid contract with the same "generous" firm.

Samuels also had evidence that other firms were hiring nonunion laborers at a low wage while receiving substantially higher payments from the government for labor costs. A former superior, unaware of an office dictaphone, had incautiously instructed Samuels on how to accept bribes for overlooking sub-par performance.

As he prepared to volunteer this information to various members of Congress, he became tense and uneasy. His family was scared and the fears were valid. It might cost Samuels thousands of dollars to protect his job. Those who had freely provided Samuels with information would probably recant or withdraw their friendship. A number of people might object to his using a dictaphone to gather information. His agency would start covering up and vent its collective wrath upon him. As for reporters and writers, they would gather for a few days, then move on to the next story. He would be left without a job, with fewer friends, with massive battles looming, and without the financial means of fighting them. Samuels decided to remain silent.

B. Engineers of Company "A" prepared plans and specifications for machinery to be used in a manufacturing process and Company "A" turned them over to Company "B" for production. The engineers of Company "B," in reviewing the plans and specifications, came to the conclusion that they included certain miscalculations and technical deficiencies of a nature that the final product might be unsuitable for the purposes of the ultimate users, and that the equipment, if built according to the original plans and specifications, might endanger the lives of persons in proximity to it. The engineers of Company "B" called the matter to the attention of appropriate officials of their employer who, in turn, advised Company "A." Company "A" replied that its engineers felt that the design and specifications for the equipment were adequate and safe and that Company "B" should proceed to build the equipment as designed and specified. The officials of Company "B" instructed its engineers to proceed with the work.

C. A recently hired assistant director of admissions in a state university begins to wonder whether transcripts of some applicants accurately reflect their accomplishments. He knows that it matters to many in the university community, including alumni, that the football team continue its winning tradition. He has heard rumors that surrogates may be available to take tests for a fee, signing the names of designated applicants for admission, and that some of the transcripts may have been altered. But he has no hard facts. When he brings the question up with the director of admissions, he is told that the rumors are un-

---

To: You
From: The Philosopher
Subject: "Ralph Nader on Whistle-Blowing"

The key question is, at what point should an employee resolve that allegiance to society (e.g., the public safety) must supersede allegiance to the organization's policies (e.g., the corporate profit) and then act on that resolve by informing outsiders or legal authorities? It is a question that involves basic issues of individual freedom, concentration of power, and information flow to the public.

founded and asked not to inquire further into the matter.

INDIVIDUAL MORAL CHOICE

What questions might those who consider sounding an alarm in public ask themselves? How might they articulate the problem they see and weigh its injustice before deciding whether or not to reveal it? How can they best try to make sure their choice is the right one? In thinking about these questions it helps to keep in mind the three elements mentioned earlier: dissent, breach of loyalty, and accusation. They impose certain requirements—of accuracy and judgment in dissent; of exploring alternative ways to cope with improprieties that minimize the breach of loyalty; and of fairness in accusation. For each, careful articulation and testing of arguments are needed to limit error and bias.

Dissent by whistleblowers, first of all, is expressly claimed to be intended to benefit the public. It carries with it, as a result, an obligation to consider the nature of this benefit and to consider also the possible harm that may come from speaking out: harm to persons or institutions and, ultimately, to the public interest itself. Whistleblowers must, therefore, begin by making every effort to consider the effects of speaking out versus those of remaining silent. They must assure themselves of the accuracy of their reports, checking and rechecking the facts before speaking out; specify the degree to which there is genuine impropriety; consider how imminent is the threat they see, how serious, and how closely linked to those accused of neglect and abuse.

If the facts warrant whistleblowing, how can the second element—breach of loyalty—be minimized? The most important question here is whether the existing avenues for change within the organization have been explored. It is a waste of time for the public as well as harmful to the institution to sound the loudest alarm first. Whistleblowing has to remain a last alternative because of its destructive side effects: it must be chosen only when other alternatives have been considered and rejected. They may be rejected if they simply do not apply to the problem at hand, or when there is not time to go through routine channels or when the institution is so corrupt or coercive that

steps will be taken to silence the whistleblower should he try the regular channels first.

What weight should an oath or a promise of silence have in the conflict of loyalties? One sworn to silence is doubtless under a stronger obligation because of the oath he has taken. He has bound himself, assumed specific obligations beyond those assumed in merely taking a new position. But even such promises can be overridden when the public interest at issue is strong enough. They can be overridden if they were obtained under duress or through deceit. They can be overridden, too, if they promise something that is in itself wrong or unlawful. The fact that one has promised silence is no excuse for complicity in covering up a crime or a violation of the public's trust.

The third element in whistleblowing—accusation—raises equally serious ethical concerns. They are concerns of fairness to the persons accused of impropriety. Is the message one to which the public is entitled in the first place? Or does it infringe on personal and private matters that one has no right to invade? Here, the very notion of what is in the public's best "interest" is at issue: "accusations" regarding an official's unusual sexual or religious experiences may well appeal to the public's interest without being information relevant to "the public interest."

Great conflicts arise here. We have witnessed excessive claims to executive privilege and to secrecy by government officials during the Watergate scandal in order to cover up for abuses the public had every right to discover. Conversely, those hoping to profit from prying into private matters have become adept at invoking "the public's right to know." Some even regard such private matters as threats to the public: they voice their own religious and political prejudices in the language of accusation. Such a danger is never stronger than when the accusation is delivered surreptitiously. The anonymous accusations made during the McCarthy period regarding political beliefs and associations often injured persons who did not even know their accusers or the exact nature of the accusations.

From the public's point of view, accusations that are openly made by identifiable individuals are more likely to be taken seriously. And in fairness to those criticized, openly accepted responsibility for blowing the whistle should be preferred to the denunciation or the leaked rumor. What is openly stated can more easily be checked, its source's motives challenged, and the underlying information examined. Those under attack may otherwise be hard put to defend themselves against nameless adversaries. Often they do not even know that they are threatened until it is too late to respond. The anonymous denunciation, moreover, common to so many regimes, places the burden of investigation on government agencies that may thereby gain the power of a secret police.

From the point of view of the whistleblower, on the other hand, the anonymous message is safer in situations where retaliation is likely. But it is also often less likely to be taken seriously. Unless the message is accompanied by indications of how the evidence can be checked, its anonymity, however safe for the source, speaks against it.

During the process of weighing the legitimacy of speaking out, the method used, and the degree of fairness needed, whistleblowers must try to compensate for the strong possibility of bias on their part. They should be scrupulously aware of any motive that might skew their message: a desire for self-defense in a difficult bureaucratic situation, perhaps, or the urge to seek revenge, or inflated expectations regarding the effect their message will have on the situation. (Needless to say, bias affects the silent as well as the outspoken. The motive for holding back important information about abuses and injustice ought to give similar cause for soul-searching.)

Likewise, the possibility of personal gain from sounding the alarm ought to give pause. Once again there is then greater risk of a biased message. Even if the whistleblower regards himself as incorruptible, his profiting from revelations of neglect or abuse will lead others to question his motives and to put less credence in his charges. If, for example, a government employee stands to make large profits from a book exposing the iniquities in his agency, there is danger that he will, perhaps even unconsciously, slant his report in order to cause more of a sensation.

A special problem arises when there is a high risk that the civil servant who speaks out will have to go through costly litigation. Might he not justifiably try to make enough money on his public revelations— say, through books or public speaking—to offset his losses? In so doing he will not strictly speaking have

profited from his revelations: he merely avoids being financially crushed by their sequels. He will nevertheless still be suspected at the time of revelation, and his message will therefore seem more questionable.

Reducing bias and error in moral choice often requires consultation, even open debate: methods that force articulation of the moral arguments at stake and challenge privately held assumptions. But acts of whistleblowing present special problems when it comes to open consultation. On the one hand, once the whistleblower sounds his alarm publicly, his arguments will be subjected to open scrutiny; he will have to articulate his reasons for speaking out and substantiate his charges. On the other hand, it will then be too late to retract the alarm or to combat its harmful effects, should his choice to speak out have been ill-advised.

For this reason, the whistleblower owes it to all involved to make sure of two things: that he has sought as much and as objective advice regarding his choice as he can *before* going public; and that he is aware of the arguments for and against the practice of whistleblowing in general, so that he can see his own choice against as richly detailed and coherently structured a background as possible. Satisfying these two requirements once again has special problems because of the very nature of whistleblowing: the more corrupt the circumstances, the more dangerous it may be to seek consultation before speaking out. And yet, since the whistleblower himself may have a biased view of the state of affairs, he may choose not to consult others when in fact it would be not only safe but advantageous to do so; he may see corruption and conspiracy where none exists.

NOTE

1. Case A is adapted from Louis Clark, "The Sound of Professional Suicide," *Barrister,* Summer 1978, p. 10; Case B is Case 5 in Robert J. Baum and Albert Flores, eds., *Ethical Problems of Engineering* (Troy, N. Y.: Rensselaer Polytechnic Institute, 1978), p. 186.

QUESTIONS

1. When and why do we have a duty to blow the whistle, according to Bok?
2. What are the constraints that govern whistleblowers?

Michael Davis | # Some Paradoxes of Whistleblowing

Michael Davis is a Senior Fellow at the Illinois Institute of Technology Center for Study of Ethics in the Professions and a professor of philosophy.

Most acts, though permitted or required by morality, need no justification. There is no reason to think them wrong. Their justification is too plain for words. Why then is whistleblowing so problematic that we need *theories* of its justification? What reason do we have to think whistleblowing might be morally wrong?

Whistleblowing always involves revealing information that would not ordinarily be revealed. But there is nothing morally problematic about that; after all, revealing information not ordinarily revealed is one function of science. Whistleblowing always involves, in addition, an actual (or at least declared) intention to prevent something bad that would otherwise occur. There is nothing morally problematic in that either. That may well be the chief use of information.

What seems to make whistleblowing morally problematic is its organizational context. A mere individual cannot blow the whistle (in any interesting sense); only a member of an organization, whether a current or a former member, can do so. Indeed, he can only blow the whistle on his own organization (or some part of it). . . .

The whistleblower cannot blow the whistle using just any information obtained in virtue of membership in the organization. A clerk in Accounts who, happening upon evidence of serious wrongdoing while visiting a friend in Quality Control, is not a whistleblower just because she passes the information to a friend at the *Tribune*. She is more like a self-appointed spy. She seems to differ from the whistleblower, or at least from clear cases of the whistleblower, precisely in her relation to the information in question. To be a whistleblower is to reveal information with which one is *entrusted*.

But it is more than that. The whistleblower does not reveal the information to save his own skin (for example, to avoid perjury under oath). He has no excuse for revealing what his organization does not want revealed. Instead, he claims to be doing what he should be doing. If he cannot honestly make that claim—if, that is, he does not have that intention—his revelation is not whistleblowing (and so, not justified as whistleblowing), but something analogous, much as pulling a child from the water is not a rescue, even if it saves the child's life, when the "rescuer" merely believes herself to be salvaging old clothes. What makes whistleblowing morally problematic, if anything does, is this high-minded but unexcused misuse of one's position in a generally law-abiding, morally decent organization, an organization that *prima facie* deserves the whistleblower's loyalty (as a burglary ring does not).

The whistleblower must reveal information the organization does not want revealed. But, in any actual organization, "what the organization wants" will be contested, with various individuals or groups asking to be taken as speaking for the organization. Who, for example, did what Thiokol wanted the night before the *Challenger* exploded? In retrospect, it is obvious that the three vice presidents, Lund, Kilminster, and Mason, did not do what Thiokol wanted—or, at least, what it would have wanted. At the time, however, they had authority to speak for the company—the conglomerate Morton-Thiokol headquartered in Chicago—while the protesting engineers, including Boisjoly, did not. Yet, even before the explosion, was it obvious that the three were doing what the company wanted? To be a whistle-

From *Business and Professional Ethics Journal* 15 (Spring 1996). Reprinted by permission of the author. Notes were deleted from the text.

blower, one must, I think, at least temporarily lose an argument about what the organization wants. The whistleblower is disloyal only in a sense—the sense the winners of the internal argument get to dictate. What can justify such disloyalty?

THE STANDARD THEORY

According to the theory now more or less standard,[1] such disloyalty is morally permissible when:

(S1) The organization to which the would-be whistleblower belongs will, through its product or policy, do serious considerable harm to the public (whether to users of its product, to innocent bystanders, or to the public at large);

(S2) The would-be whistleblower has identified that threat of harm, reported it to her immediate superior, making clear both the threat itself and the objection to it, and concluded that the superior will do nothing effective; and

(S3) The would-be whistleblower has exhausted other internal procedures within the organization (for example, by going up the organizational ladder as far as allowed)—or at least made use of as many internal procedures as the danger to others and her own safety make reasonable.

Whistleblowing is morally required (according to the standard theory) when, in addition:

(S4) The would-be whistleblower has (or has accessible) evidence that would convince a reasonable, impartial observer that her view of the threat is correct; and

(S5) The would-be whistleblower has good reason to believe that revealing the threat will (probably) prevent the harm at reasonable cost (all things considered).

Why is whistleblowing morally required when these five conditions are met? According to the standard theory, whistleblowing is morally required, when it is required at all, because "people have a moral obligation to prevent serious harm to others if they can do so with little cost to themselves."[2] In other words, whistleblowing meeting all five conditions is a form of "minimally decent Samaritanism" (a doing of what morality requires) rather than "good Samaritanism" (going well beyond the moral minimum). . . .

THREE PARADOXES

That's the standard theory—where are the paradoxes? The first paradox I want to call attention to concerns a commonplace of the whistleblowing literature. Whistleblowers are not minimally decent Samaritans. If they are Samaritans at all, they are good Samaritans. They always act at considerable risk to career, and generally, at considerable risk to their financial security and personal relations.

In this respect, as in many others, Roger Boisjoly is typical. Boisjoly blew the whistle on his employer, Thiokol; he volunteered information, in public testimony before the Rogers Commission, that Thiokol did not want him to volunteer. As often happens, both his employer and many who relied on it for employment reacted hostilely. Boisjoly had to say goodbye to the company town, to old friends and neighbors, and to building rockets; he had to start a new career at an age when most people are preparing for retirement.

Since whistleblowing is generally costly to the whistleblower in some large way as this, the standard theory's minimally decent Samaritanism provides *no* justification for the central cases of whistleblowing. That is the first paradox, what we might call "the paradox of burden."

The second paradox concerns the prevention of "harm." On the standard theory, the would-be whistleblower must seek to prevent "serious and considerable harm" in order for the whistleblowing to be even morally permissible. There seems to be a good deal of play in the term *harm*. The harm in question can be physical (such as death or disease), financial (such as loss of or damage to property), and perhaps even psychological (such as fear or mental illness). But there is a limit to how much the standard theory can stretch "harm." Beyond that limit are "harms" like injustice, deception, and waste. As morally important as injustice, deception, and waste can be, they do not seem to constitute the "serious and considerable harm" that can require someone to become even a minimally decent Samaritan.

Yet, many cases of whistleblowing, perhaps most, are not about preventing serious and considerable physical, financial, or psychological harm. For example, when Boisjoly spoke up the evening before the *Challenger* exploded, the lives of seven astronauts sat in the balance. Speaking up then was about preventing serious and considerable physical, financial, and psychological harm—but it was not whistleblowing. Boisjoly was then serving his employer, not betraying a trust (even on the employer's understanding of that trust); he was calling his superiors' attention to what he thought they should take into account in their decision and not publicly revealing confidential information. The whistleblowing came after the explosion, in testimony before the Rogers Commission. By then, the seven astronauts were beyond help, the shuttle program was suspended, and any further threat of physical, financial, or psychological harm to the "public" was—after discounting for time—negligible. Boisjoly had little reason to believe his testimony would make a significant difference in the booster's redesign, in safety procedures in the shuttle program, or even in reawakening concern for safety among NASA employees and contractors. The *Challenger*'s explosion was much more likely to do that than anything Boisjoly could do. What Boisjoly could do in his testimony, what I think he tried to do, was prevent falsification of the record.

Falsification of the record is, of course, harm in a sense, especially a record as historically important as that which the Rogers Commission was to produce. But falsification is harm only in a sense that almost empties "harm" of its distinctive meaning, leaving it more or less equivalent to "moral wrong." The proponents of the standard theory mean more by "harm" than that. De George, for example, explicitly says that a threat justifying whistleblowing must be to "life or health."[3] The standard theory is strikingly more narrow in its grounds of justification than many examples of justified whistleblowing suggest it should be. That is the second paradox, the "paradox of missing harm."

The third paradox is related to the second. Insofar as whistleblowers are understood as people out to prevent harm, not just to prevent moral wrong, their chances of success are not good. Whistleblowers generally do not prevent much harm. In this too, Boisjoly is typical. As he has said many times, the situation at Thiokol is now much as it was before the disaster. Insofar as we can identify cause and effect, even now we have little reason to believe that—whatever his actual intention—Boisjoly's testimony actually prevented any harm (beyond the moral harm of falsification). So, if whistleblowers must have, as the standard theory says (S5), (beyond the moral wrong of falsification) "good reason to believe that revealing the threat will (probably) prevent the harm," then the history of whistleblowing virtually rules out the moral justification of whistleblowing. That is certainly paradoxical in a theory purporting to state sufficient conditions for the central cases of justified whistleblowing. Let us call this "the paradox of failure."

A COMPLICITY THEORY

As I look down the roll of whistleblowers, I do not see anyone who, like the clerk from Accounts, just happened upon key documents in a cover-up. Few, if any, whistleblowers are mere third-parties like the good Samaritan. They are generally deeply involved in the activity they reveal. This involvement suggests that we might better understand what justifies (most) whistleblowing if we understand the whistleblower's obligation to derive from *complicity* in wrongdoing rather than from the ability to prevent harm.

Any complicity theory of justified whistleblowing has two obvious advantages over the standard theory. One is that (moral) complicity itself presupposes (moral) wrongdoing, not harm. So, a complicity justification automatically avoids the paradox of missing harm, fitting the facts of whistleblowing better than a theory which, like the standard one, emphasizes prevention of harm.

That is one obvious advantage of a complicity theory. The second advantage is that complicity invokes a more demanding obligation than the ability to prevent harm does. We are morally obliged to avoid doing moral wrongs. When, despite our best efforts, we nonetheless find ourselves engaged in some wrong, we have an obligation to do what we reasonably can to set things right. If, for example, I cause a traffic accident, I have a moral (and legal) obligation to call help, stay at the scene until help arrives, and render first aid (if I know how), even at substantial cost to myself and those to whom I owe my time, and even with little likelihood that anything I do will help much. Just as a complicity theory avoids the paradox of missing harm, it also avoids the paradox of burden.

What about the third paradox, the paradox of failure? I shall come to that, but only after remedying one disadvantage of the complicity theory. That disadvantage is obvious—we do not yet have such a theory, not even a sketch. Here, then, is the place to offer a sketch of such a theory.

Complicity Theory

You are morally required to reveal what you know to the public (or to a suitable agent or representative of it) when:

(**C1**) what you will reveal derives from your work for an organization;

(**C2**) you are a voluntary member of that organization;

(**C3**) you believe that the organization, though legitimate, is engaged in serious moral wrongdoing;

(**C4**) you believe that your work for that organization will contribute (more or less directly) to the wrong if (but *not* only if) you do not publicly reveal what you know;

(**C5**) you are justified in beliefs C3 and C4; and

(**C6**) beliefs C3 and C4 are true.

The complicity theory differs from the standard theory in several ways worth pointing out here. The first is that, according to C1, what the whistleblower reveals must derive from his work for the organization. This condition distinguishes the whistleblower from the spy (and the clerk in Accounts). The spy seeks out information in order to reveal it; the whistleblower learns it as a proper part of doing the job the organization has assigned him. The standard theory, in contrast, has nothing to say about how the whistleblower comes to know of the threat she reveals (S2). For the standard theory, spies are just another kind of whistleblower.

A second way in which the complicity theory differs from the standard theory is that the complicity theory (C2) explicitly requires the whistleblower to be a *voluntary* participant in the organization in question. Whistleblowing is not—according to the complicity theory—an activity in which slaves, prisoners, or other involuntary participants in an organization engage. . . .

A third way in which the complicity theory differs from the standard theory is that the complicity theory (C3) requires moral wrong, not harm, for justification. The wrong need not be a new event (as a harm must be if it is to be *prevented*). It might, for example, consist in no more than silence about facts necessary to correct a serious injustice.

The complicity theory (C3) does, however, follow the standard theory in requiring that the predicate of whistleblowing be "serious." Under the complicity theory, minor wrongdoing can no more justify whistleblowing than can minor harm under the standard theory. While organizational loyalty cannot forbid whistleblowing, it does forbid "tattling," that is, revealing minor wrongdoing.

A fourth way in which the complicity theory differs from the standard theory, the most important, is that the complicity theory (C4) requires that the whistleblower believe that her work will have contributed to the wrong in question if she does nothing, but it does *not* require that she believe that her revelation will prevent (or undo) the wrong. The complicity theory does not require any belief about what the whistleblowing can accomplish (beyond ending complicity in the wrong in question). The whistleblower reveals what she knows in order to prevent complicity in the wrong, not to prevent the wrong as such. She can prevent complicity (if there is any to prevent) simply by publicly revealing what she knows. The revelation itself breaks the bond of complicity, the secret partnership in wrongdoing, that makes her an accomplice in her organization's wrongdoing. The complicity theory thus avoids the third paradox, the paradox of failure, just as it avoided the other two.

The fifth difference between the complicity theory and the standard theory is closely related to the fourth. Because publicly revealing what one knows breaks the bond of complicity, the complicity theory does not require the whistleblower to have enough evidence to convince others of the wrong in question.

Convincing others, or just being able to convince them, is not, as such, an element in the justification of whistleblowing.

The complicity theory does, however, require (C5) that the whistleblower be (epistemically) justified in believing both that his organization is engaged in wrongdoing and that he will contribute to that wrong unless he blows the whistle. Such (epistemic) justification may require substantial physical evidence (as the standard theory says) or just a good sense of how things work. The complicity theory does not share the standard theory's substantial evidential demand (S4).

In one respect, however, the complicity theory clearly requires more of the whistleblower than the standard theory does. The complicity theory's C6— combined with C5—requires not only that the whistleblower be *justified* in her beliefs about the organization's wrongdoing and her part in it, but also that she be *right* about them. If she is wrong about either the wrongdoing or her complicity, her revelation will not be justified whistleblowing. . . .

The complicity theory says nothing on at least one matter about which the standard theory says much— going through channels before publicly revealing what one knows. But the two theories do not differ as much as this difference in emphasis suggests. If going through channels would suffice to prevent (or undo) the wrong, then it cannot be true (as C4 and C6 together require) that the would-be whistleblower's work will contribute to the wrong if she does not publicly reveal what she knows. Where, however, going through channels would *not* prevent (or undo) the wrong, there is no need to go through channels. Condition C4's if-clause will be satisfied. For the complicity theory, going through channels is a way of finding out what the organization will do, not an independent requirement of justification. That, I think, is also how the standard theory understands it.

TESTING THE THEORY

Let us now test the theory against Boisjoly's testimony before the Rogers Commission. Recall that under the standard theory any justification of that testimony seemed to fail for at least three reasons: First, Boisjoly could not testify without substantial cost to himself and Thiokol (to whom he owned loyalty). Second, there was no serious and substantial harm his testimony could prevent. And, third, he had little reason to believe that, even if he could identify a serious and considerable harm to prevent, his testimony had a significant chance of preventing it.

Since few doubt that Boisjoly's testimony before the Rogers Commission constitutes justified whistleblowing, if anything does, we should welcome a theory that—unlike the standard one—justifies that testimony as whistleblowing. The complicity theory sketched above does that:

(C1) Boisjoly's testimony consisted almost entirely of information derived from his work on booster rockets at Thiokol.

(C2) Boisjoly was a voluntary member of Thiokol.

(C3) Boisjoly believed Thiokol, a legitimate organization, was attempting to mislead its client, the government, about the causes of a deadly accident. Attempting to do that certainly seems a serious moral wrong.

(C4) On the evening before the *Challenger* exploded, Boisjoly gave up objecting to the launch once his superiors, including the three Thiokol vice presidents, had made it clear that they were no longer willing to listen to him. He also had a part in preparing those superiors to testify intelligently before the Rogers Commission concerning the booster's fatal field joint. Boisjoly believed that Thiokol would use his failure to offer his own interpretation of his retreat into silence the night before the launch, and the knowledge that he had imparted to his superiors, to contribute to the attempt to mislead Thiokol's client.

(C5) The evidence justifying beliefs C3 and C4 consisted of comments of various officers of Thiokol, what Boisjoly had seen at Thiokol over the years, and what he learned about the rocket business over a long career. I find this evidence sufficient to justify his belief both that his organization was engaged in wrongdoing and that his work was implicated.

(**C6**) Here we reach a paradox of *knowledge*. Since belief is knowledge if, but only if, it is *both* justified *and* true, we cannot *show* that we know anything. All we can show is that a belief is now justified and that we have no reason to expect anything to turn up later to prove it false. The evidence now available still justifies Boisjoly's belief both about what Thiokol was attempting and about what would have been his part in the attempt. Since new evidence is unlikely, his testimony seems to satisfy C6 just as it satisfied the complicity theory's other five conditions.

Since the complicity theory explains why Boisjoly's testimony before the Rogers Commission was morally required whistleblowing, it has passed its first test, a test the standard theory failed.

NOTES

1. Throughout this essay. I take the standard theory to be Richard T. De George's version in *Business Ethics,* 3rd

Edition (New York: Macmillan, 1990), pp. 200–214 (amended only insofar as necessary to include non-businesses as well as businesses). Why treat De George's theory as standard? There are two reasons: first, it seems the most commonly cited; and second, people offering alternatives generally treat it as the one to be replaced. The only obvious competitor, Norman Bowie's account, is distinguishable from De George's on no point relevant here. See Bowie's *Business Ethics* (Englewood Cliffs, NJ: Prentice Hall, 1982), p. 143.

2. De George, op. cit.

3. De George, p. 210: "The notion of *serious* harm might be expanded to include serious financial harm, and kinds of harm other than death and serious threats to health and body. But as we noted earlier, we shall restrict ourselves here to products and practices that produce or threaten serious harm or danger to life and health."

QUESTIONS

1. What are the paradoxes of whistle-blowing?
2. What is Davis's "complicity theory" of the morality of whistle-blowing? How does it avoid the failures of the standard theory?

Ronald Duska | # Whistleblowing and Employee Loyalty

Ronald Duska is Charles F. Lamont Post Chair of Ethics and the Professions Professor of Ethics at the American College.

There are proponents on both sides of the issue—those who praise whistleblowers as civic heroes and those who condemn them as "finks." Maxwell Glen and Cody Shearer, who wrote about the whistleblowers at Three Mile Island say, "Without the *courageous* breed of assorted company insiders known as whistleblowers—workers who often risk their livelihoods to

disclose information about construction and design flaws—the Nuclear Regulatory Commission itself would be nearly as idle as Three Mile Island. . . . That whistle-blowers deserve both gratitude and protection is beyond disagreement."[1]

Still, while Glen and Shearer praise whistleblowers, others vociferously condemn them. For example, in a now infamous quote, James Roche, the former president of General Motors said:

> Some critics are now busy eroding another support of free enterprise—the loyalty of a management

From Tom L. Beauchamp and Norman E. Bowie, *Ethical Theory and Business* (Englewood Cliffs, NJ: Prentice Hall, 2001). Reprinted by permission of the author.

team, with its unifying values and cooperative work. Some of the enemies of business now encourage an employee to be *disloyal* to the enterprise. They want to create suspicion and disharmony, and pry into the proprietary interests of the business. However this is labeled—industrial espionage, whistle blowing, or professional responsibility—it is another tactic for spreading disunity and creating conflict.[2]

From Roche's point of view, not only is whistle-blowing not "courageous" and not deserving of "gratitude and protection" as Glen and Shearer would have it, it is corrosive and impermissible.

Discussions of whistleblowing generally revolve around three topics: (1) attempts to define whistle-blowing more precisely, (2) debates about whether and when whistleblowing is permissible, and (3) debates about whether and when one has an obligation to blow the whistle.

In this paper I want to focus on the second problem, because I find it somewhat disconcerting that there is a problem at all. When I first looked into the ethics of whistleblowing it seemed to me that whistleblowing was a good thing, and yet I found in the literature claim after claim that it was in need of defense, that there was something wrong with it, namely that it was an act of disloyalty.

If whistleblowing is a disloyal act, it deserves disapproval, and ultimately any action of whistleblowing needs justification. This disturbs me. It is as if the act of a good Samaritan is being condemned as an act of interference, as if the prevention of a suicide needs to be justified.

In his book *Business Ethics,* Norman Bowie claims that "whistleblowing . . . violate(s) a *prima facie* duty of loyalty to one's employer." According to Bowie, there is a duty of loyalty that prohibits one from reporting his employer or company. Bowie, of course, recognizes that this is only a *prima facie* duty, that is, one that can be overridden by a higher duty to the public good. Nevertheless, the axiom that whistleblowing is disloyal is Bowie's starting point.[3]

Bowie is not alone. Sissela Bok sees "whistle-blowing" as an instance of disloyalty:

The whistleblower hopes to stop the game; but since he is neither referee nor coach, and since he blows the whistle on his own team, his act is seen as a *violation*

of loyalty. In holding his position, he has assumed certain obligations to his colleagues and clients. He may even have subscribed to a loyalty oath or a promise of confidentiality. . . . Loyalty to colleagues and to clients comes to be pitted against loyalty to the public interest, to those who may be injured unless the revelation is made.[4]

Bowie and Bok end up defending whistleblowing in certain contexts, so I don't necessarily disagree with their conclusions. However, I fail to see how one has an obligation of loyalty to one's company, so I disagree with their perception of the problem and their starting point. I want to argue that one does not have an obligation of loyalty to a company, even a prima facie one, because companies are not the kind of things that are properly objects of loyalty. To make them objects of loyalty gives them a moral status they do not deserve and in raising their status, one lowers the status of the individuals who work for the companies. Thus, the difference in perception is important because those who think employees have an obligation of loyalty to a company fail to take into account a relevant moral difference between persons and corporations.

But why aren't companies the kind of things that can be objects of loyalty? To answer that we have to ask what are proper objects of loyalty. John Ladd states the problem this way, "Granted that loyalty is the wholehearted devotion to an object of some kind, what kind of thing is the object? Is it an abstract entity, such as an idea or a collective being? Or is it a person or group of persons?"[5] Philosophers fall into three camps on the question. On one side are the idealists who hold that loyalty is devotion to something more than persons, to some cause or abstract entity. On the other side are what Ladd calls "social atomists," and these include empiricists and utilitarians, who think that at most one can only be loyal to individuals and that loyalty can ultimately be explained away as some other obligation that holds between two people. Finally, there is a moderate position that holds that although idealists go too far in postulating some super-personal entity as an object of loyalty, loyalty is still an important and real relation that holds between people, one that cannot be dismissed by reducing it to some other relation.

There does seem to be a view of loyalty that is not extreme. According to Ladd, "'loyalty' is taken to refer to a relationship between persons—for instance, between a lord and his vassal, between a parent and his children, or between friends. Thus the object of loyalty is ordinarily taken to be a person or a group of persons."[6]

But this raises a problem that Ladd glosses over. There is a difference between a person or a group of persons, and aside from instances of loyalty that relate two people such as lord/vassal, parent/child, or friend/ friend, there are instances of loyalty relating a person to a group, such as a person to his family, a person to this team, and a person to his country. Families, countries, and teams are presumably groups of persons. They are certainly ordinarily construed as objects of loyalty.

But to what am I loyal in such a group? In being loyal to the group am I being loyal to the whole group or to its members? It is easy to see the object of loyalty in the case of an individual person. It is simply the individual. But to whom am I loyal in a group? To whom am I loyal in a family? Am I loyal to each and every individual or to something larger, and if to something larger, what is it? We are tempted to think of a group as an entity of its own, an individual in its own right, having an identity of its own.

To avoid the problem of individuals existing for the sake of the group, the atomists insist that a group is nothing more than the individuals who comprise it, nothing other than a mental fiction by which we refer to a group of individuals. It is certainly not a reality or entity over and above the sum of its parts, and consequently is not a proper object of loyalty. Under such a position, of course, no loyalty would be owed to a company because a company is a mere mental fiction, since it is a group. One would have obligations to the individual members of the company, but one could never be justified in overriding those obligations for the sake of the "group" taken collectively. A company has no moral status except in terms of the individual members who comprise it. It is not a proper object of loyalty. But the atomists go too far. Some groups, such as a family, do have a reality of their own, whereas groups of people walking down the street do not. From Ladd's point of view the social atomist is wrong because he fails to recognize the kinds of groups that are held together by "the ties that bind." The atomist tries to reduce these groups to simple sets of individuals bound together by some externally imposed criteria. This seems wrong.

There do seem to be groups in which the relationships and interactions create a new force or entity. A group takes on an identity and a reality of its own that is determined by its purpose, and this purpose defines the various relationships and roles set up within the group. There is a division of labor into roles necessary for the fulfillment of the purposes of the group. The membership, then, is not of individuals who are the same but of individuals who have

On Secrecy and Disclosure

Joseph Pulitzer

There is not a crime, there is not a dodge, there is not a trick, there is not a swindle, there is not a vice which does not live by secrecy. Get these things out in the open, describe them, attack them, ridicule them in the press, and sooner or later public opinion will sweep them away. Publicity may not be the only thing that is needed, but it is the one thing without which all other agencies will fail.

specific relationships to one another determined by the aim of the group. Thus we get specific relationships like parent/ child, coach/player, and so on, that don't occur in other groups. It seems then that an atomist account of loyalty that restricts loyalty merely to individuals and does not include loyalty to groups might be inadequate.

But once I have admitted that we can have loyalty to a group, do I not open myself up to criticism from the proponent of loyalty to the company? Might not the proponent of loyalty to business say: "Very well. I agree with you. The atomists are short-sighted. Groups have some sort of reality and they can be proper objects of loyalty. But companies are groups. Therefore companies are proper objects of loyalty."

The point seems well taken, except for the fact that the kinds of relationships that loyalty requires are just the kind that one does not find in business. As Ladd says, "The ties that bind the persons together provide the basis of loyalty." But all sorts of ties bind people together. I am a member of a group of fans if I go to a ball game. I am a member of a group if I merely walk down the street. What binds people together in a business is not sufficient to require loyalty.

A business or corporation does two things in the free enterprise system: It produces a good or service and it makes a profit. The making of a profit, however, is the primary function of a business as a business, for if the production of the good or service is not profitable, the business would be out of business. Thus nonprofitable goods or services are a means to an end. People bound together in a business are bound together not for mutual fulfillment and support, but to divide labor or make a profit. Thus, while we can jokingly refer to a family as a place where "they have to take you in no matter what," we cannot refer to a company in that way. If a worker does not produce in a company or if cheaper laborers are available, the company—in order to fulfill its purpose—should get rid of the worker. A company feels no obligation of loyalty. The saying "You can't buy loyalty" is true. Loyalty depends on ties that demand self-sacrifice with no expectation of reward. Business functions on the basis of enlightened self-interest. I am devoted to a company not because it is like a parent to me; it is not.

Attempts of some companies to create "one big happy family" ought to be looked on with suspicion. I am not devoted to it at all, nor should I be. I work for it because it pays me. I am not in a family to get paid, I am in a company to get paid.

The cold hard truth is that the goal of profit is what gives birth to a company and forms that particular group. Money is what ties the group together. But in such a commercialized venture, with such a goal, there is no loyalty, or at least none need be expected. An employer will release an employee and an employee will walk away from an employer when it is profitable for either one to do so.

Not only is loyalty to a corporation not required, it more than likely is misguided. There is nothing as pathetic as the story of the loyal employee who, having given above and beyond the call of duty, is let go in the restructuring of the company. He feels betrayed because he mistakenly viewed the company as an object of his loyalty. Getting rid of such foolish romanticism and coming to grips with this hard but accurate assessment should ultimately benefit everyone.

To think we owe a company or corporation loyalty requires us to think of that company as a person or as a group with a goal of human fulfillment. If we think of it in this way we can be loyal. But this is the wrong way to think. A company is not a person. A company is an instrument, and an instrument with a specific purpose, the making of profit. To treat an instrument as an end in itself, like a person, may not be as bad as treating an end as an instrument, but it does give the instrument a moral status it does not deserve; and by elevating the instrument we lower the end. All things, instruments and ends, become alike.

Remember that Roche refers to the "management team" and Bok sees the name "whistleblowing" coming from the instance of a referee blowing a whistle in the presence of a foul. What is perceived as bad about whistleblowing in business from this perspective is that one blows the whistle on one's own team, thereby violating team loyalty. If the company can get its employees to view it as a team they belong to, it is easier to demand loyalty. Then the rules governing teamwork and team loyalty will apply. One reason the appeal to a team and team loyalty works so well in business is that businesses are in competition with one another. Effective motivation turns business practices into a game and instills teamwork.

But businesses differ from teams in very important respects, which makes the analogy between business and a team dangerous. Loyalty to a team is loyalty within the context of sport or a competition. Teamwork and team loyalty require that in the circumscribed activity of the game I cooperate with my fellow players, so that pulling all together, we may win. The object of (most) sports is victory. But winning in sports is a social convention, divorced from the usual goings on of society. Such a winning is most times a harmless, morally neutral diversion.

But the fact that this victory in sports, within the rules enforced by a referee (whistleblower), is a socially developed convention taking place within a larger social context makes it quite different from competition in business, which, rather than being defined by a context, permeates the whole of society in its influence. Competition leads not only to victory

The Upside of Whistle-Blowing

Jim Yardley

The nightclub sparkled under a strobe light, as dancers gyrated to "Play That Funky Music" and Court TV's guest of honor, Sherron S. Watkins, sipped wine from a glow-in-the-dark glass. The music stopped so Ms. Watkins could accept the cable channel's Scales of Justice award.

It was not quite the Nobel Prize ceremony. "Let's rock-n-roll and have a few drinks!" exclaimed Court TV's chairman, Henry Schleiff, after handing Ms. Watkins a bronze statuette. The D.J. obeyed and blasted "Shaft," as the 1970's-theme publicity party roared on.

For Ms. Watkins, the Enron vice president whose blunt-spoken warning about the company's accounting practices made her an instant celebrity, the Court TV party in New Orleans on Sunday was only one weird scene from her surreal new life. The day before, Sam Donaldson introduced her to President Bush at the White House Correspondent's Association dinner in Washington.

And this week in Houston, she has continued to do what some consider the unlikeliest thing of all—work at Enron, whose improprieties she sought to expose in the memo, now famous, she wrote to the former chairman, Kenneth L. Lay, months before the company filed for bankruptcy.

"Generally, people are surprised that she is still there," said Philip H. Hilder, Ms. Watkins's lawyer. "Some people think she has been fired. Some people thought that just on her own she had moved on."

For now, while she remains at Enron, the 42-year-old Ms. Watkins is also tip-toeing toward a public life. Her persona as an upscale Erin Brockovich has brought her book and movie deals. She is in demand on the lecture circuit, and next week she is scheduled to be the keynote speaker at a San Francisco conference that is being sponsored by Steve Forbes.

The New York Times, May 10, 2002

but to losers. One can lose at sport with precious few consequences. The consequences of losing at business are much larger. Further, the losers in business can be those who are not in the game voluntarily (we are all forced to participate) but who are still affected by business decisions. People cannot choose to participate in business. It permeates everyone's lives.

The team model, then, fits very well with the model of the free market system, because there competition is said to be the name of the game. Rival companies compete and their object is to win. To call a foul on one's own teammate is to jeopardize one's chances of winning and is viewed as disloyalty.

But isn't it time to stop viewing corporate machinations as games? These games are not controlled and are not ended after a specific time. The activities of business affect the lives of everyone, not just the game players. The analogy of the corporation to a team and the consequent appeal to team loyalty, although understandable, is seriously misleading, at least in the moral sphere where competition is not the prevailing virtue.

If my analysis is correct, the issue of the permissibility of whistleblowing is not a real issue since there is no obligation of loyalty to a company. Whistleblowing is not only permissible but expected when a company is harming society. The issue is not one of disloyalty to the company, but of whether the whistleblower has an obligation to society if blowing the whistle will bring him retaliation.

NOTES

1. Maxwell Glen and Cody Shearer, "Going After the Whistle-blowers," *Philadelphia Inquirer,* Tuesday, August 2, 1983, Op-ed page, p. 11A.

2. James M. Roche, "The Competitive System, to Work, to Preserve, and to Protect," *Vital Speeches of the Day* (May 1971): 445.

3. Norman Bowie, *Business Ethics* (Englewood Cliffs, N.J.: Prentice Hall, 1982), pp. 140–143.

4. Sissela Bok, "Whistleblowing and Professional Responsibilities," *New York University Education Quarterly* 2 (1980): 3.

5. John Ladd, "Loyalty," *The Encyclopedia of Philosophy* 5: 97.

6. Ibid.

QUESTIONS

1. Whether and when is whistle-blowing permissible, according to Duska? What moral constraints do whistle-blowers have?

2. What is the "team model"? How does it solve the problem of whistle-blowing?

David E. Soles | # Four Concepts of Loyalty

David E. Soles is an author and a philosopher.

THE IDEALIST ACCOUNT

The first view of loyalty may be called an idealist account because of the close resemblance it bears to the position developed by the American idealist, Josiah Royce. According to Royce, loyalty is

> [t]he willing and practical and thorough-going devotion of a person to a cause. A man is loyal when, first, he has some *cause* to which he is loyal; secondly, he *willingly* and *thoroughly* devotes himself to this cause; and when, thirdly, he expresses his devotion in some *sustained and practical way,* by acting steadily in the service of his cause. Instances of loyalty are: The devotion of a patriot to his country, when this devotion leads him to actually live and perhaps to die for his country; the devotion of a martyr to his religion; the devotion of a ship's captain to the requirements of his office when, after a disaster, he works steadily for his ship and for the saving of the ship's company until the last possible service is accomplished, so that he is the last man to leave the ship, and is ready if need be to go down with his ship.[1]

As Royce realizes, each of the aspects of his analysis requires further elucidation. To begin with the object of loyalty: that to which one is loyal must be something objective, external to the individual, and possessed of its own inherent value; "[i]t does not get its value merely from your being pleased with it. You believe, on the contrary, that you love it just because of its own value, which it has by itself, even if you die" (19).

By saying that loyalty requires *willing* devotion, Royce is maintaining that loyalty must be freely given; while obedience can be demanded, loyalty cannot. In part, this follows from Royce's thesis that loyalty entails devotion: devotion is a mental state not reducible to behavior, and while behavior can be demanded, mental states cannot. But while loyalty may entail devotion, devotion is never sufficient for loyalty: "[l]oyalty is never mere emotion. Adoration and affection may go with loyalty, but can never alone constitute loyalty" (18).

This follows from the claim that loyalty is practical—to be loyal is to serve a cause. Furthermore, this service is thorough-going and sustained; a loyal person does whatever is necessary to promote the cause, "ready to live or die as the cause directs" (18).

This idealist conception of loyalty is germane to discussions of business ethics in the following way. If this is the accepted conception of loyalty and if it can be established that employees ought to be loyal to their employers, then the stringent obligations sometimes placed upon employees in the name of loyalty would be perfectly justified. A loyal employee would be one thoroughly dedicated to serving the interests of his principal, ready to live or die as directed, and to say that employees should be loyal would be to advocate such dedication. It is instructive to consider some examples of the sorts of obligations this conception of loyalty could require of a loyal employee. A loyal employee would always be willing to place the interests of the principal before purely private interests, even in matters unrelated to employment; a loyal employee would be willing to sacrifice the interests of uninvolved third parties or even society at large, if doing so served the employer's interest; a loyal employee would never advocate or vote for social policies or legislation that might damage the interests of the employer; a loyal

Reprinted by permission of the author from *The International Journal of Applied Philosophy* 8 (Summer 1993). Notes were deleted from the text.

employee would never publicly criticize or oppose the actions of the employer; a loyal employee would never consider leaving the employer. That something akin to the idealist conception of loyalty is operative in some quarters is evidenced by the frequent endorsements of these claims.

Lest it be thought that I am constructing a straw man here, consider the following case which Marcia Baron discusses in *The Moral Status of Loyalty*.

> In a 1973 CBS report on Phillips Petroleum, Inc., one of its chief executives was asked to describe what sort of qualities his company looks for in prospective employees. He responded without hesitation that above all else, what Phillips wants and needs is loyalty on the part of its employees. A loyal employee, he elaborated, would buy only Phillips products. . . . Moreover, a loyal employee would vote in local, state, and national elections in whatever way was most conducive to the growth and flourishing of Phillips. And, of course, a loyal employee would never leave Phillips unless it was absolutely unavoidable. To reduce the likelihood of that happening, prospective employees were screened to make sure their respective wives did not have careers which might conflict with lifelong loyalty to Phillips.[2]

Is it true that employees have an obligation to so thoroughly dedicate themselves to the interests of their employers and, if so, what are the grounds of that obligation? . . .

It is morally irresponsible to be willing to perform any conceivable action that would further the interests of one's chosen cause; one must always reserve the option of saying that one can no longer serve a cause if it requires the performance of certain sorts of actions. . . .

If loyalty requires such total, thorough-going dedication to a cause, there are very few things worthy of loyalty; furthermore, since the interests of any two causes could conceivably come into conflict, one can be loyal to only one object. Therefore, it is incumbent upon each person to ensure that the object of his loyalty is of the highest inherent worth.

It is very unlikely that business institutions qualify as objects of the most inherent worth. To begin with, business institutions are instrumentally, not in-

herently, valuable; they are valued because they are means for providing goods and services which are valued. If we no longer cared for those goods and services or if we found better ways to obtain them, the institutions which provide them would lose much of their value. Furthermore, not all business institutions possess instrumental value: some produce more harm than good by manufacturing dangerous, inferior products, polluting the environment, engaging in illegal business practices, etc. But whether instrumentally good or evil, a business institution is not the sort of thing worthy of loyalty in the idealist sense.

In summary, if the idealist conception of loyalty were accepted as our working notion of loyalty, and if it could be established that employees ought to be loyal to their employers, then the demands placed upon employees in the name of loyalty would be justified: employees would have an obligation to place the interests of their employers before all other interests. However, it is not clear that we should accept this as our working conception of loyalty and, more importantly, even if we did, we must conclude that business institutions could not be appropriate objects of loyalty.

THE COMMON SENSE CONCEPTION

The common sense view of loyalty more satisfactorily captures the everyday conception of loyalty with which most of us are familiar. Most of us are untroubled by statements to the effect that someone is a loyal fan of the Kansas City Royals, a loyal member of the Republican party, or loyal to her alma mater, and when we hear such claims we are not inclined to suppose that the person is totally dedicated to the cause, "willing to live or die as the cause directs."

A version of the common sense view of loyalty has been formulated by Andrew Oldenquist in "Loyalties."[3] According to Oldenquist,

> . . . [w]hen I have a loyalty to something I have somehow come to view it as *mine*. It is an object of non-instrumental value to me in virtue (but not only in virtue) of its being mine, and I am disposed to feel pride when it prospers, shame when it declines, and anger or indignation when it is harmed. In general, people care about the objects of their loyalties, and

they acknowledge obligations that they would not acknowledge were it not for their loyalties. (175)

... [L]oyalty is positive and is primarily characterized by esteem and concern for the common good of one's group. (177)

On this view, there are three essential features of loyalty. First, loyalty entails having a positive attitude towards the objects of one's loyalty; a loyalty is to "an object of non-instrumental value," people "care about" the objects of their loyalties. Second, loyalty entails a disposition to serve the interests of the object to which one is loyal; loyal persons "acknowledge obligations that they would not acknowledge were it not for their loyalties." Third, both the concern and the obligations are rooted in the individual's belief that he stands in some personal relationship to the object of his loyalty; to have a loyalty to something is to somehow come to view it as one's own.

The first thing to note about this conception of loyalty is that it is not sufficient to distinguish loyalty from many other virtues.[4] While caring, acknowledging obligations, and feeling a personal relationship may be necessary features of loyalty, they also are necessary features of virtues such as love and friendship and may even characterize the relationship between some professionals and their patients, clients, students, etc. Many dedicated teachers consider their students to be objects of non-instrumental value, care about them, acknowledge supererogatory obligations, and both the concern and the obligations stem from the fact that these students are their students. Similar remarks may be made about doctors, nurses, lawyers, social workers, etc. To characterize their attitude as one of loyalty seems to be stretching the common sense notion of loyalty too far. ...

In conflating loyalty with other, distinct, virtues, Oldenquist has failed to provide the promised analysis of loyalty. Nevertheless, while this common sense account should not be construed as providing a definition of "loyalty" in terms of necessary and sufficient conditions, it may be acceptable as a rough characterization of some essential features of loyalty. Loyalty, like friendship, love, and professional interest, entails concern, obligations, and a feeling of personal identification with the object of one's loyalty. The questions that need to be asked, then, are: (1)

does one have any obligation to have such attitudes to one's employer, and (2) does the having of such attitudes justify always acting in the interests of the object of one's loyalty?

Beginning with the first question, on the common sense account, the mere fact that one happens to have been born in a particular country, happens to have attended a particular school, or happens to work for a particular institution is not sufficient for saying that one should be loyal to it. Oldenquist makes this point in maintaining that "... a loyalist doesn't value something simply because it is his. It must have features which make it worth having, and it could deteriorate to the extent that shame ultimately kills his loyalty" (178). On this conception of loyalty, one should bestow one's loyalty only on those objects which are worthy of it and loyalty bestowed upon some nations, schools or institutions would be misguided.

Furthermore, if this is our working conception of loyalty, no one has an obligation to be loyal to anything; to suppose that one has an obligation to be loyal to anything is to make a fundamental category mistake. On this view, being loyal entails having certain sorts of attitudes; to be loyal to an object one must care about it. But while persons can have moral obligations to perform certain actions and while certain attitudes may be morally desirable or indesirable, we do not have moral obligations to have certain attitudes and beliefs. Just as no one has an obligation to have feelings of love or friendship to another, no one has an obligation to have feelings of loyalty to anything. Thus, one can have no obligation to be loyal to her nation, school, or employer even if they are worthy of loyalty.

Turning to the second question, does loyalty require one to always act in the interest of that to which one is loyal? It is often suggested that loyalty is inconsistent with certain sorts of actions, for example, whistleblowing is alleged to be incompatible with loyalty. Sissela Bok, for instance, sets up the dichotomy this way.

... [T]he whistleblower hopes to stop the game; but since he is neither referee nor coach, and since he blows the whistle on his own team, his act is seen as a violation of loyalty. In holding his position, he has assumed certain obligations to his colleagues and clients. He may even have subscribed to a loyalty oath or a promise of confidentiality. Loyalty to colleagues and clients comes to be pitted against loyalty to the public interest, to those who may be injured unless the revelation is made.

Not only is loyalty violated in whistleblowing, hierarchy as well is often opposed. . . . If the facts warrant whistleblowing, how can the second element—breach of loyalty—be minimized?[5] *(my italics)*

Blind to Earned Loyalty

Robert C. Solomon and Clancy Martin

The concept of loyalty has changed from one of "blind and obligated" to one of "insightful and earned." Several generations ago, if a person worked hard and kept his nose to the grindstone, he could pretty well be assured of work for a lifetime. People were loyal to organizations because they believed organizations would be loyal to them.

The passage of "good old loyalty" may be lamented by many, but there is some good news. It has been replaced by a strong new type—namely, earned loyalty.

So, rather than lament the loss of "good old loyalty," let's focus on a loyalty that may well provide a stronger motivational force for both management and the managed. I have identified five basic elements of the new loyalty.

1. Values and Standards. Loyalty tends to be more easily earned in those organizations that have clearly-defined values and challenging standards. People are likely to be loyal to values that lead to outstanding achievements in products, services, and relationships.
2. Clear Expectations. A willingness to be specific and forthright in terms of expected behaviors does a great deal toward developing a feeling of loyalty on the part of those who will follow. It is easier for people to be loyal to what they clearly understand.
3. Frequent Feedback. People need to know where they stand and how well or poorly they have performed when evaluated against the expectations, standards, and values. People need to hear good news as well as bad. Frequent feedback is a way of increasing meaningful involvement.
4. Respect for the Individual. The new loyalty will have to be earned on the basis of respect for the individual. Respect requires trust, based on consistency in personal and interpersonal relationships; a willingness to be open with expectations and requirements; to really listen and engage in honest exchange.
5. Long-Term Commitments. This last element is probably most difficult to achieve. In what appears to many to be an atmosphere of layoffs, terminations, forced resignations, and retirements, it is difficult to convince people that long-term commitments are realistic or possible.

—From *Above the Bottom Line*

On the common sense conception, this is a very misleading way of presenting the problem for it implies that whistleblowing is a breach of loyalty, that one cannot both be loyal to an institution and blow the whistle on it. But, on the common sense view, this is surely wrong; one can view an institution as one's own, care deeply about it, assume obligations towards it, and still publicly and strenuously oppose what one takes to be unethical or illegal actions on its part. This is a feature of loyalty explicitly recognized in British politics as "the loyal opposition."

Setting up a dichotomy between loyalty and whistleblowing is not merely a misleading way to present the problem of whistleblowing, it is dangerous. Loyalty is generally perceived as a virtue and disloyalty is perceived as a vice. To say that loyalty demands a certain action is to give a prima facie reason for performing that action and to label a particular action as disloyal is to give a prima facie reason for not performing that action. Under those conditions, potential whistleblowers are encouraged to construe themselves as choosing between performing a wrong act themselves (being disloyal) or remaining silent about the performance of wrongs committed by others. When presented this way, it is not surprising that many individuals choose silence. But if whistleblowing is not construed as an instance of disloyalty, the whole complexion of the problem changes. If loyalty does not require acquiescence in wrong doing, the refusal to remain silent about known wrongs cannot be construed as an ipso facto instance of disloyalty.

Acceptance of the common sense view of loyalty, thus, would justify two conclusions both of which are anathema to many discussions of business and professional ethics. First, it is simply a mistake to suppose that individuals have an obligation to be loyal to their employers and second, loyalty is compatible with strenuously opposing actions of one's employer.

LOYALTIES AS NORMS

While he does not appear to be aware that he is doing so, Oldenquist formulates a second conception of loyalty radically different from his common sense account. According to this second view, "loyalties are norms that define the domains within which we accept the moral machinery of universalizable reasons and relevant differences" (182); alternatively, "loyalties define moral communities or domains within which we are willing to universalize moral judgments, treat equals equally, protect the common good, and in other ways adopt the familiar machinery of impersonal morality. . . . A loyalty defines a moral community in terms of a conception of a common good and a special commitment to the members of the group who share this good" (177). This seems to be incompatible with the common sense account Oldenquist formulates. Attitudes, definitions and norms are different sorts of things. If loyalty is an attitude as the common sense account maintains, then it is neither a norm nor a definition.

Perhaps the confusion here is merely verbal. Perhaps Oldenquist's claim is something like this: the class of objects to which one is loyal is delineated by, or co-extensive with, the moral communities or domains "within which we are willing to universalize moral judgments, treat equals equally, protect the common good, and in other ways adopt the familiar machinery of impersonal morality." On this reading, loyalty is not literally a norm which defines a moral community; rather, one has attitudes of loyalty towards the moral community determined by the norms.

There are two ways of interpreting this talk of loyalty to the moral community: (1) we might have feelings of loyalty to each of the members of the community defined by the norm, or (2) we might have feelings of loyalty to the community, but not necessarily to each of its members. Either alternative faces serious difficulties.

Beginning with the first interpretation, if loyalty is characterized by positive feelings of esteem and concern, a disposition to feel pride when the object of loyalty prospers, shame when it declines, and anger or hurt when it is harmed, then the moral community defined by the norms and the objects of one's loyalty might not be co-extensive. One might, for instance, define the moral community as rational, sentient beings; this would define the domain within which we are willing to universalize moral judgments, etc. One might not, however, have positive feelings of concern, esteem, etc. for all the members of this community. In that case, the community of objects to which one is loyal would not be coextensive with the moral community.

The second interpretation would avoid this conclusion by arguing that on the above example one is loyal to the class of rational sentient beings, not individual rational sentient beings; that communities and not individuals are the proper objects of loyalty. . . .

If any moral norm to which one is committed defines a moral community to which one is loyal, then loyalty can never come into conflict with any other moral standard. Suppose that I am loyal to the institution where I am employed; it is a community towards which I have positive attitudes, I have assumed special obligations to promote its interests, I treat the members of that community according to the procedures of impersonal morality, recognizing universalizable reasons, and relevant differences, etc. Suppose that I am also committed to the principle that rational beings should always be treated as ends in themselves. Suppose, finally, that I come to perceive certain policies pursued by my institution as being grossly exploitive and am torn between a desire to protect the institution and an obligation to act on my moral principles. In choosing what course of action to pursue, it would be natural to describe myself as choosing between considerations of loyalty to the institution and some other principle of morality.

On Oldenquist's view, however, the choice is merely one between a wide and a narrow loyalty; on the one hand I am loyal to the institution and on the other hand I am loyal to the moral community defined by the norm. If any moral standard which I accept defines a moral community to which I am loyal, then loyalty can never come into conflict with any other moral standard, there can only be conflicts between wide and narrow loyalties. At precisely that point loyalty becomes a vacuous, trivial moral notion.

Furthermore, to say that loyalty is a norm does not answer any ethical questions nor provide moral guidance. . . . In particular, characterizing loyalties as norms which define moral communities provides no guidance in ascertaining whether we should be loyal to our employers nor does it provide any insight into what loyalty would demand should we decide that loyalty is appropriate. Consequently, such an analysis is useless for deciding the interesting questions about loyalty that arise in the context of business and professional ethics.

THE MINIMALIST ACCOUNT

There is a fourth conception of loyalty which maintains that a loyal individual is one who meets reasonable expectations of trust; to be loyal just is to discharge one's obligations and responsibilities conscientiously. Such an attenuated view of loyalty does not demand positive feelings of affection, devotion, or respect nor does it expect one to perform supererogatory actions in promoting the interests of the object of one's loyalty. At most, loyalty demands that one act in a way that does not betray reasonable expectations of trust.

The Restatement of the Law of Agency is subject to a minimalist interpretation.[6] That Restatement maintains that a loyal agent has a duty " . . . to act solely for the benefit of the principal in all matters connected with his agency" (387). This claim that the agent is to act solely for the benefit of the principal is qualified in several important respects by the Restatement. First, an agent may act against the interests of his principal when doing so is necessary for the protection of his own interests or those of others (387b). Second, an agent has no obligation to perform acts which are illegal or unethical and " . . . in determining whether or not the orders of the principal are reasonable . . . business or professional ethics . . . are considered" (385-1a). Third, an agent is not "prevented from acting in good faith outside his employment in a manner which injuriously affects his principal's business" (387b). Finally, "[a]n agent is privileged to reveal information confidentially acquired . . . in the protection of a superior interest of himself or of a third person. Thus, if the confidential information is to the effect that the principal is committing or is about to commit a crime, the agent is under no duty not to reveal it" (395f).

Like most documents, the Restatement of Agency is subject to competing interpretations. As Blumberg has noted, the Restatement

> . . . is drafted in terms of economic activity, economic motivation, and economic advantage and formulates duties of loyalty and obedience for the agent to prevent the agent's own economic interest from impairing his judgment, zeal, or single-minded devotion to the furtherance of his principal's economic interests. The reference in section 395, Comment permitting the agent to disclose confidential information concerning a criminal act committed or planned by the principal is the sole exception to a system of analysis that is otherwise exclusively concerned with matters relating to the economic position of the parties.[7] . . .

As Blumberg rightly emphasizes, the Restatement is concerned almost exclusively with conflicts of economic interests; nevertheless, if interpreted liberally, the Restatement can be quite useful in responding to the broader issues. The discussion of criminal activity at 395f could be treated as an example of a case where the revelation of confidential material is justified by the need to protect a superior interest; it need not be read as limiting the revelation of confidential material to cases involving criminal activity. By the same token, 387b could be interpreted as maintaining that an agent is justified in acting against the interests of the principal when doing so is necessary to protect important noneconomic interests of himself or others. Interpreted thusly, either 395f or 387b could be appealed to in justifying the claim that loyalty is consistent with acting against the interests of one's employer.

On the minimalist account, loyalty would not entail a willingness to participate in, condone or remain silent about illegal activities. It would not entail willingness to participate in unethical conduct if doing so promoted the interests of one's principal. It would be compatible with acting against the interests of one's employer, even revealing confidential information, if doing so were necessary to protect important interests of the public. Finally, contrary to the opinion of the Phillips executive, loyalty would be compatible with voting in ways not conducive to the growth and flourishing of one's principal and

even compatible with seeking employment elsewhere. In this minimalist sense, simply meeting reasonable expectations of trust is sufficient for loyalty.

This, of course, raises the issue of what responsibilities it is reasonable for employers to entrust to employees. Many of these are defined and clearly stipulated in job descriptions, contracts, and codes of professional ethics and many more are informally recognized as standard acceptable practices within a profession; and, while there are bound to be grey areas and points of disagreement, there are some activities which loyalty does not enjoin.

If the minimalist conception of loyalty is accepted, it seems clear that employees ought to be loyal to their employers. That, however, merely amounts to the claim that they ought to meet reasonable, legitimate expectations of trust; it does not impose upon them the sorts of obligations that often are urged in the name of loyalty.

CONCLUSION

Much of the confusion and disagreement infecting discussions of the role of loyalty in business and professional ethics has been engendered by equivocation and ambiguity in the concept itself. This essay has briefly considered four different conceptions of loyalty and examined some of the implications of each. If the idealist conception of loyalty is accepted, loyalty to one's employer would demand the sort of behavior sometimes advocated in its name. It is not clear, however, that this account should be accepted and, if we do accept it, employers would not be appropriate objects of loyalty. If the common sense conception of loyalty is accepted, two conclusions follow: first, since loyalty is supererogatory, no one has an obligation to feel loyal to anything; second, loyalty, in this sense, does not entail placing the interests of one's principal before all other considerations and, in fact, is compatible with opposing some of the interests of one's principal. The third conception, which maintains that the adoption of any norm regulating conduct generates a loyalty, trivializes the notion of loyalty to the point where it is useless for guiding conduct. Finally, on the minimalist conception, one can justify saying that employees ought to be loyal to their employers; the minimalist view is sufficiently attenuated, however, that such a claim does not amount to much.

NOTES

1. Josiah Royce, *The Philosophy of Loyalty,* The MacMillan Co., New York, 1916, pp. 16–17. Subsequent references to this work are provided as page numbers in the text.

2. Marcia Baron, *The Moral Status of Loyalty,* Kendal Hunt, Dubuque, Iowa, 1984, p. 1.

3. Andrew Oldenquist, "Loyalties," *The Journal of Philosophy,* April, 1982, pp. 173–193. Subsequent references to this work are provided as page numbers in the text.

4. This should not be construed as a criticism of Oldenquist. His objective seems to be to advocate loyalty, not explicate the conception.

5. Sissela Bok, "Whistleblowing and Professional Responsibility," *New York University Education Quarterly,* Vol. II, 4 (1980), 2–7. Reprinted in Beauchamp and Bowie, *Ethical Theory and Business,* 2nd ed., Prentice Hall, Inc., Englewood Cliffs, New Jersey, pp. 261–269.

6. *Restatement of the Law, Second, Agency,* Vol. 2, American Law Institute Publishers, St. Paul, Minn., 1958.

7. Phillip J. Blumberg, "Corporate Responsibility and the Employee's Duty of Loyalty and Obedience," in Beauchamp and Bowie, *Ethical Theory and Business,* Prentice Hall, Inc., Englewood Cliffs, New Jersey, 1979, pp. 309–310.

QUESTIONS

1. What are the four concepts of loyalty? How do they disagree with one another?

2. What remains of loyalty after Soles concludes his analysis? What concept of loyalty do you subscribe to? Can you offer your own, original concept of loyalty?

George D. Randels

Loyalty, Corporations, and Community

George D. Randels Jr. is associate professor of social ethics in the Religious Studies Department of the University of the Pacific.

The man in the gray flannel suit. The organization man. When it comes to loyalty, American business is not without images, flawed though they may be. But these are the ghosts of business past. In spite of their hard work, long hours, and important sacrifices, they have been downsized. It is yesterday's news that this type of devotion is not necessarily rewarded, nor does such devotion necessarily indicate loyalty to a company as opposed to the company being a mere instrument for personal advantage. Three *New Yorker* cartoons reflect current trends. In one, the downsized employee is pictured as that paradigm of loyalty, the dog. "Of *course* the company appreciates your years of loyalty," says the manager to the teary-eyed employee (destined for the Humane Society?). In another, the manager s consolation includes some positive spin: "Yes, and the fact that you've been an outstanding employee for twenty-five years is going to look great on your résumé." The third cartoon's setting is the interview rather than the layoff. Here the personnel manager's statement depicts both sides of the coin: "We expect little loyalty. In return we offer little security." In the context that these cartoons portray, the "Why be moral?" question often associated

© 2001. *Business Ethics Quarterly,* Volume 11, Issue 1. ISSN 1052-1064. Notes were deleted from the text.

with discussions of business ethics becomes "Why be loyal?" There seems to be no benefit, unless loyalty is somehow its own reward. . . .

LOYALTY, DUTY, AND VIRTUE

Loyalty is often characterized as a duty that an employee owes to a corporation, or as a virtue of a good employee, but loyalty is not a duty or a virtue. It is, however, linked to both of these concepts in that loyal persons will perform certain duties and possess certain virtues. Loyalty involves a complex of passions and character traits such as commitment, with outward actions springing from them. It is thus more readily identified by character-based ethics, but is not itself an individual virtue. . . .

WHAT IS LOYALTY?

. . . Loyalty is a passion. But contrary to traditional thinking, there is not necessarily a one-to-one correspondence between passions and virtues (or vices). Loyalty seems to be the type of passion that can contribute to multiple virtues (and vices) and obviously to a multitude of ends. Ewin apparently finds loyalty so central, however, that it is the sole passion at work. He suggests that "loyalty is the emotional setting for the virtues and vices; it is not itself a virtue or a vice, but is the raw material for them."[1] Because loyalty extends beyond the self to some object, it is a social passion, and Robert Solomon likely is correct to suggest that it is a type of love.[2] But even as a type of love, loyalty is not the sole passion for the virtues, not even the moral virtues. There are, after all, other types of love, and other passions, such as fear, daring, pleasure, anger, joy, pity, pride, shame, and hope. These other loves and passions are not readily reducible to loyalty, and also provide "raw material" for virtues and vices.

Loyalty is a social passion, a type of love that extends beyond the self to some object of loyalty. As loyalty develops, this object becomes no longer strictly external, but is linked to one's self-identity and helps to provide meaning for one's life. Solomon and Fletcher both claim that it is through our loyalties that we define our sense of self, and this seems quite right.[3] Harvard or Yale, Duke or Carolina, Cubs or Sox,

Catholic or Protestant, Macy's or Gimble's, Microsoft or Netscape. While loyalties often do not involve binary choices like these or an "us v. them" mentality, they clearly do define us and link us not only to the object of loyalty but perhaps also to a group of other people who share that loyalty with us. . . .

The link between self and others is key to loyalty, and relationship is the source of this link and serves as an important conceptual tool. But relationship would need to move from the literal to the metaphorical to provide a general understanding of loyalty (as opposed to a particular type of loyalty), and even then the metaphor breaks down. When venturing beyond interpersonal loyalties, the nature of relationships will differ dramatically, and it is difficult to maintain that mutuality or reciprocity is required for all forms of loyalty as it is in the friendship relation. Just as there can be unrequited love, there can be unrequited loyalty. A person can be loyal without a literal relationship to the object of loyalty. It is possible to be a loyal Cub fan without having a relationship with Sammy Sosa, or even having his autograph or ever having seen a game at Wrigley Field. Likewise, it is possible to be a loyal customer by continuing to use a product without any contact with any person from the company (e.g., Coke or Pepsi). And one can be loyal to certain ideals regardless of the support of like-minded persons.

In the corporate context, relationship works quite well for understanding interpersonal loyalties between co-workers, loyalty to one's boss, and so on. The concept presents difficulties, however, when thinking about the prospects for loyalty to an organization. Fletcher partially addresses this concern by noting that in group loyalty, membership rather than relationship provides the basis. "Membership makes one an insider; it confers identity within a matrix of relationships both to other members and to the leadership of the organization." Entry into the group and subsequent identification with it are the two key aspects of membership. Loyalties arise from this identification.[4] Membership defined in this way is a good vehicle for characterizing loyalty to an organization like a corporation. To be loyal, an employee or manager would need to feel like a part of the organization through a matrix of relationships and identify himself or herself with the organization, typically with a positive association. A sense of membership minimizes the compartmentalization or segmentation of oneself that often happens between the workplace and the rest of one's life. There are, of course, different possible levels of membership in terms of commitment and identification (not necessarily in terms of job status), and the degree of loyalty would vary with them.

Loyalty in the corporate context would have to be based on relationships and a sense of membership. This analysis necessarily cuts against traditional business/economic theory about individualism, self-interest, and the corporation. In the next section, I will discuss loyalty in relation to this standard account of business, and then move on to discuss an alternative account in the last section.

LOYALTY AND THE STANDARD ACCOUNT OF BUSINESS

The standard account of business presents serious barriers for loyalty's prospects in the business context with its focus on the individual and self-interest in pursuit of wealth. The "spirit of capitalism," the economic mind-set, would seem to preclude loyalties except perhaps as instrumental for one's own gain. Ewin nicely presents the contrast between loyalty and the standard account of business. "A really loyal person subjugates (at least to some extent) his or her private interests to those of the object of loyalty, and that is quite different from being an entirely independent item entering a commercial relationship. Loyalty involves emotional ties and not merely commercial ties." Loyalty runs counter to commercial judgment because the latter would require one to take a better job offer from a rival company rather than stay put. Loyalty proves difficult in the business context because it would necessarily involve a "willingness *not* to follow good [commercial] judgment, at least some of the time."[5]

One must then choose between loyalty and self-interest, and in the standard account, there really could not be a choice at all. Self-interest would be the only option. There would be a very limited sense—if any—of relationship or membership, which serve as the grounding of loyalty. This is why Duska rejects a duty of loyalty in the business context, because "the kinds of relationships that loyalty requires are just the

kind that one does not find in business." The common pursuit of personal financial gain is insufficient to establish the bonds necessary for loyalty. "Loyalty depends on ties that demand self-sacrifice with no expectation of reward. Business functions on the basis of enlightened self-interest. . . . Attempts of some companies to create 'one big happy family' ought to be looked upon with suspicion. I am not devoted to it at all, nor should I be. I work for it because it pays me. I am not in a family to get paid, I am in a company to get paid." Money, not love, keeps the company together. Duska holds that loyalty to a corporation is not only not required, but is likely to be misguided when it exists. A corporation is concerned with profit, not human fulfillment. We should thus get rid of foolish romanticism about corporations. Accepting this harsh reality benefits us all, especially those loyal workers who wind up feeling betrayed. Corporate loyalty should not exist, and is a mistake when it does.[6]

. . . Insofar as a corporation operates for the sole purpose of profit making, then Duska is exactly right that such an organization does not deserve loyalty. Neither would individuals like co-workers and bosses if they were strictly rational maximizers of their own self-interest. Furthermore, if financial gain is all *I* want, then I could not be loyal anyway, whether the organization, boss, or co-workers deserve my loyalty or not. I would view it (and them) strictly in instrumental terms, even as it (and they) may also view me the same way. The grounds for loyalty would not exist.

Although Duska follows most accounts of loyalty in emphasizing self-sacrifice—and clearly loyal people sacrifice various interests, their time, and sometimes even their lives—loyalty is not strictly altruistic. The loyal person's self-interest is tied up with that of the object of loyalty. There is an important link between the self and the object of loyalty. It is not just in the company's interest or the boss's interest or my co-workers' interests that the product succeed, but *my* interest. It is not strictly a matter of sacrifice for others, although I may make sacrifices. I have invested myself and thus have a stake in the object of loyalty. In many respects, its interests *are* my interests. The necessary dichotomy between loyalty and self-interest is a false one. The standard account mistakenly assumes that they cannot co-exist in the business world.

CORPORATE LOYALTY IN THE POSTMODERN BUSINESS WORLD

What is a proper object of loyalty? Why not loyalty to a corporation, co-worker, boss, project, team, or profession? Of course, corporate loyalty might not be prudential, as the downsizing phenomenon has shown.[7] Moreover, as Duska indicates, "A company is an instrument, and an instrument with a specific purpose, the making of profit. To treat an instrument as an end in itself . . . give[s] the instrument a moral status it does not deserve."[8]

Duska is correct that a corporation is indeed an instrument, and insofar as that is all a corporation is, then his conclusion is correct. But a corporation can also be much more, . . . Robert Solomon claims that corporations are indeed much more—they are communities. The "relationships of reciprocity and cooperation . . . consist, first of all, in a shared sense of belonging, a shared sense of mission or, at least, a shared sense of mutual interest."[9] . . .

For a corporation to be a community, it would have to be more than an instrument for financial gain. It would have to contribute to human fulfillment. This is not to say, however, that a corporation needs to become the center of its employees' lives to be a community. . . . A corporation or any group need not include all of one's social relationships, values, and interests in order to be a community. Instead, a community involves "a framework of shared beliefs, interests, and commitments unit[ing] a set of *varied* groups and activities . . . that establish a common faith or fate, a personal identity, a sense of belonging, and a supportive structure of activities and relationships." For a group like a corporation, "*the emergence of community depends on the opportunity for, and impulse toward, comprehensive interaction, commitment, and responsibility.*"[10]

. . . Rather than viewing corporations strictly as instruments because they are not comprehensive communities, they can be seen as existing along a community continuum. While I would not want to see corporations all the way at the comprehensive end of the continuum, the closer they move in that direction, the greater the sharing of values, sense of membership, and identification of the self with the whole. To the extent that corporations are communities, loyalty not only is possible, but can be very much appropriate.

Whether loyalty is appropriate is a crucial question, but can receive only a cursory reply here. Good judgment is necessary to determine if and when to invest loyalty and hence oneself in an organization. The presence of community is a necessary but insufficient condition for doing so. One must consider the ideals and goals of organization and their worthiness. Do they match with my own aspirations, or do I want to modify my own to fit with its? Furthermore, are the goals and ideals adhered to, and if so, are ethically acceptable means used to attain them?

Assuming loyalty is appropriate in a corporation, as a community it involves whole persons rather than strictly their segmented interests. Unlike the organization man's singleness of purpose, however, this involvement of the whole person does not exclude loyalties to other communities and to individuals with whom we have relationships. . . . Loyalties to family, friends, religion, town, country, and corporation, among others, may happily co-exist with one another, but likely will compete from time to time. When they do compete, as Alan Wolfe indicates, "the choice is not between loyalty and disloyalty but between competing ways of being loyal. . . . The question is how we balance them, not how we choose between them."[11]

Integrity, a personal sense of wholeness, is important to the task of balancing one's loyalties. This sense of wholeness involves not an isolated self, but includes connectedness with these various others. It involves not a return to singleness of purpose, but balance. That is not to say that all loyalties are equal and so must receive identical treatment; some undoubtedly are more important than others. Corporate loyalty should be less than some loyalties, but perhaps more than some others. This balancing must be worked out in concrete cases, however, and can only be suggested in the abstract.

While the need for such balancing may cause one to question the desirability of corporate loyalty, the inability to have loyalty to a corporation itself can damage one's integrity. The impossibility of loyalty makes for a divided self and potentially compromises one's other loyalties to religion, family, friends, etc., as one engages in tasks for a purely instrumental entity. It would be far better to establish a Connection Thesis that acknowledges the legitimacy of loyalty to corporate communities.

NOTES

1. R. E. Ewin, "Loyalty and Virtues," *The Philosophical Quarterly* 42 (1992): 418.

2. Robert C. Solomon, *A Passion for Justice: Emotions and the Origins of the Social Contract* (Reading, Mass.: Addison-Wesley Publishing Co., 1990), p. 288.

3. Solomon, p. 289; George P. Fletcher, *Loyalty: An Essay on the Morality of Relationships* (New York: Oxford University Press, 1993), pp. 8–9.

4. Fletcher, pp. 33–34.

5. Ewin, pp. 410–412 (emphasis original). p. 554.

6. Ronald Duska, "Whistleblowing and Employee Loyalty," *Contemporary Issues in Business Ethics,* 2nd ed., ed. Joseph R. Des Jardins and John J. McCall (Belmont, Calif.: Wadsworth, 1990); reprinted in *Business Ethics: A Philosophical Reader,* ed. Thomas I. White (New York: Macmillan, 1993), p. 554.

7. *The Economist* contends that for prudential reasons employees should avoid loyalty to a corporation. Given the shrinking life expectancy of a Fortune 500 company and downsizing, employees might find a better focus than companies for their feelings of loyalty. "Two Cheers for Loyalty," *The Economist,* 6 Jan. 1996, p. 49.

8. Duska, p. 554.

9. Robert C. Solomon, "The Corporation as Community: A Reply to Ed Hartman." *Business Ethics Quarterly* 4 (1994): 277.

10. Philip Selznick, *The Moral Commonwealth: Social Theory and the Promise of Community* (Berkeley: University of California Press, 1992), pp. 358–359 (emphasis original).

11. Alan Wolfe, "On Loyalty," *Wilson Quarterly* 21 (1997): 52.

REFERENCES

Duska, Ronald. 1990. "Whistleblowing and Employee Loyalty." In *Contemporary Issues in Business Ethics,* 2nd ed., ed. Joseph R. Des Jardins and John J. McCall, pp. 142–146. Belmont, Calif.: Wadsworth. Reprinted in *Business Ethics: A Philosophical Reader,* ed. Thomas I. White, pp. 551–556. New York: Macmillan, 1993.

Ewin, R. E. 1992. "Loyalty and Virtues." *The Philosophical Quarterly* 42:403–419.

Fletcher, George P. 1993. *Loyalty: An Essay on the Morality of Relationships.* New York: Oxford University Press.

Freeman, R. Edward. 1994. "The Politics of Stakeholder Theory: Some Future Directions." *Business Ethics Quarterly* 4:409–421.

Haughey, John C. 1993. "Does Loyalty in the Workplace Have a Future?" *Business Ethics Quarterly* 3: 1–16.

Lewis, Michael. 1989. *Liar's Poker: Rising Through the Wreckage on Wall Street.* New York: W. W. Norton and Co.

Meyer, John P. and Natalie J. Allen. 1997. *Commitment in the Workplace: Theory, Research, and Application.* Thousand Oaks, Calif.: Sage Publications.

Nathanson, Stephen. 1993. "Fletcher on Loyalty and Universal Morality." *Criminal Justice Ethics* 12: 56–62.

Oldenquist, Andrew. 1982. "Loyalties." *The Journal of Philosophy* 79: 173–193.

Pfeiffer, Raymond S. 1992. "Owing Loyalty to One's Employer." *Journal of Business Ethics* 11: 535–543.

Pincoffs, Edmund L. 1986. *Quandaries and Virtues: Against Reductivism in Ethics.* Lawrence: University Press of Kansas.

Rachels, James. 1999. *The Elements of Moral Philosophy.* 3rd ed. Boston: McGraw-Hill College.

Reichheld, Frederick F. (with Thomas Teal). 1996. *The Loyalty Effect: The Hidden Force Behind Growth, Profits, and Lasting Value.* Boston: Harvard Business School Press.

Royce, Josiah. 1908, 1920. *The Philosophy of Loyalty.* New York: Macmillan.

Selznick, Philip. 1992. *The Moral Commonwealth: Social Theory and the Promise of Community.* Berkeley: University of California Press.

Solomon, Robert C. 1990. *A Passion for Justice: Emotions and the Origins of the Social Contract.* Reading, Mass.: Addison-Wesley Publishing Co.

————. 1992. *Ethics and Excellence: Cooperation and Integrity in Business.* New York: Oxford University Press.

————. 1994. "The Corporation as Community: A Reply to Ed Hartman." *Business Ethics Quarterly* 4: 271–285.

"Two Cheers for Loyalty." 1996. *The Economist,* Jan. 6, p. 49.

Wolfe, Alan. 1997. "On Loyalty." *Wilson Quarterly* 21: 46–6.

QUESTIONS

1. How is a corporation like a community? How do they differ?

2. Does a corporation always deserve my loyalty? A community? Why or why not? When and when not?

CASES

CASE 11.1
The One Successful Business Model
Sherron Watkins

Before the catastrophic collapse of Enron, the company congratulated itself for having "the one successful business model" in the world. This piece is excerpted from whistle-blower Sherron Watkins' book, *Power Failure*.

At 7:40 the next morning, Ken Lay, founder and longtime CEO of Enron, gave the formal welcome. Even though he, too, was dressed casually, his casual—pressed jeans and a crisp white button-down shirt—was still a little starchy, an ensemble from another time. He was fifty-eight, which was nearly elderly at Enron, and his audience treated him that way—respectfully, but just a little restively. Lay had been playing the gentle sage to Skilling's samurai for years; a balding, somewhat jowly man of average build, he spoke with a sharp midwestern twang and lately had sometimes seemed too folksy for the sleek, sharklike company he had created. Maybe he knew that, because for the last few months Lay had been orchestrating his exit. Clinton was leaving the White House, and Lay's enormous, long-term investment in the Bush family was about to pay off again. (Lay didn't wonder, in November 2000, who really won the presidential election. He was an indefatigable optimist, and a major donor to the Republican party.)

Lay had succeeded beyond his wildest dreams. He was worshiped in Houston both as a political king-maker and for his philanthropy. His was the classic American success story: He had triumphed over childhood poverty, a bad stutter, an antiquated, regu-

lated business, and enough financial setbacks to kill most companies. And now, in late middle age, he was ready to let go. He had already anointed Skilling as his successor. If he didn't join the Bush administration, maybe he would run for mayor of Houston. Whatever he did, it would be big. But on this particular morning Lay was focused solely on Enron. "Our future has never looked rosier," he told his many heirs. Enron was in businesses today it had not been in just five years earlier; he hoped that in ten years Enron would find more new business worlds to invent and dominate. At Enron it was always the future that mattered: inventing it, shaping it, ruling it.

The ashen, hung-over executives applauded politely. They'd heard this before.

And so it went for the next several hours. The editor of the hip *Red Herring* magazine extolled the glories of the Internet, followed by a pep talk from Gary Hamel, a stylishly shabby Harvard professor and the author of the best-selling *Leading the Revolution,* in which he championed the corporate innovators of the late nineties, especially Enron. "It pays to hire the best," Hamel said of the company. "You can't build a forever restless, opportunity-seeking company unless you're willing to hire forever restless, opportunity-seeking individuals." That Hamel was also a paid adviser to Enron didn't seem to bother anyone in the crowd. He was a Harvard professor, after all, and behavior that would once have been characterized as a conflict of interest was, by the late nineties, simply viewed as synergistic.

From Mimi Swartz, with Sherron Watkins, *Power Failure* (New York: Doubleday, 2003).

Finally, Skilling took the podium, and the enthusiasm in the room contracted noticeably. Skilling, like Lay, was small in stature. (In fact, almost everyone who got ahead at Enron was short.) But where Lay was soft and self-assuredly self-deprecating—almost Sunday schoolish—Skilling was sharp and cool. He was dressed casually, almost carelessly, like his troops, and he wore his hair combed off his face in the style of Hollywood producers and Wall Street financiers. He was assiduously fit; his eyes were ice blue and his gaze was steady, and he spoke in clipped, flat, supremely confident tones. Everyone at Enron knew that Jeff was twice as smart as they were—twice as smart as they could ever hope to be—and they hung on every word. It was Skilling who had made the revenues grow from $4 billion to more than $60 billion, an increase of nearly 2,000 percent. It was Skilling who had made the stock price ascend to the heavens. So it was Skilling who made Enron's troops frantic to live in fast-forward mode, who made them anxious to prove that they could deliver any concept he could dream up, who made them desperate to tag along on his extreme adventures—rock climbing, bungee jumping—around the globe. Because if Jeff Skilling thought you "got it," you really did.

Skilling's appearance onstage signaled the arrival of an annual event: his stock-price prediction. In years past he had been on the money—Enron had gone from $40 to $60 a share in 1998, and soared to $80 in 1999. Now he stood before his faithful and bowed his head, as if he had to think about what he had to say. When he looked at the crowd again, he was beaming. Enron stock, he told them, would hit $126 a share in 2001. There was just a second of stunned silence before the crowd burst into applause. No one quite knew how the stock was going to increase another 30 percent, even with the success of Broadband, which was not exactly a sure thing. Neither was Enron Energy Services, the company's foray into the management of power needs for large corporations. And a few people in the crowd had heard of problems in Fastow's finance group. But no one was that worried. They reminded themselves that they worked for Enron and, no matter what, Jeff would find a way. Because he always did.

There was, in fact, only one cautionary note sounded that morning. Skilling introduced the crowd to Tom Peters, the author of the best-selling business bible *In Search of Excellence*. Before abandoning the stage to Peters, Skilling wanted to boost morale a little higher. Enron, he reminded the crowd, had found the one successful business model that could be applied to any market.

Peters strode to the stage, abandoned his prepared speech, and started pacing back and forth. He was even sweating slightly, which made some in the audience think he might be another loser. "That's the scariest thing I've ever heard," Peters said to Skilling, his former colleague at McKinsey. What, exactly, had Enron done that was so novel? he asked. What accounted for such self-congratulation? The company had taken a model and replicated it in other fields—Enron had created markets where none had existed before, in gas, in power, probably in telecom. But everyone knew that now. Other businesses were already copying Enron, and the novelty would soon wear off. And then where would Enron be? Where were the company's new new ideas? "An excess of self-confidence kills companies," Peters warned.

In the audience, Sherron Watkins scribbled notes furiously on a pad, listing Peters' signs of a company in trouble:

1. denial of problems
2. nostalgia
3. arrogance

Listening, Skilling and Lay sat frozen in their seats, smiles locked on their faces. When Peters stopped speaking, Skilling jumped up to the dais, thanked him, and repeated himself: Remember, he said, *Enron had found the one successful business model that could be applied to any market.*

QUESTIONS

1. Should Watkins have spoken up earlier? How does a whistle-blower know when to whistle?
2. If you could go back in time and advise Enron, what would you tell them?

CASE 11.2
Would You Blow the Whistle on Yourself?
Pat L. Burr

In the course of teaching business classes through the semesters, I have been the butt of a great many accusations about the unethical behavior of American entrepreneurs, the deceptive advertising of Madison Avenue silver tongues, and even the rolling back of odometers by the local used-car dealers. I have not been personally involved in any of the activity, I hasten to add, I have simply been held accountable for it. All of it. By business students.

Enough, I said one day. I have done nothing wrong. I am not a crook. I vowed to bring the issue to the surface.

I set about my plan by inviting comments from my business students . . . about the structure of the system. The real question, as I saw it, was whether our business activity is inherently unethical or whether business persons are simply a product of our social system and therefore a reflection of our collective social values. Hogwash, they said. . . .

In pressing for more substance in their arguments, each semester I posed the same question to them at least once on written exams. I asked for detailed discussion. And on those very exams, I deliberately made grading mistakes on the numerous other questions, giving my students the advantage by two to five points. In short, I gave them grades which clearly were too high.

I turned back their papers, smugly awaiting the rush of feet to my desk to point out my error and to bring their unquestionably ethical behavior to a shining apex. I was confident of my students' motives. When none of them rushed forward, I pointed out the need for them to review my grading lest I had made a mistake on their papers. Still no comment. . . . Not one student, in my seven years of teaching, has ever come forward to point out my error in their favor. . . .

My game usually ends each semester when I nonchalantly explain my own dirty trick on the last class day, thus giving them every opportunity to come clean before final exam day. . . . "Surely, it is a hoax," they say. "For shame," I mumble under my breath, enunciating clearly so they can hear me. I had caught them. Even set the trap. They were furious.

After years of refinement of my game of "values clarification," I have arrived at several conclusions:

1. It is . . . too late to reach business students with ethics courses.
2. One dirty trick in the hand is worth two fists of mud in the bush when the entire system is under attack.
3. Our economic system is closely tied to our social system.
4. Some of our business students, particularly those I have observed after they were exposed in my little test, would make terrific drama coaches.

QUESTIONS

1. Would you have reported yourself? Why or why not? Should you have?

2. Do people ever blow the whistle on themselves? Is there something wrong with blowing the whistle on yourself? Is it irrational to do so? Explain.

Business and Society Review, #19. 1977–78

CASE 11.3
Changing Jobs and Changing Loyalties
William H. Shaw and Vincent Barry

Cynthia Martinez was thrilled when she first received the job offer from David Newhoff at Crytex Systems. She had long admired Crytex, both as an industry leader and as an ideal employer, and the position the company was offering her was perfect. "It's just what I've always wanted," she told her husband, Tom, as they uncorked a bottle of champagne. But as she and Tom talked, he raised a few questions that began to trouble her.

"What about the big project you're working on at Altrue right now? It'll take three months to see that through," Tom had reminded her. "The company has a lot riding on it, and you've always said that you're the driving force behind the project. If you bolt, Altrue is going to be in a real jam."

Cynthia explained that she had mentioned the project to David Newhoff. "He said he could understand I'd like to see it through, but Crytex needs someone right now. He gave me a couple of days to think it over, but it's my big chance."

Tom looked at her thoughtfully and responded, "But Newhoff doesn't quite get it. It's not just that you'd like to see it through. It's that you'd be letting your whole project team down. They probably couldn't do it without you, at least not the way it needs to be done. Besides, Cyn, remember what you said about that guy who quite the Altrue branch in Baltimore."

"That was different," Cynthia responded. "He took an existing account with him when he went to another firm. It was like ripping Altrue off. I'm not going to rip them off, but I don't figure I owe them anything extra. It's just business. You know perfectly well that if Altrue could save some money by laying me off, the company wouldn't hesitate."

"I think you're rationalizing," Tom said. "You've done well at Altrue, and the company has always treated you fairly. Anyway, the issue is what's right for you to do, not what the company would or wouldn't do. Crytex is Altrue's big competitor. It's like you're switching sides. Besides, it's not just a matter of loyalty to the company, but to the people you work with. I know we could use the extra money, and it would be a great step for you, but still . . ."

They continued to mull things over together, but the champagne no longer tasted quite as good. Fortunately, she and Tom never really argued about things they didn't see eye to eye on, and Tom wasn't the kind of guy who would try to tell her what she should or shouldn't do. But their conversation had started her wondering whether she really should accept that Crytex job she wanted so much.

QUESTIONS

1. What should Cynthia do? What ideals, obligations, and effects should she take into account when making her decision?

2. Would it be unprofessional of Cynthia to drop everything and move to Crytex? Would it show a lack of integrity? Could moving abruptly to Crytex have negative career consequences for her?

3. What does loyalty to the company mean, and how important is it, morally? Under what circumstances, if any, do employees owe loyalty to their employers? When, if ever, do they owe loyalty to their coworkers?

William H. Shaw and Vincent Barry, *Moral Issues in Business,* 9th ed. (Belmont, CA: Wadsworth, 2004).

CASE 11.4

The Greenhouse Effect: Putting the Heat on Halliburton

Larry Margasak

The Army extended a Halliburton Co. troop support contract over the objections of a top contracting officer, even contending—and then withdrawing—a claim that U.S. forces faced an emergency if the company didn't get the extra work.

"I wrote directly on the document the weaknesses . . . so that all could clearly see," contracting official Bunnatine Greenhouse wrote a top general this month in questioning the extended troop support contract in the Balkans.

Halliburton was formerly headed by Vice President Dick Cheney.

Greenhouse has had problems with the $2 billion ([euro]1.6 billion) contract at least since January 2002, when she wrote, "There is little or no incentive for the contractor to reduce or keep cost down."

The contracting officer has gone public with allegations of favoritism toward the company once headed by Vice President Dick Cheney. . . .

Greenhouse complained, in writing, Oct. 5 to Lt. Gen. Carl Strock, commander of the Army Corps of Engineers, that the Corps should not have halted plans to let companies compete for a successor Balkans contract. She is the Corps' top contracting officer.

Corps officials initially justified stopping the bidding by concluding that a "compelling emergency" would exist if Halliburton's work were to be interrupted.

When Greenhouse challenged the justification and sought an explanation of the emergency, however, Corps officials changed their reasoning. The new explanation was that Halliburton subsidiary KBR was the "one and only" company that could do the job.

Greenhouse wrote Strock that "the truth should be clearly explained" about the reason for halting competition.

She not only complained there was no explanation of what drove officials to cite an emergency, but, referring to the second justification, added: "It is not reasonable to believe that only one source responded to the solicitation."

Greenhouse, who has said she was frozen out of decisions on Halliburton, went public last weekend with allegations that Army officials showed favoritism to the company.

The FBI has asked Greenhouse's lawyers for an interview with her. The bureau has launched a criminal investigation of Halliburton's no-bid work.

The Associated Press has obtained dozens of documents that Greenhouse intends to provide to investigators.

The Balkans contract was to have ended May 27 but has been extended through next April.

The extension was so politically sensitive that a Corps official, William Ryals, sent a memo to Corps headquarters in July seeking high-level approval.

"The reason for sending it to (headquarters) for approval is because this is so controversial in regard to this firm," the memo said. "If it had been any other firm, we would have done this and moved forward without any further consideration. Given that the firm is KBRS (the Halliburton subsidiary) and that we are in an election year and coming up to the peak in the election season soon, I sent to (headquarters) for concurrence."

Halliburton spokeswoman Wendy Hall said, "This is very old information. The issue mentioned about the Balkans was fully dealt with and resolved several years ago, and since then KBR has received high marks from the Army on our Balkans Support Contract."

In a letter to Corps employees on Friday, Strock said the Army is investigating Greenhouse's allegations and therefore would not respond to the allegations "to ensure that a fair investigation can proceed."

The Army has cited severe problems with Halliburton's work in the Balkans, many documented in the Jan. 4, 2002, report by Greenhouse, who reviewed findings of investigators known as a "tiger" team.

"The general feeling in the theater is that the contractor is 'out of control,'" she wrote.

Greenhouse said it appeared the Halliburton subsidiary "makes the decisions of what is constructed, purchased or provided and it appears that oftentimes the products and services delivered reflect gold-plating since the contractor proudly touts that they provide the very, very best."

Greenhouse said Army contracting officials must work as a team because "divided—the contractor will 'eat our lunch.'"

QUESTIONS

1. Should no-bid contracts ever be allowed? What might be a good argument in favor of no-bid contracts?

2. Do you think a problem arises when former members of company boards acquire a great deal of political power (such as becoming vice president or president)? What is presently done to control this? What more should be done?

CASE 11.5
Whistleblowing at the Phone Company
Joseph R. Desjardins and John J. McCall

Michael J., an employee of the phone company, recognizes that he has divided loyalties. The company has treated him well and, despite some minor disagreements, he gets along quite well with upper management and his own department. However, the phone company is a public utility, regulated for the public interest by the state's Public Utility Commission (PUC). As such, Michael J. recognizes that his firm owes a loyalty to citizens that goes beyond the simple responsibility that other firms owe to their consumers.

Once a year, as part of a major fund-raising drive for a local charity, the phone company encourages its employees to donate their personal time and money to this charity. This year, however, Michael J. discovers that a significant amount of company resources are being used to support the charity. The company is printing posters and sending out mail at its own expense and is using employees on company time to promote the fund-raiser. When Michael J. brought this to the attention of his manager, the whole incident was dismissed as trivial. After all, the resources were going to charity.

After some consideration, Michael J. judged that these charitable efforts were betraying the public trust. The public, and not private individuals acting as their agents, ought to decide for themselves when to contribute to charity. As a result, he notified the PUC of this misallocation of funds. Knowing that records of calls from his desk could easily be traced, Michael J. made the calls from pay phones and from his house.

Joseph R. Desjardins and John J. McCall, *Contemporary Issues in Business Ethics*, 2nd ed. (Belmont, CA: Wadsworth, 1990).

As required by law, the PUC investigated the charges. Although the facts were as Michael J. reported, the PUC judged that the misallocation was not substantial enough to constitute a violation of the public trust. However, executives of the phone company were less willing to dismiss the incident. They were upset at what they judged to be serious disloyalty among their employees.

Although they suspected that Michael J. was the whistleblower, there was no proof that he was. A check of his office phone records showed no calls placed to the PUC. However, since this was the phone company, it was easy enough to trace calls made from Michael J.'s home and cross-check these against calls made to and from the PUC's offices.

They did so, confirmed their suspicions, and disciplined Michael J.

QUESTIONS

1. Do employees of public utilities have special responsibilities to protect the public interest? Why or why not? Should these responsibilities be extended to employees of some private firms, for example, large defense contractors?

2. Did the phone company do anything unethical in checking its own records to trace Michael J.'s phone calls? Should the PUC investigate further?

3. Would your opinion of this case change if large sums of money or something other than a charity was involved?

CHAPTER QUESTIONS

1. When should you blow the whistle?

2. How is loyalty created? What ethical demands are created by loyalty? Does loyalty ever entirely outweigh other ethical concerns? Should it?

12

Think Local, Act Global

International Business

Introduction

You have just been transferred to the international division of your company. Your new job requires you to work with company operations all over the world. Navigating various cultural customs can be tricky, but the most difficult problems you will face concern navigating different ethical norms of behavior. Sometimes it is not easy to distinguish between customs that you should follow to be polite and respectful and practices that are morally unacceptable, regardless of what appears to be common practice in the culture. As soon as you leave your home country, you find yourself grappling with variations on a major philosophical question: Are ethical principles universal, or does every culture have its own ethics? In a practical sense, when you are in Rome, should you do what the Romans do, even if it is morally repugnant? Or should you follow what you take to be the moral path, even if it makes you unpopular and is bad for your business? Sometimes, perhaps, we can be mistaken about what is really the moral path. You may not understand the situation because it is complex in ways that you have never had to deal with. In some cases, you may discover that your stereotype about the local culture and what is right in it is wrong. A Kenyan friend told me that paying small bribes is a part of everyday life in Kenya. This is not because Kenyans think bribery is acceptable, but because they cannot do anything about it. When you are in another culture, it is important to find out what people in that culture think life requires as they actually live it. It is not enough for you to imagine an idealized version of their life as it might be with a major change in their institutions. There is what is morally necessary. There is also what is morally preferable. But there is also what is morally possible, and confusing them when you are in a position of power or influence can do a lot of people a lot of harm.

At the same time, it is a good idea for you and your organization to have a clear picture of your own values and ethical standards of behavior *before* you go to do business in another country. While your company may have its rules and regulations, there is always an open question whether these rules and regulations will make sense elsewhere. (Indeed, it may be a matter of ongoing debate whether or not some of them make sense at home.) Furthermore, you also have to have your own sense of what you personally will and will not do, anywhere, as a person and as a professional. You may be able to justify paying "facilitating payments" to an official abroad, on the grounds that everyone in the culture expects it, but you should resolve ahead of time that you are unwilling to engage in the local customs of hiring children to do dangerous work, of denigrating women on the job, of physically abusing employees who fail to make their quotas, and of lying to the home office about how the work is going or to officials about the nature of the product or the services you provide. Making such decisions on the spot may be much more difficult if it is not backed up by prior understanding or, preferably, by company policy as well.

Navigating a business in a foreign culture can be confusing. How do you balance respect for other cultures with what you believe is morally right? For example, if companies in another country pay female employees less than men to do the same work, should you do the same? Businesses and individuals in some overseas countries are tempted to slip into the lax standards of health, safety, and human rights. In the name of "staying competitive," are you justified in doing the same? It isn't always easy to act on your own or to enforce your company's values in another place where the customs are going against you because an essential part of business is about gaining favor and building relationships. So the practical question is, how can you build a relationship by adhering to local expectations and preferences and, at the same time, stay true to your own and your company's values? More than anything, you will need the moral imagination to comprehend both the values of the local culture and your own in order to figure out how best to act both ethically and without seeming disrespectful, arrogant, unfriendly, or uncooperative.

Globalization intertwines the economic fates of nations and tends to promote shared values on the basis of shared business interests, but it also accentuates real differences in cultural values. People from other countries often think of Americans as ethical imperialists who try to impose their values on the world. Much worse, they tend to think of us as hypocrites who espouse values like justice, liberty, and equality but do not actually act in ways that promote these values in other countries. But global business is, ethically, a double-edged sword. On the one hand, multinational corporations can and do exploit people in poorer countries and market products and values that are undesirable, undermining whatever respect those people may have had for "our values" and our way of life. On the other hand, multinationals can be a positive force for improving the welfare and opportunities of people in other countries and prove by doing what those lofty values have promised.

The first two articles in this chapter, by Benjamin Barber and Thomas L. Friedman, look at the clash of values that is an inherent part of globalization. Both authors, in different ways, talk about how the values of material goods, progress, and freedom conflict with or pose a real or perceived threat to a culture's traditional values. The ethical challenge of business in an era of globalization is to preserve the roots (or the olive tree) of a culture, while at the same time providing it with good, jobs, and economic development (or the Lexus). But this, then, raises the question of Mary Midgley's article: Can we make ethical judgments about the traditional practices of another culture? Can we really understand other cultures? One interesting facet of human beings is our capacity to feel empathy. While we may not understand a person's language and culture, we are able to understand how that person feels when, for example, she has lost her child. As the Dalai Lama argues in his article, empathy is the basis of compassion, and compassion is a core element of morality.

The next two articles put you on the street in a foreign culture. Thomas Donaldson looks at a the practical problems that you may encounter in a foreign environment, and the *Economist* article challenges you to think about the ethical issues that are related to working in and sending employees to work in dangerous parts of the world. Last, we have included the United Nations "Universal Declaration of Human Rights." Carefully look at the declaration. If you think that it is an idealist document, you are right—even America does not live up to all its provisions. Yet, it is widely recognized as the ideal set of standards for human societies. Few people on this earth would not want to have these rights, (yet a number of leaders are bent on denying them to their people).

The cases in this chapter are about how to treat people and how to make ethical decisions in other cultures. The "Oil Rig" raises questions about respect for persons, equality, and employees' rights when operating in developing countries. "Diller's Dilemma" is about how to assess the responsibility for problems that foreign companies contribute to, but are also the result of other cultural and economic problems. In the "PureDrug" case, you will think about a company's obligations when someone from another culture knowingly wants to buy a product that could be unsafe. Whereas in the "Lomatex" case, you will consider the problem of selling a fertilizer that could be used to make weapons that will end up in dangerous hands. "Foreign Assignment" is a personal case about how you should act and what kind of treatment you should tolerate in another culture. "Consulting for Jones and Jones Pharmaceutical" is the proverbial "when in Rome" case. Whose professional practices do you follow when you are in another culture? In the end, the intent of all the readings and cases in this chapter is to help you reflect on what values and standards you want to live by, no matter where you are in the world. It helps to be clear on this point before you take a foreign assignment or a job with a multinational because you will be miserable working with an organization that does not allow you to act ethically. Furthermore, working for such an employer may be harmful to your character.

Benjamin Barber | # Jihad vs. McWorld

Benjamin R. Barber is the Gershon and Carol Kekst Professor of Civil Society and Distinguished University Professor at the University of Maryland and a principal of the Democracy Collaborative.

INTRODUCTION

History is not over. Nor are we arrived in the wondrous land of techné promised by the futurologists. The collapse of state communism has not delivered people to a safe democratic haven, and the past, fratricide and civil discord perduring, still clouds the horizon just behind us. Those who look back see all of the horrors of the ancient slaughterbench reenacted in disintegral nations like Bosnia, Sri Lanka, Ossetia, and Rwanda and they declare that nothing has changed. Those who look forward prophesize commercial and technological interdependence—a virtual paradise made possible by spreading markets and global technology—and they proclaim that everything is or soon will be different. The rival observers seem to consult different almanacs drawn from the libraries of contrarian planets.

Yet anyone who reads the daily papers carefully, taking in the front page accounts of civil carnage as well as the business page stories on the mechanics of the information superhighway and the economics of communication mergers, anyone who turns deliberately to take in the whole 360-degree horizon, knows that our world and our lives are caught between what William Butler Yeats called the two eternities of race and soul: that of race reflecting the tribal past, that of soul anticipating the cosmopolitan future. Our secular eternities are corrupted, however, race reduced to an insignia of resentment, and soul sized down to fit the demanding body by which it now measures its

needs. Neither race nor soul offers us a future that is other than bleak, neither promises a polity that is remotely democratic.

The first scenario rooted in race holds out the grim prospect of a retribalization of large swaths of humankind by war and bloodshed: a threatened balkanization of nation-states in which culture is pitted against culture, people against people, tribe against tribe, a Jihad in the name of a hundred narrowly conceived faiths against every kind of interdependence, every kind of artificial social cooperation and mutuality: against technology, against pop culture, and against integrated markets; against modernity itself as well as the future in which modernity issues. The second paints that future in shimmering pastels, a busy portrait of onrushing economic, technological, and ecological forces that demand integration and uniformity and that mesmerize peoples everywhere with fast music, fast computers, and fast food—MTV, Macintosh, and McDonald's—pressing nations into one homogenous global theme park, one McWorld tied together by communications, information, entertainment, and commerce. Caught between Babel and Disneyland, the planet is falling precipitously apart and coming reluctantly together at the very same moment.

Some stunned observers notice only Babel, complaining about the thousand newly sundered "peoples" who prefer to address their neighbors with sniper rifles and mortars; others—zealots in Disneyland—seize on futurological platitudes and the promise of virtuality, exclaiming "It's a small world after all!" Both are right, but how can that be?

We are compelled to choose between what passes as "the twilight of sovereignty" and an entropic end of all history;[1] or a return to the past's most fractious and demoralizing discord; to "the menace of global

Benjamin Barber, "Jihad vs. McWorld" (New York: Balantine Books, 1995), pp. 3–20. Notes were deleted from the text.

anarchy," to Milton's capital of hell, Pandaemonium; to a world totally "out of control."[2]

The apparent truth is that the tendencies of both Jihad *and* McWorld are at work, both visible sometimes in the same country at the very same instant. Iranian zealots keep one ear tuned to the mullahs urging holy war and the other cocked to Rupert Murdoch's Star television beaming in *Dynasty, Donahue,* and *The Simpsons* from hovering satellites. Chinese entrepreneurs vie for the attention of party cadres in Beijing and simultaneously pursue KFC franchises in cities like Nanjing, Hangzhou, and Xian where twenty-eight outlets serve over 100,000 customers a day. The Russian Orthodox church, even as it struggles to renew the ancient faith, has entered a joint venture with California businessmen to bottle and sell natural waters under the rubric Saint Springs Water Company. Serbian assassins wear Adidas sneakers and listen to Madonna on Walkman headphones as they take aim through their gunscopes at scurrying Sarajevo civilians looking to fill family watercans. Orthodox Hasids and brooding neo-Nazis have both turned to rock music to get their traditional messages out to the new generation, while fundamentalists plot virtual conspiracies on the Internet.

Now neither Jihad nor McWorld is in itself novel. History ending in the triumph of science and reason or some monstrous perversion thereof (Mary Shelley's Doctor Frankenstein) has been the leitmotiv of every philosopher and poet who has regretted the Age of Reason since the Enlightenment. Yeats lamented "the center will not hold, mere anarchy is loosed upon the world," and observers of Jihad today have little but historical detail to add. The Christian parable of the Fall and of the possibilities of redemption that it makes possible captures the eighteenth-century ambivalence—and our own—about past and future. I want, however, to do more than dress up the central paradox of human history in modern clothes. It is not Jihad and McWorld but the relationship between them that most interests me. For, squeezed between their opposing forces, the world has been sent spinning out of control. Can it be that what Jihad and McWorld have in common is anarchy: the absence of common will and that conscious and collective human control under the guidance of law we call democracy?

Progress moves in steps that sometimes lurch backwards; in history's twisting maze, Jihad not only revolts against but abets McWorld, while McWorld not only imperils but re-creates and reinforces Jihad. They produce their contraries and need one another. . . .

What then does it mean in concrete terms to view Jihad and McWorld dialectically when the tendencies of the two sets of forces initially appear so intractably antithetical? After all, Jihad and McWorld operate with equal strength in opposite directions, the one driven by parochial hatreds, the other by universalizing markets, the one re-creating ancient subnational and ethnic borders from within, the other making national borders porous from without. Yet Jihad and McWorld have this in common: they both make war on the sovereign nation-state and thus undermine the nation-state's democratic institutions. Each eschews civil society and belittles democratic citizenship, neither seeks alternative democratic institutions. Their common thread is indifference to civil liberty. Jihad forges communities of blood rooted in exclusion and hatred, communities that slight democracy in favor of tyrannical paternalism or consensual tribalism. McWorld forges global markets rooted in consumption and profit, leaving to an untrustworthy, if not altogether fictitious, invisible hand issues of public interest and common good that once might have been nurtured by democratic citizenries and their watchful governments. Such governments, intimidated by market ideology, are actually pulling back at the very moment they ought to be aggressively intervening. What was once understood as protecting the public interest is now excoriated as heavy-handed regulatory browbeating. Justice yields to markets, even though, as Felix Rohatyn has bluntly confessed, "there is a brutal Darwinian logic to these markets. They are nervous and greedy. They look for stability and transparency, but what they reward is not always our preferred form of democracy."[3] If the traditional conservators of freedom were democratic constitutions and Bills of Rights, "the new temples to liberty," George Steiner suggests, "will be McDonald's and Kentucky Fried Chicken."[4]

In being reduced to a choice between the market's universal church and a retribalizing politics of particularist identities, peoples around the globe are threatened with an atavistic return to medieval politics where local tribes and ambitious emperors together ruled the world entire, women and men united by the universal abstraction of Christianity even as they lived out isolated lives in warring fiefdoms defined by involuntary (ascriptive) forms of identity. This was a world in which princes and kings had little real power until they conceived the ideology of nationalism. Nationalism established government on a scale greater than the tribe yet less cosmopolitan than the universal church and in time gave birth to those intermediate, gradually more democratic institutions that would come to constitute the nation-state.To-day, at the far end of this history, we seem intent on re-creating a world in which our only choices are the secular universalism of the cosmopolitan market and the everyday particularism of the fractious tribe.

In the tumult of the confrontation between global commerce and parochial ethnicity, the virtues of the democratic nation are lost and the instrumentalities by which it permitted peoples to transform themselves into nations and seize sovereign power in the name of liberty and the commonweal are put at risk. Neither Jihad nor McWorld aspires to resecure the civic virtues undermined by its denationalizing practices; neither global markets nor blood communities service public goods or pursue equality and justice. Impartial judiciaries and deliberative assemblies play no role in the roving killer bands that speak on behalf of newly liberated "peoples," and such democratic institutions

---

To: You
From: The Philosopher
Subject: "Isaiah Berlin on Values"

I hear that you will be traveling all over the world in your new job. The thing I like best about traveling is comparing home to what is better and worse in other countries. Americans often think that they have the best values and people in other places have got it all wrong, but as the philosopher Isaiah Berlin argues, disagreements about values are not always about who is right and who is wrong. Berlin doesn't think it is possible or desirable for everyone to agree on the same values. He says, "These collisions of values are of the essence of what they are and what we are." But, "We are doomed to choose, and every choice may entail an irreparable loss." Berlin writes:

> What is clear is that values can clash—that is why civilizations are incompatible. They can be incompatible between cultures, or groups in the same culture, or between you and me. You believe in always telling the truth, not matter what; I do not, because I believe that it can sometimes be too painful and too destructive. We can discuss each other's point of view, we can try to reach common ground, but in the end what you pursue may not be reconcilable with the ends to which I find that I have dedicated my life. Values may easily clash within the breast of an individual; and it does not follow that, if they do, some must be true and others false. Justice, rigorous justice, is for some people an absolute value, but it is not compatible with what may be no less ultimate values for them—mercy, compassion—as arises in concrete cases.*

*Isaiah Berlin, "The Pursuit of the Ideal," *The Crooked Timber of Humanity* (Alfred A. Knopf), 1991, pp. 7–8.

have at best only marginal influence on the roving multinational corporations that speak on behalf of newly liberated markets. Jihad pursues a bloody politics of identity, McWorld a bloodless economics of profit. Belonging by default to McWorld, everyone is a consumer; seeking a repository for identity, everyone belongs to some tribe. But no one is a citizen. Without citizens, how can there be democracy?

––––––––––––

The dynamics of the Jihad-McWorld linkage are deeply dialectical. Japan has, for example, become more culturally insistent on its own traditions in recent years even as its people seek an ever greater purchase on McWorld. In 1992, the number-one restaurant in Japan measured by volume of customers was McDonald's, followed in the number-two spot by the Colonel's Kentucky Fried Chicken. In France, where cultural purists complain bitterly of a looming Sixième République ("la République Américaine"), the government attacks "franglais" even as it funds EuroDisney park just outside of Paris. In the same spirit, the cinema industry makes war on American film imports while it bestows upon Sylvester Stallone one of France's highest honors, the Chevalier des arts et lettres. Ambivalence also stalks India. Just outside of Bombay, cheek by jowl with villages still immersed in poverty and notorious for the informal execution of unwanted female babies or, even, wives, can be found a new town known as SCEEPZ—the Santa Cruz Electronic Export Processing Zone—where Hindi-, Tamil-, and Mahratti-speaking computer programmers write software for Swissair, AT&T, and other labor-cost-conscious multinationals. India is thus at once a major exemplar of ancient ethnic and religious tensions and "an emerging power in the international software industry."[5] To go to work at SCEEPZ, says an employee, is "like crossing an international border." Not into another country, but into the virtual nowhere-land of McWorld.

More dramatic even than in India, is the strange interplay of Jihad and McWorld in the remnants of Yugoslavia. In an affecting *New Republic* report, Slavenka Drakulic recently told the brief tragic love story of Admira and Bosko, two young star-crossed lovers from Sarajevo: "They were born in the late 1960's," she writes. "They watched Spielberg movies; they listened to Iggy Pop; they read John le Carré; they went to a disco every Saturday night and fantasized about traveling to Paris or London."[6] Longing for safety, it seems they finally negotiated with all sides for safe passage, and readied their departure from Sarajevo. Before they could cross the magical border that separates their impoverished land from the seeming sanctuary of McWorld, Jihad caught up to them. Their bodies lay along the riverbank, riddled with bullets from anonymous snipers for whom safe passage signaled an invitation to target practice. The murdered young lovers, as be-fits émigrés to McWorld, were clothed in jeans and sneakers. So too, one imagines, were their murderers. . . .

In Russia, in India, in Bosnia, in Japan, and in France too, modern history then leans both ways: toward the meretricious inevitability of McWorld, but also into Jihad's stiff winds, heaving to and fro and giving heart both to the Panglossians and the Pandoras, sometimes for the very same reasons. The Panglossians bank on Euro-Disney and Microsoft, while the Pandoras await nihilism and a world in Pandaemonium. Yet McWorld and Jihad do not really force a choice between such polarized scenarios. Together, they are likely to produce some stifling amalgam of the two suspended in chaos. Antithetical in every detail, Jihad and McWorld nonetheless conspire to undermine our hard-won (if only half-won) civil liberties and the possibility of a global democratic future. In the short run the forces of Jihad, noisier and more obviously nihilistic than those of McWorld, are likely to dominate the near future, etching small stories of local tragedy and regional genocide on the face of our times and creating a climate of instability marked by multimicrowars inimical to global integration. But in the long run, the forces of McWorld are the forces underlying the slow certain thrust of Western civilization and as such may be unstoppable. Jihad's microwars will hold the headlines well into the next century, making predictions of the end of history look terminally dumb. But McWorld's homogenization is likely to establish a macropeace that favors the triumph of commerce and its markets and to give to those who control information, communication, and entertainment ultimate (if inadvertent) control over human destiny. Unless we can offer an alternative to the struggle between Jihad and McWorld, the epoch on whose threshold we stand—postcommunist, postindustrial, postnational, yet sectarian, fearful, and bigoted—is likely also to be terminally postdemocratic.

NOTES

1. Francis Fukuyama, *The End of History and the Last Man,* (New York: Free Press, 1992).

2. Georgie Anne Greyer, "Our Disintegrating World: The Menace of Global Anarchy, *Encyclopedia Britanica, Book of the Year,* 1985 (Chicago: University of Chicago Press, 1985), pp. 11–25.

3. Rohatyn cited by Thomas L. Friedman, "When Money Talks, Governments Listen," *The New York Times,* July 24, 1994, p. E3.

4. George Steiner, in Granta, cited by Anthony Lewis, "A Quake Hits the Summit," *International Herald Tribune,* June 2–3, 1990.

5. National Public Radio, *All Things Considered,* December 2, 1993, from the broadcast transcription.

6. Slavenka Drakulic, "Love Story: A True Tale from Sarajevo," *The New Republic,* October 26, 1993, pp. 14–16.

QUESTIONS

1. If the market triumphs in the clash between jihad and MacWorld, what moral values will people in a culture gain, and what values will they lose?

2. If Barber is right about the conflict between jihad and McWorld, what are the practical and moral implications for multinational organizations?

| Thomas L. Friedman | # The Lexus and the Olive Tree |

Thomas L. Friedman is an author and an Op-Ed columnist for the *New York Times.*

Once you recognize that globalization is the international system that has replaced the Cold War system, is this all you need to know to explain world affairs today? Not quite. Globalization is what is new. And if the world were made of just microchips and markets, you could probably rely on globalization to explain almost everything. But, alas, the world is made of microchips and markets and men and women, with all their peculiar habits, traditions, longings and unpredictable aspirations. So world affairs today can only be explained as the interaction between what is as new as an Internet Web site and what is as old as a gnarled olive tree on the banks of the river Jordan. I first started thinking about this while riding on a train in Japan in May 1992, eating a sushi box dinner and traveling at 180 miles per hour.

I was in Tokyo on a reporting assignment and had arranged to visit the Lexus luxury car factory outside Toyota City, south of Tokyo. It was one of the most memorable tours I've ever taken. At that time, the factory was producing 300 Lexus sedans each day, made by 66 human beings and 310 robots. From what I could tell, the human beings were there mostly for quality control. Only a few of them were actually screwing in bolts or soldering parts together. The robots were doing all the work. There were even robotic trucks that hauled materials around the floor and could sense when a human was in their path and would "beep, beep, beep" at them to move. I was fascinated watching the robot that applied the rubber seal that held in place the front windshield of each Lexus.

Thomas L. Friedman, "The Lexus and the Olive Tree," *The Lexus and the Olive Tree* (New York: Anchor Books, 2000), pp. 29–34.

The robot arm would neatly paint the hot molten rubber in a perfect rectangle around the window. But what I liked most was that when it finished its application there was always a tiny drop of rubber left hanging from the tip of the robot's finger—like the drop of toothpaste that might be left at the top of the tube after you've squeezed it onto your toothbrush. At the Lexus factory, though, this robot arm would swing around in a wide loop until the tip met a tiny, almost invisible metal wire that would perfectly slice off that last small drop of hot black rubber—leaving nothing left over. I kept staring at this process, thinking to myself how much planning, design and technology it must have taken to get that robot arm to do its job and then swing around each time, at the precise angle, so that this little thumbnail-size wire could snip off the last drop of hot rubber for the robot to start clean on the next window. I was impressed.

After touring the factory, I went back to Toyota City and boarded the bullet train for the ride back to Tokyo. The bullet train is aptly named, for it has both the look and feel of a speeding bullet. As I nibbled away on one of those sushi dinner boxes you can buy in any Japanese train station, I was reading that day's *International Herald Tribune,* and a story caught my eye on the top right corner of page 3. It was about the daily State Department briefing. State Department spokeswoman Margaret D. Tutwiler had given a controversial interpretation of a 1948 United Nations resolution, relating to the right of return for Palestinian refugees to Israel. I don't remember all the details, but whatever her interpretation was, it had clearly agitated both the Arabs and the Israelis and sparked a furor in the Middle East, which this story was reporting.

So there I was speeding along at 180 miles an hour on the most modern train in the world, reading this story about the oldest corner of the world. And the thought occurred to me that these Japanese, whose Lexus factory I had just visited and whose train I was riding, were building the greatest luxury car in the world with robots. And over here, on the top of page 3 of the *Herald Tribune,* the people with whom I had lived for so many years in Beirut and Jerusalem, whom I knew so well, were still fighting over who owned which olive tree. It struck me then that the

Lexus and the olive tree were actually pretty good symbols of this post–Cold War era: half the world seemed to be emerging from the Cold War intent on building a better Lexus, dedicated to modernizing, streamlining and privatizing their economies in order to thrive in the system of globalization. And half of the world—sometimes half the same country, sometimes half the same person—was still caught up in the fight over who owns which olive tree.

Olive trees are important. They represent everything that roots us, anchors us, identifies us and locates us in this world—whether it be belonging to a family, a community, a tribe, a nation, a religion or, most of all, a place called home. Olive trees are what give us the warmth of family, the joy of individuality, the intimacy of personal rituals, the depth of private relationships, as well as the confidence and security to reach out and encounter others. We fight so intensely at times over our olive trees because, at their best, they provide the feelings of self-esteem and belonging that are as essential for human survival as food in the belly. Indeed, one reason that the nation-state will never disappear, even if it does weaken, is because it is the ultimate olive tree—the ultimate expression of whom we belong to—linguistically, geographically and historically. You cannot be a complete person alone. You can be a rich person alone. You can be a smart person alone. But you cannot be a complete person alone. For that you must be part of, and rooted in, an olive grove.

This truth was once beautifully conveyed by Rabbi Harold S. Kushner in his interpretation of a scene from Gabriel García Márquez's classic novel *One Hundred Years of Solitude:*

> Márquez tells of a village where people were afflicted with a strange plague of forgetfulness, a kind of contagious amnesia. Starting with the oldest inhabitants and working its way through the population, the plague causes people to forget the names of even the most common everyday objects. One young man, still unaffected, tries to limit the damage by putting labels on everything. "This is a table," "This is a window," "This is a cow; it has to be milked every morning." And at the entrance to the town, on the main road, he puts up two large signs. One reads "The name of our village is Macondo,"

and the larger one reads "God exists." The message I get from that story is that we can, and probably will, forget most of what we have learned in life—the math, the history, the chemical formulas, the address and phone number of the first house we lived in when we got married—and all that forgetting will do us no harm. But if we forget whom we belong to, and if we forget that there is a God, something profoundly human in us will be lost.

But while olive trees are essential to our very being, an attachment to one's olive trees, when taken to excess, can lead us into forging identities, bonds and communities based on the exclusion of others. And when these obsessions really run amok, as with the Nazis in Germany, or the murderous Aum Shinrikyo cult in Japan or the Serbs in Yugoslavia, they lead to the extermination of others.

Conflicts between Serbs and Muslims, Jews and Palestinians, Armenians and Azeris over who owns which olive tree are so venomous precisely because they are about who will be at home and anchored in a local world and who will not be. Their underlying logic is: I must control this olive tree, because if the other controls it, not only will I be economically and politically under his thumb, but my whole sense of home will be lost. I'll never be able to take my shoes off and relax. Few things are more enraging to people than to have their identity or their sense of home stripped away. They will die for it, kill for it, sing for it, write poetry for it and novelize about it. Because without a sense of home and belonging, life becomes barren and rootless. And life as a tumbleweed is no life at all.

———————————

So then what does the Lexus represent? It represents an equally fundamental, age-old human drive—the drive for sustenance, improvement, prosperity and modernization—as it is played out in today's globalization system. The Lexus represents all the burgeoning global markets, financial institutions and computer technologies with which we pursue higher living standards today.

Of course, for millions of people in developing countries, the quest for material improvement still involves walking to a well, subsisting on a dollar a day, plowing a field barefoot behind an ox or gathering wood and carrying it on their heads for five miles. These people still upload for a living, not download. But for millions of others in developed countries, this quest for material betterment and modernization is increasingly conducted in Nike shoes, shopping in integrated markets and using the new network technologies. The point is that while different people have different access to the new markets and technologies that characterize the globalization system, and derive highly unequal benefits from them, this doesn't change the fact that these markets and technologies are the defining economic tools of the day and everyone is either directly or indirectly affected by them.

The Lexus versus the olive tree, though, is just a modern version of a very old story—indeed one of the oldest stories in recorded history—the story of why Cain slew Abel. The Hebrew Bible says in Genesis: "Cain said to his brother Abel; And when they were in the field, Cain rose up against his brother Abel and killed him. Then the Lord said to Cain, 'Where is your brother Abel?' And he said, 'I do not know. Am I my brother's keeper?' And the Lord said, 'What have you done? The voice of your brother's blood is crying to me from the ground.' "

If you read this paragraph closely you notice that the Hebrew Bible never tells us what Cain actually said to Abel. The sentence reads that "Cain said to his brother Abel," and then it just stops. We are not privy to the conversation. What happened in the conversation between them that got Cain so angry that he would actually kill his brother Abel? My theology teacher, Rabbi Tzvi Marx, taught me that the rabbinic sages in Genesis Rabbah, one of the fundamental rabbinic commentaries on the Bible, give three basic explanations of what was said. One is that the two brothers were arguing about a woman—Eve. After all, there was only one woman on earth at the time, their mother, and they were arguing over which brother would get to marry her. They were arguing over sexual fulfillment and procreation. Another interpretation posits that Cain and Abel had basically divided up the world between them. Cain had all the real estate—or as the Bible says, "Cain became a tiller of the soil"—and Abel had all the movables and livestock—"Abel became a keeper of sheep." And according to this interpretation, Cain told Abel to get his sheep off Cain's property and this triggered a fight over territory that eventually ended with Cain slaying Abel in the heat of the argument. They were fighting over economic development and material fulfillment. The third interpretation is that the two brothers had already neatly divided everything in the world between them, except one critical thing that was still up for grabs: Where would the Temple be built that would reflect their particular religious and cultural identity? Each wanted to control that Temple and have it reflect his identity. Each wanted that Temple in his olive grove. They were fighting over the issue of identity, and which of them would be the keeper of their family's source of legitimacy. So, the rabbis noted, all the basic elements of human motivation are potentially there in one story: the need for sexual intimacy, the need for sustenance and the need for a sense of identity and community. I will leave matters of sex for somebody else. This book is about the other two.

That's why I like to say that information arbitrage provides the lenses we need to look into today's world, but lenses alone are not enough. We also need to know what we are looking at and for. And what we are looking at and for is how the age-old quests for material betterment and for individual and communal identity—which go all the way back to Genesis—play themselves out in today's dominant international system of globalization. This is the drama of the Lexus and the olive tree.

QUESTIONS

1. Compare and contrast Friedman's characterization of the Lexus and the olive tree with Barber's jihad versus McWorld.

2. Do you think that the Lexus will destroy the olive tree in a competitive global economy, or will there simply be a divide between those who have olive trees and those who own Lexuses?

Mary Midgley | # Trying Out One's New Sword

Mary Midgely is a prominent British philosopher.

All of us are, more or less, in trouble today about trying to understand cultures strange to us. We hear constantly of alien customs. We see changes in our lifetime which would have astonished our parents. I want to discuss here one very short way of dealing with this difficulty, a drastic way which many people now theoretically favour. It consists in simply denying that we can ever understand any culture except our own well enough to make judgements about it. Those who recommend this hold that the world is sharply divided into separate societies, sealed units, each with its own system of thought. They feel that the respect and tolerance due from one system to another forbids us ever to take up a critical position to any other culture. Moral judgement, they suggest, is a kind of coinage valid only in its country of origin.

I shall call this position "moral isolationism." I shall suggest that it is certainly not forced upon us, and indeed that it makes no sense at all. People usually take it up because they think it is a respectful attitude to other cultures. In fact, however, it is not respectful. Nobody can respect what is entirely unintelligible to them. To respect someone, we have to know enough about him to make a *favourable* judgement, however general and tentative. And we do understand people in other cultures to this extent. Otherwise a great mass of our most valuable thinking would be paralysed.

To show this, I shall take a remote example, because we shall probably find it easier to think calmly about it than we should with a contemporary one, such as female circumcision in Africa or the Chinese Cultural Revolution. The principles involved will still be the same. My example is this. There is, it seems, a verb in classical Japanese which means "to try out one's new sword on a chance wayfarer." (The word is *tsujigiri,* literally "crossroads-cut.") A samurai sword had to be tried out because, if it was to work properly, it had to slice through someone at a single blow, from the shoulder to the opposite flank. Otherwise, the warrior bungled his stroke. This could injure his honour, offend his ancestors, and even let down his emperor. So tests were needed, and wayfarers had to be expended. Any wayfarer would do—provided, of course, that he was not another Samurai. Scientists will recognize a familiar problem about the rights of experimental subjects.

Now when we hear of a custom like this, we may well reflect that we simply do not understand it and therefore are not qualified to criticize it at all, because we are not members of that culture. But we are not members of any other culture either, except our own. So we extend the principle to cover all extraneous cultures, and we seem therefore to be moral isolationists. But this is, as we shall see, an impossible position. Let us ask what it would involve.

We must ask first: Does the isolating barrier work both ways? Are people in other cultures equally unable to criticize *us?* This question struck me sharply when I read a remark in *The Guardian* by an anthropologist about a South American Indian who had been taken into a Brazilian town for an operation, which saved his life. When he came back to his village, he made several highly critical remarks about the white Brazilians' way of life. They may very well have been justified. But the interesting point was that the anthropologist called these remarks "a damning indictment of Western civilization." Now the Indian had been in that town about two weeks. Was he in a

position to deliver a damning indictment? Would we ourselves be qualified to deliver such an indictment on the Samurai, provided we could spend two weeks in ancient Japan? What do we really think about this?

My own impression is that we believe that outsiders can, in principle, deliver perfectly good indictments—only, it usually takes more than two weeks to make them damning. Understanding has degrees. It is not a slapdash yes-or-no matter. Intelligent outsiders can progress in it, and in some ways will be at an advantage over the locals. But if this is so, it must clearly apply to ourselves as much as anybody else.

Our next question is this: Does the isolating barrier between cultures block praise as well as blame? If I want to say that the Samurai culture has many virtues, or to praise the South American Indians, am I prevented from doing *that* by my outside status? Now, we certainly do need to praise other societies in this way. But it is hardly possible that we could praise them effectively if we could not, in principle, criticize them. Our praise would be worthless if it rested on no definite grounds, if it did not flow from some understanding. Certainly we may need to praise things which we do not *fully* understand. We say "there's something very good here, but I can't quite make out what it is yet." This happens when we want to learn from strangers. And we can learn from strangers. But to do this we have to distinguish between those strangers who are worth learning from and those who are not. Can we then judge which is which?

This brings us to our third question: What is involved in judging? Now plainly there is no question here of sitting on a bench in a red robe and sentencing people. Judging simply means forming an opinion, and expressing it if it is called for. Is there anything wrong about this? Naturally, we ought to avoid forming—and expressing—crude opinions, like that of a simple-minded missionary, who might dismiss the whole Samurai culture as entirely bad, because non-Christian. But this is a different objection. The trouble with crude opinions is that they are crude, whoever forms them, not that they are formed by the wrong people. Anthropologists, after all, are outsiders quite as much as missionaries. Moral isolationism forbids us to form *any* opinions on these matters. Its ground for doing so is that we don't understand them. But there is much that we don't understand in our own culture too. This brings us to our last question: If we can't judge other cultures, can we really judge our own? Our efforts to do so will be much damaged if we are really deprived of our opinions about other societies, because these provide the range of comparison, the spectrum of alternatives against which we set what we want to understand. We would have to stop using the mirror which anthropology so helpfully holds up to us.

In short, moral isolationism would lay down a general ban on moral reasoning. Essentially, this is the programme of immoralism, and it carries a distressing logical difficulty. Immoralists like Nietzsche are actually just a rather specialized sect of moralists. They can no more afford to put moralizing out of business than smugglers can afford to abolish custom regulations. The power of moral judgement is, in fact, not a luxury, not a perverse indulgence of the self-righteous. It is a necessity. When we judge something to be bad or good, better or worse than something else, we are taking it as an example to aim at or avoid. Without opinions of this sort, we would have no framework of comparison for our own policy, no chance of profiting by other people's insights or mistakes. In this vacuum, we could form no judgements on our own actions.

Now it would be odd if Homo sapiens had really got himself into a position as bad as this—a position where his main evolutionary asset, his brain, was so little use to him. None of us is going to accept this sceptical diagnosis. We cannot do so, because our involvement in moral isolationism does not flow from apathy, but from a rather acute concern about human hypocrisy and other forms of wickedness. But we polarize that concern around a few selected moral truths. We are rightly angry with those who despise, oppress or steamroll other cultures. We think that doing these things is actually *wrong*. But this is itself a moral judgement. We could not condemn oppression and insolence if we thought that all our condemnations were just a trivial local quirk of our own culture. We could still less do it if we tried to stop judging altogether.

Real moral scepticism, in fact, could lead only to inaction, to our losing all interest in moral questions,

most of all in those which concern other societies. When we discuss these things, it becomes instantly clear how far we are from doing this. Suppose, for instance, that I criticize the bisecting Samurai, that I say his behaviour is brutal. What will usually happen next is that someone will protest, will say that I have no right to make criticisms like that of another culture. But it is most unlikely that he will use this move to end the discussion of the subject. Instead, he will justify the Samurai. He will try to fill in the background, to make me understand the custom, by explaining the exalted ideals of discipline and devotion which produced it. He will probably talk of the lower value which the ancient Japanese placed on individual life generally. He may well suggest that this is a healthier attitude than our own obsession with security. He may add, too, that the wayfarers did not seriously mind being bisected, that in principle they accepted the whole arrangement.

Now an objector who talks like this is implying that it *is* possible to understand alien customs. That is just what he is trying to make me do. And he implies, too, that if I do succeed in understanding them, I shall do something better than giving up judging them. He expects me to change my present judgement to a truer one—namely, one that is favourable. And the standards I must use to do this cannot just be Samurai standards. They have to be ones current in my own culture. Ideals like discipline and devotion will not move anybody unless he himself accepts them. As it happens, neither discipline nor devotion is very popular in the West at present, Anyone who appeals to them may well have to do some more arguing to make *them* acceptable, before he can use them to explain the Samurai. But if he does succeed here, he will have persuaded us, not just that there was something to be said for them in ancient Japan, but that there would be here as well.

Isolating barriers simply cannot arise here. If we accept something as a serious moral truth about one culture, we can't refuse to apply it—in however different an outward form—to other cultures as well, wherever circumstance admit it. If we refuse to do this, we just are not taking the other culture seriously. This becomes clear if we look at the last argument used by my objector—that of justification by consent of the victim. It is suggested that sudden bisection is quite in order, *provided* that it takes place between consenting adults. I cannot now discuss how conclusive this justification is. What I am pointing out is simply that it can only work if we believe that *consent* can make such a transaction respectable—and this is a thoroughly modern and Western idea. It would probably never occur to a Samurai; if it did, it would surprise him very much. It is *our* standard. In applying it, too, we are likely to make another typically Western demand. We shall ask for good factual evidence that the wayfarers actually do have this rather surprising taste—that they are really willing to be bisected. In applying Western standards in this way, we are not being confused or irrelevant. We are asking the questions which arise *from where we stand,* questions which we can see the sense of. We do this because asking questions which you can't see the sense of is humbug. Certainly we can extend our questioning by imaginative effort. We can come to understand other societies better. By doing so, we may make their questions our own, or we may see that they are really forms of the questions which we are asking already. This is not impossible. It is just very hard work. The obstacles which often prevent it are simply those of ordinary ignorance, laziness and prejudice.

If there were really an isolating barrier, of course, our own culture could never have been formed. It is no sealed box, but a fertile jungle of different influences—Greek, Jewish, Roman, Norse, Celtic and so forth, into which further influences are still pouring—American, Indian, Japanese, Jamaican, you name it. The moral isolationist's picture of separate, unmixable cultures is quite unreal. People who talk about British history usually stress the value of this fertilizing mix, no doubt rightly. But this is not just an odd fact about Britain. Except for the very small-est and most remote, all cultures are formed out of many streams. All have the problem of digesting and assimilating things which, at the start, they do not understand. All have the choice of learning something from this challenge, or, alternatively, of refusing to learn, and fighting it mindlessly instead.

This universal predicament has been obscured by the fact that anthropologists used to concentrate largely on very small and remote cultures, which did not seem to have this problem. These tiny societies, which had often forgotten their own history, made neat, self-contained subjects for study. No doubt it was valuable to emphasize their remoteness, their extreme strangeness, their independence of our cultural tradition. This emphasis was, I think, the root of moral isolationism. But, as the tribal studies themselves showed, even there the anthropologists were able to interpret what they saw and make judgements—often favourable—about the tribesmen. And the tribesmen, too, were quite equal to making judgements about the anthropologists—and about the tourists and Coca-Cola salesmen who followed them. Both sets of judgements, no doubt, were somewhat hasty, both have been refined in the light of further experience. A similar transaction between us and the Samurai might take even longer. But that is no reason at all for deeming it impossible. Morally as well as physically, there is only one world, and we all have to live in it.

QUESTIONS

1. What are the ramifications of not making judgments about foreigners and their cultures?

2. Does the fact that people in another country have traditional practices or religious practices make them morally right there, even if they are wrong in your own country?

Dalai Lama | # The Ethic of Compassion

The Dalai Lama is the spiritual leader of all Tibetan Buddhists. He is also a Nobel Laureate.

[A]ll the world's major religions stress the importance of cultivating love and compassion. In the Buddhist philosophical tradition, different levels of attainment are described. At a basic level, compassion (*nying je*) is understood mainly in terms of empathy—our ability to enter into and, to some extent, share others' suffering. But Buddhists—and perhaps others—believe that this can be developed to such a degree that not only does our compassion arise without any effort, but it is unconditional, undifferentiated, and universal in scope. A feeling of intimacy toward all other sentient beings, including of course those who would harm us, is generated, which is likened in the literature to the love a mother has for her only child.

But this sense of equanimity toward all others is not seen as an end in itself. Rather, it is seen as the springboard to a love still greater. Because our capacity for empathy is innate, and because the ability to reason is also an innate faculty, compassion shares the characteristics of consciousness itself. The potential we have to develop it is therefore stable and continuous. It is not a resource which can be used up—as water is used up when we boil it. And though it can be described in terms of activity, it is not like a physical activity which we train for, like jumping, where once we reach a certain height we can go no further. On the contrary, when we enhance our sensitivity toward others' suffering through deliberately opening ourselves up to it, it is believed that we can gradually extend out compassion to the point where the individual feels so moved by even the subtlest suffering of others that they come to have an overwhelming sense of responsibility toward those oth-

ers. This causes the one who is compassionate to dedicate themselves entirely to helping others overcome both their suffering and the causes of their suffering. In Tibetan, this ultimate level of attainment is called *nying je chenmo,* literally "great compassion."

Now I am not suggesting that each individual must attain these advanced states of spiritual development in order to lead an ethically wholesome life. I have described *nying je chenmo* not because it is a precondition of ethical conduct but rather because I believe that pushing the logic of compassion to the highest level can act as a powerful inspiration. If we can just keep the aspiration to develop *nying je chenmo,* or great compassion, as an ideal, it will naturally have a significant impact on our outlook. Based on the simple recognition that, just as I do, so do all others desire to be happy and not to suffer, it will serve as a constant reminder against selfishness and partiality. It will remind us that there is little to be gained from being kind and generous because we hope to win something in return. It will remind us that actions motivated by the desire to create a good name for ourselves are still selfish, however much they may appear to be acts of kindness. It will also remind us that there is nothing exceptional about acts of charity toward those we already feel close to. And it will help us to recognize that the bias we naturally feel toward our families and friends is actually a highly unreliable thing on which to base ethical conduct. If we reserve ethical conduct for those whom we feel close to, the danger is that we will neglect our responsibilities toward those outside this circle.

Why is this? So long as the individuals in question continue to meet our expectations, all is well. But should they fail to do so, someone we consider a dear friend one day can become our sworn enemy the next. As we saw earlier, we have a tendency to react

Dalai Lama, "The Ethic of Compassion," *Ethics for the New Millennium,* (New York: Riverhead Books, 1999), pp. 123–127. Reprinted with permission of Riverhead Books.

badly to all who threaten fulfillment of our cherished desires, though they may be our closest relations. For this reason, compassion and mutual respect offer a much more solid basis for our relations with others. This is also true of partnerships. If our love for someone is based largely on attraction, whether it be their looks or some other superficial characteristic, our feelings for that person are liable, over time, to evaporate. When they lose the quality we found alluring, or when we find ourselves no longer satisfied by it, the situation can change completely, this despite their being the same person. This is why relationships based purely on attraction are almost always unstable. On the other hand, when we begin to perfect our compassion, neither the other's appearance nor their behavior affects our underlying attitude.

Consider, too, that habitually our feelings toward others depend very much on their circumstances. Most people, when they see someone who is handicapped, feel sympathetic toward that person. But then when they see others who are wealthier, or better educated, or better placed socially, they immediately feel envious and competitive toward them. Our negative feelings prevent us from seeing the sameness of ourselves and all others. We forget that just like us, whether fortunate or unfortunate, distant or near, they desire to be happy and not to suffer.

The struggle is thus to overcome these feelings of partiality. Certainly, developing genuine compassion for our loved ones is the obvious and appropriate place to start. The impact our actions have on our close ones will generally be much greater than on others, and therefore our responsibilities toward them are greater. Yet we need to recognize that, ultimately, there are no grounds for discriminating in their favor. In this sense, we are all in the same position as a doctor confronted by ten patients suffering the same serious illness. They are each equally deserving of treatment. The reader should not suppose that what is being advocated here is a state of detached indifference, however. The further essential challenge, as we begin to extend our compassion toward all others, is to maintain the same level of intimacy as we feel toward those closest to us. In other words, what is being suggested is that we need to strive for even-handedness in our approach toward all others, a level ground into which we can plant the seed of *nying je chenmo,* of great love and compassion.

If we can begin to relate to others on the basis of such equanimity, our compassion will not depend on the fact that so and so is my husband, my wife, my relative, my friend. Rather, a feeling of closeness toward all others can be developed based on the simple recognition that, just like myself, all wish to be happy and to avoid suffering. In other words, we will start to relate to others on the basis of their sentient nature. Again, we can think of this in terms of an ideal, one which it is immensely difficult to attain. But, for myself, I find it one which is profoundly inspiring and helpful.

Let us now consider the role of compassionate love and kind-heartedness in our daily lives. Does the ideal of developing it to the point where it is unconditional mean that we must abandon our own interests entirely? Not at all. In fact, it is the best way of serving them—indeed, it could even be said to constitute the wisest course for fulfilling self-interest. For if it is correct that those qualities such as love, patience, tolerance, and forgiveness are what happiness consists in, and if it is also correct that *nying je,* or compassion, as I have defined it, is both the source and the fruit of these qualities, then the more we are compassionate, the more we provide for our own happiness. Thus, any idea that concern for others, though a noble quality, is a matter for our private lives only, is simply shortsighted. Compassion belongs to every sphere of activity, including, of course, the workplace.

QUESTIONS

1. Why is compassion an important moral value?
2. How might one use the Dalai Lama's concept of compassion to generate a set of moral guidelines for a multinational organization?

Thomas Donaldson

Values in Tension: Ethics Away from Home

Thomas Donaldson is Mark O. Winkelman Professor of Legal Studies at the Wharton School of Business, University of Pennsylvania.

When we leave home and cross our nation's boundaries, moral clarity often blurs. Without a backdrop of shared attitudes, and without familiar laws and judicial procedures that define standards of ethical conduct, certainty is elusive. Should a company invest in a foreign country where civil and political rights are violated? Should a company go along with a host country's discriminatory employment practices? If companies in developed countries shift facilities to developing nations that lack strict environmental and health regulations, or if those companies choose to fill management and other top-level positions in a host nation with people from the home country, whose standards should prevail?

Even the best-informed, best-intentioned executives must re-think their assumptions about business practice in foreign settings. What works in a company's home country can fail in a country with different standards of ethical conduct. Such difficulties are unavoidable for businesspeople who live and work abroad.

But how can managers resolve the problems? What are the principles that can help them work through the maze of cultural differences and establish codes of conduct for globally ethical business practice? How can companies answer the toughest question in global business ethics: What happens when a host country's ethical standards seem lower than the home country's?

COMPETING ANSWERS

One answer is as old as philosophical discourse. According to cultural relativism, no culture's ethics are better than any other's; therefore there are no international rights and wrongs. If the people of Indonesia tolerate the bribery of their public officials, so what? Their attitude is no better or worse than that of people in Denmark or Singapore who refuse to offer or accept bribes. Likewise, if Belgians fail to find insider trading morally repugnant, who cares? Not enforcing insider-trading laws is no more or less ethical than enforcing such laws.

The cultural relativist's creed—When in Rome, do as the Romans do—is tempting, especially when failing to do as the locals do means forfeiting business opportunities. The inadequacy of cultural relativism, however, becomes apparent when the practices in question are more damaging than petty bribery or insider trading.

In the late 1980s, some European tanneries and pharmaceutical companies were looking for cheap waste-dumping sites. They approached virtually every country on Africa's west coast from Morocco to the Congo. Nigeria agreed to take highly toxic polychlorinated biphenyls. Unprotected local workers, wearing thongs and shorts, unloaded barrels of PCBs and placed them near a residential area. Neither the residents nor the workers knew that the barrels contained toxic waste.

We may denounce governments that permit such abuses, but many countries are unable to police transnational corporations adequately even if they want to. And in many countries, the combination of ineffective enforcement and inadequate regulations leads to behavior by unscrupulous companies that is clearly wrong. A few years ago, for example, a group of investors became interested in restoring the SS *United States,* once a luxurious ocean liner. Before the actual restoration could begin, the ship had to be stripped of its asbestos lining. A bid from a U.S. company, based on U.S. standards for asbestos removal, priced the job at more than $100 million. A company in the Ukranian city of Sevastopol offered to do the work for less than $2 million. In October 1993, the ship was towed to Sevastopol.

A cultural relativist would have no problem with that outcome, but I do. A country has the right to establish its own health and safety regulations, but in the case described above, the standards and the terms of the contract could not possibly have protected workers in Sevastopol from known health risks. Even if the contract met Ukranian standards, ethical businesspeople must object. Cultural relativism is morally blind. There are fundamental values that cross cultures, and companies must uphold them. (For an economic argument against cultural relativism, see the insert "The Culture and Ethics of Software Piracy.")

At the other end of the spectrum from cultural relativism is ethical imperialism, which directs people to do everywhere exactly as they do at home. Again, an understandably appealing approach but one that is clearly inadequate. Consider the large U.S. computer-products company that in 1993 introduced a course on sexual harassment in its Saudi Arabian facility. Under the banner of global consistency, instructors used the same approach to train Saudi Arabian managers that they had used with U.S. managers: the participants were asked to discuss a case in which a manager makes sexually explicit remarks to a new female employee over drinks in a bar. The instructors failed to consider how the exercise would work in a culture with strict conventions governing relationships between men and women. As a result, the training sessions were ludicrous. They baffled and offended the Saudi participants, and the message to avoid coercion and sexual discrimination was lost.

The theory behind ethical imperialism is absolutism, which is based on three problematic principles. Absolutists believe that there is a single list of

truths, that they can be expressed only with one set of concepts, and that they call for exactly the same behavior around the world.

The first claim clashes with many people's belief that different cultural traditions must be respected. In some cultures, loyalty to a community—family, organization, or society—is the foundation of all ethical behavior. The Japanese, for example, define business ethics in terms of loyalty to their companies, their business networks, and their nation. Americans place a higher value on liberty than on loyalty; the U.S. tradition of rights emphasizes equality, fairness, and individual freedom. It is hard to conclude that truth lies on one side or the other, but an absolutist would have us select just one.

The second problem with absolutism is the presumption that people must express moral truth using only one set of concepts. For instance, some absolutists insist that the language of basic rights provide the framework for any discussion of ethics. That means, though, that entire cultural traditions must be ignored. The notion of a right evolved with the rise of democracy in post-Renaissance Europe and the United States, but the term is not found in either Confucian or Buddhist traditions. We all learn ethics in the context of our particular cultures, and the power in the principles is deeply tied to the way in which they are expressed. Internationally accepted lists of moral principles, such as the United Nations' Universal Declaration of Human Rights, draw on many cultural and religious traditions. As philosopher Michael Walzer has noted, "There is no Esperanto of global ethics."

The third problem with absolutism is the belief in a global standard of ethical behavior. Context must shape ethical practice. Very low wages, for example, may be considered unethical in rich, advanced countries, but developing nations may be acting ethically if they encourage investment and improve living standards by accepting low wages. Likewise, when people are malnourished or starving, a government may be wise to use more fertilizer in order to improve crop yields, even though that means settling for relatively high levels of thermal water pollution.

When cultures have different standards of ethical behavior—and different ways of handling unethical behavior—a company that takes an absolutist approach may find itself making a disastrous mistake. When a manager at a large U.S. specialty-products company in China caught an employee stealing, she followed the company's practice and turned the employee over to the provincial authorities, who executed him. Managers cannot operate in another culture without being aware of that culture's attitudes toward ethics.

If companies can neither adopt a host country's ethics nor extend the home country's standards, what is the answer? Even the traditional litmus test—What would people think of your actions if they were written up on the front page of the newspaper?—is an unreliable guide, for there is no international consensus on standards of business conduct.

BALANCING THE EXTREMES: THREE GUIDING PRINCIPLES

Companies must help managers distinguish between practices that are merely different and those that are wrong. For relativists, nothing is sacred and nothing is wrong. For absolutists, many things that are different are wrong. Neither extreme illuminates the real world of business decision making. The answer lies somewhere in between.

When it comes to shaping ethical behavior, companies must be guided by three principles.

- Respect for core human values, which determine the absolute moral threshold for all business activities.
- Respect for local traditions.
- The belief that context matters when deciding what is right and what is wrong.

Consider those principles in action. In Japan, people doing business together often exchange gifts—sometimes expensive ones—in keeping with longstanding Japanese tradition. When U.S. and European companies started doing a lot of business in Japan, many Western business-people thought that the practice of gift giving might be wrong rather than simply different. To them, accepting a gift felt like accepting a bribe. As Western companies have become more familiar with Japanese traditions, however, most have

come to tolerate the practice and to set different limits on gift giving in Japan than they do elsewhere.

Respecting differences is a crucial ethical practice. Research shows that management ethics differ among cultures; respecting those differences means recognizing that some cultures have obvious weaknesses—as well as hidden strengths. Managers in Hong Kong, for example, have a higher tolerance for some forms of bribery than their Western counterparts, but they have a much lower tolerance for the failure to acknowledge a subordinate's work. In some parts of the Far East, stealing credit from a subordinate is nearly an unpardonable sin.

People often equate respect for local traditions with cultural relativism. That is incorrect. Some practices are clearly wrong. Union Carbide's tragic experience in Bhopal, India, provides one example. The company's executives seriously underestimated how much on-site management involvement was needed at the Bhopal plant to compensate for the country's poor infrastructure and regulatory capabilities. In the aftermath of the disastrous gas leak, the lesson is clear: companies using sophisticated technology in a developing country must evaluate that country's ability to oversee its safe use. Since the incident at Bhopal, Union Carbide has become a leader in advising companies on using hazardous technologies safely in developing countries.

Some activities are wrong no matter where they take place. But some practices that are unethical in one setting may be acceptable in another. For instance, the chemical EDB, a soil fungicide, is banned for use in the United States. In hot climates, however, it quickly becomes harmless through exposure to intense solar radiation and high soil temperatures. As long as the chemical is monitored, companies may be able to use EDB ethically in certain parts of the world.

DEFINING THE ETHICAL THRESHOLD: CORE VALUES

Few ethical questions are easy for managers to answer. But there are some hard truths that must guide managers' actions, a set of what I call *core human values*, which define minimum ethical standards for all companies.[1] The right to good health and the right to economic advancement and an improved standard of living are two core human values. Another is what Westerners call the Golden Rule, which is recognizable in every major religious and ethical tradition around the world. In Book 15 of his *Analects,* for instance, Confucius counsels people to maintain reciprocity, or not to do to others what they do not want done to themselves.

Although no single list would satisfy every scholar, I believe it is possible to articulate three core values that incorporate the work of scores of theologians and philosophers around the world. To be broadly relevant, these values must include elements found in both Western and non-Western cultural and religious traditions. Consider the examples of values in the [box] "What Do These Values Have in Common?"

At first glance, the values expressed in the two lists seem quite different. Nonetheless, in the spirit of what philosopher John Rawls calls *overlapping consensus,* one can see that the seemingly divergent values converge at key points. Despite important differences between Western and non-Western cultural and religious traditions, both express shared attitudes about what it means to be human. First, individuals must not treat others simply as tools; in other words, they must recognize a person's value as a human being. Next, individuals and communities must treat people in ways that respect people's basic rights. Finally, members of a community must work together to support and improve the institutions on which the community depends. I call those three values *respect for human dignity, respect for basic rights,* and *good citizenship.*

Those values must be the starting point for all companies as they formulate and evaluate standards of ethical conduct at home and abroad. But they are only a starting point. Companies need much more specific guidelines, and the first step to developing those is to translate the core human values into core values for business. What does it mean, for example, for a company to respect human dignity? How can a company be a good citizen?

I believe that companies can respect human dignity by creating and sustaining a corporate culture in which employees, customers, and suppliers are treated not as means to an end but as people whose intrinsic value must be acknowledged, and by producing safe products and services in a safe workplace. Companies can respect basic rights by acting in ways that support and protect the individual rights of employees, customers, and surrounding communities, and by avoiding relationships that violate human beings' rights to health, education, safety, and an adequate standard of living. And companies can be good citizens by supporting essential social institutions, such as the economic system and the education system, and by working with host governments and other organizations to protect the environment.

The core values establish a moral compass for business practice. They can help companies identify practices that are acceptable and those that are intol-

---

What Do These Values Have in Common?

Non-Western

Kyosei (Japanese): Living and working
  together for a Common good

Dharma (Hindu): The fulfillment of inherited duty

Santutthi (Buddhist): The importance of limited desires

Zakat (Muslim): The Muslin duty to give alms to the poor.

Western

Individual liberty

Egalitarianism

Political Participation

Human rights

erable—even if the practices are compatible with a host country's norms and laws. Dumping pollutants near people's homes and accepting inadequate standards for handling hazardous materials are two examples of actions that violate core values.

Similarly, if employing children prevents them from receiving a basic education, the practice is intolerable. Lying about product specifications in the act of selling may not affect human lives directly, but it too is intolerable because it violates the trust that is needed to sustain a corporate culture in which customers are respected.

Sometimes it is not a company's actions but those of a supplier or customer that pose problems. Take the case of the Tan family, a large supplier for Levi Strauss. The Tans were allegedly forcing 1,200 Chinese and Filipino women to work 74 hours per week in guarded compounds on the Mariana Islands. In 1992, after repeated warnings to the Tans, Levi Strauss broke off business relations with them.

CREATING AN ETHICAL CORPORATE CULTURE

The core values for business that I have enumerated can help companies begin to exercise ethical judgment and think about how to operate ethically in foreign cultures, but they are not specific enough to guide managers through actual ethical dilemmas. Levi Strauss relied on a written code of conduct when figuring out how to deal with the Tan family. The company's Global Sourcing and Operating Guidelines, formerly called the Business Partner Terms of Engagement, state that Levi Strauss will "seek to identify and utilize business partners who aspire as individuals and in the conduct of all their businesses to a set of ethical standards not incompatible with our own." Whenever intolerable business situations arise, managers should be guided by precise statements that spell out the behavior and operating practices that the company demands.

Ninety percent of all *Fortune* 500 companies have codes of conduct, and 70% have statements of vision and values. In Europe and the Far East, the percentages are lower but are increasing rapidly. Does that mean that most companies have what they need?

Hardly. Even though most large U.S. companies have both statements of values and codes of conduct, many might be better off if they didn't. Too many companies don't do anything with the documents; they simply paste them on the wall to impress employees, customers, suppliers, and the public. As a result, the senior managers who drafted the statements lose credibility by proclaiming values and not living up to them. Companies such as Johnson & Johnson, Levi Strauss, Motorola, Texas Instruments, and Lockheed Martin, however, do a great deal to make the words meaningful. Johnson & Johnson, for example, has become well known for its Credo Challenge sessions, in which managers discuss ethics in the context of their current business problems and are invited to criticize the company's credo and make suggestions for changes. The participants' ideas are passed on to the company's senior managers. Lockheed Martin has created an innovative site on the World Wide Web and on its local network that gives employees, customers, and suppliers access to the company's ethical code and the chance to voice complaints.

Codes of conduct must provide clear direction about ethical behavior when the temptation to behave unethically is strongest. The pronouncement in a code of conduct that bribery is unacceptable is useless unless accompanied by guidelines for gift giving, payments to get goods through customs, and "requests" from intermediaries who are hired to ask for bribes.

Motorola's values are stated very simply as "How we will always act: [with] constant respect for people [and] uncompromising integrity." The company's code of conduct, however, is explicit about actual business practice. With respect to bribery, for example, the code states that the "funds and assets of Motorola shall not be used, directly or indirectly, for illegal payments of any kind." It is unambiguous about what sort of payment is illegal: "the payment of a bribe to a public official or the kickback of funds to an employee of a customer. . . ." The code goes on to prescribe specific procedures for handling commissions to intermediaries, issuing sales invoices, and disclosing confidential information in a sales transaction—all situations in which employees might have an opportunity to accept or offer bribes.

Codes of conduct must be explicit to be useful, but they must also leave room for a manager to use his or her judgment in situations requiring cultural sensitivity. Host-country employees shouldn't be forced to adopt all home-country values and renounce their own. Again, Motorola's code is exemplary. First, it gives clear direction: "Employees of Motorola will respect the laws, customs, and traditions of each country in which they operate, but will, at the same time, engage in no course of conduct which, even if legal, customary, and accepted in any such country, could be deemed to be in violation of the accepted business ethics of Motorola or the laws of the United States relating to business ethics." After laying down such absolutes, Motorola's code then makes clear when individual judgment will be necessary. For example, employees may sometimes accept certain kinds of small gifts "in rare circumstances, where the refusal to accept a gift" would injure Motorola's "legitimate business interests." Under certain circumstances, such gifts "may be accepted so long as the gift inures to the benefit of Motorola" and not "to the benefit of the Motorola employee."

Striking the appropriate balance between providing clear direction and leaving room for individual judgment makes crafting corporate values statements and ethics codes one of the hardest tasks that executives confront. The words are only a start. A company's leaders need to refer often to their organization's credo and code and must themselves be credible, committed, and consistent. If senior managers act as though ethics don't matter, the rest of the company's employees won't think they do, either.

CONFLICTS OF DEVELOPMENT AND CONFLICTS OF TRADITION

Managers living and working abroad who are not prepared to grapple with moral ambiguity and tension should pack their bags and come home. The view that all business practices can be categorized as either ethical or unethical is too simple. As Einstein is reported to have said, "Things should be as simple as possible—but no simpler." Many business practices that are considered unethical in one setting may be ethical in another. Such activities are neither black nor white but exist in what Thomas Dunfee and I

have called *moral free space*.[2] In this gray zone, there are no tight prescriptions for a company's behavior. Managers must chart their own courses—as long as they do not violate core human values.

GUIDELINES FOR ETHICAL LEADERSHIP

Learning to spot intolerable practices and to exercise good judgment when ethical conflicts arise requires practice. Creating a company culture that rewards ethical behavior is essential. The following guidelines for developing a global ethical perspective among managers can help.

Treat corporate values and formal standards of conduct as absolutes. Whatever ethical standards a company chooses, it cannot waver on its principles either at home or abroad. Consider what has become part of company lore at Motorola. Around 1950, a senior executive was negotiating with officials of a South American government on a $10 million sale that would have increased the company's annual net profits by nearly 25%. As the negotiations neared completion, however, the executive walked away from the deal because the officials were asking for $1 million for "fees." CEO Robert Galvin not only supported the executive's decision but also made it clear that Motorola would neither accept the sale on any terms nor do business with those government officials again. Retold over the decades, this story demonstrating Galvin's resolve has helped cement a culture of ethics for thousands of employees at Motorola.

Design and implement conditions of engagement for suppliers and customers. Will your company do business with any customer or supplier? What if a customer or supplier uses child labor? What if it has strong links with organized crime? What if it pressures your company to break a host country's laws? Such issues are best not left for spur-of-the-moment decisions. Some companies have realized that. Sears, for instance, has developed a policy of not contracting production to companies that use prison labor or infringe on workers' rights to health and safety. And BankAmerica has specified as a condition for many of its loans to developing countries that environmental standards and human rights must be observed.

Allow foreign business units to help formulate ethical standards and interpret ethical issues. The French pharmaceutical company Rhône-Poulenc Rorer has allowed foreign subsidiaries to augment lists of corporate ethical principles with their own suggestions. Texas Instruments has paid special attention to issues of international business ethics by creating the Global Business Practices Council, which is made up of managers from countries in which the company operates. With the overarching intent to create a "global ethics strategy, locally deployed," the council's mandate is to provide ethics education and create local processes that will help managers in the company's foreign business units resolve ethical conflicts.

In host countries, support efforts to decrease institutional corruption. Individual managers will not be able to wipe out corruption in a host country, no matter how many bribes they turn down. When a host country's tax system, import and export procedures, and procurement practices favor unethical players, companies must take action.

Many companies have begun to participate in reforming host-country institutions. General Electric, for example, has taken a strong stand in India, using the media to make repeated condemnations of bribery in business and government. General Electric and others have found, however, that a single company usually cannot drive out entrenched corruption. Transparency International, an organization based in Germany, has been effective in helping coalitions of companies, government officials, and others work to reform bribery-ridden bureaucracies in Russia, Bangladesh, and elsewhere.

Exercise moral imagination. Using moral imagination means resolving tensions responsibly and creatively. Coca-Cola, for instance, has consistently turned down requests for bribes from Egyptian officials but has managed to gain political support and public trust by sponsoring a project to plant fruit trees. And take the example of Levi Strauss, which discovered in the early 1990s that two of its suppliers in Bangladesh were employing children under the age of 14—a practice that violated the company's principles but was tolerated in Bangladesh. Forcing the suppliers to fire the children would not have

ensured that the children received an education, and it would have caused serious hardship for the families depending on the children's wages. In a creative arrangement, the suppliers agreed to pay the children's regular wages while they attended school and to offer each child a job at age 14. Levi Strauss, in turn, agreed to pay the children's tuition and provide books and uniforms. That arrangement allowed Levi Strauss to uphold its principles and provide long-term benefits to its host country.

Many people think of values as soft; to some they are usually unspoken. A South Seas island society uses the word *Mokita,* which means, "the truth that everybody knows but nobody speaks." However difficult they are to articulate, values affect how we all behave. In a global business environment, values in tension are the rule rather than the exception. Without a company's commitment, statements of values and codes of ethics end up as empty platitudes that provide managers with no foundation for behaving ethically. Employees need and deserve more, and responsible members of the global business community can set examples for others to follow. The dark consequences of incidents such as Union Carbide's disaster in Bhopal remind us how high the stakes can be.

NOTES

1. In other writings, Thomas W. Dunfee and I have used the term *hypernorm* instead of *core human value.*

2. Thomas Donaldson and Thomas W. Dunfee, "Toward a Unified Conception of Business Ethics: Integrative Social Contracts Theory," *Academy of Management Review,* April 1994; and "Integrative Social Contracts Theory: A Communitarian Conception of Economic Ethics," *Economics and Philosophy,* spring 1995.

QUESTIONS

1. When should companies and/or the people who work in them attempt to assert their own moral values over the values of another culture?

2. When you have traveled to other countries, which cultural values and practices did you find more ethical than your home culture, and which ones did you find less ethical? Why?

The Economist | # Doing Business in Dangerous Places

Setting up a business abroad has always been risky, and not just financially. To create the colony of 90,000 white settlers that, in the late 17th century, earned enormous profits from growing tobacco in Virginia required the immigration of around 116,000 people. The chaps who sailed for India a century later had to endure even worse. "The variety of means by which a man could be carried off was quite bewildering," observes a recent book on the East India Company. "Malaria, typhoid or enteric fever, cholera, dysentery and smallpox were the most common diseases, and the bites of scorpions and mad dogs were frequently lethal."

Those who today run businesses in the nastier parts of the world also face a bewildering range of threats to the safety and health of their employees. Indeed, there are many more disagreeable places to choose from than there were a generation ago. In the days of the Cold War, there was usually a government to deal with, or at worst a rebel authority. These days, a growing number of countries, or large tracts of them are run (if at all) by shifting coalitions of warlords or local bullies. Such power vacuums create potentially lethal uncertainty. They also aggravate more mundane (but no less burdensome) risks, from life-threatening driving conditions to the spread of diseases such as aids and malaria.

Moreover, some of the protection once offered by a white face, a red cross, a neutral flag or the passport of a Great Power has now vanished. As a result, many places that have long been dangerous have become even more so. Last month, Médecins Sans Frontières (msf), an aid group that specialises in sending medical staff to countries in conflict, shut all its programmes in Afghanistan after five of its staff were killed in a deliberate attack on a clearly marked msf vehicle. Taliban spokesmen said that aid organi-

sations such as msf were helping the Americans, something the charity vehemently denies. Anyone doing business in a conflict zone runs similar risks: driving a truck or building a telecoms network may not seem a political act to the company that undertakes the task, but followers of Osama bin Laden think otherwise.

HOW TO BE SAFER

For most employers, health and safety issues are generally about avoiding minor injuries and malfunctions. To send employees to regions where injury or death are real possibilities involves, on the face of it, quite a different approach. Sending staff to work in Iraq or Colombia might appear to be the reverse of good health-and-safety practice. In fact, whereas some of the principles of protecting employees in dangerous places are different, others are surprisingly similar.

For example, the greatest risks even in some of the scariest parts of the world are not of kidnap or murder, but of illness, traffic accidents or violent crime. In the heyday of the East India Company, the single biggest cause of death of the company's employees was not mad dogs or scorpions, but the familiar drug of alcohol (aggravated by bad diet and lack of exercise). In Congo today, malaria is a far bigger risk for expatriates than murder. The good news: such threats are easier to deal with than the terrors of ambush or armed attack. One of the simplest ways to lessen risk is to get all expats, their families and local staff to wear seatbelts: prosaic but effective.

Employers sending people to dangerous places need, first of all, to be honest about what they are doing. That means thinking early about the risks involved. Too many companies entering markets in

The Economist, Doing Business in Dangerous Places, August 14, 2004, p. 11.

backward countries, even those not at war, greatly underestimate the cost of security. Employers also need to decide early on how big a threat to their staff would force them to withdraw. That will vary from firm to firm. KBR, part of Halliburton, has lost 42 employees in Iraq and Kuwait and yet stayed put. Many other companies would have retreated at a serious threat to just one staff member.

Being honest with employees entails—as far as possible—avoiding pressure on them to go somewhere dangerous. That is sometimes easier said than done: the oil-company engineer willing to work only in comfy places is unlikely to thrive. It also means giving staff good advance training, especially in first aid. And it means using people with experience where possible. For instance, South Africans, accustomed to working in some of the riskier parts of their continent, may understand how to deal with a threat much better than someone coming to Africa for the first time. Inexperienced staff need more specialist support, perhaps from one of the companies in the burgeoning threat-management business.

SIMMERING

Inexperienced staff may also be eager to go for the wrong reasons—to be able to boast that they have risked death for their work and survived. One constant hazard is the "boiling frog" syndrome. Where danger is mounting, as it seems to be now in Saudi Arabia, people on the ground may not realise it, or may prefer to pretend otherwise, until too late. Even if they do acknowledge the risk, they may stay on out of exaggerated loyalty to clients or misplaced zeal to outlast competitors. Wise companies make sure that the judgment of independent security experts goes to head office, not the local boss, and that risks are kept under constant review.

What about using local staff? They may have a better sense of danger and be less conspicuous than expatriates. Many employers in dangerous parts of the world try to keep the use of foreigners to a minimum. That is fine if they also take their responsibilities to local staff seriously, but not if the locals are put at greater risk than expatriates because they are considered more expendable.

Why go, if the risks are great? There are good reasons for operating in dangerous lands. There are people who need help, and countries to rebuild. But for companies, the lure is usually the one that led early Virginians to endure the privations of America or the British to colonise India: if the risks are great, then so too are the rewards. What matters is that the rewards are not earned at the cost of putting employees in more danger than, once properly informed, they choose to accept.

QUESTIONS

1. To what extent should companies be held responsible for employees who get kidnapped or murdered while working in a foreign country?

2. In an era of terrorism, are there some places or conditions under which no company should send employees?

United Nations Universal Declaration of Human Rights

On December 10, 1948 the General Assembly of the United Nations adopted and proclaimed the Universal Declaration of Human Rights the full text of which appears in the following pages. Following this historic act, the Assembly called upon all Member countries to publicize the text of the Declaration and "to cause it to be disseminated, displayed, read and expounded principally in schools and other educational institutions, without distinction based on the political status of countries or territories."

PREAMBLE

Whereas recognition of the inherent dignity and of the equal and inalienable rights of all members of the human family is the foundation of freedom, justice and peace in the world,

Whereas disregard and contempt for human rights have resulted in barbarous acts which have outraged the conscience of mankind, and the advent of a world in which human beings shall enjoy freedom of speech and belief and freedom from fear and want has been proclaimed as the highest aspiration of the common people,

Whereas it is essential, if man is not to be compelled to have recourse, as a last resort, to rebellion against tyranny and oppression, that human rights should be protected by the rule of law,

Whereas it is essential to promote the development of friendly relations between nations,

Whereas the peoples of the United Nations have in the Charter reaffirmed their faith in fundamental human rights, in the dignity and worth of the human person and in the equal rights of men and women and have determined to promote social progress and better standards of life in larger freedom,

Whereas Member States have pledged themselves to achieve, in co-operation with the United Nations, the promotion of universal respect for and observance of human rights and fundamental freedoms,

Whereas a common understanding of these rights and freedoms is of the greatest importance for the full realization of this pledge,

Now, Therefore THE GENERAL ASSEMBLY proclaims THIS UNIVERSAL DECLARATION OF HUMAN RIGHTS as a common standard of achievement for all peoples and all nations, to the end that every individual and every organ of society, keeping this Declaration constantly in mind, shall strive by teaching and education to promote respect for these rights and freedoms and by progressive measures, national and international, to secure their universal and effective recognition and observance, both among the peoples of Member States themselves and among the peoples of territories under their jurisdiction.

ARTICLE 1

All human beings are born free and equal in dignity and rights. They are endowed with reason and conscience and should act towards one another in a spirit of brotherhood.

ARTICLE 2

Everyone is entitled to all the rights and freedoms set forth in this Declaration, without distinction of any kind, such as race, colour, sex, language, religion, political or other opinion, national or social origin, property, birth or other status. Furthermore, no distinction shall be made on the basis of the political, jurisdictional or international status of the country or territory to which a person belongs, whether it be independent, trust, non-self-governing or under any other limitation of sovereignty.

ARTICLE 3

Everyone has the right to life, liberty and security of person.

ARTICLE 4

No one shall be held in slavery or servitude; slavery and the slave trade shall be prohibited in all their forms.

ARTICLE 5

No one shall be subjected to torture or to cruel, inhuman or degrading treatment or punishment.

ARTICLE 6

Everyone has the right to recognition everywhere as a person before the law.

ARTICLE 7

All are equal before the law and are entitled without any discrimination to equal protection of the law. All are entitled to equal protection against any discrimination in violation of this Declaration and against any incitement to such discrimination.

ARTICLE 8

Everyone has the right to an effective remedy by the competent national tribunals for acts violating the fundamental rights granted him by the constitution or by law.

ARTICLE 9

No one shall be subjected to arbitrary arrest, detention or exile.

ARTICLE 10

Everyone is entitled in full equality to a fair and public hearing by an independent and impartial tribunal, in the determination of his rights and obligations and of any criminal charge against him.

ARTICLE 11

(1) Everyone charged with a penal offence has the right to be presumed innocent until proved guilty according to law in a public trial at which he has had all the guarantees necessary for his defence.

(2) No one shall be held guilty of any penal offence on account of any act or omission which did not constitute a penal offence, under national or international law, at the time when it was committed. Nor shall a heavier penalty be imposed than the one that was applicable at the time the penal offence was committed.

ARTICLE 12

No one shall be subjected to arbitrary interference with his privacy, family, home or correspondence, nor to attacks upon his honour and reputation. Everyone has the right to the protection of the law against such interference or attacks.

ARTICLE 13

(1) Everyone has the right to freedom of movement and residence within the borders of each state.

(2) Everyone has the right to leave any country, including his own, and to return to his country.

ARTICLE 14

(1) Everyone has the right to seek and to enjoy in other countries asylum from persecution.

(2) This right may not be invoked in the case of prosecutions genuinely arising from non-political crimes or from acts contrary to the purposes and principles of the United Nations.

ARTICLE 15

(1) Everyone has the right to a nationality.

(2) No one shall be arbitrarily deprived of his nationality nor denied the right to change his nationality.

ARTICLE 16

(1) Men and women of full age, without any limitation due to race, nationality or religion, have the right to marry and to found a family. They are entitled to equal rights as to marriage, during marriage and at its dissolution.

(2) Marriage shall be entered into only with the free and full consent of the intending spouses.

(3) The family is the natural and fundamental group unit of society and is entitled to protection by society and the State.

ARTICLE 17

(1) Everyone has the right to own property alone as well as in association with others.

(2) No one shall be arbitrarily deprived of his property.

ARTICLE 18

Everyone has the right to freedom of thought, conscience and religion; this right includes freedom to change his religion or belief, and freedom, either alone or in community with others and in public or private, to manifest his religion or belief in teaching, practice, worship and observance.

ARTICLE 19

Everyone has the right to freedom of opinion and expression; this right includes freedom to hold opinions without interference and to seek, receive and impart information and ideas through any media and regardless of frontiers.

ARTICLE 20

(1) Everyone has the right to freedom of peaceful assembly and association.

(2) No one may be compelled to belong to an association.

ARTICLE 21

(1) Everyone has the right to take part in the government of his country, directly or through freely chosen representatives.

(2) Everyone has the right of equal access to public service in his country.

(3) The will of the people shall be the basis of the authority of government; this will shall be expressed in periodic and genuine elections which shall be by universal and equal suffrage and shall be held by secret vote or by equivalent free voting procedures.

ARTICLE 22

Everyone, as a member of society, has the right to social security and is entitled to realization, through national effort and international co-operation and in accordance with the organization and resources of each State, of the economic, social and cultural rights indispensable for his dignity and the free development of his personality.

ARTICLE 23

(1) Everyone has the right to work, to free choice of employment, to just and favourable conditions of work and to protection against unemployment.

(2) Everyone, without any discrimination, has the right to equal pay for equal work.

(3) Everyone who works has the right to just and favourable remuneration ensuring for himself and his family an existence worthy of human dignity, and supplemented, if necessary, by other means of social protection.

(4) Everyone has the right to form and to join trade unions for the protection of his interests.

ARTICLE 24

Everyone has the right to rest and leisure, including reasonable limitation of working hours and periodic holidays with pay.

ARTICLE 25

(1) Everyone has the right to a standard of living adequate for the health and well-being of himself and of his family, including food, clothing, housing and medical care and necessary social services, and the right to security in the event of unemployment, sickness, disability, widowhood, old age or other lack of livelihood in circumstances beyond his control.

(2) Motherhood and childhood are entitled to special care and assistance. All children, whether born in or out of wedlock, shall enjoy the same social protection.

ARTICLE 26

(1) Everyone has the right to education. Education shall be free, at least in the elementary and fundamental stages. Elementary education shall be compulsory. Technical and professional education shall be made generally available and higher education shall be equally accessible to all on the basis of merit.

(2) Education shall be directed to the full development of the human personality and to the strengthening of respect for human rights and fundamental freedoms. It shall promote understanding, tolerance and friendship among all nations, racial or religious groups, and shall further the activities of the United Nations for the maintenance of peace.

(3) Parents have a prior right to choose the kind of education that shall be given to their children.

ARTICLE 27

(1) Everyone has the right freely to participate in the cultural life of the community, to enjoy the arts and to share in scientific advancement and its benefits.

(2) Everyone has the right to the protection of the moral and material interests resulting from any scientific, literary or artistic production of which he is the author.

ARTICLE 28

Everyone is entitled to a social and international order in which the rights and freedoms set forth in this Declaration can be fully realized.

ARTICLE 29

(1) Everyone has duties to the community in which alone the free and full development of his personality is possible.

(2) In the exercise of his rights and freedoms, everyone shall be subject only to such limitations as are determined by law solely for the purpose of securing due recognition and respect for the rights and freedoms of others and of meeting the just requirements of morality, public order and the general welfare in a democratic society.

(3) These rights and freedoms may in no case be exercised contrary to the purposes and principles of the United Nations.

ARTICLE 30

Nothing in this Declaration may be interpreted as implying for any State, group or person any right to engage in any activity or to perform any act aimed at the destruction of any of the rights and freedoms set forth herein.

QUESTIONS

1. Which human rights would countries disagree with the most?

2. Which human rights are not respected or fully respected in your own country?

CASES

CASE 12.1
The Oil Rig
Joanne B. Ciulla

You have just taken over as the new chief executive officer of Stratton Oil Company, an exploration and drilling firm under contract to a major multinational oil company. Your enterprise has experienced ups and downs over the past few years because of the fluctuation of international oil prices and complications with overseas operations.

Many of the operational problems stem from difficulties with Stratton's offshore oil-drilling rigs. Maintenance and equipment costs have skyrocketed. You have received several reports of strained labor relations on the platforms. One incident caused such an uproar that the rig manager halted operations for over a week. In addition, there have been a number of complaints from conscientious shareholders who are concerned with the environmental impact of these rigs.

In an attempt to address these issues, you decide to get a firsthand look at the offshore drilling operations. On your first excursion, you visit a rig off the coast of Africa, dubbed the "Voyager 7." You discover that an oil rig is really a small society, separate and distinct from the rest of the world.

Stratton's Voyager 7 is a relatively small "jack-up" (a platform with legs) with dimensions of about 200 feet by 100 feet. The platform houses a crew of 150 men, made up of skilled laborers, "roustabouts" or unskilled laborers, maintenance staff, and 30 expatriates. The expatriates work as roughnecks, drillers, technicians, or administrators. The top administrator on the Voyager 7 is the "tool pusher," an expatriate who wields almost absolute authority over matters pertaining to life on the rig.

Stratton engineers modified the crew quarters on the Voyager 7 for operations in Africa. They installed a second galley on the lower level and enlarged the cabins to permit a dormitory-style arrangement of 16 persons per room. This lower level of the rig makes up the "African section" of the rig, where the 120 local workers eat, sleep, and socialize during their 28-day "hitch."

The upper level of the platform houses the 30 expatriates in an area that is equal in square footage to that of the African section. The "expatriate section" contains semiprivate quarters with baths and boasts its own galley, game room, and movie room. Although not explicitly written, a tacit regulation exists prohibiting African workers from entering the expatriate section of the rig except in emergencies. The only Africans who are exempt from this regulation are those who are assigned to the highly valued positions of cleaning or galley staff in the expatriate section. The Africans hold these positions in high esteem because of the potential for receiving gifts or recovering discarded razors and other items from the expatriates.

Several other rig policies separate the African workers from the expatriates. African laborers travel to and from the rig by boat (an 18-hour trip), whereas expatriates receive helicopter transportation. An expatriate registered nurse dispenses medical attention to the expatriates throughout the day, but the Africans have access to treatment only during shift changes or in an emergency. The two groups also receive disparate treatment when serious injuries arise. For instance, if a finger is severed, expatriates are rushed to the mainland for reconstructive surgery. However, because of the high cost of helicopter transportation, African workers must have an amputation operation performed on the rig by the medic.

The company issues gray coveralls to the Africans, while the expatriates receive red coveralls. Meals in the two galleys are vastly different: The expatriate galley serves fine cuisine that approaches gourmet quality, while the Africans dine on a somewhat more proletarian fare. Despite the gross disparity in the numbers served, the catering budgets for the two galleys are nearly equal.

Communication between the expatriates and the Africans is notably absent on the Voyager 7, since none of the expatriates speaks the native language and none of the Africans speaks more that a few words of the expatriate's language. Only the chef of the catering company knows both languages. Consequently, he acts as an interpreter in all emergency situations. In the everyday working environment, management must rely upon sign language or repetition of examples to train and coordinate efforts.

From time to time, an entourage of African government officials visits the Voyager 7. These visits normally last only for an hour or so. Invariably, the officials dine with the expatriates, take a brief tour of the equipment, and then return to shore by helicopter.

No entourage has never expressed concern about the disparity in living conditions on the rig, nor have officials ever bothered to speak with the African workers. Observers comment that the officials seem disinterested in the situation of the African workers, most of whom come from outside the capital city.

The presence of an expatriate black worker has little effect on the rig's segregated environment. The expatriate black is assigned to the expatriate section and partakes in all expatriate privileges. However, few expatriate blacks participate in the international drilling business, and the few who do are frequently not completely welcomed into the rig's social activities.

You leave the oil rig feeling uneasy. You know that there has always been a disparity in living conditions on the drilling platforms. However, you want to make Stratton a socially responsible and profitable company. You wonder how you can best accomplish your dual goals.

QUESTIONS

1. What do you think is really bothering the workers?
2. What kinds of inequalities are tolerable and intolerable on an oil rig, in operations away from home, and inside an organization at home?

CASE 12.2
Diller's Dilemma: Street Children and Substance Abuse
Karen Marquis and Joanne B. Ciulla

Walter Diller, Chief Executive Officer of B. H. Diller, Inc., faced a formidable problem. Could the company continue production of its most profitable adhesive product, Endurol, and at the same time manage to maintain its impeccable image for social responsibility?

This case was adapted by Karen Marquis and Joanne B. Ciulla from "H. B. Fuller in Hondouras: Street Children and Substance Abuse" by Norm Bowie and Stephanie Ann Lenway in 1991. It was published in *The Ethics of Business in a Global Economy,* Klewer Academic Publishers, 1993.

The executives at B. H. Diller, Inc., first became aware of the substance abuse problem back in 1986 when Honduran newspapers carried articles about police arrests of street children who drugged themselves by sniffing glue. Most of the orphaned or runaway children lived in the poorest slums of the big cities, where they scratched out a minimal existence as beggars and illegal squatters. The commonly available adhesive known as Endurol emerged as the substance of choice among these young junkies because of its low price and hallucinogenic qualities. The highly addictive glue induced immediate feelings of elation, grandeur, and power, but it also initiated irreversible liver and brain damage when used over a long period of time. Although the street children abused other substances in addition to Endurol, they soon became tagged as "Enduroleros," a name that eventually became synonymous with all street children, whether they used the drug or not.

Malena Chemical Industries, S.A., one of B. H. Diller's wholly owned subsidiaries, first introduced Endurol to the Central American market in the early 1980s. Malena manufactured and distributed more than a dozen different adhesives under the Endurol brand name in several countries. In Honduras, where Endurol was manufactured, the products had a strong market position. The adhesives were intended primarily for use in shoe manufacturing and repair, leatherwork, and carpentry. The most common forms of Endurol had properties similar to those of airplane glue or rubber cement and were readily available at household goods stores throughout the country. Malena maintained tight control over the wholesale distribution of Endurol. Nearly all glue products that reached the Enduroleros came from retail outlets, either directly of through street pushers.

In spite of the competitive challenge of operating under unstable political and economic conditions in Central America, Malena managers stressed the objective of going beyond the bottom line in their annual report:

> Malena carries out business with the utmost respect for ethical and legal principles. Its orientation is not solely directed to the customer, who has the highest priority, but also to the shareholders, to employees, and to the communities where it operates.

Diller's founder and chairman of the board, B. Howard Diller, had become a legendary figure in the local area. He had served several terms in local government and remained active in civic affairs. Diller saw the company through four decades of financial success as president and chief executive officer before handing over the managerial reigns to his son Walter in January 1989.

Three months into Walter's term as president, angry letters began to trickle in from the stockholders. Some of these individuals heard of the Endurol problem through international press releases, while others had witnessed the problem firsthand in Central America. On November 2, 1989, Diller received an irate call from a shareholder whose daughter worked with an international aid group in Honduras. The man demanded, "How can a company like B. H. Diller claim to have a social conscience and continue to sell Endurol, which is 'practically burning out the brains' of children in Latin America?" The letter's timing was uncanny. Walter was about to meet with a national group of socially responsible investors who were considering B. H. Diller's stock for inclusion in their portfolio.

Meanwhile, Walter learned that Malena management had failed to dissuade the Honduran government from regulating Endurol. As a solution to the glue-sniffing problem, the legislature mandated that oil of mustard, allyl isothiocyanate, be added to Endurol to prevent its abuse. They argued that a person attempting to sniff glue with oil of mustard included would find it too powerful to tolerate—like getting an "overdose of horseradish." However, independent toxicology reports revealed that the oil of mustard had some acute side effects. The material could prove fatal if inhaled, swallowed, or absorbed through the skin; caused severe irritation or burns; and could destroy tissues of the mucous membranes, upper respiratory tract, eyes, and skin. In addition, the Endurol with the oil of mustard included had a shelf life of only six months.

Given B. H. Diller's high visibility as a socially responsible corporation, the glue-sniffing problem had the potential for becoming a public relations nightmare. Diller's staff suggested a number of options, including withdrawal of the product from the market or altering the formula to make Endurol a water-based product. Both would solve the glue-sniffing problem. However, any formula alteration would also affect the strength and durability of the glue, its most valuable properties.

Finally, Diller decided to go to Honduras and see what was going on. Upon his return, he realized that the situation involved more than product misuse and the company's image; it had social and community ramifications as well. The issue was substance abuse by children, regardless of who manufactured the product.

The depth of poverty in Honduras exacerbated the problem. In 1989, 65 percent of all households in Honduras lived in poverty, making it one of the poorest countries in Latin America. The government remained highly unstable with a large turnover rate.

Officials usually settled for a quick fix. They seldom stayed in office long enough to manage a long-term policy. By the time of Diller's trip, the oil-of-mustard law had been on the books for several months. However, officials had yet to implement the rule, and the country had scheduled national elections in three months.

Diller wondered if his company could do much to solve this complicated social problem.

QUESTIONS

1. Is a company responsible for the misuse of its product in another culture?

2. Do companies have a duty to try and influence the way that a government addresses a social problem related to their products?

CASE 12.3

Foreign Assignment

Thomas Dunfee and Diana Robertson

Sara Strong graduated with an MBA from UCLA four years ago. She immediately took a job in the correspondent bank section of the Security Bank of the American Continent. Sara was assigned to work on issues pertaining to relationships with correspondent banks in Latin America. She rose rapidly in the section and received three good promotions in three years. She consistently got high ratings from her superiors, and she received particularly high marks for her professional demeanor.

In her initial position with the bank, Sara was required to travel to Mexico on several occasions. She was always accompanied by a male colleague even though she generally handled similar business by herself on trips within the United States. During her trips to Mexico she observed that Mexican bankers seemed more aware of her being a woman and were personally solicitous to her, but she didn't discern any major problems. The final decisions on the work that she did were handled by male representatives of the bank stationed in Mexico.

A successful foreign assignment was an important step for those on the "fast track" at the bank. Sara applied for a position in Central or South America and was delighted when she was assigned to the bank's office in Mexico City. The office had about

Case study by Thomas Dunfee and Diana Robertson, "Foreign Assignment," the Wharton School of Business, The University of Pennsylvania. Reprinted by permission of the authors.

twenty bank employees and was headed by William Vitam. The Mexico City office was seen as a preferred assignment by young executives at the bank.

After a month, Sara began to encounter problems. She found it difficult to be effective in dealing with Mexican bankers—the clients. They appeared reluctant to accept her authority and they would often bypass her in important matters. The problem was exacerbated by Vitam's compliance in her being bypassed. When she asked that the clients be referred back to her, Vitam replied, "Of course that isn't really practical." Vitam made matters worse by patronizing her in front of clients and by referring to her as "my cute assistant" and "our lady banker." Vitam never did this when only Americans were present, and in fact treated her professionally and with respect in internal situations.

Sara finally complained to Vitam that he was undermining her authority and effectiveness; she asked him in as positive a manner as possible to help her. Vitam listened carefully to Sara's complaints, then replied: "I'm glad that you brought this up, because I've been meaning to sit down and talk to you about my little game-playing in front of the clients. Let me be frank with you. Our clients think you're great, but they just don't understand a woman in authority, and you and I aren't going to be able to change their attitudes overnight. As long as the clients see you as my assistant and deferring to me, they can do business with you. I'm willing to give you as much responsibility as they can handle your having. I *know* you can handle it. But we just have to tread carefully. You and I know that my remarks in front of clients don't mean anything. They're just a way of playing the game Latin style. I know it's frustrating for you, but I really need you to support me on this. It's not going to affect your promotions, and for the most part you really will have responsibility for these clients' accounts. You just have to act like it's my responsibility." Sara replied that she would try to cooperate, but that basically she found her role demeaning.

As time went on, Sara found that the patronizing actions in front of clients bothered her more and more. She spoke to Vitam again, but he was firm in his position, and urged her to try to be a little more flexible, even a little more "feminine."

Sara also had a problem with Vitam over policy. The Mexico City office had five younger women who worked as receptionists and secretaries. They were all situated at work stations at the entrance to the office. They were required to wear standard uniforms that were colorful and slightly sexy. Sara protested the requirement that uniforms be worn because (1) they were inconsistent to the image of the banking business and (2) they were demeaning to the women who had to wear them. Vitam just curtly replied that he had received a lot of favorable comments about the uniforms from clients of the bank.

Several months later, Sara had what she thought would be a good opportunity to deal with the problem. Tom Fried, an executive vice present who had been a mentor for her since she arrived at the bank, was coming to Mexico City; she arranged a private conference with him. She described her problems and explained that she was not able to be effective in this environment and that she worried that it would have a negative effect on her chance of promotion within the bank. Fried was very careful in his response. He spoke of certain "realities" that the bank had to respect and he urged her to "see it through" even though he could understand how she would feel that things weren't fair.

Sara found herself becoming more aggressive and defensive in her meetings with Vitam and her clients. Several clients asked that other bank personnel handle their transactions. Sara has just received an Average rating, which noted "the beginnings of a negative attitude about the bank and its policies."

QUESTIONS

1. Do you think that Vitam and Tom are correct about the "realities" of the culture concerning women? If these cultural assumptions are correct, what are the ethical implications of following the "when in Rome" principle?

2. Was Sarah treated fairly in her evaluation?

CASE 12.4
The Quandry at PureDrug
Karen Marquis and Joanne B. Ciulla

You are the Chief Executive Officer of Puredrug, a large pharmaceutical company with sales and operations throughout the world. Your firm has an outstanding reputation for quality as well as a long-term record of growth and profitability. Over the past 10 years, sales grew at an average annual compound rate of 12 percent and profits increased by an average of 15 percent per annum. The company had not experienced losses since 1957, and stock prices remained consistently healthy.

In spite of Puredrug's impeccable record, by October 1991 your company is in trouble. Due to a general economic downturn and a few product development problems, the firm faces a declining market share and weakened corporate profits. Although still profitable, Puredrug fell far short of its goals established for 1990. As of the end of the third quarter of 1991, you project a $4 million loss for the year. The value of your corporate stock has already dropped by one-fifth of its 1990 year-end value, and a loss for the year could result in an even more substantial devaluation. Small investors might switch to pharmaceutical companies with better results. Even worse, a disappointing year could cause large institutional investors such as pension funds to support a takeover by one of your competitors.

In an attempt to remedy the immediate situation, you call an emergency meeting of your top managers to poll their suggestions. Charles Dunn, head of the International Export Division, reminds you that his department has an opportunity to sign an $8 million contract with the Philippine government. The contract involves the sale of Travolene, a new injectable drug, developed by Puredrug for the treatment of serious viral infections, including measles. The drug remains difficult and expensive to manufacture and has been in very short supply since its introduction. The 1991 budget did not include this sale due to the lack of product availability.

Dunn mentions that at this time Puredrug's inventory contains a large lot of Travolene, produced at a cost of about $2 million. The government rejected the batch for the domestic market on the basis of a new, very sensitive test for endotoxin. The authorities recently adopted this test in addition to the standard method that had been used for many years. The more sensitive test revealed a very low level of endotoxin in the batch of Travolene, while the old procedure uncovered no endotoxin whatsoever.

You ask Ann Doe, the company's Chief Medical Safety Officer, whether this rules out shipping the batch to the Philippines. She explains that the Philippines and many other countries still rely exclusively on the old test. Ann said, "It always takes them awhile to adopt more sophisticated practices, and sometimes they never do. Endotoxin might cause high fever when injected into patients, but I can't tell you that the level in this batch is high enough to cause trouble. Still, how can we have a double standard, one for our nation and one for Third World countries?"

Charles Dunn interrupts, "It's not our job to overprotect other countries. The health authorities in the Philippines know what they are doing. Our officials always take an extreme position. Measles is a serious illness. Last year in the Philippines half of the children who contracted measles died. It's not only good business but also good ethics to send them the only batch of Travolene we have available."

Karen Marquis & Joanne B. Ciulla "The Quandry at PureDrug" in Paul Minus, ed., *The Ethics of Business in a Global Economy* (Boston: Kluwer Academic Press, 1993), pp. 130–131.

As the other senior members of Puredrug's management begin to take sides on the issue, you contemplate your options. In the short run, the profit margin on the lot of Travolene would boost Puredrug's bottom line into the black for the year. In addition, the sale to the Philippines could foster a lucrative long-term relationship and lead to expansion into other Asian markets.

You leave the meeting with an uneasy feeling.

You have only 72 hours before you must present a plan to Puredrug's Board of Directors.

QUESTIONS

1. Is it ethical for Puredrug to practice one standard of safety at home and another in a foreign country?

2. If children in the Philippines die as the result of taking Tavolene, is Puredrug morally responsible for it?

CASE 12.5

The Conflict at Lomatex Chemical

Karen Marquis

You are the President of Lomatex Chemical, Inc., a medium-sized petrochemical company. The company manufactures a variety of chemical products for agricultural use, such as pesticides, herbicides, and fertilizers, along with a number of petroleum-based commodities.

Lomatex employs a large number of residents who live in the small community of about 40,000 where Lomatex is located. The firm enjoys a positive image in the area, and has been a stable economic force since the mid-1960s.

However, over the last few years, sales have consistently dropped in the industry. Luckily the company managed to weather the oil price instability of the 1980s. Still, the firm was forced to ride the ups and downs of the economy along with the rest of the industry. In order to temper these effects, you began to seek out new international markets for your agricultural products.

After a long search, you found the ideal person to head up the company's new international marketing division. Norman Smith was highly recommended by

a number of your most respected colleagues. He had strong connections in Europe and Northern Africa from his days as marketing director with a competing firm. You decided to target the growing pesticide and fertilizer market in Africa. With a constant population growth, many of the developing African nations had a real need for agricultural products.

Only two months after he came on board, Norman had already landed a potentially lucrative contract. He solicited an attractive order from the government of Bawumba, a small nation located in north central Africa. The Bawumba officials wanted to purchase a small quantity of several agricultural chemicals in order to test them over a period of three months. If the results proved satisfactory, then the government would grant Lomatex a multimillion dollar contract for pesticides and fertilizers. It seemed like just the break that Lomatex needed to boost its sagging earnings. However, you decide to keep the good news a secret until the contract is signed.

On the very day you expect to hear from the Bawumban government, you receive a distressed call

Karen Marquis, "The Conflict at Lomotex Chemical" in Paul Minus, ed., *The Ethics of Business in a Global Economy*, (Boston: Kluwer Academic Press, 1993), pp. 138–139.

from Bill Swan, chief chemist from the pesticide division. You have always respected Bill and maintain an open-door policy with him and his staff.

As Bill enters your office, he seems distraught. Norman Smith had just leaked the news of the pending deal to him. Bill tells you that he spent some time in Bawumba in the foreign service, and that they could not possibly need a chemical shipment this large. When he was there 15 years ago, they had a good deal of agricultural production already under way; however, a large portion of the country is unsuitable for farming.

Bill reminds you that over the last two years, a new military dictatorship has taken power in Bawumba. Relations with their neighbors have become strained. He has even heard rumors of a possible arms buildup from friends who remain in the country. Bill warns you that chemical weaponry is common in that region, and that the government may use the Lomatex chemicals to produce poisonous gas.

You are stunned. The request from the Bawumbans seemed innocent enough. However, you do recall that over 200 Western firms had been accused of helping Iraq build up its supply of chemical and other weapons. Many of those Iraqi purchase orders

appeared legitimate as well, and this fact did not release those companies from the responsibility of shipping potential weaponry to a hostile government. Recently, a number of Western firms were accused of jeopardizing their national interest.

On the one hand, you do not know if the Bawumbans have the technology to convert Lomatex chemicals into lethal weapons. Bill lived in the country many years ago. Perhaps technological development now permits the government to grow food on previously infertile land. On the other hand, you are not sure how the chemicals will be used.

As you ponder these concerns, the telephone rings. You answer, and Norman informs you that the Bawumba government has decided to grant Lomatex the contract.

QUESTIONS

1. Should Lomatex refuse to sell to the Bawumban government?

2. Is Lomatex morally responsible if the Bawumbans use their product to make weapons that harm their own people or others? Where does its ethical responsibility begin and end in this case?

CASE 12.6
Consulting for Jones and Jones Pharmaceutical
Kelley MacDougall and Tom L. Beauchamp

Ricardo D'Amato is a high-salaried executive who for four years has been on the payroll of a large international pharmaceutical company, the Jones and Jones Company. Located at the European headquarters in Sweden, D'Amato is in charge of certifying that new products are ready for the approval and reg-

istration process and for subsequent marketing. His office is responsible for sending new products to the relevant government authorities in European countries, each of which has an organization similar to the U.S. Food and Drug Administration (FDA), where drugs are tested for safety and effectiveness.

Although D'Amato's relations with his peers have been without significant strain, he now suddenly finds himself enmeshed in controversy and crisis. He has refused to authorize a $15,000 payment on a contract the company has with a consultant in Switzerland. The contract calls for the company to pay the specified fee to a distinguished pharmacologist, Dr. Helmut Koenig, for giving advice on how to obtain approval from the Swiss regulatory authorities. Dr. Koenig is uniquely qualified for this work because he is also employed by the Swiss Drug Regulatory Agency, the same agency that is responsible for approving all Swiss drug products for marketing.

Sitting on D'Amato's desk is an internal memo written by the most powerful vice-president at Jones and Jones, who arranged and then signed the contract with Dr. Koenig. The memo has a section on credentials that says, "Dr. Koenig is a vital influence and creator of opinion in the approval of drug applications in Switzerland."

D'Amato was alarmed when he discovered Dr. Koenig's position of influence and his contractual arrangement with Jones and Jones. He believes that it is unethical to make such payments to a man who is currently involved with the approval of five to ten pending product registrations for Jones and Jones. He has written Dr. Koenig to this effect. In particular, Dr. Koenig is involved with the application for Lotriprox, a drug that those who have tested it for the company believe to be more effective in the treatment of psoriasis than its main competitors. Jones and Jones had submitted the original application for approval of this drug twice; the Swiss Drug Regulatory Agency rejected both attempts. On each occasion the agency said there was a lack of evidence of the drug's effectiveness. Jones and Jones officials view the receipt of Swiss approval as vital because regulatory agencies in other countries often follow the Swiss lead.

D'Amato is an American working in Europe, but most of his fellow executives in Sweden come from various European countries. Almost all have given him their opinion on the matter. They all concur that the practice of hiring regulators as consultants is a common and accepted practice in Switzerland. They point out, correctly, that other companies that market similar products have been hiring these consultants for years. They deny that this practice involves the use of devious or special influence to get applications approved, and they emphasize Dr. Koenig's ability to properly advise pharmaceutical companies on how to proceed.

Dr. Koenig has responded in a terse letter directly to D'Amato that he knows as well as anyone how to keep his consulting work separate from his work at the regulatory agency. He notes in the letter that he has many times been in this position and that there are clear advantages to be enjoyed by both the company and the regulatory agency in his dual role. For example, he is able to keep on top of every aspect of a drug and of the approval system. He points out that the reason Jones and Jones has not previously obtained approval for Lotriprox is the company's "terrible testing" of the drug, which is precisely his professional domain.

Nonetheless, D'Amato does not accept these arguments, which he views as rationalizations prompted by a corrupt system. However, he has tried to make it clear to those with whom he has discussed his views that he is not disputing the history of the Swiss consulting process. His concern is with the practices of his company, Jones and Jones. He sees the contract with Dr. Koenig as a willing and in fact devious violation of practices that are unacceptable in the United States—and in his company, which is, after all, American.

Three weeks ago, on his own authority and without anyone's advice or approval, D'Amato wrote the Intercantonal Office of Medicaments in Switzerland to ask for an investigation. To his surprise he received a detailed and carefully crafted response. The investigators said that they did find that Jones and Jones pharmaceutical products and the products of many other companies had been consistently approved for marketing after the hiring of well-placed consultants, but they found no indication that these approvals were made under fraudulent circumstances. Unless D'Amato could submit additional evidence to the contrary, the investigators concluded there was no reason why an educated and experienced adviser could not separately render his or her services to an outside company. In fact, they advised him that it makes good practical sense for Jones and

Jones to obtain evaluations prior to submitting products for approval. As they see it, this process facilitates the production of a safer and more effective product, and it spares both the company and the regulatory agency time that would otherwise be wasted considering inferior products.

D'Amato still maintains that, even if these payments do not openly constitute bribery, Jones and Jones has abused its position of influence. Furthermore, he believes that Dr. Koenig is locked in an untenable conflict of interest. D'Amato is adamant in his view that under the Swiss system any corporation of sufficient size and financial backing could wield unfair advantage over less powerful companies.

D'Amato's supervisor, Raymond Freymaster, has now intervened in a process that he believes cannot be allowed to stalemate any longer. He has told D'Amato that the contract with Dr. Koenig is proper and therefore must be paid. Freymaster has increased the pressure by saying that if D'Amato does not authorize payment within ten days he will be fired, and Freymaster will then authorize it himself. D'Amato now sees no way to maintain both his integrity and his job.

QUESTIONS

1. Do you think it is reasonable for D'Amato to doubt Dr. Koenig when he says that he can keep his consulting separate from his work at the regulatory agency?

2. What might you do to find out if the Swiss really think this sort of practice is ethical?

CHAPTER QUESTIONS

1. What values and moral principles do you think would be understood and embraced in any culture in which you did business?

2. To what extent are the current tensions in the world about commercial values and the market system, and to what extent are they about the way that people and companies actually practice business in their own cultures and other cultures?

13

Working with Mother Nature

Environmental Ethics and Business Ecology

Introduction

Will you buy an SUV? They are very popular these days, and if you want to win the admiration or, at least, not attract the scorn of your acquaintances (including those whom you zoom past on the Interstate), you had better get one. (As opposed, say, to a staid sedan or, worse, a minivan, which singles you out as one who is utterly and hopelessly uncool). Of course, you could get a Miata or a BMW Sportster, but that puts you at risk from those who do go for the more gargantuan three-ton SUVs. But, sadly, in addition to burning a small hole in your gas allowance, driving an SUV also helps burn a hole in the ozone layer, arguably increases global warming, burns up more of an increasingly precious fossil fuel, pollutes the very air that you breathe, and puts us at the mercy of foreign, often hostile, oil producers. But politics and expense aside, you are sensitive enough to the state of the environment—as now we all are—to feel just a little bit guilty that you are now contributing to the problem. And it doesn't make you feel any better that millions of people around the globe—including the fast emerging car markets of Asia—are doing the same thing. It is little comfort to know that the air quality in Beijing is even worse than it is in Houston and Los Angeles, or that the skin cancer rate in New Zealand is increasing faster than it is in Florida.

Whether or not to buy an SUV is probably a personal decision, but it has obvious implications regarding the entire planet. It is commonly said that pollution recognizes no national boundaries, but this might be said of the environment and the state of the planet in general. There are few changes, including the depletion of one natural resource or another, in one place or another, that do not sooner or later involve the planet as a whole. In business, the same principle applies. There are few enterprises, whether they directly involve the mining or use of natural resources or the financial concerns of developers and entrepreneurs, that do not have profound environmental implications, perhaps not in their immediate, particular results, but certainly when reiterated around the globe in country after country, whether "developed" or "developing." (Are there any countries, even including those that are wretchedly poor or torn apart by civil strife, that are not developing?) The days when we could tap into our natural resources without concern and remain oblivious to the costs and

Native American Proverb

"The frog does not drink up the pond in which he lives."

effects of our behavior are now past. Every business has effects on the environment. Every business therefore involves and requires thinking about the environment. There is no such luxury as being "too small to make a difference." Our actions are imitated around the globe, and the result is literally enough to move—or remove—mountains.

The environment plays a peculiar but crucial role in business ethics. The concept of social responsibility, and even stakeholder theory, generally refers to people or groups of people who have, or potentially could have, a say in the business by buying stocks, by buying or refusing to buy products, by joining community groups, and so on. (In fact, one prominent management textbook perversely defines a stakeholder as someone who has the power to affect the *operation* of a business or a corporation.) But the environment has no "say." It does not "respond." (Of course, environmental groups may speak on its behalf, but that is not the point.) The fact is that the environment is affected by business operations, and it, in turn, affects us all. Of course, we distinguish between accidents, which, after all, will happen, and negligence, which means causing an accident that could have and should have been prevented, and producing those by-products which one knows may be harmful but are unavoidable in the production process itself, and questions concerning conservation and the depletion of resources. In the last two cases, the question should be, do we need this product or to use this resource in this way? And that, in turn, may depend on the general question of lifestyle. Americans use some 60 percent of the world's resources for less than 5 percent of its population. And then we ask the third world to cut back on their pollution and use of resources. Is that fair? But in any case, we need to look at our own lifestyles and expectations—which by now have often grown into feelings of entitlement—and ask whether our own responsibilities as consumer are as much a part of the problem as the behavior of the giant corporations.

We begin with an essay by Mark Sagoff, "At the Shrine of Our Lady Fatima *or* Why Political Questions Are Not All Economic." Sagoff argues that we err when we suppose that all public policy questions (especially public policy vis-à-vis the environment) should be settled on the basis of money. Sagoff argues that we may and often do have policy concerns that are equal to or more important than financial concerns. How, he asks, can we put a price on the diversity of wildlife in the Alaskan Wildlife Reserve? Then William F. Baxter, in "People or Penguins," argues that we should allow our relationship with the environment to be determined by our own rational, long-term interest. We do not have duties to the environment as such, but we do have duties to ourselves and to future generations of humanity. But when it is a choice between "people or penguins," we must choose people. Against this view, Peter Singer argues that not only humans, but also sentient nonhumans, are of moral concern and so must be included in our moral analyses of environmental issues. Norman Bowie then explores the ethical complexities of the automobile business in "Morality, Money, and Motor Cars." Finally, Jon Entine discusses the relationship between protecting the environment for ethical reasons and protecting the environment for reasons of corporate image in "Rain-forest *Chic*."

Mark Sagoff

At the Shrine of Our Lady Fatima *or* Why Political Questions Are Not All Economic

Mark Sagoff is a Senior Research Scholar at the University of Maryland–College Park and a Pew Fellow.

Lewiston, New York, a well-to-do community near Buffalo, is the site of the Lake Ontario Ordinance Works, where years ago the federal government disposed of the residues of the Manhattan Project. These radioactive wastes are buried but are not forgotten by the residents who say that when the wind is southerly, radon gas blows through the town. Several parents at a recent Lewiston conference I attended described their terror on learning that cases of leukemia had been found among area children. They feared for their own lives as well. On the other side of the table, officials from New York State and from local corporations replied that these fears were ungrounded. People who smoke, they said, take greater risks than people who live close to waste disposal sites. One speaker talked in terms of "rational methodologies of decisionmaking." This aggravated the parents' rage and frustration.

The speaker suggested that the townspeople, were they to make their decision in a free market and if they knew the scientific facts, would choose to live near the hazardous waste facility. He told me later they were irrational—"neurotic"—because they refused to recognize or to act upon their own interests. The residents of Lewiston were unimpressed with his analysis of their "willingness to pay" to avoid this risk or that. They did not see what risk-benefit analysis had to do with the issues they raised.

If you take the Military Highway (as I did) from Buffalo to Lewiston, you will pass through a for-

midable wasteland. Landfills stretch in all directions and enormous trucks—tiny in that landscape—incessantly deposit sludge which great bulldozers then push into the ground. These machines are the only signs of life, for in the miasma that hangs in the air, no birds, not even scavengers, are seen. Along colossal power lines which criss-cross this dismal land, the dynamos at Niagra send electric power south, where factories have fled, leaving their remains to decay. To drive along this road is to feel, oddly, the mystery and awe one experiences in the presence of so much power and decadence.

POLITICAL AND ECONOMIC DECISIONMAKING

This essay concerns the economic decisions we make about the environment. It also concerns our political decisions about the environment. Some people have suggested that ideally these should be the same, that all environmental problems are problems in distribution. According to this view, there is an environmental problem only when some resource is not allocated in equitable and efficient ways.

This approach to environmental policy is pitched entirely at the level of the consumer. It is his or her values that count, and the measure of these values is the individual's willingness to pay. The problem of justice or fairness in society becomes, then, the problem of distributing goods and services so that more people get more of what they want to buy: a condo on the beach, a snowmobile for the mountains, a tank full of gas, a day of labor. The only values we have, according to this view, are those that a market can price.

The Ninth Annual National Report on Environmental Attitudes, Knowledge, and Behaviors

National Environmental Education and Training Foundation (May 2001)

As in the previous eight years [1993–2001] a majority of Americans say that "environmental protection and economic development can go hand in hand." Of those surveyed, 63% agree with this option, rather than the alternative—that one must be chosen over the other (25%).

Americans say that a balance between the environment and the economy is required for prosperity. Fully 89% either strongly or mostly agree that "The condition of the environment will play an increasingly important role in the nation's economic future." Thus, Americans believe that environmental protection and economic development must be achieved together to ensure a vibrant nation. Still, when people are asked to choose between environmental protection and economic development, fully 71% say they would choose the environment.

There is room for improvement in our efforts to protect the environment. Close to half (46%) of Americans hold the view that current laws "do not go far enough" to protect the environment. One-third (32%) hold the view that existing laws have struck "about the right balance," while 15% contend that laws and regulations already "go too far."

How much do you value open space, a stand of trees, an "unspoiled" landscape? Fifty dollars? A hundred? A thousand? This is one way to measure value. You could compare the amount consumers would pay for a townhouse or coal or a landfill to the amount they would pay to preserve an area in its "natural" state. If users would pay more for the land with the house, the coal mine, or the landfill, then without—less construction and other costs of development—than the efficient thing to do is to improve the land and thus increase its value. This is why we have so many tract developments, pizza stands, and gas stations. How much did you spend last year to preserve open space? How much for pizza and gas? "In principle, the ultimate measure of environmental quality," as one basic text assures us, "is the value people place on these . . . services or their *willingness to pay.*"[1]

Willingness to pay: what is wrong with that? The rub is this: not all of us think of ourselves simply as *consumers.* Many of us regard ourselves *as citizens* as well. We act as consumers to get what we want *for ourselves.* We act as citizens to achieve what we think is right or best *for the community.* The question arises, then, whether what we want for ourselves individually as consumers is consistent with the goals we would set for ourselves collectively as citizens. Would I vote for the sort of things I shop for? Are my preferences as a consumer consistent with my judgments as a citizen?

They are not. I am schizophrenic. Last year, I fixed a couple of tickets and was happy to do so since I saved fifty dollars. Yet, at election time, I helped to vote the corrupt judge out of office. I speed on the highway; yet I want the police to enforce laws against speeding. I used to buy mixers in returnable bottles—but who can bother to return them? I buy only disposables now, but to soothe my conscience, I urge my state senator to outlaw one-way containers.

I love my car; I hate the bus. Yet I vote for candidates who promise to tax gasoline to pay for public transportation. And of course I applaud the Endangered Species Act, although I have no earthly use for the Colorado squawfish or the Indiana bat. I support almost any political cause that I think will defeat my consumer interests. This is because I have contempt for—although I act upon—those interests. I have an "Ecology Now" sticker on a car that leaks oil everywhere it's parked.

The distinction between consumer and citizen preferences has long vexed the theory of public finance. Should the public economy serve the same goals as the household economy? May it serve, instead, goals emerging from our association as citizens? The question asks if we may collectively strive for and achieve only those items we individually compete for and consume. Should we aspire, instead, to public goals we may legislate as a nation? . . .

SUBSTITUTING EFFICIENCY FOR SAFETY

The labor unions won an important political victory when Congress passed the Occupational Safety and Health Act of 1970.[2] That Act, among other things, severely restricts worker exposure to toxic substances. It instructs the Secretary of Labor to set "the standard which most adequately assures, to the extent feasible . . . that no employee will suffer material impairment of health or functional capacity even if such employee has regular exposure to the hazard . . . for the period of his working life."[3]

Pursuant to this law, the Secretary of Labor in 1977 reduced from ten to one part per million (ppm) the permissable ambient exposure level for benzene, a carcinogen for which no safe threshold is known. The American Petroleum Institute thereupon challenged the new standard in court. It argued, with much evidence in its favor, that the benefits (to workers) of the one ppm standard did not equal the costs (to industry).[4] The standard therefore did not appear to be a rational response to a market failure in that it did not strike an efficient balance between the interests of workers in safety and the interests of industry and consumers in keeping prices down.

The Secretary of Labor defended the tough safety standard on the ground that the law demanded it. An efficient standard might have required safety until it cost industry more to prevent a risk than it cost workers to accept it. Had Congress adopted this vision of public policy—one which can be found in many economics texts—it would have treated workers not as ends-in-themselves but as means for the production of overall utility. This, as the Secretary saw it, was what Congress refused to do.[5]

The United States Court of Appeals for the Fifth Circuit agreed with the American Petroleum Institute and invalidated the one ppm benzene standard.[6] On July 2, 1980, the Supreme Court affirmed the decision in *American Petroleum Institute v. Marshall*[7] and remanded the benzene standard back to OSHA for revision. The narrowly based Supreme Court decision was divided over the role economic considerations should play in judicial review. Justice Marshall, joined in dissent by three other justices, argued that the Court had undone on the basis of its own theory of regulatory policy an act of Congress inconsistent with that theory.[8] He concluded that the plurality decision of the Court "requires the American worker to return to the political arena to win a victory that he won before in 1970."[9]

The decision of the Supreme Court is important not because of its consequences, which are likely to be minimal, but because of the fascinating questions it raises. Shall the courts uphold only those political decisions that can be defended on economic grounds? Shall we allow democracy only to the extent that it can be construed either as a rational response to a market failure or as an attempt to redistribute wealth? Should the courts say that a regulation is not "feasible" or "reasonable"—terms that occur in the OSHA law[10]—unless it is supported by a cost-benefit analysis?

The problem is this: An efficiency criterion, as it is used to evaluate public policy, assumes that the goals of our society are contained in the preferences individuals reveal or would reveal in markets. Such an approach may appear attractive, even just, because it treats everyone as equal, at least theoretically, by according to each person's preferences the same respect and concern. To treat a person with respect, however, is also to listen and to respond intelligently to his or her views and opinions. This is not the same thing as to ask how much he or she is willing to pay for them. The cost-benefit analyst does not ask economists how much they are willing to pay for what they believe, that is, that the workplace and the environment should be made efficient. Why, then, does the analyst ask workers, environmentalists, and others how much they are willing to pay for what they believe is right? Are economists the only ones who can back their ideas with reasons while the rest of us can only pay a price? The cost-benefit approach treats people as of equal worth because it treats them as of no worth, but only as places or channels at which willingness to pay is found.

LIBERTY: ANCIENT AND MODERN

When efficiency is the criterion of public safety and health, one tends to conceive of social relations on the model of a market, ignoring competing visions of what we as a society should be like. Yet it is obvious that there are competing conceptions of what we should be as a society. There are some who believe on principle that worker safety and environmental quality ought to be protected only insofar as the benefits of protection balance the costs. On the other hand, people argue—also on principle—that neither worker safety nor environmental quality should be treated merely as a commodity to be traded at the margin for other commodities, but rather each should be valued for its own sake. The conflict between these two principles is logical or moral, to be resolved by argument or debate. The question whether cost-benefit analysis should play a decisive role in policy-making is not to be decided by cost-benefit analysis. A contradiction between principles—between contending visions of the good society—cannot be settled by asking how much partisans are willing to pay for their beliefs. The role of the *legislator,* the political role, may be more important to the individual than the role of *consumer.* The person, in other words, is not to be treated merely as a bundle of preferences to be juggled in cost-benefit analyses. The individual is to be respected as an advocate of ideas which are to be judged according to the reasons for them. If health and environmental statutes reflect a vision of society as something other

than a market by requiring protections beyond what are efficient, then this may express not legislative ineptitude but legislative responsiveness to public values. To deny this vision because it is economically inefficient is simply to replace it with another vision. It is to insist that the ideas of the citizen be sacrificed to the psychology of the consumer.

We hear on all sides that government is routinized, mechanical, entrenched, and bureaucratized; the jargon alone is enough to dissuade the most mettlesome meddler. Who can make a difference? It is plain that for many of us the idea of a national political community has an abstract and suppositions quality. We have only our private conceptions of the good, if no way exists to arrive at a public one. This is only to note the continuation, in our time, of the trend Benjamin Constant described in the essay *De La Liberte des Anciens Compare a Celle des Modernes.*[11] Constant observes that the modern world, as opposed to the ancient, emphasizes civil over political liberties, the rights of privacy and property over those of community and participation. "Lost in the multitude," Constant writes, "the individual rarely perceives the influence that he exercises," and, therefore, must be content with "the peaceful enjoyment of private independence."[12] The individual asks only to be protected by laws common to all in his pursuit of his own self-interest. The citizen has been replaced by the consumer; the tradition of Rousseau has been supplanted by that of Locke and Mill.

Nowhere are the rights of the moderns, particularly the rights of privacy and property, less helpful than in the area of the natural environment. Here the values we wish to protect—cultural, historical, aesthetic, and moral—are public values. They depend not so much upon what each person wants individually as upon what he or she thinks is right for the community. We refuse to regard worker health and safety as commodities: we regulate hazards as a matter of right. Likewise, we refuse to treat environmental resources simply as public goods in the economist's sense. Instead, we prevent significant deterioration of air quality not only as a matter of individual self-interest but also as a matter of collective self-respect. How shall we balance efficiency against moral, cultural, and aesthetic values in policy for the workplace and

Placement of box OK? No call-out. Thanks, SBI

478   HONEST WORK

The Earth and Myself Are of One Mind

Chief Joseph of the Nez Perce

The earth is our mother. She should not be disturbed by hoe or plough. We want only to subsist on what she freely gives us. Our fathers gave us many laws, which they had learned from their fathers. These laws were good. I have carried a heavy load on my back ever since I was a boy. I realized then that we could not hold our own with the white men. We were like deer. They were like grizzly bears. We had small country. Their country was large. We were contented to let things remain as the Great Spirit Chief made them. They were not, and would change the rivers and mountains if they did not suit them.

the environment? No better way has been devised to do this than by legislative debate ending in a vote. This is very different from a cost-benefit analysis terminating in a bottom line.

VALUES ARE NOT SUBJECTIVE

It is the characteristic of cost-benefit analysis that it treats all value judgments other than those made on its behalf as nothing but statements of preference, attitude, or emotion, insofar as they are value judgments. The cost-benefit analyst regards as true the judgments that we should maximize efficiency or wealth. The analyst believes that this view can be backed by reasons, but does not regard it as a preference or want for which he or she must be willing to pay. The cost-benefit analyst tends to treat all other normative views and recommendations as if they were nothing but subjective reports of mental states. The analyst supposes in all such cases that "this is right" and "this is what we ought to do" are equivalent to "I want this" and "this is what I prefer." Value judgments are beyond criticism if, indeed, they are nothing but expressions of personal preference; they are incorrigible since every person is in the best position to know what he or she wants. All valuation, according to this approach, happens *in foro interno;* debate *in foro publico* has no point. With this approach, the reasons that people give for their views do not count; what does count is how

much they are willing to pay to satisfy their wants. Those who are willing to pay the most, for all intents and purposes, have the right view; theirs is the more informed opinion, the better aesthetic judgment, and the deeper moral insight.

Economists have used this impartial approach to offer solutions to many significant social problems, for example, the controversy over abortion. An economist argues that "there is an optimal number of abortions, just as there is an optimal level of pollution, or purity. . . . Those who oppose abortion could eliminate it entirely, if their intensity of feeling were so strong as to lead to payments that were greater at the margin than the price anyone would pay to have an abortion."[13] Likewise, economists, in order to determine whether the war in Vietnam was justified, have estimated the willingness to pay of those who demonstrated against it. Following the same line of reasoning, it should be possible to decide whether Creationism should be taught in the public schools, whether black and white people should be segregated, whether the death penalty should be enforced, and whether the square root of six is three. All of these questions arguably depend upon how much people are willing to pay for their subjective preferences or wants. This is the beauty of cost-benefit analysis: no matter how relevant or irrelevant, wise or stupid, informed or uninformed, responsible or silly, defensible or indefensible wants may be, the analyst is able to derive a policy from them—a policy which is legitimate because, in theory, it treats all of these preferences as equally valid and good.

PREFERENCE OR PRINCIPLE?

In contrast, consider a Kantian conception of value.[14] The individual, for Kant, is a judge of values, not a mere haver of wants, and the individual judges not for himself or herself merely, but as a member of a relevant community or group. The central idea in a Kantian approach to ethics is that some values are more reasonable than others and therefore have a better claim upon the assent of members of the community as such. The world of obligation, like the world of mathematics or the world of empirical fact, is public not private, and objective standards of argument and criticism apply. Kant recognized that values, like beliefs, are subjective states of mind which have an objective content as well. Therefore, both values and beliefs are either correct or mistaken. A value judgment is like an empirical or theoretical judgment in that it claims to be *true* not merely to be *felt*.

We have, then, two approaches to public policy before us. The first, the approach associated with normative versions of welfare economics, asserts that the only policy recommendation that can or need be defended on objective grounds is efficiency or wealth-maximization. The Kantian approach, on the other hand, assumes that many policy recommendations may be justified or refuted on objective grounds. It would concede that the approach of welfare economics applies adequately to some questions, for example, those which ordinary consumer markets typically settle. How many yo-yos should be produced as compared to how may frisbees? Shall pens have black ink or blue? Matters such as these are so trivial it is plain that markets should handle them. It does not follow, however, that we should adopt a market or quasi-market approach to every public question.

A market or quasi-market approach to arithmetic, for example, is plainly inadequate. No matter how much people are willing to pay, three will never be the square root of six. Similarly, segregation is a national curse and the fact that we are willing to pay for it does not make it better, but only us worse. The case for abortion must stand on the merits; it cannot be priced at the margin. Our failures to make the right decisions in these matters are failures in arithmetic, failures in wisdom, failures in taste, failures in morality—but not market failures. There are no relevant markets which have failed.

What separates these questions from those for which markets are appropriate is that they involve matters of knowledge, wisdom, morality, and taste that admit of better or worse, right or wrong, true or false, and not mere economic optimality. Surely environmental questions—the protection of wilderness, habitats, water, land, and air as well as policy toward environmental safety and health—involve moral and aesthetic principles and not just economic ones. This is consistent, of course, with cost-effectiveness and with a sensible recognition of economic constraints.

The neutrality of the economist is legitimate if private preferences or subjective wants are the only values in question. A person should be left free to choose the color of his or her necktie or necklace, but we cannot justify a theory of public policy or private therapy on that basis. . . . The neutrality of economics is not a basis for its legitimacy. We recognize it as an indifference toward value—an indifference so deep, so studied, and so assured that at first one hesitates to call it by its right name.

THE CITIZEN AS JOSEPH K.

The residents of Lewiston at the conference I attended demanded to know the truth about the dangers that confronted them and the reasons for those dangers. They wanted to be convinced that the sacrifice asked of them was legitimate even if it served interests other than their own. One official from a large chemical company dumping wastes in the area told them in reply that corporations were people and that people could talk to people about their feelings, interests, and needs. This sent a shiver through the audience Like Joseph K. in *The Trial*,[15] the residents of Lewiston asked for an explanation, justice, and truth, and they were told that their wants would be taken care of. They demanded to know the reasons for what was continually happening to them. They were given a personalized response instead.

This response, that corporations are "just people serving people," is consistent with a particular view of power. This is the view that identifies power with the ability to get what one wants as an individual, that is, to satisfy one's personal preferences. When people in official positions in corporations or in the government put aside their personal interests, it would follow that they put aside their power as well. Their neutrality then justifies them in directing the resources of society in ways they determine to be best. This managerial role serves not their own interests but those of their clients. Cost-benefit analysis may be seen as a pervasive form of this paternalism. Behind this paternalism, as William Simon observes of the lawyer-client relationship, lies a theory of value that tends to personalize power. "It resists understanding power as a product of class, property, or institutions and collapses power into the personal needs and dispositions of the individuals who command and obey."[16] Once the economist, the therapist, the lawyer, or the manager abjures his own interests and acts wholly on behalf of client individuals, he appears to have no power of his own and thus justifiably manipulates and controls everything. "From this perspective it becomes difficult to distinguish the powerful from the powerless. In every case, both the exercise of power and submission to it are portrayed as a matter of personal accommodation and adjustment."[17]

The key to the personal interest or emotive theory of value, as one commentator has rightly said, "is the fact that emotivism entails the obliteration of any genuine distinction between manipulative and non-manipulative social relations."[18] The reason is that once the affective self is made the source of all value, the public self cannot participate in the exercise of power. As Philip Reiff remarks, "the public world is constituted as one vast stranger who appears at inconvenient times and makes demands viewed as purely external and therefore with no power to elicit a moral response."[19] There is no way to distinguish the legitimate authority that public values and public law create from tyranny.

"At the rate of progress since 1900," Henry Adams speculates in his *Education,* "every American who lived into the year 2000 would know how to control unlimited power."[20] . . . Yet in the 1980s, the citizens of Lewiston, surrounded by dynamos, high tension lines, and nuclear wastes, are powerless. They do not know how to criticize power, resist power, or justify power—for to do so depends on making distinctions between good and evil, right and wrong, innocence and guilt, justice and injustice, truth and lies. These distinctions cannot be made out and have no significance within an emotive or psychological theory of value. To adopt this theory is to imagine society as a market in which individuals trade voluntarily and without coercion. No individual, no belief, no faith has authority over them. To have power to act as a nation we must be able to act, at least at times, on a public philosophy, conviction, or faith. We cannot abandon the moral function of public law. The antinomianism of cost-benefit analysis is not enough.

NOTES

1. A. Freeman, R. Haveman, A. Kneese, The Economics of Environmental, Policy (1973), *supra* note 6, at 23.

2. Pub. L. No. 91–596, 84 Stat. 1596 (1970) (codified at 29 U.S.C. §§ 651–678 (1970)).

3. 29 U.S.C. $sm 655(b)(5) (1970).

4. American Petroleum Inst. v. Marshall, 581 F.2d 493 (5th Cir. 1978), *aff'd,* 448 U.S. 607 (1980) at 501. *See, e.g.,* R. Posner, Economic Analysis of Law I & II (1973). In G. Calabresi, The Costs of Accidents *passim* (1970), the author argues that accident law balances two goals, "efficiency" and "equality" or "justice."

5. American Petroleum Inst. v. Marshall, 581 F.2d 493, 503–05 (5th Cir. 1978).

6. *Id.* at 505.

7. 448 U.S. 607 (1980).

8. *Id.* at 719.

9. *Id.*

10. 29 U.S.C. §§655(b)(5) & 652(8) (1975).

11. B. Constant, De La Liberte des Anciens Comparee a Celle des Modernes (1819)

12. *Oeuvres Politiques de Benjamin Constant,* 269 (C. Louandre, ed. 1874). *quoted in* S. Wolin, Politics and Vision 281 (1960).

13. H. Macaulay & B. Yandle, Environmental Use and the Market 120–21 (1978). *See generally* Cicchetti, Freeman, Haveman, & Knetsch, *On the Economics of Mass Demonstrations: A Case Study of the November 1969 March on Washington,* 61 Am. Econ. Rev. 719 (1971).

14. I. Kant, Foundations of the Metaphysics of Morals (1969). I follow the interpretation of Kantian ethics of W. Sellars, Science and Metaphysics ch. vii (1968) and Sellars, *On Reasoning About Values,* 17 Am. Phil. Q. 81 (1980). *See* A. Macintyre, After Virtue 22 (1981).

15. F. Kafka, The Trial (rev. ed. trans. 1957). Simon applies this anology to the lawyer-client relationship. Simon, *supra* note 40, at 524.

16. Simon, *supra* note 40, at 495.

17. *Id.*

18. A. Macintyre, *supra* note 54, at 22.

19. P. Reiff, The Triumph of the Therapeutic: Uses of Faith After Freud 52 (1966).

20. H. Adams, *supra* note 1, at 476.

QUESTIONS

1. Why are some political questions *not* economic questions?

2. What are the two approaches to public policy distinguished by Sagoff? How do they arrive at different solutions to the same questions?

William F. Baxter | # People or Penguins

William F. Baxter is a professor at the Stanford University Law School.

I start with the modest proposition that, in dealing with pollution, or indeed with any problem, it is helpful to know what one is attempting to accomplish. Agreement on how and whether to pursue a particular objective, such as pollution control, is not possible unless some more general objective has been identified and stated with reasonable precision. We talk loosely of having clean air and clean water, of preserving our wilderness areas, and so forth. But none of these is a sufficiently general objective: each is more accurately viewed as a means rather than as an end.

With regard to clean air, for example, one may ask, "how clean?" and "what does clean mean?" It is even reasonable to ask, "Why have clean air?" Each of these questions is an implicit demand that a more general community goal be stated—a goal sufficiently general in its scope and enjoying sufficiently general assent among the community of actors that such "why" questions no longer seem admissible with respect to that goal.

If, for example, one states as a goal the proposition that "every person should be free to do whatever he wishes in contexts where his actions do not interfere with the interests of other human beings," the speaker is unlikely to be met with a response of "why?" The goal may be criticized as uncertain in its implications or difficult to implement, but it is so basic a tenet of our civilization—it reflects a cultural value so broadly shared, at least in the abstract—that the question of "why" is seen as impertinent or imponderable or both. . . .

Without any expectation of obtaining unanimous consent to them, let me set forth four goals that I generally use as ultimate testing criteria in attempting to frame solutions to problems of human organization. My position regarding pollution stems from these four criteria. . . .

My criteria are as follows:

1. The spheres of freedom criterion stated [two paragraphs] above.
2. Waste is a bad thing. The dominant feature of human existence is scarcity—our available resources, our aggregate labors, and our skill in

employing both have always been, and will continue for some time to be, inadequate to yield to every man all the tangible and intangible satisfactions he would like to have. Hence, none of those resources, or labors, or skills, should be wasted—that is, employed so as to yield less than they might yield in human satisfactions.

3. Every human being should be regarded as an end rather than as a means to be used for the betterment of another. Each should be afforded dignity and regarded as having an absolute claim to an even-handed application of such rules as the community may adopt for its governance.

4. Both the incentive and the opportunity to improve his share of satisfactions should be preserved to every individual. Preservation of incentive is dictated by the "no-waste" criterion and enjoins against the continuous, totally egalitarian redistribution of satisfactions, or wealth; but subject to that constraint, everyone should receive, by continuous redistribution if necessary, some minimal share of aggregate wealth so as to avoid a level of privation from which the opportunity to improve his situation becomes illusory.

The relationship of these highly general goals to the more specific environmental issues at hand may not be readily apparent, and I am not yet ready to demonstrate their pervasive implications. Recently scientists have informed us that use of DDT in food production is causing damage to the penguin population. For the present purposes let us accept that assertion as an indisputable scientific fact. The scientific fact is often asserted as if the correct implication—that we must stop agricultural use of DDT—followed from the mere statement of fact of penguin damage. But plainly it does not follow if my criteria are employed.

My criteria are oriented to people, not penguins. Damage to penguins, or sugar pines, or geological marvels is, without more, simply irrelevant. One must go further, by my criteria, and say: Penguins are important because people enjoy seeing them walk about rocks; and furthermore, the well-being of people would be less impaired by halting use of DDT than by giving up penguins. In short, my observations about environmental problems will be people-oriented, as are my criteria. I have no interest in preserving penguins for their own sake.

It may be said by way of objection to this position that it is very selfish of people to act as if each person represented one unit of importance and nothing else was of any importance. It is undeniably selfish. Nevertheless I think it is the only tenable starting place for analysis for several reasons. First, no other position corresponds to the way most people really think and act—i.e., corresponds to reality.

Second, this attitude does not portend any massive destruction of nonhuman flora and fauna, for people depend on them in many obvious ways, and they will be preserved because and to the degree that humans do depend on them.

Third, what is good for humans is, in many respects, good for penguins and pine trees—clean air for example. So that humans are, in these respects, surrogates for plant and animal life.

Fourth, I do not know how we could administer any other system. Our decisions are either private or collective. Insofar as Mr. Jones is free to act privately, he may give such preferences as he wishes to other forms of life: he may feed birds in winter and do with less himself, and he may even decline to resist an advancing polar bear on the ground that the bear's appetite is more important than those portions of himself that the bear may choose to eat. In short my basic premise does not rule out private altruism to competing life-forms. It does rule out, however, Mr. Jones' inclination to feed Mr. Smith to the bear, however hungry the bear, however despicable Mr. Smith.

Insofar as we act collectively, on the other hand, only humans can be afforded an opportunity to participate in the collective decisions. Penguins cannot vote now and are unlikely subjects for the franchise—pine trees more unlikely still. Again each individual is free to cast his vote so as to benefit sugar pines if that is his inclination. But many of the more extreme assertions that one hears from some conservationists amount to tacit assertions that they are specially appointed representatives of sugar pines, and hence that their preferences should be weighted more heavily than the preferences of other humans who do not enjoy equal rapport with "nature." The simplistic assertion that agricultural use of DDT must stop at once because it is harmful to penguins is of that type.

Fifth, if polar bears or pine trees or penguins, like men, are to be regarded as ends rather than means, if they are to count in our calculus of social organization, someone must tell me how much each one counts, and someone must tell me how these life-forms are to be permitted to express their preferences, for I do not know either answer. If the answer is that certain people are to hold their proxies, then I want to know how those proxy-holders are to be selected: self-appointment does not seem workable to me.

Sixth, and by way of summary of all the foregoing, let me point out that the set of environmental issues under discussion—although they raise very complex technical questions of how to achieve any objective—ultimately raise a normative question: what *ought* we to do? Questions of *ought* are unique to the human mind and world—they are meaningless as applied to a nonhuman situation.

I reject the proposition that we *ought* to respect the "balance of nature" or to "preserve the environment" unless the reason for doing so, express or implied, is the benefit of man.

I reject the idea that there is a "right" or "morally correct" state of nature to which we should return. The word "nature" has no normative connotation. Was it "right" or "wrong" for the earth's crust to heave in contortion and create mountains and seas? Was it "right" for the first amphibian to crawl up out of the primordial ooze? Was it "wrong" for plants to reproduce themselves and alter the atmospheric composition in favor of oxygen? For animals to alter the atmosphere in favor of carbon dioxide both by breathing oxygen and eating plants? No answers can be given to these questions because they are meaningless questions.

All this may seem obvious to the point of being tedious, but much of the present controversy over environment and pollution rests on tacit normative assumptions about just such nonnormative phenomena: that it is "wrong" to impair penguins with DDT, but not to slaughter cattle for prime rib roasts. That it is wrong to kill stands of sugar pines with industrial fumes, but not to cut sugar pines and build housing for the poor. Every man is entitled to his own preferred definition of Walden Pond, but there is no definition that has any moral superiority over another, except by reference to the selfish needs of the human race.

From the fact that there is no normative definition of the natural state, it follows that there is no normative definition of clean air or pure water—hence no definition of polluted air—or of pollution—except by reference to the needs of man. The "right" composition of the atmosphere is one which has some dust in it and some lead in it and some hydrogen sulfide in it—just those amounts that attend a sensibly organized society thoughtfully and knowledgeably pursuing the greatest possible satisfaction for its human members.

The first and most fundamental step toward solution of our environmental problems is a clear recognition that our objective is not pure air or water but

On Pollution

Milton Friedman

In fact, the people responsible for pollution are consumers, not producers. They create, as it were, demand for pollution. People who use electricity are responsible for the smoke that comes out of the stacks of generating plants.

rather some optimal state of pollution. That step immediately suggests the question: How do we define and attain the level of pollution that will yield the maximum possible amount of human satisfaction?

Low levels of pollution contribute to human satisfaction but so do food and shelter and education and music. To attain ever lower levels of pollution, we must pay the cost of having less of these other things. I contrast that view of the cost of pollution control with the more popular statement that pollution control will "cost" very large numbers of dollars. The popular statement is true in some senses, false in others; sorting out the true and false senses is of some importance. The first step in that sorting process is to achieve a clear understanding of the difference between dollars and resources. Resources are the wealth of our nation; dollars are merely claim checks upon those resources. Resources are of vital importance; dollars are comparatively trivial.

Four categories of resources are sufficient for our purposes: at any given time a nation, or a planet if you prefer, has a stock of labor, of technological skill, of capital goods, and of natural resources (such as mineral deposits, timber, water, land, etc.). These resources can be used in various combinations to yield goods and services of all kinds—in some limited quantity. The quantity will be larger if they are combined efficiently, smaller if combined inefficiently. But in either event the resource stock is limited, the goods and services that they can be made to yield are limited; even the most efficient use of them will yield less than our population, in the aggregate, would like to have.

If one considers building a new dam, it is appropriate to say that it will be costly in the sense that it will require x hours of labor, y tons of steel and concrete, and z amount of capital goods. If these resources are devoted to the dam, then they cannot be used to build hospitals, fishing rigs, schools, or electric can openers. That is the meaningful sense in which the dam is costly.

Quite apart from the very important question of how wisely we can combine our resources to produce goods and services is the very different question of how they get distributed—who gets how many goods? Dollars constitute the claim checks which are distributed among people and which control their share of national output. Dollars are nearly valueless pieces of paper except to the extent that they do represent claim checks to some fraction of the output of goods and services. Viewed as claim checks, all the dollars outstanding during any period of time are worth, in the aggregate, the goods and services that are available to be claimed with them during that period—neither more nor less.

It is far easier to increase the supply of dollars than to increase the production of goods and services—printing dollars is easy. But printing more dollars doesn't help because each dollar then simply becomes a claim to fewer goods, i.e., becomes worth less.

The point is this: many people fall into error upon hearing the statement that the decision to build a dam, or to clean up a river, will cost $X million. It is regrettably easy to say: "It's only money. This is a wealthy country, and we have lots of money." But you cannot build a dam or clean a river with $X million—unless you also have a match, you can't even make a fire. One builds a dam or cleans a river by diverting labor and steel and trucks and factories from making one kind of goods to making another. The cost in dollars is merely a shorthand way of describing the extent of the diversion necessary. If we build a dam for $X million, then we must recognize that we will have $X million less housing and food and medical care and electric can openers as a result.

Similarly, the costs of controlling pollution are best expressed in terms of the other goods we will have to give up to do the job. This is not to say the job should not be done. Badly as we need more housing, more medical care, and more can openers, and more symphony orchestras, we could do with somewhat less of them, in my judgement at least, in exchange for somewhat cleaner air and rivers. But that is the nature of the trade-off, and analysis of the problem is advanced if that unpleasant reality is kept in mind. Once the trade-off relationship is clearly perceived, it is possible to state in a very general way what the optimal level of pollution is. I would state it as follows:

People enjoy watching penguins. They enjoy relatively clean air and smog-free vistas. Their health is improved by relatively clean water and air. Each of these benefits is a type of good or service. As a society we would be well advised to give up one washing machine if the resources that would have gone into that washing machine can yield greater human satisfaction when diverted into pollution control. We should give up one hospital if the resources thereby freed would yield more human satisfaction when devoted to elimination of noise in our cities. And so on, trade-off by trade-off, we should divert our productive capacities from the production of existing goods and services to the production of a cleaner, quieter, more pastoral nation up to—and no further than—the point at which we value more highly the next washing machine or hospital that we would have to do without than we value the next unit of environmental improvement that the diverted resources would create.

Now this proposition seems to me unassailable but so general and abstract as to be unhelpful—at least unadministerable in the form stated. It assumes we can measure in some way the incremental units of human satisfaction yielded by very different types of goods. The proposition must remain a pious abstraction until I can explain how this measurement process can occur. . . . But I insist that the proposition stated describes the result for which we should be striving—and again, that it is always useful to know what your target is even if your weapons are too crude to score a bull's eye.

QUESTIONS

1. Why does Baxter think that there is a choice between people or penguins? Do you agree?

2. What does Baxter mean by "optimal" pollution? What does he say about future generations?

Norman Bowie | # Morality, Money, and Motor Cars

Norman Bowie is a professor of management at the University of Minnesota.

Environmentalists frequently argue that business has special obligations to protect the environment. Although I agree with the environmentalists on this point, I do not agree with them as to where the obligations lie. Business does not have an obligation to protect the environment over and above what is required by law; however, it does have a moral obligation to avoid intervening in the political arena in order to defeat or weaken environmental legislation. In developing this thesis, several points are in order. First, many businesses have violated important moral obligations, and the violation has had a severe negative impact on the environment. For example, toxic waste haulers have illegally dumped hazardous material, and the environment has been harmed as a result. One might argue that those toxic waste haulers who have illegally dumped have violated a special obligation to the environment. Isn't it more accurate to say that these toxic waste haulers have violated their obligation to obey the law and that in this case the law that has been broken is one pertaining to the environment? Businesses have an obligation to obey the law—environmental laws and all others. Since there are many well-publicized cases of business having broken environmental laws, it is easy to think

From *Business, Ethics, and the Environment: The Public Policy Debate,* edited by W. Michael Hoffman, Robert Frederick, and Edward S. Petry, Jr. (Westport, CT: Quorum Books, 1990). Notes were deleted from the text.

that business has violated some special obligations to the environment. In fact, what business has done is to disobey the law. Environmentalists do not need a special obligation to the environment to protect the environment against illegal business activity; they need only insist that business obey the laws.

Business has broken other obligations beside the obligation to obey the law and has harmed the environment as a result. Consider the grounding of the Exxon oil tanker *Valdez* in Alaska. That grounding was allegedly caused by the fact that an inadequately trained crewman was piloting the tanker while the captain was below deck and had been drinking. What needs to be determined is whether Exxon's policies and procedures were sufficiently lax so that it could be said Exxon was morally at fault. It might be that Exxon is legally responsible for the accident under the doctrine of respondent superior, but Exxon is not thereby morally responsible. Suppose, however, that Exxon's policies were so lax that the company could be characterized as morally negligent. In such a case, the company would violate its moral obligation to use due care and avoid negligence. Although its negligence was disastrous to the environment. Exxon would have violated no special obligation to the environment. It would have been morally negligent.

A similar analysis could be given to the environmentalists' charges that Exxon's cleanup procedures were inadequate. If the charge is true, either Exxon was morally at fault or not. If the procedures had not been implemented properly by Exxon employees, then Exxon is legally culpable, but not morally culpable. On the other hand, if Exxon lied to government officials by saying that its policies were in accord with regulations and/or were ready for emergencies of this type, then Exxon violated its moral obligation to tell the truth. Exxon's immoral conduct would have harmed the environment, but it violated no special obligation to the environment. More important, none is needed. Environmentalists, like government officials, employees, and stockholders expect that business firms and officials have moral obligations to obey the law, avoid negligent behavior, and tell the truth. In sum, although many business decisions have harmed the environment, these decisions violated no environmental moral obligations. If a corporation is negligent in providing for worker safety, we do not say the corporation violated a special obligation to employees; we say that it violated its obligation to avoid negligent behavior.

The crucial issues concerning business obligations to the environment focus on the excess use of natural resources (the dwindling supply of oil and gas, for instance) and the externalities of production (pollution, for instance). The critics of business want to claim that business has some special obligation to mitigate or solve these problems. I believe this claim is largely mistaken. If business does have a special obligation to help solve the environmental crisis, that obligation results from the special knowledge that business firms have. If they have greater expertise than other constituent groups in society, then it can

Land as a Commodity

Vine Deloria

"Every time we have objected to the use of the land as a commodity, we have been told that progress is necessary to American life. Now the laugh is ours."

—Vine Deloria,

be argued that, other things being equal, business's responsibilities to mitigate the environmental crisis are somewhat greater. Absent this condition, business's responsibility is no greater than and may be less than that of other social groups. What leads me to think that the critics of business are mistaken? . . .

Consider the harm that results from the production of automobiles. We know statistically that about 50,000 persons per year will die and that nearly 250,000 others will be seriously injured in automobile accidents in the United States alone. Such death and injury, which is harmful, is avoidable. . . . What such arguments point out is that some refinement of the moral minimum standard needs to take place. Take the automobile example. The automobile is itself a good-producing instrument. Because of the advantages of automobiles, society accepts the possible risks that go in using them. Society also accepts many other types of avoidable harm. We take certain risks—ride in planes, build bridges, and mine coal—to pursue advantageous goals. It seems that the high benefits of some activities justify the resulting harms. As long as the risks are known, it is not wrong that some avoidable harm be permitted so that other social and individual goals can be achieved. . . .

It is a fundamental principle of ethics that "ought" implies "can." That expression means that you can be held morally responsible only for events within your power. In the ought-implies-can principle, the overwhelming majority of highway deaths and injuries is not the responsibility of the automaker. Only those deaths and injuries attributable to unsafe automobile design can be attributed to the automaker. The ought-implies-can principle can also be used to absolve the auto companies of responsibility for death and injury from safety defects that the automakers could not reasonably know existed. The company could not be expected to do anything about them.

Does this mean that a company has an obligation to build a car as safe as it knows how? No. The standards for safety must leave the product's cost within the price range of the consumer ("ought implies can" again). Comments about engineering and equipment capability are obvious enough. But for a business, capability is also a function of profitability. A company that builds a maximally safe car at a cost that puts it at a competitive disadvantage and hence threatens its survival is building a safe car that lies beyond the capability of the company.

Critics of the automobile industry will express horror at these remarks, for by making capability a function of profitability, society will continue to have avoidable deaths and injuries; however, the situation is not as dire as the critics imagine. Certainly capability should not be sacrificed completely so that profits can be maximized. The decision to build products that are cheaper in cost but are not maximally safe is a social decision that has widespread support. The arguments occur over the line between safety and cost. What we have is a classical trade-off situation. What is desired is some appropriate mix between engineering safety and consumer demand. To say there must be some mix between engineering safety and consumer demand is not to justify all the decisions made by the automobile companies. Ford Motor Company made a morally incorrect choice in placing Pinto gas tanks where it did. Consumers were uninformed, the record of the Pinto in rear-end collisions was worse than that of competitors, and Ford fought government regulations. . . .

As long as business obeys the environmental laws and honors other standard moral obligations, most harm done to the environment by business has been accepted by society. Through their decisions in the marketplace, we can see that most consumers are unwilling to pay extra for products that are more environmentally friendly than less friendly competitive products. Nor is there much evidence that consumers are willing to conserve resources, recycle, or tax themselves for environmental causes.

Consider the following instances reported in the *Wall Street Journal*.[1] The restaurant chain Wendy's tried to replace foam plates and cups with paper, but customers in the test markets balked. Procter and Gamble offered Downey fabric softener in concentrated form that requires less packaging than ready-to-use products; however the concentrate version is less convenient because it has to be mixed with water. Sales have been poor. Procter and Gamble manufactures Vizir and Lenor brands of detergents in concentrate form, which the customer mixes at home in reusable bottles. Europeans will take the trouble;

Americans will not. Kodak tried to eliminate its yellow film boxes but met customer resistance. McDonald's has been testing mini-incinerators that convert trash into energy but often meets opposition from community groups that fear the incinerators will pollute the air. A McDonald's spokesperson points out that the emissions are mostly carbon dioxide and water vapor and are "less offensive than a barbecue." Exxon spent approximately $9,200,000 to "save" 230 otters ($40,000 for each otter). Otters in captivity cost $800. Fishermen in Alaska are permitted to shoot otters as pests.[2] Given these facts, doesn't business have every right to assume that public tolerance for environmental damage is quite high. . . .

Recently environmentalists have pointed out the environmental damage caused by the wide-spread use of disposable diapers. Are Americans ready to give them up and go back to cloth diapers and the diaper pail? Most observers think not. . . . Moreover, if the public wants cloth diapers, business certainly will produce them. If environmentalists want business to produce products that are friendlier to the environment, they must convince Americans to purchase them. Business will respond to the market. It is the consuming public that has the obligation to make the trade-off between cost and environmental integrity.

Data and arguments of the sort described should give environmental critics of business pause. Nonetheless, these critics are not without counter-responses. For example, they might respond that public attitudes are changing. Indeed, they point out, during the Reagan deregulation era, the one area where the public supported government regulations was in the area of environmental law. In addition, *Fortune* predicts environmental integrity as the primary demand of society on business in the 1990s.[3]

More important, they might argue that environmentally friendly products are at a disadvantage in the marketplace because they have public good characteristics. After all, the best situation for the individual is one where most other people use environmentally friendly products but he or she does not, hence reaping the benefit of lower cost and convenience. Since everyone reasons this way, the real demand for environmentally friendly products cannot be registered in the market. Everyone is understating the value of his or her preference for environmentally friendly products. Hence, companies cannot conclude from market behavior that the environmentally unfriendly products are preferred.

Suppose the environmental critics are right that the public goods characteristic of environmentally friendly products creates a market failure. Does that mean the companies are obligated to stop producing these environmentally unfriendly products? I think not. . . . There is a need, and certainly corporations that cause environmental problems are in proximity. However, environmentally clean firms, if there are any, are not in proximity at all, and most business firms are not in proximity with respect to most environmental problems. In other words, the environmental critic must limit his or her argument to the environmental damage a business actually causes. . . . But even narrowing the obligation to damage actually caused will not be sufficient to establish an obligation to pull a product from the market because it damages the environment or even to go beyond what is legally required to protect the environment. Even for damage actually done, both the high cost of protecting the environment and the competitive pressures of business make further action to protect the environment beyond the capability of business. This conclusion would be more serious if business were the last resort, but it is not.

Traditionally it is the function of the government to correct for market failure. If the market cannot register the true desires of consumers, let them register their preferences in the political arena. Even fairly conservative economic thinkers allow government a legitimate role in correcting market failure. Perhaps the responsibility for energy conservation and pollution control belongs with the government.

Although I think consumers bear a far greater responsibility for preserving and protecting the environment than they have actually exercised, let us assume that the basic responsibility rests with the government. Does that let business off the hook? No. Most of business's unethical conduct regarding the environment occurs in the political arena.

Far too many corporations try to have their cake and eat it too. They argue that it is the job of government to correct for market failure and then use their

To: You
From: The Philosopher
Subject: Who Owns the Earth?

Are we entitled to use the resources available to us? Or are we charging on an account that later generations will have to settle?

> "Treat the earth well: it was not given to you by your parents, it was loaned to you by your children. We do not inherit the Earth from our Ancestors, we borrow it from our Children."

Ancient Indian Proverb, source unknown . . . most likely oral tradition handed down over the years.

influence and money to defeat or water down regulations designed to conserve and protect the environment.[4] They argue that consumers should decide how much conservation and protection the environment should have, and then they try to interfere with the exercise of that choice in the political arena. Such behavior is inconsistent and ethically inappropriate. Business has an obligation to avoid intervention in the political process for the purpose of defeating and weakening environmental regulations. Moreover, this is a special obligation to the environment since business does not have a general obligation to avoid pursuing its own parochial interests in the political arena. Business need do nothing wrong when it seeks to influence tariffs, labor policy, or monetary policy. Business does do something wrong when it interferes with the passage of environmental legislation. Why?

First, such a noninterventionist policy is dictated by the logic of the business's argument to avoid a special obligation to protect the environment. Put more formally:

1. Business argues that it escapes special obligations to the environment because it is willing to respond to consumer preferences in this matter.
2. Because of externalities and public goods considerations, consumers cannot express their preferences in the market.

3. The only other viable forum for consumers to express their preferences is in the political arena.
4. Business intervention interferes with the expression of these preferences.
5. Since point 4 is inconsistent with point 1, business should not intervene in the political process.

The importance of this obligation in business is even more important when we see that environmental legislation has special disadvantages in the political arena. Public choice reminds us that the primary interest of politicians is being reelected. Government policy will be skewed in favor of policies that provide benefits to an influential minority as long as the greater costs are widely dispersed. Politicians will also favor projects where benefits are immediate and where costs can be postponed to the future. Such strategies increase the likelihood that a politician will be reelected.

What is frightening about the environmental crisis is that both the conservation of scarce resources and pollution abatement require policies that go contrary to a politician's self-interest. The costs of cleaning up the environment are immediate and huge, yet the benefits are relatively long range (many of them exceedingly long range). Moreover, a situation where the benefits are widely dispersed and the costs are large presents a twofold problem. The costs are large enough so that all voters will likely notice them and in certain cases are catastrophic for individuals (e.g., for those who lose their jobs in a plant shutdown).

Given these facts and the political realities they entail, business opposition to environmental legislation makes a very bad situation much worse. Even if consumers could be persuaded to take environmental issues more seriously, the externalities, opportunities to free ride, and public goods characteristics of the environment make it difficult for even enlightened consumers to express their true preference for the environment in the market. The fact that most environmental legislation trades immediate costs for future benefits makes it difficult for politicians concerned about reelection to support it. Hence it is also difficult for enlightened consumers to have their preferences for a better environment honored in the political arena. Since lack of business intervention seems necessary, and might even be sufficient, for adequate environmental legislation, it seems business has an obligation not to intervene. Nonintervention would prevent the harm of not having the true preferences of consumers for a clean environment revealed. Given business's commitment to satisfying preferences, opposition to having these preferences expressed seems inconsistent as well.

The extent of this obligation to avoid intervening in the political process needs considerable discussion by ethicists and other interested parties. Businesspeople will surely object that if they are not permitted to play a role, Congress and state legislators will make decisions that will put them at a severe competitive disadvantage. For example, if the United States develops stricter environmental controls than other countries do, foreign imports will have a competitive advantage over domestic products. Shouldn't business be permitted to point that out? Moreover, any legislation that places costs on one industry rather than another confers advantages on other industries. The cost to the electric utilities from regulations designed to reduce the pollution that causes acid rain will give advantages to natural gas and perhaps even solar energy. Shouldn't the electric utility industry be permitted to point that out?

These questions pose difficult questions, and my answer to them should be considered highly tentative. I believe the answer to the first question is "yes" and the answer to the second is "no." Business does have a right to insist that the regulations apply to all those in the industry. Anything else would seem to violate norms of fairness. Such issues of fairness do not arise in the second case. Since natural gas and solar do not contribute to acid rain and since the costs of acid rain cannot be fully captured in the market, government intervention through regulation is simply correcting a market failure. With respect to acid rain, the electric utilities do have an advantage they do not deserve. Hence they have no right to try to protect it.

Legislative bodies and regulatory agencies need to expand their staffs to include technical experts, economists, and engineers so that the political process can be both neutral and highly informed about environmental matters. To gain the respect of business and the public, its performance needs to improve. Much more needs to be said to make any contention that business ought to stay out of the political debate theoretically and practically possible. Perhaps these suggestions point the way for future discussion.

Ironically business might best improve its situation in the political arena by taking on an additional obligation to the environment. Businesspersons often have more knowledge about environmental harms and the costs of cleaning them up. They may often have special knowledge about how to prevent environmental harm in the first place. Perhaps business has a special duty to educate the public and to promote environmentally responsible behavior.

Business has no reticence about leading consumer preferences in other areas. Advertising is a billion-dollar industry. Rather than blaming consumers for not purchasing environmentally friendly products, perhaps some businesses might make a commitment to capture the environmental niche. I have not seen much imagination on the part of business in this area. Far too many advertisements with an environmental message are reactive and public relations driven. Recall those by oil companies showing fish swimming about the legs of oil rigs. An educational champaign that encourages consumers to make environmentally friendly decisions in the marketplace would limit the necessity for business activity in the political arena. Voluntary behavior that is environmentally friendly is morally preferable to coerced behavior. If business took greater responsibility for educating the public, the government's responsibility would be lessened. An educational campaign aimed at consumers would likely enable many businesses to do good while simultaneously doing very well.

Hence business does have obligations to the environment, although these obligations are not found where the critics of business place them. Business has no special obligation to conserve natural resources or to stop polluting over and above its legal obligations. It does have an obligation to avoid intervening in the political arena to oppose environmental regulations, and it has a positive obligation to educate consumers. The benefits of honoring these obligations should not be underestimated.

NOTES

1. Alicia Swasy, "For Consumers, Ecology Comes Second," *Wall Street Journal,* August 23, 1988, p. B1.

2. Jerry Alder, "Alaska after Exxon," *Newsweek,* September 18, 1989, p. 53.

3. Andrew Kupfer, "Managing Now for the 1990s," *Fortune,* September 26, 1988, pp. 46–47.

4. I owe this point to Gordon Rands, a Ph.D. student in the Carlson School of Management. Indeed the tone of the chapter has shifted considerably as a result of his helpful comments.

QUESTIONS

1. Does business have a special responsibility to protect the environment, according to Bowie? Why or why not? What is his argument?

2. Why might business serve itself well by taking responsibility for the environment?

Peter Singer | # The Place of Nonhumans in Environmental Issues

Peter Singer is professor of philosophy at Princeton University. He is America's leading voice on the question of animal rights.

I. HUMANS AND NONHUMANS

When we humans change the environment in which we live, we often harm ourselves. If we discharge cadmium into a bay and eat shellfish from that bay, we become ill and may die. When our industries and automobiles pour noxious fumes into the atmosphere, we find a displeasing smell in the air, the long-term results of which may be every bit as deadly as cadmium poisoning. The harm that humans do the environment, however, does not rebound solely, or even chiefly, on humans. It is nonhumans who bear the most direct burden of human interference with nature.

By "nonhumans" I mean to refer to all living things other than human beings, though for reasons to be given later, it is with nonhuman animals, rather

---

The first five sections of this essay are reprinted from Peter Singer, "Not for Humans Only: The Place of Nonhumans in Environmental Ethics," in K. E. Goodpaster and K. M. Sayre, eds., *Ethics and Problems of the 21st Century* (Notre Dame, Ind.: University of Notre Dame Press, 1979). Reprinted by permission. The final section is reprinted by permission from Peter Singer, "All Animals Are Equal," *Philosophic Exchange,* vol. 1, no. 5 (Summer 1974). Copyright © 1974 the Center for Philosophic Exchange. (Section headings have been added.)

than plants, that I am chiefly concerned. It is also important, in the context of environmental issues, to note that living things may be regarded either collectively or as individuals. In debates about the environment the most important way of regarding living things collectively has been to regard them as species. Thus, when environmentalists worry about the future of the blue whale, they usually are thinking of the blue whale as a species, rather than of individual blue whales. But this is not, of course, the only way in which one can think of blue whales, or other animals, and one of the topics I shall discuss is whether we should be concerned about what we are doing to the environment primarily insofar as it threatens entire species of nonhumans, or primarily insofar as it affects individual nonhuman animals.

The general question, then, is how the effects of our actions on the environment of nonhuman beings should figure in our deliberations about what we ought to do. There is an unlimited variety of contexts in which this issue could arise. To take just one: Suppose that it is considered necessary to build a new power station, and there are two sites, A and B, under consideration. In most respects the sites are equally suitable, but building the power station on site A would be more expensive because the greater depth of shifting soil at that site will require deeper foundations; on the other hand, to build on site B will destroy a favored breeding ground for thousands of wildfowl. Should the presence of the wildfowl enter into the decision as to where to build? And if so, in what manner should it enter, and how heavily should it weigh?

In a case like this the effects of our actions on nonhuman animals could be taken into account in two quite different ways: directly, giving the lives and welfare of nonhuman animals an intrinsic significance which must count in any moral calculation; or indirectly, so that the effects of our actions on nonhumans are morally significant only if they have consequences for humans. . . .

II. SPECIESISM

The view that the effects of our actions on other animals have no direct moral significance is not as likely to be openly advocated today as it was in the past; yet it is likely to be accepted implicitly and acted upon. When planners perform cost-benefit studies on new projects, the costs and benefits are costs and benefits for human beings only. This does not mean that the impact of [a] power station or highway on wildlife is ignored altogether, but it is included only indirectly. That a new reservoir would drown a valley teeming with wildlife is taken into account only under some such heading as the value of the facilities for recreation that the valley affords. In calculating this value, the cost-benefit study will be neutral between forms of recreation like hunting and shooting and those like bird watching and bush walking—in fact hunting and shooting are likely to contribute more to the benefit side of the calculations because larger sums of money are spent on them, and they therefore benefit manufacturers and retailers of firearms as well as the hunters and shooters themselves. The suffering experienced by the animals whose habitat is flooded is not reckoned into the costs of the operation; nor is the recreational value obtained by the hunters and shooters offset by the cost to the animals that their recreation involves.

Despite its venerable origin, the view that the effects of our actions on nonhuman animals have no intrinsic moral significance can be shown to be arbitrary and morally indefensible. If a being suffers, the fact that it is not a member of our own species cannot be a moral reason for failing to take its suffering into account. This becomes obvious if we consider the analogous attempt by white slave-owners to deny consideration to the interests of blacks. These white racists limited their moral concern to their own race, so the suffering of a black did not have the same moral significance as the suffering of a white. We now recognize that in doing so they were making an arbitrary distinction, and that the existence of suffering, rather than the race of the sufferer, is what is really morally significant. The point remains true if "species" is substituted for "race." The logic of racism and the logic of the position we have been discussing, which I have elsewhere referred to as "speciesism," are indistinguishable; and if we reject the former then consistency demands that we reject the latter too.[1]

It should be clearly understood that the rejection of speciesism does not imply that the different species are in fact equal in respect of such characteristics as intelligence, physical strength, ability to communicate, capacity to suffer, ability to damage the environment, or anything else. After all, the moral principle of human equality cannot be taken as implying that all humans are equal in these respects either—if it did, we would have to give up the idea of human equality. That one being is more intelligent than another does not entitle him to enslave, exploit, or disregard the interests of the less intelligent being. The moral basis of equality among humans is not equality in fact, but the principle of equal consideration of interests, and it is this principle that, in consistency, must be extended to any nonhumans who have interests.

III. NONHUMANS HAVE INTERESTS

There may be some doubt about whether any nonhuman beings have interests. This doubt may arise because of uncertainty about what it is to have an interest, or because of uncertainty about the nature of some nonhuman beings. So far as the concept of "interest" is the cause of doubt, I take the view that only a being with subjective experiences, such as the experience of pleasure or the experience of pain, can have interests in the full sense of the term; and that any being with such experiences does have at least one interest, namely, the interest in experiencing pleasure and avoiding pain. Thus consciousness, or the capacity for subjective experience, is both a necessary and a sufficient condition for having an interest. While there may be a loose sense of the term in which we can say that it is in the interests of a tree to be watered, this attenuated sense of the term is not the sense covered by the principle of equal consideration of interests. All we mean when we say that it is in the interests of a tree to be watered is that the tree needs water if it is to continue to live and grow normally; if we regard this as evidence that the tree has interests, we might almost as well say that it is in the interests of a car to be lubricated regularly because the car needs lubrication if it is to run properly. In neither case can we really mean (unless we impute

consciousness to trees or cars) that the tree or car has any preference about the matter.

The remaining doubt about whether nonhuman beings have interests is, then, a doubt about whether nonhuman beings have subjective experiences like the experience of pain. I have argued elsewhere that the commonsense view that birds and mammals feel pain is well founded,[2] but more serious doubts arise as we move down the evolutionary scale. Vertebrate animals have nervous systems broadly similar to our own and behave in ways that resemble our own pain behavior when subjected to stimuli that we would find painful; so the inference that vertebrates are capable of feeling pain is a reasonable one, though not as strong as it is if limited to mammals and birds. When we go beyond vertebrates to insects, crustaceans, mollusks and so on, the existence of subjective states becomes more dubious, and with very simple organisms it is difficult to believe that they could be conscious. As for plants, though there have been sensational claims that plants are not only conscious, but even psychic, there is no hard evidence that supports even the more modest claim.[3]

The boundary of beings who may be taken as having interests is therefore not an abrupt boundary, but a broad range in which the assumption that the being has interests shifts from being so strong as to be virtually certain to being so weak as to be highly improbable. The principle of equal consideration of interests must be applied with this in mind, so that where there is a clash between a virtually certain interest and a highly doubtful one, it is the virtually certain interest that ought to prevail.

In this manner our moral concern ought to extend to all beings who have interests. . . .

IV. EQUAL CONSIDERATION OF INTERESTS

Giving equal consideration to the interests of two different beings does not mean treating them alike or holding their lives to be of equal value. We may recognize that the interests of one being are greater than those of another, and equal consideration will then lead us to sacrifice the being with lesser interests, if one or the other must be sacrificed. For instance, if for some reason a choice has to be made between saving the life of a normal human being and that of a dog, we might well decide to save the human because he, with his greater awareness of what is going to happen, will suffer more before he dies; we may also take into account the likelihood that it is the family and friends of the human who will suffer more; and finally, it would be the human who had the greater potential for future happiness. This decision would be in accordance with the principle of equal consideration of interests, for the interests of the dog get the same consideration as those of the human, and the loss to the dog is not discounted because the dog is not a member of our species. The outcome is as it is because the balance of interests favors the human. In a different situation—say, if the human were grossly mentally defective and without family or anyone else who would grieve for it—the balance of interests might favor the nonhuman.[4]

The more positive side of the principle of equal consideration is this: where interests are equal, they must be given equal weight. So where human and nonhuman animals share an interest—as in the case of the interest in avoiding physical pain—we must give as much weight to violations of the interest of the nonhumans as we do to similar violations of the human's interest. This does not mean, of course, that it is as bad to hit a horse with a stick as it is to hit a

human being, for the same blow would cause less pain to the animal with the tougher skin. The principle holds between similar amounts of felt pain, and what this is will vary from case to case.

It may be objected that we cannot tell exactly how much pain another animal is suffering, and that therefore the principle is impossible to apply. While I do not deny the difficulty and even, so far as precise measurement is concerned, the impossibility of comparing the subjective experiences of members of different species, I do not think that the problem is different in kind from the problem of comparing the subjective experiences of two members of our own species. Yet this is something we do all the time, for instance when we judge that a wealthy person will suffer less by being taxed at a higher rate than a poor person will gain from the welfare benefits paid for by the tax; or when we decide to take our two children to the beach instead of to a fair, because although the older one would prefer the fair, the younger one has a stronger preference the other way. These comparisons may be very rough, but since there is nothing better, we must use them; it would be irrational to refuse to do so simply because they are rough. Moreover, rough as they are, there are many situations in which we can be reasonably sure which way the balance of interests lies. While a difference of species may make comparisons rougher still, the basic prob-

The Tame Land

Luther Standing Bear

Only to the white man was nature a "wilderness" and only to him was the land "infested" with "wild" animals and "savage" people. To us it was tame. Earth was bountiful and we were surrounded with the blessings of the Great Mystery.

Luther Standing Bear (1868–1939) from *Land of the Spotted Eagle,* 1933.

lem is the same, and the comparisons are still often good enough to use, in the absence of anything more precise. . . .

V.   EXAMPLES

We can now draw at least one conclusion as to how the existence of nonhuman living things should enter into our deliberations about actions affecting the environment: Where our actions are likely to make animals suffer, that suffering must count in our deliberations, and it should count equally with a like amount of suffering by human beings, insofar as rough comparisons can be made.

The difficulty of making the required comparison will mean that the application of this conclusion is controversial in many cases, but there will be some situations in which it is clear enough. Take, for instance, the wholesale poisoning of animals that is euphemistically known as "pest control." The authorities who conduct these campaigns give no consideration to the suffering they inflict on the "pests," and invariably use the method of slaughter they believe to be cheapest and most effective. The result is that hundreds of millions of rabbits have died agonizing deaths from the artificially introduced disease, myxomatosis, or from poisons like "ten-eighty"; coyotes and other wild dogs have died painfully from cyanide poisoning; and all manner of wild animals have endured days of thirst, hunger, and fear with a mangled limb caught in a leg-hold trap.[5] Granting, for the sake of argument, the necessity for pest control—though this has rightly been questioned—the fact remains that no serious attempts have been made to introduce alternative means of control and thereby reduce the incalculable amount of suffering caused by present methods. It would not, presumably, be beyond modern science to produce a substance which, when eaten by rabbits or coyotes, produced sterility instead of a drawn-out death. Such methods might be more expensive, but can anyone doubt that if a similar amount of human suffering were at stake, the expense would be borne?

Another clear instance in which the principle of equal consideration of interests would indicate methods different from those presently used is in the timber industry. There are two basic methods of obtaining timber from forests. One is to cut only selected mature or dead trees, leaving the forest substantially intact. The other, known as clear-cutting, involves chopping down everything that grows in a given area, and then reseeding. Obviously when a large area is clear-cut, wild animals find their whole living area destroyed in a few days, whereas selected felling makes a relatively minor disturbance. But clear-cutting is cheaper, and timber companies therefore use this method and will continue to do so unless forced to do otherwise.[6] . . .

VI. THE MEAT INDUSTRY

For the great majority of human beings, especially in urban, industrialized societies, the most direct form of contact with members of other species is at mealtimes: We eat them. In doing so we treat them purely as means to our ends. We regard their life and well-being as subordinate to our taste for a particular kind of dish. I say "taste" deliberately—this is purely a matter of pleasing our palate. There can be no defenses of eating flesh in terms of satisfying nutritional needs, since it has been established beyond doubt that we could satisfy our need for protein and other essential nutrients far more efficiently with a diet that replaced animal flesh by soy beans, or products derived from soy beans, and other high-protein vegetable products.

It is not merely the act of killing that indicates what we are ready to do to other species in order to gratify our tastes. The suffering we inflict on the animals while they are alive is perhaps an even clearer indication of our speciesism than the fact that we are prepared to kill them.[7] In order to have meat on the table at a price that people can afford, our society tolerates methods of meat production that confine sentient animals in cramped, unsuitable conditions for the entire durations of their lives. Animals are treated like machines that convert fodder into flesh, and any innovation that results in a higher "conversion ratio" is liable to be adopted. As one authority on the subject has said, "cruelty is acknowledged only when profitability ceases."[8] So hens are crowded four or five to a cage with a floor area of twenty inches by eighteen inches, or around the size of a single page of the *New York Times*. The cages have wire floors, since this reduces cleaning costs, though wire is unsuitable for the hens' feet; the floors slope, since this makes the eggs roll down for easy collection, although this makes it difficult for the hens to rest comfortably. In these conditions all the birds' natural instincts are thwarted: They cannot stretch their wings fully, walk freely, dust-bathe, scratch the ground, or build a nest. Although they have never known other conditions, observers have noticed that the birds vainly try to perform these actions. Frustrated at their inability to do so, they often develop what farmers call "vices," and peck each other to death. To prevent this, the beaks of young birds are often cut off.

This kind of treatment is not limited to poultry. Pigs are now also being reared in cages inside sheds. These animals are comparable to dogs in intelligence, and need a varied, stimulating environment if they are not to suffer from stress and boredom. Anyone who kept a dog in the way in which pigs are frequently kept would be liable to prosecution, in England at least, but because our interest in exploiting pigs is greater than our interest in exploiting dogs, we object to cruelty to dogs while consuming the produce of cruelty to pigs. Of the other animals, the condition of veal calves is perhaps worst of all, since these animals are so closely confined that they cannot even turn around or get up and lie down freely. In this way they do not develop unpalatable muscle. They are also made anemic and kept short of roughage, to keep their flesh pale, since white veal fetches a higher price; as a result they develop a craving for iron and roughage, and have been observed to gnaw wood off the sides of their stalls, and lick greedily at any rusty hinge that is within reach.

Since, as I have said, none of these practices cater to anything more than our pleasures of taste, our practice of rearing and killing other animals in order to eat them is a clear instance of the sacrifice of the most important interests of other beings in order to satisfy trivial interests of our own. To avoid speciesism we must stop this practice, and each of us has a moral obligation to cease supporting the practice. Our custom is all the support that the meat industry needs. The decision to cease giving it that

support may be difficult, but it is no more difficult than it would have been for a white Southerner to go against the traditions of his society and free his slaves; if we do not change our dietary habits, how can we censure those slaveholders who would not change their own way of living?

NOTES

1. For a fuller statement of this argument, see my *Animal Liberation* (New York: A New York Review Book, 1975), especially Ch. 1.

2. Ibid.

3. See, for instance, the comments by Arthur Galston in *Natural History,* 83, no. 3 (March 1974): 18, on the "evidence" cited in such books as *The Secret Life of Plants.*

4. Singer, *Animal Liberation,* pp. 20–23.

5. See J. Olsen, *Slaughter the Animals, Poison the Earth* (New York: Simon and Schuster, 1971), especially pp. 153–164.

6. See R. and V. Routley, *The Fight for the Forests* (Canberra: Australian National University Press, 1974); for a thoroughly documented indictment of clear-cutting in America, see *Time,* May 17, 1976.

7. Although one might think that killing a being is obviously the ultimate wrong one can do to it, I think that the infliction of suffering is a clearer indication of speciesism because it might be argued that at least part of what is wrong with killing a human is that most humans are conscious of their existence over time, and have desires and purposes that extend into the future—see, for instance, M. Tooley, "Abortion and Infanticide," *Philosophy and Public Affairs,* vol. 2, no. 1 (1972). Of course, if one took this view one would have to hold—as Tooley does—that killing a human infant or mental defective is not in itself wrong, and is less serious than killing certain higher mammals that probably do have a sense of their own existence over time.

8. Ruth Harrison, *Animal Machines* (Stuart, London, 1964). This book provides an eye-opening account of intensive farming methods for those unfamiliar with the subject.

QUESTIONS

1. What is the place of nonhumans in environmental issues?

2. Why should we be concerned about "nonhumans"? Isn't our first duty to ourselves?

Jon Entine | # Rain-forest *Chic*

Jon Entine is an Emmy-winning television producer, reporter, and author who specializes in ethics, business, genetics, science, and politics.

"The church used to be the dominant force in our lives."

The burly, rumpled speaker with wild hair sounds almost professorial as he builds a case for the coming New Age of profits with principles. "Then came the nation-states, where we looked to government for support and guidance. That era is ending."

Who would have thought that this ruby-faced college dropout would one day hold an audience spellbound with his version of intellectual history. "Today," says Ben Cohen, sounding now like an earnest Republican at a Rotary Club luncheon, "we are in the era of business. Business is our new universal community. We are the leaders who can turn business into a positive social force."

The crowd breaks into applause. The affection, and indeed the adulation, can be felt by everyone in the room. It is a June celebration to open the Los Angeles chapter of Business for Social Responsibility, a trade group that promotes itself as environmentally and socially progressive, and the audience has come to hear its hero. Ben Cohen, 43, and his high-school buddy, Jerry Greenfield, started mixing up batches of ice cream 16 years ago at an abandoned gas station in Burlington, Vt. Today, Chunky Monkey, Cherry Garcia and Rainforest Crunch are staples for fortysomethings everywhere. Although he no longer runs the company day to day, Cohen remains the chairman and lovable, eccentric corporate symbol of Ben & Jerry's Homemade Inc., which has seven Canadian outlets and worldwide sales of about $200 million (U.S.).

The soul of Ben & Jerry's is natural, artery-clogging ice cream and a quixotic social philosophy. It is one of the best known of a growing list of "progressive" firms such as skin-and-hair-care franchisor The Body Shop International PLC (BSI), eco-friendly apparel makers Patagonia and Esprit de Corp, and Tom's of Maine, which sells natural toothpaste and personal-care products.

Cohen's company has set an impressive standard of ethical innovation. It publishes a state-of-the-art social audit of its operations, gives an astonishing 7.5% of pretax profits to charity, buys only local dairy products to help preserve the family farm, and refuses to back down from its support of peace and social-justice causes even if that means alienating some potential customers.

Ben Cohen is more the rule than the exception among successful, New Age entrepreneurs. Many grew up in the sixties, their values shaped by civil-rights activism, Vietnam protests, free love, drugs and an unremitting belief in the moral and cultural ascendancy of the baby-boom generation. Many now run public companies that have ridden the green wave into the hearts, minds and pocketbooks of eco-consumers. Cohen and the founders of other successful eco-businesses, who in many cases are worth millions and even hundreds of millions of dollars in company stock, now jet around the world spreading the New Age gospel of anticapitalist business.

Cohen rails on to his audience about the greedy, soulless character of Corporate America, and then boasts of how a corporation has made a difference in helping save the rain forest. "The success of our Rainforest Crunch," says Cohen, "shows that harvesting Brazil nuts is a profitable alternative for Amazon natives who have seen their lands ravaged to

From *Report on Business Magazine,* Toronto, Ontario, October 1995, pp. 41–45. © 1995 Jon Entine, runjonrun@earthlink.net, http://www.jonentine.com

create grazing areas or for mining." The crowd is on its feet. It is an inspiring moment.

Yet Ben & Jerry's own 1995 annual report, released just days before, carries the not-so-socially responsible details of what some anthropologists are calling the "rain-forest fiasco." While the label of Rainforest Crunch, one of Ben & Jerry's flagship products, suggests that buying the ice cream helps preserve the Amazon's endangered rain forests, the documented social benefits of its Third World micro-project are ambiguous at best.

The popular fascination for social marketers—who have built an image as a leading force of social change—obscures a far more complex reality. Consumers with a high tolerance for pricy goods—most New Age products command a hefty premium over ordinary brands—play a modest role in raising awareness of social problems. At worst, though, cause-related marketing can be little more than baby-boom agitprop, masking serious lapses at socially conscious firms.

The small companies in the vanguard of the movement are learning that "social responsibility" is a margin game: When profits are rolling in, as they were in the 1980s, progressive gestures are painless. But now, as they face growing pains and intense worldwide competition, many of these enlightened firms are firing workers, closing inner-city stores, cutting back on charity projects, and making their products in overseas sweatshops. In other words, they are acting like most businesses when confronted with difficult bottom-line challenges. . . .

Ironically, the social and environmental contributions of New Age business pale when compared with the substantial reforms taking place in major corporations. Selling quality products, treating employees, vendors and franchisees with integrity, and upgrading their environmental practices are improvements, they have discovered, that go straight to the bottom line. And given their massive financial resources, many familiar blue-chip firms are in a better position than New Age entrepreneurs to effect social change as they quietly, but determinedly, adopt higher standards of affirmative hiring, pollution abatement and community involvement practices. "Even a tiny, 1% improvement in the environmental standards of a DuPont or a Monsanto," says corporate ethics guru Paul Hawken author of *The Ecology of Commerce,* "will have a more meaningful impact than creating a hundred new Patagonias."

We'll look at some unheralded examples of progress on the corporate social responsibility front. But first, a sobering behind-the-gloss look at some firms that have gotten rich and famous by "having a heart" and wearing it on their sleeves.

Efforts to "save the rain forest" have brought together two popular movements: the environmentalists' struggle to protect the forest against clear-cutting and the romantic quest to preserve indigenous cultures. Capitalism-on-the-Amazon as popularized by Ben & Jerry's and The Body Shop has an almost serendipitous history. In 1988, after a Grateful Dead rainforest fundraising concert, Cohen found himself at a party where a Cambridge, Mass. anthropologist explained his pet project of saving the rain forest. The anthropologist convinced Cohen that Amazon natives could achieve self-sufficiency by selling fruits and nuts instead of selling mining and logging rights. A few days later, Cohen was mixing up batches of Brazil-nut brittle ice cream in his Vermont kitchen. Simultaneously, Rainforest Crunch and the rain-forest harvest were born.

The eco-capitalism movement got a big boost the following spring when Sting, The Body Shop founder Anita Roddick and other celebrities turned that year's Amazon peoples' conference in Altamira, Brazil, into an international media event. Within months, BSI was selling rain-forest hair rinse and bath beads while Ben & Jerry's launched Rainforest Crunch. Both companies promoted their rain-forest products as eco-friendly solutions to mining and clear-cutting.

"Money from these nuts," read the label for Rainforest Crunch ice cream when it was launched in 1990, "helps to show that rain forests are more profitable when . . . cultivated for traditional harvest than when their trees are cut and burned for short-term gain." The product was an overwhelming, overnight success—at least for Ben & Jerry's, which reaped millions of dollars' worth of free publicity for showing how profits and principles can go hand in hand.

The view from Amazonia was quite different.

Amazon peoples' groups and anthropologists feared opening up this fragile area even to supposedly friendly capitalists. There also is no evidence to support the central premise of the harvest—that nuts could ever approximate the income that natives collect by selling off land rights to miners and foresters.

The anticipated source for Ben & Jerry's nuts—the Xapuri co-operative in the Amazon—never produced the necessary quality or quantity to meet exploding demand. And the description of the Xapuri co-operative as "forest peoples" was odd: The co-op is largely run by ethnic European and mixed-blood rubber tappers who arrived as contract workers at the turn of the century during an earlier wave of rain-forest exploitation.

The harvest soon proved a windfall for the landowners who have long controlled trade in this region. To meet demand, the agency purchasing nuts on Ben & Jerry's behalf, in which Cohen was a partner, was forced to buy from the commercial markets supplied by some of the most notorious, antilabour agribusinesses in Latin America, including the Mutran family, which has been linked in Brazilian press reports with the killings of labour organizers. By the spring of 1994, the Xapuri had cut off all supplies, saying their own harvesting efforts were hopelessly uneconomic. The project has run in the red for the past three years, generating none of the promised charitable contributions to the Amazonians that were to have flowed from sales of Rainforest Crunch. And there is no evidence that the harvest has provided an incentive for forest natives to curtail their auctioning of land, mining and timber rights. "It's really a disingenuous marketing strategy to say if you spend $2.99, you'll help save the rain forest," says Michelle McKinley, executive director of Cultural Survival, which used to run the project for Ben & Jerry's. "We rushed into this project recklessly. We created a fad market overnight and the hard-sell promotions have contributed to a lot of confusion. The harvest just didn't work." . . .

Ben Cohen often talks about his kinship with Anita Roddick, charismatic founder of U.K.-based The Body Shop International PLC. Cohen and Roddick, 53, are regarded as the king and queen of progressive business.

In 1976, Roddick opened a tiny shop in the faded English resort town of Brighton. It offered "one-stop ear piercing" and sold beauty products with natural-sounding names in refillable plastic bottles. It soon developed a cult following and expanded dramatically through franchising. Today, Anita Roddick and her husband, Gordon, oversee a $1-billion (sales) chain of 1,290 mostly franchised Body Shop outlets in 45 countries. Canada, with 113 stores—all of them franchises—is BSI's third-largest market.

Roddick is arguably the most successful self-made businesswoman in the world. For years, no competitor could match her two-for-one sale: Buy a bottle of non-tested-on-animals Brazil-nut hair rinse and get social justice for free. Roddick became a favourite of affluent baby boomers, a New Age feminist heroine weaned on can-do chutzpah and do-right values. "Anita," Ralph Nader told *People* magazine, "is the most progressive businessperson I know."

BSI, Ben & Jerry's and other eco-marketers have cleverly used cause-related marketing to brand what are essentially commodity products—in this case ice cream and cosmetics—and to fuel a booming niche market in so-called "green" products. They also pad their bottom lines by spending very little, if anything, on conventional advertising. Instead, they benefit from free and largely favourable media coverage of their "new way of doing business." . . . By its own calculation, BSI has racked up as many as 10,000 press mentions in a single year.

Despite glowing press, BSI has long been held in mixed regard in the corporate social responsibility movement. Roddick is almost universally admired for stirring debate on important issues: environmental degradation, the use of animal testing on cosmetics and other products, the role of corporations as model community citizens. But the firm is also known for exaggerating its progressive practices. . . .

Roddick is a study in contradictions. She is perhaps best known for her relentless campaign for a total ban on animal testing. The company does aggressively enforce its limited ban by refusing to use ingredients tested within the last five years. The practical impact of the ban is limited, however, given that most ingredients in widespread use today were once animal tested; and many of the new ones are developed first for medicinal use, which BSI says puts them outside its rule. In any event, BSI is hardly unique among the scores of major world cosmetics makers that have adopted similar bans on ingredients recently tested on animals. This reality is reflected in BSI's 1989 decision to back down from its testing-related product claims, and change its product labels to replace the slogan NOT TESTED ON ANIMALS with the vague AGAINST ANIMAL TESTING.

At the International Chamber of Commerce Conference in Cancún in 1993, Roddick lambasted the distinguished business and government leaders in the audience for trading with what she called the "torturers" and "despots" in China's political regime, who allow sweatshops to churn out cheap goods for greedy, "nomadic" capitalists who put low labour costs above ethics. Her admonition: Just say no to trading in Chinese goods. The behind-the-rhetoric reality: BSI for years had bought its popular baskets in China, and they continued to be on sale at Roddick's stores even as she spoke. . . .

While BSI was claiming it was giving away "an inordinately high percentage of pretax profits to often controversial charitable campaigns," and Roddick was saying, "What else do I do with the money than give it away?", there are no records that show BSI gave any money to charity prior to becoming a publicly traded company in 1984. And until 1994, BSI donated less than the U.S. corporate average of 1.5% of pretax profits. In the past two years, as criticism mounted, BSI donated an impressive 3% of pretax profits in 1994 and 2.3% in 1995. Roddick touts her "Trade Not Aid" program as a progressive substitute for handouts and claims she pays. "First World wages for Third World goods." In fact, BSI pays going wages and in 1994 paid only about 0.3% of worldwide sales to its Trade Not Aid producers. University of Chicago anthropologist Terence Turner, who has visited BSI's trade project with the Kayapo tribe in Brazil, calls its programs "Aid Not Trade," a play on The Body Shop slogan. "Indigenous cultures give these companies free aid in the form of their green image," Turner says, "with almost no trade in return." Stung by a growing chorus of critics, the company has revamped its ethical trading department and pledges to increase its Third World purchases. . . .

In 1993, the U.S. Federal Trade Commission launched an investigation of alleged BSI violations of the Federal Trade Commission Act in the sale of products and franchises, subpoenaing former franchisees and requesting internal documents and videotapes from BSI. The FTC, which seldom resorts to formal charges in its efforts to reform practices, issued a letter in March saying that "no further action is warranted by the Commission at this time," and that the end of the investigation should not be taken as a sign that a violation had or had not occurred.

Finally, many BSI fans are surprised to learn that BSI shares its name, many of its early products and its vaunted refilling philosophy with an earlier pioneer of socially progressive cosmetics, The Body Shop of Berkeley, Calif., which opened its doors in 1970. The founders of the tiny U.S. Body Shop chain sold the rights to its name to the Roddicks in 1987 for $3.5 million (U.S.).

Without question, it was Roddick who conquered the world with her version of the concept, but critics are put off by her image as having more or less exclusively invented the idea of progressive cosmetic marketing.

Despite its problems, BSI still has many loyal supporters. "The Body Shop is a leader in socially responsible corporate participation in Canadian society," says Beverley Wybrow, executive director of The Canadian Women's Foundation. She notes that The Body Shop Canada has used promotional campaigns to generate more than $140,000 in funds for domestic-violence prevention programs in which CWF is a partner.

BSI itself suggests that its performance is being judged against unrealistically high standards. "We *all* admit that we are retailers, pure and simple," says Margot Franssen, president of The Body Shop Canada. "We aren't exactly out to change the world, but instead to make our communities a little bit better." The company operates a state-of-the-art production facility, and it is the rare Canadian firm to offer subsidized on-site day care at its head office.

Depending on one's perspective, Roddick is either a visionary crucified for excessive enthusiasm or an exploiter of idealistic followers. The biggest problem for The Body Shop now is not performance—it has made dramatic strides in almost every area of its operations in the past two years—but credibility.

It's a rare company, of course, whose history isn't blemished by occasional inconsistencies between the founder's vision and the way that vision is played out. What's rare in this case is Roddick's strident assertion that she occupies a high moral plane shared only with some of her peers in the New Age fraternity. "Over the past decade, while many businesses have pursued what I call business as usual, I have been part of a different, smaller business movement, one that has tried to put idealism back on the agenda," Roddick told the Mexican conclave of big-business leaders, urging them to follow BSI's example. "We are creating new markets of informed and morally motivated consumers. We are succeeding and thriving as businesses and as moral forces."

Even if they lived up to their reputation as models of a new type of "virtuous capitalism," relatively small, faddish firms have little impact on the economy. In that sense, can they be regarded as being a more powerful force for good than such multibillion-dollar firms as drugmaker Merck & Co. and computer giant Hewlett-Packard Co., which for decades have quietly but conscientiously made large charitable contributions, involved themselves in the communities in which they operate, opened their corporate practices to public scrutiny, and pioneered in management practices that create intensely loyal workforces?

The urge to demonize Big Business and idolize eco-entrepreneurs caricatures the complexity of business. Most companies resemble dysfunctional families. Even the best of them make mistakes or compromise their ideals under bottom-line pressure. "Some of the best environmental programs are the creation of some of the worst polluters," notes Paul Hawken. "Innovative solutions are not the exclusive province of so-called progressive companies. We have to keep an open mind and look for solutions wherever they may be."

Many of those solutions originate with Big Business. At a time when affirmative hiring is a popular target of politicians and right-wing talk-show hosts, companies such as Polaroid Corp., Texaco Inc. and Dow Chemical Co. are more determined than ever to promote women and minorities into higher levels of management, and have done so far more aggressively than most New Age companies.

Even before the Bhopal tragedy, chemical companies were a frequent target of environmentalists. Yet the industry's Responsible Care program of scrupulous controls on the manufacture and use of toxic chemicals, largely designed in Canada and adopted by most major North American chemical producers, is an important initiative that other industries are under pressure to emulate. . . .

Just as industries long held in poor regard deserve credit for their efforts to improve, high-profile "cause-related" marketers should be viewed with caution. For "socially responsible" business, whether practiced by New Age firms or hulking multinationals, is a land of contradictions.

- Apparel giants Esprit de Corp, Levi Strauss & Co. and The Gap Inc. lavish their employees with progressive benefits, while some of their clothing is manufactured by suppliers that operate sweatshops in countries where human-rights violations are a common occurrence.
- Reebok International Ltd., frequently cited as a progressive employer, has made hopscotch its sourcing credo, moving its manufacturing operations from South Korea and Taiwan to China, Indonesia and Thailand in search of the lowest wages. It also recently paid $12.3 million to settle price-fixing charges in the United States.
- Baby boomers now seem less interested in sixties ideals of changing the world than "shopping for a better world"—the title of a popular "green" buying guide. But the inconvenient reality is that it's difficult for consumers to identify the "good guys" even with a scorecard. For instance, which companies are more "ethical" in dealing with the following two controversial issues:
- Gillette Co. and Procter & Gamble Co., which spend millions of dollars on safety-testing of their products and have pioneered in research and development into alternative cosmetics, but perform government-required animal tests; or

The Body Shop, which has stimulated a useful public debate but relies on tested-on-animals ingredients and has been attacked by former allies in the animal-rights movement for over-simplifying this complex issue for commercial gain.

- Monsanto Co. and DuPont, which have innovative pollution-control practices, yet have been guilty of environmental violations; or Ben & Jerry's, which publishes an annual audit of its corporate conduct, but sometimes ignores its most important conclusions.

There are no icons in the business world. At best we can identify firms that acknowledge their daily struggle to improve product quality, environmental practices, and worker and community relations, and which open their practices to outside scrutiny. "We are entering a new era in the world of socially responsible managing and investing," says Joan Bavaria, president of Franklin Research & Development Corp., a Boston-based social-investment firm. "It is not a black-and-white world with neat lines of demarcation. This is the real world of complex systems and internal contradictions."

A constructive response to these inevitable contradictions is to confront them. Bavaria is one of the founders of CERES, the Coalition for Environmentally Responsible Economies, which was set up by a group of social and environmental activists and public-pension-fund trustees to develop environmental standards and accounting guidelines in partnership with business. CERES has 54 members pledged to conducting internal audits of their environmental records, including Polaroid, General Motors Corp. and oil producer Sun Co., as well as Ben & Jerry's and The Body Shop. In recruiting new members, CERES looks for larger, "messier" companies that are struggling with problems, but are committed to transparency in disclosing and remedying problems.

Even modest changes in the business practices of traditional manufacturing and resource firms—and in Canada that's more than 40% of the GDP—will have far more sweeping economic impact than a handful of firms claiming no bottom-line instincts but which operate at the fringes of the economy.

Acting responsibly means being responsive to criticism. "I talked with both Ben and Jerry," says business student Ritu Kalra, who was present at a recent speech by Cohen and co-founder Jerry Greenfield at the University of Pennsylvania's Wharton business school. "Neither of them knew much about the harvest. When it came down to it, they didn't want to comment and didn't feel responsible for misleading labelling or telling half-truths."

The recent revelations about the rain-forest fiasco have hardly slowed Ben & Jerry's ice cream tour. Even though the company has ditched its references to helping aboriginal nut harvesters, not many consumers realize how few of their eco-dollars go toward helping distant Amazonian natives.

At the Los Angeles New Age business meeting, Cohen relentlessly hawks his most famous ice-cream flavour. "We *have* made a difference in the rain forest," he declares. After the speech, dozens of people crowd around Cohen as he signs napkins and dishes out bowls of Rainforest Crunch ice cream. "It's so inspiring," says a fellow entrepreneur, licking her spoon, "to know that business can make money and still do so much good."

QUESTIONS

1. Is there anything wrong with promoting environmental awareness just because it is "cool" to do so? Should "ethical" concerns always disagree with self-interest?

2. Advertising is often misleading. Why is false advertising about environmental issues any worse (or better) than other kinds of misleading advertising? What are the duties (if any) of companies who would like to claim "rain-forest *chic*"?

CASES

CASE 13.1

The Ethics of Dolphin-Human Interaction

Thomas I. White

In tales that reach back to ancient Crete, dolphins are said to be special creatures. We are told that they regularly aid lost ships, save drowning sailors, and form fast friendships with humans. Dolphins were even thought to be gods by some ancient peoples. This fascination with dolphins continues in the present. Even though we no longer consider dolphins to be divine, we have learned that they are surprisingly complex socially, emotionally, and intellectually. Accordingly, we now face a series of questions about the moral justifiability of our behavior toward them.

Research over the last two decades reveals that dolphins are more like humans than was once thought. Dolphins are air-breathing mammals, not fish, and they evidence many of the same higher characteristics as humans. The size and complexity of the dolphin brain compares favorably to that of the human brain. Dolphins can solve difficult, novel problems; they are aware of time; and they can handle abstract and relational concepts. They have a sophisticated level of language comprehension, including the ability to understand syntax, something heretofore thought to be an exclusively human ability. More than one study suggests that dolphins engage in self-reflection. Dolphins appear to experience a range of emotions and to have distinct personalities, and their actions seem to result from deliberation and choice.

At the same time, the fact that dolphins live in the ocean and have an evolutionary history much different from humans leads to important differences between the two species. Dolphins possess a sonar sense that we humans lack, a sense that is superior to anything our technology has been able to devise. They use whistles to communicate with one another at a speed and at frequencies often beyond the ability of human hearing to perceive. Their system of communication may be more nonverbal than ours is, but they live a much more intensely social life than we do.

Both the similarities and the differences between dolphins and humans raise important philosophical questions. For example, we humans have traditionally reserved for ourselves the category of "person," with its special rights and privileges. Yet the advanced characteristics of dolphins suggest that they are probably "nonhuman persons." Does this mean, then, that they have moral standing and "rights"?

The question of whether dolphins have moral standing is an interesting philosophical issue in its own right. The specifics about dolphin/human interaction, however, make it much more than that because it raises the question of the ethical justifiability of our behavior toward the dolphins. Clashes between human and dolphin interests take place daily in the fishing and entertainment industries, and dolphins generally do poorly in the exchange. For example, approximately four hundred dolphins are held in captivity in the United States alone for purposes of research and entertainment at facilities such as Sea World and Marine World. In addition, despite recent

From Thomas I. White, *Business Ethics: A Philosophical Reader,* (New York: Macmillan, 1993). Reprinted with permission.

progress regarding how tuna is caught in the eastern tropical Pacific, and despite decisions by companies such as Star-Kist to no longer sell tuna caught on dolphins, as many as three hundred dolphins still die each day in the nets of tuna boats. (In the eastern tropical Pacific, dolphins and tuna frequently school together. Tuna boats will often set their nets around a school of dolphin hoping to find tuna beneath them. Dolphins are regularly killed or injured in this process. Approximately 7 million dolphins have died because of this practice.)

The Marine Mammal Protection Act of 1972 allows 20,500 dolphins to die annually from American tuna fishing despite the fact that the original version of the bill aimed to bring the deaths to zero. The law also allows the United States to refuse to import fish from foreign boats causing too many dolphin deaths, and a federal court ordered such an embargo on Mexican tuna in 1990. Mexico objected to the U.S. action and appealed to an international trade body, arguing that the embargo was an unfair trade practice. A panel of the Geneva-based General Agreement on Tariffs and Trade (GATT) sided with Mexico, saying that a GATT member nation has no right to limit trade that harms the environment beyond its borders. For the time being, however, Mexico has agreed to table its case rather than take it to GATT's General Council.

REFERENCES

Aridjis, Homero, "Defending Dolphins," *New York Times,* October 7, 1991 A17.

White, Thomas I., "Is a Dolphin a Person?," *Discovering Philosophy* (Englewood Cliffs, NJ: Prentice Hall, 1991), 72–96.

———, "Ethics at Sea: The Dolphin/Tuna Controversy," in *Business, Ethics and the Environment: The Public Policy Debate,* edited by W. Michael Hoffman, Robert Frederick, and Edward S. Petry, Jr. (New York: Quorum Books, 1990), 233–245.

QUESTIONS

1. Do dolphins have rights? If so, which ones? Life? Liberty? Self-determination?

2. How do we evaluate situations in which there is a conflict between human interests and dolphin interests? In trying to resolve such a clash, how do we properly take account of the differences between dolphins and humans and avoid anthropocentrism, that is, irrational prejudice in favor of our own species?

3. Does our need for food and our desire for maximum profit justify the technology we currently employ in tuna fishing? Does human curiosity about dolphins defend keeping them captive for research and education? Does human pleasure at watching dolphins perform (and the ability to make a profit at this) make it ethically justifiable to keep dolphins captive?

CASE 13.2

Made in the U.S.A.—and Dumped

William H. Shaw and Vincent Barry

When it comes to the safety of young children, fire is a parent's nightmare. Just the thought of their young ones trapped in their cribs and beds by a raging nocturnal blaze is enough to make most mothers and fathers take every precaution to ensure their children's safety. Little wonder that when fire-retardant children's pajamas hit the market in the mid-1970s,

they proved an overnight success. Within a few short years more than 200 million pairs were sold, and the sales of millions more were all but guaranteed. For their manufacturers, the future could not have been brighter. Then, like a bolt from the blue, came word that the pajamas were killers.

In June 1977, the U.S. Consumer Product Safety

From William H. Shaw and Vincent Barry, *Moral Issues in Business,* 5th ed. (Belmont, CA: Wadsworth, 1996)

Commission (CPSC) banned the sale of these pajamas and ordered the recall of millions of pairs. Reason: The pajamas contained the flame-retardant chemical Tris (2,3-dibromoprophyl), which had been found to cause kidney cancer in children.

Whereas just months earlier the 100 medium- and small-garment manufacturers of the Tris-impregnated pajamas couldn't fill orders fast enough, suddenly they were worrying about how to get rid of the millions of pairs now sitting in warehouses. Because of its toxicity, the sleepwear couldn't even be thrown away, let alone sold. Indeed, the CPSC left no doubt about how the pajamas were to be disposed of—buried or burned or used as industrial wiping cloths. All meant millions of dollars in losses for manufacturers.

The companies affected—mostly small, family-run operations employing fewer than 100 workers—immediately attempted to shift blame to the mills that made the cloth. When that attempt failed, they tried to get the big department stores that sold the pajamas and the chemical companies that produced Tris to share the financial losses. Again, no sale. Finally, in desperation, the companies lobbied in Washington for a bill making the federal government partially responsible for the losses. It was the government, they argued, that originally had required the companies to add Tris to pajamas and then had prohibited their sale. Congress was sympathetic; it passed a bill granting companies relief. But President Carter vetoed it.

While the small firms were waging their political battle in the halls of Congress, ads began appearing in the classified pages of *Women's Wear Daily*. "Tris-Tris-Tris . . . We will buy any fabric containing Tris," read one. Another said, "Tris—we will purchase any large quantities of garments containing Tris." The ads had been placed by exporters, who began buying up the pajamas, usually at 10 to 30 percent of the normal wholesale price. Their intent was clear: to dump the carcinogenic pajamas on overseas markets. ("Dumping" is a term apparently coined by *Mother Jones* magazine to refer to the practice of exporting to overseas countries products that have been banned or declared hazardous in the United States.)

Tris is not the only example of dumping. In 1972, 400 Iraqis died and 5,000 were hospitalized after eating wheat and barley treated with a U.S.-banned organic mercury fungicide. Winstrol, a synthetic male hormone that had been found to stunt the growth of American children, was made available in Brazil as an appetite stimulant for children. Depo-Provera, an injectable contraceptive known to cause malignant tumors in animals, was shipped overseas to seventy countries where it was used in U.S.-sponsored population control programs. And 450,000 baby pacifiers, of the type known to have caused choking deaths, were exported for sale overseas.

Manufacturers that dump products abroad clearly are motivated by profit or at least by the hope of avoiding financial losses resulting from having to withdraw a product from the market. For government and health agencies that cooperate in the exporting of dangerous products, the motives are more complex.

For example, as early as 1971 the dangers of the Dalkon Shield intrauterine device were well documented. Among the adverse reactions were pelvic inflammation, blood poisoning, pregnancies resulting in spontaneous abortions, tubal pregnancies, and uterine perforations. A number of deaths were even attributed to the device. Faced with losing its domestic market, A. H. Robins Co., manufacturer of the Dalkon Shield, worked out a deal with the Office of Population within the U.S. Agency for International Development (AID), whereby AID bought thousands of the devices at a reduced price for use in population-control programs in forty-two countries.

Why do governmental and population-control agencies approve for sale and use overseas birth control devices proved dangerous in the United States? They say their motives are humanitarian. Since the rate of dying in childbirth is high in Third World countries, almost any birth control device is preferable to none. Third World scientists and government officials frequently support this argument. They insist that denying their countries access to the contraceptives of their choice is tantamount to violating their countries' national sovereignty.

Apparently this argument has found a sympathetic ear in Washington, for it turns up in the "notification" system that regulates the export of banned or dangerous products overseas. Based on the principles of national sovereignty, self-determination, and free trade, the notification system requires that foreign governments be notified whenever a product is banned, deregulated, suspended, or canceled by an

American regulatory agency. The State Department, which implements the system, has a policy statement on the subject that reads in part: "No country should establish itself as the arbiter of others' health and safety standards. Individual governments are generally in the best position to establish standards of public health and safety."

Critics of the system claim that notifying foreign health officials is virtually useless. For one thing, other governments rarely can establish health standards or even control imports into their countries. Indeed, most of the Third World countries where banned or dangerous products are dumped lack regulatory agencies, adequate testing facilities, and well-staffed customs departments.

Then there's the problem of getting the word out about hazardous products. In theory, when a government agency such as the Environmental Protection Agency or the Food and Drug Administration (FDA) finds a product hazardous, it is supposed to inform the State Department, which is to notify local health officials. But agencies often fail to inform the State Department of the product they have banned or found harmful. And when it is notified, its communiqués typically go no further than the U.S. embassies abroad. One embassy official even told the General Accounting Office that he "did not routinely forward notification of chemicals not registered in the host country because it may adversely affect U.S. exporting." When foreign officials are notified by U.S. embassies, they sometimes find the communiqués vague or ambiguous or too technical to understand.

In an effort to remedy these problems, at the end of his term in office, President Jimmy Carter issued an executive order that (1) improved export notice procedures; (2) called for publishing an annual summary of substances banned or severely restricted for domestic use in the United States; (3) directed the State Department and other federal agencies to participate in the development of international hazards alert systems; and (4) established procedures for placing formal export licensing controls on a limited number of extremely hazardous substances. In one of his first acts as president, however, Ronald Reagan rescinded the order. Later in his administration, the law that formerly prohibited U.S. pharmaceutical companies from exporting drugs that are banned or not registered

in this country was weakened to allow the export to twenty-one countries of drugs not yet approved for use in the United States.

But even if communication procedures were improved or the export of dangerous products forbidden, there are ways that companies can circumvent these threats to their profits—for example, by simply changing the name of the product or by exporting the individual ingredients of a product to a plant in a foreign country. Once there, the ingredients can be reassembled and the product dumped. Upjohn, for example, through its Belgian subsidiary, continues to produce Depo-Provera, which the FDA has consistently refused to approve for use in this country. And the prohibition on the export of dangerous drugs is not that hard to sidestep. "Unless the package bursts open on the dock," one drug company executive observes, "you have no chance of being caught."

Unfortunately for us, in the case of pesticides the effects of overseas dumping are now coming home. The Environmental Protection Agency bans from the United States all crop uses of DDT and Dieldrin, which kill fish, cause tumors in animals, and build up in the fatty tissue of humans. It also bans heptachlor, chlordane, leptophos, endrin, and many other pesticides, including 2,4,5-T (which contains the deadly poison dioxin, the active ingredient in Agent Orange, the notorious defoliant used in Vietnam) because they are dangerous to human beings. No law, however, prohibits the sale of DDT and these other U.S.-banned pesticides overseas, where thanks to corporate dumping they are routinely used in agriculture. The FDA now estimates, through spot checks, that 10 percent of our imported food is contaminated with illegal residues of banned pesticides. And the FDA's most commonly used testing procedure does not even check for 70 percent of the pesticides known to cause cancer.

QUESTIONS

1. Do you think dumping involves any moral issues? What are they?

2. Can a moral argument be made in favor of dumping, when doing so does not violate U.S. law? Do any moral considerations support illegal dumping? Speculate on why dumpers dump. Do you think they believe that what they are doing is morally permissible?

CASE 13.3

The Fordasaurus

William H. Shaw and Vincent Barry

Before Ford publicly unveiled the biggest sport-utility vehicle ever, the Sierra Club ran a contest for the best name and marketing slogan for it. Among the entries were "Fordasaurus, powerful enough to pass anything on the highway except a gas station" and "Ford Saddam, the truck that will put America between Iraq and a hard place." But the winner was "Ford Valdez: Have you driven a tanker lately?"

Ford, which decided to name the nine-passenger vehicle the Excursion, was not amused. Sales of sport-utility vehicles (SUVs) exploded in the 1990s, going up nearly sixfold, and the company sees itself as simply responding to consumer demand for ever larger models. Although most SUVs never leave the pavement, their drivers like knowing their vehicles can go anywhere and do anything. They also like their SUVs to be big. The Excursion is now the largest passenger vehicle on the road, putting Ford far ahead of its rivals in the competition to build the biggest and baddest SUV. The Excursion weighs 8,500 pounds, equivalent to two mid-sized sedans or three Honda Civics. It is more than 6 1/2 feet wide, nearly 7 feet high, and almost 19 feet long—too big to fit comfortably into some garages or into a single parking space.

Although the Excursion is expensive ($40,000 to $50,000 when loaded with options), it is, like other SUVs, profitable to build. Because Ford based the Excursion on the chassis of its Super Duty truck, the company was able to develop the vehicle for a relatively modest investment of about $500 million. With sales of 50,000 to 60,000 per year, Ford earns about $20,000 per vehicle.

Most SUVs are classified as light trucks. Under current rules, they are allowed to emit up to several times more smog-causing gases per mile than automobiles. In 1999, the Clinton administration proposed tighter emissions restrictions on new passenger cars, restrictions that new vehicles in the light-truck category would also have to meet by 2009. However, these rules would not affect the Excursion, which is heavy enough to be classified as a medium-duty truck.

Ford says that the Excursion, with its 44-gallon gas tank, gets 10 to 15 miles per gallon, and that its emission of pollutants is 43 percent below the maximum for its class. By weight, about 85 percent of the vehicle is recyclable, and 20 percent of it comes from recycled metals and plastics. The company thus believes that the Excursion is in keeping with the philosophy of William Clay Ford, Jr. When he became chairman in September 1998, he vowed to make Ford "the world's most environmentally friendly auto maker." He added, however, that "what we do to help the environment must succeed as a business proposition. A zero-emission vehicle that sits unsold on a dealer's lot is not reducing pollution."

The company, however, has failed to win environmentalists to its side. They believe that with the Excursion, the Ford Company is a long way from producing an environmentally friendly product. Daniel Becker of the Sierra Club points out that in the course of an average lifetime of 120,000 miles, each Excursion will emit 130 tons of carbon dioxide, the principal cause of global warming. "It's just bad for the environment any way you look at it," he says. John DeCicco of the American Council for an Energy-Efficient Economy agrees. He worries further that the Excursion is clearing the way for bigger and bigger vehicles. "This is the antithesis of green leadership."

Stung by criticism of the Excursion, William Clay Ford, Jr., has vowed to make the company a more responsible environmental citizen. Worried that if automobile producers don't clean up their act, they will become as vilified as cigarette companies, in August 2000 Ford promised it would improve the

William H. Shaw and Vincent Barry, *Moral Issues in Business,* 9th ed. (Belmont, CA: Wadsworth, 2004).

fuel economy of its SUVs by 25 percent over the next five years, smugly inviting other automakers to follow its green leadership. To this GM responded that it was the real green leader and "will still be in five years, or 10 years, or for that matter 20 years. End of story." When they aren't bragging about their greenness, however, both companies continue to lobby Congress to forbid the Department of Transportation from studying fuel economy increases.

Update:

According to media reports, yet to be confirmed by Ford, the company is planning on phasing out the Excursion after 2004.

QUESTIONS

1. Are environmentalists right to be concerned about the environmental impact of SUVs? How do you explain the growing demand for ever larger passenger vehicles?

2. In developing and producing the Excursion, is the Ford Motor Company sacrificing the environment to profits, or is it acting in a socially responsible way by making the Excursion relatively energy efficient for its vehicle class? If you had been on the board of directors, would you have voted for the project? Why/why not? Do Ford's stockholders have a right to insist that it produce the most profitable vehicles it legally can, regardless of their environmental impact?

CASE 13.4

Texaco in the Ecuadorean Amazon

Denis G. Arnold

Ecuador is a small nation on the northwest coast of South America. During its 173-year history, Ecuador has been one of the least politically stable South American nations. In 1830 Ecuador achieved its independence from Spain. Ecuadorean history since that time has been characterized by cycles of republican government and military intervention and rule. The period from 1960 to 1972 was marked by instability and military dominance of political institutions. From 1972 to 1979 Ecuador was governed by military regimes. In 1979 a popularly elected president took office, but the military demanded and was granted important governing powers. The demo-

cratic institutional framework of Ecuador remains weak. Decreases in public sector spending, increasing unemployment, and rising inflation have hit the Ecuadorean poor especially hard. World Bank estimates indicate that in 1994 35 percent of the Ecuadorean population lived in poverty, and an additional 17 percent were vulnerable to poverty.

The Ecuadorean Amazon is one of the most biologically diverse forests in the world and is home to an estimated 5 percent of Earth's species. It is home to cicadas, scarlet macaws, squirrel monkeys, freshwater pink dolphins, and thousands of other species. Many of these species have small populations, mak-

This case was prepared by Denis G. Arnold and is based on James Brooke, "New Effort Would Test Possible Coexistence of Oil and Rain Forest," *The New York Times,* February 26, 1991; Dennis M. Hanratty, Ed., *Ecuador: A Country Study,* 3rd ed. (Washington D.C.: Library of Congress, 1991); Anita Isaacs, *Military Rule and Transition in Ecuador, 1972–92* (Pittsburgh: University of Pittsburgh Press, 1993); *Ecuador Poverty Report* (Washington D.C.: The World Bank, 1996); Joe Kane, *Savages* (New York: Vintage Books, 1996); Eyal Press, "Texaco on Trial," *The Nation,* May 31, 1999; and "Texaco and Ecuador," *Texaco: Health, Safety & the Environment,* 27 September 1999, www.texaco.com/she/index .html (16 December, 1999); and *Aguinda v. Texaco, Inc.,* 142 F. Supp. 2d 534 (S.D.N.Y. 2001).

ing them extremely sensitive to disturbance. Indigenous Indian populations have lived in harmony with these species for centuries. They have fished and hunted in and around the rivers and lakes; and they have raised crops of cacao, coffee, fruits, nuts, and tropical woods in *chakras,* models of sustainable agroforestry.

Ten thousand feet beneath the Amazon floor lays one of Ecuador's most important resources: rich deposits of crude oil. Historically, the Ecuadorean government regarded the oil as the best way to keep up with the country's payments on its $12 billion foreign debt obligations. For 20 years American oil companies, lead by Texaco, extracted oil from beneath the Ecuadorean Amazon in partnership with the government of Ecuador. (The United States is the primary importer of Ecuadorean oil.) They constructed 400 drill sites and hundreds of miles of roads and pipelines, including a primary pipeline that extends for 280 miles across the Andes. Large tracts of forest were clear-cut to make way for these facilities. Indian lands, including *chakras,* were taken and bulldozed, often without compensation. In the village of Pacayacu the central square is occupied by a drilling platform.

Officials estimate that the primary pipeline alone has spilled more than 16.8 million gallons of oil into the Amazon over an 18-year period. Spills from secondary pipelines have never been estimated or recorded; however, smaller tertiary pipelines dump 10,000 gallons of petroleum per week into the Amazon, and production pits dump approximately 4.3 million gallons of toxic production wastes and treatment chemicals into the forest's rivers, streams, and groundwater each day. (By comparison, the Exxon Valdez spilled 10.8 million gallons of oil into Alaska's Prince William Sound.) Significant portions of these spills have been carried downriver into neighboring Peru.

Critics charge that Texaco ignored prevailing oil industry standards that call for the re-injection of waste deep into the ground. Rivers and lakes were contaminated by oil and petroleum; heavy metals such as arsenic, cadmium, cyanide, lead, and mercury; poisonous industrial solvents; and lethal concentrations of chloride salt, and other highly toxic

chemicals. The only treatment these chemicals received occurred when the oil company burned waste pits to reduce petroleum content. Villagers report that the chemicals return as black rain, polluting what little fresh water remains. What is not burned off seeps through the unlined walls of the pits into the groundwater. Cattle are found with their stomachs rotted out, crops are destroyed, animals are gone from the forest, and fish disappear from the lakes and rivers. Health officials and community leaders report adults and children with deformities, skin rashes, abscesses, headaches, dysentery, infections, respiratory ailments, and disproportionately high rates of cancer. In 1972 Texaco signed a contract requiring it to turn over all of its operations to Ecuador's national oil company, Petroecuador, by 1992. Petroecuador inherited antiquated equipment, rusting pipelines, and uncounted toxic waste sites. Independent estimates place the cost of cleaning up the production pits alone at 600 million dollars. From 1995 to 1998 Texaco spent 40 million dollars on cleanup operations in Ecuador. In exchange for these efforts the government of Ecuador relinquished future claims against the company.

Numerous international accords—including the 1972 Stockholm Declaration on the Human Environment signed by over 100 countries, including the United States and Ecuador—identify the right to a clean and healthy environment as a fundamental human right and prohibit both state and private actors from endangering the needs of present and future generations. Ecuadorean and Peruvian plaintiffs, including several indigenous tribes, have filed billion-dollar class-action lawsuits against Texaco in U.S. courts under the Alien Tort Claims Act (ACTA). Enacted in 1789, the law was designed to provide noncitizens access to U.S. courts in cases involving a breach of international law, including accords. Texaco maintains that the case should be tried in Ecuador. However, Ecuador's judicial system does not recognize the concept of a class-action suit and has no history of environmental litigation. Furthermore, Ecuador's judicial system is notoriously corrupt (a poll by George Washington University found that only 16 percent of Ecuadoreans have confidence in their judicial system) and lacks the infrastructure necessary to handle the case (e.g., the city in which the case would be tried lacks a courthouse). Texaco defended its actions by arguing that it is in full compliance with Ecuadorean law and that it had full approval of the Ecuadorean government.

In May 2001 U.S. District Judge Jed Rakoff rejected the applicability of the ACTA and dismissed the case on grounds of forum non conveniens. Judge Rakoff argued that since "no act taken by Texaco in the United States bore materially on the pollution-creating activities," the case should be tried in Ecuador and Peru. In October 2001 Texaco completed a merger with Chevron Corporation. Chevron and Texaco are now known as Chevron Texaco Corporation.

In August 2002 the U.S. Court of Appeals for the Second Circuit upheld Judge Rakoff's decision.

QUESTIONS

1. Given the fact that Texaco operated in partnership with the Ecuadorean government, is Texaco's activity in the Amazon morally justifiable? Explain.

2. Does Texaco (now Chevron Texaco) have a moral obligation to provide additional funds and technical expertise to clean up areas of the Amazon it is responsible for polluting? Does it have a moral obligation to provide medical care for the residents of the Amazon region who are suffering from the effects of the pollution? Explain.

CHAPTER QUESTIONS

1. What duties do we have to the environment? To future generations? How do we draw the line between our pressing needs and the needs of those who will come after us? What about our needs versus the needs of nonhuman animals? Or should only humans count?

2. Is it hip to be green? Or is it only hip to say you're green while you go on consuming more or less like everyone else? What sacrifices are you willing to make for the environment? And how can we change society's behavior? Who should decide how society ought to behave, vis-à-vis the environment?

14

The Gift that Keeps on Asking

Reciprocity and Conflicts of Interest

Introduction

Imagine that you are a regional manager of a large multinational manufacturing concern who oversees operations in several African countries. A year ago, you promoted a talented, hard-working, local employee to run one of your factories. You are touring the region and decide to stop in and visit the factory. When you arrive at the manager's office, you notice that the secretary has the same last name as the manager. You mention this to him, and he tells you that she is his sister. He takes you on a tour of the plant, and as you walk around, the manager is greeted by various people working there as "uncle," "cousin," and "father." You ask him. "Are all these people your relatives?" He replies that they are. You then discover that out of the 80 employees on the payroll, over half are members of the manager's extended family. Is this sort of nepotism unethical, or is this just a cultural difference in the way people do business?

Now let's cut to the 2000 presidential election in the United States. It pitted a son of a president against the son of a senator. When George W. Bush won, he made Michael Powell, son of Secretary of State Colin Powell, the chairman of the Federal Communications Commission. He made Elaine Cho, wife of Senator Mitch McConnell, the secretary of labor, and he appointed Eugene Scalia, son of Supreme Court Justice Antonin Scalia, the chief labor attorney. In addition to these appointments, Bush appointed the vice president's daughter, Elizabeth Cheney, deputy assistant secretary of state and her husband chief council for the Office of Management and Budget. At the request of Senator Strom Thurmond, Bush made Thurmond's 28-year-old son, Strom Thurmond, Jr., the U.S. attorney for South Carolina. Other family legacies in races that election year included three senators—Hilary Rodham Clinton, the wife of President Clinton; Jean Carnahan, who had taken her dead husband's seat; and Elizabeth Dole, wife of another former senator. It would appear that even in the United States, the Chinese proverb holds that "When a man becomes an official, his wife, children, dogs, cats, and even chickens fly up to heaven."

One may argue that politics is different from business, but think again. Contrary to the impression sometimes given in business schools, the majority of businesses in the world are not publicly held corporations; they are family businesses. Almost 95 percent of American businesses are family owned, including 40 percent of the Fortune 500 companies. Lachlan Murdoch runs a publishing concern for his father Rupert's company, William Ford is CEO of the Ford motor company, Jane Lauder heads up Estée Lauder, and Bill Wrigly manages his family's chewing gum business. No one seems to complain about nepotism in these businesses. The lists of who's who in nepotism in business, politics, the arts, and sports go on and on. (In Hollywood, the second generation of actors and actresses rules the big screen and video, too.)

Nepotism in family businesses, especially large businesses, raises a number of ethical questions. The interests of the family may conflict with the interests of the business and its stakeholders. Family members may not be the best people to manage the company. (Almost every family has an idiot son or daughter in it somewhere, and that idiot may well turn up at the helm.) Nepotism and cronyism can make organizations less transparent and breed corruption. But then again, a privately held family business should have the right to hire its relatives. As a matter of fact, one of the main reasons why, throughout history, people have started businesses is so that they could employ their relatives and pass the businesses on to future generations. Family businesses are different from our initial example because in that case, the manager did not own the firm. Yet, even when it is a family business or when a relative is clearly the best person for the job, nepotism can make other employees and even the stockholders uneasy. The problem of favoritism will always be foremost in their minds.

Biologists argue that altruism in humans emerges with the family. Family members in a wide variety of species do whatever they can to promote the well-being of their offspring. The same is true of humans. Most people feel a strong desire and obligation to help their families and close friends before they help strangers. These natural obligations are something we *feel.* They do not depend on abstract ethical theories or exotic religious teachings. The obligations that tie us to others are also based on reciprocity. This, too, is probably inherited and in our genes. In reciprocity, people (and many animals) feel an obligation to each other because of some gift, favor, or other kindness. In business, these feelings of obligation, especially within families (but also between close friends) are both natural and problematic. Reciprocity is the very basis of business. (Buyers and sellers each expect to gain something from the transaction.) But when family (and friendship) obligations get in the way of more straight business-like bonds of reciprocity (for instance, a nonfamily worker doing an excellent job and expecting an appropriate reward), or when family (or friendship) bonds interfere with sound business judgments or interfere with a work environment that is based on merit and not on connections or unfair influence, then these relationships become a problem.

We noted earlier that friendships can be as problematic as family ties when it comes to matters of fairness in business. But these problems are not limited to friends and family. When you do casual acquaintances or strangers a favor, they will usually remember your kindness, and even if they never get to repay the favor, they will probably feel obligated to you. Thus the pervasive problem of gift giving. You know how a gift from someone you do not know or do not like can make you feel uncomfortable? That is because you then feel this uncomfortable sense of obligation. You also know how it feels to get a present from someone whom you neglected to get a present for at Christmas? This same uncomfortable sense of obligation is why gift giving raises a number of ethical questions in business. Gifts or favors can create a conflict of interest or the appearance of it. Gifts create an atmosphere of favoritism. And gifts that are used to gain favors sometimes slide into the category of bribes. That is why so many corporations have strict rules about receiving gifts, not matter how "personal." Gifts create obligations, and obligations create conflicts of interest. A loan officer at a bank may welcome the 45-pound turkey for Thanksgiving or the $200 bottle of French Bordeaux for Christmas, but he or she is unlikely to treat that gift-giving customer with the same objective scrutiny after the holidays. Which is, very likely, precisely the point of the gift.

Unlike a gift, a bribe is explicitly offered to gain favor or to get what you want or need. While gifts can be innocent tokens of appreciation, bribes are never just this. Fairness in business demands that people conduct transactions on the basis of quality, merit, and price, not on obligations or relationships that are based on gifts or bribes. Bribes, in addition to being unfair (both to the party who is forced to pay them and the customers who will get poorer or more expensive products), corrupt the market and, accordingly, the whole society. But while most people know that bribery is wrong, even in countries where it is widely practiced, the dynamics of giving and getting gifts are far subtler because of the feelings that are engendered. Gifts and favors can easily give the appearance of a conflict of interest or become a real conflict of interest. The same is true for nepotism or favoritism with friends. This is, of course, to say nothing against family and friends, nor is it to say that there is anything wrong with gift giving as such, where business (and politics and grades) are not involved. Family, friends, gifts, and kindnesses are some of the best things in life, but they can also be problematic in business.

In many business ethics texts, issues about bribery and nepotism are in the chapter on international business. We decided to make a separate chapter for them because, as Adam Bellow demonstrates in his article, "Nepotism in American Business," nepotism, cronyism, and the like are not just found in other places, and as John T. Noonan, Jr., tells us in "A Quick Look at the History of Bribes," bribery has been considered unethical in most cultures for a long time. Bribery can be large scale, as in the case of the famous Lockeed scandal of the 1970s, or it can be petty and annoying. The last article, by Mark Pastin and Michael Hooker, is about the Foreign Corrupt Practices Act, which, among other things made it illegal to pay bribes, but still left plenty of gray areas for "grease payments." The first case in this chapter is about the Regis family, owners of Adelphia Communications. It demonstrates not only the ethical problems of a family business, but how they are complicated when the family business becomes a public company. Next we have a bribery case concerning a construction project. It is made more difficult because it takes place in a foreign country, but a variation of this situation could also happen in the United States. The last case is a simple case about the conflict between obligations to family and to the organization.

Adam Bellow | # Nepotism in American Business

Adam Bellow is the former editorial director of the Free Press and is currently an editor-at-large for Doubleday.

No one can pick up the phone these days and get their kid a job, a record deal, or a spot on the national ticket. But more and more, such intervention isn't necessary. Growing up around a business or vocation—learning how it works, getting to know the people in it—creates a powerful advantage that is tantamount to nepotism, and when exercised unworthily it carries a similar stigma.

If all of this can be called nepotism—and it can—it is clearly a new kind of nepotism, a modern or (if you will) postmodern nepotism that adapts an ancient impulse to contemporary cultural conditions. This new, postmodern nepotism works subtly and invisibly, creating opportunities for those who have connections in a given field, and increasingly excluding those who don't. All that is required to profit from this kind of opportunity is a willingness to take advantage of it. Indeed, the New Nepotism differs from the Old in being not so much a matter of parents hiring or getting jobs for children as of children themselves choosing to follow in their parents' footsteps. To that extent, the successor phenomenon looks a lot less like nepotism on the part of mothers and fathers than it does opportunism on the part of sons and daughters.

Dictionaries trace the word "nepotism" to the Latin *nepos,* meaning nephew or grandson. But while technically accurate, this etymology is misleadingly narrow. The word actually derives from the Italian *nepote,* which can refer to any family member, of any generation, male or female. The term *nepotismo* was coined sometime in the fourteenth or fifteenth century to describe the corrupt practice of appointing papal relatives to office—usually illegitimate sons described as "nephews"—and for a long time this ecclesiastical origin continued to be reflected in dictionaries. (Even today, some dictionaries list the subordinate definition of "nephew" as "illegitimate child of an ecclesiastic.") The modern definition of nepotism is "favoritism based on kinship," but over time the word's dictionary meaning and its conventional applications have diverged. Most people today define the term very narrowly to mean not just hiring a relative, but hiring one who is grossly incompetent—though technically one would have to agree that hiring a relative is nepotism whether he or she is qualified or not. But nepotism has also proven to be a highly elastic concept, capable of being applied to a much broader range of relationships than simple consanguinity. Many practices that are in fact nepotistic don't look like nepotism, while practices that seem normal and acceptable to some look like nepotism to others.

To understand the nature of a thing it is best to begin with its critics. Thus, from the workingman's perspective nepotism means hiring or promoting the boss's son-in-law, nephew, or girlfriend over the heads of more qualified candidates. This violates our basic sense of fairness and elicits strong reactions of revulsion, both for those who practice nepotism and (even more perhaps) for those who profit from it. Yet nepotism is often the rule in family businesses, and it is usually accepted as "the way things are" by everyone involved. Such nepotism appears to be a problem only when the beneficiary is manifestly unqualified. Even then, whatever damage may result usually hurts only the nepotist himself.

Economists view nepotism as an obstacle to healthy change in business firms, promoting waste and inefficiency. Yet some acknowledge that nepo-

Adam Bellow, "Nepotism in American Business" in *In Praise of Nepotism: A Natural History* (New York, Doubleday, 2002), pp. 10–15. Notes were deleted from the text.

tism may be a rational practice, since engaging in extensive talent searches is a cost that might well be avoided. Still others argue that hiring family members is the best way to promote important values of trust and solidarity within a business enterprise. And despite official nepotism policies, most large companies admit that they prefer to hire the relatives of existing employees, since the proven conduct of a relative is the best guide to the behavior of a prospective worker.

Most Americans see nepotism as a means for the rich to warehouse their unemployable sons while keeping the lower classes in their place. In this view, nepotism appears as part of a strategy of class and elite domination. There is much to be said for this argument. Historically, most elites that have risen through merit of one kind or another normally seek to keep their gains within the family and contrive various ways to pass on property and status to their children. Yet systematic nepotism has been practiced just as widely by the poor and working classes: there are multigenerational families of cops and firemen, and so-called father-son unions still dominate the building trades. In fact, the Old Nepotism has been practiced more or less continuously by both the upper and lower classes as a rational group strategy. It was the middle class that pushed the merit principle, and this is one of the things that makes the New Nepotism such a surprising development: the fact that it is essentially a middle class phenomenon.

In politics, nepotism has appeared in various forms: that of hereditary family rule under a monarchy, the domination of a landed or commercial oligarchy, and (in democratic societies) as a species of corruption linked to patronage. The American Revolutionaries wanted nothing to do with hereditary rule from abroad and feared the dynastic ambition of rich and powerful men in their own country. Early American politics was obsessed with such fears, and the result has been a long struggle to free our political system from its lingering entanglement with the family. The tension between birth and merit was most famously articulated in the debate between Adams and Jefferson about the prospects for a "natural aristocracy." Both wished to see the nation governed by an elite of talent rather than birth, but disagreed on

whether this could be achieved. Though we seem to have gone pretty far toward realizing Jefferson's dream of a true meritocracy, we have not been able to do away with nepotism and patronage completely. While some might object that patronage and nepotism are two different things, there is really a good deal of overlap. Nepotism itself is a species of patronage directed at family members. Wherever patronage exists, moreover, nepotism rarely lags behind. . . .

Proponents of economic globalism decry the role of nepotism in fostering bureaucratic corruption and crony capitalism in Africa, Asia, and Latin America; and everyone rejects the resurgent ethnic nationalism that has led to genocidal violence in India, Rwanda, and the Balkans—a violent form of particularism that ultimately springs from the nepotistic preference for one's own cultural, linguistic, or religious group. Even the Dalai Lama comes down on nepotism in *Ethics for the New Millennium,* where he includes the stubborn preference for our own families, communities, and ethnic groups in a list of man-made evils that we must strive to overcome in the twenty-first century. From this angle, nepotism is not just a legal, moral, or political infraction, but a spiritual one as well.

These perspectives reflect the prevailing negative view of the Old Nepotism: it burdened the economy, corrupted government, reduced women and children to chattels, disadvantaged blacks and other minorities, throttled meritocracy, promoted amoral selfishness, and reinforced the American class system. The New Nepotism is clearly different, and it elicits different reactions. For one thing, the American social environment has become more competitive; the playing field is much more level than it was one hundred, fifty, or even twenty years ago, and it is no longer possible for nepotism to be practiced indiscrimately, or in a way that masks incompetence. Time and again we hear that while a famous name may get you in the door, you have to prove your worth or face the consequences.

It is worth dwelling for a moment on the differences between the Old Nepotism and the New. The Old Nepotism involved parents hiring their children outright or pulling strings on their behalf. It was also highly coercive—obedient daughters married according to their parents' wishes, and dutiful sons allowed their fathers to chart their careers and often to select suitable brides for them as well. Since then there has been a great civil rights revolution that has completed the liberation of women and children from patriarchal control. Coming on the other side of this revolution, the New Nepotism operates not (so to speak) from the top down but from the bottom up: it is voluntary, not coercive; it springs from the motives of children, not the interest of parents; it tends to seem natural rather than planned. It reverses the flow of energies in the nepotistic equation, so that instead of parents holding themselves out as examples for their children, today's children validate their parents by following in their footsteps. While not nepotism in the classic sense, it is rightly called nepotism because it involves exploiting the family name, connections, or wealth. The method may be different, but the result is much the same.

Mainly, however, the new nepotism differs in combining the privileges of birth with the iron rule of merit in a way that is much less offensive to democratic sensibilities. This is what explains the astonishing latitude—in effect, the room to fail—that we seem perfectly willing to grant the new successor generation. Americans increasingly feel that there is nothing wrong with hiring a relative, so long as he or she is qualified. We even say that when we hire a relative or pull strings to help relatives who *are* qualified, that is not really nepotism. But this leaves us in the logically inconsistent position of saying that hiring a relative is or is not nepotism depending on the relative's performance.

The reason we have tied ourselves in knots around this question is really quite simple: there is a missing distinction in our lexicon between *good* nepotism and *bad*. Of course, in order to recognize such a distinction we would have to completely revise our view of nepotism as bad by definition. But this should not be difficult, because our negative view of nepotism is not a natural or God-given law but a cultural artifact, the result of several centuries of social and cultural history.

Europeans in general have a much more relaxed and balanced view of nepotism. Despite the occasional scandal—such as the forced resignation in 1999 of twenty EU commissioners charged with blatant nepotism—they tend to accept it as part of the fabric of things. In contrast, the extreme antipathy to nepotism is an American phenomenon. Moreover, it is an attitude that America has been busily exporting to the rest of the world (with mixed success) for the last fifty years, along with the whole complex of values and practices associated with modern technocratic liberalism.

QUESTIONS

1. From an ethical point of view, what problems stem from nepotism, patronage, and other forms of cronyism in business?

2. Do you agree with Bellow's distinction between good nepotism and bad nepotism?

John T. Noonan, Jr. | A Quick Look at the History of Bribes

John T. Noonan, Jr., is a judge in the United States Ninth Circuit Court of Appeals.

First. Bribes—socially disapproved inducements of official action meant to be gratuitously exercised—are ancient, almost as ancient as the invention in Egypt of scales which symbolized and showed social acceptance of the idea of objective judgment.

Second. The bribe has a history, divisible into discernible epochs. From approximately 3000 B.C. to 1000 A.D. the idea of nonreciprocity struggles against the norms of reciprocation which cement societies whose rulers are both judges and the recipients of offerings. In the second period from, say, 1000 A.D. to 1550 A.D., the antibribery ideal is dominant in religious, legal, and literary expressions; its active enforcement is attempted in successive waves of reformation. The third period of the idea, as far as English-speaking people are concerned, begins in the sixteenth century with its domestication in English bibles and English plays and English law and ends in the eighteenth century with its proclamation as a norm for the English empire. The fourth stage is the American, when the heirs of the successive reformations and of English politics begin to apply it and then to expand its sway until it is asserted as an American norm around the earth; and the rest of the world—not merely as a result of American influence but because of the general expansion of the Western moral tradition—makes at least verbal acknowledgment of the norm.

Third. Bribes are today universal; that is, every culture, with insignificant exceptions, treats certain reciprocities with officials as disapproved.

Fourth. The bribe is a concept running counter to normal expectations in approaching a powerful stranger. Linguistic ambiguity in the term for bribe in Hebrew, Greek, and Latin marks the cultural resistance encountered by the concept. Historically, the limitation of the concept to one class of officials—judges—is a second sign of the resistance. Reluctance to apply the concept against the bribegiver is a third. Lack of specific sanctions against the bribetaker is a fourth indication of the precarious hold the concept, historically, has enjoyed.

Fifth. The bribe in its origins depends on religious teaching. Reciprocity is so regularly the norm of human relations that the conception of a transcendental figure, a Judge beyond the reach of ordinary reciprocities, was of enormous importance for the idea that certain reciprocities with earthly officials were intolerable. That conception of a transcendental Judge was shaped in the ancient Near East. Communication of this image to the West was largely dependent on religion. Accepted as divine revelation, Scripture by commandment and paradigm inculcated a teaching on impartial judgment. The concept of the bribe was cast in a biblical mold.

Sixth. Religion—Jewish, Christian, pagan—has been, however, profoundly ambivalent in its teaching on reciprocity. The Judge beyond influence has been placated by pagans, offered prayers and slaughtered animals by Jews, and seen by Christians as accepting a special redeeming sacrifice. Religion can be viewed as bribery on a grand scale, organized for the highest end, man's salvation, and practiced to persuade the Supreme Authority. Indulgences, systematized to support enterprises from basilicas to bridges, constitute an especially striking example of this kind of religion. Even in its most primitive form, Christianity rests on a transaction carried out between God and the Son of God which theology labeled the Buy Back, a term in Roman civilization often used to mean payoff to a judge to escape punishment. Job

John T. Noonan, Jr. "A Quick Look at the History of Bribes" in *Bribes* (New York: MacMillan Publishers, 1984), pp. xx–xxiii.

and Jesus himself to the contrary, religion can be read as reinforcement of the iron law, "I give that you may give," a law requiring reciprocity with every power-holder including God.

Seventh. The double message conveyed by the several religious traditions is paralleled in Western cultures by the elimination of certain reciprocities as bribes and the retention of others as acceptable quid pro quos. Words alone seem to mark the distinction between certain acceptable and condemned offerings. In sixteenth-century Europe payment to obtain a spiritual favor was the sin of simony; a *contributio* to obtain an indulgence was legitimate. In twentieth-century America, payment to a candidate for his vote is a penal offense; a licensed contribution to a campaign committee is lawful. In some instances, there is only verbal camouflage; in some instances, the verbal distinction points to a real difference.

Eighth. Although the definition of a bribe depends on the conventions of the culture, so that ceremony and context, form and intention, determine whether an exchange counts as a crime or a virtuous act, ultimately the distinction between bribe and gift has become fundamental. Without this distinction the condemnation of bribes appears arbitrary, and intermediate offerings such as a tip or a campaign contribution are indiscriminately lumped into a single category which includes all reciprocities. With bribe and gift set at polar opposites, a spectrum with shades of discrimination exists. For our culture—Western culture, now the dominant world culture—the difference between bribe and gift has been most powerfully developed by reflection, theological and literary, on the Redemption.

Ninth. Bribes come openly or covertly, disguised as an interest in a business, as a lawyer's fee, or, very often, as a loan. Bribes come directly, paid into the waiting hands of the bribee or, more commonly, indirectly to the subordinate or friend performing the nearly indispensable office of bagman. Bribes come in all shapes as sex, commodities, appointments, and, most often, cash. In the shape of sex, bribes have been both male and female: a slave, a wife, a noble boy. As commodities, they have included bedspreads, cups, dogs, fruits, furniture, furs, golf balls, jewels, livestock, peacocks, pork, sturgeon, travel, wine—the gamut of enjoyable goods. As appointments, they have often been rationalized or justified by the merits of the appointee—a double effect, one good, one bad, being achieved by the bribe. As cash they have come as contingent payments and down payments, as payments for the life of the contract and payments for the life of the recipient and as cash on the spot. They have come at the rate of so much a car towed, so much a prostitute undisturbed, so much a plane purchased, so much a guinea spent, at such a percentage, and at a flat rate. They have been as little as 1 percent of a contract and as high as 20 percent or more. They have been as small as $2.50 for a Connecticut voter and as much as $12,000,000 for the prime minister of Japan and his associates. . . .

Tenth. Bribers have included every variety of business, from very small to multinational; all the professions; every manner of criminal defendant; and the ordinary citizen in line for an inheritance or in need of a traffic ticket being fixed. Bribees have ranged from constables and sheriffs to the Speaker of the House (U.S., nineteenth century), the Speaker of the House of Commons (U.K., seventeenth century), the president of Honduras, the president of Italy, the prime minister of Japan, the prince-consort of the Netherlands, the Lord Chancellor of England (seventeenth century). Bribe-takers and bribegivers are not distinguished by any of the characteristics commonly associated with criminality. Sometimes they are oppressed and bribe to escape harassment. Sometimes they are oppressed and therefore accept bribes. Often they are possessed of high office and comfortable income, bribe to maintain or expand their power or wealth, and accept bribes given as tributes to their power or wealth. Their crimes have not been shown to depend on any oedipal fixation, sexual need or malfunction, or uncontrollable instinct. They are not vicious in all respects; they are often otherwise decent individuals. They are of all nationalities and sects and have been in the past more often men than women.

Eleventh. The bribe is ideologically neutral—that is, charges of bribery can be made by an established class attacking a new class (John Randolph pursuing the Yazoo speculators; George Templeton Strong scorning the Tweed Ring); by a new class attacking

Havamal

Business is based on reciprocity. The exchange of gifts and contracts has always been an important part of human relationships. Gifts bind people together and create webs of obligation. An old Scandinavian poem called the "Havamal" celebrates gift giving and the bonds that come with it.

> With weapons and clothes
> Friends must give pleasure to one another;
> Everyone knows that for himself
> Those who exchange presents with one another
> Remain friends the longest
> If things turn out successfully . . .
>
> You know, if you have a friend
> In whom you have confidence
> And if you wish to get good results,
> Your soul must blend with his
> And you must exchange presents
> And frequently pay him visits . . .
>
> Noble and valiant men
> Have the best life;
> They have no fear at all
> But a coward fears everything:
> The miser always fears presents . . .
>
> It is better not to ask
> Than t sacrifice too much
> A present given always expects one in return.
> It is better not to bring any offering
> Than to spend too much on it.*

*Quotes in Marcel Mauss, *The Gift,* trans. W.D. Halls, (W. W. Norton, 1990), pp. 1–2.

---

an old class (the Protestants assailing the papacy; Andrew Jackson censuring Adams and Clay); and in intraclass warfare (Coke against Bacon; the Carter administration against the Abscam defendants). The bribe is a concept which can be effectively evoked by "the center" or existing hierarchy, as fourth-century Roman emperors and popes like Gregory I, Gregory VII, and Innocent III illustrate. It is a concept which is useful to "the border" or sectarian groupings within a society, as is shown by the writings of John Wyclif and Jan Hus.

Twelfth. Enforcement of law against bribes has nearly always been a function of prosecutorial discretion. Prosecutions for bribery have often depended on motivations distinct from the desire to punish the bribe. The watershed for widespread federal prosecution of bribery occurred in the 1960s. Whatever social causes account for it, at this time the pursuit of bribery became a national enterprise in the United States. Watergate is the consequence not the cause of this phenomenon. In the Orwellian prophecy for the year 1984, sexual Puritanism is the rule, enforced by electronics. In the actual America of 1984, it is the purity of political reciprocities that is enforced by wire taps, tape recordings, and television cameras.

Thirteenth. The commonest sanctions against bribes are moral—the invocation of guilt before God and shame before society, guilt and shame being equally relied on. Political sanctions—repudiation at the polls, forced resignation from office, loss of promotion—are frequently invoked. Sanctions prescribed by law are more often indirect than direct—not the crime of bribery itself but a related offense is usually punished. Until very recent times application of direct criminal sanctions to highly placed bribetakers was rare.

Fourteenth. Prosecutors, politicians, and journalists are those most attentive to contemporary corruption. Academic lawyers, anthropologists, psychoanalysts, and theologians have had little to say. Political scientists and sociologists, intent on understanding the function of social practices, sometimes give little weight to the moral impact of corruption. Biographers and historians, despite a tendency at times to act as advocates or apologists, give a kind of secular last judgment on the corrupt. Those who have most powerfully articulated the antibribery ethic are the masters of Western literature—above, all, Chaucer, Dante, and Shakespeare

Fifteenth. The material injury bribers and bribees inflict is often undemonstrable. Their actions always subvert the trust that accompanies public office and distinguishes office from power. For Jews, for Christians, for those who share their moral heritage, the bribe is not a morally neutral concept.

Writing at this interesting time in the history of the bribe, I venture a prediction that is a projection of my values. That will come at the end. History itself is not prediction but the selection of significant actions, words, and characters to be remembered—drama more than process. "Remember! Remember! Remember!"—Burke's incantation after his prosecution of Warren Hastings had ended in defeat. If all that is collected here survives in memory, this account has been worth making.

QUESTIONS

1. How would you delineate the difference between a bribe and a gift?

2. What is it about a bribe that makes it such a prevalent ethical problem in history? Why has bribery been discredited for so long in so many places?

Mark Pastin and Michael Hooker

Ethics and the Foreign Corrupt Practices Act

Mark Pastin is president of the Health Ethics Trust and Council of Ethical Organizations. Michael Hooker was a philosophy professor at Harvard.

Not long ago it was feared that as a fallout of Watergate, government officials would be hamstrung by artificially inflated moral standards. Recent events, however, suggest that the scapegoat of post-Watergate morality may have become American business rather than government officials.

One aspect of the recent attention paid to corporate morality is the controversy surrounding payments made by American corporations to foreign officials for the purpose of securing business abroad. Like any law or system of laws, the Foreign Corrupt Practices Act (FCPA), designed to control or eliminate such payments, should be grounded in morality, and should therefore be judged from an ethical perspective. Unfortunately, neither the law nor the question of its repeal has been adequately addressed from that perspective.

HISTORY OF THE FCPA

On December 20, 1977 President Carter signed into law S.305, the Foreign Corrupt Practices Act (FCPA), which makes it a crime for American corporations to offer or provide payments to officials of foreign governments for the purpose of obtaining or retaining business. The FCPA also establishes record keeping requirements for publicly held corporations to make it difficult to conceal political payments proscribed by the Act. Violators of the FCPA, both cor-

porations and managers, face severe penalties. A company may be fined up to $1 million, while its officers who directly participated in violations of the Act or had reason to know of such violations, face up to five years in prison and/or $10,000 in fines. The Act also prohibits corporations from indemnifying fines imposed on their directors, officers, employees, or agents. The Act does not prohibit "grease" payments to foreign government employees whose duties are primarily ministerial or clerical, since such payments are sometimes required to persuade the recipients to perform their normal duties.

At the time of this writing, the precise consequences of the FCPA for American business are unclear, mainly because of confusion surrounding the government's enforcement intentions. Vigorous objections have been raised against the Act by corporate attorneys and recently by a few government officials. Among the latter is Frank A. Weil, former Assistant Secretary of Commerce, who has stated, "The questionable payments problem may turn out to be one of the most serious impediments to doing business in the rest of the world."[1]

The potentially severe economic impact of the FCPA was highlighted by the fall 1978 report of the Export Disincentives Task Force, which was created by the White House to recommend ways of improving our balance of trade. The Task Force identified the FCPA as contributing significantly to economic and political losses in the United States. Economic losses come from constricting the ability of American corporations to do business abroad, and political losses come from the creation of a holier-than-thou image.

The Task Force made three recommendations in regard to the FCPA:

- The Justice Department should issue guidelines on its enforcement policies and establish procedures by which corporations could get advance government reaction to anticipated payments to foreign officials.
- The FCPA should be amended to remove enforcement from the SEC, which now shares enforcement responsibility with the Department of Justice.
- The administration should periodically report to Congress and the public on export losses caused by the FCPA.

In response to the Task Force's report, the Justice Department, over SEC objections, drew up guidelines to enable corporations to check any proposed action possibly in violation of the FCPA. In response to such an inquiry, the Justice Department would inform the corporation of its enforcement intentions. The purpose of such an arrangement is in part to circumvent the intent of the law. As of this writing, the SEC appears to have been successful in blocking publication of the guidelines, although Justice recently reaffirmed its intention to publish guidelines. Being more responsive to political winds, Justice may be less inclined than the SEC to rigidly enforce the Act.

Particular concern has been expressed about the way in which bookkeeping requirements of the Act will be enforced by the SEC. The Act requires that company records will "accurately and fairly reflect the transactions and dispositions of the assets of the issuer." What is at question is the interpretation the SEC will give to the requirement and the degree of accuracy and detail it will demand. The SEC's post-Watergate behavior suggests that it will be rigid in requiring the disclosure of all information that bears on financial relationships between the company and any foreign or domestic public official. This level of accountability in record keeping, to which auditors and corporate attorneys have strongly objected, goes far beyond previous SEC requirements that records display only facts material to the financial position of the company.

Since the potential consequences of the FCPA for American businesses and business managers are very serious, it is important that the Act have a rationale capable of bearing close scrutiny. In looking at the foundation of the FCPA, it should be noted that its passage followed in the wake of intense newspaper coverage of the financial dealings of corporations. Such media attention was engendered by the dramatic disclosure of corporate slush funds during the Watergate hearings and by a voluntary disclosure program established shortly thereafter by the SEC. As a result of the SEC program, more than 400 corporations, including 117 of the Fortune 500, admitted to making more than $300 million in foreign political payments in less than ten years.

Throughout the period of media coverage leading up to passage of the FCPA, and especially during the hearings on the Act, there was in all public discussions of the issue a tone of righteous moral indignation at the idea of American companies making foreign political payments. Such payments were ubiquitously termed "bribes," although many of these could more accurately be called extortions, while others were more akin to brokers' fees or sales commissions.

American business can be faulted for its reluctance during this period to bring to public attention the fact that in a very large number of countries, payments to foreign officials are virtually required for doing business. Part of that reluctance, no doubt, comes from the awkwardly difficult position of attempting to excuse bribery or something closely resembling it. There is a popular abhorrence in this country of bribery directed at domestic government officials, and that abhorrence transfers itself to payments directed toward foreign officials as well.

Since its passage, the FCPA has been subjected to considerable critical analysis, and many practical arguments have been advanced in favor of its repeal. However, there is always lurking in back of such analyses the uneasy feeling that no matter how strongly considerations of practicality and economics may count against this law, the fact remains that the law protects morality in forbidding bribery. For example, Gerald McLaughlin, professor of law at Fordham, has shown persuasively that where the legal system of a foreign country affords inadequate protection against the arbitrary exercise of power to the disadvantage of American corporations, payments to foreign officials may be required to provide a compensating mechanism against the use of such arbitrary power. McLaughlin observes, however, that "this does not mean that taking advantage of the compensating mechanism would necessarily make the payment moral."[2]

The FCPA, and questions regarding its enforcement or repeal, will not be addressed adequately until an effort has been made to come to terms with the Act's foundation in morality. While it may be very difficult, or even impossible, to legislate morality (that is, to change the moral character and sentiments of people by passing laws that regulate their behavior), the existing laws undoubtedly still reflect the moral beliefs we hold. Passage of the FCPA in Congress was eased by the simple connection most Congressmen made between bribery, seen as morally repugnant, and the Act, which is designed to prevent bribery.

Given the importance of the FCPA to American business and labor, it is imperative that attention be given to the question of whether there is adequate moral justification for the law.

ETHICAL ANALYSIS OF THE FCPA

The question we will address is not whether each payment prohibited by the FCPA is moral or immoral, but rather whether the FCPA, given all its consequences and ramifications, is itself moral. It is well known that morally sound laws and institutions may tolerate some immoral acts. The First Amendment's guarantee of freedom of speech allows individuals to utter racial slurs. And immoral laws and institutions may have some beneficial consequences, for example, segregationist legislation bringing deep-seated racism into the national limelight. But our concern is with the overall morality of the FCPA.

The ethical tradition has two distinct ways of assessing social institutions, including laws: *End-Point Assessment* and *Rule Assessment*. Since there is no consensus as to which approach is correct, we will apply both types of assessment of the FCPA.

The End-Point approach assesses a law in terms of its contribution to general social well-being. The ethical theory underlying End-Point Assessment is utilitarianism. According to utilitarianism, a law is morally sound if and only if the law promotes the well-being of those affected by the law to the greatest extent practically achievable. To satisfy the utilitarian principle, a law must promote the well-being of those affected by it at least as well as any alternative law that we might propose, and better than no law at all. A conclusive End-Point Assessment of a law requires specification of what constitutes the welfare of those affected by the law, which the liberal tradition generally sidesteps by identifying an individual's welfare with what he takes to be in his interests.

Considerations raised earlier in the paper suggest that the FCPA does not pass the End-Point test. The argument is not the too facile one that we could propose a better law. (Amendments to the FCPA are now being considered.[3]) The argument is that it may be better to have *no* such law than to have the FCPA. The main domestic consequences of the FCPA seem to include an adverse effect on the balance of payments, a loss of business and jobs, and another opportunity for the SEC and the Justice Department to compete. These negative effects must be weighed against possible gains in the conduct of American business within the United States. From the perspective of foreign countries in which American firms do business, the main consequence of the FCPA seems to be that certain officials now accept bribes and influence from non-American businesses. It is hard to see that who pays the bribes makes much difference to these nations.

Rule Assessment of the morality of laws is often favored by those who find that End-Point Assessment is too lax in supporting their moral codes. According to the Rule Assessment approach: A law is morally sound if and only if the law accords with a code embodying correct ethical rules. This approach has no content until the rules are stated, and different rules will lead to different ethical assessments. Fortunately, what we have to say about Rule Assessment of the FCPA does not depend on the details of a particular ethical code.

Those who regard the FCPA as a worthwhile expression of morality, despite the adverse effects on American business and labor, clearly subscribe to a rule stating that it is unethical to bribe. Even if it is conceded that the payments proscribed by the FCPA warrant classifications as bribes, citing a rule prohibiting bribery does not suffice to justify the FCPA.

Most of the rules in an ethical code are not *categorical* rules; they are *prima facie* rules. A categorical rule does not allow exceptions, whereas a prima facie rule does. The ethical rule that a person ought to keep promises is an example of a prima facie rule. If I promise to loan you a book on nuclear energy and later find out that you are a terrorist building a private atomic bomb, I am ethically obligated not to keep my promise. The rule that one ought to keep promises is "overridden" by the rule that one ought to prevent harm to others.

A rule prohibiting bribery is a prima facie rule. There are cases in which morality requires that a bribe be paid. If the only way to get essential medical care for a dying child is to bribe a doctor, morality requires one to bribe the doctor. So adopting an ethical code which includes a rule prohibiting the payment of bribes does not guarantee that a Rule Assessment of the FCPA will be favorable to it.

The fact that the FCPA imposes a cost on American business and labor weighs against the prima facie obligation not to bribe. If we suppose that American corporations have obligations, tantamount to promises, to promote the job security of their employees and the investments of shareholders, these obligations will also weigh against the obligation not to bribe. Again, if government legislative and enforcement bodies have an obligation to secure the welfare of American business and workers, the FCPA may force them to violate their public obligations.

The FCPA's moral status appears even more dubious if we note that many of the payments prohibited by the Act are neither bribes nor share features that make bribes morally reprehensible. Bribes are generally held to be malefic if they persuade one to act against his good judgement, and consequently purchase an inferior product. But the payments at issue in the FCPA are usually extorted *from the seller.* Further it is arguable that not paying the bribe is more likely to lead to purchase of an inferior product than paying the bribe. Finally, bribes paid to foreign officials may not involve deception when they accord with recognized local practices.

In conclusion, neither End-Point nor Rule Assessment uncovers a sound moral basis for the FCPA. It is shocking to find that a law prohibiting bribery has no clear moral basis, and may even be an immoral law. However, this is precisely what examination of the FCPA from a moral perspective reveals. This is symptomatic of the fact that moral conceptions which were appropriate to a simpler world are not adequate to the complex world in which contemporary business functions. Failure to appreciate this point often leads to righteous condemnation of business, when it should lead to careful reflection on one's own moral preconceptions.

NOTES

1. *National Journal,* June 3, 1978: 880.

2. Gerald T. McLaughlin, "The Criminalization of Questionable Foreign Payments by Corporations," *Fordham Law Review,* Vol. 46: 1095.

3. "Foreign Bribery Law Amendments Drafted," *American Bar Association Journal,* February 1980: 135.

QUESTIONS

1. Do you think that the Foreign Corrupt Practices Act makes American businesses less competitive?

2. Do you believe there is not a sufficient ethical justification for the act?

CASES

CASE 14.1
Family Values at Adelphia
Barry Meier

The government rested its case against the Rigas family after 10 weeks of testimony about an alleged scheme to hide $2 billion in debts from investors of Adelphia, a Greenwood Village, Colorado-based company with 5.3 million cable subscribers. Prosecutors contended that the defendants lied to investors and used fraudulent bookkeeping to hide more than $3 billion in debt from shareholders. They alleged that Rigas, 79, and sons Michael and Timothy—bachelors who live with their parents on the family estate in Coudersport, Pa.—reduced the company to their "private piggy bank" and took more than $100 million from the company. The defendants claim that, at worst, they were guilty of lapses in judgment.

John Rigas, the son of a Greek immigrant, a military veteran, and a former movie theater owner, struck it rich by investing in the cable industry in its infancy. It was in Coudersport, PA starting in the 1950's, that Mr. Rigas began to build Adelphia from the ground up. Several experts said that it was not unusual for a founder of a company to perceive it as his own, even after he reached retirement age or after it went public, as Adelphia did in 1986. A short man with silver hair and a quick smile, he has projected the image of a protective—if not bewildered—old patriarch at the trial." I wish I could do something as a parent," Rigas told reporters.

"It is hard for them to make the distinction between the business and themselves," said James Lea, a professor of family medicine at the University of North Carolina at Chapel Hill, who advises family businesses. That certainly seemed to be the case for John Rigas. According to testimony, he often took cash advances—as much as $1 million a month—from the company to pay for personal interests like operating an area farm that produced products like maple syrup. And while Mr. Rigas was known as a very generous contributor to community causes, he was not above hitting employees up for cash.

The witnesses said that John Rigas' demands for cash advances were so frequent that Timothy Rigas intervened and set a $1 million a month limit, but was unable to keep his father to it. Wayne Rivers, the president of the Family Business Institute, says that it takes tremendous courage for a son to face down his father in a business setting because of potential ripple effects in the family. "It may not only affect the dad but also the relationship with his own mother," Mr. Rivers said. Whether the Rigas family had any such confrontations is not known.

Timothy Rigas was also charged with tapping company funds to pay for extravagances. Golf pro Lisa Lynn Scally testified that Timothy Rigas, 47, hired her to help clients with their swings. She detailed a $7,000 junket to the famed Pebble Beach course in California, saying she was asked to take her brother along to preserve a reservation for four. "Once you have a tee time, if you don't use it, you lose it," she explained. Timothy used $700,000 from company funds to cover the cost of a golf-club membership. He later had Adelphia pay $13 million to build his own golf course,"

Adapted from Barry Meier, "The Portrait of a Family, as Painted at a Fraud Trial, *New York Times,* May 30, 2004, Sec. 3, p. 5.

Also taking the stand at the Regas trial was George Cretekos, who managed a private fleet of jets that made 1,000 flights a year. The trips included deliveries of eggs, paper towels and toilet paper to John Rigas' daughter, Ellen, he said. About $6,000 was spent on flight time devoted to the delivery of two Christmas trees from Pennsylvania to the daughter's New York home in 2000. The second tree was flown in after her husband "objected to the (first) tree because it was too short," Cretekos said. Ellen Rigas Venetis, and her husband, Peter, were given two rent-free apartments in New York City. According to the company, Adelphia loaned $3.7 million to set up two film companies and help Ellen Rigas Venetis produce the film *Songcatcher*. In 1997, she also released a country music CD called "God's Country."

Also prominent on the list of frequent fliers was Peta Wilson, sultry star of cable's "La Femme Nikita." She told jurors that Timothy Rigas sent a jet to take her home from the Caribbean so she could star in an opening ceremony at a hockey game of the Rigas-owned Buffalo Sabres. The actress also was treated to trips to Los Angeles and Jamaica. Asked if she was ever required to pay, she said, "I think I may have tipped the pilots."

Another government witness testified that the family shelled out hundreds of thousands of dollars in company money on antiques, golf memberships and mortgage payments. In another incident, Timothy Rigas once returned from a business trip and told an assistant to buy a pair of hotel slippers he liked with company funds. When it turned out that the slippers were only sold in packages of 100, Mr. Rigas told her to buy an entire package at the cost $268.

Peter Fleming, an attorney for John Rigas, maintained the Rigases didn't loot the cable company they controlled, as the U.S. government has alleged, but borrowed money they planned to repay. "If you borrow money with the intent and ability to repay, is that looting, or is that borrowing money?" "This isn't a case where John Rigas or any of the Rigases walked off with millions and left Adelphia or any of its employees high and dry," said Mr. Fleming.

The Rigases have all denied any wrongdoing. And Professor Lea, the family-business adviser, said it was possible that the Rigases did not perceive the use of Adelphia proceeds to finance their personal businesses or hobbies as crimes. "To them, this probably did not appear like embezzlement or malfeasance of any kind," he said. "It was more like you go to work in the store in the morning, you spend what you make and Adelphia was their family-owned store."

QUESTIONS

1. For the Regis family, how is Adelphia different from a family-owned store?
2. How does the involvement of a family members in a business change the way that they think about business?

CASE 14.2
The Moza Island Project
Karen Marquis and Joanne B. Ciulla

THE PROJECT

You are owner and President of Gulf Trading Company. Your firm became involved in the Moza Island Project back in the early 1980s through collaboration with a large, influential multinational corporation located in the Middle East. The joint venture, known as Gulf Sargam, hoped to use Gulf Trading Company's contacts to secure large construction contracts. Meanwhile, the multinational provided all the technical, administrative and support staff, including the General Manager Joe Fernandes. Gulf Trading and the multinational had initially contributed capital of 51% and 49%, respectively, but profits were divided into 55% and 45% shares, respectively.

In January of 1983, the regional government decided to modernize the living facilities on Moza Island. Located 150 miles to the southeast of the nation's capital, Moza contained most of the country's major liquefied petroleum gas plants. The government invited bids from international construction firms in early 1983.

In April, the government awarded the mechanical subcontract to Gulf Sargam for $3 million. This contract amounted to almost ten times the company's original capital of $305,000. You felt that the estimated profit of $300,000 seemed dangerously low for a project spanning 18 months in a remote location. However, Joe, your General Manager, persuaded you to go ahead with the project because of the potential for future work. Joe then selected Tom Johnson to serve as Moza Island Project Manager for Gulf Sargam.

To protect its interests, the government employed a prominent consulting firm to supervise the Moza Island Project. Habib Sharif was Construction Consultant. He had final authority on every aspect of the project, including approvals of equipment, finish work, variations and change orders. Disagreements between the contractors and the construction consultant could only be resolved through a complex civil arbitration system administered by the government at its mainland capital.

CONTRACT EXECUTION

From the beginning, Tom, your Project Manager, noticed that Habib Sharif, the government's Construction Consultant, often went out of his way to enforce the contract specifications for Gulf Sargam. At Moza Island, Habib consistently interpreted contract clauses to the advantage of the government, insisting upon absolute compliance with even the smallest details. Habib routinely delayed Gulf Sargam's construction drawings and then returned them for correction of minute flaws. Only rarely did Habib approve Gulf's work the first time. In defense, Tom filed claims for reimbursement of the additional costs incurred by Gulf Sargam due to these delays.

On the other hand, Habib seemed extremely tolerant with the general contractor and each of the other subcontractors. He approved their work from his office without even visiting the job site. A year into the job, a space frame structure that was made of lightweight aluminum erected by the general contractor crashed to the ground. Fortunately, no one was hurt. Habib attributed the mishap to metal fatigue and not to shoddy workmanship.

A familiar picture began to unfold. Most construction consultants in the region expected to gain

Karen Marquis and Joanne B. Ciulla, eds., "The Moza Island P.) in Paul Minus, ed., *The Ethics of Business in a Global Economy* (Boston: Kluwer Academic Press, 1993), pp. 142–145.

personally from their work, but none asked for an outright bribe. The consultant normally initiated the move with subtle "feelers" and awaited a response from the contractor. If a favorable reaction did not materialize, the consultant sent stronger signals, each causing more disruption to the contractor's work than the earlier one. However, Tom had faced this situation in several earlier projects and managed to avoid paying a bribe in each case through a combination of diplomacy and skill.

As owner and President of Gulf Trading Co., you had strong feelings on the subject. The fact that gratuities were often paid in the Middle East did not seem to you to make it right to pay them. The practice existed simply because corporations paid when asked. No law said that you must pay. Taking part in a corrupt system seemed immoral and served only to perpetuate the corruption. Giving in would set a precedent for all your other operations. You had to make it clear to Habib Sharif that the company would not play by those rules. Perhaps if you held fast, the man would see that you meant it. He would come around.

However, by June 1985, Gulf Sargam had incurred costs on an additional 9,000 man hours due to delays in approval of drawings and rejection of site work by Habib. Gulf had filed variation claims totalling $300,000, but not a single one had been approved. By early 1986, the delays imposed on the firm had slowed the entire Moza Island Project, but Habib refused to waver. Tom's crew found themselves six months behind schedule with the situation worsening every day.

At a chance meeting at the island club, Tom decided to confront Habib directly in order to resolve the matter before the end of the contract. Habib remarked that the general contractor and the other "subs" had taken "good care" of him and he had reciprocated their gesture accordingly. He expressed surprise that Gulf Sargam had not followed the same policy, a common Middle Eastern practice that remained essential for the smooth execution of a project.

But Habib claimed that it was not too late for Gulf Sargam. He had the authority to approve variation claims up to a total of $800,000 and Gulf Sargam could still make a profit. The cost of the consideration would equal $80,000, or ten percent of the claims approved for payment. Habib also pointed out that he had every right to enforce the contract agreement on Gulf Sargam, including an imposition of the contract's ten percent penalty clause should Gulf Sargam fail to complete the job on time. Tom repeated company policy on such financial arrangements, but said he would relay Habib's information to higher authorities.

CONTRACT COMPLETION

In June of 1986, you review this scenario. Gulf Sargam has completed the Moza Island contract six months behind schedule. Habib might impose the contract's penalty clause, adding another potential $300,000 to the firm's losses. Even without the penalty, your net loss amounts to $575,000 against an estimated profit of $300,000. Tom considered the situation hopeless. He said the firm must accede to Habib's request in order to recover its losses.

Joe Fernandes agreed. He reminded you that as an employee of the multinational he was obliged to take all possible steps to avoid losses to his parent company. Since Gulf Sargam had exhausted all other avenues, Joe told you to endorse the payment to Habib. He then underscored his government's interest in the performance of joint ventures. The government monitored financial results regularly, and a loss of this size would be difficult to explain. Joe's arguments are compelling but you do not feel comfortable with them.

QUESTIONS

1. Are there circumstances under which payments of this kind are not questionable?

2. How would you handle a situation like this one in which your moral reservations may cost the company money and you, your job, bonus, or promotion?

CASE 14.3
Personal Luxury or Family Loyalty?
Motorola University

Joe was a native of *Ganzpoor,* a megacity in the developing nation of *Chompu.* Joe entered this life as the first of five children of an impoverished cloth peddler. Against all odds, by means of sheer guts, hard work and ability, Joe had brought himself to the United States and managed to earn a prestigious degree in engineering from *Cornford University.* Motorola snapped him up a week after graduation, and during the next five years gave him challenging assignments in Florida, Phoenix, Scotland and Mexico. Joe had thoroughly "bought into" the Motorola Culture. Or so it seemed.

Meanwhile, Motorola's business in Chompu began taking off. The Chompu Group was eager for more engineers. But the Human Resources Office was having great difficulty finding candidates willing to accept assignment to Ganzpoor. The news of all this reached Joe, who soon began a vigorous campaign for a transfer. "Look," he argued, "I speak native Ganzpoori and near-native Chompunese, and can hit the ground running." HR saw him as a guy too good to be true: qualified both professionally and culturally. Joe got his transfer.

Upon his assignment to Ganzpoor, Joe was informed in writing that he was expected to reside in a safe and seemly residence of his choice, and would be reimbursed for the actual cost of his rent and servants, up to a maximum of $2,000 per month. "Joe, just give us your landlord's and servants' receipts, and we'll get you promptly reimbursed," explained *Pierre Picard,* a French Motorolan assigned as financial controller for Motorola/Chompu.

Joe found a place to live, but even months later, other Motorolans were not sure exactly where it was because he never seemed to entertain at home. Some of his colleagues thought this was a bit strange, but then realized that Joe hardly had time for entertain-

ing, given his executive responsibility for sourcing contracts for the construction of a new office and factory complex.

Each month Joe would send Pierre a bill for $2,000, accompanied by a rental and service receipt for exactly that amount, duly signed by his landlord. Each month Pierre would reimburse Joe accordingly. This went on for several months, until one day, a traditionally dressed Chompunese man came to see Pierre. He complained bitterly that Joe was his Master, and that Master had cheated him of his servant's wages for the past three months. At this point Pierre, despite his personal regard for Joe, had no alternative but to check into the facts of Joe's living arrangements.

Pierre and the local HR manager, *Harry Hanks,* had trouble getting the facts of the case, so finally they got a car and driver and went looking for Joe's address. It took almost two hours. The address turned out to be on the edge of a slum area of Ganzpoor, where houses were poorly marked. When they finally got there, they were shocked. Joe was living in what was, by Western standards, not much more than a shack.

Their first concern was for Joe's safety. In this part of the world, there were good reasons why transpatriates chose not to live in slums. Also, they felt, Joe's unseemly residence was hardly good for Motorola's image. Aside from these considerations, though, was the fundamental matter of simple integrity.

Harry felt he had no choice but to report the case to the regional HR director, who had no choice but to order a full-scale investigation.

When Joe learned that he was under investigation, he exploded in fury. He complained to HR that his right to personal privacy was being invaded. Further, he argued that his receipts were legitimate, despite

From R. S. Moorthy, Richard T. De George, Thomas Donaldson, William J. Ellos, Robert C. Solomon, and Robert B. Textor, *Uncompromising Integrity: Motorola's Global Challenge* (Schaumburg, IL: Motorola University Press, 1998) p. 88–89.

the fact that the investigation revealed that rent plus service in so humble a dwelling could not possibly have cost Joe more than $400 a month, and probably cost much less.

Joe finally explained: Yes, it was true that he actually paid "less than" $2,000 a month (though he refused to say how much less). But, he argued, just because he was willing to "make sacrifices" should not mean that he should receive less than the full $2,000, which "all of my fellow Motorolans receive." To clinch his defense, Joe argued, "Look, I'm a Chompunese as well as a Motorolan, and here in Chompu this kind of thing happens all the time."

The hearings officer pressed further. Finally Joe, near tears, explained that all four of his younger siblings were now of college or high school age, and that he was putting all four of them through school with the reimbursements he received from Motorola, plus a sizeable chunk of his salary. "Look," said Joe, "My family is *poor*—so poor in fact that most Westerners wouldn't believe our poverty even if they saw it. This money can mean the difference between hope and despair for all of us. For me to do anything less for my family would be to defile the honor of my late father.

"Can't you understand?"

A week later Joe was asked to step into the director's office to learn his fate. . . .

QUESTIONS

1. Do employees have a right to spend their living allowance in a foreign country any way they want?

2. If you were the director, what would you do with Joe?

CHAPTER QUESTIONS

1. What is the relationship between bribery and nepotism? What factor makes them both lead to unethical behavior?

2. What can a business do to help employees avoid conflicts of interest between their self-interest and the interests of their families, friends, and communities?

15

When the Buck Stops Here

Leadership

Introduction

Imagine that you've finally made it to the top. As CEO, you are now in a position of leadership. Leadership is a funny thing. Some people lead without holding positions of power, and some people hold positions of power but do not really lead. You are probably familiar with the "airport" how-to books on leadership and those numerous biographies and autobiographical books about famous businesspeople. They often tend to make leadership sound easy, a matter of personality or a matter of mastering a few simple techniques. But leadership is about much more than style, expertise, and technique. Leadership is ethically challenging. It requires an enormous amount of self-knowledge and self-control. Power and success can do strange things to people. They can give you a sense of entitlement or make you feel that you no longer have to play by the same rules as others. Many people dream of leading, but the truth is that not everyone is up to the job. No doubt you have noticed how some people, when given authority over others, immediately turn into petty dictators: a teacher's aide when you were in elementary school, one of your playmates who was made captain of your team or leader of your group, a graduate teaching assistant running his or her first class. It is no different in business except that the money tends to be much better. While business leadership brings with it power, money, perks, and prestige, it also brings with it the dangers of overreaching and the burdens of responsibility for the welfare of your company and all its stakeholders. Those who love the perks and ignore or neglect the burdens of caring for the company often fall hard, and the company frequently suffers, sometimes fatally (and too often the abusers float away on "golden parachutes, an enduring blot on the integrity of business and the merits of the market). Attentive leadership is time consuming and stressful. It can take its toll on you and your loved ones. It is not just a chance to enjoy power and its perks.

Corporate leaders do matter. One need only look at business scandals to see how much damage a few executives can do to a company and the people in it. By contrast, a good leader can turn around a failing organization by formulating a compelling vision for the organization. A vision is different from a goal. A company may have the goal of increasing profits by

10 percent in the next year, but the vision is about producing a more environmentally friendly and affordable product, about becoming the powerhouse leader in the industry, about reinventing the way people live or do business or get around town. Behind every vision is some notion of a greater good. It is this moral component that often motivates people in organizations. As a leader, you will not only run a company. You will model the ethical values of the company in your own behavior and demonstrate them in the people with whom you choose to surround yourself. As the leader, you will set the *ethos,* the lifestyle and the customs, as well as the ethics of the company, and set an example for the lives of your employees and perhaps even your customers. It will not be enough for you to be ethical. A corporate leader is responsible for making the company and the people in it flourish and live well. You will have to make sure that everyone who works for you understands the meaning and the moral parameters of their jobs. Managing the moral environment is one of the greatest challenges of leadership in large organizations. While you cannot micromanage or know everything, you have a moral obligation as the leader to have a good sense of what is going on. If the company gets in trouble, you are accountable, even if you did not know about the problem. It is therefore imperative that you keep informed or have a way of sniffing out trouble before it hits the market or the newspapers. We don't mean to take the joy out of your promotion, but people sometimes forget that with power and privilege comes moral responsibility. That is why it is important that you think seriously about the moral challenges of leadership before you get the job that you will probably have worked so hard all those years to get. Until you do actually make it to the top, remember that people at all levels of an organization sometimes exercise leadership, especially when it comes to questions of right and wrong. You will have many years to practice your own leadership and observe firsthand the strengths and weaknesses of how others lead, so practice, watch, and learn.

The first two articles in this chapter are about the relationship between ethics and effectiveness. We all know that good leaders get the job done. Joanne B. Ciulla argues that we have to ask for more from our leaders—they have to do the right thing, the right way, with the right intentions. Often leaders are ethical in some areas, but not in others. In a different way, Machiavelli was concerned with the same issues, only he is willing to sacrifice the fine points of ethics to get the job done. The second two readings are about the personal discipline and intentions of leaders. In "The Bathsheba Syndrome," the authors use the famous biblical story to talk about why success can make leaders not only less ethical, but less effective on the job. The last three articles in this chapter focus on the leader-follower relationship. Norman E. Bowie applies Kantian ethical principles to the practice of leadership. James MacGregor Burns and Robert Greenleaf both offer models of leadership that are based on respect for persons and on the idea that leaders are there not only to benefit their constituents, but to make their constituents morally better human beings.

The first two cases in this chapter are about the relationship between leaders and followers. We begin with George Orwell's famous short story about an elephant. For our purposes, it's about how large noisy crowds can make leaders do things that they don't want to do. When you read it, think about what personal resources leaders need to have to resist outside pressures to do things that they do not think are right. Abraham Zeleznick's description of General Patton slapping a soldier offers an opportunity to talk about the boundaries of a leader's behavior. Is it ever right for a leader to slap, yell at, insult, humiliate, or otherwise harm a subordinate in the course of his or her work? We then have a look at someone who has been regarded as a successful leader. Jack Welsh was lionized in the business press as a great business leader who made GE a profitable company year after year. In Alejo José G. Sisson's article, we see that when ethics enters into our assessment, the story of Welsh as a leader is not as impressive as the press that he has gotten in the over the years.

The next two articles are about leaders who were celebrated for doing the right thing. The first is Aaron Feuerstein, who kept paying his employees after his factory burned down, and the second is Roy Vagelos, the head of Merck, who made the decision to donate to the poorest of the poor a drug that cures river blindness. Both of these cases show that the ethics of leaders really can make a difference in people's lives. We end this chapter with the case study of Jack Stack. Norman Bowie might call Stack a "Kantian leader." Stack's leadership rests on his natural inclination to treat people with dignity; respect; or, as Kant would say, as ends. The Stack case illustrates how ethical behavior can translate into the development of innovative and highly successful organizations. This is an important story because, as we said earlier, the main challenge of leadership is to find ethical ways to be effective.

Joanne B. Ciulla | # What Is Good Leadership?

The moral triumphs and failures of leaders carry a greater weight and volume than those of nonleaders. In leadership we see morality and immorality magnified, which is why ethics is fundamental to our understanding of leadership. Ethics is about right and wrong and good and evil. It's about what we should do and what we should be like as human beings, members of a group or society, and in the different roles that we play in life. Leadership entails a particular kind of role and moral relationship between people. By understanding the ethics of leadership we gain a better understanding of what constitutes good leadership.

The point of studying leadership is to answer the question, What is good leadership? The point of teaching it is to develop good leaders. The use of the word *good* here has two senses: morally good and technically good (or effective). The problem with this notion of good leadership is that it is sometimes difficult to find both qualities in the same person. Some people are ethical, but not very effective; others are effective, but not very ethical. History only makes things more difficult. Historians don't write about the leader who was ethical but didn't do anything of significance. They rarely write about a general who was a very moral person but never won a battle. Most historians write about leaders who were winners or who changed history, for better or for worse. While leaders usually bring about change or are successful at doing something, the ethical questions waiting in the wings are: What were the leader's intentions? How did the leader go about bringing change? And was the change itself good? Leadership educators and educators in professional

Joanne B. Ciulla, "What is Good Leadership?" Center for Public Leadership Working Papers, John F. Kennedy School of Government, Harvard University, Spring, 2004, pp. 116–122. (Author holds copyright.)

schools face the challenge of seamlessly teaching students to do things right and do the right thing.

OUR FASCINATION WITH PIZZAZZ

Leadership scholars have spilled a lot of ink about the effectiveness of charismatic leaders. But as Rakesh Khurana argues in his book *Searching for a Corporate Savior: The Irrational Quest for Charismatic CEOs,* the mythical belief in the powers of charismatic leaders is overestimated when it comes to their actual effect on corporate performance.[1] Our fascination with charismatic leaders blurs the line between leaders and celebrities. As we have seen in politics, it is almost impossible for a highly competent but dry and boring person to be elected. It's certainly more fun to work with charismatic leaders, and they are more interesting to study, but it's not clear that they are always more effective than leaders with less pizzazz.

American writers used to pay more attention to the moral virtues of leaders than to their personality traits. Benjamin Franklin argued that good character was necessary for success. In his autobiography he listed eleven virtues needed for success in business and in life: temperance, silence, order, resolution, sincerity, justice, moderation, cleanliness, tranquility, chastity, and humility.[2] This list does not describe the ideal political candidate or the business leaders who frequently grace the cover of *Fortune* magazine.

In the nineteenth century, William Makepeace Thayer specialized in biographies of business and political leaders. His books focused on how the moral values that leaders formed early in life contributed to their success. Thayer summed up the moral path to success this way: "Man deviseth his own way, but the Lord directeth his steps."[3] Other eighteenth- and nineteenth-century writers preached that strong moral character was the key to leadership and wealth. By the early twentieth century the emphasis on moral character shifted to an emphasis on personality. In Dale Carnegie's 1936 classic *How to Win Friends and Influence People,* personality, not morality, was the key to success in business.[4] Until recently, this was true in the leadership research as well. Scholars were more interested in studying the personality traits of leaders than their ethics.

IT'S GREAT TO BE KING!

When you really think about it, the issue is not that leaders should be held to a *higher* moral standard, but that they should be held to the *same* standards as the rest of us. What we want and hope for are leaders who have a higher rate of success at living up to those standards than the average person. History is littered with leaders who didn't think they were subject to the same rules and standards of honesty, propriety, etc., as the rest of society. Leaders sometimes come to think that they are exceptions to the rules. It's easy to see why, given the perks and privileges that we give to leaders, whether in business, politics, or government. For example, Tyco's former CEO L. Dennis Kozlowski didn't seem to think that he should have to pay $1 million in New York State taxes on $13 million worth of art that he bought for his Fifth Avenue apartment. He simply arranged to have empty boxes and the invoices for the artwork sent to the Tyco headquarters in Exter, New Hampshire.[5] Commentators have described Kozlowski's behavior in terms of an overblown sense of entitlement or plain and simple greed. But he may have decided that he no longer had to live by the rules.

THE CHALLENGE OF CONSISTENCY

There are some areas, such as moral consistency, where leaders have to be more meticulous than ordinary people—first, because a leader's moral inconsistencies are public and more noticeable than other people's, and second, because a leader's credibility rests on some level of consistency. When leaders' actions do not match their espoused values, they lose the trust they need to be effective with various stakeholders.

Moral consistency is so important to a leader that moral *inconsistency* is the weapon of choice for character assassination. Consider the case of Tim Eyman, leader of the citizen group Permanent Offence. This group has sponsored a number of successful citizen ballot initiatives aimed at holding politicians accountable for how they spent taxpayers' dollars. In February 2002, the *Seattle Post-Intelligencer* revealed that Eyman had paid himself $45,000 of the money raised for one of his ballot initiatives. While this is not illegal, the politicians whom Eyman had often called "corrupt" seized on the issue to damage his credibility and the credibility of the causes that his organization supported. Eyman must have realized how hypocritical he looked because when confronted with the allocations, he denied that he had paid himself the money. He later confessed, saying, "I was in lie mode."[6] We generally think of hypocrites as people who express strong moral values that they do not hold and then act against them. But hypocrites are not always liars. Some really want to live up to the values they talk about, but fail to do so, either intentionally or unintentionally. This may have been Eyman's problem. Sometimes people find it difficult to live up to their own values.

MACHIAVELLIANISM AND ROBINHOODISM

We characterize effective leaders largely in terms of their ability to bring about change, for better or worse. This creates a divide between the ethics of a leader and the ethics of what the leader does. Machiavelli was disgusted by Cesare Borgia the man, but impressed by Borgia as the resolute, ferocious, and cunning prince. Borgia got the job done, but the way he did it was morally repugnant.[7] This is the classic problem of the ends justifying immoral means. Leaders don't have to be evil, greedy, or power hungry to have this moral problem. It even rears its head in charitable organizations. The fact that Robin Hood stole from the rich to give to the poor doesn't get him off the moral hook. Stealing for a good cause looks better than stealing for a bad one, but stealing is still stealing. Robinhoodism is simply Machiavellianism for nonprofits.

There are cases where leaders use appropriate means to serve the needs of some of their constituents effectively, but their beliefs are morally suspect in other areas. Trent Lott's departure as Senate majority leader offers a compelling example of this. Lott was forced to step down from his position because of insensitive racial comments that he made during a speech at the late Senator Strom Thurmond's birthday party. After the incident, some of his African American constituents were interviewed on the news. Several of them said that they would vote for Lott again, regardless of his racist beliefs, because Lott had used his power and influence in Washington to bring jobs and money to the state. In politics, the old saying "He may be a son-of-a-bitch, but he's *our* son of a bitch," captures the trade-off between ethics and effectiveness. In other words, as long as Lott accomplishes the part of the job we're interested in, we don't care about his ethics in other areas. This morally myopic view of a leader explains why people sometimes get the leaders they deserve when their "son-of-a-bitch" turns out to be a *real* son-of-a-bitch.

THE INTERSECTION OF ETHICS AND EFFECTIVENESS

The distinction between ethics and effectiveness is not always a crisp one. In certain cases being ethical *is* being effective and sometimes being effective *is* being ethical. Sometimes simply being regarded as ethical and trustworthy makes a leader effective, and at other times simply being effective makes a leader ethical. Given the limited power and resources of the secretary-general of the United Nations, it would be very difficult for someone in this position to be effective on the job if he or she did not behave ethically. In some jobs, personal integrity is a leader's sole or primary currency of power and influence. Business leaders have other sources of power that allow them to be effective, but in some situations acting ethically boosts their effectiveness. In the famous Tylenol case, manufacturer Johnson and Johnson actually increased sales of Tylenol by pulling the product off the shelves after some Tylenol had been poisoned. The leaders at Johnson and Johnson were effective at boosting sales of Tylenol *because* of the ethical way that they handled the problem.

In other cases the sheer competence of a leader has a moral effect. There were many examples of heroism in the aftermath of the terrorist attack on the World Trade Center. The most inspiring and frequently cited were the altruistic acts of rescue workers. Yet consider the case of Alan S. Weil, whose law firm, Sidley, Austin, Brown, & Wood, occupied five floors of the World Trade Center. Immediately after watching the towers fall to the ground and checking to see whether his employees got out safely, Weil got on the phone and within three hours had rented four floors of another building for his employees. By the end of the day he had arranged for an immediate delivery of eight hundred desks and three hundred computers. The next day the firm was open for business with a desk for almost every employee who wanted to work.[8] We don't know whether Mr. Weil's motives were altruistic or avaricious. Mr. Weil may have worked quickly to keep his law firm going because he didn't want to lose a day of billing, but in doing so he also filled the firm's obligations to various stakeholders. We may not like his personal reasons for acting, but in this scenario, the various stakeholders might not care because they benefited.

UNETHICAL OR STUPID?

So what can we say about leaders who do ethical things but for selfish or unethical reasons? In modernity we often separate the inner person from the outer person. John Stuart Mill saw this split between an individual's ethics and the ethics of his or her actions clearly. He said the intentions or reasons for an act tell us something about the morality of the person, but the ends of an act tell us about the morality of the action.[9] This solution doesn't really solve the ethics-and-effectiveness problem. It simply reinforces the split between the personal morality of a leader and what he or she does as a leader. If the various stakeholders knew that Weil had selfish intentions, they would, as Mill said, think less of him but not less of his actions. This is sometimes the case in business. When a business runs a campaign to raise money for the homeless, it may be doing so to sell more of its products or improve its public image. Yet it would be harsh to say that the business shouldn't hold the charity drive and raise needed funds for the homeless.

Sometimes it is unethical (and just mean spirited) to demand perfect moral intentions. Nonetheless, personally unethical leaders who do good things for their constituents are still problematic. Even though they might provide for the greatest good, once their unethical intentions are public, people can never really trust them, even if they benefit.

In some situations it is difficult to tell whether leaders are unethical or stupid. They can be incompetent in terms of their knowledge or skill or incompetent in terms of their ability to identify, solve, or prioritize moral problems. There are times when leaders get their facts wrong or think that they are acting ethically when, in fact, they are not. For example, in 2000, President Thabo Mbeki of South Africa issued a statement saying that it was not clear that HIV caused AIDS. He believed the pharmaceutical industry was just trying to scare people so that it could increase its profits.[10] Coming from the leader of a country where about one in five people tests positive for HIV, this was a shocking statement. His stance outraged public health experts and other citizens. Mbeki understood the scientific literature but chose to put political and philosophical reasons ahead of scientific knowledge. (He has since backed away from this position.) When leaders do things like this, we want to know whether they are unethical or misinformed. Mbeki was not misinformed. He knew the AIDS literature but chose to focus on work by researchers who held this minority opinion. His actions appeared unethical, but he may have thought he was taking an ethical stand; however, it was the wrong ethical stand on the wrong ethical issue. His comments demonstrated a misplaced sense of moral priorities. Political concerns about big business and the way the world sees South Africa may have led him to recklessly disregard his more pressing obligations to stop the AIDS epidemic.

In other situations leaders act with moral intentions, but because they are incompetent, the way they solve a problem creates an unethical outcome. For instance, consider the unfortunate case of the Swiss charity Christian Solidarity International. Its goal was to free an estimated 200,000 Dinka children who were enslaved in Sudan. The charity paid between $35 and $75 a head to free the enslaved children. The unintended consequence of their actions was that by creating a market for slavery, they actually encouraged it. The price of slaves and the demand for them went up. Also, some cunning Sudanese found that it paid to pretend that they were slaves; they could make money by being liberated again and again.[11] This deception made it difficult for the charity to distinguish those who really needed help from those who were faking it. Here the charity's intent and the means it used to achieve its goals were not unethical in relation to alleviating suffering in the short run; however, in the long run, the charity inadvertently created more suffering.

BLINDING MORALITY

We want leaders who possess strong moral convictions, but there are times when leaders' moral convictions are too strong and they undercut both their ethics and their effectiveness. Leaders with overzealous moral convictions can be far more dangerous than amoral or immoral leaders. Consider the recent response of the Catholic Church hierarchy to cases of sexual abuse. Many Church leaders still held the medieval view that they could play by different rules than the rest of society, in part because they were the "good guys." The sexual abuse of children is one of the most heinous crimes in our society; however, some church leaders treated it differently because it involved people who "do God's work." Overly moralistic leaders sometimes confuse working for God with being God, usually with disastrous results.

Self-righteousness can also blind leaders to the more mundane things that they need to do in order to be effective. They become so impassioned with the moral rightness of their cause that they forget what they have learned in other areas of life or fail to get the expertise they need to do their job. This is as true today as it was in the past. The story of Magellan, the first navigator to circumvent the globe, is one such case. Magellan led his three ships down the South American coast and on a 12,600-mile journey across the Pacific Ocean. When he arrived in the Philippines, he took up the Spanish cause of spreading Christianity. He began baptizing native leaders and gaining their allegiance to Spain. Magellan's religious fervor became so great that he started to think that he could perform miracles. He then took up the cause of a baptized chief in an unnecessary battle against an unbaptized chief on the island of Mactan. Magellan's seasoned marines would not join him in the battle, so he organized a ragtag group of cooks and other apprentices to fight. The battle was a disaster. Before attacking the island, Magellan failed to get information on the tides. Hence, one of the greatest navigators in the world met his demise waist deep in water, weighed down by heavy armor and unprotected by his ships, which were helplessly anchored outside the reef, too far away to provide him with cover.[12] All this because he thought mundane details and planning were not necessary when you had God on your side.

The story of Magellan shows us how even brilliant leaders can believe so much in the moral rightness of their goals that they don't listen to others or take mundane precautions to achieve their goals. This case is a dramatic way to think about the mistakes that nonprofit leaders sometimes make, such as having earnest but unqualified volunteers keep the books or assuming that when providing meals for the homeless, it is not necessary to follow standard health procedures in the kitchen. Leaders have a moral obligation to consult with experts, get their facts straight, and take care in planning. This is where ethics and effectiveness converge. The line between being incompetent and unethical is often very thin.

Professional schools are good at teaching students what they know, but they are not as good at teaching them what they don't know. Leadership requires a mixture of confidence and humility. It is about how well leaders understand the limitations of their knowledge and personal perspective. Good leadership calls for people who are confident enough to ask for help, admit they are wrong, and invite debate and discussion. Good leadership also requires humility. Leaders are imperfect human beings who are put in jobs where the moral margin of error is much smaller because the effect of their actions on others is greater. That is why good leaders need knowledge, self-knowledge, ethics, confidence, humility, and a lot of help from people who will tell them the truth.

NOTES

1. Khurana, Rahesh. (2002). *Searching for the Corporate Savior/The Irrational Quest for Charismatic CEOs.* (Princeton): Princeton University Press.

2. Franklin, Benjamin (1964). *The Autobiography of Benjamin Franklin,* ed. Leonard W. Larabee, et.al. (New Haven): Yale University Press.

3. Thayer, quoted in Huber, R. M. (1971). *The American Idea of Success* (New York): McGraw-Hill, p. 53.

4. Carnegie, Dale. (1981). *How to Win Friends and Influence People.* (New York): Pocket Books.

5. Maremont, M., & Markon, J. "Ex-Tyco Chief Evaded $1 Million in Taxes on Art, Indictment Says," *Wall Street Journal,* June 5, 2002, A1.

6. "A Watchdog Who Got Watched," *The Economist,* February 9, 2002, p. 29.

7. Prezzolini Giuseppe. (1928). Ralph Roeder (trans.) *Nicolo Machiavelli, the Florentine.* (New York): Brentanos.

8. Schwartz, J. "Up from the Ashes, One Firm Rebuilds," *New York Times,* September 16, 2001: Section 3, p. 1.

9. Mill, John Stuart (1987). "What Utilitarianism Is." Alan Ryan (ed), *Utilitarianism and Other Essays,* (New York): Penguin Books, 276–297.

10. Garrett, L. "Added Foe in AIDS War: Skeptics," Newsday, March 29, 2000: News Section, A6.

11. "A Funny Way to End the Slave trade; Slavery in Sudan," *The Economist,* February 9, 2002, p. 42.

12. Manchester, W. (1993). *A World Lit Only by Fire.* (Boston): Little, Brown.

QUESTIONS

1. How is ethical leadership related to effective leadership in business?

2. Is it unethical for an incompetent person to hold a leadership position?

Niccolo Machiavelli | # Is It Better to Be Loved than Feared?

Niccolo Machiavelli was the most influential political philosopher of the Italian Renaissance.

And here comes in the question whether it is better to be loved rather than feared, or feared rather than loved. It might perhaps be answered that we should wish to be both; but since love and fear can hardly exist together, if we must choose between them, it is far safer to be feared than loved. For of men it may generally be affirmed that they are thankless, fickle, false, studious to avoid danger, greedy of gain, devoted to you while you are able to confer benefits upon them, and ready, as I said before, while danger is distant, to shed their blood, and sacrifice their property, their lives, and their children for you; but in the hour of need they turn against you. The Prince, therefore, who without otherwise securing himself builds wholly on their professions is undone. For the friendships which we buy with a price, and do not gain by greatness and nobility of character, though they be fairly earned are not made good, but fail us when we have occasion to use them.

Moreover, men are less careful how they offend him who makes himself loved than him who makes himself feared. For love is held by the tie of obligation, which, because men are a sorry breed, is broken on every whisper of private interest; but fear is bound by the apprehension of punishment which never relaxes.

Nevertheless a Prince should inspire fear in such a

Niccolo Machiavelli, *The Prince,* translated by Hill Thompson, (The Limited Editions Club, 1954), pp. 123–124 and 127–129.

fashion that if he do not win love he may escape hate. For a man may very well be feared and yet not hated, and this will be the case so long as he does not meddle with the property or with the women of his citizens and subjects. And if constrained to put any to death, he should do so only when there is manifest cause or reasonable justification. But, above all, he must abstain from the property of others. For men will sooner forget the death of their father than the loss of their patrimony. Moreover, pretexts for confiscation are never to seek, and he who has once begun to live by rapine always finds reasons for taking what is not his; whereas reasons for shedding blood are fewer.

But when a Prince is with his army, and has many soldiers under his command, he must needs disregard the reproach of cruelty, for without such a reputation in its Captain, no army can be held together or kept under any kind of control. Among other things remarkable in Hannibal this has been noted, that having a very great army, made up of men of many different nations and brought to fight in a foreign country, no dissension ever arose among the soldiers themselves, nor any mutiny against their leader, either in his good or in his evil fortunes. This we can only ascribe to the transcendent cruelty, which, joined with numberless great qualities, rendered him at once venerable and terrible in the eyes of his soldiers; for without this reputation for cruelty these other virtues would not have produced the like results.

Unreflecting writers, indeed, while they praise his achievements, have condemned the chief cause of them; but that his other merits would not by themselves have been so efficacious we may see from the case of Scipio, one of the greatest Captains, not of his own time only but of all times of which we have record, whose armies rose against him in Spain from no other cause than his too great leniency in allowing them a freedom inconsistent with military strictness. With which weakness Fabius Maximus taxed him in the Senate House, calling him the corrupter of the Roman soldiery. Again, when the Locrians were shamefully outraged by one of his lieutenants, he neither avenged them, nor punished the insolence of his officer; and this from the natural easiness of his disposition. So that it was said in the Senate by one who sought to excuse him, that there were many who knew better how to refrain from doing wrong themselves than how to correct the wrong-doing of others. This temper, however, must in time have marred the name and fame even of Scipio, had he continued in it, and retained his command. But living as he did under the control of the Senate, this hurtful quality was not merely disguised, but came to be regarded as a glory.

Returning to the question of being loved or feared, I sum up by saying, that since his being loved depends upon his subjects, while his being feared depends upon himself, a wise Prince should build on what is his own, and not on what rests with others. Only, as I have said, he must do his utmost to escape hatred.

Be it known, then, that there are two ways of contending, one in accordance with the laws, the other by force; the first of which is proper to men, the second to beasts. But since the first method is often ineffectual, it becomes necessary to resort to the second. A Prince should, therefore, understand how to use well both the man and the beast. And this lesson has been covertly taught by the ancient writers, who relate how Achilles and many others of these old Princes were given over to be brought up and trained by Chiron the Centaur; since the only meaning of their having for instructor one who was half man and half beast is, that it is necessary for a Prince to know how to use both natures, and that the one without the other has no stability.

But since a Prince should know how to use the beast's nature wisely, he ought of beasts to choose both the lion and the fox; for the lion cannot guard himself from the toils, nor the fox from wolves. He must therefore be a fox to discern toils, and a lion to drive off wolves.

To rely wholly on the lion is unwise; and for this reason a prudent Prince neither can nor ought to keep his word when to keep it is hurtful to him and the causes which led him to pledge it are removed. If all men were good, this would not be good advice, but since they are dishonest and do not keep faith with you, you, in return, need not keep faith with

To: You
From: The Philosopher
Subject: "Lao Tzu and *Tao-te-ching*"

Now that you've moved to the corner office, you're going to have to get used to having people dislike you—as a matter of fact, some people will hate you. That's part of the job. People hate leaders when they behave unethically and sometimes even when they behave ethically. Leaders have to focus on doing the right thing, not trying to please everyone. That is one reason why Machiavelli said that it is better to be feared than to be loved, but the ancient Chinese philosopher Lao Tzu disagreed with him. Lao Tzu believed that leaders should be loved and that they should respect their followers.

> The best (rulers) are those whose existence is (merely) known by the people.
> The next best are those who are loved and praised.
> The next are those who are feared.
> And the next are those who are despised.
> It is only when one does not have enough faith in others that others have no faith in him.*

Lao Tzu also realized that when people get power, they act like arrogant jerks. That's why he thinks that "lovable leaders" are modest. He writes:

> He who stands on tiptoe is not steady.
> He who strides forward does not go.
> He who shows himself is not luminous.
> He who justifies himself is not prominent.
> He who boasts of himself is not given credit.
> He who brags does not endure for long.**

*Lao Tzu, "The Lao Tzu (Tao-te-ching)" from Wing-Tist Chan (ed.), *A Source Book in Chinese Philosophy* (Princeton, N.J.: Princeton University Press, 1963), p. 148.

**Ibid., p. 152.

them; and no prince was ever at a loss for plausible reasons to cloak a breach of faith. Of this numberless recent instances could be given, and it might be shown how many solemn treaties and engagements have been rendered inoperative and idle through want of faith in Princes, and that he who was best known to play the fox has had the best success. It is necessary, indeed, to put a good colour on this nature, and to be skilful in simulating and dissembling.

But men remain so simple, and governed so absolutely by their present needs, that he who wishes to deceive will never fail in finding willing dupes. One recent example I will not omit. Pope Alexander VI had no care or thought but how to deceive, and always found material to work on. No man ever had a more effective manner of asseverating, or ever made promises with more solemn protestations, or observed them less. And yet, because he understood this side of human nature, his frauds always succeeded.

It is not essential then, that a Prince should have all the good qualities which I have enumerated above, but it is most essential that he should seem to have them; I will even venture to affirm that if he has and invariably practices them all, they are hurtful, whereas the appearance of having them is useful. Thus, it is well to seem merciful, faithful, humane, religious, and upright, and also to be so; but the mind should remain so balanced that were it needful not to be so, you should be able and know how to change to the contrary.

QUESTIONS

1. What moral qualities does Machiavelli think a leader should have?

2. In today's world, is it enough for leaders simply to appear ethical?

Dean C. Ludwig
and Clinton O. Longnecker

The Bathsheba Syndrome: The Ethical Failure of Successful Leaders

Dean C. Ludwig and Clinton O. Longnecker teach at the University of Toledo.

THE STORY OF DAVID AND BATHSHEBA

Most individuals are at least vaguely familiar with the story of David and Bathsheba, but we would especially like to point out some of the details leading up to David's violation and point out how in many ways the story of David and Bathsheba is paradigmatic for many of the ethical failures of successful leaders which we witness today. How did David, a good, talented, and successful leader, get entangled in this downward spiral of events? The scriptural accounts provide some insight, and offer food for thought for today's leaders.

David loses strategic focus in success. The story of David and Bathsheba begins by noting that David is not where he is supposed to be, doing what he is supposed to be doing. His recent successes in battle have apparently left David complacent—complacent that his overall strategy did not need revision for the time being and complacent that his subordinates were capable of executing the current strategy on their own. Instead of leading his troops into battle as was his role as king, he stayed home, leaving the direction of his troops during critical battles to his right hand man, Joab. David was apparently comfortable that Joab would be able to handle things.

How often today we see executives lead their organizations to the top of the competitive heap, displaying exceptional courage, energy, and leadership, only then to put their organizations on autopilot, kick-back, and indulge themselves for all of the sacrifices they have made along the way. Their set-up for ethical failure begins by not being where they are supposed to be. Not only does this expose the *leader* to potential conflict, but by not being with the troops through a time of crisis and competition, it opens the door to questionable ethical behavior by subordinates.

David's failure of leadership is certainly not that he delegated (though the accounts indicate that it was a king's duty to be with his troops in battle). Rather,

Journal of Business Ethics **12**:265–273, 1993. © 1993 *Kluwer Academic Publishers. Printed in the Netherlands.* References were deleted from the text.

David delegated and then ignored what was happening. He did not give supervision to Joab. In addition, David seemed to be delegating not out of a sense of necessity but out of a sense of self-indulgence. That is, David was delegating not because he needed to free time for other duties, but because he wanted more time for leisure (the accounts indicate that David was just rising from bed as evening came). David may have felt he needed or deserved a break after his earlier conquests; it is interesting that he did not feel his troops also needed or deserved to share in this break.

David's success leads to privileged access. As was mentioned, David's leisure allowed him the opportunity, literally, to look around. He was not focused on organizational decision making. Instead, his lack of pre-occupation allowed him to see things he otherwise wouldn't have noticed. Second, his privileged position, high atop the roof of the palace, allowed him to see things that were sheltered to those at lower levels. It would have been clear to someone at a lower level that violation of Bathsheba's privacy was wrong, for they would have somehow had to circumvent the wall that separated her bath from public view. It was easy, however, for David to forget that it was not his right to view this beautiful woman at bath. His privileged vantage point was designed to give him a perspective—a view—that would help him lead his people, not a view that would feed his self-indulgence. By this point, David's lack of involvement in the leadership combined with his privileged position, allowed him to shift his focus to the satisfaction of personal wants.

Many of the scandals we have witnessed in recent years have evolved from privileged access to information, people and objects and from leaders' apparent inability to understand that their privileged position is supposed to give them a perspective from which they can more effectively lead—not from which they can more effectively satisfy personal wants.

David's success leads to control of resources and inflated belief in personal ability to control outcomes. The story of David and Bathsheba unfolds through a degenerative progression of indulgence and cover-up. As the story of David and Bathsheba develops, David sends servants to investigate who this beautiful woman was that he saw from his roof.

When he found that she was not only married, but married to one of his officers, he knew it would be a grave offense to take her to his bed. Yet, her husband was off in battle, and the servants, knowing the consequences, could certainly be counted on for silence. David sends for Bathsheba, sleeps with her, and she become pregnant.

In the hopes of covering this violation, David brings Bathsheba's husband in from the battlefield under the false pretense of finding out the state of battle. After months in the field, he hopes Uriah will sleep with his wife, but noble Uriah decides it would be inappropriate while his comrades are still in battle. David then gets Uriah drunk in the hope that he will sleep with his wife, but he doesn't. Finally, David gives Uriah a message to carry back to Joab, the commander of the battle. The message is Uriah's death sentence—it tells Joab to send Uriah to the front of the fiercest battle and then withdraw, leaving Uriah and other innocents to die. After Uriah's death, David sent word to Joab not to let what had just happened seem evil in his sight. Smug in his cover-up, David then took Bathsheba into his house as his wife. It was the prophet Nathan, an outsider to the events, who finally exposed David.

David, in short, chose to do something he knew was clearly wrong in the firm belief that through his personal power and control over resources he could cover up. David's inflated, self-confident belief in his own personal ability to manipulate the outcome of this story is probably representative of the attitude of many of today's professionally trained managers of business. Trained in attitude and technique to "get things done" and "make things happen," today's business school graduates often possess a dangerously inflated self-confidence. Reinforced by success, given increasing control of resources, and subjected to decreasing levels of supervision, these managers too often stumble as they move into leadership roles.

SUCCESS AS AN ANTECEDENT TO ETHICAL FAILURE

We have outlined four by-products of success—loss of strategic focus, privileged access, control of resources, and inflated belief in ability to manipulate

	Positive/Benefit	Negative/Disadvantage
Personal Level	**Privileged Access** Position Influence Status Rewards/Perks Recognition Latitude Associations Access	**Inflated Belief in Personal Ability** Emotionally Expansive Unbalanced Personal Life Inflated Ego Isolation Stress Transference Emptiness Fear of Failure

Organizational Level	**Control of Resources**
	
	No Direct Supervision
	Ability to Influence
	Ability to set Agenda
	Control Over
	    Decision Making
		Loss of Strategic Focus
		
		Org on Autopilot
		Delegation without
		    Supervision
		Strategic Complacency
		Neglect of Strategy

Figure 2   Possible outcomes experienced by successful leaders.

outcomes—and we have looked at the dynamics of these by-products in the life of David. We have noted that privileged access and control of resources are, when kept within reason, positive, justified, strategic perquisites of success. Privileged access is essential for comprehensive strategic vision. Control of resources is necessary for the execution of strategy.

On the other hand, we have suggested that the other two by-products—loss of strategic focus and inflated belief in personal ability to control outcomes—are essentially negative. Further, we suggest (as shown in Figure 2) that privileged access and inflated belief in personal ability are primarily personal issues, while control of resources and loss of strategic focus are primarily organizational issues.

We suggest that several explosive combinations can be found within this matrix. First, when loss of strategic focus is coupled with privileged access, the door is opened for real abuse of some of the personal perquisites associated with success. Position and status are suddenly used to promote non-strategic, non-organizational purposes. An even more explosive combination occurs when control of resources is coupled with an inflated belief in personal ability to manipulate outcomes.

THE DARK SIDE OF SUCCESS

Success is the goal of every leader—both personal success and organizational success. Very often the two are intimately intertwined. Paradoxically, embedded in success may be the very seeds that could lead to the downfall of both the leader and the organization.

On a *personal* level the *benefits* of success to a leader are obvious to even the casual observer. Greater power and influence, increased status, a heightened sense of personal achievement, greater rewards and perks, and more personal latitude on the job are all by-products that come to leaders who can make things happen in their organization. We have summed all of these under the heading "privileged access." When a leader has proven him or herself to the organization, a host of *organizational* benefits tend to accompany this status. Leaders are granted greater control of resources and decision processes; they have increased access to information, people, and things; they are permitted to set their own agendas and have every worker's dream come true— no direct supervision. The combination of personal and organizational benefits that accompany success are indeed the very reasons all of us want to be successful. In a nutshell, success leads to increasing levels of power, influence, rewards, status, and control. None of these should in and of themselves be seen as negative.

Less readily apparent is the personal "dark side" of success—a side that is only recently being addressed by executive psychologists and is still seldom talked about. When leaders climb the organizational ladder and appear to have it all, they are confronted with a host of negatives that affect them on a very personal level. These negatives come in a variety of shapes and forms and affect leaders differently. The negatives of success may not appear to be obvious to most of us, but they nonetheless come with the territory of successful leadership. Collectively, they might be labeled as factors that are associated with an unbalanced personal life and a loss of touch with reality. In this paper we have focused on one of their major manifestations: an inflated sense of personal ability (and sometimes desire) to manipulate outcomes.

Literature on executive psychology describes a variety of negative dynamics associated with success. Successful leaders can often become emotionally expansive, which is to say that their appetite for success, thrills, gratification, and control becomes insatiable. Thus they lose their ability to be satisfied with their current status and they desire more of everything. Secondly, they can experience personal isolation and a lack of intimacy in their lives. Inability to share their problems and long hours away from home can cause leaders to be isolated from their families and friends, losing a valuable source of personal balance. In addition, leaders find themselves without peers at work and can find making friends at work difficult. Many of these leaders literally lose touch with reality.

Furthermore, the status can bring with it increased stress and, at times, the fear of failure which can cause a leader to experience extreme levels of anxiety. It is one thing to make it to the top, but many leaders are not prepared for what it takes to stay there. At the same time leaders can experience the "emptiness syndrome"—after working hard for years and finally "making it," they take a step back and ask themselves "is this all there is to success?" They have success, but they don't experience it in a meaningful way on a personal level which can cause them to seek other ways to satisfy their needs.

Many times all of this simply adds up to an inflated sense of ego. This egocentricity can cause the leader to become abrasive, close-minded, disrespectful, and prone to extreme displays of negative emotion, all of which are warning signs along the road to megalomania (or the "I am the center of the universe phenomenon").

We are not suggesting that all successful leaders fall prey to these negatives that are frequently associated with success, but rather want to make the case that success can bring with it some very negative emotional baggage. When we couple these negatives that affect leaders on a very personal basis with the organizational benefits of success discussed earlier, they create a rather potent combination for unethical behavior on the part of the successful leader. When we combine extreme organizational autonomy and control with a personal emotional state that is possibly inflated, isolated, or emotionally expansive, it is not hard to see how successful leaders frequently make unethical choices which not only harm them personally but contain the potential to destroy or severely damage the organizations they are responsible for protecting.

In in the case of King David, we see both of these propensities in operation. We see a leader with complete free rein and a man who was apparently more concerned with personal gratification (at this particular moment in time) than with the responsibilities of being an effective leader. David clearly believed in his own ability to cover-up his wrong-doing. And as was addressed at length earlier in this paper, we also saw in David the explosive combination of privileged access combined with a loss of focus. David's inability to handle the by-products of success left him extremely vulnerable to ethical failure.

This ethical failure cost David dearly: the death of the child he bore with Bathsheba; the loss of his commander, Joab, who would later betray him; internal strife and conflict in his household for years to come; the loss of respect in his kingdom that led to future leadership problems; the loss of valuable fighting men and morale among his troops; and extreme personal guilt that he was continually forced to live with.

All of these dynamics created even less balance in David's life. David was finally confronted with his ethical failure by the prophet Nathan (who was in this case the equivalent of a modern day whistle-blower) who led David to realize that his cover-up had been a failure. Even kings who fail to provide ethical leadership are eventually found out.

Whenever a modern leader falls prey to the Bathsheba Syndrome they are knowingly setting themselves and their organizations up for a fall whether they believe it or not. The lessons from David's sad experience are obvious:

1. Leaders are in their positions to focus on doing what is right for their organization's short-term

---

To: You
From: The Philosopher
Subject: "Plato on Why Ethical People Don't Want to be Leaders"

I think that you've wanted to move up into this job for a long time, but you've been very careful not to say it out loud. You've probably noticed that people are sometimes uncomfortable with those who seem a little too eager to take on leadership roles. Plato said that we are uneasy with such people because we worry that they are in it for their own interests, not the interests of their constituencies. According to Plato, ethical people have to be compelled to lead. Here is what he says:

> Therefore good people won't be willing to rule for the sake of either money or honor. They don't want to be paid wages openly for ruling and get called hired hands nor take them in secret from their rule and be called thieves. And they won't rule for the sake of honor, because they aren't ambitious honor-lovers. So, if they are willing to rule, some compulsion or punishment must be brought to bear on them—perhaps that's why it is thought shameful to seek to rule before one is compelled to. Now, the greatest punishment, if one isn't willing to rule, is to be ruled by someone worse than one-self. And I think that it's fear of this that makes decent people rule when they do. They approach ruling not as something good or something to be enjoyed, but as something necessary, since it can't be entrusted to anyone better than—or even as good as—themselves. In a city of good men, if it came into being, citizens would fight in order not to rule, just as they do now in order to rule. There it would be quite clear that anyone who is really a true ruler doesn't by nature seek his own advantage, but that of his subjects. And everyone knowing this, would rather be benefited by others than take the trouble to benefit them.

—Plato (*Republic,* 347b3–347e5)

and long-term success. This can't happen if they aren't where they are supposed to be, doing what they are supposed to be doing.

2. There will always be temptations that come in a variety of shapes and forms that will tempt leaders to make decisions they know they shouldn't make. With success will come additional ethical trials.

3. Perpetrating an unethical act is a personal, conscious choice on the part of the leader that frequently places a greater emphasis on personal gratification rather than on the organization's needs.

4. It is difficult if not impossible to partake in unethical behavior without implicating and/or involving others in the organization.

5. Attempts to cover-up unethical practices can have dire organizational consequences including innocent people getting hurt, power being abused, trust being violated, other individuals being corrupted, and the diversion of needed resources.

6. Not getting caught initially can produce self-delusion and increase the likelihood of future unethical behavior.

7. Getting caught can destroy the leader, the organization, innocent people, and everything the leader has spent his/her life working for.

CONCLUSIONS

In closing, some advice to successful leaders is warranted. First, it could happen to you. David was an intelligent, principled individual. So, too are many of your colleagues that you read about in the paper these days. It is not simply the unprincipled and those under competitive pressure who fall victim to ethical violation. Stand forewarned of David's painful experience and read the papers for constant reminders that the chances of being caught have never been greater. Second, realize that living a balanced life reduces the likelihood of the negatives of success causing you to lose touch with reality. Family, relationships, and interests other than work must all be cultivated for

long-term success to be meaningful. Third, understand that your primary function is to provide strategic direction and leadership at all levels. Avoid becoming complacent with strategic direction and current performance. Strategic direction is never "set," no matter how successful. The privilege and status that has been granted to you is designed to enhance your strategic vision. It is not simply reward for a job already accomplished. Likewise, control of organizational resources has been given to you so that you can execute strategy—not to feed personal gratification. Fourth, build an ethical team of managers around you who will inspire you to lead by example and who will challenge or comfort you when you need either. Finally, ethical leadership is simply part of good leadership and requires focus, the appropriate use of resources, trust, effective decision making, and provision of model behavior that is worth following. Once it is lost it is difficult if not impossible to regain.

Several observations are also in order for boards of directors and others responsible for overseeing organizational leaders. First, board involvement should include concern for the leader's personal/psychological balance. Support for the leader's psychological well-being can be displayed via forced vacations, outside activities, and periodic visits to counselors and/or psychologists to help the leader keep both feet firmly planted on the ground. Second, boards should erect guard-rails. Detection is the primary factor that deters unethical behavior. Organizations should thus make prudent use of such devices as regularly scheduled audits of critical organizational decision processes and resources. Organizations should also consider the use of ombudsmen for employees who might be willing to uncover unethical acts. Third, boards must clearly establish and implement ethical codes of conduct for organizational leaders and take steps to regularly heighten both the awareness and compliance with such standards. Clearly even successful leaders need both the input, direction, and support of a governing body to be prevented from falling into the dark side of success.

Finally, for those engaged in business ethics training we suggest a broadened understanding of why leaders/managers sometimes abandon their own principles. Do we too quickly focus on the maintenance of ethical behavior in the face of competitive pressure? Should we also discuss the maintenance of ethical behavior in the face of success? Is adherence to principle in either the face of competitive pressure or the wake of success a matter of ethics or of virtue? If success leads to increased levels of power, then we must take steps to deal with the phenomenon that "power corrupts." Researchers and academicians must look

for creative ways to prevent this from occurring while not limiting the ability of leaders to lead.

QUESTIONS

1. In the story of David and Bathsheba, where does King David most abuse his power as a leader?

2. In recent business and political scandals, what leaders seem to have fallen prey to the Bathsheba syndrome?

Norman E. Bowie | # A Kantian Theory of Leadership

Norman E. Bowie is a professor of management at the University of Minnesota.

One might think that a Kantian theory of leadership is as much an oxymoron as business ethics itself. After all, it is a conceptual truth that a leader must have followers. Moreover, people tend to think that a follower is of lesser rank than a leader. For many the term "leader" has hierarchical and even élitist connotations. Kant's moral philosophy, on the other hand, is basically egalitarian. It is Kant who provides the intellectual justification for the respect for persons principle. Kant points out that each person thinks of himself or herself as a rational creature who is entitled to dignity and respect. Consistency then requires that each person recognize the rational nature of other persons and thus recognize that other persons are also entitled to be treated with dignity and respect. This is why Kant argues that one cannot use another as a means merely. In yet another formulation of the categorical imperative Kant argues that in a community or organization we are bound by rules but by rules that we ourselves would accept as rational legislators. Thus in

such communities, which Kant calls kingdoms of ends, the members are all equally subject and sovereign. Given these egalitarian commitments, how can Kant provide a theory of leadership when "leadership" has connotations of élitism and hierarchy? Suggesting a way out of this dilemma is the subject of this paper.

———

In this section I defend the claim that Kantian leadership supports the development of autonomy both in his or her followers as well as in himself or herself. The implementation of such a view requires that the leader turn followers into leaders. In other words the leader transforms the relationships in an organization so that those who had been followers could now be considered leaders.

Thus far the Kantian theory of leadership I have presented has been negative. I have shown that certain well-received views of leadership are not acceptable on Kantian grounds. Prominent among these failed views are charismatic leadership, servant leadership, and instrumental leadership. Theories of

The Leadership & Organization Development Journal 21/4 [2000] 185–193 © MCB University Press [ISSN 0143-7739] Notes and references were deleted from the text.

transformational leadership and the leader as teacher have proved more promising, but only if constrained by certain features of Kant's moral philosophy. However, I think a Kantian theory of leadership is more robust than standard transformational or leader as teacher theories. I believe that Kantian moral theory provides the tools to construct a positive theory of leadership that shares many features with transformational leadership and with the model of the leader as a teach but that is unique in its own right.

I propose that the kingdom of ends formulation of the categorical imperative is the key to a positive theory of leadership just as the second formulation was the key for a negative theory (a theory of telling us what leadership is not). The kingdom of ends formulation asserts that "One should act as one were a member of an ideal kingdom of ends in which one was subject and sovereign at the same time". Kant recognized that human beings interacted with other human beings (ends). Thus the arena of interaction was called a "kingdom of ends". A business organization, like any other organization, is composed of individual persons and since persons are moral creatures, the interaction of persons in an organization are moral interactions and thus are subject to moral law. On Kant's view a business relationship cannot be simply economic; business interactions are interactions among person and thus they are always subject to morality as well. And as we have seen the relation between leaders and followers cannot simply be transactional.

What are the laws, which govern those interactions? Kant maintained that since those interactions were the interactions of human beings and not billiard balls, laws made by human beings themselves should govern them. Thus the laws should reflect the fact that the members of the organization are autonomous and rational in the practical sense. The laws that govern the interactions of persons should be self-legislated. Of course those laws ought to be consistent with the requirements of morality as spelled out in the first two formulations of the categorical imperative. Thus the laws must be capable of being universally applied and respect the humanity in a person as an end rather than as a means merely.

Subjection to moral law equally applies when the interaction is within an organization including business organizations. Leaders interact with followers and thus these interactions are subject to moral rules. From the negative point of view or in the sense of things forbidden, leadership interactions cannot violate the categorical imperative. But interactions between leaders and followers need more guiding norms than that. The third formulation of the categorical imperative provides the moral requirement for adopting these other norms. It provides a positive view of what the norms governing a kingdom of ends should be. Basically it says these norms cannot be simply imposed on the basis of power or superiority of position. The norm must be the kind of norm that could in principle receive the assent of all rational moral beings. Thus there is a sense in which the norms that govern an organization must be acceptable to all. That is what it means to say that all individuals including leaders and followers are both subject and sovereign with respect to the norms that govern them.

The third formulation acts as a significant restraint on leadership as it is traditionally understood. Many think of the leader as the boss—as the person who makes the decisions. A Kantian does not accept that view. To be consistent with the kingdom of ends formulation of the categorical imperative, the leader is a decision proposer rather than a decision imposer. The leader in an organization can propose ends as well as means for reaching those ends. He or she can propose decision-making rules as well. But the leader should not order these things or impose them on the basis of his or her power. In management terms the leader creates the conditions for participative management. In less scholarly terminology, the Kantian leader gets buy-in. But the buy-in is not based on charisma. Neither is it based on power or position. Rather it is based on the merits of the proposal. The rules that govern human interactions should be rules that are acceptable to all.

But isn't participative management the abandonment of leadership? And even if it weren't, wouldn't such leadership lead to chaos. If you need universal buy-in for every decision that is made in an organization, you have anarchy and the organization will surely fail. That is certainly true, but universal buy-in is not required for every decision under a Kantian theory of leadership. We need to distinguish among the following:

1. the individual decision, e.g. how many motors should we order,
2. the norm for making a decision, e.g. should that decision be left to the purchasing department; and
3. how should we decide how the norms in (2) should be made.

At a minimum I think a Kantian theory of leadership requires that the norms in (3) meet the conditions of the third formulation of the categorical imperative. Respecting a legislator in the kingdom of ends requires at least that much. Moreover, I think that as an ideal the Kantian leader should get assent for norms and decisions as often as possible and as far down into the organization as possible. The following principles may guide a leader as he or she attempts to transform an organization into a kingdom of ends:

1. The leader should consider the interests of all the affected stakeholders in any decision it makes.
2. The leader should have those affected by the firm's rules and policies participate in the determination of those rules and policies before they are implemented.
3. It should not be the case that the leader always gives the interests of one stakeholder group priority.
4. When a situation arises where it appears that the humanity of one set of stakeholders must be sacrificed for the humanity of another set of stakeholders, the leader cannot make the decision on the grounds that there is a greater number of people in one stakeholder group than in another.
5. Every leader must in cooperation with others in the organization establish procedures to ensure that relations among stakeholders are governed by rules of justice.

The first principle is a straightforward requirement that leaders take respect for persons seriously. The criterion says that leaders should take the moral point of view. Most philosophers agree that the moral point of view involves at least the commitment to take into account the interests of those affected by our actions. It seems to me that it is a principle that all rational persons would adopt.

The second principle provides a practical way for the leader to respect the autonomy of followers. Rather than simply give orders, the leader encourages followers to participate and thus the leader begins the transformation from mere followers, that is from followers who follow blindly, to persons who can coordinate their goals and interests with others so that the objectives of the organization are obtained.

The third principle functions as a principle of legitimacy. It insures that all those involved in the firm receive some minimum benefit from being part of the organization. The principle reminds us that the task of the leader is not to use participants to achieve the greater good when those participants receive no benefit from the public good.

The fourth principle is an anti-utilitarian criterion and principle 5 ensures that where there is disagreement about the laws or norms that should govern an organization, the disagreement should be settled on grounds of justice. Principle 5 is a further check on authoritarian tendencies in leaders. Some believe that it is the task of the leader to resolve such disagreements. But not a Kantian. The Kantian leader assists in the resolution of disagreement, but he or she does not make the decision herself. To do so would violate the autonomy of the other members of the organization. It seems to me that these criteria for leadership could win universal assent and would meet Kant's requirement that they be norms to which all members of the community may be both subject and sovereign.

What I am really arguing is that the basis of a Kantian theory of leadership is autonomy. What should the relation of a Kantian leader to his or her followers be? The leader should enhance the autonomy of his or her followers. At the extreme the leader transforms followers into leaders. The leader drives leadership down through the organization by making people at lower levels in the hierarchy decision-maker leaders themselves rather than mere followers.

The Harvard Business School case, ABB's Relays Business, is often used as a case study for the development of the matrix organization but it can also be used as a case study for a Kantian theory of leadership. Here is how the case unfolds: the CEO of Asea Brown Boveri (ABB) is Percy Barnevik, the most cited non-American international business leader in American leadership literature. In this case, Barnevik is the person who exemplifies leadership. Yet after page two, Barnevik disappears and is never heard from again. However this HBR case is 12 pages long excluding appendices. If this case is about Barnevik's leadership, where is he? By page two, the actor on center stage is Goran Lindahl, Asea's executive vice-president. As the case unfolds, it is clear Barnevik has made Lindahl a leader. For example Lindahl is responsible for communicating the new philosophy and principles including the guiding principle of decentralization. He also wanted to emphasize the importance of individual accountability. He delegated a series of tasks to managers at lower levels. By page six Lindahl disappears and Ulf Gundemark who becomes ABB's business head for the worldwide relay business is at the center of action. Leadership is being pushed down the organizational chart. A focal point event in the case centers on the allocation of export markets. The Swiss company had been given responsibility for coordinating sales into Mexico but a dispute arose concerning shortening the company's lines to its customers and minimizing the non-value added work in the system. Gundemark delegated this to a team of four marketing managers. After much negotiation they reported back to Gundemark that they could not reach a decision. Rather than make the decision himself, Gundemark sent them back for further discussion. Several days later after exhausting negotiations, they reported they had reached a majority decision of three to one. Gundemark wanted a unanimous decision and sent them back yet again. Finally after three more days of intense negotiation, the marketing team comes back with a unanimous recommendation. Talk about a decision where you are subject and sovereign at the same time. A Kantian leader, contrary to a popular stereotype, is not one to whom you look for a decision. The Kantian leader empowers others in the organization to take responsibility for making a deci-

sion. In so doing Barnevik, at least in part, exemplifies what it means to be a Kantian leader.

Yet another Kantian leader is Jan Carlzon former head of SAS airlines. When Carlzon took over as CEO of SAS, the company had lost its way and was floundering. He undertook a number of steps that brought popularity and thus profitability to the airline. A characteristic of his leadership style was to empower others in the organization to make decisions. One story in particular reflects Carlzon's leadership style. Carlzon realized he had not succeeded in providing adequate leadership for the company when he finally went on vacation. Throughout his vacation there were constant phone calls asking him to make a decision. Carlzon realized that he would only succeed when he went on vacation and no one called to seek his advice. His job as a leader was to encourage subordinates to make decisions on their own. In that way they increased their autonomy on the job. Eventually he went on vacation and no one called. Carlzon begins his book *Moments of Truth* with the following quotations:

> Everyone needs to know and feel that he is needed. Everyone wants to be treated as an individual. Giving someone the freedom to take responsibility releases resources that would otherwise remain concealed. An individual without information cannot take responsibility; an individual who is given information cannot help but take responsibility.

These two cases illustrate the central thesis of a Kantian theory of leadership. A central task of the leader is to respect and enhance the autonomy of followers. In many organizational contexts, especially in business, having the followers become leaders themselves enhances autonomy. The Kantian leader teaches followers to become leaders.

QUESTIONS

1. What are the obstacles to being a Kantian leader in business?

2. What personal qualities would a leader need to practice Kantian leadership?

James MacGregor Burns | # What Is Transforming Leadership?

James MacGregor Burns is a Pulitzer Prize-winning presidential biographer and a pioneer in the study of leadership.

My own uncertainty over the anatomy of causation spurred me to explore Franklin D. Roosevelt's presidency as a case study in change. I did so not as a theoretician of change but as a biographer of a man who had enormously affected the lives of millions of Americans, including my own. He was the president my college dormitory friends and I had listened to raptly over the radio. In the fall of 1940, I had looked down on him from the balcony of the Boston Garden as he painfully inched his way to the rostrum to assure "the mothers and fathers of America" that "your boys are not going to be sent into any foreign wars." Soon he would become my commander in chief in World War II.

FDR was most intent on producing change—from the campaign days of 1932 and throughout his years in the White House. "The country needs and, unless I mistake its temper, the country demands bold, persistent experimentation. It is common sense to take a method and try it: If it fails, admit it frankly and try another."

Striving to understand his pursuit of change, I found his first two years in office puzzling. He alternated between the bold steps he had promised and a baffling conservative caution. Thus he pressed for economizing in the budget even while proposing large and costly changes in dozens of policy areas. Even more puzzling were his rousing appeals to the voters coupled with endless wheeling and dealing with Democratic congressmen, progressive Republicans, city bosses, western agrarians, southern conservatives. To reflect his doublesidedness, I decided to subtitle my 1956 book, with a steal from Machiavelli, *The Lion and the Fox*.

I found FDR's second term still more fascinating than his first, because in 1937–38 he pursued institutional as well as policy changes. The reason was clear: he had been frustrated by a fragmented Congress, a rising Republican opposition, and the ancient checks and balances of the Constitution, notably the vetoes of key New Deal bills by a reactionary Supreme Court. He proposed a "court-packing" bill that aroused bitter feeling, and later he tried to "purge" Congress of several anti—New Deal Democrats. Yet the closer I studied these "bold moves," the more they struck me as expedient, high-level brokerage. Thus he sought to manipulate the membership of the Supreme Court rather than alter its constitutional mandate, and he tried to oust his congressional foes without a broad-reaching grass-roots strategy that might have mobilized Democrats to fight for a more decisively liberal party. The best word for this practical, give-and-take leadership was "transactional."

It was only years later, when I came to study FDR's war presidency for a second volume of my biography, that I found "transactional" leadership an inadequate tool of analysis for the broader and deeper dimensions of his actions. The foundation for leadership had markedly changed during—and because of—the war. After Pearl Harbor, FDR had the backing of an aroused and united people. Goals were now clear—beat the Axis—and they were set in defense of the great public values threatened by the Nazis and their allies. Change, planned and unplanned, was so pervasive that it reached into every sector of the nation. Arguing that a healthy, well-housed, properly trained, and well-paid population was vital to the war effort,

James MacGregor Burns, "What is Transforming Leadership?" *Transforming Leadership* (New York: Atlantic Monthly Press, 2003), pp. 22–29.

the president engineered social programs far broader than anything he had achieved with the New Deal. He proclaimed an "Economic Bill of Rights" that in effect laid out the domestic programs of Democratic presidencies over the next quarter century.

Of course behind the façade of war unity politicians conducted the same old transactional leadership. But it seemed clear to me that FDR, driven by the new situation, was following a governing strategy significantly different from that of the prewar years. It was not simply a souped-up version of transactional leadership. He boasted that he was shifting from Dr. New Deal to Dr. Win-the-War. He—and the war effort he conducted—was fundamentally changing the country. He had become what his example inspired me to call a *transforming* leader, just as Lincoln had midway through the Civil War. He had been both a lion and a fox, but now the lion prevailed.

This realization—this new analytical tool of transforming leadership—made me take another look at episodes earlier in FDR's presidency where the lion might have outpaced the fox. Perhaps they were not as marked as during the war, but were there not strong strands of transforming leadership in the extraordinary outpouring of legislation in the "Second Hundred Days" of 1935? And could they not be found even amid the ill-planned effort to transform the Democratic party into a reliable vehicle for "continuous liberal government"?

During the past two decades both transactional and transformational leadership have become a focus of research and of controversy. Transactional leadership seemed fairly easy to define, if only because it was the basic, daily stuff of politics, the pursuit of change in measured and often reluctant doses. The transactional leader functioned as a broker and, especially when the stakes were low, his role could be relatively minor, even automatic. But what did it mean to *transform?* Was there a decisive difference between transactional and transforming leadership or were they variations on a spectrum?

We must distinguish here between the verbs "change" and "transform," using exacting definitions. To change is to substitute one thing for another, to give and take, to exchange places, to pass from one place to another. These are the kinds of changes I attribute to transactional leadership. But to transform something cuts much more profoundly. It is to cause a metamorphosis in form or structure, a change in the very condition or nature of a thing, a change into another substance, a radical change in outward form or inner character, as when a frog is transformed into a prince or a carriage maker into an auto factory. It is change of this breadth and depth that is fostered by transforming leadership.

In broad social and political terms, transformation means basic alterations in entire systems—revolutions that replace one structure of power with another, or the constitutional changes America achieved in the late eighteenth century. Bernard Bass of the Binghamton group has distinguished between the "first order of change," or changes of degree, and a "higher order of change," constituting alterations in "attitudes, beliefs, values, and needs." Quantitative changes are not enough; they must be qualitative too. All this does not mean total change, which is impossible in human life. It does mean alterations so comprehensive and pervasive, and perhaps accelerated, that new cultures and value systems take the places of the old.

Is transforming leadership measured simply by the number of alterations achieved? The more transactions, in short, the more transformational change? No, the issue is the nature of change and not merely the degree, as when the temperature in a pot of water is gradually raised to produce a transformation, boiling. Time—timing—can be crucial. Continual transactions over a long period can produce transformation. If such incremental changes take lifetimes, how long should people wait?

Is transforming leadership simply a new version of the Great Man theory, thinly disguised in academic clothing? Work on transforming leadership did occur during the "age of the titans"—from Churchill and Attlee in Britain to Margaret Thatcher, from FDR and Truman to JFK and LBJ, from Stalin to Khrushchev and Gorbachev, from Mao to a host of remarkable postcolonial leaders in the Third World. But for leadership students the rise and fall of luminaries—many of them, indeed, more rulers and tyrants than leaders—dramatized the basic leadership issue of *agency* versus *structure,* the relation between the leaders' character and qualities and the social and political context in which they operated, and the role of each in change. FDR, we noted, was a prime example. Winston Churchill was another. Despite his long-honed political skills, the British leader was a much-frustrated politician in peacetime who flowered in the demanding circumstances of two world wars. Charles de Gaulle could not have assumed leadership in 1940 and 1958 without the collapse of transactional politics-as-usual. And the limited transactional skills of Mao Tse-tung were nearly irrelevant to the dire needs of the followers who instead put their trust in his transforming powers.

Vigorous interaction between transforming leaders and their followers is itself a powerful causal force for change. By the 1990s almost all leadership scholars emphasized the role of *followers;* a few even argued that leaders and followers merged in interdependent collectivities in which it was difficult to discern the differences between the roles—in effect, denying a distinct leadership function. But this was a mistake. Leaders take the initiative in mobilizing people for participation in the processes of change, encouraging a sense of collective identity and collective efficacy, which in turn brings stronger feelings of self-worth and self-efficacy, described by Bernard Bass as an enhanced "sense of 'meaningfulness' in their work and lives." By pursuing transformational change, people can transform themselves.

The word for this process is *empowerment.* Instead of exercising power over people, transforming leaders champion and inspire followers. Tension can develop in this process. As leaders encourage followers to rise above narrow interests and work together for transcending goals, leaders can come into conflict with followers' rising sense of efficacy and purpose. Followers might outstrip leaders. They might become leaders themselves. That is what makes transforming leadership participatory and democratic.

The use of such subjective terms as "self-worth" and "meaningfulness" in leadership analysis poses the question of the place of emotions in the relationship between leaders and followers. This side of it has usually been identified with charisma, and studies of this phenomenon burgeoned in the twentieth century, in part from the urgency to understand the recurrence of demagogues who goaded their "masses" to extremes of racial and ethnic hatred, ideological extremism, religious fanaticism. Early in the century, Max Weber described charisma as "the greatest revolutionary force," capable of producing "a completely new orientation" through followers' "complete personal devotion" to leaders they perceived as endowed with almost magical—"supernatural, superhuman"—qualities and powers.

Following Weber, leadership scholar Ann Ruth Willner viewed charisma as based in worshipful emotions of "devotion, awe, reverence, and blind faith," while Robert Tucker, another student of leadership, saw followers responding to charismatic leaders with "fervent loyalty" because the "promise of salvation from distress" fulfilled urgently felt needs. Indeed, psychoanalyst Erik Erikson recognized that people might become "charisma hungry" in times of fear and crisis, when the old values that had upheld social structures and personal identity dissolved.

So the crucial elements of emotion and faith, as well as mysticism, irrationality, and psychological need, in the bond between leaders and followers have long been recognized. Yet hard questions arise. How much weight is to be put on these factors, among all those that define leadership? Weber and others sought to isolate a "pure" charismatic leadership, in which the irrational was the central defining feature. But how was such leadership to accomplish rational, planned transformational change—real, comprehensive, durable change, changes that advanced the great public values? And how was it to be analyzed, evaluated, in real-world terms? Leaders who fill bellies can be tested on the basis of how many bellies filled. How to test leaders defined in terms of the satisfaction of an array of murky psychological needs, of "hungers" of the "mind and spirit"?

"Pure" charismatic leadership also distorts constructive and mutually empowering leader-follower relationships. Followers are portrayed as so loyal or obeisant that, even when measured in the millions, they can have little impact on the leader beyond gratifying his own psychological hungers. The creative leader-follower interaction, in which the leader offers initiatives that followers pick up, amplify, reshape, and direct back onto the leader, is lacking. Just as charismatic leadership fails to empower followers, so leaders are not empowered by subservient followers. Mutual empowerment means exactly that: the empowering of one makes possible the other's empowerment.

At best, charisma is a confusing and undemocratic form of leadership. At worst, it is a type of tyranny. It should be studied, I think, as an exotic or lopsided form of transforming leadership that does not exclude the subjective but integrates it with multiple other factors, which as a whole produce a "completely new orientation" capable of pursuing significant social change. Organization scholars David A. Nadler and Michael L. Tushman argue that the strongest components of charismatic leadership are envisioning, energizing, and enabling. These are even more the functions of transforming leadership, which it achieves not by enslaving followers but by liberating and empowering them.

QUESTIONS

1. To what extent can a business leader be a transforming leader to his or her employees? Can you think of a transforming business leader?

2. What are the potential ethical pitfalls of transforming leadership?

Robert Greenleaf

Servant Leadership: A Journey into the Nature of Legitimate Power and Greatness

Robert Greenleaf was a pioneer in leadership studies. He taught and consulted at the Harvard Business School and the Ford Foundation.

Servant and leader—can these two roles be fused in one real person, in all levels of status or calling? If so, can that person live and be productive in the real world of the present? My sense of the present leads me to say yes to both questions. This chapter is an attempt to explain why and to suggest how.

The idea of *The Servant as Leader* came out of reading Hermann Hesse's *Journey to the East.* In this story we see a band of men on a mythical journey, probably also Hesse's own journey. The central figure of the story is Leo who accompanies the party as the *servant* who does their menial chores, but who also sustains them with his spirit and his song. He is a person of extraordinary presence. All goes well until Leo disappears. Then the group falls into disarray and the journey is abandoned. They cannot make it without the servant Leo. The narrator, one of the party, after some years of wandering finds Leo and is taken into the Order that had sponsored the journey. There he discovers that Leo, whom he had known first as *servant,* was in fact the titular head of the Order, its guiding spirit, a great and noble *leader.*

From Robert Greenleaf, *Servant Leadership: A Journey into the Nature of Legitimate Power and Greatness* (New York: Paulist Press, 1977), pp. 213, 217–19

WHO IS THE SERVANT-LEADER?

The servant-leader *is* servant first—as Leo was portrayed. It begins with the natural feeling that one wants to serve, to serve *first*. Then conscious choice brings one to aspire to lead. That person is sharply different from one who is *leader* first, perhaps because of the need to assuage an unusual power drive or to acquire material possessions. For such it will be a later choice to serve—after leadership is established. The leader-first and the servant-first are two extreme types. Between them there are shadings and blends that are part of the infinite variety of human nature.

The difference manifests itself in the care taken by the servant-first to make sure that other people's highest priority needs are being served. The best test, and difficult to administer, is: Do those served grow as persons? Do they, *while being served,* become healthier, wiser, freer, more autonomous, more likely themselves to become servants? *and,* what is the effect on the least privileged in society; will they benefit, or, at least, not be further deprived?

As one sets out to serve, how can one know that this will be the result? This is part of the human dilemma; one cannot know for sure. One must, after some study and experience, hypothesize—but leave the hypothesis under a shadow of doubt. Then one acts on the hypothesis and examines the result. One continues to study and learn and periodically one re-examines the hypothesis itself.

Finally, one chooses again. Perhaps one chooses the same hypothesis again and again. But it is always a fresh open choice. And it is always an hypothesis under a shadow of doubt. "Faith is the choice of the nobler hypothesis." Not the *noblest;* one never knows what that is. But the *nobler,* the best one can see when the choice is made. Since the test of results of one's actions is usually long delayed, the faith that sustains the choice of the nobler hypothesis is psychological self-insight. This is the most dependable part of the true servant.

The natural servant, the person who is *servant first,* is more likely to persevere and refine a particular hypothesis on what serves another's highest priority needs than is the person who is *leader first* and who later serves out of promptings of conscience or in conformity with normative expectations.

My hope for the future rests in part on my belief that among the legions of deprived and unsophisticated people are many true servants who will lead, and that most of them can learn to discriminate among those who presume to serve them and identify the true servants whom they will follow.

EVERYTHING BEGINS WITH THE INITIATIVE OF AN INDIVIDUAL

The forces for good and evil in the world are propelled by the thoughts, attitudes, and actions of individual beings. What happens to our values, and therefore to the quality of our civilization in the future, will be shaped by the conceptions of individuals that are born of inspiration. Perhaps only a few will receive this inspiration (insight) and the rest will learn from them. The very essence of leadership, going out ahead to show the way, derives from more than usual openness to inspiration. Why would anybody accept the leadership of another except that the other sees more clearly where it is best to go? Perhaps this is the current problem: too many who presume to lead do not see more clearly and, in defense of their inadequacy, they all the more strongly argue that the "system" must be preserved—a fatal error in this day of candor.

But the leader needs more than inspiration. A leader ventures to say: "I will go; come with me!" A leader initiates, provides the ideas and the structure, and takes the risk of failure along with the chance of success. A leader says: "I will go; follow me!" while knowing that the path is uncertain, even dangerous. One then trusts those who go with one's leadership.

Paul Goodman, speaking through a character in *Making Do,* has said, "If there is no community for you, young man, young man, make it yourself."

WHAT ARE YOU TRYING TO DO?

"What are you trying to do?" is one of the easiest to ask and most difficult to answer of questions.

A mark of leaders, an attribute that puts them in a position to show the way for others, is that they are better than most at pointing the direction. As long as one is leading, one always has a goal. It may be a goal arrived at by group consensus, or the leader, acting on inspiration, may simply have said, "Let's go this way." But the leader always knows what it is and can articulate it for any who are unsure. By clearly stating and restating the goal the leader gives certainty and purpose to others who may have difficulty in achieving it for themselves.

The word *goal* is used here in the special sense of the overarching purpose, the big dream, the visionary concept, the ultimate consummation which one approaches but never really achieves. It is something presently out of reach; it is something to strive for, to move toward, or become. It is so stated that it excites the imagination and challenges people to work for something they do not yet know how to do, something they can be proud of as they move toward it.

Every achievement starts with a goal—but not just any goal and not just anybody stating it. The one who states the goal must elicit trust, especially if it is a high risk or visionary goal, because those who follow are asked to accept the risk along with the leader. Leaders do not elicit trust unless one has confidence in their values and competence (including judgment) and unless they have a sustaining spirit (entheos) that will support the tenacious pursuit of a goal.

Not much happens without a dream. And for something great to happen, there must be a great dream. Behind every great achievement is a dreamer of great dreams. Much more than a dreamer is required to bring it to reality; but the dream must be there first.

QUESTIONS

1. How is a servant leader different from a transforming leader?

2. Is servant leadership a viable model for business leaders today?

CASES

CASE 15.1
Shooting an Elephant
George Orwell

In Moulmein, in lower Burma, I was hated by large numbers of people—the only time in my life that I have been important enough for this to happen to me. I was subdivisional police officer of the town, and in an aimless, petty kind of way anti-European feeling was very bitter. No one had the guts to raise a riot, but if a European woman went through the bazaars alone somebody would probably spit betel juice over her dress. As a police officer I was an obvious target and was baited whenever it seemed safe to do so. When a nimble Burman tripped me up on the football field and the referee (another Burman) looked the other way, the crowd yelled with hideous laughter. This happened more than once. In the end the sneering yellow faces of young men that met me everywhere, the insults hooted after me when I was at a safe distance, got badly on my nerves. The young Buddhist priests were the worst of all. There were several thousands of them in the town and none of them seemed to have anything to do except stand on street corners and jeer at Europeans.

All this was perplexing and upsetting. For at that time I had already made up my mind that imperialism was an evil thing and the sooner I chucked up my job and got out of it the better. Theoretically—and secretly, of course—I was all for the Burmese and all against their oppressors, the British. As for the job I was doing, I hated it more bitterly than I can perhaps make clear. In a job like that you see the dirty work of Empire at close quarters. The wretched prisoners huddling in the stinking cages of the lock-ups, the gray, cowed faces of the long-term convicts, the scarred buttocks of the men who had been flogged with bamboos—all these oppressed me with an intolerable sense of guilt. But I could get nothing into perspective. I was young and ill educated and I had had to think out my problems in the utter silence that is imposed on every Englishman in the East. I did not even know that the British Empire is dying, still less did I know that it is a great deal better than the younger empires that are going to supplant it. All I knew was that I was stuck between my hatred of the empire I served and my rage against the evil-spirited little beasts who tried to make my job impossible. With one part of my mind I thought of the British Raj as an unbreakable tyranny, as something clamped down, in *saecula saeculorum,* upon the will of prostrate peoples; with another part I thought that the greatest joy in the world would be to drive a bayonet into a Buddhist priest's guts. Feelings like these are the normal by-products of imperialism; ask any Anglo-Indian official, if you can catch him off duty.

One day something happened which in a roundabout way was enlightening. It was a tiny incident in itself, but it gave me a better glimpse than I had had before of the real nature of imperialism—the real motives for which despotic governments act. Early one morning the subinspector at a police station the other end of the town rang me up on the phone and said that an elephant was ravaging the bazaar. Would I please come and do something about it? I did not know what I could do, but I wanted to see what was happening and I got on to a pony and started out. I took my rifle, an old .44 Winchester and much too small to kill an elephant, but I thought the noise might be useful *in terrorem.* Various Burmans stopped me on the way and told me about the elephant's doings. It was not, of course, a wild elephant, but a tame one which had gone "must." It had been chained up, as tame elephants always are when their attack of "must" is due, but on the previous night it had broken its chain and escaped. Its mahout, the only person who could manage it when it was in that state, had set out in pursuit, but had taken the wrong direction and was now twelve hours' journey away, and in the morning the elephant had suddenly reappeared in the town. The Burmese population had no weapons and were quite helpless against it. It had already destroyed somebody's bamboo hut, killed a cow and raided some fruit-stalls and devoured the stock; also it had met the municipal rubbish van and, when the driver jumped out and took to his heels, had turned the van over and inflicted violences upon it.

The Burmese subinspector and some Indian constables were waiting for me in the quarter where the elephant had been seen. It was a very poor quarter, a labyrinth of squalid bamboo huts, thatched with palm-leaf, winding all over a steep hillside. I remember that it was a cloudy, stuffy morning at the beginning of the rains. We began questioning the people as to where the elephant had gone and, as usual, failed to get any definite information. That is invariably the case in the East; a story always sounds clear enough at a distance, but the nearer you get to the scene of events the vaguer it becomes. Some of the people said that the elephant had gone in one direction, some said that he had gone in another, some professed not even to have heard of any elephant. I had almost made up my mind that the whole story was a pack of lies, when we heard yells a little distance away.

There was a loud, scandalized cry of "Go away, child! Go away this instant!" and an old woman with a switch in her hand came round the corner of a hut, violently shooing away a crowd of naked children. Some more women followed, clicking their tongues and exclaiming; evidently there was something that the children ought not to have seen. I rounded the hut and saw a man's dead body sprawling in the mud. He was an Indian, a black Dravidian coolie, almost naked, and he could not have been dead many minutes. The people said that the elephant had come suddenly upon him round the corner of the hut, caught him with its trunk, put its foot on his back and ground him into the earth. This was the rainy season and the ground was soft, and his face had scored a trench a foot deep and a couple of yards long. He was lying on his belly with arms crucified and head sharply twisted to one side. His face was coated with mud, the eyes wide open, the teeth bared and grinning with an expression of unendurable agony. (Never tell me, by the way, that the dead look peaceful. Most of the corpses I have seen looked devilish.) The friction of the great beast's foot had stripped the skin from his back as neatly as one skins a rabbit. As soon as I saw the dead man I sent an orderly to a friend's house nearby to borrow an elephant rifle. I had already sent back the pony, not wanting it to go mad with fright and throw me if it smelled the elephant.

The orderly came back in a few minutes with a rifle and five cartridges, and meanwhile some Burmans had arrived and told us that the elephant was in the paddy fields below, only a few hundred yards away. As I started forward practically the whole population of the quarter flocked out of the houses and followed me. They had seen the rifle and were all shouting excitedly that I was going to shoot the elephant. They had not shown much interest in the elephant when he was merely ravaging their homes, but it was different now that he was going to be shot. It was a bit of fun to them, as it would be to an English crowd; besides they wanted the meat. It made me vaguely uneasy. I had no intention of shooting the elephant—I had merely sent for the rifle to defend myself if necessary—and it is always unnerving to have a crowd following you. I marched down the hill, looking and feeling a fool, with the rifle over my shoulder and an ever-growing army of people jostling at my heels. At the bottom, when you got away from the huts, there was a metaled road and beyond that a miry waste of paddy fields a thousand yards across, not yet plowed but soggy from the first rains and dotted with coarse grass. The elephant was standing eight yards from the road, his left side toward us. He took not the slightest notice of the crowd's approach. He was tearing up bunches of grass, beating them against his knees to clean them, and stuffing them into his mouth.

I had halted on the road. As soon as I saw the elephant I knew with perfect certainty that I ought not to shoot him. It is a serious matter to shoot a working elephant—it is comparable to destroying a huge and costly piece of machinery—and obviously one ought not to do it if it can possibly be avoided. And at that distance, peacefully eating, the elephant looked no more dangerous than a cow. I thought then and I think now that his attack of "must" was already passing off; in which case he would merely wander harmlessly about until the mahout came back and caught him. Moreover, I did not in the least want to shoot him. I decided that I would watch him for a little while to make sure that he did not turn savage again, and then go home.

But at that moment I glanced round at the crowd that had followed me. It was an immense crowd, two thousand at the least and growing every minute. It blocked the road for a long distance on either side. I looked at the sea of yellow faces above the garish clothes—faces all happy and excited over this bit of fun, all certain that the elephant was going to be shot. They were watching me as they would watch a conjurer about to perform a trick. They did not like me, but with the magical rifle in my hands I was momentarily worth watching. And suddenly I realized that I should have to shoot the elephant after all. The people expected it of me and I had got to do it; I could feel their two thousand wills pressing me forward, irresistibly. And it was at this moment, as I stood there with the rifle in my hands, that I first grasped the hollowness, the futility of the white man's dominion in the East. Here was I, the white man with his gun, standing in front of the unarmed native crowd—seemingly the leading actor of the piece; but in reality I was only an absurd puppet pushed to and fro by the will of those yellow faces behind. I perceived in this moment that when the white man turns tyrant it is his own freedom that he destroys. He becomes a sort of hollow, posing dummy, the conventionalized figure of a sahib. For it is the condition of his rule that he shall spend his life in trying to impress the "natives," and so in every crisis he has got to do what the "natives" expect of him. He wears a mask, and his face grows to fit it. I had got to shoot the elephant. I had committed myself to doing it when I sent for the rifle. A sahib has got to act like a sahib; he has got to appear resolute, to know his own mind and do definite things. To come all that way, rifle in hand, with two thousand people marching at my heels, and then to trail feebly away, having done nothing—no, that was impossible. The crowd would laugh at me. And my whole life, every white man's life in the East, was one long struggle not to be laughed at.

But I did not want to shoot the elephant. I watched him beating his bunch of grass against his knees with that preoccupied grandmotherly air that elephants have. It seemed to me that it would be murder to shoot him. At that age I was not squeamish about killing animals, but I had never shot an elephant and never wanted to. (Somehow it always seems worse to kill a *large* animal.) Besides, there was the beast's owner to be considered. Alive, the elephant was worth at least a hundred pounds; dead, he would only be worth the value of his tusks, five pounds, possibly. But I had got to act quickly. I turned to some experienced-looking Burmans who had been there when we arrived, and asked them how the elephant had been behaving. They all said the same thing: he took no notice of you if you left him alone, but he might charge if you went too close to him.

It was perfectly clear to me what I ought to do. I ought to walk up to within, say, twenty-five yards of the elephant and test his behavior. If he charged, I could shoot; if he took no notice of me, it would be safe to leave him until the mahout came back. But also I knew that I was going to do no such thing. I was a poor shot with a rifle and the ground was soft mud into which one would sink at every step. If the elephant charged and I missed him, I should have about as much chance as a toad under a steam-roller. But even then I was not thinking particularly of my own skin, only of the watchful yellow faces behind. For at that moment, with the crowd watching me, I was not afraid in the ordinary sense, as I would have been if I had been alone. A white man mustn't be frightened in front of "natives"; and so, in general, he isn't frightened. The sole thought in my mind was that if anything went wrong those two thousand Burmans would see me pursued, caught, trampled on, and reduced to a grinning corpse like that Indian up the hill. And if that happened it was quite probable that some of them would laugh. That would never do. There was only one alternative. I shoved the cartridges into the magazine and lay down on the road to get a better aim.

The crowd grew very still, and a deep, low, happy sigh, as of people who see the theater curtain go up at last, breathed from innumerable throats. They were going to have their bit of fun after all. The rifle was a beautiful German thing with cross-hair sights. I did not then know that in shooting an elephant one would shoot to cut an imaginary bar running from ear-hole to ear-hole. I ought, therefore, as the elephant was sideways on, to have aimed straight at his ear-hole; actually I aimed several inches in front of this, thinking the brain would be further forward.

When I pulled the trigger I did not hear the bang or feel the kick—one never does when a shot goes home—but I heard the devilish roar of glee that went up from the crowd. In that instant, in too short a time, one would have thought, even for the bullet to get there, a mysterious, terrible change had come over the elephant. He neither stirred nor fell, but every line of his body had altered. He looked suddenly stricken, shrunken, immensely old, as though the frightful impact of the bullet had paralyzed him without knocking him down. At last, after what seemed a long time—it might have been five seconds, I dare say—he sagged flabbily to his knees. His mouth slobbered. An enormous senility seemed to have settled upon him. One could have imagined him thousands of years old. I fired again into the same spot. At the second shot he did not collapse but climbed with desperate slowness to his feet and stood weakly upright, with legs sagging and head drooping. I fired a third time. That was the shot that did for him. You could see the agony of it jolt his whole body and knock the last remnant of strength from his legs. But in falling he seemed for a moment to rise, for as his hind legs collapsed beneath him he seemed to tower upward like a huge rock toppling, his trunk reaching skyward like a tree. He trumpeted, for the first and only time. And then down he came, his belly toward me, with a crash that seemed to shake the ground even where I lay.

I got up. The Burmans were already racing past me across the mud. It was obvious that the elephant would never rise again, but he was not dead. He was breathing very rhythmically with long rattling gasps, his great mound of a side painfully rising and falling. His mouth was wide open—I could see far down into caverns of pale pink throat. I waited a long time for him to die, but his breathing did not weaken. Finally I fired my two remaining shots into the spot where I thought his heart must be. The thick blood welled out of him like red velvet, but still he did not die. His body did not even jerk when the shot hit him, the tortured breathing continued without a pause. He was dying, very slowly and in great agony, but in some world remote from me where not even a bullet could damage him further. I felt that I had got to put an end to that dreadful noise. It seemed dreadful to see the great beast lying there, powerless to move and yet powerless to die, and not even to be able to finish him. I sent back for my small rifle and poured shot after shot into his heart and down his throat. They seemed to make no impression. The tortured gasps continued as steadily as the ticking of a clock.

In the end I could not stand it any longer and went away. I heard later that it took him half an hour to die. Burmans were bringing dahs and baskets even before I left, and I was told they had stripped his body almost to the bones by the afternoon.

Afterward, of course, there were endless discussions about the shooting of the elephant. The owner was furious, but he was only an Indian and could do nothing. Besides, legally I had done the right thing, for a mad elephant has to be killed, like a mad dog, if its owner fails to control it. Among the Europeans opinion was divided. The older men said I was right, the younger men said it was a damn shame to shoot an elephant for killing a coolie, because an elephant was worth more than any damn Coringhee coolie. And afterward I was very glad that the coolie had been killed; it put me legally in the right and it gave me a sufficient pretext for shooting the elephant. I often wondered whether any of the others grasped that I had done it solely to avoid looking a fool.

QUESTIONS

1. Why was the policeman unable to do what he thought was right?

2. Did the policeman fail as a leader?

CASE 15.2

General Patton and the Sicilian Slapping Incident
Abraham Zeleznick

"Whenever Patton felt the need to bolster his own morale," his biographer writes, "he would visit the nearest hospital because he gained solace and inspiration from the sight of men whose badge of courage was their wounds."

As much as he needed these visits to reassure him-

Abraham Zeleznick, "The Slapping Incident," in *Learning Leadership: Cases and Commentaries on Abuse of Power in organizations* (Chicago, IL: Bonus Books, 1993), pp. 375–380.

self, he thought the men needed him even more to lighten their sufferings. Patton regarded these visits as the high points of his command and his noblest task. He was always gratified to see that he was a tonic for the maimed men.

To take his mind off the bad news, he had called on Colonel Daniel Franklin, the Seventh Army's Surgeon, on August 2, and—with a load of 40 Purple Hearts—visited the patients at the Base Hospital. He walked from bed to bed and talked with easy familiarity with the men.

"Where did you get it, boy?" he asked a soldier whose bandage was concealed under the cover.

"In the chest, sir."

"Well," Patton said, raising his voice, for he wanted the whole ward to hear his pep talk, "it may interest you to know that the last German I saw had no chest and no head either. To date you have captured or killed over 80,000 s.o.b.'s—that's the official figure, but as I travel around, my nose tells me that the figures are much bigger and before the end they will double that. Get well quickly, boy—you want to be in on that final kill." He made a different speech at each ward, another to the nurses, still another to the doctors.

Just before leaving, he walked up to a bed in which a soldier was breathing heavily under an oxygen mask. When Patton realized that the man was unconscious, he took off his helmet, knelt down, pinned a Purple Heart on the pillow, whispered something into the ear of the dying man, then stood up at attention. If it was a corny performance, it did not seem so to the nurses on the ward. "I swear there wasn't a dry eye in the house," wrote his aide, Colonel Codman, who witnessed the impromptu drama.

Patton was so overcome by the experience that he went straight to a chapel to pray before he returned to his quarters.

On August 3, the military situation showed no improvement and Patton spent his first day at the front encouraging and exhorting the men—doing the job he reserved for himself and which he thought he was best qualified to perform. This was what he meant when he wrote in his diary on the eve of the landing in Morocco, "I feel that my claim to greatness hangs on an ability to lead and inspire." Now, in

the pressure-cooker of Sicily, he put it more plainly. "I am the best damn butt-kicker in the whole United States Army," he told General Bradley, who, under the circumstances, was not so enthusiastic about this aspect of Patton's technique of command.

"In the unhappy part of his career," Bradley later wrote, "George's theatrics brought him much contempt, and his impetuousness outraged his commanders . . . In Sicily, Patton, the man, bore little resemblance to Patton, the legend."

In front of Troina, as he mingled with the men, even his most inspired butt-kicking did not seem to work. He was appalled by what he found in the First Division. Having borne the brunt of two campaigns, the division had become temperamental, and even insubordinate. Discipline was lax, rules were disregarded, superiors were disobeyed. The commander, General Allen, "too much of an individualist to submerge himself without friction in the group undertakings of war," appeared to be either unable or disinclined to do anything about it. Discouraged by the hard going and left to brood about their fate in Allen's *laisser-aller* regime, his men developed too much pride in their past achievements and too much self-pity in their present plight.

Casualties had left gaping holes in the line, and Patton saw a tangible connection between them and his difficulties. Moreover, he was told that an increasing number of men had gone to the hospital with nothing but combat fatigue, a form of neurosis for which he had neither understanding nor sympathy. The departure of these men from the tough battle for Troina was felt seriously by the hard-pressed regiments, which were in any case becoming substantially reduced by *bona fide* casualties. Since no replacements could be obtained, every man was indispensable.

It was with the fresh memories of his visit to the First Division boiling in him, on this August 3, that Patton spied signs on the road to Mistretta showing directions to the Fifteenth Evacuation Hospital. He told Sergeant George Mims, his driver, "Take me to that Evac," not so much to seek solace this time but to see for himself how crowded it was with those combat-neurosis cases.

The Fifteenth Evac, a typical forward hospital

under canvas, was headed by Lieutenant Colonel Frank Y. Leaver. Leaver and his staff respected Patton's obviously sincere concern for the wounded, and appreciated his profound interest in the medical facilities of his Army. Nonetheless they viewed him with somewhat jaundiced eyes because of lingering memories of his strict disciplinarian regime in Tunisia.

In Tunisia Patton had no sooner taken command than an order of his appeared on the bulletin board of the hospital threatening fines of up to $25 for not wearing a steel helmet at all times, or going without leggings. "Since it was impossible for a doctor to get a stethoscope in his ears while wearing a helmet," wrote Major Max S. Allen with tongue in cheek, "and still worse to attempt to operate while wearing a helmet, the order had to be ignored inside the tents, but everyone wore his helmet on going from one tent to another."

Though Patton's visit was unexpected, the Fifteenth Evac was up to Patton's strictest standards when Mims drove him through its improvised gate to the tent where Colonel Leaver had his office. The colonel escorted the general to the receiving tent, where they were greeted by Lieutenant Colonel Charles N. Wasden, the receiving officer.

The grand round inside the tent cheered Patton, because the men appeared to be legitimate casualties so far as he could judge from the abundance of bandages evident. He talked effusively with the patients, and was particularly pleased to meet the first sergeant of the Thirty-ninth infantry Regiment because its commander, Colonel Harry Albert "Paddy" Flint, was one of his best friends. Flint was an eccentric soldier in Patton's own mold. With helmet, a black silk scarf and rifle in hand, he led his men on Troina stripped to the waist "so that he might be more easily identified." Patton spent some time at the bedside of the sergeant, talking about "Paddy," and telling the noncom how proud he ought to be to serve under such a valiant leader.

He was about to leave the tent when his eyes fell on a boy in his mid-twenties who was squatting on a box near the dressing station with no bandage on him to indicate that he had been wounded. He was Private Charles Herman Kuhl, ASN 35536908, of Mishawaka, Indiana, a bright-faced, good-looking young soldier eyeing the general with what Patton thought was a truculent look.

"I just get sick inside myself," Patton later told his friend, Henry J. Taylor, a millionaire businessman who doubled as a war correspondent in Sicily, "when I see a fellow torn apart, and some of the wounded were in terrible, ghastly shape. Then I came to this man and asked him what was the matter.

"The soldier replied: 'I guess I can't take it.'

"Looking at the others in the tent, so many of them badly beaten up, I simply flew off the handle."

What happened next was described the day after by Kuhl himself in a letter to his father. "General Patton slapped my face yesterday," he wrote, "and kicked me in the pants and cussed me. This probably won't get through, but I don't know. Just forget about it in your letter."

The letter passed the censor, but the Kuhls in Mishawaka—his parents and his wife Loretta—did exactly as Charley advised. They "forgot" about "it," probably because they were inclined to give the general the benefit of the doubt.

A carpetlayer in civilian life, Kuhl had been in the Army eight months, with the First Division about 30 days, serving in L Company of the Twenty-sixth Infantry Regiment. He had been admitted to the aid station of the Third Battalion at 2:10 p.m. on August 2, with a diagnosis of "exhaustion" made by Lieutenant H.L. Sanger of the Medical Corps. He was then evacuated to the First Medical Battalion, well to the rear, where a note was made on his emergency medical tag that he "had been admitted to this place three times during the Sicilian campaign."

Kuhl then was sent on to the clearing company by Captain J.D. Broom, was put in "quarters" there and given sodium amytal on a prescription signed by Captain Ralph S. Nedell.

On August 3, he was examined by Captain T. P. Covington, who wrote on Kuhl's medical tag: "Psychoneurosis anxiety state, moderately severe. Soldier has been twice before in hospital within 20 days. He can't take it at the front evidently. He is repeatedly returned."

As Taylor reconstructed the incident on the basis of his first-hand information, "Patton squared off in front of the soldier. He called the man every kind of a loathsome coward and then slapped him across the face with his gloves. The soldier fell back. Patton grabbed him by the scruff of the neck and kicked him out of the tent."

When Patton was through, he turned to Colonel Wasden.

"Don't admit this sonuvabitch," he yelled. "I don't want yellow-bellied bastards like him hiding their lousy cowardice around here, stinking up this place of honor." Then turning to Colonel Leaver and still shouting at the top of his high-pitched voice, he ordered:

"Check up on this man, Colonel. And I don't give a damn whether he can take it or not! You send him back to his unit at once—you hear me, you gutless bastard," he was now shrieking at Kuhl again, "you're going back to the front, *at once!*"

Kuhl was picked up by a group of corpsmen attracted to the scene by the noise. They took him to a ward, where he was found to have a temperature of 102.2 degrees. It also developed that he had been suffering from chronic diarrhea ever since he joined the First Division at the front. A blood test then showed that he had malaria.

Neither the medical staff, nor Kuhl nor his family in Mishawaka followed up the incident, and that seemed to close the case. Patton himself dismissed it from his mind after issuing the following General Order:

"To: Corps, division and separate unit commanders.

"It has come to my attention that a very small number of soldiers are going to the hospital on the pretext that they are nervously incapable of combat. Such men are cowards and bring discredit on the army and disgrace to their commanders, whom they heartlessly leave to endure the dangers of battle while they, themselves, use the hospitals as a means of escape. You will take measures to see that such cases are not sent to the hospital but are dealt with in their units. Those who are not willing to fight will be tried by court-martial for cowardice in the face of the enemy."

QUESTIONS

1. What do you think of Patton's motivational techniques?

2. How would you assess Patton's motivation for slapping the soldier?

CASE 15.3
Neutralizing "Neutron Jack"
Alejo José G. Sison

John (Jack) Francis Welch, Jr was born in Salem, MA—a working-class town north of Boston—in 1936. He was an only child. His father worked as a conductor for the Boston & Maine Railroad Company. The biggest influence in his early years, however, came by way of the tough-love lessons he received from his devout and determined mother, Grace.

In the first chapter of his autobiography, *Jack. Straight from the Gut* (Welch and Byrne 2001) he related the following story. Jack used to play for the local hockey team of Salem High, and once, after having been defeated at overtime by their traditional rivals, he blew his top and flung his stick across the rink. A few minutes later, when the team was already in the locker room, Grace Welch suddenly burst in

From Alejo José G. Sison, *The Moral Capital of Leaders: Why Virtue Matters* (Northampton, MA: Edward Elgar, 2003), pp. 129–138.

through the door. She then grabbed Jack by the shoulders and yelled at him in the presence of his coach and teammates, saying, "You punk! If you don't know how to lose, you'll never know how to win. If you don't know this, you shouldn't be playing." In other emotionally less-charged moments, whenever Jack would express his perplexity over events, she would tell him, "Don't kid yourself. That's the way it is." Jack found guidance dwelling on these thoughts each time he faced the challenge of ridding people of false illusions about business: "I found it hard to get people to see a situation for what it is and not for what it was, or what they hoped it would be. My mother's admonition to me many years ago was just as important for GE."

Later on, in a fitting tribute to his mother, Jack Welch went as far as saying, "my basic management beliefs—things like competing hard to win, facing reality, motivating people by alternately hugging and kicking them, setting stretch goals, and relentlessly following up on people to make sure things get done—can be traced to her as well." When pressed to specify just what exactly was his mother's most important contribution to the shaping of his personality, he responded: "Perhaps the greatest single gift she gave me was self-confidence. It's what I've looked for and tried to build in every executive who has ever worked for me. Confidence gives you courage and extends your reach. It lets you take greater risks . . . My mother never managed people, but she knew all about building self-esteem."

After leaving his hometown, Jack went on to earn a B.S. in chemical engineering from the University of Massachusetts in 1957, an M.S. then a Ph.D. in chemical engineering, both from the University of Illinois, in 1960.

Jack Welch joined General Electric (GE) in 1960, working as a junior chemical engineer for its plastics division in Pittsfield, MA and earning a salary of $10,500 a year. A little over a year later he wanted to quit his job because he felt stifled by the company's bureaucracy, underappreciated by his boss, and somewhat insulted by the $1,000 raise he had just been offered for what he considered to be extraordinary efforts (Byrne 1998). Furthermore, he had recently received an attractive offer at International Minerals & Chemicals, based in Skokie, Ill. Reuben Gutoff, then a young executive a level above Welch at GE, got wind of his plans and desperately tried to dissuade him from leaving. Over dinner at a restaurant with Welch and his wife, Carolyn, Gutoff vowed that henceforth he would protect Jack from being entangled in the web of the GE red tape. He also promised to create for Jack a congenial work atmosphere in GE that combined small-company smugness with big-company resources. Guttoff remembered having pleaded, "Trust me. As long as I am here, you are going to get a shot to operate with the best of the big company and the worst part of it pushed aside." Gutoff won Welch over and remained as his boss until 1973. At around that time, Welch had already earned his wings at GE and was bold enough to write in his annual performance review that his long-term goal was to become the company's CEO.

Welch was elected GE's youngest vice president in 1972 and was named vice chairman in 1979. In April 1981, he succeeded Reginald H. Jones as the eighth chairman and CEO in GE's 121-year history. GE traced its beginnings to the Edison Electric Light Company, founded by Thomas A. Edison in 1878. A merger between the Edison General Electric Company and the Thomson-Houston Electric Company in 1892 gave birth to the General Electric Company (GE), as it began to be called. As of June 2002, GE was the only company from the original Dow Jones Industrial Index of 1896 that still existed. It had become a diversified services, technology and manufacturing firm, operating in more than 100 countries worldwide and employing approximately 313,000 people.

An authority no less than Warren Bennis, from the University of Southern California's Marshall School, affirmed that although it was Alfred P. Sloan who invented the concept of the modern corporation, it was Jack Welch that made it work. Bennis wrote: "It is no exaggeration to say that Welch is at least partly responsible for the amazing resurgence of the American economy over the past 15 years. And few would dispute that he has been the role model for many other CEOs or that his thinking underpins many of the best and most esteemed of today's business practices. His preeminence is well deserved" (Bennis

2002: 96). In heaping accolades over Welch, Bennis was simply joining a roster of business writers who declared Welch to be "the world's greatest business leader," "the manager of the century," "the CEO of the century"; or as *Fortune* magazine would unabashedly say, "the most widely admired, studied, and imitated CEO of his time" (Walker 2001).

Such claims of course, would always be controversial. But what seemed beyond doubt was that no other business personality had been the object of as much media coverage and attention as Welch. At least nine full-length books have been written about him. Foremost among them was his autobiography, *Jack. Straight from the Gut,* published in September 2001, which immediately jumped to the number 1 spot on bestseller lists from *The New York Times, The Wall Street Journal,* Amazon.com, *USA Today* and the Association of Independent Booksellers. This book earned Welch an incredible $7.1 million author's fee. . . .

Besides all these reams of printed paper, what else was there behind Welch? Did he really have the achievements to deserve all the publicity?

In 1980, the year before Welch became chairman and CEO, GE reported $1.5 billion in profits. From 1981, during Welch's first five years at the helm, he fired one out of every four people working in the firm (Auletta 2001). This earned him the worthy moniker of "Neutron Jack," referring to his uncanny capability to get rid of people while leaving the company's physical plant intact. Throughout his 41-year career at GE, 20 of which were spent at the top office, he had downsized more than 100,000 employees. By the end of Welch's watch in 2001, profits at the company had grown to $14.1 billion (GE 2002).

For at least the past 20 years, share prices at GE had risen at an average rate of 21 per cent each year. This record was about 50 per cent faster than the Standard & Poor's 500 stock index. The company's market capitalization also grew from $13 billion, in 1981, to almost $500 billion, in 2001 (*Knowledge at Wharton* 2001b). For all of these reasons, GE was Wall Street's darling and consistently ranked first in surveys among the world's most admired and most respected companies. How was Welch able to accomplish all this?

First among Welch's recipes for success was the strategy that every GE product should be "number 1, number 2 or abandoned" (*Knowledge at Wharton* 2001a). Later on, Welch refined it after he had learned that many of the company's managers were defining their markets so narrowly that practically all of their products became number 1. The revised version then ordered that each product account for no more than 10 per cent of the market share. This simple directive seemed to have opened the door to enormous gains, as what initially appeared to be mature markets were suddenly transformed into astounding growth opportunities.

No less important was the 20/70/10 people management philosophy that Welch instilled in GE (*Knowledge at Wharton* 2001a). The company went through an annual appraisal system in which every manager was ranked in the top 20 per cent, in the vital middle 70 per cent, or at the bottom 10 per cent. After all this effort at differentiation, needless to say, the bottom 10 per cent got fired. The top 20 per cent got a grade of A, meaning that they both "made the numbers and embodied GE values" (Bennis 2002). The bulk making up the 70 per cent obtained a grade of B, meaning that they either made the numbers or embodied GE values; however, they had the company's commitment that it would help them to achieve both. The official template of executive excellence at GE was comprised of four E's, which stood for energy, energize, edge—the capacity to make tough decisions in the firm's lingo—and execute.

At an Information Technology conference in the spring of 2002, Welch spoke of the need to spot good workers with positive values, while quickly doing away with poor managers, regardless of how much they apparently contributed to the bottom line:

> It's a sin to lose a top performer. The managers who lose top performers should be removed themselves. The way you find out where the horses' asses are is you see they're losing people. In addition, giving false kindness to those workers, especially over age 50, who are not contributors, is unfair. I think it counts so much to let people know where they stand. You have no right to BS people (Russell 2002).

Primarily for this reason, Welch spent at least 60 per cent of his time choosing, developing and of course, firing people (Bennis 2002). So committed was he to the task that he personally interviewed every single promising candidate for the top 500 positions at GE. The company also had a marvelous executive training program that rivaled those of elite business school in terms of quality, intensity and relevance. It maintained a campus, or a "GE people factory" in Crotonville, NY. And according to a rough estimate, about 3 per cent of its payroll was earmarked for staff development and training.

Welch immediately realized that knowledge and information were the company's primary strategic resources, and that it had to invest in them in order to succeed in the future (*Knowledge at Wharton* 2001a). GE became one of the first global companies to appoint a chief knowledge and learning officer who reported directly to Welch. This move was in line with Welch's initiative to transform the firm into a "boundaryless organization" where knowledge and information freely flowed. He developed operating procedures that eliminated barriers and helped knowledge to be shared widely not the least through his famous "work out" sessions. As he once remarked: "Taking everyone's best ideas and transferring them to others is the secret. There is nothing more important. But there is also nothing more difficult" (*Knowledge at Wharton* 2001a).

This emphasis on the "soft stuff" did not mean, however, that Welch did not make use of financial rewards to drive behavior; quite the contrary (Byrne 1998). In 1998, for example, base salaries could rise—depending on one's performance—by as much as 25 per cent, even without a promotion. Cash bonuses could increase by as much as 150 per cent, equivalent to between 20 and 70 per cent of one's base pay. And stock option plans were likewise broadly expanded from very senior executives alone to nearly a third of Ge's professional employees.

Finally, Welch also proved to be a consummate master in the art of negotiating deals (*Knowledge at Wharton* 2001b). During his tenure, GE successfully made close to 1,000 acquisitions and more than 400 divestments. His strategy in acquiring new businesses did not always consist in driving the hardest possible bargain. Rather, Welch was always careful

to leave something on the negotiating table and try to build on that to have a fruitful long-term relationship with the new subsidiary.

Despite Welch's two acknowledged failures—the pollution of the Hudson River by PCBs released by GE plants and the botched acquisition of Honeywell due to opposition from the European Commission—he left the chief executive's office in September 2001 bathed in an almost supernatural aura. But the business downturn triggered first by the bursting of the Internet bubble, then followed by the Enron scandal invited a more critical revisiting of Welch's supposed merits and accomplishments at GE.

Welch was often painted by hagiographers not only as a "self-made man," but also as a "rebel" or "revolutionary" who single-handedly transformed stodgy GE into a lithe and nimble firm. He was supposed to have been the one primarily responsible for the company's blessed fortune. A few business analysts and commentators, however, begged to disagree.

Contrary to the popular belief that Welch inherited a moribund company from Reginald Jones in 1981, things were already sailing along quite smoothly for GE even then. Between 1972, when Jones began his stint at the top, and 1981, when he handed the baton over to Welch, revenue had already been growing at an annual rate of 12 per cent, and earnings at 16 per cent (Walker 2001). In fact, the average annual earnings growth throughout Welch's tenure at 12 per cent was even lower than Jones's, although it had reached about 15 per cent in Welch's last eight years.

Another popular benchmark of a company's strength is its return on equity (ROE), or earnings as a percentage of shareholder equity. This figure measures the efficiency with which management uses shareholder capital to create profits. Under Welch, GE registered an average annual ROE of 25.8 per cent. However, when compared to the pre-tax ROE figures of the seven previous CEOs at GE, Collins and Porras found that Welch merely ranked third.

The truth of the matter, therefore, was not so much that GE was the house that Jack Welch built, as GE being the house that built Jack Welch.

Certainly, with Welch, GE shares traded well above the Standard & Poor's average, at 38 times their earnings. This led many to embrace what had come to be the core belief of Welch fans, that he had made shareholders far richer than anyone else ever had. Except for the fact that this just wasn't true, unfortunately.

Even a magazine as favorable to Welch as *Fortune* acknowledged that in the decade of the 1990s GE ranked 55th in annual rate of return to investors (Walker 2001). The same magazine took note that over 17 years, Colgate-Palmolive shares consistently outperformed those of GE. That record was pegged to the tenure of Colgate-Palmolive's CEO, Reuben Mark, who unfortunately for him, was not half as media-friendly as Welch.

Of course there are other better indicators to gauge a company's performance than raw stock market gains. Collins and Porras suggested that one compare the performance of a firm's stocks to that of the market in general during a given period (Collins and Porras 1997). They calculated that between 1981 and 1995, GE stocks under Welch beat the market by a factor of 2.4 to 1. Nevertheless, eleven other companies fared better than GE by this benchmark. Between 1971 and 1991, for example, Kimberly-Clark shares, under the leadership of Darwin E. Smith, outperformed the market by a ratio of 4.1 to 1. So was there really more puff than stuff to Jack Welch's legend?

Hard to say, but one thing clear was that the general public's relationship with business leaders had radically changed during Welch's time (Walker 2001). Aside from Welch, other corporate icons such as Bill Gates and Steve Jobs began to receive far more attention than they used to, thanks to the advent of networks like CNBC, for example, dedicated to live business and stock-market coverage.

What Welch had really mastered was the fine art of having an extraordinarily thriving relationship with Wall Street. Under Welch, GE gave Wall Street exactly what it wanted, predictable increases in earnings, quarter by quarter, without any surprises. When Welch took over, GE was trading at a price to earnings (P/E) ratio of 8, which was broadly in line with the market average (Walker 2001). Normally, a

firm's P/E ratio shrank as its revenues and earnings increased. With Welch, however, GE did the exact opposite, with the market apparently believing that the company's growth potential had become greater than it was in 1981. Welch's GE incredibly chalked up this record through more than a hundred consecutive quarters. How did he do it?

Six months after Welch's retirement from GE, serious questions began to surface regarding the veracity of the company's numbers and the credibility of the accomplishments of its former CEO (Brady 2002). First to raise the red flag was Bill Gross, an influential executive of Pacific Investment Management Co., the world's largest bond fund. On 20 March 2002, Gross issued a report in which he accused GE of dishonesty, basically because it used cheap commercial paper and stock to buy growth. In consequence, he said that he would no longer by the firm's short term debt. Gross wiped off a full 6 per cent of GE's share price and caused the value of its $233 billion debt to plummet, sharply raising the company's interest costs. Those new interest costs were now supposed to reflect the firm's true riskiness more accurately. Whereas GE's superb reputation rested on its industrial powerhouse, with products ranging from light bulbs to aircraft engines, it had in fact become a financial company, according to Gross. But unlike other financial firms, GE's risks were heavily disguised, Gross said.

Gross voiced a common fear that GE was actually 'managing' or 'smoothing' its earnings, rather than reporting them faithfully, so as to keep an impressive record of profit growth (*The Economist* 2002). . . .

"Managing" earnings was one thing, but another more serious charge was that GE was in fact covering up a slump in growth by claiming to earn more money that it actually was . . .

In August 2000, a month before Welch's departure, GE shares were fetching $60 a piece. As a result of all these doubts raised, by the middle of June 2002, they were going at almost half the price, at $31. Despite the new CEO, Jeffrey R. Immelt's, offer to give investors more information than Welch ever gave, the market remained skeptical. By the end of the first semester of 2002, GE's share price had fallen by 25 per cent since the beginning of the year, dropping about twice as much as the Standard & Poor 500 index (Leonhardt 2002). A reassessment of Welch's tenure at GE was definitely in order.

In a sense, the same may be said not only of Welch's stint at the GE top office, but also of the impact of GE on Welch's personal life. Welch himself had expressed his regret that due to his work at GE he had "obviously been marginal on marriage" (Russell 2002). It was a thinly veiled acceptance of his failure to find a balance between career and family life: his professional success had cost him no less than two divorces.

In a chapter on "Divorce and marriage" in the work *Jack Welch. My Personal History* (Welch 2001) he wrote: "Unfortunately, while I was doing the biggest deal of my professional career, the biggest merger in my personal life was ending" (Welch 2001). This was in reference to his 28 years of marriage with his first wife, Carolyn. Welch admitted to being the ultimate workaholic throughout his GE years. As a result, the burden of raising their four children fell squarely on his wife's shoulders. At the time of their divorce in April 1987, their oldest, Katherine, was at Harvard Business School, while their other daughter, Anne, was also about to enter the Harvard School of Architecture for her master's degree. Their older son, John, was working through his chemical engineering degree at the University of Virginia, while their youngest, Mark, was already then a freshman at the University of Vermont. On this count, undeniably, Carolyn did a mighty fine job, even without her husband's help.

However, after seeing their children through school, Carolyn wanted to develop a new career for herself, while Welch wanted her to remain at home as a full-time housewife. Welch's having reached the top position at GE did not help their relationship at all and soon enough they parted ways. Eventually, Carolyn became a lawyer and married her former boyfriend during undergraduate years.

In October 1987, six months after his divorce, Welch met Jane Beasley on a blind date arranged by common friends. She was an attorney working in New York, 17 years his junior. Two years later, in April 1989, they were wed. But this did not happen

until, in a very Welch-like manner, they first struck out a deal. As Welch himself recounted:

> I told her it bothered me that she didn't ski or play golf. She told me it bothered her that I didn't go to the opera. We made a deal: I agreed to go to the opera if she agreed to ski and golf. I really wanted a full-time partner, someone who would be willing to put up with my schedule and travel with me on business trips. Jane would have to give up her career. She took a leave of absence to try it out and, luckily for me, decided to make this her full-time occupation . . . Jane won the club championships at Sankaty Head in Nantucket four years in a row and I won it twice. She's become the perfect partner (Welch 2001).

Whatever happened between Jack Welch and Jane Beasley from then on until March 2002 could be anybody's guess. But the fact was that towards the middle of that month Jane filed for a divorce and hired Raoul Felder, one of New York's top lawyers, to assure her fair half of Jack's fortune, estimated at about $900 million in outstanding GE stock options alone (Hogg 2002). A big factor in Jane's favor was that the once happy couple's pre-nuptial contract had already expired.

The estranged couple's divorce papers revealed that aside from a lifetime retainership of $86,000 a year from GE, Jack Welch would also continue to have—after his retirement—full access to company services and facilities, including a Boeing 737 jet, a luxurious Manhattan apartment with its attendant costs, dining privileges at exclusive restaurants and court-side seats to New York Knicks and US Open games. It is certainly hard to justify such a lavish outpouring of shareholder money on someone who, like Welch, is already in retirement. Furthermore, the issue remains of who should be paying taxes for such monies. In principle, Welch should be paying and GE could write the corresponding amount off, but only if the company could show that these are ordinary and necessary expenses of doing business.

The 66-year-old Welch's new love was Suzy Wetlaufer, a 42-year-old divorcee and mother of four. They first met when Wetlaufer, the editor in chief of *Harvard Business Review,* requested an interview in October 2001. Over a series of meetings during which Welch revised Wetlaufer's article, the pair found out that they had good rapport. The closeness she had developed with her subject put Wetlaufer's journalistic objectivity in question, so she pulled her story out of the *Harvard Business Review*'s February 2002 issue. Later on, as her affair with Welch became more public, Wetlaufer was somewhat forced to take a leave of absence from her $250,000 a year job. Eventually Wetlaufer got reinstated, although no longer as editor in chief but as "editor at large," that is, minus the managerial responsibilities. But this was too much for some of her co-workers, two of whom resigned from their posts as senior editors in protest. The normally boisterous and media-friendly Jack Welch surprisingly gave no comments, for he considered these recent developments to be a purely personal matter.

REFERENCES

Bennis, W. (2002), 'Will the legacy live on?' *Harvard Business Review,* February.

Brady, D. (2002), 'The education of Jeff Immelt,' *Business Week,* 29 April.

Collins, James C. and Jerry I. Porras (1997), *Built to Last: Successful Habits of Visionaary Companies,* New York: Harper Business.

GE (2002), 'GE fact sheet,' *www.ge.com,* 19, June.

Knowledge at Wharton (2001a), 'Life according to Jack,' 8 November.

Knowledge at Wharton (2001b), 'The Jack Welsh show,' 7 December.

Hogg, A. (2002), 'Jack Welsh's new squeeze,' *Moneyweb,* 13 March.

Leonhardt, D. (2002), 'The imperial chief executive is suddenly in the cross hairs,' *The New York Times,* 24 June.

The Economist, (2002), 'General Electric. The Jack and Jeff show loses its luster,' 4 May.

Russell, J. (2002), 'Jack Welsh on success, regrets, and values,' *VAR Business,* 21 March.

Walker, R. (2001), 'Overvalued: Why Jack Welsh isn't God,' *www.robwalker.net,* 11 June.

Welsh, Jack and John A. Bryne (2001), '*Jack straight from the gut*' Boston: Warner Business Books.

QUESTIONS

1. How does Jack Welch measure up as a leader in terms of ethics and effectiveness?

2. Is Welch a good role model for business leaders today?

CASE 15.4

Aaron Feuerstein: Not a Fool, Not a Saint

Thomas Teal

Malden Mills owner Aaron Feuerstein was both ridiculed and canonized when he kept his 1,000 employees on the payroll after a fire burned down his factory last Christmas. But now he's proving that treating workers well is just plain good business.

At a European trade show in Brussels during the first week of September, Malden Mills of Lawrence.

Massachusetts, introduced a broad new line of high-end upholstery fabrics. Buyers snapped up the sleek material, derived from the company's hugely successful line of Polartec and Polarfleece apparel knits. A victory, certainly. And one more step in an uphill comeback by a factory that suffered one of the biggest industrial fires in New England history less than a year ago, a factory whose owner achieved heroic stature by keeping more than 1,000 jobless employees at full pay for several months after the blaze.

Yet Aaron Feuerstein, owner, president, and CEO of Malden Mills, has good reason to feel unappreciated. It's true that his work force adores him, that almost every newspaper, TV station, and business magazine in the U.S. has sung his praises, that Bill Clinton invited him to Washington for the State of the Union address, and that columnists, unions, and religious leaders all across the country have declared him a saint. But much of this celebrity is based on the misleading premise that this 70-year-old acted selflessly, against his own best interests, which is another way of saying that he acted the way a saint might act: irrationally.

In fact, it seems pretty clear that some people call Feuerstein a saint because they don't quite have the courage to call him a fool. They don't think he should be rebuilding his mill, at least not in Lawrence. They think he should have pocketed the insurance proceeds, closed the business, and walked away. Or else they think he should have grabbed the chance to move the company to some state or country with lower labor costs.

Some commentators have even accused him of risking the very survival of his business with a lot of grandstanding magnanimity that served no purpose but self-advertisement. There's a suggestion that real businessmen are tougher than Feuerstein, that responsible owners never pay any employee a dime more than they have to, and that no factory owner could possibly have done what Feuerstein has done unless he'd been touched by God or is just touched, period. These people, for instance, argue that Feuerstein certainly could have skipped the grand gesture of paying out some $15 million in wages and benefits to already overpaid workers when they no longer had a place to work. One business school professor has suggested pointedly that not everyone should look to him as a model.

Most of this carping is nonsense. But in a way, so is much of the praise. Why in the world should it be a sign of divinely inspired nuttiness to treat a work force as if it was an asset, to cultivate the loyalty of employees who hold the key to recovery and success,

to take risks for the sake of a large future income stream, even to seek positive publicity? These are the things Aaron Feuerstein has done, and most people stand in amazement as if they were witnessing a miracle or a traffic accident.

I was one of them until I discovered that Feuerstein is at heart a hard-nosed businessman. He has some minor eccentricities—a weakness for little bursts of Shakespeare, a tendency to wander off into far corners of the room as he thinks and talks—and his Old Testament intensity and biblical pronouncements can be slightly intimidating, despite his warmth. The two hours I spent with him, however, convinced me that he is as tough-minded as he is righteous, a man entirely up to the job of running a factory for profit.

Take downsizing. Would anyone have guessed that Feuerstein was a devotee? At one point, as he was warming to an attack on the unconscionable Al Dunlap (the man who dismantled Scott Paper and fired a third of its work force), I interrupted to suggest that maybe Scott Paper was overstaffed and Feuerstein surprised me: "If one-third of the people in that company were wastefully employed, then Dunlap did the right thing." And then the new patron saint of working Americans surprised me some more. "Legitimate downsizing as the result of technological advances or as a result of good industrial engineering? Absolutely. I'm in favor of it. And we do it here all day long. . . . We try to do it in such a way as to minimize human suffering, but the downsizing must be done." Under the benevolent, angular exterior lurks a businessman—a businessman who understands labor. The trick, he told me, is to keep growing fast enough to give new jobs to the people technology displaces, to weed out unnecessary jobs "without crushing the spirit of the work force." If all you're after is cutting costs, if you "just have a scheme to cut people—that sort of thing is resented by labor, and you're never forgiven." Feuerstein has a union shop, has long invested heavily in technology that eliminates jobs, and has never had a strike—not exactly the hallmarks of a fool.

Or take the insurance question. Feuerstein could certainly have closed the factory, sold the business, pocketed the proceeds, and spent the rest of his days in a hammock. But men in their 70s who still come to work every day for the sheer exhilaration of the job don't turn to hammocks in a crisis. His decision to rebuild seems to have been spontaneous and immediate, made more or less by the light of the flames and without much thought to the insurance proceeds. And still it was a rational decision Factories are insured for their replacement cost and if you don't replace them you may have to settle for the depreciated value of the lost building and machinery, in this case a lot of modern machinery and several antediluvian buildings. You can solve this equation without the higher math. An insurance payoff is likely to be much larger when it's taken as a contribution toward a state-of-the-art manufacturing facility, partly because it has the potential to produce income for your family for two or three generations to come. Last year's pre-fire, pretax profit was $20 million on sales of $400 million. Twenty million times two or three generations comes to an awful lot of money.

Or take self-advertisement. Feuerstein has not been shy with the media. Malden Mills has been featured everywhere from *People* to *Dateline* to the Land's End catalogue, and it's all been free. What's more, if the insurance settlement should wind up in court—not wildly improbable—will it hurt Feuerstein's chances of winning that half the people in the country worship the ground he walks on? Do insurance companies care about their reputations? You bet.

As for the idea that he might relocate the company somewhere with lower wages. Feuerstein moved the company to Lawrence (from Malden, just outside Boston) in 1956, at a time when New England textile mills thought local labor too expensive and were streaming south like carpetbaggers. A great many of those companies failed anyway, despite the lower wages they spent so much money to find, and Feuerstein is sure he knows why: They gave too much attention to costs and not enough to quality. He responds with contempt to suggestions that Malden Mills should move offshore (Labor in the South is no longer such a bargain.)

"Why would I go to Thailand to bring the cost lower when I might run the risk of losing the advantage I've got, which is superior quality?" In any case, he goes on, lower wages are a temporary advantage. Quality lasts. At least it can last if you focus hard on

expertise and the freedom to innovate. But to do that, you have to focus hard on employees. When Feuerstein came to Lawrence, he wasn't looking for cheap labor but for skilled labor—capable, experienced textile designers, engineers, and workers who could give him the edge he needed to compete more effectively.

It's here he has shown his real genius. Any idiot with a strong enough stomach can make quick money, sometimes a lot of it, by slashing costs and milking customers, employees, or a company's reputation. But clearly that's not the way to make a lot of money for a long time. The way to do that is to create so much value that your customers wouldn't dream of looking for another supplier. Indeed, the idea is to build a value creation system of superior products, service, teamwork, productivity, and cooperation with the buyer. Reduced to its essence, that means superior technology and superior employees. Reduced still further, as Aaron Feuerstein can tell you, it means superior employees. The correlation between loyal customers and loyal employees is no coincidence.

For Malden Mills, the first test and the breakthrough came in the early 1980s with the total collapse of the market for what was then a company mainstay—artificial furs. It was the R&D and production employees who saved the company over the next few years, using their superior expertise in synthetic fibers, napping, and finishing to create a series of lightweight, thermal, resilient, woollike fabrics under the brand names Polarfleece and Polartec. They look good, feel good, wick well, don't pill, and hold up to repeated washing. Moreover, they're all engineered to order. The retailer wants, say, a fabric for cyclists that's windproof and light but also soft, absorbent, and quick-drying. Malden's ability to satisfy such orders has made Polartec a favorite of upscale retailers like Land's End, L. L. Bean, Patagonia, the North Face, Eddie Bauer, and a dozen more.

Best of all, these customers are loyal. Customer retention at Malden Mills runs roughly 95%, which is world class. Employee retention runs above 95%, which is prodigious but can hardly come as a surprise to anyone familiar with Feuerstein's approach to personnel. As for productivity, from 1982 to 1995, revenues in constant dollars more than tripled while the work force barely doubled. Compare that with an overall productivity increase for the U.S. of a little better than 1% per year. Thanks to its employees, Malden Mills has risen from at least one five-alarm crisis in the past. No wonder Aaron Feuerstein loves those employees enough to risk $15 million to keep them available and motivated and to help him rise from the literal ashes of last year's catastrophe. This isn't the work of a saint or a fool, it's the considered and historically successful policy of a genial manufacturing genius who might serve as a model for every man and woman in business.

QUESTIONS

1. In what ways were Aaron Feuerstein's assumptions about business different from those of other business leaders?

2. What elements of Fauerstain's background and personality contributed to the way that he ran his business?

CASE 15.5

Merck and Roy Vagelos: The Values of Leaders

Joanne B. Ciulla

Prior to becoming CEO, Vagelos was director of Merck Sharp & Dohme's research laboratories.[1] In 1979 a researcher named William Campbell had a hunch that an antiparasite drug he was working on called Ivermectin might work on the parasite that caused river blindness, a disease that threatens the eyesight and lives of 85 million people in 35 developing countries. He asked Vagelos if he could have the resources to pursue his research. Despite the fact that the market for this drug was essentially the poorest people in the world, Vagelos gave Campbell the go ahead. While the decision was Vagelos's, it was also reinforced by Merck's axiom "health precedes wealth."

Campbell's hunch about Ivermectin proved to be right, and he developed a drug called Mectizan, which was approved for use by the government in 1987. By this time Vagelos had become the CEO of Merck. Now that the drug was approved, he sought public underwriting to produce Mectizan. Vagelos hired Henry Kissenger to help open doors for Merck. They approached several sources, including the U.S. Agency for International Development and the World Health Organization, but couldn't raise money for the drug. Merck was left with a drug that was useful only to people who couldn't buy it. Vagelos recalled, "We faced the possibility that we had a miraculous drug that would sit on a shelf."[2] After reviewing the company's options, Vagelos and his directors announced that they would give Mectizan away for free, forever, on October 21, 1987. A decade later, the drug give-away cost Merck over $200 million. By 1996 Mectizan had reached 19 million people. In Nigeria alone it saved 6 million people from blindness.

Few business leaders ever have the opportunity to do what Vagelos did. When asked how he could commit his company to produce a product that cost rather than generated money, he said he had "no choice. My whole life has been dedicated" to helping people, and "this was *it* for me."[3] His values guided his decisions in this case, but so did the values of the founder. George C. Merck, son of the company's American founder, said that from the very beginning, Merck's founders asserted that medicine was for people, not profits. However, he quickly added that they also believed that if medicine is for people, profits will follow.[4]

Like many corporate mission statements, Merck's says its mission "is to provide society with superior products and services." The statement goes on to assert, "We are in the business of preserving and improving human life. . . . All of our actions must be measured by our success at achieving this goal." It concludes that "We expect profits from work that satisfies customer needs and that benefits humanity.[5] Merck's corporate leaders acted on and hence instilled and reinforced these values long before Vagelos donated Mectizan. After World War II, tuberculosis thrived in Japan. Most Japanese couldn't afford to buy Merck's powerful drug, Streptomycin, to fight it. Merck gave away a large supply of the drug to the Japanese public. The Japanese did not forget. In 1983 the Japanese government allowed Merck to purchase 50.02 percent of Banyu Pharmaceutical. At the time, this was the largest foreign investment in a Japanese company. Merck is currently the largest American pharmaceutical company in Japan. The story makes Merck's mission statement come alive. It is the kind of story that employees learn and internalize when they come to work there.

Vagelos' moral leadership in this case extended beyond his organization into the industry. As Michael Useem pointed out, Merck has become the benchmark by which the moral behavior of other pharmaceutical companies are judged. Sometimes the moral actions of one CEO or company set the bar higher for others. Useem observed that the message hit home at Glaxo. In comparing Glaxo to Merck, a business writer once called Glaxo "a hollow enterprise lacking purpose and lacking soul."[6] Merck's values seemed to inspire Glaxo's new CEO Richard Sykes. In 1993 Glaxo invested in developing a drug to combat a form of tuberculosis that is connected to AIDS and found mostly among the poor. In 1996 Glaxo donated a potent new product for malaria. Similarly, Dupont is now giving away nylon to filter guinea worms out of drinking water in poor countries, and American Cyanamid is donating a larvacide to control them.

A cynic might regard Merck's donation of Streptomycin and Mectizan as nothing more than public relations stunts. But what is most interesting about the actions of Merck's leaders is that while they believed that "by doing good they would do well," at the time that they acted, it was unclear exactly when and how the company would benefit. Neither the Japanese after the war nor the poor people of the world who are threatened by river blindness seemed likely to return the favor in the near future. While this wasn't an altruistic act, it was not a purely self-interested one either. Since it was unclear if, when, and how Merck would benefit, it is reasonable to assume that Merck's leaders and the values upon which they acted were authentic. They intentionally acted on their values. Any future benefits required a leap of faith on their part.

Business leaders' values matter to the organization only if they act on them. In business ethics and in life, we always hope that doing the right thing, while costly and sometimes painful in the short run, will pay off in the long run.

NOTES

1. The information about this case is from Michael Useem, *The Leadership Moment* (New York: Times Business Books, 1998), chap. 1.

2. Ibid., p. 23.

3. Ibid., p. 42.

4. Ibid., p. 29.

5. Ibid., p. 29.

6. Ibid., p. 31.

QUESTIONS

1. What was it about the corporate culture and Vagelos that made it possible for Merck to donate the drug Mectizan?

2. What does this case tell you about the impact of moral leadership inside and outside the organization?

CASE 15.6
Jack Stack
Kirk O. Hanson

Jack Stack started in the mailroom at International Harvester in 1968, at the age of 18. Expelled from both college and a seminary for disciplinary reasons, and fired by General Motors Corporation, Jack Stack's job as mail clerk at International Harvester represented a fresh beginning. The 4,000-employee Melrose Park factory of International Harvester, with 26 acres under one roof (one mile in each direction) was a living archetype of another management era. "We spoke four different languages in the factory, and drew from three different states," said Stack. "Management and employees communicated with each other with a 632-page union document. I was the least senior employee, and one of the first baby-boomers to enter into this particular job market."

A plant that once made airplanes for World War II, the Melrose Park facility was steeped in traditions of secrecy and bureaucratic hierarchy. Work was parceled into discrete functions, and employees, for national security reasons, were forbidden from knowing what other departments were doing. Exemplary employees did their jobs—nothing more, nothing less—and were neither told nor encouraged to consider how the enterprise might be functioning as a whole. That was for the top managers to know. "I was the only person, apart from the plant manager, who actually had permission to visit any department in that organization—because I was the *mailboy!*" Stack quips.

"When I had my first promotion, from mailboy to forecasting clerk," he recalled, "I replaced somebody who had been in his job for 26 years. He had never

been out into the factory! He had not actually seen the products he was forecasting. No one in our company ever saw the big picture. We were totally divided and segmented in our job responsibilities."

Stack's business education continued when, at age 20, he was made head of the purchasing department. Shortly thereafter, he was made manager of production control, a job that once again gave him a holistic view of the plant's operations. "Once I went out to shop floor and saw workers flipping through bins looking for parts. I said, 'Why are you doing this ridiculous job? And he said, 'Some jerk in purchasing last year said this was the new policy, and we've been doing it ever since!' "That jerk in purchasing," Stack confessed, "was me".

The lesson was driven home again in his next position as manager of machining. "I was trying to figure out why I couldn't get enough stock for my machines," Stack said. "It turned out that the inventory control policies I had put in at my last position were to blame. They were also demoralizing the work force. So I began to see the interplay from one department to another. It was absolutely scary!"

The real epiphany came after Stack got another promotion, becoming, at age 28, superintendent of the least productive of seven company divisions, machining. The division's five general foremen and 500 union workers turned out 300 heavy-duty truck engines a day. It was a rough blue-collar environment in which workers grumbled at the daily grind and were often careless about quality. The structure of people's jobs was largely determined by industrial

This case was prepared by Kirk O. Hanson, senior lecturer at the Stanford Graduate School of Business, based on research and writings by David Bollier. Copyright © 1993 by The Business Enterprise Trust. The Business Enterprise Trust is a national non-profit organization that honors exemplary acts of courage, integrity and social vision in business. No part of this publication may be reproduced, stored in a retrieval system, or transmitted in any form or by any means—electronic, mechanical, recording, or otherwise—without the permission of The Business Enterprise Trust. Harvard Business School Publishing is the exclusive distributor of this publication.

engineers who used latter-day versions of Taylorite scientific management, a mindset that Stack found asinine. "Whenever we would change one engine on the assembly line," said Stack, "we had to re-allocate all 275 jobs. That's how tightly we had those assembly lines run. When you're running one engine every three minutes, you can imagine how many times we were in the industrial engineering department allocating basic workloads. To ensure fairness and balance within the organization, under the union contract, we couldn't add one minute to one section of that line without changing every single job."

Unfortunately, no matter how much tinkering the industrial engineers did, Stack's division consistently underperformed the company's other divisions. "Every single Friday we used to walk into the plant manager's office," Stack recalls with distaste, "and he would pound on the table and say we had to make more profits. The trouble is, we only got evaluated on how fast we got a part to the assembly line, our housekeeping, our safety record, work stoppages, and so on. No one had ever stopped and told us how to make profits or generate cash flow. The plant manager's whole theory of management was 'Numbers are power, and the numbers are mine.'"

So Stack embarked upon his own guerrilla management tactics. It turned out that an engineering friend had his own computer system containing production and financial data that closely paralleled those of the company comptroller. Stack learned that his own division, while indeed seventh of seven, was capable of performing at a productivity output rate of $10 a person higher than it usually did. Armed with that knowledge, he challenged his work crew to exceed that higher productivity rate the next week, as measured by his friend's computer data.

"I told everyone on the assembly line, if you beat your all-time high, I'll buy all of you coffee. And if you beat it a second week, you'll get coffee *and* rolls. And if you beat it a third week, I'll have everyone over to my house for pizza and beers."

"At the end of three weeks," Stack deadpans, "my wife and I entertained 200 people (the entire first shift) for a two-week period of time. It was the first time that anyone in management had ever gone to the organization and actually told them how they were

really being evaluated." What made his little trick work, Stack realized, was that it satisfied an utterly basic human need: "People just love to have little wins. They love to play little games and feel good about what they're doing. And they will contribute— *if* you trust them."

Stack's wacky competitions were only the beginning. "When our division rose from the bottom, the top division went after it. We improved our productivity from $48 to $70 a person. We were the hottest thing going. Once we had a $500 bet on the line with the heat-treat department that we could beat their productivity," he said. "Ironically, by Thursday, the race came down to the biggest over-achiever in our department for the past 30 years—this poor guy who gave 115 percent day in, day out. We needed to get to $72.10 productivity per person, and we were at $72.08. This guy had been withdrawn all week. We said we'd do anything if he would help. 'What do you need?' I asked him."

And he told Stack, "Promise me that if I give you the best that I ever can, you won't have that industrial engineer coming up here and cranking up my time study, and changing the rates. I cannot always be the best in this department."

"I said, *you got it!*" Stack exclaimed. And the John Henry of the line hunkered down and increased his output from $72.10 all the way to $78 for the day, propelling Stack's division to victory.

Stack learned a sobering lesson from the episode. *"All that guy was asking us to do was to always give him the ability to succeed,"* Stack says. Give employees a carrot, not a stick. Appeal to their best selves, their highest aspirations, their latent desires to do something excellent and deserving of pride, and you will elicit superior performance. Management will get more from employees by giving them the whole, unvarnished truth than by weaving a tangled web of half-truths and manipulations.

This was illustrated to Stack when he learned, at a secret management meeting, that the company would soon pay a huge cash penalty for every day it went beyond an October 1st deadline for shipping hundreds of tractors to the Soviet Union. "We were 800 tractors short with just 20 working days to go, and we were only making about five tractors a day," Stack told a reporter. "At that rate we'd still be about 700 tractors short. Everybody at the meeting was trying to figure out how to cover their rear ends. And everybody agreed heads were going to roll and that the whole mess was a secret best kept to ourselves."

Stack's had a different idea. He told his assembly line the truth, and posted a sign outside his office: "Our goal: 800 tractors." When line workers, accustomed to meeting the bare demands of their narrowly defined jobs, suddenly were presented with a collective goal toward which their individual performance *mattered,* productivity took off. Freed of rigid job descriptions and inspired by a tangible challenge, Stack's workers rallied to the challenge, and began cranking out 55 tractors a day. By October 1st, 808 tractors had been assembled and shipped, to Moscow's and Harvester's great surprise.

It was from such episodes that Stack began to build his own people-driven philosophy of management: a philosophy that treated employees as whole human beings who want to *give* of their intelligence, creativity and energy. But to elicit those qualities, Stack learned, employees need something in return: genuine respect, a sense of community based on trust and open communication, and a larger common vision to unite all parts of the enterprise. Leadership was not a way of talking. It was a way of acting, boldly and fairly, on behalf of everyone, giving them the tools and encouragement they need to do their best.

As division superintendent at Harvester, Stack was shocked to learn that his division had no idea what happened to their engines once they left the factory. "Workers never got the feeling that they were building engines for trucks that would carry goods throughout the United States. They never got to understand that they were building engines that went into farm tractors that brought food to people's tables. They never got to *feel,* or participate, in anything! Why? Because we had industrially engineered all the intelligence and all the skills out of their jobs. We just asked them to do their jobs, nothing more, nothing less."

Stack's solution was to obtain every brochure, marketing document and merchandising giveaway that the sales department had ever used to market the engines. He showered these on the assembly line to show everyone how important their work really was, to the company and to the world. As a result, Stack said, "Everybody had this tremendous amount of pride and satisfaction, because work was no longer a matter of putting 2,000 washers on 2,000 bolts. People were *participating* in something. They were asked to contribute."

"Probably the highlight of my life at that time," Stack said, "was when somebody came up to me and said, 'You know, I was riding down the highway the other day and my child was in the car. This big truck pulled up next to me, and it had a DT-466 engine on the right side, and I said to my son, 'Your daddy built that engine.' The more we taught people the big picture, the more productivity rose. The more we showed them the end result, the fewer engines hit the floor. And I said to myself, 'This is the job I want for the rest of my entire life!' "

STACK'S EXPERIENCE AT SPRINGFIELD RENEW

Stack's bosses at International Harvester had different ideas, however. In the late 1970s the company was having serious problems with the small engine remanufacturing plant in Springfield, Missouri, 550 miles south of Chicago. The Springfield ReNew Center, was bleeding at the rate of $300,000 a year. Workers were so demoralized that two unions were vying to organize the plant. While the plant, with about $21 million in sales, was no jewel in the crown of a company with $8 billion-plus sales, Harvester brass figured the troubled Springfield operation might at least provide a learning experience for the brash and clever 29-year-old manager. And besides, how could a comer like Jack Stack turn down the chance to be the youngest plant manager in the long history of this illustrious company? Even though Stack would supervise fewer employees, the new job as plant manager represented a promotion within the Harvester hierarchy, largely because he would in effect be running a standalone business, not working within a large bureaucracy. With an assignment to turn the factory around or close it down, Stack, his wife and two babies departed for Springfield in 1979.

Before leaving, a Harvester executive grabbed Stack by the shoulder and gave him a bit of friendly advice. "Be sure to buy a house in an area where you can resell it real fast," he warned. "Like in six months."

Stack received a dramatic demonstration of this fact when he first visited the plant. For the two days of his visit, he noticed that the same partially assembled engine block sat on its stand. Back at the Melrose Park plant, a new engine rolled off the assembly line every three minutes. But that was only the half of it, Stack recalls. The shop floor was a shambles. Inventory was grossly disorganized. Productivity was abysmal, contributing to a backlog of orders. Employees were so disgruntled they had invited both the Teamsters and the United Auto Workers to organize the plant; the election was slated for March 10, two months away. "Back then, you just were kind of mushrooms," said William "Bus" Bryant, who now works in the service engineering department. "They kind of fed you and kept you in the dark."

Stack's first priority was pragmatic: keep the union out. It was not that Stack wanted a free hand to squeeze the workforce with a new regime of authoritarian discipline and wage rollbacks. Stack believed the traditional adversarialism between management and unions worked to everyone's detriment, at least in his experiences at Melrose Park. Both workers and management jockeyed for political advantage and clung to contract legalisms while business productivity and employee morale spiraled downward. What was needed now at the ReNew Center was healing.

"People ask me how I won the union election," Stack recounts. "The reality was, we got down on our hands and knees and begged them to trust us. We groveled!" His sincerity won the day, and workers, while still dissatisfied with their jobs and the company, voted 3-to-1 against unionizing. Employees sensed they had a different breed of manager to lead them.

Slowly, in fact, things did change. The most basic problems, such as safety, inventory control and production routines, were addressed. Improvements were made in delivery time, inventories, quality, even profits. A new discipline took root. But as a near-forgotten appendage of the Harvester empire, the ReNew Center could not get the capital investment or top management attention it deserved.

SPRINGFIELD RENEW FOR SALE

The ongoing tumult and decline at Harvester headquarters was felt even at the remote, nearly forgotten Springfield ReNew Center. "Every single day when the employees of this factory came to work, they would come up to me and ask, 'Should I buy a car? Should I get married? Should I have a kid? What am I going to do with my life?' " Stack recalls. "Unemployment was running at around 11 percent. The company froze wages for a long period of time. We saw other factories close. Everybody was scared. People would look at me as the plant manager, that I should have the answers. All they knew was that they were wage-labor and I was their supervisor. They didn't realize that the guys in Chicago [at Harvester headquarters] were creating our problems. I was the plant manager. They thought I was the guy!

"I'd go to bed at night and think about how I was going to execute 119 people (attrition had reduced the workforce from 170 to 119)," reported Stack. I had virtually spent my entire 14 years with the company without laying anybody off. I had always figured out how to maintain full employment, because I totally believe that when you bring people into your workforce, they're taking on debt, they're building families. They're trying to go forward in terms of their lives. To pull that out from under them is probably one of the biggest disgraces I could ever imagine!"

Realizing that he might soon be commanded to lay off everyone before being "taken out to a field and shot" himself, Stack and his fellow managers, hanging out one evening in a basement rec room, came up with a crazy idea: *Why not buy the plant ourselves?* The idea was born of pure frustration and the dismal prospects for change.

Stack and his buddies drafted a five-page purchase proposal and sent it to Harvester in May 1981. "We didn't get a lawyer. We didn't get a CPA firm. We just wrote this letter saying, 'Duh. We're just a bunch of people down here in Missouri. We'd like to buy our factory. Would you mind selling us the business?' "

After the letter had wended its way through bureaucratic channels, Harvester had a swift, decisive response. Six internal auditors wearing dark suits and carrying big black bags arrived unannounced at Stack's office one day. Harvester executives suspected financial shenanigans at their lackluster manufacturing outpost. Why else would its managers want to *buy* such a woebegone operation? After a thorough audit which uncovered no wrongdoing, Harvester showed little serious interest in the managers' proposal to buy the ReNew Center.

The proposal did prod Harvester to shop around over the next two years for other buyers, however. "One day I picked up the *Wall Street Journal* and discovered that our plant was for sale. So I called my boss in Chicago and asked him, did he know we're for sale? And he said, 'Oh yeah, I forgot to tell you that we put it on the market.' 0" One weekend, Stack was shocked to learn that Dresser Industries, another maker of heavy-duty trucks and earth-moving equipment, had purchased the Springfield ReNew Center as part of a larger purchase of properties from Harvester. The deal was so close to completion that Dresser representatives started installing dedicated modem lines from the plant to Dresser headquarters in Dallas, and another Dresser official asked Stack to turn over his financial records. Stack believed, however, that the new corporate owner had little interest in improving wages, working conditions or job security for his employees. And Stack had no interest in being a tool of such a regime.

Fate dictated an abrupt reversal of fortunes, however, on the Thursday before Christmas 1982. The chief negotiator for Harvester called to inform Stack that negotiations with Dresser had broken off; the deal had fallen through. "Would you be able to come up with one million dollars more than their offer [a total of $9 million]?" the negotiator asked. "We'll sell the plant to you."

FINANCING THE BUY-OUT

Stack groans in recollection of that crazy Christmas. "I had to try to raise equity, float a loan and find an attorney, all by January 1, 1983, when they wanted to close the deal." For the previous two years, since the first proposal to buy the plant, Stack had been on a cross-country odyssey to find a bank that would finance their purchase. "We were turned down in excess of 50 times for loans by the safest financial institutions in America," Stack recalls.

Though grueling, the process gave him an invaluable education in corporate finance and how financial markets can be as critical to the success of a manufacturing operation as production, marketing or labor relations. "We began to see how somebody can be a lending officer, literally controlling the lives of hundreds of thousands of people, through the loans they make," said Stack. "We admired the fact that these lending officers could be running seven companies but they didn't go to bed at night worrying about payroll or about laying off people. Now, coming from a manufacturing background and being trained to always look for productivity increases, it was here that we learned if this was the end of all ends—being part of some loan portfolio—then maybe what we ought to do is take this whole concept of loan evaluation and put it back as an evaluation system within our business."

As Harvester teetered toward bankruptcy between 1980 and 1982, Stack intensified his search for a bank that would give him a loan—and finally found one. Stack asked his fellow managers and employees how much money they could contribute toward a down payment on the plant purchase. The total from 119 employees was $67,540, or more than $8.9 short of the $9 million purchase price. After giving everyone the weekend to think the deal over, Stack asked a second time. The total dropped to $65,000. "Some guy's wife thought it was the worst deal she had ever seen, and dragged $2,000 out of the pot," Stack said with an amused grin.

But the loan officer refused to take the loan to his loan committee, saying that it didn't even meet the bank's minimal financial ratios. Besides, he complained, if the loan went bad, the bank did not want to have to chase down the collateral of dozens of employees, each holding tiny slices of equity. The only way the loan would be feasible, said the officer, was if it had the backing of the personal assets of the top 13 managers. That collective sum, Stack discovered after the loan officer opened 13 envelops with confidential financial data, totaled only $96,000— and these assets did not offset the managers' personal debts.

"Let's round it up to $100,000," Stack gamely suggested. The loan officer, astonishingly, agreed with personal "performance guarantees" to help work out the loan if it went bad, the loan officer took the deal to the loan committee, which approved it.

On February 1, 1983, Stack and his 12 managers closed on the $9 million deal. With 89 parts debt ($8.9 million) to one part equity ($100,000), and an interest rate of three percentage points over prime, which then stood at 15 percent, the deal represented one of the most highly leveraged buyouts in corporate history.

At the closing at the bank's legal offices, Stack was surprised that his loan officer was nowhere to be seen. Minutes later a bank official called up to inform Stack that the loan officer had been fired that very day for making the loan. And furthermore, the official said, the bank wanted to renegotiate the terms of the loan.

"So I made my first major management decision," said Stack. "I had to bluff him. I said, 'O.K. Sue me, because I'm going to sue you. Now what are you going to do?'" The bank official relented, but promised that it would look forward to sending the liquidation trailers to the plant. The loan was made, and the deal consummated.

Stack and his hardy co-investors had cleared the first hurdle. They owned an unremarkable 68,000 square-foot heavy-duty engine remanufacturing plant and its inventory at 480 Maple Street. Most of the original plant employees, who had officially been fired the day before in order to close the deal, were re-hired as fast as the paperwork could be processed, or about 30 per day. But the factory began with only 60 percent of its previous customer base because Dresser Industries, which had unsuccessfully bid on the plant, abruptly withdrew its engine remanufacturing business from the new company.

STACK'S PROPOSAL

What Stack proposed at this critical moment in SRC's creation seemed naive to many. Each element echoes some "lesson" Stack thought he had learned in his years at International Harvester. Stack urged his fellow managers, who had risked their total net worth on the leveraged buyout, to:

1. Create a work culture of "open-book management," making every aspect of the business visible to every employee, indeed to anyone who cared to know;
2. Invest a substantial amount of time and effort

training every employee in financial management so that they could follow, in detail, the weekly operating and financial reports of the company and other information they would see; and
3. Offer employees a significant share in the equity gains they helped achieve through a participatory stock ownership program.

The concept of "open-book management" seemed to many the riskiest part of the proposal. Stack proposed to share with every employee every scrap of operating and financial data the company had, to use information to teach people to work together to achieve common goals. He felt that information should never be used as a power tool to intimidate, control or manipulate people. Traditionally, managers are concerned that such a system of sharing of performance data may put a demoralizing spotlight on individuals and groups who miss goals, or that competitors might gain access to critical confidential information.

Stack's proposed participative stock ownership program would "give away" one-third of the company to employees through an Employee Stock Ownership Plan (ESOP), a mechanism whereby some portion is financed by reduced corporate taxes. Stack also proposed that the small group of managers who had put themselves at such risk would permit employees later to put additional amounts of money into the company by purchasing stock on a favorable basis.

The management group at the fledgling company met to discuss whether to accept Stack's ideas, how far to take each of them, and the practicalities of trying to implement even one while trying to keep the company in business.

QUESTIONS

1. What is the relationship to ethics and effectiveness in Jack Stack's leadership?

2. How would you characterize Jack Stack's leadership? Is he a Kantian leader, a servant leader, and/or a transforming leader?

CHAPTER QUESTIONS

1. Why is it difficult to be an ethical and effective leader in business?
2. What ethical challenges are distinctive to people who hold positions of leadership?

16

Who's Minding the Store?

The Ethics of Corporate Governance

Introduction

It is an old question: Who will guard the guardians? In our giant corporations, many of which are larger and more powerful than most state and national governments, who will see to it that they obey the rules and see to the public interest as well as their own profits? The answer is supposed to be corporate directors, whose job it is to ensure that the corporation follows the rules and acts responsibly. But who keeps an eye on the directors? What assures us that they, too, follow the rules and keep a perspective larger than the corporation and its chief executives? It is difficult enough to govern the corporate superstars that many CEOs have become in today's celebrity-driven media. (Even the business pages read like "lives of the rich and famous" these days.) CEOs today enjoy rock star-like celebrity status and salaries that even rock stars cannot reach, and they develop gigantic (if only sometimes justified) egos to match. To complicate matters even more, a good number of CEOs started their companies themselves. They have a privileged attitude toward their creations, which were once private companies, in which they could, in effect, make all of the rules and formulate uncontradicted policies. When they took those companies public, however, a whole new set of rules and responsibilities came to govern how they could operate and how they could spend the money that now came from their investors. Dennis Koslowski, the extravagant CEO of Tyco who threw multimillion-dollar parties and lived in several multimillion-dollar homes and apartments, all on the company tab (and not declared to his stockholders as part of his compensation), is only a particularly egregious example of what is not an uncommon problem. But imagine, if you were one of Tyco's directors, trying to manage Dennis Koslowski. How do you get him to produce results for the company and serve the public when he is, at least in his mind, the monarch, rather than a mere "officer" of the corporation? You remember, too, that he has an important, if not definitive, say in your own compensation for being a board member as well as on whether or not you continue to serve on the board. Now how do you feel about criticizing his behavior or overseeing his decisions? No matter how conscientious you are, if there is no serious insulation between the executives and the board, it is evident that your views are going to be pressured or compromised.

In response to this problem of interlocking executives and board members, some corporate analysts believe that stockholders, stakeholders, and employees (three groups that should be distinguished and might well disagree) ought to have a strong voice in corporate governance. But this has its problems, too. Democracy may be the best kind of government when it comes to running nations, but successful corporations often have to be swift moving and decisive. There is sometimes no time to debate the issues, form a committee, or take a vote. Furthermore, most successful large companies are run by a single authoritative person or perhaps a small group (a CEO, a COO, and a CFO), not a large group of people with many different voices. We want dissent and disagreement in a democracy, but do we want the same in a large corporation? Most executives, needless to say, want unity, "everybody on the same page." The more dissident voices they try to include in decisions, the more difficult that unity is to achieve. They think, how can a hundred or a thousand only somewhat-informed people make a better decision about the direction of a company than a single expert—or a handful of experts—who made that company the success that it is? On the other hand, multiple perspectives often make decisions more rational. From the executive or director's high perch, the view of the company might be impressive, but it is also limited. A worker on the floor or a line manager may see problems much more clearly than any executive could. And in terms of fairness, too, should a person who has $20,000 invested in a company after working for the company for 30 years have no say in the company's future while someone who recently invested $10 million (and so earned a seat on the board) gets to call the shots?

In this chapter we consider these problems of corporate governance, some of the recent spectacular failures of governance, and some proposals for better models of guiding corporations and their leaders. We are particularly concerned with the kinds of pressures that are placed on corporations, their boards and their CEOs, and how those pressures may be counterbalanced by regulations or other forms of systematic corporate control.

Ralph Nader, Mark Green and Joel Seligman consider the problem of how power should be exerted in corporation, by whom and on what grounds. They suggest criteria for controlling directors and monitoring the responsibility of directors. Irving Shapiro surveys the recent "state of play" of corporate boards. Mintzberg analyzes many possible models for control in corporations. Finally, John McCall argues for a strong employee voice in corporate governance.

Ralph Nader, Mark Green, and Joel Seligman

Who Rules the Corporation?

For years Ralph Nader has been one of the most powerful voices in corporate reform. He is also a prominent independent political figure. Mark Green is a leading democratic author and thinker. His most recent work is *The Book on Bush*. Joel Seligman is dean and Ethan A.H. Shepley University Professor at Washington University School of Law.

All modern state corporation statutes describe a common image of corporate governance, an image pyramidal in form. At the base of the pyramid are the shareholders or owners of the corporation. Their ownership gives them the right to elect representatives to direct the corporation and to approve fundamental corporate actions such as mergers or bylaw amendments. The intermediate level is held by the board of directors, who are required by a provision common to nearly every state corporation law "to manage the business and affairs of the corporation." On behalf of the shareholders, the directors are expected to select and dismiss corporate officers; to approve important financial decisions; to distribute profits; and to see that accurate periodic reports are forwarded to the shareholders. Finally, at the apex of the pyramid are the corporate officers. In the eyes of the law, the officers are the employees of the shareholder owners. Their authority is limited to those responsibilities which the directors delegate to them.

In reality, this legal image is virtually a myth. In nearly every large American business corporation, there exists a management autocracy. One man—variously titled the President, or the Chairman of the Board, or the Chief Executive Officer—or a small coterie of men rule the corporation. Far from being chosen by the directors to run the corporation, this chief executive or executive clique chooses the board of directors and, with the acquiescence of the board, controls the corporation.

The common theme of many instances of mismanagement is a failure to restrain the power of these senior executives. A corporate chief executive's decisions to expand, merge, or even violate the law can often be made without accountability to outside scrutiny. There is, for example, the detailed disclosures of the recent bribery cases. Not only do these reports suggest how widespread corporate foreign and domestic criminality has become; they also provide a unique study in the pathology of American corporate management. . . .

The key to management's hegemony is money. Effectively, only incumbent management can nominate directors—because it has a nearly unlimited power to use corporate funds to win board elections while opponents must prepare separate proxies and campaign literature entirely at their own expense. . . .

REVAMPING THE BOARD

The modern corporation is akin to a political state in which all powers are held by a single clique. The senior executives of a large firm are essentially not accountable to any other officials within the firm. These are precisely the circumstances that, in a democratic political state, require a separation of powers into different branches of authority. As James Madison explained in the *Federalist No. 47:*

> The accumulation of all powers, legislative, executive, and judiciary, in the same hands, whether of

one, a few or many, and whether hereditary, self-appointed, or elective, may justly be pronounced the very definition of tyranny. Were the federal constitution, therefore, really chargeable with this accumulation of power, or with a mixture of powers, having a dangerous tendency to such an accumulation, no further arguments would be necessary to inspire a universal reprobation of the system.

A similar concern over the unaccountability of business executives historically led to the elevation of a board of directors to review and check the actions of operating management. As a practical matter, if corporate governance is to be reformed, it must begin by returning the board to this historical role. The board should serve as an internal auditor of the corporations, responsible for constraining executive management from violations of law and breach of trust. Like a rival branch of government, the board's function must be defined as separate from operating management. Rather than pretending directors can "manage" the corporation, the board's role as disciplinarian should be clearly described. Specifically, the board of directors should:

- establish and monitor procedures that assure that operating executives are informed of and obey applicable federal, state, and local laws;
- approve or veto all important executive management business proposals such as corporate by-laws, mergers, or dividend decisions;
- hire and dismiss the chief executive officer and be able to disapprove the hiring and firing of the principal executives of the corporation; and
- report to the public and the shareholders how well the corporation has obeyed the law and protected the shareholders' investment.

It is not enough, however, to specify what the board should do. State corporations statutes have long provided that "the business and affairs of a corporation shall be managed by a board of directors," yet it has been over a century since the boards of the largest corporations have actually performed this role. To reform the corporation, a federal chartering law must also specify the manner in which the board performs its primary duties.

First, to insure that the corporation obeys federal and state laws, the board should designate executives responsible for compliance with these laws and require periodic signed reports describing the effectiveness of compliance procedures. Mechanisms to administer spot checks on compliance with the principal statutes should be created. Similar mechanisms can insure that corporate "whistle blowers" and nonemployee sources may communicate to the board—in private and without fear of retaliation—knowledge of violations of law.

Second, the board should actively review important executive business proposals to determine their full compliance with law, to preclude conflicts of interest, and to assure that executive decisions are rational and informed of all foreseeable risks and costs. But even though the board's responsibility here is limited to approval or veto of executive initiatives, it should proceed in as well-informed a manner as practicable. To demonstrate rational business judgment, the directorate should require management "to prove its case." It should review the studies upon which management relied to make a decision, require management to justify its decision in terms of costs or rebutting dissenting views, and, when necessary, request that outside experts provide an independent business analysis.

Only with respect to two types of business decisions should the board exceed this limited review role. The determination of salary, expense, and benefit schedules inherently possesses such obvious conflicts of interest for executives that only the board should make these decisions. And since the relocation of principal manufacturing facilities tends to have a greater effect on local communities than any other type of business decision, the board should require management to prepare a "community impact statement." This public report would be similar to the environmental impact statements presently required by the National Environmental Policy Act. It would require the corporation to state the purpose of a relocation decision; to compare feasible alternative means; to quantify the costs to the local community; and to consider methods to mitigate these costs. Although it would not prevent a corporation from making a profit-maximizing decision, it would require the corporation to minimize the costs of relocation decisions to local communities.

To accomplish this restructuring of the board requires the institutionalization of a new profession: the full-time "professional" director. Corporate scholars frequently identify William O. Douglas' 1940 proposal for "salaried, professional experts [who] would bring a new responsibility and authority to directorates and a new safety to stockholders" as the origin of the professional director idea. More recently, corporations including Westinghouse and Texas Instruments have established slots on their boards to be filled by full-time directors. Individuals such as Harvard Business School's Myles Mace and former Federal Reserve Board chairman William McChesney Martin consider their own thoroughgoing approach to boardroom responsibilities to be that of a "professional" director.

To succeed, professional directors must put in the substantial time necessary to get the job done. One cannot monitor the performance of Chrysler's or Gulf's management at a once-a-month meeting; those firms' activities are too sweeping and complicated for such ritual oversight. The obvious minimum here is an adequate salary to attract competent person to work as full-time directors and to maintain the independence of the board from executive management.

The board must also be sufficiently staffed. A few board members alone cannot oversee the activities of thousands of executives. To be able to appraise operating management, the board needs a trim group of attorneys, economists, and labor and consumer advisors who can analyze complex business proposals, investigate complaints, spot-check accountability, and frame pertinent inquiries.

The board also needs timely access to relevant corporate data. To insure this, the board should be empowered to nominate the corporate financial auditor, select the corporation's counsel, compel the forwarding and preservation of corporate records, require all corporate executives or representatives to answer fully all board questions respecting corporate operations, and dismiss any executive or representative who fails to do so.

This proposed redesign for corporate democracy attempts to make executive management accountable to the law and shareholders without diminishing its operating efficiency. Like a judiciary within the corporation, the board has ultimate powers to judge and sanction. Like a legislature, it oversees executive activity. Yet executive management substantially retains its powers to initiate and administer business operations. The chief executive officer retains control over the organization of the executive hierarchy and the allocation of the corporate budget. The directors are given ultimate control over a narrow jurisdiction: Does the corporation obey the law, avoid exploiting consumers or communities, and protect the shareholders' investment? The executive contingent retains general authority for all corporate operations.

No doubt there will be objections that this structure is too expensive or that it will disturb the "harmony" of executive management. But it is unclear that there would be any increased cost in adopting an effective board. The true cost to the corporation could only be determined by comparing the expense of a fully paid and staffed board with the savings resulting from the elimination of conflicts of interest and corporate waste. In addition, if this should result in a slightly increased corporate expense, the appropriateness must be assessed within a broader social context: should federal and state governments or the corporations themselves bear the primary expense of keeping corporations honest? In our view, this cost should be placed on the corporations as far as reasonably possible.

It is true that an effective board will reduce the "harmony" of executive management in the sense that the power of the chief executive or seniors executives will be subject to knowledgeable review. But a board which monitors rather than rubber-stamps management is exactly what is necessary to diminish the unfettered authority of the corporate chief executive or ruling clique. The autocratic power these individuals presently possess has proven unacceptably dangerous: it has led to recurring violations of law, conflicts of interest, productive inefficiency, and pervasive harm to consumers, workers, and the community environment. Under normal circumstances there should be a healthy friction between operating executives and the board to assure that the wisest possible use is made of corporate resources. When corporate executives are breaking the law, there should be no "harmony" whatsoever.

ELECTION OF THE BOARD

Restructuring the board is hardly likely to succeed if boards remain as homogeneously white, male, and narrowly oriented as they are today. Dissatisfaction with current selection of directors is so intense that analysts of corporate governance, including Harvard Laws School's Abram Chayes, Yale political scientist Robert Dahl, and University of Southern California Law School Professor Christopher Stone, have each separately urged that the starting point of corporate reform should be to change the way in which the board is elected.

Professor Chayes, echoing John Locke's principle that no authority is legitimate except that granted "the consent of the governed," argues that employees and other groups substantially affected by corporate operations should have a say in its governance:

> Shareholder democracy, so-called, is misconceived because the shareholders are not the governed of the corporations whose consent must be sought. . . . Their interests are protected if financial information is made available, fraud and overreaching are prevented, and a market is maintained in which their shares may be sold. A priori, there is no reason for them to have any voice, direct or representational, in [corporate decision making]. They are no more affected than nonshareholding neighbors by these decisions. . . .
>
> A more spacious conception of 'membership,' and one closer to the facts of corporate life, would include all those having a relation of sufficient intimacy with the corporation or subject to its powers in a sufficiently specialized way. Their rightful share in decisions and the exercise of corporate power would be exercised through an institutional arrangement appropriately designed to represent the interests of a constituency of members having a significant common relation to the corporation and its power.

Professor Dahl holds a similar view: "[W]hy should people who own shares be given the privileges of citizenship in the government of the firm when citizenship is denied to other people who also make vital contributions to the firm?" he asks rhetorically. "The people I have in mind are, of course, employees and customers, without whom the firm could not exist, and the general public, without whose support for (or acquiescence in) the myriad protections and services of the state the firm would instantly disappear. . . ." Yet Dahl finds proposals for interest group representation less desirable than those for worker self-management. He also suggests consideration of co-determination statutes such as those enacted by West Germany and ten other European and South American countries under which shareholders and employees separately elect designated portions of the board.

From a different perspective, Professor Stone has recommended that a federal-agency appoint "general public directors" to serve on the boards of all the largest industrial and financial firms. In certain extreme cases such as where a corporation repeatedly violates the law, Stone recommends that the federal courts appoint "special public directors" to prevent further delinquency.

There are substantial problems with each of those proposals. It seems impossible to design a general "interest group" formula which will assure that all affected constituencies of large industrial corporations will be represented and that all constituencies will be given appropriate weight. Even if such a formula could be designed, however, there is the danger that consumer or community or minority or franchisee representatives would become only special pleaders for their constituents and otherwise lack the loyalty or interest to direct generally. This defect has emerged in West Germany under codetermination. Labor representatives apparently are indifferent to most problems of corporate management that do not directly affect labor. They seem as deferential to operating executive management as present American directors are. Alternatively, federally appointed public directors might be frozen out of critical decision-making by a majority of "privately" elected directors, or the appointing agency itself might be biased. . . .

The homogeneity of the board can only be ended by giving to each director, in addition to a general duty to see that the corporation is profitably administered, a separate oversight responsibility, a separate expertise, and a separate constituency so that each important public concern would be guaranteed at least one informed representative on the board. There might be nine corporate directors, each of whom is elected to a board position with one of the following oversight responsibilities:

1. Employee welfare
2. Consumer protection
3. Environmental protection and community relations
4. Shareholder rights
5. Compliance with law
6. Finances
7. Purchasing and marketing
8. Management efficiency
9. Planning and research

By requiring each director to balance responsibility for representing a particular social concern against responsibility for the overall health of the enterprise, the problem of isolated "public" directors would be avoided. No individual director is likely to be "frozen out" of collegial decision-making because all directors would be of the same character. Each director would spend the greater part of his or her time developing expertise in a different area; each director would have a motivation to insist that a different aspect of a business decision be considered. Yet each would simultaneously be responsible for participating in all board decisions, as directors now are. So the specialized area of each director would supplement but not supplant the director's general duties.

To maintain the independence of the board from the operating management it reviews also requires that each federally chartered corporation shall be directed by a purely "outside" board. No executive, attorney, representative, or agent of a corporation should be allowed to serve simultaneously as a director of that same corporation. Directorial and executive loyalty should be furthered by an absolute prohibition of interlocks. No director, executive, general counsel, or company agent should be allowed to serve more than one corporation subject to the Federal Corporate Chartering Act.

Several objections may be raised. First, how can

we be sure that completely outside boards will be competent? Corporate campaign rules should be redesigned to emphasize qualifications. This will allow shareholder voters to make rational decisions based on information clearly presented to them. It is also a fair assumption that shareholders, given an actual choice and role in corporate governance, will want to elect the men and women most likely to safeguard their investments.

A second objection is that once all interlocks are proscribed and a full-time outside board required, there will not be enough qualified directors to staff all major firms. This complaint springs from that corporate mentality which, accustomed to 60-year-old white male bankers and businessmen as directors, makes the norm a virtue. In fact, if we loosen the reins on our imagination, America has a large, rich, and diverse pool of possible directorial talent from academics and public administrators and community leaders to corporate and public interest lawyers.

But directors should be limited to four two-year terms so that boards do not become stale. And no director should be allowed to serve on more than one board at any one time. Although simultaneous service on two or three boards might allow key directors to "pollinize" directorates by comparing their different experiences, this would reduce their loyalty to any one board, jeopardize their ability to fully perform their new directorial responsibilities, and undermine the goal of opening up major boardrooms to as varied a new membership as is reasonable.

The shareholder electoral process should be made more democratic as well. Any shareholder or allied shareholder group which owns .1 percent of the common voting stock in the corporation or comprises 100 or more individuals and does not include a present executive of the corporation, nor act for a present executive, may nominate up to three persons to serve as directors. This will exclude executive management from the nomination process. It also increases the likelihood of a diverse board by preventing any one or two sources from proposing all nominees. To prevent frivolous use of the nominating power, this proposal establishes a minimum shareownership condition.

Six weeks prior to the shareholders' meeting to elect directors, each shareholder should receive a ballot and a written statement on which each candidate for the board sets forth his or her qualifications to hold office and purposes for seeking office. All campaign costs would be borne by the corporation. These strict campaign and funding rules will assure that all nominees will have an equal opportunity to be judged by the shareholders. By preventing directorates from being bought, these provisions will require board elections to be conducted solely on the merit of the candidates.

Finally, additional provisions will require cumulative voting and forbid "staggered" board elections. Thus any shareholder faction capable of jointly voting approximately 10 percent of the total number of shares cast may elect a director.

A NEW ROLE FOR SHAREHOLDERS

The difficulty with this proposal is the one that troubled Juvenal two millennia ago: *Quis custodiet ipsos custodes,* or Who shall watch the watchmen? Without a full-time body to discipline the board, it would be so easy for the board of directors and executive management to become friends. Active vigilance could become routinized into an uncritical partnership. The same board theoretically elected to protect shareholder equity and internalize law might instead become management's lobbyist.

Relying on shareholders to discipline directors may strike many as a dubious approach. Historically, the record of shareholder participation in corporate governance has been an abysmal one. The monumental indifference of most shareholders is worse than that of sheep; sheep at least have some sense of what manner of ram they follow. But taken together, the earlier proposals—an outside, full-time board, nominated by rival shareholder groups and voted on by beneficial owners—will increase involvement by shareholders. And cumulative voting insures that an aroused minority of shareholders—even one as small as 9 or 10 percent of all shareholders—shall have the opportunity to elect at least one member of the board. . . .

Shareholders are not the only ones with an incentive to review decisions of corporate management; nor, as Professors Chayes and Dahl argue, are shareholders the only persons who should be accorded corporate voting rights. The increasing use by American corporations of technologies and materials that pose direct and serious threats to the health of communities surrounding their plants requires the creation of a new form of corporate voting right. When a federally chartered corporation engages, for example, in production or distribution of nuclear fuels or the emission of toxic air, water, or solid waste pollutants, citizens whose health is endangered should not be left, at best, with receiving money damages after a time-consuming trial to compensate them for damaged property, impaired health, or even death.

Instead, upon finding of a public health hazard by three members of the board of directors or 3 percent of the shareholders, a corporate referendum should be held in the political jurisdiction affected by the health hazard. The referendum would be drafted by the unit triggering it—either the three board members or a designate of the shareholders. The affected citizens by majority vote will then decide whether the hazardous practice shall be allowed to continue. This form of direct democracy has obvious parallels to the initiative and referendum procedures familiar to many states—except that the election will be paid for by a business corporation and will not necessarily occur at a regular election.

This type of election procedure is necessary to give enduring meaning to the democratic concept of "consent of the governed." To be sure, this proposal goes beyond the traditional assumption that the only affected or relevant constituents of the corporation are the shareholders. But no longer can we accept the Faustian bargain that the continued toleration of corporate destruction of local health and property is the cost to the public of doing business. In an equitable system of governance, the perpetrators should answer to their victims.

QUESTIONS

1. Is corruption at the highest levels of the corporation inevitable? How can it be guarded against?

2. Why do corporations and corporate boards so often encounter ethical dilemmas?

Irving S. Shapiro	Power and Accountability: The Changing Role of the Corporate Board of Directors

Irving S. Shapiro was a prominent attorney.

Are corporations suitably controlled, and to whom or what are they responsible?

One school of opinion holds that corporations cannot be adequately called to account because there are systemic economic and political failings. In this view, nothing short of a major overhaul will serve. What is envisioned, at least by many in this camp, are new kinds of corporate organizations constructed along the lines of democratic political institutions. The guiding ideology would be communitarian, with the needs and rights of the community emphasized in preference to profit-seeking goals now pursued by corporate leaders (presumably with Darwinian abandon, with natural selection weeding out the weak, and with society left to pick up the external costs).

BOARDS CHANGING FOR BETTER

Other critics take a more temperate view. They regard the present system as sound and its methods of governance as morally defensible. They concede, though, that changes are needed to reflect new conditions. Whether the changes are to be brought about by gentle persuasion, or require the use of a two-by-four to get the mule's attention, is part of the debate.

This paper sides with the gradualists. My position, based on a career in industry and personal observation of corporate boards at work, is that significant improvements have been made in recent years in corporate governance, and that more changes are coming in an orderly way; that with these amendments, corporations are accountable and better monitored than ever before; and that pat formulas or proposals

for massive "restructuring" should be suspect. The formula approach often is based on ignorance of what it takes to run a large enterprise, on false premises as to the corporate role in society, or on a philosophy that misreads the American tradition and leaves no room for large enterprises that are both free and efficient.

The draconian proposals would almost certainly yield the worst of all possibilities, a double-negative tradeoff: They would sacrifice the most valuable qualities of the enterprise system to gain the least attractive features of the governmental system. Privately owned enterprises are geared to a primary economic task, that of joining human talents and natural resources in the production and distribution of goods and services. That task is essential, and two centuries of national experience suggest these conclusions: The United States has been uncommonly successful at meeting economic needs through reliance on private initiative; and the competitive marketplace is a better course-correction device than governmental fiat. The enterprise system would have had to have failed miserably before the case could be made for replacing it with governmental dictum.

Why should the public have any interest in the internal affairs of corporations? Who cares who decides? Part of the answer comes from recent news stories noting such special problems as illegal corporate contributions to political campaigns, and tracking the decline and fall of once-stout companies such as Penn Central. Revelations of that kind raise questions about the probity and competence of the people minding the largest stores. There is more to it than this, though. There have always been cases of corporate failures. Small companies have gone under too,

Excerpted from a paper presented in the Fairless Lecture Series. Carnegie-Mellon University, October 24, 1979. Reprinted by permission. Notes were deleted from the text.

at a rate far higher than their larger brethren. Instances of corruption have occurred in institutions of
all sizes, whether they be commercial enterprises or
some other kind.

Corporate behavior and performance are points of
attention, and the issue attaches to size, precisely
because people do not see the large private corporation as entirely private. People care about what goes
on in the corporate interior because they see themselves as affected parties whether they work in such
companies or not.

There is no great mystery as to the source of this
challenge to the private character of governance.
Three trends account for it. First is the growth of very
large corporations. They have come to employ a
large portion of the workforce, and have become key
factors in the nation's technology, wealth and security. They have generated admiration for their
prowess, but also fear of their imputed power.

The second contributing trend is the decline of
owner-management. Over time, corporate shares
have been dispersed. The owners have hired managers, entrusted them with the power to make decisions, and drifted away from involvement in corporate affairs except to meet statutory requirements (as,
for example, to approve a stock split or elect a slate
of directors).

That raises obvious practical questions. If the
owners are on the sidelines, what is to stop the managers from remaining in power indefinitely, using an
inside position to control the selection of their own
bosses, the directors? Who is looking over management's shoulder to monitor performance?

The third element here is the rise in social expectations regarding corporations. It is no longer considered enough for a company to make products and
provide commercial services. The larger it is, the
more it is expected to assume various obligations that
once were met by individuals or communities, or
were not met at all.

With public expectations ratcheting upward, corporations are under pressure to behave more like
governments and embrace a universe of problems.
That would mean, of necessity, that private institutions would focus less on problems of their own
choice.

If corporations succumbed to that pressure, and in
effect declared the public's work to be their own, the
next step would be to turn them into institutions
accountable to the public in the same way that units
of government are accountable.

But the corporation does not parallel the government. The assets in corporate hands are more limited
and the constituents have options. There are levels of
appeal. While the only accountability in government
lies within government itself—the celebrated system
of checks and balances among the executive, legislative, and judicial branches—the corporation is in a
different situation: It has external and plural accountability, codified in the law and reinforced by social
pressure. It must "answer" in one way or another to
all levels of government, to competitors in the marketplace who would be happy to have the chance to
increase their own market share, to employees who
can strike or quit, and to consumers who can keep
their wallets in their pockets. The checks are formidable even if one excludes for purposes of argument
the corporation's initial point of accountability, its
stockholders (many of whom do in fact vote their
shares, and do not just use their feet).

The case for major reforms in corporate governance rests heavily on the argument that past governmental regulation of large enterprises has been impotent or ineffectual. This is an altogether remarkable
assertion, given the fact that the nation has come
through a period in which large corporations have
been subjected to an unprecedented flood of new legislation and rule making. Regulation now reaches
into every corporate nook and cranny—including
what some people suppose (erroneously) to be the
sanctuary of the boardroom.

Market competition, so lightly dismissed by some
critics as fiction or artifact, is in fact a vigorous force
in the affairs of almost all corporations. Size lends no
immunity to its relentless pressures. The claim that
the largest corporations somehow have set themselves above the play of market forces or, more
likely, make those forces play for themselves, is
widely believed. Public opinion surveys show that.
What is lacking is any evidence that this is so. Here
too, the evidence goes the other way. Objective studies of concentrated industries (the auto industry, for

instance) show that corporate size does not mean declining competitiveness, nor does it give assurance that the products will sell.

Everyday experience confirms this. Consider the hard times of the Chrysler Corporation today, the disappearance of many once-large companies from the American scene, and the constant rollover in the membership list of the "100 Largest," a churning process that has been going on for years and shows no signs of abating.

If indeed the two most prominent overseers of corporate behavior, government and competition, have failed to provide appropriate checks and balances, and if that is to be cited as evidence that corporations lack accountability, the burden of proof should rest with those who so state.

The basics apply to Sears Roebuck as much as to Sam's appliance shop. Wherever you buy the new toaster, it should work when it is plugged in. Whoever services the washing machine, the repairman should arrive at the appointed time, with tools and parts.

Special expectations are added for the largest firms, however. One is that they apply their resources to tasks that invite economies of scale, providing goods and services that would not otherwise be available, or that could be delivered by smaller units only at considerable loss of efficiency. Another is that, like the elephant, they watch where they put their feet and not stamp on smaller creatures through clumsiness or otherwise.

A second set of requirements can be added, related not to the markets selected by corporations individually, but to the larger economic tasks that must be accomplished in the name of the national interest and security. In concert with others in society, including big government, big corporations are expected to husband scarce resources and develop new ones, and to foster strong and diverse programs of research and development, to the end that practical technological improvements will emerge and the nation will be competitive in the international setting.

Beyond this there are softer but nonetheless important obligations: To operate with respect for the environment and with careful attention to the health and safety of people, to honor and give room to the personal qualities employees bring to their jobs, including their need to make an identifiable mark and to realize as much of their potential as possible; to lend assistance in filling community needs in which corporations have some stake; and to help offset community problems which in some measure corporations have helped to create.

Advice for Corporate Directors

Immanuel Kant

1. Act only on the maxim [intention] whereby you can at the same time will that it should become a universal law.
2. Act as if the maxim of your action were to become by your will a universal law of nature.
3. Always act so as to treat humanity, whether in yourself or in others, as an end in itself, never merely as a means.
4. Always act as if to bring about, and as a member of, a Kingdom of Ends *[that is, an ideal community in which everyone is always moral]*.

—*Fundamental Principles of the Metaphysics of Morals*

This is not an impossible job, only a difficult one. Admitting that the assignment probably is not going to be carried out perfectly by any organization, the task is unlikely to be done even half well unless some boundary conditions are met. Large corporations cannot fulfill their duties unless they remain both profitable and flexible. They must be able to attract and hold those volunteer owners; which is to say, there must be the promise of present or future gain. Companies must have the wherewithal to reinvest significant amounts to revitalize their own capital plants, year after year in unending fashion. Otherwise, it is inevitable that they will go into decline versus competitors elsewhere, as will the nation.

Flexibility is no less important. The fields of endeavor engaging large business units today are dynamic in nature. Without an in-and-out flow of products and services, without the mobility to adapt to shifts in opportunities and public preferences, corporations would face the fate of the buggywhip makers.

Profitability and flexibility are easy words to say, but in practice they make for hard decisions. A company that would close a plant with no more than a passing thought for those left unemployed would and should be charged with irresponsibility; but a firm that vowed never to close any of its plants would be equally irresponsible, for it might be consigning itself to a pattern of stagnation that could ultimately cost the jobs of the people in all of its plants.

The central requirement is not that large corporations take the pledge and bind themselves to stated actions covering all circumstances, but that they do a thoughtful and informed job of balancing competing (and ever changing) claims on corporate resources, mediating among the conflicting (also changing) desires of various constituencies, and not giving in to any one-dimensional perspective however sincerely felt. It is this that describes responsible corporate governance. . . .

Once roles are defined, the key to success in running a large corporation is to lay out a suitable division of labor between the board and the management, make that division crystal clear on both sides, and staff the offices with the right people. Perhaps the best way to make that split is to follow the pattern used in the U.S. Constitution, which stipulates the powers of the Federal Government and specifies that everything not covered there is reserved to the states or the people thereof. The board of directors should lay claim to five basic jobs, and leave the rest to the paid managers.

The duties the board should not delegate are these:

1. The determination of the broad policies and the general direction the efforts of the enterprise should take.
2. The establishment of performance standards—ethical as well as commercial—against which the management will be judged, and the communication of these standards to the management in unambiguous terms.
3. The selection of company officers, and attention to the question of succession.
4. The review of top management's performance in following the overall strategy and meeting the board's standards as well as legal requirements.
5. The communication of the organization's goals and standards to those who have a significant stake in its activities (insiders and outsiders both) and of the steps being taken to keep the organization responsive to the needs of those people.

The establishment of corporate strategy and performance standards denotes a philosophy of active stewardship, rather than passive trusteeship. It is the mission of directors to see that corporate resources are put to creative use, and in the bargain subjected to calculated risks rather than simply being tucked into the countinghouse for safekeeping.

That in turn implies certain prerequisites for board members of large corporations which go beyond those required of a school board member, a trustee of a charitable organization, or a director of a small, local business firm. In any such assignments one would look for personal integrity, interest and intelligence, but beyond these there is a dividing line that marks capability and training.

The stakes are likely to be high in the large corporation, and the factors confronting the board and management usually are complex. The elements weighing heavily in decisions are not those with which people become familiar in the ordinary course of day-to-day life, as might be the case with a school board.

Ordinarily the management of a corporation attends to such matters as product introductions, capital expansions, and supply problems. This in no way reduces the need for directors with extensive business background, though. With few exceptions, corporate boards involve themselves in strategic decisions and those involving large capital commitments. Directors thus need at least as much breadth and perspective as the management, if not as much detailed knowledge.

If the directors are to help provide informed and principled oversight of corporate affairs, a good number of them must provide windows to the outside world. That is at least part of the rationale for outside directors, and especially for directors who can bring unique perspective to the group. There is an equally strong case, though, for directors with an intimate knowledge of the company's business, and insiders may be the best qualified to deliver that. What is important is not that a ratio be established, but that the group contain a full range of the competences needed to set courses of action that will largely determine the long-range success of the enterprise.

BOARDS NEED WINDOWS

The directors also have to be able and willing to invest considerable time in their work. In this day and age, with major resources on the line and tens of thousands of employees affected by each large corporation, there should be no seat in the boardroom for people willing only to show up once a month to pour holy water over decisions already made. Corporate boards need windows, not window dressing!

There are two other qualities that may be self-evident from what has been said, but are mentioned for emphasis. Directors must be interested in the job and committed to the overall purpose of the organization. However much they may differ on details of accomplishment, they must be willing to work at the task of working with others on the board. They ought to be able to speak freely in a climate that encourages open discussion, but to recognize the difference between attacking an idea and attacking the person

who presents it. No less must they see the difference between compromising tactics to reach consensus and compromising principles.

Structures and procedures, which so often are pushed to the fore in discussions of corporate governance, actually belong last. They are not unimportant, but they are subordinate.

Structure follows purpose, or should, and that is a useful principle for testing some of the proposals for future changes in corporate boards. Today, two-thirds to three-quarters of the directors of most large corporations are outsiders, and it is being proposed that this trend be pushed still farther, with the only insider being the chief executive officer, and with a further stipulation that he not be board chairman. This idea has surfaced from Harold Williams, and variations on it have come from other sources.

The idea bumps into immediate difficulties. High-quality candidates for boards are not in large supply as it is. Conflicts of interest would prohibit selection of many individuals close enough to an industry to be familiar with its problems. The disqualification of insiders would reduce the selection pool to a still smaller number, and the net result could well be corporate boards whose members were less competent and effective than those now sitting.

Experience would also suggest that such a board would be the most easily manipulated of all. That should be no trick at all for a skillful CEO, for he would be the only person in the room with a close, personal knowledge of the business.

The objective is unassailable: Corporate boards need directors with independence of judgment; but in today's business world, independence is not enough. In coping with such problems as those confronting the electronics corporations beset by heavy foreign competition, or those encountered by international banks which have loans outstanding in countries with shaky governments, boards made up almost entirely of outsiders would not just have trouble evaluating nuances of the management's performance; they might not even be able to read the radar and tell whether the helmsman was steering straight for the rocks.

If inadequately prepared individuals are placed on corporate boards, no amount of sincerity on their part can offset the shortcoming. It is pure illusion to suppose that complex business issues and organizational problems can be overseen by people with little or no experience in dealing with such problems. However intelligent such people might be, the effect of their governance would be to expose the people most affected by the organization—employees, owners, customers, suppliers—to leadership that would be (using the word precisely) incompetent.

It is sometimes suggested that the members of corporate boards ought to come from the constituencies—an employee-director, a consumer-director, an environmentalist-director, etc. This Noah's Ark proposal, which is probably not to be taken seriously, is an extension of the false parallel between corporations and elected governments. The flaw in the idea is all but self evident: People representing specific interest groups would by definition be committed to the goals of their groups rather than any others; but it is the responsibility of directors (not simply by tradition but as a matter of law as well) to serve the organization as a whole. The two goals are incompatible.

If there were such boards they would move at glacial speed. The internal political maneuvering would be Byzantine, and it is difficult to see how the directors could avoid an obvious challenge of accountability. Stockholder suits would pop up like dandelions in the spring.

One may also question how many people of ability would stand for election under this arrangement. Quotas are an anathema in a free society, and their indulgence here would insult the constituencies themselves—a woman on the board not because she is competent but only because she is female; a black for black's sake; and so on ad nauseam.

A certain amount of constituency pleading is not all bad, as long as it is part of a corporate commitment. There is something to be said for what Harold Williams labels "tension," referring to the divergence in perspective of those concerned primarily with internal mattes and those looking more at the broader questions. However, as has been suggested by James Shepley, the president of Time, Inc., "tension" can lead to paralysis, and is likely to do so if boards are packed with groups known to be unsympathetic to the management's problems and business realities.

As Shepley commented, "The chief executive would be out of his mind who would take a risk-laden business proposition to a group of directors who, whatever their other merits, do not really understand the fine points of the business at hand, and whose official purpose is to create 'tension.' "[1]

Students of corporate affairs have an abundance of suggestions for organizing the work of boards, with detailed structures in mind for committees on audit, finance, and other areas; plus prescriptions for membership. The danger here is not that boards will pick the wrong formula—many organization charts could be made to work—but that boards will put too much emphasis on the wrong details.

The idea of utilizing a committee system in which sub-groups have designated duties is far more important than the particulars of their arrangement. When such committees exist, and they are given known and specific oversight duties, it is a signal to the outside world (and to the management) that performance is being monitored in a no-nonsense fashion.

It is this argument that has produced the rule changes covering companies listed on the New York Stock Exchange, calling for audit committees chaired by outside directors, and including no one currently active in management. Most large firms have moved in that direction, and the move makes sense, for an independently minded audit committee is a potent instrument of corporate oversight. Even a rule of that kind, though, has the potential of backfiring.

Suppose some of the directors best qualified to perform the audit function are not outsiders? Are the analytical skills and knowledge of career employees therefore to be bypassed? Are the corporate constituencies well served by such an exclusionary rule, keeping in mind that all directors, insiders or outsiders, are bound by the same legal codes and corporate books are still subject to independent, outside audit? It is scarcely a case of the corporate purse being placed in the hands of the unwatched.

Repeatedly, the question of structure turns on the basics: If corporations have people with competence and commitment on their boards, structure and process fall into line easily; if people with the needed qualities are missing or the performance standards are unclear, corporations are in trouble no matter whose guidebook they follow. Equally, the question drives to alternatives: The present system is surely not perfect, but what is better?

By the analysis presented here the old fundamentals are still sound, no alternative for radical change has been defended with successful argument, and the best course appears to be to stay within the historical and philosophical traditions of American enterprise, working out the remaining problems one by one.

NOTE

1. Shepley, *The CEO Goes to Washington,* Remarks to Fortune Corporation Communications Seminar, March 28, 1979.

QUESTIONS

1. How is the role of the board of directors changing?
2. What is the relationship between power and accountability? Why do they go hand in hand?

Henry Mintzberg | # Who Should Control the Corporation?

Henry Mintzberg is Cleghorn Professor of Management Studies at McGill University in Montreal.

Who should control the corporation? How? And for the pursuit of what goals? Historically, the corporation was controlled by its owners—through direct control of the managers if not through direct management—for the pursuit of economic goals. But as shareholding became dispersed, owner control weakened; and as the corporation grew to very large size, its economic actions came to have increasing social consequences. The giant, widely held corporation came increasingly under the implicit control of its managers, and the concept of social responsibility—the voluntary consideration of public social goals alongside the private economic ones—arose to provide a basis of legitimacy for their actions.

To some, including those closest to the managers themselves, this was accepted as a satisfactory arrangement for the large corporation. "Trust it" to the goodwill of the managers was their credo; these people will be able to achieve an appropriate balance between social and economic goals.

But others viewed this basis of control as fundamentally illegitimate. The corporation was too large, too influential, its actions too pervasive to be left free of the direct and concerted influence of outsiders. At the extreme were those who believed that legitimacy could be achieved only by subjecting managerial authority to formal and direct external control. "Nationalize it," said those at one end of the political spectrum, to put ultimate control in the hands of the government so that it will pursue public social goals. No, said those at the other end, "restore it" to direct share holder control, so that it will not waiver from the pursuit of private economic goals.

Other people took less extreme positions. "Democratize it" became the rallying cry for some, to open up the governance of the large, widely held corporation to a variety of affected groups—if not the workers, then the customers, or conservation interests, or minorities. "Regulate it" was also a popular position, with its implicit premise that only by sharing their control with government would the corporation's managers attend to certain social goals. Then there were those who accepted direct management control so long as it was tempered by other, less formal types of influence. "Pressure it," said a generation of social activists, to ensure that social goals are taken into consideration. But others argued that because the corporation is an economic instrument, you must "induce it" by providing economic incentives to encourage the resolution of social problems.

Finally, there were those who argued that this whole debate was unnecessary, that a kind of invisible hand ensures that the economic corporation acts in a socially responsible manner. "Ignore it" was their implicit conclusion.

This article is written to clarify what has become a major debate of our era, *the* major debate revolving around the private sector: Who should control the corporation, specifically the large, widely held corporation, how, and for the pursuit of what goals? The answers that are eventually accepted will determine what kind of society we and our children shall live in. . . .

As implied earlier, the various positions of who should control the corporation, and how, can be laid out along a political spectrum, from nationalization at one end to the restoration of shareholder power at the other. From the managerial perspective, however, those two extremes are not so far apart. Both call for direct control of the corporation's managers by specific outsiders, in one case the government to ensure the pursuit of social goals, in the other case the shareholders to ensure the pursuit of economic ones. It is the moderate positions—notably, trusting the corporation to the social responsibility of its managers—that are farthest from the extremes. Hence, we can fold our spectrum around so that it takes the shape of a horseshoe.

Figure 3 shows our "conceptual horseshoe," with "nationalize it" and "restore it" at the two ends. "Trust it" is at the center, because it postulates a natural balance of social and economic goals. "Democratize it," "regulate it," and "pressure it" are shown on the left side of the horseshoe, because all seek to temper economic goals with social ones. "Induce it" and "ignore it," both of which favor the exclusive pursuit of economic goals, are shown on the right side. . . .

"NATIONALIZE IT"

Nationalization of the corporation is a taboo subject in the United States—in general, but not in particular. Whenever a major corporation runs into serious difficulty (i.e., faces bankruptcy with possible loss of many jobs), massive government intervention, often including direct nationalization, inevitably comes up as an option. . . .

From a managerial and organizational perspective, the question is not whether nationalization is legitimate, but whether it works—at least in particular, limited circumstances. As a response to concerns about the social responsibility of large corporations, the answer seems to be no. The evidence suggests that social difficulties arise more from the size of an organization and its degree of bureaucratization than from its form of ownership. On the other hand, contrary to popular belief in the United States, nationalization does not necessarily harm economic efficiency. When people believe that government ownership leads to interference, politicization, and inefficiency, that may be exactly what happens. However, when they believe that nationalization has to work, then state-owned enterprises may be able to attract the very best talent in the country and thereby work well.

But economic efficiency is no reason to favor nationalization any more than is concern about social responsibility. Nationalization does, however seem to make sense in at least two particular circumstances. The first is when a mission deemed necessary in a society will not be provided adequately by the private sector. . . . The second is when the activities of an organization must be so intricately tied to government policy that it is best managed as a direct arm of the state. . . .

Thus, it is not rhetoric but requirement that should determine the role of this position as a solution to who should control the corporation. "Nationalize it" should certainly not be embraced as a panacea, but neither should it be rejected as totally inapplicable.

"DEMOCRATIZE IT"

A less extreme position—at least in the context of the American debate—is one that calls for formal devices to broaden the governance of the corporation. The proponents of this position either accept the legal fiction of shareholder control and argue that the cor-

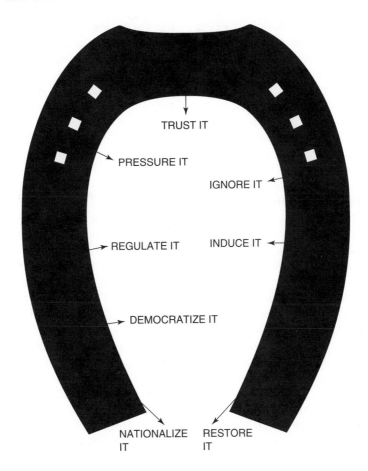

TRUST IT

PRESSURE IT

IGNORE IT

REGULATE IT   INDUCE IT

DEMOCRATIZE IT

NATIONALIZE   RESTORE
IT   IT

Figure 3   The Conceptual Horseshoe

poration's power base is too narrow, or else they respond to the emergent reality and question the legitimacy of managerial control. Why, they ask, do stockholders or self-selected managers have any greater right to control the profound decisions of these major institutions than do workers or customers or the neighbors downstream.

This stand is not to be confused with what is known as "participative management." The call to "democratize it" is a legal, rather than ethical one and is based on power, not generosity. Management is not asked to share its power voluntarily; rather, that power is to be reallocated constitutionally. That makes this position a fundamental and important

one, *especially* in the United States with its strong tradition of pluralist control of its institutions.

The debate over democratization of the corporation has been confusing, in part because many of the proposals have been so vague. We can bring some order to it by considering, in organizational terms, two basic means of democratization and two basic constituencies that can be involved. As shown in Table 1, they suggest four possible forms of corporate democracy. One means is through the election of representatives to the board of directors, which we call *representative democracy*. The other is through formal but direct involvement in internal decision making processes, which we call *participatory democ-*

racy. Either can focus on the workers—either all the employees or just those in operating tasks—or else on a host of outside interest groups, the latter giving rise to a *pluralistic* form of democracy. These are basic forms of corporate democracy in theory. With one exception, they have hardly been approached—let alone achieved—in practice. But they suggest where the "democratize it" debate may be headed. . . .

Critics . . . have pointed out the problems of defining constituencies and finding the means to hold elections. "One-person, one-vote" may be easily applied to electing representatives of the workers, but no such simple rule can be found in the case of the consumer or environmental representatives, let alone ones of the "public interest." Yet it is amazing how quickly things become workable in the United States when Americans decide to put their collective mind to it. Indeed, the one case of public directors that I came across is telling in this regard. According to a Conference Board report, the selection by the Chief Justice of the Supreme Court of New Jersey of 6 of the 24 members of the board of Prudential Insurance as public directors has been found by the company to be "quite workable."[1]

Despite its problems, representative democracy is crystal clear compared with participatory democracy. What the French call "auto-gestion" (as opposed to "co-gestion," or co-determination) seems to describe a kind of bottom-up, grassroots democracy in which the workers participate directly in decision making (instead of overseeing management's decisions from the board of directors) and also elect their own managers (who then become more administrators than bosses). Yet such proposals are inevitably vague, and I have heard of no large mass production or mass service firm—not even one owned by workers or a union—that comes close to this.

What has impeded worker participatory democracy? In my opinion, something rather obvious has stood in its way; namely, the structure required by the very organizations in which the attempts have been made to apply it. Worker participatory democracy—and worker representative democracy too, for that matter—has been attempted primarily in organizations containing large numbers of workers who do highly routine, rather unskilled jobs that are typical of most mass production and service—what I have elsewhere called Machine Bureaucracies.[2] The overriding requirement in Machine Bureaucracy is for tight coordination, the kind that can only be achieved by central administrators. For example, the myriad of decisions associated with producing an automobile at Volvo's Kalmar works in Sweden cannot be made by autonomous groups, each doing as it pleases. The whole car must fit together in a particular way at the end of the assembly process. These decisions require a highly sophisticated system of bureaucratic coordination. That is why automobile companies are struc-

Table 1   Four Basic Forms of Corporate Democracy

		Groups Involved	
		Internal Employees	External Interest Groups
Focus of Attention	Board of Directors	Worker Representative Democracy (e.g., "co-determination" or worker ownership)	Pluralistic Representative Representative Democracy (e.g., "public interest" directors)
	Internal Decision-Making Process	Worker Participatory Democracy (e.g., works councils)	Pluralistic Participatory Democracy (e.g., outsiders on new product committees)

tured into rigid hierarchies of authority, not because their managers lust for power (though lust for power some of them no doubt do). . . .

Participatory democracy is approached in other kinds of organizations. These are not the large, mass output corporations, but rather the autonomous professional institutions such as universities and hospitals, which have very different needs for central coordination. . . . But the proponents of democracy in organizations are not lobbying for changes in hospitals or universities. It is the giant mass producers they are after, and unless the operating work in these corporations becomes largely skilled and professional in nature, nothing approaching participative democracy can be expected.

In principal, the pluralistic form of participatory democracy means that a variety of groups external to the corporation can somehow control its decision-making processes directly. In practice, of course, this concept is even more elusive than the worker form of participatory democracy. To fully open up the internal decision-making processes of the corporation to outsiders would mean chaos. Yet certain very limited forms of outside participation would seem to be not only feasible but perhaps even desirable. . . . Imagine telephone company executives resolving rate conflicts with consumer groups in quiet offices instead of having to face them in noisy public hearings.

To conclude, corporate democracy—whether representative or participatory in form—may be an elu-

Corporate-Governance Reform

The certification of company accounts by senior executives should be a non-event. After all, financial statements were always supposed to be true and complete, and lying has long been deemed fraudulent. But in the wake of Enron, WorldCom and a slew of other scandals, America no longer trusts its corporate leaders to tell the truth without being warned by the sound of prison doors slamming. Thus, new rules requiring chief executives and chief financial officers to sign off on their accounts have become the stuff of headlines. All the headlines this week concerned August 14th, the SEC's deadline for the bosses of 695 listed American companies with annual revenue of more than $1.2 billion to swear by their financial statements or admit to problems. They are not the only ones under the microscope. Another 250 or so firms (those that do not have a calendar year-end) are expected to vouch for their numbers later in the year. And under America's new Sarbanes-Oxley act, the senior executives of all 14,000 firms listed in the United States, including those based overseas, will have to certify their accounts from August 29th. As people logged on in their thousands to the SEC's website to check which companies had made the cut—and as the treasury secretary, Paul O'Neill, called business honesty "the new patriotism"—it became clear that several firms would unpatriotically miss the deadline. Not surprisingly, the battered energy and telecoms sectors produced the most laggards (including CMS, Dynergy and Qwest). A big trucking group, Consolidated Freightways, also asked for more time. The penalties these companies face are still not clear.

—The Economist,
Saturday, August 17, 2002

sive and difficult concept, but it cannot be dismissed. It is not just another social issue, like conservation or equal opportunity, but one that strikes at the most fundamental of values. Ours has become a society of organizations. Democracy will have decreasing meaning to most citizens if it cannot be extended beyond political and judicial processes to those institutions that impinge upon them in their daily lives—as workers, as consumers, as neighbors. This is why we shall be hearing a great deal more of "democratize it."

"REGULATE IT"

In theory, regulating the corporation is about as simple as democratizing it is complex. In practice, it is, of course, another matter. To the proponents of "regulate it," the corporation can be made responsive to social needs by having its actions subjected to the controls of a higher authority—typically government, in the form of a regulatory agency or legislation backed up by the courts. Under regulation, constraints are imposed externally on the corporation while its internal governance is left to its managers. . . .

To some, regulation is a clumsy instrument that should never be relied upon; to others, it is a panacea for the problems of social responsibility. At best, regulation sets minimum and usually crude standards of acceptable behavior; when it works, it does not make any firm socially responsible so much as stop some from being grossly irresponsible. Because it is inflexible, regulation tends to be applied slowly and conservatively, usually lagging public sentiment. Regulation often does not work because of difficulties in enforcement. The problems of the regulatory agencies are legendary—limited resources and information compared with the industries they are supposed to regulate, the cooptation of the regulators by industries, and so on. When applied indiscriminately, regulation either fails dramatically or else succeeds and creates havoc.

Yet there are obvious places for regulation. A prime one is to control tangible "externalities"—costs incurred by corporations that are passed on to the public at large. When, for example, costly pollution or worker health problems can be attributed directly to a corporation, then there seems to be every reason to

force it (and its customers) to incur these costs directly, or else to terminate the actions that generate them. Likewise, regulation may have a place where competition encourages the unscrupulous to pull all firms down to a base level of behavior, forcing even the well-intentioned manager to ignore the social consequences of his actions. Indeed, in such cases, the socially responsible behavior is to encourage sensible regulation. "Help us to help ourselves," businessmen should be telling the government.

Although the public has generally been sympathetic to it, "regulate it," even in highly limited form, has hardly been the position of businessmen . . . Most discouraging is Theodore Levitt's revelation some years ago that business has fought every piece of proposed regulatory or social legislation throughout this century, from the Child Labor Act on up. In Levitt's opinion, much of that legislation has been good for business—dissolving the giant trusts, creating a more honest and effective stock market, and so on. Yet, "the computer is programmed to cry wolf."[3] One reason why so much legislation has been excessive and ineffective may be because it has been enacted with the support of the general public but over the obstinate resistance of businessmen.

In summary, regulation is a clumsy instrument but not a useless one. Were the business community to take a more enlightened view of it, regulation could be applied more appropriately, and we would not need these periodic housecleanings to eliminate the excesses.

"PRESSURE IT"

"Pressure it" is designed to do what "regulate it" fails to do: provoke corporations to act beyond some base level of behavior, usually in an area that regulation misses entirely. Here, activists bring ad hoc campaigns of pressure to bear on one or a group of corporations to keep them responsive to the activists' interpretation of social needs. . . .

"Pressure it" is a distinctively American position. While Europeans debate the theories of nationalization and corporate democracy in their cafés, Americans read about the exploits of Ralph Nader et al. in their morning newspapers. Note that "pressure it," unlike "regulate it," implicitly accepts management's right to make the final decisions. Perhaps this is one reason why it is favored in America.

While less radical than the other positions so far discussed, "pressure it" has nevertheless proved far more effective in eliciting behavior sensitive to social needs. . . .

Activist groups have pressured for everything from the dismemberment of diversified corporations to the development of day care centers. Of special note is the class action suit, which has opened up a whole new realm of corporate social issues. But the effective use of the pressure campaign has not been restricted to the traditional activist. President Kennedy used it to roll back U.S. Steel price increases in the early 1960s, and business leaders in Pittsburgh used it in the late 1940s by threatening to take their freight-haulage business elsewhere if the Pennsylvania Railroad did not replace its coal burning locomotives to help clean up their city's air.

"Pressure it" as a means to change corporate behavior is informal, flexible, and focused; hence, it has been highly successful. Yet it is irregular and ad hoc, with different pressure campaigns sometimes making contradictory demands on management. Compared to the positions to its right on the horseshoe, "pressure it," like the other positions to its left, is based on confrontation rather than cooperation.

"TRUST IT"

To a large and vocal contingent, which parades under the banner of "social responsibility," the corporation has no need to act irresponsibly, and therefore there is no reason for it to either be nationalized by the state, democratized by its different constituencies, regulated by the government, or pressured by activists. This contingent believes that the corporation's leaders can be trusted to attend to social goals for their own sake, simply because it is the noble thing to do. (Once this position was known as *noblesse oblige,* literally "nobility obliges.")

We call this position "trust it," or, more exactly, "trust the corporation to the goodwill of its managers," although looking from the outside in, it might just as well be called "socialize it." We place it in the center of our conceptual horseshoe because it alone postulates a natural balance between social and economic goals—a balance which is to be attained in the heads (or perhaps the hearts) of responsible businessmen. And, as a not necessarily incidental consequence, power can be left in the hands of the managers; the corporation can be trusted to those who reconcile social and economic goals.

The attacks on social responsibility, from the right as well as the left, boil down to whether corporate managers should be trusted when they claim to pursue social goals; if so, whether they are capable of pursuing such goals; and finally, whether they have any right to pursue such goals.

The simplest attack is that social responsibility is all rhetoric, no action. E.F. Cheit refers to the "Gospel of Social Responsibility" as "designed to justify the power of managers over an ownerless system. . . .

Other argue that businessmen lack the personal capabilities required to pursue social goals. Levitt claims that the professional manager reaches the top of the hierarchy by dedication to his firm and his industry; as a result, his knowledge of social issues is highly restricted.[4] Others argue that an orientation to efficiency renders business leaders inadept at handling complex social problems (which require flexibility and political finesse, and sometimes involve solutions that are uneconomic). . . .

Milton Friedman writes that social responsibility amounts to spending other people's money—if not that of shareholders, then of customers or employees. Drawing on all the pejorative terms of right-wing ideology, Friedman concludes that social responsibility is a "fundamentally subversive doctrine," representing "pure and unadulterated socialism," supported by businessmen who are "unwitting puppets of the intellectual forces that have been undermining the basis of a free society these past decades." To Friedman, "there is one and only one social responsibility of business—to use its resources and engage in activities designed to increase its profits so long as it stays within the rules of the game."[5] Let businessmen, in other words, stick to their own business, which is business itself.

The modern corporation has been described as a rational, amoral institution—its professional managers "hired guns" who pursue "efficiently" any goals asked of them. The problem is that efficiency really means measurable efficiency, so that the guns load only with goals that can be quantified. Social goals, unlike economic ones, just don't lend themselves to quantification. As a result, the performance control systems—on which modern corporations so heavily depend—tend to drive out social goals in favor of economic ones. As Robert Ackerman concluded in a study of performance control systems:

> The financial reporting system may actually inhibit social responsiveness. By focusing on economic performance . . . such a system directs energy and resources to achieving results measured in financial terms. It is the only game in town, so to speak, at least the only one with an official scorecard.[6]

Even when the chief executive is personally committed to social goals, the control systems he must rely upon to manage far flung operations may preclude him from doing anything about them. Thus, while he sings the praises of social responsibility, his employees are forced to march to the tune of economic performance. And then they respond to questionnaires with complaints about having to compromise their ethics.

How, then, is anyone to "trust it"?

The fact is that we have to trust it, for two reasons. First, the strategic decisions of large organizations inevitably involve social as well as economic consequences that are inextricably intertwined. The neat distinction between economic goals in the private sector and social goals in the public sector just doesn't hold up in practice. Every important decision of the large corporation—to introduce a new product line, to close an old plant, whatever—generates all kinds of social consequences. There is no such thing as purely economic decisions in big business. Only a conceptual ostrich, with his head deeply buried in the abstractions of economic theory, could possibly use the distinction between economic and social goals to dismiss social responsibility.

The second reason we have to "trust it" is that there is always some degree of discretion involved in corporate decision making, discretion to thwart social needs or to attend to them. Things could be a lot better in today's corporation, but they could also

be an awful lot worse. It is primarily our ethics that keep us where we are. If the performance control systems favored by diversified corporations cut too deeply into our ethical standards, then our choice is clear: to reduce these standards or call into question the whole trend toward diversification.

To dismiss social responsibility is to allow corporate behavior to drop to the lowest level, propped up only by external controls such as regulation and pressure campaigns. Solzhenitsyn, who experienced the natural conclusion of unrestrained bureaucratization, warned us (in sharp contrast to Friedman) that "a society with no other scale but the legal one is not quite worthy of man . . . A society which is based on the letter of the law and never reaches any higher is scarcely taking advantage of the high level of human possibilities."[7]

This is not to suggest that we must trust it completely. We certainly cannot trust it unconditionally by accepting the claim popular in some quarters that only business can solve the social ills of society. Business has no business using its resources without constraint in the social sphere—whether to support political candidates or to dictate implicitly through donations how non-profit institutions should allocate their efforts. But where business is inherently involved, where its decisions have social consequences, that is where social responsibility has a role to play: where business creates externalities that cannot be measured and attributed to it (in other words, where regulation is ineffective); where regulation would work if only business would cooperate with it; where the corporation can fool its customers, or suppliers, or government through superior knowledge; where useful products can be marketed instead of wasteful or destructive ones. In other words, we have to realize that in many spheres we must trust it, or at least socialize it (and perhaps change it) so that we can trust it. Without responsible and ethical people in important places, our society is not worth very much.

"IGNORE IT"

"Ignore it" differs from the other positions on the horseshoe in that explicitly or implicitly it calls for no change in corporate behavior. It assumes that social needs are met in the course of pursuing economic goals. We include this position in our horse-shoe because it is held by many influential people and also because its validity would preempt support for the other positions. We must, therefore, investigate it alongside the others.

It should be noted at the outset that "ignore it" is not the same position as "trust it." In the latter, to be good is the right thing to do; in the present case, "it pays to be good." The distinction is subtle but important, for now it is economics, not ethics, that elicits the desired behavior. One need not strive to be ethical; economic forces will ensure that social needs fall conveniently into place. Here we have moved one notch to the right on our horseshoe, into the realm where the economic goals dominate. . . .

"Ignore it" is sometimes referred to as "enlightened self-interest," although some of its proponents are more enlightened than others. Many a true believer in social responsibility has used the argument that it pays to be good to ward off the attacks from the right that corporations have no business pursuing social goals. Even Milton Friedman must admit that they have every right to do so if it pays them economically. The danger of such arguments, however—and a prime reason "ignore it" differs from "trust it"—is that they tend to support the status quo: corporations need not change their behavior because it already pays to be good.

Sometimes the case for "ignore it" is made in terms of corporations at large, that the whole business community will benefit from socially responsible behavior. Other times the case is made in terms of the individual corporation, that it will benefit directly from its own socially responsible actions. A popular claim in the 1960s, for example, was that satisfied workers lead to greater productivity. "Treat them well, get them involved, and you will make money," we were told by a generation of industrial psychologists. This particular claim has been largely discredited, but many others have taken its place—for example, that companies that are good neighbors by polluting less are more profitable. Others make the case for "ignore it" in "social investment" terms, claiming that socially responsible behavior pays off in a better image for the firm, a more positive relationship with customers, and ultimately a healthier and more stable society in which to do business.

Then, there is what I like to call the "them" argument: "If we're not good, *they* will move in"—"they" being Ralph Nader, the government, whoever. In other words, "Be good or else." The trouble with this argument is that by reducing social responsibility to simply a political tool for sustaining managerial control of the corporation in the face of outside threats, it tends to encourage general pronouncements instead of concrete actions (unless, of course, "they" actually deliver with pressure campaigns). . . .

The "ignore it" position rests on some shaky ground. It seems to encourage average behavior at best; and where the average does not seem to be good enough, it encourages the status quo. In fact, ironically, "ignore it" makes a strong case for "pressure it," since the whole argument collapses in the absence of pressure campaigns. Thus while many influential people take this position, we question whether in the realities of corporate behavior it can really stand alone.

"INDUCE IT"

Continuing around to the right, our next position drops all concern with social responsibility per se and argues, simply, "pay it to be good," or, from the corporation's point of view, "be good only where it pays." Here, the corporation does not actively pursue social goals at all, whether as ends in themselves or as means to economic ends. Rather, it undertakes socially desirable programs only when induced economically to do so—usually through government incentives. If society wishes to clean up urban blight, then let its government provide subsidies for corporations that renovate buildings; if pollution is the problem, then let corporations be rewarded for reducing it.

"Induce it" faces "regulate it" on the opposite side of the horseshoe for good reason. While one penalizes the corporation for what it does do, the other rewards it for doing what it might not otherwise do. Hence these two positions can be direct substitutes: pollution can be alleviated by introducing penalties for the damage done or by offering incentives for the improvements rendered.

Logic would, however, dictate a specific role for each of these positions. Where a corporation is doing society a specific, attributable harm—as in the case of pollution—then paying it to stop hardly seems to make a lot of sense. If society does not wish to outlaw the harmful behavior altogether, then surely it must charge those responsible for it—the corporation and, ultimately, its customers. Offering financial incentives to stop causing harm would be to invite a kind of blackmail—for example, encouraging corporations to pollute so as to get paid to stop. And every citizen would be charged for the harm done by only a few. . . .

CONCLUSION: IF THE SHOE FITS . . .

I believe that today's corporation cannot ride on any one position any more than a horse can ride on part of a shoe. In other words, we need to treat the conceptual horseshoe as a portfolio of positions from which we can draw, depending on circumstances. Exclusive reliance on one position will lead to a narrow and dogmatic society, with an excess concentration of power. We have learned about the dangers of unrestrained government ownership. No less menacing is the unrestrained pursuit of the economic interests of the shareholders, or of the oligarchy of ostensibly "socially responsible" managers. Lord Acton taught us that absolute power corrupts absolutely. In contrast, the use of a variety of positions can encourage the pluralism I believe most of us feel is necessary to sustain democracy. If the shoe fits, then let the corporation wear it.

I do not mean to imply that the eight positions do not represent fundamentally different values and, in some cases, ideologies as well. Clearly they do. But I also believe that anyone who makes an honest assessment of the realities of power in and around today's large corporations must conclude that a variety of positions have to be relied upon. Anyone can tilt to the left, right, or center of our horseshoe, favoring popular, shareholder, or managerial control, along with social or economic goals or both in balance. But even the most devoted adherent of conventional economic theory cannot, for example, dismiss regulation totally, any more than the most flaming radical can deny the place of economic goals in the corporation.

I tilt to the left of center, as has no doubt been obvious in my comments to this point. Let me summarize my own prescriptions as follows, and in the process provide some basis for evaluating the relevant roles of each of the eight positions.

First "Trust It," or at Least "Socialize It." Despite my suspicions about much of the rhetoric that passes for social responsibility and the discouraging evidence about the behavior of large contemporary organizations (not only corporations), I remain firmly convinced that without honest and responsible people in important places, we are in deep trouble. We need to trust it because, no matter how much we rely on the other positions, managers will always retain a great deal of power. And that power necessarily has social no less than economic consequences. The positions on the right side of our horseshoe ignore these social consequences while some of those on the left fail to recognize the difficulties of influencing these consequences in large, hierarchical organizations. Sitting between these two sets of positions, managers can use their discretion to satisfy or to subvert the wishes of the public. Ultimately, what managers do is determined by their sense of responsibility as individual members of society.

Although we must "trust it," we cannot *only* "trust it." As I have argued, there is an appropriate and limited place for social responsibility—essentially to get the corporation's own house in order and to encourage it to act responsibly in its own sphere of operations. Beyond that, social responsibility needs to be tempered by other positions around our horseshoe.

Then "Pressure It," Ceaselessly. As we have seen, too many forces interfere with social responsibility. The best antidote to these forces is the ad hoc pressure campaign, designed to pinpoint unethical behavior and raise social consciousness about issues. . . .

In fact, "pressure it" underlies the success of most of the other positions. Pressure campaigns have brought about necessary new regulations and have highlighted the case for corporate democracy. As we have seen, the "ignore it" position collapses without "pressure it." Indeed, what if not a pressure campaign is the media blitz of Milton Friedman to "restore it."

After That, Try to "Democratize It." A somewhat distant third in my portfolio is "democratize it," a position I view as radical only in terms of the current U.S. debate, not in terms of fundamental American values. Democracy matters most where it affects us directly—in the water we drink, the jobs we perform, the products we consume. How can we call our society democratic when many of its most powerful institutions are closed to governance from the outside and are run as hierarchies of authority from within?

As noted earlier, I have no illusions about having found the means to achieve corporate democracy. But I do know that Americans can be very resourceful when they decide to resolve a problem—and this is a problem that badly needs resolving. Somehow, ways must be found to open the corporation up to the formal influence of the constituencies most affected by it—employees, customers, neighbors, and so on—without weakening it as an economic institution. At stake is nothing less than the maintenance of basic freedoms in our society.

Then, Only Where Specifically Appropriate, "Regulate It" and "Induce It." Facing each other on the horseshoe are two positions that have useful if limited roles to play. Regulation is neither a panacea nor a menace. It belongs where the corporation can abuse the power it has and can be penalized for that abuse—notably where externalities can be identified with specific corporations. Financial inducements belong, not where a corporation has created a problem, but where it has the capability to solve a problem created by someone else.

Occasionally, Selectively, "Nationalize It" and "Restore It," but Not in Friedman's Way. The extreme positions should be reserved for extreme problems. If "pressure it" is a scalpel and "regulate it" a cleaver, then "nationalize it" and "restore it" are guillotines.

Both these positions are implicitly proposed as alternatives to "democratize it." One offers public control, the other "shareholder democracy." The trouble is that control by everyone often turns out to be control by no one, while control by the owners—even if attainable—would remove the corporation even further from the influence of those most influenced by it.

Yet, as noted earlier, nationalization sometimes makes sense—when private enterprise cannot provide a necessary mission, at least in a sufficient or appropriate way, and when the activities of a corporation must be intricately tied in to government policy.

Finally, Above All, Don't "Ignore It." I leave one position out of my portfolio altogether, because it contradicts the others. The one thing we must not do is ignore the large, widely-held corporation. It is too influential a force in our lives. Our challenge is to find ways to distribute the power in and around our large organizations so that they will remain responsive, vital, and effective.

REFERENCES

1. From J. Bacon and J. K. Brown, *Corporate Directorship Practices: Role, Selection and Legal Status of the Board* (The Conference Board and the American Society of Corporate Secretaries, Inc., 1975), p. 48.

2. See Henry Mintzberg, *Structure in Fives: Designing Effective Organizations* (Englewood Cliffs, NJ: Prentice Hall, 1983).

3. T. Levitt, "Why Business Always Loses," *Harvard Business Review* (March/April 1968), p. 83.

4. Ibid.

5. Milton Friedman, "A Friedman Doctrine: The Social Responsibility of Business is to Increase its Profits," *The New York Times Magazine,* September 13 1970, pp. 33, 126.

6. Robert W. Ackerman, *The Social Challenge to Business* (Cambridge, MA: Harvard University Press, 1975), p. 56.

7. Aleksander Solzhenitsyn, from "Why The West Has Succumbed to Cowardice," *The Montreal Star News and Review,* June 10, 1978, p. B1.

QUESTIONS

1. How does Mintzberg answer his own question? Who should control the corporation? Why?

2. Explain Mintzberg's "conceptual horseshoe" characterization of the corporation. Be sure to explain all the pressures on the corporation. Can you add new pressures? Do you think some pressures should be increased, reduced, or eliminated (through regulation, taxation, or governance)?

John J. McCall

Employee Voice in Corporate Governance: A Defense of Strong Participation Rights

John J. McCall is professor of economics at the University of California at Los Angeles.

INTRODUCTION

Participative Management." "Employee Involvement." "Flattened Hierarchies." "Employee Voice." As these current buzzwords of management literature indicate, the topic of employee participation decision making has arrived in the U.S. Once a mantra of left-wingers that was inaudible in mainstream discussions of corporate governance, concern with employee participation promises to spread in the current economic and political climate. It is urged by former Clinton administration players (Labor Secretary Robert Reich and chief economist Laura D'Andrae Tyson), promoted as an essential element of the future American workplace by the blue ribbon "Dunlop Commission on the Future of Labor-Management Relations" and embraced by some labor leaders.

DEFENSES

Employee participation rights can be defended on a number of grounds.

Dignity

First, most approaches to morality that emphasize rights do so because their adherents believe that persons somehow have inherent value and should be treated with dignity. A long tradition explains that inherent value as deriving from the ability to deliberate rationally and choose freely how to live, that is, from autonomy. Traditional hierarchical patterns of work organization, of course, treat employees as anonymous and replaceable "human resources" that are to be "managed" for the goal of corporate profit. An authentic social commitment to the dignity and autonomy of individuals would challenge that tradition. Since we spend one-third to one-half of our adult lives at work, since our work experience influences the character of even our non-working hours and since work in our culture plays such a dominant role in defining us as individuals and in establishing our social worth, a commitment to dignity and autonomy should urge that workers have some ability to exercise control over their work lives. . . . That control can only be more than token when it is possessed in amounts equal to that of management.

Fairness

Second, participation rights can be derived from modern Western moral norms that profess a commitment to the *equal* dignity of each person. While no social system could guarantee that all the interests of it members are accommodated, the commitment to equality requires that decisions affecting those interests, and especially decisions affecting important or basic interests, be made fairly. Clearly, many policy decisions made in corporations are capable of great impact on the most basic interests of workers. What more effective guarantee of fairness and accountability could there be than allowing workers to represent their own interests in the decision-making process . . . ? In order for that guarantee to be effective, however, the mechanism of participation must provide real authority. And, since a balanced and fair consideration of all interests is more likely when opposing parties have roughly equal institutional power, em-

From *Business Ethics Quarterly*, Vol. 11, Issue 1, pp. 195–213. Reprinted with permission. References were deleted from the text.

ployees deserve an amount of authority that enables them to resist policies that unfairly damage their interests. That, of course, means a right to co-determine policy at all levels.

Self-Respect

Third, it is now a psychological commonplace that a person's sense of self-worth is largely conditioned by the institutional relationships she has and by the responses from others she receives in those relationships. Of course, in contemporary America, the development of both the division of labor and hierarchical authority structures leaves little room for most workers to exercise their autonomy or to feel that their opinions are influential. The frequent consequence of such work structures is worker burnout and alienation. Workers dissociate themselves from a major portion of their lives, often with the consequence of a sense of impotence and unimportance. However, these results are less likely when workers are given opportunities for autonomous action and for the exercise of judgment. Since participation in decision making can reaffirm the employees' sense of influence and self worth, there is a presumptive reason for implementing it in the workplace.

It should be noted that this defense of participation rights does not require that those rights be rights to co-determine policy. The concerns expressed by this defense could potentially be satisfied by forms of participation that were merely advisory, if those advisory mechanisms in fact increased employees' subjective sense of influence and self-worth. It is also worth noting, however, that purely advisory mechanisms of participation carry the danger that workers, after an initial decrease in feelings of alienation, might become cynical about the real impact of the participatory structures. Cases of this abound in corporations that implemented quality circles without a strong commitment to altering traditional hierarchical and autocratic structures. . . .

Health

Fourth, if as was just suggested, contemporary work organization is an important cause of alienation, work may provide the stressors that lead to both physical and mental health problems. Some evidence indicates, however, that stress is inversely related to perceived control over one's work environment . . . Thus, if employees were granted some measure of control over workplace decisions, stress and attendant health difficulties might be reduced. In fact, data exist which show increased levels of work satisfaction when workers believe they are able to influence corporate policies. Additionally, there is evidence that employee voice in the workplace through participatory committees makes more effective regulatory initiatives aimed at health and safety. . . . Since health is a basic interest, there are presumptive reasons for programs, such as employee participation, that might reduce threats to it.

Democracy

Finally, some have argued that only by increasing citizens' sense of power over more local and immediate aspects of their lives will we be able to reverse trends toward voter apathy and disengagement from active participation in the political process, trends that so threaten the vitality of our democracy. . . . Of course, the workplace is a prime example of the kind of environment where persons can learn lessons either of impotence or efficacy. Hence, participation mechanisms can be instrumental in protecting the health of democratic politics by encouraging people toward greater civic involvement. . . .

PROPERTY RIGHTS OBJECTIONS

. . . Some objections to strong forms of worker participation arise from efficiency concerns. The most serious objections from a moral perspective, however, derive from property rights claims and it is on those that the remainder of this paper focuses.

The property objection presents a serious obstacle (at least rhetorically) to the acceptance of a manifesto right to strong employee participation. That objection asserts that extending to workers partial control over enterprise decisions is a violation of the corporate owners' property rights. Clearly, if property rights mean anything, they mean that the title holder has more or less exclusive rights to control the use of property. Of course shareholders might allow their agents, management, to introduce participatory schemes if that were a beneficial strategy. That, however, is a far cry from claiming that employees are entitled to participation as a matter of right. Since rights to private property are so central to the ideology of our culture, this objection has a rhetorical seriousness that threatens to undermine the presumptive grounds for participation.

Some reject this corporate property rights argument on the basis of a fact that . . . in contemporary corporations, ownership is separated from control. Some might suggest that since owners have already ceded control to management, there is no conflict between shareholders' property rights and an employee share of decision-making control.

. . . While it is true that contemporary corporate forms separate owners from substantial control of their property, there are still a number of reasons why corporate property rights might be seen as in conflict with strong employee participation rights.

First, even if owners have ceded control, they arguably have done so under the assumption that management will act as their fiduciary and will promote the interests of shareholders alone. Some ongoing debates about corporate control and the agency problems of corporate structures indicate that there is a serious concern that management might not focus sufficiently on shareholder benefit and might instead opportunistically use their powers to promote their own financial gain. . . . Thus, the mere separation of ownership and control does not necessarily make it any easier to defend mechanisms of participation, especially if those mechanisms might force corporate decisions to give more consideration to the interests of employees.

Second, one could imagine, as the law sometimes seems to, that the property is the corporation's and that management has a quasi-ownership right to control the corporate assets. . . . Under this interpretation, the right to control decisions is still vested in another constituency whose interests are in potential conflict with the interests of employees. A defense of strong employee participation rights must still, then, confront a property rights objection.

However . . . private property has traditionally been justified by appeals to autonomy, democracy, fairness and utility. Private possession of property has been defended as providing the greatest incentive for people to work and invest, thus raising the total amount of economic activity and goods produced and, in turn, increasing the aggregate standard of living (utility). It has been described as the only approach that rewards labor properly because it allows one who "mixes his labor with nature" to enjoy the fruits of that labor (fair return). It has been urged as an external check on government abuse that protects democracy by providing a countervailing locus of power. And it has been presented as maintaining autonomy by allowing property owners to have a stable and secure material base that frees them from over-reliance on the largesse of others.

Whatever one thinks of these traditional defenses of private property, the important thing for our purposes is that they reveal property rights to . . . have the same moral foundations as do the manifesto right of employee participation. As a consequence, it will not be possible for opponents of participation rights to brush them aside by an appeal to owner's rights to control property.

ADJUDICATING THE RIGHTS CONFLICT

What form must such further argument take? When two claimed rights rest on the same moral grounds, a theoretical defense for the priority of one over the other must show that the justifying values are more centrally at stake in the one taking priority. . . . We must ask whether the values promoted by the property rights would be compromised seriously by allowing encroachment in order to sustain another person's competing right claim. Can it be shown that property will take priority over participation rights, that autonomy, fairness and utility are more jeopardized by granting participation rights than by denying them?

Autonomy

Certainly, there seems little threat to owners' autonomy from the marginal decrease in the owners' con-

Does Governance Need Government?

As the astonishing wave of corporate scandals continues, the public's distaste for corporate misconduct deepens. The CBS poll, for example, shows just 16 percent of the public expressing a "great deal" or "quite a lot" of confidence in big business. This is the lowest level recorded since pollsters began asking this question in 1986.

More amazing still, 67 percent say that most corporate executives are not honest, compared to only 27 percent who say they are. That is not "some"; that is "most," which is quite an indictment. In addition, 79 percent believe questionable accounting practices are widespread, compared to a mere 16 percent who feel these are isolated instances limited to a few companies. Similar questions about CEOs of large companies and investment professionals also show lopsided majorities believing that wrongdoing is widespread, not confined to isolated instances. Finally, more than half (57 percent) endorse the notion that "committing white-collar crimes to make a dishonest profit for themselves and their companies" happens very often in American business, not just occasionally (39 percent) or hardly ever (2 percent).

Related to these feelings, the public is changing its views about the relationship between government and business. In an intriguing result from the Gallup poll, big business is increasingly seen as the biggest threat to the country in the future. Thirty-eight percent now believe this is the case, compared to 47 percent who believe that big government is the biggest threat. This might not seem so bad until one looks at the trend data and realizes this is the highest "threat" reading for big business since pollsters started asking this question way back in 1965; it also is the smallest gap between big business and big government recorded in those thirty-seven years.

Similarly, since 1981 pollsters have been asking whether there is "too much, too little or about the right amount of government regulation of business and industry." In the Gallup poll, 33 percent said "too little," 32 percent said "too much," and 30 percent said the "right amount." That is the highest "too little" reading since the question was first asked.

The CBS poll shows the same feelings about government regulation of business—in fact, in this instance a little stronger. Thirty-seven percent feel the federal government regulates business too little, 30 percent think too much, and 24 percent say the right amount. This is a turnaround from results of the same question in February, which showed 26 percent believing there was too little regulation and 35 percent saying too much.

Feelings are even stronger about federal regulation of businesses' accounting practices. Seventy-one percent believe the federal government should be doing more to regulate these practices, compared to just 7 percent (!) who think it should be doing less and 17 percent who feel it is doing enough.

—CBS Poll of 685 Adults. Released July 11, 2002 (conducted July 8–9, 2002); Gallup Poll of 1,013 Adults for CNN/USA Today. Released July 11, 2002 (conducted July 5–8, 2002); http://www.rcf.org/Opinions/Public_Opinion_Watch/July8–12.html

trol over their property that would be required to recognize a workers' right to co-determine corporate policy. For even if workers were given a right to co-determination, owners still would have a large bundle of rights associated with share ownership. In addition to a significant right to control through voting privileges, and a representation of their interests by management, owners retain the ability to sell their shares. Further, the evidence indicates that a well-designed program of participation does no necessary damage to productivity or profitability. There is increasing empirical and theoretical evidence that employee participation either improves productivity and/or profitability or is at least neutral with regard to those. (See citations in the immediately following paragraph). And, so, corporate property owners would still have the financial "cushion" of their investment. Since the autonomy promoting aspect of corporate share ownership is the greater economic independence and greater control over life-choices that such ownership provides, employee participation rights seem to pose no substantial threat to owners' autonomy. . . .

Fairness

One could imagine an argument that with strong participation rights workers gain greater guarantees that their interests will be considered fairly, and individual owners retain rights over their corporate assets substantial enough to provide for a fair return on investment. At the very most, owners might suffer some loss of profits returned as dividends if workers were better able to protect their interests (e.g., by gaining more safety equipment). But in assessing the fairness of this, one could argue that workers with co-determination rights assure a fairer distribution of surplus revenue than would be the case under traditional arrangements where management alone determines the distribution.

The typical replies to this suggestion are that investors deserve the return either because they took the risk or because their investment created the enterprise. This, however, ignores the facts that employees face substantial risks at work and are also essential contributors to the enterprise. Neither risk exposure nor contribution, as we will see presently, will pro-

vide grounds sufficient for the claim that investors deserve sole rights to control.

Clearly, shareholders and employees are both necessary contributors to the enterprise; the absence of either would mean the corporation would cease to exist. Some might suggest, though, that, since they initiated the process that created the organization, shareholders deserve control over the enterprise. For most contemporary corporations, however, stockholders are not temporally prior participants in the organization. I would hazard that most stock now owned was obtained after the firm was actively involved in production. In any case, it is not clear that being temporally first in involvement with the organization would carry sufficient moral weight to justify exclusion of other contributors from a say in the operation of the firm. What seems more relevant is that the contributions of both constituencies are logically necessary for any production to occur.

As for risk, it is often suggested that shareholders, as the residual risk bearers, deserve greater control. Employees, it is claimed, have already been compensated for their risks by the wage they negotiated. This position, however, fails on a number of grounds. Employees face risks to life and health at work. These risks are differentially distributed across and within occupational categories. No evidence suggests, though, that there is a risk premium given to all whose work is more risky, as this position would imply. . . .

Employees also face risks that the firm will lose money and that they will then be out of a job. While shareholders can diversify against such risk by owning a broad portfolio of stock, employees generally cannot have simultaneous careers in multiple corporations. . . . Hence, there is reason for finding that employees, too, face significant economic risk in choosing to work for a given corporation.

More importantly, it is problematic to claim that employees have been compensated for their risk and efforts by their past wages. This claim ignores the importance of internal labor markets for understanding the economics of employment. Typically, workers, after some job-hopping while young, develop long-term relationships with firms. . . . As workers stay in a firm's employment for longer periods, they gradually and increasingly make "investments" in the firm. Clearly, workers develop social attachments in their workplaces that are not easily replaced. They acquire firm specific skills that are not easily transferable nor as valuable in the external labor market as they are within the firm. They also typically gain seniority benefits (increased wages, first preference for new positions, greater opportunities for promotion, less exposure to layoffs when there are cyclic downturns in demand) and pension vesting. Given these firm-specific investments, it is not surprising that evidence indicates that the costs of being laid-off rise with the length of a worker's job tenure. . . . Workers with all these investments are likely to have a difficult time matching their old income and benefits in a new job, especially since new jobs will often begin at the lowest seniority levels.

Recent economic and industrial relations analyses explain the presence of some of these internal job characteristics by pointing out the benefits firms achieve by structuring their internal labor market in these ways. . . . Many of these practices serve to bond the worker to the firm by making quitting more expensive. Firms thus reduce the possible loss of hiring and training costs when a worker leaves voluntarily. Firms that increase wages or that increase the value of pension benefits over a worker's job tenure also solve problems associated with monitoring a worker's performance. If future earnings are likely to rise, firms create an incentive mechanism that decreases a worker's probability of slacking on the job while simultaneously decreasing the need for constant and costly performance monitoring. Since workers have more to lose if they are fired for insufficient performance, the frequency of monitoring may be reduced. Essentially, firms promise delayed, future compensation as a vehicle for achieving high productivity at reduced management costs. Thus, the longer workers remain with a firm, the more they have invested in their jobs.

These employee investments, however, are subject to predatory and opportunistic abuse by employers. The implicit bargain of higher future wages and/or benefits for current effort and loyalty to the firm is not an enforceable one. For instance, in recent cases, moneys invested in corporate pension funds on the basis of actuarial projections of future earnings of workers (so

as to assure that pension benefits were based on wage levels just before retirement) were raided during hostile takeovers because of a technicality in pension law. After the takeover, employees lost substantial value in the expected pension. . . . Similarly, in plant closings and layoffs, discharged workers are denied the implicitly promised future benefits. If we recognize, as economists and industrial relations specialists increasingly do, that the promise of higher wages and benefits in the future is part of an economic bargain that employers strike for their own benefit, it is very clear that employees have quite a bit at risk in the corporation. It is also clear that past wages and benefits cannot be seen as sufficient compensation for employees' effort and risk. The claim that they are sufficient treats labor markets as ordinary commodity markets. The above characteristics of internal labor markets, however, cannot be explained if the markets are viewed as simple commodity markets.

Thus, it does not seem that the value of fairness, whether it is understood as grounded in contribution or in risk, can provide easy theoretical grounds for a claim that property rights "trump" the manifesto right of employees to co-determination. Rather, it seems that since risk and contribution are shared between owners and employees, then both ought to be able to exercise control over corporate decisions. That, of course, is tantamount to recognition of co-determination rights for employees. . . .

Utility

The outcome of analysis is substantially the same for the two remaining values that underlie both property and participation: utility and democracy. Whether utility is substantially increased by strong participation rights will depend on data about work satisfaction, health and economic results. There is an emerging literature, both theoretical and empirical, which addresses the consequences of employee involvement for efficiency, profitability and productivity. An adequate assessment of that literature is, however, beyond the scope of this paper and will have to wait for another day.

But even without pursuing that full assessment of consequences, one could argue that the marginal

Advice to Outside Auditors

Warren Buffett

1. If the auditor were solely responsible for preparation of the company's financial statements, would they have been done differently? If "differently," the auditor should explain both management's argument and his own.
2. If the auditor were an investor, would he have received the information essential to understanding the company's financial performance during the reporting period?
3. Is the company following the same internal audit procedure that the auditor would if he himself were CEO. If not, what are the differences and why?

From *Fortune* magazine, August 22, 1999

change in current understandings of property rights that would be required to recognize participation rights will not significantly change the incentive to produce or, more to the point for this issue, invest. For, investment in U.S. would be attractive because of the stability and productivity of the economy and because of the sheer size of the American market. Moreover, as the evidence in sources cited above indicates, participatory mechanisms can contribute to a firm's efficiency. If it would not substantially alter the investment incentive, the traditional utility-based argument for private property would provide no bar to recognizing rights to co-determine corporate policy.

Democracy

Perhaps least clear is the relation between the two claimed rights (property and participation) and the vitality of democracy. The benefits of participatory processes at work for the health of democracy are speculative at best. However the contemporary role of private corporate property in promoting true democracy is also open to question. Some will claim that in a culture with strongly embedded constitutional rights against government, the real threat to democracy is in concentrated ownership of corporate wealth and its

ability to influence the outcome of public debate. (Recall that the distribution of wealth is even more skewed than is the distribution of income.) Whatever may be the case for the respective impacts on democracy of participation rights or marginally changed property rights, I doubt that those impacts, given all of the preceding, would be sufficient to tip the scales away from extending a right to participate.

CONCLUSION

The argument of this paper has been that an employee right to co-determine corporate policy has presumptive force. Its force is based on the very same values that have traditionally been used to support a right to private property. While the former right is not currently recognized, the moral commitments of the culture dictate that it ought to be. Such a recognition sets up a potential conflict between participation and property as it is now understood. I have argued that conflict should be resolved by asking which has the greater impact on the underlying values: rejecting the right to co-determination or marginally changing current understandings of corporate property rights. I have also argued both that the marginal change to property rights does least violence to those underlying values and that those who claim that participatory rights are unnecessary for achieving the underlying values are mistaken.

I would preliminarily conclude, then, since the two rights have the same underlying values and since those underlying values have not been shown more crucially at stake in the case of corporate property rights, that we are obliged to extend recognition to the manifesto right of employees to co-determine corporate policy. That would seem the only theoretically legitimate compromise between the competing rights claims.

I offer this conclusion as only preliminary for several reasons. First, as noted above, some of the arguments presented depend on beliefs that strong employee participation will not have seriously harmful economic consequences. There is solid evidence,

much of it from the performance of European firms with employee participation, to support that belief. I have not in this limited space, however, done justice to the debates about that evidence. Second, and relatedly, some questions remain about the possibility of transferring labor market institutions from one environment to another. Serious practical questions, then, must be answered before my arguments are more than preliminary.

QUESTIONS

1. Why should employees have a voice in corporate governance? What are the limits of that voice?

2. Explain the "property rights objections" to strong forms of worker participation. Do you agree with them? Why or why not?

CASES

CASE 16.1
Selling Your Sole at Birkenstock
Michael Lewis

One day this spring, two students from the Haas Business School, imbued with the values of public corporate life, traveled to a small private company to explain why it should reconsider its ways. The company was Birkenstock Footprint Sandals, or, as the employees like to call it, Birkenstock USA. Just to say the name, of course, is to hear the sound of granola crunching and the rustle of female underarm

hair in the wind. The shoe company of choice for hippies is slightly more complicated than its reputation. It was founded in 1966 by a woman named Margot Fraser to sell orthopedic shoes manufactured by the German shoemaker Birkenstock. In the beginning the only retail outlets that would stock the sandals Fraser imported were health-food stores (then novel), and so the company's first customers had a counter-

Michael Lewis, "The Irresponsible Investor," Reprinted with permission.

cultural flavor. The American distributor now sells many different kinds of shoes, including a line for the striving office worker. It has a strain of hippie in it, but other strains too.

At any rate, Birkenstock USA is still a private company, subject to ordinary market forces but immune to pressures from outside investors. When the Haas Business School students went into the company's headquarters in Novato, Calif., they found something of a mess, at least by public corporate standards. Birkenstock had been doing good works, willy-nilly, for 30 years. It paid employees to volunteer and gave away sacks of cash to worthy causes without telling a soul about it. The company was reluctant to disclose the recipients of its philanthropy; after all, wouldn't it violate the spirit of good works to publicize them? But the business-school students were able to uncover a few specifics. For instance, they discovered that Birkenstock gave money to the Elizabeth Glaser Pediatric AIDS Foundation. And that, from the investor-driven corporate point of view, was a problem: sick kids are nice and all, but what do they have to do with selling shoes, especially if you don't spend a lot of time explaining to them why they should be grateful to you?

The students recommended that Birkenstock ditch most of their good works and put all of their energy into a single very public act that connected up naturally to footwear. They shrewdly recommended that Birkenstock sponsor walks for causes. The cause did not matter so much as the fact that potential customers would be walking many miles on its behalf, and, somewhere along the line, encounter a giant sign that said BIRKENSTOCK.

The C.E.O. of Birkenstock, Matt Endriss, listened politely to what the business-school students had to say. "I wrestle with the words and phrases they throw around," he said afterward. " 'Formalize' . . . 'standardize' . . . 'best practices' . . . 'bang for your buck.' Those words don't live in this organization on a daily basis. A lot of them are words we try to abolish." He tells me, "There's a lot of discussion inside Birkenstock about 'authenticity.' " While that concept is notoriously hard to define, its opposite is not. It is inauthentic to seem not to care too much about making money in the interest of making even more of it. It is inauthentic to go bragging about corporate

goodness, in hopes of selling more shoes. When you are honest only because honesty pays, says Birkenstock's C.E.O., you risk forgetting the meaning of honesty. When you are socially responsible only because social responsibility pays, you lose any real sense of what responsibility means.

Put another way: the instinct to give quietly to a pediatric AIDS foundation is second cousin to the instinct not to use slave labor to make your shoes, or not to manipulate your earnings. It is part of a struggle against the market's relentless pressure on the business executive to behave a bit too selfishly—to become one of those corporate villains whom investors can one day profitably sue. "The whole concept of marketing corporate social responsibility seems odd," Endriss says. "Hit folks over the head and tell them how good we are and, in exchange, there's a monetary return for us."

But the matter is clearly not so simple: the people on the receiving end of Birkenstock's social conscience may be grateful, and there's no law to prevent them from telling others what the company has done. Word spreads. And it's possible that the brand Birkenstock is actually strengthened by a less conventionally corporate approach—that is, that the company, in the long run, makes more money by doing its good works on the sly. "People subconsciously think that the company is doing the right thing," Endriss says. "But you ask them, 'Why do you think it's a good company?' And they can't tell you." If it somehow pays for Birkenstock not to publicize its good works—if stealth charity is just a clever strategy for marketing to hippies—then the company is simply strolling down a different path to the biggest pot of gold. But if so, the path is long and poorly marked. "We're not as profitable as we could be," Endriss says, and then goes on to say that if he wanted to maximize the company's earnings he would fire 60 percent of the workers (the ones who build long-term relationships with customers and vendors) and jack up the price of the shoes.

"Maximizing our profits is not our chief goal," Endriss says. "The exchange of goods and services for money—Birkenstock feels it's here for different reasons." Those reasons can be summarized in a sappy sentence: the happiness of employees and customers and a feeling that it is contributing to the general well-being of the world around it. Make money, yes, but don't make a fetish of it. "If the company were compelled to answer to shareholders," the C.E.O. says, "it would destroy us."

This kind of talk is daft to most investors. Birkenstock USA has existed for nearly 40 years, but it still has only about $120 million in annual sales. It has grown slowly, generating steady but modest profits and exhibiting no great ambition to grow a lot faster. Who'd want to invest in that? To the financial market these guys are a bunch of mediocrities. But that's the idea: when you make a point of behaving extremely well you are unlikely to make as much money as when you don't. A few highly desirable companies (Google?) might be able to dictate morality to investors, but most cannot. The highest moral standards have a price, and most investors do not wish to pay it. But businesspeople who don't have distant, amoral shareholders to answer to are able to pay whatever price they can afford, for the sake of some other goal. And these goals can include behavior so admirable as to make an investor weep.

Three years ago, the founder of Birkenstock, Margot Fraser, by then a septuagenarian, realized that for

her company to survive her it would r owner. She controlled 60 percent of t shares, and the question was what to Rather than take them into the public ma the highest bidder—who would, of course, demand the fastest-rising share price—Fraser decided that she wanted to sell them all to the company's employees in a way that turned just about every employee into an owner. To calculate the price of her shares, the board, aware of the founder's desires, took the current fair-market value, then reduced it as much as they could without making the price so ridiculously low that it could be construed as a gift. But when they presented her with a price for her shares, Fraser's only question was, "Why can't you make it lower?"

QUESTIONS

1. Should you be honest only when honesty pays? How does that risk destroying the meaning of honesty? The culture of honesty?

2. What do you predict for the future of Birkenstock, with the shares in the hands of the employees? Do you think policies will change? How and why?

CASE 16.2
The Good Old Boys at WorldCom
Dennis Moberg and Edward Romar

2002 saw an unprecedented number of corporate scandals: Enron, Tyco, Global Crossing. In many ways, WorldCom is just another case of failed corporate governance, accounting abuses, and outright greed. But none of these other companies had senior executives as colorful and likable as Bernie Ebbers. A Canadian by birth, the six foot three inch former basketball coach and Sunday School teacher emerged from the collapse of WorldCom not only broke but with a personal net worth as a negative nine-digit number.[1] No palace in a gated community, no stable of racehorses, or multi-million dollar yacht to show for the telecommunications giant he created. Only debts and red ink—results some consider inevitable given his unflagging enthusiasm and entrepreneurial flair. There is no question that he did some pretty bad stuff, but he really wasn't like the corporate villains of his day: Andy Fastow of Enron, Dennis Koslowski of Tyco, or Gary Winnick of Global Crossing.

Personally, Bernie is a hard guy not to like. In 1998 when Bernie was in the midst of acquiring the telecommunications firm MCI, Reverend Jesse Jackson, speaking at an all-black college near WorldCom's Mississippi headquarters, asked how Ebbers could afford $35 billion for MCI but hadn't donated funds to local black students. Businessman LeRoy Walker, Jr., was in the audience at Jackson's speech, and afterwards set him straight. Ebbers had given over $1 million plus loads of information technology to that black college. "Bernie Ebbers," Walker reportedly told Jackson, "is my mentor."[2] Rev. Jackson was won over, but who wouldn't be by this erstwhile milkman and bar bouncer who serves meals to the homeless at Frank's Famous Biscuits in downtown Jackson, Mississippi, and wears jeans, cowboy boots, and a funky turquoise watch to work.

It was 1983 in a coffee shop in Hattiesburg, Mississippi that Mr. Ebbers first help create the business concept that would become WorldCom. "Who could have thought that a small business in itty bitty Mississippi would one day rival AT&T?" asked an editorial in Jackson, Mississippi's *Clarion-Ledger* newspaper.[3] Bernie's fall and the company's was abrupt. In June, 1999 with WorldCom's shares trading at $64, he was a billionaire, and WorldCom was the darling of The New Economy. By early May of 2002, Ebbers resigned his post as CEO, declaring that he was "1,000 percent convinced in my heart that this is a temporary thing."[4] Two months later, in spite of Bernie's unflagging optimism, WorldCom declared itself the largest bankruptcy in American history.

THE GROWTH THROUGH ACQUISITION MERRY-GO-ROUND

From its humble beginnings as an obscure long distance telephone company WorldCom, through the execution of an aggressive acquisition strategy,

evolved into the second largest long distance telephone company in the United States and one of the largest companies handling worldwide Internet data traffic. According to the WorldCom website, at its high point the company:

- Provided mission-critical communications services for tens of thousands of businesses around the world
- Carried more international voice traffic than any other company
- Carried a significant amount of the world's Internet traffic
- Owned and operated a global IP (Internet Protocol) backbone that provided connectivity in more than 2,600 cities, and in more than 100 countries
- Owned and operated 75 data centers . . . on five continents." [Data centers provide hosting and allocation services to businesses for their mission critical business computer applications.

WorldCom achieved its position as a significant player in the telecommunications industry through the successful completion of 65 acquisitions. Between 1991 and 1997, WorldCom spent almost $60 billion in the acquisition of many of these companies and accumulated $41 billion in debt.[5] Two of these acquisitions were particularly significant. The MFS Communications acquisition enabled WorldCom to obtain UUNet, a major supplier of Internet services to business, and MCI Communications gave WorldCom one of the largest providers of business and consumer telephone service. By 1997, WorldCom's stock had risen from pennies per share to over $60 a share. Through what appeared to be a prescient and successful business strategy at the height of the Internet boom, WorldCom became a darling of Wall Street. In the heady days of the technology bubble Wall Street took notice of WorldCom and its then visionary CEO, Bernie Ebbers. This was a company "on the make," and Wall Street investment banks, analysts and brokers began to discover WorldCom's value and make "strong buy recommendations" to investors. As this process began to unfold, the analysts recommendations, coupled with the continued rise of the stock of the stock market, made World-

Com stock desirable and the market's view of the stock was that it could only go up. As the stock value went up, it was easier for WorldCom to use stock as the vehicle to continue to purchase additional companies. The acquisition of MFS Communications and MCI Communications were, perhaps, the most significant in the long list of WorldCom acquisitions. With the acquisition of MFS Communications and its UUNet unit, "WorldCom (s)uddenly had an investment story to offer about the value of combining long distance, local service and data communications."[6] In late 1997, British Telecommunications Corporation made a $19 billion bid for MCI. Very quickly, Ebbers made a counter offer of $30 billion in WorldCom stock. In addition, Ebbers agreed to assume $5 billion in MCI debt, making the deal $35 billion or 1.8 times the value of the British Telecom offer. MCI took WorldCom's offer making WorldCom a truly significant global telecommunications company.

All this would be just another story of a successful growth strategy if it wasn't for one significant business reality-mergers and acquisitions, especially large ones, present significant managerial challenges in at least two areas. First, management must deal with the challenge of integrating new and old organizations into a single smooth functioning business. This is a time-consuming process that involves thoughtful planning and a considerable amount of senior managerial attention if the acquisition process is to increase the value of the firm to both shareholders and stakeholders. With 65 acquisitions in six years and several of them large ones, WorldCom management had a great deal on their plate. The second challenge is the requirement to account for the financial aspects of the acquisition. The complete financial integration of the acquired company must be accomplished, including and accounting of asset, debts, good will and a host of other financially important factors. This must be accomplished through the application of generally accepted accounting practices (GAAP).

In July 2002, WorldCom filed for bankruptcy protection after several disclosures regarding accounting irregularities. Among them was the admission of im-

properly accounting for operating expenses as capital expenses in violation of generally accepted accounting practices (GAAP). WorldCom has admitted to a $9 billion adjustment for the period from 1999 thorough the first quarter of 2002.

SWEETHEART LOANS TO SENIOR EXECUTIVES

Bernie Ebbers' passion for his corporate creation loaded him up on common stock. Through generous stock options and purchases Ebbers' WorldCom holdings grew and grew, and he typically financed these purchases with his existing holdings as collateral. This was not a problem until the value of WorldCom stock declined, and Bernie faced margin calls (a demand to put up more collateral for outstanding loans) on some of his purchases. At that point he faced a difficult dilemma. Because his personal assets were insufficient to meet the substantial amount required to meet the call, he could either sell some of his common shares to finance the margin calls or request a loan from the company to cover the calls. Yet, when the board learned of his problem, it refused to let him sell his shares on the grounds that it would depress the stock price and signal a lack of confidence about WorldCom's future.

Had he pressed the matter and sold his stock, he would have escaped the bankruptcy financially whole, but Ebbers honestly thought WorldCom would recover. Thus, it was enthusiasm and not greed that trapped Mr. Ebbers. The executives associated with other corporate scandals sold at the top. In fact, other WorldCom executives did much, much better than Ebbers. Bernie borrowed against his stock. That course of action makes sense if you believe the stock will go up, but it's the road to ruin if the stock goes down. Unlike the others, he intended to make himself rich taking the rest of the shareholders with him. In his entire career, Mr. Ebbers sold company shares only half a dozen times. Detractors may find him irascible and arrogant, but defenders describe him as a principled man.

The policy of boards of directors authorizing loans for senior executives raises eyebrows. The sheer magnitude of the loans to Ebbers was breathtaking. The $341 million loan the board granted Mr. Ebbers is the largest amount any publicly traded company has lent to one of its officers in recent memory.[7] Beyond that, some question whether such loans are ethical. "A large loan to a senior executive epitomizes concerns about conflict of interest and breach of fiduciary duty," said former SEC enforcement official Seth Taube.[8] Nevertheless, 27% of major publicly traded companies had loans outstanding for executive officers in 2000 up from 17% in 1998 (most commonly for stock purchase but also home buying and relocation). Moreover, there is the claim that executive loans are commonly sweetheart deals involving interest rates that constitute a poor rate of return on company assets. WorldCom charged Ebbers slightly more than 2% interest, a rate considerably below that available to "average" borrowers and also below the company's marginal rate of return. Considering such factors, one compensation analyst claims that such lending "should not be part of the general pay scheme of perks for executives . . . I just think it's the wrong thing to do."[9]

WHAT'S A NOD OR WINK AMONG FRIENDS?

In the autumn of 1998, Securities and Exchange Commissioner Arthur Levitt, Jr. uttered the prescient criticism, "Auditors and analysts are participants in a game of nods and winks.[10] It should come as no surprise that it was Arthur Andersen that endorsed many of the accounting irregularities that contributed to WorldCom's demise.[11] Beyond that, however, were a host of incredibly chummy relationships between WorldCom's management and Wall Street analysts.

Since the Glass-Steagall Act was repealed in 1999, financial institutions have been free to offer an almost limitless range of financial services to its commercial and investment clients. Citigroup, the result of the merger of Citibank and Travelers Insurance Company, who owned the investment bank and brokerage firm Salomon Smith Barney, was an early beneficiary of investment deregulation. Citibank regularly dispensed cheap loans and lines of credit as a means of attracting and rewarding corporate clients for highly lucrative work in mergers and acquisi-

tions. Since WorldCom was so active in that mode, their senior managers were the target of a great deal of influence peddling by their banker, Citibank. For example, Travelers Insurance, a Citigroup unit, lent $134 million to a timber company Bernie Ebbers was heavily invested in. Eight months later, WorldCom chose Salomon Smith Barney, Citigroup's brokerage unit, to be the lead underwriter of $5 billion of it's bond issue.[12]

But the entanglements went both ways. Since the loan to Ebbers was collateralized by his equity holdings, Citigroup had reason to prop up WorldCom stock. And no one was better at that than Jack Grubman, Salomon Smith Barney's telecommunication analyst. Grubman first met Bernie Ebbers in the early 1990's when he was heading up the precursor to WorldCom, LDDS Communications. The two hit it off socially, and Grubman started hyping the company. Investors were handsomely rewarded for following Grubman's buy recommendations until stock reached its high, and Grubman rose financially and by reputation. In fact, *Institutional Investing* magazine gave Jack a Number 1 ranking in 1999,[13] and *Business Week* labeled him "one of the most powerful players on Wall Street.[14]

The investor community has always been ambivalent about the relationship between analysts and the companies they analyze. As long as analyst recommendations are correct, close relations have a positive insider quality, but when their recommendations turn south, corruption is suspected. Certainly Grubman did everything he could to tout his personal relationship with Bernie Ebbers. He bragged about attending Bernie's wedding in 1999. He attended board meeting at WorldCom's headquarters. Analysts at competing firms were annoyed with this chumminess. While the other analysts strained to glimpse any tidbit of information from the company's conference call, Grubman would monopolize the conversation with comments about "dinner last night."[15]

It is not known who picked up the tab for such dinners, but Grubman certainly rewarded executives for their close relationship with him. Both Ebbers and WorldCom CFO Scott Sullivan were granted privileged allocations in IPO (Initial Public Offering) auctions. While the Securities and Exchange Commission allows underwriters like Salomon Smith Barney to distribute its allotment of new securities as it sees fit among its customers, this sort of favoritism has angered many small investors. Banks defend this practice by contending that providing high net worth individuals with favored access to hot IPOs is just good business. Alternatively, they allege that greasing the palms of distinguished investors creates a marketing "buzz" around an IPO, helping deserving small companies trying to go public get the market attention they deserve. For the record, Mr. Ebbers personally made $11 million in trading profits over a four-year period on shares from initial public offerings he received from Salomon Smith Barney.[16] In contrast, Mr. Sullivan lost $13,000 from IPOs, indicating that they were apparently not "sure things."[17]

There is little question but that friendly relations between Grubman and WorldCom helped investors from 1995 to 1999. Many trusted Grubman's insider status and followed his rosy recommendations to financial success. In a 2000 profile in *Business Week,* he seemed to mock the ethical norm against conflict of interest: "what used to be a conflict is now a synergy," he said at the time. "Someone like me . . . would have been looked at disdainfully by the buy side 15 years ago. Now they know that I'm in the flow of what's going on."[18] Yet, when the stock started cratering later that year, Grubman's enthusiasm for WorldCom persisted. Indeed, he maintained the highest rating on WorldCom until March 18, 2002 when he finally raised its risk rating. At that time, the stock had fallen almost 90% from its high two years before. Grubman's mea culpa was to clients on April 22 read, "In retrospect the depth and length of the decline in enterprise spending has been stronger and more damaging to WorldCom than we even anticipated."[19] An official statement from Salomon Smith Barney two weeks later seemed to contradict the notion that Grubman's analysis was conflicted, "Mr. Grubman was not alone in his enthusiasm for the future prospects of the company. His coverage was based purely on information yielded during his analysis and was not based on personal relationships."[20] Right.

On August 15, 2002 Jack Grubman resigned from Salomon where he had made as much as $20 million per year. His resignation letter read in part, "I under-

stand the disappointment and anger felt by investors as a result of [the company's] collapse, I am nevertheless proud of the work I and the analysts who work with me did."[21] On December 19, 2002, Jack Grubman was fined $15 million and was banned for securities transactions for life by the Securities and Exchange Commission for such conflicts of interest.

The media vilification that accompanies one's fall from power unearthed one interesting detail about Grubman's character—he repeatedly lied about his personal background. A graduate of Boston University, Mr. Grubman claimed a degree from MIT. Moreover, he claimed to have grown up in colorful South Boston, while his roots were actually in Boston's comparatively bland Oxford Circle neighborhood. What makes a person fib about his personal history is an open question. As it turns out, this is probably the least of Jack Grubman's present worries. New York State Controller H. Carl McCall sued Citicorp, Arthur Andersen, Jack Grubman, and others for conflict of interest. According to Mr. McCall, "this is another case of corporate coziness costing investors billions of dollars and raising troubling questions about the integrity of the information investors receive."[22]

NOTES

1. This is only true if he is liable for the loans he was given by WorldCom. If he avoids those somehow, his net worth may be plus $8.4 million according to the *Wall Street Journal* (see S. Pulliam & J. Sandberg [2002]. Worldcom Seeks SEC Accord As Report Claims Wider Fraud [November 5], A-1).

2. Padgett, T., & Baughn, A. J. (2002). The Rise and Fall of Bernie Ebbers. *Time, 159,* (19 [May 12]), 56+.

3. Morse, D., & Harris, N. (2002). In Mississippi, Ebbers is a Man to be Proud Of. *Wall Street Journal,* May 2, 2002, B-1.

4. Young, S., & Solomon, D. (2002). WorldCom Backs Chief Executive For $340 Million. *Wall Street Journal* (February 8), B-1.

5. Romero, Simon, & Atlas, Rava D. (2002). WorldCom's Collapse: The Overview. *New York Times,* (July 22), A-1.

6. Eichenwald, Kurt (2002). For WorldCom, Acquisitions Were Behind its Rise and Fall, *New York Times,* (August 8), A-3.

7. Salomon, D., & Sandberg, J. (2002). Leading the News. *Wall Street Journal* (November 6), A-3, report that Bernie used 8% of this load for personal use, an uncharacteristically self-serving move for Mr. Ebbers.

8. Young, S. (2002). Big WorldCom Loan May Have Spurred Inquiry. *Wall Street Journal* (March 14), A-3.

9. Lublin, J. S., & Young, S. (2002). WorldCom Loan to CEO of $341 Million is the Most Generous in Recent Memory. *Wall Street Journal* (March 15), A-4.

10. Byrne, J. A. (2002). Fall from grace: Joe Berardino Presided over the Biggest Accounting Scandals Ever and the Demise of a Legendary Firm. *Business Week* (August 12), 50+.

11. These amounted to over $9 million in overstated income. For an explanation as to how some of this was done, see Elstrom, P. (2002). How to Hide $3.8 Billion in Expenses. *Business Week* (July 8), 41+.

12. Morgenson, G. (2002). More Clouds over Citigroup in Its Dealings with Ebbers. *New York Times* (November 3), 1.

13. Smith, R., & Salomon, D. (2002). Heard on the Street Ebbers' Exit Hurts WorldCom's Biggest Fan. *Wall Street Journal* (May 3), C-1.

14. Rosenbush, S. (2002). Inside the Telecom Game. *Business Week* (August 5), p. 34+.

15. Ibid.

16. Craig, S. (2002). Offerings Were Easy Money for Ebbers. *Wall Street Journal* (September 3), C-1.

17. Ibid.

18. Rosenbush, op. cit., 34.

19. Smith, op. cit., C-1.

20. Ibid.

21. Editors (2002), Salomon's Jack Grubman Resigns. *United Press International* (August 15), 10082777w0186.

22. Weil, J. (2002). Leading the News: An Ebbers Firm Got Citigroup loans. *Wall Street Journal* (October 14), A-3.

QUESTIONS

1. Was Ebbers greedy or just misguided? If you could go back in time and give Ebbers advice—if you were his corporate consultant—what would you tell him?

2. Could ethics have helped Ebbers and the others who were involved? How?

CASE 16.3
CEO Compensation at Qwest
Sasha Lyutse

In April 2002, despite posting a net loss of $4 billion for the previous year and being strained by a $25 billion debt, Qwest Communications awarded its CEO, Joseph Nacchio, a yearly compensation and benefits package of $217.3 million, including pay and potential gains from stock option grants. At the time of this writing, Qwest shares were 83 percent off their 52-week high.

In 2001 Nacchio received a salary of almost $1.2 million, a 27 percent increase over 2000, but his bonus dropped 32 percent to $1.5 million. In addition, he obtained at least $74.5 million from exercising stock options and long-term incentive pay of $24.4 million. Other compensation of $229,705 included a $136,745 allocation for use of corporate aircraft. However, stock options, with a potential future value of $115.6 million, became worthless by September 2002, according to the Investor Responsibility Research Center, since Qwest's share price dropped lower that the $16.81 exercise price of the options. So, as of September 2002, the actual worth of the compensation and benefits package for the year was approximately $101.7 million.

According to the Investor Responsibility Research Center, this was one of the top pay packages for 2001, based on an analysis of CEO pay at 267 companies with revenue of $1 billion or more. A Qwest spokesperson, however, said that Nacchio's pay is on a scale with other firms trying to retain officers and that Qwest has outperformed many competitors. (See *USA TODAY,* April 10, 2002.)

In 2002, despite a 30-month-long stock market slump, there appeared to remain a wide disjuncture between CEO pay and company performance. There was at the time little evidence of substantial CEO-pay-package cuts even in companies that performed poorly. Executive salaries generally rose, despite an economic climate of low stock prices and greater scrutiny of directors and executives as a result of corporate financial and fraud scandals. While average worker salaries were rising just above 3.6 percent, many CEOs were receiving double-digit salary increases, bonuses, stock option grants potentially worth millions, and benefits such as company-owned apartments.

QUESTION

1. Is Joseph Nacchio's yearly compensation and benefits package of $217.3 million fair, unfair, or neither fair nor unfair?

CHAPTER QUESTIONS

1. Why do corporations and the leaders of corporations go morally astray? What are the pressures? Does power corrupt? And does absolute power corrupt absolutely? Why do we need corporate governance? Who should make the rules for the "governors," and how?

2. Who has a right to govern the corporation? How are governance rights established? Whose interest should the "governors" of corporations serve? How should the governors balance competing interests?

17

Is Everything for Sale?

The Future of the Free Market

Introduction

The enthusiasm for market economies may be justified, but should it have it limits? From the outskirts of medieval towns to the center of downtown today, the market has changed from a marginal activity to an essential social enterprise. Local commercial life has given way to global capitalism, and the question is no longer "does this society have a market economy?" but "what kind of a market economy does this society have and how efficient is it?" Commercial life has expanded and infiltrated almost all human activities, so that virtually everything now may be said to have a market value. To take an obvious but awkward example, the value of a human life is now set in dollar terms for the sake of insurance or in lawsuits. (Ford settled Pinto deaths at a rate of $200,000 per person. Malpractice suits sometimes calculate the value of a life in terms of the loss of expected lifetime income.) But "money can't buy happiness," we are told, and "money can't buy love." To be sure, such bits of folk wisdom have their amusing retorts, but we readily recognize what is right about them. Money can't buy everything. Not everything is part of the market. What is most personal about us is not part of the market—and when it becomes part of the market, it is no longer personal. Prostitution is an example. What is wrong is not the sex or even the promiscuity, but the commercialization of something that should not be commercialized. (Thus, "marrying for money" is often subject to the same charge.) When a person "sells out," he or she gives up part of what is most dear and personally precious. We rightly object when commercialization infects religion, and we certainly should object a lot more than we do when it pervades politics.

Is everything for sale? Most of us would surely say no. But what are the limits? Does the market rule everything? Again, most of us would surely say no. But what are the exceptions? This not an all-or-nothing question. After a devastating hurricane in Florida recently, some local merchants jacked up their prices. They were accused of "price-gouging," in other words, taking advantage of the desperate and distorted demands in an emergency situation and ignoring their obligations to the community. No one objected to the merchants charging a "fair" price for such things as bottled water, batteries, and flashlights, covering their costs and giving them a reasonable profit. But taking advantage of situation was another matter, and at some point (a matter of considerable debate), their sense of solidarity with their neighbors should have kicked in. (If only for the sake of future business. No doubt those neighbors will not be good customers after this.) Religion is off-limits, but from the sale of Indulgences that Luther railed against in the sixteenth century to the obscene mix of religion, politics, and commercialism today, the distinction between the spiritual and the commercial has not always been easy to discern.

The readings in this chapter are necessarily abstract in that they consider the nature of economies in general, rather than the particular workings of any one of them. But they raise a central question of special importance in a society that has confidence in the free market to solve all sorts of social problems. We begin, accordingly, with the great philosopher Aristotle writing about a noncapitalist society, ancient Athens. Aristotle expresses considerable doubt about the virtues of what we call "business" and the motivation of those who practice it. We balance this selection with a reading from the "father" of the modern market economy, Adam Smith, who defends the benefits of the free market in his *Wealth of Nations* and an analysis of Smith by contemporary business ethicist, Patricia Werhane. We then balance these selections with an excerpt from one of the most famous critics of capitalism, Karl Marx, and the reflections of a contemporary Marxist, Robert Heilbroner, on the "Triumph of Capitalism." Nineteenth-century philosopher-economist John Stuart Mill makes the connection between laissez-faire economics and education. Then we turn to a different conception of the market economy with "small is beautiful" author E. F. Schumacher, who defends what he calls "Buddhist Economics." Nobel prize winner Amartya Sen speaks on the "The Economics of Poverty," and, by way of contrast, economist Thorstein Veblen comments on our status seeking in "Pecuniary Emulation," from his *Theory of the Leisure Class*. Finally, Daniel Bell discusses "the cultural contradictions of capitalism" and Robert Kuttner discusses the issue that is the title of this chapter, "Everything for Sale."

Aristotle | # Two Kinds of Commerce

Aristotle was one of the two greatest Greek philosophers of ancient times and arguably the first economist. But in his *Politics,* his ethics is wholly devoted to an examination of happiness (eudaimonia) and the good life.

Of the art of acquisition then there is one kind which by nature is a part of the management of a household, in so far as the art of household management must either find ready to hand, or itself provide, such things necessary to life, and useful for the community of the family or state, as can be stored. They are the elements of true riches; for the amount of property which is needed for a good life is not unlimited, although Solon in one of his poems says that

No bound to riches has been fixed for man.

But there is a boundary fixed, just as there is in the other arts; for the instruments of any art are never unlimited, either in number or size, and riches may be defined as a number of instruments to be used in a household or in a state.

There is another variety of the art of acquisition which is commonly and rightly called an art of wealth-getting, and has in fact suggested the notion that riches and property have no limit. Being nearly connected with the preceding, it is often identified with it. But though they are not very different, neither are they the same. The kind already described is given by nature, the other is gained by experience and art.

Let us begin our discussion of the question with the following considerations:

Of everything which we possess there are two uses: both belong to the thing as such, but not in the same manner, for one is the proper, and the other the improper or secondary use of it. For example, a shoe is used for wear, and is used for exchange; both are uses of the shoe. He who gives a shoe in exchange for money or food to him who wants one, does indeed use the shoe as a shoe, but this is not its proper or primary purpose, for a shoe is not made to be an object of barter. The same may be said of all possessions, for the art of exchange extends to all of them, and it arises at first from what is natural, from the circumstance that some have too little, others too much. Hence we may infer that retail trade is not a natural part of the art of getting wealth; had it been so, men would have ceased to exchange when they had enough. In the first community, indeed, which is the family, this art is obviously of no use, but it begins to be useful when the society increases. For the members of the family originally had all things in common; later, when the family divided into parts, the parts shared in many things, and different parts in different things, which they had to give in exchange for what they wanted, a kind of barter which is still practised among barbarous nations who exchange with one another the necessaries of life and nothing more; giving and receiving wine, for example, in exchange for corn, and the like. This sort of barter is not part of the wealth-getting art and is not contrary to nature, but is needed for the satisfaction of men's natural wants. The other or more complex form of exchange grew, as might have been inferred, out of the simpler. When the inhabitants of one country became more dependent on those of another, and they imported what they needed, and exported what they had too much of, money necessarily came into use. For the various necessaries of life are not easily carried about, and hence men agreed to employ in their dealings with each other something which was intrinsically useful and easily applicable to the purposes of life, for example, iron, silver, and the like. Of this the value was at first

from Aristotle, *Politics,* trans. W. S. Ross (Oxford University Press, 1916).

measured simply by size and weight, but in process of time they put a stamp upon it, to save the trouble of weighing and to mark the value.

When the use of coin had once been discovered, out of the barter of necessary articles arose the other art of wealth-getting, namely, retail trade; which was at first probably a simple matter, but became more complicated as soon as men learned by experience whence and by what exchanges the greatest profit might be made. Originating in the use of coin, the art of getting wealth is generally thought to be chiefly concerned with it, and to be the art which produces riches and wealth; having to consider how they may be accumulated. Indeed, riches is assumed by many to be only a quantity of coin, because the arts of getting wealth and retail trade are concerned with coin. Others maintain that coined money is a mere sham, a thing not natural, but conventional only, because, if the users substitute another commodity for it, it is worthless, and because it is not useful as a means to any of the necessities of life, and, indeed, he who is rich in coin may often be in want of necessary food. But how can that be wealth of which a man may have a great abundance and yet perish with hunger, like Midas in the fable, whose insatiable prayer turned everything that was set before him into gold?

Hence men seek after a better notion of riches and of the art of getting wealth than the mere acquisition of coin, and they are right. For natural riches and the natural art of wealth-getting are a different thing; in their true form they are part of the management of a household; whereas retail trade is the art of producing wealth, not in every way, but by exchange. And it is thought to be concerned with coin; for coin is the unit of exchange and the measure or limit of it. And there is no bound to the riches which spring from this art of wealth-getting. As in the art of medicine there is no limit to the pursuit of health, and as in the other arts there is no limit to the pursuit of their several ends, for they aim at accomplishing their ends to the uttermost (but of the means there is a limit, for the end is always the limit), so, too, in this art of wealth-getting there is no limit of the end, which is riches of the spurious kind, and the acquisition of wealth. But the art of wealth-getting which consists in household management, on the other hand, has a limit; the unlimited

acquisition of wealth is not its business. And, therefore, in one point of view, all riches must have a limit; nevertheless, as a matter of fact, we find the opposite to be the case; for all getters of wealth increase their hoard of coin without limit. The source of the confusion is the near connexion between the two kinds of wealth-getting; in either, the instrument is the same, although the use is different, and so they pass into one another; for each is a use of the same property, but with a difference: accumulation is the end in the one case, but there is a further end in the other. Hence some persons are led to believe that getting wealth is the object of household management, and the whole idea of their lives is that they ought either to increase their money without limit, or at any rate not to lose it. The origin of this disposition in men is that they are intent upon living only, and not upon living well; and, as their desires are unlimited, they also desire that the means of gratifying them should be without limit. Those who do aim at a good life seek the means of obtaining bodily pleasures; and, since the enjoyment of these appears to depend on property, they are absorbed in getting wealth: and so there arises the second species of wealth-getting. For, as their enjoyment is in excess, they seek an art which produces the excess of enjoyment; and, if they are not able to supply their pleasures by the art of getting wealth, they try other arts, using in turn every faculty in a manner contrary to nature. The quality of courage, for example, is not intended to make wealth, but to inspire confidence; neither is this the aim of the general's or of the physician's art; but the one aims at victory and the other at health. Nevertheless, some men turn every quality or art into a means of getting wealth; this they conceive to be the end, and to the promotion of the end they think all things must contribute.

Thus, then, we have considered the art of wealth-getting which is unnecessary, and why men want it; and also the necessary art of wealth-getting, which we have seen to be different from the other, and to be a natural part of the art of managing a household, concerned with the provision of food, not, however, like the former kind, unlimited, but having a limit.

And we have found the answer to our original question, Whether the art of getting wealth is the business of the manager of a household and of the statesman or not their business?—viz. That wealth is presupposed by them. For as political science does not make men, but takes them from nature and uses them, so too nature provides them with earth or sea or the like as a source of food. At this stage begins the duty of the manager of a household, who has to order the things which nature supplies;—he may be compared to the weaver who has not to make but to use wool, and to know, too, what sort of wool is good and serviceable or bad and unserviceable. Were this otherwise, it would be difficult to see why the art of getting wealth is a part of the management of a household and the art of medicine not; for surely the members of a household must have health just as they must have life or any other necessary. The answer is that as from one point of view the master of the house and the ruler of the state have to consider about health, from another point of view not they but the physician; so in one way the art of household management, in another way the subordinate art, has to consider about wealth. But, strictly speaking, as I have already said, the means of life must be provided beforehand by nature; for the business of nature is to furnish food to that which is born; and the food of the offspring is always what

remains over of that form which it is produced. Wherefore the art of getting wealth out of fruits and animals is always natural.

There are two sorts of wealth-getting, as I have said; one is a part of household management, the other is retail trade: the former necessary and honourable, while that which consists in exchange is justly censured; for it is unnatural, and a mode by which men gain from one another. The most hated sort, and with the greatest reason, is usury, which makes a gain out of money itself, and not from the natural object of it. For money was intended to be used in exchange, but not to increase at interest. And this term interest, which means the birth of money from money, is applied to the breeding of money because the offspring resembles the parent. Wherefore of all modes of getting wealth this is the most unnatural.

QUESTIONS

1. What is the difference between the art of wealth getting and retail trade?

2. Is the art of wealth getting the business of the statesman? Why or why not?

| Adam Smith | The Benefits of Capitalism |

Adam Smith was the great classical economist who wrote *An Inquiry into the Nature and Causes of the Wealth of Nations* and invoked the tantalizing image of an "invisible hand" that would organize the sum of (more or less) self-interested economic actions into common prosperity.

Everybody must be sensible how much labor is facilitated and abridged by the application of proper machinery. It is unnecessary to give any example. I shall only observe, therefore, that the invention of all those machines by which labor is so much facilitated and abridged seems to have been originally owning to the division of labor. Men are much more likely to discover easier and readier methods of attaining any object when the whole attention of their minds is directed toward that single object than when it is dissipated among a great variety of things. But in consequence of the division of labor, the whole of every

From Adam Smith, *An Inquiry into the Nature and Causes of the Wealth of Nations* (New York: Hafrer, 1948), pp. 6–9.

man's attention comes naturally to be directed toward some one very simple object. It is naturally to be expected, therefore, that some one or other of those who are employed in each particular branch of labor should soon find out easier and readier methods of performing their own particular work, wherever the nature of it admits of such improvement. A great part of the machines made use of in those manufactures in which labor is most subdivided were originally the inventions of common workmen, who, being each of them employed in some very simple operation, naturally turned their thoughts toward finding out easier and readier methods of performing it. Whoever has been much accustomed to visit such manufactures must frequently have been shown very pretty machines which were the inventions of such workmen in order to facilitate and quicken their own particular part of the work. In the first fire-engines, a boy was constantly employed to open and shut alternately the communication between the boiler and the cylinder, according as the piston either ascended or descended. One of those boys, who loved to play with his companions, observed that, by tying a string from the handle of the valve which opened this communication to another part of the machine, the valve would open and shut without his assistance, and leave him at liberty to divert himself with his play-fellows. One of the greatest improvements that has been made upon this machine, since it was first invented, was in this manner the discovery of a boy who wanted to save his own labor.

All the improvements in machinery, however, have by no means been the inventions of those who had occasion to use the machines. Many improvements have been made by the ingenuity of the makers of the machines, when to make them became the business of a peculiar trade; and some by that of those who are called philosophers or men of speculation, whose trade it is not to do anything, but to observe everything; and who, upon that account, are often capable of combining together the powers of the most distant and dissimilar objects. In the progress of society, philosophy or speculation becomes, like every other employment, the principal or sole trade and occupation of a particular class of citizens. Like every other employment too, it is subdivided into a great number of different branches, each of which affords occupation to a peculiar tribe or class of philosophers; and this subdivision of employment in philosophy, as well as in every other business, improves dexterity, and saves time. Each individual becomes more expert in his own peculiar branch, more work is done upon the whole, and the quantity of science is considerably increased by it.

It is the great multiplication of the productions of all the different arts, in consequence of the division of labor, which occasions, in a well-governed society, that universal opulence which extends itself to the lowest ranks of the people. Every workman has a great quantity of his own work to dispose of beyond what he himself has occasion for; and every other workman being exactly in the same situation, he is enabled to exchange a great quantity of his own goods for a great quantity, or, what comes to the same thing, for the price of a great quantity of theirs. He supplies them abundantly with what they have occasion for, and they accommodate him as amply with what he has occasion for, and a general plenty diffuses itself through all the different ranks of the society.

Observe the accommodation of the most common artificer or day laborer in a civilized and thriving country, and you will perceive that the number of people of whose industry a part, though but a small part, has been employed in procuring him this accommodation, exceeds all computation. The woolen coat, for example, which covers the day laborer, as coarse and rough as it may appear, is the produce of the joint labor of a great multitude of workmen. The shepherd, the sorter of the wool, the wool-comber or carder, the dyer, the scribbler, the spinner, the weaver, the fuller, the dresser, with many others, must all join their different arts in order to complete even this homely production. How many merchants and carriers, besides, must have been employed in transporting the materials from some of those workmen to others who often live in a very distant part of the country! how much commerce and navigation in particular, how many ship-builders, sailors, sail-makers, rope-makers, must have been employed in order to bring together the different drugs made use of by the dyer, which often come from the remotest corners of the world! What a variety of labor too is necessary in order to produce the tools of the meanest of those workmen! To say nothing of such complicated machines as the ship of the sailor, the mill of the fuller, or even the loom of the weaver, let us consider only what a variety of labor is requisite in order to form that very simple machine, the shears with which the shepherd clips the wool. The miner, the builder of the furnace for smelting the ore, the feller of the timber, the burner of the charcoal to be made use of in the smelting-house, the brick-maker, the brick-layer, the workmen who attend the furnace, the mill-wright, the forger, the smith, must all of them join their different arts in order to produce them. Were we to examine, in the same manner, all the different parts of his dress and household furniture, the coarse linen shirt which he wears next his skin, the shoes which cover his feet, the bed which he lies on, and all the different parts which compose it, the kitchen grate at which he prepares his victuals, the coals which he makes use of for that purpose, dug from the bowels of the earth, and brought to him perhaps by a long sea and a long land carriage, all the other utensils of his kitchen, all the furniture of his table, the knives and forks, the earthen or pewter plates upon which he serves up and divides his victuals, the different hands employed in preparing his bread and his beer, the glass window which lets in the heat and the light, and keeps out the wind and the rain, with all the knowledge and art requisite for preparing

that beautiful and happy invention, without which these northern parts of the world could scarce have afforded a very comfortable habitation, together with the tools of all the different workmen employed in producing those different conveniencies; if we examine, I say, all these things, and consider what a variety of labor is employed about each of them, we shall be sensible that without the assistance and co-operation of many thousands, the very meanest person in a civilized country could not be provided, even according to what we very falsely imagine the easy and simple manner in which he is commonly accommodated. Compared, indeed, with the more extravagant luxury of the great, his accommodation must no doubt appear extremely simple and easy; and yet it may be true, perhaps, that the accommodation of an European prince does not always so much exceed that of an industrious and frugal peasant, as the accommodation of the latter exceeds that of many an African king, the absolute master of the lives and liberties of ten thousand naked savages.

QUESTIONS

1. How does Smith explain the improvements in machinery? Why does that matter?

2. Why does Smith discuss the "woolen coat" of a workman? Why is he concerned about the complexity and organization of labor?

Patricia Werhane

Adam Smith's Relevance to Contemporary Economic Theory

Patricia Werhane teaches business ethics at the University of Virginia and currently holds the Wicklander Chair in Business Ethics and is director of the Institute for Business and Professional Ethics at De Paul University in Chicago. She is the author of *Adam Smith and His Legacy for Modern Capitalism* (Oxford University Press, 1991).

Some commentators find Smith to be a utopian whose laissez-faire model is an ideal impossible to realize. Typical of this view is Gunnar Myrdal's statement: "A sunny optimism radiates from Smith's writing. He had no keen sense of social disharmonies, for interest conflicts. . . . On the whole, it is true to say that he was blind to social conflicts. The world is for him harmonious. Enlightened self-interest ultimately increases social happiness."[1] But as I have suggested, this interpretation belies much of what Smith worries about in the *WN*. He finds fault with the fate of labor when it is allocated to small repetitive tasks; he sees problems with collusion between merchants and manufacturers; he details countless situations in which business people act against the public interest; he knows that property ownership yields inequalities; and he recognizes that unfair disadvantages occur even under the condition of perfect liberty. Smith, then, is hardly a "sunny" utopian.

In Smith's documentation of the failures of capitalism, Robert Heilbroner finds what he calls a "dark side" to Smith's analysis. Heilbroner argues that Smith himself predicted the moral decay and decline of capitalism, that his aim for any society is the "natural progress toward improvement" of both liberty and material conditions. Yet paradoxes that result from perfect liberty show that Smith allegedly developed a pessimistic view of capitalism, finding that his ideal political economy would eventually create economic and moral decay, for both capitalists and laborers. According to Heilbroner, Smith did not see a solution for these paradoxes, but he did see the problems that advanced capitalism might create.[2]

Heilbroner interprets Smith's analysis of the four stages of the development of property and civil government as four progressive stages in the historical evolution of economic growth that describe a model for all economic evolution. Our natural desire to "better our condition" is such that "in favourable circumstances society both *will* and *should* pass through these stages in sequence,"[3] according to Heilbroner's reading of Smith. In an earlier chapter I questioned such an interpretation of Smith's so-called philosophy of history. But given that reading, Heilbroner then criticizes Smith for truncating the description of the historical process of economic development by concluding that the last stage is an age of commerce. Smith did not do justice to his own insights, according to Heilbroner, because he himself saw the eventual decline of an unregulated private property system.

It is true that although Smith is a strong advocate of economic growth and finds that the age of commerce—with freedom, industrialization, and specialization of labor—provides the conditions for such growth, he does not paint a completely optimistic picture of the future of a commercial society. For example, he sees perfect liberty as leading to the improvement of standards of living for the laborer and sees the demand for labor as raising wages and thus reducing capital and economic growth. In a

From Patricia Werhane, *Adam Smith and His Legacy for Modern Capitalism* (New York: Oxford University Press, 1991). Reprinted with permission.

nation where there is full employment and wages continue to rise because of the demand for labor, Smith predicts that profits will fall and that capital will be unavailable for reinvestment. He sees that in a prosperous society the population increases; the demand for higher wages reduces stocks; and eventually both wages and stock decline. Alternatively, if there is too much capital for reinvestment in proportion to the demand for goods, the competition for goods will lower profits. Smith does not detail these possibilities but merely implies their likely occurrence in the distant future. Nevertheless, in such cases economic growth halts, and the economy becomes stagnant or static and eventually declines.

> In a country fully peopled in proportion to what either its territory could maintain or its stock employ, the competition for employment would necessarily be so great as to reduce the wages of labour to what was barely sufficient to keep up the number of labourers, and, the country being already fully peopled, that number could never be augmented. In a country fully stocked in proportion to all the business it had to transact. . . . [t]he competition, therefore, would everywhere be as great, and consequently the ordinary profit as low as possible. [The] usual market rate of interest . . . would be so low as to render it impossible for any but the very wealthiest people to live upon the interest of their money. . . . It would be necessary that almost every man should be a man of business, or engage in some sort of trade.[4]

Certainly this is not a positive outlook toward economic and social happiness. Smith, however, reveals in the next paragraphs that in such a situation, low prices of commodities produced by such cheap labor would place that country in an advantageous trade position with its neighbors, thereby eventually improving that economic situation.

Heilbroner points out that Smith sees a "dark side" on the microeconomic level as well. The division of labor, essential to industrial capitalism, also raises wages, but Smith also recognizes that the division of labor with the repetitiveness of its tasks also impairs the moral character and intelligence of the workers. Therefore, Heilbroner argues, we have the first recognition of what later came to be known as the alienation of labor resulting from industrialization.

Smith also predicted overpopulation problems. A well-paid laboring class produces more children, who expand the work force and thus contribute to a decline in wages. Smith noticed, too, that excess profits lead to both avarice and the moral decay of capitalists and even of the poor. Landholders, and even manufacturers and merchants, seldom take into account the public interest and often collude with one another to control wages or prices. Smith's ideal of perfect liberty, then, as Heilbroner sees it, when linked to a laissez-faire economy and economic growth, eventually leads to moral and economic decay.

Heilbroner makes little of the fact that although Smith acknowledges these problems, he also proposes solutions. Smith thinks that a civil government that enforces laws of justice and develops public works can both ameliorate private activities not in the public interest and preserve the ideal of competition. One of the public works that government should undertake is the education of every citizen, for it is education, according to Smith, that will improve the plight of the laborers. And one must not forget that Smith sees the demand for goods and the division of labor as means to liberate human beings from their reliance on agriculture, to force laborers to become independent of the charity of their landlords, and, more importantly, to expedite the development of the laborers' liberty from their labor. This can be realized only through economic growth, thus the division of labor functions to improve both the liberty and the economic status of laborers.

Heilbroner interprets Smith as a pessimist because, he argues, Smith sees free enterprise both as the last stage in economic progress and as having its own built-in disintegration. According to Heilbroner, Smith predicts the decline of capitalism, yet he could not find solutions to these paradoxes. Heilbroner traces Smith's failure to find solutions to his inability to imagine a solution to population growth and the finite availability of capital. Moreover, Smith could not see beyond capitalism to envision further historical-economic progress, a fifth stage in historical-economic evolutionary development.

Contrary to Heilbroner, I believe that although Smith found problems and even paradoxes in his ideal political economy, he saw solutions to these paradoxes within the system he proposed. According to Smith, an unregulated commercial and industrial economy is an ideal system—better than mercantilism or other forms of regulated economy because of its basis in natural liberty and justice and its promise of economic growth. But the system and thus the invisible hand work best only when the five conditions I cited earlier—perfect liberty, internal self-restraint, coordination, laws of justice, and perfect competition—are operative. The proposed system, then, is an ideal, because perfect liberty is seldom achieved; not every individual is willing to restrain his or her self-interests; cooperation is not always in the public interest; laws of justice are not always complete or fairly enforced; and perfect competition is rarely achieved, because advantages are not usually distributed similarly among competing parties. The division of labor, essential to the economic well-being of an economy, reaches its ends only when in addition to the foregoing conditions, there is available capital for investment, an unsatisfied market demand for goods, and an opportunity for an expanding market. Smith's lists of failures of laissez-faire are not "acknowledged exceptions" but, rather, failures of the ideal to be realized. He is somewhat pessimistic because he finds these failures to exist, but he is not pessimistic about his ideal. For if these conditions could be achieved, a "natural harmony in the economic order" would be possible. Therefore, Smith is neither a utopian nor a pessimist about his ideal of a political economy.

Smith presents an optimal scheme for a realizable political economy that balances private and public interests, that maximizes natural liberty and opportunity for laborers and the poor as well as the wealthy, while also increasing economic well-being. Because his political economy is not utopian, there are trade-offs that may not be acceptable to all economic thinkers, but for Smith such trade-offs are balanced by a generally improved climate of natural liberty and economic welfare. If one considers his political economy in its eighteenth-century economic political context and if one analyzes his scheme in its totality rather than abstracting self-interest, individualism, the invisible hand, property rights, the division of labor, or nonregulation as representative of his theses, then Smith's political economy becomes a viable possibility in that context, and he can be seen as an alternative to both Marxism and the radical individualism of the nineteenth-century social Darwinists.

NOTES

1. Gunnar Myrdal, *The Political Element in the Development of Economic Theory* (1953), p. 107.

2. Robert Heilbroner, "The Paradox of Progress." in A. Skinner and T. Welson, eds. *Essays on Adam Smith* (Oxford: Clarendon, 1975) p. 524.

3. Ibid., p. 526.

4. *Wealth of Nations,* I ix 20.

QUESTIONS

1. Is Smith a utopian? Give detailed examples in your response. What does Heilbroner think (according to Werhane)?

2. What are the five conditions that Werhane identifies as essential to the just operation of an unregulated economy? Why does she need all five?

| Karl Marx | Commodity Fetishism |

Karl Marx was a brilliant but often misused philosopher-economist in the nineteenth century. His great tome was the three-volume *Das Kapital,* published in 1887, which laid out the ground rules for Marxism and then communism in the twentieth century.

The wealth of those societies in which the capitalist mode of production prevails, presents itself as "an immense accumulation of commodities," its unit being a single commodity. Our investigation must therefore begin with the analysis of a commodity.

A commodity is, in the first place, an object outside us, a thing that by its properties satisfies human wants of some sort or another. The nature of such wants, whether, for instance, they spring from the stomach or from fancy, makes no difference. Neither are we here concerned to know how the object satisfies these wants, whether directly as means of subsistence, or indirectly as means of production.

Every useful thing, as iron, paper, &c., may be looked at from the two points of view of quality and quantity. It is an assemblage of many properties, and may therefore be of use in various ways. To discover the various use of things is the work of history. So also is the establishment of socially-recognised standards of measure for the quantities of these useful objects. The diversity of these measures has its origin partly in the diverse nature of the objects to be measured, partly in convention.

The utility of a thing makes it a use-value. But this utility is not a thing of air. Being limited by the physical properties of the commodity, it has no existence apart from that commodity. A commodity, such as iron, corn, or a diamond, is therefore, so far as it is a material thing, a use-value, something useful. This property of a commodity is independent of the amount of labour required to appropriate its useful qualities. When treating of use-value, we always assume to be dealing with definite quantities, such as dozens of watches, yards of linen, or tons of iron. The use-values of commodities furnish the material for a special study, that of the commercial knowledge of commodities. Use-values become a reality only by use or consumption: they also constitute the substance of all wealth, whatever may be the social form of that wealth. In the form of society we are about to consider, they are, in addition, the material depositories of exchange value.

Exchange value, at first sight, presents itself as a quantitative relation, as the proportion in which values in use of one sort are exchanged for those of another sort, a relation constantly changing with time and place. Hence exchange value appears to be something accidental and purely relative, and consequently an intrinsic value, *i.e.,* an exchange value that is inseparably connected with inherent in commodities, seems a contradiction in terms. . . .

If . . . we leave out of consideration the use-value of commodities, they have only one common property left, that of being products of labour. But even the product of labour itself has undergone a change in our hands. If we make abstraction from its use-value, we make abstraction at the same time from the material elements and shapes that make the product a use-value; we see in it no longer a table, a house, yarn, or any other useful thing. Its existence as a material thing is put out of sight. Neither can it any longer be regarded as the product of the labour of the joiner, the mason, the spinner, or of any other definite kind of productive labour. Along with the useful qualities of the products themselves, we put out of sight both the

From *Capital* Vol. I, ???.

Au: Provide a complete source/permission note.

useful character of the various kinds of labour embodied in them, and the concrete forms of that labour; there is nothing left but what is common to them all; all are reduced to one and the same sort of labour, human labour in the abstract.

Let us now consider the residue of each of these products; it consists of the same unsubstantial reality in each, a mere congelation of homogeneous human labour, of labour-power expended without regard to the mode of its expenditure. All that these things now tell us is, that human labour-power has been expended in their production, that human labor is embodied in them. When looked at as crystals of this social substance, common to them all, they are—Values.

We have seen that when commodities are exchanged, their exchange value manifests itself as something totally independent of their use-value. But if we abstract from their use-value, there remains their Value as defined above. Therefore, the common substance that manifests itself in the exchange value of commodities, whenever they are exchanged, is their value. The progress of our investigation will show that exchange value is the only form in which the value of commodities can manifest itself or be expressed. For the present, however, we have to consider the nature of value independently of this, its form.

A use-value, or useful article, therefore, has value only because human labour in the abstract has been embodied or materialised in it. How, then, is the magnitude of this value to be measured? Plainly, by the quantity of the value-creating substance, the labour, contained in the article. The quantity of labour, however, is measured by its duration, and labour-time in its turn finds its standard in weeks, days, and hours. . . .

We see then that that which determines the magnitude of the value of any article is the amount of labour socially necessary, or the labour-time socially necessary for its production. Each individual commodity, in this connexion, is to be considered as an average sample of its class. Commodities, therefore, in which equal quantities of labour are embodied, or which can be produced in the same time, have the same value. The value of one commodity is to the value of any other, as the labour-time necessary for the production of the one is to that necessary for the

production of the other. "As values, all commodities are only definite masses of congealed labour-time."

A commodity appears, at first sight, a very trivial thing, and easily understood. Its analysis shows that it is, in reality, a very queer thing, abounding in metaphysical subtleties and theological niceties. So far as it is a value in use, there is nothing mysterious about it, whether we consider it from the point of view that by its properties it is capable of satisfying human wants, or from the point that those properties are the product of human labour. It is as clear as noon-day, that man, by his industry, changes the forms of the materials furnished by Nature, in such a way as to make them useful to him. The form of wood, for instance, is altered, by making a table out of it. Yet, for all that, the table continues to be that common, every-day thing, wood. But, so soon as it steps forth as a commodity, it is changed into something transcendent. It not only stands with its feet on the ground, but, in relation to all other commodities, it stands on its head, and evolves out of its wooden brain grotesque ideas, far more wonderful than "table-turning" ever was.

The mystical character of commodities does not originate, therefore, in their use-value. Just as little does it proceed from the nature of the determining factors of value. For, in the first place, however varied the useful kinds of labour, or productive activities, may be, it is a physiological fact, that they are functions of the human organism, and that each such function, whatever may be its nature or form, is essentially the expenditure of human brain, nerves, muscles, &c. Secondly, with regard to that which forms the groundwork for the quantitative determination of value, namely, the duration of that expenditure, or the quantity of labour, it is quite clear that there is a palpable difference between its quantity and quality. In all states of society, the labour-time that it costs to produce the means of subsistence must necessarily be an object of interest to mankind, though not of equal interest in different stages of development. And lastly, from the moment that men in any way work for one another, their labour assumes a social form.

Whence, then, arises the enigmatical character of

the product of labour, so soon as it assumes the form of commodities? Clearly from this form itself. The equality of all sorts of human labour is expressed objectively by their products all being equally values; the measure of the expenditure of labour-power by the duration of that expenditure, takes the form of the quantity of value of the products of labour; and finally, the mutual relations of the producers, within which the social character of their labour affirms itself, take the form of a social relation between the products.

A commodity is therefore a mysterious thing, simply because in it the social character of men's labour appears to them as an objective character stamped upon the product of that labour; because the relation of the producers to the sum total of their own labour is presented to them as a social relation, existing not between themselves, but between the products of their labour. This is the reason why the products of labour become commodities, social things whose qualities are at the same time perceptible and imperceptible by the senses. In the same way the light from an object is perceived by us not as the subjective excitation of our optic nerve, but as the objective form of something outside the eye itself. But, in the act of seeing, there is at all events, an actual passage of light from one thing to another, from the external object to the eye. There is a physical relation between physical things. But it is different with commodities. There, the existence of the things *qua* commodities, and the value relation between the products of labour which stamps them as commodities, have absolutely no connexion with their physical properties and with the material relations arising therefrom. There it is a definite social relation between men, that assumes, in their eyes, the fantastic form of a relation between things. In order, therefore, to find an analogy, we must have recourse to the mist-enveloped regions of the religious world. In that world the productions of the human brain appear as independent beings endowed with life, and entering into relation both with one another and the human race. So it is in the world of commodities with the products of men's hands. This I call the Fetishism which attaches itself to the products of labour, so soon as they are produced as commodi-

ties, and which is therefore inseparable from the production of commodities.

This Fetishism of commodities has its origin, as the foregoing analysis has already shown, in the peculiar social character of the labour that produces them.

As a general rule, articles of utility become commodities, only because they are products of the labour of private individuals or groups of individuals who carry on their work independently of each other. The sum total of the labour of all these private individuals forms the aggregate labour of society. Since the producers do not come into social contact with each other until they exchange their products, the specific social character of each producer's labour does not show itself except in the act of exchange. In other words, the labour of the individual asserts itself as a part of the labour of society, only by means of the relations which the act of exchange establishes directly between the products, and indirectly, through them, between the producers. To the latter, therefore, the relations connecting the labour of one individual with that of the rest appear, not as direct social relations between individuals at work, but as what they really are, material relations between persons and social relations between things. It is only by being exchanged that the products of labour acquire, as values, one uniform social status, distinct from their varied forms of existence as objects of utility. This division of a product into a useful thing and a value becomes practically important, only when exchange has acquired such an extension that useful articles are produced for the purpose of being exchanged, and their character as values has therefore to be taken into account, beforehand, during production. From this moment the labour of the individual producer acquires socially a two-fold character. On the one hand, it must, as a definite useful kind of labour, satisfy a definite social want, and thus hold its place as part and parcel of the collective labour of all, as a branch of a social division of labour that has sprung up spontaneously. On the other hand, it can satisfy the manifold wants of the individual producer himself, only in so far as the mutual exchangeability of all kinds of useful private labour is an established social fact, and therefore the private useful labour of each producer ranks on an equality with that of all others. The equalisation of the most different kinds of labour can be the result only of an abstraction from their inequalities, or of reducing them to their common denominator, viz., expenditure of human labour power or human labour in the abstract. The two-fold social character of the labour of the individual appears to him, when reflected in his brain, only under those forms which are impressed upon that labour in everyday practice by the exchange of products. In this way, the character that his own labour possesses of being socially useful takes the form of the condition, that the product must be not only useful, but useful for others, and the social character that his particular labour has of being the equal of all other particular kinds of labour, takes the form that all the physically different articles that are the products of labour, have one common quality, viz, that of having value.

QUESTIONS

1. Why do we tend to "fetishize" commodities?
2. What is the distinction Marx draws between "exchange-value" and "use-value"?

Robert Heilbroner

Reflections on the Triumph of Capitalism

Robert Heilbroner teaches at the New School for Social Research in New York. He wrote the classic *The Worldly Philosophers* and has written widely on "the future of capitalism."

Less than seventy-five years after it officially began, the contest between capitalism and socialism is over: capitalism has won. The Soviet Union, China, and Eastern Europe have given us the clearest possible proof that capitalism organizes the material affairs of humankind more satisfactorily than socialism: that however inequitably or irresponsibly the marketplace may distribute goods, it does so better than the queues of a planned economy; however mindless the culture of commercialism, it is more attractive than state moralism; and however deceptive the ideology of a business civilization, it is more believable than that of a socialist one. . . .

Yet I doubt whether the historic drama will conclude, like a great morality play, in the unequivocal victory of one side and the ignominious defeat of the other. The economic enemy of capitalism has always been its own self-generated dynamics, not the presence of an alternative economic system. Socialism, in its embodiments in the Soviet Union and, to a lesser degree, China, [was] a military and political competitor but never an economic threat. Thus, despite the rout of centralized planning . . . one would have to be very incautious to assume that capitalism will now find itself rid of its propensity to generate both inflation and recession, cured of its intermittent speculative fevers, or free of threatening international economic problems. Nevertheless, in one very important respect the triumph of capitalism alters the manner in which we must assess its prospects. The old question "Can capitalism work?"

to which endless doubting answers have been given by its critics, becomes "Can capitalism work well enough?" which is quite another thing.

. . . Modern-day economists sedulously avoid scenarios of long-term capitalist development—a caution that was not shared by the great economists of the past, virtually all of whom wrote boldly about prospects for the system. What is perhaps more surprising is that, although they disagreed about many things, those economic thinkers were near-unanimous in depicting the prospects as gloomy. Adam Smith, for example, believed that the society of his time, which had not yet been named capitalism, would have a long run but would end up in decline. Marx, of course, expected the demise of the system, but so did John Stuart Mill, whose *Principles of Political Economy* was published in 1848, the year of Marx's *Manifesto*. The most important Victorian economist, Alfred Marshall, warned against socialism and unconsidered changes, but his very Victorianism—he called for "economic chivalry"—makes us squirm a little as we read the exhortative concluding words of his *Principles*. His pupil and protégé, John Maynard Keynes, was of a different mind. Only a "somewhat comprehensive socialization" of investment, he wrote, would rescue the system from intolerable levels of unemployment. Even Joseph Schumpeter, the most conservative (and the least publicly known) of these magisterial economists, asked in his famous *Capitalism, Socialism and Democracy,* in 1942, "Can capitalism survive?" and answered, "No. I do not think it can." . . .

Keynes . . . based his prognosis not on material limitations of the system but on economic ones—not on the intrinsic lack of any need for a second line from London to York but on the lack of enough purchasing power to buy all the tickets on the first line and thereby establish a possible demand for a second. Quixotically, this lack of purchasing power was itself the result of a failure on the part of business to undertake enough investment projects—railways and others. A pessimistic appraisal of the investment outlook led to insufficient employment on investment projects; and this, in turn, resulted in an insufficiency of the purchasing power needed to make such projects profitable. Given this catch-22, which is one of

Keynes's enduring contributions to economic theory, it is not surprising that he looked to the "socialization" of investment as necessary to avoid economic stagnation.

Marx's scenario was not hobbled by a static view of the capacity of the system for inventing new technologies and developing new commodity wants, but it, too, had its catch-22s. These were based on inherent conflicts—contradictions, Marx called them—between the needs of individual enterprises and the working requirements for the system as a whole. One of them was the tendency of capitalism to undercut the buying power of the working class by the continuous introduction of labor-saving machinery, to which business was driven by the pressures of competition. Each enterprise thereby sought to steal a march on its competitors, but instead all enterprises found themselves facing a condition of underconsumption. It is summed up in the perhaps apocryphal story of Henry Ford II walking through a newly automated engine factory with Walter Reuther, the legendary organizing figure of the United Automobile Workers, and asking, "Walter, how are you going to organize these machines?"—to which Reuther is supposed to have answered, "Henry, how are you going to sell them cars?" Another contradiction foreseen by Marx was the erosion of profit rates—not purchasing power—which stemmed from this same substitution of machinery for labor. According to Marx's analysis, labor power was the goose that laid the golden eggs of profits, because employers were able to extract more value from their workers than they paid out as wages. The replacement of living labor by machinery constricted the base from which profit arose, and thus ultimately reduced the rate of return on capital.

. . . The decisive factor in determining the fate of capitalism must be political, not economic. Schumpeter, for example, expected capitalism to disappear, but not because of any strictly economic difficulties. The stumbling block was cultural. "Capitalism," he wrote, "creates a critical frame of mind which, after having destroyed the moral authority of so many other institutions, in the end turns against its own; the bourgeois finds to his amazement that the rationalist attitude does not stop at the credentials of kings and popes but goes on to attack private property and the whole scheme of bourgeois values." Schumpeter anticipated a painless metamorphosis of capitalism into socialism, by which he meant a presumably democratic, planned economy run by the former managers of capitalism. Marx would have scoffed at Schumpeter's low appraisal of capitalism's self-esteem, but he, too, laid its ultimate downfall on the doorstep of political, not economic, events. Capitalism would be progressively weakened by its economic crises, but, in the famous words of *Capital,* the "knell of capitalist private property" would not sound or the "expropriators" be "expropriated" until the working class arose to take things into its own hands.

Schumpeter obviously did not anticipate the present-day resurgence of conservative self-confidence, nor did Marx expect that working-class attitudes and politics would become middle class. Despite their recognition of the importance of mustering and holding the faith of its participants, neither man fully grasped the capacity of the system to do so. This is so, I believe, because neither sufficiently appreciated that capitalism is a social order built upon a deeply embedded and widely believed principle expressed in the actions and beliefs of its most important representatives. From such a viewpoint it is comparable to imperial or aristocratic or Communist regimes, with their universally accepted principle of

kingship or aristocracy or socialism, embodied in the personages of monarchs or lords or sacred texts. Capitalism is not normally thought of as possessing such a principle, but its largely uncritical worship of the idea of economic growth is as central to its nature as the similar veneration of the idea of divine kingship or blue blood or doctrinal orthodoxy has been for other regimes. Suggesting that capitalism can be likened to a "regime" rubs our sensibilities the wrong way, but the word is useful in forcing us to consider capitalism as an order of social life, with distinctive hierarchies, imperatives, loyalties, and beliefs. It is this regime-like aspect of capitalism that turns Schumpeter's feared rational skepticism of its privileges into a rationalization of its rights, and makes the working class, far from the opposition that Marx hoped it would become, into stalwart supporters.

QUESTIONS

1. What does Heilbroner mean when he writes that "the decisive factor in determining the fate of capitalism must be political, not economic"? Use examples from his analysis of economic history in your response.

2. Does Heilbroner favor capitalism as an economic system? Is he suspicious of it? Or does he resist such "normative" claims altogether? Why might he adopt a "descriptive" stance toward economic systems?

John Stuart Mill | # Laissez-faire and Education

John Stuart Mill was perhaps the greatest philosopher and political economist in England in the nineteenth century. The following is from his *Principles of Political Economy.*

We have now reached the last part of our undertaking; the discussion, so far as suited to this trea-

tise . . . of the limits of the province of government: the question, to what objects governmental intervention in the affairs of society may or should extend, over and above those which necessarily appertain to it. No subject has been more keenly contested in the present age: the contest, however, has chiefly taken place round certain select points, with only flying

From *Principles of Political Economy,* D. Appleton & Co., 1887.

excursions into the rest of the field. Those indeed who have discussed any particular question of government interference, such as state education (spiritual or secular), regulation of hours of labour, a public provision for the poor, &c., have often dealt largely in general arguments, far outstretching the special application made of them, and have shown a sufficiently strong bias either in favour of letting things alone, or in favour of meddling; but have seldom declared, or apparently decided in their own minds, how far they would carry either principle. The supporters of interference have been content with asserting a general right and duty on the part of government to intervene, wherever its intervention would be useful: and when those who have been called the *laisserfaire* school have attempted any definite limitation of the province of government, they have usually restricted it to the protection of person and property against force and fraud; a definition to which neither they nor any one else can deliberately adhere, since it excludes . . . some of the most indispensable and unanimously recognised of the duties of government. . . .

We must set out by distinguishing between two kinds of intervention by the government, which, though they may relate to the same subject, differ widely in their nature and effects, and require, for their justification, motives of a very different degree of urgency. The intervention may extend to controlling the free agency of individuals. Government may interdict all persons from doing certain things; or from doing them without its authorization; or may prescribe to them certain things to be done, or a certain manner of doing things which it is left optional with them to do or to abstain from. This is the *authoritative* interference of government. There is another kind of intervention which is not authoritative: when a government, instead of issuing a command and enforcing it by penalties, adopts the course so seldom resorted to by governments, and of which such important use might be made, that of giving advice, and promulgating information; or when, leaving individuals free to use their own means of pursuing any object of general interest, the government, not meddling with them, but not trusting the object solely to their care, establishes, side by side with their arrange-

ments, an agency of its own for a like purpose. Thus, it is one thing to maintain a Church Establishment, and another to refuse toleration to other religions, or to persons professing no religion. It is one thing to provide schools or colleges, and another to require that no person shall act as an instructor of youth without a government licence. There might be a national bank, or a government manufactory, without any monopoly against private banks and manufactories. There might be a post-office, without penalties against the conveyance of letters by other means. There may be a corps of government engineers for civil purposes, while the profession of a civil engineer is free to be adopted by every one. There may be public hospitals, without any restriction upon private medical or surgical practice.

It is evident, even at first sight, that the authoritative form of government intervention has a much more limited sphere of legitimate action than the other. It requires a much stronger necessity to justify it in any case; while there are large departments of human life from which it must be unreservedly and imperiously excluded. Whatever theory we adopt respecting the foundation of the social union, and under whatever political institutions we live, there is a circle around every individual human being, which no government, be it that of one, of a few, or of the many, ought to be permitted to overstep: there is a part of the life of every person who has come to years of discretion, within which the individuality of that person ought to reign uncontrolled either by any other individual or by the public collectively. That there is, or ought to be, some space in human existence thus entrenched around, and sacred from authoritative intrusion, no one who professes the smallest regard to human freedom or dignity will call in question: the point to be determined is, where the limit should be placed; how large a province of human life this reserved territory should include. I apprehend that it ought to include all that part which concerns only the life, whether inward or outward, of the individual, and does not affect the interests of others, or affects them only through the moral influence of example. With respect to the domain of the inward consciousness, the thoughts and feelings, and as much of external conduct as is personal only, involving no consequences, none at least of a painful or injurious kind, to other people; I hold that it is allowable in all, and in the more thoughtful and cultivated often a duty, to assert and promulgate, with all the force they are capable of, their opinion of what is good or bad, admirable or contemptible, but not to compel others to conform to that opinion; whether the force used is that of extra-legal coercion, or exerts itself by means of the law.

———————

Now, the proposition that the consumer is a competent judge of the commodity, can be admitted only with numerous abatements and exceptions. He is generally the best judge (though even this is not true universally) of the material objects produced for his use. These are destined to supply some physical want, or gratify some taste or inclination, respecting which wants or inclinations there is no appeal from the person who feels them; or they are the means and appliances of some occupation, for the use of the persons engaged in it, who may be presumed to be judges of the things required in their own habitual employment. But there are other things, of the worth of which the demand of the market is by no means a test; things of which the utility does not consist in ministering to inclinations, nor in serving the daily uses of life, and the want of which is least felt where the need is greatest. This is peculiarly true of those things which are chiefly useful as tending to raise the character of human beings. The uncultivated cannot be competent judges of cultivation. Those who most need to be made wiser and better, usually desire it least, and if they desired it, would be incapable of finding the way to it by their own lights. It will continually happen, on the voluntary system, that, the end not being desired, the means will not be provided at all, or that, the persons requiring improvement having an imperfect or altogether erroneous conception of what they want, the supply called forth by the demand of the market will be anything but what is really required. Now any well-intentioned and tolerably civilized government may think, without presumption, that it does or ought to possess a degree of cultivation above the average of the community which it rules, and that it should therefore be capable of offering better education and better instruction to the people, than the greater num-

ber of them would spontaneously demand. Education, therefore, is one of those things which it is admissible in principle that a government should provide for the people. The case is one to which the reasons of the non-interference principle do not necessarily or universally extend.

With regard to elementary education, the exception to ordinary rules may, I conceive, justifiably be carried still further. There are certain primary elements and means of knowledge, which it is in the highest degree desirable that all human beings born into the community should acquire during childhood. If their parents, or those on whom they depend, have the power of obtaining for them this instruction, and fail to do it, they commit a double breach of duty, towards the children themselves, and towards the members of the community generally, who are all liable to suffer seriously from the consequences of ignorance and want of education in their fellow-citizens. It is therefore an allowable exercise of the powers of government, to impose on parents the legal obligation of giving elementary instruction to children. This, however, cannot fairly be done, without taking measures to insure that such instruction shall be always accessible to them, either gratuitously or at a trifling expense.

It may indeed be objected that the education of children is one of those expenses which parents, even of the labouring class, ought to defray; that it is desirable that they should feel it incumbent on them to provide by their own means for the fulfilment of their duties, and that by giving education at the cost of others, just as much as by giving subsistence, the standard of necessary wages is proportionally lowered, and the springs of exertion and self-restraint in so much relaxed. This argument could, at best, be only valid if the question were that of substituting a public provision for what individuals would otherwise do for themselves; if all parents in the labouring class recognised and practised the duty of giving instruction to their children at their own expense. But inasmuch as parents do not practise this duty, and do not include education among those necessary expenses which their wages must provide for, therefore the general rate of wages is not high enough to bear those expenses, and they must be borne from some other source. And this is not one of the cases in which the tender of help perpetuates the state of things which renders help necessary. Instruction, when it is really such, does not enervate, but strengthens as well as enlarges the active faculties: in whatever manner acquired, its effect on the mind is favourable to the spirit of independence: and when, unless had gratuitously, it would not be had at all, help in this form has the opposite tendency to that which in so many other cases makes it objectionable; it is help towards doing without help.

In England, and most European countries, elementary instruction cannot be paid for, at its full cost, from the common wages of unskilled labour, and would not if it could. The alternative, therefore, is not between government and private speculation, but between a government provision and voluntary charity: between interference by government, and interference by associations of individuals, subscribing their own money for the purpose, like the two great School Societies. It is, of course, not desirable that anything should be done by funds derived from compulsory taxation, which is already sufficiently well done by individual liberality. How far this is the case with school instruction, is, in each particular instance, a question of fact. The education provided in this country on the voluntary principle has of late been so much discussed, that it is needless in this place to criticise it minutely, and I shall merely express my conviction, that even in quantity it is, and is likely to remain, altogether insufficient, while in quality, though with some slight tendency to improvement, it is never good except by some rare accident, and generally so bad as to be little more than nominal. I hold it therefore the duty of the government to supply the defect, by giving pecuniary support to elementary schools, such as to render them accessible to all the children of the poor, either freely, or for a payment too inconsiderable to be sensibly felt.

One thing must be strenuously insisted on; that the government must claim no monopoly for its education, either in the lower or in the higher branches; must exert neither authority nor influence to induce the people to resort to its teachers in preference to others, and must confer no peculiar advantages on those who have been instructed by them. Though the government teachers will probably be superior to the average of private instructors, they will not embody all the knowledge and sagacity to be found in all instructors taken together, and it is desirable to leave open as many roads as possible to the desired end. It is not endurable that a government should, either *de jure* or *de facto,* have a complete control over the education of the people. To possess such a control, and actually exert it, is to be despotic. A government which can mould the opinions and sentiments of the people from their youth upwards, can do with them whatever it pleases. Though a government, therefore, may, and in many cases ought to, establish schools and colleges, it must neither compel nor bribe any person to come to them; nor ought the power of individuals to set up rival establishments, to depend in any degree upon its authorization. It would be justified in requiring from all the people that they shall possess instruction in certain things, but not in prescribing to them how or from whom they shall obtain it.

QUESTIONS

1. What two kinds of government intervention does Mill distinguish between? Why does he distinguish between them?

2. Why is education an example of legitimate government "interference"? Can you think of other, similar forms of legitimate government interference?

E. F. Schumacher | # Buddhist Economics

E. F. Schumacher was an iconoclastic economist who wrote the classic, *Small Is Beautiful.*

"Right Livelihood" is one of the requirements of
the Buddha's Noble Eightfold Path. It is clear, therefore, that there must be such a thing as Buddhist
economics.

Buddhist countries have often stated that they
wish to remain faithful to their heritage. So Burma:
"The New Burma sees no conflict between religious
values and economic progress. Spiritual health and
material well-being are not enemies: they are natural
allies." Or: "We can blend successfully the religious
and spiritual values of our heritage with the benefits
of modern technology." Or: "We Burmans have a
sacred duty to conform both our dreams and our acts
to our faith. This we shall ever do."

All the same, such countries invariably assume
that they can model their economic development
plans in accordance with modern economics, and
they call upon modern economists from so-called
advanced countries to advise them, to formulate the
policies to be pursued, and to construct the grand
design for development, the Five-Year Plan or whatever it may be called. No one seems to think that a
Buddhist way of life would call for Buddhist economics, just as the modern materialist way of life has
brought forth modern economics.

Economists themselves, like most specialists, normally suffer from a kind of metaphysical blindness,
assuming that theirs is a science of absolute and
invariable truths, without any presuppositions. Some
go as far as to claim that economic laws are as free
from "metaphysics" or "values" as the law of gravi-
tation. We need not, however, get involved in arguments of methodology. Instead, let us take some fundamentals and see what they look like when viewed
by a modern economist and a Buddhist economist.

There is universal agreement that a fundamental
source of wealth is human labour. Now, the modern
economist has been brought up to consider "labour"
or work as little more than a necessary evil. From the
point of view of the employer, it is in any case simply
an item of cost, to be reduced to a minimum if it cannot be eliminated altogether, say, by automation.
From the point of view of the workman, it is a "disutility"; to work is to make a sacrifice of one's leisure
and comfort, and wages are a kind of compensation
for the sacrifice. Hence the ideal from the point of
view of the employer is to have output without
employees, and the ideal from the point of view of the
employee is to have income without employment.

The consequences of these attitudes both in theory
and in practice are, of course, extremely far-reaching.
If the ideal with regard to work is to get rid of it,
every method that "reduces the work load" is a good
thing. The most potent method, short of automation,
is the so-called division of labour and the classical
example is the pin factory eulogised in Adam
Smith's *Wealth of Nations.* Here it is not a matter of
ordinary specialisation, which mankind has practised
from time immemorial, but of dividing up every
complete process of production into minute parts, so
that the final product can be produced at great speed
without anyone having had to contribute more than a
totally insignificant and, in most cases, unskilled
movement of his limbs.

The Buddhist point of view takes the function of
work to be at least threefold: to give a man a chance
to utilise and develop his faculties; to enable him to

overcome his ego-centredness by joining with other people in a common task; and to bring forth the goods and services needed for a becoming existence. Again, the consequences that flow from this view are endless. To organise work in such a manner that it becomes meaningless, boring, stultifying, or nerve-racking for the worker would be little short of criminal; it would indicate a greater concern with goods than with people, an evil lack of compassion, and a soul-destroying degree of attachment to the most primitive side of this worldly existence. Equally, to strive for leisure as an alternative to work would be considered a complete misunderstanding of one of the basic truths of human existence, namely that work and leisure are complementary parts of the same living process and cannot be separated without destroying the joy of work and the bliss of leisure.

From the Buddhist point of view, there are therefore two types of mechanisation which must be clearly distinguished: one that enhances a man's skill and power and one that turns the work of man over to a mechanical slave, leaving man in a position of having to serve the slave. How to tell the one from the other? "The craftsman himself," says Ananda Coomaraswamy, a man equally competent to talk about the modern west as the ancient east, can always, if allowed to, draw the delicate distinction between the machine and the tool. The carpet loom is a tool, a contrivance for holding warp threads at a stretch for the pile to be woven round them by the craftsmen's fingers; but the power loom is a machine, and its significance as a destroyer of culture lies in the fact that it does the essentially human part of the work." It is clear, therefore, that Buddhist economics must be very different from the economics of modern materialism, since the Buddhist sees the essence of civilisation not in a multiplication of wants but in the purification of human character. Character, at the same time, is formed primarily by a man's work. And work, properly conducted in conditions of human dignity and freedom, blesses those who do it and equally their products. The Indian philosopher and economist J. C. Kumarappa sums the matter up as follows:

If the nature of the work is properly appreciated and applied, it will stand in the same relation to the

higher faculties as food is to the physical body. It nourishes and enlivens the higher man and urges him to produce the best he is capable of. It directs his free will along the proper course and disciplines the animal in him into progressive channels. It furnishes an excellent background for man to display his scale of values and develop his personality.

If a man has no chance of obtaining work he is in a desperate position, not simply because he lacks an income but because he lacks this nourishing and enlivening factor of disciplined work which nothing can replace. A modern economist may engage in highly sophisticated calculations on whether full employment "pays" or whether it might be more "economic" to run an economy at less than full employment so as to ensure a greater mobility of labour, a better stability of wages, and so forth. His fundamental criterion of success is simply the total quantity of goods produced during a given period of time. "If the marginal urgency of goods is low," says Professor Galbraith in *The Affluent Society,* "then so is the urgency of employing the last man or the last million men in the labour force." And again: "If . . . we can afford some unemployment in the interest of stability—a proposition, incidentally, of impeccably conservative antecedents—then we can afford to give those who are unemployed the goods that enable them to sustain their accustomed standard of living."

From a Buddhist point of view, this is standing the truth on its head by considering goods as more important than people and consumption as more important than creative activity. It means shifting the emphasis from the worker to the product of work, that is, from the human to the subhuman, a surrender to the forces of evil. The very start of Buddhist economic planning would be a planning for full employment, and the primary purpose of this would in fact be employment for everyone who needs an "outside" job: it would not be the maximisation of employment nor the maximisation of production. Women, on the whole, do not need an "outside" job, and the large-scale employment of women in offices or factories would be considered a sign of serious economic failure. In particular, to let mothers of young children work in factories while the children run wild would be as uneconomic in the eyes of a Buddhist economist as the employment of a skilled worker as a soldier in the eyes of a modern economist.

While the materialist is mainly interested in goods, the Buddhist is mainly interested in liberation. But Buddhism is "The Middle Way" and therefore in no way antagonistic to physical well-being. It is not wealth that stands in the way of liberation but the attachment to wealth; not the enjoyment of pleasurable things but the craving for them. The keynote of Buddhist economics, therefore, is simplicity and non-violence. From an economist's point of view, the marvel of the Buddhist way of life is the utter rationality of its pattern—amazingly small means leading to extraordinarily satisfactory results.

For the modern economist this is very difficult to understand. He is used to measuring the "standard of living" by the amount of annual consumption, assuming all the time that a man who consumes more is "better off" than a man who consumes less. A Buddhist economist would consider this approach excessively irrational: since consumption is merely a means to human well-being, the aim should be to obtain the maximum of well-being with the minimum of consumption. Thus, if the purpose of clothing is a certain amount of temperature comfort and an attractive appearance, the task is to attain this purpose with the smallest possible effort, that is, with the smallest annual destruction of cloth and with the help of designs that involve the smallest possible input of toil. The less toil there is, the more time and strength is left for artistic creativity. It would be highly uneconomic, for instance, to go in for complicated tailoring, like the modern west, when a much more beautiful effect can be achieved by the skillful draping of uncut material. It would be the height of folly to make material so that it should wear out quickly and the height of barbarity to make anything ugly, shabby or mean. What has just been said about clothing applies equally to all other human requirements. The ownership and the consumption of goods is a means to an end, and Buddhist economics is the systematic study of how to attain given ends with the minimum means.

Modern economics, on the other hand, considers consumption to be the sole end and purpose of all economic activity, taking the factors of production—land, labour, and capital—as the means. The former,

in short, tries to maximise human satisfactions by the optimal pattern of consumption, while the latter tries to maximise consumption by the optimal pattern of productive effort. It is easy to see that the effort needed to sustain a way of life which seeks to attain the optimal pattern of consumption is likely to be much smaller than the effort needed to sustain a drive for maximum consumption. We need not be surprised, therefore, that the pressure and strain of living is very much less in, say, Burma than it is in the United States, in spite of the fact that the amount of labour-saving machinery used in the former country is only a minute fraction of the amount used in the latter.

Simplicity and non-violence are obviously closely related. The optimal pattern of consumption, producing a high degree of human satisfaction by means of a relatively low rate of consumption, allows people to live without great pressure and strain and to fulfill the primary injunction of Buddhist teaching: "Cease to do evil; try to do good." As physical resources are everywhere limited, people satisfying their needs by means of a modest use of resources are obviously less likely to be at each other's throats than people depending upon a high rate of use. Equally, people who live in highly self-sufficient local communities are less likely to get involved in large-scale violence than people whose existence depends on world-wide systems of trade.

From the point of view of Buddhist economics, therefore, production from local resources for local needs is the most rational way of economic life, while dependence on imports from afar and the consequent need to produce for export to unknown and distant peoples is highly uneconomic and justifiable only in exceptional cases and on a small scale. Just as the modern economist would admit that a high rate of consumption of transport services between a man's home and his place of work signifies a misfortune and not a high standard of life, so the Buddhist economist would hold that to satisfy human wants from faraway sources rather than from sources nearby signifies failure rather than success. The former tends to take statistics showing an increase in the number of ton/miles per head of the population carried by a country's transport system as proof of economic progress, while to the latter—the Buddhist economist—the same statistics would indicate a highly undesirable deterioration in the *pattern* of consumption.

Another striking difference between modern economics and Buddhist economics arises over the use of natural resources. Bertrand de Jouvenel, the eminent French political philosopher, has characterised "western man" in words which may be taken as a fair description of the modern economist:

> He tends to count nothing as an expenditure, other than human effort; he does not seem to mind how much mineral matter he wastes and, far worse, how much living matter he destroys. He does not seem to realise at all that human life is a dependent part of an ecosystem of many different forms of life. As the world is ruled from towns where men are cut off from any form of life other than human, the feeling of belonging to an ecosystem is not revived. This results in a harsh and improvident treatment of things upon which we ultimately depend, such as water and trees.

The teaching of the Buddha, on the other hand, enjoins a reverent and non-violent attitude not only to all sentient beings but also, with great emphasis, to trees. Every follower of the Buddha ought to plant a tree every few years and look after it until it is safely established, and the Buddhist economist can demonstrate without difficulty that the universal observation of this rule would result in a high rate of genuine economic development independent of any foreign aid. Much of the economic decay of south-east Asia (as of many other parts of the world) is undoubtedly due to a heedless and shameful neglect of trees.

Modern economics does not distinguish between renewable and non-renewable materials, as its very method is to equalise and quantify everything by means of a money price. Thus, taking various alternative fuels, like coal, oil, wood, or water-power: the only difference between them recognised by modern economics is relative cost per equivalent unit. The cheapest is automatically the one to be preferred, as to do otherwise would be irrational and "uneconomic." From a Buddhist point of view, of course, this will not do; the essential difference between non-renewable fuels like coal and oil on the one hand and renewable fuels like wood and waterpower on the other cannot

be simply overlooked. Non-renewable goods must be used only if they are indispensable, and then only with the greatest care and the most meticulous concern for conservation. To use them heedlessly or extravagantly is an act of violence, and while complete nonviolence may not be attainable on this earth, there is nonetheless an ineluctable duty on man to aim at the ideal of nonviolence in all he does.

Just as a modern European economist would not consider it a great economic achievement if all European art treasures were sold to America at attractive prices, so the Buddhist economist would insist that a population basing its economic life on non-renewable fuels is living parasitically, on capital instead of income. Such a way of life could have no permanence and could therefore be justified only as a purely temporary expedient. As the world's resources of non-renewable fuels—coal, oil, and natural gas—are exceedingly unevenly distributed over the globe and undoubtedly limited in quantity, it is clear that their exploitation at an ever-increasing rate is an act of violence against nature which must almost inevitably lead to violence between men.

This fact alone might give food for thought even to those people in Buddhist countries who care nothing for the religious and spiritual values of their heritage and ardently desire to embrace the materialism of modern economics at the fastest possible speed. Before they dismiss Buddhist economics as nothing better than a nostalgic dream, they might wish to consider whether the path of economic development outlined by modern economics is likely to lead them to places where they really want to be. Towards the end of his courageous book *The Challenge of Man's Future,* Professor Harrison Brown of the California Institute of Technology gives the following appraisal:

> Thus we see that, just as industrial society is fundamentally unstable and subject to reversion to agrarian existence, so within it the conditions which offer individual freedom are unstable in their ability to avoid the conditions which impose rigid organisation and totalitarian control. Indeed, when we examine all of the foreseeable difficulties which threaten the survival of industrial civilisation, it is difficult to see how the achievement of stability and the maintenance of individual liberty can be made compatible.

Even if this were dismissed as a long-term view there is the immediate question of whether "modernisation," as currently practised without regard to religious and spiritual values, is actually producing agreeable results. As far as the masses are concerned, the results appear to be disastrous—a collapse of the rural economy, a rising tide of unemployment in town and country, and the growth of a city proletariat without nourishment for either body or soul.

It is in the light of both immediate experience and long-term prospects that the study of Buddhist economics could be recommended even to those who believe that economic growth is more important than any spiritual or religious values. For it is not a question of choosing between "modern growth" and "traditional stagnation." It is a question of finding the right path of development, the Middle Way between materialist heedlessness and traditionalist immobility, in short, of finding "Right Livelihood."

QUESTIONS

1. What are "Buddhist economics"?
2. For Schumacher and Buddhism, what is the importance of character in ethics?

Amartya Sen	The Economics of Poverty

Amartya Sen is based at Trinity College Cambridge and won the Nobel Prize for his work on welfare economics and the causes of famine.

PHIL PONCE: Professor, when one thinks of the field in which Nobel winners in economics often work, it's oftentimes something like money, markets, the capital, and yet you seem to be more interested in how events affect people. Why is that?

AMARTYA SEN: Well, economics is a very broad subject, and the money and capital and the operation of the stock market, these are matters of interest to economists, as well as matters of—the way the lives of people go, and I happen to be concerned primarily with the latter and in particular with the down side of the latter, namely the people who seem to have a worse time than others—the poor, the unemployed, the hungry, the starving, and so on. So this has been something I've been concerned with for a long time.

PHIL PONCE: Professor, one of the specific issues that the Nobel citation talks about is your interest in understanding famine, and it says that your best-known work has to do with understanding that famine isn't just caused by a shortage of food but by other things like unemployment, drop in income. Why the specific interest in famine?

AMARTYA SEN: Well, there are many reasons, of course, because famines are unfortunately still a real phenomenon in the world. And lots of people die from it, systematically, in different parts of the world, but in my case the personal interest arose also from the fact that I happened to observe from inside a major famine of the 20th century—the Bengal famine, which occurred in Indian in 1943—in fact, the last famine that occurred in India, in which close to 3 million people died. And I was a nine-and-a-half-year-old boy at that time. It had very impressionable—certainly very striking memories I have from that period, and the people who starved, they came from a particular group—in this care rural laborers—but that's a characteristic I later found of many famines, indeed, sometimes food supply may fall, sometimes not. Food supply fell in the Irish

Credit: From the NewsHour with Jim Lehrer transcript. McNeil NewsHour transcript, Oct. 15, 1998. Reprinted with permission.

famine of the 1840's. It did not fall in the Bengal famine of '43, and it was at a peak height in the Bangladesh famine of '74. But a section of the community lose their ability to command food by not having jobs—not having enough wage and then they cannot buy food and that's what happened—not a really large proportion usually—but it can still kill millions of people.

PHIL PONCE: According to a report that I read, you personally, when you were a boy, personally fed people who were starving refugees

AMARTYA SEN: Well, my parents—you know—since we [were] relatively prosperous, still not rich, lower middle class family—still not rich—a lower middle class family—but quite committed on social matters and come from an academic background. My father was a professor; my grandfather was a professor—we were quite involved in that so I was committed to give anyone who asked for food, a tin, a cigarette tin of rice. But since there are many people asking, I was also told that that's what I could give to anyone. I obviously felt very moral in trying to give as much as I could. And it's a very harrowing experience. Obviously, this didn't do anything to solve the famine, but it's a question that got even more strongly engrained in my mind because of the small participation that I happened to do in this context.

PHIL PONCE: Professor, what does winning this prize mean to you personally?

AMARTYA SEN: Well, I was particularly pleased that the prize was given with the citation about social—about welfare economics and social choice because these are areas in which very interesting, very important work has occurred, and I'm very proud of what others have done and I've learned from them. I think I was led on to that subject by Kenneth Arrow—a great figure in modern economics. And I had very good students and very good colleagues working in this area. So when they mentioned this area, I took that to be a recognition of the importance of that area, and even though I was lucky enough to get the prize, I did think that it was a much wider recognition and in the way it tried to be more appropriate and fair, if the prize was widely shared. But many people have contributed in this area, and this gives me an opportunity to think

about them and to the extent to which my own work has been influenced by and dependent on the work that others have done.

PHIL PONCE: Professor, there is this world economic crisis, a lot of turmoil in the markets, and it's adding a lot of new people to poverty, millions of people. How much do economists know? How much can economists explain what is happening now?

AMARTYA SEN: I think economists—if they set their mind to it—can explain a lot. You know, I think it's really a question of concentrating, the questions—the inquiries—appropriately. We know the nature of the success that some of these economies—for example, the East Asian economies, which are in turmoil now, had. We know the basis of their success, which included using the market mechanism efficiently but open-mindedly, non-dogmatically, letting the government do its job in expanding educational base, doing land reform, helping with the health care. It's a partnership of the public and market arrangement. Now they did not work out pretty well. The financial regularities and there were a lot of lacunae and some of the economies there like Indonesia it didn't work out, what would happen if the economy were to go into a slump, namely, how to deal with those who've been thrown out of the system and given to the wolves, and the kind of social safety net that you need didn't exist. There's a lot to learn from the experience of these countries, both positively as to what they have achieved, as well as negatively as to what to avoid. So I think economists—if they analyze these issues—will have various things to offer. And, indeed, there are a lot of economists who are interested in it. And I would not accept that economists really don't have very much to say on this question.

PHIL PONCE: Professor, do you think people have lost faith in economists because of the current world financial crisis?

AMARTYA SEN: Well, you know, I think the—economics is not a kind of business whereby you could eliminate these problems. You know, it's—odd thing is that earlier on in late 19th century and early 20th century—one of the subjects people studied was business cycle. From time to time you have slump, and at times you have boom. The job of the economist was meant to be to understand why they are caused, rather than to eliminate them. Now I think it would be nice to eliminate them and, indeed, it is possible certainly to reduce them and eliminate it to a great extent. But the fact that sometimes these things would happen does not indicate that these times of economics is worth nothing. What it does indicate is that we have to pay much more attention than often happens to some of these problems, and since I've spent most of my life on the side of economics, I'm very sympathetic to the view that the economy should spend more time in dealing with the predicament of people who are thrown into turmoil when things go wrong, and also the fact that while there are successes of market economies, there are also needs for supplementation in other fields in terms of public intervention, in terms of political par-

ticipation, and so forth. So it's a question of taking an adequately broad view of economics, along with its neighboring discipline, and it's also a question of paying more attention to those who are most likely to lose when a crisis hits.

PHIL PONCE: Professor Sen, thank you very much. And, again, congratulations.

AMARTYA SEN: Thank you very much.

QUESTIONS

1. Why does poverty exist, according to Sen? How is it encouraged? Can it be defeated? How? Who has a duty to combat it? Why?

2. Why does Sen have a specific interest in famine? What ethical problems does famine pose to us, as (comparatively) wealthy Westerners?

Thorstein Veblen

Pecuniary Emulation and Conspicuous Consumption

Thorstein Veblen published his classic *The Theory of the Leisure Class* in 1899.

Wherever the institution of private property is found, even in a slightly developed form, the economic process bears the character of a struggle between men for the possession of goods. It has been customary in economic theory, and especially among those economists who adhere with least faltering to the body of modernised classical doctrines, to construe this struggle for wealth as being substantially a struggle for subsistence. Such is, no doubt, its character in large part during the earlier and less efficient phases of industry. Such is also its character in all cases where the "niggardliness of nature" is so strict

as to afford but a scanty livelihood to the community in return for strenuous and unremitting application to the business of getting the means of subsistence. But in all progressing communities an advance is presently made beyond this early stage of technological development. Industrial efficiency is presently carried to such a pitch as to afford something appreciably more than a bare livelihood to those engaged in the industrial process. It has not been unusual for economic theory to speak of the further struggle for wealth on this new industrial basis as a competition for an increase of the comforts of life,—primarily for an increase of the physical comforts which the consumption of goods affords.

The end of acquisition and accumulation is con-

From *The Theory of the Leisure Class,* Macmillan, 1899.

ventionally held to be the consumption of the goods accumulated—whether it is consumption directly by the owner of the goods or by the household attached to him and for this purpose identified with him in theory. This is at least felt to be the economically legitimate end of acquisition, which alone it is incumbent on the theory to take account of. Such consumption may of course be conceived to serve the consumer's physical wants—his physical comfort—or his so-called higher wants—spiritual, aesthetic, intellectual, or what not; the latter class of wants being served indirectly by an expenditure of goods, after the fashion familiar to all economic readers.

But it is only when taken in a sense far removed from its naïve meaning that consumption of goods can be said to afford the incentive from which accumulation invariably proceeds. The motive that lies at the root of ownership is emulation; and the same motive of emulation continues active in the further development of the institution to which it has given rise and in the development of all those features of the social structure which this institution of ownership touches. The possession of wealth confers honour; it is an invidious distinction. Nothing equally cogent can be said for the consumption of goods, nor for any other conceivable incentive to acquisition, and especially not for any incentive to the accumulation of wealth.

It is of course not to be overlooked that in a community where nearly all goods are private property the necessity of earning a livelihood is a powerful and ever-present incentive for the poorer members of the community. The need of subsistence and of an increase of physical comfort may for a time be the dominant motive of acquisition for those classes who are habitually employed at manual labour, whose subsistence is on a precarious footing, who possess little and ordinarily accumulate little; but it will appear in the course of the discussion that even in the case of these impecunious classes the predominance of the motive of physical want is not so decided as has sometimes been assumed. On the other hand, so far as regards those members and classes of the community who are chiefly concerned in the accumulation of wealth, the incentive of subsistence or of physical comfort never plays a considerable part. Ownership

began and grew into a human institution on grounds unrelated to the subsistence minimum. The dominant incentive was from the outset the invidious distinction attaching to wealth, and, save temporarily and by exception, no other motive has usurped the primacy at any later stage of the development.

Property set out with being booty held as trophies of the successful raid. So long as the group had departed but little from the primitive communal organisation, and so long as it still stood in close contact with other hostile groups, the utility of things or persons owned lay chiefly in an invidious comparison between their possessor and the enemy from whom they were taken. The habit of distinguishing between the interests of the individual and those of the group to which he belongs is apparently a later growth. Invidious comparison between the possessor of the honorific booty and his less successful neighbours within the group was no doubt present early as an element of the utility of the things possessed, though this was not at the outset the chief element of their value. The man's prowess was still primarily the group's prowess, and the possessor of the booty felt himself to be primarily the keeper of the honour of his group. This appreciation of exploit from the communal point of view is met with also at later stages of social growth, especially as regards the laurels of war.

But so soon as the custom of individual ownership begins to gain consistency, the point of view taken in making the invidious comparison on which private property rests will begin to change. Indeed, the one change is but the reflex of the other. The initial phase of ownership, the phase of acquisition by naïve seizure and conversion, begins to pass into the subsequent stage of an incipient organisation of industry on the basis of private property (in slaves); the horde develops into a more or less self-sufficing industrial community; possessions then come to be valued not so much as evidence of successful foray, but rather as evidence of the prepotence of the possessor of these goods over other individuals within the community. The invidious comparison now becomes primarily a comparison of the owner with the other members of the group. Property is still of the nature of trophy, but, with the cultural advance, it becomes more and more a trophy of successes scored in the game of ownership carried on between the members of the group under the quasi-peaceable methods of nomadic life. . . .

. . . With the growth of settled industry, the possession of wealth gains in relative importance and effectiveness as a customary basis of repute and esteem. Not that esteem ceases to be awarded on the basis of other, more direct evidence of prowess; not that successful predatory aggression or warlike exploit ceases to call out the approval and admiration of the crowd, or to stir the envy of the less successful competitors; but the opportunities for gaining distinction by means of this direct manifestation of superior force grow less available both in scope and frequency. . . . It becomes indispensable to accumulate, to acquire property, in order to retain one's good name. When accumulated goods have in this way once become the accepted badge of efficiency, the possession of wealth presently assumes the character of an independent and definitive basis of esteem. The possession of goods, whether acquired aggressively by one's own exertion or passively by transmission through inheritance from others, becomes a conventional basis of reputability. The possession of wealth, which was at the outset valued simply as an evidence of efficiency, becomes, in popular apprehension,

itself a meritorious act. Wealth is now itself intrinsically honourable and confers honour on its possessor. By a further refinement, wealth acquired passively by transmission from ancestors or other antecedents presently becomes even more honorific than wealth acquired by the possessor's own effort. . . .

What has just been said must not be taken to mean that there are no other incentives to acquisition and accumulation than this desire to excel in pecuniary standing and so gain the esteem and envy of one's fellow-men. The desire for added comfort and security from want is present as a motive at every stage of the process of accumulation in a modern industrial community; although the standard of sufficiency in these respects is in turn greatly affected by the habit of pecuniary emulation. To a great extent this emulation shapes the methods and selects the objects of expenditure for personal comfort and decent livelihood.

QUESTIONS

1. What is "pecuniary emulation"?
2. Why do you want an SUV? A Rolex? (If you do). What would Veblen say? Is wanting something because everyone else wants one necessarily bad? Why might it be a good thing?

Daniel Bell

The Cultural Contradictions of Capitalism

Daniel Bell taught for many years at Harvard University and wrote, among many other works, *The Cultural Contradictions of Capitalism.*

The relationship between a civilization's socioeconomic structure and its culture is perhaps the most complicated of all problems for the sociologist. A

nineteenth century tradition, one deeply impregnated with Marxist conceptions, held that changes in social structure determined man's imaginative reach. An earlier vision of man—as *homo pictor,* the symbol-producing animal, rather than as *homo faber,* the tool-making animal—saw him as a creature uniquely able to prefigure what he would later "objectify" or construct in reality. It thus ascribed to the realm of

From Daniel Bell, *The Cultural Contradictions of Capitalism* (New York: Basic Books, 1976).

culture the initiative for change. Whatever the truth of these older arguments about the past, today culture has clearly become supreme; what is played out in the imagination of the artist foreshadows, however dimly, the social reality of tomorrow.

Culture has become supreme for two complementary reasons. First, culture has become the most dynamic component of our civilization, outreaching the dynamism of technology itself. There is now in art—as there has increasingly been for the past hundred years—a dominant impulse towards the new and the original, a self-conscious search for future forms and sensations, so that *the idea* of change and novelty overshadows the dimensions of actual change. And secondly, there has come about, in the last fifty years or so, a legitimation of this cultural impulse. Society now accepts this role for the imagination, rather than—as in the past—seeing it as establishing a norm and affirming a moral-philosophic tradition against which the new could be measured and (more often than not) censured. Indeed, society has done more than passively accept—it has provided a market which eagerly gobbles up the new, because it believes it to be superior in value to all older forms. Thus, our culture has an unprecedented mission: it is an official, ceaseless searching for a new sensibility.

It is true, of course, that the idea of change dominates the modern economy and modern technology as well. But changes in the economy and technology are constrained by available resources and financial cost. In politics, too, innovation is constrained by existing institutional structures, by the veto power of contending groups, and to some extent by tradition. But the changes in expressive symbols and forms, difficult as it may be for the mass of people to absorb them readily, meet no resistance in the realm of culture itself.

What is singular about this "tradition of the new" (as Harold Rosenberg has called it) is that it allows art to be unfettered, to break down all genres and to explore all modes of experience and sensation. Fantasy today has few costs (is *anything* deemed bizarre or opprobrious today?) other than the risk of individual madness. And even madness, in the writings of such social theorists as Michel Foucault and R. D. Laing, is now conceived to be a superior form of

truth! The new sensibilities, and the new styles of behavior associated with them, are created by small coteries which are devoted to exploring the new; and because the new has value in and of itself, and meets with so little resistance, the new sensibility and its behavior-styles diffuse rapidly, transforming the thinking and actions of larger masses of people.

————

Bourgeois society, justified and propelled as it had been in its earliest energies by these older ethics, could not easily admit to the change. It promoted a hedonistic way of life furiously—one has only to look at the transformation of advertising in the 1920's—but could not justify it. It lacked a new religion or a value system to replace the old, and the result was a disjunction.

The "new capitalism"—the phrase was used in the 1920's—continued to demand a Protestant Ethic in the area of production—that is, in the realm of work—but to stimulate a demand for pleasure and play in the area of consumption. The disjunction was bound to widen. The spread of urban life, with its variety of distractions and multiple stimuli; the new roles of women, created by the expansion of office jobs and the freer social and sexual contacts; the rise of a national culture through motion pictures and radio—all contributed to a loss of social authority on the part of the older value system.

The Puritan Ethic might be described most simply by the phrase "delayed gratification," and by restraint in gratification. It is, of course, the Malthusian injunction for prudence in a world of scarcity. But the claim of the American economic system was that it had introduced abundance, and the nature of abundance is to encourage prodigality rather than prudence. The "higher standard of living," not work as an end in itself, then becomes the engine of change. The glorification of plenty, rather than the bending to niggardly nature, becomes the justification of the system. But all of this was highly incongruent with the theological and sociological foundations of nineteenth century Protestantism, which was in turn the foundation of the American value system.

————

From a *cultural* point of view, the politics of the 1920's to 1960's was a struggle between tradition and modernity. In the 1960's a new cultural style appeared. Call it psychedelic or call it, as its own protagonists have, a "counter-culture." It announced a strident opposition to bourgeois values and to the traditional codes of American life. "The bourgeoisie," we are told, "is obsessed by greed; its sex life is insipid and prudish; its family patterns are debased; its slavish conformities of dress and grooming are degrading; its mercenary routinization of life is intolerable. . . ."[1]

What is quixotic about such pronouncements is the polemical and ideological caricature of a set of codes that had been trampled on long ago—beginning sixty years earlier, with the Young Intellectuals. Yet such a caricature is necessary to make the new counter-culture seem more daring and revolutionary than it is. The new sensibility, with its emphasis on psychedelic experience, sexual freedom, apocalyptic moods and the like, thinks of itself as being against "bourgeois" culture. But in truth, bourgeois culture vanished long ago. What the counter-culture embodies is an extension of the tendencies initiated sixty years ago by political liberalism and modernist culture, and represents, in effect, a split in the camp of modernism. For it now seeks to take the preachments of personal freedom, extreme experience ("kicks," and "the high") and sexual experimentation, to a point in *life-style* that the liberal culture—which would approve of such ideas in *art and imagination*—is not prepared to go. Yet liberalism finds itself uneasy to say why. It approves a basic permissiveness, but cannot with any certainty define the bounds. And this is its dilemma. In culture, as well as in politics, liberalism is now up against the wall.

Liberalism also finds itself in disarray in an arena where it had joined in support of capitalism—in the economy. The economic philosophy of American liberalism had been rooted in the idea of growth. One forgets that in the late 1940's and 1950's Walter Reuther, Leon Keyserling, and other liberals had attacked the steel companies and much of American industry for being unwilling to expand capacity and had urged the government to set target growth figures. Cartelization, monopoly, and the restriction of pro-duction had been historic tendencies of capitalism. The Eisenhower administration consciously chose price stability over growth. It was the liberal economists who instilled in the society the policy of the conscious planning of growth through government inducements (e.g., investment credits, which industry, at first, did not want) and government investment. The idea of potential GNP and the concept of "shortfall"—the posting of a mark of what the economy at full utilization of resources could achieve compared to the actual figure—was introduced in the Council of Economic Advisors by the liberals. The idea of growth has become so fully absorbed as an economic ideology that one realizes no longer, as I said, how much of a liberal innovation it was.

The liberal answer to social problems such as poverty was that growth would provide the resources to raise the incomes of the poor. The thesis that growth was necessary to finance public services was the center of John Kenneth Galbraith's book *The Affluent Society*.

And yet, paradoxically, it is the very idea of economic growth that is now coming under attack—and from liberals. Affluence is no longer seen as an answer. Growth is held responsible for the spoliation of the environment, the voracious use of natural resources, the crowding in the recreation areas, the densities in the city, and the like. One finds, startlingly, the idea of zero economic growth—or John Stuart Mill's idea of the "stationary state"—now proposed as a serious goal of government policy. Just as the counter-culture rejects the traditional problem-solving pragmatism of American politics, it now also rejects the newer, liberal policy of economic growth as a positive goal for the society. But without a commitment to economic growth, what is the *raison d'etre* of capitalism?

TWO CRISES

American society faces a number of crises. Some are more manifest—the alienation of the young, the militancy of the blacks, the crisis of confidence created by the Vietnam war. Some are structural—the creation of a national society, a communal society, and a post-industrial phase—which are reworking the occupational structure and the social arrangements of the society. These are all aspects of a political torment in the social system. Yet these crises, I believe, are manageable (not solvable; what problems are?) if the political leadership is intelligent and determined. The resources are present (or will be, once the Vietnam war is ended) to relieve many of the obvious tensions and to finance the public needs of the society. The great need here is *time,* for the social changes which are required (a decent welfare and income maintenance system for the poor, the reorganization of the universities, the control of the environment) can only be handled within the space of a decade or more. It is the demand for "instant solutions" which, in this respect, is the source of political trouble.

But the deeper and more lasting crisis is the cultural one. Changes in moral temper and culture—the fusion of imagination and life-styles—are not amenable to "social engineering" or political control. They derive from the value and moral traditions of the society, and these cannot be "designed" by precept. The ultimate sources are the religious conceptions which undergird a society; the proximate sources are the "reward systems" and "motivations" (and their legitimacy) which derive from the arena of work (the social structure).

American capitalism, as I have sought to show, has lost its traditional legitimacy which was based on a moral system of reward, rooted in a Protestant sanctification of work. It has substituted in its place a hedonism which promises a material ease and luxury, yet shies away from all the historic implications which a "voluptuary system"—and all its social permissiveness and libertinism—implies.

This is joined to a more pervasive problem derived from the nature of industrial society. The characteristic style of an industrial society is based on the principles of economics and economizing: on efficiency, least cost, maximization, optimization, and functional rationality. Yet it is at this point that it comes into sharpest conflict with the cultural trends of the day, for the culture emphasizes anticognitive and anti-intellectual currents which are rooted in a return to instinctual modes. The one emphasizes functional rationality, technocratic decision-making, and meritocratic rewards. The other, apocalyptic moods and antirational modes of behavior. It is this disjunction which is the historic crisis of Western society. This cultural contradiction, in the long run, is the deepest challenge to the society.

NOTE

1. T. Roszak, *The Making of a Counter-Culture* (Doubleday, 1969), p. 13.

QUESTIONS

1. What are the cultural contradictions of capitalism?
2. How has the "Puritan Ethic" influenced American capitalism and culture?

Robert Kuttner | # Everything for Sale

Robert Kuttner is cofounder and coeditor of *The American Prospect*.

The ideal of a free, self-regulating market is newly triumphant. The historical lessons of market excess, from the Gilded Age to the Great Depression, have all but dropped from the collective memory. Government stands impeached and impoverished, along with democratic politics itself. Unfettered markets are deemed both the essence of human liberty, and the most expedient route to prosperity.

In the United States, the alternative to laissez-faire has never been socialism. Rather, the interventionist party, from Hamilton and Lincoln, through the Progressive era, Franklin Roosevelt and Lyndon Johnson, sponsored what came to be known as a "mixed economy." The idea was that market forces could do many things well—but not everything. Government intervened to promote development, to temper the market's distributive extremes, to counteract its unfortunate tendency to boom-and-bust, to remedy its myopic failure to invest too little in public goods, and to invest too much in processes that harmed the human and natural environment.

Since the constitutional founding, however, the libertarian strain in American life has often overwhelmed the impulse toward collective betterment. Today, after two decades of assault by the marketizers, even the normal defenders of the mixed economy are defensive and uncertain. The last two Democratic presidents have been ambivalent advocates for the mixed economy. Mostly, they offered a more temperate call for the reining in of government and the liberation of the entrepreneur. The current vogue for deregulation began under Jimmy Carter. The insistence on budget balance was embraced by Bill Clinton, whose pledge to "reinvent government" soon became a shared commitment merely to reduce government. And much of the economics profession, after an era of embracing the mixed economy, has reverted to a new fundamentalism cherishing the virtues of markets.

America, in short, is in one of its cyclical romances with a utopian view of laissez-faire. Free markets are famous for overshooting. Real-estate bubbles, tulip manias, and stock-market euphorias invariably lead to crowd psychologies and painful mornings-after. The same, evidentially, is true of ideological fashions.

So this is a good moment for a sober sorting out. How does the market, whose first principle is one-dollar/one-vote, properly coexist with a political democracy whose basic rule is "one person/one vote"? When does the market run riot? What are the proper boundaries of market principles? What should not be for sale?

II

Even in a capitalist economy, the marketplace is only one of several means by which society makes decisions, determines worth, allocates resources, maintains a social fabric, and conducts human relations. Actual capitalist nations display a wide variation in the blend of market and nonmarket. A basically capitalist system is clearly superior to a command economy. But the nations where markets have the freest rein do not invariably enjoy the most reliable prosperity, let alone the most attractive society.

In this age of the resurgent market, we are promised that technology, ingenuity, and freedom from the dead hand of government will revive economic efficiency and material progress. Yet, despite the triumph of market principles, market society is no

From Robert Kuttner, *Everything for Sale: The Virtues and Limits of Markets* (New York: Knopf, 1998).

Utopia. Compared with the golden era of the postwar boom and the mixed economy, this is a time of broad economic unease. As society becomes more marketized, it is producing stagnation of living standards for most people, and a fraying of the social fabric that society's best-off are all too able to evade. One thing market society does well is to allow its biggest winners to buy their way out of its pathologies.

Even as the market enjoys new prestige, ordinary people are uneasy with many of the results. With greater marketization comes not just opportunity but opportunism; a society that prizes risk also reaps insecurity. Taken to an extreme, markets devalue and diminish extra-market values and norms—on which viable capitalism depends.

The promise of growth has also run into questions of sustainability. Even mainstream economists wonder about the effect on the natural environment if the third world were to enjoy even half the living standards and the claim on natural systems of the United States and Europe. The standard economic calculus does not know how to measure the costs of depletion of natural systems, since these are not accurately captured in current prices. And in market logic, by definition, what is not reflected in the price system does not exist.

All of this should cast serious doubt on the presumption, so fashionable of late, that the natural form of capitalism is laissez-faire. Beyond a certain point, excessive marketization may not be efficient *even for economic life.* . . .

III

The mixed economy of a generation ago was constructed on the ruins of depression and war. It produced a quarter-century of unprecedented growth and prosperity. It allowed a blend of dynamism and stability, of market and political community. When economic growth faltered after 1973, a new, radically classical economics gradually gained influence in the academy and in politics. Resurgent business groups, once cowed by the New Deal-Great Society era, became unabashed crusaders for laissez-faire. The increasing marketization of global commerce undermined the institutional capacity of nation-states to manage a mixed economy, and discredited center-left parties.

The period of "stagflation" discredited economic management and conferred new prestige on laissez-faire. If further confirmation were needed, the erosion and collapse of communism impeached not just state socialism, but European social democracy and American neo-Keynesianism as well. The political counterrevolution that culminated in the 1980 election of Ronald Reagan enjoyed a rendezvous with an intellectual reversion that had been sweeping the economics profession for at least a decade. Each drew strength from the other.

In scholarly economics, theorists such as Milton Friedman, who had been marginal, became central. The concrete study of economic history and economic institutions became archaic. The smartest rising economists used ever more complex mathematics, based on the premise of a "general equilibrium"—a concept that presumed a smoothly self-correcting market and implicitly urged that markets become purer and that more realms of society become markets. Newly self-confident conservative economic theorists colonized other academic disciplines. Market concepts became widespread in law, political science, and economic history. As experts on public policy, these economists became the intellectual champions of privatization, deregulation, and liberation of the global marketplace. It all boiled down to one very simple core precept: market is better.

I begin with the working hypothesis that a capitalist system is a superior form of economic organization, but even in a market economy there are realms of human life where markets are imperfect, inappropriate, or unattainable. Many forms of human motivation cannot be reduced to the market model of man.

There is at the core of the celebration of markets a relentless tautology. If we begin, by assumption, with the premise that nearly everything can be understood as a market and that markets optimize outcomes, then everything else leads back to the same conclusion—marketize! If, in the event, a particular market doesn't optimize, there is only one possible inference: it must be insufficiently marketlike. This epistemological sleight of hand is an astonishing blend that blurs the descriptive with the normative. It is a no-fail system for guaranteeing that theory trumps evidence. Should some human activity not, in fact, behave like an efficient market, it must be the result of some interference that should be removed or a stubborn human refusal to appreciate markets. It cannot possibly be that the theory fails to specify accurately how human behavior works. The thrust of free-market economics for a quarter-century has been a search to narrow the set of special cases where market solutions cannot be found for market failures. Today, the only difference between the utopian version and the mainstream version is degree.

In interpreting political economy, parsimony—Occam's celebrated razor—is the most overrated tool in the scholarly medicine cabinet. The beauty of the market model is its elegant simplicity. A perfect market can be modeled; the analyst can perform neat simulations, using very sophisticated mathematics. But the more complex the departures from a perfect market, the less relevant is the cherished analytic apparatus or the Platonic ideal of a pure market.

Academic champions of the market concede, often with irritation, that real-world institutions are messy; that labor markets are not like product markets, whose merchandise "clears" based on adjustments of price; that actual bundles of capital equipment are "lumpy," and not prone to smooth, frictionless equilibration as in the algebra. But as the economist ventures into the institutional thicket,she strays from the norms of her profession. She had better be tenured first. Thus, in part because of the attractiveness of its own core model, academic economics has lately become a purer version of itself—almost a lobby for the idea that the real economy should strive to emulate the model. The Cambridge economist John Eatwell once remarked, facetiously, "If the world is not like the model, so much the worse for the world."

. . . I am a believer in a balance between market, state, and civil society. I arrive at this belief primarily from a reading of economic and political history, which suggests that pure laissez-faire is socially and even economically unsustainable. Although defenders of a mixed economy often argue their case on equity grounds, there is significant evidence that,

quite apart from questions of distributive justice, the very stability of the system requires departures from laissez-faire. My previous books have all treated, in different ways, the intersection of economics, politics, policy, and ideology. They have all dealt with the boundaries between state, market, and society. In these earlier works, I challenged one of the central claims of the marketizers—that equality necessarily comes at the expense of efficiency. I also examined the corrosive influence of international laissez-faire on the project of operating a mixed economy at home. And I explored the practical political difficulty of center-left parties serving their natural constituency in an era of limited budgets and resurgent laissez-faire.

. . . Where, really, do markets perform roughly as advertised? Where is the market model a reasonable approximation of human motivation, and where is it misleading? By what criteria are we to know when the market has overstepped its proper bounds? How do different kinds of markets fail to optimize outcomes? What patterns of failure recur? How are we to know when we are in a realm where markets produce rough efficiency and rough justice, versus one where markets produce avoidable calamities? When is the best response to market failure to contrive procedures or outcomes that are more "marketlike"? When does that approach only make things worse? Where is the proper boundary between market and nonmarket?

In the search for principles on which to reinvent a mixed economy, one must begin by according great respect to the market. For markets do many things very well. . . . It is evident that command economies are not viable; that prices are indeed potent signals of what it costs to produce a good or a service and what consumers will pay; that when prices unreasonably depart from market discipline they yield too many of the wrong goods or too few of the right ones, and insulate producers from the bracing tonic of competition—leading to stagnation. The trouble is that markets do not reliably yield such results; on the contrary, markets sometimes produce perverse outcomes for fairly prolonged periods.

The quest for a viable mixed economy necessarily leads back to government and politics, for the democratic state remains the prime counterweight to the market. Marketization, of late, has swamped the polity. The dynamics are cumulative. Government has less popular legitimacy, and fewer resources with which to treat escalating problems. The less government is able to achieve, the more it seems a bad bargain. American liberals and European social democrats often seem unable to offer more than a milder version of the conservative program—deregulation, privatization, globalization, fiscal discipline, but at a less zealous extreme. Few have been willing to challenge the premise that nearly everything should revert to a market.

To rebuild an alternative philosophy of political economy, one must first shake the hegemony of the laissez-faire market. I hope to accomplish this with evidence, not tautology. The last intellectual refuge of the marketizer is the claim that, even if markets some-

times fail, political interferences are likely only to compound those failures. Here, also, we must get down to cases. Governments seek to override markets for a variety of purposes—to stabilize, to promote growth, to limit detrimental side effects, to temper inequalities, to cultivate civic virtues. But governments also operate in a political crucible, and require political consent and fiscal resources. In the search for strategies to temper and tame the market, we need to seek ones that are within the competence of the state, that restore vitality to the enterprise of politics, and nourish rather than overload civil society.

QUESTIONS

1. What are some reasons we might be uneasy about the socials results of the market?

2. How does Kuttner argue for a balance between market, state, and civil society?

CASES

CASE 17.1
Blood for Sale
William H. Shaw and Vincent Barry

Sol Levin was a successful stockbroker in Tampa, Florida, when he recognized the potentially profitable market for safe and uncontaminated blood and, with some colleagues, founded Plasma International. Not everybody is willing to make money by selling his or her own blood, and in the beginning Plasma International bought blood from people addicted to wine. Although innovative marketing increased Plasma

International's sales dramatically, several cases of hepatitis were reported in recipients. The company then began looking for new sources of blood.

Plasma International searched worldwide and, with the advice of a qualified team of medical consultants, did extensive testing. Eventually they found that the blood profiles of several rural West African tribes made them ideal prospective donors. After

From William H. Shaw and Vincent Barry, *Moral Issues in Business*, 5th ed. (Belmont, CA: Wadsworth, 1996).

negotiations with the local government, Plasma International signed an agreement with several tribal chieftains to purchase blood.

Business went smoothly and profitably for Plasma International until a Tampa paper charged that Plasma was purchasing blood for as little as fifteen cents a pint and then reselling it to hospitals in the United States and South America for $25 per pint. In one recent disaster, the newspaper alleged, Plasma International had sold 10,000 pints, netting nearly a quarter of a million dollars.

The newspaper story stirred up controversy in Tampa, but the existence of commercialized blood marketing systems in the United States is nothing new. Approximately half the blood and plasma obtained in the United States is bought and sold like any other commodity. About 40 percent is given to avoid having to pay for blood received or to build up credit so blood will be available without charge if needed. By contrast, the National Health Service in Britain relies entirely on a voluntary system of blood donation. Blood is neither bought nor sold. It is available to anyone who needs it without charge or obligation, and donors gain no preference over nondonors.

In an important study, economist Richard Titmuss showed that the British system works better than the American one in terms of economic efficiency, administrative efficiency, price, and blood quality. The commercialized blood market, Titmuss argued, is wasteful of blood and plagued by shortages. Bureaucratization, paperwork, and administrative overhead result in a cost per unit of blood that is five to fifteen times higher than in Britain. Hemophiliacs, in particular, are disadvantaged by the American system and have enormous bills to pay. In addition, commercial markets are much more likely to distribute contaminated blood.

Titmuss also argued that the existence of a commercialized system discourages voluntary donors. People are less apt to give blood if they know that others are selling it. Philosopher Peter Singer has elaborated on this point:

> If blood is a commodity with a price, to give blood means merely to save someone money. Blood has a cash value of a certain number of dollars, and the importance of the gift will vary with the wealth of the recipient. If blood cannot be bought, however, the gift's value depends upon the need of the recipient. Often, it will be worth life itself. Under these circumstances blood becomes a very special kind of gift, and giving it means providing for strangers, without hope of reward, something they cannot buy and without which they may die. The gift relates strangers in a manner that is not possible when blood is a commodity.

This may sound like a philosopher's abstraction, far removed from the thoughts of ordinary people. On the contrary, it is an idea spontaneously expressed by British donors in response to Titmuss's questionnaire. As one woman, a machine operator, wrote in reply to the question why she first decided to become a blood donor: "You can't get blood from supermarkets and chain stores. People themselves must come forward; sick people can't get out of bed to ask you for a pint to save their life, so I came forward in hopes to help somebody who needs blood."

The implication of this answer, and others like it, is that even if the formal right to give blood can coexist with commercialized blood banks, the respondent's action would have lost much of its significance to her, and the blood would probably not have been given at all. When blood is a commodity, and can be purchased if it is not given, altruism becomes unnecessary, and so loosens the bonds that can otherwise exist between strangers in a community. The existence of a market in blood does not threaten the formal right to give blood, but it does away with the right to give blood which cannot be bought, has no cash value, and must be given freely if it is to be obtained at all. If there is such a right, it is incompatible with the right to sell blood, and we cannot avoid violating one of these rights when we grant the other.

Both Titmuss and Singer believe that the weakening of the spirit of altruism in this sphere has important repercussions. It marks, they think, the increasing commercialization of our lives and makes similar changes in attitude, motive, and relationships more likely in other fields.

QUESTIONS

1. Is Sol Levin running a business "just like any other business," or is his company open to moral criticism? Defend your answer by appeal to moral principle.

2. What are the contrasting ideals of the British and American blood systems? Which system, in your opinion, best promotes human freedom and respect for persons?

3. Examine the pros and cons of commercial transactions in blood from the egoistic, the utilitarian, and the Kantian perspectives.

4. Are Titmuss and Singer right to suggest that the buying and selling of blood reduces altruism? Does knowing that you can sell your blood (and that others are selling theirs) make you less inclined to donate your blood? Do we have a right to give blood that cannot be bought?

5. Many believe that commercialization is increasing in all areas of modern life. If this is so, is it something to be applauded or condemned? Is it wrong to treat certain things—like human organs—as commodities?

6. Did Plasma International strike a fair bargain with the West Africans who supplied their blood to the company? Or is Plasma guilty of exploiting them in some way? Explain your answer.

7. Do you believe that we have a moral duty to donate blood? If so, why and under what circumstances? If not, why not?

CASE 17.2

Cocaine at the Fortune-500 Level

Tom L. Beauchamp, Jeff Greene, and Sasha Lyuste

Roberto, a pure libertarian in moral and political philosophy, is deeply impressed by his reading of Robert Nozick's account of justice. He lives in Los Angeles and teaches philosophy at a local university. Roberto is also a frequent user of cocaine, which he enjoys immensely and provides to friends at parties. Neither he nor any of his close friends is addicted. Over the years Roberto has become tired of teaching philosophy and now has an opportunity, through old friends who live in Peru, to become a middleman in the cocaine business. Although he is disturbed about the effects cocaine has in some persons, he has never witnessed these effects firsthand. He is giving his friends' business offer serious consideration.

Roberto's research has told him the following: Selling cocaine is a $35 billion plus industry. Although he is interested primarily in a Peruvian connection, his research has shown conclusively that the Colombian cartel alone is large enough to place it among the Fortune 500 corporations. Cocaine production in Peru and Bolivia in 1995 represented about

90 percent of the world's cocaine base; the remaining 10 percent was produced in Columbia (*Journal of Inter-American and World Affairs, 1997*). Cocaine is Latin America's second largest export, accounting for 3–4 percent of the GDP of Peru and Bolivia, and up to 8 percent of that of Columbia. The cocaine industry employs close to half a million people in the Andean region alone. Columbian coca cultivation rose 11 percent in 2000.

Former Peruvian President Alan Garcia once described cocaine as Latin America's "only successful multinational." It can be and has been analyzed in traditional business categories, with its own entrepreneurs, chemists, laboratories, employment agencies, small organizations, distribution systems, market giants, growth phases, and so forth. Cocaine's profit margins have narrowed in some markets, while expanding in others. It often seeks new markets in order to expand its product line. For example, in the mid-1980s "crack," a potent form of smoked cocaine, was moved heavily into new markets in

This case was prepared by Tom L. Beauchamp and updated by Jeff Greene and Sasha Lyutse; it relies in part on accounts in *The Wall Street Journal* and *The Economist*.

Europe. Between the mid-1960s and the late 1990s the demand for cocaine grew dramatically (weathering some up and down markets) because of successful supply and marketing. Middlemen in Miami and Los Angeles were established to increase already abundant profits. Heavy investments were made in airplanes, efficient modes of production, training managers, and regular schedules of distribution. In the late 1980s there was a downturn in cocaine consumption after the deaths of two prominent athletes. In the early 1990s the market recovered slightly before slipping again in the mid-1990s. However, cocaine remains an enormously powerful industry in many countries.

Roberto sees the cocaine industry as not being subject to taxes, tariffs, or government regulations other than those pertaining to its illegality. It is a pure form of the free market in which supply and demand control transactions. This fact about the business appeals to Roberto, as it seems perfectly suited to his libertarian views. He is well aware that there are severe problems of coercion and violence in some parts of the industry, but he is certain that the wealthy clientele whom he would supply in Los Angeles would neither abuse the drug nor redistribute it to others who might be harmed. Roberto is confident that his Peruvian associates are honorable and that he can escape problems of violence, coercion, and abusive marketing. However, he has just read a newspaper story that cocaine-use emergencies—especially those involving cocaine-induced heart attacks—have tripled in the last five years. It is only this fact that has given him pause before deciding to enter the cocaine business. He views these health emergencies as unfortunate but not unfair outcomes of the business. Therefore, it is his humanity and not his theory of justice that gives him pause.

QUESTIONS

1. Would a libertarian—such as Roberto—say that the cocaine business is not unfair so long as no coercion is involved and the system is a pure function of supply and demand?

2. Does justice demand that cocaine be outlawed, or is this not a matter of justice at all? Are questions of justice even meaningful when the activity is beyond the boundaries of law?

3. Is the distinction Roberto draws between what is unfortunate and what is unfair relevant to a decision about whether an activity is just?

CHAPTER QUESTIONS

1. Should everything be for sale? What should *not* be for sale (are there some things that should *never* be for sale)? How would you distinguish between those things that ought to be subject to market forces and those that should never be subject to the market?

2. Francis Fukuyama argued that history has effectively come to an end because free markets and free societies are the natural goal of humankind. Do you agree? Has Western society discovered (more or less) the ideal economic and political form? Does a free society depend upon free markets? And is capitalism the best—or only—form that free markets can take?